The SAGE Handbook of
# Historical Theory

The editors have assembled a large and outstanding group of historians and other theorists who examine and represent theories of historical knowledge from every angle. The collection is comprehensive, scholarly, and full of new insights.
**David Carr, Professor Emeritus, Emory University, USA**

The challenges of the use of theory in history is analysed and interrogated in significant and exciting ways in this work. In drawing on the insights of leading scholars, this indispensable volume broadens the parameters of our investigation of the past and deepens our interpretation and understanding of historical knowledge.
**Joy Damousi, Professor of History, University of Melbourne, Australia**

Nancy Partner and Sarah Foot have brought together a comprehensive and up-to-date collection of essays on historical theory. The special feature is that more than half the contributions are written by working historians with their feet on the ground. The book will be invaluable both to students of historiography and seasoned practitioners.
**John Tosh, Professor of History, University of Roehampton, UK**

This is an important overview and critical analysis of the present state of history writing. Starting with history's modernist foundations in the 19th century, the Handbook succinctly explains how the rise of postmodernism has brought about our present-day post-postmodernist predicament with its broad variety of historical genres.
**Chris Lorenz, Professor of German Historical Culture and Historical Theory, VU University Amsterdam and Amsterdam University College, The Netherlands**

# The SAGE Handbook of
# Historical Theory

Edited by

## Nancy Partner
and **Sarah Foot**

Los Angeles | London | New Delhi
Singapore | Washington DC

Los Angeles | London | New Delhi
Singapore | Washington DC

SAGE Publications Ltd
1 Oliver's Yard
55 City Road
London EC1Y 1SP

SAGE Publications Inc.
2455 Teller Road
Thousand Oaks, California 91320

SAGE Publications India Pvt Ltd
B 1/I 1 Mohan Cooperative Industrial Area
Mathura Road
New Delhi 110 044

SAGE Publications Asia-Pacific Pte Ltd
3 Church Street
#10-04 Samsung Hub
Singapore 049483

Editor: Katie Metzler
Editorial assistant: Anna Horvai
Production editor: Vanessa Harwood
Project manager: Jill Birch
Copyeditor: David Hemsley
Proofreader: Jill Birch
Indexer: Gary Birch
Marketing manager: Ben Griffin-Sherwood
Cover design: Wendy Scott
Typeset by: C&M Digitals (P) Ltd, Chennai, India
Printed by: MPG Books Group, Bodmin, Cornwall

Editorial arrangement © Nancy Partner and Sarah Foot 2013

Parts I, II, III introductions © Nancy Partner 2013
Chapter 1 © Michael Bentley 2013
Chapter 2 © Lutz Raphael 2013
Chapter 3 © Jan van der Dussen 2013
Chapter 4 © Joseph Tendler 2013
Chapter 5 © Donald R. Kelley 2013
Chapter 6 © Brian Lewis 2013
Chapter 7 © Robert Doran 2013
Chapter 8 © Kalle Pihlainen 2013
Chapter 9 © Robert M. Stein 2013
Chapter 10 © Hans Kellner 2013
Chapter 11 © Clare O'Farrell 2013
Chapter 12 © Ann Rigney 2013
Chapter 13 © Ann Curthoys and John Docker 2013
Chapter 14 © Brian Lewis 2013
Chapter 15 © Judith P. Zinsser 2013
Chapter 16 © Bonnie G. Smith 2013
Chapter 17 © Karen Harvey 2013
Chapter 18 © Amy Richlin 2013
Chapter 19 © Michael Roper 2013
Chapter 20 © Kevin Foster 2013
Chapter 21 © Gilbert B. Rodman 2013
Chapter 22 © Patrick H. Hutton 2013
Chapter 23 © Benjamin Zachariah 2013
Chapter 24 © John H. Zammito 2013
Chapter 25 © Frank Ankersmit 2013
Chapter 26 © Judith Keilbach 2013
Chapter 27 © Valerie Johnson and David Thomas 2013
Chapter 28 © David Gary Shaw 2013
Chapter 29 © Nancy Partner 2013

First published 2013

**Library of Congress Control Number: 2012935850**

**British Library Cataloguing in Publication data**

A catalogue record for this book is available from the British Library

ISBN 978-1-4129-3114-4

# Contents

# List of contributors

**Frank Ankersmit** was Professor for Intellectual History and Philosophy of History at Groningen University from 1992 until his retirement in 2010. He has published some 15 books and more than 200 articles in the fields of philosophy of history, political philosophy and aesthetics. His next book, entitled *Meaning, Truth and Reference in Historical Representation*, will be published in Spring 2012. His writings have been translated into many languages. He is founder and chief editor of the *Journal of the Philosophy of History* and has an honorary degree in the humanities of the University of Ghent.

**Michael Bentley** is Professor of Modern History at the University of St Andrews. His major research interests are in the political and intellectual history of Britain in the nineteenth and twentieth centuries, and in the philosophy of history, and historiography. His publications include *The Liberal Mind, 1914–1929* (1977); *Politics without Democracy, 1815–1914* (1984, 1996); *The Climax of Liberal Politics* (1987); *A Companion to Historiography* (1997); *Modern Historiography* (1999); *Lord Salisbury's World* (2001); and *The Life and Thought of Herbert Butterfield: History, Science and God* (2011). He is currently writing a comparative analysis of Western historiography since the Enlightenment.

**Ann Curthoys** is Australian Research Council Professorial Fellow at the University of Sydney, and Fellow of the Academy of Social Sciences of Australia and the Australian Academy of the Humanities. Her research is in Australian history, as well as history and theory, and historical writing. Major publications include *Freedom Ride: A Freedomrider Remembers* (2002); *How to Write History that People Want to Read* (2009), with Ann McGrath; *Rights and Redemption: History, Law, and Indigenous People*, with Ann Genovese and Alexander Reilly (2008); and *Is History Fiction?*, with John Docker (2005, rev. edn 2010). She is currently working on a project titled: 'The British Empire, Indigenous Peoples, and Self-government for the Australian Colonies'.

**John Docker** is Honorary Professor in the School of Philosophical and Historical Inquiry at the University of Sydney, where his research is in the field of intellectual and cultural history. His publications include *The Origins of Violence: Religion, History and Genocide* (2008); *1492: The Poetics of Diaspora* (2001); *Postmodernism and Popular Culture: A Cultural History* (1994); and, with Ann Curthoys, *Is History Fiction?* (2005, rev. edn 2010). He is currently working on a book titled *Sheer Folly and Derangement: Disorienting Europe and the West*, as well as other projects.

**Robert Doran** is James P. Wilmot Assistant Professor of French and Comparative Literature at the University of Rochester (USA). His main areas of specialization are aesthetics, literary theory, continental philosophy, intellectual history and nineteenth-century French literature. He is the editor of the collected essays of Hayden White, *The Fiction of Narrative: Essays on History, Literature and Theory, 1957–2007* (2010), and of the anthology, *Philosophy of History after Hayden White* (London: Bloomsbury, 2013). He is also the editor of *Mimesis and Theory:*

*Essays on Literature and Criticism 1953–2005* (2008), by René Girard. His monograph, *The Theory of the Sublime from Longinus to Kant,* is under review.

**Jan van der Dussen** is Professor (emeritus) of Humanities at the Open University of The Netherlands. His publications include *History as a Science: The Philosophy of R.G. Collingwood* (1981); with Lionel Rubinoff, editor of *Objectivity, Method and Point of View: Essays in the Philosophy of History* (1991); editor of the revised edition of R.G. Collingwood, *The Idea of History* (Oxford, 1993); with W.H. Dray editor of *R.G. Collingwood: The Principles of History and Other Writings in Philosophy of History* (1999); revised edition of *History as a Science: The Philosophy of R.G. Collingwood* (2012).

**Sarah Foot** is the Regius Professor of Ecclesiastical History at Christ Church, University of Oxford. Her research is on Anglo-Saxon monasteries, women and religion, the invention of the English, and in historiography and historical theory. Her publications include *Veiled Women: The Disappearance of Nuns from Anglo-Saxon England* (2 vols, 2000); *Monastic Life in Anglo-Saxon England c. 600–900* (2006); *Æthelstan: the First English Monarch* (2011); 'Plenty, portents and plague: Anglo-Saxon readings of the natural world', in *The Church and the Natural World*, ed. Peter Clarke and Tony Claydon (2010); 'Church and monastery in Bede's Northumbria', in *The Cambridge Companion to Bede*, ed. Scott De Gregorio (2010). She is currently working on an edition of the Anglo-Saxon Charters of Bury St Edmunds Abbey for the British Academy.

**Kevin Foster** is an Associate Professor in the School of English Communications and Performance Studies at Monash University where he teaches Media Studies. He has written widely on cultural history and national identity with a particular focus on war and conflict. His work has appeared in a range of international journals including *Cultural Studies, Modern Fiction Studies, Third Text* and *The Journal of Popular Culture*. He is the author of *Fighting Fictions: War, Narrative and National Identity* (1999) and *Lost Worlds: Latin America and the Imagining of Empire* (2009). He has also edited *What are we doing in Afghanistan? The Military and the Media at War* (2009) and *The Information Battlefield: Representing Australians at War* (2011).

**Karen Harvey** is Senior Lecturer in Cultural History at the University of Sheffield. She has published widely on gender, sexuality and material culture, with a particular interest in the history of masculinity. She uses a wide range of written, visual and material sources in her research, and is committed to interdisciplinarity. Her books include *Reading Sex in the Eighteenth Century: Bodies and Gender in English Erotic Culture* (2004); and as editor, *The Kiss in History* (2005) and *History and Material Culture*, ed. (2009). Her most recent book is *The Little Republic: Masculinity and Domestic Authority in Eighteenth-Century Britain* (2012). This reconstructs men's experiences of the house, examining the authority that accrued to mundane and everyday household practices and employing men's own concepts to understand what men thought and felt about their domestic lives.

**Patrick H. Hutton** is Professor of History (emeritus) at the University of Vermont, where he teaches in the Integrated Humanities Program. His books include: *The Cult of the Revolutionary Tradition* (1981); *History as an Art of Memory* (1993); and *Philippe Ariès and the Politics of French Cultural History* (2004); as editor, *A Historical Dictionary of the Third French Republic* (1986); and as co-editor, *Technologies of the Self: A Seminar with Michel Foucault* (1988).

**Valerie Johnson** is Head of Research at The National Archives. Prior to that, she worked as Research Officer on a history project based at the University of Cambridge History. She holds an MA with Distinction in Archive Administration, and was awarded the Alexander R Myers Memorial Prize for Archive Administration. She also has a PhD in History for her thesis, 'British multinationals, culture and empire in the early twentieth century' (2007), for which she won the 2008 Coleman Prize. She has worked as an archivist and a historian in the academic, corporate and public sectors.

**Judith Keilbach** is Assistant Professor of Television History in the Media and Culture Studies Department of Utrecht University (Netherlands). Her research focuses include television history and theory, the relation of media technology and historiography, archives, aerial photography and animals. Her book on *Geschichtsbilder und Zeitzeugen* (historical images and witness) analyzes how German television documentaries represent the National Socialist past. She has published a number of English articles on that topic, amongst others in *New German Critique* and *The Leo Baeck Yearbook*. She is co-editor of *Grundlagentexte zur Fernsehwissenschaft* and *Die Gegenwart der Vergangeheit* and of the journal *Montage AV*.

**Donald R. Kelley** is the James Westfall Thompson Professor (emeritus) of History at Rutgers University. His research interests are in the history of Western historiography, European Intellectual history, and the history of Law. Among his many publications are *The Faces of History: Historical Inquiry from Herodotus to Herder* (1998); *The Descent of Ideas: The History of Intellectual History* (2002); *The Writing of History and the Study of Law* (1997); as editor, *Versions of History: From Antiquity to the Enlightenment* (1990); *History and the Disciplines: The Reclassification of Knowledge in Early Modern Europe* (1997); and *Fortunes of History: Historical Inquiry from Herder to Huizinga* (in press).

**Hans Kellner** is Professor of English at North Carolina State University, and a member of the Communications, Rhetoric, and Digital Media Program. He is the author of *Language and Historical Representation: Getting the Story Crooked* (1989). He is also co-editor of *A New Philosophy of History* (with F.R. Ankersmit) (1995) and *Re-figuring Hayden White* (with F.R. Ankersmit and E. Domanska) (2009). He is the author of many articles in historical theory, rhetorical theory, history of rhetoric and historiography.

**Brian Lewis** is Associate Professor of History at McGill University. He is the author of *The Middlemost and the Milltowns: Bourgeois Culture and Politics in Early Industrial England* (2001); *'So Clean': Lord Leverhulme, Soap and Civilization* (2008). He is guest editor of a special edition of the *Journal of British Studies* on queer history (July 2012), and editor of *British Queer History: New Approaches and Perspectives* (forthcoming). He is currently working on a book titled *The First Queer Revolution: George Ives and Homosexuality in Britain from Wilde to Wolfenden*.

**Clare O'Farrell** is a Senior Lecturer in the School of Cultural and Language Studies in Education at the Queensland University of Technology in Brisbane, Australia. She studied philosophy in Paris in the early 1980s and attended Foucault's lectures. She has written two books on Foucault, *Foucault: Historian or Philosopher?* (1989) and *Michel Foucault* (2005), and has edited a large collection of essays on his work, *Foucault the Legacy* (1997). She was one of the founding editors of the journal *Foucault Studies*. She also runs a resource website on Foucault, http://michel-foucault.com (online since 1997) and a blog titled Foucault News.

**Nancy Partner** is Professor of History at McGill University. Her research interests are medieval historical writing, applications of psychoanalysis for history, and historical theory with emphasis on narrative theory and epistemology. Her publications include the edited books, *Studying Medieval Women: Sex, Gender, Feminism* (1993), and *Writing Medieval History* (2005), to which she contributed 'The hidden self: psychoanalysis and the textual unconscious'. Recent articles include: 'The linguistic turn along post-postmodern borders: Israeli/Palestinian narrative conflict' in *New Literary History* (2009); 'Narrative persistence: the post-postmodern life of narrative theory', in *Refiguring Hayden White*, ed. by Frank Ankersmit, et al. (2009), and 'Our history/your myths: narrative and national identity', in *Storia della Storiografia* (2012). She is currently working on the topic of narrative construction and European identity.

**Kalle Pihlainen** is an Academy of Finland Research Fellow based at the Department of Philosophy, Åbo Akademi University, as well as Adjunct Professor in Philosophy of History at the Department of Contemporary History, University of Turku, Finland. He holds a PhD in History from the University of Turku, where he also taught and worked at the Department of Cultural History. He has published articles on narrative theory and the philosophy of history in various anthologies and in journals including *Clio, Historein, New Literary History, Rethinking History* and *Storia della Storiografia*. His work to date has primarily focused on literary and performance theory, existentialism and poststructuralism, as well as the ethics of narrative representation particularly in relation to Hayden White and Jean-Paul Sartre. Ongoing research projects investigate the representational strategies employed by Sartre in 'L'Idiot de la Famille' as well as the question of embodiment in contemporary narrative theory.

**Lutz Raphael** is Professor of Contemporary History at the University of Trier (Germany). One of his main fields of research has been the history of modern Historiography starting with a study on the French Annales School after the Second World War, *Die Erben von Bloch und Febvre. Annales-Historiographie und nouvelle histoire in Frankreich 1945–1980* (1994), later extending his field of interest towards comparative studies like: 'Flexible response? Strategies of academic historians towards larger markets for national historiographies and increasing scientific standards', in *KVHAA Konferenser*, Vol. 49 (2000), 127–47; and 'Experiments in modernization: social and economic history'. He has written a synthesis of international trends in twentieth-century historiography, *Geschichtswissenschaft im Zeitalter der Extreme: Theorien, Methoden, Tendenzen von 1900 bis zur Gegenwart* (2nd edn, 2010); and has edited (with Ilaria Porciani), *Atlas of European Historiography: The Making of a Profession 1800–2005* (2009). His second field of research is the comparative history of European societies since 1900. Publications on this topic include (with Anselm Doering-Manteuffel), *Nach dem Boom. Perspektiven auf die Zeitgeschichte seit 1970* (2nd edn, 2010); and *Imperiale Gewalt und mobilisierte Nation. Europa 1914–1945* (2011). He is a member of the editorial board of the *Journal of Modern European History*.

**Amy Richlin** is Professor of Classics at UCLA. She has published widely on the history of sexuality, on Latin literature, and on Roman women's history; her books include *The Garden of Priapus* (1983, rev. edn 1992); *Rome and the Mysterious Orient: Three Plays by Plautus* (2005); and *Marcus Aurelius in Love* (2006). She has edited *Pornography and Representation in Greece and Rome* (1992) and co-edited *Feminist Theory and the Classics* (1993). She is revising a book on epistolarity, the end of the ancient sex/gender system, and the circulation of knowledge about that system in the nineteenth and early twentieth centuries, with the working title *How Fronto's Letters Got Lost: Reading Roman Pederasty in Modern Europe*. A book of her collected essays on Roman women's history is forthcoming from University of Michigan Press. Other current interests include Roman comedy as slave theatre and the teaching of classical literature to Native Americans in the seventeenth and eighteenth centuries.

**Ann Rigney** is Professor of Comparative Literature at Utrecht University where she also directs the university research area Cultures & Identities. She was elected a member of the Netherlands Academy of Arts and Sciences in 2005. She has written widely in the field of narrative theory and memory cultures of the nineteenth and twentieth centuries, and directed the research project The Dynamics of Cultural Remembrance (2006–2010) funded by the Dutch Research council. Her many publications include *The Rhetoric of Historical Representation* (1990); *Imperfect Histories* (2001); and as co-editor (with Astrid Erll), *Mediation, Remediation, and the Dynamics of Cultural Memory* (2009). A new book, *The Afterlives of Walter Scott: Memory on the Move*, examines the social life of Scott's work over a period of two centuries (2012). See further www.rigney.nl.

**Gilbert B. Rodman** is Associate Professor of Communication Studies at the University of Minnesota. His research and teaching focuses on cultural studies, media studies, popular culture, media technologies, intellectual property, and the politics of race and ethnicity. He is the author of *Elvis After Elvis: The Posthumous Career of a Living Legend* (1996) and *Why Cultural Studies?* (forthcoming); one of the co-editors of *Race in Cyberspace* (2000); and the editor of *The Race and Media Reader* (forthcoming). He is currently working on a book about Stuart Hall. He is the founder and manager of CULTSTUD-L (the largest and longest-running international listserv devoted to cultural studies); sits on the editorial boards of the journals *Cultural Studies*, *Communication and Critical Cultural Studies* and the *European Journal of Cultural Studies*; and serves as the Chair of the Association for Cultural Studies.

**Michael Roper** is a social and cultural historian of twentieth-century Britain, based in the Sociology Department at the University of Essex. His most recent book is *The Secret Battle: Emotional Survival in the Great War* (2009) and he has published numerous articles on personal sources and the use of psychoanalysis in historical research on subjectivity. He has a particular interest in the Kleinian psychoanalyst and First World War veteran Wilfred Bion, and is currently working on a history of 'the generation between' in Britain, which explores the psychological impact of the First World War on the children born between the wars.

**David Gary Shaw** is the Dean of the Social Sciences and Interdisciplinary Programs and Professor of History at Wesleyan University. He teaches medieval history, British history until 1700, as well as historiography and the theory of history. His research first focused on urban communities in medieval England and then the nature of the social self, a subject that has drawn him far from his medieval beginnings. At present, he is researching a book on the circulation of people (and their sentient side-kicks), information and ideas in later medieval England. He is also continuing to examine the shifting nature of historical agency among people, animals, and other possible actors. He is an associate editor of *History and Theory*. While at the journal he edited special issues on Religion, Agency and Evolutionary Theory. He is currently working on another themed issue about animals and history, which should be published in 2013. His publications include *The Creation of a Community: The City of Wells in the Middle Ages* (1993); *The Return of Science: Evolution, History, and Theory,* edited with Philip Pomper (2002); and *Necessary Conjunctions: The Social Self in Medieval England* (2005).

**Bonnie G. Smith** is Board of Governors Professor of History at Rutgers University, where her research interests focus on women's history in a global perspective. Among her many publications are: *Ladies of the Leisure Class: The Bourgeoises of Northern France in the Nineteenth Century* (1981); *Changing Lives: Women in European History since 1700* (1989); *The Gender of History: Men, Women, and Historical Practice* (1998); *Global Feminisms since 1945*, edited (2000); *Women's and Gender History in Global Perspective* (2003–4); and the *Encyclopedia of Women in World History* (2008).

**Robert M. Stein** is Doris and Carl Kempner Distinguished Professor in the Humanities at Purchase College, SUNY, and Adjunct Senior Research Scholar in the Department of English and Comparative Literature at Columbia University. He has written on contemporary critical theory, including articles on Walter Benjamin and Erich Auerbach, as well as on medieval historiography and romance. His recent publications include *Reading Medieval Culture*, a festschrift for Robert Hanning, which he edited with Sandra Pierson Prior (2005), and *Reality Fictions: Romance, History, and Governmental Authority, 1025–1180* (2006). He is currently at work on an English translation, with introduction and commentary, of *La Vie de St Edmond le Rei* and the Anglo-Norman Pseudo-Turpin Chronicle for the French of England Project.

**Joseph Tendler** completed his doctorate at the University of St Andrews. His research and teaching interests centre on the historiography and intellectual history of the Atlantic world, as well as historical theory, broadly conceived. A first monograph, *Against the Tide: Opponents of the Annales School in Comparative Perspective, 1900–1970*, will challenge previous depictions of the Annales School of historians by examining their methodologies from the point of view of their opponents across Western Europe and the United States of America. He has also contributed book chapters on the French historian Jacques Droz and Annales historians' contested transformations of the practice of local history writing. Recent articles include a study of the forefathers of contemporary trends in historical interpretations of the French Revolution, an exposition of the political consensus advanced by constitutional historians in Europe during the first Cold War and the now-forgotten significance of the Nebraska School of historians in establishing in communication with European scholars the practice of professional history in America around 1900. His post-doctoral project is on the international impact of Benedetto Croce's historical writing. He also reviews work on the history of historiography for *German History*.

**David Thomas** is Director of Technology at the National Archives, a post he has held since 2005. Prior to that he held a variety of posts at the National Archives and has led their IT operations since 1995. He is currently working on the development of new systems to capture, preserve and make available digital and digitised records. He holds a PhD in History for his thesis on the crown lands under Elizabeth I. Until recently he served on the Council of the Royal Historical Society.

**Benjamin Zachariah** read history at Presidency College, Calcutta, and at Trinity College, Cambridge, and is currently Professor of History at Presidency University, Calcutta. His research interests centre on the intellectual history of modern South Asia, on historiography and historical theory, and on the global movement of ideas. He is the author of a biography of the first Indian Prime Minister, Jawaharlal Nehru (2004); *Developing India: an Intellectual and Social History, c. 1930–1950* (2005); and *Playing the Nation Game: the Ambiguities of Nationalism in India* (2011). He is currently working on international networks of fascists and India.

**John H. Zammito** is John Antony Weir Professor of History at Rice University. His research focuses on the philosophy of Immanuel Kant and of his student and rival, Johann Gottfried Herder, as well as on the history and philosophy of science both as a methodology and with specific reference to developments in the eighteenth century. He has also written extensively on the philosophy of history. His current research involves the germination of biology as a special science in Germany in the eighteenth century. His key publications are *The Genesis of Kant's Critique of Judgment* (1992); *Kant, Herder, and the Birth of Anthropology* (2002); and *A Nice Derangement of Epistemes: Post-Positivism in the Study of Science from Quine to Latour* (2004); plus numerous articles in *Studies in History and Philosophy of Science* and in *History and Theory*.

**Judith P. Zinsser**, Professor emerita of History at Miami University (Ohio), wrote *Emilie Du Châtelet: Daring Genius of the Enlightenment* (2006). Her articles on the marquise have appeared in journals in the USA and Europe. Most recently she collaborated on a translation of Du Châtelet's writings for the series, 'The Other Voice of Early Modern Europe' (2009). Zinsser has written articles on the relationship between feminism and biography, on gender and world history, and in *A Glass Half Full* (1994) on the impact of feminism on the practice of history and the workings of the historical profession. She is co-author of the two-volume classic, *A History of Their Own: Women in Europe from Prehistory to the Present* (1999).

# PART I

# Foundations: Theoretical Frameworks for Knowledge of the Past

Nancy Partner

## INTRODUCTION

Historical theory is a coherent yet flexible framework which supports the analysis of historical knowledge, and assists our understanding of what kind of knowledge we can have of the past, and precisely how that knowledge is constructed, assembled, and presented. In this sense of a framework of conceptual instruments for examining our knowledge of the past, theory is metahistorical: it does its work as an adjunct operation opening out the reach of critical self-awareness we bring to our assumptions and practices as historians. Theory is metahistorical also in that in its strongest versions it applies to the entire discipline of history, all time periods, and specialized topics. The focus and coverage of historical theory differentiate it from methodology and techniques, and from traditional philosophy of history, and situate it closer to hermeneutics.

In the very *longue durée* of the history of history, by the conventional measure beginning with Herodotus, theory in this self-scrutinizing sense is quite new, chiefly a product of the later twentieth century; the development of historical theory marks a clear stage in the modern maturity of history as an intellectual and cultural practice.

The terminology we have available for these metahistorical frameworks for examining historical knowledge tends to merge the edges of philosophy and theory, especially when questions of epistemology are involved, but there are substantial differences between older approaches to big historical concerns and the contemporary project of understanding what exactly 'history' is. Philosophy of history, in its many formulations, attempted to discern the shape and direction of very large scale changes in human collective life over long stretches of time. Well-known variants range from cyclical repetitions attributed to Thucydides and other Greeks of antiquity, medieval Christian millennial ideas, to Marxist and Hegelian dialectical history. Everything potentially enters into these sort of ambitious enterprises to encompass and intellectually control the enormous variety of human activity (culture, politics, war, economics, social organization, religion) collected under the rubric of 'history' with the exception of 'history' itself – that is, exactly what we mean by 'history' as a form of knowledge and how this knowledge is formulated and conveyed in any stable form. Philosophy of history in its several variants can be speculative or analytical but, at its core, the ontological entity 'history' is assumed, not interrogated. The history whose movements are explained in these large scale guises is some cumulative, accepted version of what historians have offered, especially in long-form histories of nations, empires, the rise and fall of dynastic powers, and economic and cultural hegemonies.

The assembly and presentation of this information in written form (the histories that make up 'History') is taken for granted as offering trustworthy material of past reality which awaits organization by philosophers of history into cycles, spirals, dialectic encounters, or revolutionary upheavals. Historical theory, in contrast, homes in on the 'history' itself, asking: Exactly what sort of representations are offered as true information about past reality? How does the category-language of description work? What operations produce the intelligible linguistic structures of events-in-time which are, in the end, what we really mean by 'history'? It is this difference of focus and object of interrogation which marks the distinction between philosophy of history and theory.

Why should history, a discipline committed to verifiable factuality, need theory? What is intrinsic to history, to what we really mean by history, that invites and even requires an extra theoretical discussion? The short answer is 'writing.' Historical theory is summoned by the tension set up between the

concentration on factuality (locating the sources of accurate information of the past, the technical handling of documents and other artifacts, establishing the web of verification around historical information, and articulating and securing consistent standards for historical work) and the larger structures of language that alone can convey the complex meanings historians see 'in' well-established facts. A tension of incommensurate standards arises between facts and linguistic forms. Events become facts (or 'facts' in our self-conscious usage) when they are subject to descriptions or predications, and the factuality of small-scale historical knowledge is subject to verification. Verification, in the modern discipline, is a set of procedures for measuring statements against the evidence supporting them. The methods and standards involved in adjudicating the truth-value status of specific assertions about past actuality (this happened, this way, at this time and place) is modern in its scientific aspirations and rational framework. But the forms of language that hold together assemblages of factual information in relations and sequences that are comprehensible and meaningful are, in their base elements, literally ancient and 'literary' in genre.

History is narrative in form, virtually by definition, because narrative is what brings the seriatim stream of time under control for intelligible, meaningful comprehension; but the narrative constructions necessary to historical knowledge are not themselves susceptible to verification as discreet facts are. The linguistic form for statements about single events is totally different in scale, complexity, and argumentation from long-form narrative. The epistemological force of our procedures of verification applies with maximal effect on small-scale facts, but verification attenuates as history expands beyond statement level, and the complex relationships that express the meaning of events over controlled stretches of time are not really susceptible to verification at all in the same way. That is where historical theory intersects with historical work: at the level of interpretation, narrative emplotment, the complex configuration of events in time, in writing. These incommensurate yet interlinked forms (statement vs. narrative) invite scrutiny, and this scrutiny opens the way to historical theory.

Historical theory does not mean '*a theory of history*,' some unified system explaining or predicting the course of world events in the manner of older styles of philosophy of history; theory does not gesture at world historical movements pictured as ascents and declines, or cycles, or dialectical antitheses, and it emphatically does not aim at disciplinary parameters that would govern or restrict the possibilities of interpretation of the past. History, the word, is part of our common vocabulary, so we continue to use 'history' to cover an overlapping array of other ideas ranging from the entirety of past actuality to something more like a story ('they have a history …'), but only those writings adhering to contemporary protocols for historicity can be subjected to analysis *as history* in a systematic way. Thus, the history that generates historical theory as its metadiscourse takes written form, works describing and interpreting the past which are offered as serious contributions to knowledge – *works of history* rather than 'history' as an abstract gesture towards the real past. The purpose of theory directed to written history is the deep analysis of this historical knowledge, for the sake of intellectual transparency and disciplinary self-reflection, and if theory is the category term collecting together the instruments of analysis, it requires a stable defined object on which to work. A theoretical scrutiny addresses the procedures and operations involved in the making of written history above the level of its constituent statement-facts and trains an intense light on the construction of chronology, causal trajectories, selection and emphasis, value-laden language, and interpretation in the fullest sense.

Historical theory, then, provides a framework that supports the investigations of what we mean by historical knowledge, the interpretive operations that turn traces of the past into 'evidence of' some larger set of meanings that emerge over time. Even if not *a system*, historical theory does have to be sufficiently systematic in the sense that its operative concepts work together coherently, and it does point to a certain level of abstraction because its object is history, the whole domain of written history. This breadth of application is what earns historical theory its title to being 'theory': it addresses foundational elements of historical knowledge of all times and places; thus it is co-extensive with history in its entirety. The test of a strong concept in historical theory is whether it applies usefully and aptly across fields and specialities, and times and places. Because knowledge of the past is produced as cultural artifacts made of language – alias: *histories* in the plural – theoretical analysis applies to the histories of all chronological periods, and all societies available for historical research. The complex formulations of language historians construct to turn observation, memory, evidentiary traces of the past, documents, and material artifacts into *histories* – truth-claim texts – require this level of self-reflexive scrutiny if history is to be a fully matured discipline. The need for rigorous self-reflection is where theory is summoned up, to do this self-critical work. Theory, in this sense, confronts history in its most concrete and lucid form, what historians actually do, the written work that formulates their research and interpretation.

## MODERNITY AND HISTORY: THE PROFESSIONAL DISCIPLINE

History's modernity began with its entry into the university as a teaching and research subject in the nineteenth century; the university-based historian was, for the first time, a trained professional who had mastered the difficult techniques of archival research. The enthusiasm and respect generated by contemporary scientific advance exerted a compelling attraction and drew the first generations of research historians to define their work also as a 'science,' and try to claim a place, albeit a marginal one, for history within the boundaries of scientific endeavor.

The professionalization of history in the nineteenth century directed attention to research, method, rigor, and the relationship between archival collections and the historian's restatement of information grounded in primary sources. The new methodology, rigorous and critical, was its own self-explanation: the in-text/out-of-text structure of verification displayed this method visibly in every history book with footnotes. The footnoted page was the distinctive expression of the archival research that provided its foundation. Professionalized history felt scientific to most of its credentialed practitioners; as Michael Bentley notes, 'History, that is to say, had become a form of culturally-acceptable historical science; it had become "technical"; it had learned to require "training"; it celebrated its professors who were now "experts".'

During the formative stages of professionalization when so much effort had to be directed at developing exacting techniques for research, and the concomitant necessity for a demanding course of training for historians, the discipline as a whole was absorbed by the core task of producing reliable factual information about the past. Empiricist assumptions – that empirical methods correctly reflected an empirical world – did not seem to invite questions. The new 'scientific' emphasis on factuality as a standard, and the defining element of history, tended to concentrate attention on having procedures and tests for separating out facts as those assertions about the past that could sustain a critical inspection by other credentialed professionals, a testing process only possible with some common protocols for verification shared and accepted by all historians. Archives, especially collections of administrative, financial, diplomatic, and other non-narrative records, were the arena for the exercise of professional research.

Unlike the erudite amateur of previous centuries, the professional's mastery of evidence was to be encompassing, in depth and breadth, grounding the final written history in a stable base prepared for the critical inspection of other professionals – verification. This regime of verification in which the same standards, procedures, the same high level of acquired technical skills (languages, paleography, philology, diplomatics, and more) could be assumed as the entry credential shared by the cadre of truly professional historians is what seemed at first to align history with science.

Science in a general preview offered a methodology based in replicable conditions for research projects, credentialed researchers trained in similar institutional centers, research results opened to critical inspection by specialist experts, the discipline-wide acceptance of verification, criticism, peer-reviewed results published in professional journals, testing, revision. This view of science appeared capacious enough to include a place for history, albeit a marginal place in view of the irreducibly specific, event-detailed nature of the historical material, and the persistence of narrative form for the end presentation of historical research. Methodological rigor was a big idea, a defining idea inculcated through serious training whose effects extended through all aspects of the now-professional historian's research and newly professional life. And it seemed for a long time enough, enough at least to define history as an aspiring science, or science-like activity. But the commonsense variety of empiricism equated with bias-free objectivity, accepted by most historians, was not a static or universal premise. The historian's version of empiricism based in positivist assumptions about language and reality was facing revision and scepticism even in the nineteenth century, all of which accelerated into the twentieth. The empiricist link between history and past actuality has proved, as Lutz Raphael demonstrates, to be highly contested as both history and empiricism itself have undergone redefinition.

Major contributions to academic history's expanding domain of subject fields with their inherent demands for new approaches and new conceptions of evidentiary adequacy must include the work of R. G. Collingwood, whose influential philosophy of history sought to connect an evidence-based definition of science, applicable to history, with acts of imagination and empathy, as Jan van der Dussen explains. Historians of the *Annales* school stretched traditional ideas of comprehensible chronology to *longue durée* periods and almost indiscernible 'events,' as Joseph Tendler puts it: 'the slowest-paced motors of change; conjunctural, medium-speed, mutations in population sizes and growth, economic cycles and evolutions in social tastes.' Intellectual history defined a practice that came into maturity by the 1950s, evolving from a rich prehistory antedating the term, and extended the range of historically suitable topics into philosophy, folklore, religious belief, arts, and beyond. Donald Kelley notes that attentiveness to the variations over time in the meaning of salient words (culture, experience, medieval, modern) marks intellectual history as an important predecessor to the linguistic turn. Probably the most notable change to the dominant subject matters and viewpoint of academic history was accomplished by social history, introducing the history of everyday life, labor history, non-elite people, or history 'from the bottom up' – a total change of perspective. Within the historians' guild, Brian Lewis describes how the post-war democratizing impulse took academic form in social history's emphasis on mass action and economics, incorporating an implicit materialist causality and preference for quantifiable evidence.

The conceptual 'place' where the generating of facts in sufficient quantity left off, and the very non-scientific business of constructing complex accounts of the past with the non-scientific instrument of language took up the work was not marked for special attention during the decades when commonsense empiricism was taken for granted. The anti-rhetorical plain style favored by the profession

suggested that factuality prevailed in this literary-free zone. The old, but still lingering, idiom of 'writing it up' captures this attitude: the real work of research in all its demanding rigor comes first, followed, merely for the sake of human communication, by 'writing it up' (with 'it' standing for all the thought, argument, constructed patterns, all the 'history' compacted into a spectacularly ambiguous pronoun). All things considered, it did not take historians very long to recognize that the physical sciences grounded in quantifiable data, replicable experiments, and the quest for predictive laws made an incommensurate fit with history, grounded in questions of chronology, specific events, non-replicable situations, social and cultural particularity, and presented in prose compositions wholly unlike laws or models or paradigms. But quietly backing off from 'science' descriptions for the discipline of history does not mean that history would remain a practice without a metadiscourse, lacking the instruments for self-reflection and self-definition. The development of historical theory marks this next stage in the maturity of history as an intellectual and cultural project.

## POSTMODERNISM: THE LINGUISTIC TURN AND HISTORICAL KNOWLEDGE

The 'post' of postmodern is less a precise location in time than a passage into a new constellation of interests: postmodernism restored language to a primary place in the foundational elements of history. Eventually, and this is more a stage in a thoughtful process than a precise time, it was too clear that the science-dominated conception of history would not work, the theoretical language of science did not apply. The laboratory model with controlled experiments was not how history was done, and an historian's research projects were not tried out over and over in the same way by other historians to see if they too would arrive at the same results – essentially write the same articles and books. Historians do come to consensus acceptance of well-founded historical work as fully researched and persuasive accounts of specific times and situations are produced, which then motivate further studies that extend, add depth and nuance, and locate variations, around a generally accepted picture, and this process is analogous to the stages of scientific advance described by Thomas Kuhn. But replicable results, on a scientific model, are not what historians mean by the advance of historical knowledge.

Most importantly, even as historians seek causes and patterns beyond the 'thingness' of one-time events, history remains irreducible if it is to remain history. History does not boil down to abstract predictive descriptions (theories or laws, or paradigms or models) leaving behind the textured detail of recorded life, the irreducible concreteness of social, cultural, and political events, and all the significant detritus of lives lived in particular times in particular places. The historical account, narrative in form, whose generalizing argument is expressed *in and through* all the specificity of past actuality, *is* history – all of it. To say that 'power tends to corrupt' is a conclusion proven by multitudes of historical examples from numberless times and places, and on every scale from small to great, may be to say something true, but it is not saying something historical. The historical instances of certain kinds of power acquired by particular persons or groups in a place, at a time, attended by all the deep context and circumstantial detail specific to *this* power, used in *these* ways, are history, even when a banal truism can be abstracted from it.

In any case, the procedures for scrutinizing and controlling the evidentiary base for history (primary research/establishing facts) that come closest to scientific inquiry outside the humanities take place at a point logically prior to, or are subsumed within, the historical work that 'theory,' in the newer sense, takes as its domain. Theory in this sense confronts history at the level of its greatest complexity: where the historian deploys the now-verifiable information, described in value-saturated language, into long intelligible

sequences whose connections and emphases make the reader see the meaning immanent in events-in-time. The historian's work is to expose meanings residing 'in,' and yet concealed in, the simultaneity and onward push of everything that happens by transforming mere sequence into narrative, narrative that is 'about' something more than the events that make it up.

The philosopher Louis O. Mink's term for this is 'configurational comprehension,' one of the three fundamental modes of comprehension by which we organize and grasp reality. The other two, in Mink's indispensable analysis, are the deductive theoretical mode of science, which comprehends things as instances of a formula or law, and the categoreal mode typical of philosophy, which collects defined objects into categories. The mode of comprehending the world through complex sets of concrete relationships and configurations, characterizes history and literature, and is a primary way of giving structure and intelligibility to the world of specific persons in social organization and cultural surrounds, causing and reacting to events. Theoretical analysis is drawn to this level, the complex configuration, because the historian makes this artifact of language and offers it as knowledge. The configuration of relations over time, one of the irreducible modes of knowledge, is the written history, in its entirety.

The idea of history in the precise sense of a 'cultural artifact of language' is the premise of all postmodern approaches: the linguistic turn of postmodernism returned language to the foreground of attention and recognized the power of language to constitute as well as reflect reality. It should be evident, by now, that this enhanced respect for language does not diminish or undermine the epistemological status of history, or deny its ability to produce reliable knowledge, nor does it sever the referential connection to the actuality of the past of this highly evolved and rigorous artifact of language. All information offered as a genuine contribution to knowledge (regarded as justified belief) has to take verbal form or it cannot undergo verification or systematic criticism. The concept of history as a cultural artifact of language is stable and comprehensible once we recognize that our history has to meet the standard for history in the modern discipline. The term 'cultural' points directly to those standards – ours, not those of Herodotus or even Gibbon.

More than any other single scholar, Hayden White has brought the full meaning of this recognition to the discipline of history: that history is made of language – language in complex, meaning-fraught formulations that emanate from the active mind of the historian-writer, and are not passively copied from the world. 'History,' its narrative form and its meanings, always *feels* found, and always is made; the many facets of this radical insight have been explored by White with unequalled depth and precision. The necessity for historians to understand and use literary critical concepts and modes of exegesis to grasp the textuality of documents; the essential recognition that narrative is made, and not found; and the cultural origins of what feel like 'inevitable' plot types for history – these near-universally accepted practices speak to the deep influence of White's work. The essays by Robert Doran and Kalle Pihlainen examine the elements of White's thought that have opened out the very self-definition of history to include tropological language, the ways that meaning is caught in figuration, the structural components of narrative form, and the plots shared between fictional literature and history. The influence of Jacques Derrida should be considered here as well, as an essential part of the challenge to empiricist assumptions posed by the linguistic turn of postmodernism. Most often associated with deconstruction, a concept and hermeneutic addressed to linguistic signification, Derrida's thought is often considered difficult and paradoxical, often misunderstood. Robert Stein presents Derrida primarily through his reflections on historical agency, causality, and change. Classical rhetoric, an essential stream of conceptual language-about-language,

revived for contemporary use by the linguistic turn, remains the source for our basic conceptual instruments for analysing representation on every scale, and argumentation in the fullest sense. Hans Kellner places the procedures that construct the persuasive argument, all of them systematically laid out in rhetorical concepts, in the foreground of his essay, aligning the writing of history with its rhetorical instruments.

Michel Foucault's impact on historical interpretation remains strong, albeit complicated, with certain of his contributions absorbed almost totally into the taken-for-granted assumptions of historians; the very word, 'power,' in historical usage invokes his presence. Clare O'Farrell traces his career and impact on history. Not a professional historian in training or research method, Foucault characterized his work as philosophical in focus while historical in materials, working out original approaches to historical problems such as punishment and control, incarceration, medical diagnosis, and management. His work on sexuality in antiquity has influenced the formation of a new field of inquiry, demonstrating how bodies and sexual acts could be 'read' as texts of hierarchy and power relations.

The sharpened attention to narrative, a form shared by history and fiction, to rhetorical tropes as the very shapes of meaning, to rhetorical techniques for persuasive argument, and the entire panoply of language-based concepts centrally involved with historical knowledge, has meant that the distinction between history and fiction has had to be redrawn more carefully. Narrative theory, the systematic examination of how narratives are constructed, how plots are organized and causality or agency located, covers fiction and history equally, but historians rightly remain concerned to establish a stable truth-claim for their accounts. Thus, as Ann Rigney recognizes, what is at stake for historians is 'its [narrative's] functionality in the production of historical knowledge.' The boundaries and intersections of history and fiction, examined here by Ann Curthoys and

John Docker, remain nodes sensitive to threat and instability, especially when the *longue durée* of historical writing is surveyed, with tensions intensifying as the linguistic turn reached history. 'History,' Cuthoys and Docker note, 'has a double character; it both partakes of the world of literary forms, and at the same time is a rigorous intellectual practice which seeks to achieve historical truth.

This double character … is also perhaps the secret of history's cunning as an inventive, self-transforming discipline ….' The framework of historical theory holds together the instruments provided by narrative theory, rhetoric, discourse analysis, and related domains of the linguistic turn for continuing analysis of history as a cultural artifact of language with a compelling truth-claim.

# Modernity and History:
# The Professional Discipline

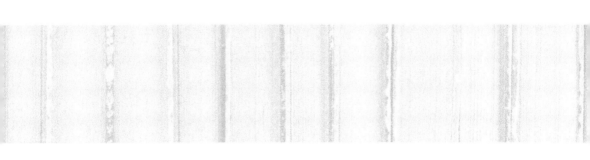

# 1

# The Turn Towards 'Science': Historians Delivering Untheorized Truth

Michael Bentley

A certain unease has always characterized historians' relation to theory in the West and no single period has shown itself free from that discomfiture. But perhaps one can identify an extended moment in western historical discourse – one running from around 1870 to at least the First World War and possibly the Second – when new currents of excitement over the possibility of unending discovery surrounded historical writing and captivated a young historical profession desperate to assert its cultural authority. Never had the exuberance of 'scientists' (an 1830s word) been so marked, never their achievements so remarkable by 1870. No century had produced so many scientific advances as the nineteenth. It was not simply that Darwinist biology had placed human and natural history in a novel and compelling frame since 1859, with many implications for the nature of historical development as a whole. Spectacular feats of engineering and technology, from iron ships to transatlantic cables to the first, unsteady flights of man-made machines accelerated the sense of time

itself as space reduced seemingly to a conquerable sphere.[1] The city, with its new ethnicities and social problems, declared its primacy as a unit of analysis to which the new disciplines of sociology and anthropology turned their eye and made historians quarrel over their own apparent failure to look in that direction. Economies, in an era of first and second industrial revolutions, became urgent objects of study as 'political economy' lost its impressionistic gentility from 1870 and became a science quite as mathematical as it was dismal. Class and popular unrest in the wake of the Paris Commune and the first Russian revolution scarcely fitted whig complacencies about social harmony or the everlasting progress promised by an invisible hand. Even theology demonstrated that nothing was sacred with it historicized Christ, its patter of 'hermeneutics', its search for deeper, more authentic narrative and exegesis. The world demanded new forms and levels of answer to the questions its radical nature implicitly posed; and those demands invaded more than the laboratories and consulting rooms of a Curie or a Freud. Present urgencies informed each section of the past believed relevant to understanding it and historians found themselves faced with a dilemma: whether to prosecute the subject in its traditional modes – biography, constitutional narrative, uplifting accounts of burgeoning democracy and freedom – or to face into the wind, rethink and retool. We shall see that the dilemma produced no uniform pattern in the response of historians but that, whatever it produced, it left behind a sense of the historical enterprise that felt different from those depicted by previous generations – one receptive to analysis, untainted by subjectivity, licensed by scientific credential.

All of this owed something to changing structures imposed by a new 'profession' and those developments prompt a pause in any study of historical theory because the structures carried a theoretical imprimatur that made itself no less persistent (or dangerous) for its lacking self-awareness. Coincidental with Darwin's *Origins* (1859), the foundation of Berlin's *Historische Zeitschrift* marked a significant departure in systematizing knowledge and offered an example of what a more professional forum might look like. And indeed the German academy established a clear leadership in the movement to establish chairs of history and turn Berlin, Göttingen, Bonn, Leipzig into significant nodes of historical 'research' – itself a concept drawn from the natural sciences – that drew to the German historical schools promising young men from France, Britain and the United States.[2] So often in the biographies of major historians who flourished in the half-century after 1860 one finds among the experiences of their early life a period of study in German universities where young scholars learned the language, absorbed the culture and sometimes the Idealism of their new environment and brought home both a training in the scientific treatment of sources – *Quellenkritik* – and a role-model in the century's greatest historical genius, Leopold von Ranke (1795–1886). Yet, one after the other,

those other countries followed where Germany had led in establishing their own professoriate and opening graduate schools in which their students could be home-grown. By the turn of century, Johns Hopkins and Columbia had asserted the nativism of graduate study in their new schools aimed at retaining the best of the new generation at home. By 1885 Paris had established an academic regime in history that already threatened to overtake the German establishment.[3] By 1900 the Universities of Oxford and Cambridge had made significant strides in developing a new cadre of British historians, though the real energy-centres for the move came in the newer, technological universities that emerged in the context of economic depression after 1885, apart from their pioneer institution, Owens College, that would shortly become the University of Manchester with its formidable intellectual leader in the medievalist Thomas Frederick Tout (1855–1929).[4]

That each of these trajectories towards establishing a salaried historical profession led their societies in significant directions and guided the kinds of education available to their young seems obvious enough. Less apparent may be the degree to which this climate of historical work was not theoretically neutral. It formed in reaction to a style of historical writing carried out by the gentlemen scholars of a more sedate epoch, the expansive age of Bancroft, Motley, Macaulay, Carlyle and Michelet. These romantic narrators had not merely assumed but self-consciously theorized that the point of writing lay in communicating a story with a plot to readers who resided mostly outside the academy. The cliché that reminds us that Macaulay wanted his historical books to grace the lady's dressing table along with the latest three-decker novel is relevant to the theme but misses the seriousness of his intention. It was not a matter of selling books or becoming famous – though both had their attractions; he wanted to insist rather that history *consisted* in that presentation of pictures to the imagination that his earlier essays had asserted as fundamental to the historical enterprise. Evidence mattered, to a degree, though imagination could infuse it in ways that laboratory study would declare illegitimate. Equally, knowledge – understood as the accumulation of certified facts – would remain the precondition for all successful historical evocation. Joining all these prescriptions together in a seamless fabric of the created past, however, the idea of narrative played a central role and with it the art (it could be no less) of constructing it in a form that satisfied the objective of stimulating the reader's sense of being there among the events portrayed, seeing them happen in the mind's eye as might a fascinated observer watching through a window. The past became compelling by its having been rendered into a present through which author and reader could experience its immediacy, share the thrill of great figures, exciting panoramas. In that way the present discovered, too, an explanation of itself: how we got from how things were then to where they are now. So history had learned to reconnect readers to a real but transient state of affairs in the past and by so doing deepened their self-location and understanding in a vision that struck many as noble and satisfying.

The new dispensation did not abolish that vision but rather introduced protocols for limiting it. Training in the rigours of source-criticism militated against emotional excess. 'Imagination' began its long and tortuous journey away from a recommendatory term with its own adjective ('imaginative') to a negative term with a contemptuous one ('imaginary'). Astonishing strides in laboratory and natural sciences beckoned history forward to a better-grounded future, one that rested on a fresh conception of *method* that would focus on a revised notion of appropriate content. Quite how frictionless the process might become depended to an extent on which culture attempted it. For the Anglophone world it would always prove slow and partial. So rich was the 'whig' heritage that no matter how scientistic prominent historians might turn out to be, a recalcitrant minority would always hold out for the older model of communicative sympathy and drama.[5] For the French it fed from a very different

stream. The espousal of science as an historian's objective ran back into the first half of the century and the generation of Guizot.[6] The age of Gabriel Monod and Hyppolyte Taine had but to deepen an existing cultural tendency. Americans, meanwhile, had whigs of their own but picked up some of the new movements after the foundation of their own specialist journal, the *American Historical Review*, in 1895 and the emergence of a self-conscious New History some years later. Italians had no whigs but plenty of Hegelians and Marxists, which kept them out of the laboratory for longer than most.

This horizon dominated by an emerging conception of 'science' merits a moment of reflection to consider just three texts from these divergent nations that commented in a very direct way on the new development. To place Britain first feels paradoxical but then everything about Henry Thomas Buckle (1821–62) attracts paradox: the eccentricities of a gentleman scholar, the combination of vision and madness that infused his unfinished *History of Civilization in England* (1857–8), the echoes of Comte and the younger Mill, the undertow of animus against the history of kings and queens, the premature death. Yet Buckle mattered for his status as a pioneer of a strain of thought that others would take forward, often by bouncing off his passionate text. The world of 1850s rationalism leaps from every page and showed how the world did not need to wait for *On the Origin of Species*, which appeared in the following year, to anticipate the call for making history the study of laws of development made accessible to the intellect by a reformed historical method that would rise above describing contingency to find regularity:

This expectation of discovering regularity in the midst of confusion is so familiar to scientific men that among the most eminent of them it becomes an article of faith: and if the same expectation is not generally found among historians, it must be ascribed partly to their being of inferior quality to the investigators of nature, and partly to the great complexity of those social phenomena with which their studies are concerned.[7]

That few thought his programme feasible or desirable does not detract from Buckle's significance as a major irritant. Lord Acton's review of him was, as always, masterly and, more than usually, conclusive. Its terms bear recalling because they announce the frame of the discussion that would so often surround the discourse of history as a *Naturwissenschaft* for the next hundred years. Lord Acton's famous review of Buckle pinned him to the board like a dead insect, alleging that history would degenerate into 'tabular views of births, deaths, marriages, diseases, prices, commerce, and the like; and the historian would be chiefly useful in providing grocers with cheap paper to wrap up butter in'.[8] For all that, thoughtful commentators on the place of science in history frequently began their thinking with Buckle if only to transcend him.

One who certainly felt his influence lived far away in Florence. Italian culture is often marginalized through linguistic ignorance but any temptation to ignore Pasquale Villari (1826–1917) would mislead any student of the scientific turn. Best known for his political career – Villari committed himself impressively to the ideals of the *Risorgimento* and the politics of Garibaldi in 1859–60, with a senatorial and ministerial career later in his life – he became simultaneously the historian of Florence, of Savonarola, of Machiavelli. What he brought to these studies was a peculiarly Italian sense of materialism as the basic drive of action and a view of method that would capture that drive in a systematic way. He found Buckle stimulating in this quest and wrote an essay about him in 1883. But the text for which he deserves to be remembered is a long essay called 'Is history a science?', which he wrote shortly before completing a term as Minister of Public Instruction and that was published in 1891. Reverting to Buckle but also now to J.R. Seeley, Regius Professor of Modern History at Cambridge, Villari felt his early radicalism confirmed in recent controversy and reiterated his stress on science as the key to historical method:

In reality, the scientific method is the only true method, the literary method a false one. The former – unknown before the present day – seeks the *principles* of politics, the *laws* of events, and these can be learned from history alone.[9]

The historian's task becomes threefold when pursuing this agenda: to discover facts, to learn presentation ('a literary labour') but most importantly to seek 'the logical connection of events, the laws by which they are ruled'.[10] Yet he had moved on from the early, crude assertions about history as a nomothetic – i.e. law-seeking – form of enquiry and his Italian cultural background with its continuing emphasis on the relevance on Hegel, reinforced by the genius of Benedetto Croce,[11] and the urgency of Marxist analysis, such as that epitomized in Labriola,[12] prevented him from espousing in later life the mechanical prescriptions of Buckle or Wilhelm Wundt or his own contemporary and critic, de Sanctis.[13] The title of his essay ended in a question mark, after all, and Villari's ultimate position is one that fretted about *reducing* history to science. He urged historians to 'desist from ... futile attempts to go beyond social and moral facts' and realize that their subject 'can never be converted into a philosophical system, nor into a natural or mathematical science'.[14] As Maria Luisa Cicalese perceptively notes, Villari found himself trapped *between* scientific positivism and Italian Idealism: he wanted both to defend scientific method and a conception of history that protected social, religious and above all patriotic values.[15] Science would never satisfy the ultimate needs of man and never penetrate to the inner of world of individual intention. Villari's world retains its reflection of Croce's: individual and world are not separable and individuality embodies universality.

From a very different direction the search for science in a world characterized by ungovernable, chaotic individuals also found a voice in the French historian Paul Lacombe whose treatise *De l'Histoire Considerée Comme Science* followed three years after Villari's in 1894. The first explosion of a

Durkheimian 'sociology' had already left its scars on the Parisian intellectual landscape. Indeed Lacombe toyed with the idea of writing a book about that instead of history and might have done so had not the new sociology come to feel 'un peu exclusive' though its penchant for studying only 'les peoples sauvages et barbares'.[16] He wanted to assert a method and content that would relate to modern society, not Aborigines and Zulus, and the reclamation of its past. In order to do that one would need to break some eggs.

> What, then, is my basic plan? In the first place to show that history can be placed on a scientific footing and, second, that it can only be so placed if it concentrates on certain kinds of material at the expense of others and preference certain methodological procedures, recognizing the insufficiency of some other procedures currently better thought of ....[17]

It was a brave manifesto and also an authoritative one, coming as it did from the Inspector General of Libraries and Archives. But the tone of the volume hardly reflected the *mentalité* of bookstack and folio. From the first page Lacombe recalls Buckle and Taine with wild swipes at existing practice and unevidenced assertions about the forces that control how people behave. These are twofold. For the individual they are psychological and he echoes his more distinguished contemporary, Wilhelm Dilthey, in crediting history with the power to become the true psychology that would reveal a vertical list of drives that begin with food and go down through reproduction to lesser forces. For the social individual they are economic. These forces should become the target-content of history and the historian should see as the primary task of the discipline in the evocation of 'l'homme général' who is the solution to the problem of individual randomness found in anecdotal accounts. Of course, Lacombe knows that it is those discrete individuals who make things happen in the world. 'That is why so many people announce that history cannot be a science. They are absolutely right if we make the individual and individuality

[*l'individu et l'individuel*] one and the same or, to put it another way, if the individual does not always embody those elements that make him similar and equivalent to other individuals.'[18] But (s)he always does, in Lacombe's account. A fundamental objection to his notion of a scientific history thus drops away because he contends that it is possible to study man as opposed to men and to do so historically provided that this expanded individual is placed in a frame that combines space and time. 'The real object of a scientific history is man set in time and space, temporal man or what one might call historical man ...' [19] Like economic man, moreover, this constructed human being is amendable to *hypothesis* since he only has three characteristics – wealth, morality and intelligence – and that incision opens the possibility of a science that will avoid all the messiness of induction of the kind that one finds in conventional historical theory, and reveals a comparative, deductive model of human behaviour that will lend its results something approaching certainty.[20]

Each of these texts conveys a flavour of the scientific moment of the late nineteenth century: the suffusive environment of evolutionary language, the urgency of new methodologies and the reflections of a science of economics that had supplanted the older styles of political economy. The nations that gave rise to them say something, too, about the European currents that would inform discussion of history-as-science for the next half-century. As that argument ran forwards from the 1890s, however, its texture derived less from Britain or Italy or France than from the most avidly-professionalizing historical culture in Europe. Germany was different. Germany had everything: a deep seam of Idealist philosophy running back to Kant and Hegel that would always contradict scientific method; an obsessive commitment to biology, chemistry and psychology that would contradict any other way of proceeding; and a panoply of great literature that insisted on the centrality of *Kultur*, an explosion of empirical discovery that insisted no less loudly on making science culture's vehicle. It could only end in tears when the dominance of Rankean historical tools came under challenge in the decade after the great man's death in 1886. Not for nothing do we use a German theoretical vocabulary in thinking about the *Methodenstreit* of the 1890s. The quarrel over method, for it exceeded debate or argument, permeated all aspects of German intellectual life and in retrospect it focused many of the strands of discussion about the future of history that every country of the West had been facing, each in its own way.

Because other cultures had their own story to tell about the nature of historical enquiry, there is some justification for seeing the *Methodenstreit* as simply a German manifestation of a more general theoretical malaise among those concerned about the future of the humanities in the 1890s. Current scholars tend to have a *penchant* for finding such links and crossovers, moreover, so it is hardly surprising that a mood of reduction has entered the literature in thinking about the bitter German quarrels that historians once read as specific and unique. Georg Iggers has reminded us, for example, that a significant Austrian element should not be ignored: the foundation of Vienna's *Zeitschrift für Sozial- und Wirtschaftsgeschichte* in 1893 brought that voice into the German discussion and underlined the mistake of treating (say) Karl Lamprecht – of whom more shortly – as an isolated case of revolt against established practices.[21] Or one might recur to the French case and individuals such as Durkheim and Simiand and outlets that propagated the new approaches: one thinks at once of Henri Berr's *Revue de Synthèse* (1900) and the *Société d'Histoire Moderne* (1901–3).[22] It brooks no denial that some form of tectonic movement within European and American historical culture had begun by 1890 and that it would have exerted serious influences on historical writing even if the German arguments had proved less vocal than they were. Like all explanations of change, however, this view of the matter may be overworked. German academia did have distinctive features, structures

and assumptions; and the argument over method reached a degree of focus and passion that other countries felt only in more minor key. One can always find analogous developments when thinking about comparative intellectual or cultural history whose protagonists read foreign languages and attend international colloquia. What gives each country or state its particular flavour none the less is the modulations and personalities that gave the arguments and personalities their relevance for that culture. Every state in Europe could in principle have produced a Lamprecht and a Weber; it was the Germans who did and for largely German reasons.

The soil from which a seed of this kind might spring had a peculiar richness and depth. In the 40 years before Lamprecht burst on the national historiographical consciousness, German historians had taken positions which prepared the way for the events of the 1890s. Their godfather – Leopold von Ranke – dominated the stage until the 1880s with a degree of authority that promised, one day, a backlash and a turn to move in directions of which he had disapproved. Darwinian science had made its presence felt and been denounced by those committed to forms of empiricist positivism, such as Georg Waitz, and by those no less committed to literary paradigms of historical representation – Mommsen, Droysen, Ranke himself – so historians knew long before the 1890s about reactions to 'scientism' as a form of procedure.[23] On the other side of the argument the new German economic history associated with Schmoller, Roscher, Knies and others had begun, however tentatively, the characterization of the past in terms of typologies. Indeed it was not accidental that the original instigation of the *Methodenstreit* – the word dates from the early 1880s – can be traced to a robust critique of Schmoller by the Austrian economist Carl Menger arguing against the new 'historical' school. That argument produced a discussion of models and typologies that in their turn became stepping-stones for Max Weber, it has been argued, on his way to thinking through how types might illuminate reality rather than conceal it.[24] No less influential was the force of psychology and an assumed relationship with a kind of socio-biological determinism. Its most extreme proponent, Wilhelm Wundt, reduced intentionality to a raft of external, invisible causes. 'Everything occurs mechanically,' he said, 'and customs produce moral consequences without the latter having been either wished or foreseen.'[25] That Lamprecht met him when he studied in Leipzig in the late 1870s may well have been formative. What remains certain is that the appearance of the early volumes of Lamprecht's *Deutsche Geschichte* lit the bonfire that these previous decades had helped pile.

Karl Lamprecht (1856–1915) occupies a prominent place in the story of 'scientific history', not because of what he achieved but rather through the manner of his failure. Originally an economic historian of the middle ages, he turned in his middle years to the development of ideas about comparative history across societies but also an enhanced social psychology as a way of investigating them internally. The former he brought into play through his edition of a series to which he invited, among others, the great Belgian historian Henri Pirenne to contribute.[26] His concern with social psychology penetrated, with an increasing shrillness, his own contribution, his massive *Deutsche Geschichte* that appeared in 14 volumes between 1895 and 1909. A new edition of the first volume in 1894 gave rise to controversy through its emphasis on collective forces and typologies: the need to apply what nowadays might be called 'social holism' to historical problems by conceiving a society to be more than just the sum of its parts or the actions of individuals. Explanation on this level involved more than description or evocation; it demanded that the historian search for deep causal structures and show how they operated over time.[27] The year 1894 turned out to be a signal one for such pronouncements. In that year, in a lecture at Strasbourg, the philosopher Wilhelm Windelband[28] spoke about 'History and the Natural Sciences' and

popularized a distinction that became part of the controversy in which Lamprecht had implicated himself – that between a 'nomothetic' discipline or area of study and an 'idiographic'one – between subjects whose content allowed explanation resting on laws and others where only a sophisticated form of depiction or evocation would remain possible. Which one worked for history? Lamprecht explicitly called for explanation couched in the language of covering laws and deprecated historians, even and especially Ranke, who had contented themselves with a form of mystical connection with the past through the minds and intentions of individuals. Unsurprisingly, these contentions brought a storm of criticism from professional historians who felt that not only their role-model but their entire discipline had been traduced by a nobody from the University of Leipzig, hardly the centre of German academica. Lamprecht replied in a considered and important statement of his position by contrasting conventional modes of approaching history with the 'new directions' in which he believed history must go.[29] Seeking only a 'Debatte über die Prinzipien unserer Wissenschaft', he walked into a wall of professional resistance.[30]

The details of that resistance have a grim fascination but need not detain us here. It will be enough to understand that through the second half of the 1890s Lamprecht became vilified and marginalized. Not that the argument lay completely on his side. Very few historians today would endorse the scientism that Lamprecht wanted to visit on the profession and some of the reservations expressed by his contemporaries seem both intelligent and necessary. More to the point, however, is the style of his undoing by a rising class of *Jungrankianer* – ambitious young professionals making their way in a competitive and hierarchically structured environment, determined to crush Lamprecht because he threatened the kind of history that they had been taught to write and the career that they expected their writing to generate. Lamprecht himself failed to see what was happening to him and returned continually to the unfairness of his critics in not understanding his intellectual case. He would rail to his friend Pirenne about his treatment and receive soothing letters in beautiful French: 'Il m'a semblé que l'auteur n'avait compris ni votre but, ni votre méthode, et les traits qu'il lance tombent sans vous atteindre'[31]; or, most perceptively, following an attack by Finke in 1897, 'une fois de plus, votre adversaire se dérobe dès que la question théorique se pose. Il y a là une véritable masque d'impuissance.'[32] But in fact Lampecht's critics had a good deal of *puissance*, which derived not from their ideas or intellects but from their location within the most professionalized structure in Europe. Lamprecht never recovered, even when he became an apologist for the aggressive Wilhelmine state in 1914. He remained an isolated and bitter figure who had championed 'science' of one kind only to be defeated by a different understanding of 'historical science' – one that turned on conventions established in the second half of the nineteenth century and which pretended to hold out the promise of historical truth rather than the manipulation of arbitrary 'theories'. Lamprecht's perceptive biographer records the situation in sad but accurate resignation:

> Of the *Methodenstreit* it suffices here to note that Lamprecht's ambitions foundered on constraints that were stronger than he. These took the form of historiographical traditions and conventions of argument that were tenaciously defended by men who, although they were less imaginative than Lamprecht, were far more adept at moving within the established boundaries of the profession, where the issue was ultimately decided.[33]

Or so it seemed to those whose eyes had focused on the *Lamprechtstreit* rather than the wider picture. Not only did the issues raised after 1891 continue to ripple outwards in the historical profession, but one theme dominating those issues – that of the relation of individual and society as subjects of historical investigation – also proved of permanent significance because of its later treatment by one of the most powerful minds produced in the human sciences in the last two centuries.

We have to move south-west, from Leipzig to Freiburg. There the theoretical problem posed by trying to encapsulate individual human action within a conceptual framework deeply exercised the philosopher Heinrich Rickert who had come to believe that individuals, conceived as random agents, would always escape the compass of any concept, however sophisticated. He reacted against the individualist psychology of the Berlin philosopher Wilhelm Dilthey who sought to construct a process of empathetic communication or *Einfühlung* between historical individuals and the investigating historian.[34] But he reacted no less strongly against trying to subsume the vagaries of individual actors with all their randomness and irrational purposes under the categories of a conceptual scheme. Instead he sought a redefinition of 'individuality' in the style of Lacombe and tried to produce a conceptual basis for enquiry in the human sciences. The result was hardly a best-seller and it is a reasonable guess that most historians never looked at it. *Die Grenzen der Naturwissenschaftlichen Begriffsbildung* (1902), or *The Limits of Forming Scientific Concepts*, had its own significance all the same, partly for its thesis but more so for the discussions of its theme that Rickert conducted with a colleague who was almost his exact contemporary, an economist with a compelling historical mind that nursed the ambition of achieving conceptual schemata that would take him beyond Rickert. His name was Max Weber.[35]

Reluctantly at first, but then with increasing conviction, Weber came to accept the force of Rickert's objection to an unproblematized history of individual action while sharing his sense that history must operate both conceptually at some level yet with a purchase on contingent behaviour. The mental space between these two convictions became the domain within which Weber's mature thought expressed itself, leading eventually to his master-work *Wirtschaft und Gesellschaft* [*Economy and Society*] but also to his most important venture in applying concepts to a specific historical problem in his famous essay on *The Protestant Ethic and the Spirit of Capitalism*.[36] Neither Rickert nor Weber had played a direct role in the *Methodenstreit* but they took its message forward and produced a synthesis that would prove of lasting importance within the theory of historical study. The crude notion found in Buckle or Villari or Lacombe that individual behaviour could be rendered explicable in nomothetic statements Weber firmly rejected. Instead he sought to create a new category of concepts that he called, following the phraseology of the German jurist and sociologist Georg Jellinek, an 'ideal type'. 'Ideal' in this formulation did not correspond to a sense of best-possible; rather, it reflected a German emphasis on ideality as a world of mental constructs. The ideal type did not exist in the world as a demonstrable *thing*: in Weber's own dialect it had the nature of a *ratio cognoscendi* as opposed to that of a *ratio essendi*. It arose in the mind of the historian after an immersion in empirical evidence, not as an explanation of the evidence but as a form of classification from which the deviations of individual instances could be read as significant. If an ideal type did not subsume all items of historical knowledge, neither could any piece of that knowledge in itself disprove the ideal type. It was thus a style of concept-formation that side-stepped the difficulty that Rickert had identified many years before since its point often lay precisely in identifying instances which did *not* fit the typology in order to move towards a better-structured account of causation in an historical problem. It functioned as a control-mechanism which responded to what he called 'the basic duty of scientific self-control'.[37] So an ideal type had to be understood, Weber said, as 'an ideal limiting concept with which the real situation, or action, is compared,' rather than as a description of the reality itself; and it would show, not what had to happen or what actually happened, but rather 'what course human action of a certain kind *would* take if it were strictly purposive – rationally oriented, undisturbed by error or emotions,

and if, furthermore, it were unambiguously oriented towards one single, especially an economic, purpose'.[38]

'Economic' deserves its stress as a qualifier of Weber's historical theory because the ideal type inevitably brings to mind thoughts of economic 'models' and the often dubious accounts of 'economic man' that have arisen from them. What rescued Weber's conception was its relation to empirical investigation and its celebration of the Type as a suggestive instrument rather than a lowest common denominator of reality. He wanted to produce a 'pattern', certainly; he accepted an element of 'rationalization'. Both ambitions, however, had to take their subordinate place in a schema that sought 'observed deviations' from that 'ideal typical construction of rational action'.[39] Here was a view of the subject that had none of *a priorism* that historians saw in Lamprecht. It becomes noticeable, indeed, that the disciples of Ranke who had eviscerated the Leipzig historian found much to admire in Weber. The same Friedrich Meinecke who had played so negative a role in the *Methodenstreit* expressed warm views about him. Otto Hintze, another critic of Lamprecht, went on to deploy some of Weber's methodology in his own work on European constitutional history.[40] To write off the *Methodenstreit* as a minor quibble among historians misses the point, therefore, in a major way. Once we move away from the idea that the issues concerned only Germany (and then only between 1891 and 1898) it becomes plain that the turn to science involved more than a reduction of history to scientific method along the lines pioneered by writers over-fascinated by Darwin. But what *kind* of science? The availability by 1914 of a sophisticated sense of 'scientific' enquiry with a conceptual essence may lead one to expect that historians would espouse it. The historical problem consists in explaining why they did not.

Professionalization, we saw at the outset of this discussion, brought its own view of science, one that sat awkwardly with the recommendations of its more radical members who wanted to move toward an explicitly 'scientific' method. It is hard to turn a profession towards science when it believes itself already to have turned. It is especially hard when professional orthodoxy hardens into a view that it, and it alone, embodies a scientific methodology appropriate to its subject matter. One reason why the German crisis over method seems so significant in retrospect lies among the arguments provided by the *opponents* of change. Meinecke, von Below, Finke, Lenz all had detailed criticisms to make of Lamprecht but the primary one concerned his failure to understand that history already had its own conception of scientific method – the one pioneered by their master, Leopold von Ranke. As von Below put it at the end of an 80-page thrashing, Lamprecht's system was right only in the parts that were not new. The bits that were genuinely new were also completely wrong.[41] History, that is to say, had become a form of culturally acceptable historical science; it had become 'technical'; it had learned to require 'training'; it celebrated its professors who were now 'experts'. Each issue of the *Historische Zeitschrift* or *Revue Historique* or the *English Historical Review* or *American Historical Review* breathed a confidence that the subject had moved on from romantic narratives in the direction of 'analysis' and 'research' – terms drawn from the discourse of natural science. Rather than helping that process forward, a sympathy with Lamprecht's social psychology or Durkheim's sociology, or Frazer's anthropology threatened to retard and redirect it. Of course there were important dissenting voices. No one in Paris could glance at Berr's *Revue de Synthèse* without sensing the excitement of conceiving the human sciences as interpenetrative.[42] It was another matter to expect professional historians to envisage being penetrated. When some of these ideas reached the American Historical Association in 1903, the record of the proceedings showed, among the abuse, an alarmed coterie anxiously resisting the tide.[43] Despite the imagination of James Harvey Robinson and his colleagues in fomenting a 'new history',[44] the old retained

its grip through a professional cadre now raised in American graduate schools. In England the serenity remained mostly unbroken. This complacency, for such it was, owed much to *not* experiencing a *Methodenstreit* outside the new field of economics. When one professor with European inclinations tried to tell the Oxford History Faculty to move in the direction of undergraduate research and compulsory dissertations, on the lines that Tout had introduced at Manchester University, he not only failed but was also made to apologise to the Faculty for implying criticism of their methods.[45] Oxford thus joined hands with Berlin and Baltimore in promoting a conception of history and its young audience to which only a professional guild could effectively minister.

The guild rejected theory while simultaneously embodying one. Essentially, it rested on a view of what knowledge amounted to and a certainty that the gaining of that knowledge formed the purpose historical teaching and study. Valuable knowledge resided in certain areas of discussion: constitutional history, the history of the state and statesmanship, the history of religion and the military history that so often showed how things turned out the way they did. Knowledge of this kind was available, its proponents said, and accessible. It could be disseminated through general textbooks that covered a wide period and include a ballast of relevant 'facts' which the historian had 'discovered'. And it was available in the first place – the fundamental assumption – because the world was roughly how it seemed when investigated empirically. It did not hide behind a veil; there was no sense of concealment. Truth was visible to the naked eye or, if that failed, to the microscope or telescope. What got in the way of it was blindness. Sometimes the blindness acted as a screen for stupidity: you had to be bright, or at least attentive, to do history. More often it had a willful character that could be expressed in a word that typified this epistemological model. It suggested 'bias'. Once introduced into historical thought through a version of 'common sense' philosophy, this devastating term and its antonym 'objectivity' formed the minds of young people as it still does a hundred years later. Historians learned and taught that knowledge was available and accessible so long as they did not fall victim to 'bias' and remained 'objective' in their work. All pre-conceptions must be set aside; all value-judgments must be suspended; politics and religion should be shuffled-off at the study door. Historians took down from the hook at the back of that door the white coat of science that would clothe their history as completely as it clothed their body.

A second feature followed from the first. History could not emerge from ideas, concepts, theories, hypotheses, questions. These obviously carried the stains of those very preconceptions from which the subject needed to free itself: they bore the marks of an author when the exercise recommended, as Ranke had indeed taught, that the author should 'dissolve' at the desk. So an 'objective' history had to begin elsewhere with things that existed in the real world and on which everybody could focus scientific attention. Thus began the notion that history began with the 'evidence' and that the evidence lay in the past among the 'sources'.[46] This move further cemented professional solidarity and self-regard because only those students trained in *Quellenkritik*, or source-criticism, could hope to make sense of a very technical and demanding subject. Good German would come into play even in the study of modern periods of history. (French was assumed.) For all previous periods Latin and perhaps Greek or Hebrew would prove a *sine qua non* for serious analysts. Historians could thus hold up their heads when they entered Faculty meetings with the scientists whose fields – biology, chemistry, physics, cosmology – now exploded with significant and 'objective' conclusions. Perhaps that was the point.

Whatever its rationale, an intra-professional theory buttressed the rising cadre of historians in the universities of the West in the first half of the twentieth century, blocking serious intrusions from more radical (and often better-grounded) persuasions. Interesting challenges emerged, as they always will among intelligent people. The *Annales* School in France, with its exciting research agendas and attempts to overturn epistemological premises, made some headway into the Parisian establishment after 1930 and became itself hegemonic after 1950. In America during the Depression, Carl Becker and Charles Beard tried, with less success, to pull the American Historical Association towards a more sceptical account of historical factuality.[47] British historical thought would have received a shot in the arm during the same years, had it not missed, from the astringencies of Robin Collingwood and Michael Oakeshott. Italian, German and Iberian historians had problems of their own and saw their subject bent into the opposite of objectivity by Fascist and Nazi rednecks. Standing back from all these complications, an observer of 'science' in its many forms and dialects sees perhaps two epochs in the ongoing argument after 1870. The first, running to about 1960 or 1970, displayed a preoccupation with prophylactics against science unless it took the form that the professional class of historians deemed congruent with an objectivity/bias model of the subject. The second, dating from the 1960s but distorted in its responses by the 'linguistic turn' and its consequences, has espoused science of the kind that radical spirits before the First World War identified as important to understanding the past – anthropology, sociology, global perspectives. That adoption has produced a theoretical subject in the place where once historians thought they had control over an empirical one. Many of the theories have turned out, in their turn, to be weird, unworkable or dead ends. But at least the subject has now shed the false dignity of imagining itself a repository of unshakable truth-claims resting on crystalline 'facts'. In shedding it, moreover, historians have not merely arranged their lives in a better relationship with science; they have also come to terms, arguably for the first time in this complicated relationship, with what scientists themselves believe scientific work to involve. The real turn to science has followed from turning a face towards those questions, hypotheses and reflections to which historians were once wont only to turn a blind eye.

## NOTES AND REFERENCES

1   Stephen Kern, *The Culture of Time and Space 1880–1918* (1983).
2   The use of 'men' is, of course, deliberate. Only after the turn of the century did women begin in any numbers to follow the same paths. For the context of this issue see Bonnie G. Smith, *The Gender of History: Men, Women and Historical Practice* (Cambridge, MA, 1998).
3   See William R. Keylor, *Academy and Community: The Foundation of the French Historical Profession* (Cambridge, MA, 1975). For the German profession over a similar period, see Wolfgang Weber, *Priester der Klio: Historisch-sozialwissenschaftliche Studien zur Herkunft und Karriere deutscher Historiker und zur Geschichte der Geschichtswissenschaft 1800–1970* (Frankfurt am Main, 1984).
4   Peter Slee, *Learning and a Liberal Education: The study of Modern History at the Universities of Oxford, Cambridge and Manchester* (Manchester, 1986); Reba Soffer, *Discipline and Power: The University, History and the Making of an English Elite 1870–1930*; Michael Bentley, 'The organization and dissemination of historical knowledge', in Martin Daunton (ed.), *The Organization of Knowledge in Victorian England* (Oxford, 2005), 173–98.
5   See M. Bentley, *Modernizing England's Past: English Historiography in the Age of Modernism 1870–1970* (Cambridge, 2005), esp. 92–116.
6   'Nothing could be more scientific,' writes one of his students, 'than his detached and objective style.' Douglas Johnson, *Guizot: Aspects of French History 1787–1874* (1963), 327.
7   T.H. Buckle, *The History of Civilization in England*, 2nd edn (Vol. 1, 1858), 6.
8   Lord Acton in *The Rambler* (1858), printed in Acton, *Essays on the Liberal Interpretation of History: Selected Papers*, ed. W.H. Mc Neill (Chicago, IL, 1967), 3–21 at 18.
9   *La Storia è una Scienza?* (1894), reprinted in English translation in *Studies: Historical and Critical* (1907), 4–5.
10  Ibid., 45.
11  B. Croce, *What is Living and What is Dead of the Philosophy of Hegel?* (trans. Douglas Ainslie, 1915).
12  Antonio Labriola, *La Concezzione Materialistica della Storia* (Bari, 1942).
13  For the intellectual currents surrounding Villari in these years see Fulvio Tessitore, 'La storiografia come scienza', *Storia della Storiografia*, 1 (1982), 48–88, esp. 69–75.
14  *Is History a Science?*, 108.
15  Maria Luisa Cicalese, 'La storia è una scienza? Villari fra positivismo e idealismo', *Rassegna Storica Toscana*, 44 (1998), 91–112.
16  Paul Lacombe, *De l'Histoire Considérée Comme Science* (Paris, 1894), viii.
17  Ibid., xiii. My translation.
18  Ibid., 249. My translation.
19  Ibid., 52. My translation.
20  Ibid., 53–63, 131–5.
21  Georg Iggers, 'The "Methodenstreit" in international perspective. The reorientation of historical studies at the turn from the nineteenth to the twentieth century', *Storia della Storiografia*, 6 (1984), 21–32 at 26–7.
22  See Lutz Raphael's impressive critique of too 'national' a frame for the *Methodenstreit* in an important article, 'Historikerkontroversen im Spannungsfeld zwischen Berufshabitus, Fächerkonkurrenz und sozialen Deutungsmustern: Lamprechtstreit und französicher Methodenstreit der Jahrhundertwende in vergleichender Perspektive', *Historische Zeitschrift*, 251 (1990), 325–63, esp. 327–8.
23  For a development of this point, see Michael Maclean, 'German historians and the two cultures', *Journal of the History of Ideas*, 49 (1988), 473–94.
24  Cf. Manfred Schön, 'Gustav Schmoller and Max Weber', in Wolfgang Mommsen and Jürgen Osterhammel (eds), *Max Weber and his Contemporaries* (1989), 60–61.
25  Quoted in Steven Lukes, *Emile Durkheim, His Life and Work: A Historical and Critical Study* (Harmondsworth, 1975), 91. This cosmic utterance was announced in 1887, four years before the appearance of Lamprecht's infamous first volume of the German history.
26  This was the origin of Pirenne's renowned *Histoire de Belgique* (Brussels, 7 vols., 1900–32).
27  See Hans Schleier, 'Karl Lamprecht als Initiator einer intensivierten Forschung über die Geschichte der Geschichtsschreibung', *Storia della Storiografia*, 2 (1982), 38–56, esp. 40–41.
28  Wilhelm Windelband (1848–1915), Professor at Strasbourg (German after 1871) from 1882 to 1903 and then at Heidelberg.
29  *Alte und neue Richtungen in der Geschichtswissenschaft* (Berlin, 1896)
30  For a detailed discussion of the responses see Karl Metz, 'Der Methodenstreit in der deutsche Geschichtswissenschaft: Bemerkungen zum sozialen Kontext wissenschaftlicher Auseinandersetzungen', *Storia della Storiografia*, 6 (1984), 3–19.
31  'It seems to me that the author has understood neither your objective nor your method and the spears that he throws fall short of reaching you.' Pirenne to Lamprecht, 19 Feb. 1896, in Bryce Lyon, 'The letters of Henri Pirenne to Karl Lamprecht (1894–1915)', in *Bulletin de la Commission Royale d'Histoire*, 132 (1966), 161–231 at 196.
32  'Once more your opponent runs away as soon as the question of theory arises. In that there is a true concealment of weakness.' Pirenne to Lamprecht, 31 Jan. 1897, ibid., 206.

33  Roger Chickering, 'Young Lamprecht', *History and Theory*, 28 (1989), 210; and the same author's magisterial biography, *Karl Lamprecht: A German Academic Life 1856–1915* (Atlantic Highlands, NJ, 1993).

34  For Dilthey's vision of the historical process see in particular *The Formation of the Historical World in the Human Sciences* (ed. A. Makkreel and F. Rodi). Selected Works, Vol. 3 (Princeton, NJ, 2002).

35  Max Weber (1864–1920). Raised in Berlin where his father was a lawyer and National Liberal Deputy. Studied at Heidelberg, Berlin and Göttingen; doctorate in medieval commercial law. Professor of Economics at Freiburg, then Heidelberg. But his health was always fragile. Private scholar and statesman until appointed Professor of Economics at Munich in the year before his death.

36  Originally published serially in 1904–5. The English translation was produced by Talcott Parsons with an introduction by R.H. Tawney (London, 1930). It is worth recalling that *Geist* had quotation marks around it in the original.

37  The 'elementare Pflicht der wissenschaftlichen Selbstkontrolle'. Quoted in Jürgen Kocka, 'Zwischen Elfenbeimturm und Praxisbezug: Max Weber und die "Objektivität" der Kulturwissenschaften', in Christian Gneuss and Jürgen Kocka (eds.), *Max Weber: Ein Symposium* (Munich, 1998), 189.

38  Weber, *Economy and Society*, quoted in W.J. Cahnman and A. Boskoff (eds.), *Sociology and History: Theory and Research* (New York, 1964), 116.

39  The phrases are Weber's, quoted in Leonard Krieger, *Time's Reasons: Philosophies of History Old and New* (Chicago, IL, 1989), 127–8.

40  For these and other illustrations, see W.J. Mommsen and J. Osterhammel (eds.), *Max Weber and his Contemporaries* (2006), 2–4.

41  Georg von Below, 'Die neue historische Methode', *Historische Zeitschrift*, 45 (1898), 193–273.

42  For an introduction see Peter Burke, *French Historical Revolution: The Annales School 1929–89* and a more critical account in François Dosse, *Histoire en Miettes: Des 'Annales' à la 'Nouvelle Histoire'* (Paris, 1987).

43  See the report printed in the *American Historical Review*, 9 (1903–4), 437–55, esp, 448–50.

44  James Harvey Robinson, *The New History: Essays Illustrating the Modern Historical Outlook* (New York, 1912).

45  See C.H. Firth's infamous inaugural lecture on *The Historical Teaching of History* (Oxford, 1904), which drew a sharp attack from Sir Charles Oman in his own inaugural two years later.

46  I have discussed the pervasive consequences of this view in my Wiles Lectures, *Modernizing England's Past*, esp. 5–18.

47  Their addresses were printed in the *American Historical Review*, e.g. Carl Becker, 'Everyman his own historian', *AHR*, 37 (1932), 221–36 and C.A. Beard, 'Written history as an act of faith', *AHR*, 39 (1934), 219–31. Beard's more celebrated address called 'That Noble Dream' forms the platform for Peter Novick's compelling account of American historians in *'That Noble Dream': The 'Objectivity' Question and the American Historical Profession* (Cambridge, 1988).

# 2

# The Implications of Empiricism for History

Lutz Raphael

In the world of Anglo-American historians, empiricism has become a current concept that defines one side in the ongoing controversy between those historians who defend their discipline as based on common sense assumptions about facts and historical truth and those that espouse postmodern theories that emphasise the literary qualities of history and criticise the scientific self-understanding of professional historians. In many other countries (e.g. France, Germany or Italy) postmodernism has no larger an audience among historians than in Great Britain or the United States, but its theory is refuted on the basis of other epistemological arguments that often combine hermeneutic views of history with (moderate) constructivist arguments about scientific knowledge in general. In every case, the last 30 years have seen a renewal of epistemic disputes among historians where many arguments echoed older controversies about historical truth and objectivity, the specificity of the historical method and the place of the discipline in the public sphere. Empiricism always did play a certain role in these quarrels although, from an international perspective, it was far from being the one dominant epistemic model as often suggested

by Anglo-American defenders of established norms and current practice, as when Stephen Davies declared: 'For the last 200 years at least, most historians have drawn their professional ideas and beliefs from one theory. This is empiricism. The central doctrine of empiricism, that true knowledge of the world comes ultimately from sense impressions, underlies most of the practices and arguments of professional historians.'[1]

On the contrary, a historical assessment of empiricism in history has to cope with different national or international schools and cultures of historiography, such as German or Italian historicism (Historismus, storicismo), French positivism, American scientific history or Marxism, German Society history (historische Sozialwissenschaft) or the French Annales School. It has to take into account an epistemological pluralism that prevailed among the majority of professional historians over more than two hundred years and informed their arguments against the recurrent criticism of their discipline from the standpoints of relativism, scepticism or science.

Therefore, before looking for the traces of empiricism inside the discipline itself, it seems necessary to spell out what empiricism meant in epistemology and how its meaning has changed since its invention in the seventeenth century.

## EMPIRICISM AND ITS CONFIGURATIONS IN THE HISTORY OF EPISTEMOLOGY

The philosophical doctrine or school of empiricism starts from the argument that knowledge and especially scientific knowledge is dependent on experience, that it is only the more or less sophisticated result of observation and sense impressions. This argument attempts to give an epistemic foundation to the problem of certainty.[2] Empiricism developed in the seventeenth and eighteenth centuries based on the works and arguments of Francis Bacon, John Locke, George Berkeley and David Hume in sharp opposition to the rationalism of Descartes and others who insisted on the importance of a priori, innate ideas as the essential basis of rational, true knowledge. The first philosopher who developed an empiricist programme of scholarly knowledge was Francis Bacon (1561–1626), whose arguments were systematised by his followers. The collection of facts must be the foundation and starting point of every kind of scientific knowledge and these data of observation, when accumulated and logically analysed, are the basic materials for inductive reasoning. Theories and general laws can be derived at the end of a long process of data gathering and inductive conclusions. Therefore, the main task of the single scientist or scholar is to discover new facts or to compare those already observed in order to come to a higher degree of abstraction or generalisation. Empirical methods can be organised as a kind of a collective work in progress in which any single fact of observation has to be regarded as an elementary unit of scientific knowledge.

The empiricists of the eighteenth century were divided on the issue of certainty: scepticism opposed the mainstream optimistic creed on the virtues of sensory observation, and still more the emerging scientific methods of processing measurable data. But the empiricist argument was reformulated and transformed by the critical contribution of Immanuel Kant. He reflected in detail on the mental activity of processing sensory data and tried to combine the older arguments about the two sources of human knowledge (mental and empirical) in an 'idealistic' model. Thus the anti-Cartesian empiricism seemed to be absorbed in a new synthesis. The new scientific techniques of producing new insights by systematic observation and experimentation were explained as the encounter of empirical and aprioristic sources of evidence and certainty. After Kant, at least for many continental schools of philosophy, empiricism has become a philosophical school of the past; its arguments were seen as refuted or reformulated in a new context. Even the epistemology of the natural sciences that followed the Baconian programme with ever increasing success since the end of the eighteenth century borrowed from Kantian idealism to better explain the important role of abstract concepts and mathematics in the natural sciences.

Thus empiricism survived in weaker or stronger forms as a kind of basic epistemological argument about sensory data or experience as a necessary condition for scientific or error-free true statements about the world. This basic empiricist argument became part of larger epistemological models during the nineteenth and the twentieth century. A genuine empiricist tradition was established in Britain and later in the United States whose most prominent thinkers were John Stuart Mill, Bertrand Russell and Alfred Julius Ayer.[3] Positivism, Neo-Kantianism, Pragmatism, Logical Positivism – all took up empiricist arguments in their own way and all these currents added new arguments and made them part of larger theories about human or scientific knowledge.

Internationally, the most important strand was that of positivism, which started from the impulses of eighteenth-century empiricists to build up a unified system of scientific knowledge starting from the sensorial data, from 'positive' facts. Positivism in all its different versions joined the epistemological basis of empiricism to a realistic argument about the existence of the outside world and its accessibility to human knowledge. Augmented by materialism, positivism formed the opposition to the idealistic epistemologies that still dominated in the academic philosophy of the nineteenth century. Together, positivism and materialism gave birth to elaborated philosophies of history from Comte to Marx and Spencer that had a strong impact on the concepts of historiography and the social sciences throughout the nineteenth and the twentieth centuries.[4] The decades from 1890 to 1920 can be regarded as a time of revolutionary change in epistemology. Neither science nor the humanities fit the old models any longer and a series of new epistemic programmes tried to take up the challenge of the paradoxes and uncertainties that new theories and discoveries in scholarly knowledge produced during this time. It was mainly the tradition of logical positivism that gave empiricism new vigour in twentieth-century philosophy. In a period when the main epistemological schools dealing with the humanities, such as Neo-Kantianism, sociology of knowledge, phenomenology, vitalism or hermeneutics, preferred idealistic or aprioristic answers, neo-positivism defended objectivity and its foundation in empirical data or facts and their logical combination.[5]

Since Quine's criticism of the dogmatism of empiricism, analytic philosophy has developed positions that deny the logical relevance of the old difference between empiricism and apriorism or idealism. 'Neutralists' started to criticise the dichotomy between 'idealistic constructivism' and 'empiricist realism' as meaningless. Essential arguments of empiricism have been refuted, including the foundationalist idea of sensory data as the secure basis of knowledge and the idea that single assertions in a larger set of theoretical or practical models of reality can be isolated and subjected to the test (or verification) of falsification. The position of Wittgenstein, that there is no fundamental difference between the change of meanings and the growth of knowledge, undermined the search for certainty that had been the driving force of logical positivism in epistemology. Thus in recent epistemological discussions, neither pure or classic empiricism (that sensory data or facts are the solid anchors of truth and scientific knowledge) nor radical scepticism (often taken up by postmodernism) seemed to fit the new sophisticated arguments of epistemology. New schools of thought, such as system theory or evolutionary theories of cognition, have developed new arguments and new modes of description that transcend the old dichotomies that had situated empiricism as one of only two possible answers.[6]

## EMPIRICISM AND THE EPISTEMIC CULTURE OF HISTORIANS

The discipline of history echoed these epistemological developments in a more or less distorted, more or less weakened form. Like many other disciplines in the humanities and the sciences, history identified itself by refuting philosophy with its manifold theoretical models of Polity, Morality, Society or universal history, an antitheoretical stance that continued throughout the nineteenth and twentieth centuries. The number of historians who engaged in discussions about the epistemological foundations of their discipline was always limited. Solemn anniversaries or other academic celebrations occasioned speeches and texts that mainly supported the community in their assumptions and avoided deeper reflection on abstract problems. In the course of professionalisation, academic teaching about the theory and methodology of history played only a minor role and the more technical aspects of research soon dominated. But we do not really know enough about the frequency and the contents of these courses to come to valuable conclusions in a comparative view.[7] Systematic debate about the theoretical framework of the historical discipline did continue (the results will be documented and analysed in detail in the following chapters of this handbook), but there is another level of less articulated assumptions about historians' methods and ideas.

As far as historical knowledge and its techniques are concerned these arguments, attitudes and professional habits can be subsumed under the term of 'epistemic culture,' a concept borrowed from the history and sociology of science. Change on this level does not follow the agitated rhythm of the theoretical debates – it has its own pace. This difference may explain why certain debates are repeated several times over without any essential change in the arguments. But on the international level, the different epistemic cultures of the discipline have not yet been studied profoundly so that we have to approach this question more or less indirectly. One possible indicator of change in epistemic cultures are the ways that intellectual controversies are reflected in introductions, handbooks or manuals that try to redefine the conventions and the consensus among historians after disputes. We can discern four great waves of significant and lasting influence in the form of regularly cited articles or introductions into the methods and theories of history that served as textbooks for more than one generation. A first wave started in the decades between 1830 and 1860 when the discipline was shaped and a European discussion about its methods, topics and philosophical background took place. The Rankean model (we will see how ambiguous it was) emerged more or less victorious from this contest of ideas. The next wave occurred around 1900, which saw controversies about the theory and method of history in all greater national communities; in every case it was the new social sciences and the public quest for social and economic history that was a starting point for controversy.[8] The most influential introductions or handbooks that defended the orthodox view or the conventional wisdom of the discipline under attack, those of Langlois–Seignobos and of Bernheim,[9] were published at this time, and they served as authorities for more than two generations of professional historians. We have to wait more

than 60 years before a new wave of discussions and texts arrived. Again the social sciences set the agenda but this time the philosophical issues were much broader. Once again, a number of influential textbooks were the lasting outcome of this conjuncture.[10] The next high tide of theoretical dispute is still building, or is perhaps just ebbing: it started in the 1980s and culminated at the end of the twentieth century when a series of pamphlets and textbooks discussed the methods and theory of history in the face of postmodernism.[11] In these moments of open dispute we can see more precisely what epistemic positions circulate among historians and the relevance of empiricist arguments.

In the case of history, we are dealing with an epistemic culture where the basic concepts of epistemology were often taken for granted and more or less unconsciously joined to often unspoken assumptions behind them. Thus we will meet once again with 'combinations of logically disparate elements'.[12] A look back to the fate of the empiricist tradition in modern historiography has to take account of this hidden agenda behind the theoretical arguments. Recurrent concerns of this agenda were the social norms and cultural images of 'science' or 'certainty'. Thus we have to take into account the institutional and social circumstances that gave meaning and relevance to arguments about abstract theoretical problems that normally are of very little concern to professional historians. One effect of history's specific epistemic culture is that terms such as 'empiricism', 'Faktenpositivismus', 'objectivism' (the term more often used in German, French or Italian studies) or 'objective empiricism'[13] have to be used in the broad sense of a common designation for a set of similar attitudes or arguments historians make about their professional knowledge, its object and purpose, attitudes that coexist with somewhat different epistemic theories such as historism, positivism or social science history. We can identity a group of core arguments concerning different epistemological problems that inform this kind of 'basic' or 'trivial empiricism', as we will call it from now on, in order to differentiate it from the empiricism of epistemological theory and its offshoots like 'positivism', 'logical' or 'Neo-positivism'. These core arguments of 'trivial empiricism' include:

1   The essential empiricist argument that all knowledge comes from experience is accepted. But for history, this proposition is rather ambiguous and had to be adapted because there is no direct observation of the past available for historians. 'Experience' has been replaced by the historical method or source-criticism.
2   Among historians, trivial empiricism is generally linked with another realistic argument in ontology that the world does exist independently of the human mind and that this outer world is accessible to our knowledge. The past does exist independently of present knowledge, and historical documents are transparent to past reality that can therefore be 'reconstructed' or re-narrated in an 'objective' manner. The correspondence theory of truth was probably the most widespread common sense argument on this issue among empiricist historians.
3   In the epistemology of scientific knowledge, empiricism defends the idea that in science single facts or data can be verified independently from the theoretical framework they refer to or within which they have been scientifically generated. For the trivial empiricism we are describing here, historical 'facts' are independent of theories or concepts that the human mind may add in the process of pursuing knowledge. They can be critically tested as far as their 'truth' is concerned; therefore 'facts' are primary elements of historical knowledge. In order to reconstruct these 'facts', the historian has to keep him/herself free from subjective, personal and, especially, moral judgements and preferences; he/she has to develop a sense of 'impartiality' in order to avoid errors and anachronisms.
4   Empiricism defends the logic of induction as the best way to develop more general concepts or to detect regular patterns. In history, this argument underpins the position that the main task of the historian is the accumulation of historical facts by scrutinising new or unexamined sources. Belief in the virtues of inductive logic is often linked to the conviction that abstract concepts should be avoided and

that premature generalising or the use of general theories or models risks distorting the object of inquiry.

We will see that this kind of 'basic' or 'trivial' empiricism has been articulated in many different formulations. It served different functions or purposes in different professional contexts. It found its emblematic formula in the Rankean dictum: 'It [= history] wants only to show what actually happened [wie es eigentlich gewesen]'.[14] Many historians continue to subscribe to all or some of these assumptions. Thus it makes sense to distinguish radical from moderate empiricists, and we can further distinguish 'naive' from sophisticated ones according to their capacity or willingness to defend these arguments by borrowing from more elaborated epistemologies of their time.

## HISTORICAL METHOD AND EMPIRICISM: THE BIRTH OF AFFINITIES IN THE EIGHTEENTH AND NINETEENTH CENTURIES

Empiricist epistemology was a kind of natural ally for historians of the Enlightenment. Their place in society and academe was still uncertain, their discipline merely a component part of other disciplines. Empiricism ennobled historiography and historical research in many ways. Attacking the dogma of Cartesianism with its emphasis on inborn/innate ideas as the only pure and certain basis of human knowledge, it legitimated historiography as a practical yet rational enterprise useful for many kinds of human affairs, from politics to economics. Hume defended the case of history against any radical scepticism or logical criticism on the basis of common sense arguments about the logic of human understanding and communication. It is quite interesting to see that his own scepticism was more scathing against dogmatic scientific certainties than against the 'fabric of history'.[15] The pragmatic argument had become one of the pillars of empiricist convictions. Thus empiricism encouraged critical inquiries about the past that went beyond the small-scale microscopic and specialised erudition of antiquarians and it legitimated the scholarly work of those gentleman historians who were the pioneers of the new historiography of the enlightenment. Until the end of the eighteenth century, 'Science' or 'Wissenschaft' was not analysed within the terms of this new epistemology that referred to human knowledge in general.

Around 1800 a new epistemic situation emerged when the techniques of philological criticism of ancient texts were combined with the new critical spirit that the new historiography of the Enlightenment had propagated throughout Europe. History established itself as an academic discipline in more or less open dispute with two older traditions of historiography: it refuted the generalisations of the philosophers of history who, during the nineteenth century, were popular, very ambitious and very loquacious. Secondly, it had to distance itself from the literary forms of historiography that emerged from the traditions of rhetoric closely linked to history in the unreformed universities, modes of historical writing that flourished along with classicism and romanticism as the great literary movements in Europe between 1780 and 1830. In both cases the empiricist arguments served as a useful weapon. The empirically confirmed 'facts' (*Tatsachen*) did not fit the great narratives of literary historiography or the big theories of philosophy. The deconstruction of these two great narrative traditions was one side of the new methodology. The other side was that of the reconstruction of a new kind of narrative where the single event, the particulars of a broader complex of facts, get more attention and a far greater relevance. 'Individuality' was the philosophical concept developed by Herder, and the German idealism that informed this aspect of the new discipline on the continent added a hermeneutic and idealistic dimension beyond empiricism.

It was of vital importance for the further development of the epistemological concepts in the German-speaking area that the philological and historical disciplines established their new methods slightly in advance of the natural sciences, and that both were subsumed under the new heading of 'Wissenschaft' to become part of the reformed universities inspired by the spirit of neo-humanism. Thus, what Dilthey at the end of the nineteenth century named 'Geisteswissenschaften' (humanities, sciences humaines) early on developed an epistemological separatism which refused to accept the empiricist and later positivist model as an inappropriate domination by methods suitable only for the natural sciences. At the same time, history was established as an autonomous discipline in the new faculties of philosophy.

Niebuhr and Ranke, who established the new norms, were not at all followers of empiricist philosophy. Niebuhr, a specialist in Roman history and a well-trained philologist who was one of the first to use the new term, 'Geschichtsforscher' (researcher), developed and expressed his own new scholarly practice of combining source criticism, search for systematic connections between the facts and a proper narrative of Roman history in terms of the Kantian epistemology of empirical knowledge: the critique (of sources, of traditional epistemic positions) was also a new synthesis, a new system of knowledge. He recurred to metaphors of observation and experience like 'Anschauung' (view) or 'Vergegenwärtigung' (representation) or 'imagination' to explain his new method.[16]

Ranke too was a philosophical idealist and a Protestant historian who saw 'God's work' in history: displayed in his romantic piety before the past as a meaningful tradition; and his idealistic confidence in the continuity between the historical world and the present time. This creed shaped his epistemic model of historical research that strongly stressed the basic empiricist tenets of close observation and objective knowledge. For him the historian is a passive, but very attentive, observer of the past that can be discovered thanks to the new type of archival sources that allow the historian to see past politics in the making. Ranke's favourite sources, the diplomatic records of the Venetian ambassadors, had a great influence upon him. But critical assessment of the 'positive' facts was only one part of the Rankean model, the other part was his idealistic confidence in the continuity of the historical world.[17] The new 'historical method' was nothing other than the recombination of techniques known and continually developed since humanism with the writing of history itself. The criticism of documents became an integral part of the new scholarly reconstruction of the past that culminated in historiography as a new style of historical narration. The unification of these three elements – collection and criticism of the sources; rearrangement/reconstruction of the past; and the writing of a story, a history – gave highest relevance to the sources where the procedures started and to which even the narrative should return whenever it is possible. More and more, this new epistemic objective became the vital centre of the epistemic culture of the new discipline in its formation.

Thus in the first half of the nineteenth century, the historical practice that developed first and with greater speed in the German-speaking countries than elsewhere was theorised in a new, specific language that borrowed much from contemporary idealistic philosophy. It differed from the older empiricist idiom by its constructivist view which underlined the active role of the mind (both as the subject and the object of historical knowledge) in surpassing the older forms of antiquarian erudition and philosophical generalisation.

A new situation arose between 1850 and 1880 when the newly professionalised discipline in Central Europe and France, Britain and the United States grew and established its institutions of research, teaching and communication: public archives, source editions, journals and university chairs. The relationship between the various specialised disciplines and philosophy, between science and religion, was hotly discussed and new models or systems of knowledge and new epistemologies proposed. Empiricism split into two divergent idioms: the first followed the trend of the natural sciences and tried to establish a comprehensive model of science. This tendency gave birth to different systems of 'positivist scientism' by defining all scientific disciplines by their goal of establishing general 'laws' on the basis of systematic and controllable observation. The discovery and verification of regularities and 'causal chains' became the essential part of this programme. The second strand of empiricism was sceptical about the possibility or the utility of such a unified model both for natural and 'moral' sciences. Instead, it defined the emergent new disciplines by their methods: the construction of positive facts and inductive logic became essential elements in this definition.

The task of the historian was to reconstruct the particulars of the past, such as events, epochs or nations, producing true facts about the past that could serve as elements in any larger synthesis of historical knowledge. Facts and original research on the basis of new sources were the essentials of this second version of empiricism. It defended the special nature of history as a discipline in two directions: against the natural sciences and against the newly emerging social sciences. Both versions were united in their rejection of older forms of literary historiography and of speculative forms of great narratives about the past that were typical of the philosophy of history. Whereas the second form of empiricism gained strength everywhere, the first model had a less successful fate. In France where the natural sciences had advanced quickly and gained general acceptance since 1789, the new epistemology of scientific positivism emerged. Saint-Simon, Comte and his followers borrowed heavily from empiricist philosophy of the eighteenth century but they went further in their methodological exigencies for the new 'sciences': empirical data and inductive logic should pave the way to a general system of scientific knowledge based on the discovery and the practical use of natural or moral laws understood as regularly recurring and verifiable phenomena which were interpreted as causes. Positivism gained acceptance easily in Europe and the Americas, later in the century in Asia.

Generally it profited much from the discoveries of Darwin and the popularity of evolutionism. Thus in a period when the new professional historiography was just developing, positivism was discussed widely in the intellectual and academic circles where the works and theses of gentlemen researchers (themselves outsiders of the university system and the still small world of professional historians) had a great impact. The British author and amateur historian, Henry Thomas Buckle, was internationally the most influential single voice.[18] His ambitious programme for a new science of history insisted on the systematic search for regularities in human action of the past.[19] This new nomothetic (law-seeking) approach was based on the empiricist epistemology of John Stuart Mill. The observation of mass phenomena, the use of statistical documentation and the inductive method of generalisation were to be the main intellectual tools to discover these laws of development. Prognostics and political advice should be the outcome of such a discipline. Buckle's new historiography was widely discussed at an international level (with translations into French, German, Spanish, Italian, Russian, Portuguese and Japanese) but its echo among historians was ambiguous.[20]

In some countries this new programme became an important element in the professionalisation of history and became part of the new language that professional historians adopted when reflecting on or defending their own practice. But more often the professional historians remained sceptical of this version of scientism. In France the nomothetic model did not gain acceptance among the first generation of professionals who began organising their discipline in the 1860s, with great success in the first two decades of the Third Republic. Positivism as a philosophical doctrine itself and its scientific programme found only a few followers.[21] Instead, the pioneers of a 'scientific' history endorsed the general demand for a 'méthode positive' as a common ground for all scholarly disciplines, accepting the more advanced natural sciences and their methods as a kind of scientific ideal. But it

was the historical method in its established form that served as the criterion of internal evaluation within the profession, and the German practice served as a source of external legitimation. None of the new historians would accept a return to older forms of universal history with their speculative laws of development; the new monographs of the successful German school served as models. The 'méthode positive' consisted in the production of undeniable, sure facts of the past, whose interpretation was mainly a process of categorisation or classification. French historians such as Monod or Fustel de Coulanges agreed with Buckle and other positivists on the virtues of induction as the only way to arrive at more complex 'theories'. But the 'méthode positive' served first of all to guard against the risks of false information resulting from gaps in the sources or missing archival studies.

In Britain and the United States the general conditions for a positive reception of Buckle's ideas were quite good. Positivism won a place in the academic philosophy of both countries supported by its continuity with empiricist epistemology. 'Baconism' as a kind of 'definitive account of the scientific method'[22] served as a starting point; John Locke's passive/inscriptive or blank-slate model of knowledge acquisition gave a kind of psychological evidence, and John Stuart Mill's System of Logic provided a general model of explicit reasoning.

In Germany, positivism had to contend with stronger criticism. From Kant to Hegel, the idealistic epistemology had acquainted the learned public with a German distinction between natural sciences and the humanities. The sharp political and ideological confrontation between materialism or naturalism and idealism that had characterised debate in the 1840s added further material to the controversies. Therefore the disputes about positivism were very hot and Buckle was unacceptable to the leading German historians. Droysen sharpened his own theory of hermeneutics, expanding his concept of 'forschendes Verstehen' (investigative understanding by research) into an explicitly alternate epistemic

programme for the discipline.[23] This 'hermeneutic turn' in the 1860s did not prevent
other prominent German historians, such as
Sybel, from borrowing from this new positivist epistemology, stressing the exactitude
of the historical method and the necessity to
search for causal explanations. Thus as in the
French case, but in a less explicit way, positivism infiltrated the German community of
historians, especially among those who were
engaged in editing sources.[24]

When we draw a kind of balance at the end
of the nineteenth century, when the institutional settings of history were established in
Europe and Northern America, and began to
be introduced in Japan and China, positivist
epistemology had gained a wider audience
especially among the newly professional
historians of the United States, Italy, or Japan,
but it served often as a kind of external legitimation for a professional self-understanding
that relied on the historical method. In all
languages the new professional historians
saw themselves less as scientists than as
craftsmen; the medieval terms of Zunft,
mestiere, métier or guild circulated as desig-
nations for the new 'history men'.

Recent studies show us in detail the transformation in learning and research that may
better explain these trends. Eventually, documents or sources became the well defined
'epistemic objects'[25] necessary to any research
activity of professional historians. Their adequate 'manipulation' needed a set of sophisticated techniques and a new professional
socialisation for the young scholars who had
to learn how to regard their sources correctly
('Quellenblick').[26] It was medieval history
that became the focus of these operations that
encompassed a new training and a new ethos
for those young scholars who decided to
devote their lives to the service of history and
the archives. It is quite obvious that the social
construction of the new discipline centred
around this epistemic object: the primary
source. It is therefore no surprise that the
professional priests of this scholarly service
were very inclined to reserve a central place
for these sources when they were forced or

invited to reflect on the epistemic grounds of
their exacting discipline. There still was a
range of options concerning the interpretation
of the epistemological status of this new epistemic object, but we can observe a general
trend culminating in a kind of objectivism
based on three assumptions: (1) the facts
(Sachverhalte) established by the methodical
scrutiny of the sources correspond or come
closest to what happened in the past; (2) the
historian has to do his/her work of reconstruction of the past with patience and impartiality
(both qualities became part of a professional
ethos or habitus); (3) those historians who
master their sources thoroughly will discover
the causes and motives that enable the correct
story of the past to be discerned in the mass
of evidence. The sources thus 'speak' to the
well-trained historian, and any kind of previously held theory or hypothesis will tend to
destroy the intimate relationship between
historian and archival material.

Thus objectivity became one of the idols
of the new profession – it was more or less
taken for granted by the generations of scholars
studying history in the new seminars or institutes. The language used to express this professional conviction varied from country to
country, but everywhere the Rankean phrase,
*wie es eigentlich gewesen* ('the past as it
actually was'), became the password for this
conviction. That an international cult developed around the 'father of the discipline' is the
best proof for this kind of empiricist orthodoxy. Ranke has been described in the language of empiricism by Anglo-American
scholars since the end of the nineteenth century, thus completely obscuring the fact that
his own methodology is a classical example
of idealist historicism. Peter Novick showed
how American historians translated the
Rankean model into a 'scientific' model that
was really more informed by Mill and
Bacon, but adhered to the new norms of
obligatory archival research, complete bibliography, and impartiality. Thus it could be
stated: 'the fundamental principle of Ranke's
method ... was ... No generalisation, no
interpretation and little exercise of native

intuition – only the one question, "what really happened".'[27] This kind of 'naturalisation' occurred not only in England and the United States but also in Japan or China.[28] It helped to express professional values and conventions in a common language of objectivity, political neutrality and dedication to the scholarly ethos of impartial study of numerous archival sources. But it should be remembered that there was no necessary link between this conventional or 'trivial positivism' and a rigorously empiricist epistemology.

Typical of this shift towards methodology as the foundation for scientific legitimacy of history were the two handbooks or introductions by Langlois–Seignobos and Bernheim, both of which had great international influence. Both started from slightly different epistemic points of view, the French authors using an empiricist language, the German author defending the hermeneutic view even when he enlarged it. But both books devoted the major part of their text to the exposition of source-criticism as the essential part of the historical method. In the mirror of these introductions, the discipline of history resembled more a craft whose professional skills lay in the distillation of 'facts' by means of the critical assessment of all kinds of documents, with the aid of a large range of 'auxiliary sciences' (Hilfswissenschaften). Here Bernheim and Langlois–Seignobos went hand in hand. Both books certified in written form the kinds of academic socialisation and professional training that were practiced in different institutional settings, such as the German seminars or institutes at the universities, the French Ecole des Chartes or the IV section of the Ecole Pratique des Hautes Etudes, or the famous Institut für Österreichische Geschichtsforschung at Vienna.

When the two books approach epistemic problems we see the different languages and traditions at work. Langlois and Seignobos distanced themselves from the ontological realism often connected with empiricism: 'En histoire, on ne voit rien de réel que du papier écrit … elle n'est qu'un procédé abstrait, une opération purement intellectuelle.'[29] They emphasise that the historian has to study subjective documents in order to reconstruct facts: 'Au lieu d'observer directement des faits, elle opère indirectement en raisonnant sur des documents. Toute connaissance historique étant indirecte, l'histoire est essentiellement une science de raisonnement. Sa méthode est une méthode indirecte, par raisonnement. C'est une méthode évidemment inférieure, une méthode d'expédient.'[30] The main task of the historian is to collect and classify facts using universal categories of human behaviour and social institutions: facts are first to be stated and then catalogued. The construction of broader patterns ('construction des formules générales') such as causal linkage is seen from an atomistic point of view as the assembly (assemblage) of single facts. This version of empiricism strongly argues for methodological individualism and rejects energetically any kind of holism ('un monde d'êtres imaginaires s'est ainsi créé derrière les faits historiques').[31] Thirdly, the French authors defend a very narrow and limited form of historical synthesis: general laws are not discernable or only at the price of vague abstractions; comparison is seen sceptically as a rarely usable tool of analysis. Relating linear changes in the course of events fits best with this epistemological scheme.

Bernheim's epistemology is more sophisticated. He insists on the ideographic character of history and the genetic perspective which combines descriptive or narrative elements with more general causal explanations as the proper feature of history that justifies it in being considered as a science in its own right. The historian's job of building a synthesis is described in the same way as in the description by Langlois and Seignobos of the construction of larger logical units by assembling single facts. We should not forget that 'trivial empiricism' alone did not accomplish this high degree of self-confidence typical of the profession at the end of the nineteenth century. It was the more or less common credo for both (liberal) progress and (conservative) continuity between past and present that gave cultural and political meaning to the worship of facts and to the hardships of rigorous erudition and archival research. This epistemic culture went along with a shared belief that the facts of the past could and should inform the morale and the polity of the present. Relativism had not yet shattered the political convictions of most of the professional historians. Their greatest disputes were about concepts, the philosophical ideas about the (ontological) connection between past and present: evolution or revolution, materialistic or idealistic models of past and present were at stake. Some strong ideological presuppositions hid behind the basic empiricism that shaped the historiographic output of this generation but these were generally excluded from any critical reflection.

Around 1900 we can observe a first climax in the international diffusion of 'trivial empiricism' throughout the different national epistemic cultures of the discipline. The cult of impartiality, the new antirhetorical style of historical writing and a mistrust of sociological or philosophical theories were common among the new generations of professional historians, adopted uncritically from their senior colleagues. In their autobiographical writings, the younger generation of professional historians trained at this time often write of the 'well-established path of the historical method' that gave them a strong sense of self confidence and self sufficiency – attitudes that provoked irritation and protest among a yet younger generation of historians who experienced first the intellectual innovations in the decades after 1890, then the upheavals of the First World War and the interwar years.[32]

## EMPIRICISM UNDER ATTACK: NEW EPISTEMOLOGIES FOR A CHANGING PRACTICE

The successful books by Bernheim and Langlois–Seignobos were published when the certainties they spelled out were under attack. Their arguments could be effectively used in defence of current historical practice against new challenges coming mainly from within the 'scientific' world, and in the name of the new social sciences like sociology, psychology or political science. There culminated a series of controversies about methods and epistemology around 1900. The German dispute between Karl Lamprecht[33] and the defenders of Rankean orthodoxy followed the same path that polemics against Buckle had taken in Germany. Lamprecht's proposals for a new methodology opening the field of historical research to social, economic and cultural mass phenomena, and including serial data were refused in the name of the singularity of historical facts and individuals, the leading role of political history, and against 'positivistic' methodology in history. The epistemological idealism and established practice of German historism were defended against 'naturalism', 'materialism' and a new social and cultural history. But at the same time the customary assumptions of trivial empiricism were upset by the new trends. The young heirs of Rankean orthodoxy attacked Lamprecht on the ground of his professional practice, and tried to delegitimise him as a serious scholar by enumerating logical fallacies and empirical mistakes. At the same time they articulated their hostility against any kind of 'sociological' generalisations and theories.[34]

In the German case, Rankean orthodoxy fought side by side with neo-Kantian philosophers like Rickert or Windelband against 'positivism' and 'collectivism'. In these debates, the established scheme of classification – science versus humanities – was overthrown by a more sophisticated scheme placing the nomothetic over against the ideographic disciplines, that is, the disciplines that seek general laws as distinct from those that analyse particular non-repeatable events.[35] Rickert added a secondary, material opposition. He distinguished between disciplines dealing with things whose existence does not depend on cultural values like the natural sciences, and others dealing with objects whose identity is linked to meaning and cultural value.[36] This double (formal and material) differentiation at first hand justified the orthodox view of history as a discipline which deals with single, meaningful events of the past. But this epistemological proposal opened up the field for reflections about the relationship between historians and the cultural values of their own society and secondly, about the possibilities of a new kind of history including nomothetical views, albeit without adopting the positivistic programme.

In the French debates positivist arguments were of much greater importance. The debate opposed defenders of the established discipline to reformers from inside and outside history who insisted on a more scientific approach to history. Nearly simultaneously, around 1894, new contributions to the methodology of history were published pleading for a more scientific approach, inviting historians to search for continuities and regularities in the past by turning to new objects of study (institutions, society and economy) and by using new methods such as comparison and statistics.[37] The most influential contribution was that of François Simiand, who took up these arguments in an attack against the shortcomings of the empiricist orthodoxy.[38] He identified three Baconian 'idols' or wrong ideas engrained in French historiography: (1) the habit of treating history as the history of individuals (the idol of individuality); (2) looking for the origins of a phenomenon instead of studying its 'normal' type (the idol of chronology); (3) and excessive attention to political events (the idol of politics).[39] Simiand criticised the methodological individualism of the French school arguing that social facts were facts *sui generis* that could not be treated as simple amalgams of individual facts. Similar to the other critiques, he proposed a new comparative history of institutions, and the use of serial data over longer periods. Seignobos answered in the same positivistic language but refused the ambitions of the sociologist, insisting on the secure grounds but modest ambitions of history. For him, history could only get access to the past indirectly; it could not fully realise all the conditions of a positive science. He reminded colleagues that by renouncing the ambitions of a nomothetic

science, history had gained its own methodological certainty and achieved a great quantity of positive knowledge about the past that distinguished it from all other social sciences.[40]

It was surely a very successful defence of his discipline that Seignobos presented before the Society of Philosophy in 1906 but he could not prevent the history of events ('histoire evenementielle') he was defending from losing more and more credit, or prevent it from seeming old fashioned and less 'scientific' than that of its more ambitious critics. In many respects, this controversy was the starting point of the new directions in French historiography organised around Lucien Febvre and Marc Bloch, the founders of the future 'Annales School', whose 'official' start came in 1929 with the foundation of their journal, *Annales d'Histoire Economique et Sociale*.

In Britain and the United States, these controversies were only distantly echoed; the certainties of the empiricist credo were not shattered by reports of the debates abroad.[41]

In these countries, basic empiricism came under attack after the First World War. It was historians' observation of the manipulation of historical scholarship for the purpose of national propaganda that undermined their traditional high esteem for German erudition and historiography, but doubt was equally cast on their own practice. The interwar years saw an unprecedented amount of interventions on behalf of relativistic ideas in both countries: in the United States, Beard and Becker were the two leading figures of an epistemological critique of conventional views, introducing hermeneutics and historism into the American debates.[42] In Britain it was Collingwood who developed a clearly anti-positivist epistemology for history, one that took up many arguments that continental theories of history since Dilthey and Croce had developed in defence of a new hermeneutic epistemology of history.

It is quite interesting to see how new tendencies in the sciences blurred the empiricist attitude during this period. In physics, Einstein's theory of relativity and new discussions in theoretical physics shattered the image of the natural sciences as exemplary models of empiricism. The new social sciences, from sociology to psychology, produced new knowledge and new methods that undermined the certainties of 'scientific' history based on a quite simple form of inquiry. The criteria for being scientific had changed and become more sophisticated. Instead of general or universal laws debates turned around types and typologies, evolutionary (or revolutionary) stages of development or 'processes' as specific patterns of change in the different sectors of one civilisation like society, economy or culture. All these proposals introduced the new element of construction and modelling in the 'fabric of history'. The arena was opened for new epistemic problems, as for example that of the relationship between the singular 'data' extracted from the sources and treated as indicators or traces of larger phenomena, and the explanatory scheme or model.

Before the First World War, Max Weber's methodological articles had criticised the basic empiricism dominating the German historical discipline. But it was a very polite and unsystematic attack coming from an economist who wrote about historical subjects but was no historian. Weber started from the classical hermeneutic argument that the understanding of the past differs from the observation of natural facts because of the psychological and intellectual character of the traces of human action. But for Weber explanatory understanding is possible when the researcher combines systematic observation informed by the construction of rational models or ideal types, with the interpretation of human actions and attitudes. All these techniques of inquiry could be submitted to internal scientific control and therefore for Weber, justify the humanities as 'scientific' enterprises. But he criticised the idea of objectivity in the realm of values. The social and cultural differences between historians were not neutral in their construction of historical objects.[43] Weber's attack on the well established objectivist consensus was only effective in the long

run; it took time to infiltrate the historical field. But his theory quickly spread among intellectuals, philosophers and sociologists who discussed the problem of partiality and relativism as the 'crisis of historism'.[44]

Internationally, positivism and empiricism lost ground to other schools of thought inspired by the 'crisis of historism' that shattered the well established world of the 'Geisteswissenschaften' (humanities) on the continent and to a lesser degree in the Anglo-American world. Relativism and scepticism were the common enemy of all orthodoxies in these disciplines. Both empiricist common sense and the historians' belief in the power of ideas in past and present lost credit or came under attack after the disasters of the First World War and the social, political and cultural upheavals between the wars. Behind the epistemological problems we discern economic and political insecurity, as well as social and cultural changes that threatened the status and the identity of the profession as a whole, and of the individual historian. Naturally, the depth and outcome of these crises varied sharply from one country to the other. The European continent and East Asia were more deeply involved than Britain or the United States, but we can find traces of intellectual uncertainty and upheaval everywhere.[45] It was this constellation that produced exactly the same kind of opposition as would appear 70 years later when postmodernist relativism seemed to undermine the methodological certainties of the discipline.

Debate over the appropriate style for historical writing broke out in Germany when the young medievalist, Ernst Kantorowicz, published his first book on Emperor Frederic II in a poetic literary style that was far from the literary conventions of academic writing. In the United States, Becker and Beard publicly articulated their doubts about the objectivity of history, each in his presidential address to the American Historical Association: Becker in 1931 with 'Everyman His Own Historian'; Beard two years later with 'Written History as an Act of Faith.'[46] In France, right-wing gentlemen historians such as Gaxotte and

Bainville attacked the impartiality of their academic colleagues when it came to the lessons of the past for the national future.

Everywhere the professional assumption of objectivity seemed old-fashioned or politically incorrect. The new dictatorships that gained strength and spread worldwide in the interwar years openly declared partisanship and partiality to be the virtues of the professional historian who has to serve the cause of the regime in the name of the nation or the working class. 'Objectivity besieged'[47] may well describe the epistemic discussions and the political situation of history in this period but it is more complicated to assess if and how far this new perspectivism entered the working habits of historians or eroded their well-entrenched empiricism. Under authoritarian regimes, those historians who were in political dissent found their niche in defending the historical method and worshipping the cult of pure facts and objectivity, but distancing themselves from more ambitious or politically sensitive subjects. The empiricist mood of the 'epistemic cultures' was in retreat. Alternative epistemic arguments were advanced: values were no longer seen as the indisputable results of progress or history itself. The impact of values on the selection of sources and facts, their relevance for the choice of themes and concepts, became apparent to a growing number of historians. The growth of sociology and social theories and concepts that were not taken from the pure speculation of philosophers set a new agenda for the discussion of theoretical models and concepts in history.

The currents that took shape in this period, like the Annales school or the variants of Volksgeschichte,[48] had clear-cut ideas about new methods and new approaches to the past but were much more ambiguous about epistemological questions. Lucien Febvre polemicised against the myopic nature of 'scientific history' and ridiculed the empiricist programme of Seignobos[49] borrowing his own epistemic positions from Bergson and Durkheim. Marc Bloch followed a refined version of Durkheimian positivism and

defended a position that was close to that of his colleague Maurice Halbwachs: for him, the facts of history were basically 'psychological', which meant products of human action, intention and imagination. To understand and explain them requires hermeneutics and theories; thus, his version of 'critical rationalism' comes very near to the position of Max Weber.

## THE RETURN OF OBJECTIVISM AND EMPIRICISM: COLD WAR AND THE TIDE OF SOCIAL SCIENCES

From 1914 onward, 'objectivity' became a moral battleground for historians who defended their mastery of facts and the integrity of their method against those members of the discipline who pleaded for political mobilisation and professional partisanship. But metanarrative, expansive histories or larger synthesis tended to impose themselves against the particulars of the sources. Their 'right of veto' of the sources[50] seemed to be at stake. Thus the French historian, Marc Bloch, defended in his own introduction to historical theory and method the virtues of the historical method in the battle against forgery of facts and the manipulation of the public. As a young scholar he had seen his senior colleagues intervene in defence of Dreyfus as experts who could identify the papers of Henry as falsifications.[51]

This argument became very popular among Western scholars during the Cold War. Novick has shown how the American historians forgot the arguments of their sceptical colleagues, Beard and Becker, and returned to a rather naive cult of truth and objectivity in the 1940s and 1950s. According to him, 'The disparagement of ideology and the concomitant celebration of American Empiricism were among the forces which in the postwar years returned historiographical thought in the United States to older norms of objectivity.'[52] The Marxist-communist historiography of Soviet or East European origin served as the counter-model. In Western

Europe this confrontation was equally strong; in every country, the majority of historians identified themselves with an unideological, 'objective' practice. Thus they defended at the same time their conventional professional practice against the 'New French School' that emerged on the international scene in 1950 at the international Congress in Paris.[53] Empiricism stood in sharp opposition to Marxist epistemology, although both had much in common throughout the nineteenth century. Logical positivism refuted historical materialism as a meaningless metaphysics that could not be verified by empirical research. Mainstream historians rejected Marxist historiography for its use of theoretical models and concepts and its partisan bias.

Internationally, the 1950s and 1960s of the twentieth century saw the rise of social and economic history and, with it, the development of new methods of research; statistical or serial studies of mass phenomena over longer periods of time, and the establishment of historical demography and econometric methods were part of this shift in interest. This went along with an intensification of contacts with the social sciences, which resulted in methodological borrowings and a theoretical reorientation towards the dominant empirical western sociology. A special type of 'instrumental positivism'[54] spread among one group of social historians: the ideal of nomological science should be realised by the meticulous practice of quantification and statistical methods of research or other 'objective' methods; theories or general explanations (middle range laws) should be generated by induction. An axiomatic premise of this epistemology was the strict separation of scientific statements about facts from value judgements. The increase of factual knowledge and the refinement of methodology were the pillars of this scientific practice. 'Quantification' was the methodological issue which raised the highest ambitions for a transformation of historical practice into 'objective' social science.

It is evident that this form of positivism fit within the empiricist traditions of history. Historians' sceptical distance from any kind of great theory, the ideal of cumulative increase of historical knowledge by specialisation, and the atomistic view of the historical facts found a new theoretical frame. The impact of positivism was strong in the Anglo-American world but also on the European continent when we look at France or Scandinavia. (As, for example, Michelle Perrot: 'C'est qu'en outre nous croyions à la Science. Sous l'influence d'un néo-positivisme diffus, et en dépit de tous nos sarcasmes pour Seignobos, nous rêvions confusement de "physique sociale", de laboratoires historiques, peuplés de chercheurs en blouse blanche construisant les "faits".'[55]) The Annales School offers the most spectacular examples of the practical outcome of this empiricism and may illustrate its shortcomings. In order to organise a coordinated research programme for the history of social classes of the Ancien Regime in 1959, the young historians of the Centre de Recherches Historiques proposed to use a list of contemporary socio-professional categories as the basis of their quantitative analysis without considering the effect this classification produced on the data under scrutiny. Immediately a heated debate over the character of French society under the Ancien Regime broke out.[56] On the theoretical level (when only a minority of historians were present or participated actively in the debates), the empiricist arguments of logical positivism dominated the scene: 'explanation' became the central item and authors like C.H. Hempel and E. Nagel adopted Hume's definition of laws as regularities between two or more observable facts discovered by the cumulative effect of methodical observation and the logic of induction. The 'covering law' model was the undisputed norm of causal explanation for history but it soon became apparent that the practice of historians did not fit this model because their explanations (the famous 'why?' question) and descriptions (how and what) were interrelated because historians were interested in the particular case, not the general laws that could be observed in it. The debates among neo-positivist philosophers of science left only small traces on the historical discipline; the arguments and problems of philosophers were very distant from historians' actual practice. Thus the neo-positivist definition of historical knowledge did not have much effect on the internal debates among historians, or their self-image.

Much closer to historians' concerns was the revisionism of Edward Carr whose 1961 book, *What Is History?*, was one of the most influential for the generations entering the discipline in the 1960s and 1970s. Carr broke with the antitheoretical tradition and accepted social theory as a new element that ended the dominance of the old inductive logic. He gave relativism a place in historical practice, and accepted its inevitability, but sought to minimise its costs and risks. His revisions of conventional assumptions were taken up later by many authors who refined the arguments and elaborated more complex models. There is no detailed study of the international reception of Carr's book, but in many respects he was a forerunner of the many revisions that can be found in the handbooks and introductions of the 1970s and 1980s that tried to assimilate the empiricist credo to the new conditions of research and debate: everywhere social theory and perspectivism were integrated as new elements of professional practice. These arguments were familiar to Marxists who were in this period the greatest single current in historiography, and whose western branch participated in the weakening of the basic empiricist aspect of the epistemic culture by combining their material research in social, cultural or economic history with theoretical contributions.[57]

The defence of the standard empiricist arguments on behalf of history's 'scientific' methods (echoing the positions of Langlois and Seignobos) became the voice of the conservatives among historians. The most ferocious and eloquent was Geoffrey Elton in 1967, but its impact outside the British isles was rather weak. Elton's warnings against the import of social theories and the methods of social sciences went along with his defence of political history as the backbone of the

discipline. His strong empiricism upheld a conventional epistemic culture whose defenders became a minority during the next two decades, but it still had strongholds in many national historical cultures, rather more numerous among ancient and medieval historians than in modern fields.

## THE FATE OF EMPIRICISM AFTER THE END OF EPISTEMIC FOUNDATIONALISM

After the 1960s the tide of instrumental positivism in the social sciences subsided and in epistemology neo-positivist arguments were criticised from many sides: internal criticism via Quine and Wittgenstein; critical theory via Habermas; and new Heideggerian hermeneutics via Derrida. In history, the New Cultural History began its rise in the 1980s and together with social history attracted most attention among those historians engaged in epistemological problems.[58] It is not the task of this chapter to give a critical introduction to all these new currents and positions.[59] I would just like to underline some common features of these new trends with regard to empiricism: firstly, they rejected the objectivist positions common to neo-positivism and older forms of empiricism. The problems of 'truth' and 'objectivity' were replaced by a set of interrelated concepts such as intersubjectivity, rational explication and scope of validity. This revision addressed both the difference between facts and value judgements, and the distinction between theories and facts. The new theories argued for gradualism and for interdependance between these different operations and artefacts of historical research. Most strikingly, the new theories refused any foundationalist answer to the questions of truth and certainty, and proposed arguments for a purely social or cultural legitimation of historical research and scientific practice in general. The quest for final certainties was rejected in favour of establishing a set of historically proven criteria for scientific methods. In a certain sense, the 'empiricist stance' against Cartesianism has been reaffirmed but on the basis of other arguments. The constructivist character of historical research was no longer ignored, especially when facts are selected and particular aspects of the past are chosen as relevant for historical inquiry.

The most visible rupture with objectivist traditions can been seen in the fact that the writing of history has attracted much more attention. Historical writing, especially narrative composition, became a privileged object of reflection and literary study. Narratologies of many kinds have resulted from this shift of scholarly attention to the linguistic form of historical knowledge. Here empiricism has never developed any deeper theoretical attention, treating the writing as a kind of personal technique or the refuge of artistic skills.[60]

The outcome of these epistemological reorientations differs from country to country. No new international orthodoxy has emerged. On the contrary, the common resistance to postmodernist theories of literary criticism as a new platform for the discipline did not inaugurate a new empiricist mainstream. We do not yet know enough about how the present epistemic cultures of the discipline have integrated these new theories and models of historical knowledge. For Britain, Alun Munslow may be right in saying: 'Most historians today accept a middle position that rejects extreme empiricism (i.e. rationalism), maintaining that we observe but we also mentally process information deploying a priori knowledge and categories of analysis as appropriate and helpful ... Today most historians do not accept that history can be known through an exact correspondence of knowing and being. Most historians these days regard themselves as sophisticated empiricists who judge the reality of the past by a measure of understanding based upon sense-data as filtered through the grid of mental structures pre-existing in our minds ... Few historians today would defend a crude sceptical empiricism.'[61] Naturally in many other countries, most historians, as in the past, would not call themselves

'sophisticated empiricists', but the position that Munslow describes as acceptable for a hypothetical majority of his British colleagues may be shared by them too.

## NOTES AND REFERENCES

1  S. Davies, *Empiricism and History* (London, 2003), p. 1.
2  D.W. Hainlyn, Empiricism, in P. Edwards (ed.), *The Encyclopedia of Philosophy*, vol.1 (New York/London, 1972), pp. 499–505.
3  S. Priest, The British Empiricists (London, 1990), pp. 173–247.
4  W.M. Simon, *European Positivism in the Nineteenth Century* (Ithaca, NY, 1963); C. Bryant, *Positivism in Social Theory and Research* (London, 1985), pp. 1–56.
5  Bryant, *Positivism*, op. cit., pp. 109–32.
6  P. Baumann, *Erkenntnistheorie* (Stuttgart, 2006); M. Willaschek et al. (eds), *Realismus* (Stuttgart, 2000).
7  For Germany see: H.W. Blanke, *Historiographiegeschichte als Historik* (Stuttgart-Bad Canstatt, 1991); for France and the USA: G. Lingelbach, *Klio macht Karriere. Die Institutionalisierung der Geschichtswissenschaft in Frankreich und den USA in der zweiten Hälfte des 19. Jahrhunderts* (Göttingen, 2003), pp. 438–59, 543–55.
8  G.G. Iggers, The Methodenstreit in international perspective, *Storia della storiografia* **6** (1984), pp. 21–32; E. Fuchs, Englischer Methodenstreit und Lamprechtkontroverse in vergleichender Perspektive, in G. Diesener (eds.), *Karl Lamprecht Weiterdenken* (Leipzig, 1993), pp. 242–57; L. Raphael, Historikerkontroversen im Spannungsfeld zwischen Berufshabitus, Fächerkonkurrenz und sozialen Deutungsmustern, *Historische Zeitschrift* **251** (1990), pp. 325–63.
9  V. Langlois and C. Seignobos, *Introduction aux Études Historiques* (Paris, 1898; English transl. London, 1898); E. Bernheim, *Lehrbuch der historischen Methode und der Geschichtsphilosophie* (Leipzig, 1889; 3rd edn Leipzig, 1903).
10  E.H. Carr, *What is History* (London, 1961), G.R. Elton, *The Practice of History* (Sydney, 1967); K.G. Faber, *Theorie der Geschichtswissenschaft* (München, 1971).
11  J. Appleby, L. Hunt and M. Jacob, *Telling the Truth about History* (New York, 1994); R. Evans, *In Defense of History* (London, 1997); A. Prost, *Douze Leçons sur l'Histoire* (Paris, 1996); C. Lorenz, *Konstruktion der Vergangenheit* (Köln, Weimar, Wien, 1997); A. Munslow, *The Routledge Companion to Historical Studies* (London, New York, 2000).
12  P. Bourdieu, *Homo Academicus* (Frankfurt, 1988), p. 125.
13  A. Marwick, *The Nature of History* (London 1970), p. 18.
14  Ranke cited in F. Stern, *The Varieties of History* (London, 1970), p. 57.
15  R.G. Collingwood, *The Idea of History* (London, 1970), p. 76.
16  G. Walter, *Niebuhrs Forschung* (Stuttgart, 1993), pp. 106–13, 200–4.

17  U. Muhlack, Von der philologischen zur historischen Methode, in C. Meier and J. Rüsen (eds), *Historische Methode* (München, 1988), pp. 154–80; R. Vierhaus, Rankes Begriff der historischen Objektivität, in R. Koselleck, W.J. Mommsen and J. Rüsen (eds), *Objektivität und Parteilichkeit* (München, 1977), pp. 63–76.

18  E. Fuchs, *Henry Thomas Buckle. Geschichtsschreibung und Positivismus in England und Deutschland* (Leipzig, 1994).

19  H.T. Buckle, *The History of Civilization in England*, 2 vols (London, 1857, 1861).

20  Fuchs, *Buckle*, op. cit., pp. 230–9.

21  C.-O. Carbonell, Les historiens dits positivists, *Romantisme* **21–22** (1978), pp. 173–85; Histoire narrative et histoire structurelle dans l'historiographie positiviste du XIXe siècle', *Storia della Storiografia* **10** (1986), pp. 153–61.

22  P. Novick, *That Noble Dream. The 'Objectivity Question' and the American Historical Profession* (Cambridge, 1988), p. 34.

23  J.G. Droysen, *Historik* (München, 1937); J. Rüsen, *Begriffene Geschichte. Genesis und Begründung der Geschichtstheorie* (Padernborn, 1969); Fuchs, *Buckle*, op. cit., pp. 306–13, 316–21.

24  Fuchs, *Buckle*, op. cit., pp. 311–13.

25  H.-J. Rheinberger, *Experimental Systems and Epistemic Objects* (1997).

26  D. Saxer, Die Schärfung des Quellenblicks. Die geschichtswissenschaftliche Forschungspraxis in Wien und Zürich (1840–1914), Ph.D., Zürich (2005).

27  Dodd cited in Novick, *That Noble Dream*, op. cit., pp. 29, 26–31.

28  *Leopold von Ranke and the Shaping of the Historical Discipline*, edited by G. Iggers and J.M. Powell (Syracuse, NY, 1990).

29  Langlois and Seignobos, *Études Historiques*, op. cit., p. 178ff.

30  C. Seignobos, *La Méthode Historique Appliquée aux Sciences Sociales* (Paris, 1909), p. 5.

31  Langlois and Seignobos, *Études Historiques*, op. cit., p. 234.

32  E. Schulin, Weltkriegserfahrung und Historikerreaktion, in W.Küttler, J.Rüsen and E.Schulin (eds), *Geschichtsdiskurs*, vol. 4 (Frankfurt, 1997), pp. 165–88.

33  On Lamprecht see: R. Chickering, *Karl Lamprecht: A German Academic Life* (Atlantic Highlands, 1993); L. Schorn-Schütte, *Karl Lamprecht: Kulturgeschichtsschreibung zwischen Wissenschaft und Politik* (Göttingen, 1984).

34  Raphael, Historikerkontroversen, op. cit.

35  W. Windelband, *Geschichte und Naturwissenschaft* (Strassburg, 1900).

36  H. Rickert, *Science and History: A Critique of Positivist Epistemology* (Princeton, NJ, 1962), translated from *Kulturwissenschaft und Naturwissenschaft* (1899).

37  P. Lacombe, *De l'Histoire Considérée Comme Science* (Paris, 1894); E. Durkheim, *Règles de la Méthode*

*Sociologique* (Paris, 1895), first published as an article in 1894; L. Bourdeau, *L'histoire et les Historiens. Essai critique sur l'histoire considérée comme science positive* (Paris, 1888).

38  F. Simiand, Méthode historique et science sociale, *Revue de Synthèse Historique* **6** (1903), pp. 1–22, 129–57.

39  Ibid., pp. 154, 155.

40  Seignobos, *La Méthode historique*, op. cit..

41  Fuchs, *Buckle*, op. cit., pp. 335–44; Novick, *That Noble Dream*, op. cit., pp. 86–108

42  Novick, *That Noble Dream*, op. cit., pp. 206–49.

43  Bryant, *Positivism*, op. cit., pp. 76–98

44  G. Scholz, Zum Strukturwandel in den Grundlagen kulturwissenschaftlichen Denkens, in W. Küttler, J. Rüsen and E. Schulin (eds), *Geschichtsdiskurs*, vol. 4 (Frankfurt, 1997), pp. 19–50.

45  L. Raphael, *Geschichtswissenschaft im Zeitalter der Extreme. Theorien, Methoden, Tendenzen von 1900 bis zur Gegenwart* (Munich, 2003), pp. 81–95.

46  Novick, *That Noble Dream*, op. cit., pp. 252–64.

47  Ibid., p. 109.

48  *Volksgeschichten im Europa der Zwischenkriegszeit*, edited by M. Hettling (Göttingen, 2003).

49  L. Febvre, *Combats pour l'Histoire* (Paris, 1953).

50  R. Koselleck, Standortbindung und Zeitlichkeit. Ein Beitrag zur historiographischen Erschließung der geschichtlichen Welt, in R. Koselleck, W.J. Mommsen and J. Rüsen (eds), *Objektivität und Parteilichkeit* (München, 1977), pp. 17–46, here p. 45.

51  M.Bloch, *Apologie pour l'Histoire ou Métier d'historien* (Paris, 1993), pp. 153–5.

52  Novick, *That Noble Dream*, op. cit., p. 300.

53  K.D. Erdmann, *Toward a Global Community of Historians: The International Historical Congresses and the International Committee of Historical Sciences 1898-2000* (New York, Oxford, 2005).

54  Bryant, *Positivism* op.cit.

55  M. Perrot, *Les Ouvriers en grève*, 2 vols (Paris, La Haye, 1974), vol. 1, p. 5ff.

56  L. Raphael, *Die Erben von Bloch und Febvre, Annales-Historiographie und Nouvelle histoire in Frankreich 1945–1980* (Stuttgart, 1994), p. 291.

57  E. Hobsbawm, *On History* (London, 1997); E.P. Thompson, *The Poverty of Theory and Other Essays* (London, 1978).

58  As well as the titles cited in note 11 see: P. Ricoeur, *Time and Narative*, 3 vols (Chicago, 1984–1985); *A New Philosophy of History*, edited by F. Ankersmit and H. Kellner (London, 1995)

59  For a detailed analysis see Chapters 7–13 of this handbook.

60  H. White, *Metahistory: The Historical Imagination in Nineteenth-Century Europe* (Baltimore, OH, 1974).

61  Munslow, *Companion to Historical Studies*, op. cit., p. 81–2.

# 3

# The Case for Historical Imagination: Defending the Human Factor and Narrative

Jan van der Dussen

## INTRODUCTION

In debates on the status of the historical discipline the views of the English philosopher, historian and archaeologist R.G. Collingwood (1889–1943) play a prominent part. In the English-speaking world Collingwood is undoubtedly the most well-known and influential philosopher of history of the twentieth century. He is especially known for his posthumously published book *The Idea of History* (1946), which in 1995 appeared on a list in *The Times Literary Supplement* with the hundred most influential books since the Second World War.[1] This is not without reason, for *The Idea of History*, and the debates it has aroused since its appearance, has initiated a particular interest in the philosophy of history among both historians and philosophers. This is a remarkable phenomenon in itself, since until then philosophers in the English-speaking world had hardly shown any interest in the subject, whereas this had only occasionally been the case with historians.

From the second half of the nineteenth until the beginning of the twentieth century, the theory and philosophy of history was a subject in which primarily German authors like Droysen, Dilthey, Windelband and Rickert had played a prominent part, but also the Italian philosophers Croce and Gentile should be mentioned. The influence of the latter was limited outside Italy, however. The German contributions to the theory of history ended in fact with the Nazi-era, Karl Heussi's *Die Krisis des Historismus* (1932) being the last study in this field. It was only with *Wahrheit und Methode* (1960) by Gadamer that an important new German contribution to the theory of history appeared.

Since the Second World War the debates on the theory and philosophy of history have been focused within the English-speaking world. The interest in this field of study has not only been initiated by Collingwood's *The Idea of History*, but also by Karl Popper's *The Open Society and its Enemies* (1945) and the voluminous *A Study of History* (1934, 1939, 1954) by Arnold Toynbee. When we

concentrate in the following on Collingwood's views on history this is not without
reason. For these views have not only been
highly influential, but also have aroused until
the present day many lively debates. Without
exaggeration one could say that for many
decades there has hardly been a study on the
theory or philosophy of history in the English-
speaking world in which Collingwood's
name or views are not referred to.

## COMPLEXITIES IN INTERPRETING COLLINGWOOD'S PHILOSOPHY OF HISTORY

In explaining Collingwood's philosophy of
history one is confronted with some paradoxes and complexities. In the first place *The
Idea of History*, the book his fame as a philosopher of history is primarily based upon,
would not have been published in its present
form by Collingwood. After his premature
death it was posthumously put together by
his pupil and literary executor T.M. Knox
from various sources, ranging from 1935 to
1939, and consisting of lectures, some previously published articles, and parts of a
manuscript of an unfinished book. It should
furthermore be noted that it has become clear
that in editing *The Idea of History* Knox has
not always been as careful as one could have
wished, and that he has made changes of his
own in the text.

In the second place, since 1978 a large
amount of manuscripts of Collingwood
(some 4000 pages) has become available,
some important ones being on philosophy of
history. Besides these, the manuscript of his
unfinished book *The Principles of History*
(1939) was discovered in 1995 in the archives
of Oxford University Press. The most important manuscripts on philosophy of history
have only recently been published, respectively in 1993 and 1999.[2] They are not only a
most valuable supplement to *The Idea of
History*, but also evidence the all-round nature
of Collingwood's philosophy of history. Since

they are only recently available, this means
that Collingwood's views on history, instead
of being a voice from the past, should rather
be seen as one whose significance can in fact
only at present be fully digested. For the
manuscripts make clear that *The Idea of History* gives a deficient picture of Collingwood's philosophy of history. This is indeed
a unique phenomenon in the history of ideas
with an author who died almost 70 years ago.
In anticipation of what will be said in the following about Collingwood's views on history, I would say that they are of great current
interest. For his views on the ideality of history and the historical imagination not only
anticipated positions taken by the postmodernist 'linguistic turn', initiated by Hayden
White's *Metahistory* (1973), but, in contrast
to the latter, he did pioneer work as well on
'modernist' topics, like historical evidence,
historical interpretation and understanding,
historical reasoning, and causality.

Another complication in interpreting
Collingwood's work is his exceptional broad
scope of mind, covering various fields and a
bewildering amount of subjects. Since the
many areas in which he worked cannot be
seen as isolated endeavours, this means that
his views on history should be seen within
the context of his thought in other fields.

Collingwood was both a philosopher, historian and accomplished archaeologist. In all
three areas he has published extensively and
has made important contributions. Whereas
Collingwood is at present known primarily
as a philosopher, during his life he was
chiefly appreciated as the main expert on
Roman Britain, specializing, among other
things, on the intricate problems related to
Hadrian's Wall. As a philosopher he was seen
as a more or less extravagant figure, being
not in line with the realism and positivism of
his day. 'I find myself writing gloomily,' he
wrote to his friend the Italian philosopher de
Ruggiero in 1927. 'For four months I have
been deep in historical studies, and there I
find myself among friends and willing collaborators; the return to philosophy means a

return to a work in which I become more and more conscious of being an outlaw.'

In spite of his premature death Collingwood has left behind an impressive oeuvre. He has written 15 books, three of which have appeared posthumously. Nine books are on philosophical subjects, two on Roman Britain, and two on archaeology. Besides these he has written more than 150 articles and book reviews on the most diverse subjects. As a philosopher Collingwood has dealt with a great variety of subjects. Besides his posthumous *The Idea of History* he has written books on the philosophy of religion, art, nature, and politics, on metaphysics, and philosophical method. Besides these, his unpublished manuscripts deal among others with ethics, cosmology, and anthropology. Some of the manuscripts have been published in the meantime, the most recent being the ones on folklore, anthropology, and several other topics.[3]

It is rather puzzling that Collingwood, whose publications are so extensive, never wrote a major study on the philosophy of history, and that even his articles on the subject are relatively scanty, dealing also with rather diverse topics. It is certainly not because he was not interested in the subject. For on various occasions Collingwood made it explicitly clear that he not only considered the philosophy of history most important, but also that he regarded it as his main task to realize an improvement of the thought on the subject. In the chapter 'The need for a philosophy of history' in his autobiography, Collingwood refers to the great value he attached to the subject, saying: 'My life's work hitherto, as seen from my fiftieth year, has been in the main an attempt to bring about a *rapprochement* between philosophy and history' (Aut, 77).[4] And returning from a trip through the Dutch East-Indies, he writes in the spring of 1939 in a letter to his friend, the archaeologist F.G. Simpson, about *The Principles of History* he had begun to write, saying that it 'is the book which my whole life has been spent in preparing to write. If I can finish that, I shall have nothing to grumble at.'

Because of ill-health and various other projects he worked on ever since, Collingwood never managed to finish his book on philosophy of history. His observation, however, that it would be the book 'which my whole life has been spent in preparing to write' may give a clue for the reason that it had not been written before. For during his career Collingwood indeed constantly had the philosophy of history in mind. But since his views on the subject permanently developed they were never given shape to in a final form. These circumstances add to the complications involved in giving a proper interpretation of Collingwood's philosophy of history, which in fact has to be reconstructed from bits and pieces.

Notwithstanding these difficulties, it is possible, however, to show a 'figure in the carpet', as Louis Mink observed about the variety of Collingwood's books.[5] For Collingwood himself used to emphasize the unity of mind, and there is no reason that this should not hold for the development of his views on history as well.

## THE CONCEPT OF HISTORY AND ITS PHILOSOPHY

In Collingwood's view philosophy is related to the particular problems a specific age is confronted with. The Greeks were especially concerned about the problems of mathematics, and accordingly their philosophy was in search of their foundations; the Middle Ages were concerned with theology and reflected on the relations between God and man; in the modern age, from the sixteenth century, attention was focused on the natural world and the way this world could be known through knowledge of its laws. But from the eighteenth century arises a specific interest in history and the epistemological problems related with it (IH, 4–5, 232–3).

We are still living in the age of history, Collingwood avers, but the influence of the preceding age, with its focus on nature and the principles of natural science, is still haunting it. He is of the opinion that because of this our understanding of the present 'historical' age is seriously hampered. The starting-point of Collingwood's philosophy of history therefore is, one could say, to further a better understanding of the idea of history and the way it is – or rather ought to be – studied. This basic conviction is the guiding principle which frames the unity of Collingwood's thought on history.

In *Speculum Mentis* (1924), his first major book on philosophy, Collingwood explicitly pays attention to history, it constituting a part within the overall argument of the book. Its theme is the question of the unity and diversity of mind. Within mind Collingwood makes a distinction between art, religion, science, history, and philosophy as 'forms of experience'. These exhibit a logical relation of a dialectical nature, its essence being that what is implicit at one level within a form of experience becomes explicit at the next. With philosophy the highest stage is reached: mind has here only itself as object and arrives in this way at explicit self-knowledge.

History as a form of experience is also described by Collingwood as, among other things, 'historical consciousness' and 'the historical conception of reality'. Like the other forms of experience, history exhibits a development. Its 'highest sense', also called by him history 'in the special sense of the word', came into being, Collingwood says, in the eighteenth century 'and shot up to a gigantic stature in the nineteenth'. 'It is an absolutely new movement in the life of mankind,' he continues. 'In the sense in which Gibbon and Mommsen were historians, there was no such thing as an historian before the eighteenth century' (SM, 203). So we see here Collingwood putting what he also calls the 'historians' history' – that is, the study of the past – within the wider context of history as a form of experience, it being in fact the most advanced realization of the latter.

After *Speculum Mentis* Collingwood paid special attention to the philosophy of history as the study of the past. He lectured on the subject from 1926 to 1931 and wrote a few articles about it.[6] Though he did not come back to the idea of history as a form of experience, he refers to it in another wording on two occasions, when he explains how a philosophy of history should be conceived.[7] In this connection the distinction he makes between philosophical and empirical concepts is crucial. Philosophy deals, Collingwood contends, with the universal and necessary aspects of the things we think about. As with the previous forms of experience, he gives among others art, science and history as examples. History is a universal and necessary concept, 'because everything that exists is an historical fact' (IH, 352), and 'everything has a past; everything has somehow come to be what it is'.[8] So history is seen by Collingwood as a universal and necessary aspect of reality, our thought about it accordingly being of the same nature. It is, in other words, a certain way of looking at the world; a way, moreover, that cannot be refrained from.

History, however, is also an object of study, practised by historians. In this sense it is an empirical concept, since 'it means that activity which distinguishes persons called historians from others called scientists, trombone-players, or ophthalmic surgeons' (IH, 355). As a form of knowledge, the study of the past is not done haphazardly, however, but according to certain principles. What type of knowledge it is and which principles are involved are also questions of a philosophical nature. 'The philosophy of history, so understood,' Collingwood says, 'means bringing to light the principles used in historical thinking, and criticizing them; its function is to criticize and regulate these principles, with the object of making history truer and historically better' (IH, 346). It is in particular this reflection on the empirical concept of history Collingwood is interested in.

In the introduction to *The Idea of History* another explication is given of the philosophy of history. Collingwood there characterizes philosophy as 'thought of the second degree', meaning by it that it is not only thinking about an object, but also about the thought about that object. Thought of the first degree, in contrast, is only aimed at a specific object. Philosophy is also not focused on thought by itself, this being the specific object of psychology as thought of the first degree. Applied to the philosophy of history this means that 'the fact demanding attention is neither the past by itself, as it is for the historian, nor the historian's thought about it by itself, as it is for the psychologist, but the two things in their mutual relation' (IH, 2). The philosophy of history as conceived by Collingwood should therefore be seen as a reflection on the way historians think when studying the past.

## THE HISTORIAN AND HIS/HER OBJECT

Collingwood used to emphasize that the study of history is of a special nature, since it deals with the past, that is, a vanished and therefore non-existing reality. In this it differs from other studies – in particular natural science – that focus on an existing reality, or a reality manipulated through experiments. With history, however, this is not the case. Since we can have no direct acquaintance with a no longer existing past, we have to use other methods than the ones of natural science in order to acquire knowledge of it.

The problem, however, is that because of the influence and prestige of natural science its epistemology still has a heavy bearing on our thought. With history this has in various ways resulted in the idea that the 'reality' of the past should be recovered in one way or another. Philosophers of history like Hegel and Marx, for instance, were aimed at comprehending the overall pattern of the historical process. Historians, on the other hand, looked for the historical 'facts' as the foundation upon which our knowledge of the past should be based. In this way the past could be known, in the famous words of Ranke, '*wie es eigentlich gewesen*'.

Collingwood is very critical of the latter view that has especially been influential among German theorists and philosophers of history in the nineteenth century. He sees it as an illustration of a form of positivism originating from natural science.[9] Summarizing his criticism of 'the German school of *Geschichtsphilosophie*', Collingwood contends: 'It has always regarded history as an object confronting the historian in the same way in which nature confronts the scientist: the task of understanding, valuing, or criticizing it is not done by itself for itself, it is done to it by the historian standing outside it' (IH, 176).

The idea of historical 'facts' being the foundation of historical knowledge, with the historical realism implied by it, had been very influential until well into the twentieth century. Being critical of it and considering it a relic of positivistic thought, Collingwood developed a theory of his own, put down in his essay 'Outlines of a philosophy of history' of 1928 (IH, 426–96).

Starting from the observation that history means both a special kind of knowledge and a special kind of object, Collingwood contends in its introduction that both are closely interwoven. Based on his 'doctrine of the ideality of history', this means that *history a parte subjecti* as knowledge of the past cannot be separated from *history a parte objecti*, the past as object of knowledge. This implies that any idea of a 'real' past is put aside, since the past should always be seen as being equivalent to the historian's thought about it, or, as Collingwood puts it, 'historical fact, as known to the historian, is essentially relative to the thought that knows it' (IH, 429).

The close relationship between *history a parte subjecti* and *history a parte objecti* entails that what is said about the former is relevant for the latter and vice versa. Therefore Collingwood attaches much value not only to the methodology of history, but also to what he calls the 'metaphysics' of history, that is, the view on the nature of the past. An incorrect understanding of one of these aspects will impair a proper understanding of history in general. To give an example, Collingwood is not only opposed to the influence of natural science on the methodology of history, but is also of the opinion that an historical process should be conceived as being different from processes in nature.

At the end of his preface to 'Outlines of a philosophy of history' Collingwood aptly summarizes his theory on the relation between the historian and his/her object:

> The gulf which, on an empiricist or positivistic philosophy, separates historical thought from historical fact, has disappeared. Historical thought and its object are seen to be inseparable, the latter having only an ideal existence in and for the former; and therefore a methodological theory of the necessary forms of historical thought is also a metaphysical theory of the necessary forms of historical fact.[10] (IH, 429–30)

In the first chapter of the essay Collingwood gives an exposition of his theory. It is here that he develops his doctrine of the re-enactment of the past, undoubtedly the theory he is primarily known for, and certainly the most widely discussed aspect of his philosophy of history. It should be noted, however, that these discussions were not based on Collingwood's exposition of the theory in 'Outlines of a philosophy of history', for this essay was only published in 1993.

## RE-ENACTMENT OF THE PAST: COLLINGWOOD'S EXPOSITION

Collingwood begins 'Outlines of a philosophy of history' with a perspicuous description of the problem of the reality of the past: 'History *a parte objecti*, the object of historical thought, is of course in some sense real, for if it were not, there would be no sense in which historical judgements could be true, or indeed false. But in what sense are historical facts (using that term to denote the objects of historical thought) real?' (IH, 439).

After this Collingwood begins with discussing the concept of reality, equating it

with actuality. The latter can refer either to the existence of things or the occurrence of events. Historical events are events that have occurred, and are therefore not actual but ideal. 'This proposition I shall call *the Ideality of History*,' Collingwood says, adding:'[b]y the word ideality I intend to signify the quality of being an object of thought without having actuality', whereas actuality 'implies simultaneity with the thought in question' (IH, 440). Collingwood makes a distinction between a thing and an event in that the first may be both ideal and actual, this not being possible with an event. The Matterhorn as I remember it ten years ago, he gives as example, is ideal, but is the same as I see now as being actual. With past occurrences, in contrast, this is not possible, they accordingly being wholly and only ideal.

Having said this, Collingwood makes a curious twist in his argument. For he points out that for an historian of music his object is not only ideal as past music, but may also be actual in present performances of it, adding to it that the latter is necessary: '[h]e must have listened to Bach and Mozart, Palestrina and Lasso, and possess personal acquaintance with their works.' 'We may therefore boldly say,' Collingwood concludes a little further, 'that the *sine qua non* of writing the history of past music is to have this past music *re-enacted in the present*' (IH, 441).

After this, Collingwood surprisingly avers:

> Similarly, to write the history of a battle, we must re-think the thoughts which determined its various tactical phases: we must see the ground of the battlefield as the opposing commanders saw it, and draw from the topography the conclusions that they drew: and so forth. The past event, ideal though it is, must be actual *in the historian's re-enactment* of it. In this sense, and this sense only, the ideality of the object of history is compatible with actuality and indeed inseparable from actuality. (IH, 441–2)

The way the argument for his famed re-enactment doctrine is developed here is rather curious. For the analogy between the performance of past music and the re-thinking of past thoughts as embodied in past actions is far from obvious. The only plausible explanation is to see the first as a metaphor for the second. What it makes clear, one could say, is to illustrate how a past occurrence can become actual in the present. This is in itself is, of course, a significant observation. For in contrast with Collingwood's initial contention, this means that a past occurrence has not only the quality of being ideal, but can be actualized in the present as well. It should be added, however, that, in Collingwood's view, this only holds – leaving the performance of past music aside – for thoughts.

The corollary is that only the thought-side of the past is capable of being actualized in the present. And this is indeed Collingwood's contention. 'Not only is the history of thought possible,' he avers, 'but, if thought is understood in its widest sense, it is the only thing of which there can be history. Nothing but thought can be treated by the historian with that intimacy without which history is not history; for nothing but thought can be re-enacted in this way in the historian's mind.' This brings Collingwood to the conclusion that '[a]ll history, then, is the history of thought, where thought is used in the widest sense and includes all the conscious activities of the human spirit' (IH, 444–5).

The way Collingwood formulates his position is misleading in the sense that it seems to imply that he is of the opinion that thoughts as such are the specific object of historical study. This, however, is strictly speaking not the case. For in his later writings Collingwood emphasizes that human actions are the object of history. In *The Idea of History*, for instance, it is stated, in answer to the question what the object of history is, 'that history is the science of *res gestae*, the attempt to answer questions about human actions done in the past' (IH, 9). As we will see, this is underlined as well in *The Principles of History*, Collingwood's unfinished and last writing on history. What the historian studies, he there explicates, are the thoughts as embodied in and expressed by

human actions. It is in this sense that all history is the history of thought, and not in the sense that history proper should be conceived as intellectual history. It is Collingwood's position that it is only by understanding thoughts – implying the re-enactment of them – that actions can be understood or explained. Since it is hardly possible to conceive of a history without human actions being involved, Collingwood's re-enactment doctrine does not imply a restriction, therefore, as regards the objects to be studied.[11] It should also be noted that this doctrine should not be conceived as a kind of methodological device for obtaining knowledge of the past, as many commentators have initially interpreted it: it is a theory on the transcendental conditions of historical knowledge and not a theory on how this knowledge should be obtained.

As we will see, 'this new conception of history', as Collingwood described it (Aut, 110), was initially not endorsed by most interpreters. This is understandable, however, when it is taken into account that 'Outlines of a philosophy of history' was as yet not known.

## HISTORY AS THE HISTORY OF THOUGHT

Based on what Collingwood says about the re-enactment of past thought and all history being the history of thought in *The Idea of History*, but also in *An Autobiography*, these topics have attracted the attention of both historians and philosophers and have been widely discussed.

The comments on the idea of all history being the history of thought have been mainly critical. It was seen as implying an unacceptable limitation of the historian's object, it being only relevant for intellectual history, but excluding, for instance, social and economic history. By others it was seen as a defect that it entailed a too rationalistic view of humankind, not taking into account unreasonable actions, but also their irrational aspects like feelings and emotions. It was also criticized for being only relevant for individual actions, but not for group- or mass-behaviour. This argument also has a bearing, of course, on the supposed lack of relevancy for social and economic history. Finally, it was seen as a shortcoming that it did not take into consideration 'objective conditions', like geographical factors, playing a part in history.

If these objections would be valid, Collingwood's theory of history could only be considered extravagant, even to the degree of hardly deserving serious consideration. On closer examination, however, Collingwood did not hold certain views imputed to him, or these should be seen within the context of other positions held by him, which should accordingly be taken into consideration. A more inclusive investigation of Collingwood's views on history requires, moreover, that it is not confined to *The Idea of History* and *An Autobiography*, but takes notice of the recently available manuscripts as well. But also philosophical studies like *The Principles of Art* (1937) and *The New Leviathan* (1942) are of importance, since they explicitly deal with, among others things, the relation between thought, feeling and emotion, this being relevant for Collingwood's allegedly rationalistic view.

The position that all history is the history of thought is part of Collingwood's view on the object of history, being, as said, human actions done in the past: 'Historians think and always have thought that history is about *Res Gestae*, deeds, actions done in the past' (PH, 40). Being the object of history it is important how an action is conceived. Collingwood is unambiguous about this, and maintains that its pivotal aspect is the thought it embodies. That is, actions should be seen as expressions of thoughts, implying their rationality. In this human beings differ from animals, Collingwood avers, and it is accordingly this attribute the study of history is aimed at.

Though in human life its 'animal' aspects, such as being born, eating, sleeping, begetting

children, becoming ill, and dying, are most important, Collingwood says in *The Principles of History*, it is not in these aspects in themselves that historians are interested. They are interested in the institutions that have arisen from them and the various rituals that surround them. People eat and die, 'but the history of dining is not the history of eating, and the history of death-rituals is not the history of death'. After referring to the classical definition of human being as *animal rationale*, Collingwood summarizes his viewpoint saying: '[o]n a foundation of animal life his rationality builds a structure of free activities' (PH, 46).

His examples of thought as embodied in human actions clearly illustrate that thought should indeed be conceived in a wide sense. In contrast to the criticism concerned it indicates in particular that it is not limited to individual actions, not overtly rationalistic, and social history is not excluded.

But it is interesting to note that in *The Principles of History* Collingwood also explicitly anticipates another criticism, to wit that his position would exclude unreasonable actions. For after saying that *res gestae* should be seen as 'actions done by reasonable agents in pursuit of ends determined by their reason', he continues:

> These include – is it necessary to add? – acts done by an unreasonable agent in pursuit of ends (or in the adoption of means) determined by his unreason; for what is meant by unreason, in a context of this kind, is not the absence of reasons but the presence of bad ones; and a bad reason is still a reason. A brute that wants discourse of reason does not make a fool of itself. The actions traditionally studied by history are actions in this narrower sense of the word: actions in which reason, in a high or a low degree, reason triumphant or reason frustrated, wise thought or foolish thought, is not only at work but recognizably at work.[12] (PH, 47)

With regard to the argument developed by Collingwood on the rationality of actions, W.H. Dray has made the appropriate distinction between subjective and objective rationality. In the first an action is found rational 'in the sense of viewing its implicit argument as sound'. But since that argument may be derived from erroneous beliefs and is related to the purposes the agent in fact had, 'no matter how foolish or even monstrous they may have been,' Dray argues, 'the claim to understand the action by grasping the soundness of its argument is clearly compatible with the judgment that, objectively speaking, the action is very irrational indeed.'[13] As Dray correctly observes, it is the subjective rationality that Collingwood has in mind when considering the rationality implied in actions. That is, what is at issue is the agent's point of view, its subjective rationality being part of it, and not a supposedly objective rationality.

This position is related to the topic of the role of 'objective conditions' in history as well, that can be seen as the counterpart of the idea of an assumed objective rationality. For in the case of objective conditions Collingwood emphasizes as well its 'subjective' relevance, that is, its thought-side. To put it plainly, it is his position that natural conditions in themselves do not determine human conduct, but only influence it through the way they are conceived.

In a chapter entitled 'Nature and action' this subject is extensively discussed by Collingwood in *The Principles of History*. In this case the idea that history traditionally occupies 'a position of pupilage' under natural science is taken as starting-point. This 'historical naturalism' is, Collingwood avers, exemplified, among other things, by emphasis being put on the influence of natural conditions like geography and climate on history. But '[i]t is not nature as such and in itself (where nature means the natural environment) that turns man's energies here in one direction, there in another,' Collingwood declares, 'it is what man makes of nature by his enterprise, his dexterity, his ingenuity, or his lack of these things.' The sea is given as example, which 'estranges only people who have not learnt to sail on it. When they have discovered the art of navigation, and become reasonably skilled mariners, the sea no longer estranges, it unites. It ceases to be an obstacle,

it becomes a highway' (PH, 93). So it is not nature in itself that influences the course of history, but 'the beliefs about nature, true or false, entertained by the human beings whose actions are in question' (PH, 96).

Collingwood even extends this principle to any supposedly 'brute force' people might be confronted with. If, for instance, the troops of a weak nation yield to the stronger ones of an aggressor, '[w]hat makes them yield ... is not the situation's being what it is "in itself", but their knowledge that the situation is like that. ... A defeated army is an army that thinks it is no use going on fighting.' 'The phrase hard facts, in the mouth of an historian,' Collingwood concludes, 'refers to the facts of how certain human beings on certain occasions think' (PH, 96).

However Collingwood's position on the role of 'objective' conditions or situations in history may be valued, it cannot be denied that the issue raised by him is not only of importance for the theory of history, but has repercussions for historiographical practice as well. One could also observe that the criticism that the doctrine of all history being the history of thought does not take objective conditions or situations into account is in fact begging the question, actually assuming what is at issue.

That Collingwood's theory would be limited to individual actions is rather curious, since there is more reason to assume that he would – on account of his archaeological practice – underline the opposite. For it is typical for archaeological remains that they are the products of anonymous actions. In his celebrated article 'The purpose of the Roman wall', for instance, Collingwood gave a reconstruction of the thoughts embodied in the building of Hadrian's Wall, these being totally anonymous.[14] After rejecting in *The Principles of History* biographies as a serious form of historiography, Collingwood explicitly states his position on the subject: 'the history of a thought has nothing to do with the names of the people who think it' (PH, 75). Besides his writings on archaeology, the manuscripts on folklore and anthropology evidence as well that this position was taken seriously by Collingwood.[15] This does not mean, however, that he was not interested in the thoughts implied in individual actions. For both in theory and practice there is ample evidence to the contrary.

Reviewing the preceding considerations concerning the various criticisms levelled against Collingwood's doctrine of all history being the history of thought, the conclusion is justified that it is not as extravagant as so many commentators have thought it to be. Though it has a certain air of provocation, it cannot be denied that it is challenging as well. In Collingwood's view, however, it is also related to the doctrine of the re-enactment of the past.

## THE RECEPTION OF THE RE-ENACTMENT DOCTRINE

We have seen how Collingwood developed his doctrine of the re-enactment of past thought in his 'Outlines of a philosophy of history' in 1928. However, since this essay was only available in print in 1993, in the preceding decades the comments on this doctrine were only based on *The Idea of History*.

In the beginning of the chapter 'History as re-enactment of past experience' in *The Idea of History*, Collingwood gives the reading of the Theodosian Code as an illustration of what he understands re-enactment of past thought to mean. In order to know its historical significance merely reading the words and being able to translate them does not suffice, the historian 'must envisage the situation with which the emperor was trying to deal, and he must envisage it as that emperor envisaged it'. After this Collingwood continues:

> Then he must see for himself, just as if the emperor's situation were his own, how such a situation might be dealt with; he must see the possible alternatives, and the reasons for choosing one rather than another; and thus he must go through the process which the emperor went through in deciding on this particular course.

> Thus he is re-enacting in his own mind the experience of the emperor; and only in so far as he does this has he any historical knowledge, as distinct from merely philological knowledge, of the meaning of the edict. (IH, 283)

This passage indeed describes the substance of the re-enactment doctrine: it is only through the re-enactment of past thought that historical knowledge is achieved.

As with the theory of all history being the history of thought, the comments on the re-enactment doctrine initially have been mainly critical, especially since it was seen as an inappropriate methodological directive for attaining historical knowledge. The philosopher W.H. Walsh, one of the first to comment on Collingwood's theory, expressed what in the first instance has been the general opinion: it claimed 'that history involves a unique and direct form of understanding which raises it above other kinds of knowledge'.[16] This direct form of understanding was generally seen as implying a kind of intuition. It is not surprising that this was not considered a convincing theory of historical knowledge, implying a subjectivist theory of truth, but also being non-inferential and unscientific.

The interpretation of the re-enactment doctrine as being a methodology involving an intuitive capacity came under heavy fire, however, by the philosophers A. Donagan and W.H. Dray. They argued that it should not be conceived as a methodology for acquiring historical knowledge, but as the answer to the philosophical question how historical knowledge is possible.[17] With the availability of 'Outlines of a philosophy of history' one can definitely state that this is indeed the correct interpretation of the re-enactment doctrine. For we have seen how in that essay the capacity of re-enacting past thoughts is put forward as a solution to the problem of how knowledge of a non-existing past is possible.

Dray has shown how the re-enactment doctrine viewed in this way has repercussions for the way the study of the past is conceived. For in his *Laws and Explanation in History* (1957) he develops the 'rational explanation model' for explaining actions, contrasting it with the 'covering law model' as advocated by Carl Hempel and Karl Popper. This has started a lively debate not only in the philosophy of history, but in the philosophy of science in general as well. Since Dray's rational explanation model is based on Collingwood's re-enactment doctrine the latter has indirectly played a major part in the discussions on the nature of explanation in history and the social sciences. In his book on Collingwood's philosophy of history, written almost 40 years after *Laws and Explanation in History*, Dray still refers to the rational explanation model, saying of Collingwood's idea of re-enactive understanding that the historian elicits 'from the performance of an action an implied practical argument which represents what was done as the thing to have done, given the agent's point of view'.[18] Though this interpretation of Collingwood's re-enactment doctrine is certainly correct, it should be observed, however, that it does not cover all aspects implied by this doctrine. For, in Collingwood's view, its relevance is not limited to explaining or understanding individual actions, and is, besides this, also relevant for the interpretation of human artefacts.

## THE PHILOSOPHICAL DIMENSION OF THE RE-ENACTMENT DOCTRINE

In spite of the fact that the methodological interpretation of Collingwood's re-enactment doctrine, let alone the intuitive version of it, has been definitely refuted, this does not mean, though, that it is no subject of debate anymore. For it is still widely discussed and commented upon. This is not without reason, for – though this has hardly been realized – it should be noted that as a philosophical theory the re-enactment doctrine raises some important philosophical issues. This is the case, in the first place, with the concept of thought, being an essential part of the re-enactment doctrine. For this concept is ambiguous in the sense that it can refer both to the act of thought and its content. Collingwood

was well aware of this distinction, but this has been less the case with his interpreters, this being to a large degree the background of the methodological interpretation given to the re-enactment doctrine.

An act of thought is strictly individual and occurs, Collingwood says, 'at a certain time, and in a certain context of other acts of thought, emotions, sensations, and so forth'. Thought in this sense he calls thought 'in its immediacy'. He emphasizes that the immediate, as such, cannot be re-enacted, including the thought involved: 'thought itself can never be re-enacted in its immediacy' (IH, 297). With the content of thought the situation is different, however. Though Collingwood does not refer to it explicitly, he has this in mind when he says that 'an act of thought, in addition to actually happening, is capable of sustaining itself and being revived or repeated without loss of its identity' (IH, 300). Elsewhere this is phrased differently, when Collingwood refers to 'the way in which thought, transcending its own immediacy, survives and revives in other contexts' (IH, 303). Thought in this sense he calls thought 'in mediation', in contrast to thought in its immediacy (IH, 300-1).

These references to the different senses of the concept of thought are made by Collingwood in passing, and are therefore easily disregarded. He touches, however, on an important philosophical issue, that has been profoundly worked out by the German logician and philosopher Gottlob Frege in his celebrated article *Der Gedanke. Eine logische Untersuchung* ('Thought. A logical inquiry'), published in 1918.[19] Frege argues that thought is what is expressed by a sentence, the thought being its sense, but it is also something for which the question of truth arises. Frege emphasizes the public character of thought, and as such sharply distinguishes it from what he calls *Vorstellungen* ('ideas'). The latter are private and belong to the content of one's consciousness; they need an owner and can only have one owner ('no two men have the same idea').[20]

Thoughts, in contrast, differ from ideas in that they do not need an owner to the contents of whose consciousness they belong. Giving the thought expressed in the Pythagorean theorem, Frege gives as example, is not an idea, since '[i]f other people can assent to the thought I express in the Pythagorean theorem just as I do, then it does not belong to the content of my consciousness, I am not its owner'.[21] A little further Frege expands on the difference between an idea and thought:

> Not everything is an idea. Thus I can also acknowledge thoughts as independent of me; other men can grasp them just as much as I; I can acknowledge a science in which many can be engaged in research. We are not owners of thoughts as we are owners of our ideas. We do not *have* a thought as we have, say, a sense impression, but we also do not *see* a thought as we see, say, a star. So it is advisable to choose a special expression; the word 'grasp' suggests itself for the purpose. To the grasping of thoughts there must then correspond a special mental capacity, the power of thinking. In thinking we do not produce thoughts, we grasp them … The grasp of a thought presupposes someone who grasps it, who thinks. He is the owner of the thinking, not of the thought.[22]

Collingwood was not acquainted with the writings of Frege, but it is remarkable how the latter in fact describes in his article the philosophical foundation of the re-enactment doctrine. What Collingwood calls thought 'in mediation' Frege simply calls thought. Both emphasize the public nature of thought,[23] in contrast with the private nature of what is called by Collingwood thought 'in its immediacy' and by Frege 'ideas'. The 'grasping' of thoughts, as conceived by Frege, can be seen, furthermore, as the equivalent of Collingwood's idea of re-enacting thoughts. Collingwood would also endorse an observation made by Frege at the end of his article, saying: 'The influence of man on man is brought about for the most part by thoughts … Could the great events of world history have come about without the communication of thoughts?'[24]

Frege has written another famous article, *Über Sinn und Bedeutung* ('On sense and meaning') (1892),[25] parts of which are also relevant for a proper understanding of the re-enactment doctrine. In this article Frege develops an authoritative argument about the distinction between sense and meaning as regards words and sentences. In a sentence the thought it contains is its sense, Frege argues, its meaning being constituted by its truth value, that is, the circumstance of its being either true or false.

There is a problem, however, with sentences which refer in a subordinate sentence to a thought. For in this case the subordinate sentence does not have its truth value as meaning, as is the case with normal sentences, Frege maintains, but a thought, its sense being the one of the words 'the thought, that …'. A main sentence referring to a subordinate one containing a thought occurs, Frege says, 'after "say", "hear", "be of the opinion of", "be convinced", "conclude", and similar words'.[26] He gives as example the two sentences 'Copernicus believed that the planetary orbits are circles', and 'Copernicus believed that the apparent motion of the Sun is produced by the real motion of the Earth'.[27] In this case the two main sentences are true, though of the subordinate sentences the first one is false and the second one true. This means that in cases like this, in which reference is made to a thought, not the truth value of the latter is at issue, but only the sense of the thought concerned.

It should be noted, however, that though in the subordinate sentence only its sense is at issue, this does not preclude, of course, that a judgement can be made on its truth value. That is, in the examples given of Copernicus' beliefs, that the first one is false. This means that statements about thoughts are layered in the sense that both the sense of the latter are grasped and an assessment is made of them. Collingwood calls this the principle of the 'incapsulation' of thoughts, formulated by him as follows: 'Historical knowledge is the re-enactment of a past thought incapsulated in a context of present thoughts which, by contradicting it, confine it to a plane different from theirs' (Aut, 114).[28]

Sentences referring to thoughts are called by Frege 'indirect speech' ('*ungerade Rede*'). The problems involved with it have aroused a voluminous literature in semantics, and is also known as the problem of propositional attitudes, *oratio obliqua*, or oblique contexts.

It is obvious that the issue concerned is highly relevant for Collingwood's thesis that all history is the history of thought. For taking this as starting-point, one could say that the language of historians may be characterized as specifically consisting of sentences containing indirect speech, that is, expressing thoughts about thoughts. That this is indeed the case, is illustrated by an historical example of indirect speech given by Frege:

> If, toward the end of the battle of Waterloo, Wellington was glad that the Prussians were coming, the basis for his joy was a conviction. Had he been deceived, he would have been no less pleased so long as his illusion lasted; and before he became so convinced he could not have been pleased that the Prussians were coming – even though in fact they might have been already approaching.[29]

This example also illustrates the correctness of Collingwood's position with regard to the influence of objective conditions, to wit that what is at issue is not these conditions in themselves, but how they are conceived.

But the idea of indirect speech is relevant for the re-enactment doctrine in another sense as well. For it has been a point of debate to what extent Collingwood's claim is plausible that in re-enacting past thoughts 'the same thoughts' are re-thought. In connection with this issue it is relevant that in indirect speech the truth of the main sentence is not dependent on the literal expression as used in the embedded sentence. A concept or idea may not even have been expressed explicitly, as is the case, for instance, with beliefs. As it is formulated by the philosopher Peter Geach: '*Oratio obliqua* serves to give us, not the actual words that somebody said, but rather their gist or purport.'[30] Dray refers to the same

principle, when he says: 'what ... [the agent] *was* explicitly aware of thinking need not be re-thought by the historian in precisely the way it was originally thought by the agent, there being as many ways of thinking the same thought as there are ways of expressing it.'[31]

The foregoing makes clear that the positions as developed by Collingwood in his re-enactment doctrine are not only related to some intricate philosophical problems, but also have a sound philosophical foundation.

## HISTORICAL METHODOLOGY

Whereas the doctrines of the re-enactment of the past and all history being the history of thought are the best known and most widely discussed topics of Collingwood's philosophy of history, it is notable that his own conception of the nature of a philosophy of history was primarily aimed at the methodological aspects of the study of history. Though the two doctrines mentioned are an essential element of Collingwood's view of history, his main interest was focused on comprehensive issues related to the study of history.

In his first lectures on the subject, given in 1926, he describes philosophy of history as 'bringing to light the principles used in historical thinking, and criticizing them', adding to it that 'so understood, [it] is the methodology of history' (IH, 346-7). The doctrines Collingwood is especially known for did indeed play a part in the methodological principles of historical thought he was primarily interested in – they partly providing their philosophical foundation – but the latter cannot outright be reduced to the former. The views Collingwood developed on the methodology of history therefore deserve attention in themselves. The concepts and subjects Collingwood's views on the methodology of history are especially related to are the logic of question and answer, historical evidence and its interpretation, and the narrative aspect of history. In the following attention will successively be paid to these aspects.

## THE LOGIC OF QUESTION AND ANSWER

The essence of knowledge should in Collingwood's view not be seen, in accordance with the empiricist tradition, as the assertion of facts, but as a process of question and answer. 'Questioning is the cutting edge of knowledge,' he says in *Speculum Mentis*, 'assertion is the dead weight behind the edge that gives it driving force' (SM, 78). In *An Autobiography* Collingwood explicitly returns to the subject. The context within which this is done is notable, since Collingwood explains that it has been the 'laboratory of knowledge' of his archaeological practice that has taught him the lesson of the importance of the question and answer approach (Aut, 24). What he refers to is that an archaeological digging should always be undertaken with a specific question in mind, in the hope or expectation that the digging will provide the answer. This 'selective digging' is put against the practice of 'blind digging'. It was especially in his excavations and research related to Hadrian's Wall that Collingwood has put the question and answer approach into practice.

The interesting point, however, is that Collingwood extends the lesson learnt from archaeology to knowledge in general, on the principles of Bacon and Descartes, that 'knowledge comes only by answering questions, and that these questions must be the right questions and asked in the right order' (Aut, 25). In *The Idea of History* as well Collingwood refers to the importance Bacon attached to the questioning activity. This time it is put within the context of the rise of experimental natural science finding 'its proper method when the scientist, in Bacon's metaphor, puts Nature to the question, tortures her by experiment in order to wring from her answers to his own questions' (IH, 237).

What Collingwood in *An Autobiography* calls the 'logic of question and answer' is in his opinion the pivotal characteristic of science. Since this feature is also exhibited in the study of history in its advanced stage, Collingwood without reserve considers history to be a science: 'generically it belongs to what we call the sciences: that is, the forms of thought whereby we ask questions and try to answer them' (IH, 9). This argument, claiming that natural science and history correspond in having the same basis is noteworthy, especially since it is hardly to be found with other authors on the theory and philosophy of history.

The relation between question and answer is not only relevant for historical research as regards asking specific questions, but in another sense as well. For any statement should be seen, in Collingwood's view, as an answer to a specific question, and can accordingly only be understood if the question it was meant to answer is taken into account. '[N]ever think you understand any statement made by a philosopher,' he says, 'until you have decided, with the utmost possible accuracy, what the question is to which he means it for an answer' (Aut, 74). Likewise certain actions should be seen as solutions to particular problems. The tactical problem that Nelson set himself at Trafalgar, Collingwood gives as example, can only be discovered 'by studying the tactics he pursued in the battle. We argue back from the solution to the problem' (Aut, 70). The observation should be made, though, that this approach apparently cannot be realized in cases where the solution of a problem has failed. In occasions like these certain relevant conditions and circumstances will have to be taken into account, this making an understanding or explanation more complicated, including discerning the nature of the problem concerned.

Notwithstanding the problems that may be involved in practice, the principles implied by the logic of question and answer as put forward by Collingwood are of importance for the study of history for two reasons, being related to two aspects that may be distinguished. In the first place it serves as a directive for historical inquiry, the principle being that historical research should always be guided by specific questions. Secondly, it implies a theory of historical interpretation – that is, as a hermeneutical principle – in that the past should be interpreted within the context of a question and answer complex.

As a theory of inquiry the logic of question and answer is relevant for the activity of the historian – history *a parte subjecti* – his or her research being seen as part of a question and answer process. As a theory of hermeneutics it is relevant for interpreting the past, *history a parte objecti*. In the first, as has been noted by Louis Mink, one looks forward, the historian being part of a question and answer process that is prospectively open, whereas in the second a question and answer process is traced backward, it being retrospectively determinate.[32]

## HISTORICAL METHOD: THE IMPORTANCE OF EVIDENCE

As said, Collingwood claims, in contrast to almost all theoreticians and philosophers of history, that history is a science. But he also emphasizes that it is a science of a special kind. As has been explained above, this position is based on the specific object of the study of history, it accordingly having a specific methodology of its own, evidence playing a pivotal part in it. The fact that the first chapter of *The Principles of History*, Collingwood's endeavour to write a 'final' book on the philosophy of history, is about historical evidence, indicates the importance he attached to the subject. It is the only chapter of the manuscript of the book that has been included by Knox in *The Idea of History* (249–82).[33]

In this chapter the role of evidence is explained in an argument putting the study of history against natural science and the exact sciences. In this connection attention is paid in particular to the kind of inferences used. Whereas in natural science and the exact sciences the inferences made are respectively

inductive and deductive, for history neither of these is appropriate, Collingwood argues. But he claims that history is inferential as well, meaning by it that it is, as with the other sciences, based on particular grounds leading to specific conclusions.[34] These grounds are provided by evidence. This is a necessary characteristic of history, since it deals with a vanished reality, in contrast to natural science, which is based on observation and experiments. This brings Collingwood to the following definition of the study of history:

> History, then, is a science, but a science of a special kind. It is a science whose business is to study events not accessible to our observation, and to study these events inferentially, arguing to them from something else which is accessible to our observation, and which the historian calls 'evidence' for the events in which he is interested. (IH, 251–2)

That Collingwood considered the use of evidence as the all-important characteristic of history is manifested time and again in his writings. In his article 'The limits of historical knowledge' (1928), for instance, it is the central topic of his argument, evidence being described as the limit the historian cannot transcend.[35] The first 'rule of the game' of history, he says, 'runs thus: "You must not say anything, however true, for which you cannot produce evidence"'.[36] Likewise in *An Autobiography* Collingwood maintains that 'no historian is entitled to draw cheques in his own favour on evidence that he does not possess, however lively his hopes that it may hereafter be discovered. He must argue from the evidence he has, or stop arguing' (Aut, 139).

Whereas in these statements evidence is put forward as a formal requirement for historical knowledge, Collingwood emphasizes its material significance as well. In the draft of his inaugural lecture (1935) he says about it:

> [T]he advancement of historical knowledge and the improvement of historical method comes about mainly through discovering the evidential value of certain kinds of perceived fact which hitherto historians have thought worthless to them. The discovery of new kinds of evidence may have

two functions: it may help to answer old questions, or it may solve new problems about which,
if only because there was no evidence bearing
upon them, historians have not previously
thought. (PH, 164)

An interesting example of exploring new
kinds of evidence is given by Collingwood in
his manuscripts on folklore and anthropology, which discuss fairy tales, myths and
customs as evidence for reconstructing the
historical life of societies. He calls it 'in
effect a new kind of archaeology', which in
contrast to archaeology in the ordinary sense
does not study fragments of material objects,
but 'fragments of ... customs and beliefs
handed down in traditional stories'.[37]

## EMPIRICAL AND PURE METHODOLOGY

Collingwood's involvement with the topic of
evidence in history is not limited to indicating its importance, however. For in his
'Lectures on the philosophy of history' the
chapters 'The sources of history' and 'The
interpretation of sources' extensively deal
with the subject (IH, 368–90).[38] The way the
topics of sources and their use as evidence is
discussed is of great interest for historians.
The essay is especially striking as an exem-
plification of the way Collingwood's experience as an archaeologist and historian gives
substance and authenticity to his philosophical arguments.

Collingwood emphasizes that historical
sources should be interpreted according to
principles. These principles have their origin,
he says, 'not in the facts as we observe them,
but in the thought which we bring to bear
upon them' (IH, 384). For this reason they
should be justified a priori, that is, 'made into
objects of critical study and discussion by a
scientific methodology of history' (IH, 385).
Within this a distinction is made between
'empirical' and 'general or pure' methodology.[39]
The first is concerned with the peculiarities of
different kinds of evidence and exemplified
by sciences as palaeography, diplomatics,

epigraphy, numismatics, historical architecture, 'and all the ramifications of archaeology
in its application to various kinds of imple-
ments and relics' (IH, 386).

General or pure methodology, in contrast,
'is concerned with problems of method which
are never absent from any piece of historical
thinking'. Collingwood considers this a
'much more important part of historical methodology', giving the problem of the argument
from silence as example (IH, 388).[40]

Collingwood has made substantial contributions to both the 'empirical' and 'pure'
methodology of history. Though he is nowadays especially known for the latter, that is,
his philosophy of history, during his life he
was in particular known for his contributions
to the empirical methodology of history. His
masterpiece in this field has been *The Archaeology of Roman Britain* (1930), the first and
for decades the only handbook on the subject.[41]
In 16 chapters the various sources relevant for
the history of Roman Britain are discussed,
from roads, villas, and coins to brooches.
Even for people not knowledgeable about the
subject some parts of it are a delight to read.
This is the case, for instance, with the paragraph on 'Coins as archaeological evidence',
describing the principles involved in the interpretation of coins as evidence.[42] Collingwood's
expertise, however, was in the field of epigraphy. He worked on it from 1920, 'travelling
about the country and drawing Roman
inscriptions' (Aut, 145). It made Collingwood
an internationally acknowledged expert on
Roman epigraphy, but it was only in 1965 that
the results of his work in this field were posthumously published.[43]

## THE RELEVANCE OF ARCHAEOLOGY FOR HISTORY

From his archaeological practice Collingwood
derived certain principles for history in general, that is, for its 'pure' methodology. They
are based on the idea that in his opinion the
distinction between unwritten and written
sources is invalid. In the first instance written

sources may appear to be more informative, but in Collingwood's view this is deceptive, since they should be critically studied in the same way as unwritten sources.

As has been explained above, the logic of question and answer is the driving force of this critical approach. In archaeology this not only means that one should start a digging with a certain question in mind, but also more specifically, that with certain objects definite questions should be asked in terms of purposes. 'Whenever you find any object you must ask, "What was it for?",' Collingwood avers, 'and, arising out of that question, "Was it good or bad for it? i.e. was the purpose embodied in it successfully embodied in it, or unsuccessfully?" These questions, being historical questions, must be answered not by guesswork but on historical evidence' (Aut, 128). In *The Principles of History* Collingwood gives the example of certain objects that are interpreted as being loom-weights. 'At this point they speak to him as an historian,' Collingwood says, because they tell him something about the thoughts of the people concerned: they wove and therefore produced textiles (PH, 66–7).

That the interpretative principle implied by the logic of question and answer is not only valid for archaeology, but for history in general as well, is stated explicitly by Collingwood: 'The principle applies not merely to archaeology, but to every kind of history. Where written sources are used, it implies that any action attributed by the sources to any character must be understood in the same way' (Aut, 130–1). He gives the example that the explanation of the fact that Julius Caesar did not mention in his *Commentaries* his intention for invading Britain was that 'whatever his purpose had been he had failed to achieve it'. Collingwood comments on this that he has reasons for believing that Caesar must not have intended a mere punitive expedition, but the complete conquest of the country (Aut, 131). Whatever the quality of this interpretation ('this view of mine may be mistaken,' Collingwood says), the methodological point he wants to make is

clear: by asking certain questions about written sources they may even be informative about aspects that are not referred to.

What Collingwood in fact has in mind is to transfer the principles of archaeological practice, which in his view heavily relies on the logic of question and answer, to the study of history in general. For this reason in 'Historical evidence' the relation between asking questions and evidence is emphasized: '[q]uestion and evidence, in history, are correlative,' Collingwood maintains. About the nature of evidence, however, nothing can be said in general, for 'everything in the world is potential evidence for any subject whatever' (IH, 281, 280). Questions, in contrast, must have two qualities: they must be sensible ('[t]o ask questions which you see no prospect of answering is the fundamental sin in science') and specific ('nothing is evidence except in relation to some definite question'). For this reason Collingwood endorses Lord Acton's 'great precept', 'Study problems, not periods' (IH, 281).

## THE INTERPRETATION OF EVIDENCE IN *THE PRINCIPLES OF HISTORY*

As said before, 'Historical evidence', being part of *The Idea of History*, is in fact the first chapter of the manuscript of *The Principles of History*. In a paragraph of the second chapter of the manuscript, entitled 'Evidence and language', Collingwood expands on the subject, however, saying that 'our previous examination of historical method has not gone far enough'. Referring to the concrete objects like footprints, paint-smears, etc., described as evidence in the detective story used in the previous chapter as example of the question and answer approach, Collingwood observes that 'strictly speaking evidence consists not in these things themselves but in something else which may be roughly defined as "what they say"'. 'The relation between historical evidence and the conclusions drawn from it, historical knowledge,' he says, 'is the relation between what such things "say" and "what it means"' (PH, 48–9). The nature of historical evidence therefore needs a more refined explanation.

This is done by Collingwood in a subsequent passage, in which evidence is related to thoughts as expressed in actions, the latter being the specific object of history. This time he uses the more or less traditional example of interpreting an historical document. If an historian has a certain charter of Henry I, Collingwood argues, he should go through four stages in its interpretation: he must satisfy himself that the copy is a true one; he must satisfy himself that the original was genuine, and not a forgery; he must read it and find out what it says; and finally 'he must decide what it means, that is to say, what Henry I was "driving at" when he issued that charter' (PH, 51).

Of these four stages Collingwood considers the first one an affair of 'practical judgment', and the second of textual scholarship. They should therefore not be seen, Collingwood says, as examples of historical thinking. But even the third stage is in his view not yet history, though it is 'an essential preliminary' of it. Its relation to history can be defined, he says, 'as apprehending or discerning the evidence' (PH, 52). It is only at the fourth stage that the import of the charter as historical evidence is grasped.

This clarification of the nature of historical evidence is an emendation of what was said on the subject in the preceding chapter. For there it was stated that evidence is observed, whereas it is now emphasized that a historian should be able to 'read' what evidence 'says'. It is curious that no attention is paid to the inferential aspect of historical knowledge, this being explicitly put forward in 'Historical evidence'. It is only mentioned in the summary of the chapter, when Collingwood says about the relation between the third and fourth stage of interpretation: 'The perceptible "evidence" is in the nature of language or of a notation of language, and the historian must treat it as such before he can use its message as the starting-point of an inference' (PH, 76).

It is also remarkable that no mention is made of the 'empirical methodology' of the 'archaeological sciences' of history, that is, the auxiliary sciences. For the critical study of sources, though belonging to the earlier stages of Collingwood's four-stage theory of historical interpretation, is, as we have seen, highly valued by Collingwood in his 'Lectures on the philosophy of history' of 1926 and 1928. 'These archaeological sciences are a *sine qua non* of critical history,' he says in 'Outlines of a philosophy of history', 'They are not themselves history; they are only methods of dealing with the sources of history … They form, as it were, the bones of all historical thinking. History itself must be flexible, but it must have rigid bones' (IH, 490–1).

Discussing the interpretation of historical evidence in the second chapter of *The Principles of History* Collingwood focuses on its final stage of making known its meaning within an historical argument. This is considered by him history in the proper sense of the word. It is indeed flexible and inferential, but the part played by the 'archaeological sciences' as its rigid bones is left out of account in his exposition. As with other aspects of Collingwood's philosophy of history, his view on the interpretation of evidence has to be reconstructed from bits and pieces.

## HISTORY: FROM SCISSORS-AND-PASTE TO CRITICAL HISTORY

In the foregoing an exposition has been given of Collingwood's considered views on the study of history. In putting forward these views he contrasted them with what he regarded as false conceptions of history. Collingwood saw the scientific study of history as the outcome of an historical process, beginning with the ancient Greeks. It is extensively described by him in the first four parts of *The Idea of History*, from Greco-Roman historiography to scientific history (IH, 14–204). In this account, especially in the part on scientific history, Collingwood frequently refers to what in his judgement are mistaken or fallacious ideas of history.

But these false conceptions of history, seen from an historical perspective, are also dealt with by Collingwood in a systematic way. Since in criticizing these views he develops his own position, it deserves special attention. This approach is in particular actualized in 'The historical imagination' (1935), Collingwood's inaugural as Waynflete Professor of Metaphysical Philosophy at Magdalen College in Oxford. It is reprinted in *The Idea of History* (IH, 231–49), but a draft of it is one of the manuscripts added to the edition of *The Principles of History*.[44] Though the draft covers the same ground as the inaugural lecture, parts of it are quite different, and for this reason of interest. In addition to the inaugural and its draft, Collingwood also discusses the flaws of past views on history in parts of 'Historical evidence'.

'The historical imagination' is aimed at explaining the characteristics of history as a science. With a view to this Collingwood begins with a description of the flaws of what he calls the 'common-sense' theory of history. This theory is based on the view that the grounds of historical knowledge are memory and authority. That is, someone must have been acquainted with an aspect of the past and its recollection transmitted, which subsequently is accepted by another person as true. 'History is thus the believing some one else when he says that he remembers something,' Collingwood says, 'The believer is the historian; the person believed is called his authority' (IH, 234–5).

This theory breaks down, Collingwood argues, for three reasons. In the first place a selection has to be made from the information given by the authorities, since they often tell him not only too little, but too much (PH, 144–5). The selection an historian inevitably has to make is based on the idea of what he or she thinks of importance, and this is the starting-point of critical history. But there are also other aspects making critical history necessary. For the testimonies of authorities may conflict, or they may assert things to have happened which the historian believes

to be impossible (PH, 146). In the third place an historian makes interpolations in the testimonies of authorities, Collingwood argues, for instance, when facts are concealed or not known (PH, 147–8).

This brings Collingwood to the conclusion that the common-sense view of history gives an altogether inadequate picture of historical knowledge. 'Throughout the course of his work the historian is selecting, constructing, and criticizing,' he says, adding to it that 'it is only by doing these things that he maintains his thought upon the *sichere Gang einer Wissenschaft*' (IH, 236). The essence of scientific history is, as compared with the common-sense view, that the tables are turned on the status of authorities: instead of the historian relying on his or her authorities, 'the historian is his own authority and his thought autonomous, self-authorizing, possessed of a criterion to which his so-called authorities must conform and by reference to which they are criticized' (IH, 236). Following Kant in his characterization of his theory of knowledge, Collingwood speaks in this connection of 'a Copernican revolution in the theory of history'.

In 'Historical evidence' Collingwood develops the same argument, the common-sense view of history being named differently, however: 'History constructed by excerpting and combining the testimonies of different authorities I call scissors-and-paste history' (IH, 257). This notion has become a well-known slogan of Collingwood's philosophy of history. In 'Historical evidence', but also the subsequent chapters of *The Principles of History*, Collingwood is extremely critical of scissors-and-paste history, even saying that 'it is not really history at all' (IH, 257). Conceptions of history he repudiates Collingwood accordingly usually typifies as being examples of scissors-and-paste history. Biography, for instance, 'is not history, because … [i]ts methods are scissors-and-paste' (PH, 77), and historical naturalism is rejected, because it 'presupposes that history is a scissors-and-paste affair and can never be anything else' (PH, 108).

The idea of scissors-and-paste history is used by Collingwood as a contrast to explain his conception of scientific history. Authorities lose their traditional status and are turned into sources that should be critically studied and put in the 'witness-box'. In scientific history, Collingwood avers, no use is made of ready-made statements, since statements are not treated as statements, but as evidence used by the historian to find answers for his or her own questions.

## CONSTRUCTIVE HISTORY AND IMAGINATION

In critical history the historian goes beyond the information offered by authorities and extracts from it answers to specific questions. But there is another way as well in which an historian goes beyond his or her authorities. Collingwood calls it the constructive one, saying of it that it is 'still higher and more important than critical history' (PH, 150). The peculiar features of it are that interpolations are made and that it is inferential, but more importantly, that both are based on imagination. It is the imaginative aspect of historical thought that comprises the main argument of 'The historical imagination', but its draft is more comprehensive about the issue.

Imagination is, Collingwood says – again following Kant – an *a priori* faculty of the human mind, that is, it is a universal and necessary aspect of it. He gives perception as an example, since it always imaginatively 'sees' more than is actually perceived: 'the under-side of this table, the back of the moon, the inside of a unopened egg' (PH, 166). The *a priori* imagination is also at work, Collingwood says, with 'the pure or free, but by no means arbitrary, imagination of the artist' (IH, 242).

Historical imagination is put forward by Collingwood as a third kind of imaginative activity. It presents us a past that cannot be perceived, but through imagination becomes an object of our thought. He gives the simple example of our authorities telling that Caesar was in Rome at one day and in Gaul on a later day. Though nothing is said about the journey, one may safely interpolate that he travelled from one place to the other. The 'web of imaginative construction' that provides the historian's picture of his or her subject, should not be seen, however, as pegged down to certain fixed facts supplied by authorities. For we have seen that the latter should be examined critically. It is pegged down, therefore, 'to the conclusions at which [the historian] has arrived by criticizing his authorities, or rather, interpreting his sources'. After this Collingwood comments: 'The element of given fact has disappeared altogether. Our common-sense theory maintained that in history everything is given; the conclusion which we have now reached is that nothing is given' (PH, 154). What Collingwood wants to make clear is that the imaginative and constructive activity of the historian should be seen as the guiding directive in relation to the facts, and not the other way around. Of the web of imaginative construction he maintains that '[s]o far from relying for its validity upon the support of given facts, it actually serves as the touchstone by which we decide whether alleged facts are genuine' (IH, 244).

Though in his criticism of the common-sense theory of history Collingwood mainly focuses on the role of so-called authorities as source, it is obvious that historical sources are not limited to these. For in archaeology authorities are out of the question, with the consequence that in a history based on archaeological sources the imaginative and constructive activity of the historian is obviously manifest. It can even recover facts that were unknown to contemporaries, Collingwood says, giving the example of Gaulish potters who supplied most of the western Roman Empire with their products without knowing it (PH, 149). This example is illustrative for the web of imaginative construction as practised by historians. It should be added, however, that it not only holds for ancient history based on archaeological remains, but for history in general. For in Collingwood's view all history consists of all kinds of imaginative constructions based on all kinds of sources.

What Collingwood's theory of constructive history based on imagination in fact explicates, is the common practice of historians to see the subject of their studies as a coherent whole, that is, as a synthesis, in which certain events, actions, situations, conditions etc. are sorted out and connected in a comprehensive way. This practice has become familiar as 'colligation', a term used by W.H. Walsh, borrowing it from the nineteenth-century logician Whewell.[45] He means by it the process of '"colligating" events under "appropriate conceptions"' in order that the historian makes 'a coherent whole out of the events he studies', giving notions like the Enlightenment, the Romantic movement, the age of reform in nineteenth-century England, and the rise of monopoly capitalism as examples.[46]

## THE HISTORICAL NARRATIVE

Since the *a priori* imagination is not only at work in history, but also in art, Collingwood pays special attention to their relation. He sees a certain likeness between the historian and the artist, this being especially the case with the novelist, since '[t]he historian and the novelist are alike in that each of them tells a story'. But also the nature of the stories are similar in that in both characters are analysed, motives displayed, and situations described. '[T]he same generation which has revolted against the idea of the novelist as a mere story-teller,' Collingwood observes, 'has revolted against the idea of history as mere narrative' (PH, 161). The aim of both novelists and historians, he concludes, is to compose in their narratives a picture 'as a single coherent whole', which is 'displayed by the imagination to the imagination' (PH, 161–2).

The difference between the novelist and the historian, however, Collingwood avers, is that the picture of the past as given by the latter is meant to be true, a claim that can only be realized to the extent that it is based on evidence. There is only one way to assess the truth of an historian's picture of the past, Collingwood says: 'by doing his work over again for ourselves, that is, by reconsidering the evidence upon which his picture is based and, exercising upon this evidence our own historical imagination, finding that we are led to the same result' (PH, 164).

It is not surprising that Collingwood does not give a definition of historical truth, for it indeed cannot be given. Since the past does not exist anymore, there is no reality with which a description, let alone a picture, of the past can be compared. The imaginary picture of the past is therefore always a construction based on the inferences made from evidence. About the nature of this inferential relation Collingwood is conspicuously vague, however, merely saying that 'it is one of a peculiar kind' (PH, 165).[47] It is indeed peculiar, when Collingwood says that in drawing conclusions from evidence 'everything that the historian knows may enter either as additional premises or as controlling principles: knowledge about nature and man, mathematical knowledge, philosophical knowledge and so forth. The whole sum of his mental habits and possessions is active' (PH, 165, see also IH, 248). Collingwood even goes so far to conclude from this that 'since these are never quite the same in any two men, it is not to be expected that two men will necessarily draw exactly the same conclusion from the same evidence'. He comments, though, that this does not make history arbitrary or irrational, no more than 'the difference in apparent shape of the same body seen from various directions and distances proves the irrationality of visual perception' (PH, 165).

Though Collingwood emphasizes that in contrast to novelists the pictures of the past as given by historians are meant to be true, it is obvious that no definite rules can be given to ensure the latter. It should rather be seen as a regulative idea guiding the historian's work. In his inaugural lecture Collingwood refers in this connection to 'three rules of method, from which the novelist or artist in general is free', mentioning besides the reliance on evidence, that the historian's picture must be localized in space and time, and that all history must be consistent with itself: 'Purely imaginary worlds cannot clash and need not agree; each is a world to itself. But there is only one historical world' (IH, 246).

The preceding gives a rather abstract account of the similarities and differences between the imaginative pictures given by novelists and historians. It is in particular not clear how the 'meant to be true' claim of the latter should be conceived, let alone be realized. But in 'Outlines of a philosophy of history' Collingwood discusses the subject within the context of historiographical practice in a clarifying way. In the chapter 'Relation' he examines the nature of an historical monograph that illustrates the idea of what he would later call a web of imaginative construction as being typical for constructive history. An historical monograph, Collingwood says, 'has both a unity and a plurality in its composition'. 'As a unity, it is a single narrative, artistically and logically bound up into a whole; subjectively, it is one treatise; objectively, it is about one thing' (IH, 472). As examples he mentions the French Revolution, the Wars of the Roses, or the Evolution of the Pointed Arch.

The monograph as a whole, Collingwood maintains, 'is a sum of parts, each part being so designed as to make its proper contribution to the whole, and the whole being simply the organized system of parts ... Thus the whole must precede the part, in this sense, that the part must be thought out in relation to the whole. The converse is not true.' The practical consequence of this is that 'in composing an historical work, the first thing to do is to decide upon a subject' (IH, 473). This is illustrated in the following way:

> For instance, we should describe the battle of Trafalgar in different ways according as we were composing a treatise on naval tactics, on the Napoleonic Wars, on the life of Nelson, or on the influence of sea-power on history. Or we might be simply composing a monograph on the battle of Trafalgar, which would demand a different treatment again. (IH, 473)

The historian must therefore 'begin with the idea of his work as a whole, and develop every part in relation to this whole'. This is not enough, however, since the various parts of a treatise 'are not only related to the whole: they are related to each other'. That is, 'they are related chronologically: they state a temporal sequence and therefore constitute a narrative'. But '[t]hey constitute not merely a sequence but a process. Each part leads to the one which follows and rests on the one which precedes' (IH, 473–4).

The question of the assessment of an historical study is put by Collingwood in the context of viewing the study of history as a collective enterprise by peers, aimed at solving particular historical problems.[48] When an historian wants to solve a specific historical problem, he must therefore 'find out where he stands, and what his problem exactly is, by looking into the history of the problem itself: that is, into the history of research concerning the subject' (IH, 462). Collingwood calls this the history of history, or second-order history, which he considers an indispensable element of history, since it implies 'the historian's consciousness of how he has arrived at the particular problem which confronts him' (IH, 464).[49] This notion is in fact placed within the context of the logic of question and answer, when Collingwood refers to the example of a monograph on the Peasants' Revolt. For in this case not the vague and general question 'what was the Peasants' Revolt?' is asked, but 'I am asking for answers to certain definite and specific questions about it; and these are the questions which have been raised by previous inquiry' (IH, 463).

It is noticeable how much Collingwood's notion of the constructive imagination and his views on the historical narrative correspond to the positions put forward within the 'linguistic turn'. Hayden White was well aware of this, and though he was not acquainted with Collingwood's writings on the historical narrative, he is highly appreciative of Collingwood's notion of constructive imagination,[50] saying also of him that he 'insisted that the historian was above all a story teller'.[51] White refers in particular to Collingwood's inaugural lecture 'The historical imagination', and the importance he attaches to this notion is illustrated by *The Historical Imagination in Nineteenth-Century Europe* being the subtitle of *Metahistory*. There is every reason, therefore, that, in contrast to the received view, Collingwood could rather be considered a precursor of the 'linguistic turn' instead of his views being opposed to it. In any case, as regards Collingwood's assertion that 'the idea of the historical imagination … [is] a self-dependent, self-determining, and self-justifying form of thought' (IH, 249), it could be maintained that it is certainly in line with Hayden White's position.[52]

## CONCLUSION

Because of Collingwood's unusual background and career it is not easy to give a final appraisal of Collingwood's contribution to the theory and philosophy of history. It should first of all be noted that, notwithstanding his great interest in the subject, Collingwood was not known as a philosopher of history during his life, and accordingly has not been influential in this field in the interwar years. This is exemplified by the fact that in a *Festschrift* for Ernst Cassirer, entitled *Philosophy and History*, published in 1936, Collingwood is not among the 21 contributors.[53] Collingwood was primarily known as an expert on Roman Britain and its archaeology. As a philosopher he was considered more or less extravagant, being not in line with the British philosophical climate of his time. The few scattered articles he wrote on the philosophy of history only confirmed this position.

It was only after the Second World War, with the posthumously published *The Idea of History*, that Collingwood became well-known as a philosopher of history. This book attracted much attention, and triggered off lively debates among both historians and philosophers. It is no overstatement to assert that *The Idea of History* has had a decisive influence in making the theory and philosophy of history an acknowledged field of study in the English-speaking world.

From the 1970s the central position of Collingwood within the philosophy of history has been undermined by the 'linguistic turn' in this field, incarnated in the theories of, among others, Hayden White, Foucault, and Derrida. At the same time a growing interest developed in other aspects of Collingwood's philosophy, such as his theory of metaphysics, his view on the nature of philosophy, political philosophy, and philosophy of art. Besides this, the availability of his manuscripts, covering several thousand pages, opened up new vistas to the exploration of Collingwood's exceptional broad scope of mind.

Because of these developments it has increasingly become clear that Collingwood's philosophy of history cannot exclusively be based on *The Idea of History*, and that his other philosophical writings, both published and unpublished, should be taken into account as well. It should be added that this also applies to Collingwood's writings on Roman Britain and archaeology, which have been insufficiently taken notice of until now.

This means that Collingwood's philosophy of history, but also other aspects of his philosophy, is in fact still in process of being disclosed.[54] This is a rather unusual circumstance for an author 70 years after his death. It is like an ancient civilization, as the Egyptian, its existence being known, but knowledge about it only being developed at a relatively late date, after the disclosure of newly discovered sources. Similarly in the case of Collingwood there are many new sources, throwing new light on his views.

In this chapter an attempt has been made to give a picture of Collingwood's theory and philosophy of history, based on the scattered sources on the subject. In accordance with Collingwood's own methodological principles, it has been guided by the directives of trying to find the questions Collingwood was aimed at answering, and of focusing on what he meant by certain assertions. With hindsight one could say that this approach has initially been insufficiently put into practice by the interpreters of Collingwood's philosophy of history. This resulted in a misconceived methodological interpretation of the doctrines of the re-enactment of past thought and history being the history of thought, whereas Collingwood's actual methodological views were hardly taken into account. Because of this a proper interpretation of Collingwood's philosophy of history has protractedly been impaired.

What assessment can in conclusion be made of Collingwood's place within the development of the thought on the theory and philosophy of history? One might say that it epitomizes the latest and most well-considered manifestation of its 'modernist' phase, starting in the nineteenth century. The basic question Collingwood had in mind was to find an answer to the question – as Kant had done with natural science – 'how is historical knowledge possible?'. He concurs in this with Dilthey's project to develop a *Kritik der historischen Vernunft*. But Collingwood was critical of the way Dilthey tried to find an answer to the questions raised as regards this project, especially since he relied in his opinion too much on psychology and intuition. But other German theorists and philosophers of history are criticized by Collingwood as well, among others for their intuitive approach, for seeing historical facts as isolated and not as part of an historical process, and for having in his view a mistaken conception of the dissimilarity of natural science and history. The most notable difference between the German conception of history and Collingwood's, however, is that Collingwood without hesitation, and even emphatically, considered history a science and not part of a separate *Geisteswissenschaften* or *Kulturwissenschaften*.

Collingwood's philosophy of history was a consistent fight against the influence of natural science on the study of history, his aim being to free the latter of being, as he used to call it, 'under pupilage' of the former. Nowadays this is not considered a major problem in the theory and philosophy of history anymore, as it was in Collingwood's days, with the exception perhaps in the shape of a positivistically conceived social science.

The present discussions on the theory and philosophy of history are to a large extent related to topics raised within the postmodern 'linguistic turn'. As has been argued above, Collingwood's views are far from being inconsistent with this movement, and could in some respects rather be seen as an anticipation of it. The main difference between the approach of the linguistic turn and the one of Collingwood is, however, that the latter does not confine himself to the 'superstructure' of historical narratives, that is, the finished products of historical research, but is focused on the 'infrastructure' of historical research in all its ramifications, both theoretical and practical, as well.

The importance of history for self-knowledge and understanding society was the basic background of Collingwood's engagement in history and its philosophy. The views he developed in this field are not only important, but still of current interest.

## NOTES AND REFERENCES

1   *The Times Literary Supplement*, Oct. 6 (1995), 39.
2   'The idea of a philosophy of something, and, in particular, a philosophy of history' (1927), 'Lectures on the philosophy of history' (1926), 'Outlines of a philosophy of history' (1928), in: R.G. Collingwood, *The Idea of History*, rev. edn, with Lectures 1926–1928, Jan van der Dussen ed. (Oxford, 1993), 335–496; *R.G. Collingwood. The Principles of History and Other Writings in Philosophy of History*, W.H. Dray and W.J. van der Dussen eds. (Oxford, 1999).
3   *R.G. Collingwood. The Philosophy of Enchantment. Studies in Folktale, Cultural Criticism, and Anthropology*, D. Boucher, W. James, and Ph. Smallwood eds. (Oxford, 2005).
4   In the text the following abbreviations are used for Collingwood's works: SM: *Speculum Mentis* (Oxford, 1924); Aut: *An Autobiography* (Oxford, 1939); IH: *The Idea of History*, rev. edn (Oxford, 1993; 1st ed. 1946); PH: *The Principles of History and Other Writings in Philosophy of History* (1999).
5   L.O. Mink, *Mind, History, and Dialectic. The Philosophy of R.G. Collingwood* (Middletown, CT, 1968), 3.
6   Reprinted in: *Essays in the Philosophy of History by R.G. Collingwood*, William Debbins ed. (Austin, TX, 1965).
7   R.G. Collingwood, 'The idea of a philosophy of something, and, in particular, a philosophy of history', in: IH,

335–58; idem, 'The philosophy of history', in: *Essays*, Debbins ed., 121–39.

8   *Essays*, Debbins ed., 124.

9   See the chapters on 'Positivism' and 'Germany' in IH, 126–33, 165–83.

10  This position offers a drastic and revolutionary solution to the problem of historical realism, especially if one takes into account that Hayden White calls 'the nature of "realistic" representation … *the* problem for modern historiography' (*Metahistory*, 3). In his discussion on historical narratives in the same essay Collingwood makes clear that this position has consequences for historiography, saying that '[g]ranted the ideality of history … the truth about an event is relative to the point of view from which one approaches it' (IH, 474). One could see this as an anticipation of the position of the 'linguistic turn', referred to above. The only difference is that the latter speaks about the language used by historians, whereas Collingwood speaks of their thoughts. But, as Collingwood explains in *The New Leviathan* (1942), 40–6, language and thought cannot be separated.

11  That economic history, for instance, is not ruled out is illustrated by the fact that Collingwood has extensively written on the subject (R.G. Collingwood, 'Roman Britain', in: *An Economic Survey of Ancient Rome*, Tenney Frank ed., vol. 3 (Paterson, 1937), 7–118.

12  In a passage crossed out in the manuscript Collingwood develops the same argument in another phrasing. 'One of the most fashionable modern superstitions is to be frightened of the word reason,' he says. In answer to the objection that most actions studied by history 'obviously proceed from the extremest unreason', Collingwood retorts: 'But this is to pick a quarrel about a word. I mean by reason, as people have meant for a good many centuries now, thinking. My critic, to dignify him by that name, calls thinking unreason when he personally disagrees with it. I do not object. I will admit that Ethelred the Unready behaved unreasonably when he paid blackmail to the Danes. But an unreasonable reason is still a reason, though a bad one. A beast that wants discourse of reason does not pay blackmail' (PH, 46).

13  W.H. Dray, *History as Re-enactment. R.G. Collingwood's Idea of History* (Oxford, 1995), 116.

14  R.G. Collingwood, 'The purpose of the Roman wall', *The Vasculum* 8 (1921), 4–9. Collingwood refers to this article in Aut, 128–9.

15  *The Philosophy of Enchantment*, Boucher et al. eds, 115–287.

16  W.H. Walsh, 'The character of a historical explanation', *Aristotelian Society*, Supplementary Volume 21 (1947), 51–68, there 55.

17  A. Donagan, 'The verification of historical theses', *The Philosophical Quarterly* 6 (1956), 193–208; W.H. Dray, *Laws and Explanation in History* (Oxford, 1957), 128; idem, 'R.G. Collingwood and the Acquaintance Theory of Knowledge', *Revue Internationale de Philosophie* 11 (1957), 420–32; idem, 'Historical understanding as re-thinking', *University of Toronto Quarterly* 27 (1958), 200–15.

18  Dray, *History as Re-enactment*, 323.

19  Translated in: *The Frege Reader*; Michael Beany ed., (Oxford, 1997), 325–45.

20  Ibid., 335.

21  Ibid., 336. Likewise, Collingwood calls the Pythagorean theorem 'a thought that constitutes a permanent addition to mathematical knowledge' (IH, 218).

22  Ibid., 341–2.

23  '[T]ought is always and everywhere *de jure* common property', Collingwood maintains in 'Outlines of a philosophy of history', 'and is *de facto* common property wherever people at large have the intelligence to think in common' (IH, 450).

24  *The Frege Reader*; Beany ed., 344.

25  Translated in: *The Frege Reader*; Beany ed., 151–71.

26  Ibid., 160.

27  Ibid.

28  Collingwood refers to this principle when he observes about reading Dante: 'For Dante, the *Commedia* was his whole world. For me, the *Commedia* is at most half my world, the other half being all those things in me which prevent me from literally becoming Dante' (IH, 447).

29  *The Frege Reader*; Beany ed., 161.

30  P. Geach, *Mental Acts* (London, 1957), 79.

31  W. Dray, *Perspectives on History* (London, 1980), 26.

32  Mink, *Mind, History, and Dialectic*, 132, 192. Mink is otherwise of the opinion that Collingwood's logic of question and answer 'might more properly have been called the *dialectic* of question and answer' (132).

33  It has also been reprinted in PH, 3–37, to which a 'summary' is added from the manuscript (37–8).

34  Collingwood does not expand on the specific nature of an historical inference. It is notable, however, that it corresponds to the notion of a 'hypothetical inference' as conceived by the American philosopher Ch. Peirce, also called by him 'abduction'. Like Collingwood, Peirce puts it forward as a third kind of inference, besides deduction and induction, being explanatory in a specific way. In Peirce's view abductive reasoning applies to science in general. For the conformity of Collingwood's views on history as a science – using a specific kind of reasoning – with Peirce's views, see: Jan van der Dussen, 'Collingwood's claim that history is a science', *Collingwood and British Idealism Studies* 13,2 (2007), 5–30.

35  R.G. Collingwood, 'The limits of historical knowledge', in: *Essays*, Debbins ed., 90–103.

36  Ibid., 97.

37  *The Philosophy of Enchantment*, Boucher et al. eds, 129–30.

38  Though Collingwood in this essay also speaks of evidence, the word 'source' is used for referring to the raw material out of which history is made. In 'Historical evidence', however, where the theoretical aspects of the use of sources as evidence are discussed, Collingwood is critical of the word 'source'. '[A] source means something from which water or the like is drawn ready made,' he says, apparently having in view that this metaphor too much implies the suggestion that information 'wells up' from sources. He therefore says that '[i]f history means

scientific history, for "source" we must read "evidence"' (IH, 277, 279).

39   In 'Outlines of a philosophy of history' they are called respectively 'archaeological sciences' and 'philosophy of history' (IH, 490–2, 496).

40   The question at issue is how far it is justified to say that a certain event did not happen since we have no evidence for it. On the one side, Collingwood says, one can claim it is not, but on the other side it may be argued 'that all historians always do rely on the argument from silence when they accept a narrative based on a certain source because they have no other sources and therefore cannot check the one which they possess' (IH, 388).

41   R.G. Collingwood, *The Archaeology of Roman Britain* (London, 1930). Reprint (London: Bracken Books, 1996).

42   Ibid., 185–93.

43   R.G. Collingwood and R.P. Wright, *The Roman Inscriptions of Britain*, vol. 1, *Inscriptions on Stone* (Oxford, 1965).

44   R.G. Collingwood, 'Inaugural: rough notes', PH, 143–69.

45   W.H. Walsh, '"Colligation" in history', in: idem, *An Introduction to Philosophy of History* (London, 1951), 59–64, there 62.

46   Ibid., 62, 60.

47   As with the interpretation of evidence, historical imagination could be seen as being part of abductive reasoning (see n. 34).

48   'It is only by his peers that any claimant to knowledge is judged', Collingwood says in 'Historical evidence' (IH, 252).

49   In Aut, 132, second-order history is put forward as a third principle of historical thinking, besides the 'logic of question and answer' and the identification of the thoughts of historical agents.

50   Hayden White, *Tropics of Discourse* (Baltimore, OH, 1978), 59–61.

51   Ibid., 83.

52   When White points out the importance of a kind of 'configurational' comprehension 'that we get from any historical narrative worthy of the name, that is to say, comprehension of the ways that traditionally provided modes of storytelling function to inform us of the ways that our own culture can provide a host of different meanings for the same set of events', he adds: 'It is here, I think, that Collingwood's "constructive imagination" is really active in the best historical work. This, rather than either storytelling itself or argument, is what we mean by interpretation. And it is the place where narrative capability pays off most profitably in the great historians, past and present' (*The Fiction of Narrative* (Baltimore, OH, 2010), 125). It is interesting to note that there is a special link between Hayden White and Collingwood through Louis Mink, a close associate and friend, who was a prominent Collingwood scholar. Samuel James says that 'Mink was influenced by the philosophy of R.G. Collingwood, while he was himself an important influence on Hayden White' ('Louis Mink, "postmodernism", and the vocation of historiography' (*Modern Intellectual History* 7 (2010), 151–84, there 151). On the relation between Louis Mink and Hayden White, see also: Richard T. Vann, 'Louis Mink's linguistic turn', *History and Theory* 26 (1987), 1–14.

53   R. Klibansky and H.J. Paton ed., *Philosophy and History. Essays presented to Ernst Cassirer* (Oxford, 1936).

54   As Marnie Hughes-Warrington observes, '[p]resent-day Collingwood scholars are only just beginning to chart and understand [his] extraordinary wide vision of history' (*Fifty Key Thinkers on History*, 2nd edn (London, 2008), 43).

# 4

# The *Annales* School: Variations on Realism, Method and Time

Joseph Tendler

The *Annales* School has enjoyed more success, and exerted greater influence on professional and public opinion, than comparable schools; it has also courted controversy. But so unavoidable has it become that, particularly in the Anglophone world, historians sometimes attribute to *Annales* other schools' approaches.[1] Observers also deploy the collective noun metonymically: the *Annales* School stands sometimes for an 'informal network' of historians, who provide 'mutual assistance' to each other; at other times it is an *esprit*, a 'paradigm', 'a new social and economic history', a 'movement' or a 'current of thought'.[2] According to its founders, however, *Annales* never constituted a school in any of these senses.[3] This chapter provides a synoptic examination of the *Annales* phenomenon, first of its constituent parts, then of its development. It then assesses the coherences and cleavages in evidence across that conspectus, and concludes with a reflection on current perceptions of *Annales* now and attempts to envision its future.

Certain historians associate themselves with a notional *Annales* School. Marc Bloch and Lucien Febvre resound as founders today because they established the journal *Annales* in 1929. Fernand Braudel, Pierre and Huguette Chaunu and Charles Morazé led a cohort of historians who both continued it and secured institutional shelter for its collaborators in organisations unique to France: the Sixth Section of the *École Pratique des Hautes Études* founded in 1946, the *Centre des Recherches Historiques* in 1949, the *Laboratoire de Démographie Historique*, 1972, and the *Fondation Maison des Sciences de l'Homme*, 1975.[4] Jacques Le Goff, Pierre Nora, Emmanuel Le Roy Ladurie and Jean-Marie Pesez thereafter diversified collective projects prosecuted within the *Annales* community. Into the new millennium, Bernard Lepetit and, following Lepetit's untimely demise in 1996, Roger Chartier and Jacques Revel, offered a reformed version of *Annales* historical enquiry. These, according to certain observers, comprise the four principal 'generations' formative of an intellectual tradition. But André Burgière described such categorisation as 'uncertain and somewhat ridiculous'.[5] Better then, perhaps, to see a series of moments at and across which *Annales* historians have lent nuance and direction to an historiographical undertaking.

Surveying these historians' endeavours nevertheless reveals shared substantive preoccupations. They have contributed to, and altered, understandings of the early-modern period. From Febvre's studies of Reformation history through Braudel's work, *La Meditérranée et le Monde Mediterránéen à l'Époque de Philippe II*, and George Duby's analysis of mediaeval feudalism to Chartier on cultural dissemination, *annalistes* have shaped the way in which historians view the foundations of modernity.[6] Other specialisms have impinged. The history of France, for example – Ernest Labrousse and Braudel's co-edited seven-volume *opus* makes the point – as well as the fields of ancient history and archaeology.[7]

Nor have *Annales* historians sleepwalked into theory.[8] Alongside discursive histories, they have advanced precepts, differing between, as well as within, authors' *oeuvre*. The effort to describe, analyse and understand the past in its totality prevailed from the creation of *Annales d'Histoire Économique et Sociale* until the end of the Second World War. Bloch and Febvre's formulations, *histoire totale* and *histoire problème*, encapsulated the tenet. Holism might come through examination of interactions between environment and institutions with a composite social fabric – the collective will – as productive of objective conditions – the cost of living, social customs as well as psychological and geographic factors.[9] The problems historians resolved arose from their present. Why, for example, had diplomats perceived a border region in the Rhine valley after 1918; to what extent had commodity prices in wheat played a decisive role in forming public attitudes toward government fiscal policy; in what ways had the feudal divisions of land determined rural production?[10] History thus revealed the story of humanity in time, not in the past.[11]

This output borrowed from Henri Berr and his circle's cognitive registers. Berr had reprised Diderot's Baconian project to provide a comprehensive record of worldly, secular knowledge by ensuring that practitioners of science – any organised body of knowledge – communicated the results of their work to each other through his *Revue de Synthèse Historique*.[12] Synthesis in Berr's lexicon had foundational historical qualities: knowledge evolved, so awareness of its historicity became a *sine qua non* of understanding the experienced world.[13] *Belle époque* developments in economics, ethnography, linguistics, psychology and sociology also informed the endeavour: François Simiand's 'positive economics' provided a model of methodological stringency. It proposed the formulation and testing of hypotheses, thereafter revising, and so advancing, understanding.[14] Scientism of this sort thus continued the masculine-imprinted 'professionalism' of the nineteenth century.[15] Contemporaneous to Graham Wallas's work in England, Émile Durkheim led efforts to use social science techniques in order to establish the characteristics and mechanisms animating the social organism.[16] Lucien Lévy-Bruhl's insistence that pre-modern groups exhibited regulated, predictable but unconscious behaviour, and Charles Blondel and Henri Wallon's development of this conceptual tool, *mentalité*, in the field of personal psychology in turn gave Bloch and Febvre the idea that communities created distinctive ideas of their world.[17] The syntactical cadences by which past communities recorded and evoked their surroundings exposed a series of relations, structures in Antoine Meillet's linguistics, which demarcated past meanings and values.[18] Emphasis on psychology as revelatory of a lost world also drew Febvre, as well as Bloch, to Paul Vidal de la Blache's conception of human geography, which outlined how human beings shaped their environment, not contrariwise, through the generation of geographical concepts.[19] Landscape and its interpretation thus became a category of analysis with historical interest. And comparative procedure also spurred the *annaliste* project. Bloch, following other economic historians such as Henri Pirenne, engaged with the idea that an historian could superimpose the organisational facets of English enclosures on French land distribution in order to reveal analogous features otherwise concealed by native records.[20] He added that comparison of pre-modern societies from all parts of the globe would deepen understandings of the social organisation characteristic of a feudal 'phase', thus dispelling political historians' ideas that feudalism resembled 'an event that arrived once in the world'.[21] His agenda in that sense chimed with the anxiety of historians after 1918 to distance themselves from national politics, the perceived anathema with which the historians' *Zunft* in Germany had become involved on the eve of the First World War.[22]

Braudel, the Chaunus and Morazé adopted these tenets, but they altered Bloch and Febvre's notion of historical time. Braudel provided a touchstone of difference in his article, 'Histoire et sciences sociales'. He insisted that achievement of total history required a sense of the recondite processes active over the *longue durée* because the patterns and trends constitutive of material histories operated according to their own logic to determine events in human life. Short periods and specific events ought not, therefore, to arrogate the ground on which historians based their interpretations; instead, the *longue durée* provided the matrix in which all objects of historical analysis met. This not only meant that history connected all of its neighbouring disciplines in a *rassemblement* but that it also led them, because without *longue durée* analysis the work of the human sciences became incoherent.[23] History, by this account, assumed an hegemonic position, so it comes as little surprise that Braudel described the human sciences as an history-led *rassemblement*, a word deployed by de Gaulle to christen the super-party into which he attempt to incorporate his supporters.

As a result, *Annales* historians looked at geological and geographical evolutions, the slowest-paced motors of change; conjunctural, medium-speed, mutations in population sizes and growth, economic cycles and evolutions in social tastes; as well as the dynamic of political events, confined to the volatile short-term. This triptych provided the structure for Braudel's *Méditerranée* and also informed analyses of modern civilisation

offered by Ladurie, Morazé and Georges Duby.[24] The analytical form, strengthened with quantitative technique, meant to achieve the total resurrection of the past, irrespective of its established association with a particular research team or institution, so breaking specialisation boundaries within universities, by exposing the patterns of conjunctural mutations.[25] This enabled a total history in Febvre and Bloch's sense that combined a multi-perspectival examination of social formations with an exhaustive examination, factually and thematically, of entire civilisations.

As late as the 1970s, a decade after Braudel retired as editor-in-chief of *Annales*, anthropological methods assumed particular importance.[26] Renewed efforts followed to construct the role of conscious agency in explaining events. Le Goff's former post at the *École des Hautes Études en Sciences Sociales* became that of *Directeur d'Études en Anthropologie Historique du Monde Médiéval* in 1975.[27] Claude Lévi-Strauss's challenge to history's pre-eminence (on the basis that the only difference between anthropology and history came from their respective foci on unconscious and conscious factors) also stimulated the movement of mind and teaching.[28] But, by 1978, and in addition to Braudel's *longue durée*, *annalistes* had a translation of Norbert Elias at their disposal and emulated Clifford Geertz's observational techniques as well as West-German historians' reassessment of *Alltagsgeschichte*.[29]

Agency and environment competed with each other in the new disposition. Emmanuel Le Roy Ladurie's work displayed the conflicted *aggiornamento*. In his inaugural lecture at the *Collège de France*, he had spoken of an 'immobile' history, which charted slow-moving natural, economic and population developments.[30] Accordingly, in 1973, Ladurie predicted that future historians would become 'computer programmers' because they would compile data-series about such subjects electronically for interpretation by specialists in other social sciences. Yet the young mediaevalist also hoped to reconstruct agency with recourse to its imprint on context: the peculiarities of one group's social customs, for example.[31] A special issue of *Annales*, 'Histoire et Structure', also signalled the persistence of structuralist axioms that a nexus of invisible relations between psychological concepts and objective conditions determined historical reality.[32] But *Annales* historians simultaneously heeded Michel De Certeau and Georges Duby's warnings that, although statistics and structures lent the appearance of science to historical research, mathematicisation and its search for regularities and rules threatened to unleash an unruly successor to an old doctrine, 'neo-positivism'.[33]

These hesitations arose partly from uncertainties about history's status in the French curriculum. *Annales' grand nom* historians had an international audience in the 1980s: Ladurie's *Montaillou* enjoyed unprecedented success in America, and Anglophone publishers sought opportunities to translate a volume of Pierre Goubert or Braudel.[34] But in France, history ceded its place in the hierarchy of disciplines deemed desirable by employers to mathematics and science owing to the provisions of the *réforme Fouchet* of 1966.[35] Braudel's success in defending Clio's resources, by convincing Paul Berger, the Finance Minister, and the Rockefeller Foundation that *Annales* history could help politicians organise, nurture and prolong economic growth, social integration and cosmopolitanism, all of which would benefit post-war reconstruction, thus ended.[36] Industrial unrest in support of student-led demands for democratisation in 1968 had also generated audiences for 'protest histories' about rebel heroes and groups.[37] The reorganisation of *Annales'* own editorial board along corporate lines reflected these social readjustments, played out within the *silvas academi* by the influx of younger staff.[38] For the first time, *Annales* became a polyphonic review, no longer obedient to its 'traditionally imperious editorial line'.[39]

Polyphony, however, echoed contestation. Whereas outsiders such as Jacques Rougerie had criticised Labrousse for losing the overview in regional studies of pre-1789 history,

*annalistes* now worried about it too.[40] François Furet, in a moment of conversion to neo-liberalism during his directorship of the *Écoles des Hautes Études en Sciences*, alleged that practitioners of *nouvelle histoire* had become so preoccupied with the minutiae of cultural worlds that they had lost sight of the past.[41] Arguments from a philosopher peripheral to, but not ignored by, historians of the *Annales* School, Paul Ricoeur, and from Lawrence Stone, Carlo Ginzburg and Paul Veyne, as well as Hayden White by the end of the 1980s, simultaneously reasserted the importance of narrative as a way to present complex historical topics.[42]

The *nouvelle histoire* experiment also witnessed a softening of the distinctions that *annalistes* invoked to differentiate their work from rival approaches to the past. An awareness of memory grew up, thanks to Pierre Nora's depiction of the symbolic *loci* constructed and referred to in social life.[43] Chartier's turn to collective representations reconfigured perception as both function and creator of socio-economic as well as political history, in open dialogue with American historians' *New Cultural History*.[44] The real and its representation remained separable for Chartier, who, like Dominique Julia and Revel, defended that contextualist distinction as foundational in their socio-cultural history.[45] This they counter-posed to Robert Darnton's argument that social and professional auto-definitional categories existed in advance of their articulation by using Certeau and Michel Foucault's idea of the distinction between discursive and non-discursive practices.[46]

Alternative styles of research, meanwhile, gained ground: political history had, for example, returned, enriched by interdisciplinary and conceptual advances; historians now returned to the proposition that biography provided a useful tool; and researchers breathed new life into military history by explaining how cultural markers littered the battlefields that they scoured.[47] The end of the Algerian War in 1962 also thrust politics and its histories into the limelight because historians contributed to public discussions about France's colonial heritage.[48] As memory, memorialisation and research interacted and clashed, ideological contest became more frequent; President Mitterand even spoke of the need for the country to unite around its history, thus voicing the implication of Furet, Ladurie and Maurice Agulhon's *Histoire de France*.[49] Marcel Gauchet, proponent of a political history of the concepts informing past actors' *Weltanschauungen*, argued that 'the *Annales* paradigm', eviscerated, he thought, by opponents of its own making, must fall; historians on the Right even blamed *annalistes* in *Le Figaro Magazine* for the lability of historical debates, accusing them of cluttering the subject with extraneous details; and François Dosse and Hervé Coutau-Bégarie, for the Left and Right respectively, described (and regretted) fracture.[50] Where, they all asked in different ways, had Bloch, Febvre and Braudel's aspiration to a total history gone? From which book could a student, familiar even in the 1980s with Ernest Lavisse and Albert Malet's survey-histories, find what Henri Bergson had called 'the overall picture'?[51]

The *tournant critique* instigated by Bernard Lepetit from inside the *annaliste milieu* sought change in the 1990s. Numerically, historians had no majority in directing the re-evaluation. Even on *Annales*' editorial board, a mixture of economists and sociologists as well as young historians prevailed: Luc Boltanski, Laurent Thévenot, André Orléan, Jean-Yves Grenier, Jocelyne Daklia and Michael Werner. Whereas Bloch and Febvre had used social history to complete the representation of past periods that they thought political historians had previously defined in narrow legal-constitutional terms, and Braudel had seen it as one layer of a multi-temporal system, social history according to Lepetit now displayed a *complete* picture.[52] The legitimation of *annalistes'* epistemology thus responded to charges that they had chopped up the past as a chef shreds parsley.[53] Lepetit ran the project from the *École des Hautes Études en Sciences*

*Sociales*, still a home to *Annales* historians but more ecumenical now that the *Centre de Recherches Politiques Raymond Aron* disseminated René Rémond's political history.[54] He insisted that historical agents inhabited instrumentalist worlds, where past peoples' concepts and actions combined to prefigure and control their experience of reality. The interpretative stance accepted Pierre Bourdieu's idea that social systems reproduced themselves because actors settled on and observed a set of rules governing their interaction.[55] Boltanski, Orléan and Thévenot's description of the economy of conventions – practices accepted throughout a community and embodied in organisations and legal codes – and the competence of actors to interpret them, also provided part of the analytic framework.[56] With this actor-centric vision in mind, Lepetit interpreted *Annales* historiography since 1945 as a period of 'l'oublie de l'acteur'.[57]

Today, the *Annales* School operates amongst an ever-greater plurality of historiographical formations fuelled by growing numbers of applicants for a static number of university posts, a situation that compels aspirant researchers to raise their scientific profile, in order to bolster their employment prospects, by establishing a media presence.[58] The journal continues to sponsor radical empiricism: the study of sexuality as constructive of social attitudes, histories of ecological variables and the continuing expansion of cultural history. Drawing on the work of anthropologists Marshall Sahlins, theorist Reinhart Koselleck, Paul Ricoeur and Pierre Nora, François Hartog and ethnologist Gérard Lenclud have continued Lepetit's idea of *régimes d'historicité*, the study of what in the 1950s had been described as 'a general relation that people entertain with both the past and the future'.[59] They want to achieve three things: to reflect on the role of memory, to examine changing modes of speaking and thinking and to assess the difficulties of creating and defining past and present.[60] Stasis of any kind recedes in favour of contextual essentialism, the effort to recover basic, even unjustified beliefs supporting frameworks of understanding.[61] Similarly, Michael Werner and Bénédicte Zimmermann have pioneered the notion of entangled history, *histoire croisée*, in order to examine the interaction of concepts and notions as they exist in time and space, both in the past and the present as determinants of historians' own assumptions.[62] A consensus on history's relation to observational science has also emerged: historians in varying degrees assert that history makes truth-claims, but that their provisionality distinguishes them from conclusions in natural science.[63] They therefore follow Jean-Claude Passeron and Gilles-Gaston Granger in describing their practice in a manner they trace back to Bloch's *Métier d'historien* rather than 'philosophising'.[64]

The temptation to reiterate Georges Bourgin's expression of mystification about the point of history according to *Annales* historians might by now have become difficult to resist.[65] Coherences and cleavages run, however, throughout *Annales'* productions of theory. First amongst them is the articulation by *Annales* historians of a firm defence of historical realism. Chartier provided its latest incarnation in arguments at first against then in conversation with Paul Riceour about narrative. Historians and past societies co-exist in a shared experiential space, Chartier proposed, that allows scholars to recover and relay historical events.[66] In that communion of experience, time poses few problems because analytical technique opens past realities to scrutiny.[67] Narrative, Chartier suggested in opposition to Ricoeur, superimposed a chronological rationale on recondite and manifest processes rather than exposing their morphology.[68] That concern later ceded its place to the proposition common to Chartier and Ricoeur's vision of professional history, namely that historians grappled with vanished realities on their own terms.[69] Literary theorists' semiotic challenge, inside France, and the 'linguistic turn' in the Anglophone world, stimulated agreement about the need for realism. As had Bourdieu, Chartier

maintained that linguistic determinism, phenomena as an effect produced by the interplay of symbols and inflexions, could not suppress experienced realities.[70] He instead proposed that the past resembled a 'palimpsest', as had Bloch and Febvre in the troubled 1930s: discussion of the world *sub specie praeteriorum* required rational explication of present phenomena in terms of predecessors, revealed by peeling back layers of discursive and objective reality.[71]

Putting human beings *in* time, as Bloch and Febvre insisted grounded such realism, Braudel took to extremes and subsequent *annalistes* continued, transformed historical thought into a contemplation of presence, notably witness of any or all features of the historian's spatial, objective world. Few *Annales* historians invoked chronology, either as historians at the *École des Chartes* saw it – a way of marshalling stories of contingent origins and developments to the present (and future) – or as an aesthetic division of distinctive epochs in politics, ideas, cultures or civilisations. Most followed Febvre's dismissal of the associated Bergsonian irrationalism, the past as a creative process produced by the unconscious and conscious acts resulting from fusions of familiar and unwonted sensations yielded by the passing of time. Instances of this recurred in the reception *annalistes* gave to philosophers' historical theories, as in Febvre's denunciation of the 'chattering' Alexandru-Dmitrie Xénopol or the limited response to the work of hermeneuticists, Certeau or Paul Veyne (also an historian).[72]

Epistemological reflection, however, did give *Annales* historians methodological self-awareness inasmuch as they examined historical enquiries against methodological criteria: they asked what historians can know and how they arrive at comprehension. The *Annales* School continued in this way the work of a *milieu* of prominent historians, congregated in the *Sorbonne*, the *École des Chartes* and the *Archives Nationales*, nicknamed (unrepresentatively) '*méthodiques*' because of their preoccupation with history as an impartial method imitative of observational scientists' procedures.[73] Yet Febvre and like-minded historians had criticised Julien Benda, Henri Jassemin and Charles Seignobos for failing to justify their assumption that political histories incorporated, without examining the interrelations of, the spectrum of activities and beliefs in a given community in the 1930s.[74] But *Annales* historians surmised, and practised, refinements of a central *méthodique* proposition: historians applied a method, one of a growing number in the case of *annalistes*, in order to exploit 'certain materials hitherto unknown'.[75]

This project of discovering different facets of reality in greater depth fuelled attempts to forge original paths to them. The Braudel–Labrousse generation of researchers took to unprecedented lengths the aspiration to know about invisible processes; Le Goff, Ladurie and the Chaunus translated it into new methods. The arrival of the computer, the installation of research teams using quantification at the *École des Hautes Études en Sciences Sociales* and the accessibility of assembled statistics made it possible for *annalistes* to use theoretical models to evaluate data as graphical representations. The burgeoning of hybrid techniques, combining statistics with model-driven analyses, thus spurred on the search to vindicate hypotheses. The problem that this posed for critics presented itself as a suspicion similar to that raised in opposition to the new science of ecosystems in the 1930s: that no cognitive or methodological advance had taken place but rather *Annales* historians had 'invented' concepts and categories of analysis by 'playing around with words' and imposing them onto selected, not necessarily pertinent, facts.[76] An intuitive historian such as Louis Chevalier saw that as a form of fabrication.[77]

A theoretical inconsistency also emerged in these innovations. For Simiand, Bloch, Braudel, Goubert, Le Goff or Lepetit, an explicit discourse about the nature of the past itself remained unarticulated. Ricoeur, by contrast, showed how memory, history and forgetting constituted core operations of the human historical condition, an admission itself reflecting Lepetit's definition of social history. History in that vision brings together discursive histories; it sees the past as an interaction of traces, memory and research with a present always slipping from grasp and future potentiality.[78] But Ricoeur's philosophising attracted few supporters until Hartog and his circle formulated the notion termed regimes of historicity.[79] Yet, like *histoire croisée*, a regime of historicity examines a relational past, a past expressed in terms of remembered entities, but omits to conceptualise the ontological identity of these absences, past *qua* past.

Braudel's modelling of historical knowledge into temporal layers predicted the dilemma. The *longue durée* weighted historical analysis in favour of environmental and conjunctural factors, 'self-reproducing automata' obedient to surmised systems of variables summed up by mathematical formulae, as indicators of historical realities.[80] Chaunu's serial history, sequences of facts relating to features of an investigated object, implied a comparable objectivist leaning; its author's attempt to minimise a perceived de-humanisation made that much clear.[81] In both cases, the past becomes information carried by matter through time, the slowest form of which, in Braudel's system, occurs at a planetary level. Mind becomes incidental to the overall picture: past decisions and attitudes in the chaos of the short-term result from conjunctural mechanics, itself a correlate of developments in the natural realm; equally, in their present, historians reveal, measure and compile transmitted facts. Two difficulties impinge when conceptualising the past in this way. The first, a complaint well-rehearsed by the Earl of Shaftesbury, seems facile: the *longue durée* constitutes a system. Who, therefore, could prove that discursive history ought to observe the logic of the *longue durée*, and how?[82] To accept Braudel's proposition is, from that angle, to make a commitment, not to revere uncovered truth. That in its turn suggests that the *longue durée* in fact compromises the realism purveyed by the

School's founders because, as a system, it diminishes the immediacy of past to present worlds implicit in Bloch and Febvre's *histoire problème* or Chartier's defence of a trans-temporal communion of experience. To unsympathetic observers of the *Annales* School it heralded the 'collapse' of the past itself under the weight of ruminations exogenous to its morphology.[83] And Lepetit's conception of the social world as an encoded domain with its own conventions may also continue the systematic impulse to which Braudel's work responded, despite Lepetit's attempt to distance himself from the neglect of actors.

Another contention arises from the logic of Braudel's historical understanding. Whereas Braudel made mind incidental, explanations based on the *longue durée* actually suggest the contrary: that environment and objective matter are as much characteristic of consciousness as mind is of the material world. Explanatory regressions internal to the *longue durée* framework yield the clue: the actions of the short-term, dominated by great men and events that Braudel himself saw as one attraction of historical study, always relate back to the conjuncture and the long time-span.[84] Critics saw this as entrapping humanity in circumstances beyond their control and denying them, and power-relations, a constructive role in events.[85] However, if historians can write the history of the objective environment based on its features communicated to them, either through records or as social or physical formations, mind could inhere in matter. Without that possibility, Braudel would not have distinguished the human from the physical realm nor would the differentiation become conceivable.[86]

Braudel's speculative understanding also hints at an explanatory ambivalence running throughout the *Annales* School: a tendency to waver between methodological individualism and holism. At every turn of *Annales'* history its adherents have reconstructed complex entities. But their accounts of the findings have a kinetic emphasis, at one moment displaying the internal complexity and individuation of the whole, and at another suggesting its

regularity. Percy Ernst Schramm's response to Bloch's *Les Rois Thaumaturges*, or Jean-Louis Flandrin's to Philippe Aries's *L'Enfant et la Vie Familiale*, signalled the difficulty: Bloch and Ariès had probed public attitudes to mediaeval legends of 'royal touch' could heal scrofula and the extent to which societies provided education exclusively to children in the late-mediaeval and early-modern period. Schramm and Flandrin accepted, indeed admired, the range of source-material supporting both accounts. But Schramm alleged that Bloch had not examined the differentiation in communal and geographically specific responses and Flandrin wondered whether Ariès's notion that childhood became a phase of human development only when education by age-cohort began rang true given the uneven development of Europe's educational institutions.[87] This individual-collective tension never rivalled, however, covering-law debates raging in those Anglophone journals that carried North-American and British theoretical work.[88] It nevertheless indicates some strain within the realism purveyed by *Annales* historians. That point becomes clear from the intellectual evolution of the *Annales* phenomenon from founding notions of total histories of delimited subjects and actors, to global histories of everything, and then back again.

*Annales* history may, in addition, not enjoy such distinctiveness as historians associated with it have claimed. The genesis of Le Goff and Rémond's co-edited *Histoire de la France Religieuse*, for example, attests to the interpenetration of *annalistes'* theoretical suppositions with those emanating from other historians' approaches.[89] Henri Hubert and Mauss had suggested evaluating the prominence of religions *per enumeratium simplicem* in 1903.[90] Fernand Boulard mapped religious practice in the troubled years of the Second World War, as Catholics questioned the Papacy's attitude to the Third Reich.[91] Gabriel Le Bras and André Siegfried's work with members of the *Société de l'Histoire de l'Église en France*, beginning in the 1930s, came to fruition in the *Répertoire des Visites Pastorales* in 1977.[92] As that research began, Febvre's work on Reformation Europe appeared, emphasising a need to contextualise in order to understand the radicalism (or lack thereof) of theologians' treatise and to view reform movements on a comparative-European scale rather than as the work of isolated great men.[93]

After 1945, universities incorporated the subject into their history departments. André Latreille, who preceded Emmanuel Le Roy Ladurie as author of the *Chroniques Historiques* at *Le Monde* (in which he ignored the *Annales* historians altogether), and Émile Léonard offered survey-histories of Catholicism and Protestantism in France.[94] The *Sorbonne* appointed Henri-Irénée Marrou, critic of Morazé, and Charles-Henri Pouthas to chairs devoted to the history of Christian Antiquity and Nineteenth-Century Religious Life.[95] Its Academic Senate also inaugurated the *Centre de Recherches sur la Civilisation de l'Europe Moderne* in 1958, and Latreille, then dean at the University of Lyon, followed suit with the *Centre de Recherche d'Histoire Religieuse* in 1962. One of its early students, Michel Vovelle, close to *annalistes* and to Marxists, whose interpretation of the French Revolution as a class conflagration created by an enterprising *bourgeoisie* he shared, completed his doctoral dissertation there in 1971.[96] And Alphonse Dupront, Gabriel Le Bras and Émile Poulat, all in limited ways interested by *annalistes'* new approaches, occupied three of the seven chairs in the subject created between 1957 and 1964 in the Fifth Section of the *École Pratiques des Hautes Études*.[97] Certeau also contributed to the effort at the moment when his hermeneutic explanation of the past contravened mainstream *Annales* historians' preoccupations with computer-driven serial and quantitative history. The *Groupe de la Bussière*, from 1958, reconnected theoretical innovations in the human sciences, from semiotics, psychoanalysis and ethnology, in order to emphasise the importance of texts and their heterogeneity of meaning.[98] So, in a century-long perspective on applied theory, and not purely on *annalistes'* own terms as a distinctive

approach renovating entrenched professional habits, *Annales* history shares more with other approaches than investigation of a School might suggest.

Recent ruminations on *Annales* now dwell on the *dépassement* of its paradigm and see an opportunity usefully to reflect on Durkheim, Mauss, Bloch and other founders' work as part of contemporary historical debates.[99] The two sentiments are not mutually exclusive. Nor are they any longer contested, if indeed they ever had been. The variety of authors at any one moment and across the *Annales'* history, both in terms of specialism and approach, makes the idea of a paradigm difficult to justify.[100] *Annalistes* themselves often spoke of the distinctiveness of their approach but they deployed a taxonomy of novelty in part to promote their claims to pre-eminence amongst the social, or human, sciences; the assumption of 'strongly-normative positions, designed to stigmatise rival and competing approaches, or to declare obsolete older practices' in any case characterised historiography in France until Guy Bourdé and Henri Martin's work returned the subject to the realm of research, so *Annales* historians' combative self-descriptions require invigilation.[101]

Recent publications also testify that those school-forming tactics, and the differences they manufactured, create less of an effect now. When Bloch and Febvre adopted a semi-biological attitude toward the social as an investigable organism, revolution in Russia and world war accompanying financial collapse haunted analytical registers used within disciplinary history and demanded their renovation.[102] When Braudel, Chaunu, Morazé, Ladurie and Goubert proposed to show the curvature of all historical developments, the Second World War, visions of European integration and technological developments made the envisaged and traversable world smaller for historians, who as a result had access to archival repositories previously inaccessible to them.[103] The liberalized France of Presidents Giscard d'Estaing and Mitterrand, by contrast, changed the relationship between the government and the citizen, who required a new role in an evolving context at the time of the turn to anthropology.[104] And, in the twenty-first century, heterogeneous historical epistemologies, understandings, methods and explanations advanced by *annalistes* and non-*annalistes* alike are themselves perceived to suffer assaults from the Executive, newly-active in educational and intellectual affairs. The *Comité de Vigilance Face aux Usages Publiques de l'Histoire*, historians' petitions to remove legislation such as the *loi Gayssot* because they think that it allows government to regulate history-teaching as well as public commemorations and concern expressed by historians, including Le Goff, at President Sarkozy's plans to create an institution devoted to national history, privileged to the detriment of new transnational and comparative visions, all testify to a climate in which historians in France fear for Clio's future.[105] So the possibility, perhaps the purpose, of singling out a distinctive *Annales* School available to its adherents, admirers or critics has diminished. So too have the overt Left–Right confrontations of the 1960s and 1970s in which *annalistes* played a part.[106] As in French politics and society, historians can no longer construct an hegemonic image without admitting debts to competing styles of enquiry, particularly in the field of cultural history.

A glance towards the future in turn suggests the outstanding need to envision the past. The repetitive tension between claims of realism mixed with systematic understandings and spatial epistemologies leaves unresolved the lingering issue of time. Research into historicities remains a programme without fulfilment.[107] It and *histoire croisée* could, in order to achieve coherence against their own realist standards, think about the meaning that they invest in terms such as 'past' as have, for example, Ricoeur and Levinas.[108] Seeing the past as dynamic and discursive rather than spatial may require readings of Martin Heidegger and Benedetto Croce, both criticised or ignored in France, especially by Braudel.[109] They may also require attention to scientists' changing vision of multi-directional time, where the

past, present and future animate exceptional moments of experience of a world construed as energy embodied.[110] Curiously, Eduard Meyer, an ancient historian, observed an analogous need but Berr, whose own idea of synthesis also presupposed the centrality of time by positing that knowledge evolved, condemned it as Romantic irrationalism.[111] In short, a coherent *Annales* School with a unified theoretical output remains as possible today as Bloch and Febvre might have hoped it would become in 1929. It also remains as distant.

## NOTES AND REFERENCES

1  Philippe Poirrier, *Les Enjeux de l'Histoire Culturelle* (Paris, 2004), 218–19.
2  Georges Debien, 'Marc Bloch and rural history', *American Historical Review*, 21 (1947): 187–9, 189; Hugh Trevor-Roper, 'Fernand Braudel, the *Annales* and the Mediterranean', *American Historical Review*, 44 (1972): 468–479, 468; Lynn Hunt, 'French history in the last twenty years: the rise and fall of the Annales paradigm', *Journal of Contemporary History*, 21 (1986): 209–24; Garrett Mattingly, review of Fernand Braudel, *La Méditerranée et le Monde Méditerranéen à l'Époque de Philippe II*, *American Historical Review*, 55 (1950): 349–51, 350; Jean-Pierre V. M. Herubel, '"The Annales movement" and its historiography: a selective bibliography', *French Historical Studies*, 18 (1993): 346–55; Christian Delacroix, 'Le moment de l'histoire-science sociale des années 1920 aux années 1940', in Christian Delacroix, François Dosse and Patrick Garcia, eds, *Les Courants Historiques en France, XIXe–XXe Siècle* (Paris, 2005), 200–95.
3  Fernand Braudel, 'Les *Annales* continuent ...', *Annales: Économies, Sociétés, Civilisations*, 12 (1957): 1–2, 1; Martin Fugler, 'Fondateurs et collaborateurs, les débuts de la *Revue de Synthèse Historique (1900–1910)*', in Agnès Biard, Dominique Bourel and Eric Brian, eds, *Henri Berr et la Culture du XXe Siècle* (Paris, 1997), 188; Armando Sapori, 'Necrologio: Lucien Febvre 1878–1957', *Archivio Storico Italiano*, 65 (1957): 131–2, 131.
4  Lutz Raphael, 'Orte und Ideen der kollektiven Geschichtsforschung: Einer vergleichenden Blick auf die ersten Jahrzehnte des Centre de recherches historiques und die Praktiken in Westdeutschland (1945–1975)', in Matthias Middell, Gabriele Lingelbach and Frank Hadler, eds, *Historische Institut im Internationelen Vergleich* (Leipzig, 2001), 378.
5  André Burgière, *The Annales School: An Intellectual History*, translated by Jane Marie Todd (Ithaca, 2009; originally published in French in 2006), 9.

6   Lucien Febvre, *Philippe II et la Franche-Comté: Étude d'Histoire Politique, Religieuse et Sociale* (Paris, 1912), *Martin Luther: Un Destin* (Paris, 1928); Fernand Braudel, *La Méditerranée et le Monde Méditerranée à l'Époque de Philippe II* (Paris, 1949); Georges Duby, *L'Économie Rurale et la vie des Campagnes dans l'Occident Médiéval* (2 vols; Paris, 1962); Roger Chartier, *Inscrire et Effacer: Culture Écrite et Littérature (XIᵉ–XVIIIᵉ Siècle)* (Paris, 2004).

7   Fernand Braudel and Ernest Labrousse, eds, *Histoire Économique et Sociale de la France* (4 vols; Paris, 1970–1980); John Bintliff, ed., *The Annales School and Archaeology* (London, 1991); Jean-Marie Pesez, *L'Archéologie: Mutations, Missions, Méthodes* (Paris, 2007).

8   Georg Iggers, *Historiography in the Twentieth Century: From Scientific Objectivity to the Postmodern Challenge* (Middletown, 2005; originally published in 1997), 51.

9   The 'social fabric' came to *annalistes* through Durkheim's use of T.H. Green, *Lectures on the Principles of Political Obligation*, edited by Paul Harris and John Morrow (Cambridge, 1986), 14–15; Marc Bloch and Lucien Febvre, 'À nos lecteurs', *Annales d'Histoire Économique et Sociale*, 1 (1929): 1–2; Lucien Febvre, 'Pro domo nostra: à quoi sert la critique?', ibid., 8 (1936): 54–6, 55; Lucien Febvre, 'Tours d'horizons mondiaux ou Européens', ibid., 41 (1936): 580–2, 581.

10  Lucien Febvre and Albert Demangeon, *Le Rhin: Problèmes d'Histoire et d'Économie* (Paris, 1935), x, 126–50, 293; Lucien Febvre, 'Le problème des prix', *Annales d'Histoire Économique et Sociale*, 1 (1929): 67; Marc Bloch, *La Société Féodale* (2 vols; Paris, 1939–40).

11  Marc Bloch, *Apologie pour l'Histoire ou Métier d'Historien*, edited by Étienne Bloch (Paris, 2007; originally published in 1949), 57–66; Lutz Raphael, 'The present as a challenge for the historian: the contemporary world in the "Annales E.S.C.", 1929–1949', *Storia della Storiografia*, 21 (1992): 25–44.

12  Henri Berr, 'Sur notre programme', *Revue de Synthèse Historique*, 1 (1900): 1–8, 2.

13  Henri Berr, *La Synthèse en Histoire* (Paris, 1911), 308.

14  François Simiand, 'Méthode historique et science sociale: étude critique d'après les ouvrages récents de M. Lacombe et de M. Seignobos', *Revue de Synthèse Historique*, 2 (1902): 1–22; 128–77, *La Méthode Positive en Science Économique* (Paris, 1912), 57, 80–81. See also Massimo Mastrogregori, 'Note su simiand metodologo: esiste una terza via tra storicismo e empirismo?', *Rivista Storica Italiana*, 101 (1989): 237–50.

15  Bonnie G. Smith, *The Gender of History: Men, Women, and Historical Practice* (Harvard, 1998), 6–8, 213–15.

16  Graham Wallas, *The Great Society: A Psychological Analysis* (London, 1914); Émile Durkheim, *Les Règles de la Méthode Sociologique* (Paris, 1895), vii–viii, 5–19, 75.

17  Lucien Lévy-Bruhl, *La Mentalité Primitive* (Paris, 1922); Charles Blondel, *Introduction à la Psychologie Collective* (Paris, 1924); Henri Wallon, *Principes de Psychologie Appliquée* (Paris, 1930).

18  Antoine Meillet, *La Méthode Comparative en Linguistique Historique* (Paris, 1928).

19  Paul Vidal de la Blache, *Tableau de la Géographie de la France* (Paris, 1903), 20.

20  Marc Bloch, 'Pour une histoire comparée des sociétés européennes', *Revue de Synthèse Historique*, 46 (1928): 15–50, 21–24.

21  Bloch, *Société Féodale*, ii. 252.

22  Henri Pirenne, *Ce Que Nous Devons Désapprendre de l'Allemagne* (Gent, 1922). But German methodology remained important, see Peter Schöttler, 'Henri Pirenne, historien européen entre la France et l'Allemagne', *Revue Belge de Philologie et de l'Histoire*, 76 (1998): 875–83.

23  Fernand Braudel, 'Histoire et science sociales: la longue durée', *Annales: Économies, Sociétés, Civilisations*, 13 (1958): 725–53, 738, 728, 726, 'Histoire et sociologie', in Fernand Braudel, *Écrits sur l'Histoire* (2 vols; Paris, 1969), i. 105.

24  Emmanuel Le Roy Ladurie, *Histoire du Climat Depuis l'an Mil* (2 vols; Paris, 1967); Jacques Le Goff, *La Civilisation de l'Occident médiéval* (Paris, 1964); Charles Morazé, *Essai sur la Civilisation de l'Occident* (2 vols; Paris, 1950–67).

25  Fernand Braudel and Ruggiero Romano, *Navires et Marchandises à l'entrée du port de Livourne (1547–1611)* (Paris, 1951); Pierre and Huguette Chaunu, *Séville et l'Atlantique (1504–1560)* (12 vols; Paris, 1955–59); Pierre Chaunu, 'Manille et Macao, face à la conjoncture des XVIᵉ et XVIIᵉ siècles', *Annales: Économies, Sociétés, Civilisations*, 17 (1962): 555–80; Jean Meuvret, 'Conjoncture et crise au XVIIIᵉ siècle, l'exemple des prix milanais', ibid., 8 (1953): 215–19.

26  Jacques Le Goff and Jacques Revel, eds, *La Nouvelle Histoire* (Paris, 1978).

27  Lucette Valensi and Nathan Wachtel, 'L'anthropologie historique', in Jacques Revel and Nathan Wachtel, eds, *Une École pour les Sciences Sociales: De la VIᵉ Section à l'École des Hautes Études en Sciences Sociales* (Paris, 1996), 252.

28  Claude Lévi-Strauss, 'Histoire et ethnologie', originally published in 1949, reprinted in Claude Lévi-Strauss, *Anthropologie Structurale* (2 vols; Paris, 1958), i. 28; Claude Lévi-Strauss, *La Pensée Sauvage* (Paris, 1962), 345.

29  Roger Chartier, 'Elias: Une Pensée des relations', *EspacesTemps*, 53–54 (1993): 43–60, 'Pour un Usage libre et respectueux de Norbert Elias', *Vingtième Siècle*, 106 (2010): 37–52; Mathieu Lepetit, 'Un regard sur l'historiographie allemande: Les Mondes de l'*Alltagsgeschichte*', *Revue d'Histoire Moderne et Contemporaine*, 45 (1998): 466–86.

30  Emmanuel Le Roy Ladurie, 'L'histoire immobile', *Annales: Économies, Sociétés, Civilisations*, 29 (1974): 673–82.

31  Emmanuel Le Roy Ladurie, *Les Paysans de Languedoc* (2 vols; Paris, 1966), i. 11.

32  André Burgière, 'Présentation', *Annales: Économies, Sociétés, Civilisations*, 3–4 (1971): 1–7.

33  Ricoeur enumerated five characteristics of 'positivism' in French historical theory: a call to observational science objectivity; critique of documents; erudition in order to uncover facts; the past as interrelated accidents; methodological individualism. Paul Ricoeur, *The*

*Contribution of French Historiography to the Theory of History* (Oxford, 1980), 8; Michel De Certeau, *Histoire et Psychanalyse entre Science et Fiction* (Paris, 1987), 77–78; Georges Duby, *Dialogues* (Paris, 1980), 53.

34  Lewis Bateman to Braudel, 24 May 1976, Colin Franklin, Routledge Kegan Paul Ltd, to Braudel, 2 July 1965, Braudel Archive, Bibliothèque de l'Institut de France, Paris.

35  Antoine Prost, *L'École et la Famille dans une Société en Mutation (Depuis 1930)* (Paris, 2004), 331–32.

36  Hervé Coutau-Bégarie, *Le Phénomène 'Nouvelle Histoire': Grandeur et Décadence de l'École des 'Annales'* (Paris, 1989), 280; Brigitte Mazon, *Aux Origines de l'ÉHESS. Le Rôle du Mécénat Américain* (Paris, 1988), 44, 115, 318; Lutz Raphael, *Die Erben von Bloch und Febvre: 'Annales'-Geschichtsschreibung und 'Nouvelle Histoire' in Frankreich 1945–1980* (Stuttgart, 1994), 43.

37  Joan Borell, Arlette Farge, Geneviève Fraisse and Jacques Rancière, *Les Revoltes Logiques*, *Forum histoire* and *Le Peuple Français* (now *Gavroche*), edited by Jean Saudrin; Suzanne Citron, *L'Histoire de France autrement* (Paris, 1992).

38  Alain Norvez, *Le Corps Enseignant et l'Évolution Démographique* (Paris, 1978), 121.

39  Braudel to Mandrou, 4 June 1962, Braudel Archive.

40  Jacques Rougerie, 'Faut-il départementaliser l'histoire de France?', *Annales: Économies, Sociétés, Civilisations*, 21 (1966): 178–93; Philippe Minard, 'Les recherches récentes en histoire économique de la France de l'époque moderne (XVIe–XVIIIe siècle)', *Historiens et Géographes*, 378 (2002): 149–64.

41  François Furet, 'En marge des *Annales*: histoire et sciences sociales', *Le Débat*, 17 (1981): 112–26.

42  Paul Ricoeur, *Temps et Récit* (3 vols; Paris, 1983–85); Lawrence Stone, 'The revival of narrative: reflections on a new old history', *Past and Present*, 85 (1979): 3–24; Carlo Ginzburg, *Le Fromage et le Vers. L'Univers d'un Meunier du XVIe Siècle*, translated by Monique Aymard (Paris, 1980; originally published in Italian in 1976); Paul Veyne, *Comment On Écrit l'Histoire* (Paris, 1971), especially 13–28; Hayden White, *Metahistory: The Literary Imagination in Nineteenth-Century Europe* (Baltimore, 1973).

43  Pierre Nora, *Les Lieux de Mémoire* (7 vols; Paris, 1984–92).

44  Roger Chartier, 'Le Monde comme représentation', *Annales: Économies, Sociétés, Civilisations*, 6 (1989): 1505–20, 'L'histoire culturelle aujourd'hui', *Genèses*, 15 (1994): 115–29; see also, Arlette Farge, 'L'histoire sociale', in François Bédarida, ed., *L'Histoire et le métier d'historien en France 1945–1995* (Paris, 1995), 281–300; Georges Vigarello, *Le Sain et le Malsain. Santé et Mieux-être Depuis le Moyen Âge* (Paris, 1993).

45  Dominique Julia, 'L'historien et le pouvoir des clés', *Le Débat*, 99 (1988): 34–52, 41–42; Jacques Revel, *Un Parcours Critique. Douze Exercices d'Histoire Sociale* (Paris, 2006), 18–22.

46  Robert Darnton, *Le Grand Massacre des Chats: Attitudes et Croyances dans l'Ancienne France*, translated by Marie-Alyx Revellat (Paris, 1985; originally published in English in 1984); Roger Chartier, 'Writing the practices',

*French Historical Studies*, 21 (1998): 255–64. Prost shares in kind Chartier's view, see Antoine Prost, *Douze Leçons sur l'Histoire* (Paris, 1996), 292–3.

47  René Rémond, 'Le retour du politique', in Agnès Chauveau and Philippe Tétart, eds, *Questions à l'Histoire des Temps Présents* (Brussels, 1992), 55–64; Pierre Rosanvallon, 'Pour une histoire conceptuelle du politique', *Revue de Synthèse*, 1–2 (1986), 93–105; Jean-Noël Jeanneney, 'Vive la biographie!', *L'Histoire*, 13 (1979): 80–3; Jacques Le Goff, 'Saint Louis a-t-il existé?', *L'Histoire*, 40 (1981): 90–9; Pascal Brioist, Hervé Drevillon and Pierre Serna, eds, *Croiser le Fer: Violence et Culture de l'épée dans la France Moderne* (Paris, 2002).

48  Pierre Albertini, *L'École en France XIXe–XXe Siècle* (Paris, 1992), 152; Suzanne Citron, 'Chronique d'une impossible réforme', *EspacesTemps*, 66–67 (1998): 20–33.

49  Jacques Revel, 'Au pied de la falaise: retour aux pratiques', *Le Débat*, 103 (1999): 154–61.

50  Marcel Gauchet, 'Changement de Paradigme en sciences sociales?', *Le Débat*, 50 (1988): 165–70; Alain Decaux, 'On n'apprend plus l'histoire à vos enfants!', *Le Figaro Magazine*, 20 Oct. 1979; Coutau-Bégarie, *Phénomène 'Nouvelle Histoire'*; François Dosse, *L'Histoire en Miettes: Des 'Annales' à la 'Nouvelle Histoire'* (Paris, 1987).

51  Fernand Braudel, *Grammaire des Civilisations* (Paris, 1987; originally published in 1963), 25–7; Henri Bergson to Louis Madelin, 16 Dec. 1934, Bergson to Madelin, 7 Sept. 1938, Madelin Archive, Archives Nationales, Paris, AP/355.

52  Bernard Lepetit, *Les Formes de l'Expérience. Une Autre Histoire Sociale* (Paris, 1995), 28.

53  Delio Cantimori, *Studi di Storia* (3 vols; Turin, 1959), i. xix.

54  Lepetit's social history competed with 'university' social histories: Antoine Prost, 'Où Va L'Histoire sociale?', *Le Mouvement Social*, 174 (1996): 15–21; Gareth Stedman-Jones, 'Une Autre Histoire sociale?', *Annales: Histoire, Sciences Sociales*, 2 (1998): 383–94.

55  Pierre Bourdieu and Jean-Claude Passeron, *La Reproduction* (Paris, 1970).

56  Luc Boltanski and Laurent Thévenot, *De La Justification. Les Économies de la Grandeur* (Paris, 1987), 177–81; André Orléan, ed., *Analyse Économique des Conventions* (Paris, 1994), 87–93.

57  Jean-Yves Grenier and Bernard Lepetit, 'L'expérience historique. À propos de C.-E. Labrousse', *Annales: Économies, Sociétés, Civilisations*, 6 (1989): 1337–60.

58  Pierre Bourdieu, *Homo Academicus* (Paris, 1984), 112, 324; Jean Boutier and Dominique Julia, 'Ouverture: à quoi pensent les historiens?', *Autrement*, 150 (1995): 13–53; Christophe Charle, 'Être historien en France: une nouvelle profession?', in Bédarida, ed., *L'Histoire et le Métier Historien*, 21–44; Gérard Noiriel, *Sur le 'Crise' de l'Histoire* (Paris, 1996), 43–6; Daniel Roche, 'Les historiens aujourd'hui. Remarques pour un débat', *Vingtième Siècle*, 12 (1986): 3–20.

59  François Hartog and Gérard Lenclud, 'Régimes d'historicité', in Alexandre Dutu and Norbert Dodille, eds, *L'État des Lieux en Science Sociales* (Paris, 1993),

18–38; François Hartog, *Régimes d'Historicité. Présentisme et Expériences du Temps* (Paris, 2003); Claude Lefort, 'Sociétés sans histoire et historicité', *Cahiers Internationaux de Sociologie*, 12 (1952): 91–114.

60 Marcel Detienne, *Comparer L'Incomparable* (Paris, 2000), 65; Jean-Clément Martin, 'Histoire, mémoire, oubli. Pour un autre régime d'historicité', *Revue d'Histoire Moderne et Contemporaine*, 47 (2000): 783–804.

61 Keith DeRose, 'Assertion, Knowledge, Context', *Philosophical Review*, 111 (2002): 167–203, *The Case for Contextualism: Knowledge Scepticism and Context* (Oxford, 2009), i. 47–49.

62 Michael Werner and Bénédicte Zimmermann, 'Penser l'histoire croisée: entre empirie et réflexivité', *Annales: Histoire, Sciences Sociales*, 58 (2003): 7–36.

63 Prost, *Douze Leçons*, 287; François Bédarida, 'L'historien régisseur du temps? Savoir et responsabilité', *Revue historique*, 605 (1998): 3–23; François Hartog, 'L'historien et la conjoncture historiographique', *Le Débat*, 112 (1998): 4–10.

64 Gilles-Gaston Granger, 'La spécificité des actes humains', *EspacesTemps*, 84 (2004): 51–61; Jean-Claude Passeron, 'Formalisation, rationalité et histoire', in Jean-Yves Grenier, Claude Grignon and Pierre Michel Menger, eds, *Le Modèle et le Récit* (Paris, 2001), 215–82; Gérard Noiriel, *Penser Avec, Penser Contre. Itinéraire d'un Historien* (Paris, 2003), 15–16.

65 Georges Bourgin, 'L'orientation actuelle des travaux d'histoire contemporaine: discussion', in *Relazioni del X Congresso Internazionale di Scienze Storiche* (7 vols; Rome, 1955), ii. 248.

66 Roger Chartier, *Au Bord de la Falaise: L'Histoire entre Certitudes et Inquiétude* (Paris, 1998), 161, 195, 'Paul Ricoeur', *Esprit*, 7–8 (1988): 258–63.

67 Roger Chartier, 'La vérité entre histoire et fiction', in Antoine de Baecque and Christian Delage, eds, *De L'Histoire au Cinéma* (Brussels, 1998), 42, 'L'histoire culturelle', 126, 'Histoire, littérature et pratiques', *Le Débat*, 103 (1999): 162–8, 162.

68 Christian Delacroix, 'Ce que Ricoeur fait des *Annales*: méthodologie et épistémologie dans l'identité des *Annales*', in Christian Delacroix, François Dosse and Patrick Garcia, eds, *Paul Ricoeur et les Sciences Humaines* (Paris, 2007), 222.

69 Paul Ricoeur, *La Mémoire, l'Histoire, l'Oubli* (Paris, 2000), 292.

70 Pierre Bourdieu, *La Distinction: Critique Sociale du Jugement* (Paris, 1979), 494–5.

71 Burguière uses this metaphor in *The Annales School*, 24.

72 Febvre as cited in Suzanne Citron, 'Positivisme, corporatisme et pouvoir dans la société des professeurs d'histoire de 1910 à 1947', *Revue Française de Science Politique*, 27 (1977): 691–716, 714.

73 Scholars disagree about both the intellectual commitments signalled by the label and their variation between *méthodique* historians' works. For a selection of views, William R. Keylor, *Academy and Community. The Foundation of the French Historical Profession* (Cambridge, MA, 1975), 68–74, 172–3; Guy Bourdé, 'L'école méthodique', in Guy Bourdé and Hervé Martin, eds, *Les Écoles Historiques* (Paris, 1983), 181–214; Charles-Olivier Carbonell, *Histoire et Historiens: Une Mutation Idéologique des Historiens Français, 1865–1885* (Toulouse, 1976), 409–18; Patrick Garcia, 'Le moment méthodique', in Delacroix, Dosse and Garcia, eds, *Courants Historiques*, 96–199, 172–6; Isabel Noronha-DiVanna, *Writing History in the Third Republic* (Newcastle-upon-Tyne, 2010), 1–8.

74 Lucien Febvre, 'Entre l'histoire à thèse et l'histoire manual; deux esquisses récentes d'histoire de France: M. Benda, M. Seignobos', *Revue de Synthèse*, 5 (1933): 205–36, 'Une histoire politique de la Russie moderne: histoire-tableau ou synthèse historique?', *Annales d'Histoire Économique et Sociale*, 7 (1934): 29–36, review of Henri Jassemin, *Chambre des Comptes de Paris au XVᵉ Siècle*, ibid., 6 (1934): 148–53, 149.

75 The emblematic formulation comes from Leopold von Ranke, *Die Römischen Päpste* (3 vols; Berlin, 1844–45), i. xi.

76 Peder Anker, *Imperial Ecology: Environmental Order in the British Empire, 1895–1945* (Cambridge, MA, 2001), 118–57.

77 Louis Chevalier, 'Du rôle de l'histoire dans l'étude contemporaine de Paris', *Revue des Travaux de l'Académie des Sciences Morales et Politiques*, 110 (1957): 1–8, 5, 'A reactionary view of urban history', *Times Literary Supplement*, 8 Sept. 1966: 832. Also, Federico Chabod, *Storia della Politica Estera Italiana dal 1870 al 1896* (3 vols; Bari, 1951), i. xiii.

78 Ricoeur, *La Mémoire*, 274.

79 Hartog, *Régimes d'Historicité*, 26–8.

80 John von Neumann, *Theory of Self-Reproducing Automata*, edited by Arthur W. Burks (Chicago, 1966; originally published in 1951); on the echoes of Neumann's version of science as mathematical model-building in Braudel's work, Giorgio Israel, 'Modèle récit ou récit modèle?', in Jean-Yves Grenier, Claude Grignon and Pierre-Michel Menger, eds, *Le Modèle et le Récit* (Paris, 2001), 375.

81 Pierre Chaunu, 'Une histoire religieuse sérielle', *Revue d'Histoire Moderne et Contemporaine*, 1 (1965): 5–34.

82 Seignobos made the same point about comparison without naming any author in Charles-Victor Langlois and Charles Seignobos, *Introduction aux Études Historiques* (Paris, 1898), 235. On Shaftesbury, Douglas J. Den Uyl, 'Shaftesbury and the modern problem of virtue', *Social Philosophy and Policy*, 15 (1998): 275–316.

83 Gaston Brière to Pierre Caron, 24 Oct. 1948, Caron Archive, Archives Nationales, Paris, AB/XIX/4404/1/3, Brière to Caron, 18 May 1949, ibid., AB/XIX/4404/1/18; further examples include, Delio Cantimori, report on Braudel, *Civiltà e imperi*, 22 May 1949, in Luisa Mangoni, ed., *Delio Cantimori. Politica e Storia Contemporanea: Scritti 1927–1942* (Turin, 1991), 796; Maurice Cowling, 'A view of history', *The Times* (London), 14 Jan. 1983; Jacques Droz,

'Hauptprobleme der französischen Forschungen zur neueren Geschichte', *Die Welt als Geschichte*, 14 (1954): 109–18, 'Gegenwärtige Strömungen in der neueren französischen Geschichtschreibung', *Geschichte in Wissenschaft und Unterricht*, 3 (1952): 177–81; Geoffrey Elton, 'Historians against history', *The Cambridge Review*, 18 Nov. 1983: 286–92; Rodney Hilton, review of Emmanuel Le Roy Ladurie, *Les Paysans de Languedoc*, *English Historical Review*, 82 (1967): 791–5, 792; H.G. Koenigsberger, review of Pierre Chaunu, *Séville et l'Atlantique*, ibid., 76 (1961): 675–81, 678; Gerhard Ritter to Braudel, 16 Dec. 1958, Ritter Archive, Bundesarchiv Koblenz, N1166/348, 'Zum Begriff der "Kulturgeschichte". Ein Diskussionbeitrag', *Historische Zeitzchrift*, 171 (1951): 293–302.

84 Fernand Braudel, 'Positions de l'histoire en 1950', in Braudel, *Écrits*, i. 22.

85 For example, Jean-Paul Sartre, 'Questions de méthode: existentialisme et marxisme', *Les Temps Modernes*, 139–40 (1957): 1–37; Klingenstein referred to it as Braudel's 'morose' tendency, see Greta Klingenstein, 'Kultur- und universalgeschichtliche Aspekte in strukturaler Sicht', review of Braudel, *Civilisation Matérielle et Capitalisme*, *Archiv für Kulturgeschichte*, 52 (1970): 280–96, 288.

86 This argument owes a debt to Conor Cunningham, *Darwin's Pious Idea: Why the Ultra-Darwinists and Creationists Both Get it Wrong* (Cambridge, 2010).

87 Percy Ernst Schramm, *Der König von Frankreich: Das Wesen der Monarchie vom 9. zum 16. Jahrhundert. Ein Kapitel aus der Geschichte des abendländischen Staates* (2 vols; Weimar, 1939), i. 152–5, ii. 75; Jean-Louis Flandrin, 'Enfance et société', review of Philippe Ariès, *L'Enfant et la vie Familiale*, *Annales: Économies, Sociétés, Civilisations*, 19 (1964): 322–29.

88 Murray G. Murphy, 'Explanation, causes, and covering laws', *History and Theory*, Beiheft 25 (1986): 43–57.

89 Jacques Le Goff and René Rémond, eds, *Histoire de la France Religieuse* (4 vols; Paris, 1998–92).

90 Henri Hubert and Marcel Mauss, 'Esquisse d'une théorie de la magie', *Année Sociologique*, 7 (1903): 1–146.

91 Canon Fernand Boulard, *Carte Religieuse de la France* (Paris, 1952).

92 Gabriel Le Bras, François de Dainville, Jean Gaudemet and André Latreille, *Répertoire des visites pastorales de la France* (Paris, 1977); also, Michel Froeschlé-Chopard and Marie-Hélène Froeschlé-Chopard, *Atlas de la Réforme Pastorale en France: De 1550 à 1790* (Paris, 1986).

93 Febvre, *Martin Luther*, vii.

94 André Latreille, ed., *Histoire du Catholicisme en France* (3 vols; Paris, 1957–62); Émile Léonard, ed., *Histoire Générale du Protestantisme* (3 vols; Paris, 1961–64).

95 On Marrou's debates with Morazé, see Pierre Riché, *Henri Irénée Marrou: Historien Engagé* (Paris, 2003), 174.

96 Michel Vovelle, *Piété Baroque et Déchristianisation en Provence au XVIII<sup>e</sup> siècle* (Paris, 1973).

97 Dosse, 'Expansion et fragmentation', 465.

98 Filippi Bruna, 'Le Groupe "de la Bussière": Quelques étapes d'un parcours collectif', *Revue de l'Histoire de l'Église en France*, 86 (2000): 735–45.

99 Delacroix, Dosse and Garcia, *Courants Historiques*, 633; Burgière, *The Annales School*, 1, 258.

100 Hunt, 'French History', 212–13.

101 Matthias Middell, 'Die unendliche Geschichte', in Matthias Middell and Steffen Sammler, eds, *Alles Gewordene hat Geschichte: Die Schule der Annales in ihren Texten 1929–1992* (Leipzig, 1994), 7–40; Poirrier, *L'Histoire Culturelle*, 218; Bourdé and Martin, eds, *Les Écoles*.

102 René Pillorget, 'From a classical to a serial and quantitative study of history: some new directions in French historical research', *Durham University Journal*, 149 (1976–77): 207–16, 208.

103 Felix Gilbert, John Higham and Leonard Krieger, *History* (Englewood, 1965), 256.

104 Rod Kedward, *La Vie en bleu: France and the French Since 1900* (London, 2005), 541–51.

105 Pascal Blanchard et Sandrine Lemaire, eds, *Culture Impériale. Les Colonies au Cœur de la République, 1931–1961* (Paris, 2004), 26–7; François Bonnet, Pierre Vidal-Naquet and Nicolas Weill, 'Analyse des relais dont disposent les négationnistes', *Le Monde*, 4 May 1996; Isabelle Backouche, Christophe Charle, Arlette Farge, Jacques Le Goff, Gérard Noiriel, Nicolas Offenstadt, Michèle Riot-Sarcey, Daniel Roche, Pierre Toubert and Denis Woronoff, 'Le Maison de l'histoire est un projet dangereux', *Le Monde*, 21 Oct. 2010.

106 Brian Anderson, *Raymond Aron: The Recovery of the Political* (Oxford, 1997), 167–74; Jonathon Bourg, *From Revolution to Ethics: May 1968 and Contemporary French Thought* (Montreal, 2007), 29.

107 On the unresolved notion of time in *Annales*, Marina Cedriono, 'Profilo delle "Annales" attraverso le pagine delle "Annales"', in Marina Cedriono, Furio Diaz and Carla Russo, eds, *Storiografia Francese di Ieri e di Oggi* (Naples, 1997), 35. Bernard Lepetit, 'Une logique du raisonnement historique', *Annales: Économies, Sociétés, Civilisations*, 5 (1993): 1209–19, 1213.

108 Emmanuel Levinas, *Autrement De L'Être, ou au-delà de l'Essence* (Paris, 1974), xvi–xviii; see also, Michael Bentley, 'Past and "presence": revisiting historical ontology', *History and Theory*, 45 (2006): 349–61.

109 Graziella Pagliano, 'Ricerche sulla fortuna di Benedetto Croce in Francia', *Revue des Études Italiennes*, 10 (1964): 272–301; Robert Paris, 'Benedetto Croce en France', *Annales: Économies, Sociétés, Civilisations*, 20 (1965): 273–301.

110 Max Tegmark, 'The mathematical universe', *Foundations of Physics*, 38 (2008): 101–50.

111 Eduard Meyer, *Geschichte des Ältertums* (5 vols; Stuttgart, 1907), §112, i. 198; Henri Berr, review of Eduard Meyer, *Zur Theorie und Methodik der Geschichte*, *Revue de Synthèse Historique*, 6 (1903): 371–6, 373.

# 5

# Intellectual History: From Ideas to Meanings

Donald R. Kelley

'Intellectual History' is a practice and a theory, or set of theories, that has been bound up with the 'history of ideas' for generations. Its boundaries are still not certain, though the latter has usually inclined more to the history of philosophy and, to some extent, the history of 'science' in a broad sense, and the former with the history of 'culture.'[1] In either form the field has had a certain integrity ever since the Enlightenment and even the Renaissance, when the 'encyclopedia' of all the arts and sciences was revived in the age of print and the beginning of what Ann Blair calls 'information overload.' Central to this revival was the revival of interest in Greek philosophy. The debate over the primacy of Plato or Aristotle was the central problem of the history of philosophy and so also of intellectual history, which began the task of investigating the rivals and successors of these masters.[2] These 'isms' – both magisterism and disciplularism – took over the history of intellectual history as well as the history of philosophy, disciples learning from masters and adapting and revolting from them.

In the middle ages intellectual history flourished *ante literam* in the so-called Carolingian renaissance with the revival of Latin literature under the aegis of Alcuin, and more especially in what C.H. Haskins called the 'renaissance of the twelfth century,' when Greek science and philosophy, centering on Aristotle and his commentators, were revived via Arabic translations, and including Latin historical scholarship.[3] In effect intellectual history was promoted in the faculties of philosophy and liberal arts through the study of major 'authors' and scholastic commentaries, later with encyclopedic compilations. The rise of the 'republic of letters' gave an institutional foundation to such studies and the Latin language became the language of intellectual communication and exchange. Scholasticism, which is to say Aristotelian dialectic, dominated medieval learning. In his Etymologies Isidore of Seville was in effect a historian of encyclopedic thought, though his method was topical and not chronological. In his introduction to divine and human readings Cassiodorus celebrated all the arts and sciences, including history. In his *Metalogicon* John of Salisbury had defended the role of the arts, including grammar and rhetoric, which became the center of wisdom and the humanist movement in a later period, and Nicolas of Cusa praised written learning and the process by which 'the disciplines have grown incrementally.'[4] In effect this marks the first 'linguistic turn' in intellectual history.

In the wake of Renaissance learning came what one scholar has called the 'light of philosophy reborn,' produced not only by scholastic philosophers but by humanists like Petrarch, Ficino, Pico, Valla, Erasmus, Campanella, and others who brought a 'new philosophy' to the modern world.[5] Scholars like Ficino and Pico built on the past, especially on Plato, but in the sixteenth century thinkers like Campanella and Bacon began to strike on their own toward a 'new philosophy,' a move reinforced by the revival of skepticism.'[6] Such was the positions of the 'Moderns' in their quarrel with the 'Ancients' in the seventeenth century, the whole legacy of ancient learning being at stake.[7] As one observer remarked, 'Sects are numerous, and every day new forms appear. The whole state is divided among philosophers, medical doctors, jurists, historians, mathematicians, orators, grammarians, and poets and each has its own laws.'[8] From philosophy and theology disciplinary independence had been declared by many arts and sciences.

The first beneficiary was apparently the history of natural science, though of course it had its own medieval roots, going back to the 'calculatores' of medieval philosophy, who raised the prestige of mathematics in the encyclopedia of learning as the humanists had raised that of the liberal arts and philology.[9] Galileo was a beneficiary of this revival of mathematics, and not only his laws of motions but his world view rested on the notion that 'mathematics was the language of nature.' As grammar resisted the primacy of philosophy, so mathematic took up the challenge and the science of Galileo and Kepler was one result, as indeed was Newton's, though he tried to work within the old encyclopedia of knowledge, as was shown by his work on biblical studies. Yet through the ideas of Descartes and Bacon natural science

began to free itself and indeed to dominate this old encyclopedia – although other disciplines began to come into their own.[10]

With the invention of printing came the rise of 'literary history' (*historia literaria*), meaning everything set in the written word, which G.J. Vossius defined as 'the lives and writings of learned men and the invention and progress of the arts.'[11] A few key texts illustrate the practice of what amounts to intellectual history, among them Polydore Vergil's *De Inventoribus Rerum* (1496), Christophe Milieu's *De Scribendis Universitatis Rerum Historia* (1551), and Louis Le Roy's *La Vicissitude des Choses en l'Univers* (1575). As Francis Bacon wrote in his *Advancement of Learning*, to the history of natural science, 'Let there be added the sects and most celebrated controversies that have occupied the learned; by which they suffered; the praises and humors with which they were decorated. Let there be noted the principal authors, the most famous books, the successors, the academies, the societies, the colleges, their orders.'[12] Seventeenth-century encyclopedists like Johann Alstred and Daniel Morhof carried on this project under the motto that 'philosophy is knowledge of all that is knowable'; and the 'quarrel of the ancients and the moderns' was carried on in this fashion, by the 'ancients' at any rate. But this is *avant la lettre*; the field really begins, at least nominally, with J.J. Brucker's *Historia Doctrinae de Ideis* (1723), which surveyed the Platonic doctrine, and Vico's criticism, which rejected the idea of a Greek monopoly on ideas.[13] But Vico was swimming against the current, for down to the time of Kant and Hegel the 'way of ideas' was coming into fashion and idealist philosophers denigrated the 'pedantry' of the history of philosophy. 'Intellectual history' in modern usage came much later.

As Felix Gilbert showed, 'intellectual history' is a peculiar American coinage, albeit one with counterparts in other European languages, and it defined a practice that came into maturity by the 1950s, though the phrase already was part of the 'new history' of James Harvey Robinson in 1912.[14] But the practice far antedated the terminology. As Dilthey and Cassirer have shown, the eighteenth century was an age not only of science, as D'Alembert said, but also of history.[15] The primary example of this was the 'new science' of Giambattista Vico, who founded his new vision on philology and law and the study of the 'true Homer.' For Vico, writing in an anti-Cartesian mode, a review of history was the proper way to approach not only biography but also humanity, the world of the gentes, in general. The true was to be found not in what the individual thinks but what the human race has made (*verum factum*), and Vico associated *verum* also with *verbum*, and not only etymologically. Thus Vico was led to his grand theories about cultural cycles and recycles (*corso-ricorso*) over the long process of history from barbarism to a 'new barbarism.' As Vico (in effect) wrote about intellectual history, 'Philology is the study of speech, and it treats of words and their history, shows their origin and progress .... But since the ideas of things are represented by words, philology must first treat the history of things. Whence it appears that philologists must study human governments, customs, laws, institutions, intellectual disciplines, and the mechanical arts.' For according to one of his axioms, 'the order of ideas must follow the order of institutions.'[16]

In the later eighteenth century J.G. Herder seems quite in the spirit of Vico, though there is apparently no historical connection. Herder's interests, too, centered on the relations between language and thought, as he made clear in his 'metacriticism' of Kantian idealism.[17] Kant erred, according to Herder, by isolating reason from other faculties, especially that of language. For Herder 'The human mind thinks with words' (*Die menchliche Seele denkt mit Worten*), and reason was a process of experience in specific (not absolute) time and space, which was to say in history. Kant's ideal of a priori science which would be 'above all possible experience' would need to be above all possible languages, too; nor did Kant ever pose the crucial historical question asked by Herder and Irwing

before him, 'How did human concepts of understanding arise and develop?' What Herder offers, in his rejection of philosophical fashion, is not only an epistemological metacritique of the empty abstractions of critical philosophy but also, at least implicitly, a justification of intellectual history as the more comprehensive and human access to a critique of reason – for human reason is indeed all we can know.

One of Herder's like-minded contemporaries was Christoph Meiners, who published many works on religion, philosophy, literature, education, and history, as well as an early *Revision der Philosophie* (1772), which argued that philosophy depended not only on reason but also 'on the condition of learning and the spirit [*genius*] of the times.'[18] Like everything else, Meiners noted, philosophy changes and cannot be finalized. Moreover – and here is the revisionism – philosophy ought to be exoteric and not esoteric, that is, devoted not only to truth but also to the public good and 'improving' (*menschenbessere*) philosophy, siding with the 'popular philosophers' (*Populärphilosophen*) against the academics, and offering as models not Aristotle and Leibniz but rhetorical-minded scholars like Cicero, Erasmus, and Melanchthon.[19] It was this attitude that turned Meiners into an intellectual historian, his *History of Humanity* (1786) presenting a veritable manifesto of intellectual and cultural history, which for him included not only spiritual achievements but also the bodily needs of people contributing to the progress and what he called the 'revolutions' of the 'human spirit' underlying enlightened reason.[20]

In 1793 Meiners rephrased the prize question to emphasize his contrasting position: 'Was ist wahre Aufklärung?' ('What is true enlightenment?').[21] For Meiners Enlightenment was the product of and not an escape from history. Nor was human reason itself 'pure'; rather it was a cultural development from ancient times renewed in the period of Reformation, especially in the liberation theology of Luther and in the tradition of 'reformed philosophy' culminating in the work of Leibniz and Christian Wolff. Meiners was also interested, often in a comparative way, not only in the history of science and the economic base of culture (*Luxus*) but also questions of race (drawn from New World encounters), sexual behavior, especially Greek homosexuality (*Männerliebe*), and gender, including a multi-volume *History of the Female Sex*, translated into English in 1808.[22] 'True Enlightenment' began with Dante, Petrarch, and the Renaissance humanists and turned away from Aristotle, who was admired by the majority (according to an old motto), to Plato, who was followed by the wisest and the best; and it continued with champions of the new science and of human progress until the turning point supposedly marked by the French Revolution.

In the early nineteenth century Victor Cousin began a new movement in the history of philosophy which was at the same time old, that is, 'eclecticism,' which had predecessors also in Brucker and Diderot as well as the semi-legendary 'Potamon' of antiquity and his successors, Christian as well as Roman and Greek.[23] Modern eclecticism was provoked in part by the rise of skepticism and the idea of the 'liberty of philosophy,' that is, free choice in the choice of doctrinal masters. Cousin's eclecticism drew on many and intellectual and philosophical traditions, and he was responsible for the revival of Vico and Herder in France. He had his own disciples, among them some women, as well as critics in mid-century France. In the name of doing philosophy Cousinian eclectics such as Jules Simon in fact investigated its history and principal authors. More influential in a long term was Friedrich Nietzsche, who had something to say about practically all aspects of history, and especially the consideration that all historical statements are interpretations.

The nineteenth century was the age of ideologies, revolutionary and otherwise. Nationalism was the most successful of these ideologies and remained dominant until the era of Woodrow Wilson and after. The French Revolution was based on a vision of a 'perfect society' and a transforming 'social science,' and later thinkers followed the patterns and suggestions of that transformation, resisted always by conservatives who found their ideals in the 'old regime.' Like Kant, Hegel literally idealized the world, holding that history was the dialectical coming of humanity to its full consciousness and freedom and that the real is the ideal and the ideal is the real. Marx altered the pattern by arguing that the dialectic had a 'material base' and that history needed revolutionary and socialist change. Other varieties of 'socialism' sprang up and like most conservatism rejected rampant individualism and the chaos of bourgeois capitalism. August Comte also tried to establish a science of society as well as a philosophy of history, based on the idea of progress as was virtually every other system of thought. Planned economy, whether from a proletarian or an authoritarian base, was looked to by ideologies left and right to mitigate class warfare. Darwin, on the other hand, taught that nature was based on struggle, and that evolution, itself a form of progress, had to be embraced, not resisted; and his view was systematized by Herbert Spencer. Disciples of all these views produced their own versions and followers. Another product of these ideologies, including Romanticism, was an emphasis on historical studies, which of course included intellectual history.[24]

In the nineteenth century intellectual history was practiced by scholars attached the many other disciplines, including literature, linguistics, political science, and the history of science. In France Ernst Renan, Hippolyte Taine, and Charles-Augustin Sainte-Beuve were pioneering intellectual as well as literary historians who explored the context and background of literary works to the extent that Marcel Proust charged the latter with ignoring the work of art itself.

Sainte-Beuve was not only a major critic but was a historian of Port-Royal as an initiator of the modern age. His younger contemporary Renan was inspired by the 'oriental renaissance' and turned to philology as the central discipline in the humanities and he remarked, 'The science of languages is the history of languages; the science of literature and philosophy is the history of literature and philosophy; the science of the human spirit is the history of the human spirit, not merely abalysis of the mechanics of the soul.' Taine devised the famous contextualist trinity – *race, moment, milieu* – as a framework for his historical interpretations of French and English literature. Like Renan and Sainte-Beuve he turned also to the history of civilization, a field that had been opened by Cousin's colleague François Guizot, following philosophers like Voltaire, Condorcet, and Dugald Stewart.

In Germany *Literaturwissenschaft* was also basically historical, as was *Sprachwissenschaft*, as practiced by the brothers Grimm. For Karl Vossler language shows its 'super-social' presence as 'a vast soliloquy of the human mind which unfolds itself in untold millions of persons and characters'; and he illustrated his search for a literary world view in his study of Dante, a book whose English translation entitles it 'medieval civilization.'[25] Since literature 'is nothing but its language as this is written down by its elite speakers,' asked Vossler's Viennese colleague Leo Spitzer, 'can we perhaps not hope to grasp the spirit of a nation in the language of its outstanding works of literature?' Spitzer pursued his kind of intellectual history (*Geistesgeschichte*) through many studies in what he termed 'stylistics.'[26] Eric Auerbach also followed a linguistic path to intellectual history, as in his study of the fortunes of the word *figura* in antiquity and the middle ages in order 'to show how on the basis of its semantic development a word may grow into a historical situation and give rise to structures that will be effective for many centuries.' Elsewhere he wrote, 'My purpose in always to write history,' and this was an underlying purpose of his study of literary efforts of 'mimesis,' expressing what he called 'aesthetic historicism.'[27] Finally, Ernst Curtius envisioned surveying Goethe's old project of a 'world-literature,' and he achieved this in

part in his great work on 'European literature and the Latin middle ages' as well as his essays on modern literature.[28]

Among notable intellectual historians in Britain were T.H. Buckle, W.E.H. Lecky, Leslie Stephen, J.T. Merz, and the Scot Robert Flint. Buckle wrote a monumental history of English literature under the influence of Comte's positivism and the scientistic ideas of Taine, grounding works of art in social and cultural context, while Merz surveyed the history of European thought with similar naturalistic presuppositions. Stephen and Lecky were more concerned with the tradition of moral thought, especially as related to religion, and Lecky also wrote a study of the rise of rationalism in Europe. Robert Flint wrote a major history of the philosophy of history in France, in which Vico figured prominently, along with many other French scholars. In the United States the physiologist J.W. Draper, who was an evolutionist before Darwin, interpreted the 'intellectual development of Europe' in terms of Darwinian theory and in a positivist spirit denying the force of free will, for 'law is everlasting.' As Draper concluded, 'The object of this book is to impress upon its reader a conviction that civilization does not proceed in an arbitrary manner or by chance, but that it passes through a determinate succession of stages, and is a development according to law.'[29] This was a view that was often followed by late nineteenth- and early-twentieth-century scholars in search of formal regularities in history, most prominently perhaps John Fiske.

In the 'generation of 1914' Europe entered a period of crisis as doubt began to infect many fields of thought, not only science but also the social and human sciences and literature. Central to this crisis was the revolt against old-fashioned positivism. One of the results of the theory of relativity was the conviction that there was no 'objective' observation or conclusion because the observer was always part of the process. For the human sciences Wilhelm expressed this insight this way, that 'the first condition for the possibility of a human science lies in the consciousness that ... the one who examines history also makes history' – and this applies not only to *Geisteswissenschaft* but also to *Geistesgeschichte* – intellectual history. Literary Modernism, according to Friedrich Karl, was the age of 'the sovereignty of the artist 1885–1925. This located just the moment when James Harvey Robinson issued his manifesto for the 'new history' (1912), in which his 'reflections on intellectual history' appeared.[30] Of this, he wrote, 'It not only enables us to reach a clear perception of our duties and responsibilities by explaining the manner in which existing problems have arisen, but also promotes that intellectual liberty upon which progress fundamentally depends.

Robinson's 'new history' rejected the view that that history was merely 'past politics,' and he popularized the interdisciplinary 'new interests' that had been appearing in the previous century. His new history was followed by the publications of Charles Beard and Carl Becker. Intellectual history was given significant promotion by this movement of educational reform. There were other 'new histories' at this time, notably in the work of Karl Lamprecht in Germany, Benedetto Croce in Italy, Johann Huizinga in the Netherlands, and Henri Berr, Lucien Febvre, Marc, Bloch, and their colleagues in France. Reinforcing the 'new history' was the interdisciplinary movement of the 'history of ideas' led by the philosopher Arthur O. Lovejoy from the 1920s.[31] Lovejoy often came under criticism for an idealist view of ideas, but in fact he did stress external and 'irrational' factors. The disciplines he listed in 1983 defined the limits of the 'history of ideas' but may be taken as well as the range of intellectual history: the history of philosophy, of science, 'folklore and some parts of ethnography,' the history of language, of religious beliefs, literary history, 'what is unhappily called 'comparative literature,' the history of arts, economic history the history of education, political and social history, and a certain part of sociology. And for Rene Wellek, 'the

history of criticism ... is simply a branch of the history of ideas.'[32]

What J.W. Burrow calls the 'crisis of reason' involved also an intensive examination of the self and self-consciousness, and of course the unconscious. Freudianism led to inquiry into not only the motives of intellectuals but into their inner drives and even to the new field of 'psychohistory.' Nietzsche had already rejected the excesses of rationalism and others pursued the critique of reason. Nietzsche traced the unconscious 'Dionysian' spirit from ancient Greece to modern times, and through Nietzsche, Freud, and Carl Jung mythology was restored to European thought. 'Modernism' threatened the Church, too, and religion went on the defensive against many of the new movements of scientism and 'historicism,' which threatened the old absolutes of western civilization, as did the infiltration of oriental ideas. This was also the golden age of the social sciences, and the work of Max Weber, Emile Durkheim, Villefredo Pareto, and many others rivalled Marxism for leadership in this field.[33] Yet it was in literature that modernism was most thoroughly apparent.

The past is a foreign country perhaps, but early twentieth-century scholars proposed to overcome this limitation. 'Is it possible that the Middle Ages should speak to us,' asked Henry Osborn Taylor, 'as through a common humanity?'[34] This is what he and younger colleagues like E.K. Rand set out to do. They assumed the continuity of history, for, as Rand wrote, not only does 'the culture of the present day springs from many a medieval root' but 'the Middle Ages drew their own strength from the past.' These authors traced medieval intellectual history from the Augustinian Christian turn to Thomas Aquinas and Dante's 'medieval synthesis.' C.H. Haskins added to this survey the achievements of medieval science and scholarship, and other scholars added other specialties through their studies of religion, law, economics, and language to complete the encyclopedic synthesis. With this fuller weight of knowledge Marcia Colish rehearsed the arguments of Taylor and Rand, likewise emphasizing intellectual continuities, though without neglecting the way in which medieval patterns of thought were superseded by modern ones.[35]

Renaissance intellectual history was traced in a most thorough fashion by Wallace K. Ferguson in 1948 from late medieval origins down to the time of Jacob Burckhardt and the later 'revolt of the medievalists' and deniers of the 'renaissance' like Taylor.[36] Modern founders of Renaissance scholarship included Alfred von Martin, Hans Baron, Felix Gilbert, P.O. Kristeller, and centered at first on Florence and the theme of 'civic humanism' in political thought, though deviating little from Burckhardt's vision of 'the civilization [Kultur] of the Renaissance in Italy.' Studies of art history and economics buttressed this evolving view, as did studies of the 'northern Renaissance.' Wilhelm Dilthey and Ernst Cassirer carried investigations into the field of philosophy, whose modern form in the shape of the 'problem of knowledge' was located there.[37] Other scholars have tried to fix the origins of the Renaissance in the national traditions of France or Germany, but the older debates continue, and Ferguson regards them as themselves a fundamental part of intellectual history.

The Protestant Reformation has been an even richer source of controversies for centuries, to the extent that I (following John Adams) called the resistance ideas of the Germans, French, and Dutch in the sixteenth century the 'beginning of ideology.' Debates over the Reformation have followed generally confessional lines, or else tracing secular themes such as the idea of toleration.[38] Despite the 'ideological' tendencies genuine contributions have been made by Protestant scholars like Roland Bainton and Catholic scholars like Hubert Jedin and students of the 'radical Reformation' like G.H. Williams. Intellectual history covered the efforts of religious scholars like the later Jaroslav Pelikan, who published a multivolume study of the theological tradition in the spirit (or shadow) of Adolf von Harnack.

Many studies not only of Luther and his teachings and struggles but of independent national traditions, such as Augustin Renaudet's work on humanism and pre-reform in Paris, of sermon literature, and of biblical scholarship have filled out the story of Luther's head-line revolt; and tracing of later repercussions and carry-overs have projected Reformation scholarship forward in political terms.

In recent years the 'Scientific Revolution' has attracted a lot of attention, beginning first with the intellectual history, as in E.A. Burtt's *Metaphysical Foundations of Modern Science* and E.J. Dijksterhuis's *Mechanization of the World Picture*, and moving on the social and institutional context; and again it has become the center of debate and even 'culture wars.'[39] Herbert Butterfield pioneered in the search for the medieval roots of the thought of Kepler and Galileo, but a vast literature has piled up since then, of which the major contribution is perhaps A.C. Crombie's *Styles of Scientific Thinking in the European Tradition*. Again research has often followed national lines, as Porter's and Teich's collection spells out, but attention has also been paid to the 'thematic origins' of modern science.[40] In the work especially of Joseph Needham and Marshall Clagett the contributions of the Chinese and the medieval Arabs have come into comparative perspective.

But the most heated debate has been carried on between the 'internalist' and the 'externalist' interpretations over whether science is a matter of finding or of making discoveries, that is, whether regularities are 'out there' in nature independently of the observer of whether the observer has a central role in constructing the laws of nature, as argued by Shapin and Schaffer in their *Leviathan and the Air Pump*.[41] 'Constructivism' is the method that has been followed by an increasing number of historians, most notably Hayden White's 'metahistorical' view. Contributing, too, to the externalist argument is Thomas Kuhn's *Structure of Scientific Revolutions*, which provided a 'role for history' in the process of scientific discovery. The history of science has proceeded among these contrasting points of view, and others.

The Enlightenment has likewise been the object of debate, most famously perhaps between Carl Becker's argument that it was a secular repetition of the medieval 'heavenly city' of the philosophers and those of Peter Gay that it was essentially a revival of paganism.[42] For Gay the secular political values of the twentieth century, especially of the Weimar Republic, were rooted in the ideas of Voltaire and the philosophes. A more serious answer to Gay's position in that of Horkheimer's and Adorno's *Dialectic of the Enlightenment*, which tried to show the totalitarian implications and disastrous consequences of the application of rationality to the human condition in the twentieth century, for the domination of reason can entail the worst of tyrannies, the subordination of men to system. Adding to the confusion is Isaiah Berlin's notion of a 'counter-Enlightenment' opposing the age of reason from within, plausible as such a view is. More confusion is added when the Enlightenment is confronted by postmodern scholars, though one author suggests that much of the postmodern 'turn' was anticipated by Carl Becker.[43]

The Enlightenment is commonly seen as the progenitor of the French Revolution, and so Daniel Mornay sought its 'intellectual origins' in the pamphlet literature of the eighteenth century, while I explored similar material for an earlier period to trace a larger tradition of resistance or 'revolution,' which Napoleon called 'ideology.'[44] But in the post-1989 generation 'revolution' has acquired the status not of a political program or a global goal but of a myth with only fitful and local appearances in the past, impressive and influential though these have been – ranging from well- and badly-intentioned efforts to renew the world to mindless violence. The Revolution has joined other events not as historical agency but as on the *lieux de mémoire* deserving commemoration. Paul Hazard looked more broadly into literary sources for the 'crisis of European consciousness' in the early eighteenth century.[45] Others, in the wake

of the decline or disappearance of Marxist explanations have shifted from politics to 'culture' to follow the fortunes of the Revolution. For the most part intellectual history, like political and literary history, has followed national lines and has focused on national themes, though a few scholars have ranged more widely. Ever since the time of Herder scholars have looked to language, via literature, as the key to history, institutions, and national character, and of the 'world of nations.' One enduring practice of intellectual historians has been tracing the history of particular words. This underlies what scholars from Raymond Williams to Martin Jay have practiced, though dictionaries of 'received ideas' can be traced back to the eighteenth century.[46] Many terms, such as 'culture,' 'experience,' 'medieval,' 'modern,' 'representation,' and 'revolution' have been subjected to historical examination over the centuries, especially regarding their origins; and this has been part of the aim, too, of *Begriffsgeschichte*. One of the terms most often associated with history is 'postmodernism,' though there is far from any consensus about what it represents – any more than about 'ist' terms (post-western, post-structuralist, post-historical, post-human) that try to identify a chronological position that in effect denies chronology. According to Lyotard, for example, 'the essay (Montaigne) is postmodern, and the fragment (the *Athenaeum* [the Schlegels]) is modern.'[47] 'What are we calling postmodernity?' Foucault once asked; 'I'm not up-to-date.'[48]

Political thought has had to re-establish ties with history from time to time, and in the work of Quentin Skinner, John Pocock, and John Dunn it has done just that, taking a necessary 'linguistic turn' as well. Pocock and Skinner both reached back to the middle ages in their interpretations – the first in his work on the 'ancient constitution' and in his *Machiavellian Moment*, the second in his book on the foundations of political theory – though both also projected their view forward toward the modern world – the first in his concern with 'discourse,' the second in his emphasis on rhetoric.[49] Without denying that political agents were doing serious 'thinking,' Pocock insists that what is left for the historian to ponder are the words, and specifically the political languages in which the words occur, the historian thus appearing in the role of archeologist attempting to reconstitute languages from that foreign country that is the past. Another illustration of the current emphasis on language is the *Begriffsgeschichte* of Reinhard Koselleck, who has traced the changes in vocabulary in the generations before and after the French Revolution.[50] Koselleck himself is an admirer of the more radical views of Hayden White (in the wake of Northrup Frye, I.A. Richards, Kenneth Burke, and – what else? – the 'new rhetoric') about the functions of rhetoric.

In 1980 Dominick LaCapra and Steven Kaplan held a conference at Cornell called 'the future of intellectual history' and published it under the less defiant title of 'reappraisals and new perspectives' three years later, though many aspects of their agenda have in fact been followed by the field in subsequent years.[51] In this conference Hayden White was a central, though absent figure, and in fact his *Metahistory* of 1973 has shone a bright light, or cast a long shadow, over the practice of (at least 'imagined') intellectual history in the past generation. Roger Chartier, Martin Jay, Keith Baker, Hans Kellner, and Peter Jellavich are among the authors gathered in this collection, whose purpose was among other things to challenge the primacy of social history with a new intellectual history. La Capra in particular has led the emigration of scholars from what might be called 'normal history' into literohistory, which in effect takes the world itself as a text to be analyzed with the methods of literary criticism. White's concern has been especially to study history not as a heuristic practice inferred from 'sources' but as a form of narrative to be investigated for itself and to 'rethink' historiography from within.[52] History is 'discourse' or metaphor, not 'what really happened,' and historiography is thus a form of literary criticism, not to say autobiography.

In the recurrent search for novelty the 'new philosophy of history' of Frank Ankersmit and Hans Kellner (1995) is one example, of which Ankersmit suggests White's *Metahistory* as a 'progenitor.'[53] The 'linguistic turn' is here revisited, as is narrative, 'discourse,' 'point of view,' 'subjectivity,' and museology. Alan Megill notes the multiplicity of narratives, grand and small, and does not believe that historiography can reach a consensus about the proper to be told. Ankersmit himself celebrates history as an art, as a literary form. In an earlier age historiography and historical theory had the great eighteenth- and nineteenth-century historical narratives to work on, as Aristotle had Greek literature for his art of poetry, but today's theorists have mainly themselves to consider. In any case there seems to be agreement that history should lower its sights and focus instead on itself and the patterns of its 'discourse.' But as one of the authors, Nancy Partner, asks, 'Is there anything new here?'

Intellectual history has gathered momentum in the twentieth century and taken many forms as different sources have been explored. Ever since the eighteenth century 'cultural history' (*Kulturgeschichte*) attracted historians like Herder and Meiners who began essentially as intellectual historians, and that legacy was pursued by many scholars in the nineteenth century until the time of Karl Lamprecht and his students, when it was adopted in the universities. 'Culture,' a term of anthropology also, added context to text, material to intellectual activity and there is still less new in the 'new cultural history' of even the 'new historicism.' One of the great works of intellectual history is Werner Jaeger's survey of ancient 'paideia,' which is the equivalent of culture in an intellectual sense.[54] In any case intellectual history continues to thrive in fashions old and new, in journals old and new, in an old and a new 'dictionary of the history of ideas'; and Ulrich Schneider has been busy compiling a 'dictionary of intellectual historians' of the past century which will be continually renewed.

One of the monuments of intellectual history of the past century was Perry Miller's *New England Mind*, which was a study of key Puritan ideas as reflected in the sermons and writings of the seventeenth century, and though it did not escape criticism from socio-economic historians it has retained its classic status. Perhaps the greatest source of modern intellectual history, however, has come from Europe, especially the generation of Weimar scholars and their successors, including Marxists and Critical Theorists as well as philosophers, historians, and literary scholars too numerous to mention. Historians like Anthony Grafton, Joseph Levine, Martin Jay, Leonard Krieger, and myself are products of this group, although many other disciplines are represented. Much of this influence has come from Germany via exiles like Kristeller, Ernst Kantorowicz, Hand Baron, Felix Gilbert, Peter Gay, Hajo Holborn, and Fritz Stern; but the French impact has also made itself thought through the *Annaliste* school and such concepts as that of *mentalité*; and Roger Chartier and Jacques Le Goff are its main current representatives – although Michelet is as likely to be invoked as Berr, Febvre, Bloch, or Braudel.

In the past generation the important figures in intellectual history have been Martin Heidegger, Michel Foucault, and Jacques Derrida. For Heidegger and his follower H.G. Gadamer, language is the 'house of being,' and the 'fore-structures' of being dictate the course of thought beyond any metaphysics. History, then, was a matter of interpretation within particular horizons, and going beyond those horizons required feats of translation. Foucault built on Heidegger, though uncertainly, as did Derrida in his deconstructive criticism. Foucault proposes and 'archeology of knowledge,' in which intellectual history is not a matter of finding but of 'representing' material in discourse (and not in the intention of a putative author). Derrida continues this view by arguing 'that historicity itself is tied to the possibility of writing.' and so writing supplements speech as law supplements nature. The problem of living in the 'house'

that language represents is that humans are not in control of that house and on the contrary are imprisoned in it. So intellectual history itself is not a matter of inference but of creating the past out of words.

History has always been a search for meaning, and this is the case especially with intellectual history, since it explored what men and women have thought about their world. But they have not always recognized that meaning is itself a part of history, though localized the changing with the times. Every historian has his or her own place in space and time and so his or her own fore-structure, to use Heidegger's term, in terms of which to interpret his world. In everyday life and in the sciences we speak of this world in the present tense, but in intellectual history we have to revise our conclusions as time passes, and as Goethe said, history itself had to be rewritten every so often, not because of accumulating knowledge but from changing viewpoints. Like plain old 'history' itself, intellectual history is continually caught between the extremes of literary narrative and philosophical theory and more or less conventional practice, though enticements from other fields, especially 'cultural studies,' continue to attract. In an age of 'information overload' my horizons are too limited to notice more than prominent figures whom I appreciate, short of resorting to bibliography; and I suppose that makes this a 'personal statement,' but what could be more appropriate in this age of what Linda Orr calls 'the revenge of literature'? But now intellectual history merges with the old, yet renewed, tradition of cultural history, which had emerged in the Enlightenment and now returns with new claims.

And what of 'postmodernism'? Rudolf Pannwitz's work on 'the crisis of European culture' of 1917 linked Nietzsche and his *Übermensch* with nihilism, decadence, and what he called 'postmodern humanity' (*postmodernen Menschen*).[55] This term has become an inescapable part of current literary and philosophical jargon. As a German critic has remarked, 'The word "postmodern" belongs to a network of "postist" concepts and ways of thinking' – and so a new species of '-isms' for the young to throw in the face of the old, or (at least in earlier times) the left to throw in the face of the right. Postmodernism is a beginning, as it were, that is defined as an ending; a historical category that affects to deny history. It is a sort of life of the mind after the death of the subject and the demise of the comforting metanarratives which used to give meaning – a single, stable meaning – to human life. In general, I believe, postmodernism is a product of the excesses of Modernism, and it is hard to draw a line (or find a turning point) between the two, especially as 'postmodernism' resists the sort of historicizing definitions made in the first part of the term itself. Like St Paul, postmodernism is all things to all men, and women. It defines a turning point in only a most subjective or generic sense, or rather encompasses multiple turning points in the thought of a post-Marxist, post-Nietzschean, post-Foucauldian age.

To intellectual historians postmodernism is a process of unbuilding, of undermining foundations, and denial of metanarratives; but in this connection it seems less a new point of departure than a radical extension of such modernist and anti-foundationalist lines of thought as Heidegger's destruction of metaphysics, Niels Bohr's principle of complementarity, Werner Heisenberg's indeterminism, Hans Vaihinger's philosophy of 'as if,' Kurt Gödel's critique of metalogic, and new fashions in what has been called the 'new scientific revolution' of chaos and complexity theory.[56] In this general perspective postmodernism may indeed be seen as a continuation of the negative aspect of the 'Enlightenment project' – and what a modern philosopher has called the 'modern project to rigor' from Descartes to Nietzsche – that is, skepticism, criticism, and metacriticism, which each generation seems to take up afresh.[57] Reason completed, the turn is to imagination, or history; memory and emotions exhausted, it is to science; Positivism ineffective, to the human sciences; Modernism spent, to Postmodernism – and so what comes next?

Where can we turn? Each generation has its turning, or returning, and its turning away, or turning against, or overturning – and who knows where and when the next turning point will appear, or who will take or be given credit for it? We have come to the end, and now the beginning, of a millennium, and maybe this is a turning point too, but from and to what we are not yet in a position to say. Yet surely it will be a part of intellectual history.

## NOTES AND REFERENCES

1  D.R. Kelley, *The Descent of Ideas: The History of Intellectual History* (Burlington, 2002).

2  David Bradshaw, *Aristotle East and West* (Cambridge, 2004), and Charles Schmitt, *Aristotle and the Renaissance* (Cambridge, 1983).

3  *Twelfth-Century Europe and the Foundations of Modern Society*, ed. Clagett, Post, Reynolds (Madison, 1966).

4  Cassiodorus, *An Introduction to Divine and Human Readings*, tr. L. Jones (New York, 1946), John of Salisbury, *The Metalogicon*, trans. Daniel D. McGarry (Berkeley, 1962), and Nicolas of Cusa, *Wisdom and Knowledge*, tr. J. Hopkins (Minneapolis, 1996).

5  P.O. Kristeller, *Eight Philosophers of the Renaissance* (Stanford, 1962).

6  R.H. Popkin, *The History of Scepticism* (Oxford, 20003), and Brendan Dooley, *The Social History of Skepticism* (Baltimore, 1999); Kelley, *Descent*, ch. 3.

7  Joseph M. Levine, *The Battle of the Books* (Ithaca, 1991).

8  [Noel d'Argonne], *Melanges d'Histoire et de Litterature* (Paris, 1740), 154.

9  A.C. Crombie, *Augustine to Galileo* (Cambridge, Mass., 1959), and Ernan McMullin, *Galileo Man of Science* (New York, 1967).

10  D.R. Kelley (ed.), *History and the Disciplines* (Rochester, 1997).

11  Nicholas Wickenden, *G.J. Vossius and the Humanist Concept of History* (Assen, 1993), 73; Kelley, *Descent*, ch. 6.

12  Bacon, *Works*, ed. Spedding et al. (Boston, 1816), II, 199.

13  G. Vico, *The New Science*, tr. Bergin and Fisch (Ithaca, 1984), par. 347.

14  Felix Gilbert and Stephen Graubard (ed.), *Historical Studies Today* (New York, 1972), 141.

15  E. Cassirer, *The Philosophy of the Enlightenment*, tr. Koelln, Pettegrove (Princeton, 1951), 197.

16  Vico, *New Science*, par. 314.

17  Heder, *Metakritik: Sammtliche Werke* (Stuttgart, 1853), xxxvii.

18  *Revision der Philosophie* (Göttingen, 1772), 4 (published anonymously).

19  See H. Holzey, 'Popularphilosophie,' *Handwörterbuch der Philosophie*, VII, 1094; Johan van der Zande, 'In the

image of Cicero: German philosophy between Wolff and Kant,' *Journal of the History of Ideas*, 56 (1995), 419-42; and Frederick Beiser, *The Fate of Reason: German Philosophy from Kant to Fichte* (Cambridge, MA, 1987), 75, 167.

20  *Geschichte der Menschheit* (Lemgo, 1793).
21  *Historische Vergleichung der Sitten und Verfasssungen, des Gesetz und Gewerbe, des Handels, und der Religion, der Wissenschaften, und Lehranstalten des Mittelalters mit denen unsers Jahrhunderts in Rücksicht auf die Vortheile und Nachteile der Aufklärung* (Hannover, 1793), II, 465.
22  *History of the Female Sex*, tr. Frederic Schobert (4 vols; London, 1808).
23  Kelley, *Descent of Ideas*, ch. 1, ch. 5.
24  J.W. Burrow, *The Crisis of Reason, European Thought, 1848–1914* (New Haven, 2000).
25  K. Vossler, *The Spirit of Language in Civilization*, tr. O. Geser (London, 1932), 13.
26  L. Spitzer, *Linguistics and Literary History* (Princeton, 1948).
27  E. Auerbach, *Literary Language and its Public in the Middle Ages*, tr. R. Manheim (New York, 1965), 6.
28  E. Curtius, *European Literature and the Latin Middle Ages*, tr. W. Trask (Princeton, 1953).
29  J.W. Draper, *The Intellectual Development in Europe* (New York, 1876).
30  J.H. Robinson, *The New History* (New York, 1912), 101.
31  D.R. Kelley (ed.), *The History of Ideas: Canon and Variations* (Rochester, 1990).
32  R. Wellek, *A History of Modern Criticism 1750–1950* (Cambridge, 1981), I, 7.
33  H.S. Hughes, *Consciousness and Society* (New York, 1958); Kelley, *Descent*, ch. 8.
34  H.O. Taylor, *The Medieval Mind* (New York, 1919), I, ix.
35  M. Colish, *Medieval Foundations of the Western Intellectual Tradition 400–1400* (New Haven, 1997).

36  W.K. Ferguson, *The Renaissance in Historical Thought* (Cambridge, MA, 1948).
37  Kelley, *Descent*, ch. 9.
38  A.G. Dickens and John M. Tonkin, *The Reformation in Historical Thought* (Cambridge, MA, 1985).
39  Kelley, *Descent*, ch. 7.
40  Gerald Holton, *Thematic Origins of Scientific Thought* (Cambridge, MA, 1983).
41  Jan Golinski, *Making Natural Knowledge* (Cambridge, 1998), and Keith Parsons (ed.), *The Science Wars* (Amherst, 2003).
42  P. Gay, *The Enlightenment* (New York, 1966).
43  Daniel Gordon (ed.), *Postmodernism and the Enlightenment* (New York, 2001), 161.
44  Kelley, *The Beginning of Ideology* (Cambridge, 1981).
45  P. Hazard, *The European Mond 1680–1715* (New York, 1963).
46  M. Jay, *Cultural Semantics* (Amherst, 1998).
47  *The Postmodern Explained* (Minneapolis, 1992), 15.
48  'Structuralism and poststructuralism,' *Telos*, 55 (1983), 204.
49  J. Pocock, 'The concept of language and the metier d'historien,' in *The Languages of Political Theory in Early-Modern Europe*, ed. A. Pagden (Cambridge, 1987), 19–38.
50  R. Koselleck, *The Practice of Conceptual History* (Stanford, 2002); also German Historical Institute pamphlet 1996.
51  D. LaCapra and S. Kaplan (eds), *Modern European Intellectual History* (Ithaca, 1982); Kelley, Descent, ch. 10.
52  H. White, *Metahistory* (Baltimore, 1973).
53  F. Ankersmit and H. Kellner (eds). *A New Philosophy of History* (London, 1995).
54  W. Jaeger, *Paideia*, tr. G. Highet (Oxford, 1939)
55  R. Pannwitz, *Die Krisis der Europäischen Kultur* (Nürnberg, 1917), 674.
56  Mitchell Waldrop, *Complexity: The Emerging Science at the Edge of Order and Chaos* (New York, 1992).
57  Patrick Madigan, *The Modern Project to Rigor: Descartes to Nietzsche* (Lanham, MD, 1986).

# 6

# Social History: a New *Kind* of History

Brian Lewis

Social history, like hardcore pornography, is easier to recognize than to define: its boundaries are just as porous, its scope just as contested.[1] But the practitioners of the 'new' social history in the 1960s could agree on one thing: it was not (or should not be) what George Macaulay Trevelyan said it was. Trevelyan, Regius Professor of Modern History at Cambridge and Master of Trinity College, the last of the great Whig political historians, had turned his attention to social history during the Second World War. His *English Social History* of 1944 is remembered, if it is remembered at all, for its initial declaration: 'Social history might be defined negatively as the history of a people with the politics left out.'

This is not quite so crass as it sounds. Read on in the same paragraph and the qualifications considerably soften this reckless opening gambit. Trevelyan conceded that it was perhaps difficult to leave politics out, but since most histories of politics largely ignored their social environments it would perhaps be useful to reverse the bias and help redress the balance. Moreover, the rise of a flourishing economic history in his lifetime

had greatly assisted the serious study of social history; for 'the social scene grows out of economic conditions, to much the same extent that political events in their turn grow out of social conditions. Without social history, economic history is barren and political history is unintelligible.' For him the scope of social history included the daily life of inhabitants in the past, the human and economic relations between classes, the character of family and household life, the conditions of labour and leisure, the attitude of man to nature and the culture of each age as expressed in religion, literature, music, architecture, learning and thought.[2]

Although his perception of the social as playing an intermediary role between the economic and the political was a rather more nuanced and sophisticated interpretation than his critics granted, Trevelyan became a useful scapegoat for the supposed inadequacies of the 'old' social history. But this 'traditional' social history, in reality, came in a number of different guises. One such was the history of everyday life, entirely devoid of political content and unrelated to social structures or contexts. This might be termed

Onanistic history: pleasurable and personally satisfying but of no benefit to anyone else. It was much derided by the new wave of scholars as antiquarian, journalistic, 'pots and pans' or 'food and clothing' history, based largely on literary sources – a kind of fluffy history that in no way sought to rival or challenge the 'important' history of politics and statecraft.[3]

Two additional variants of traditional social history were the product of the rapid industrialization and urbanization of the nineteenth century. The first was in a subordinate relationship to economic history, which was able to establish an institutional footprint in universities and journals from the 1890s because the need to understand economic growth was pressing and the historians who pursued it were 'apolitical' and uncontroversial (read: non-socialist). The 'social question' – the nexus of poverty, revolutionary potential and increasing demands of proletarians and peasants for the rights of citizenship – spawned the second of these variants. Here the focus was on the history of labour movements, labour pioneers, trades unions and other sub-state institutions. Whether drawing on Marx and Engels or cleaving to more reformist strategies, this history was often anti-capitalist or socialist in inspiration. In Britain, the work of Sidney and Beatrice Webb, John L. and Barbara Hammond and G.D.H. Cole was representative. In the alternative labour universe of the US, the Progressive historians Charles Beard and Carl Becker produced socially based, Depression-era studies of the rise of American democracy. Much of this type of social history was intensely political, since its subject was the struggle of the people for power. As Elizabeth Fox-Genovese and Eugene Genovese put it, 'History "from the bottom up" incorporated a heavy and healthy dose of blood and iron.'[4]

It would be a mistake to downplay these social history antecedents and unduly to accentuate the differences between old and new: the battle against the hegemony of elitist political history was several decades old by the mid-twentieth century, even if it had made little impact in the academy. Yet propagandists in the postwar period were to make claims of an entirely different order for the centrality of social history. This rising generation of Young Turks had a message, a method and an approach that sought to revolutionize the study of history as a whole. If they had prewar role models they found them in the first generation of the *Annales* School in France, in particular Lucien Febvre and Marc Bloch. And if there was one text above all that pointed to the future, that was indicative of the variety of history they sought to write, it was Bloch's *Feudal Society*. This remarkable study attempted to lay bare the scaffolding of an entire society, to explain how power and authority worked at every level. It offered vastly more than the daily lives of ordinary people while dramatically complicating any history that purported to explain how the House of Capet ruled simply in terms of court and chancellery politics.[5]

The new social history, building on such work after the Second World War, was powerfully propelled by a democratizing impulse. In place of fully self-aware Great Men (politicians, diplomats, businessmen) making calculations, taking decisions and deciding the fate of millions, social history sought to uncover the traces, experiences and impact of ordinary people. Requiring a good deal of entrepreneurial drive and proselytizing zeal to pummel it into shape, against considerable scepticism and opposition, it did not emerge naturally and inevitably at a certain stage of historical development; but the times for its development were propitious: its flowering during the 'golden age of capitalism' in the West was no coincidence. The postwar corporatist world of economic management and growth, full employment and expanding welfare states, all underpinned by American economic and military might, seemed to promise endless, replicable progress. The social polity was no longer at the mercy of uncontrollable economic forces, or so it seemed: the common folk could take control of their destinies. All this was fertile soil for varieties of modernization theory.

In addition, and very much related, the social-democratic compromise growing out of the 'people's war' helped promote a 'people's history' – a history of the people, for the people and maybe even to some extent (in the newly expanding universities, through adult education and in the increasing popularity of self-guided local and family history) by the people. The new plateglass colleges and universities in particular were open to innovative approaches, and fresh cohorts of working-class, ethnic and female students sought or welcomed a history that better reflected their diverse, non-privileged backgrounds. Economic prosperity and, especially in the United States, the political mobilization surrounding the battle for civil rights, also underwrote the 'permissive moment' of the 1960s and the mood of student-led radical-liberationist optimism.[6] Against this backdrop, historians massively extended the range of legitimate topics to explore. The new social history gleefully dissected and amassed information on social classes, demographic variations, work and leisure patterns, families and lifecycles, social institutions and organizations, mentalities and customs, the standard of living, everyday life, crime and punishment, underworlds and underclasses, riots and revolutions, urban space and much else besides.[7]

This history from the bottom up largely reversed the arrow of causality: historical change could be explained not by the actions of individuals and elites, not through the primacy of politics, but by the actions of the masses and the primacy of economics.[8] Much social history paid little attention to theoretical concerns, yet the explicit or implicit working model for many social historians was one in which material conditions and an individual's position in the social structure determined his or her actions. In the strongest such formulations, 'structure' existed objectively and independently of individuals,

base determined superstructure.[9] The tension between ordinary people taking control of their lives and this denial of individual or collective agency was palpable.

In spite of its universalizing pretensions to explain the ramifications of large economic processes at all times and in all places, this type of social history – the 'social history project' – developed distinctive national variations. In France, the *Annaliste* paradigm, developed by Febvre and Bloch to displace political with structural history and traditional intellectual history with the study of mentalities, moved into its Braudelian or second-generation phase. This variant, which held sway in the 1960s and 1970s, posited a history of layers moving at markedly different speeds: the practically immobile *longue durée*, the medium-term conjunctural and the relatively inconsequential froth of *l'histoire événementielle*, the history of events and experience. War and diplomacy, politics and power, the machinations of elites – all the things that had loomed so large in traditional historiography – were downgraded to surface epiphenomena. The model was materialist, structuralist and one-way: the deeper layers determined the shallower. Consequently, the historian's principal task in explaining change over time was to analyze the structure rather than be distracted by 'men and events'.[10]

This primacy of the material, and the sense that people are powerfully constricted by the economic and social structures within which they find themselves, was one of the strongest organizing principles of social history in its heyday. So was an aligning of history with other social sciences – initially economics, increasingly sociology – and a reliance on quantification. As part and parcel of the rescue of the common people and the denigration of the impact of the individual, it stood to reason that the statistical analysis of census data, parish registers, trade figures, price fluctuations and the like could capture the economic and social fortunes of collective historical subjects who had left few other personal or literary traces. Quantification was a staple of *Annaliste* analysis, but it perhaps reached its apogee in the United States, particularly in relation to the study of urban populations but stretching as far as the investigation of communal protest and of slavery.[11] The American social historian Paul E. Johnson captures this moment vividly:

> I began graduate study at UCLA in 1967 and found colleagues whose own trajectories had taken them to where I was: we wanted to be historians, and we wanted to Serve the People. The new Social History reached UCLA at about that time, and I was trained as a quantitative social science historian. I learned that 'literary' evidence and the kinds of history that could be written from it were inherently elitist and untrustworthy. Our cousins, the *Annalistes*, talked of ignoring heroes and events and reconstructing the more constitutive and enduring 'background' of history. Such history could be made only with quantifiable sources. The result would be a 'History from the Bottom Up' that ultimately engulfed traditional history and, somehow, helped to make a Better World. Much of this was acted out with mad-scientist bravado. One well-known quantifier said that anyone who did not know statistics at least through multiple regression should not hold a job in a history department. My own advisor told us that he wanted history to become 'a predictive social science'.[12]

The West German variant of the 'social history project', principally associated with Hans-Ulrich Wëhler and Jürgen Kocka, postulated a modernization theory that owed much to Max Weber. Understandably obsessed with the rise of National Socialism, these historians deployed statistical methodology and a rigorous sense of social control (lower-class people powerless in the face of unbending structures and manipulating elites) to explain Germany's *Sonderweg* – why the country followed a deviant course rather than the 'correct' route to modernity.[13] Since East German historians continued to churn out the most rigorously mechanistic of Marxist histories, their colleagues in the Federal Republic had little to do with or say about Marx. Marxist or marxisant social history did prove to be the most mobile across national borders, but in West German historiography it was primarily British Marxist historians like Tim Mason and Geoff Eley who argued that the dominant social-history explanation (relying heavily on the supposed persistence of 'feudal' elements) let capitalism off the hook. They brought a Marxian, class-based analysis to the study of the rise of the radical right.[14]

Meanwhile, in explaining another of the colossal events of modern world history, the French Revolution, French Marxist historians continued in the prewar tradition of Georges Lefebvre to hold the commanding heights, impatiently swatting away or ignoring the empiricist challenge of Alfred Cobban, Norman Hampson and others from across the English Channel.[15] But it was the British humanist Marxists, scholars like R.H. Hilton, Christopher Hill, E.P. Thompson and Eric Hobsbawm, mostly writing about English history, who did the most to rejuvenate or resuscitate a Marxist interpretation across multiple areas and periods. They never formed a majority of social historians in Britain, but their influence stretched far beyond their numbers and ensured that they set the agenda for the conduct of the principal debates. In the US, social historians like Paul E. Johnson were increasingly uncomfortable with the ways in which quantification in alliance with social theory (principally Marx, Weber and Durkheim) imprisoned their subjects within categories of the historian's own devising. The attempt to historicize ordinary people – to make sense of their lives, to resurrect what they said and did – by locating them within social structures and long-term trends, was all well and good, laudable and noble; but something was being lost. They turned to the British Marxists with some relief.[16]

E.P. Thompson was most influential of all, at home and abroad, and served as a pointer to the debates to come. His work on class formation and the transition from the 'moral economy' to the 'market economy' rejected Parsonian structural functionalism, which had a powerful appeal in America, and more importantly the mechanistic notion propagated by more orthodox, 'scientific' Marxists that class consciousness arose unproblematically and inevitably out of class position, that the superstructure automatically reflected the base. He maintained instead that class is a *relationship* and not a *thing*, and that classes cannot simply be 'read off'. In restoring individual agency, in arguing that classes are *made* over *time* through *struggle*, Thompson's plea was for a focus on the experience and culture of the common people. But he stopped short of breaking the link between economic base and class. His argument was that the achievement of class consciousness would vary depending on the nature of the local struggle and a host of contingent factors, but he did not doubt that it would be achieved in the end. His work therefore remained within the capacious boundaries of the new social history paradigm.[17]

In his preface to *The Making of the English Working Class*, Thompson penned one of the most memorable and frequently cited passages in the historical canon:

> I am seeking to rescue the poor stockinger, the Luddite cropper, the 'obsolete' hand-loom weaver, the 'utopian' artisan, and even the deluded follower of Joanna Southcott, from the enormous condescension of posterity. Their crafts and traditions may have been dying. Their hostility to the new industrialism may have been backward-looking. Their communitarian ideals may have been fantasies. Their insurrectionary conspiracies may have been foolhardy. But they lived through these times of acute social disturbance, and we did not. Their aspirations were valid in terms of their own experience ...[18]

This was not the main purpose of his book, of course, which was to describe the forging of working-class consciousness through struggle against oppression and immiseration. But, with considerable humanity, expressed in his familiar mellifluous cadences, Thompson also set himself the task of capturing the lives of the flotsam and jetsam, those swept aside or drowned by the tide of history. Yet his language remained judgmental and (in spite

of himself) condescending. Their aspirations were valid only 'in terms of their own experience', not of the deeper forces of historical change. To distance himself from received wisdom, the 'obsolescence' and 'utopianism' of the hand-loom weavers and artisans were protected by scare-quotes; but their ideas (preceded only by a more equivocal 'may have been') remained 'backward-looking', 'foolhardy' 'fantasies'. And Southcott's supporters were simply deluded, without any prophylactic literary armature. There were two things at work here, and in the book as a whole, exemplifying much of the new social history in its heyday: a bid to record the unrecorded, however insignificant and peripheral to the forward march of history, whether they got it right or wrong in the opinion of posterity; and a drive to further the social history project, the anatomy of large-scale social processes – in Thompson's case, class formation – to explain the teleology of humanity.

By no means all the crusaders for the social history project were swept along by the Marxist tide – indeed, the biggest fault-line within social history (as in the historical profession more broadly), at least in Britain and North America, remained that between the Marxists and the non-Marxists. As early as 1955, J.H. Hexter – defining social history as 'that sort of history-writing that makes social groupings and especially socioeconomic classes the focus of its attention' – in characteristically provocative language lamented the choices most social historians made. Some operated without scaffolding, he wrote, choosing 'accuracy and incoherence in describing chaos'; others chose the stultifying framework of dialectical materialism, favouring 'intelligibility and coherence in describing a myth', and then baptizing the myth as history. But even many of those historians of the pre-industrial era who pretended to sell their wares loose were in fact bad Marxists, since they unconsciously glued their bits and pieces of social history together, using as their adhesive the ceaseless conflict of the rising business class against the landed class, to which all economic, social, political, religious and intellectual processes could ultimately be related. He did not deny the concepts of class interest and class conflict; he did see the need for a tentative type of scaffolding that could be readily extended or torn down; but he rejected the attempt to discover proofs for prefabricated theories, holding to the principle that 'History is what happened to happen' and that the historian must take social and economic groupings as he found them.[19]

It is worth pausing to look at the contrasting careers, thinking and stocktaking of two leading entrepreneurs for the new social history, Harold Perkin and Eric Hobsbawm, one a social democrat, the other a Marxist. Perkin, born into a working-class family in a two-up, two-down terraced house in the Potteries, made it to Cambridge on a scholarship. His background was indicative of the expansion of the postwar university down the social scale, but he was never persuaded that any Marxian schema could capture the slipperiness of class position, his own or anyone else's. The first lecturer in social history in Britain (at the University of Manchester, in 1951), the first Professor of Social History (at the University of Lancaster, in 1967) and the main impetus behind and first president of the Social History Society (in 1976), Perkin was strongly influential in defining and promoting the field. He made his name with *The Origins of Modern English Society, 1780–1880*, a pioneering example of the total history of society that he advocated.[20]

In 1962 Perkin described social history as the Cinderella of English historical studies. Its institutional footprint was tiny: no chairs, no departments, no academic journals, no real textbooks. Since the new social history he was promoting was not a field of study like economic or political history but all of history from a social point of view, fencing off a new plot was not really an option. But simply trespassing on others' land or being hired as a journeyman labourer by several

masters at once was not appealing either. For him social history was more, much more, than mere antiquarianism with no central unifying theme – more than 'the kitchen, the wardrobe, the sports-field, the ballroom, the garden-party, the tap-room, and the green circle around the maypole', unrelated to the wider world of which they formed a part. It was more than the recovery of the lives of the common people: the social origins of the peerage and the social connections of City merchants and financiers cried out for systematic investigation, and fell just as much within the purview of the social historian. It was 'nothing more and nothing less than the history of society.' But it was less than total history, the pursuit of everything, which could only induce exhaustion (some social historians were to dispense with this modesty later on) and, in its concern about concrete events fixed in past time and space, it was not simply a branch of sociology.

In terms of its sources, Perkin claimed, anything was grist to the social historian's mill: from love letters to census returns, clothes to cooking pots, temples to miniature paintings, lost villages to landscape architecture. Social historians could never hope to gain expertise in all the areas and sub-disciplines impacted by their terms of inquiry, but – in addition to being skilled researchers – they should be like ideally educated readers of *The Times* or the *Guardian*: able to peruse and understand every page with intelligence, whether dealing with politics, law, finance, fashion-design, literary criticism, advertising, marriage guidance or life insurance. But, armed with this formidable remit and given carte blanche to wander at will amidst all the traces of the recoverable past, was Cinderella ready to step up from handmaiden to princess? She had already occupied centre stage in the great academic brouhaha of the time, the gentry controversy, an attempt to explain the origins of the English Civil War in terms of the social upheavals of the preceding century (even if, one might add, not all the participants realized or were prepared to acknowledge that they were, with Molière's Monsieur Jourdain, 'speaking prose'). And now some of the missing support apparatus was slowly being erected: the publication of the *International Review of Social History* by the *International Instituut voor Sociale Geschiedenis* in Amsterdam since 1956; the appointment of Asa Briggs to a chair in social studies at the new University College of Sussex; and the beginnings of a number of series in social (or social and economic) history, edited by J.H. Plumb (Hutchinson), H.L. Beales and O.R. MacGregor (Heinemann), Briggs (Longmans, Green and Co.) and Perkin himself (Routledge and Kegan Paul). Social history was clearly on the move.[21]

A decade and a half later, Perkin noted the institutional advances in Britain. These included seven chairs in social history dotted around the country, in redbrick as well as plateglass universities (with nearly all existing chairs in economic history upgraded to 'and social' when their occupants were replaced); two postgraduate centres for the study of social history, at Warwick (E.P. Thompson) and Lancaster (Perkin), plus the Cambridge Group for the History of Population and Social Structure (Peter Laslett, E.A. Wrigley and Roger Schofield); two new journals, *Social History* and *History Workshop* (which grew out of Raphael Samuel's working-class oral history workshops at Ruskin College, Oxford), in addition to older and more specialized journals like H.J. Dyos's *Urban History Newsletter* (later *Yearbook*) at Leicester (1963) and Paul Thompson's *Oral History* at Essex (1971); the new Social History Society (1976); Routledge and Kegan Paul's commissioning of a seven-volume social history of England series, co-edited by Perkin; the flourishing of local history (at Leicester); and the on-going rude good health of labour history (at Warwick, Ruskin, Hull, Birkbeck and elsewhere). But social historians still had their work cut out to capture the immense range of human experience (the history of sexuality was particularly ripe for attention) and all of

society's constituent groups (women, children, elites and the middle classes all demanded more serious study). And, while no longer Cinderella, social history remained an institutional orphan as she contemplated the tension at the heart of the discipline between the wish to carve out space and a desire to conquer all:

> From some points of view, perhaps, it has been too successful. There is now scarcely a political, economic or intellectual historian who would not claim to place his specialism firmly in a social context: 'We are all social historians now.' Everything happens in society; *ergo*, everything is a social happening.[22]

Eric Hobsbawm grew up among the Jewish bourgeoisie of interwar Vienna and Berlin, joined the exodus to England in 1933 and gravitated at an early age towards Marxism and Communist politics. As a student in prewar Cambridge, economic history (in particular as purveyed by the medievalist M.M. Postan) provided intellectual succour for him and other young Marxists in contrast to what they saw as the provincialism and parochialism of political history. After the War, he dates the first section of any historical congress to be held on social history to an international congress of historical sciences in Paris in 1950. This drew together a heterogeneous collection of Marxists, *Annalistes* and others, united in their opposition to 'positivism' (the belief that all one needs to do is get the 'facts' right and the correct conclusions will follow), against traditional top-down political and military history and in favour of 'a much broadened or democratized as well as methodologically sophisticated field of history.' The modernizers – chiefly Marxists in Britain, especially through the medium of the journal *Past and Present*, founded in 1952; the non-Marxist *Annalistes* in France (only the historians of the French Revolution looked mainly to Marx for inspiration); and the Weberians in Germany – were just beginning to build up a head of steam and push the traditionalists on to the defensive.

Hobsbawm's own contributions to the burgeoning literature in the 1950s and 1960s revolved around studies of labouring men, rebels and bandits.

By 1970, at a meeting organized by the American journal *Daedalus* to assess the state of history, the modernizers were clearly in the ascendant. As Hobsbawm puts it in his autobiography:

> By that time a common flag had been found for the far from homogeneous popular front of the innovators: 'social history'. It fitted in with the political radicalization of the dramatically expanding student population of the 1960s. The term was vague, sometimes misleading, but as I wrote at the time, noting the 'remarkably flourishing state of the field': 'It is a good moment to be a social historian. Even those of us who never set out to call ourselves by this name will not want to disclaim it.'[23]

In his journal article growing out of this conference, Hobsbawm rested his explanation for this rapid development and growing emancipation of social history on two main factors. The first was academic redefinition and professional shifts – for example, the rise of a mathematically sophisticated 'new economic history' designed to fit in with developing economic theory and analysis drove many erstwhile economic historians, including Marxists, into social history's welcoming embrace. The second was the historicization of the social sciences, strongly linked to the wave of decolonization and the need by academics, governments and policy-makers to come to terms with the transformation of social structures – that is, with the history of societies – domestically and internationally. For him, the most interesting work of the past decade or so clustered around demography and kinship (particularly family reconstitution from parish registers); urban history (becoming institutionalized as a distinct field, but a central concern of social historians); the history of classes and social groups (in all aspects of their social existence, relations and behaviour); and mentalities (primarily of 'the common people', especially the inarticulate, undocumented and obscure, conservative as well as militant).[24]

If it is asserted that social history is the history of society, and is an approach rather than a discrete area of study, maximilizing claims follow closely behind. Whatever their differences, Hobsbawm was no different in this regard to Perkin. 'Social history can never be another specialization like economic or other hyphenated histories because its subject matter cannot be isolated', was how he phrased it; 'the social or societal aspects of man's being cannot be separated from the other aspects of his being, except at the cost of tautology or extreme trivialization.'[25] And yet, in retrospect, Hobsbawm dates the highpoint of the new social history to about this period, the early 1970s. Even before the postmodern onslaught of the eighties he detects a waning of confidence in historians' ability to answer the big questions: a shift from structure to culture, from telescope to microscope, from Braudel and the Mediterranean to Clifford Geertz and his 'thick description' of a Balinese cockfight.[26]

Any such creeping doubts at the time scarcely rippled the mood of self-congratulation. The opening editorial to *Social History*, the first dedicated journal of social history in Britain, launched under the editorship of Janet Blackman and Keith Nield at the University of Hull in 1976, rehearsed a by-now familiar refrain:

> Social history is not simply another specialism in process of professional formation, a relatively new splinter of historical knowledge to be defined by its separate institutions and narrowed to a handful of interests which rarely trespass into fields 'proper' to other specialisms. For social history is not a new *branch* of historical scholarship, but, in Lucien Febvre's words, a new kind of history. Social history must be at once iconoclastic, corrosive of received explanations; creative in producing new concepts and devising new methods; and aggressive, encouraging incursions into all fields of historical analysis.

That said – while recognizing the strong contributions of the British Marxists and the French *Annalistes* and the brilliance of maestros like Bloch, Braudel, Hobsbawm and Thompson – the editors noted that social history had no dominant central core or organizing concept akin to the economic historians' 'industrialization' or 'growth'. This, somewhat paradoxically, was for them a matter for congratulation, since it enabled a welcome diversity of approach and range of methods and explanations.[27]

At the end of 1976, a health-check by the *Journal of Social History*, the flagship for social history in the US, gave a more measured sense of how this gawky adolescent, with its gargantuan appetite and rebellious spirit, was faring. Peter Stearns, who had edited the journal since its inception in 1967, celebrated the number of practitioners, journals, associations, courses, methodological innovations and new topics in social history. And he gave this ringing endorsement:

> Social history *is* history, an approach to the entirety of the past. It is not a topic, like intellectual history, or even a set of topics (the Mulligan stew syndrome). It is panoramic, asking questions broader than those most historians have previously raised and dealing with an unprecedented combination of familiar sources and materials essentially untapped before. The established topical fields of history – political, intellectual, even military … are all aspects of social history.

But his enthusiasm was tempered. Alongside such triumphalism he lamented the smorgasbord (or Mulligan stew) quality to the field, the fact that in the US and Britain there were still relatively few social historians (only in France and in some German and central European institutions had social history triumphed within the academy) and that in some vital areas (such as demography, kinship studies, urban studies and quantitative methods in general) there was a danger of methodologically or source-driven research losing sight of the bigger social picture. He also feared that the more traditional historians were succeeding in cubby-holing social history rather than recognizing its totalizing ambitions. The only solution, he argued, was

the creation of a separate discipline with its own identity in distinct departments.[28]

This was surprising advice, perhaps, if social history sought hegemony, if it refused to be corralled and rendered docile in a separate paddock in history's backyard. But it is indicative of some of the tension even in social history's self-confident heyday, when its maximilizing claims reached their zenith. In the same state-of-the-field collection, Theodore Zeldin noted that social history was the most ambitious form of history but that it had most difficulty articulating its subject and that, because of its success, it had rather lost its way. He thought that the *histoire sociale* of Febvre and Bloch, the study of the whole of life, had in practice contracted in the hands of most of their less ambitious followers ever since.[29] Michelle Perrot similarly commented that imprecision bedevilled the field. 'If any branch of history lacks certainty in its object and methodology,' she wrote, 'if any manages to be at once proliferous [*sic*] and deprived, nebulous and fragmented, it is "social" history.' It had been at the centre or at the margins of most historical scholarship over the previous decade, but its openness left it without clear definition or purpose.[30]

The strongest critique, however, came from further to the Left. Elizabeth Fox-Genovese and Eugene Genovese argued that much of the new social history, departing from Marxian theoretical models, had succeeded in obscuring class struggle and the key question of political power; it was 'steadily sinking into a neoantiquarian swamp presided over by liberal ideologues'. They concluded:

> History … is primarily the story of who rides whom and how. To the extent that social history illuminates this essentially political process, we should all aspire to be social historians. To the extent that it provides new and sophisticated, or alternatively more populist, forms of evasion and obfuscation, we should recognize it for what it is: merely the latest version of liberal or even 'radical' bourgeois cant.[31]

By the end of the decade Tony Judt was polemically announcing in *History Workshop*, reversing Hobsbawm's verdict, 'This is a bad time to be a social historian'. Social history, he claimed, had become severely polluted; a constant striving for 'scientific' status had caused its practitioners to borrow indiscriminately from other disciplines. These unscholarly historians, 'bereft of ideas and subtlety', had become obsessed with method and technique, had abandoned theory and had lost touch with historical events. In jettisoning politics, in refusing to dissect power, they had succeeded in rendering whole areas of human experience incomprehensible. 'We are witnessing the slow strangulation of social history,' he wrote, 'watching while a high fever is diagnosed as blooming good health.' The solution was to return to important questions and significant problematics, to reinsert politics and ideology as central to social history.[32]

Some liberal historians, too, picked up on the allegation that historical practice and social history had become balkanized by the end of the seventies.[33] Lawrence Stone, one of the leading practitioners of prosopography in the new English social history, was vocalizing increasing doubts about 'scientific' models (Marxist economic or French ecological-demographic) and cliometric methods. His call for a return to narrative registered disillusionment with economic and demographic determinism, and disappointment with the failure of teams of data-crunchers to match expectations. But the big beasts in the field did not take such critiques lying down. For example, in a robust response, Charles Tilly drew on a range of examples – among them Stone's own work; Keith Wrightson and David Levine's study of Terling, Essex, from 1525 to 1700; and Braudel's three-volume synthesis of capitalism and material life – to demonstrate that quantitative, demographic and social science methods had succeeded in connecting individual experience with large social processes more clearly, precisely and fully than ever before. Quoting an earlier statement of Stone, he concluded that the mission of social history was still to 'tie the exciting developments in intellectual

and cultural history down to the social, economic, and political bedrock.'[34]

None of these squabbles and tensions should detract from a narrative of the rise of social history to impressive heights. Increasing numbers of scholars called themselves social historians; social history's institutional presence had become entrenched; few political, economic or any other type of historians could any longer ignore 'the social'. Social history as field and as approach had both succeeded. Asa Briggs seemed to sum this up when, nearly four decades after Trevelyan published his social history of England, he brought out his own synthesis with a similar title. Briggs, from a small-town Yorkshire background – and at various times in his long career Professor of Modern History at the University of Leeds; Dean of Social Studies and Vice-Chancellor of the University of Sussex; Provost of Worcester College, Oxford; Chancellor of the Open University; and, from 1976, Lord Briggs of Lewes – embodied the penetration of social history into the academic establishment. In the introduction to his book he spelled out the distance the discipline had travelled. Social history appealed to him not only because it rescued the nameless and the powerless but because it concerned itself with the powerful too. 'For me, as for a new generation of social historians,' he reflected, 'social history is the history of society. It is concerned with structure and processes of change. Nothing is irrelevant to it. Nor can any evidence, even the most ephemeral, be ignored.'[35] The totalizing claims and the self-confidence remained intact; few suspected that social history was about to undergo an existential crisis and that such superb self-assurance would begin to unravel.

## NOTES AND REFERENCES

1   In the obscenity case of Jacobellis v. Ohio in 1964, US Supreme Court Justice Potter Stewart famously remarked that hardcore pornography is difficult to define, but 'I know it when I see it.'

2   G.M. Trevelyan, *English Social History* (London: Longmans, Green and Co., 1944), vii.

3   See Mario S. DePillis, 'Trends in American social history and the possibilities of behavioral approaches', *Journal of Social History* 1 (Fall 1967): 37–8. DePillis points out that *A History of American Life Series*, ed. Dixon Ryan Fox and A.M. Schlesinger, Jr, 13 vols (New York: Macmillan, 1927–48), the greatest monument to 'pots and pans' history, at least opened up many new topics for historical study.

4   *Encyclopedia of American Social History*, ed. Mary Kupiec Cayton, Elliott J. Gorn and Peter W. Williams (New York: Charles Scribner's Sons, 1993), vol. I, 'Preface', xvii; Werner Conze, 'Social History', *Journal of Social History* 1 (Fall 1967): 11–13; A.J.C. Rüter, 'Introduction', *International Review of Social History* 1 (1956): 1–7; Patricia Clavin, 'Is economic history no longer fashionable?' in *Writing Contemporary History*, ed. Robert Gildea and Anne Simonin (London: Hodder Education, 2008), 25–6; Elizabeth Fox-Genovese and Eugene D. Genovese, 'The political crisis of social history: a Marxian perspective', *Journal of Social History*, 10, 2 (Winter 1976): 206.

5   E.J. Hobsbawm, 'From social history to the history of society', *Daedalus* 100, 1 (Winter 1971): 21–2; Fox-Genovese and Genovese, 'The political crisis of social history': 205–7; Marc Bloch, *La société féodale*, 2 vols. (Paris: 1939).

6   William H. Sewell, Jr, 'Crooked lines', in '*AHR* Forum: Geoff Eley's *The Crooked Line*', *American Historical Review* 113, 2 (April 2008): 396, 399–400; Rüter, 'Introduction': 7; Mike Savage, *Identities and Social Change in Britain Since 1940: The Politics of Method* (Oxford: Oxford University Press, 2010), 129.

7   Richard J. Evans, *In Defense of History* (New York: Norton, 1999), 144–5.

8   Robert Mandrou, 'Primat de l'histoire sociale: propos sans paradoxes', *Histoire Sociale-Social History* 1 (April 1968): 7–8.

9   See, for example, Christopher Lloyd, *Explanation in Social History* (Oxford: Blackwell, 1986), 16 and *passim*; Miguel A. Cabrera, *Postsocial History: An Introduction*, tr. by Marie McMahon (Lanham, MD: Lexington Books, 2005), 2–3.

10  Peter Burke, *The French Historical Revolution: The Annales School 1929–89* (Oxford: Polity Press, 1990).

11  For example, Stephan Thernstrom, *Poverty and Progress: Social Mobility in a Nineteenth Century City* (Cambridge, MA: Harvard University Press, 1964); Robert W. Fogel and Stanley L. Engerman, *Time on the Cross* (Boston and Toronto: Little, Brown, 1974); and Charles Tilly's extensive repertoire.

12  Paul E. Johnson, 'Reflections: looking back at social history', *Reviews in American History* 39, 2 (June 2011): 380.

13  For example, Hans-Ulrich Wehler, *The German Empire, 1871–1918*, tr. by Kim Traynor (Dover, NH: Berg, 1985).

14  Eley, *A Crooked Line*, 69–83.

15  Georges Lefebvre, *Quatre-Vingt-Neuf* (Paris: 1939); Ernest Labrousse, *La Crise de l'Économie Française à la fin de l'Ancien Régime et au Début de la Révolution* (Paris: Presses universitaires de France, 1944); Albert Soboul, *La Révolution Française* (Paris: Gallimard, 1962); Alfred Cobban, *Social Interpretation of the French Revolution* (Cambridge: Cambridge University Press, 1964); Norman Hampson, *A Social History of the French Revolution* (London: Routledge and Kegan Paul, 1963).

16  Johnson, 'Reflections': 380–1.

17  Edward Thompson, *The Making of the English Working Class* (London: Gollancz, 1980 [1963]), 10–12; Geoff Eley, 'Edward Thompson, social history and political culture: the making of a working-class public, 1780–1850', in *E.P. Thompson: Critical Perspectives*, ed. Harvey J. Kaye and Keith McClelland (Philadelphia: Temple University Press, 1990).

18  Thompson, *The Making*, 14.

19  J.H. Hexter, 'A new framework for social history', *Journal of Economic History* 15, 4 (December 1955): 415–17.

20  Harold Perkin, *The Making of a Social Historian* (London: Athena Press, 2002); *idem*, *The Origins of Modern English Society, 1780–1880* (London: Routledge and Kegan Paul, 1969); David Cannadine, obituary of Perkin, *Guardian*, 23 October 2004; Jeffrey Richards, obituary of Perkin, *Independent*, 2 November 2004.

21  Perkin, 'Social history', in *Approaches to History*, ed. H.P.R. Finberg (Toronto: University of Toronto Press, 1962), 51–82.

22  Perkin, 'Social history in Britain', *Journal of Social History* 10, 2 (Winter 1976): 129–43 (quotation p. 136).

23  Eric Hobsbawm, *Interesting Times: A Twentieth-Century Life* (London: Allen Lane, 2002), chap. 17 (quotations pp. 288, 290) and *passim*; *idem*, *Primitive Rebels: Studies in Archaic Forms of Social Movement in the 19th and 20th Centuries* (Manchester: Manchester University Press, 1959); *idem*, *Labouring Men: Studies in the History of Labour* (London: Weidenfeld and Nicolson, 1964); *idem*, *Bandits* (London: Weidenfeld and Nicolson, 1969); *idem* and George Rudé, *Captain Swing* (London: Lawrence and Wishart, 1969).

24  Hobsbawm, 'From social history to the history of society': 20–45.

25  Hobsbawm, 'From social history to the history of society': 24–5.

26  Hobsbawm, *Interesting Times*, 294.

27  *Social History* 1, 1 (January 1976): 1–3.

28  Peter N. Stearns, 'Coming of age', *Journal of Social History* 10, 2 (Winter 1976): 246–55 (quotation p. 252).

29  Theodore Zeldin, 'Social history and total history', *Journal of Social History* 10, 2 (Winter 1976): 237–45.

30  Michelle Perrot, 'The strengths and weaknesses of French social history', *Journal of Social History* 10, 2 (Winter 1976): 166.

31  Fox-Genovese and Genovese, 'The political crisis of social history': 209–10, 214 (1st quotation), 219 (2nd quotation).

32  Tony Judt, 'A clown in regal purple: social history and the historians', *History Workshop Journal* 7, 1 (1979): 66–94

(quotations on p. 66 and p. 89 respectively). For another such lament, see Geoff Eley and Keith Nield, 'Why does social history ignore politics?' *Social History* 5, 2 (May 1980): 249–71.

33   Chris Waters, 'Is there still a place for social history?', in *Writing Contemporary History*, ed. Gildea and Simonin, 3.

34   Charles Tilly, 'The old new social history and the new old social history', *Review* VII, 3 (Winter 1984): 365–8, 377–95; Lawrence Stone, *The Crisis of the Aristocracy,* *1558–1641* (Oxford: Clarendon Press, 1965); Keith Wrightson and David Levine, *Poverty and Piety in an English Village; Terling, 1525–1700* (New York: Academic Press, 1979); Fernand Braudel, *Civilisation Matérielle, Éonomie et capitalisme, XVe–XVIII siécle*, 3 vols. (Paris: A. Colin, 1967–79); Lawrence Stone, 'Prosopography', in *Historical Studies Today*, ed. Felix Gilbert and Stephen R. Graubard (New York: W. W. Norton, 1972), 134.

35   Asa Briggs, *A Social History of England* (London: Weidenfeld and Nicolson, 1983), 8.

# Postmodernism: The Linguistic Turn and Historical Knowledge

# 7

# The Work of Hayden White I: Mimesis, Figuration and the Writing of History

Robert Doran

Unambiguous referentiality may be established for specific words and phrases not longer than the sentence, but discourse differs from the specific sentence and any simple list of sentences by virtue of the meaning with which it endows its referents through techniques of figuration, a process of giving the odor of literalness to metaphorical utterances – which logicians castigate as the principal source of error in imprecise thinking. (Hayden White[1])

It would of course be impossible to discuss historical theory without examining a thinker who, more than any other, has placed theoretical questions at the forefront of debates surrounding history and historiography. Over a 50-year career (and counting), Hayden White has relentlessly questioned conventional thinking in historical studies. His assertion that all narrative, including the narration of real or historical events, is 'emplotted' and thus is in some fundamental way 'fictional' has unnerved many of his colleagues, provoking scathing rebukes but also genuine admiration.[2] White's most elaborate presentation of his controversial ideas, *Metahistory: The Historical Imagination in*

*Nineteenth-Century Europe* (1973), continues to be considered one of the seminal works of historical theory, though its influence has also been felt in literary studies, philosophy, media and film studies, and art history, to name only a few of the fields White's work has impacted. With respect to this wider intellectual context, *Metahistory* should also be seen in terms of its contribution to the critical theory genre that emerged in the late 1960s. Like such influential tomes as Jacques Derrida's *Of Grammotology* and René Girard's *Violence and the Sacred* (also published by Johns Hopkins University Press in the 1970s), White's magnum opus was an exemplar of wide-ranging interdisciplinary scholarship, heralding an era of unprecedented self-reflection and re-evaluation in the humanities.

At issue during this period was the relationship of the traditional humanistic disciplines to science, particularly to the emergent social sciences or 'sciences of man.' In the late nineteenth and early twentieth centuries, scientific positivism had come to embody the ideal of objective, value-free knowledge. In an effort to professionalize and garner prestige for their field, historians of the latter half of the nineteenth century, led by Leopold von Ranke (1795–1886), adopted this epistemological credo as their own. Ranke's efforts to ground historiography in an empirical methodology that stood in stark contrast to the theoretical and ideological speculations of the philosophy of history (Hegel, Marx), while at the same time distancing historical writing from its association with the literary genres and rhetoric, were gradually institutionalized, forming the basis for modern historical scholarship, particularly in the United States. *Metahistory* was in many ways a response to the Rankean idea that history should aspire to scientific objectivity, i.e., that it was possible for the historian to uncover the truth of the past and tell us 'how it actually was.'[3]

## METAHISTORY AND TROPOLOGY

In *Metahistory* White sought to develop the notion that history was identical with historical *writing*, thereby refuting the main presupposition of historical objectivism: the idea that history could be treated as ontologically distinct from its recounting. This, however, did not mean that White had abandoned the very concept of historical knowledge or historical truth. In fact, White spoke of historical writing in terms of its capacity to express a 'specifically human truth.'[4] By qualifying historical truth as human truth, White subtly shifts the epistemological ground from a question of objective knowledge to one of (individual or collective) self-knowledge. White derives this conception of human truth from the philosophy of Giambattista Vico – perhaps White's most important influence – whose famous *verum-factum* principle (literally: 'the true is the made') states that man can really know only what he himself has made and thus can aspire to a kind of knowledge of human affairs (and therefore of history) that is qualitatively different from his knowledge of nature.[5] White writes:

[Vico's] theory [of *verum-factum*] is called 'maker's knowledge,' and it holds that, since nature was made by God, human beings can never hope to have the kind of knowledge of it that only God could possess. However, the theory also says, since culture is a distinctively human creation, human beings can aspire to a knowledge of culture of a kind and degree utterly different from that which they can have of the rest of nature. And since history is the record of this process of cultural creation, human beings can legitimately aspire to a knowledge both of history and of themselves as the agents of a specifically historical mode of existence that is both truer and more certain than any knowledge they can ever hope to have of nature. Historical knowledge, in short, is human self-knowledge and specifically knowledge of how human beings make themselves through knowing themselves and come to know themselves in the process of making themselves.[6]

In other words: man 'makes' history, both literally (in act) and figuratively (in writing). The implication of this Vichian perspective is that history is best understood as a *creative* enterprise shaped by the historian's *imaginative* grasp of the human content embodied in the historical record and conditioned by the historian's socio-cultural predispositions. Writing history, then, is an act of personal and collective self-affirmation and self-making.

Inspired by Vico's use of rhetorical figures to describe modes of human consciousness, White develops, in a lengthy methodological introduction to *Metahistory*, a theory of tropes – a tropology – by which he aims to explore the 'deep structure' of historical writing. The tropes – metaphor, metonymy, synecdoche, and irony (the same list as found in Vico) – function as primordial discursive forms or strategies, upon which three other discursive levels – those of Emplotment, Argument, Ideological Implication – each with its own four-fold structure, are stacked, as it were. White sees these interactive or combinatory possibilities of the different levels as describing the diversity of historiographical styles. However, White makes it clear that the tropes are primary (prior to ideological, logical, and aesthetic concerns) insofar as they define or organize the discursive tendency of a particular approach to history, which can in turn be analyzed in terms of its relation to other tropological tendencies evolving over time.[7] Thus White can, for example, characterize a particular historian's approach as being informed fundamentally by metaphor, which does not simply mean that the historian may exhibit a strong preference for metaphors in his or her writing, but that his or her entire manner of grasping historical reality is determined 'pre-critically' (unconsciously) by the trope-structure of metaphor (i.e., by relations of similitude).[8] In effect, White is saying that the tropes are the building blocks of all formed thought (discursivity), and as such cannot correspond to reality in the way that literal language is thought to refer to the world – that is, in a direct, simple, or unmediated way. Tropes produce or 'make' historical reality because they prefigure (condition) the semantic field in which they are inevitably fulfilled (made manifest). This Kantian dimension of White's thought – which White freely acknowledges – has been much commented on.[9] For Kant, knowledge of the world is conditioned by the forms of human cognition (such as space and time), rather than the other way around. This was his 'Copernican revolution.' White's tropological approach to historical writing is no less sweeping in its aim to reorient historical studies toward a more linguistically (or rhetorically) conscious stance.

In addition to its tropological methodology, one of the major innovations of *Metahistory* is the rapprochement White effects between the philosophy of history and history proper, two types of historical writing that stood opposed to one another during the nineteenth century. Through his analyses of four philosophers (Hegel, Marx, Nietzsche, Croce) and four historians (Michelet, Tocqueville, Ranke, Burckhardt), White reveals structural identities based on common tropological processes, concluding that 'every philosophy of history contains within it the elements of a proper history, just as every proper history contains within it the elements of a full-blown philosophy of history.'[10] This rapprochement also shows how White contests

Aristotle's famous assertion that, unlike poetry and philosophy, which are concerned with universals, history is concerned only or mostly with particulars.[11] In philosophizing history, Hegel and Marx had attempted to demonstrate that history could indeed be conceived in terms of universal categories – exactly the kind of a priori theorizing that practicing historians found anathema. But in showing how writing history – whether philosophically or empirically grounded – is essentially a *poetic* (creative) enterprise, White demonstrates that history is as concerned with universals as with particulars, even if, in the case of history, the particulars are given rather than invented.[12]

Though White would continue to elaborate on aspects of his tropological theory in his next book, *Tropics of Discourse: Essays in Cultural Criticism* (1978), he soon decided to shift the emphasis from the tropes to the idea of narrative 'emplotment,' which he had developed in *Metahistory*.[13] Thus, in his two subsequent works, *The Content of the Form: Narrative Discourse and Historical Representation* (1987) and *Figural Realism: Studies in the Mimesis Effect* (1999), White focuses more specifically on issues of historical representation and narrative.

## EMPLOTMENT AND NARRATIVE FORM

White sees narrative as essential to historical writing, for even when the historian eschews storytelling – as with the French *Annalistes*, who disparaged what they called 'event history' (*l'histoire événementielle*) – White holds that some sort of *narrativization* is inescapable: 'one cannot historicize without narrativizing, because it is only by narrativization that a series of events can be transformed into a sequence, divided into periods, and represented as a process in which the substances of things can be said to change while their identities remain the same.'[14] While White agrees with those who, like Roland Barthes and the *Annalistes*, see in the 'dramatic' nature of historical narrative a kind of mythification, he considers the proposed remedies – the abandonment of history altogether, on one extreme, or its assimilation to social science, on the other – as misguided attempts to skirt an ineluctable problem: namely, how to live with the knowledge that history is as much a product of the imagination as it is of the 'facts.' All of White's work is an attempt to grapple with this problematic.

Whether one sees narrative dramatization as introducing extrinsic elements that obscure historical reality or as bringing alive a story that inheres in the data itself, one is cleaving to the same ontological position: that history 'exists' apart from its recounting. For White, on the contrary, there is no being of history other than the ontological *effect* – the reality or mimesis effect – produced by historical discourse. Hence the inevitable objection: to what extent can history claim to be telling us about events that actually happened? Or, to put it another way, how to respond to Polybius's ancient injunction: 'history, if truth be taken away, is but a useless tale.'[15]

To answer this question we must delve into White's theory of historical emplotment, which differs from the vast majority of narrative theories in its concern with the problem of referenciality or indexicality. Since the study of narrative or narratology was developed within the armature of literary studies – which tends to treat the idea of referentiality as an interesting intellectual conundrum rather than as a do-or-die, existential question, as the historian must – there had been, prior to White, little thought devoted to how formalist and historicist approaches to narrative could intertwine (in fact, they were thought to be irreconcilable). Thus for all of White's vaunted 'structuralism' and 'formalism,' it is in fact his ability to credibly address how narrative form interacts with historical content to produce historical discourse that makes his approach to narrative theory pertinent and unique.

Given that White derives his theory of emplotment from Northrop Frye's theory of narrative archetypes (*mythoi*), we should not be surprised if the literary critic sees nothing particularly controversial in the notion of emplotment as it applies to literature, even if he or she does not embrace Frye's theory *in toto* (that there are only four basic types, etc.).[16] The literary critic readily accepts the conventionality of plot, genre, etc., in the sense that, for example, Balzac 'emplotted' *Le père Goriot* by adapting the *Bildungsroman* story-type to a specifically French context. However, White's use of the term 'emplotment' implies a *polemical* stance concerning *real life*: biographies, autobiographies, memoirs, and, more specifically, histories. By asserting that the recounting of real events necessarily entails the introduction of plot-types which, because of their inherent conventionality, cannot be found in the historical record or in individual lives, White is arguing that a story is a product (*factum, poiesis*) of the human imagination, mediated by cultural and aesthetic traditions and norms:

> Stories are not lived; there is no such thing as a real story. Stories are told or written, not found. And as for the notion of a true story, this is virtually a contradiction in terms. All stories are fictions. Which means, of course, that they can be true only in a metaphorical sense and in the sense in which a figure of speech can be true. Is this true enough?[17]

More particularly, White is challenging the idea of *lived narratives*, a view articulated by historical theorists such as Paul Ricoeur and David Carr, who hold that an individual experiences life as a story. According to this view, first-person accounts should thus be seen as reproducing the form of experience as well as its content. White comments: 'As thus envisaged, historical narrative is a peculiar kind of discourse, the product of a process of verbal *figuration* that insofar as the story told conforms to the outline of the story lived in real life, is to be taken as *literally* true.'[18] But, as White continues, this collapse of the figurative into the literal merely puts us back into the position of historical objectivism: 'if that were the case, the task of the historian would be what it has always been thought to be, namely, to discover the "real" story or stories that lie embedded within the welter of "facts" and to retell them as truthfully and completely as the documentary record permits.'[19]

According to White, historical discourse emplots real events by endowing them with a particular meaning-structure – a story *of a particular kind* (for there is no such thing as narration-in-general, as if a story could be completely bereft of conventional structure). The very act of introducing even the barest outline of a story-form (e.g., beginning–middle–end) is thus an extrinsic act of construction. The supposed resemblance between real life and stories is simply a recognition of the importance of stories in our *retrospective* organization of events. Now one might, for example, assert that birth and death are 'natural' starting and ending points that are not constructed but inhere in the life of every individual. But what biography starts with birth and ends with death? (And of course the memoir, as a first-person account, cannot make use of such reference points as narrative bookends.) In fact, most biographies of famous individuals begin with a family history that precedes the individual's birth and end at a point long after the individual's death (since, presumably, an individual worth writing about has had an important posthumous impact). Furthermore, there is no reason why a segment of an individual's life cannot be coherently represented without necessarily framing itself in terms of birth and death (many films take this route). Thus the internal logic of a story is not the logic of the facts recounted but that of the aesthetic form employed: telling a story is therefore always, in some fundamental way, a fictionalization – which does not thereby mean that the facts or events are invented but that the meaning and significance given to them by the story-form is necessarily a product of that (fictional) form.[20] Put another way: the very presence of 'storiness' in a historical account is tantamount to a fictionalization; for it organizes and confers meaning on a set of facts according to a 'story-logic': i.e., relations between beginning, middle, and

end; plot coherence; dramatic devices such as climaxes and denouements; and so on.

Hence White's assertion that the same data or facts can be variously emplotted according to the meaning the historian wishes to impart to them: 'the demonstration that a given set of events *can be* represented as a comedy implicitly argues for the possibility of representing it with equal plausibility as a tragedy, romance, farce, epic, and so on.'[21] White's reputation as a relativist stems from his contention that the historian can tell a variety of different stories about the same events, without thereby violating the 'facts,' which White defines as 'singular existential statements.'[22] Thus White is a peculiar kind of relativist, since, particularly in his later writings, he insists on the irreducible facticity of historical discourse:

> This is not to say that a historical discourse is not properly assessed in terms of the truth value of its factual (singular existential) statements taken individually and the logical conjunction of the whole set taken distributively. For unless a historical discourse acceded to assessment in these terms, it would lose all justification for its claim to represent and provide explanations of specifically real events.[23]

White's relativism is thus not of the postmodern (Nietzschean) variety, which consists in saying that there are no facts, only interpretations, that what is called a 'fact' is always already an interpretation. For this is simply an inversion of Rankean historical objectivism: there are no interpretations, only facts; the facts speak for themselves. As White observes:

> The distinction between facts and meanings is usually taken to be the basis of historical relativism. This is because in conventional historical inquiry, the facts established about a specific event are taken to be the meaning of that event. Facts are supposed to provide the basis for arbitrating among the variety of different meanings that different social groups can assign to an event for different ideological or political reasons. But the facts are a function of the meaning assigned to events, not some primitive data that determine what meanings an event can have.

Thus despite his reputation for extremism, White actually steers a middle course between postmodernist relativism and historical objectivism, both of which seek to dissolve the distinction between fact and interpretation. Nevertheless, in the eyes of many critics, White's belated insistence on the sanctity of facts smacks of a desire to have it both ways: he advocates a relativism of interpretation while maintaining the truth of facts; yet his notion of 'human truth' has very little to do with facts or historical data and everything to do with interpretation. Furthermore, White's forced marriage of fact (subject to scientific verification) and fictional form (conventional form), is, for many historians, like mixing oil and water.

## MIMESIS AND HISTORICAL REPRESENTATION

This brings us to the vexed problem of *mimesis*, of how discourse refers to the world, for White insists on the specificity of the representational practices of historical discourse, even as he notes its formal and structural affinities with imaginative literature. However, since prior to the nineteenth century historical writing was considered a literary genre and more particularly a branch of rhetoric, it is important to approach the development of the verbal arts holistically.

One can certainly read the history of mimesis in Western culture, both pictorial and verbal, in terms of an evolution toward a richer, more powerful, and more vivid depiction of reality – that is, in terms of a *better apprehension* of the way things actually are, through ever more effective mimetic technics (culminating in the devices of mechanical reproduction: photography, cinema, the phonograph, and so on). Whether we are speaking of the shift from two- to three-dimensional perspective painting in the Renaissance or the advent of detailed physical and psychological description in the nineteenth-century novel, much of what was produced in the verbal and the visual arts prior to the twentieth century aspired to be judged according its fidelity to reality or its *realism*. Now the meaning of 'realism' is far from univocal; its principal denotations include: exactitude in description or detail; non-idealization; everydayness (democratization of subject matter); authenticity (documentary truth); verisimilitude (*appearing* to be true as opposed to being *actually* true); or conventionalized conceptions of any of the foregoing (e.g., the idea of the 'used future' in science fiction films to render them more 'realistic,' even though by definition they cannot refer to anything actual or historical). One is tempted to say that all realism is conventional in the sense that it must conform to some degree to the reader's/spectator's expectations of what realistic representation should consist of at a particular moment in time (as in the seventeenth-century controversy surrounding Corneille's *Le Cid*: though Corneille's account of a woman who marries her father's killer was historically accurate, it was condemned as unrealistic – as lacking in verisimilitude – and thus as unworthy of *poetic* representation). The inclusion of negative or sordid aspects of reality has also been considered a hallmark of realism (e.g., Zola's novels), but only because it appears to resist standards of taste that place arbitrary limits on representation and not because reality is inherently 'sordid.'

Since the historian must strive for the most realistic presentation of historical reality possible, the kind of presentation that most effectively mirrors (to employ an overused metaphor) its object, it is no wonder that objectivist historiography comes into its own at the very moment when realistic representation in literature, epitomized in the novel, reaches its apogee. It is as if historians wished to freeze this moment in the history of verbal mimesis, raising it to an eternal standard of historical verisimilitude. As White remarks in his seminal article 'The burden of history' (1966): 'when historians claim that history is a combination of science and art, they generally mean that it is a combination of *late nineteenth-century* social science and *mid nineteenth-century* art.'[24] (In his later works, White often recommended that historians broaden their stylistic palette to include modernist forms, a move that White thinks may be more efficacious in dealing with more recent history.)[25] Of course, historians may feel that they can ignore the extent to which their practice relies on literary conventions developed by nineteenth-century novelists, for this 'stylistic' dimension is seen as having no real effect on historical knowledge. Discursive realism is considered merely a convenient vehicle or medium for the expression of historical content, facilitating or enhancing the reader's grasp of historical reality. As we have seen, White insists that narrative form (plot-type), is inseparable from the overall meaning conveyed – i.e., the form has a 'content,' even as the content must have a form (hence the title of one of White's books: *The Content of the Form*). However, it is difficult to evaluate plot-types in terms of their degree of realism; in fact, White's theory precludes such an attempt, for he holds that plots are *made* (crafted by the historian) not found (in the historical record), and thus no particular plot-structure can be said to be inherently more 'realistic,' no closer to reality, than any other.[26]

## FIGURALISM

White's view of realistic representation is largely inspired by Erich Auerbach's literary historicism, as expounded in his *Mimesis: The Representation of Reality in Western Literature*, published just after the Second World War. Admiring Auerbach's ability to take a dynamic, external view of the history of realistic representation (in a kind of Hegelian, philosophy of history mode), as opposed to treating different instances of realism in a purely relativistic or contingent manner, White sees in Auerbach's practice an implicit theory of representation.[27]

In an article entitled 'Auerbach's literary history: figural causation and modernist historicism,' White argues that Auerbach's

*Mimesis* is based on the concept of *figuralism*, which means not only that it is a 'history of a specific kind of literary representation, that is, figuralism, but is also a history conceived as a sequence of figure-fulfillment relationships.'[28] In other words, figuralism is both the subject and *method* of Auerbach's literary history and as such provides a model of how the historical and formal levels of critical discourse interact – a model that White himself emulates in *Metahistory*.[29]

Figuralism, which Auerbach had discussed at length in an article entitled 'Figura' (1939), is a type of interpretation that connects two or more events (often far removed in time and space) by way of a retrospective bestowal of meaning.[30] Thus an earlier event is seen as prefiguring and as being fulfilled in a later event, which in turn reveals the significance (latent meaning) of the earlier event. Figural interpretation was originally developed by Christian exegetes as a way of revealing the hidden unity between seemingly disconnected events and persons, especially between the Old and New Testaments, without sacrificing the Bible's literal truth. For unlike symbolic or allegorical interpretation, which denies or negates the literal level of language, figuralism treats persons and events as concrete and historical; their literal sense is preserved. In this manner, the Bible could function as both religion and history, so that Christianity came to be to a large extent identified with the meaning of its history conceived as a series of prefigurations and fulfillments.

White sees Christian figuralism as proto-historical in its ability to synthesize the literal and figurative dimensions of language (fact and interpretation) while maintaining their distinctness. However, what in the theological interpretation were taken to be intrinsic (i.e., necessary, causal) relations between two events or persons – relations vouchsafed by divine providence – are, in specifically historical interpretation, conceived *aesthetically* as extrinsic relations stemming from the historian's or historical agent's freedom of choice. White observes:

There is no necessity at all governing the relation between, say, Italian Renaissance culture and classical Greek-Latin civilization. The relationships between the earlier and the later phenomena are purely retrospective, consisting of the decisions on the parts of a number of historical agents, from the time of Dante or thereabouts on into the sixteenth century, to choose to regard themselves and their cultural endowment as if they had actually descended from the earlier prototype.[31]

White's debt to Sartrean existentialism is apparent here and in particular to the section entitled 'My past' in *Being and Nothingness*, wherein Sartre states:

Who shall decide whether that mystic crisis in my fifteenth year 'was' a pure accident of puberty or, on the contrary, the first sign of a future conversion? I myself, according to whether I shall decide – at twenty years of age, at thirty – to be converted. The project of conversion by a single stroke confers on an adolescent crisis the value of a premonition which I had not taken seriously.[32]

Through present choices, I valorize or negate past actions. I change their meaning by fulfilling or not fulfilling them and by endowing them retroactively with the force of prefiguration or of insignificance. My choice thus gives the appearance of a direct causal link, but this is of course an illusion. And thus with societies and civilizations, as well as with historical writing itself. Sartre writes that 'human history would have to be *finished* before a particular event, for example the taking of the Bastille, could receive a definitive *meaning*.'[33] Since there is no such stopping point, historical meaning is by nature open ended; it is made and remade according to the needs of each era.

White thus effectively fuses Sartre's existential voluntarism (to 'will the past')[34] with Auerbach's redemptive figuralism. Historical agents are able to choose their own past and, by their very act, their own present. They choose a model that they not only seek to emulate and repeat, but also one that they see as being fully realized only in themselves; for in a prefiguration-fulfillment relation, the two events are always conceived as mutually determining: the earlier event bears a meaning that will become fully apparent only in the

later event. White sees history or 'the historical system' as being constituted by these *genealogical* relations (in the sense of figural or 'backward' causation), as opposed to the *genetic* relations (efficient causation) that characterize biological systems.[35] However, 'figural causation,' though 'fictional' (aesthetic), is no less real than efficient causation, for it has equally real effects. As Hans Kellner comments: 'If a generation fails to find any figures adequate to their legitimate needs and desires in the models that an existing culture offers it, they will turn away from their historical culture and create another by choosing a different past. This is a cultural revolution.'[36] Thus the creation of a historical consciousness is a dynamic process of making and remaking; the old is paradoxically the source of the new.

The implications of the prefiguration-fulfillment model for the understanding of narrative, and of historical narrative in particular, are enormous. For this model describes how the temporal dislocations of narrative are brought together into a signifying whole, though relations that are in effect *self-fulfilling*. White observes:

It is the fulfilled figure that casts its light back – retrospectively and, in the narrative account, retroactively – on the earlier figurations of the character or process being related. It is the figure-fulfillment model of narrativity that lends credence to the commonplace that the historian is a prophet but one who prophesies 'backward.' It is what justifies the notion that the historian, as against the historical characters he studies, occupies a privileged position of knowledge in virtue of the fact that, coming after a given set of events have run their course, 'he knows how events actually turned out.' But what can 'actually turned out' mean here? It can only mean that the historian has treated his enfiguration of a given set of events as an 'ending-as-fulfillment' which permits him to 'recognize' in earlier events in the sequence dim and imperfect anticipations of 'what will have been the case' later on. The meaning-effect of the narrative account of the sequence is produced by the technique of relating events in the order of their occurrence, construing them as 'clues' of the plot-structure which will be revealed only at the end of the narrative in the enfiguration of events as a 'fulfillment.'[37]

Thus emplotment should also be understood as 'enfiguration': that is, to give historical data the significance of a plot is ipso facto to introduce relations of prefiguration and fulfillment, relations that, as we have seen, possess their own internal logic, which cannot be a product of the facts (as if facts could have their own *telos*). Hence figuralism represents, for White, the principal way of conceiving the convergence of fictional form (interpretation) and empirical fact (singular existential statements), under the aegis of mimesis.

## FACTICITY AND DISCURSIVITY

This brings us to one of the most obvious objections to White's distinction between fact and interpretation, namely that it appears to be based on a more fundamental dichotomy that White takes great pains to subvert or deny in his work: that between the literal and the figurative (literal facts and figurative meanings). Seen in this light, White's insistence on the separation between fact and interpretation appears to violate his view that all language use is inherently figurative or tropological. But here we must be nuanced in our analysis.

First of all, White believes in the dialectical tension between the notions of the literal and the figurative, that a statement that can be seen *as* literal can be so considered without thereby negating its figural import. All literal statements are thus figures *in potentia*, to the extent that they are incorporable in a discourse. Indeed, the performative act of uttering a singular existential statement would necessarily bring to the fore the discursive context activated by that performance.[38] White is thus positing the *coincidence* of the literal and figurative levels of language, even if, *discursively* speaking, the figurative or tropological level is the deepest or most fundamental. Narrative in particular, but discursive language in general, is inherently interpretative, meaningful, creative. Non-discursive language use, such as one finds in

a chronicle, for example, consists of simple, unconnected statements, bereft of any conventionalized structure other than that of the chronicle itself.[39] It is by *writing*, that is, by organizing and imposing meaning on a congeries of facts, that the historian activates conventions that come to be known as historical discourse, and thus as history. The dream of stringing together facts without any discursive intervention on the part of the historian is, as White suggests, simply self-delusion.

White does not see any justification or utility in denying the truth of facts, as a certain brand of relativism advocates, except to the extent that scientific results can themselves be relativized, as invariably happens with the advent of new technologies and methods (DNA analysis, carbon dating, etc.). White does believe in science, even if he denies that history can ever be scientific. Nevertheless, the 'truth' of facts is a small 't' and not a capital 'T' truth, i.e., historical truth. Historical truth can only be a matter of discourse; and disparate facts, while they provide the raw material for a historical discourse, have no specifically historical meaning prior to their discursive elaboration.

## CONCLUSION

White's thesis about 'making history,' which I have attempted to elucidate in these pages, should not be misconstrued to mean that history is 'fictional' in the sense that it would be impossible to distinguish it from propaganda or revisionism – that is, from the attempt to distort or ignore the facts. When White says that historical writing contains an inexpugnable fictional element, he is merely saying that the story-form itself is necessarily or inherently fictional, and that this fictionality is not incidental but essential to the production of specifically historical meaning. Relating one event to another in a coherent chronological sequence – i.e., narrative – is the work of discourse and thus of interpretation; if this were not the case, all accounts of a particular historical reality based on the same information would be, for all intents and purposes, identical, and could be judged like mathematical equations or scientific theorems: as being either right or wrong. But there are no human events about which a strictly literal account could be written, both because any account, by virtue of its discursivity, is figural or tropological through and through, and because a human act or event is multivalent by its very nature and is thus irreducible or refractory to a unidimensional literality. On the other hand, if one were to deprive history of its factual basis, of its literality, it would cease to function as an investigation into the past. According to White, we must instead seek to understand history as an expression of a particular way of being-in-the-world, one that tells us as much about the producers and consumers of such writing as it does about its ostensible object.

Historical discourse is a hybrid of fictional and factual elements, and it is this very hybridity that many have difficulty in coming to terms with. Of course, it is possible for historians to lie even as it is possible for them to tell the truth. However, it is a matter of being clear on what we mean when we invoke notions of *historical truth*, *historical knowledge*, or *historical reality*. A historian who, for example, denies the existence of the Holocaust (to use a neuralgic example), is manifestly in bad faith, for he or she is denying the evidence, and is rightfully condemned on both moral and epistemological grounds.[40] On the other hand, a historian who *interprets* or *emplots* the Holocaust in ways that we may find morally offensive (e.g., by making it continuous with other historical genocides, or by 'redeeming' it dialectically à la Hegel) cannot be indicted on purely scientific grounds, for interpretation/emplotment is not subject to scientific verification.[41] Of course, one's interpretative acumen can always be questioned, but this is not a matter of empirical truth or falsity but of the relevant norms and protocols that govern the hermeneutic practices of one's particular area of inquiry (whether juridical, literary, historical,

political, and so on). In proposing his theory of historical writing, White has sought to uncover the basic presuppositions of historical interpretation, those that historians unconsciously live by.

## NOTES AND REFERENCES

1 Hayden White, *The Fiction of Narrative: Essays on History, Literature, and Theory, 1957–2007*, ed. Robert Doran (Baltimore: Johns Hopkins University Press, 2010), 198.

2 See in particular the following books by Hayden White: *The Fiction of Narrative: Essays on History, Literature, and Theory, 1957–2007*; *Figural Realism: Studies in the Mimesis Effect* (Baltimore: Johns Hopkins University Press, 1999); *The Content of the Form: Narrative Discourse and Historical Representation* (Baltimore: Johns Hopkins University Press, 1987); *Tropics of Discourse: Essays in Cultural Criticism* (Baltimore: Johns Hopkins University Press, 1978); and *Metahistory: The Historical Imagination in Nineteenth-Century Europe*, (Baltimore: Johns Hopkins University Press, 1973). See also the recently published monograph on White by Herman Paul: *Hayden White: The Historical Imagination* (Cambridge: Polity Press, 2011, Key Contemporary Thinkers).

3 'Man hat der Historie das Amt, die Vergangenheit zu richten, die Mitwelt zum Nutzen zukünftiger Jahre zu belehren, beigemessen: so hoher Ämter unterwindet sich gegenwärtiger Versuch nicht: er will blos zeigen, wie es eigentlich gewesen' (Leopold von Ranke, Preface to *Geschichten der romanischen und germanischen Völker* [originally published in 1824] [Duncker & Humblot, 1885], vii).

4 White, *The Content of the Form*, 57. Cf. the last paragraph of the Introduction to *Tropics of Discourse*: 'I have tried to show that, even if we cannot achieve a properly scientific knowledge of human nature, we can achieve another kind of knowledge about it, the kind of knowledge which literature and art in general give us in easily recognizable examples. [...] My aim has been to show that we do not have to choose between art and science, that indeed we cannot do so in practice, if we hope to speak about culture as against nature – and moreover speak about it in ways that are responsible to all the various dimensions of our specifically *human* being' (original emphasis, 23).

5 White has written extensively about Vico. See the volume White co-edited with Giorgio Tagliacozzo entitled *Giambattista Vico: An International Symposium* (Baltimore: Johns Hopkins University Press, 1969), as well as the following essays: 'What is living and what is dead in Croce's criticism of Vico' (included in the aforementioned collection, and reprinted in *Tropics of Discourse*, 218–29); 'The tropics of history: the deep structure of the *New Science*,' in G. Tagliacozzo and D. Verene, eds., *Giambattista Vico's Science of Humanity* (Baltimore: Johns Hopkins

University Press, 1976, reprinted in *Tropics of Discourse*, 65–85); 'Vico and the radical wing of structuralist/post-structuralist thought today,' *New Vico Studies* 1 (1983), 63–8 (reprinted under a slightly modified title in *The Fiction of Narrative*, 203–7); and an encyclopedia entry: 'Vico, Giovanni Battista,' in *International Encyclopedia of the Social Sciences*, vol. 16, ed. David L. Sills (New York: The Macmillan Company and The Free Press, 1968), 313–16.

6  White, *The Fiction of Narrative*, 266. The essay is entitled 'Northrop Frye's place in contemporary cultural studies.'

7  Vico held that the primary tropes reflected evolutionary stages in human consciousness: from metaphor (age of gods), to metonymy (age of heroes), to synecdoche (age of men), and finally, to irony (age of decadence and dissolution). In Vico's theory, this cycle repeats itself in ascending and descending movements he calls *corso* and *ricorso*, though the overall movement of the cycles is upward. Following Vico, White also uses the tropes to describe the evolution of nineteenth-century historical consciousness: beginning with metaphor, continuing through metonymy and synecdoche, and culminating in irony. There is, however, a tension between the interpretative freedom implied in the tropological choice of the historian (supposedly open-ended) and the constraining relationship White posits between the tropological tendency of a given society (its evolutionary state of consciousness) and the one adopted by the historian. With regard to tropological choice, White writes: 'historians and philosophers will then be freed to conceptualize history, to perceive its contents, and to construct narrative accounts of its processes in whatever modality of consciousness is most consistent with their own moral and aesthetic aspirations' (*Metahistory*, 434). However, White also contends that only those historians who are in tune with the dominant trope of their age will be seen as relevant: 'A historian such as Burkhardt, who was precritically committed to a prefiguration of the historical field in the Ironic mode, has no authority in a public which is precritically committed to the prefiguration of the historical field in the Metonymical mode' (*Metahistory*, 430). The tension between the interpretative freedom of the individual historian and the tropological influence of the era is not easy to reconcile in White's work.

8  In *Figural Realism* (11), White defines the tropological functions thus: similitude (metaphor), contiguity (metonymy), identification (synecdoche), and opposition (irony). But in *Metahistory*, White described them somewhat differently: representational (metaphor), reductionist (metonymy), integrative (synecdoche), and negational (irony).

9  See Hans Kellner, 'Hayden White and the Kantian discourse: freedom, narrative, history,' in *The Philosophy of Discourse*, ed. C. Sills and G. Jensen, (Portsmouth, NH: Boynton/Cook, 1992), 246–67.

10  White, *Metahistory*, 428.

11  See Aristotle's *Poetics* (1451b), as translated by Stephen Halliwell: 'poetry is more philosophical and more elevated than history, since poetry relates more of the universal, while history relates particulars' (*Aristotle* Poetics, *Longinus* On the Sublime, *Demetrius* On Style, Loeb Classical Library [Cambridge: Harvard University Press, 1995], 59).

12  In his *New Science*, Vico articulates the idea of 'Imaginative Universals' as a prototype of the rational concept.

13  Though he tends to deemphasize the tropes in his later work, White is still essentially keeping them alive through the types of emplotment, with which they apparently form a dyadic relationship. Thus in *Figural Realism* White comments: 'The tropological structures of metaphor, metonymy, synecdoche, and irony (and what I take – following Northrop Frye – to be their corresponding plot types: romance, tragedy, comedy and satire), provide us with a much more refined classification of the kinds of historical discourse than that based on the conventional distinction between linear and cyclical representations of historical processes' (11).

14  White, 'Historical discourse and literary writing,' in *Tropes for the Past*, ed. Kuisma Korhonen (Amsterdam: Rodopi, 2006), 30.

15  Quoted in G.M.A. Grube, *The Greek and Roman Critics* (Indianapolis, IN: Hackett Publishing Company, 1965), 157.

16  Thus White's typological reduction to the four *mythoi* described by Frye – Tragedy, Comedy, Romance, Satire (corresponding to the four tropes) – is perhaps less important that the simple assertion of narrative conventionality. White himself observes: 'I do not wish to suggest that Frye's categories are the sole possible ones for classifying genres, modes, *mythoi*, and the like, in literature; but I have found them especially useful for the analysis of historical works. [...] Precisely because the historian is not (or claims not to be) telling the story "for its own sake," he is inclined to emplot his stories in the most conventional forms... [...] Historians in general, however critical they are of their sources, tend to be naïve storytellers' (*Metahistory*, 8, n. 6).

17  White, *Figural Realism*, 9.

18  Ibid., original emphasis.

19  Ibid.

20  This contention has prompted some commentators to assert that White is separating content from form. This may be true, heuristically speaking, but if so, White separates them only to bring them into closer unity.

21  White, 'Historical pluralism and pan-textualism,' in *The Fiction of Narrative*, 232, original emphasis.

22  Furthermore, following Arthur Danto, White sees facts as 'events under a description.' However, the distinction between fact and event is potentially problematic. Even a sympathetic reader such as Richard Vann has called the notion of event 'the most under-analyzed term' in White's work (Vann, 'The reception of Hayden White,' *History and Theory* 37, no. 2 [1998], 154). In this context I could relay a comment White makes in his essay, 'Historical pluralism': 'the meaning of an event like "English Romanticism," the occurrence of which is hardly

to be doubted, is variously interpretable; and this means ... that we can tell equally plausible, alternative, and even contradictory stories about it without violating rules of evidence or critical standards commonly held across a wide variety of disciplines or philosophical or even ideological positions' (*The Fiction of Narrative*, 231). The problem is that the term 'event' can refer to simple occurrences like the fall of the guillotine's blade as well as complex realities such as the French Revolution. Thus it would have been better, I think, if White had not said that the 'event' of English Romanticism is 'hardly to be doubted'; for 'English Romanticism' is merely a conventionalized way of organizing a set of particulars, a discursive creation which is the *result* of an interpretation, not the basis for one. The same goes for 'The French Revolution' or any other complex event. It is not 'English Romanticism' that is inviolable but the facts on which this convention is based, facts like someone by the name of Shakespeare wrote a play called *Hamlet*, and so forth. Thus the statement 'Shakespeare is a Renaissance author' is not a statement of fact, but an assertion of convention. This may be what he meant to say, but White's use of the term 'event' is highly ambiguous, and commentators are not unfair to question it. What White needs, I think, is a distinction between complex and simple events. Thus construed, the complex 'event' – the historical event – is the end result of a posterior interpretation of a multitude of simple events. In a recent article, 'The historical event' (2008), White has attempted a more nuanced approach to the question; he now seems to prefer 'fact' to 'event' even when speaking about larger amalgamations: 'So, let us grant that there are events and there are facts. Let us grant, too, that there are series of events and structures of events that can be factualized, which is to say, dated, placed, described, classified, and named well enough to permit a distinction between "atomic" or individual facts and something like "molar" or macro-facts – "large" facts such as "The Russian Revolution of 1917" or "big" facts such as "The Renaissance." This would allow us to imagine a wide range of "historical facts" that would make up that "history" that is the object of study of "historians"' ('The historical event,' *differences: A Journal of Feminist Cultural Studies* 19, no. 2 [2008], 14).

23  White, *Content of the Form*, 45. Though White does say in the above quote that factual statements, like stories, 'belong to the order of discourse,' this is somewhat misleading, since what White means is that factual statements can be abstracted from the historical discourse of which they are a necessary part and be subjected to verification, not that they are inherently meaningful taken in isolation or prior to their inclusion in a discourse.

24  White, *Tropics of Discourse*, 43, original emphasis.

25  See the first four essays of *Figural Realism*.

26  This said, Auerbach's notion of realism, which, as we see in the next section, greatly influenced White, appears to privilege tragedy as an indicator of realism; for tragedy exemplifies the kind of seriousness that dignifies everyday reality.

27  Auerbach himself asserts that his method is relativistic. However, as I have written elsewhere, it is difficult to take Auerbach at his word, as when he writes: 'in the historical forms themselves, we gradually learn to find the flexible, always provisional, categories we need.' See Robert Doran, 'Literary history and the sublime in Erich Auerbach's *Mimesis*,' *New Literary History* 38, no. 2 (2007), 354.

28  White, *Figural Realism*, 91. Auerbach was well known for eschewing theoretical vocabulary, presenting his work as 'historical' as opposed to 'critical' or 'theoretical.' See the previous note.

29  The first paragraph of White's Introduction to *Metahistory* reads as follows: 'This book is a *history* of historical consciousness in nineteenth-century Europe, but it is also meant to contribute to the current discussion of the *problem of historical knowledge*. As such, it represents both an account of the development of historical thinking during a specific period of its evolution and a general theory of the structure of that mode of thought which is called "historical."' (1, original emphasis).

30  Auerbach's 'Figura' essay has been translated and collected in Erich Auerbach, *Scenes from the Drama of European Literature* (Minneapolis: University of Minnesota Press, 1984), 11–78.

31  White, *Figural Realism*, 89.

32  Jean-Paul Sartre, *Being and Nothingness*, trans. Hazel Barnes (New York: Washington Square Press, 1992), 640. Commenting on Sartre, H.J. Blackham writes: 'The past does not determine the future. Rather one must say: If you want to have such a past, act in such a way. I can choose and continue a tradition, repudiate or fulfill an engagement ... and in such ways I freely act on my past and convert it into motives by my choice of the future' (H.J. Blackham, *Six Existentialist Thinkers* [London and New York: Routledge, 1951], 132).

33  Sartre, *Being and Nothingness*, 643, original emphasis.

34  Ibid., 646.

35  White, *Figural Realism*, 89. This idea had been a part of White's thought since his essay 'What is a historical system?' (given as a lecture in 1967, but not published until 1972), in which he observes something very similar: 'What happened between the third and eighth centuries [in Christian civilization] was that men *ceased to regard themselves as descendents of their Roman forebears and began to treat themselves as descendents of their Judeo-Christian predecessors*. And it was the constitution of this *fictional* cultural ancestry which signaled the abandonment of the Roman sociocultural system. When Western European men began to act *as if* they were descended from the Christian segment of the ancient world; when they began to structure their comportment *as if* they were *genetically* descended from their Christian predecessors; when, in short, they began to honor the Christian past as the most desirable model for creation of a future uniquely their own, and ceased to honor the Roman past as *their* past, the Roman sociocultural system ceased to exist' (*The Fiction of Narrative*, 132, original emphasis).

36 Hans Kellner, Introduction to *Refiguring Hayden White*, ed. Frank Ankersmit, Ewa Domanska, and Hans Kellner (Stanford, CA: Stanford University Press, 2009), 4.

37 White, 'History as fulfillment', in *Philosophy of History after Hayden White*, ed. Robert Doran (London: Bloomsbury, 2013), chapter 1.

38 For example, the statement 'Sadam Hussein is dead,' or 'Sadam Hussein died on such and such a date,' can be seen as a literal statement of fact on which everyone can agree. However, as stated by former President George W. Bush, it brings with it a whole host of figurative meanings: a justification for the war in Iraq in the absence of other justifications; an assertion or reminder of American power in the midst of seeming impotence in the face of an out-of-control insurgency. Phrased by a Sunni tribesman or a Shiite politician the sentence would reveal an altogether different range of figurative connotations. Even my use of the phrase here in this essay as an example gives the statement a discursive context, thus de-literalizing it. Nonetheless, despite the figurative multiplicity, the singular fact remains irreducible: Sadam Hussein is, in fact, dead.

39 One can also see the chronicle as a narrative in embryo, that is, as containing narrative elements that can be weaved into a discursive structure.

40 For a discussion of some of the controversy surrounding White's work as it pertains to the Holocaust, see *Probing the Limits of Representation: Nazism and the 'Final Solution,'* ed. Saul Friedlander (Cambridge, MA: Harvard University Press, 1992), especially the essays by Carlo Ginzburg and Martin Jay, as well as Friedlander's introduction. White's essay 'Historical emplotment and the question of truth' appears in the collection (and was later republished in *Figural Realism*, 26–42).

41 The *Historikerstreit* (Historian's Debate) in Germany is a good example. In this debate, philosopher Jürgen Habermas criticized the attempt by German historians to minimize the exceptional nature of the Holocaust by comparing it with other historical massacres and genocides.

# 8

# The Work of Hayden White II: Defamiliarizing Narrative

Kalle Pihlainen

For Hayden White, historians are (in most ways at least) just like everyone else. Thus, while their methodological and professional practices sometimes lend them the appearance of detached investigators, they too can be seen as intent on finding (human) meaning, on creating stories that might answer fundamental questions of the type we all face in our everyday lives, questions involving what White calls 'the great themes of human existence: heroism, love, death, violence, compassion, and so on' (Domanska 2008, 13). So, while hard-core reconstructionist historians as well as those with merely an antiquarian interest in the past may deny involvement in such speculation, their reliance on narrative undermines any professed 'neutral' position. After all, narration as a cognitive category is our primary way of relating with a world of meanings and use of narrative form insistently presents us with just these kinds of questions. Crucially, then, while narration in a broad sense of the word – as *emplotment* and *figuration* – appears to be a natural, near-automatic process, the first thing historians need to learn is that it involves them in an imposition of values. To rely on

White, historical narratives are moral arguments simply because narrative (aesthetic) closure of any kind is ultimately a moral closure too: 'When it is a matter of recounting the concourse of real events, what other "ending" could a given sequence of such events have than a 'moralizing' ending? What else could narrative closure consist of than the passage from one moral order to another?' (White 1987, 23). This realization obviously leads the theorist of narrative (as it should the historian) to important ethical, ideological and political questions, as opposed to more straightforward epistemological ones.

The familiarity of narrative presents a double challenge for historians: where our everyday experiences are guided by our experiencing and simultaneous sense-making of them and thus instinctively appear to conform to comprehensible, ego-centric structures, the past is unavailable to such experience. Following from the combination of our instinct for meaning and the inaccessibility of the past, the presence of comprehensible stories becomes all the more important in forming any relation to the past. This desire for an experience of the past as in someway real – the historian's *phenomenological yearning* – is an essential factor in shaping what I take to be White's theoretical agenda. It necessarily moves the focus from the epistemological difficulties involved to questions of representational form. For historical texts to have significance, for the concreteness of the past to have any meaning, these accounts need to provide moving experiences that can convince us of their (however unjustified) position as truth-bearers. Despite epistemological limits, such conviction becomes possible because narratives are, first and foremost, arguments *for* something, ostensible lessons in the way(s) the world works.[1] So, instead of focusing (exclusively) on the truth of the past, they provide 'metaphorical insight' and a 'narrative truth' that satisfies the desire for meaning, much like literary works. This has long been overlooked because, as White explains,

the dual conviction that truth must be represented in literal statements of fact and explanation must conform to the scientific model or its common-sensical counterpart has led most analysts to ignore the specifically literary aspect of historical narrative and therewith whatever truth it may convey in figurative terms. (1987, 48)

Again, this emphasis on figuration and form involves the ethical and the ideological at least as much as – and much more interestingly than – the epistemological. It should, thus, be enough to show that historical objectivity is – even as desire – a futile cause.

Given these kinds of underlying beliefs and motivations, historical accuracy (or, for that matter, demonstrating the lack of it) cannot be the primary concern of a Whitean theory of history and historical representation – even though this is precisely what discussions of it far too often centre on. Indeed, White is adamant that while professional concerns and fidelity to the sources play a major, and initial, role in narrative decisions, the constraints provided by simple 'historical methodologies' are insufficient in determining the emphases of any resulting narrative.[2] Even after allowing for all such formal

considerations, there remains a great deal of latitude in the emplotment and stylistic choices, and hence the moral and political ramifications, of the final text.[3] And it is, of course, the focus on this *content of the form* for which White is most famous.

In striving to establish the narrative itself as an object for historians' attentions, then, White has brought to light a number of previously largely neglected issues. Before tackling these, it is necessary to emphasize that White has to my knowledge never denied the reality of the past (an absurd opinion sometimes attributed to him), claiming only that we have no access to any overall *truth* about it. In practice this means that, as Alun Munslow nicely formulates it, when faced with the epistemological challenge presented by history, '[t]he historian either goes into denial or gets on with it by acknowledging history is not "the real thing"' (Munslow 2007, 15). This sentiment is shared by White; his interest is never in the past *as such* but in its meaning for us in the present, hence historical *writing* is not concerned primarily with truth. At times it even appears that – employing a slightly stronger formulation by David Roberts – 'for White, truth is no longer at issue once we move from the archive and the chronicle into the narrative telling' (cited in Jenkins 1999, 119). Having made this starting-point clear, a caveat is necessary: White is difficult to pin down and I am undoubtedly in part reading my own agenda into his. As Richard Vann notes, even though White 'is generally free of the cruder sorts of inconsistency and incoherence, his thought has always been on the move' (Vann 1998, 145). In part consequence of his so 'being on the move', White has been presented variously as a humanist, a structuralist, a poststructuralist and a postmodernist, to mention just some of the more commonly applied labels. Despite the seeming contradiction, White's views are, I believe, largely compatible: he is pragmatic regarding reality, structuralist toward texts, poststructuralist and existentialist in his ethics, and postmodernist (and sometime Marxist and left-wing intellectual) in his dealings with society.[4] (Importantly, White is not unduly afraid of so-called logical inconsistencies because he is concerned firstly with *praxis*.)

## HISTORICAL NARRATIVES AS 'FICTION' AND IDEOLOGY

White has received heaps of criticism from professional historians, most of it in some way claiming that his views inevitably lead to the abandonment or disappearance of history.[5] Based on a limited understanding (and what at times seems a careless reading) of his arguments, some critics even think that he maintains historical texts are *just* a form of literary invention, dismissively: 'fiction'. While White has admittedly expressed his views quite polemically on occasion, his thinking appears carefully measured on this issue. Together with Roland Barthes' seminal essay 'The discourse of history' (1967), White's *Metahistory* (1973) is often taken to mark the beginning of the history–literature debate (and the polarization of the related fact–fiction debate), yet it makes few radical statements regarding the literary nature of history, performing instead a close reading of the narrative political and ideological choices made by the historians and philosophers of history it examines.[6] White has, however, been quite forceful about this in other early texts, particularly in 'The burden of history' (1966, reprinted in White 1978b) and 'The historical text as literary artifact' (1974, reprinted in White 1978a and 1978b).[7] Especially the latter may have prejudiced more conservative historians and inspired critique. In the most commonly cited version of this essay, White states:

> By the very constitution of a set of events in such a way as to make a comprehensible story out of them, the historian charges those events with the symbolic significance of a comprehensible plot structure. Historians may not like to think of their works as translations of 'fact' into 'fiction'; but this is one of the effects of their works. (1978a, 53)

While only partially justifying later critique (the conflation of 'fiction' and 'literature' remains largely unfounded), the idea that 'history is fiction' seems to be the most enduring of White's claims among the many affronted historians one meets today. Georg Iggers, for example, has fairly recently taken White to task on this: 'In my opinion White's error is that he argues that because all historical accounts contain fictional elements they are basically fictions and not subject to truth controls' (Iggers 2000, 383).[8] White may have intended to temper such misunderstandings early on, however, as another reprinted version (in *Tropics of Discourse*, also in 1978) presents a small but significant amendment to the phrasing: here historical writings have become, somewhat more moderately, 'translations of fact into fiction*s*' (1978b, 92; emphasis added). Replacing the scare quotes with a formulation that is perhaps harder to misquote (and misread) does nothing, however, to change his views regarding the similarity of the process of emplotment in all kinds of prose narrative. Indeed, he goes on to acknowledge that his 'insistence on the fictive element in all historical narratives is certain to arouse the ire of historians who believe that they are doing something fundamentally different from the novelist by virtue of the fact that they deal with "real," while the novelist deals with "imagined," events' (1978a, 60; 1978b, 98). Although neglecting here to emphasize the commitment of historical *research* to truth, in fact completely avoiding the issue of the past and focusing instead only on the question of presentation, he explains his position on 'fiction' carefully:

> to say that we make sense of the real world by imposing upon it the formal coherence that we customarily associate with the products of writers of fiction in no way detracts from the status as knowledge that we ascribe to historiography. ... In my view, we experience the 'fictionalization' of history as an 'explanation' for the same reason that we experience great fiction as an illumination of a world that we inhabit along with the author. In both we re-cognize the forms by which consciousness both constitutes and colonizes the world it seeks to inhabit comfortably. (White 1978a, 61)

Saddled with the controversial reputation of claiming history to be no different from literature, White's more nuanced arguments have, by and large, been ignored – even though he has been quite specific regarding most of them. The rub for many critics comes, of course, from their extreme either–or assumption that the 'fictionalization' of history entails viewing it as *only* story and – by an incredible interpretive stretch – the past as *unreal*. Yet, as Chris Lorenz pointed out during an extended debate on the fact–fiction issue in *History and Theory* in the 1990s: 'the *same* statement can fulfill *different* functions at the *same time*.' Thus, since 'descriptive statements can also be interpreted as normative statements ... the "fundamental difference" between judgements of fact and judgements of value can no longer be taken for granted' (Lorenz 1994, 323). The content of the form does not preclude there being content to the content, then.[9]

So what does White intend? In contrast to advocates of narratives as existing somehow 'out there', as inseparable from particular experiences or ways of being, philosophers like Alasdair MacIntyre and David Carr for instance,[10] White's emphasis is on narrative as a purely linguistic or theoretical construct, not as something essential to the world itself. There are, for White and like-minded theorists of history, no stories *in* the world, independent of our fashioning and constant refashioning of them. Yet, at the same time, there are suasive literary and ideological *conventions* in play: tropes, emplotments, argumentative strategies and so on.[11] Storytelling is thus a similarly ethicopolitical endeavour for White as it is for antirepresentationalists like Richard Rorty, for example.[12] And, although it largely remains unarticulated, White's political orientation is similarly poststructuralist in its fundamentals; he summarizes this stance in *Content of the Form* (1987) – to me the *tour de force* of his oeuvre to date – as follows: 'it is often overlooked that the conviction that one can make sense of history stands on the same level of epistemic plausibility as the conviction that it makes no sense whatsoever. ... I am inclined to think that a visionary politics can proceed only on the latter conviction' (White 1987, 73).

Narrative is in no way a simple thing, then. Although natural to our human ways of thinking, narratives have no 'natural' structural correspondence to the world and their content is in no way determined. They are an imposition of cognitive processes – guided by our particular desires and yearnings – on a world that is essentially unstructured. A world that, as poststructuralism emphasizes, is in constant flux, and, further, too complex for any single, however convoluted, explanation. Here narrative choices are always also ideological ones, either conscious or unthinkingly accepted and adopted. *As conventions*, they are detrimental to the formulation of ethicopolitical commitments, preventing the emplotment of representations for purposes of liberation and empowerment, and always serving the status quo. Whitean historians thus remain conscious of the added content brought by choices of form and use this knowledge for purposes that agree with their commitments. They are also acutely aware of the ease with which accepted representational forms and narrative choices can lead to conservative (and repressive) stories that uphold received beliefs: 'Nothing is better suited to lead to a repetition of the past than a study of it that is either reverential or convincingly objective in the way that conventional historical studies tend to be' (White 1987, 82).

Even though White has not generally jumped on the *petits récits* bandwagon of so much contemporary historical writing and theory (think microhistory and cultural history, for instance), there is an evident affinity with Jean-François Lyotard too; the resistance of the grand narrative – both in the form of the overarching historical interpretations and the more generalized belief in historical texts as unduly authoritative forms of talking about the past – is a thoroughly poststructuralist sentiment. Yet, in spite of his fundamentally poststructuralist epistemology and consequent ethical orientation, the past as context (and sometimes even the author and intentionality) remains significant for White. In this, the underlying referential commitment of historical writing still has consequences for his thinking; the limitations, intentions and conventions governing the writing of a historical document (think of a letter instead of a literary work, for example) still provide the most natural – if at times troubled – means of justifying any reference to a broader context. Thus, while history – at its best – is poststructuralist in its political commitments, it cannot be strictly textualist in its practical and methodological outlook. This is not, however, to say that the epistemological commitments history relies on need differ from poststructuralist ones; instead, it points out that poststructuralism and extreme forms of textualism (literary-type deconstruction) must be more clearly distinguished.[13]

White clarifies his position in a 1982 essay 'The context in the text' (reprinted as the closing essay of *The Content of the Form*) with a very concrete – and quite rare – methodological example of how narrative theory can contribute to the reading of a text for historical purposes. He tackles literary narrative theory in detail here, performing an excellent reading of the 'significance' and semiological content of Henry Adams' autobiography *The Education of Henry Adams*. As the investigation reveals, purely literary analysis has its limitations and White, even at his most textual, happily goes beyond the text to the context – as any historical investigation must – noting that, done on the terms established by the text, such an approach is quite justified; the justification for this move indeed already clearly stated in the title of the piece: the context *in* the text. Writes White: 'I have suggested that [the text-context] problem becomes resolvable from the semiological perspective to the extent that what conventional historians call the context is

already in the text in the specific modalities of code shifting by which [it] produces its meanings' (White 1987, 212).

## FROM RECEIVED IDEOLOGIES TO LIBERATION AND CRITICAL HISTORIOGRAPHY

Despite so often being termed a theorist of historical narrative, the central issue for White, as I see it, is that of history's political – or, if you will, practical or social – role. In other words, what and who history is for. Regardless of any linguistic or literary interests, his concern with narrative is primarily in pointing out how it necessarily conveys ideological content; this 'debunking' constitutes, however, as Nancy Partner notes, only 'a preliminary step on the way to someplace else' (Partner 1998, 168). (And his approach is thus far from being merely 'linguistic'.) It is the advocacy of political responsibility – after the loss of epistemological authority – which is undoubtedly the source of most of the controversy regarding the theory of history *à la* White. At the same time, its importance to White's thinking cannot be overstated. As he writes: 'On this question turns what might be called the ethics and possibly the politics of the discipline. To what is the historian responsible, or rather, to what *should* one be responsible?' (White 1987, 188). Further, White's focus on a 'practical historiography' is, it should be noted, a new concern, no longer centred on the fact–fiction debate, or in fact even on the broader issues of emplotment and narrative imposition. History's epistemological standing (or falling) is not an interesting question in terms of political efficacy or, indeed, its political orientation. Rather, history's contribution to the world is – ideally – a subjective, ethical choice on the part of historians who have got over the original epistemological dilemma and on with whatever it is they seek to accomplish. (See White 2005b.) On an abstract level this again begs the question of what we need history for. Why not simply draw on other 'imaginaries' for our pragmatic and political needs, as Keith Jenkins for example urges we do? From White's perspective – which values history on a practical basis – this is not sufficient, of course, since it leaves more stubborn historians free to continue writing 'authoritative' accounts which trade in an epistemological currency that remains accepted by many. Hence the 'ethical turn' he takes is not only about assuming responsibility for the little narratives and their protagonists but also about acquiring (and propagating) the theoretical insight needed to resist authoritarian posing. Further, *it is independent of the debate concerning history as 'fictional'* (if most intimately linked to it). Contradictory though it may seem, then, White's emphasis on the political is intended as a justification for continuing with the practice of history. This is important because resistance to narrative theorizing should not automatically lead to ignorance on all counts.

Yet, even though White's constructivism clearly has a political motivation (and, more importantly, succeeds in justifying his turn toward society and the effects of representations), his political views are rarely expounded. This goes, of course, hand-in-hand with his existentialist-poststructuralist commitments: we are all responsible for our own actions and prescriptive thought is just that, the antithesis of choice and responsibility. (This general strand of thought has been elegantly argued by Jenkins in his *Refiguring History*, 2003, mainly with reference to Jacques Derrida.) As morally responsible – or more precisely ethical – individuals we have no recourse to received opinions and choice can never be anything other than individual.[14] As one commentator presents White's 'ideology':

> Such an ideology would avoid claiming that it has a monopoly on truth – since it believes that reality is too complex to be fully grasped by one worldview – while simultaneously aiming at overcoming the [kind of ideological] irony White wanted to eliminate. ... So, instead of allowing historians to

choose whatever moral perspectives they would like – including 'dogmatic,' non-ironical ideological positions – White wanted them to be converted to an ideology that emphasizes reality's complexity and the importance of a moral commitment.' (Paul 2006, 43)[15]

This general disillusionment with history as of any practical significance (echoing Nietzsche's *Use and Abuse of History*) was already obvious in his 1966 essay, 'The burden of history'. According to White, history has lost its 'dignity' because it is 'bad' in both scientific and artistic terms. History remains stuck in outdated forms that have no scientific value and no significance for contemporary readers. For this reason, then,

> the burden of the historian in our time is to re-establish the dignity of historical studies on a basis that will make them consonant with the aims and purposes of the intellectual community at large, that is, transform historical studies in such a way as to allow the historian to participate positively in the liberation of the present from *the burden of history*. (White 1978b, 41)

White's specific politics are directed at emancipation and even, at times, the psychological needs of the individual. Primarily, they appear to involve a liberation *for* self-realization (see e.g. Domanska 2008, 13). For him, 'ideologies deprive history of the kind of meaninglessness that alone can goad living human beings to make their lives different for themselves and their children, which is to say, to endow their lives with a meaning for which they alone are fully responsible' (White 1987, 72). Hence White's calls for a 'politics of historical interpretation' are necessarily substantially non-prescriptive. Historians *should* work toward 'liberation', the reduction of suffering, the empowerment of the oppressed, and focus – first and foremost – on revealing the automatic assumptions and received ideologies transmitted and propagated by texts.

This same emphasis informs White's thought throughout; with reference to what he calls modernist events, he later reiterates: 'precisely insofar as the story is identifiable as a story, it can provide no lasting mastery of such events' (1999, 81). While this avoidance of 'mastery' – rationalization, intellectual mastery, ideological appropriation, closure – is, to me, the key to understanding White, it somehow remains problematic for some historians even on this more straight-forward level of the *effects* of representation. At this point too, more insistent critics continue to argue that denying a history text status as something other than a story effectively leads to a devaluation of history as a profession or, indeed, as a justifiable pursuit in terms of *research* and reference. But the critics seem to have the wrong end of the stick here. Although this argument would be perfectly valid in connection with the kind of epistemological scepticism presented by Keith Jenkins (who does not wish to privilege history), for instance, White's point of departure makes it an odd conclusion to reach: after all, his interest is in (at least partially) rescuing history from such objections.[16] His argument consistently begins from the premise that history writing has a social role and assumed responsibilities (never forgetting its commitment to truthfulness). Whether this is because of traditions that have led up to the present situation or because of naïve beliefs among the general public – the consumers of history texts, perhaps uninitiated into the intricacies concerning the availability of 'truth' (although, more likely, simply uncaring about such quibbling) – is not the issue. Historians – having assumed the mantle of professionals – have a responsibility for the attitudes and beliefs they come to legitimate, and history – due to its central role in society – is still looked to for insight and guidance in many instances. Even more importantly, history (as representing the past) remains central to people's identity formation – despite the challenges with this in strictly logical, epistemic terms.[17]

So, how can we acknowledge the continued existence of a shared historical imagination – without hiding our heads in the sands of reconstructionist history – *and* avoid the damaging and colonizing aspects of representation?

How, that is, can we hold on to history? The first move is to accept that history writing does not make sense as an epistemological pursuit but that, despite this senselessness, and *because people continue engaging in it*, historians – and perhaps even more urgently their readers – need to be made aware of the problems it involves. In other words, the story-nature of historical narratives needs to be foregrounded, and these narratives need to be de-naturalized. This, ideally, pre-empting authority and ideological control. The second move is to foreground the *effects* of a narrative over and above the redundant epistemological discussion. While it should be accepted by most historians today – some four decades into the debate – that apparently innocent choices (where a story begins and ends, what elements are selected, what if any causal links are posited between them, and so on) are of crucial significance to the interpretations imposed on the past, the importance of seeing these choices in terms of present-day needs often remains unrecognized. Many historians are still blinded by a faith in a 'natural' way of presenting their material that somehow exempts them from responsibility. Hence White's hope that:

> By drawing historiography nearer to its origins in literary sensibility, we should be able to identify the ideological, because it is the fictive, element in our own discourse. We are always able to see the 'fictive' element in those historians with whose interpretations of a given set of events we disagree; we seldom perceive that element in our own prose. So, too, if we recognized the literary or fictive element in every historical account, we would be able to move the teaching of historiography onto a higher level of self-consciousness than it currently occupies. (White 1978a, 61)

## THE IMPORTANCE OF LITERARY FORM FOR EFFECTIVE PRESENTATIONS

Even though it lies at the core of White's thinking, the comparison of history to literature has clearly often been poorly understood. It is not to be viewed as concerned primarily with objective reality, correspondence, reference, and so on, and nor does it centre on the epistemological question of fact or fiction as so many historians would have it. As a distinctly revolutionary move in its original context, the comparison was perfect for introducing the linguistic turn to history, and hence greatly facilitated the epistemological questioning effected by both. The problem is that, due to the close relation of all these in White's work, they too often remain conflated: his thought is too easily viewed as dependent on seeing history as a second-order literature, the linguistic turn is taken to say that everything is simply fiction, the epistemological challenges history faces are understood in terms of an either–or between objectivity and total abandonment of reference, and so on. While this 'total' challenge to the historical profession has been effective in spreading word of the debate far and wide, even to such historians as are not interested in working through the intricacies of theory, it has also caused the kinds of over-reactions mentioned, as well as a general refusal to think about these matters further among a significant chunk of the history profession.

In making finer distinctions, the epistemological problems facing historians need to be recognized as being at least twofold: historians are challenged in both their access to the past and in their representing it. The past cannot be treated as an object of study in any scientific sense simply because its object-nature is denied to us. There is no past available to our inspection; which does not mean to say that the existence of the past is denied, as the most extreme critics take it. This is a limit that should be obvious to all historians, whatever their orientation.[18] The second issue is at the core of the linguistic turn: Whatever knowledges we may have of the past, language (understood quite broadly) can never adequately represent it. This difficulty is not exclusive to history, of course, as the point is that language can never adequately represent reality. Yet, as Rorty so well puts it, 'language is the only game in town' and (linguistic) figuration is the only

means we have of dealing with reality. After these points are acknowledged one might well ask what else is gained with the comparison of history to literature? The answer depends on what is sought, of course. The comparison does nothing more in terms of history's epistemological standing. But it is crucial for White's project of showing *how* historians assume and propagate ideologies in their work. It is, in other words, an extremely good example of what these epistemological difficulties really signify for historians. In the practical task of making way for an emancipatory politics, White's intention has not, however, been to show that historical writing is somehow necessarily inferior but rather to show why this is so often the case and also, more importantly, *what historians might do about it.*

So what does it *really* mean for history to be literary? As noted, although questions of truth and reference play a role here, they are not at the core of this claim. White introduces the idea of history as a literary pursuit in order to underline the centrality of linguistic figuration to historical writing and, from there, to challenge authoritarian ideologies. Put so simply this all sounds self-evident of course. The difficulties in accepting it among historians are not due to obtuseness alone, however. Partial responsibility can be placed on White: in the course of his writing his terminology has shifted from the more controversial 'translations of fact into fiction' (made worse by most often being quoted in this manner, without the scare quotes of the original), 'the fictionalization of history', 'the historical text as literary artifact', to 'the content of linguistic form', 'symbolic structures', 'intensionality' and 'linguistic figuration'.[19] A more important reason for the rejection of White's claims, of course, is that many historians continue to be interested in the past 'for its own sake' rather than as something that holds contemporary meaning. And they perceive these concerns as somehow mutually exclusive, thus closing their minds to the unavoidable presentist drive of White's brand of narrativism.[20] (In other words, they refuse to make the same leap to the political as he does.) Yet this presentism constitutes in many ways the most interesting aspect of his thought: having questioned the authority of history by pointing out its innate nature as ideological and 'fictional', White's only means for rescuing it are in showing its effectiveness on completely different terms (and this is so even if his interest is, mistakenly, seen to involve history only as a form of political engagement and nothing more). White's call to political involvement would, after all, have little significance if history was judged as being in all ways unimportant. So, the only way to rescue history is to concentrate effort on effects – if all representations are equal, historical accounts need to command interest and respect on aesthetic grounds. Historical accounts need to *affect* readers. This argument is central in White's work from 'The burden of history' to *The Content of the Form*.

Following his turn to the political, White's rescue of history thus necessarily takes us back to considerations of form, albeit in a very different sense (and direction) than the structuralist critique of traditional historical narratives. To better understand this, we need to remember that these traditional forms are motivated by and cater to a desire for non-contradiction and clarity. (We might also note, with interest, that this is a counter-force to the general yearning for reality that drives historians.) The appeal of narratives is largely due to the way they simplify the world. They pare down our alternatives to a single path along which events transpire, thus lending greater significance to the choices and decisions and coincidences that won out, glossing over the problematic moments, the uncertainties and absence. This neglect (of the 'feel' and inherent unstructuredness of experience) is the worst aspect of traditional, 'realist' narratives for White. It leads to ideological simplification and, by such narrative means, to a glorification of dominant values. Although White's talk of narrative has various objectives, then, it can quite usefully be read as centrally aimed at opposing this

desire for non-contradiction. Or, to formulate it positively, at providing historians the opportunity of accounting for the experience of agency and being overwhelmed that is central to ordinary experience but missing from typical narrative accounts of the past. Given this goal, it is perhaps more understandable why his emphasis is so often on 'modernist' literature and experimental art forms. After all, such work strongly thematizes hesitation and doubt and, by better (re)producing the complexity of experience, might thus at least partially satisfy the general phenomenological yearnings we have regarding the past.[21]

Beginning from his 1966 'Burden of history', White has often taken the creation of experience as desirable in terms of producing meaningfulness for the reader of the historical representation. Here he uses Norman O. Brown's *Life Against Death* (1959) as an example of the routes such alternative representations might take:

> He reduces all of the data of consciousness, past as well as present, to the same ontological level, and then, by a series of brilliant and shocking juxtapositions, involutions, reductions, and distortions, forces the reader to see with new clarity materials to which he has become oblivious through sustained association, or which he has repressed in response to social imperatives. In short, in his history Brown achieves the same effects as those sought by a 'Pop' artist or by John Cage in one of his 'happenings'. (White 1978b, 45)

This same ideal motivates his latest move from discussions of straightforward emplotments and narrative to modernist 'non-narrative', what he has called 'antinarrative nonstories' (White 1999, 81). By utilizing 'modernist techniques of representation', new, inventive forms of historiography could

> provide the possibility of defetishizing both events and the fantasy accounts of them which deny the threat they pose in the very process of pretending to represent them realistically and clear the way for that process of mourning which alone can relieve the burden of history and make a more if not totally realistic perception of current problems possible. (White 1999, 82)

It can be understood, then, that White's defamiliarization of narrative has at least two goals. Narrative itself needs to be understood as a choice, something we construct and impose (albeit effortlessly out of habit, practice and proclivity) but not, however, as the only alternative; and certainly not as somehow transparent. Following this kind of detachment – permitting a sense of awe, as it were – an encounter with a past that remains foreign instead of being domesticated becomes (at least theoretically) possible. The second aspect of *defamiliarization* can then come into play: narratives that are not 'easy' to assimilate and appropriate serve to remind us of the distance between their speaking about something and the reality of that something; this, to me, is the reason for White's emphasis on literary modernism. Understood in this way, the primary task of historians as writers, then, is the constant defamiliarizing of narrative *for the reader,* best achieved through a continuous renewal of the representational form. (And if this seems to transfer and impose the poststructuralist ideal of constantly choosing onto the reader and the reading process, it is no coincidence.)

## HISTORY GOES PUBLIC

It seems that White's emphases have shifted in recent years, perhaps in part in relation to the level of acceptance for his ideas. It is no longer as necessary to be controversial in presentation since the debate has reached a fairly stable point: those who are willing to listen have understood and those who refuse to do so won't. The linguistic turn and the destabilization of meaning need very little defence; what is at issue now are the consequences. In addition to being less polemic in his terminology regarding fictionalization, there is a change in his attitude to narrative: he now detaches narrative from an implicit replication of conservative ideology; instead narrative necessarily – even when written from a conservative viewpoint – poses the

question: 'how is action possible? It may answer this question by a negative result: alas, action is not possible; or a positive one: yes, it is possible. But by raising the question, narrative itself is positive – it answers the question: is it possible to ask whether action is possible?' (White 2006, 30). Form, it seems, is less responsible for the transmission of repressive ideology than before. More broadly, White's focus has moved from narrative theory and textual analysis to modernist literary representation and practical historiography.

Such concessions do not mean that White has dulled his oppositional edge, however. His claims in his 1999 collection of essays, *Figural Realism* make him much more radical in terms of solutions to the problems faced by history than ever before. In a way White is thus, despite the less polemical terminology, more involved in discounting the hegemony of history than in his earlier work. This can be explained, I believe, by accepting that he is no longer as interested in (or perhaps hopeful of) rescuing history in an *institutional* sense (perhaps out of some deeper realization that historians simply do not care about the intricacies of historical theory, or, for that matter, of changing their present). Instead, he seems to have shifted responsibility more and more to the consumers of historical presentations and increasingly emphasises the practical uses of the past and the kinds of presentations that are not subject to professional regulation.

In *Figural Realism* and since, White appears indeed to have more fully embraced the consequences of his emphasis on social commitment and a progressive, practical or even 'radical' historiography.[22] The foremost of his new commitments, I would say, is an emphasis on the reading and reception process itself. While he does not explicitly tackle reader reception theory and the like (and has of course touched on it in several early essays), his emphasis in *Figural Realism* is more on the consumption and ownership of history by the general public (for more on this, see Pihlainen 2008). This, quite naturally, follows from his interest in history writing and opinion as a social and political motive force outside academia. Where he has previously mainly focused on professional history and its troubles and responsibilities, the central essay of *Figural Realism*, 'The modernist event', shifts his social emphasis from academic historical writing to what he calls 'postmodernist parahistorical representations'; popular, mass-mediated conceptions of events that have significance for public historical consciousness, public history. For the White of such parahistorical representation, the practical significance of representations of the past – their sociopolitical effect – is brought even more forcefully to the fore. In this, a tension is introduced in the move from *Content of the Form* to *Figural Realism*, however: from the perspective of popular, parahistorical representations it seems we require narratives that are about our self-understanding and focused on presenting things to us in terms that are familiar and recognizable; narratives that permit us to inhabit the world comfortably, as White poeticizes. At other times – in his long-standing emphasis on modernist non-narratives – White's interest is in the effects form can have on the reader through *unfamiliarity*; while it is easy enough to make a point in traditional narrative form, utilizing contemporary literary devices to make these points is much more effective. With the qualification, of course, that readers be conversant in these more complex representations.

This tension can be explained, in part, by noting that White's focus is increasingly on the changes that technological innovations and not only literary developments have brought to presentational form. A central issue that he introduces in this connection is the way in which historical materials have become less subject to linguistic rendering. The fact that so much material is available in visual form is clearly an important factor in allowing presentations to become less determining. Because materials can be made available to viewers in a more accessible

format than written records, and because these materials are capable of conveying much more information in a 'direct' fashion, emphasis is no longer on their representation as much as on presentation (White 1999, 66 ff.; see also White 1988).

The form historical presentations take, then, is dependent on the sensibilities of the intended audience, whether professional historians or viewers of 'docudrama' and 'infotainment'. So, while White's basic position remains focused on providing a history that can serve practical purposes in an ethical – as opposed to unreflective and dogmatic – way, the means he presents for achieving this have become more varied. Yet, the underlying emphasis on history as being *for* something – directed toward the reduction of suffering, for example, as White has on occasion stated – denies these representations any pretensions to objectivity. By showing objectivity as simply an excuse for not getting involved, as another instance of moral cowardice, one would expect this emphasis on linguistic figuration to have led to a landslide of ethically emphatic and aware histories (much along the lines of the tendency in documentary film, for instance). This, however, despite the oft-mentioned ethical turn in historical studies, appears not to have been the case. Critiques of traditional objectivist histories remain essentially that: critiques and opposition. Where 'alternative' histories have found institutional acceptance – cultural, feminist and microhistorical ones, for instance – they have largely done so only by first marginalizing themselves in terms of their subject matter, by directing attention to themes and materials that do not threaten 'history proper'.[23]

White's example of Oliver Stone's film *JFK* (1991) is illuminating here: despite its parahistorical status, criticism against it seemingly hinged on the idea of misrepresentation. According to more fierce critics the interpretation presented by the film was simply untrue or distorted.[24] Further, it was motivated by Stone's own politics, whereas more conventional (and conforming) representations

could, inexplicably, be seen as free of political interest and hence as more 'objective'.
Interestingly, factual discrepancies and ideological intent here condemned the work as a
whole whereas one might expect them to
simply have been accepted as 'mistakes' and
'subjective opinions' in a less controversial
case, say, *W*, the 2008 Oliver Stone film on
George W. Bush. This does not, once again,
imply that professional practices, including
fidelity to sources, fairness, inclusiveness
and so on, do not figure in the evaluation of
(what are agreed to be historical) representations. What is implied, however, is that historical fidelity is not the crucial issue (both
generally as much as in the case of *JFK*).
Rather, controversy rages over who decides
what interpretations are acceptable and how
such decisions are made. In the case of parahistorical representations, critique seldom
meets its target of course: professional consensus among historians is not a relevant
standard for such work. Hence even more
understandable are historians' worries about
people being misled.

Although he seldom emphasizes it, White
appears to rely strongly on the competence of
readers to interpret representations in terms
of their overall 'meaning'; that is, both in
terms of reference and in terms of metaphorical significance or 'narrative truths.'
Thus, while language is in theory problematic, our linguistic competence can transcend
these difficulties – and is indeed quite pragmatically assumed by White and others to do
so with relative ease. This assumption plays
a crucial role in the discussion concerning
parahistorical representations: the utilization
of the radically different (re)presentational
genre of *infotainment*, for example, demands
that readers/viewers be able to make reasonably clear distinctions between fact and fiction. Interestingly, this would seem well in
line with White's early emphasis on the trope
of *irony* and his claim regarding its prevalence in contemporary modes of thought: it
seems irony offers the best means to bracket
epistemological issues and sidestep factual
discrepancies while still holding on to some

idea of reference and significance. (Admittedly
there is something of Rorty's liberal ironist in
my formulation here.)

## CONCLUSION: PRESENTING HISTORY AS EXPERIENCE

What does White not say, though? And what
implications might his thoughts have that are
not followed up in his own writing? Given
his very broad range of interests and expertise he obviously suggests many things to
many people, depending on their particular
concerns and knowledge. In terms of narrative representation, the main points of interest, for me, follow from the apparent
centrality of 'experience' to his arguments. In
my view, White's particular phenomenological yearning regarding history – and his
consequent emphasis on the effects of alternative and experimental historical narratives –
centres on a desire to reach a non-appropriating,
non-colonizing experience of the 'inside' of
historical events, 'their possible meanings or
significances' (White 1999, 79). By this he
seems to be driving at something more than
'understanding,' hence his persistent emphasis on 'classic' (as opposed to documentary)
texts and artistic representational forms
alongside the more popular parahistorical
ones. Artistic means, and the achievement of
'worklikeness', to borrow a Heideggerian
formulation from Dominick LaCapra (1982),
are, it seems, characteristic of a content to the
form that goes beyond the merely ideological
or entertaining. Yet this presents interesting
problems. Most pressingly: when and why
does the ideological become artistic, work-
like and somehow universally human? The
short answer, of course, is simply this: when
it resonates with our particular moral and
aesthetic sensibilities. A more involved
answer appeals to a range of narrative and
aesthetic theories. Although a great deal of
interest has been on selection and emplotment and the 'literariness' of historical narratives, continued emphasis on the fact–fiction
problematic appears limiting. What such

theorizing fails to acknowledge is the uniqueness and strengths of historical representation. Seen in strictly structuralist or textualist (literary) terms, history will always remain only a second-order literary endeavour. Similarly, seen from a purely poststructuralist (philosophy) point of view, its commitment to reference (and simultaneous denial of the availability of truth) will always prevent history from taking its political role seriously and foregrounding *effects* over and above consensus. It is only White's pragmatism and the occasionally precarious mix of positions it leads to that permit any rescue of the genre after the original recognition of epistemological failure.

White's goal, then, can be understood as a history that emulates the kind of *lived experience* we have in our habitual – non-literary and (I would argue) *non-totalizing* – engagements with the world. As this seems to be a natural course to follow once a constructivist approach is adopted, it is no wonder that discussions among theorists of history often also turn to new presentational forms and ideas of worklikeness and presence. What is surprising, however, is that linguistic figuration (the issue of history as story and the related epistomological worries) and the ethicopolitical aspect of historical representation (what history is for; how it should be written) continue to be so indistinguishable in many of these debates. New forms do not, in themselves bring any real substance to the presentation (albeit they are certainly 'oppositional' in terms of challenging previous presentational traditions) and achieving worklikeness is also largely independent of the political ends intended. The creation (or simulation) of lived experience would, on the other hand, permit the historian to address the *private* and subjective of the reader: history would, in practice too, begin to *communicate with* rather than simply *to* its readers. And in this sense, the need for an author (as authority) would properly disappear.

Where history's entailments cause particular conflict is in the context of linguistic constructivism turned textualism. Viewed

from the perspective of state-of-the-art literary creation, historical writing is most often deficient in terms of both form and style. (If for no other reason than for the fact that historians respect the professional limits they are faced with. Again, this is not a matter of epistemological issues as such.) On the other hand, the 'classic' text 'gives us insight into a process that is universal and definitive of human species-being in general, the process of meaning production' (White 1987, 211). As White writes of classic historical works:

> A historical interpretation, like a poetic fiction, can be said to appeal to its readers as a plausible representation of the world by virtue of its implicit appeal to those 'pre-generic plot-structures' or archetypal story-forms that define the modalities of a given culture's literary endowment. ... This mythic element ... is recognizable in those historical accounts, such as Gibbon's *Decline and Fall*, which continue to be honored as classics long after the 'facts' contained in them have been refined beyond recognition by subsequent research. (White 1978b, 58)

It is not the historical accuracy or scientific usefulness of such texts, he argues, that lend them contemporary significance as they have long since become outdated as historical research. Rather, their status as classics stems from their having become accepted into the canon of literary works – or at least from their having become exemplars of literary historical writing. Most historical writing, however, is impaired in this sense, and unlikely – I think – to find its way into the corpus of literary classics. To explain: as a result of its entailments to truth and reference as well as its professional and methodological practices, historical writing proceeds from the vantage point of reality with a body of materials that it needs to include for it to be acceptable as historical research. Historical stories – the narratives produced – are thus determined not by any free process of linguistic figuration but first and foremost by their commitment to accommodate particular materials in a specifically historical way. Once again, the content of the content interferes with the aesthetic.[25] This difficulty, I would say, is a prime reason for White's move away from institutional history and toward popular forms.

White's topmost priority *now* – as I conceive of him here – is for historians to focus on creating emotional impact, taking the professional constraints they conduct their research under as a given. At least to the extent to which they can be so taken. In addition to the emphasis on effectiveness, the creation of aesthetic experience, a state of awe, that is more in the sphere of art than of entertainment seems important. This, admittedly, is White at his most radical: the White who advocates the expressionist poetic style of Norman O. Brown or even postmodern parahistorical representations *à la* Oliver Stone's *JFK*. The White who, less concerned with the processes of historical meaning making, is intent on history's achieving particular effects following (and independent of) the establishment of the facts by historical research. Focus is thus on practical purposes that may at times take us beyond the limits of professional history. While such presentations are undoubtedly useful in terms of social impact and, what is more, undeniably free of the limitations of (and the narrative 'impairment' I would attribute to) historical writing in the strict sense, they are, in other words, vulnerable to the critique of no longer being within the scope of history in a disciplinarily meaningful sense. Of course, this is not necessarily a bad thing, and White's varying stance on the extent to which the past can be handed over to the public appears to be modulated by his view of readers' competence and, always, driven by his interest to rescue history in one form or another.

## NOTES

1    In this way historical narratives are – in epistemic terms – best seen as 'models of interpretive thought' (White 1999, 6) and as 'points of view' onto the past (Ankersmit 1983, 26). At the same time narrativity remains, as noted, 'intimately related to, if not a function of, the impulse to moralize reality, that is, to identify it with the social system that is the source of any morality that we can imagine' (White 1987, 14).

2    In addition to emphasizing the role of professional standards and consensus, White also affirms that sources can be used to ascertain the truth-value of individual existential statements, the facts. For more on this, see notes 8 and 9. White is critical of any historical 'methodology', however. As he says: 'a methodology? For historical studies in general? I don't think so' (see Domanska 2008, 12). If there is any room for methodology in White's philosophy of history it is certainly only on the side of research methods as well as text analysis (or discourse analysis as he calls it), not in the process of linguistic figuration and ideological emplotment. Historical methodologies and prescriptive theories can sensibly be provided only for research of the past (if even there), not for the narrative presentation of the results of that research.

3    His approach at times suggests that historical materials do not limit the range of different narrative emplotments. To me, too much has been made of the idea of competing interpretations, however; see e.g. Novick 1988, 600 ff. and Evans 1999, esp. 86–7. See also Kansteiner 1993. This relates also to White's (varying) stance on whether the research stage is separable from that of emplotment and presentation. While White often separates them for descriptive purposes, Nancy Partner is right to note that '[i]n practice, this virtually never happens. The narrativizing process is in action prior to and all during the "research," recognizing and recording what may count as salient "facts," and it never feels as if anything so artificial as emplotment is taking place – although it is' (Partner 1997, 108–9).

4    See also A. Dirk Moses, who argues for 'a fundamental unity of purpose and continuity of theme' in White's oeuvre (2005a, 316). Definitions of White's positions abound: For Ewa Domanska, 'Hayden White appears as a modernist where modernism is understood as certain literary and artistic movements. When examining philosophy, I discover a realist, but one idealistically oriented and preoccupied by existential concerns' (Domanska 1998, 174). On White as a 'poststructuralist postmodernist', see Breisach 2003, 73 ff. White on occasion acknowledges his own postmodernism: 'We postmodernists are serious about our need for meaning, even if we are scientistically ironic about the possibility of ever finding meaning in the congeries of things we call "reality"' (White 2005a, 151). Although rarely developed in detail, White's Marxism is also often brought up in his own speech as well as by commentators. White provides many excellent summaries of his own thought; for the most recent of these, see e.g. White 1999, 1–26, White 2000 and Rogne 2009.

5    Examples of the critique directed at White's thinking can be found in Novick 1988, in the Ginzburg–White debate (see Friedlander 1992), and in the Marwick–White debate in the *Journal of Contemporary History* (1995–1996, issues 30:1, 30:2 and 31:1). Ankersmit (1998, 185) rightly dismisses Arthur Marwick's critique – 'an absolute low in the perennial battle of the historical discipline against the scourge of theory' – as 'inane and silly.'

6  I will not go into this in any detail as White's idea of tropes seems to me now to be mainly an example or application of his broader view of history as linguistically figured; hence attempting to present it here would only cloud this more essential point. The brief theoretical framework presented in the preface to *Metahistory* provides a concise summary to White's overall philosophy of history (see White 1973, ix–xii) and the ideas of emplotment and troping are explained in more detail in the introduction, entitled 'The poetics of history'. For more on *Metahistory* and White's tropological model, see also e.g. White's 1973 essay entitled 'Interpretation in History' (reprinted in White 1978b, pp. 51–80); Kellner 1980; Ankersmit 1998; Domanska 1998, esp. 173–5; Vann 1998; Jenkins 1999, 126 ff.; and Paul 2006 and 2011. For other more recent views, see also the essays in Ankersmit, Domanska and Kellner 2009.

7  The context of White's breakthrough as well as his earlier work and influences are presented in detail by Domanska 1998; Vann 1998; Moses 2005a, 2005b; and Paul 2008. For Domanska, '[t]here was nothing new or original in ["The burden of history"] in comparison with his earlier works, although many scholars consider "The Burden" to be White's first important piece. It contains motifs that have appeared over and over again since White began to publish' (Domanska 1998, 180). For White's early essays, see also White 2010.

8  In answer to Iggers' critique, White once again attempts to correct such misunderstandings: 'It is true that I have spoken of histories as products of a process of invention more literary or poetic than scientific and conceptual; and I have spoken of histories as fictionalizations of fact and of past reality. But, to be quite frank, I intended the notion of fiction ... as a hypothetical construct and an "as if" consideration of a reality which, because it was no longer present to perception, could only be imagined rather than simply referred to or posited' (White 2000, 398).

9  White has made this abundantly clear on many occasions: 'This is not to say that a historical discourse is not properly assessed in terms of the truth value of its factual (singular existential) statements taken individually and the logical conjunction of the whole set of such statements taken distributively. For unless a historical discourse acceded to assessment in these terms, it would lose all justification for its claim to represent and provide explanations of specifically real events. But such assessment touches only that aspect of the historical discourse conventionally called its chronicle' (White 1987, 45). And, earlier, in the 'Historical text as literary artifact': 'This is not to say that we cannot distinguish between good and bad historiography, since we can always fall back on such criteria as responsibility to the rules of evidence, the relative fullness of narrative detail, logical consistency, and the like to determine this issue' (White 1978b, 97).

10  For a brief discussion of this position as presented by MacIntyre, see e.g. Ricoeur 1992, 158 ff. For Carr, see his *Time, Narrative and History* (1986).

11  As White states: 'It is frequently forgotten or, when remembered, denied that no given set of events attested by the historical record comprises a *story* manifestly finished and complete. ... We do not *live* stories, even if we give our lives meaning by retrospectively casting them in the form of stories' (White 1978b, 90; see also White 1999, 9 and Munslow 1997, 140 ff). The kind of *impositionalism* or *constructivism* advocated by White aims at making this a fundamental reality for historians. Roland Barthes, Louis O. Mink, Paul Ricoeur, Hans Kellner and Dominick LaCapra, all of whom have similarly influenced the current narrative theory of history discussion, occupy a more or less identical constructivist position – a position which, following Munslow (2007, 17), can be more accurately termed one of '*narrative constructivism*'. A useful introduction to this broader debate is to be found in Munslow's *The New History* (2003).

12  The affinities between White and Rorty have been discussed in detail by Keith Jenkins in his *On 'What is History?'* (1995).

13  In criticizing Michael Riffaterre's idea of locating the 'original' meaning of the text in its original readers, White defends mapping 'the socio-psychological matrix of the author's experience' (White 1970, 178). On many occasions, he presents some form of intertextuality as providing context, particularly for investigations in intellectual history (esp. White 1987, 185 ff.; see also Pihlainen 2006). Seeing historical conditions, for example, in terms of 'texts' seems an unnecessary stretch of this terminology, however. At least for those who, like White, wish to hold on to the idea of history. (Again, this is not in any way to belittle the epistemological difficulties involved.) Despite differing interpretations, contextual readings are not denied by poststructuralist approaches, of course: think of Foucault's work if in doubt. Further, as is so often noted, Derrida's notorious 'there is nothing outside the text' is perhaps one of the most misunderstood statements in the debate concerning the linguistic turn. For a succint discussion of this in the context of history, see e.g. Jenkins 2000.

14  To follow up on White's existentialism, see e.g. Kellner 1980 and Paul 2006.

15  In a recent formulation of White's own: 'the antipostmodernist handwringers are wrong when they say that the postmodernists are "against" history, objectivity, rules, methods, and so on. What we postmodernists are against is a professional historiography, in service to state apparatuses that have turned against their own citizens, with its epistemically pinched, ideologically sterile, and superannuated notions of objectivity' (White 2005a, 152).

16  Ankersmit (1998, 182) and Daddow also note White's interest in rescuing history. Writes Daddow: 'His aim was not to explode history for the sake of it or to do away with the discipline of history altogether. By contrast, White's aim has been clear throughout: to make history more relevant to us in our daily lives by reconnecting it to the poetic and artistic ways of representing reality. Only then would he consider the discipline worthy of salvation' (2008, 53).

17  Hence the question of control remains acute: 'the crucial problem, from the perspective of political struggle, is not whose story is the best or truest, but who has the power to make his story stick as the one that others will choose to live by or in' (White 1982, 12–13). For more on this, see also e.g. White 2010, 136 ff.

18  Even as extreme a theorist as Keith Jenkins makes it clear that this is a completely unnecessary (if not in fact absurd) claim. See e.g. Jenkins 2000, 184. Instead, we need to see 'knowledge not as a matter of getting reality right but of acquiring pragmatic habits allowing us to cope with the contingencies of "our worded world"' (Jenkins 2000, 185). Herman Paul (2006) elaborates on White's politics in *Metahistory*, showing how White employs *epistemological* irony to refute *ideological* irony to the same effect (irony being equatable with relativism/scepticism). In undermining claims to ultimate authority and truth in this way, White opens history up to responsibility, not chaos: 'I conceive relativism to be the basis of social tolerance, not a license to "do as you please." ... the socially responsible interpreter can do two things: (1) expose the fictitious nature of any political program based on an appeal to what "history" supposedly teaches and (2) remain adamantly "utopian" in any criticism of political "realism"' (White 1987, 227).

19  Richard Vann also draws attention to White's sometime terminological ambiguity, explaining that 'in stating his basic positions in a number of different contexts and to different implied readers, he has avoided repeating himself *verbatim*, with the consequence that various formulations of these positions – and not always cautious ones – have appeared' (Vann 1998, 145).

20  As Patrick Finney (2008, 104) notes, 'it is easy to see why his message is unpalatable. Historians usually find White's scepticism entirely counter-intuitive intellectually and emotionally. It simply fails to chime with their lived experience of fruitful archival toil.'

21  For more on this, see e.g. Pihlainen 2006 and 2007.

22  For more on White as a 'radical historian', see Jenkins 2008. On the shift in White's thinking presented by *Figural Realism*, see Pihlainen 2006.

23  This is not to be understood too harshly, of course: much groundbreaking work has been carried out in all these fields. My worry is that the codification of earlier experimental and politically motivated work into replicable 'methodological approaches' – focusing on some insignificant if previously unexplored and institutionally disdained detail of the past, for example – can lead to similar retreats from moral responsibility and *engagement* as has the illusion of objectivity. Choice is given up when methodologies are allowed to take over.

24  For a thorough discussion of *JFK*, see Sturken 1997.

25  Referentiality is perhaps unduly seen as only a weakness (as it is from a strictly textualist point of view). Crucially, this depends on the readership. For history to emphasize its referential nature successfully, it is imperative that readers first become properly aware of the epistemological limitations involved and adopt an 'ironic' stance concerning history's truthfulness and/or reproduction of ideology. When written for such ironic readers, history might become free to make use of referentiality as a disruptive and alienating strategy, for instance.

# REFERENCES

Ankersmit, F.R. 1983. *Narrative Logic: A Semantic Analysis of the Historian's Language*. The Hague: Martinus Nijhoff Publishers.

Ankersmit, F.R. 1998. Hayden White's appeal to the historians. *History and Theory* 37 (2), 182–93.

Ankersmit, Frank, Ewa Domanska and Hans Kellner (eds). 2009. *Re-Figuring Hayden White*. Stanford: Stanford University Press.

Breisach, Ernst. 2003. *On the Future of History: The Postmodernist Challenge and Its Aftermath*. Chicago: University of Chicago Press.

Carr, David. 1986. *Time, Narrative, and History*. Bloomington, Indiana: Indiana University Press.

Daddow, Oliver. 2008. Exploding history: Hayden White on disciplinization. *Rethinking History* 12 (1), 41–58.

Domanska, Ewa. 1998. Hayden White: beyond irony. *History and Theory* 37 (2), 173–81.

Domanska, Ewa. 2008. A conversation with Hayden White. *Rethinking History* 12 (1), 3–21.

Evans, Richard J. 1999. *In Defense of History*. New York: W.W. Norton.

Finney, Patrick. 2008. Hayden White, International history and questions too seldom posed. *Rethinking History* 12 (1), 103–23.

Friedlander, Saul (ed.). 1992. *Probing the Limits of Representation: Nazism and the 'Final Solution'*. Cambridge, Mass.: Harvard University Press.

Iggers, Georg G. 2000. Historiography between scholarship and poetry: reflections on Hayden White's approach to historiography. *Rethinking History* 4 (3), 373–90.

Jenkins, Keith. 1995. *On 'What is History?' From Carr and Elton to Rorty and White*. London: Routledge.

Jenkins, Keith. 1999. *Why History? Ethics and Postmodernity*. London: Routledge.

Jenkins, Keith. 2000. A postmodern reply to Perez Zagorin. *History and Theory* 39 (2), 181–200.

Jenkins, Keith. 2003. *Refiguring History: New Thoughts on an Old Discipline*. London: Routledge.

Jenkins, Keith. 2008. 'Nobody does it better': radical history and Hayden White. *Rethinking History* 12 (1), 59–74.

Kansteiner, Wulf. 1993. Hayden White's critique of the writing of history. *History and Theory* 32 (3), 273–95.

Kellner, Hans. 1980. A bedrock of order: Hayden White's linguistic humanism. *History and Theory* 19 (4), 1–29.

LaCapra, Dominick. 1982. Rethinking intellectual history and reading texts, in Dominick LaCapra and Steven L. Kaplan (eds) *Modern European Intellectual History: Reappraisals and New Perspectives*. Ithaca: Cornell University Press, 47–85.

Lorenz, Chris. 1994. Historical knowledge and historical reality: a plea for 'internal realism'. *History and Theory* 33 (3), 297–327.

Moses, A. Dirk. 2005a. Hayden White, Traumatic nationalism, and the public role of history. *History and Theory* 44 (3), 311–32.

Moses, A. Dirk. 2005b. The public relevance of historical studies: a rejoinder to Hayden White. *History and Theory* 44 (3), 339–47.

Munslow, Alun. 1997. *Deconstructing History*. London: Routledge.

Munslow, Alun. 2003. *The New History*. Harlow: Pearson.

Munslow, Alun. 2007. *Narrative and History*. Basingstoke: Palgrave Macmillan.

Novick, Peter. 1988. *That Noble Dream: The 'Objectivity Question' and the American Historical Profession*. London: Cambridge University Press.

Partner, Nancy. 1997. Hayden White (and the content and the form and everyone else) at the AHA. *History and Theory* 36 (4), 102–10.

Partner, Nancy. 1998. Hayden White: the form of the content. *History and Theory* 37 (2), 162–72.

Paul, Herman. 2006. An ironic battle against irony: epistemological and ideological irony in Hayden White's philosophy of history, 1955–1973, in Kuisma Korhonen (ed.) *Tropes for the Past: Hayden White and the History/Literature Debate*. Amsterdam: Rodopi, 35–44.

Paul, Herman. 2008. A Weberian medievalist: Hayden White in the 1950s. *Rethinking History* 12 (1), 75–102.

Paul, Herman. 2011. *Hayden White*. London: Polity Press.

Pihlainen, Kalle. 2006. The confines of the form: historical writing and the desire that it be what it is not, in Kuisma Korhonen (ed.) *Tropes for the Past: Hayden White and the History/Literature Debate*. Amsterdam: Rodopi, 55–67.

Pihlainen, Kalle. 2007. Performance and the reformulation of historical representation. *Storia della Storiografia* 51, 3–16.

Pihlainen, Kalle. 2008. History in the world: Hayden White and the consumer of history. *Rethinking History* 12 (1), 23–39.

Ricoeur, Paul. 1992. *Oneself as Another*. Translated by Kathleen Blamey. Chicago: University of Chicago Press.

Rogne, Erlend. 2009. The aim of interpretation is to create perplexity in the face of the real: Hayden White in conversation with Erlend Rogne. *History and Theory* 48 (1), 63–75.

Sturken, Marita. 1997. Reenactment, fantasy, and the paranoia of history: Oliver Stone's docudramas. *History and Theory* 36 (4), 64–79.

Vann, Richard T. 1998. The reception of Hayden White. *History and Theory* 37 (2), 143–61.

White, Hayden. 1970. Literary history: the point of it all. *New Literary History* 2 (1), 173–85.

White, Hayden. 1973. *Metahistory: The Historical Imagination in Nineteenth-Century Europe*. Baltimore: Johns Hopkins University Press.

White, Hayden. 1978a. The historical text as literary artefact, in Robert H. Canary and Henry Kozicki (eds) *The Writing of History: Literary Form and Historical Understanding*. Wisconsin: University of Wisconsin Press, 41–62.

White, Hayden. 1978b. *Tropics of Discourse: Essays in Cultural Criticism*. Baltimore: Johns Hopkins University Press.

White, Hayden. 1982. Getting out of history. *Diacritics* 12 (3), 2–13.

White, Hayden. 1987. *The Content of the Form: Narrative Discourse and Historical Representation*. Baltimore: Johns Hopkins University Press.

White, Hayden. 1988. Historiography and historiophoty. *American Historical Review* 93 (5), 1193–9.

White, Hayden. 1999. *Figural Realism: Studies in the Mimesis Effect*. Baltimore: Johns Hopkins University Press.

White, Hayden. 2000. An old question raised again: is historiography art or science? (Response to Iggers). *Rethinking History* 4 (3), 391–406.

White, Hayden. 2005a. Introduction: historical fiction, fictional history, and historical reality. *Rethinking History* 9 (2/3), 147–57.

White, Hayden. 2005b. The public relevance of historical studies: a reply to Dirk Moses. *History and Theory* 44 (3), 333–8.

White, Hayden. 2006. Historical discourse and literary writing, in Kuisma Korhonen (ed.) *Tropes for the Past: Hayden White and the History/Literature Debate*. Amsterdam: Rodopi, 25–33.

White, Hayden. 2010. *The Fiction of Narrative: Essays on History, Literature, and Theory, 1957—2007*. Edited and with and introduction by Robert Doran. Baltimore: Johns Hopkins University Press.

# 9

# Derrida and Deconstruction: Challenges to the Transparency of Language

Robert M. Stein

In 1987, the publication in the *American Historical Review* of John Toews' review essay, 'Intellectual history after the linguistic turn: the autonomy of meaning and the irreducibility of experience,' marked a decisive moment in the development of Anglo-American historiography.[1] The very title of this important essay announced the accomplishment in the profession of history of the large-scale shift in emphasis that had been variously taking place for perhaps two decades throughout the human sciences. In brief, that shift involved a definitive turning of attention to the ways that experience is perceived as meaningful by individual and collective social actors and to the complex and multiple social and psychological operations that take place throughout all levels of culture and society to produce the sense of meaning in action. Most important for the profession of history is that the turn toward the analysis of culture, most broadly construed, as the sphere of meaning production in society foregrounds the fact of language both as an analytic necessity and as a problem:

language could no longer be taken for granted as a simple medium that transparently delivered reality to consciousness, for the production and dissemination of meaning takes place entirely within the symbolic sphere of expression and communication.

This direct engagement of historical practice with language moreover occurred at the very moment that the study of language itself was being subject to a most thorough interrogation in which the work of the philosopher Jacques Derrida played a central role in at least three ways. First, Jacques Derrida's work published in France during the late 1960s was translated into English in the 1970s and 1980s[2] where in its English dress it was quickly lumped together as 'French Theory' with a group of writings in several very different disciplines. Among others, Jacques Lacan's reconsideration of the fundamentals of Freudian psychoanalytical theory and practice, the earlier linguistically based writings of Michel Foucault, and the sociological analysis of Pierre Bourdieu all seemed at that time to promise an alternative to the prevailing empiricist and legalist framework of Anglo-American research in the humanities and social sciences.[3] Within the context of 'French Theory' Derrida's writing of the 1960s constituted the most far-reaching and thorough meditation on the systematic effects that language (the medium) has on cognition and representation.[4] Besides opening a set of questions regarding the effects of language as a symbolic system, Derrida's approach fast became seen as a methodology. Involving as it did a sustained and close reading of important texts in the European tradition of philosophy and literature, Derrida's work seemed to promise a model that could be codified into a set of duplicable procedures and techniques. It seemed, that is, to be the working out of a method that could be taught as a methodology and practiced by anyone. This is the second role played by Derrida's work: something called 'deconstruction' rapidly became 'deconstructionism.' One found it in English Departments being practiced for good or ill by 'deconstructionists' whose work could be spread abroad in handbooks, imitated, taught to students, celebrated, denounced, or ignored. As one methodology among others, it could be picked up or put down at will. This institutionalization is still the prevailing view of Derrida's work in America.[5] The third and most serious relevance of Derrida's work to historical theory and practice involves a much deeper set of reflections in the philosophy of history, a set of reflections that, rigorously pursued, radically calls into question the logic and meaning of a multitude of concepts necessary to historical investigation itself, historical agency, causality, and purposive change among them.

Perhaps we can best think of Derrida as a key figure in twentieth-century philosophical and artistic high modernism. The simultaneously destructive and creative project of deconstruction bears deep affinities with the work of Schoenberg and Picasso in the dismantling of tonality and the illusionistic representational system loosely called realism. It is manifestly connected to currents in philosophy that include the work of Wittgenstein and Russell as well as the continental philosophers, especially Heidegger, with whom Derrida associates himself directly by quotation and critique. The inescapably paradoxical conceptual structures of quantum physics, topology, Gödel's mathematics, Heisenberg's physics, and the divorce between 'science' and any conceivable commonsense view of the world are no less difficult than the difficult line of thought that Derrida worked through to the end of his life. Decisive are a set of developments in modern continental philosophy that are most particularly evident in the writings of Edmond Husserl and Martin Heidegger. These issues cannot be adequately discussed in the confines of this chapter. Suffice it to note that Derrida opened a specific critique of phenomenology as a 'philosophy of presence,' whose measure of truth is grounded on the activity of an autonomous subject discoursing with itself in the 'silence of the soul.' The most advanced instances of epistemology and ontology, Derrida argued, even in the guise of a critique of traditional metaphysics, thus recapitulate a tenet of the theory of knowledge fundamental to philosophy since the time of Plato.[6] The measure of truth was the self-certainty of a knowing subject, present to the contents of his own consciousness. That is to say, certainty in the western tradition of philosophy always involves not only knowing something but also knowing that one knows: this is a constant from the dawn of philosophy among the Greeks to Descartes' *cogito* – where Descartes found that he was able to call everything into doubt except the absolute certainty that he was calling everything into doubt – and beyond. This measure of certainty had, by the early twentieth century, already been called into question by Nietzsche's critique of metaphysics and its logic of truth and especially by Freud's demonstration of the role of the unconscious in psychic life, which showed that vast and important aspects of one's 'self' could never be present to one's consciousness. Thus Husserl's phenomenology, the subject of Derrida's earliest writing, claimed to be

able to deliver the thing itself to consciousness without mediation, and Heidegger, even
though calling for the 'destruction' of metaphysics by way of a profound critique of its
history so that one could go directly 'to the
things themselves,' also relies on a similar
measure of truth.[7] Derrida demonstrates thoroughly, in other words, that even the phenomenological critiques of Husserl and Heidegger
depend on and thus reinstate a subject with a
spurious independence from any system of
mediation. And from the side of the object
that is known, these critiques proceed from an
assumption that one thing can transparently
and directly be presented to consciousness
without the intervention of another thing – the
most basic definition of a sign – and especially without the mediation of the signifying
system itself.

## FROM STRUCTURALISM TO
## DECONSTRUCTION

In the works written in the late 1960s, Derrida
opened a profound investigation of the fundamental questions that seemed to escape or
even threaten to upset the systematic procedures and conclusions of the state of contemporary philosophy. In focusing on the issue of
presence – the presence of the object to consciousness, the presence of the knowing subject to itself – Derrida was led to consider
various problems of representation and fundamentally, the place of language itself,
which Saussure as early as 1909 had proposed as the model of any system of signs.
Most Anglo-American readers will have met
this aspect of Derrida's work by reading the
English translation of 'La structure, le signe
et le jeu dans le discours des sciences
humaines,' originally given as a paper in 1966
and published in English in 1970 in the
hugely influential book, *The Structuralist
Controversy*. Difficult as it is to paraphrase, it
will be worthwhile to consider the opening of
this essay at some length for it can both show
us what deconstruction is and also how it
became transformed into a method.

Presented at the conference that essentially
introduced structuralist theory to America at
the very moment that the limitations of structuralism were being seriously questioned in
Europe, Derrida begins by subjecting the
notion of structure itself to serious critique.
Whether in Claude Lévi-Strauss's approach
to anthropology or Roman Jakobson's elaboration of linguistics, structure abstracts 'a
realm of pure signification out from the complex messiness of social life' as William
Sewell eloquently puts it, and specifies 'its
internal coherence and deep logic.'[8] Derrida
begins by noting that identifying anything as
a structure always entails the existence of a
governing point, a center without which a
structure does not exist as such. This center
provides the coherence of the elements that
comprise the structure, puts them into play,
and both makes possible and limits the extent
of their transformations, substitutions, and
permutations. This center, as a governing
point, itself is always necessarily presupposed to escape these very transformations,
and is thus paradoxically both inside and
outside the structure.[9] Any apprehension of
formal coherence in the world, any formal
system or way of grasping and mentally controlling the multiplicity of reality, had to proceed from some stable point. Something has
to hold still for anything else to be understood
in relation to it. Logically contradictory, this
stable center that is both inside and outside,
Derrida argues, has always been indifferently
conceived of as either an origin or an end
(*archè* or *telos*) while governing the transformations and substitutions whose structural
play constitutes a 'history of meaning' whose
beginning can always be recalled or whose
end can be anticipated in the form of presence. Hence, 'one could perhaps say that the
movement of every archeology, like that of
every eschatology, is complicit in this reduction of the structurality of structure and tries
always to consider structure as ultimately
arising out of a full presence beyond play.'[10]
In fact, all the words that signify a basis,
principle, or center 'have always named the
invariant of presence: *eidos, archè, telos,*

*energeia, ousia* (essence, existence, substance, subject), *aletheia,* the transcendental, conscience, God, man, etc.'[11]

These words are the key terms of the history of philosophy in western culture. Over time, one has as it were replaced the next. Thus the very concepts that designate 'full presence beyond play' are themselves nothing other than a chain of signifiers, one appearing after another. They are metaphors signifying something that, if it can be said to exist at all, either seems always to have passed or is always yet to come. And they trace a history – the history of philosophy, or even more broadly, the intellectual history of western culture, would be a history of these metaphors. And yet, these terms cannot at all be said to be metaphors in the strict sense because there is no 'proper' meaning standing outside this chain of substitutions that each term really stands in place of; there is no proper meaning that could name this center once for all or ever become fully present to consciousness. There is no 'transcendental signified,' no proper designation for any of these terms that remains untouched by the play of associations consequent to each of these terms: to name this governing point 'God' is very different from saying 'man' or from saying 'governing point' for that matter. 'This is thus the moment,' writes Derrida, 'when language invades the field of universal doubt; it is the moment when, in the absence of a center or origin, everything becomes discourse – on condition that we are in agreement about this word – that is to say, a system in which the central, original or transcendental signified is never absolutely present outside of a system of differences. The absence of a transcendental signified extends the field and play of signification to infinity.'[12]

## 'WHEN EVERYTHING BECOMES DISCOURSE'

We must here follow Derrida in this essay one step further. The system of differences is inescapable and interminable. Derrida illustrates

this precisely by very briefly tracing the history of critical philosophy (connected to the names Nietzsche, Freud, and Heidegger) that makes the problem of signification visible as he has been presenting it. In this presentation, he notes that each of these critical discourses are caught in a circle: 'The circle is unique and it describes the relation between the history of metaphysics and the destruction of the history of metaphysics ...We have no other language available – no syntax and no lexicon – that are foreign to this history; we cannot utter a single destructive proposition that has not already had to slip into the form, the logic, and the formulations implicit in that very same thing that one wished to contest.'[13] And to complete this observation, Derrida adduces precisely his own procedure up to this point of the essay. To destabilize the metaphysics of presence, Derrida has made use of the concept of the sign. Now, what is involved in calling something a 'sign?' To call something a 'sign' necessarily implies something else 'out there' that is referred to or signified by the sign. Thus, thinking of anything as a sign immediately smuggles in the assumption of an 'out there,' a reality outside the sign system, that is being referred to and that remains absolutely independent and untouched by the whole apparatus of signifying. But from the moment that one suggests that there is no transcendental signified, that the signified is constituted by the same play of differences that constitutes the signifier, the whole symbolic system reaches an impasse or *aporia* that threatens the notion of coherency itself. This same impasse is visible in Lévi-Strauss's effort to 'transcend the opposition between the sensible and the intelligible' by operating entirely on the level of signs, whereas, as Derrida points out, the whole concept of the sign is determined precisely by the opposition between the sensible signifier (heard in the stream of speech) and the intelligible signified (the mental concept that the signifier delivers as its referent) and the assurance that the signified exists as such fixed outside the process of signification and untouched by the signifier that delivers it. 'We cannot renounce this metaphysical complicity without at the same moment renouncing the critical work that we would direct against it.'[14]

Two points emerge here with the utmost clarity. First, a rigorous analysis of the concept of structure is in fact a rigorous analysis of the language in which 'structure' has been formulated: there is nothing else to analyze; there is no concept that consciousness can seize on independently, just as there is no 'thinking' that can go on outside the system of signs and structure of logic in which and with which 'the concept' has been and continues to be represented.[15] Representation is thus not secondary; there is no 'thing itself' to go to and 'grasp' outside the system of representation and its mode of operation. Second, to say that representation is not secondary, however, brings us to the same impasse that we noted a moment ago in Derrida's discussion of the sign, for the very notion of representation, like the notion of a sign, depends on the notion of the existence of something that can be represented – a *representation of something else, a sign of its referent, a signifier of a signified,* etc. – without which the term is strictly meaningless. This impasse, this continual threat of meaninglessness, is 'deconstruction,' which as Derrida has repeated in several places throughout his career, is not something that someone does but rather something that happens. Deconstruction is the unraveling at a crucial point of critique of the very logic that makes critique possible and necessary.[16]

## THE PRIMACY OF WRITING

In the related essays and in the book *De la Grammatologie,* all written within just a few years of each other, these two points – that no 'thinking' goes on outside the system and logic of signification and that pursuing the logic of signification to the end takes one not to a point of closure but rather to a moment, a deconstruction, at which logic threatens to become undone – became

the central occupation of Derrida's writing. He approached them by an extremely close reading of texts in which the act of writing was a central preoccupation – Freud's essay on writing, Saussure's *Cours Générale,* Lévi-Strauss's wonderful chapter on 'the writing lesson,' and Rousseau's reflections on writing in both the *Confessions* and the essay on the origin of Language.[17] In each of these works, Derrida examined the moment of deconstruction in which the coherence of a theoretical domain began to unravel. The act of writing occupied a central place in the critique of presence since throughout the history of the theory of language, the sonic substance of speech was always considered the primary signifier that delivered the signified concept in an intimacy so close to both the concept and the speakers that the sonic substance seemed to vanish, whereas the written mark was merely the sign of a sign. And yet, throughout this same history of linguistic theory, writing also seems to pose a fearful threat, whether formulated as the Socratic loss of memory, or the Saussurean 'false' norms of pronunciation caused by the spelling system. Using the logic of this contradiction – the written mark, the graph, is merely supplementary to speech; the written mark threatens the integrity of the speech system – as a wedge, Derrida's analysis pries open the deconstructive moment in which the system seems to invert itself: if there is no 'transcendental signified' then all signs are as it were secondary, and anything in experience that appears to be a signified 'thing' at all seems to be the outcome of what can only be thought of as a logically prior act of writing. Any single sign bears the trace of the never present 'primary' sign which is itself always the trace of another.[18]

The primacy of writing calls into question or causes to deconstruct the central place of thought (logocentrism) in all philosophical discourse and its intimate connection to the ideal of face-to-face argument (phonocentrism). [19] It thus makes inroads on what seem to be the most fundamental points of the western philosophical tradition – and this was exactly Derrida's point. Derrida's method of analysis during this period involved extremely close reading of texts from the philosophical and also literary traditions. This close reading was especially sensitive to the places where the logic that maintains the coherence of both the individual text and a textual tradition begins to break down, and it pursued that logical breakdown into a kind of unthinkable territory filled with entities that, like quarks in theoretical physics, bore a certain resemblance to concepts but did not behave as concepts traditionally behave. Many of his first American readers, especially those encountering his difficult texts made even more difficult by translation into English, rather quickly lined up as either partisans or detractors of what looked like a new method of reading, yet one with strong affinities to strains of extreme skepticism or fideism that had always been part of western philosophy and was particularly attractive among those thinkers who for various reasons were being lumped together as postmodern. Among the partisans, deconstruction rather rapidly became identified with a set of repeatable moves (an operational syntax) and a set of key words (a lexicon). Among these key words were writing, supplementarity, dissemination, and above all difference, especially in Derrida's coinage *différance*, a noun formed from the two verbs *to differ* and *to defer* and therefore carrying both meanings simultaneously, where the replacement of the second *e* by *a* can only be perceived visually in writing and not in speech. In rather short order, a new methodology, deconstructionism, was born.

## FROM DECONSTRUCTION TO DECONSTRUCTIONISM

Derrida himself, as he later acknowledged, was by no means entirely outside this appropriation of his work that turned deconstruction into a set of techniques although he was always critical of it. Here he summarizes a key part of the methodology as well as any student handbook:

One could even formulate or formalize (and I applied myself in this way at first) a certain consistency in these laws which made possible reading processes at once critical and critical of the idea of critique, processes of close reading, which could reassure those who in or outside the wake of New Criticism or some other formalism, felt it necessary to legitimize this ethics of close reading or internal reading. And among the examples of these procedural and formalizing formulae that I had proposed, and which were circulating precisely as possibilities, new possibilities offered by deconstruction, there was the reversal of a hierarchy. After having reversed a binary opposition, whatever it may be – speech/writing, man/woman, spirit/matter, signifier/signified, signified/signifier, master/slave, and so on – and after having liberated the subjugated and submissive term, one then proceeded to the generalization of this latter in new traits, producing a different concept, for example, another concept of writing such as trace, différance, gramme, text, and so on .... Although I am the last to find this useless, illegitimate, or contingent, I would say, nevertheless – I was already saying – that this slightly instrumentalizing implementation tended to reduce the impetus or the languages, the desire, the arrival so to speak, the future, of deconstructions ... [to] a body of possibilities, of faculties, indeed of facilities, in a word, a body of easily reproducible means, methods, and technical procedures, hence useful, utilizable; a body of rules and knowledge; a body of powerful know-how that would be at once understandable and offered for didactic transmission, susceptible of acquiring the academic status and dignity of a quasi-interdisciplinary discipline. For deconstructions migrate, hence the plurality, from philosophy to literary theory, law, architecture, et cetera.[20]

Taken as a method, what I am calling deconstructionism seemed to supply a repertory of questions and analytic operations for the historian at just the opportune moment. These operations and questions were relevant to some fundamentals of historical work that had grown seriously complicated within the context of the linguistic turn: 'evidence' and 'context' could no longer be discussed as if writing itself were incidental to their meaning. Moreover, it could similarly no longer be considered merely incidental that what the professional historian actually does, in order to do history at all, is write something, be it a book, an essay, a review, a conference paper, or a class lecture. The operations of routine historical work thus involve writing at every level. The techniques of deconstructionism first of all offered a new protocol for treating textual evidence that, put positively, promised to liberate its meaningfulness, extending the relevance of a piece of evidence into ever new domains. This possibility was extremely desirable in the context of the rise of social history and the search for an evidentiary basis for recovering the full experience of individuals and groups silenced by the documentary record as conventionally understood and conventionally analyzed by the profession. A strong protocol for the analysis of any system of signs, moreover, opened the way for cultural history.

Put negatively, deconstructionism seemed to suggest that there *was no meaning out there in the world*, that no text could provide any documentary evidence but merely proliferated empty semblances of meaning to infinity.[21] The deconstructionists, it was said, maintained that the historian's claim to be able to produce a verifiable account of the past out of a rigorous scrutiny of evidence was based on nothing more than a rhetorical trope; there was no escape from Nietzsche's famous prison house of language. The past seemed to recede forever out of the historian's grasp. If everything was language, the lived experience of the past threatened to disappear into mere chains of signifiers leading nowhere.

The threat to the stability of historical knowledge is of course more complicated and nuanced than the previous paragraph would suggest. From the perspective of deconstruction neither the individual piece of evidence nor its context is a separable entity but each individually and together form a network of complex and crossing relationships. For texts, too, are thoroughly permeated by the play of multiple systems of signification: rather than forming a bordered, and isolatable whole, any piece of writing is rather permeated by the whole system that makes writing possible. The individual text marks a position in relation to other texts and bears their traces. Just as a phoneme's meaning is constituted by its difference from other

possible phonemes so a text's meaning arises from its relation to other texts and the traces of these absent texts are an intrinsic part of it. This is true if only because no text is ever composed free of texts that pre-exist it and supply its writer with a conceptual apparatus, a way of speaking, and a provocation to write. These 'pre-texts' include especially but not exclusively those texts of which the text in question takes a direct account. They are cited, rewritten, avoided, dismissed, revised, or even ignored and silenced more or less overtly, more or less deliberately, and more or less consciously by the writer in order to make the new text. In this way the new text is inescapably the bearer of the traces of many others. On reflection, it is these others that are its context, and thus, while the context seems to stand outside the text as other, it is perhaps more precise to see the context as inside the text, organized by it, and informing its every level. What looks like two domains, a text contained by its larger context, is rather an intertextual relation, a set of points in a series that increases exponentially beyond comprehension, and thus beyond definitive closure within any possible meaning system.

One professional reaction to this theoretical challenge has been to see deconstruction not as something that happens but rather as a set of operations that one can pick and choose among and use pragmatically.[22] Another, and perhaps the most frequent, is to adopt what we can call a weak form of deconstruction. This primarily involves continuing to do the analytic and synthetic work of history, in the Kuhnean sense of operating within the professional paradigm, while being especially sensitive to the logical or meta-historical operations that make the professional paradigm possible. The embrace of deconstruction in the weak sense is especially apparent among those historians who identify themselves as heirs to the linguistic turn especially as exemplified by the anthropological thick description associated with the pioneering work of Clifford Geertz. In this work, however, the phrase *deconstructing something* frequently means little more than analyzing it although usually with the added resonance of taking the process of analysis into conscious account. Thus Gabrielle Spiegel, a historian as sensitive as any to the implications of postmodern theoretical developments, makes a strong contrast between two historical operations. On the one hand, the historian's principal act is *constructive*, for perhaps uniquely among the disciplines the object of inquiry, the past, is not given at the beginning of inquiry but constructed as its end. On the other hand, Spiegel argues, work the historian performs on any material text that has to be read is necessarily *deconstructive*. In this distinction she contrasts the historical work of constructing the context as 'writing' with the work of deciphering the meaning of a document as 'reading.'[23] Deconstruction certainly stimulated Spiegel's nuanced and important reflections on what de Certeau calls 'the historical operation,'[24] but from the perspective of deconstruction, the logic of Spiegel's argument is untenable. The contrasts here between construction and deconstruction, reading and writing, transparent document and self-conscious literary text all are all based on the fundamental propositions of metaphysics that deconstruction has already undermined.

## DECONSTRUCTION BEYOND METHODOLOGY

The deeper critique that a rigorous deconstruction raises has more to do with the metaphysical underpinnings of any sense of 'meaning' in history than with the local questions raised by attention to genre, intertextuality, and the pressure of other texts – which include any sort of structured symbolic activities such as kinship systems or ritual practices – on the archival or evidentiary basis of historical analysis. These metaphysical underpinnings include but are not limited to all distinctions between the sensible and intelligible, the empirical and conceptual, the social and cultural, etc. They are obviously at the core of philosophical idealism including Hegelian and historicist 'philosophy of history,' which are underwritten by a history of philosophy understood as the progressive revelation, unveiling, or uncovering of the truth of human existence. And they are equally obviously at the core of all other versions of progressive revelation, such as narratives of the triumph of capitalism or of the rise of the nation state that still haunt academic disciplines such as art history, musicology, and literary studies that have their roots in classical philology. Less obviously, these same metaphysical underpinnings seem to be inescapable in any sense of meaningfulness in the historian's attempt to 'understand the past.' That is, while most working American or Anglo-American historians would vehemently deny that there is any place in their work for 'a grand narrative' – an ultimately theological or mythic 'big story' implicitly claiming to be the progressive revelation of a truth in time – any account of 'change over time,' or any claim that a partial reconstruction of 'the past,' even one rigorously based on archival evidence, is a meaningful index of human life, still needs a whole conceptual and a priori logical apparatus. Notions of cause, varying levels of causation, relations of part to whole, notions of agency both individual and collective, the difference between appearance and reality, indeed the whole apparatus of understanding itself, all absolutely inseparable from historical work at its most basic level, have been deeply structured by the assumptions of metaphysics as they have historically been developed from, say, Plato to Heidegger. Once this tradition of philosophical idealism is seen as a moment in the history of philosophy rather than as 'the rules of truth itself' it becomes deeply suspect as being the generator of the very 'truth' that it claims to reveal.

For the historian, the full appreciation of Derrida's critique of the fundamentals of the western philosophical tradition leads to a sense of historical possibility much different from the caricatural notion that Derrida claims that meaning does not exist. Above all, Derrida's work does not supply a 'new' technique of reading, nor a 'new' conceptual vocabulary, although his work certainly was, for a time, used this way by others who picked up certain key terms that did little more than signal that their users were insiders in the coterie. Nevertheless, Derrida has also provided a powerful example of close reading that has opened narrative evidence to new kinds of historical analysis. No longer could a medieval chronicle, for example, be read as a primarily 'unreliable' compendium of facts scattered about in a fabulous plot based on a superstitious and credulous world-view that the historian must ignore. Rather, the analysis of genre, rhetorical conventions, the formal and structural operations that shape the text and associate it with myriad other texts, in brief, the analysis of the whole textual system of which the chronicle is a part, has yielded important positive knowledge about the living historical actors who produced and used the text in question.[25] As noted above, the intense focus on the fundamental workings of symbolic systems of all sorts was vital to the new ways of construing evidence by social and cultural historians that made possible a much fuller account of those whose lives were not documented archivally in conventional ways. This evidentiary opening coincides with a renewed sense of the provisionality of all accounts of the past that claim to be coherent. From this perspective, all historical work is necessarily revisionary, and no word will ever be the last word. The sense of the interminable openness of the past to those who come after is a direct outcome of derridean critique.

All Derrida's work arises out of his confrontation with the past of philosophy, and it develops from extremely attentive and powerful readings of the texts that constitute that past. Derrida's later work, however, was overtly addressed to the future or rather to the possibility of a future. Manifestly written within the tradition of ethical and political philosophy, this later work reveals that it was ethical questions and political engagement that drove Derrida's work from its earliest day.[26] The critique of the past, addressed to its most fundamental questions, was not at all

motivated by what Heidegger called the basic question of ontology – why are there beings at all rather than nothing?[27] It was always motivated by the ethically and politically engaged question, what is to come?[28] Can we imagine, let alone achieve, a society without structural injustice? What is the place of violence in human experience? To what are we appealing when we refer to a 'democracy to come,' obviously different from whatever it is that we call democracy now? In brief, Derrida's profound critical engagement with the past has always been in the service of the engaged attempt to open the future to the possibility of differing in some essential way from the past, of a humanity not being sentenced to reiterate the past, and especially past atrocity, without end. In the service of this future, the work is itself deeply historical even as it has called into question the possibility of historical understanding. In the discussion after the presentation of 'Structure, Sign and Play' at Johns Hopkins, Jean Hippolyte noted the possible parallel between Derrida's paper and certain developments in natural science, adducing among others, Einsteinian relativity and the play of chance in biological mutation. At the beginning of his long intervention he asked 'is that what you are tending toward?' and then continued to speak at some length. Finally, Derrida replied: 'But you were asking a question. I was wondering myself if I know where I am going. So I would answer you by saying, first, that I am trying, precisely to put myself at a point so that I do not know any longer where I am going.'[29] Derrida's work was a life-long journey into philosophy to the end of the line.

## NOTES AND REFERENCES

1   John E. Toews, 'Intellectual history after the linguistic turn: the autonomy of meaning and the irreducibility of experience,' *American Historical Review* 92 (1987). From the vantage point afforded by the passage of more than another two decades since the appearance of that essay, it is striking that the title placed the essay most definitely 'after' the linguistic turn, while in the body of the work Toews worried constantly whether or not history *should*

take a linguistic turn, as if it were both a matter of individual choice and an avoidable institutional contingency. That the linguistic turn constituted an irrevocable and irreversible alteration in the practice of history is undeniable.

2 Jacques Derrida, *De la Grammatologie* (Paris: Editions de Minuit, 1967); *L'Écriture et la Différence* (Paris: Editions du Seuil, 1967); 'La différance,' in *Théorie d'Ensemble, Collections Tel Quel* (Paris: Éditions du Seuil, 1968); 'Le puits et la pyramide: introduction à la sémiologie de Hegel,' in *Hegel et la Pensée Moderne; Séminaire sur Hegel Dirigé par Jean Hyppolite au Collège de France (1967–1968)*, ed. Jacques d'Hondt (Paris: Presses Universitaires de France, 1970); and 'Ousia et grammé: note sur une note de Sein und Zeit,' in *L'Endurance de la Pensée* (Paris: Plon, 1968).

3 A key event in the American formation of French Theory was the symposium, 'The languages of criticism and the sciences of man' at the Johns Hopkins University in 1966 intended to introduce structuralism to the American academy. The conference consisted of papers in several languages, primarily English and French, and the proceedings were published entirely in English in 1970 and then again in 1972 as Richard Macksey, Eugenio Donato, and Johns Hopkins University Humanities Center, *The Structuralist Controversy: The Languages of Criticism and the Sciences of Man*, Johns Hopkins paperback (Baltimore: Johns Hopkins University Press, 1972). The paperback publication was a bombshell. While the Americans were grappling with Wayne Booth (*Rhetoric of Fiction*, 1961) and Northrop Frye (*Anatomy of Criticism*, 1957), the French philosophers had already subjected structuralism to a serious and sustained critique. Derrida's contribution to this symposium, 'La structure, le signe, et le jeu,' will be discussed later in this chapter.

4 For two particularly brilliant readings of this aspect of Derrida see Edward Said, 'Criticism between culture and system,' in *The World, The Text, and The Critic* (Cambridge, MA: Harvard University Press, 1983) and Gayatri Chakravorty Spivak, *A Critique of Postcolonial Reason: Toward a History of the Vanishing Present* (Cambridge, MA: Harvard University Press, 199), 248–69, 423–31.

5 See for example, William H. Sewell, 'The concept(s) of culture,' in *Beyond the Cultural Turn: New Directions in the Study of Society and Culture*, ed. Victoria E. Bonnell and Lynn Hunt (Berkeley: University of California Press, 1999). For the last 15 years, Bedford Publications has commissioned a series of pedagogical handbooks treating canonical works of literature. Each volume includes a Marxist, a psychoanalytic, and a 'deconstructionist' essay among others, each commissioned especially for the handbook and intended to illustrate critical methodologies to be emulated by undergraduate students. Most egregious was the unfortunate *New York Times* obituary, Jonathan Kandell, 'Jacques Derrida, abstruse theorist, dies at 74,' *The New York Times*, 10 October 2004; in *Le Monde* Derrida was treated as a public intellectual of wide interest.

6 See especially Jacques Derrida, *La Voix et le Phénomène, Introduction au Problème du Signe dans la Phénoménologie*

*de Husserl*, Epiméthée (Paris: Presses universitaires de France, 1967); Jacques Derrida and Edmund Husserl, *Edmund Husserl, L'Origine de la Géométrie*, Epiméthée (Paris: Presses universitaires de France, 1962).

7 'The term "phenomenology" expresses a maxim that can be formulated: "To the things themselves!" It is opposed to all free-floating constructions and accidental findings; it is also opposed to taking over concepts only seemingly demonstrated; and likewise to pseudo-questions which often are spread abroad as "problems" for generations.' Martin Heidegger, *Being and Time*, trans. Joan Stambaugh (Albany: State University of New York, 2010), 26.

8 Sewell, 'The concept(s) of culture,' 44. The notion of 'the autonomy of meaning' that Toews makes reference to in his title evokes precisely that aspect of structuralist analysis that Derrida will subject to critique.

9 'On a donc toujours pensé que le centre, qui par définition est unique, constituait, dans une structure, cela même qui commandant la structure, échappe à la structuralité. C'est pourquoi, pour une pensée classique de la structure, le centre peut être dit, paradoxalement, dans la structure et hors de la structure.' Jacques Derrida, 'La structure, le signe et le jeu dans le discours des sciences humaines,' in *L'Écriture et la Différence* (Paris: Editions du Seuil, 1967), 410. Unless otherwise noted, all translations are my own.

10 Ibid. 'C'est pourquoi on pourrait peut-être dire que le mouvement de toute archéologie, comme celui de toute eschatologie, est complice de cette réduction de la structuralité de la structure et tente toujours de penser cette dernière depuis une présence pleine et hors jeu.'

11 Ibid., 411.

12 Ibid. 'C'est alors le moment où le langage envahit le champ problématique universel; c'est alors le moment où, en l'absence de centre ou d'origine, tout devient discours – à condition de s'entendre sur ce mot – c'est-à-dire système dans lequel le signifié central, originaire ou transcendantal, n'est jamais absolument présent hors d'un système de différences: l'absence de signifié transcendantal étend à l'infini le champ et le jeu de la signification.'

13 Ibid., 412. 'Ce cercle est unique et il décrit la forme du rapport entre l'histoire de la métaphysique et la destruction de l'histoire de la métaphysique ... nous ne disposons d'aucun langage – d'aucune syntaxe et d'aucun lexique – qui soit étranger à cette histoire; nous ne pouvons énoncer aucune proposition destructrice qui n'ait déjà dû *se glisser dans la forme, dans la logique et les postulations implicites de cela même qu'elle voudrait contester.*' It is noteworthy here that Derrida is still using the closest French analog to Heidegger's *Destruktion* or *Abbau*. *Deconstruction* only enters Derrida's vocabulary in 1967 or 1968. It is a rare word in French, referring primarily to taking apart something such as a large machine for purposes of transportation. The closest literal English translation of it would have been 'dismantling.' Derrida explained that he was dissatisfied with *destruction* as the translation of *Abbau* since the French word always has the strong implication of *annihilation* not part of the German sense. On Derrida's choice of

deconstruction see his 'Lettre à un ami japonais', in *Psyche: Inventions de l'Autre* (Paris: Galilée, 2003). See also Spivak, *Critique of Postcolonial Reason*: 423–5.

14　Derrida, 'La structure, le signe et le jeu,' 413.

15　In the most down to earth terms, what we call, say, Kantian philosophy is in fact a series of written texts that themselves conform to the particular generic protocols that distinguish them from such things as social history or romantic novels. On this point the working historian J.H. Hexter was as good a Derridean as Derrida when, in an article that he said he would have preferred to title 'Footnotes, Quotations, and Name-lists,' he discussed the stylistic characteristics that identify history writing as what it is and distinguish it from the report of a physicist or a lyric poem. J.H. Hexter, 'The rhetoric of history,' in *History and Theory: Contemporary Readings*, ed. Brian Fay, Philip Pomper, and Richard T. Vann (Malden, MA: Blackwell, 1998).

16　To take two examples of the insistence among many, 'Deconstruction is not a method or some tool that you apply to something from the outside. Deconstruction is something which happens and which happens inside: there is a deconstruction at work within Plato's work, for instance.' Jacques Derrida and John D. Caputo, 'Deconstruction in a nutshell: A conversation with Jacques Derrida,' in *Perspectives in Continental Philosophy* (New York: Fordham University Press, 1997).The paper was originally delivered by Derrida in English as published. A second example: 'First, very quickly, it was shown that *deconstruction*, if this word has a sense that does not let itself be appropriated, was indissociable from a process and a law of expropriation or ex-appropriation proper that resists in the last instance, in order to challenge it, every subjective movement of appropriation of the following sort: *I* deconstruct, or *we* deconstruct, or we have the *power* and the *method* that make it possible. Deconstruction, if there be such a thing, happens; it is what happens, and this is what happens: it deconstructs itself, and it can become neither the power nor the possibility of an "I can." I insist here on the "it happens" because what I would like to make clear later on is this affirmation of the event, of the arrival or the future at the beating heart of a reflection on the impossible.' Jacques Derrida, 'Deconstructions: the im-possible,' in *French Theory in America*, ed. Sylvère Lotringer and Sande Cohen (New York: Routledge, 2001), 20. This was originally given in French as a paper at NYU in 1997. The translation here by Michael Taormina seems to be the only remaining record of the paper since the original has been lost.

17　See above note 2.

18　Cf. François Wahl, 'Without *origin*. There it is, the theme *par excellence* of Derrida's thought. In order for a play of differences to function, every difference must be retained (traced) in the others: the play is suspended from a trace, but each trace only exists as the trace of another trace, and there is no first one of them. "*The trace is the absolute origin* of meaning in general": that is to say that "*there is no absolute origin* of meaning in general"

[quoting *De la Grammatologie*, 95].' François Wahl, 'La philosophie entre l'avant et l'après du structuralisme,' in *Qu'est-ce que le Structuralisme?*, ed. François Wahl (Paris: Éditions du seuil, 1968), 429. Emphasis in the original.

19　Cf. Derrida's eloquent presentation of intimacy of voice with thought throughout the history of philosophy: 'The concept of the sign (signifier/signified) carries in itself the necessity of privileging the phonic substance and of raising up linguistics as the "patron" of semiology. The *phoné* is in effect the signifying substance that *offers itself to consciousness* as the signified concept most intimately close-knit to thought. From this point of view, the voice is consciousness itself. When I speak, not only am I conscious of being present to what I think, but also of keeping as close as possible to my thought or to the concept a signifier that does not fall into the world, a signifier that I understand as soon as I emit it, which seems to depend on my pure and free spontaneity, which does not require the use of any instrument, or any accessory, or of any force grasped in the world. Not only do the signifier and the signified seem to be united, but, in this confounding the signifier seems to vanish or become transparent in order to let the concept present itself by itself as that which is, without referring to anything other than its own presence. The exteriority of the signifier seems reduced. Naturally, this experience is an illusion, but it is an illusion on whose necessity a whole structure or a whole epoch has organized itself. On the foundation of this epoch a whole semiology is constituted whose concepts and fundamental presuppositions are very precisely recoverable from Plato to Husserl, passing by way of Aristotle, Rousseau, Hegel, etc.' ('Le concept de signe (signifiant/signifié) porte en lui-même la nécessité de privilégier la substance phonique e d'ériger la linguistique en "patron" de la sémiologie. La phoné est en effet la substance signifiante qui se donne à la conscience comme le plus intimement unie à la pensée du concept signifié. La voix est, de ce point de vue, la conscience elle-même. Quand je parle, non seulement j'ai conscience d'être présent à ce que je pense, mais aussi de garder au plus proche de ma pensée ou du "concept" un signifiant qui ne tombe pas dans le monde, que j'entends aussitôt que je l'émets, qui semble dépendre de ma pure et libre spontanéité, n'exiger l'usage d'aucun instrument, d'aucun accessoire, d'aucune force prise dans le monde. Non seulement le signifiant et le signifié semblent s'unir, mais, dans cette confusion, le signifiant semble s'effacer ou devenir transparent pour laisser le concept se présenter lui-même, comme ce qu'il est, ne renvoyant à rien d'autre qu'à sa présence. L'extériorité du signifiant semble réduite. Naturellement, cette expérience est un leurre, mais un leurre sur la nécessité duquel s'est organisée toute une structure, ou toute une époque; sur le fonds de cette époque une sémiologie s'est constituée dont les concepts et les présupposés fondamentaux sont très précisément repérables de Platon à Husserl, en passant par Aristote, Rousseau, Hegel, etc.' Jacques Derrida and Henri Ronse, *Positions; Entretiens avec Henri Ronse, Julia Kristeva, Jean-Louis Houdebine,*

*Guy Scarpetta*, Collection 'Critique' (Paris: Éditions de Minuit, 1972), 32–3.

20 Derrida, 'Deconstructions: the im-possible,' 18–20.

21 For a thorough and nuanced presentation of both the positive and negative reception of deconstruction in the profession of history see Gabrielle M. Spiegel, 'History, historicism, and the social logic of the text,' in *The Past as Text: The Theory and Practice of Medieval Historiography* (Baltimore: Johns Hopkins University Press, 1997), especially 10–21.

22 To cite one example among many, William Sewell, whose contributions to the philosophy of history are far reaching, finds what he calls the 'deconstructionist argument' that linguistic meaning is always unstable due to 'the signifying mechanism of language itself' 'entirely compatible with a [social] practice perspective on culture' interested in the way social actors negotiate among conflicting structures – economic, political, etc. – that affect social practice. In a footnote he adds: 'This is not, of course, the usual conclusion arrived at by deconstructionists, who would insist that these "other structures" are no less textual than semiotic structures and that making sense of them is purely a matter of intertextuality. This epistemological and perhaps ontological difference between my position and that of deconstruction should make it clear that I am appropriating from deconstruction specific ideas that I find useful rather than adopting a full-scale deconstructionist position.' Sewell, 'The concept(s) of culture,' 50–1 and note 29.

23 'Since the historical text is not given but must be constructed, the historian of texts is a writer in his or her function of constituting the historical narrative, but a reader of the already materially existent text. The task facing the one is broadly constructive; the other, broadly deconstructive.' Spiegel, 'Social logic,' 22. What little of deconstruction remains here vanishes completely when later in the same paragraph Spiegel contrasts texts read within the discipline of literary criticism, 'commonly distinguished as "literary" (self-reflective)' those read by historians as 'documentary (in theory, transparent).' If deconstruction has shown us anything it is that not a single one of these distinctions is tenable. One turns a text into a document, for example, by a very particular professional protocol of reading. A rigorous deconstruction calls the axiomatics of that protocol profoundly into question.

24 Michel de Certeau, *The Writing of History*, trans. Tom Conley (New York: Columbia University Press, 1988), 56–115.

25 See for example the ground-breaking work of Natalie Zemon Davis collected in Natalie Zemon Davis, *Society and Culture in Early Modern France: Eight Essays* (Stanford, Calif.: Stanford University Press, 1975). See also her *Fiction in the Archives: Pardon Tales and Their Tellers in Sixteenth-Century France*, The Harry Camp lectures at Stanford University (Stanford, Calif.: Stanford University Press, 1987). For medieval examples see Thomas N. Bisson, *Tormented Voices: Power, Crisis, and Humanity in Rural Catalonia, 1140–1200* (Cambridge, Mass.: Harvard University Press, 1998); Felice Lifshitz, *The Name of the Saint: The Martyrology of Jerome and Access to the Sacred in Francia, 627–827*, Publications in Medieval Studies (Notre Dame, Ind.: University of Notre Dame Press, 2006); Felice Lifshitz, *The Norman Conquest of Pious Neustria: Historiographic Discourse and Saintly Relics, 684–1090*, Studies and Texts (Toronto, Ontario: Pontifical Institute of Mediaeval Studies, 1995); Gabrielle M. Spiegel, *Romancing the Past* (Berkeley: University of California Press, 1993).

26 Among the most directly politically and ethically centered later works see especially the following by Jacques Derrida: *Politiques de l'Amitié; Suivi de L'Oreille de Heidegger*, Collection La Philosophie en Effet (Paris: Galilée, 1994); *Donner la Mort* (Paris: Galilee, 1999); and *Spectres de Marx: L'état de la Dette, le Travail du Deuil et la Nouvelle Internationale*, Collection La Philosophie en Effet (Paris: Editions Galilée, 1993). For a bibliography of Derrida's work see Peter Zeillinger, *Jacques Derrida: Bibliographie der Französischen, Deutschen und Englischen Werke* (Wien: Turia + Kant, 2005).

27 Martin Heidegger, *Introduction to Metaphysics*, trans. Gregory Fried and Richard Polt (New Haven: Yale University Press, 2000), especially 1–7.

28 Throughout his writings, of the two words that signify futurity in French (*futur* and *avenir*), Derrida has always preferred *avenir* because of the concrete, experiential force of its etymology, *a-venir*, to come.

29 Macksey, Donato, and Johns Hopkins University Humanities Center, *The Structuralist Controversy: The Languages of Criticism and the Sciences of Man*, 267. Cf. the whole last section of Derrida, 'Deconstructions: the im-possible,' 23–7; especially 'If an event is possible, that is, if it inscribes itself within the conditions of possibility, if it does nothing but make explicit, unveil, reveal, accomplish what is already possible, then it is not an event. For an event to take place, for it to be possible, as event, as invention, it must be the arrival of the impossible. There we see a poor proof, an evidence that is nothing less than evident' (27); and 'This means that the event of invention, if there be such a thing, can never present itself as such to a theoretical or observing judgment, to a historical judgment of the observing sort, a determining judgment, permitting itself to say: invention exists, it presents itself; it falls to this subject, to this community of subjects capable of claiming it as their own, of reappropriating it for themselves' (24).

# 10

# The Return of Rhetoric

Hans Kellner

To speak of the return of rhetoric brings to mind at once the 'linguistic turn' that has for decades preoccupied most of the human sciences, and notably history. This attention to the role of language in the conceptual shaping of scholarly discourses of reality should in fact be seen as poetics, a sub-category of rhetoric. The talk of a 'linguistic turn' in historical studies and throughout the human sciences has been notably imprecise. References to linguistics are rarely made, nor are the basic disciplinary distinctions among the discourses that take the functional uses of language as their realm often honored. Thus, poetics, rhetoric, and discourse analysis may be invoked, but without the goal of either advancing those fields or of rigorously practicing their methods.

The revived interest in the discursive aspects of history (and of non-literary prose in general) has occluded the traditional distinctions among linguistics, poetics, rhetoric, and discourse studies. Because the thrust of these discussions has been toward identifying the nature of history rather than the capabilities of the tools involved, and because the scholars who pursued such questions were not literarily, let alone rhetorically, trained, the so-called Linguistic Turn had little concern for separating the properly rhetorical

from the poetic or linguistic in general. Indeed, the lessening of distinctions (such as the one between fiction and its others), in order to benefit from the perspectives thus obtained, has been the effect, if not explicitly the goal, of the whole enterprise. A broad discussion of discourse and history is found in Robert Berkhofer's *Beyond the Great Story* (1995), Philippe Carrard's *Poetics of the New History* (1992) examined the French *Annales* School from the perspective of stucturalist poetics, and Ann Rigney's *The Rhetoric of Historical Representation* (1990) focused on the representation of certain events of the French Revolution to deploy an array of linguistic tools. Yet rhetoric in its fundamental, broader sense as a meta-discourse is only partly addressed by the linguistic turn. Indeed, the force of rhetorical developments in history may at times lead away from language; it certainly involves a whole panoply of issues not usually understood as part of the linguistic turn. To think of the linguistic turn without regard to the shaping power of rhetoric in its broader sense is to miss the inter-connection of developments in historical studies. It ratifies the 'restricted' sense of rhetoric proposed by the Renaissance, endorsed by the Enlightenment, institutionalized by literary theory in the nineteenth century, but rejected in the latter part of the twentieth, when a return to the fullest sense of rhetoric took place.

## RESPONSES TO THE OLD DEBATES

In 1958 discourse about history asked the questions: to what extent is history a science? If it is a science, what kind of science? And how can this be demonstrated? A new journal, *History and Theory*, was a leader in this questioning; the social sciences model was then regnant. Carl Hempel had proposed that historical explanations were covered by general laws in an influential article of 1942; for decades, his problematic had to be addressed. Fifteen years later, the philosopher Alan Donagan still divided historical explanation into Hempelian Theory and Non-Hempelian Theories (Donagan 1959, 428–43). The dialect of discussion was philosophical; actual written history appears, if at all, in the form of brief exemplary statements. For example, one might find:

> Luchaire, after discussing various famines in twelfth-century France, says: 'Famine produced brigandage.' The illustration suits our point very well. No doubt the generalization involved is not very clear, and one might hesitate before saying that all famines are followed by brigandage. Nevertheless, whatever qualifications are necessary to make the generalization involved true, the resulting statements would contain the terms 'famine' and 'brigandage.' (M. White 1959, 366)

Any link between this philosophy of history and the discourse of historians was obscure. Historical disagreements stubbornly resisted the solvent powers of logic from this viewpoint. The ideological divides of the postwar world were no less wide than those that preceded it, after all. History still wasn't telling an agreed-upon tale or providing a basis for moral decision.

One philosopher who found his empirical tools inadequate to the task of studying justice wrote:

> Similarly, if experience and calculation, combined according to the precepts of logical empiricism, leave no place for practical reason and do not enable us to justify our decisions and choices, must we not seek out other techniques of reasoning for that purpose? In other words, is there a logic of value judgments that makes it possible for us to reason about values instead of making them depend solely on irrational choices, based on interest, passion, prejudice, and myth? (Perelman 2001, 1389)

What Chaim Perelman discovered was that he lacked a theory of argument, and that such a theory existed in ancient rhetoric, which he realized had been grossly misrepresented. Misled by the school lessons presenting a rhetoric of ornament and artful expression, he came to realize that rhetoric provided a full description of human behavior and the sort of thing he needed in order to think about intractable positions.

Shortly after Perelman had published his *New Rhetoric* (with L. Olbrecht-Tyteca, 1958), largely a re-encounter with the old rhetoric, Northrop Frye set forth a vision of history's place in the world of words. Citing the term 'metahistory' (used to describe Toynbee), to refer to the grand mythic works that have the greatest impact on the public, Frye maintained that such works resemble poetry, particularly in their use of large-scale analogies such as the solar analogy of *The Decline of the West* (Spengler, 1934). Yet when he turned to the work of the 'historian proper,' at the other end of the spectrum from the poetic metahistory, he used language clearly drawn from ancient poetics. 'We notice also that the historian proper tends to confine his verbal imitations of action to human events. His instinct is to look always for the human cause; he avoids the miraculous or the providential. The poet, of course, is under no such limitation' (Frye 1963, 54). The fact that some regarded metahistory as 'bastard history,' in the same sense that some logicians may view metaphysics as bastard logic, creates a certain symmetry; but it fails to underscore the failure to recognize that literature is an element of the whole spectrum, because it is 'an area of verbal imitation mid-way between events and ideas,' facing the world of action in one direction and the conceptual world in the other (Frye 1963, 55).

The third step in the background I am sketching here came at the end of the 1960s, when the prestige of linguistics and its attention to structures convinced Roland Barthes and others that a science of discourse might be possible. It would provide an understanding of the toughest problem of all: how meaning can be drawn from reality. Barthes explicitly calls his tools a 'second linguistics,' a tribute to ancient rhetoric, which he took to be the first. He asks whether historical discourse, 'the narration of past events,' differs from imaginary narration as found in the standard literary genres (Barthes 1986, 127). Barthes uses an array of Jakobsonian linguistic devices to show that reality is an effect of narrative; when we find narrative, we take it to be a sign of the real, and that reality is itself proven by its narrative form. Barthes adds that the structural histories of the 'New History' mark the death of narrative because 'the sign of history is no longer the real but the intelligible' (Barthes 1986, 140). Among the rhetorical/linguistic terms that entered Barthes's essay were a pair that had been known to linguists since Roman Jakobson had used them to describe forms of aphasia. Metaphor and metonymy became two poles of discourse organization, and Barthes uses them to distinguish the 'lyric and symbolic' Michelet from the functional epic tendency of Augustin Thierry (Barthes 1986, 136–7).

In Perelman, Frye, and Barthes we find exemplars of the revival of rhetoric, poetics, and an invigorated linguistics; it was the displacement of logical empiricism by an attention to argument and audience, the notion that discourse could best be understood by its place in a total spectrum of archetypal forms, the demonstration that the meaning of all stories was produced by the same devices, whether the stories related the real or something else. The appearance in 1966 of an issue of the French journal *Communications* devoted to 'L'analyse structurale du récit' solidified the

edifice of narrative theory. Barthes, Greimas, Bremond, Eco, Metz, Todorov, and Genette contributed important essays, establishing the new rhetorical focus. I say rhetorical, and yet it is undeniable that these – Frye, Barthes, and the French group – usually referred to their work as a poetics. Poetics, of course, is almost as old as rhetoric, and shares an Aristotelian framework. Traditionally, however, poetics deals with the work as an object, a thing of form in itself; rhetoric, on the other hand, stresses its practical roots in conflict and two-sided debate. Poetics studies texts; rhetoric emphasizes production for a particular audience at a given time. Neither truth nor beauty is the point. Winning is, and the joy of performance. It would seem, then, that the return of rhetoric is misnamed. Even when Barthes, for example, explicitly writes about rhetoric, it is for poetic purposes. And yet, I shall insist, the wave of interest that begins in the 1960s, crests in the 1970s and 1980s, and takes a new form by the end of the century, is thoroughly rhetorical, because poetics is a branch of rhetoric.

In what follows, I shall show in a brief and incomplete way how the developments in historical theory and practice can be plotted over some of the basic elements of rhetoric in its classic form. Most important, perhaps, is the idea that historical *argumentation* is a primary factor, even the guiding force, in historical writing; research, in other words, is guided by the argument that defines what is relevant and not. Because arguments are made locally, for specific audiences at specific moments, it is important to understand the nature of the historical *audience*, although this is an area that has received relatively little attention. Audiences will be persuaded by the perceived authority of the historian, his or her *ethos*; historical ethos is what is at stake in all the discussions about the historian's objectivity, or personal partisanship. These core discussions of argumentation, audience, and ethos are thoroughly rhetorical, although they have little to do with formal considerations and are rarely understood as part of the linguistic turn. Beyond this, however, I shall demonstrate that the five *canons* of rhetoric, as antique as they may seem, remain a remarkably vital and comprehensive way of looking at a discourse such as history. In *invention, arrangement, style, memory,* and *delivery,* we find a theory of discourse with more than merely historical interest, despite several thousand years of service. What the canons can teach us is that there is a certain unity to the many disparate historical manifestations mentioned here – the unity of human intentions and motivations. To deploy even a few of the tools of rhetoric is to remind ourselves that historical discourse is also a form of historical, that is to say rhetorical, action.

## ARGUMENTATION: IT'S ALWAYS *SOMEONE'S* ARGUMENT

Historical argument takes itself out of the realm of science, even so mild a form of science as social science, and into the space of human life, which is just the space it claims to address. Argument is always partial, always someone's argument, always a form of special pleading. It is rhetoric, no more and no less, governed and propelled by the maligned canons and figures that first formalized discourse two and a half millennia ago. It is no surprise that rhetoric has been an unwelcome guest at the celebrations of historical virtue. Argument is itself an embarrassment; it is always many-sided, of the moment, aimed at a specific target, playful, and virtuosic. Yet argumentation, the heart of rhetoric, has come to the fore of historical theory, challenging the notion that historical discourse presents past events, rather than practicing persuasion.

The question may be put thus: does historical discourse essentially report or argue? Here, the traditional hierarchy of forms representing past events comes into play: annals, chronicle, and history demonstrate a movement toward argument and rhetoric. That is to say, the annals, which gathers recorded events and places them in order without a governing plan beyond sequence, is close to a pure report of 'what happened,' without regard for questions of meaning. Chronicles have a governing center, usually an institution or a ruling group, but what meaning there is remains highly restricted. Despite the French-inspired anti-narrative productions of the second half of the twentieth century, full historical treatment of the past, as defined for two centuries, is fundamentally narrative, dependent upon, and embedded within, a story that is always understood. What a narrative provides, as Aristotle stressed, is a plot, *mythos*, which gives an organic form and meaning to the whole. In other words, it makes an argument.

In the last quarter of the twentieth century, discussions of historical theory have returned again and again to issues of history as persuasive discourse. The heart of any rhetoric is the relationship between the audience and the speaker, areas that have been but little addressed by historians, who often take for granted the interests, needs, and capacities of the historical reader and the professionalization, competency, and impartiality of the historian. Before looking to the canon of rhetoric that defines the nature of the historical work, we must attend to the receptivity of the historical reader, the audience, and to the *ethos*, or authority of the historian.

Hayden White described the 'de-rhetoricization' of historical studies as a reaction to the realization, noted by Kant, that a rhetorically self-aware historical studies would be inherently antithetical to firm judgments about the basic questions regarding human existence:

The important point is that the variety of uses to which written history's subordination to rhetoric permitted it to be put exposed historical thinking to the threat of being conceived solely in terms of Kant's third type, the farce: as long as history was subordinated to rhetoric, the historical field itself (that is, the past or the historical process) had to be viewed as a chaos that made no sense at all or one that could be made to bear as many sense as wit and rhetorical talent could impose on it. Accordingly, the disciplining of historical thinking that had to be undertaken if history considered as a kind of knowledge was to be established as arbitrator of the realism of contending political programs, each attended by its own philosophy of history, had first of all to consist of a rigorous de-rhetoricization. (H. White 1987, 65)

This de-rhetorization was, in White's view, an attempt to create a new kind of audience for history, an audience that would accept the past as a given thing with a given meaning that figured forth an inescapable political and social regime. A rhetorical view of the past as a field of competing arguments to reflect upon – the older vision of an eighteenth-century audience – was taken to be a dangerous thing.

## AUDIENCE: WHO READS HISTORY?

As Reinhart Koselleck has reminded us, until the mid-eighteenth century, one spoke of histories, in the plural, rather than history as a singular thing; in the same way, freedom as a universal notion replaced the freedoms of designated groups, justice replaced rights, progress became a singular force, and the Revolution superseded the normal cyclical revolutions of things (Koselleck 1985, 31). In the case of history, this change certified that history would cease to be understood as a rhetorical performance in the interest of some wider and interested argument, and would become, at least in principle, a transparent and disinterested attempt to represent the past, without the 'colors' and partisanship of the past. So a new historical reader was manufactured, one with a new perspective.

According to Lionel Gossman, the frequent eighteenth-century comparisons between historical narrative and history painting underlined the peculiarly rhetorical perspectival placement of the audience in both genres. Instead of being placed in immediate relation to the object of narration, the reader, like the narrator, was to be placed at a distance from it, so that it appeared to him as if it were situated in a framed and closed space upon which he could look out, as through a window (Gossman 1990, 238).

The advantage of this artistic strategy was to subordinate the part, the detail or fact or personality, to the whole, which could be grasped by stepping back to survey the entire narrative canvas, as it were. Different members of the audience might well relate differently to this presentation: the aristocrat, who may have participated in the action depicted or known the protagonists, would dwell on details, while the bourgeois reader, not yet a potent historical actor in the eighteenth century, would have the ability to survey and master the whole picture, to truly read it by reducing it to a meaningful thing, neither too small with detail, nor too vast with philosophical or theological pleading (Gossman 1990, 238–9):

> What was important was not so much the truth of the narrative so much as the activity of reflecting about the narrative, including that of reflecting about its truth. History, in the eighteenth century, raised questions and created conditions in which the individual subject, the critical reason, could exercise and assert its freedom. (Gossman 1990, 244)

Gossman's depiction of eighteenth-century reader-response prefigures Frank Ankersmit's call for a renewed emphasis on historical reflection, rather than endless historical production. He describes an overwhelming flood of historical research, far beyond the capacity of any audience to digest, and suggests that we turn our attention to understanding:

> The wild, greedy, and uncontrolled digging into the past, inspired by the desire to discover past reality and reconstruct it scientifically, is no longer the historian's unquestioned task. We would do better to examine the result of a hundred and fifty years' digging more attentively and ask ourselves more often what all this adds up to. The time has come for us to *think* about the past, rather than *investigate* it. (Ankersmit 1994, 179)

In other words, the historical audience should step back, as we might in a picture gallery, to look at the 'big picture,' and then, perhaps, to compare pictures, recognizing that the strengths and weaknesses we find in each one is a sign of our own expectations and desires at a moment in time. This attention to audience shows its ethical dimension in

David Harlan's assertion that each of us must create a personal line to the past. The image is taken from Wallace Stegner's description of a line of lariats tied between a snow-bound house to the barn so as to make possible the journey 'from shelter to responsibility and back again' (quoted in Harlan 1997, xxxii). Harlan deplores the de-emphasis on ethical responsibility in professional historical studies. We need our own heroes and exemplars of right and wrong, and it is history that can best offer us choices:

> The best way to think through our own values is to think through our predecessors' values – and to think of ourselves as the latest in a long tradition of such thinkers. History is a line we ourselves must rig up, to a past we ourselves must populate. (Harlan 1997, xxxiii)

Harlan wants to bring a sense of history out of the tight frame that Gossman described and tie it to individual experience, rather than the ingrained consciousness of groups, but finally, it is history as a form of transformational experience that he, like Ankersmit, advocates.

It is, however, a different kind of experience from the eighteenth-century version of an experience from which lessons were to be taken. This historical experience, Count Reinhard wrote to Goethe, always comes too late, if at all. He wrote: 'This is because past experience presents itself concentrated in a single focus, while that which is yet to be experienced is spread over minutes, hours, days, years, and centuries; thus similitude never seems to be the same, for in the one case one sees the whole, and in the other only individual parts' (Koselleck 1985, 34). We note the visual metaphors for the textualization of the past; the single focus cannot but mean that written history is a thing, always already emplotted to some extent, while lived experience is not.

This lived experience of the audience, the readers, of history is a relatively neglected topic in the rhetorical discourse of history. Notable exceptions are Michel Isenberg's discussion of the reading of history in *Puzzles of the Past* (1985), and Linda Orr's reflections in *Headless History* (1990) on her own experience of reading the vast corpus of nineteenth-century French romantic historians of the Revolution. Orr offers a remarkably personal, even physical, response to the authority of Michelet, Lamartine, and Tocqueville, and in so doing suggests how individual the response to a historical text always is, even after allowing for gender, ideology, class and the many other variables that affect the reader (Orr 1990, 2–6). Eisenberg presents for us the recorded experiences of many writers – such as John Hicks, James Truslow Adams, Malcolm X, and Harry Truman – who have commented on their experience of reading history. He also notes that reading history is rarely the first sort of reading that a child does, but rather grows out of an early-developed love of reading itself, because 'an interest in history implies reading in history' (Isenberg 1985, 22). Obvious as this may seem, it is an important start to any thought of the historical audience.

## ETHOS: WHO WRITES HISTORY?

The ethos of the historian has long focused on the representation of the past as an object without an addition of extraneous or tendentious factors that belong to the subjectivity of the historian. Allan Megill (1994) has enumerated the types of objectivity to clarify the ethical confusion arising from them, and Peter Novick (1988) has traced the development of the complications of the 'objectivity question,' that have made the goal of objectivity seem 'a noble dream,' but the tendency has persisted to view this objectivity as a certain neutrality regarding political and social attitudes. Frank Ankersmit, however, has challenged the idea of subjectivity as the intrusion of the political or social opinions held by the historian. Why, he asks, are these the things that brand a historian as subjective, rather than other, more personal and more subjective things, like preferences for particular subjects or methods, or a simple lack of intelligence or creativity? These are also subjective factors that find their way into historical writing all the time, but don't seem to count in the way that politics does; they influence a sense of the past at least as surely as individual political or social preferences.

François Furet has written that the historian must choose between personal commemoration and analysis. Linda Orr replies that 'each historian presents his or her commemoration as analysis and makes it stick' (Orr 1990, 158). 'Making it stick,' of course, is accomplished rhetorically, by the establishment of ethos. One aspect of this that has changed a bit is the use of the first-person reference by historians. Philippe Carrard not only remarks on the extensive use of the overt historical narrator among the French *Annales* School, he also describes the functions that these appearances of the self serve (Carrard 1992, 86–7). Ethos is above all the establishment of a sense of belonging or identification between author and reader, and this identification may take many forms. When, for example, David Harlan, writes of 'a choice of inheritance,' in the sense that we are free to choose our intellectual forebears and thus to lay down the basis for identification with a group of readers, he stresses precisely the ethical dimension of the rhetoric of history (Harlan 1997, 157).

While the communicative relation between the historian and the reader of history may be the first order of rhetorical attention (and an area that deserves much more attention than it has received), the historical work itself in its many forms is the principal focus of rhetorical attention to history. The five canons of rhetoric – invention, arrangement, style, memory, and delivery – offer a remarkably pertinent picture of the development of historical theory in the last 50 years. The example of history is particularly revealing of the ways in which even the 'forgotten' canons, memory and delivery, have acquired a renewed relevance.

## INVENTION: THE DISCOVERY OF HISTORICAL TOPICS

Although it is axiomatic that historians are 'not free to invent,' as Ann Rigney (1990,

xii) put it, referring to the presentation of falsified evidence, invention is the crucial rhetorical starting point for any historical work. Rhetorical invention is the discovery of arguments within the given materials of discourse; it uses topics as the guide. Historical invention, similarly, depends on topics to make arguments that are recognizably historical. The nineteenth century emergence of a historical profession was based on the understanding that the topics of history were states, nations, peoples, wars, parties, revolutions, and things of this public and political nature. The archivalization and publication of mountains of political documents made these topics appear the inevitable generator of historical argument. The expansion of topics began with the emergence of social and economic history, followed by increasingly targeted sub-fields – labor history and business history, the history of women and various minorities, the history of childhood, among many others. Each of these fields has its journals, professional associations, and canons. Beyond groups of people, however, we must mention the historicization of aspects of the human body, such as food and eating, sexuality, childhood, obesity, illness, and death. Abstractions can be historicized, as in Mary Poovey's *A History of the Modern Fact* (1998) or Stephen Kern's *History of Space and Time* (2003) and *A Cultural History of Causality* (2006).

The tools of rhetorical invention, according to Aristotle, are enthymeme (informal reasoning or methodology) and example. Example clearly corresponds to the new forms of evidence to be found in most areas of history today. The use of photographs, films, audio recordings, pamphlets, political cartoons, or digital data pose new and special challenges for historical invention. The rhetorical enthymeme describes the informal logical assumptions that comprise a historical methodology, and these methodologies are also proliferating. In this area of historical invention, the work of Keith Jenkins demands attention; he has confronted the intricately self-reflexive logic of post-structuralist theory and proposed a practice of history at once skeptical and aware that the past can be 'infinitely redescribed' (Jenkins 1991, 65). Jenkins agrees with Ankersmit that the value of historical reflection in our time is precisely in examining and pondering the mass of historical interpretations in their great variety, rather than recklessly adding to them. Students should undertake 'an analysis of why the history you are getting is the one you are getting and why you are getting it in the way you are and not in any other' (Jenkins 1991, 69).

It is difficult to see the end of this inventive explosion, the point beyond which one cannot venture. In the traditional humanistic notion of history, death appeared to be the topic that could not be exceeded (Kellner 1990, 235), but recently historians like Ewa Domanska are noting a 'return to things,' which will provide a voice to the voiceless Other (things) and create counter-discourses; her conclusion is that the biography of objects actually reinstates the human obsession with origins and offers a reassuring stability compared to human life (Domanska 2006, 171–85).

## ARRANGEMENT: THE FORCE OF HISTORICAL NARRATIVE

The arrangement of parts of historical discourse has traditionally followed chronology, and taken one of several forms, including annals, chronicle, and narrative. The latter genre became the form of a maturing profession in the nineteenth century, but was challenged as unscientific by an influential French historical school led by Fernand Braudel, whose classic *The Mediterranean and the Mediterranean World in the Age of Philip II* (1996) downplayed the narrative of events in favor of what he called deep structures, geographical and anthropological forces that hardly change within the span of a human life and so remain largely invisible to the actors in history, whose role is much reduced. This anti-narrative prejudice became influential in the 1960s, and story-telling, now described as an outmoded, merely traditional form, became

suspect. As Jacques LeGoff wrote: 'Every conception of history that identifies it with narrative seems to me unacceptable today' (LeGoff 1992, 117). This, however, overlooks the basic narrative form of all human understanding; meaning itself is grasped narratologically. Hans Kellner demonstrated that even Braudel's *Mediterranean*, the avatar of non-narrative history, has discernable narrative shape (Kellner 1989). And Nancy Partner writes:

> All past events, persons, and phenomena, however abstractly defined, emerge into identity only as part of a formal pattern which controls time. 'Tick' = origins, causes, predisposing factors, fundamental premises. 'Tock' = results, effects, achievements, recovered meanings. In the 'middle,' our plot enables us to identify manifestations, symptoms, developments, characteristics. The most rigorously eventless, characterless, 'non-narrative' history has to tell something, has to begin somewhere and proceed and conclude.' (Partner 1986, 93)

The American philosopher Louis Mink argued that narrative was more than a vehicle of meaning, but a cognitive instrument itself, and that it prevented history from becoming a cumulative science because it did not produce the sort of 'detachable conclusions' that such sciences require. The conclusions to be found in historical narrative are not places in the narrative so much as the ingredients from which its argument is made, and which cannot be separated from the narrative into which it is woven. 'Articulated as separate statements in a grand finale, they are not conclusions, but reminders to the reader (and to the historian himself) of the topography of events to which the entire narrative has given order' (Mink 1987, 79). Another work of the 1960s, Arthur Danto's *Analytical Philosophy of History*, was largely concerned with narrative, and was renamed *Narrative and Knowledge* when republished with additions in 1985. Danto noted that whatever laws history could claim were unvarying narrative laws; histories were thus invariant in form; like sonnets, their marvelous variety in no way altered the essential explanatory form.

Hayden White found historical narrative to be anything but an innocent form, because its production of meaning depended upon emplotment, the presentation of one or another particular kind of arrangement and choice of beginnings and conclusions. Histories might report tragic dissolutions of institutions or the comic rise of nations or groups, or the absurd uselessness of human plans, but the form itself would always present a meaning via its plot, even if the meaning was the assertion of the meaninglessness of human affairs and aspirations. Thus all narrative is inherently ideological because the real can be presented as true only if it can be given some narrative form:

> The historical narrative, as against the chronicle, reveals to us a world that is putatively 'finished,' done with, over, and not yet dissolved, not falling apart. In this world, reality wears the mask of a meaning, the completeness and fullness of which we can only imagine, never experience. Insofar as historical stories can be completed, can be given narrative closure, can be shown to have had a plot all along, they give to reality the odor of the ideal. This is why the plot of a historical narrative is always an embarrassment and has to be presented as 'found' in the events rather than put there by narrative techniques. (H. White 1987, 20–1)

Therefore, '"what takes place" in a narrative is from the referential (reality) point of view literally *nothing;* what happens is language alone, the adventure of language, the unceasing celebration of its coming' (Barthes 1977, 124). It is not reality, but meaning that narrative produces.

French philosopher Paul Ricoeur, in a monumental three-volume study, *Time and Narrative* (1984–88), found narrative to be the human solution to the paradox of time described by Augustine – it is both an internal, phenomenological apprehension and an external succession of events. The poetics of narrative reconciles these conflicting experiences of time by 're-figuring' time into a narrative form. In other words, narrative converts what we intuit 'in here' into an object that can be examined 'out there.'

By 1979, when Lawrence Stone wrote of a 'revival of narrative' in historical studies, the terrain had shifted. To be sure, grand narrative histories were still published, and the majority of historical works had never lost their narrative form. In that same year, however, Jean-François Lyotard published *La Condition Postmoderne*, a work about the logic of temporal arrangement. The postmodern, he argued, occurs when a happening occurs for which we have no concept. Only later will the happening be integrated into a story that gives it meaning; at that point it becomes modern. 'A work can become modern only if it is first postmodern' (Lyotard 1979/1984, 79). Lyotard argued that narrative was an oppressive force when it claimed to be a representation of totality; 'grand narratives' became ideologically suspect, in the same way that philosophy of history has been suspect to historians. They are both over-plotted. Instead, he called for small narratives – necessary, but not to be tied into a large vision.

## STYLE: HISTORICAL METAPHOR AS COGNITIVE FOUNDATION

Crucial to what has been called the linguistic turn in history has been the inflation of the traditional devices of style, the metaphoric family of figures of speech, into forms of pre-linguistic organizing principles, a 'bedrock of order' for the analysis of historiography and an 'aggressive move to turn historical thought from a logical to a rhetorical form …' (Kellner 1989, 226). The expansion of the third of the rhetorical canons, style, may be seen by comparing Peter Gay's *Style in History* (1974), with Hayden White's *Metahistory* (1973) or Frank Ankersmit's *History and Tropology* (1994). Gay takes the conventional view that 'style' is a quality that some historians have and others lack. He mentions 'a few mechanical tricks of rhetoric' (Gay 1974, 3) but shows no sense that they are worthy of the historian's attention. Style is 'the bridge to substance' (Gay 1974, 156), but in no way constitutive of historical substance. The 'stylist' may seem to be putting order on the events of the past, but this is only a formal procedure. 'The order itself is something the historian does not make; he finds it. So controversial an activity as the carving out of a historical period is not a construction but a discovery. The order, the period, are there' (Gay 1974, 217). Like J.H. Hexter, who suggests that the historian's style is not just 'icing on the cake,' but is 'mixed right into the batter,' Gay sees an inevitable reality that must be represented in language (Hexter 1971, 247). Style does this.

Hayden White took the four tropes of renaissance rhetoric and found in them the 'deep structures' of historical discourse. These tropes – that is, the figures of speech metaphor, metonymy, synecdoche, and irony – once the basis of stylistic ornament, became in White's hands cognitive forms. In this inflation of tropes into concepts much larger than the surface devices of poetics, White was following the work of such thinkers as the rhetorician Kenneth Burke and the linguist Roman Jakobson. The tropes, traditionally seen as matters of style, became epistemological functions, as they had been for Vico; to organize the historical field, for example, by reduction, as metonymy does, is to posit the human world as law-bound, as Marx or Tocqueville might understand it. The Marxist-metonymist may choose prose figures of any sort, preferring, say metaphors to metonymies. This is a surface matter. At the deeper level, metonymic reduction organizes things (White 1973, 281).

Each trope offered a different way in which parts can be related to wholes, so the fundamental description of the historical field of information must be organized at a basic level in one of these ways. The historical thing itself, whether period, nation-state, revolution, class, battle, or any other topic, is constituted in advance of its study by the preference of the researcher for one mode of construction or another. What counts as a fact in the historical edifice is not a given for White. The facts themselves only appear as facts when the initial figuration of the whole has been made, tropologically. In this view, inquiry and research do indeed discover

documentary evidence and backing for various claims, but since the process as a whole has been prefigured at a very basic level the resulting facts and the discursive form they take are a fulfillment of the trope. Ankersmit takes this enlarged sense of metaphor further. The historical narrative itself is 'a sustained metaphor' in a number of senses, not least because it serves as a substitute for what is not present, the past (Ankersmit 1994, 40). In addition, he argues that the best history is the most metaphorical one because it offers the finest 'belvedere,' the broadest panorama of insight (Ankersmit 1994, 41).

Discussions of the linguistic turn are many; among them, Elizabeth A. Clark's *History, Theory, Text: Historian's and the Linguistic Turn*, begins a study of recent theoretical developments with references to those who see this turn as the end of history – a position that she firmly rejects (Clark 2004, 1). Nevertheless, the figures who comprise the standard anthology of recent historical theory, *The Postmodern History Reader*, edited by Keith Jenkins, sometimes describe an enterprise quite different from contemporary scholarly practices.

## MEMORY – COLLECTIVE EXPERIENCE, TRAUMA, AND THE HISTORICAL SUBLIME

The last two canons of rhetoric – memory and delivery – are often spoken of as the forgotten canons. The *letteraturizzazione* of rhetoric, the transformation from an oral to a primarily written form, began the decay of memory (as Socrates lamented in Plato's *Phaedrus*) and delivery. History as Hegel understood it excluded the 'Legends, Ballad-stories, and Traditions' from the proper 'Temple of Mnemosyne,' which requires writing for its existence (Hegel 1956, 1–2). Writing as the technology of delivery and written documentation as the substance of history seemed pure common sense. This has changed. Memory has taken new forms and inspired new interrogation. Delivery has broadened with images, film, and popular forms that must be taken seriously.

The relation of personal memory and the memoir-testimony to history has always been troubled, but the institutionalization of memory via oral histories and video archives has added new dimensions to this canon of rhetoric. It is in the study of the Holocaust that memory has provided a large and various theoretical field. The remembered testimonies of survivors, perpetrators, even later generations now fill archives and pose important questions. Steven Spielberg's *Shoah* Foundation, for example, has amassed a large archive of survivor's testimonies, some of which are readily available on the internet. Should historical discourse avoid memory and the ethical positions it implies, or take memory as the center of its focus? Or, asks Dominick LaCapra, 'is there a more complex and nuanced interaction between history and memory?' (LaCapra 1998, 1). For LaCapra, an important part of the study of memory is the Freudian dynamic by which trauma may be worked through so that the anxiety-producing sense of absence may be replaced with a more realistic sense of loss, which 'is situated on a historical level and is the consequence of particular events' (La Capra 2001, 64). Nostalgia is a danger faced by historical memory, but historicization can itself be a threat to memory, as Saul Friedlander points out (Friedlander 1993, 100).

Ankersmit's work of the 1990s focuses on the direct experience of the historical past, bypassing the suasions of text and representation. In turning away from the linguistic, Ankersmit hoped to set aside the obsession with words and their mediating role. Beyond language, he finds ineffable, sublime, experience.

This experience of the past is personal and beyond any notion of truth or falsehood. Experience is what must be given up or forgotten when historicization takes place. History in its textual form is a forgetting, but Ankersmit believes that in historical experience one has 'a recognition of what I had always known, but forgotten, and of a confrontation with what was both strange and alien to me' (Ankersmit 2005, 276).

Experience, forgetting, and trauma are also forms of collective memory, a topic much discussed. *Realms of Memory*, the grand seven-volume project led by Pierre Nora (1997), has the original title *Lieux de Mémoire*, which may just as well refer to the *lieux rhetorique*, the topoi where arguments are to be found. It is a profoundly rhetorical concept. The sites are the symbolic things by which a community is constituted as an entity with a past that unites it. Examples of these topoi are memorials, museums, cathedrals, and cemeteries, as well as objects (foundational texts, monuments, inheritances), and social practices and rituals. Just as the rhetor used these remembered places to stimulate arguments, so the member of a historical community uses them as reminders of the identity provided by their social world.

## DELIVERY: BEYOND THE HISTORICAL TEXT

Much of the commemoration depends on new media and technologies, new forms of delivery. The final canon of rhetoric, delivery, seems the least promising part of the classical tradition to contribute to a new discourse of history. Print technology has been crucial to the historical consciousness of the West for centuries; indeed, it seems to mark the progression from memory toward history proper. However, the new media of the late twentieth century have sparked a considerable discourse on modes of delivery. Film, in particular, but also television and, increasingly, the internet, now reach far more people and deliver all sorts of historical messages which must be considered.

The history theme park is far from the text-based norm of historical delivery, and it sometimes disturbs historical purists (and others) in its commercialism and need to entertain. (An example of this resistance was behind Disney's cancellation of plans for a history theme park in Virginia, see http://

query.nytimes.com/gst/fullpage.html?res=99
01E3D7113AF93AA1575AC0A96298260.)
However, such parks do create a form of
historical awareness and presence that can
have positive civic benefit. In Japan, a number of such parks have spurred an awareness
of local history and stimulated the civic life of
regional cities like Takefu (Witteveen 2003).

*Medieval World, USA,* advertises its
authenticity: 'This unique community is a
complete permanent assembled heritage
landscape dedicated to re-creation of the 12th
century, the Middle Ages and renaissance
periods spanning the 3rd through the 14th
centuries. Historically accurate and authentically replicated in every detail. A living history legacy to pass-on for generations to
come.'(http://www.medievalworld.us/)

Museums have been an important type of
historical delivery for centuries, but the serious study and critique of museums as institutions has flourished in our time. Stephen
Bann's 'Poetics of the museum' (1984),
which explored the implications of different
ways of arranging artifacts, is a classic in this
regard, while his *The Inventions of History*
(1990) extends beyond the museum to maps,
art, and film. In film, history has found its
most important modern expression. It is with
film that discussions of historical delivery
have been most concerned; the debates over
the place of non-written historical presentation remain totally unresolved, despite such
validations as the American Historical Association Film Festivals. The work of Robert
Rosenstone (1994, 2006) on history and film
and the journal *Film and History* offer a fine
introduction to an expanding area of study in
the fifth canon of rhetoric.

Hayden White has suggested that there is a
new sort of event that cannot be grasped by
the traditional narrative modes of history; he
calls it the 'modernist event,' in which the
occurrence of the event is delivered as an
instantaneous representation that first de-
realizes it and then converts it into an image
before it can be experienced as reality. White
mentions the Challenger explosion and the
O.J. Simpson chase and trial as examples,

and cites Christopher Browning's statement
that the events of the Holocaust struck people
as unbelievable' because they had no experiential reference to appeal to. White's response
to this new form of experience is that modernist ways of writing the event restore to
it the sense of radical newness by the disruption of traditional patterns of meaning (H.
White 1998, 74).

A more pessimistic vision of this situation
was expressed by Jean Baudrillard:

> So far as history is concerned, its telling has
> become impossible because that telling (*re-
> citatum*) is, by definition, the possible recurrence
> of a sequence of meanings. Now, through the
> impulse for total dissemination and circulation,
> every event is granted its own liberation; every act
> becomes atomic, nuclear, and pursues its trajec-
> tory into the void. In order to be disseminated to
> infinity, it has to be fragmented like a particle. This
> is how it is able to achieve a velocity of no-return
> which carries it out of history once and for all.
> Every set of phenomena, whether cultural totality
> or sequence of events, has to be fragmented,
> disjointed, so that it can be sent down the circuits;
> every kind of language has to be resolved into a
> binary formulation so that it can circulate, not in
> our memories, but in the luminous, electronic
> memory of the computers. No human language
> can withstand the speed of light. No event can
> withstand being beamed across the whole planet.
> No meaning can withstand acceleration. No his-
> tory can withstand the centrifugation of facts or
> their being short-circuited in real time.... (Baudrillard
> 1997, 40)

Delivery of events and representations in
'real time' is the challenge for history, as
written (a modernist genre?), or as museum,
film, or painting (recalling that 'history
painting' was a key concept in art history).

The return of rhetoric is more than the
linguistic turn. The intensification of the role
of language and its protocols in the creation
of historical arguments and simulacra was
undoubtedly a momentous reflection of the
intellectual climate of the twentieth century,
but the full scope of rhetoric – which I have
only suggested in this chapter – better reflects
the many developments in what we call history. What counts as history is in dispute as
the dominance of print gives way to many

other media, as the relation of reader to writer changes, and as events perceived to be unprecedented bring forth symbolic models that are without example. This is not the place for any call to a new practice of anything. It is worth our while, however, to consider that the scope of rhetoric, suggested by the traditional five canons, can open for us a vision, a belvedere, of the richness of historical discourse in our time, and the boldness and variety of the questions it poses.

# REFERENCES

Ankersmit, Frank (1994). *History and Tropology: The Rise and Fall of Metaphor.* University of California Press: Berkeley.

Ankersmit, Frank (2005). *Sublime Historical Experience.* Stanford University Press: Stanford.

Bann, Stephen (1984). 'Poetics of the museum,' in *The Clothing of Clio: a study of the representation of History in Nineteenth-Century Britain and France.* Cambridge & New York: Cambridge University Press.

Bann, Stephen (1990). *The Inventions of History: Essays on the Representation of the Past.* Manchester University Press: Manchester and New York.

Barthes, Roland (1977). 'Introduction to the structural analysis of narratives,' in *Image, Music, Text,* trans. S. Heath. Hill and Wang: New York.

Barthes, Roland (1986). *The Rustle of Language,* trans. Richard Howard. Hill and Wang: New York.

Baudrillard, Jean (1997). 'The illusion of the end,' in *The Postmodern History Reader,* ed. K. Jenkins. Routledge: London and New York, 1997.

Berkhofer, Robert Jr (1995). *Beyond the Great Story: History as Text and Discourse.* Cambridge, Mass. Harvard University Press.

Braudel, Fernand (1996). *The Mediterranean and the Mediterranean World in the Age of Philip II,* tr. Siân Reynolds. University of California Press: Berkeley and New York.

Carrard, Philippe (1992). *Poetics of the New History: French Historical Discourse from Braudel to Chartier.* Johns Hopkins University Press: Baltimore.

Clark, Elizabeth (2004). *History, Theory, Text: Historians and the Linguistic Turn.* Harvard University Press: Cambridge, MA.

Danto, Arthur (1985). *Narration and Knowledge: Including the Integral Text of Analytical Philosophy of History.* Columbia University Press: New York.

Domanska, Ewa (2006). 'The return to things,' *Archaeologia Polona,* Vol. 44.

Donagan, Alan (1959). 'Explanation in history' (1957), in Gardiner, Patrick, *Theories of History,* Free Press: New York.

Friedlander, Saul (1993). *Memory, History, and the Extermination of the Jews of Europe.* Indiana University Press: Bloomington.

Frye, Northrop (1963). *Fables of Identity.* Harcourt, Brace & World: New York.

Gay, Peter (1974). *Style in History.* Basic Books: New York.

Gossman, Lionel (1990). *Between History and Literature.* Harvard University Press, Cambridge, MA.

Harlan, David (1997). *The Degradation of American history.* University of Chicago Press: Chicago.

Hegel, Georg Friedrich Wilhelm (1956). *The Philosophy of History,* trans. J. Sibree. Dover: New York.

Isenberg, Michael T. (1985). *Puzzles of the Past: An Introduction to Thinking about History.* Texas A&M University Press: College Station.

Hexter, J.H. (1971). *The History Primer.* Basic Books: New York and London.

Jenkins, Keith (1991). *Re-Thinking History.* Routledge: London.

Kellner, Hans (1989). *Language and Historical Representation: Getting the Story Crooked.* University of Wisconsin Press: Madison and New York.

Kellner, Hans (1990). '"As real as it gets...": Ricoeur and Narrativity,' *Philosophy Today,* Vol. 34, No. 3.

Kern, Stephen (2003). *The Culture of Time and Space, 1880–1918,* 2nd edn. Harvard University Press: Cambridge MA.

Kern, Stephen (2006). *A Cultural History of Causality: Science, Murder Novels, and Systems of Thought.* Princeton University Press: Princeton.

Koselleck, Reinhart (1985). *Futures Past: On the Semantics of Historical Time,* trans. Keith Tribe. MIT: Cambridge.

LaCapra, Dominick (1998). *History and Memory After Auschwitz.* Cornell University Press: Ithaca.

LaCapra, Dominick (2001). *Writing History, Writing Trauma.* Johns Hopkins University Press: Baltimore and London.

LeGoff, Jacques (1992). *History and Memory,* trans. S. Rendall and E. Claman. Columbia University Press: New York.

Lyotard, Jean-François (1984). *The Postmodern Condition: A Report on Knowledge,* trans. by G. Bennington and B. Massumi. University of Minnesota Press: Minneapolis (originally published 1979).

Megill, Allan (1994). *Re-thinking Objectivity.* Duke University Press: Durham, NC and London.

Mink, Louis O (1987). *Historical Understanding*, ed. B. Fay, E.O. Golub, and R.T. Vann. Cornell University Press: Ithaca and London.

Nora, Pierre (1997), *Realms of Memory*, 7 vols., ed. L. Kritzman, trans. A Goldhammer. Columbia University Press: New York.

Novick, Peter (1988). *That Noble Dream: The 'Objectivity Question' and the American Historical Profession*. Cambridge University Press: Cambridge UK.

Orr, Linda (1990). *Headless History: Nineteenth-Century French Historiography of the Revolution*. Cornell University Press: Ithaca.

Partner, Nancy (1986). 'Making up lost time: writing on the writing of history,' *Speculum*, Vol. 61, No. 1.

Perelman, Chaim (2001). 'The new rhetoric,' in Patricia Bizzell and Bruce Herzberg, *The Rhetorical Tradition: Selected Readings*. Bedford/St. Martins: Boston and New York.

Perelman, Chaim and Olbrecht-Tyteca, Lucie (1958). *The New Rhetoric: A Treatise on Argumentation*. New York.

Poovey, Mary (1998). *A History of the Modern Fact*. University of Chicago Press: Chicago and London.

Ricoeur, Paul (1984–88). *Time and Narrative* (*Temps et Récit*), 3 vols., trans. Kathleen Blamey and David Pellauer. University of Chicago Press: Chicago.

Rigney, Ann (1990). *The Rhetoric of Historical Representation*. Cambridge University Press: Cambridge.

Rosenstone, Robert, ed. (1994). *Revisioning History: Film and the Construction of a New Past*. Princeton University Press: Princeton.

Rosenstone, Robert (2006). *History on Film/Film on History*. Longman: New York.

Spengler, Oswald (1934). *The Decline of the West*. Tr. Charles Francis Atkinson. Alfred A. Knopf: New York.

Stone, Lawrence (1979). 'The revival of narrative: reflections on a new old history,' *Past and Present*, Vol. 85.

White, Hayden (1973). *Metahistory: The Historical Imagination in Nineteenth-Century Europe*. Johns Hopkins University Press: Baltimore and London.

White, Hayden (1987). *The Content of the Form. Narrative Discourse and Historical Representation*, Johns Hopkins: Baltimore & London: 1987.

White, Hayden (1998). *Figural Realism: Studies in the Mimesis Effect*. Johns Hopkins University Press: Baltimore and London.

White, Morton (1959). 'Historical explanation' (1943), in Gardiner, Patrick, *Theories of History*. Free Press: New York.

Witteveen, Guven Peter (2003). *The Renaissance of Takefu: How People and the Local Past Changed the Civic Life of a Regional Japanese Town*. Routledge: London.

# 11

# Michel Foucault: The Unconscious of History and Culture

Clare O'Farrell

The French thinker, Michel Foucault (1926–84), is noted for his extensive and controversial forays into the historical disciplines. When his work first began to circulate in the 1950s and 1960s, historians did not quite know what to make of it and philosophers resented the appearance of what they saw as the importation of the tedium of concrete events into the pure untainted realm of ideas. If these responses to his work remain alive and well decades after Foucault's death, the uptake of his work has become far more complex. To restrict ourselves to the discipline of history here: if one very visible and vocal camp of historians remains deeply ambivalent about his work, this merely disguises the fact that a far larger contingent of historians of all kinds – not just those located in history departments – use his ideas quite unremarkably as they go about their daily business. Further, in areas of specialist institutional history and the history of the professions, Foucault has had a wide-ranging impact. Indeed, he has made the very idea of a history possible in some of these domains – where previously they had existed in an ahistorical limbo. He has also done much to historicise the sciences and to throw into question their claim to an unchanging and superior truth which sets the benchmark for all other forms of knowledge.

## HISTORY AS A PHILOSOPHICAL EXERCISE

Foucault's work demonstrates all the hallmarks of historical investigation: archival research, dates, beginning and ends, the description of events and periods, and references to historical figures and movements. Why is it, then, that historians are often so suspicious of his work? The most general answer to this question, perhaps, is that Foucault's work challenges the boundaries, rules and assumptions which trained mainstream historians use to organise the past and to construct what is recognised by the profession as valid historical discourse. As Hayden White puts it, Foucault challenges the notion that professional historians own history and the idea that anybody who wants to provide a valid account of the past needs to pass through their narrow and strictly policed doors.[1]

But rather than indulging in the clichés, which as Foucault put it rather nicely himself, set the painstaking cataloguer of empirical historical detail against the philosophical purveyor of grand and vague ideas, it might be more worthwhile to look at what he has to offer in general to all those interested in the interpretation of the past. Foucault observed that his approach was not that of the professional historian, which traditionally consisted in the description and analysis of a historical period or society or a variety of social institutions. Instead, he preferred to select a specific 'problem' – usually one with significant resonances in the present – and see how people had attempted to deal with it in the past.[2] This type of focused approach is of course, not unfamiliar to the historians of science and historians of ideas with whom Foucault found both common cause and notable divergences. Further, Foucault characterised his work as philosophical in its focus rather than historical in the traditional understanding, in that his interest was in 'the question of truth', which he described as 'the question of philosophy itself'.[3] At the same time he was careful to distinguish himself from traditional institutional philosophy.[4] He was not seeking to arrive at a fixed definition of an eternal truth and the classification of knowledge into rigid categories, rather, his aim was to examine how divisions had been drawn between the true and the false in history.[5] Rather than the traditional philosophical question 'what is truth?, Foucault asked, 'how has the division between the true and the false been constructed differently over time?'

This points to a strong positivist streak in Foucault's work and one that he shared wholeheartedly with the historical profession. Intellectually, we can only deal with the evidence that is presented to us in the concrete form of documentary and physical traces left behind by the past, and thought and ideas are amongst the things that leave historical traces. 'I don't do anything *but* history', he protested when accused of doing away with history in his work.[6] On being further taxed with 'positivism' by French critics in the 1960s, Foucault responded that he didn't see this as a problem, and that on

the contrary he was quite content to be a positivist.[7] Thought and the concern for truth, he argued, were not divorced from the everyday run of concrete historical events. Instead we can see the empirical workings of thought in the most everyday of physical gestures and institutional structures.[8]

Talking to the historian Arlette Farge about Philippe Ariès, while reflecting on their respective projects, he noted:

> What I wanted to do was in the order of philosophy: can one reflect philosophically on the history of knowledge as historical material rather than reflecting on a theory or a philosophy of history. In a rather empirical and clumsy fashion, I envisaged a work as close as possible to that of historians, but in order to ask philosophical questions, concerning the history of knowledge. I hoped for the good will of historians.[9]

Foucault chose history as a way of answering particular philosophical questions and in so doing forged a new way of thinking about both philosophy and history. Examining questions such as 'what is rationality?', 'how do we define truth?', or 'what counts as valid knowledge?', 'what is madness?', 'what is sexuality?', within a historical context and showing that the responses to these questions are by no means fixed, undermine traditional philosophical claims about the transhistorical eternity of certain ideas and categories. At the same time, Foucault's use of historical material to analyse these questions forces historians to think closely about their own assumptions in terms of the selection and organisation of the material that forms their own raw empirical data.

In writing about Foucault and history, one of the difficulties is that Foucault scholarship is now so vast that it is impossible to do justice to all the aspects of his work that have been taken up within the historical field. Sometimes a comment thrown out in passing, or a couple of paragraphs in his work, have generated entire industries. A case in point is Edward Said's influential work *Orientalism*,[10] published in 1978 provoked by a brief paragraph in the 1961 preface to Foucault's work *The History of Madness*.[11]

As a consequence, rather than concentrating on the finer empirical detail of his output, this chapter will focus on general ideas and themes in Foucault's work and illustrate these with a few chosen examples.

## CHRONOLOGY OF FOUCAULT'S WORK

One notable problem faced by both commentators and readers of Foucault's work is where to begin. Foucault's output is so layered and so complex that unless one is drawing a quite specific tool or concept from his work the multiplicity of entry points can be baffling. A chronological account does not entirely solve these problems but it can provide a useful set of reference points to begin with. In this section, I will briefly deal with each major work in turn, outlining the period of history and subject matter which is the focus of each work, going on to mention the key concepts that have been taken up most extensively in the secondary literature.

### The 1950s and early 1960s

Foucault's first publication in 1954 was a long introduction to an essay by Swiss existential psychologist Ludwig Binswanger.[12] This introduction was a somewhat arcane study of the history of western dream interpretation and the imagination with a number of phenomenological and existential notions to the fore, but even at this early stage, Foucault's insistence on the historical dimension of human experience was apparent. In the same year he published a small volume titled *Mental Illness and Personality* which was subsequently revised and republished as *Mental Illness and Psychology* in 1962.[13]

This and his 1961 work *History of Madness* offer histories of the practices and ideas surrounding the experience of madness in western history from the Renaissance to the nineteenth century. The latter work, massive in its scope, dealt with the philosophical, scientific, literary, historical and institutional views and practices which have contributed to the emergence of contemporary definitions of madness and what has come to be characterised as mental illness. Foucault argued that mental illness was but a restricted subset of an earlier much broader notion of madness. This book, which remains controversial to this day, has become a seminal text in the history of psychiatry.

In 1963, Foucault published a further two books: *The Birth of the Clinic,* a history of clinical medicine in France, as well as a spectacularly obscure essay on an even more obscure early twentieth-century French surrealist writer, Raymond Roussel.[14] *The Birth of the Clinic* examined the origins of clinical medicine in France between 1769 and 1825, drawing close links between the formation of modern medical knowledge, institutional and social practices and political decision making. Foucault also operated his characteristic reversal of received historical interpretation, eschewing popular notions of the triumph of enlightened science over ignorance, superstition and blind faith in the texts of the Ancients. Instead, he argued that it was more a question of a change in the rules that produce knowledge that was regarded as valid and true. This shift was the result of a complex interaction between political and institutional factors and changes in medical knowledge during and after the French revolution at the end of the eighteenth century. In his discussion Foucault introduced his notion of the 'gaze' which has since been widely adopted by commentators across a range of fields.[15]

Foucault argued that new definitions of the relation between doctor and illness came to the fore at the end of the eighteenth century. Thus visual observation practised by a '*looking* subject' (sujet *regardant*)[16] became the exclusive way of acquiring valid knowledge, and was practised at the expense of listening to the words and bodies of patients, and also at the expense of interpreting and decoding the texts of the Ancients. These older methods were thus disqualified as practices capable of generating true knowledge. The notion of visibility, of bringing things out into the light was also extended to the social and political spheres. The gaze was consequently capable not only of curing bodily ills but social ills as well.

## Structuralism

Foucault frequently used the word 'structure' in the original edition of *The Birth of the Clinic* but removed many of these references after the rise in popularity of what the media dubbed the structuralist movement.[17] Essentially, structuralism marked a shift from forms of knowledge which sought to define what things were in their essence – things such as Man, history, beauty, existence, truth and the subject – to an examination of how different elements interrelated and formed structures. It was the relation between elements (such as words in language) which could reveal the way things worked, not what discrete things (or words) meant in themselves. The structuralist movement was the subject of much discussion in the public media in France and celebrity status was conferred on those perceived to be its practitioners across a number of fields notably anthropology, literary theory, philosophy linguistics, psychoanalysis, Marxism and history. These structuralist celebrities included Claude Lévi-Strauss, Roland Barthes, Jacques Derrida, Louis Althusser, Foucault, Jacques Lacan as well as others. Foucault, however, entertained an ambivalent relationship with structuralism precisely because of his primary focus on history. He was initially enthusiastic about the movement and happy to be counted as one of its members,[18] but when it became clear that mainstream structuralist practice was more interested in devising ahistorical formal templates for universal application, he rejected the label. As he explained: 'Unlike those who are labelled "structuralists", I'm not really interested in the formal possibilities afforded by a system such as language … my object is not language but the archive, which is to say, the accumulated existence of discourses. Archaeology [Foucault's name for his historical methodology], … is the analysis of discourse in its *archival* form.'[19]

## The late 1960s

In 1966 during the heyday of the structuralist movement, Foucault published *The Order of Things*, which somewhat surprisingly became an instant best seller.[20] This book traced the formation of the disciplines of economics, linguistics and biology dealing with the period from the fifteenth century to the mid nineteenth century. The final chapter dealt with the nineteenth century origins of the human sciences including history, sociology, psychoanalysis and ethnology. Given the difficulty and the specialist nature of this work, few could have read it from cover to cover. But what drew public attention was its inflammatory statements that Marxism was no more than a storm in a children's paddling pool[21] and that 'Man was dead', that is, the humanist 'Man' so extolled by the humanists was doomed to disappear like 'a face drawn in the sand at the edge of the sea'.[22] For numbers of critics a landscape without 'Man' could only be one of nihilist amorality. If there was no 'Man' to fight for and believe in (especially since the 'death of God') – what other moral and political options were there left other than anarchy? Of equal interest to the readers and the media was the notion of successive discrete and seemingly disconnected historical periods, which Foucault labelled 'epistemes'. It was argued that such radical discontinuity 'killed history' and undermined the possibility of a progressive politics and revolution, which in their Marxist formulation relied heavily on a Hegelian dialectical view of history which proceeded inevitably and continuously via a process of progressive rationalisation to the end point of the classless State and the dictatorship of the proletariat. Foucault was impatient with these critiques that he had done away with history, countering with some exasperation that 'you can't kill history, but as for killing [a certain old-fashioned view of] history for philosophers – absolutely – I certainly wanted to kill it'.[23]

In 1969 Foucault published *The Archaeology of Knowledge*, which purported to explain the historical methodology he had used in his earlier works.[24] This is probably Foucault's best-known and most comprehensive foray into historiography. The ideas he put forward in this work were also dealt with in a number of shorter articles and interviews he published between 1967 and 1971. Foucault was quite explicit in these writings about the ways his practice of history differed from the way mainstream history was written. At the same time, however, he made clear his sympathies for the work of the more radical schools of history, such as the Annales school, the Cambridge and Russian Schools, and specialist historians such as the historian of science Georges Canguilhem and the historian of comparative philology and mythology Georges Dumézil. He remarked: 'I certainly cannot be considered as someone who has innovated, as many professional historians have for a long time been performing analyses of the type that figure in *The Order of Things*.'[25]

The introduction to *The Archaeology of Knowledge* included an enthusiastic endorsement of the work of the contemporary school of Annales historians. The historian Jacques Revel noted in response that 'the first two chapters ... are in fact a veritable eulogy to history and the historians of today, I must say they surprised a certain number of historians.'[26] If Foucault's most extensive and focused discussions of historiography emerged in the work he published between 1967 and 1971 and then later towards the end of the 1970s, historiographical remarks are in fact scattered throughout his entire oeuvre, as he constantly reworked and rethought his categories – giving them different names – archaeology, genealogy, the history of the present, the history of thought, the historical a priori, the unconscious of history, the archive. All these terms have been used to wide effect in the secondary literature.

## The 1970s

In 1970, Foucault was elected to a Chair of the History of Systems of Thought at France's elite research institution, the Collège de France. His inaugural speech, published as 'The order of discourse', is usually singled out by commentators as the text that marked the transition from 'discourse' to 'power' in his work.[27] Foucault later explained that this shift towards a more politically engaged and activist stance was provoked by his experiences and involvement in the student uprisings in 1968 in Tunis where he was posted as a professor of philosophy.[28]

His next major book, *Discipline and Punish*,[29] was not to appear until 1975, but during the intervening period he published a number of shorter pieces, gave interviews and conducted his public lectures at the Collège de France. He was also heavily involved in a range of militant activities in support of prisoners, immigrants and health workers. *Discipline and Punish* traced the historical background to some of the contemporary problems that Foucault had observed while engaged in this activity. Its gory opening makes for a gripping read, describing the execution of the regicide Damiens in 1757. Foucault then contrasted this theatrical event with the description of a routine prison timetable in 1838. Foucault's argument was that this period marked a transition between public and spectacular forms of punishment and new forms of punishment which involved incarceration and the deprivation of liberty, in other words the prison.

We can see resonances with his earlier work here. In the *History of Madness*, it was a matter of the confinement of marginal and economically unproductive populations, and *The Birth of the Clinic* tracked the transition from one form of knowledge and one institutional set of arrangements to another. As in his previous work, in *Discipline and Punish* Foucault deployed his favourite tactic of challenging received interpretations concerning particular historical transitions. The accepted interpretation regarding the change in the regime of punishment at the end of the eighteenth century had been that people had become more 'civilised', sensitive and humane. Foucault, however, attributed the change to the fact that the old methods were simply no longer working as a way of managing the population and public order. Indeed, the old spectacular approach of public punishment was actually giving rise to even more disorder in the form of riots at executions and providing an opportunity for other crimes such as petty theft. But prisons were chosen as the new form of punishment, not because they worked, and generally it was agreed by reformers and legal theorists at the time that they did not, but because they fitted in with a general movement which Foucault described as the rise of the 'disciplinary society'. The aim of 'discipline' was to manage the population through a variety of techniques for training bodies and behaviours that could be disseminated and policed by a variety of institutions such as the school, the army, factories, hospitals, asylums and prisons.

A very important element in the production of the disciplined 'docile body'[30] was surveillance and Foucault used eighteenth-century British philosopher Jeremy Bentham's design for a model prison, the Panopticon, as a metaphor to describe how this system of surveillance worked. Bentham's Panopticon was a circular building which grouped cells around a central tower. Those in the tower were able to see into the cells, but prisoners were unable to see into the tower. As a consequence, the prisoners never knew whether or not they were being watched and to avoid punishment they were forced to act as though they were constantly under observation. The intention was that this behaviour would eventually be internalised and become automatic and that the prisoners would self-regulate, producing an efficient and organised system.

If *Discipline and Punish* dealt ostensibly with a remote period of history, its readers have understood it as a critique of contemporary society and have extended its ideas far beyond its original historical focus. The Panopticon, power-knowledge (that is, practices of knowledge such as census keeping and report making which were devised to more efficiently facilitate the exercise of power) and the disciplinary society have all become theoretical commonplaces across a wide

range of literature spanning the humanities, the social sciences and a variety of applied disciplines such as education, management, architecture and the health sciences.[31]

Foucault's next book in 1976, *The History of Sexuality: Volume 1*, was the first volume in a proposed six-volume history.[32] This book was his shortest to date and probably the least dense in content, and along with *Discipline and Punish* remains one of his most widely read and most influential volumes. Foucault traced attitudes towards sexuality in Western Europe from the seventeenth century to the late nineteenth century. Again turning received interpretations on their head, he argued that, contrary to popular perception, this period did not represent a massive movement of repression and censorship in relation to sexuality. Instead, it saw the proliferation of an enormously detailed body of knowledge on sexual conduct as well as the formation of particular identities that had their foundation in sexual preferences and behaviour, most notably homosexuality. One of the aims in creating this meticulously catalogued collection of knowledge was to control and organise the life cycle and health of populations. Foucault coined the term 'biopower' to describe this management of the population through its biological parameters of reproduction, births and deaths. The term biopower has found particular fortune in the secondary literature of the new millennium, particularly through the reconceptualisations of this notion offered by the Italian philosopher and political theorist Giorgio Agamben.[33] Also of particular note in the first volume of *The History of Sexuality* are Foucault's definitions of power and resistance which he explained in easy to use format for the readers. At the time it was published, however, the book was poorly received. This made quite an impact on Foucault, who admitted later that he had written the book off 'the top of his head' and that the response to the book had made him realise that he needed to continue to produce work which challenged both his own way of thinking as well as that of others.[34] The reception of the book was certainly a contributing factor to Foucault's next major change of direction towards a focus on ethics and subjectivity.

During the 1970s, in addition to his formal publications, Foucault was also delivering his annual lectures reporting on his current research at the Collège de France. These lectures were not published until long after his death, the first volume appearing in French in 1997[35] with subsequent volumes appearing at more regular intervals after 2003 in French and then translated into other languages. Publication was delayed by disputes over the terms of Foucault's will, which stipulated no posthumous publication. But the addition of this somewhat uneven work to Foucault's opus has been capital, particularly with regards to a more expanded discussion on his extremely influential notion of 'governmentality' and to valuable additions to his ideas on truth and on biopower.

In 1978, one of these lectures was published as a separate article with the title 'Governmentality'.[36] This article was to have an enormous impact, inspiring large bodies of historical and theoretical work, but some of its argumentation was to remain obscure, to those who didn't have access to the taped lectures at least, until the publication of the entire series of lectures in 2004, which fleshed out some of its ideas at more length. Foucault went on to offer a number of definitions of governmentality in the late 1970s and early 1980s. He began by focusing on State and institutional 'techniques and procedures for directing human behavior',[37] but gradually broadened his definition to include techniques of governing the self.[38]

### The 1980s

It was not until a month before his death in 1984 that Foucault's next books appeared. These were volumes 2 and 3 of *The History of Sexuality*, and to the surprise of his readers abandoned his usual focus on the early modern period in favour of the Ancient Greek and early Christian eras.[39] Foucault examined a number of prescriptive texts in relation to sexuality and techniques of self-construction, asking 'why is sexual conduct, why are the activities and pleasures that attach to it, an object of moral solicitude?'[40] These two works were somewhat empirical in focus and it is the shorter works and lectures that Foucault produced in the 1980s that have been more productive in terms of methodological ideas in relation to ethics and the government of self and others. Foucault's foray into yet another specialised area once again provoked productive controversy amongst specialists in the field who used his work both to rethink some of the received ideas in the field and to further develop existing interpretations.

## FOUCAULT'S OPPOSITIONAL HISTORIOGRAPHY

Much has been made of the existence of three different 'phases' in Foucault's work – generally conveniently characterised as a focus on 'discourse' and the history of science up until 1970, then a focus on 'power' and the history of institutions and the State until 1980, and finally 'subjectivity' and the history of systems of ethics and self-formation. For all this, Foucault's approach was actually quite consistent throughout his career and there is a discernable philosophical framework which underpins his entire oeuvre.[41] This consistency also emerged in his approach to the treatment of history in spite of differences of terminology, empirical material and changes of emphasis across his work.

Foucault often usefully characterised the historical practice he engaged in as being in opposition to traditional views of history and philosophy. This oppositional approach can be used as a springboard for structuring an overview of how he wrote history. He often proceeded by providing a negative outline both in terms of his methodology and also in terms of his subject matter. Indeed, some commentators have described this approach as analogous to negative theology.[42] This meant that in order to define what he was doing, he spent considerable space defining what he was *not* doing. Further, in order to demarcate his historical methodology from standard history of ideas and Hegelian historicist practices he dubbed what he was doing 'archaeology', then 'genealogy' and finally 'the history of thought'.

Thus Foucault took traditional history and the history of ideas to task in five broadly related areas and proposed alternative viewpoints of his own. These areas cover:

1   The ethical and political uses of history
2   Subject matter and sources
3   The organisation of time
4   The subject and history
5   Truth and power in history

Of course this division into five categories is to some extent arbitrary as they are all closely intertwined in Foucault's work and difficult to separate neatly, but they are nonetheless useful ways of organising the discussion.

## 1 The ethical and political uses of history

We have already argued that Foucault's very choice of history was a philosophical one. Foucault started from the basic position that human existence was fundamentally historical. Every event, human action, thought, system of knowledge and cultural arrangement existed in time and had a finite beginning and end.

He was thus actively opposed to philosophical systems which posited transcendent and ahistorical ideas which govern human behaviour and history from outside. He rejected versions of history which reduced history to something else and explained away difference and change, either seeking to make them part of a grand evolutionary plan, or the expression of essences such as human nature, or other forces existing outside of history like destiny, Reason or God's plan, or the dialectical progression to the classless State. Instead, Foucault saw history as continual 'difference'. In *The Archaeology of Knowledge*

he described his 'archaeology', not as something that sought to establish a grand theory, or find the central or original truth of everything, but rather as something that 'is trying to deploy a dispersion that can never be reduced to a single system of differences ... its task is to *make* differences ... it is continually making *differentiations*, it is a *diagnosis.*'[43]

This is not to say that Foucault regarded history as unintelligible assemblages of purely random changes. Rather he was proposing a different way of organising how we see the past and its relation to the present, in other words he was seeking to establish 'a plethora of intelligibilities, a deficit of necessities'.[44] He further explained, 'the histories that I undertake are not explanatory, they never show the necessity of something, but rather show a series of shifts through which the impossible is produced ... Everything that is irregular, risky, unpredictable in a historical process is of considerable interest to me.'[45]

He wanted to make history capable of serving many agendas, not just the agenda of those in power. He postulated that history was a complex interaction between a myriad number of levels and processes that needed to be examined meticulously by the historian, not with a view to reducing them to one thing, but to finding ever more finely grained differences and multiple relations between those differences.[46]

Foucault wanted to give as much space as possible to allow for the 'undefined work of freedom',[47] declaring that his research rested 'on a postulate of absolute optimism'.[48] History becomes a tool invested with an optimistic hope that we can do better and that things can be changed. For many, Foucault's self-description as an optimist comes as a surprise. He has frequently been accused of being a gloomy pessimist, a political nihilist and determinist. But Foucault argued that his historical analysis revealed 'the precariousness, the nonnecessity, and the instability of things' and was 'flabbergasted that people are able to see in my historical studies the affirmation of a determinism from which one cannot escape'.[49] But perhaps this perception is more to do with the subject matter he dealt with, notably some of western society's most oppressive institutions as well as socially marginalised groups, not to mention subjects such as illness and death, deviant sexuality and other behavioural aberrations. If Foucault wrote about the dubious origins of some institutions and about some less than edifying human practices, it was to expose them to the light of day, in order that people might recognise that the present was not the result of an inevitable process or of enlightened progress but the result of past human decision making, struggles for power, chance and indeed pure accident.[50] It is a process that continues to occur in the present.

No system of order, in Foucault's view, should ever be taken for granted or regarded as fixed and therefore should, as a consequence, be subject to constant challenge in terms of its relation to truth and to the effects of power it is exercising. Foucault through his practice of history wanted to help people see that they were able to make choices rather than simply resigning themselves to living out cast-iron historical traditions or bowing down under the weight of inflexible institutional structures. If every human cultural situation can be shown to be limited and subject to change, then this means that everybody, no matter what their situation, has some room for manoeuvre. Foucault noted that he 'firmly believe[d] in human freedom',[51] and in the capacity to make choices, no matter how restricted, in any given situation. Foucault's goal was to show through his histories that current cultural and social arrangements had been gradually created over time by many people and as a consequence could be undone and replaced by other arrangements.

If Foucault had very firm ideas on the use of history to promote social justice and freedom, he stopped short of prescribing exactly what kind of action people should undertake:

My books don't tell people what to do … People have to build their own ethics, taking as a point of departure the historical analysis, sociological analysis and so on that one can provide for them. I don't think that people who try to decipher the truth should have to provide ethical principles or practical advice at the same moment, in the same book and the same analysis. All this prescriptive network has to be elaborated and transformed by people themselves.[52]

This position infuriated critics who believed that Reason was the sole way of accessing the truth and that intellectuals were its prophets, and Foucault was frequently – and continues to be – taken to task for his non-performance on this front. His work, however, was precisely about the failure of Reason to provide solutions to human ills and indeed about its destructive force when applied on a large scale. He argued in the *History of Madness* that it was precisely the formulation of Reason as the essential truth of what a human was which led to the exclusion of 'irrational' people (which included not only those who were mad, but those who did not obey a whole panoply of social rules: the debauched, defrocked priests, single mothers, the unemployed) and to the inevitable conclusion that they were somehow less than human. Foucault went on to argue in his later work, notably *Discipline and Punish*, that the same process had been applied historically to criminals. Crime was an affront to rational society – therefore its perpetrators must somehow be less than human: 'monstrous'. Such sub-human elements represented a danger to rational society and had to be either eliminated or undergo radical methods of retraining.[53] Foucault's view was that the tendency of such systems which provide one size fits all solutions – no matter how radical – has always been to exclude some people. The women dutifully providing tea and sandwiches (and things to throw) to their revolutionary male comrades on the barricades in 1968 were certainly able to attest to this.[54] As for those prophets of reason – the intellectuals – they were but one element in a collective process of historical and social reform in which all participated. As Foucault stated quite categorically, 'history has no spectators'.[55] 'History' is not made by a privileged elite while the rest exist on the sideline merely preoccupied with the day to day biological survival of the species.

Perhaps one of the things that most worries some historians about Foucault's practice of history is that his very choice of history was deliberately – and indeed militantly – philosophical with a strong ethical goal. He was not simply a 'scientist' like Ranke's objective historian dispassionately gathering data about one particular area of human experience bounded by particular dates. He was not seeking to provide as comprehensive and neutral an account of the past as possible, or offering exhibits to add to the museums for the curious. Mainstream historians have often preferred to leave their philosophical assumptions about history very much in the background, to the point that sometimes they are not even aware of the philosophical underpinnings of their own enterprise. History, for a number of these historians, is about empirical objectivity and science, the careful collection of data in a particular field of enquiry with a view to discovering 'what really happened' and finally unveiling the truth of the past. Foucault, of course, was not alone in mounting a challenge to this view of history, but the old Rankian objectivist view of history dies hard and substantial remnants of it still survive in the contemporary practice of many professional historians.

## 2 Subject matter and sources

### The margins of experience

Foucault's philosophical and ethical position on history had a certain number of methodological consequences. This was apparent in his choice of subject matter, and his approaches to historical source material. There is for instance his decision to focus on the margins of experience and society. He noted that if the usual path taken by historians was to try and pin down the identity of a society and culture and to describe what it valued, he wanted to follow a less common approach by looking at what particular societies

rejected and marginalised – madness, illness, death, delinquency, the abnormal and the monstrous. He remarked: 'It seemed to me interesting to try to understand our society and civilization in terms of its systems of exclusion, of rejection, of refusal, in terms of what it does not want, its limits, the way it is obliged to suppress a number of things, people, processes.'[56] Foucault was, of course, part of a larger general and cultural movement which from the late 1960s concentrated on marginal groups and experiences and his own work made a considerable contribution to the success of this movement. It is important to note, however, that although Foucault's work was often used to support identity movements which sought to redress the injustices suffered by those who had been socially marginalised, he saw the notion of identity as restrictive, in terms of the way it fixed and policed the boundaries of how people chose to define themselves.[57]

### Subjugated knowledges

Foucault also advocated the unearthing of 'subjugated knowledges', namely historical content that had been discarded and rendered invisible by the present configurations of formalised knowledge (disciplines) and by the systematic way contemporary institutions worked. He argued that it was research which had drawn attention to the historical processes surrounding the foundation of institutions such as asylums and prisons, that had led to effective critique and change. It was change that was not brought about by disciplines such as semiology or sociology, but rather by erudite research in historical archives and bringing to light what had been discredited, repressed, forgotten or no longer regarded as knowledge which was true. Foucault described this practice of history as 'genealogy'.[58]

Methodologically genealogy operated in exactly the same way as 'archaeology', except it was endowed with a more directly political focus. The idea was not to practise scholarship and accumulate erudition in the antiquarian mode of a collector, but to remind people that the knowledge that had been given the official imprimatur by powerful social institutions, the official accounts of how we came to be where we are today, were not the only possible story.

### Historical objects

One of the early observations made about Foucault's practice of history was that he dealt with different objects from those of the traditional historian. But the difference goes further than this. He historicised objects that historians and others had previously unproblematically accepted as unchanging. Instead of assuming that it was a matter of describing the discovery and unveiling of scientific truth about pre-existing objects – such as madness, disease, the functioning of the body, criminality, the State, sexuality and so on, it was a matter of looking at how these objects were actually created (not discovered) at quite particular points in history. These objects came into being at the intersection of complex relations between 'institutions, economic and social processes, behavioural patterns, systems of norms, techniques, [and] types of classification'.[59]

### The history of thought

Foucault noted that from the nineteenth century until roughly around 1960, the object of history was narrowly defined as 'reality' or 'society' and that the mission of this kind of history was to provide a totalising account of the whole of a society.[60] But it was a version of history, which for all its inclusive pretensions, was restricted to the narrow materialism of social, economic and political events. It was a view which excluded thought from the historical account, relegating the history of knowledge and ideas to a kind of vaguely ahistorical superstructure which was somehow removed from the real hustle and bustle of history. But Foucault, rejecting this division into material infrastructure and intellectual and cultural superstructure,[61] argued that people's 'behaviour, attitudes and practices are all inhabited by thought',[62] and that thought had a history as much as any physical event or process.[63]

### Documents and sources

Foucault's choice of historical documents has often been met with disapproval by historians. This is in spite of the fact that Foucault clearly shared with historians the love of the archive – the pleasure of unearthing obscure and unread documents and bringing them to the light of day. This pleasure in the archive was particularly visible in a proposal he put forward for a project that aimed to collect fragmentary documents from the seventeenth and eighteenth centuries, which revealed 'obscure and unfortunate' lives whose only historical trace was left by their interactions with mechanisms of power in the form of legal documents, denunciations to the authorities and so on.[64]

But the issue for historians was Foucault's challenge to accepted methods of organising this documentary evidence – not only in terms of the way the documents related to the events they described – but also in terms of commonly accepted hierarchies of ranking their importance. Let us look first at what Foucault had to say about the ontological status of historical documents. He argued that documents have traditionally been seen as signposts to an external reality with the goal being to interpret these documents in order to reconstitute what actually happened. Foucault rejected this view, arguing words and documents needed to be considered as material objects which existed in relation to other material objects. Documents existed alongside other physical traces we inherit from the past and as such they need to be treated in the same way as archaeological artefacts.[65] They needed to be treated both in terms of their relation to each other and their relation to non documentary traces. Further, historians needed to do away with hierarchies of importance amongst documents and treat them all at the same level. There should be no 'privileged choices', which meant that 'one will take up *Don Quixote*, Descartes and a decree by Pomponne de Bellièvre about houses of internment in the same stroke … One ought to read everything'.[66] Foucault made this statement in 1966, but eventually (and unsurprisingly) later in his career proposed the notion of 'problematisation' – the examination of specific historical 'problems' – as a way of limiting the investigation within realistic boundaries.[67]

## 3 The organisation of time

One of the most widely discussed elements of Foucault's historiography approaches has been his organisation of historical time. On the basis of his view that history should be about the enactment of continual difference, Foucault rejected any notion that would smooth out the differences produced by the passage of time. Traditional historians have made a number of assumptions about how humans live and relate to time and have used a number of categories to organise and explain how historical occurrences relate to each other. These include cause, effect, influence, eternal essences, progress, teleology, tradition, 'spirit of the age' and progress, all of which have the effect of linking the past and the present smoothly together in a continuous flow. Changes that are particularly difficult to explain away using these terms are labelled 'crises', or are the result of the intervention of 'geniuses' or 'great men'. Foucault, however, suggested a different perspective on the way human beings live in time. History was an assemblage of discontinuities, he argued, and indeed, the very idea of history presupposed discontinuity, in that the past was by definition different from the present.[68] Foucault defined his task as being 'to diagnose the present, to say what our present is and, how our present is different and absolutely different, from all that is not it, that is to say our past',[69] describing himself as a 'historian of the present'.[70]

In order to challenge continuist views of history which sought to subordinate change to fixed constants in history, Foucault proposed a variety of different rules relating to periodisation and the 'event', splitting history into multiple levels of intelligibility which linked to each other in highly complex ways.

### Periodisation

Foucault readily admitted the notion of 'period' was 'confused',[71] adding that the period was not the ultimate goal or guiding principle of his analysis. He remarked: 'The Classical age which has often been mentioned in archaeological analyses, is not a temporal figure that imposes its unity and empty form on all discourses; it is the name that is given to a tangle of continuities and discontinuities ... discursive formations that appear and disappear'.[72] Nonetheless, with the exception of volumes 2 and 3 of *The History of Sexuality* and his lectures in the 1980s which focused on Antiquity, Foucault offered a fairly standard set of periods: the Middle Ages, the Renaissance, the Classical Age, the Modern Age and the contemporary post-Second World War period. He rejected the popular label of 'postmodern' as a description for this latter period as being too vague and ill-defined.[73] Depending on what subject matter Foucault was dealing with – madness, illness, the history of punishment, the birth of biopower – he located the boundary dates between these periods differently. He explained this in an interview in 1967 where he observed that 'each level of events calls for its own periodisation', describing this as part of the 'complex methodology of discontinuity'.[74] Historians and other commentators have of course quibbled over the dates of these boundaries. Of particular interest to historians has been what Foucault describes in the *History of Madness* as the 'Great Confinement', symbolically marked in 1656 by the foundation of the Hôpital Général in Paris.[75] This event saw the establishment of houses of internment across Europe aimed at enclosing deviant and 'unreasonable' members of the population with a view to reducing the danger they posed to the rest of the population and attempting to make them economically productive. Some less favourably disposed historians, however, have argued that this event did not occur at all, or occurred much earlier or much later.[76]

Foucault was particularly interested in the changes that occurred between the seventeenth and nineteenth centuries, returning to this period again and again in his various works on madness, clinical medicine, prisons and on the origins of the social sciences. As he said in 1975: 'Basically I only have one object of historical study and that is the threshold of modernity ... From this threshold European discourse developed gigantic powers of universalisation'.[77] A year earlier, he drew attention to his deliberate avoidance of Ancient Greece and his objections to histories and analyses which ignored more recent history in order to locate the origins of all contemporary culture within Antiquity.[78] His readers were therefore more than a little surprised when he departed radically from his usual historical terrain in the early 1980s and directed his attention to Ancient Greece and Rome. He explained this shift stating that in order to pursue his interest in the links between sexuality and the relation to the self and in order to say something new he was forced to go further and further back into history: 'it became obvious that I should study the period in late antiquity when the principal elements of the Christian ethic of the flesh were being formulated'.[79]

### The episteme

The main problem that historians and others have had with Foucault's periodisation is not so much the specific dates he used to divide these rather conventional historical periods, but the suddenness and abruptness of the transition from one period to another. This surfaced most clearly in The Order of Things with his famous notion of the 'episteme' and in The Archaeology of Knowledge with its lengthy championing of the notion of discontinuity. Discontinuity operated in Foucault's work at both an empirical and a philosophical level. It is something that he observed in the train of events and it was also a tool he employed to challenge Hegelian and historicist views of history. Foucault's idea of discontinuity, of sudden historical breaks, led to heated controversy in the 1960s and early 1970s and to accusations of political quietism as history, of course, should be marked by

incremental progress towards either the classless state or a perfectly rational and Enlightened society. Yet, the notion of discontinuity had already long been one of the working tools of the history of science and the concepts of 'break' and difference were very much 'in the air' when Foucault was writing in the 1960s. Foucault acknowledges Gaston Bachelard, Canguilhem and Michel Serres in the areas of the history and philosophy of science.[80] Louis Althusser also borrowed Bachelard's notion of the 'epistemological break' to apply to his own theories of structuralist Marxism. The philosopher of science, Thomas Kuhn, also came up with the famous notion of the paradigm in 1962,[81] predating Foucault's idea of the episteme. Foucault, however, stated he didn't read Kuhn's 'admirable and definitive work' until the end of 1963, just after he had finished writing the manuscript of The Order of Things.[82]

The episteme is a notion that has been much discussed and widely used by historians and others. Foucault defines it as the 'unconscious' system of order, the rules which underlies the production of scientific knowledge in a particular time and place.[83] Unfortunately he is rather vague and somewhat inconsistent in his use of the term. In The Order of Things the episteme is only referred to in the singular as the 'western episteme' which adopted different 'configurations' at different periods in history. However, statements in The Order of Things, such as 'in any given culture and at any given moment there is always only one episteme that defines the conditions of possibility of all knowledge',[84] and later definitions have led commentators to assume the existence of successive epistemes corresponding roughly to the standard historical periods of the Renaissance, the Classical Age and so on. Even Foucault himself was to eventually use it in the plural.[85] In work subsequent to The Order of Things, Foucault specified that the episteme referred only to scientific knowledge, which was only one form of knowledge amongst others.[86] The episteme was in fact a subset of what Foucault describes more generally as 'the historical a priori'. This was a concept that described the underlying structures which governed the production of all knowledge in a particular epoch and culture.[87] If one examined what Foucault described as the 'archive' of a culture, namely the collection of all material traces left behind by a particular historical period, one could deduce the historical a priori of that period. It is important to note that neither the historical a priori nor its scientific subset the episteme had predictive value – they were descriptions of limited historical orders, the historically changeable rules or conditions which allowed knowledge to function as valid and true at a particular period. For example, during the Renaissance the underlying system of order was 'resemblance', thus all knowledge was organised by noting resemblances between things. The changeover between each configuration was rather abrupt and Foucault was accused of being deliberately provocative in positing these sudden breaks, but as he notes on a couple of occasions, these breaks were a problem for him as well and he spent considerable time and effort analysing the detail of just how these transitions occurred.[88]

### The event

The fortunes of the episteme, however, were short lived in Foucault's work. Except for a few definitional statements in later writings, it only ever appears extensively in *The Order of Things*. From a focus on macro discontinuities, Foucault shifted his emphasis to more finely grained discontinuities, particularly as embodied in the 'event'. The event was something that had a beginning and an end, and in Foucault's view, every human activity, cultural practice, discourse, thought and idea could be treated as an event. These events left material traces which could then be examined by the historian. Foucault described this process of treating history as a series of events, as 'eventialisation'.[89] He expressed a particular admiration for the work of the Annales school in this regard and referred to Marc Bloch, Fernand Braudel,[90]

Emmanuel Le Roy Ladurie[91] and Huguette and Pierre Chaunu.[92] In identifying with the positions of these 'new' historians he once again distinguished his views from traditional understandings.[93] The 'event' was not just a significant political or social occurrence, such as the inauguration of a new king, or a war.[94] Events occurred at the most mundane level, for example a ship entering and leaving a harbour,[95] a committee putting together a list of rules for the running of a school or a prison, or the slate taken out by school children in early nineteenth-century France at 9.04 am every weekday morning.[96] These events were significant at different levels and these levels interacted with each other in complex ways. As Foucault remarked in a discussion about the work of the Annales school: 'history is not one duration, but a multiplicity of durations which interlink, and envelop each other'.[97] These views lead to a radically non-reductive view of history. There is no threshold whereby some events are significant and worthy of historical notice, whereas others deserve only to be consigned to oblivion. Each event, whether in the realm of ideas, or in the realm of physical practice, is significant at a particular level of existence which it is the job of the historian to trace and render intelligible. As Foucault observed: 'Some doctor who said something asinine about madness belongs to history just as the battle of Waterloo does', also noting in the same discussion, 'Of course these are not the same types of events but they *are* events.'[98]

Further, if each event has a discrete beginning and end, it does not exist on its own, it can only exist in relation to other events and other levels of events. An event when it begins is already part of a history and a social and cultural structure. It both perpetuates and marks a break or difference – no matter how small – from those structures. To use the language of philosophy, it is both the Same and the Other. Foucault applied an identical process to his discussion of the formation of the self. The self was also an 'event'. We are born into a language, culture and historical situation and we are trained by, and train ourselves, with the tools produced by our history and culture. At the same time, however, we have the capacity to modify how we belong, to make a unique contribution – even if that contribution is destined to remain unchronicled in the annals of history.

This fragmentation of history into events and multiple non-hierarchical levels, rather than smooth chains of causes, big ideas and significant events has been extremely productive. Histories of areas in the sciences and professions which had previously been deemed as without history or not worthy of serious attention have proliferated in the wake of the work done by Foucault and the Annales School. Traditional history of science had the habit of relegating all knowledge that went before the formal 'birth' of the science to quaint errors best forgotten. The thinking and work that preceded the birth of any given science only had value in so far as it produced and led up to this event. From this perspective, other lines of investigation, other practices became simply odd and amusing wanderings providing nothing more than simple entertainment value once a science was established in all its rigour. Foucault's approach allowed these superseded and silenced forms of knowledge to be once again restored to a valued place in the history of human endeavour.

## 4 The subject and history

In *The Archaeology of Knowledge,* Foucault noted: 'Making historical analysis the discourse of the continuous and making human consciousness the original subject of all historical development and action are the two sides of the same system of thought.'[99] Categories such as genius and the great man were traditionally used to explain away and anchor historical change. The human 'subject' – an entity who was self-aware and capable of making choices – had an eternal essence that escaped history, thus, in order to discover the truth about oneself and human existence in general one needed to strip away

one's own history. History was nothing but a confusing veil over the truth. Foucault rejected the humanist subject in the 1960s precisely because it sought to remove itself from history and stand as a central point of unchanging truth. 'Man' had become a central reference point in the modern era, both an empirical truth to be studied by science and also that which allowed knowledge to be created. Foucault described this in *The Order of Things* as the paradoxical 'empirico-transcendental doublet' which lay at the heart of the human sciences such as sociology and psychology and justified their existence.[100]

Foucault was not the only thinker to challenge the centrality of the humanist subject. Indeed it was precisely this point which united the diverse researches of the so-called 'structuralists' – Lévi-Strauss, Lacan, Althusser, Barthes and Derrida. These theorists argued that the description of broad historical and cultural structures had more explanatory value than an existential and phenomenological excavation of the interior workings of discrete individual subjects. In addition to this, humanist and modernist views of subjectivity tended to suggest that only certain subjects counted in the production of history and social and cultural change. The great man and the genius, the man of vision were what moved history along. Foucault, on the other hand, insisted that every subject counted and that hierarchies of power in the construction of who had value in history needed to be challenged.

Foucault later admitted that he had tended to identify the ahistorical humanist subject with the subject in general, going on in the early 1980s to develop a far more nuanced position which allowed for a historical version of the subject. A number of critics have read Foucault's later interest in the subject as a conservative denial of his earlier radical views, but they miss the crucial point that his views on the historicity of human experience remained constant. It was not so much the subject per se that was at issue, but the existence of a category that stood outside history. Close examination of Foucault's work in fact reveals references to the possibility of a historical subject which long predate the detailed work he undertook in this area in the early 1980s. One of his first publications, 'Dream and existence', referred to 'a dream subject' that only existed at the precise moment of dreaming. It had no existence beyond that.[101]

Foucault contended that there have been three models which have governed the relation of the subject to truth and knowledge in western history, namely self-discovery, self-transformation and the scientific model. The latter makes the claim that the truth can be arrived at by the accumulation of data rather than transformative work on the self.[102] Foucault was most interested in the second model, which allowed for an ongoing and historical modification of the self/subject, observing: 'in the course of their history, men have never ceased to construct themselves in an infinite, multiple series of subjectivities that will never have an end'.[103]

### The construction of the moral subject

Foucault also proposed what has become a popular four-tiered model which can be used to analyse how individuals are historically invited to construct themselves as the moral and ethical subjects of their own actions:[104]

1 The first step consists in noting the part of the individual that needs to be worked on in order to be moral. Foucault provided some historical examples of this: for the Ancient Greeks it was acts, for the early Christians it was desire and for contemporary people it is feelings.
2 The second tier of the analysis addresses the cultural incentives which make an individual want to be moral. Historically these have included the word of God as found in the Bible and other scriptures, the desirability of making one's life an example to others (the Greeks) or the self-evidence of rationality (post-Enlightenment atheists).
3 The third part of the analysis concerns the tools individuals might use to achieve their ethical and moral goals – these can include various practices of diet and exercise and

techniques of mental discipline, such as meditation, or intellectual practices of writing.[105]
4 Finally one might ask what the aim of all these activities is – what kind of person is the individual aiming to be through the performance of moral and ethical actions? Again, the responses to this question have varied according to geography and historical period. The end point might be eternal salvation in a glorious afterlife, or it might be self-mastery or achieving happiness within this life.

What is interesting about this schema is its historicity. If Foucault argued that moral codes tended to stay relatively – but not completely – stable – the ethical relation to oneself and others and how one activates particular principles varies considerably.[106] It is a form of analysis which allows people more freedom to decide how far the specific ethical systems they have been exposed to are appropriate for their own existences.

## 5 Truth and power in history

Questions of truth and power are central to Foucault's work. He was described by *Time* magazine in 1981 as 'France's philosopher of power'[107] and continues to be best known for his theories on power. Controversies over his approach to truth also erupt at regular intervals in the popular intellectual press[108] and thrive endlessly in the academic literature.

Once again, Foucault deliberately undermined accepted understandings, removing both power and truth from the transcendental sphere and locating them firmly in history. Further, he asserted that power and truth were not mutually exclusive. These positions have led to endless discussion and moral outrage at what has been perceived as a cynically amoral view which holds that truth is relative and that what we call truth is simply what those in a position of power want us to believe. Foucault's position was in fact far more nuanced and complex. As he frequently pointed out, humans are historically limited beings who are born and who die and who occupy a specific space. They cannot occupy the whole of the territory, so they have to 'move around to gather information' and 'move things relative to another in order to make them useful'.[109] In short, people, given their limitations, are constantly reorganising both words and things in their attempts to understand and manage their social and physical environments.

Nonetheless, for all this flexibility, not just any arrangement is possible. Foucault is careful to point out that there are limits to the ways in which concepts can be formulated. This is perhaps best demonstrated by comparing his position on madness to that of the anti-psychiatrists. If anti-psychiatrists argued that madness only existed as the result of exclusionary social practices, Foucault insisted that there was a real physical basis for madness. What was variable was how this condition was defined and treated historically and the social status of those exhibiting particular symptoms. Further to this, even if Foucault described what he was writing as 'fictions' – that is, constructed stories about the past which provoked a certain 'experience' in the reader – this did not mean he was writing novels. Citing the *History of Madness* as an example, he claimed that in order for people to have an experience which allowed them to change their views of madness, mental illness and the history of psychiatry his demonstrations needed 'to be true in terms of academic, historically verifiable truth'.[110] It is also worth quoting Foucault here on the question of truth and the history of science, as this has been a source of particular confusion in relation to his work:

> There isn't *one* truth – which doesn't mean that this history is irrational or that science is illusory. Rather, it confirms the presence of a real and intelligible history, of a series of collective rational experiences conforming to a set of precise, identifiable rules and resulting in the construction of both the knowing subject and the known object.[111]

Truth is not simply the product of power relations. For Foucault truth and power existed in a highly complex relationship that was the subject of constant negotiation through history.

Foucault offered numerous definitions of power in his work, eventually arriving at the position that power was the capacity of one structure of actions to modify another structure of actions, and that the exercise of power was dependent on the freedom – that is, the capacity to make choices – of all involved.[112] A participant in an exercise of power could always say no, even if the end result was violence or slavery. But when it reached these extremes, the exercise of power had reached its limits and had become a different kind of relation.[113]

Once again, as with other categories in his work, in defining power Foucault used a process of negative definition. Power was not a thing that some people possessed and others did not – rather it was a relation, it only existed when it was being exercised. Neither was it simply something that said no, piling up endless prohibitions and repressions. Nor was it simply invested in the State and government or in the hands of the ruling classes: instead it operated at every level of social existence – within families, within local communities, within institutions such as hospitals and the schools and at macro-levels such as government taxation.[114] There was no one 'source' of power.[115] If 'states of domination' existed these were the result of historically traceable actions by large numbers of individuals.[116] Tracking the operations of power and tracing the origins of structures of domination allowed people to see that contemporary configurations of power relations were not immutable. Where there was power there was necessarily resistance; indeed Foucault suggested that any analysis of power relations should use resistance as its starting point.[117] Constant processes of negotiation were always taking place in terms of how actions were modified, in other words the deployment of power was 'strategic'.[118] Towards the end of the 1970s, Foucault began to use the term 'governmentality' in order to refine his discussion and introduce notions of subjectivity into his analysis of power relations. This term described the various techniques used to guide and modify people's conduct at every level of the social body. If initially Foucault was interested in how this occurred at the administrative level of the State, he gradually extended his analysis to include the examination of how subjects modified their own behaviour at an individual level in relation to others.[119]

The effect of defining power as a relation that only existed when it was being practised was to make power thoroughly historical. It was something that only existed through quite specific and describable historical actions and events. This meant that it was not a matter of waiting for historical destiny, revolution or charismatic individuals to change configurations of domination. Every individual at some level participated in how relations of power and resistance were played out historically.

## CONCLUSION

Foucault's contribution to contemporary historiography has been pivotal. He deliberately set out to challenge a number of taken-for-granted ideas – most particularly those which sought to universalise and dehistoricise certain aspects of human existence. It is important to remember that he was not working in isolation. He shared much in common with radical historians of science and with the Annales school in his efforts to demonstrate that history did not simply apply to a select number of human activities and experiences and that participation in the historical process was not simply the province of a privileged few. His work continues to provide a wealth of tools – both methodological and empirical – which historians and others have not hesitated to employ across a wide range of specialities in the humanities, social sciences and vocational disciplines. Foucault's work stands at the intersection of philosophical and historical investigation and this is perhaps one of the keys to its broad appeal. Indeed perhaps, he summed up his entire philosophical approach to the conundrum of human existence

right at the beginning of his career, when he declared that what is most human about humanity is history.[120]

## NOTES AND REFERENCES

1 Hayden White, 'Foucault historian?', paper presented at 'Foucault Across the Disciplines' conference, University of California, Santa Cruz, 1–2 March 2008, available at http://humweb.ucsc.edu/foucaultacrossthedisciplines/10_White.mp3.

2 Michel Foucault, 'La poussière et le nuage', in *Dits et Écrits: 1954–1988, Vol. IV*, ed. Daniel Defert, François Ewald and Jacques Lagrange (Paris: Gallimard, 1994 [1980]), 13. The date in square brackets is the date of original publication. Given that Foucault continually developed and changed his ideas, it is important to know the original publication dates of his writings.

3 Michel Foucault, 'Questions of method', in *Power*, ed. James D. Faubion (New York: The New Press, 2000 [1980]), 223.

4 Michel Foucault, 'Interview with Michel Foucault', in *Power*, [1980], 240. Foucault notes: 'If philosophy is memory or a return to origin, what I am doing cannot, in any way, be regarded as philosophy.' Michel Foucault, *The Archaeology of Knowledge*, trans. A.M. Sheridan Smith (London: Tavistock, 1972 [1969]), 206.

5 See for example: Michel Foucault, 'The end of the monarchy of sex', in *Foucault Live Interviews, 1961–1984*, ed. Sylvère Lotringer (New York: Semiotext(e), 1996 [1977]), 222.

6 Foucault, 'Interview with MF', 278.

7 Foucault, *The Archaeology*, 125.

8 Incidentally Foucault has never been accused of 'positivism' by English language critics or historians. On the contrary, he is more commonly seen as far too vaguely philosophical. For a more expanded discussion on these debates see Clare O'Farrell, *Foucault: Philosopher or Historian?* (London: Macmillan, 1989), 58.

9 Michel Foucault, 'Le style de l'histoire', in *Dits et Écrits, IV*, [1984], 652. Cf. Michel Foucault, *The Use of Pleasure. The History of Sexuality: Volume Two*, trans. Robert Hurley (Harmondsworth, Middlesex: Penguin, 1992 [1984]). 30.

10 Edward W. Said, *Orientalism* (Harmondsworth: Penguin, 1985).

11 Foucault notes in *History of Madness*, ed. Jean. Khalfa, trans. Jonathan Murphy and Jean Khalfa (London: Routledge, 2006 [1961]), p. xxx: 'In the universality of the Western *ratio*, there is a division which is the Orient ... The Orient is for the Occident everything that it is not, while remaining a place in which its primitive truth must be sought. What is required is a history of this great divide.' Said also uses Foucault's archaeological method and his book is noteworthy as one of the first extended applications of Foucault's work in English.

12  Michel Foucault and Ludwig Binswanger, 'Dream, imagination, and existence', in *Dream and Existence*, ed. K. Hoeller (Atlantic Highlands, NJ: Humanities Press, 1993 [1954]).

13  Michel Foucault, *Mental Illness and Psychology*, trans. A.M. Sheridan Smith (New York: Harper and Row, 1976 [1962]).

14  Michel Foucault, *The Birth of the Clinic: An Archaeology of Medical Perception*, trans. A. M. Sheridan Smith (London: Tavistock, 1973 [1963]); Michel Foucault, *Death and the Labyrinth: The World of Raymond Roussel*, trans. Charles Ruas, intro. by John Ashbery (London: Athlone, 1986 [1963]).

15  The gaze is an idea which ties in with the notions of surveillance that Foucault was to employ extensively in his later work, *Discipline and Punish: The Birth of the Prison*, trans. A. M. Sheridan Smith (Harmondsworth, Middlesex: Penguin, 1991 [1975]).

16  Michel Foucault, 'History, discourse and discontinuity', in *Foucault Live* [1968], 37.

17  James William Bernauer, *Michel Foucault's Force of Flight: Toward an Ethics for Thought* (London: Humanities Press International, 1990), appendix 2, 188–92.

18  Michel Foucault, 'Entretien avec Madeleine Chapsal', in *Dits et Écrits: I*, [1966], 517–18.

19  Michel Foucault, 'On the ways of writing history', in *Aesthetics, Method and Epistemology. The Essential Works of Michel Foucault 1954–1984*, ed. James D. Faubion (Harmondsworth, Middlesex: Allen Lane, Penguin, 1998 [1967]), 289–90.

20  Michel Foucault, *The Order of Things: An Archaeology of the Human Sciences*, trans. A.M. Sheridan Smith (London: Tavistock, 1970 [1966]).

21  Foucault, *The Order of Things*, 262.

22  Foucault, *The Order of Things*, 387.

23  Michel Foucault, 'Foucault responds to Sartre', in *Foucault Live*, [1968]), 55, trans. mod. For Foucault's remarks on the historicist reductionism of the Hegelian dialectic see Michel Foucault, 'Theatrum philosophicum', in *Aesthetics* [1970], 358.

24  Foucault, *The Archaeology*.

25  Michel Foucault, 'Who are you, Professor Foucault?', in *Religion and Culture*, ed. Jeremy R. Carrette (Manchester: Manchester University Press, 1999 [1967]), 92. Cf. Michel Foucault, 'A conversation with Michel Foucault', in *Foucault Live*, [1971], 68 and Foucault, 'Writing history', 281, 285.

26  Jacques Revel, 'Foucault et les historiens', *Magazine Littéraire*, no. 101 (1975), 10.

27  Michel Foucault, 'The order of discourse', in *Untying the Text: A Post-Structuralist Reader*, ed. Robert Young (Boston: Routledge and Kegan Paul, 1981 [1970]).

28  See Foucault, 'Interview with MF', 279–81; Michel Foucault, '"Je suis un artificier." A propos de la méthode et de la trajectoire de Michel Foucault', in *Michel Foucault, Entretiens*, ed. Roger-Pol Droit (Paris: Odile Jacob, 2004), 119–20. Interview conducted in 1975.

29  Foucault, *Discipline*.

30  Foucault, *Discipline*, 135–69.

31  For a detailed account of the uptake of Foucault's treatment of Bentham's Panopticon and the impact that this has had in terms of the reception of Bentham's original work see Anne Brunon-Ernst, ed., *Beyond Foucault. New Perspectives on Bentham's Panopticon* (London: Ashgate, 2012).

32  Michel Foucault, *The History of Sexuality: Volume 1*, trans. Robert Hurley (Harmondsworth, Middlesex: Penguin, 1990 [1976]).

33  Giorgio Agamben, *Homo Sacer: Sovereign Power and Bare Life*, trans. Daniel Heller-Roazen (Stanford: Stanford University Press, 1998).

34  Michel Foucault, 'The concern for truth', in *Foucault Live*, [1984], 455.

35  Michel Foucault, *'Society Must Be Defended': Lectures at the Collège de France, 1975–1976*, trans. David Macey (New York: Picador, 2003 [1997]).

36  Michel Foucault, 'Governmentality', in *Power*, [1978], 201–22.

37  Michel Foucault, 'On the government of the living', in *Ethics: Subjectivity and Truth. The Essential Works of Michel Foucault 1954–1984*, ed. Paul Rabinow (Harmondsworth, Middlesex: Allen Lane, Penguin, 1997 [1980]), 81. Cf. Michel Foucault, 'The subject and power', in *Power*, [1982b], 341–2.

38  Michel Foucault, 'Technologies of the self', in *Ethics*, [1988]), 225.

39  Foucault, *Use of Pleasure*; Michel Foucault, *The Care of the Self. The History of Sexuality: Volume 3*, trans. Robert Hurley (Harmondsworth, Middlesex: Penguin, 1990 [1984]).

40  Foucault, *Use of Pleasure*, 10.

41  See Clare O'Farrell, *Michel Foucault* (London: Sage, 2005), 54ff.

42  For discussions of this comparison see Jeremy R. Carrette, *Foucault and Religion: Spiritual Corporality and Political Spirituality* (London and New York: Routledge, 2000), 89ff and James William Bernauer and Jeremy R. Carrette, *Michel Foucault and Theology. The Politics of Religious Experience* (Aldershot, Burlington: Ashgate, 2004), 88–9.

43  Foucault, *The Archaeology*, 205–6.

44  Foucault, 'Questions', 228.

45  Foucault, 'Je suis un artificier', 133–4.

46  Foucault, *Society*, 5–13.

47  Michel Foucault, 'What is enlightenment?', in *Ethics*, [1984], 316.

48  Foucault, 'Interview with MF', 294.

49  Michel Foucault, 'Interview with Actes', in *Power*, [1984], 399.

50  Michel Foucault, 'Nietzsche, genealogy, history', in *Aesthetics*, [1971], 374.

51  Foucault, 'Interview with Actes', 399.

52  Michel Foucault, 'An interview by Stephen Riggins', in *Ethics*, [1983], 131–2.

53  Michel Foucault, 'About the concept of the "dangerous individual" in nineteenth-century legal psychiatry', in *Power*, [1978], 176–200.

54  See Claire Duchen, *Women's Rights and Women's Lives in France 1944–1968* (London: Routledge, 1994), 194–5.
55  Michel Foucault, 'Le savoir comme crime', in *Dits et Écrits: III*, [1976], 80.
56  Michel Foucault, 'Rituals of exclusion', in *Foucault Live*, [1971], 69.
57  'The insistence on identity and the injunction to make a break both feel like impositions, and in the same way'. Michel Foucault, 'For an ethic of discomfort', in *Power*, [1979], 444.
58  Foucault, *Society*, 8–12. Foucault readily admitted that history occupied a privileged position in his enquiries. History was able to play 'the role of an internal ethnology of our culture and our rationality'. Foucault, 'On the ways', 293.
59  Foucault, *The Archaeology*, 45.
60  Foucault, 'La poussière', 15.
61  Michel Foucault, 'L'âge d'or de la lettre de cachet', in *Dits et Écrits: IV*, [1982], 351.
62  Foucault, 'Le style', 654.
63  Foucault, 'The concern', 456, trans. mod.
64  Michel Foucault, 'The life of infamous men', in *Power*, [1977], 157–75. This project resulted in Foucault's involvement in the publication of two collections of documents: Michel Foucault, *Herculine Barbin (Being the Recently Discovered Memoirs of a Nineteenth Century French Hermaphrodite)*, trans. Richard McDougall (New York: Pantheon, 1980 [1978]) and a collaboration with the historian Arlette Farges dealing with *lettres de cachet*, Michel Foucault and Arlette Farges, eds., *Le Désordre des Familles: Lettres de Cachet des Archives de la Bastille au XVIIIe siècle* (Paris: Gallimard, Julliard, 1982).
65  Foucault, *The Archaeology*, 7.
66  Michel Foucault, 'The order of things', in *Aesthetics*, [1966], 262–3.
67  Foucault, 'La poussière', 13. See also Foucault, 'The concern', 456–7; Michel Foucault, 'Problematics', in *Foucault Live*, [1994], 416–22. Interview originally conducted in 1983.
68  Foucault, *The Archaeology*, 9.
69  Foucault, 'Foucault responds to Sartre', 53.
70  Michel Foucault, 'The end of the monarchy', 222.
71  Foucault, *The Archaeology*, 148.
72  Foucault, *The Archaeology*, 176.
73  See Michel Foucault, 'Structuralism and post-structuralism', in *Aesthetics*, [1983], 447–8; Foucault, 'What is enlightenment?', 309.
74  Foucault, 'On the ways', 280–1. Cf. Foucault, *The Archaeology*, 3–5.
75  See Robert Forster and Orest Ranum, eds., *Deviants and the Abandoned in French Society: Selections from the Annales: Économies, Sociétés, Civilisations, Vol 4* (Baltimore: Johns Hopkins University Press, 1978). As early as 1973, Roger Chartier commented on 'the already classical framework' of confinement offered by Foucault. 'Pauvreté et assistance dans la France moderne: l'exemple de la généralité de Lyon', *Annales: Économies, Sociétés, Civilisations* 28, no. 2 (1973), 578.
76  See Lawrence Stone, 'Madness', *New York Review of Books*, 16 December 1982, 28. For a summary of early English language and German critiques of Foucault's periodisation and notion of the Great confinement see J.G. Merquior, *Foucault* (Berkeley: University of California Press, 1987), 26–9. For a more recent and detailed discussion of the reception by historians of this book see Gary Gutting, *The Cambridge Companion to Foucault*, 2nd edn (Cambridge: Cambridge University Press, 2006), 49–73.
77  Foucault, 'Je suis un artificier', 127.
78  Michel Foucault, 'Prisons et asiles dans le mécanisme du pouvoir', in *Dits et Écrits: II*, [1974], 521–2.
79  Michel Foucault, 'Preface to The History of Sexuality, Volume II', in *Ethics*, [1984], 340.
80  Foucault, *The Archaeology*, 4–5.
81  Thomas S. Kuhn, *The Structure of Scientific Revolutions*, 3rd edn (Chicago: University of Chicago Press, 1996 [1962]).
82  Michel Foucault, 'Foucault responds', *Diacritics* 1, no. 2 (1971), 60.
83  O'Farrell, *Michel Foucault*, 134.
84  Foucault, *The Order of Things*, 168.
85  Foucault, 'Preface', 203.
86  The 'episteme of a period [is] not the sum of its knowledge, nor the general style of its research, but the departures, the distances, the oppositions, the differences, the relations of its multiple scientific discourses … [It is] not a slice of history common to all the sciences'. Foucault, 'History, discourse', 35, trans. mod.
87  Foucault, *The Order of Things*, 158; Foucault, *The Archaeology*, 126–31.
88  'This break, it's my problem not my solution. If I put so much emphasis on this break, it's because it's a hell of a puzzle, and not a way of solving things', Foucault, 'Je suis un artificier', 124.
89  Foucault, 'Questions', 226–9.
90  Michel Foucault, 'La scène de la philosophie', in *Dits et Écrits: III*, [1978], 580.
91  Michel Foucault, 'Le retour de Pierre Rivière', in *Dits et Écrits: III*, [1976]), 119.
92  Michel Foucault, 'Return to history', in *Aesthetics*, [1972], 427.
93  For a manifesto and collection of work done by the 'new historians' see Jacques Le Goff, Roger Chartier and Jacques Revel, eds., *La Nouvelle Histoire*, Les Encyclopédies du Savoir Moderne (Paris: CEPL, 1978).
94  Foucault refers approvingly to the interest of contemporary historians in the everyday and in anonymous individuals. Foucault, 'Le retour', 119.
95  Foucault, 'Return', 427.
96  Foucault, *Discipline*, 150.
97  Foucault, 'Return', 430, trans. mod.
98  Foucault, 'Interview with MF', 277.
99  Foucault, *The Archaeology*, 12.
100  Foucault, *The Order of Things*, 318–22.
101  Foucault, 'Dream', 57. For further discussion on this topic see O'Farrell, *Michel Foucault*, 111–13.

102 Michel Foucault, *The Hermeneutics of the Subject: Lectures at the Collège de France, 1981–1982*, ed. Frédéric Gros, François Ewald and Alessandro Fontana (New York: Palgrave-Macmillan, 2005 [2001]), 460–1.

103 Foucault, 'Interview with MF', 276. See also Michel Foucault, 'The ethics of the concern for the self as a practice of freedom', in *Ethics*, [1984], 291.

104 Foucault, *The Use*, 26–7, 38; Michel Foucault, 'On the genealogy of ethics: an overview of work in progress', in *Ethics*, [1983].

105 Michel Foucault, 'Self-writing', in *Ethics*, [1983].

106 Michel Foucault, 'Usage des plaisirs et techniques de soi', in *Dits et Écrits: IV*, [1983], 560–1.

107 Otto Friedrich and Sandra Burton, 'France's philosopher of power', *Time*, 16 November 1981, 92–4.

108 For some random examples see Raymond Tallis, 'The truth about lies. Foucault, Nietzsche and the Cretan paradox', *The Times Literary Supplement*, 21 December 2001; Patrick West, 'The philosopher as dangerous liar', *New Statesman*, 28 June 2004; Julian Baggini, 'This is what the clash of civilisations is really about', *The Guardian*, 14 April 2007.

109 Michel Foucault, 'Life: experience and science', in *Aesthetics*, [1978], 475.

110 Foucault, 'Interview with MF', 243. See also Michel Foucault, 'À propos des faiseurs d'histoire', in *Dits et Écrits: IV*, [1983], 414.

111 Foucault, 'Interview with MF', 254.

112 Foucault's most useful definitions of power can be found in Michel Foucault, 'Power and strategies', in *Power/Knowledge: Selected Interviews and Other Writings 1972–1977*, ed. Colin Gordon (New York: Pantheon Books, 1980 [1977]); Michel Foucault, '"Omnes et singulatim": toward a critique of political reason', in *Power*, [1981]; Foucault, 'The subject and power'; Foucault, *History of Sexuality, v.1*, 92–102.

113 Foucault, 'Omnes', 324.

114 On the 'microphysics of power' see Foucault, *Discipline*, 26, 160.

115 Michel Foucault, 'Space, knowledge and power', in *Power*, [1982], 356.

116 'Relations of power are not in superstructural positions ... Major dominations are the hegemonic effects that are sustained by all these confrontations', Foucault, *The History of Sexuality*, *Vol. 1*, 94. See also Foucault 'The ethics', 283.

117 Foucault, 'The subject', 329.

118 For definitions of strategy in relation to power see Foucault, 'The subject', 346–8.

119 For extended discussions on governmentality see Michel Foucault, *Security, Territory, Population: Lectures at the Collège de France, 1977–78*, ed. Michel Senellart, François Ewald and Alessandro Fontana (Basingstoke: Palgrave-Macmillan, 2007 [2004]).

120 Michel Foucault, 'La psychologie de 1850 à 1950', in *Dits et Écrits: I*, [1957], 137.

# 12

# History as Text: Narrative Theory and History

Ann Rigney

On 22 July 2011, 32-year-old Anders Breivik exploded a bomb in the centre of Oslo killing eight people, and then travelled disguised as a police officer to the island of Utøya, the site of a Labour Party youth camp, where he opened fire and killed another 69. In the hours and days that followed, there was inevitably much speculation on the meaning of this horrendous and seemingly 'senseless' act. For some, Breivik's actions over a period of a couple of hours made sense as the culmination of an individual life that had derailed and lost touch with reality; it was the tragic result of an individual pathology. For others, the slaughter made sense as part of the growing influence of radical right-wing thinking in Europe and of an increasing willingness to resort to violence as an alternative to democratic discussion; as such, it was not the result of the derailing of an individual, but part of a more worrying and more widespread movement. But either way, making sense of this unique event in July 2011 and explaining why it occurred when it did meant placing it within the framework of a longer-term development and connecting it to earlier events. Or to put this in terms of our topic: it

meant interpreting the bloody events of 22 July 2011 by turning them into a narrative. It transpired when Breivik's self-presentation on the internet came to light, that he too had already imagined his actions as part of a narrative, as the latest episode in the ongoing story of European crusaders struggling against Islam.

As this case suggests, telling stories about events, both retrospectively and prospectively, is integral to the way in which people make sense of them. This applies to actors as they make their plans and to journalists as they depict ongoing events. As discussions over the last half century have made clear, it also applies to historians as they retrospectively realign particular events in light of later ones as part of larger developments.[1] This chapter offers an overview of these discussions, particularly as they have addressed the question whether or not the narratives produced by historians resemble other sorts of storytelling, from journalism, to the work of creative writers and film-makers, to the self-representations of actors themselves. As we will see, not only have the answers to this question differed, but in the process the concept of 'narrative' itself has shifted in conjunction with the invention of new ways of storytelling.

The notion that the meaning of 'narrative' shifts may come as a disappointment to those who expect a stable relationship between concepts and empirical phenomena. The common-sense view is that 'concepts' should be clearly defined once and for all, so that they can be used unambiguously in debate and analysis. Following this logic, 'narrative' should mean the same thing in 2010 as in 1960, and the same thing among historians and literary scholars. The reality is that it doesn't. Given this fact, the present chapter will not present 'narrative' in abstract, ahistorical terms as something that is eternally the same and whose definition can be fixed once and for all. It starts rather from the assumption that concepts such as 'narrative' are heuristic tools and that their fruitfulness lies, not so much in the fact that they allow us to categorise things once and for all in an unambiguous way, but that their deployment continues to generate new insights regarding cultural practices that are themselves changing.[2] For all parties, reflection on narrative is work in progress: it involves an ongoing set of theoretical discussions where the emphasis shifts in reaction to new challenges emanating from within the theory itself, from the broader cultural context, and from the choices made by often creative practitioners.

## GENEALOGY OF A CONCEPT

The good news is that variations in conceptualisations of 'narrative' occur within a certain bandwidth and they do so with reference to a core meaning, a basic understanding of 'narrative' as the representation of a set of chronologically and logically connected events. (It is in this common-sense way that I used the term above with reference to the events in Oslo in July 2011.) Although there is discussion as to the boundaries of the phenomenon referred to as 'narrative', the combination of a 'set of events' (what can loosely be called

plot) and 'representation' (the use of some medium) seems to be common to all definitions. Starting from this basic understanding, more extensive and systematic accounts of narrativity have elaborated, for example, on the nature of plot and what it takes for events to be seen as connected, the importance of the depiction of human actors in an imaginable story-world, or the 'virtuality' of that world and the role of mediation in its evocation. As we shall see, the basic definition allows for elaboration in different directions and accordingly the emphasis in scholarly discussions of 'narrative' has shifted in the course of the last 50 years along these various lines, partly in response to formal and thematic innovations in story-telling, partly in response to the development of new media.

Fifty years? Although variations on the word 'narrative' have been around for a long time (derived from the *narratio* of classical rhetoric and ultimately from the proto-Indo-European *gna*, meaning 'knowledge') the term as such has been a relative latecomer on the scene of cultural theory. The current preoccupation with 'narrative' dates from the 1960s when it became the most widespread umbrella term to talk about representations of connected events in a way that was specific neither to particular genres (for example, journalism, novels, history) nor to particular media (the spoken and written word, film, drama), and that was in principle indifferent to ontological status. Whether the events in question are real (as the events of July 2011 in Norway) or imaginary (as say, much of what happens in Kurt Vonnegut's novel *Slaughterhouse-Five*, 1969) is in principle irrelevant to the definition of narrative.[3] Unlike its first cousin 'storytelling', then, the term 'narrative' became important because it offered an ostensibly neutral framework for analysing the similarities between artistic and scholarly practices as instances of a common cultural form, if not indeed cultural universal. As it developed in practice and became current in a whole range of disciplines, 'narrative' also offered a constantly renewed challenge to rethink the nature of the difference, if any, between narratives that claim to produce knowledge ('to tell the truth') and those that appeal instead to the ludic principles of fiction ('to make-believe').[4] Most fundamentally for our concerns here, it revealed narrative to be a constitutive part of the production of knowledge, including history, and thus invited the analysis of the latter as both a source of insight and a cultural form.

The emergence of the concept of 'narrative' across a range of disciplines was linked to the development of a new interdiscipline called 'narratology' within the broader field of cultural studies. Discussions of narrative among historians have intersected at points with those in narratology or 'narrative theory' as it has later come to be known.[5] But by and large, debates among historians have taken place independently and been shaped by specifically disciplinary concerns. This means that when cultural theorists and historical theorists may be ostensibly talking about the same thing, in fact their conceptualisation of narrative differs in ways that reflect their divergent priorities: while historians are concerned primarily with historical knowledge and how best to produce it (at stake is not the nature of narrative as such, which is taken as a given, but its functionality in the production of historical knowledge), literary theorists are concerned with cultural representations per se, and how best to analyse them. Given these differences it is all the more remarkable that developments in the two fields have followed roughly parallel tracks even in cases when there seems to have been no direct mutual influence. The recognition that historical narrative is open to analysis *as* a historically variable cultural form has led in more recent years to a growing willingness to study it comparatively alongside other modes of storytelling and ways of engaging with the past. [6]

## NARRATIVE IN HISTORICAL THEORY

The interest in 'narrative' among historians, like the emergence of narratology, can be dated to the 1960s, and was occasioned by the growing realisation that since 'writing up' history was as important a part of the historian's job as doing archival research, more theoretical attention needed to be paid to it. It was no longer enough to reduce the conversion of research into text to a matter of 'packaging' as traditional handbooks had done: it was more than the superficial icing on the historiographical cake, as it were, but the very cake itself. After all, historians do more than list their findings as individual, verifiable propositions ('facts'); they produce articles and books that, as Frank Ankersmit among others put it, are more than the sum of their individual propositions about the past.[7] Gathering data is, literally, only half the story. As the case of Breivik already illustrated, the known details have to be pieced together, framed and connected in order to make sense. So how to theorise the role of narrative in the production of historical knowledge? The very posing of this question meant already assuming a defamiliarising distance towards narrative and questioning its self-evident status within historiographical practice. Attempts to answer it have led theorists in several directions.

It is worth noting from the outset that those debating the role of narrative in historiography have generally emphasised the represented world (*what* do historians choose to evoke) rather than the representation itself (*how* they do so: a particular concern of literary theorists). Within this bandwith, moreover, the emphasis has swung back and forth between plot (how events are linked together as part of a chronological and logical whole) and experientiality (how storytelling can evoke the lived realities of earlier ages and their singularities), with occasional nods in the direction of mediation as such (how language shapes our understanding of the world). Above all, the meaning of 'narrative' has depended on the various alternatives it is being opposed to and the perceived choices open at a given moment to historians.

In spite of this semantic elasticity (or perhaps because of it), the term 'narrative' has been one of the benchmarks by which historical theorists have regularly calibrated their epistemological position since the early 1970s. Judging by the relative number of publications with 'narrative' and its variants in the title, there seems to have been some relaxation in the attention paid to the subject in more recent years, suggesting that a certain consensus has been reached or that other issues have become more pressing and other concepts more conducive to furthering new debates on methods and goals in historiography. Four issues in particular have shaped the debate so far, reflecting shifts of priorities and concerns within the discipline itself: (1) Should historians focus on structures or events? (2) Does narrative offer a distinct form of knowledge? (3) Are there alternatives to it? (4) Does narrative turn history into literature, and is this a bad thing? At the present time, a new discussion is emerging about how historians should respond to changes in the media landscape: (5) What happens to historical narrative in a digitised world?

Central in many of these discussions is the figure of Hayden White whose work, especially *Metahistory* (1973) and *The Content of the Form* (1987), has been of immense importance in initiating and calibrating the discussion, and in provoking controversy.[8] There have been many other theorists who have made important contributions, but there is no single writer with an impact to equal that of White who, over a period of more than 30 years, has continued to formulate new positions. He is arguably the only historical theorist, with a background and institutional affiliation as a historian, whose work on narrative has made it across the disciplinary divide to become influential within the broader field of narrative theory. In this chapter, White will accordingly be a recurrent figure, though it should be noted from the outset that his ideas do not constitute theory, but rather a form of theoretical activism, a life-long and hence evolving engagement with the nature of representation and of the choices open to historians. In the course of this engagement he has sometimes been conceptually fickle, but he has repeatedly

touched the raw nerve of fundamental questions regarding the nature and purpose of historiography, challenging historians to think about works of history as cultural – indeed, as literary – products that are shaped in a particular way, but that might have been shaped differently.

## STRUCTURES AND/OR INDIVIDUAL AGENTS?

A particular debate about narrative was generated by the so-called 'new historians' associated with the Annales School, beginning in the late 1940s and reaching a high point in the 1970s. Ironically, 'narrative' came to the fore in this debate as a negative point of reference, as something to be dismissed. As is explained in greater detail elsewhere in this collection (see Chapter 4), the Annales project entailed a re-orientation towards long-term structures and a breaking away from 'narrative' as the preferred outcome of historical research. By narrative was meant in this case, then, the traditional focus on individual agents and on particular sequences of events as they unfolded over what was usually a fairly limited period of time. Proponents of the 'new history' rejected this 'event-based' or figurative approach to history on the grounds that it stuck too close to particulars and, in the name of a greater scientific rigour, they defined their own primary focus in terms of the investigation of the underlying social, economic, and even environmental structures that lay behind punctual events. These structures, if not quite stable and unchanging, shifted by way of such long-term and impersonal processes that they could barely be seen as 'event-like'. Seen in this light traditional narrative history came over as less scientific and literally more anecdotal than histories focussed on impersonal structures. (In turning away from event-based sequences, these new 'structuralist' historians were ironically making common cause with first-generation structuralist narratologists who around the same time were busy developing a-chronic models to describe the underlying logic of plots.[9])

The canonical example of non-event-based history is Fernand Braudel's *La méditerranée et le monde méditerranéen à l'époque de Philippe II* (1949), which establishes a hierarchy of relative importance between the slowly changing landscape around the Mediterranean, the long-term economic development of the region, and the comparatively 'breathless' pace of short-term political events in which individuals play a part; this hierarchy is then reflected in the three-part structure of the work that, instead of simply moving in one single account across time, turns back on itself every time it moves to a different level. The relative lack of importance of chronology, an emphasis instead on spatial description as an organising principle, and a relative absence of individual agents in whose lives we can become involved: all of these are reasons to see Braudel's work, at the very least, as a non-traditional narrative. Does this also make it a non-narrative?

While some proponents of the 'new history' presented its practices as a radical break with narrative as such, this view has been nuanced by later commentators. While Braudel's work is innovative and non-traditional (though not without precedents) it does maintain some narrative features.[10] The tri-partite structure does not represent an Aristotelian beginning, middle and end focussed on a single action, but the narration itself follows distinct, interconnected stages and the transformation of the Mediterranean world, however slow, is a basic point of concern. As importantly, the impact of Braudel's work and its canonical status as an example of the 'new history' is arguably linked to this particular historian's imaginative and literary capacity to evoke a world through words and images (a capacity which is less evident in some other works of the new history, for example in Emmanuel Le Roy Ladurie's *Histoire du climat depuis l'an mil*, 1967). Finally, if we take 'world-making' in a very general sense as one of the features of narrative alongside plot then Braudel's work could

also count as narrative since it draws its readers into its imaginative reconstruction of the ecological and human world of the Mediterranean. For all these reasons, it might be seen as a new variation on narrative rather than as something so entirely different that it no longer deserves the name at all.[11]

In the first instance, however, the new departure in historiography associated with the Annales school was construed as a move away from narrative as such. This meant that subsequent new departures could present themselves as a return to it. Thus Lawrence Stone, in an oft-quoted article from 1979, celebrated 'The revival of narrative' as a new alternative to the non-event-based history practised by the Annalists.[12] Set up as it was in opposition to structuralist tendencies in historiography, Stone's notion of narrative is as idiosyncratic as it is telling of the state of play within the discipline: the revival he envisaged was not a matter of a renewed interest in 'plot' and in the plotting characteristic of the world of politics, but rather of an interest in the lived experience of individuals. Set up in opposition to the focus on structure and on long-term social processes and inspired by the anthropological model of thick description, Stone's 'narrative' was synonym for a focus on individual actors and their everyday lives, the topics that at the time of his writing were emerging as central to the new cultural history. Thus 'narrative,' with the emphasis now on world-making and experientiality, functioned once again as a polemic touchstone. Works of cultural history were 'narrative', according to Stone and others, primarily because of their focus on the lives of individuals – literally, their figurative dimension – and not because of the prominence of sequentiality and plot. Stone's particular priorities explain why his chief example of new-style *narrative* history, Le Roy Ladurie's *Montaillou, village occitan de 1294 à 1324* (1975) has actually little to offer in the way of plot: instead, the emphasis is on the unchanging patterns of everyday life among individuals in a particular place. (As Stone remarked, the book does not offer a story but instead 'rambles around inside people's heads' in the manner of the modern novel.[13]) Much of what passes as 'narrative' history from the realm of cultural history is often only narrative in the sense that it is not about long-term impersonal processes, but evokes instead individual actors and people's private lives. 'Narrative' in the stronger meaning of 'presenting a plot' features only in a reduced form in such discussions of world-making (the world described is known to have changed later, but the change is not the central topic of the account). Defining narrativity by world-making may seem odd in view of the traditional association between narrative and plot, but as we shall see below, this shift of emphasis parallels a new orientation in narrative theory towards our interactions with virtual realities.

In his magisterial attempt to synthesise discussions about narrative in the fields of history, literary studies, and philosophy, Paul Ricoeur argued in *Temps et récit* (1983–85) that the impersonal and non-event-based works of the 'new history' in the Annales tradition should indeed be seen as a form of narrative since, however slowly the phenomena they describe change and however much it is space rather than time that governs their composition, they too structure information in such a way as to make sense of the world across a period of time. Ricoeur's point was supported by Philippe Carrard's detailed analysis of the poetics of the new history and the way its practitioners continued to follow tripartite models that are derived from the basic beginning–middle–end of storytelling.[14] In this desire to reconcile the apparently opposing parties, however, Ricoeur overstated the similarities between 'structure-oriented' and 'actor-oriented' narratives. These do not outweigh the obvious differences between, for example, Braudel's history of the Mediterranean (where the central subject is a geographical area over a long period of time), Le Roy Ladurie's *Montaillou* (a thick description of a particular community at a given period), and a work like Thomas Pakenham's *The Boer War* (1979)

which focuses on individual agents and describes how they acted over a period of time. While all three works are arguably narratives in a very general sense, they are not all characterised by narrativity to the same degree, and to elide these differences, as Ricoeur tended to do, may yield a rather blunt analytical tool. Indeed, discussions among all parties have sometimes become unnecessarily murky because of a tendency to use 'narrative' as a 'one-size-fits-all' concept, instead of thinking of narrativity as a matter of the degree to which the work represents the experiences and actions of people as part of a plot. Ultimately, the discussion between 'structure' and 'narrative', which was first conducted in either-or terms, now seems to have resolved itself into a matter of relative emphasis. All histories are founded on a degree of narrativity since they deal with change and singular circumstances, but this does not mean that they are necessarily fully fledged narratives in the strong sense of being not only highly emplotted, but also focussed on individual experience and written in an engaging way. Although theorists have for too long tended to treat it as a single property, it seems more fruitful to conclude that there are degrees of narrativity, just as there are degrees of heat.[15]

## NARRATIVE AND/OR KNOWLEDGE?

The second set of discussions on narrative and history ran in part parallel to the first one, and concerns the epistemological status of narrative as a form of explanation. Here the most salient feature of narrative was taken to be 'plot', that is, the depiction of a minimum set of chronologically and logically connected events. Once again, the debate arose in response to the idea that there might be an alternative to (traditional) narrative. The gravitation towards social science models on the part of historians, who hoped to increase their scientific credentials by using quantitative methods and focussing on long-term processes, provoked this new defence of narrative as a 'cognitive' instrument.[16] As Louis O. Mink among others argued, narrative is not only a legitimate mode of explanation in that it shows how one situation evolves from another; it is also what distinguishes history from other types of knowledge. In the case of history, individual phenomena are explained by being made observable as part of a plot (as part of a beginning–middle–end sequence), whereas in other disciplines, they are explained nomothetically as exemplifications of general laws.[17] The more phenomena the plot could accommodate as necessary elements in understanding how an initial situation evolves into a final one the better the historical explanation.[18] (Using these criteria it is possible to say that the story of Breivik as a 'lone wolf' is less powerful as a historical account than the narrative which places him as a part of a larger tendency since it would fail to explain, for example, that he drew on an anti-Islamic discourse to justify his act.)

The idea that historical knowledge is fundamentally narrative in character, because it is fundamentally about defining developments and explaining change, echoed fairly traditional ideas as formulated, for example, by Wilhelm Dilthey at the beginning of the twentieth century. The interest in narrative as a knowledge-producing form became more controversial, however, in combination with constructivism: the realisation that narrative structure is not a property of events themselves (it is not a matter of 'uncovering' a pre-existing plot) but a product of the verbal representation which, by making certain selections and organising information in particular ways, invites us to see a particular coherence in events. This constructivist view formed the basis of what is sometimes referred to as 'narrativism' in historical theory, to use a term coined by Frank Ankersmit.[19] As one might expect, debate on these issues intersected with broader epistemological discussions relating to the nature of historical knowledge, and to the extent that narrativism involved putting the constructedness of all discursive knowledge on the agenda, it fell into step with what is known as the 'linguistic turn' in the Human sciences.

As Mink argued, narrativity is not a property of history itself, but of the way we represent events and, in the process, interpret them. 'There can in fact be no untold stories at all,' he wrote, 'just as there can be no unknown knowledge.'[20] Historians transform events into objects of knowledge when they represent them in the form of a story: 'An event may take five seconds or five months, but in either case whether it is one event or many depends not on a definition of "event" but on a particular narrative construction which generates the event's appropriate description.'[21] Although narrative is the form traditionally taken by histories in the modern period, then, it is not merely a reproductive mirror, but a heuristic instrument or, to use Mink's term, a 'cognitive' one. Events do not dictate the stories we tell about them, but in trying to re-present them as stories we make sense of them. When they are narrated and placed within the framework of some plot, events become part of 'known knowledge' in the sense both of becoming intelligible and becoming accessible to third parties. In selecting, organising and verbalising data, narrators build up a case for looking at the connections between events in a particular way.

From a narrativist perspective, 'beginnings' and 'endings' are the result of a (well-informed and judicious) framing on the part of historians. As the many versions of the French Revolution indicate, for example, neither its beginning nor its ending are self-evident; both are subject to keen debate. Indeed, it is the very possibility of being able to relate the same set of events in various ways that makes the need to narrate them in one way rather than another all the more urgent.[22] Whether the French Revolution 'ended' in 1794 with the death of Robespierre (as in Michelet's version) or with Napoleon's coup d'état (as in Carlyle's), or in 1870 with the foundation of the Third Republic (as in Furet's) is a matter of interpretation and of the particular story being told. In the course of narrating events, historical narrators not only establish beginnings and endings, they also have to define the central subject of the narrative, whose ambitions and ability to realise them form the focus of the drama. Whether the storming of the Bastille is told from the perspective of those defending it, or those attacking it, is again a matter of interpretation that reflects priorities and affiliations, along with a basic understanding of how power worked in the situation being described. The historian's division of actantial roles among particular figures, to borrow a term from the narratologist Algirdas Greimas, expresses a particular understanding of agency and value.[23] In thus shaping their image of events, historians build up a case for looking at them in one way rather than another and, in the process, they *add* something to the information they have garnered. Their accounts generate something new, a narrative logic that the empirical data did not possess in itself. The fact that this emplotment of events is a constructive activity, however, should not be taken to mean that it is necessarily fraudulent or valueless. On the contrary: narrating history is the royal way to understanding how events occur the way they do. Knowledge, like a cooked meal, is made, not found.

This perspective on historical narrative, as formulated by Mink and others, was elaborated further in a radicalised form in the work of Hayden White. In his *Metahistory* (1973), White argued that historians not only 'emplot' events into beginnings–middles–ends; they do so by adopting traditional plot models (romance, comedy, tragedy, satire) that have been developed by creative writers dealing with imaginary events. It is interesting to note that White, although following an independent track and working with rather eclectic sources, took very much a structuralist approach in this early work by assuming that all narratives were produced on the basis of a limited number of models, in total four, relating to each of the four aspects of historiographical explanation: emplotment, figures of thought or

'tropes', ideological positions, and styles of argumentation. The modes of emplotment that White referred to in this four-by-four formula were based on the archetypal plots described by the Canadian scholar Northrop Frye in his proto-structuralist *Anatomy of Criticism: Four Essays* (1957). White made no extensive reference, either then or subsequently, to the other plot models with a greater degree of specificity being developed in the parallel world of predominantly French narratology. In practice, the actual models that White invoked in this four-by-four poetics were to prove of limited analytic value and White himself rarely returned to them.

Despite these limitations, White's attempt to define the 'poetics of historiography' through his readings of several historians and philosophers meant that a number of new issues were placed firmly on the theoretical agenda. Firstly, that the relationship between the chosen mode of emplotment and particular events may be an arbitrary one (the same events could potentially be emplotted in different ways depending on the preference of the narrator). Secondly, that historical narratives represent unique events but do so while drawing on templates abstracted from earlier stories. Thirdly, that the way historians emplot particular events, for example as comedy, may be closely tied up with their 'metahistorical' or philosophical view on the nature of History as such: each particular story is a miniature version of an implicit 'grand narrative' encompassing all of time. Finally, and most importantly for our discussion later, that historical narration may be a poetic act (in the original meaning of poiesis: making), and that historical narratives more closely resemble the purely imagined stories produced by poets than they do other forms of science.

As the subtitle of *Metahistory* indicates, White's theory supposed that historians need *imagination* as much as they need skills in gathering information. His idea that historical narratives are basically conceived as wholes, and that they are constructed according to poetic models affecting the work as a whole, implied further that narratives are persuasive because of their general sweep rather than because of the verifiable content of their individual propositions. Criticism was accordingly a matter of accepting or rejecting the narrative as a whole rather than of being persuaded by details. This meant that narratives on the same topic could not really be compared critically with each other since the preference for one over the other was based on metahistorical and aesthetic preferences affecting the work as a whole rather than on the validity of particular details. White's poetics of historiography has thus far-reaching implications for the very possibility of critical debate within the field of history.

White's basic point about the essentially poetic character of historiographical composition continues to generate discussion. He himself went on to elaborate on the ideas first put forward in *Metahistory*, but from the outset a certain structural tension can be observed in his approach between, on the one hand, the power he attributed to the historian's imagination and discourse and, on the other hand, the historians' self-imposed task to represent particular sets of events and not just their own aesthetico-philosophical preferences. In emphasising above all the power of the historian's discourse, White left himself open to the charge of an inverted positivism, in which the referential dimension of historiography (its commitment to representing particular events) was as conspicuous in its absence as narration had been in earlier views. It seemed as if historians were free to impose any shape on events they liked, their only limitations lying in the number of models at their disposal. This position became particularly problematic when White later came to discuss representations of the Holocaust and found himself hard put to convince others that he could reconcile his view of narration with an event that, for ethical as well as cognitive reasons, is perceived as 'unmasterable', resisting all attempts to mould it into traditional models.[24] He later conceded that the 'holocaustal' events of the twentieth century

called for a different way of writing, one that was more germane to the experiments of modernist fiction writers than to the realist aesthetics of the nineteenth century.[25]

One way to move beyond the apparent standoff between imagination (the freedom to depict the world at will) and realism (the claim to represent the world as it is) was to take more into account the practical constraints under which historians work. While historical narratives are indeed constructed using the verbal, poetic and intellectual means at the historian's disposal, they are also constrained, as my *Rhetoric of Historical Representation* (1990) showed, both by the nature of the events themselves and by the importance of convincing others of the validity of the interpretation.[26] Thus if someone wants to construe genocide or the *Terreur* as comedy and still be recognised as a source of knowledge, he or she will have to struggle with the resistance both of the known facts and of the alternative interpretations of the same events; and may indeed fail in the end either to impose the form envisaged or to convince others. The poetic character of historical interpretation makes debate difficult and fraught, but it does not obviate the fact that narratives do not just exist in isolation but also compete with each other.

## TO NARRATE OR NOT?

In 1980 White published an article called 'The value of narrativity in the representation of reality' in which he reflected on the fundamental question: why did narrative become the privileged form for representing historical events?[27] Since the form in which history is written is not dictated by events themselves, why choose narrative? After all, the importance of annals and chronicles in earlier periods provided proof of the fact that the later predominance of narrative was the outcome of history and not of necessity. The emergence of narrative as the privileged form of representation was dependent, White argued, on the parallel development of the idea of a secular collective subject (the state or nation) whose struggles to realise its values in the political sphere, its successes and failures in achieving justice, provided the basis for the historian's plotting of temporal experience. Narrating history became thus implicitly a way of moralising in that it showed whether the achievement of certain values was possible or not given the distribution of power in the period being described (crudely put: did the forces of good prevail?).

In explaining the tenacious appeal of narrative in modern historiography, then, White pointed to its usefulness both as a cognitive and as a socialising instrument. Even more fundamentally, in keeping with his belief that all representations of particular events are informed by an implicit philosophy of history (what he called 'metahistory'), White linked the 'value of narrativity' to our deep-seated, meta-historical desire to believe that history is coherent; that it makes sense 'in itself'. In short, narrative has been so important in historiography not just because it explains events by emplotting them, but because it appeals to our deepest desires for the consolation of living in an ordered world. By re-presenting historical reality in an emplotted form, and hence with a moral relating to the relative distribution of value and power, narrative historians also reassure us with the metahistorical implication that, even if things don't always work out for the good, there is at least an order to the world and that the realm of the secular – that is, history itself – can be a source of meaning and guidance. As White put it in a passage characteristically dotted with speculative questions marks:

> What I have sought to suggest is that this value attached to narrativity in the representation of real events arises out of a desire to have real events display the coherence, integrity, fullness, and closure of an image of life that is and can only be imaginary. The notion that sequences of real events possess the formal attributes of the stories we tell about imaginary events could only have its origin in wishes, daydreams, reveries. Does the world really present itself to perception in the form of well-made stories, with central subjects, proper beginnings, middles, and ends, and a coherence that permits us to see 'the end' in every beginning? Or does it present itself more in the forms that the annals and chronicle suggest, either as mere sequence without beginning or end or as a sequence of beginnings that only terminate and never conclude? And does the world, even the social world, ever really come to us as already narrativized, already 'speaking itself' from beyond the horizon of our capacity to make scientific sense of it? Or is the fiction of such a world, capable of speaking itself and displaying itself as a form of story, necessary for the establishment of that moral authority without which the notion of a specifically social reality would be unthinkable.[28]

Modern historiography has traditionally set itself the goal of imposing a narrative structure on otherwise chaotic information, according to White, but narrative is in fact a purely conventional choice which ultimately ends up as much restricting our view of history as enabling us to understand it. In this sense, the chosen form (emplotment) has itself content: the reassuring promise of sense and order in history and the exclusion of the possibility of having to live with contingency (not for nothing has White been described as an existentialist).[29] Following this line of argument in another essay, he polemically proposed to 'de-discipline' history, that is, to encourage historians *not* to 'reduce' events to a coherent narrative so that people reading them would be left more aware of historical contingency and the multiplicity of possible interpretations of any given event. To refrain from narration would help provoke a more critical attitude on the part of the public to their own world and to the 'grand narratives' which give them a sense of false security and blind them to other points of view. (That Anders Breivik should have justified his actions with reference to the story of the age-long struggle between Crusaders and Islam offers support to White's position on the negative potential of narrative and the dangers of looking for meaning *in* history.)

It is of course a moot point whether a historian can ever choose *not* to make sense and still write a book. It is also a moot point whether making sense through narrative, and imposing coherence on events is ever as easy as White suggested (see above). But the most important thing to note here is that White's highly suggestive discussion of the 'value of narrativity' was based on a 'one-model-fits-all' approach to storytelling. Not only does this presuppose an almost Aristotelian view of plot, with its emphasis on closure and imaginary coherence. It also presupposes that narration gravitates towards full-blown 'narrativisation'. This is the term White coined to designate the way in which narrators may do their best to ensure the full-scale immersion of their readers so as to give the illusion that the story is telling itself: where some narrators merely report on the past from a position in the present and do nothing to conceal their own role as interpreters, 'narrativising' narrators do their utmost to evoke the past in such vivid terms that events seem to be happening as a ready-made story; that the narrative coincides with history itself. White implied that narration always gravitates towards narrativisation since the value of narrativity lies essentially in the illusion that the world *is* a story and that it has closure. In making this point, he took nineteenth-century realism as his prototype, and construed this as a naïve belief in the possibility of narrators holding up a mirror to the world (realists like Balzac were less naïve than this bad reputation suggests). Had White's prototype here been modernist narrative, where the emphasis is on montage, fragmentation and spatial forms, or postmodernist narrative, with its self-conscious narrators happy to draw defamiliarising attention to their own activities and do without a tightly structured plot, then the picture would have been different. In fact, the option as White presented it – to narrate or not – was in practice an unacknowledged choice between a realist 'narrativising' aesthetic and other styles of writing with more room for reflection on the activity of representation itself. (In his later work, as we have seen, he acknowledged the existence of other aesthetics, but did not connect this back to his earlier arguments on the value of narrativity.)[30]

Although highly narrativised accounts of the world continue to be produced (in Hollywood for example), other options have become available. Indeed, White's own critique of narrativisaton roughly coincided with a widespread cultivation of alternatives among cultural practitioners in various media, including creative writers, film-makers and indeed historians. The well-wrought plot that he took as his basic model in identifying the value of narrativity has been giving way to a new interest in multiple storylines, self-reflexive representation and a form of narration that is based on the invitation to virtually participate in an open-ended story-world rather than on the expectation of closure. Take the case of works consisting of various, juxtaposed short stories rather than of a single plot: Julian Barnes' fictional *History of the World in 10½ Chapters* (1989), based on multiple short stories, or Paul Haggis' film *Crash* (2004), on intersecting lives in contemporary Los Angeles, have had some parallels within the field of history – for example, in Natalie Zemon Davis' *Women on the Margins* (1995), which is organised around the separate lives of three individuals in the seventeenth century, or Hans Ulrich Gumbrecht's *In 1926: Living at the Edge of Time* (1997), a cultural history made up of multiple short chapters that invites its reader to follow different pathways through its pages.

Theorists of postmodern culture such as Jean-François Lyotard have explained this growing reluctance to see individual and collective experience as part of one converging 'grand' narrative as a result of the world-shattering experiences of twentieth-century history, which no longer fits the traditional models we have for describing it.[31] Others have put the rejection of traditional narrative more positively, seeing it as a reflection of a nascent ability on the part of more recent generations, the 'children of chaos', to live without the imagined coherence referred to by White or as evidence of a new openness to seeing multiple points of view and multiple possible subjects in history.[32] One way or another, once it is accepted that narrative does not necessarily lead to full-blown 'narr-ativisation', as White in his early work implied it did, it becomes apparent that there are more choices open to historians than that between either creating the illusion of coherence or refraining from making sense at all. There is also the option of exploring new ways of using narrative as a cognitive instrument without creating the illusion that the story is telling itself, or of exploring new ways of structuring information so that it does not necessarily converge into a single point of view.

## HISTORIOGRAPHY AND/OR LITERATURE?

Just as a convicted criminal finds it hard to shake off a reputation for unreliability, so too has 'narrative' found it difficult to shake off its association with literature. After all, questions regarding storytelling and plots originated in the study of texts and performances that do not make any claim to veracity. So while the concept of 'narrative' became widespread for its neutrality with respect to the imagined or actual character of the events represented, in practice, discussions continually slide along a slippery semantic slope towards fictional 'storytelling' based on the principle of make-believe and serving the purposes of aesthetic pleasure. Since modern historiography has consistently defined itself in *opposition* to imaginative literature and often as a liberation from it, anything leading to a new convergence was guaranteed to raise hackles and meet resistance.[33] Against this background, the foregrounding of 'narrative' in history has been construed, both by proponents and critics, in terms of a controversial choice between literature or science.

The controversy was fuelled by White's polemical insistence on the similarities between history and literature. The provocative titles of his essays 'The fictions of factual representation' (1976) and 'The historical work as literary artefact' (1978) speak volumes, both regarding his main theses and his readiness to go on the offensive against all those who might believe that historians simply 'find' their narratives in the archives rather than make them themselves. In emphasising the comparability of history-writing and works of imaginative literature, White threw down a gauntlet to those theorists who had been emphasising their affinities with the social sciences or the distinctness of history as a scholarly discipline with its own traditions and norms.

Janus-like historiography faces towards other forms of writing and cultural production, on the one hand, and towards other forms of scholarship, on the other. In which direction should one look for kindred spirits? Narrativism encouraged its sympathisers and challenged its opponents to think about the side which had been neglected since the mid nineteenth century: the literary. Whether moved by a desire to provoke debate or redress the imbalance, narrativists have tended to stress the affinities between history and literature, at the risk of conflating history and literature or, more generally, history and art.[34] Thus White complained on one occasion of the 'general reluctance to consider historical narratives as what they most manifestly are – verbal fictions – the contents of which are as much invented as found and the forms of which have more in common with their counterparts in literature than they have with those in the sciences.'[35] For those who believe in the high seriousness of literature and see no stigma at all in being a literary artist, this association is not necessarily a problem and is indeed a compliment rather than a put-down. But it still begs the question of the significant differences, if any, between the two modes of writing.

There is a lot to be said for taking seriously the resemblances between literary writing and historical writing, not least because of the parallel developments within these two fields of cultural production. Not only have historians' topics changed in the course of time, but also the narrative techniques and narrative designs for treating those topics. Indeed, the invention of new topics goes hand in glove with the development of new forms of expression with which to deal with them.[36] As mentioned earlier, there are grounds for comparison between postmodern fiction and contemporary historiography when it comes to the rejection of a central 'classical' plot, while there were earlier parallels (as Stone pointed out) between the investigation of consciousness in modern fiction and in works of cultural history where the narrators also went 'rambling around inside people's heads'. Indeed, Braudel's history of the Mediterranean might be seen as a historiographical counterpart of the spatial form developed in James Joyce's *Ulysses* (1922), with both being forerunners of the spatial organisation dominant in recent fiction.[37] Or, to take another example, Saul Friedlander's multiperspectival and multivocal *The Years of Extermination* (2007) has been described as a work of historiographical modernism answering to the particular challenges posed to representation by the horrors of the Holocaust (Friedlander, 2007; Kansteiner, 2009). The very fact that events do not dictate the stories we tell about them, to recall Mink, means that we need to continuously invent new ways of talking about a world that is itself subject to change and new ways of giving expression to changing interpretations of it: in that sense, literary and historiography remain closely related activities.

But despite such fascinating parallels and cross-currents, White's assertion that the contents of history are as much 'invented as found' seems exaggerated. Although White himself has always insisted that he respects the importance of evidence in historiography and that his analysis simply targets another level, his polemical courting of the relationship with literature left narrativism as such open to the accusation of an 'anything goes' attitude in which the distinction between historical narration (based on a systematic inquiry into what actually happened) and novelistic narration (in which the writer is free to invent) was no longer relevant: 'Telling it as you like it' was picked up and thrown back as an insult.[38] So where to draw the line

between the work of the creative writer and that of the historian? And why draw it at all?

Part of the confusion was caused by the emotive charge (the 'red rag to a bull' effect) of the word 'fiction' when used in relation to historiography. The impact was aggravated by the polyvalence within the word 'fiction' itself, which meant that a polemicist could play simultaneously both on its weaker and its stronger meanings. In its most neutral or 'weak' usage, 'fiction' simply means 'things that have been fashioned': in this sense all narratives are *fictive* since they have been put together by historians. In its strongest and most everyday meaning, 'fiction' refers to a subcategory of narrative works in which the principle of make-believe is operative. These works are not just fictive (in the sense of being artefacts), but *fictional*; that is, they invite readers or viewers to suspend their disbelief while using their imagination. From this point of view, there is in principle a fundamental difference between the attitude one has to fictional narratives (suspend disbelief; make-believe; do not criticise errors) and to historical narratives (believe provisionally; if no justification by evidence, then criticise). The context and the packaging of a text usually give a strong signal as to its genre (the cover, the title, the position in bookstore or library). In practice, of course, it may sometimes be difficult for the reader to classify a text with certainty or, in the course of reading it, to distinguish in a clear-cut way with relation to specific sections of a work between what the writer has invented and what has been documented in the archives. But the fact that people sometimes do not know with certainty whether they are dealing with imagined or documented cases, does not mean that the distinction as such becomes irrelevant. On the contrary, dealings with historiography can be defined precisely by a readiness to believe provisionally what is said while being alert to possible gaps between the narrative and the evidence on which it is based or the evidence available elsewhere. Indeed, as Louis O. Mink already pointed out in 1970, the concept of fiction and the concept of history thrive precisely on the perceived difference between them: it is because they resemble each other so much and operate sometimes in each other's sphere of influence that historians attach so much importance to differentiating between them.[39] Because the difference is both highly important and rarely clear-cut, it is continuously being re-negotiated. Hybrid forms – historical novels, historical movies, experimental historiography – are thus par for the course and exceptions that create a new rule: they have a structural role in blurring distinctions and hence regularly force people to re-articulate norms, expectations and priorities.

Studies of reception by literary scholars have shown what historical theory has overlooked: namely, what readers 'do' with texts is an important element in their cultural impact. To consider the writing of narrative in isolation from its reception is again only half the story. Only if historians or their public were to become indifferent to the evidential basis of a narrative, could it be said that the 'fictional' and the 'historical' had become merged. And it is highly unlikely that academic historians will stop worrying since this would be to undermine their own raison d'être. The public at large is another matter since, as Nancy Partner has warned, indifference to the relation between image and evidence (or disbelief all around) may be one of the by-products of the mass media and their manipulation of evidence, leading to all-round cynicism and a general alienation from the sense of a shared history.[40] This blurring in the public sphere of the distinction between evidence-based narratives and imagination-based ones raises in itself new sorts of issues for historians, but these have less to do with the relationship between history and literature as such, than with the relationship between academic history and the mass media (see below).

Nor are the differences between historiography and literature only a matter of the way they are subsequently evaluated, but also of the constraints in which they operate. As cultural practices, literature and history bring different skills and expectations into play and play distinct roles in the general circulation of stories in society. Crudely put: historians can draw on the authority of their scholarship, but they lack the freedom to say what they want; in contrast, creative writers and film-makers lack the authority of scholarship and the backing of the academy, but they are free to invent, have the expressive skills to do so, and can thus appeal to a larger public. The case of Kurt Vonnegut's *Slaughterhouse-Five* illustrates, for example, that the toolbox of the novelist includes, along with historical information, such devices as irony, humour, understatement, hyperbole and fantasy. Indeed, as Geoffrey Hartman has written, literature at its best may help explain what has happened and is happening in the world, but above all it offers new reasons for living and new grounds for hope; in contrast, the role of the historian is, no more and no less, than to explain how things happened and to clear the world of misunderstanding: a role that is more critical than constructive.[41] But both are needed and to reduce one to the other does justice to neither. One could debate the particular terms of Hartman's comparison but this would not diminish the theoretical point it allows one to make: seen together as part of the circulation of stories at large and the cultural production of memory, historical and fictional narratives supplement, imitate, reinforce, but also deviate from each other in ways that are crucial for the fertilising of critical debate.[42] In short: while historical narratives and fictional narratives, along with the hybrid variations between these categories, 'make sense', they do not make sense in the same way or with the same goal in mind. And luckily so.

## IN A NEW MEDIA LANDSCAPE?

Behind all the discussions summarised above is the idea that there is no 'natural' or pre-given way of writing history, and that how you write history is a matter of choice, convention and imagination. In short, 'narrative' has been defamiliarised as the default form in which history should be written since the current wave of discussions began a half-century ago. At the same time as theorists have been 'getting the story crooked', to use Hans Kellner's phrase,[43] the concept of 'narrative' itself has continued to shift focus in relation to the various 'non-narrative' alternatives to which it has been opposed: a focus on individual lives versus long-term social and economic structures; a way of evoking worlds versus telling plots; explanation by plot versus by covering laws; presenting the world as coherent versus as contingent; a form of poetry versus scholarship. At the present time, a new set of discussions is appearing on the horizon in response to the changing media landscape in which historians are now operating and to new challenges to historians to engage with alternative modes of communication.[44]

Since discussion about narrative and history first arose in the 1960s, it was been very much an academic affair, that is, focussed on historiographical practice within the framework of the academy. This is not itself so surprising since the priority of the debaters was with establishing and explicating norms and models for producing the best history possible. Perhaps inevitably given the level of abstraction at which such debates were conducted, there was little ink wasted on the varieties within historiographical practice, stretching from the lavishly footnoted and unpublished dissertation, the closely argued monograph, but also – moving from academic history as such, to more popularising works – to combinations of history and journalism, to experimental types of history that border on imaginative literature, to well-told and engrossing tales for a general public such as William Dalrymple's *The Last Mughal: The Fall of a Dynasty, Delhi, 1857* (2006) or Ken Burns' documentary *The Civil War* (1990). In the last half-century, the issue of how to reach a broader public, and whether indeed this should be part of the core business of an academic historian, has also become a theoretical issue, fanned by the possibility of

using the mass medium of television to reach an audience, by publishers' promotion of the general-interest book and, most recently and for the present context most importantly, by the rival presence of informal digital forums where non-professionals also practice history. Although academic historians are chief stakeholders in the production of historical knowledge, they are not its gatekeepers: with amateurs free to browse the internet and with the means to generate and disseminate content, 'everyman is becoming his own historian', to echo Carl Becker's famous phrase.[45] With mixed results, as the anti-Islamic myth-making of a Breivik indicates.

When all of the discussions summarised above began, print and writing were the self-evident media for historical representation, and literature the most obvious alternative. Looking back now on those debates from the perspective of a digitised world in which images, sound and words can be so easily reproduced and transformed, it is striking how conceptualisations of narrative were so closely bound to the written word and the medium of print. The cultural salience of audio-visual media, the emergence of computer gaming and interactive media, digitisation and networking – all of these have challenged narratologists to broaden their understanding of narrative so as to account for these new forms. As a result there has been a new interest among narrative theorists in the formative influence of particular media on the production of narratives (writing, film, photography, social networking sites) along with a shift of emphasis away from plot as a key feature of narrative to that of immersivity (digitisation having provided new technologies for evoking virtual worlds) and interactivity (digitisation having afforded new agency to users).[46] Add to this the fact that the hypertextual organisation of information and the availability of visual materials are generating new forms of semantic organisation, and new possibilities for producers and users to link events in ways that seem quite far removed from the core definition of narrativity given earlier. For lack of a better name, we may still call this a form of narrativity, but as Lev Manovich warns: 'in the world of new media, the word narrative is often used ... to cover up the fact that we have not yet developed a language to describe these new strange objects.'[47]

Unsurprisingly, historians have not remained unaffected by these major cultural and technological changes, and it is already apparent that the availability of digital resources and possibilities for online collaboration are generating new modes of presentation alongside print-based ones (with books themselves already becoming more multimedial and more often illustrated). Inevitably, it will also generate new modes of making sense whose contours we are only now beginning to see. So rather than become lost in speculation about an enormously complex set of volatile issues, let us return to the central concern here: what might be the value of narrativity for historians to come?

One possible scenario is that new modes of representing and interpreting events will emerge that are indeed so far removed from what has traditionally been known as 'narrative' that the concept itself may one day have outlived its usefulness and other enabling concepts will emerge. Against this possible obsolescence speaks cultural history itself: as we have seen, narrative practices have changed shape in the past, from highly emplotted to more open-ended and multiple, and the conceptualisation of narrative has adapted in response. Thus 'narrative' is already no longer exclusively linked to the production of a coherent plot with a clearly defined beginning, middle and end, but also extends to include mediated ways of virtually engaging in other people's lives without these forming a 'plot' in the conventional sense.

Another scenario, not necessarily incompatible with the first one, is that narrative as the cultural practice of emplotment may actually gain in importance precisely in reaction to the developments sketched above. Despite all reflection and experimentation in the avant-garde margins, a glance through recent works of historiography from various fields suggests that the basic underlying narrative structure of showing how one situation developed into another continues to inform historiographical practice across the board.[48] This might be read as evidence of the conservatism of most historians when it comes to writing. But it can also be read in more positive terms as a reflection of the undiminished importance of their core business: to explain what happened and why things happened the way they did. We have been released from any naïve belief in the world 'as' story, but we continue to face the challenge of conceiving new ways of writing about social, cultural and political changes in such a way that they not only make sense, but that they make the best sense possible in view of what we know to have been the case. Being able to explain how and why something happened, be this a bloodbath in Norway or a famine in Somalia, by placing it within the framework of some larger development will arguably become all the more important as a counter-force to the viral spread of myths and to the fragmentation of perspectives on history that has been the downside of the digital age. Whether those future narratives will also only take the form of a written narrative is another matter. That historians now face the challenge of using new media to bring across their stories is beyond question.

## NOTES

1  The idea of historical narrative as 'retroactive re-alignment' draws on Danto (1985).
2  This view of concepts draws on Bal (2002), (2009).
3  General surveys of narratology are provided in Bal (2004); Herman et al. (2005).
4  On discussions regarding narrative and knowledge production in different fields, see Kreiswirth (2000), Bal (2004), Herman et al. (2005) and Nash (1990).
5  In designating this field of research there has been a recent preference for 'narrative theory' over 'narratology' because of the overly structuralist connotations of the latter: McQuillan (2000).
6  See for example the theme issues of *History and Theory* 47 (2009) and 48 (2009).
7  Ankersmit (1983).

8   The work of White has been subject to extensive commentary and exegesis; most notably in the special issues of *Storia della Storiografia* (1993) and *History and Theory* (1998), marking the 20th and 25th anniversaries of the appearance of *Metahistory* (1973); also noteworthy are the discussions in Kellner (1987), Kramer (1989), Kansteiner (1993), Jenkins (1995), (1999) and Paul (2011).

9   For examples of structuralist plot models, see Barthes (1977); Culler (1975).

10  The geographical *tableau* can be seen as belonging to the French tradition of historical geography; Kellner (1989), 102–23.

11  Ricoeur (1983–85), 1: 146–52.

12  Stone (1979).

13  Stone (1979), 90.

14  Carrard (1992).

15  On degrees of narrativity see Rigney (1991), also Kellner (1987), 29.

16  Mink (1978).

17  Dray (1954); Danto (1985); Veyne (1971); Kocka and Nipperdey (1979).

18  Gallie (1964).

19  Ankersmit (1988).

20  Mink (1978), 147.

21  Ibid.

22  The idea that historical narration is inherently linked to interpretive conflict is advanced in White (1987), 19.

23  This point is elaborated in Rigney (1990), chapter 2.

24  See Friedlander (1992) for both White's contribution to the UCLA conference on 'The Limits of Representation' and some of the responses to it; White's article, entitled 'Historical emplotment and the problem of truth,' is also reproduced in White (1999), 27–42.

25  White, 'The modernist event' in White (1999), 66–86.

26  For a more extensive account of this argument see Rigney (1990).

27  In White (1987), 1–25. This is arguably the most influential of White's essays among narrative theorists and is often reproduced in general anthologies.

28  White (1987), 24–5.

29  Paul (2011).

30  White (1999), 66–86.

31  Lyotard (1979).

32  On the new conceptualisation of time, see Ermarth (1991); Jenkins (1995); Heise (1997); the phrase 'children of chaos' is from Rushkoff (1997). On the desirability of a more inclusive history using multiple perspectives, see Berkhofer (1995).

33  Gossman (1990), 227–56.

34  The pictorial analogy is central for example in Ankersmit (1994).

35  White (1978), 42.

36  This point is more fully developed in Rigney (2001), 59–98. The existence of a category like 'unconventional history' (the title of a 2002 theme issue of *History and Theory*) or 'experiments' (a regular section of the journal *Rethinking History*) indicates a new readiness to see experimentation with ways of writing history as a structural, if necessarily marginal, part of normal historical practice.

37  Amin Maalouf's *Balthasar's Odyssey* (2002), for example, is a rewriting of Homer's work, but also an imaginative survey of the Mediterranean world in the seventeenth century.

38  Himmelfarb (1992).

39  Mink (1970).

40  Partner (1995), 39.

41  Hartman (1995).

42  More on the interactions between novel-writing and history in Rigney (2009).

43  Kellner (1989).

44  A more extended version of this final section can be found in Rigney (2010).

45  Becker (1932).

46  According to Fludernik (1996), becoming virtually involved in the lives of others is a more essential feature of narrative than following an action to its completion; see further Ryan (2001); Ryan (2004).

47  Manovich (2001), 226.

48  Randomly selected examples: Mark Munn, *The School of History: Athens in the Age of Socrates* (2000), is divided into three parts following chronologically 'The Spirit of Democratic Athens, 510–425', 'The Crisis of Athens, 415–403' and 'Resurrecting Athens, 403–395'. Simon Maclean, *Kingship and Politics in the Late Ninth Century: Charles the Fat and the End of the Carolingian Empire* (2003) moves chronologically through the career of Charles the Fat, the end of the Carolingian Empire, and ends with responses to it. Mark Mazower, *Salonica, City of Ghosts: Christians, Muslims and Jews 1430–1950* (2004) follows a chronologically ordered three-part structure marking the islamisation of Salonica, its contacts with Europe in the later period, and the final process of 'Making the City Greek', followed by an epilogue on the contemporary remembrance of the earlier periods. Finally, Tony Judt, *Postwar: A History of Europe since 1945* (2005) also follows a chronologically ordered, four-part structure: setting the scene ('The legacy of war: 1945–1953'); the complication ('Prosperity and its discontents: 1953–1971'); the reversal ('Recessional: 1971–1989') and aftermath ('After the fall: 1989–2005'). For pointing out these other examples I am grateful to my colleagues in the history department at Utrecht University: Josine Blok, Ido de Haan, Mayke de Jong, Ed Jonker and Maarten Prak.

# REFERENCES

Ankersmit, F.R. *Narrative Logic: A Semantic Analysis of the Historian's Language*. The Hague: Martinus Nijhoff, 1983.

Ankersmit, F.R. 'Twee vormen van narrativisme', *Tijdschrift voor filosofie* 50 (1988): 40–82.

Ankersmit, F.R. *History and Tropology: The Rise and Fall of Metaphor*. Berkeley, CA: University of California Press, 1994.

Bal, Mieke. *Travelling Concepts in the Humanities: A Rough Guide*. Toronto: University of Toronto Press, 2002.

Bal, Mieke, ed. *Narrative Theory: Critical Concepts in Literary and Cultural Studies*. 4 vols. London: Routledge, 2004.

Bal, Mieke. 'Working with concepts', *European Journal of English Studies* 13(1) (2009): 13–23.

Barthes, Roland. 'Introduction à l'analyse structurale des récits' [1966], in *Poétique du récit*. Paris: Seuil, 1977: 7–57.

Barnes, Julian. *History of the World in 10½ Chapters*. London: Cape, 1989.

Becker, Carl. 'Everyman his own historian', *American Historical Review* 37(2) (1932): 221–36.

Berkhofer, Robert F. *Beyond the Great Story: History as Text and Discourse*. Cambridge, MA: Harvard University Press, 1995.

Braudel, Fernand. *La méditerranée et le monde méditerranéen à l'époque de Philippe II*. 2 vols. Paris: Armand Colin, 1949.

Carrard, Philippe. *Poetics of the New History: French Historical Discourse from Braudel to Chartier*. Baltimore, MD: Johns Hopkins University Press, 1992.

Culler, Jonathan. *Structuralist Poetics: Structuralism, Linguistics and the Study of Literature*. Ithaca, NY: Cornell University Press, 1975.

Dalrymple, William. *The Last Mughal: The Fall of a Dynasty, Delhi, 1857*. 2006.

Danto, Arthur C. *Narration and Knowledge (Including the Integral Text of 'Analytical Philosophy of History')*. New York: Columbia University Press, 1985.

Davis, Natalie Zemon. *Women on the Margins*. Cambridge, MA: Harvard University Press, 1995.

Dray, William. 'Explanatory narrative in history', *The Philosophical Quarterly* 4(14) (1954): 15–27.

Ermarth, Elizabeth Deeds. *Sequel to History: Postmodernism and the Crisis of Representational Time*. Princeton, NJ: Princeton University Press, 1991.

Fludernik, Monika. *Towards a Natural Narratology*. London: Routledge, 1996.

Friedlander, Saul, ed. *Probing the Limits of Representation: Nazism and the Extermination of the Jews of Europe*. Cambridge, MA: Harvard University Press. 1992.

Friedlander, Saul. *The Years of Extermination: Nazi Germany and the Jews, 1939–1945*. New York: HarperCollins, 2007.

Frye, Northrop. *Anatomy of Criticism: Four Essays*. Princeton, NJ: Princeton University Press, 1957.

Gallie, W.B. *Philosophy and the Historical Understanding*. London: Chatto and Windus, 1964.

Gossman, Lionel. *Between History and Literature*. Cambridge, MA: Harvard University Press, 1990.

Gumbrecht, Hans Ulrich. *In 1926: Living at the Edge of Time*. Cambridge, MA: Harvard University Press, 1997.

'Hayden White: twenty-five years on', special issue of *History and Theory*, 37(2) (1998).

'Hayden White's *Metahistory* twenty years after', special issues of *Storia della Storiografia* 24 and 25 (1993).

Hartman, Geoffrey H. 'Public memory and its discontents', in Marshall Brown, ed. *The Uses of Literary History*. Durham, NC: Duke University Press, 1995, 73–9.

Heise, Ursula K. *Chronoschisms: Time, Narrative, and Postmodernism*. Cambridge: Cambridge UP, 1997.

Herman, David, Manfred Jahn and Marie-Laure Ryan, eds. *Routledge Encyclopedia of Narrative Theory*. London: Routledge, 2005.

Himmelfarb, Gertrude, 'Telling it as you like it: postmodernist history and the flight from fact', *Times Literary Supplement*, 16 October 1992, 12–15.

Jenkins, Keith, *On 'What is History?' From Carr and Elton to Rorty and White*. London: Routledge, 1995.

Jenkins, Keith, *Why History? Ethics and Postmodernity*. London: Routledge, 1999.

Joyce, James. *Ulysses*. Paris: Shakespeare & Co., 1922.

Judt, Tony. *Postwar: A History of Europe since 1945*. New Brunswick, NJ: Rutgers University Press, 2005.

Kansteiner, Wulf. 'Hayden White's critique of the writing of history', *History and Theory* 32(3) (1993): 273–95.

Kansteiner, Wulf. 'Success, truth, modernism in Holocaust historiography: reading Saul Friedlander thirty-five years after the publication of *Metahistory*.' *History and Theory, Theme Issue 47* (May 2009): 25–53.

Kellner, Hans. 'Narrativity in history: post-structuralism and since', *History and Theory* supp. 26 (1987): 1–29.

Kellner, Hans. *Language and Historical Representation: Getting the Story Crooked*. Madison, WI: University of Wisconsin Press, 1989.

Kocka, Jürgen and Thomas Nipperdey, eds. *Theorie und Erzählung in der Geschichte*. Theorie der Geschichte: Beiträge zur Historik, 3. Munich: Deutscher Taschenbuch Verlag, 1979.

Kramer, Lloyd, 'Literature, criticism, and historical imagination: the literary challenge of Hayden White and Dominick LaCapra', in Lynn Hunt, ed. *The New Cultural History*. Berkeley, CA: University of California Press, 1989, 97–128.

Kreiswirth, Martin. 'Merely telling stories? Narrative and knowledge in the human sciences', *Poetics Today* 21(1) (2000): 293–318.

Le Roy Ladurie, Emmanuel. *Histoire du climat depuis l'an mil*. Paris: Flammarion, 1967.

Le Roy Ladurie, Emmanuel. *Montaillou, village occitan de 1294 à 1324*. Paris: Gallimard, 1975.

Lyotard, Jean-François. *La Condition postmoderne: Rapport sur le savoir*. Paris: Minuit, 1979.

Maalouf, Amin. *Balthasar's Odyssey*. Paris: Editions Grasset, 2002.

Maclean, Simon. *Kingship and Politics in the Late Ninth Century: Charles the Fat and the End of the Carolingian Empire*. Cambridge: Cambridge University Press, 2003.

Manovich, Lev. *The Language of New Media*. Cambridge, MA: MIT Press, 2001.

Mazower, Mark. *Salonica, City of Ghosts: Christians, Muslims and Jews 1430–1950*. London: HarperCollins, 2004.

McQuillan, Martin, ed. *The Narrative Reader*. London: Routledge, 2000.

Mink, Louis O. 'History and fiction as modes of comprehension', *New Literary History* 1 (1970): 541–58.

Mink, Louis O. 'Narrative form as a cognitive instrument', in Robert H. Canary and Henry Kozicki, eds. *The Writing of History: Literary Form and Historical Understanding*. Madison, WI: University of Wisconsin Press, 1978, 129–49.

Munn, Mark. *The School of History: Athens in the Age of Socrates*. Berkeley, CA: University of California Press, 2000.

Nash, Christopher, ed. *Narrative in Culture: The Uses of Storytelling in the Sciences, Philosophy, and Literature*. London: Routledge, 1990.

Pakenham, Thomas. *The Boer War*. London: Weidenfeld and Nicolson, 1979.

Partner, Nancy. 'Historicity in an age of reality-fictions', in F.R. Ankersmit and H. Kellner, eds. *A New Philosophy of History*. London: Reaktion, 1995, 21–39.

Paul, Herman. *Hayden White: The Historical Imagination*. Cambridge: Polity Press, 2011.

Ricoeur, Paul. *Temps et récit*. 3 vols. Paris: Seuil, 1983–85.

Rigney, Ann, *The Rhetoric of Historical Representation: Three Narrative Histories of the French Revolution*, Cambridge: Cambridge University Press, 1990.

Rigney, Ann. 'Narrativity and historical representation', *Poetics Today* 12(3) (1991): 591–605.

Rigney, Ann, *Imperfect Histories: The Elusive Past and the Legacy of Romantic Historicism*, Ithaca, NY: Cornell University Press, 2001.

Rigney, Ann. 'All this happened, more or less: what a novelist made of the bombing of Dresden', *History and Theory, Theme Issue* 47 (May 2009): 5–24.

Rigney, Ann. 'When the monograph is no longer the medium: historical narrative in the online age', *History and Theory, Theme Issue* 49 (December 2010): 100–117.

Rushkoff, Douglas. *Children of Chaos: Surviving the World as We Know It*. London: HarperCollins, 1997.

Ryan, Marie-Laure. *Narratives as Virtual Reality: Immersion and Interactivity in Literature and Electronic Media*. Baltimore, MD: Johns Hopkins University Press, 2001.

Ryan, Marie-Laure, ed. *Narrative Across Media*. Lincoln, NB: University of Nebraska Press, 2004.

Stone, Lawrence. 'The revival of narrative: reflections on a new old history', *Past and Present* 85 (1979): 3–24.

Veyne, Paul. *Comment on écrit l'histoire: Essai d'epistémologie*. Paris: Seuil, 1971.

Vonnegut, Kurt. *Slaughterhouse-Five: Or, the Children's Crusade*. New York: Delacorte Press, 1969.

White, Hayden. *Metahistory: The Historical Imagination in Nineteenth-Century Europe*. Baltimore, MD: Johns Hopkins University Press, 1973.

White, Hayden. 'The fictions of factual representation', in Angus Fletcher, ed. *The Literature of Fact: Selected Papers from the English Institute*. New York: Columbia University Press, 1976, 21–44.

White, Hayden. 'The historical text as literary artefact', in Robert H. Canary and Henry Kozicki, eds. *The Writing of History: Literary Form and Historical Understanding*. Madison, WI: University of Wisconsin Press, 1978, 41–62.

White, Hayden. *The Content of the Form: Narrative Discourse and Historical Representation*. Baltimore, MD: Johns Hopkins University Press, 1987.

White, Hayden. *Figural Realism: Studies in the Mimesis Effect*. Baltimore, MD: Johns Hopkins University Press, 1999.

# 13

# The Boundaries of History and Fiction

Ann Curthoys and John Docker

The relationship between history and fiction is a lively and troubled one. Historians insist that what they write is not fiction, as it must retain a fidelity to the available historical sources, those residues from the past we have inherited in the form of documents, images, memories, stories, rituals, material objects, landscapes, and recorded sounds. At the same time, they sometimes envy fiction writers' abilities to imagine and perhaps reconstruct the emotional and intimate aspects of the past that historians find it so hard to recover in the archive. Many of us yearn to be novelists as well, and a surprising number of historians turn their hands to fiction-writing on the side or on their retirement. For their part, fiction writers find what historians do useful but frequently unimaginative, and they resent historians' claims to ownership of the past.

Some of these tensions came to the surface in 2005, with the publication of Kate Grenville's popular and Booker-Prize-short-listed novel, *The Secret River*.[1] Although it dealt with British settlers' dispossession of Indigenous peoples in Australia, it attracted very little of the conservative anger and vituperation that had come the way of the historians who had portrayed these events as violent and destructive. Conservatives, who had attacked and denounced these historians for 'fabrication', ignored the novel as mere fiction, just as they were to do in response to a later and equally harsh historical novel dealing with the violent destruction of Tasmanian Indigenous society, Rohan Wilson's *The Roving Party*.[2] Yet if conservatives ignored these novels as 'mere fiction', thousands of readers did not, and they have generated serious debate about their value as history.

One of the key issues in these debates has been about the otherness of the past. In an interview in July 2005, Kate Grenville contrasted historians' and novelists' treatment of the past by saying while historians battle over the empirical details, the task of novelists was to empathise and understand, to think 'what would I have done in that situation, and what sort of a person would that make me?'[3] When several historians criticised her for putting twenty-first-century emotions and ideas into nineteenth-century people, and for under-estimating the extent to which the past and present are different,[4] Grenville replied that the charge was beside the point – she was not a historian, and she did not claim to write history. Yet, to a historian, she continued to seem undecided on how she wanted her book to be read. She pointed out: 'I did an enormous amount of research. This book isn't history, but it's solidly based on history. Most of the events in the book "really happened" and much of the dialogue is what people really said or wrote'.[5] Later, in a companion book, *Searching for the Secret River*, which described how *The Secret River* was originally meant to be a non-fiction book about her ancestors but had gradually been transformed into a historical novel, Grenville still saw her novel as true to the past: 'This wasn't quite how it was in the documents, but making a sequence out of these scenes wouldn't distort what had "really happened" in any significant way.'[6] In these discussions of historical fiction, an increasingly popular genre, we can thus see embedded some very old concerns with the relationship between truth and fiction, and past and present.

We were intrigued by these debates – our book, *Is History Fiction?*, which had appeared the year before, having traversed these very issues.[7] In that book, we explore the intellectual history of the discipline of history, from Herodotus and Thucydides as its founders in antiquity, to Ranke from the 1820s helping establish the institutional practices of modern professional history, and then through to the present, including discussion of how debates about Holocaust denialism bear on the question of postmodernism and history. We suggest a continuing contrast for over two millennia now between the 'Herodotean' and the 'Thucydidean' as competing modes of historical writing. The 'Herodotean' we see as open and capacious, exploring truth through the narration of many stories, fables, and parables, and engaging with histories that are social, cultural, religious, gendered, sexual, and erotic, as well as diplomatic, political, and military. 'Thucydidean' history is much narrower, confining itself to the diplomatic, political and military, to states and the interaction of states, a focus where women rarely figure; it offers a single authoritative account

in a magisterial tone. We see these two traditions as continuing right up to the present, with the Thucydidean emphasis on political and military history and a single authoritative account usually dominant, but the Herodotean surging at times, especially with the rise of social, cultural, and women's history in the 1970s and 1980s.

In *Is History Fiction?* we also explored the attempted separation of history from fiction especially since Ranke, noting both the ideal of objective scientific history on the one hand, and the continuing doubts about the project of making history scientific on the other. History cannot, we argued, escape its literary nature because it cannot escape itself. Rather, we proposed, history has a double character; it both partakes of the world of literary forms, and at the same time is a rigorous intellectual practice which seeks to achieve historical truth. This double character, we suggest, gives history ample room for uncertainty and disagreement, yet is also perhaps the secret of history's cunning as an inventive, self-transforming discipline; its nature is never settled; its two dimensions can never be resolved into a single character. From the tension between its literary form and its commitment to rigorous scrutiny of the historical archive comes a discipline that is both practical and aesthetic, which crosses the boundaries between art and science. The literary or fictional aspects of historical writing (calling on resources of rhetoric like genre, tone, narrative, allegory, and metaphor), are not to be considered mere surface features, but are themselves part of the search for truth; they help provide explanations, playing a role in the ways historians suggest what happened, and how and why. In other words, our aim was not so much to draw boundaries between fiction and history as to suggest that while such boundaries are forever being drawn and redrawn they are less interesting than the intersections, crossovers, borrowings, influences, and imbrications that both history and fiction find themselves in and which are constitutively part of the long history of historical writing.

In this chapter we focus on just one part of this long history of tension over the problem of history and fiction, and that is the linguistic turn and its critics, or what might otherwise be termed the debates over postmodernism and anti-postmodernism that dominated discussion over the nature of history from the 1970s to the 1990s. We investigate the rise of postmodernism and poststructuralism, and the ways these were interpreted (and often misinterpreted) by historians. We consider some of the attempts by historians to write experimental and postmodern history, and then look at the hostile responses from historians and others to these experiments and to the linguistic turn more generally. Finally, we attempt to assess which aspects of the linguistic turn still influence historical practice today, and which have been rejected and why. In our view, history's double character continues and persists, but the forms of the contest between art and science within history continue to change, and will always do so. Today we see new concerns, with guilt, reparation, memory and notions of the honour of nations and civilisations, and the growth of world and environmental histories interested in humanity as a species and our interactions both with other species and the planet as a whole. We ask how those earlier debates over postmodernism, relativism, and truth have helped shape these recent historical preoccupations.

## HISTORY'S RHETORIC BEFORE POSTMODERNISM

While a concern with the language of history is generally attributed to postmodernism, there were some historians who had already thought about it earlier. The English tradition, for one, never quite gave up its sense of the importance of historical imagination and literary form for historical writing. History became a scene of tension and conflict. As early as 1828, Thomas Babington Macaulay, later to become famous as author of the multi-volume *The History of England*, complained

that history was becoming boring and dull. In an essay, 'On history', he criticised those historians who 'miserably neglect the art of narration, the art of interesting the affections and presenting pictures to the imagination'.[8] Historians should not forget the importance of writing in an engaging exciting way. His own histories were to become hugely popular, partly for their writing style, and partly for the inspiring and ultimately celebratory tales they told English readers about their history.

Seventy-five years later, his great-nephew, George Macaulay Trevelyan (1876–1962), wrote passionately on the same theme. Trevelyan was responding to the proclamation in 1903 by J.B. Bury (1861–1927) in his inaugural lecture as Regius professor of history at Cambridge, that history is a 'science, no less and no more'. For Bury, those who regressively insisted on seeing history as art, in particular as a branch of literature, were impeding recognition of history's scientific character.[9] The young Trevelyan resented Bury's call to arms as an insult to his great-uncle, and wrote a reply, 'Clio, a muse' (1903).[10] He derided Bury's characterisation of history as a science to be shaped in the spirit of Ranke, and protested against what he perceived as the aping of German history whose spirit was alien to the 'free, popular, literary traditions' of England. With the great historians like Carlyle, he wrote, we know that the historian's first duty is 'to tell the story', to attend to 'the art of narrative'.[11] We should recognise history as part of literature in the way writing of all kinds, including history, was recognised in the seventeenth and eighteenth centuries and also much of the nineteenth. Sir Walter Scott, he noted, 'did more than any professional historian to make mankind advance towards a true conception of history', by his stress on history's complexity and his point that history never repeats itself but 'ever creates new forms differing according to time and place'.[12]

In a similar vein, Herbert Butterfield, in *The Whig Interpretation of History* (1931), was deeply conscious that when historians wrote about the past, they were engaged in art as much as science. History, he wrote, 'is a story that cannot be told in dry lines, and its meaning cannot be conveyed in a species of geometry'. Butterfield is critical of historians who forget that historical writing is a creative act, involving imaginative sympathy to make the past intelligible to the present, and a kind of historical awareness or 'historic sense'. The greatest sin in historical composition is to 'abstract events from their context and set them up in implied comparison with the present day, and then to pretend that by this "the facts" are being allowed to "speak for themselves"'.[13]

From the late 1960s, the French poststructuralist tradition also pondered the question of history's form, producing an assemblage of perspectives that became known as the 'linguistic turn'. Barthes, Foucault, and Derrida all wrote works that challenged historians to think about their discipline in new ways. Their challenge met with very different responses, from enthusiastic acceptance to hostile rejection. Many of the rejections are based on either a very sketchy reading of these theorists or more often no reading at all but rather a reading of their followers. As a result, it is important to spend some time examining these foundational thinkers, to establish just what the 'linguistic turn' meant, at least for them.

Here we must make some careful distinctions, for the terms postmodernism and poststructuralism are used more loosely by historians than by literary and cultural critics. In the latter decades of the twentieth century, we can track *postmodernism* as emerging from arguments in North America against a modernist heritage of art and architecture, perceived as frozen in orthodoxy, where the supposedly new had become institutionalised and respectable. In literary and cultural theory, postmodernism challenged an early twentieth-century modernist worldview which had created a hierarchy of genres, where tragedy or a tragic effect was at the summit of aesthetic achievement. Postmodern culture opened itself out to any genre,

whether previously despised or not as 'mass', 'low', 'popular', and 'female'.[14] *Poststructuralism*, on the other hand, explores how much in language meanings can be uncertain and indeterminate, stressing heterogeneity, difference, and contradictoriness. In relation to history specifically, it is poststructuralism that draws attention to history's fictive elements, its use of narrative, allegory, and metaphor, and which asks historians and other scholars to openly acknowledge themselves as narrators in the staged world of their texts.[15] Poststructuralists are not necessarily postmodernist in matters of culture, though they may be.[16]

However, postmodernism, denoting a mode of thinking about history and truth that is to be feared and despised, became in historiographical debate the shorthand term for those who opposed poststructuralism and postmodernism alike.

## BARTHES

A key intervention that helped establish the 'linguistic turn' is Roland Barthes' essay, 'Historical discourse', or 'The discourse of history', first published in 1967. Though crucial, it is not well known to most historians, and its semiotic language, of signifieds and signifiers and shifters and the like, is at times very technical and not easily accessible to non-specialists. Yet its implications are profound. Barthes is best known as one of the founders of the modern discipline of cultural studies; in the highly influential *Mythologies* (1957), he applied the techniques of linguistic and textual analysis to a wide variety of mass culture texts and events, from a Parisian wrestling match to an advertisement to plastic toys.[17] In his essay on historical discourse he applies these techniques to conventional historical writing and attempts to discern what historical discourse shares with other forms of literature and what is specific to it. Barthes finds that historical writing, while it presents itself as a normal scholarly practice, is very odd indeed.

In conventional historical writing, Barthes quizzically observes, the author stands aside, omits any reference to his own time or to the fact of his historical discourse. Just as Herbert Butterworth in 1931 had been critical of historians for their pretence that the facts speak for themselves, Barthes similarly reflects, with irony and perplexity at its impossibility, that in historical writing the past is made to appear as if speaking for itself: 'the history seems to be telling itself all on its own'.[18] Barthes notes how historical discourse shares this technique with the realist novel; both believe they are 'objective' because they suppress any mention of 'I' in their discourse. Barthes finds himself wondering if this kind of 'objective' discourse is not actually a form of psychopathology. It shares with schizophrenic discourse a radical censorship of the act of uttering: 'no-one is there to take responsibility for the utterance'.[19]

So far, Barthes has described what history and the realist novel have in common. He then explores what is distinctive to history. In historical writing, the elimination of the fact of narration ostensibly allows the 'real' and its expression to come together, producing a 'realistic effect'.[20] Historical discourse from the nineteenth century saw in the pure and simple relation of the facts the best proof of those facts; truth came from careful narration. In the hands of the positivist historians, narrative structure, originally developed in the 'cauldron of fiction (in myths and the first epics)' becomes 'at once the sign and the proof of reality'.[21] Against this illusion or delusion, Barthes draws attention to historical discourse as a form of writing which 'oscillates between two poles', the indexical (metaphoric) and the functional (metonymic), or in our terms, history has a double character, the literary and the scientific. Somewhat in the spirit of Benedetto Croce's essay 'History and chronicle' (1917),[22] Barthes distinguishes between annals and chronology (or chronicles) and history, regarding the former as an unstructured series of notations, and the latter as a form of discourse which connects these notations, giving them

meaning. The historian organises facts 'with the purpose of establishing positive meaning and filling the vacuum of pure, meaningless series'.[23] What seems to conventional historians to be pure description is actually an interpretation.

Barthes asked historians, then, to consider that what they took to be some kind of transcription of the actual events of the past into readable form was in fact a form of discourse which had its own metaphoric and functional meanings, a discourse marked by a 'reality effect'. He was implicitly asking them to be more self-conscious about the kind of texts they were producing, and to recognise the gap between themselves, their forms of discourse, and the pasts they narrated.

## DERRIDA

French poststructuralism in the work of Jacques Derrida took some of these issues a little further. Derrida does not address historical discourse explicitly in the way Barthes does, but he is important to the 'linguistic turn' for his attention to textual reading and the nature of texts, and for defining poststructuralism itself. His major works, *Writing and Difference* and *Of Grammatology* appeared in the same year as Barthes' 'The discourse of history'. Especially important in *Writing and Difference* was his essay 'Structure, sign and play in the discourse of the human sciences', which radically challenged the prevailing French structuralist tradition and proposed a deconstructionist or poststructuralist approach. Where structuralism presupposes that every phenomenon has a hidden structure that, once discovered, will explain the nature of the phenomenon, poststructuralism refuses essentialist notions of a centre or origin. Instead, we should think of a play of alternative structurings, a play of interpretation where truth is searched for but never finally arrived at, and where the writing is highly self-reflexive, calling attention to its own theorising, its own theoretical and methodological operations.[24] In *Of*

*Grammatology*, Derrida studies at length the question of the text. He argues that in human history, writing comes before speech, interpreting 'writing' in a much broader sense than is usually understood, so that it denotes everything that gives rise to inscription – the pictographic, ideographic, hieroglyphic, cuneiform, aural, and musical, that is, a trace of any kind.[25] In history from its beginning, such traces form together to constitute chains of signification, systems, and texts. There is, however, no original trace, no origin from which all history unfolds; there is only the play of differences, of interpretations and reinterpretations, ever disputed and involved with power and violence; a play of meanings and values which can never yield complete certainty or final truths.[26]

*Of Grammatology* is the book in which Derrida wrote, exceedingly controversially: 'There is nothing outside of the text [there is no outside-text; *il n'y a pas de hors-texte*]'.[27] So notorious has this emphasised phrase become that we might dwell for a moment on the passage of argument in which it occurs. Derrida is doing what he always does, reading a text, in this case, Rousseau's *Confessions*. In particular, he is discussing how *The Confessions* reveals and explores the ways Rousseau's lover, Thérèse, is a replacement, supplement, substitute, for Rousseau's mother. Derrida takes the opportunity to make some general observations on method and the protocols of reading and interpretation. In common with a great deal of twentieth-century literary criticism, Derrida argues that while Rousseau's own life, and the lives of his mother and Thérèse, are certainly of 'prime interest', what we know about Rousseau's actual mother or the life of Thérèse or his own personal biography can be known only from Rousseau's text, and from other texts interested in those histories. In particular, to know Rousseau's real mother now becomes impossible; all we can do is explore the traces, substitutions, and supplements 'to infinity', in their textual richness.[28]

In view of the way poststructuralism has been understood and rejected by many historians as meaning anything goes, it is important to note that Derrida says here that we cannot develop an interpretation 'in any direction at all', as if we could 'say almost anything'.[29] In the same vein, he says in 'Plato's Pharmacy' in *Dissemination* (1972), in a long contemplation of the *Phaedrus*, that the critic enters into a particular relationship with the text in which he cannot 'add any old thing'. The game of reading, the 'logic of *play*', proceeds with rigour; it is not careless or haphazard or made up.[30] Scrupulous reading demands, first of all, establishing the protocols of reading. When we look at what these protocols are, they turn out to be those familiar to historians, such as questioning the specific provenance of the text as a historical event.[31] In our view, then, while Derrida insists on the endless play of interpretation and the impossibility of a final incontestable truth, he most certainly does not see interpretation as 'made up', as free. To suggest otherwise is a serious misrepresentation.

## HEXTER

It was not only French poststructuralists who drew attention to history's specific rhetoric. Surprisingly similar points were being made by historians coming from a much more pragmatic Anglo-American historical tradition. In 1968, the year after Barthes's essay on historical discourse and Derrida's *Of Grammatology* appeared, J.H. Hexter, an American historian of early modern Europe, published the rather truculent 'The rhetoric of history', an essay which would become well known. Drawing on the strong American tradition of rhetoric study,[32] he argued for the distinctiveness of history's rhetoric, and against the attempts of others, especially analytical philosophers, to impose an inappropriate 'denotative rhetoric' on historians, to reduce historical writing to a single dimension. Historians, unlike scientists, Hexter suggested, happily sacrifice exactness in the interests of 'evocative force', which helps them advance the 'understanding of the past'.

As a form of communication, historical rhetoric, more like that employed in the 'fictive arts' rather than the rhetoric of the sciences, is 'not only permissible but on occasion indispensable'. Nevertheless, for Hexter a major difference remains between history and the fictive arts and that is the 'overriding commitment of historians to fidelity to the surviving records of the past'. The difference between Conrad's *Nostromo* and Oscar Handlin's *The Uprooted* is that the standard of judgement of the latter, a historical work, must ultimately be 'extrinsic'. It must communicate knowledge of 'the actual past congruent with the surviving record'.[33]

Rhetoric, he insists, is not a superficial aspect of history – it is not merely 'aesthetic', nor is it 'intellectual slatternliness', as analytical philosophers would have historians believe.[34] Rhetoric is part of history's 'essential function', its rigorous manly Rankean capacity to 'convey knowledge of the past as it really was', to further 'knowledge, understanding, truth, and meaning'. Narrative, for example, is the common mode of explanation that historians deploy in order to answer historical questions, those that Hexter refers to as the *how* and *why* questions concerning what happened in the past. In concluding, Hexter makes a plea for a 'paradigm shift' where it may 'now be desirable and even necessary' for historians to arrive at a kind of inclusive self-understanding concerning their discipline, to foreground questions of the relations between rhetoric, connotation, necessary incompleteness, similarity to fictive arts, characterisation, explanation, meaning, and truth.[35]

While Hexter shares none of the French poststructuralist epistemological concern to question our ability to know what actually happened, the congruence on the question of historical discourse and rhetoric between an Anglo-American largely empiricist historian and French anti-empiricist poststructuralism and semiotics gives us a hint, perhaps, of why poststructuralist ideas began to have an impact on Anglo-American scholarship.

## HAYDEN WHITE AND MIKHAIL BAKHTIN

In the latter decades of the twentieth century, the historian who did most to draw attention to the literary nature of historical texts was the American Hayden White, an expert in European intellectual history. In many essays and key books – *Metahistory* (1973), *Tropics of Discourse* (1978), *The Content of the Form* (1987), and *Figural Realism* (1999)[36] – he provocatively argued that historians inevitably write a certain kind of fiction, and he especially focussed on their narrative strategies and techniques, their uses of plot and character, voice and tone. Hayden White's ideas were to prove both very attractive to and deeply troubling for historians, and remain so to this day. On the one hand, he stimulated at least some historians' recognition that they actually wrote texts themselves, constructed narratives and analyses that were embedded in language and literary form, and that the particular nature and form of their texts arose from the present in which they were written rather than as a direct expression of the past. On the other, he was perceived as forgetting the referentiality of historical writing, its relation to the past or at least to its traces in the present. It is perhaps this apparent distance from a concern with what historians would call 'the past itself' that led many of them to fail to see the importance of his key point, that narrative is made, not found.

In 'The historical text as literary artifact' (1974), White suggests that historians fail to recognise that they inevitably and unavoidably use fictional techniques to narrate the past. Creative writers are highly conscious of their techniques and narrative strategies, but historians seem to genuinely believe that they have found the form of their narrative in the events themselves. It is a fiction of historians, says White, that the various states of affairs that they constitute as the beginning, the middle, and the end of a course of development are all actual or real and that they are merely recording what happened. In fact, both beginning and ending are poetic constructions chosen by the historian. Historians use a range of time-honoured narrative techniques: highlighting some details and subordinating others, repeating a symbol or motif, varying the tone and point of view to indicate the difference in perspective of different characters, and describing people and places in an interesting way. He shocked – and still shocks – many historians by insisting that the relationships between people or between events that *appear* to be inherent in the past have actually been imposed by the historian.[37]

Like Hexter, White reminds historians that the literary aspects of what they do are crucial, not subsidiary, to the historical enterprise. In White's view, historians not only use narrative technique to suggest relationships and bring logic to their stories; they also write within a quite limited number of narrative genres. Historians, he says, gain part of their explanatory effect by making stories through 'emplotment', the placing of 'fact' or 'data' found in the chronicle as components of specific kinds of plot structures. Readers only make sense of events within a recognisable genre, such as the tragic, comic, romantic, ironic, epic, or satirical. When readers recognise to which genre a story belongs, they experience the effect of having the unfolding events in the story explained to them. Nevertheless, White contends, 'most historical sequences can be emplotted in a number of different ways'. Historical situations are 'not *inherently* tragic, comic, or romantic'. A different genre will yield a different understanding or explanation of the past. White gives as an example Marx's *Eighteenth Brumaire*: what is tragic from one perspective is farcical from another. Figurative elements such as choice of metaphor also help constitute meaning. White called for historians to move to a 'higher level of self-consciousness' in recognising the 'literary or fictive element in every account'.[38]

While we think White's main argument, the constructed nature of historical discourse and narrative form, is important, we are critical of certain aspects of his approach to historical

theory. One problem is his reliance on Northrop Frye, from whom he derived his notion of genre. A North American literary critic best known for *Anatomy of Criticism* (1957), Frye was associated with myth or archetype criticism, which constructed literature as a vast system made up of a limited number of genres: comedy, romance, tragedy, irony, and satire. Each genre is held to possess an essential meaning, for example, the isolation of the hero in tragedy, or the 'integration of society' in comedy. Further, for Frye such genres and forms are, in Jungian terms, archetypes lodged in the collective unconscious.[39] White's originality was to extend Frye's method to the analysis of historical as well as literary forms of writing. Yet he was adopting an approach to literature that was being increasingly rejected by literary critics, who by this time generally saw Frye's approach as deterministic, denying any particular text its individuality, nuance, subtle difference, its own tone, rhythm, voice, grain, markings, and oddities.[40]

Furthermore, White's attention to a multiplicity of genres was perhaps a little misplaced, for, as Barthes had already pointed out, most historical writing worked – wittingly or unwittingly – within only one genre, that of the realist novel. This was a form in which the omniscient author/narrator told the story in such a way that only one point of view, one interpretation, was possible. The chosen genre was rarely tragedy, comedy, romance, irony, or satire, but simply that of realism. Modern professional historians from the nineteenth century on had a certain kind of realist prose style firmly in their grasp, and they were never going to easily entertain a notion that alternative genres were possible or relevant.[41]

Rather than Northrop Frye, there is in our view another literary thinker who is much more interesting for historians, and that is Mikhail Bakhtin. One of the most important cultural theorists and philosophers of the twentieth century, Bakhtin's work came to the notice of Anglophone scholars in the 1970s. He had, however, written his work decades earlier. After participating as a young scholar in the intellectual ferment of the Soviet Union in the 1920s, debating prominent theories of the time – Russian Formalism, Freud, Marxism, the philosophy of language – Bakhtin published his pathbreaking *Problems of Dostoevsky's Poetics* in 1929. Arrested that year during a purge of Leningrad intellectuals, he remained in exile in various provincial towns for the rest of his working life. Young Soviet scholars began to take renewed interest in his work in the early 1960s; the Dostoevsky book was republished in 1963, and followed two years later by *Rabelais and His World*. Another landmark publication was the appearance of *The Dialogic Imagination* with its essays on the history of the novel. Translations of his work began to appear in France in the late 1960s, followed by English translations in the 1970s. By the 1980s, scholars internationally welcomed Bakhtin's writings for their fruitful notions of genre, monologic, dialogic, polyphony, heteroglossia, chronotope, carnival, and carnivalesque.[42]

Bakhtin was critical of the essentialised conception of character one finds in the realist novel, in which characters are presented as psychologically coherent individuals. He drew attention to the many ways characters might be textually represented in a diverse range of genres throughout cultural history. Sometimes characters are fixed (as in the hero and heroine of ancient romances, or figures like the clown, trickster, rogue, crank, the forerunners of modern figures like the detective) and the interest lies in the narrative excitements, complications, dangers, and perils into which they have entered. Sometimes characters such as the rogue, crank, fool, and trickster are important as outsider figures, needed to provide a fresh, amused, bemused, questioning sceptical eye. At other times, in narratives ancient and modern, characters go through various transformations and metamorphoses. Furthermore, Bakhtin made an important distinction between two kinds of novel, the dialogic and the monologic. In the dialogic novel, there is a play of voices, where each character represents a different troubled worldview, and where the clash of characters, and therefore of different worldviews, is never finalised or completed. The monologic novel insists, by contrast, on one pervading set of values. For Bakhtin the dialogic and the monologic novel were ideal types, different bookends (as it were) of a continuum; and he recognised that in any one novel there would be competition and mixing between them. Bakhtin thus made available to history a sophisticated approach to the literary aspects of historical texts.[43]

In short, if we combine Barthes' attention to historical discourse with White's observations on the literary nature of historical texts and Bakhtin's dynamic conception of genre, character, and narrative, we begin to have a basic framework for thinking about historical texts *as* texts. To this framework, we might profitably add the insights of Michel Foucault and Edward Said, to whom we now turn.

## MICHEL FOUCAULT AND EDWARD SAID

Foucault's books began appearing in 1961, with *Madness and Civilisation* and continued with *The Birth of the Clinic* (1963) and *The Order of Things* (1966). Three years later, in the extraordinarily influential *The Archaeology of Knowledge* (1969), Foucault expressed concern that his own earlier work may have been too structuralist; in *The Order of Things*, he now feels, he may have given the impression that he was conducting his analyses in terms of notions like 'cultural totality'.[44] In *The Archaeology of Knowledge*, by contrast, Foucault argues strongly against total history, the assumption of seamless connections between phenomena; in total history, the traditional historian is preoccupied with long periods, where stable patterns can be discerned. Clearly, Foucault is opposing the Annales school of historians (though he doesn't name them) then dominant in France. The traditional historian, he says, in terms not dissimilar from those of Barthes, always wishes to link the disparate and dispersed, to perceive continuity and causal relationships between events, to find their overall significance, with the eventual hope of establishing the desired total history. In this desire for totality and coherence, traditional history was, however, lagging behind the new thinking in other fields, where attention was turning to notions of 'threshold, rupture, break, mutation, transformation'.[45] For Foucault, the new history would establish not continuity and connectedness but rather *discontinuity*. The historian, though, recognises that he cannot escape imposing himself on his material; even the emphasis on discontinuity would be a 'deliberate operation on the part of the historian', rather than a 'quality of the material with which he has to deal'.[46]

Two years later, in his essay 'Nietzsche, genealogy, history' (1971), Foucault again addressed the complex problem of the connection between the historian and the past. He admires Nietzsche's notion of genealogy, which connects the past and the present; it seeks to write a history from the present to the past, drawing out myriad lines of connection.[47] Traditional history, Foucault points out, sees itself as neutral in terms of values, 'committed solely to truth'. Yet, in its 'will to knowledge', traditional history conceals what might be its own motives and desires. The genealogist, on the other hand, will openly admit his perspectives, his preferences in a controversy. He will attempt to understand his own motives and desires, fears and forebodings; his own situation within a specific historical context. The genealogist understands that the will to knowledge will never 'achieve a universal truth'. History can never achieve absolute knowledge.[48]

Foucault, unlike Barthes and Derrida, paid little attention to language and rhetoric.[49] In an interview conducted in 1976 published as 'Truth and power', his lack of interest in linguistic form is quite explicit. He insists that the 'history which bears and determines us has the form of a war rather than that of language'. We should talk, he says, about

'relations of power, not relations of meaning'; we should refuse to analyse the 'symbolic field' or the 'domain of signifying structures'.[50] Truth, he says in this interview, is not 'outside power, or lacking in power'. Each society, he points out, 'has its regime of truth', its 'general politics' of truth: that is, the types of discourse which it accepts and makes function as true; the mechanisms and instances which enable one to distinguish true and false statements, the means by which each is sanctioned; the techniques and procedures accorded value in the acquisition of truth; the status of those who are charged with saying what counts as true. This has often been taken to mean that Foucault believes there is no truth, and like Derrida as suggesting that anything goes, we can interpret the past any way we like. We do not read him in this way. He seems to us simply to be offering a sociology of knowledge, reminding us that there is no neutral or objective or non-discursive place from which to view the past, or write about it in the present. After all, in 'Nietzsche, genealogy, history', Foucault does commit himself to a notion of truth, recommending we possess a 'true historical sense'.[51]

Foucault proved inspiring not only for the development of the relatively new fields of history of the body and history of sexuality, but also for the development and flourishing of postcolonial theory. Edward Said noted in the introduction to his great work *Orientalism*: 'I have found it useful here to employ Michel Foucault's notion of a discourse, as described by him in *The Archaeology of Knowledge* and in *Discipline and Punish*, to identify Orientalism.' Foucault's notion of discourse, Said suggests, helps us understand the 'enormously systematic discipline by which European culture was able to manage – and even produce – the Orient politically, sociologically, militarily, ideologically, scientifically, and imaginatively' during the post-Enlightenment period of the nineteenth century and then into the twentieth, the period particularly of English and French imperial power. Said qualifies his use of Foucault, however, in one important respect.

Where Foucault in Said's view believes that the individual text or author counts for very little when discussing a discourse, Said considers that individual writers left their 'determining imprint', and accordingly he will employ 'close textual readings' to reveal the interweavings of individual text or author and Orientalism as a complex collective discursive formation.[52] We agree with Said's critical qualification here, and ourselves have attempted to present the linguistic turn through an examination of specific writers and texts, in our book, *Is History Fiction?*, in this chapter, and elsewhere.[53]

## POSTMODERN EXPERIMENTATION

The poststructuralist emphasis on language, discourse, narrative, and speaking position, and also on the play of interpretation and the impossibility of a final truth, inspired some historians to rethink their own practice. Many had absorbed from the poststructuralists a new interest in form, and began exploring new modes of writing history and developing more self-consciousness about the consequences for their argument of the particular form of their texts. Perhaps they might find ways to present the results of their research in writing which does not rely on the hidden narrator who apparently knows everything, but rather draws attention to the fact that historical knowledge is constructed in the present. Historians could be more self-conscious in terms of acknowledging the process of research itself, the difficulty of knowing what happened in the past, the fact of interpretation and re-interpretation, and the complex relation between the historian (and reader) in the present and the past events narrated by the historian.

Historians in the 1980s and 1990s engaged in formal experimentation to a striking degree. They wrote imaginative micro-narratives, experimented with multiple points of view, and played with fragmentation, montage, and genre-crossing. At the same time, many writers of fiction were turning to history, plundering historical records and the works of historians to create historical fictions. In some they blended created characters with real historical figures, ascribing to the latter entirely invented actions and words and speeches. The boundaries between history and fiction that had held for so long were being breached.

In his 1991 essay, 'History of events and the revival of narrative', Peter Burke reported on and encouraged these developments. Burke was interested in attempts to avoid the omniscient narrator by directly representing competing or alternative points of view. Invoking Bakhtin's notion of heteroglossia, or multivocality, he suggested that multi-voiced story telling would 'allow an interpretation of conflict in terms of a conflict of interpretations'.[54] He discussed various narrative modes that might prove useful for historians: the self-conscious foregrounding of the fact of narration, unreliable first-person narrators, and non-chronological narration through a variety of techniques, drawn from novels and film. He drew attention to the rise of micro-narratives or micro-histories, the telling of a story about 'ordinary people in their local setting', akin to 'thick description' (in Clifford Geertz's tireless phrase). Historians of French and Italian history had, Burke noted, developed the art of micro-history to a high level.[55] Through use of official and especially legal sources, historians seemed to have found a way to narrate the lives and thoughts of the relatively unknown, the ordinary and powerless people of the past. Particularly famous instances of the genre were Carlo Ginzburg's *The Cheese and the Worms* (1976) and Emmanuel Le Roy Ladurie's *Montaillou* (1978).[56]

Burke stressed how much historians could learn, in terms of narrative form, from novelists and filmmakers. They could emulate the early twentieth-century moderns like James Joyce, Marcel Proust, and Virginia Woolf, with their decomposing of temporal continuity, or novelists like William Faulkner and Lawrence Durrell who tell their stories from more than one viewpoint. Or they could learn from film how to play with chronology and multiple points of view while still maintaining a sense of historical sequence, through techniques such as montage, flashbacks, and flashforwards. Historians could, perhaps, write history backwards, as Norman Davies had done in *Heart of Europe* (1984), a history of Poland which started with the post World War II period and moved back, chapter by chapter, through to earlier times. Burke proposed experiments, influenced in part by his reading of Hayden White, such as offering alternative endings, along the lines of John Fowles' novel, *The French Lieutenant's Woman*. The historian might give the reader a number of endings according to the date chosen to end the story; a narrative history of World War I ending in 1919 will give a different impression from one ending in 1933 or 1939. Alternative endings, Burke suggested, could make the work more 'open' in the sense of encouraging readers to reach their own conclusions.[57] Burke thought, however, that certain forms of experimentation were 'best avoided by historians', including invented speech and the 'inventions of someone's stream of consciousness'.[58] He was advocating the use of fictional techniques to produce new and more complex meanings, not the introduction of 'made-up' elements to historical writing.

In the *fin de siècle* of the 1980s and 1990s, historians especially took up the idea of more openly foregrounding what they did not know, and their own processes of trying to decipher documents and to decide what might have happened. Such an approach re-introduces the historian as a first-person narrator in his or her own text, established as a detective figure attempting to work out from the (incomplete and sometimes contradictory) evidence what may have occurred in the past. In an experimental work not discussed by Burke, *Mirror in the Shrine* (1988), Robert Rosenstone foregrounded his involvement in the stories he was telling, creating a character called 'the biographer' who would complain of the problems involved in writing the book. At one point, talking of a young American in

Japan, the biographer quotes from some diary entries and letters, then comments:

> There it is, the whole story. Or at least all the available evidence. We are at the mercy of a single firsthand report from a witness who can hardly be neutral, one who already bent evidence on similar sensitive issues – drinking, Sunday parties, prostitution. How we wish for more … What we want are those lost, secret moments …[59]

We can also think of innovative works like John Demos' *The Unredeemed Captive* (1995), with its invented speech and dialogue, and three different endings.[60]

## ANTI-POSTMODERNISM

Some historians found the effervescent mood of literary experimentation and adventurous risk-taking as it began to flourish in the latter 1980s and early 1990s disturbing. These opponents of what they usually comprehensively labelled 'postmodernism' crossed all usual boundaries; they included Marxists, feminists, 'anti-theory' 'working historians', ex-Marxists turned conservative, and militant positivists. In particular, they defended the idea of a single knowable truth about the past. An empiricism and faith in objectivity was reasserted with a vigour rarely seen since the 1960s. Yet these rejoinders of the 1990s and 2000s were by no means a simple return to the postwar period; they framed the debate in new ways. We take two widely read texts of the 1990s as emblematic of this response: both accept certain aspects of postmodernism, while vehemently rejecting others.

In *Telling the Truth about History* (1994), Joyce Appleby, Lynn Hunt, and Margaret Jacob set out to explain the strengths and weaknesses of postmodernism and the linguistic turn for the history profession. Directed at an American student audience, and subsequently one of the most commonly used texts in courses on history and historiography, *Telling the Truth about History* concedes some ground to postmodernism and the linguistic turn. It takes the postmodernist point that historians' use of omniscient narration conceals historians' own interests, partiality, and viewpoints, and welcomes the fact that historians influenced by the linguistic turn have 'alerted an unwary public, as well as their peers, to how the different perspectives of historians enter into their books'. The authors acknowledge that the historian 'is stuck in time present, trying to make meaningful and accurate statements about time past'; curiosity about the past derives from the preoccupations of the present, and the traces of the past 'never speak for themselves'. And they sound mightily like Hayden White when they agree that 'the flow of time does not have a beginning, middle, and end; only stories about it do'. On the other hand, they see postmodernists as denying 'our ability to represent reality in any objectively true fashion'. Foucault, they claim, made 'truth nothing more than the will to power within discourse', while Derrida, they suggest, questioned the enterprise of seeking truth altogether. Postmodernists have in their view offered a new kind of determinism – 'linguistic determinism', reducing 'the social and natural world to language'. Against the meta-narratives or master narratives they criticise – the idea of progress, nationalism, modernism, Marxism, and liberalism – postmodernists have unwittingly developed a master narrative of their own.[61]

The equivalent English text, appearing a few years later, is Richard J. Evans' *In Defence of History* (1997). Like the authors of *Telling the Truth about History*, Evans believes some of the effects of postmodernism on history have been positive. He is quite happy with the literary experimentation generated by postmodernism's impact on history: he thinks that as a result of the influence of the social sciences most history books had become 'hopelessly unreadable', and he largely welcomes the work of people like Simon Schama, Natalie Zemon Davis, and Robert Darnton. Yet, in our view, he misinterprets Derrida and Foucault in much the same way as Appleby et al. do, contending that postmodern history exhibits an extreme

relativism which leaves the door open to fascist or racist views of history, with no way of saying these ideas are false: 'Total relativism provides no objective criteria by which fascist or racist views of history can be falsified.' Consequently, postmodernism paved the way for Holocaust denialism. The 'increase in scope and intensity of the Holocaust deniers' activities since the mid-1970s', he contends, reflects the 'postmodernist intellectual climate'.[62]

Both these texts seriously misinterpret French poststructuralism. Holocaust denialism, nonetheless, does pose real questions for historians, somewhat similar to those posed to scientists by creationism. How do we insist on truth about the past, while still acknowledging the inevitability of competing interpretations? Unease that relativism is disabling for historians in debates over calamitous events – not only the Holocaust, but also instances of war, genocide, and gross abuses of human rights more generally – has led many historians to reject what we consider are valuable postmodern insights. We would argue that postmodernism is *not* a ground for Holocaust denialism, or even for the kind of relativism that sees all versions of the past as equally plausible and acceptable. Pointing to the impossibility of finalising the search for truth does not mean rejecting that search or the protocols and rules by which we seek to understand the past and represent it to readers in the present. We support the view of Dan Stone, who in his *Constructing the Holocaust* (2003) takes issue with those who charge that postmodernists create an atmosphere conducive to Holocaust denialism. There is nothing, Stone writes, in postmodern awareness of the importance of subjectivity, perspective, and speaking position that disallows a commitment to truth and rigorous reliance on the evidence.[63] He also directly answers *Telling the Truth about History*, which contends that the kind of cultural relativism that postmodernism allegedly exhibits had already been evident in Nazism and the Holocaust: in the words of *Telling the Truth about History*, 'cultural relativism had reached its limits in the death camps'; the Holocaust demonstrates that in history 'absolute moral standards' are 'necessary'.[64] Stone passionately replies:

> This is an astonishing assertion. Surely the opposite is the case? Nazism was anything but a form of cultural relativism. ... Nazism showed exactly how far the desire to impute one absolute meaning to History can go.

In Stone's view, in the wake of the Holocaust, it is only a 'multiplication of interpretations of the meaning of history' that can 'safeguard historical freedom'.[65]

Debate about the Holocaust is also important to the linguistic turn for another reason. As Stone reflects, the Holocaust, in making us 'aware of general problems of representation that are normally passed by with ease', challenges us to change the way we write history. The problem of how to represent the Holocaust historically, he argues, is most fruitfully explored by postmodernism (at its best and most rigorous) because of its sophisticated understanding of texts and its imaginativeness and adventurousness of interpretation of the meanings of the past.[66]

## HISTORY IN THE TWENTY-FIRST CENTURY

The linguistic turn and mood of formal experimentation it encouraged seem to have subsided in the new millennium. In its place is the increased profile of history in public and especially political life. History has become increasingly entangled with questions of national honour, apology, and reparation. Of course, history has long been closely associated with the nation state, and we can see Ranke as the prime theorist and example of this relationship.[67] What has changed, perhaps, is not history as a discipline or history's relation to the nation state, but rather the way various publics now interact with the past. We might call this the new politics of memory.

In 2000 Elazar Barkan, in his *The Guilt of Nations: Restitution and Negotiating Historical Injustices*, commented on 'the sudden appearance of restitution cases all over the world', which he saw as suggesting 'a potentially new international morality'.[68] What Barkan particularly noticed was that demands for restitution arose not only when citizens of one country or ethnic group charge others with human rights abuses, but also as a result of self-examination.[69] Barkan was struck by the 'willingness of the perpetrators to engage and accommodate the victims' demands'.[70] National leaders, he noted, from Clinton to Chirac, Blair to Schroeder, were offering apologies for 'gross historical crimes in their own countries'.[71] Apologies and demands for restitution have occurred mainly in relation to three key areas: wartime atrocities (German reparation to Jews, the treatment of Japanese Americans, the Japanese use of 'comfort women', and Switzerland's restitution of funds to Holocaust victims who lost their money in Swiss banks), colonialism (especially in North America, Hawaii, Australia, and New Zealand), and slavery (United States, Brazil).[72] For Barkan, the growing politicisation of history has been closely connected with the influence of postmodernism: 'as history has become increasingly malleable, it has simultaneously become more central to our daily life ... being subject to interpretation, it has also become a space for contesting perspectives'.[73]

Yet the notion of conflicting perspectives is itself contested. In the courtroom, for example, historians find that only a strong assertion of a single historical truth will satisfy the court. Historians have been assisting courts since at least the *Brown* vs *Board of Education* desegregation case of 1954, but never more than now, especially in cases involving Indigenous peoples' land and other claims. Time and again, historians have found the experience of dealing with legal teams and especially of cross examination in court very difficult. Many would agree with David Rothman when he writes, 'To enter the courtroom is to do many things, but it is not to do history. The essential attributes that we treasure most about historical inquiry have to be left outside the door.'[74] Or, to take another example, Helen Hornbeck Tanner writes with some pathos and irony: 'My experience has taught me that the law is opposed to history; that history and the law are in a state of perpetual warfare in the courts of law. As a historian, I feel that every time I have gone into a courtroom, I have been flung into an arena where I might be chewed up by the legal lions before I can get out alive.'[75] There are many issues here, but one of the most fundamental is that courts must decide on one account being true, and adversarial legal processes will tend to push historians to do the same. The law's need to resolve a dispute and therefore to decide on a single account of what happened sometimes pushes historians to be more certain than they would like, and many have later regretted putting forward a much more definitive case than they really felt the evidence could sustain.[76]

In other words, when history becomes significant either in politics or the law, historians are pushed to provide unambiguous narratives. They have in practice to decide on one account being true, if not 'beyond reasonable doubt' (the criterion of criminal law), then at least on civil law's 'balance of probabilities'. In this context, there appears to be little place for uncertainty, playfulness, ambiguity, or alternative endings. The attention to literary form, and the open recognition of the difficulty of knowing what really happened in the past, that characterised the linguistic turn and the almost carnivalesque experimentalism of late twentieth-century historical writing, becomes subdued in these political and legal contexts.

History does not operate, however, only in the political and legal spheres. Far from it. It continues both as a popular practice in its own right, in the form of history books and essays and on film and television, and as a source for fiction, in the ever-popular historical novel.[77] One of the most historically conscious of recent novels is the exceedingly popular Harry Potter series, largely set in a high school teaching witchcraft. J.K. Rowling's fantasy novels include entertaining discussions

of why conventional history can be so unengaging, rather in the spirit of Jane Austen's *Northanger Abbey*, and reminding us again of Croce's call, in his essay 'History and chronicle', that 'only an interest in the life of the present can move one to investigate past fact', for 'past fact' comes alive when it is 'unified with an interest in the present life'. Until the historian is interested and begins enquiring, the narratives and documents of the past are mere chronicle, not history as such.[78] The 'History of Magic', we learn in volume 5, *Harry Potter and the Order of the Phoenix* (2003), 'was by common consent the most boring subject ever devised by wizard kind', and this theme is repeated later in the novel in a wonderful account of the History of Magic exam.[79] In contrast to this irrelevant dead History, chronicle in Croce's terms, the logic of the story through the Potter novels is always that one can only go forward by going back. One has to learn one's enemy's formation, to truly understand and thereby confront him. To know the past is essential in order to negotiate the present, and past and present have a dynamic relationship. The present is a consequence of past events, and the characters in these novels learn in different ways to recognise how those events continue to influence and shape the future. As Edmund Kern points out, each volume not only takes the story forward, but also takes it back into the past as well.[80] In order to survive the dangers that beset them, key characters like Harry and Hermione become historical detectives, motivated by urgent present needs.

The seventh and final volume in the series, *Harry Potter and the Deathly Hallows* (2007), deals with history in another sense. In our view, it allegorically evokes the growing terror for Jews and others in Germany in the 1930s, as notions of 'race' were used to round up, exclude, silence, imprison, and kill those who were designated enemies of the state, and in response to which many Jews fled Germany. The evil wizard Voldemort puts in place a puppet government, and his troops, who bring to mind Hitler's Brownshirts, set out to destroy all opposition. Where they had previously been a paramilitary force, now they are government troops, suggesting sinister and ruthless military forces such as the SS. They take over the leading newspaper, and then move against those of human rather than wizard parentage (the 'Muggle-born'). The Muggle-borns, who are now all under suspicion for their identity and ancestry rather than for any actions they may have engaged in, are brought in to the Ministry for questioning. '[Y]ou should all go home and go into hiding with your families,' Harry urgently tells the Muggle-borns who are waiting to be interrogated. 'Go abroad if you can. Just get well away from the Ministry.'[81] The novel creates a drama where we ponder how much authoritarianism, including extreme authoritarianism, can recur in history, and how much, how desperately, how resourcefully and resolutely, it needs to be resisted.[82]

In the latter part of the twentieth century and into the twenty-first, world history, including environmental history, has, to use Dan Stone's terms, become important as requiring imaginative and adventurous forms of historical understanding and writing. For the second edition of *Is History Fiction?*, published in 2010, we added a new chapter, 'Is a history of humanity possible?', where we draw attention to a rapid acceleration of interest in supra-national histories, from the popularity of transnational approaches to histories on a grand scale, as in world, global, 'Big', and environmental histories.[83] One of the most important of the world historians is Janet Abu-Lughod, author of *Before European Hegemony: The World System AD 1250–1350* (1989), who has critiqued Eurocentrism both in historical methodology and world history narratives. In *Before European Hegemony*, Abu-Lughod challenges, and provides an alternative to, interpretations of the development of Europe which consider only internal forces and events. She shows how, in medieval times, Europe joined already existing economies to become part of a vibrant trading world that stretched from Moorish Spain in the west to China in the east. For a lengthy period Europe was but a minor player, with everything to gain from the association.[84]

In a 1995 essay, 'The world-system perspective in the construction of economic history', Abu-Lughod reflects on her own world history approach. The world-history practitioner, she suggests, should engage in what the philosopher Hans Gadamer, in his *Truth and Method*, refers to as a capacity for 'reflexivity and self-conscious awareness', especially as an antidote to hubris, to believing one has arrived at a complete explanation. Abu-Lughod values the kind of personal vision, inspired by eccentricity, ideology, and idiosyncrasy, that leads to the finding of a particular pattern in history. *Eccentricity* is a form of de-centred thinking, and enables the historian to combat ethnocentric tendencies in one's explanations. As an example of using eccentricity in this way, she says that in her study of the thirteenth-century world system in *Before European Hegemony* she tried whenever possible to pair evocations of the Crusades by Muslim and Christian writers: 'I was trying to de-center accounts, to view them ex-centrically.' *Ideology*, Abu-Lughod writes, must always be held up for scrutiny: rather than deducing historical reality from the 'deep sets of beliefs about how the world works' in one's own culture, the historian should strive to be self-reflexive about the nature and sources of one's own ideology. By *idiosyncrasy*, Abu-Lughod means the personal voice of the historian, which will be closely related to the individual historian's biography. In world history, idiosyncrasy, as the major source of new vision is especially important; 'many of the major transformations in how we think about the world' have been inspired by those working at the edge of established disciplinary assumptions and practices.[85]

Janet Abu-Lughod's thinking here about methodology resonates with Edward Said, not only his longstanding interest in a 'contrapuntal' method drawn from music,[86] but also his musing on the productive possibilities of 'late style'. In his *Freud and the Non-European*

(2003), Said suggests that everything about Freud's highly eccentric 1939 book *Moses and Monotheism* reveals 'not resolution and reconciliation' but a 'willingness to let irreconcilable elements' remain as they are: 'episodic, fragmentary, unfinished (i.e. unpolished)'.[87]

Within world history, the field of environmental history is growing fast, in response to the serious challenges to humanity posed by human-generated climate change. In the course of their necessarily close association with the natural sciences, environmental historians have to face in a new way some old questions of historical truth and representation, and the nature and status of their own knowledge. In 2005, a collaborative project, the Integrated History and future Of People on Earth (IHOPE), was launched. Under the auspices of the International Council of Scientific Unions, an international group of scientists directly concerned with the effects of human-induced climate change, IHOPE is seeking to map biophysical and human system change over the last 100,000 years. A contributor to the project is Paul Crutzen, the scientist who coined the term 'Anthropocene' to describe the epoch we have now entered, in which humans are changing the climate. While there is room for argument as to when the Anthropocene began and the Holocene ended, Crutzen nominates the invention of the steam engine in 1784, which led to the rapid growth of carbon dioxide and methane concentrations in the late eighteenth century. The idea of the Anthropocene is attracting increasing attention, strengthening desires for an integration of biophysical and human history. In their illuminating essay 'History for the Anthropocene', Libby Robin and Will Steffen propose that any history of humanity needs to be 'reflexive and transparent about why we need such a history, and open-minded about who "we" are'. They see this kind of history as morally necessary, as being 'in the service of human co-operation in the interests of the planet'.[88]

History operates in many very different contexts: in politics, the courts, universities and schools, museums, the mass media, in novel, and in film. As such, the questions addressed by the linguistic turn, of history's form and the nature of historical knowledge, are no less important now than they ever were. As histories are told for interested (in every sense) audiences, the ways they create meaning grows, not diminishes, in significance. Under pressure from all sides, historians need, perhaps, to find a way to inform their audiences about the existence and inevitability of competing interpretations and at the same time firmly to offer one of their own. Perhaps our next challenge is to develop the forms of historical discourse and narration that will best assist us in this delicate balancing act.

## NOTES AND REFERENCES

1  These debates are also discussed in Ann Curthoys and Ann McGrath, *How to Write History that People Want to Read* (Palgrave Macmillan, Basingstoke, 2011), pp. 180–1.
2  Rohan Wilson, *The Roving Party* (Allen and Unwin, Sydney, 2011).
3  www.abc.net.au/rn/arts/bwriting/stories/s1414510.htm.
4  John Hirst, 'How sorry can we be?', in *Sense and Nonsense in Australian History* (Black Inc, Melbourne, 2005), pp. 80–106. See also Mark McKenna, 'Writing the past', *Australian Financial Review*, 16 December 2005; Inga Clendinnen, *The History Question. Who Owns the Past?*, Quarterly Essay, issue no. 23, 2006, the relevant pages are pp. 16–28.
5  www.users.bigpond.com/kgrenville/TSR/RedersSR.htm.
6  Kate Grenville, *Searching for the Secret River* (Text Publishing, Melbourne, 2006), p. 185.
7  Ann Curthoys and John Docker, *Is History Fiction?* (The University of Michigan Press, Ann Arbor, and UNSW Press, Sydney, 2005). This chapter draws on that book.
8  Extract from Macaulay's essay 'On history', first published in the *Edinburgh Review*, May 1828, online at www.blupete.com/Literature/Essays/Best/MacaulayModHistorian.htm.
9  See Harold Temperley (ed.), *Selected Essays of J.B. Bury* (Cambridge University Press, Cambridge, 1930), pp. 3–22; also published in Fritz Stern (ed.), *The Varieties of History: From Voltaire to the Present* (Meridian, Cleveland, 1966), pp. 210–23.
10  See Richard Evans, *In Defence of History* (Granta Books, London, 1997), pp. 24–5.
11  Fritz Stern (ed.), *The Varieties of History*, pp. 228–35. 'Clio, a muse' was originally published in December 1903 in the *Independent Review*. See also G.M. Trevelyan, *An Autobiography and Other Essays* (Longmans, Green and Co., London, 1949).

12  Fritz Stern (ed.), *The Varieties of History*, pp. 239–43. See also Trevelyan's essay 'Influence of Sir Walter Scott on history', in *An Autobiography and Other Essays*, pp. 200–5.

13  Herbert Butterfield, *The Whig Interpretation of History* (1931; G. Bell and Sons, London, 1950), pp. 68, 91, 105.

14  See the classic essay by Andreas Huyssen, 'Mass culture as woman: modernism's other', in Tania Modleski (ed.), *Studies in Entertainment* (Indiana University Press, Bloomington, 1986). See also John Docker, *Postmodernism and Popular Culture: A Cultural History* (Cambridge University Press, Melbourne, 1994), chapters 7 and 8.

15  Docker, *Postmodernism and Popular Culture*, pp. 143–5; also Ann Curthoys and John Docker, 'Popular romance in the postmodern age', *Continuum*, Vol. 4, No. 1, 1990, pp. 22–36.

16  Cf. Cornell West, 'Black culture and postmodernism', in Barbara Kruger and Phil Mariani (eds), *Remaking History* (Bay Press, Seattle, 1989), p. 88.

17  Docker, *Postmodernism and Popular Culture*, pp. 52–5.

18  Roland Barthes, 'The discourse of history', trans. Stephen Bann, *Comparative Criticism*, Vol. 3, No. 1, 1981, pp. 7–20. The essay was first published in *Social Science Information* in 1967.

19  Barthes, 'The discourse of history', p. 14.

20  Barthes, 'The discourse of history', p. 17.

21  Barthes, 'The discourse of history', p. 18.

22  Benedetto Croce, *History: Its Theory and Practice*, trans. Douglas Ainslie (Harcourt, Brace, and Co., New York, 1921), pp. 11–26, reprinted as 'History and chronicle', in Hans Myerhoff (ed.), *The Philosophy of History in Our Time* (Doubleday Anchor, New York, 1959), pp. 45–56; Curthoys and Docker, *Is History Fiction?*, pp. 91–3.

23  Barthes, 'The discourse of history', p. 16.

24  Jacques Derrida, *Writing and Difference*, trans. Alan Bass (1967; University of Chicago Press, Chicago, 1978), chapter 10, pp. 278–93.

25  Jacques Derrida, *Of Grammatology*, trans. Gayatri Chakravorty Spivak (1967; Johns Hopkins University Press, Baltimore, 1976), pp. 3, 9, 68, 87, 89, 129.

26  *Of Grammatology*, pp. 7–8, 60–2, 65–6, 68, 73, 89, 106, 109–12, 127–8.

27  *Of Grammatology*, p.158; cf. Curthoys and Docker, *Is History Fiction?*, p.148.

28  *Of Grammatology*, pp. 157–9.

29  *Of Grammatology*, pp. 157–9. See also Barbara Johnson's discussion of 'There is nothing outside the text *[il n'y a pas de hors-texte]*' in her introduction to Derrida, *Dissemination*, trans. and introd. Barbara Johnson (The University of Chicago Press, Chicago, 1981), pp. xiii–xv.

30  Derrida, *Dissemination*, pp. 63–4. We would like to acknowledge the value of discussions with Ned Curthoys on Derrida.

31  *Dissemination*, pp. 67–9.

32  Hexter, 'The rhetoric of history', in *Doing History* (George Allen and Unwin, London, 1971), pp. 19, 21, 24, 29.

33  Hexter, 'The rhetoric of history', pp. 47–8.

34  Cf. Bonnie G. Smith, *The Gender of History: Men, Women, and Historical Practice* (Harvard University Press,

Cambridge, MA, 1998), p. 119; Curthoys and Docker, *Is History Fiction?*, pp. 99–100.

35  Hexter, 'The rhetoric of history', pp. 68, 75–6.

36  Hayden White, *Metahistory: The Historical Imagination in Nineteenth-Century Europe* (Johns Hopkins University Press, Baltimore, 1973); *Tropics of Discourse: Essays in Cultural Criticism* (Johns Hopkins University Press, Baltimore, 1978); *The Content of the Form: Narrative Discourse and Historical Representation* (Johns Hopkins University Press, Baltimore, 1987); *Figural Realism: Studies in the Mimesis Effect* (Johns Hopkins University Press, Baltimore, 1999).

37  Hayden White, 'The historical text as literary artifact', in *Tropics of Discourse*, pp. 81–100.

38  White, 'The historical text as literary artifact', pp. 83–6, 88, 92–4, 97, 99.

39  Northrop Frye, *Anatomy of Criticism* (1957; Princeton University Press, Princeton, 1973), pp. 43, 54, 243.

40  Cf. Frank Lentricchia, *After the New Criticism* (Athlone Press, London, 1980), ch.1, 'The place of Northrop Frye's *Anatomy of Criticism*', pp. 2–26.

41  Cf. Nancy Partner, 'Making up lost time: writing on the writing of history', *Speculum*, Vol. 6, No. 1, 1986, p. 94.

42  Mikhail Bakhtin, *Problems of Dostoevsky's Poetics*, edited and trans. Caryl Emerson (Manchester University Press, Manchester, 1984); Mikhail Bakhtin, *Rabelais and His World*, trans. Helene Iswolsky (Indiana University Press, Bloomington, 1984); Mikhail Bakhtin, *The Dialogic Imagination*, edited by Michael Holquist, trans. Caryl Emerson and Michael Holquist (University of Texas Press, Austin, 1981). See also Katerina Clark and Michael Holquist, *Mikhail Bakhtin* (Harvard University Press, Cambridge, MA, 1984).

43  See the thinking about Bakhtin in Dominick LaCapra, *Rethinking Intellectual History: Texts, Contexts, Language* (Cornell University Press, Ithaca, NY, 1983) and *Soundings in Critical Theory* (Cornell University Press, Ithaca, NY, 1989); also Curthoys and Docker, *Is History Fiction?*, pp. 194–6.

44  Michel Foucault, *Madness and Civilization: a History of Insanity in the Age of Reason*, trans. Richard Howard (Pantheon, New York, 1965); Michel Foucault, *The Birth of the Clinic: An Archaeology of Medical Perception*, trans. A.M. Sheridan (Routledge, London, 2003); Michel Foucault, *The Order of Things: An Archaeology of the Human Sciences* (Routledge, London, 2002); Michel Foucault, *The Archaeology of Knowledge*, trans. A.M. Sheridan Smith (1969; Harper Colophon, New York, 1972), Introduction, pp. 15–16.

45  Foucault, *The Archaeology of Knowledge*, pp. 3–6.

46  Foucault, *The Archaeology of Knowledge*, pp. 7-9.

47  Michel Foucault, 'Nietzsche, genealogy, history' (1971), in *Language, Counter-Memory, Practice: Selected Essays and Interviews*, ed. and introd. Donald F. Bouchard (1977; Cornell University Press, Ithaca, NY, 1986), pp. 153, 159–60.

48  Michel Foucault, 'Nietzsche, genealogy, history', pp. 157, 162–3.

49  Cf. Alan Sheridan, *Michel Foucault: The Will to Truth* (1980; Tavistock, London, 1984), p. 90.

50   Michel Foucault, *Power/Knowledge: Selected Interviews and Other Writings 1972–1977*, ed. Colin Gordon (Harvester Wheatsheaf, London, 1980), p. 114.

51   Foucault, 'Nietzsche, genealogy, history', pp. 153–6, 159–60; Curthoys and Docker, *Is History Fiction?*, pp. 184–6.

52   Edward W. Said, *Orientalism* (1978; Routledge and Kegan Paul, London, 1980), pp. 3–4, 23–4. Cf. Foucault, *Language, Counter-Memory, Practice*, essay on 'What is an author?'.

53   See Ann Curthoys, 'Mary Wollstonecraft revisited', in Ned Curthoys (ed.), *Key Thinkers and Their Legacy*, special issue of *Humanities Research*, Vol. XVI, No. 2, 2010, pp. 29–48, and John Docker, *The Origins of Violence: Religion, History and Genocide* (Pluto, London, 2008).

54   Peter Burke (ed.), *New Perspectives on Historical Writing* (Polity Press, London, 1991), 'History of events and the revival of narrative', pp. 238–9.

55   Burke, 'History of events and the revival of narrative', p. 241. See Clifford Geertz, *Interpretation of Cultures* (Basic Books, New York, 1973), pp. 3–31; Carlo M. Cipolla, *Cristofano and the Plague: A Study of the History of Public Health in the Age of Galileo* (University of California Press, Los Angeles, 1973); Natalie Zemon Davis, *The Return of Martin Guerre* (Harvard University Press, Cambridge, MA, 1983).

56   Carlo Ginzburg, *The Cheese and the Worms: The Cosmos of a Sixteenth-Century Miller* (1976; Penguin, London, 1992), and Emmanuel Le Roy Ladurie, *Montaillou: The Promised Land of Error* (1978; G. Braziller, New York, 1978). See also Robert Darnton, *The Great Cat Massacre and Other Episodes in French Cultural History* (Vintage, New York, 1985); LaCapra, *History and Criticism* (Cornell University Press, Ithaca, NY, 1985), pp. 45–69.

57   Burke, *New Perspectives on Historical Writing*, pp. 240–6. Cf. Ann Curthoys, 'Sex and racism in Australia in the 1960s', in Jane Long, Jan Gothard, and Helen Brash (eds), *Forging Identities: Bodies, Gender and Feminist History* (University of Western Australia Press, Perth, 1997).

58   Burke, *New Perspectives on Historical Writing*, p.238.

59   Robert A. Rosenstone, *Mirror in the Shrine: American Encounters with Meiji Japan* (Harvard University Press, Cambridge, MA, 1988), p. 112. See also pp. xii–xiii, 137, 202–3.

60   John Demos, *The Unredeemed Captive: A Family Story from Early America* (Knopf, New York, 1995); Curthoys and Docker, *Is History Fiction?*, pp. 203, 205.

61   Joyce Appleby, Lynn Hunt, and Margaret Jacob, *Telling the Truth about History* (W.W. Norton, New York, 1994), pp. 208, 213, 230, 236–7, 246, 253–55, 265.

62   Richard J. Evans, *In Defence of History* (Granta Books, London, 1997), pp. 70, 238–9.

63   Dan Stone, *Constructing the Holocaust: A Study in Historiography* (Vallentine Mitchell, London and Portland, OR, 2003), pp. 15–16.

64   Appleby, Hunt, and Jacob, *Telling the Truth about History*, p. 7.

65   Stone, *Constructing the Holocaust*, p. 16.

66   Stone, *Constructing the Holocaust*, pp. 27, 233.

67   Curthoys and Docker, *Is History Fiction?*, pp. 53–4.

68   Elazar Barkan, *The Guilt of Nations: Restitution and Negotiating Historical Injustices* (W.W. Norton and Co., New York, 2000), p. ix.

69   Barkan, *The Guilt of Nations*, p. vii.

70   Barkan, *The Guilt of Nations*, p. ix.

71   Barkan, *The Guilt of Nations*, p. xvii.

72   Barkan, *The Guilt of Nations*, passim.

73   Barkan, *The Guilt of Nations*, p. x.

74   David J. Rothman, 'Serving clio and client: the historian as expert witness', *Bulletin of the History of Medicine*, Vol. 77, No. 1, 2003, p. 44.

75   Helen Hornbeck Tanner, 'History vs. the law: processing Indians in the American legal system', *University of Detroit Mercy Law Review*, Vol. 76, 1999, p. 698.

76   For an extended examination of these issues see Ann Curthoys, Ann Genovese, and Alex Reilly, *Rights and Redemption: History, Law, and Indigenous Peoples* (UNSW Press, Sydney, 2008).

77   See Ann Curthoys, 'Crossing over: academic and popular history', *The Australasian Journal of Popular Culture*, Vol. I, No. 1, 2012, pp. 7–18.

78   Croce, 'History and chronicle', pp. 45, 51–2.

79   J.K. Rowling, *Harry Potter and the Order of the Phoenix* (Bloomsbury, London, 2003), pp. 206–7, 639.

80   See Edmund M. Kern, 'The phoenix in Harry Potter: the metaphoric power of the past', in *Proceedings of the Accio Conference on the Harry Potter Series*, 29–31 July 2005, University of Reading, http://accio.org.uk/05/proc/edkern.pdf.

81   J.K. Rowling, *Harry Potter and the Deathly Hallows* (Bloomsbury, London, 2007), p. 216.

82   See Ann Curthoys, 'Harry Potter and historical consciousness: reflections on history and fiction', *History Australia*, Vol. 8, No. 1, 2011, pp. 7–22.

83   Ann Curthoys and John Docker, *Is History Fiction?*, 2nd edition (UNSW Press, Sydney, 2010), pp. 238–66.

84   Janet L. Abu-Lughod, *Before European Hegemony: The World System AD 1250–1350* (Oxford University Press, New York, 1989), pp. 6, 11–12, 15–16, 33.

85   Janet Abu-Lughod, 'The world-system perspective in the construction of economic history', *History and Theory*, Vol. 34, No. 2, 1995, pp. 89–96.

86   See Ben Etherington, 'Said, Grainger and the ethics of polyphony', in Ned Curthoys and Debjani Ganguly (eds), *Edward Said: The Legacy of a Public Intellectual* (Melbourne University Press, Melbourne, 2007), pp. 221–38.

87   Edward W. Said, *Freud and the Non-European* (Verso, London, 2003), p. 28.

88   Libby Robin and Will Steffen, 'History for the Anthropocene', *History Compass*, Vol. 5, No. 5, 2007, pp. 1699, 1711–12.

# PART II

# Applications: Theory-intensive Areas of History

Nancy Partner

## INTRODUCTION

The impress of historical theory has left its mark on the professional practice of history throughout all the specialized subject fields, albeit some more than others. A generalized awareness that complex meanings and interpretive assertions are not passively uncovered 'in' historical archives but are constructed in the course of the historian's research and writing has become part of the very atmosphere of advanced training in research universities. As modern academic historians, we take for granted that empirically grounded research, with its stringent standards of accuracy, transparency, and sufficiency, is part of a complex process of pattern-seeking, scaling up and down through analogues, and other active interpretive work by which events become facts, and facts are integrated into structures of language. In this sense, all historical fields are susceptible to a theoretical analysis in which their conceptual premises and underlying frameworks can be brought to the foreground and described. Some particular fields of history have benefitted

very noticeably from techniques and modes of interpretation opened up by historical theory, and some fields owe their very existence as defined areas of history to language-based modes of handling evidence. These are the areas of history chosen for this section of the handbook: applications. It was not possible to be exhaustive in coverage here, but the areas chosen highlight the ways in which theoretical self-consciousness and language-focused interpretation have expanded the ability of historians to 'see' subjects previously without historical presence, and to bring critical clarity to subjects that otherwise could not 'have a history.'

By theory-intensive areas of history, we mean specialized fields primarily identified by their historical subjects, but whose methodology draws intensively on insights and techniques that grew out of fairly recent theoretical projects, and whose practitioners show a high degree of awareness of the premises and epistemology underlying their work. Discourse analysis, understanding the textuality of documentary evidence, applying literary critical techniques to nonfiction documents, unpacking the cultural stereo-types in the language of 'natural' description, perceiving the narrative operations that pro-duce collective protagonists like nations, and many more kinds of sophisticated interpreta-tion beyond the literal levels of meaning fig-ure importantly in theory-intensive fields. In some instances, the special subject matters and interpretive concepts developed within these fields have made such a powerful impact in the discipline that they have acquired the titles of independent theories in their own right: gender theory, postcolonial theory, memory theory, are prominent exam-ples of specialized fields often called 'theo-ries.' Psychoanalysis, whose place here is assured by its theoretical depth and univer-salist applications, is an intellectual domain both separate from and deeply linked to his-tory and literary studies with a longstanding claim to autonomous theory.

The scope of these more narrowly special-ized 'theories' is limited by their focus on, say, the cultural meanings layered onto bio-logical sex, or the occulted power relations in colonial situations. This concentration gives them sharpness and impact. The arguments formed with the conceptual instruments of special-subject 'theories' have been able to demonstrate that subjects such as gender, subaltern status, the implicit politics of cul-tural production, among others, are real, are 'there' in the historical record with as much actuality as the traditional areas of military and constitutional history. Even 'women,' had to become 'theorized,' the subject of specialized techniques addressed to primary sources before women's history could suc-cessfully claim its place as a major historical field. The theory-intensive fields tend to be special applications of insights and tech-niques associated generally with the linguis-tic turn, with special emphasis on discourse analysis of documents, applied to specialized subject matter, like postcolonial history. There is nothing wrong with calling these sophisticated specialities 'theories' in recog-nition of their evolved conceptual vocabu-lary, finely tuned interpretive techniques, and

epistemological self-consciousness, but for the sake of intellectual clarity it is worth not-ing that specialized field 'theories' do not have the capacity to establish a basic frame-work covering all areas of history with con-cepts that apply across chronological and other borders, as do narrative theory and tropology.

Social history marked the first major 'new' subject matter for history in its entirety, intro-ducing not only previously non-historical actors and areas of social life to historical attention, but altering the very point of view of historical writing. Brian Lewis takes up the later (or newer) evolution of social his-tory as the field encountered postmodernist challenges to its basic approaches and fre-quently declared itself 'in crisis.' Cultural history, in all its many variations, invited historians to turn a fascinated gaze on mean-ings and experience, turning away from materialist determinants and aggregated data in favor of experience-as-text, an approach that, among other effects, ushered women and sexual minorities to the historical fore-ground. The cultural and linguistic turns 'rejected the commonsensical notion that the biological begat the economic begat the political begat the cultural: culture did not reflect social experience but constituted it; the causal arrow pointed both ways.'

Many of the subject matters, interpretive techniques, and ideological concerns of the most theory-intensive fields of history are shared among them, with notably deep over-lap in areas concerning women, gender, and sexuality – all historical interests still new enough to feel 'new' while supporting a matured and extensive scholarship. The four essays in this grouping proceed from the still recent struggle of scholars inspired by the feminist movement to win acceptance for 'women' as a legitimate research topic, to the morphing of the subject from biological females to feminine gender, onward to the expansion of gender theory to encompass males and masculinity, and to sexuality itself as a valid subject for historical research and analysis.

Judith Zinsser points out the almost incredible fact that in the 1970s it was possible to read *everything* historical written about women in English and other European languages. The number of historians, research projects and publications about women's history accelerated from that time, as women's history gained intellectual traction and brought with it a characteristically polydisciplinary methodology drawing on anthropology, sociology, economics, and psychology. Women's history as a new subject matter, bringing into visibility an entire hitherto effaced human population, also brought theoretical challenges as historians of women dismantled traditional claims to accuracy, disinterestedness and objectivity, as well as assumptions about the 'natural' order of human society. Bonnie Smith, writing on the transition from women's history to gender history, notes that the conceptual foundations of gender theory were begun long before gender became a category of analysis among professional historians. Gender, understood with analytic instruments drawn from French theorists from Simone de Beauvoir to Foucault and Lacan, extended sex-linked meanings beyond the biologic body to institutions and the state. In the postmodern formulation focused on cultural meanings, gender dissolves into power when subjected to discursive analysis. And in its most recent advances, gender has ceased to belong only to women; Karen Harvey traces the disciplinary and conceptual steps that brought men into gender's optic: 'Coming after the massive changes that women's and feminist history had made to the discipline, and also after the first key theoretical statements about gender, masculinity is a field of history produced out of the productive tensions between poststructuralist theory, social history, feminist theory, women's history, but also (and often less acknowledged) the area of study often known as "Men's Studies."' Masculine gender (usually expressed in the plural of 'masculinities' to underscore its historical variability) a growth field since the 1990s, has shown rich possibilities for transforming traditional subject matter, from the presumably natural category of the body to politics and power.

'Like women and the body, sex has not seemed, to most historians since historians began, to have a history at all. What changed?' Amy Richlin offers a complex answer compounded of the desire for history on the part of excluded minorities; the historian's duty to the dead and the true reality of their lives; the lifting of moral regulation of permitted subjects; and postmodernist competition for place at the cutting edge of intellectual and social movements, among other factors. Further, she asks, and answers: 'What is the history of sexuality good for? Why does it matter? To whom? And, if it matters, how can it be written? What is it a history *of*? In acquiring a history, sexuality has become a theorized field of exceptional sophistication and acrimony since all of its terminology (sexuality, identity, homosexuality, etc.) has had to be formulated anew at the most basic level. This heightened awareness of the fraught and fungible nature of basic concepts and the difficulties involved in representation itself when there is little agreement on the nature or even existence of sexual identities, makes sexuality a field rich in open debate over its theoretical framework.

Psychoanalysis is a theoretically mature discipline with strong implications for historical use. As a mode of analysis addressed specifically to language and the processes of symbolization by which unconscious ideation leaves its impress on the language of consciousness, the psychoanalytically informed historian has fine instruments for delaminating the layers of meaning in evidence, historical assertions, and his or her own procedures. Michael Roper here turns this critical optic away from its usual subjects located in the past, and back onto the historian in the very process of making history: '... onto the historian, to think about the residues of the past to which we expose our feelings as well as our minds in doing history. How, I will ask, does the historian's unconscious bear upon his or her efforts to make sense of the past?' This is a use of psychoanalytic techniques eminently suited to the discipli- nary introspection that characterizes histori- cal theory in general, extended in this essay to classic social history, women's history, oral history, and the 'cultural turn.' In a strikingly complementary study, Kevin Forster lays out a case study in applications of narrative the- ory, inflected with psychoanalytic insight, to imperial/national narratives of Britain in rela- tion to Latin America. Awareness of the rela- tion of latent to manifest levels of meaning, and reading techniques that are equal to the task, show how 'the English, and Britons as a whole, have often thought most penetratingly about themselves when ostensibly thinking about others.'

Cultural studies, memory studies, and postcolonial studies all occupy places at the intersection of multiple disciplinary tradi- tions and new theoretical influences, result- ing in complex, sophisticated areas of study, deeply grounded in history but not entirely defined by it, all theory-intensive to a high degree. As Gilbert Rodman candidly explains: 'Over the past two or three decades, numer- ous people and institutions have tried (and continue to try) to stuff the square peg of cul- tural studies into the round hole of normative disciplinarity ... but such efforts fundamen- tally misunderstand what cultural studies is.' Driven by a frankly acknowledged political engagement, the extraordinary diversity of cultural studies also operates as a testing ground for the theoretical instruments and concepts it deploys to examine the relation between the real world and mediated repre- sentations of reality. Memory studies is another area that both invites and defies clear definition: memory both promises a closer, more direct access to past experience while evading the techniques of verification, highly problematic for history. Its central concept of collective memory is difficult to define but is indispensable to the study of social identity at every level from individual to national – a topic of compelling interest to historians now. Patrick Hutton tracks the intellectual evolution of this fraught conceptual entity as scholars bring to its examination the full theoretical repertoire. Postcolonial studies occupies one of these disciplinary nodes where objects of study and approaches meet without neat edges: 'Postcolonialism is a label worn uneasily by practitioners of "post- colonial theory", of "postcolonial history", "postcolonial criticism" or (more noncom- mittally) of "postcolonial studies".' As Ben- jamin Zachariah notes, the historical subject matter suggested by the postcolonial direc- tive invites in its wake a thickly populated debate over theoretical framing: from Marxist materialist readings to issues of identity (and memory) and the linguistic turn signalled by the 'post' of postmodernism.

# 14

# The Newest Social History: Crisis and Renewal

Brian Lewis

Is social history dead? Patrick Joyce raised the question in an article in the mid-1990s as the passionate debates over the impact of the linguistic and cultural turns began to abate.[1] Has a triumphalist cultural history killed it? When the Social History Society in Britain in 2004 launched a new journal, *Cultural and Social History*, the desire to hang on to the social moniker was understandable for a proud, flagship organization less than three decades old, but at best 'social' now had equal billing with 'cultural', or perhaps the placing of 'cultural' first really signified greater primacy than the merely alphabetical. In the introductory editorial to this journal, Asa Briggs, President of the Social History Society, wrote that, 'many social historians, like myself, who were I believe pioneers of social history in Britain, have for many years come to consider themselves principally as cultural historians.'[2] If this is not quite the dousing of the flame of social history by one of its most distinguished guardians, it scarcely signals a strenuous effort to keep it alight.

It is a far cry from the heyday of social history and its hegemonic ambitions from the 1960s to the early 1980s, when Eric Hobsbawm in Britain famously announced, in his pursuit of 'the history of society', 'This is a good time to be a social historian'; when Fernand Braudel in France laid claim to *histoire totale* through social historical means; when Hans-Ulrich Wëhler in West Germany proclaimed the need for 'analysis of society in its entirety'; and when Charles Tilly in the US sought to map out *Big Structures, Large Processes, Huge Comparisons* (1984).[3] Peter Stearns, perhaps the most sustained American champion of social history, captured the totalizing claim – and the pride before the fall – with his statement in the *Journal of Social History* in 1976: 'social history *is* history.'[4] Contrast this with Geoff Eley's *cri de coeur* in 2005:

'Social history' simply isn't available anymore, whether in its most coherent and self-conscious materialist versions (Marxist, Annaliste, social-scientific) or in the more amorphous, but still aggrandizing, forms of the 1970s. In the form of the original project, 'social history' has ceased to exist. Its coherence derived from the sovereignty of social determinants within a self-confident materialist paradigm of social totality, grounded in the primacy of class. But since the early 1980s, each part of that framework has succumbed to relentless and compelling critique. In the process, its prestige as the natural home for the more radi-cal, innovative, and experimental spirits dissolved, particularly for younger people entering the pro-fession. The 'new cultural history' took its place.[5]

So how did this happen? What has 'gone wrong'? *Is* social history ... well, history – that is, defunct, passé, superseded?

As we saw in Chapter 6, the new social his-tory, circa 1980, was facing a barrage of criti-cism for alleged trivialization, for ignoring power and politics and for settling on balkani-zation (social history as topic or field) rather than living up to its totalizing ambitions (social history as approach): for being, in short, noth-ing but a 'clown in regal purple'.[6] The barbs were sharply pointed and touched some raw nerves; but the self-confidence of most social historians was not, as yet, profoundly shaken. Some important 'cultural' interpretations – relying more on anthropology than sociology, the chief sister discipline for the new social historians – were, however, already prefigur-ing the cultural turn of the 1980s. Inspired by key writers such as Raymond Williams and E.P. Thompson in Britain and Clifford Geertz in America, the third generation of *Annalistes* in France, the microhistorians in Italy and the *Alltagsgeschichte* historians in Germany were all registering varying degrees of disquiet with modernization models. Starting with Thompson's deluded followers of Joanna Southcott, Emanuel Le Roy Ladurie's Albigensian crusaders in Montaillou, Carlo Ginsburg's heretical miller in Milan, Natalie Zemon Davis's imposter in a Pyrenean village and Robert Darnton's cat-killing apprentices in Paris were all, in their rather different ways, products of a desire to return agency to ordi-nary people.[7] While quantitative methods reduced lived lives to numbers and *longue durée* schema threatened to efface individuals entirely, this crop of historians, mainly in the late 1970s and early 1980s, latched on to the key concept of 'experience'. This was all ammunition for those critics who angrily denounced such approaches for focusing on the weird and marginal, inventing uncorrobo-rated explanations and losing sight of the big

questions. But the Italian microhistorians, for example, did not reject the structuralist para-digm and argued that they were merely explor-ing individual choice constrained by social and economic structures.[8] Still, the signs were there that a new phase in the struggle to understand structure and agency was about to begin – and, with it, a challenge to the whole notion of the legitimacy of the social history project itself.

Caveats against reductionism duly noted, quickening doubts played out against a back-drop of substantial socio-economic and politi-cal change. The confident postwar phase of corporatist capitalism shuddered to a halt in the early 1970s and the developed world entered a period of profound economic restructuring over the next quarter century characterized by considerably greater workplace insecurity, the rise of neo-liberal politics, galloping globaliza-tion, the information revolution and a boom in consumption. In the 1980s, with the resurgence of right-wing politics in a number of Western countries and the decline of a blue-collar work-ing class predominantly supporting socialist, social democratic, or labour parties and trade unions, the whole concept of class – especially of classes as the key to historical change – came into greater question.[9] And, as we shall see, the debate over the concept of class is one of the clearest examples of the problems beset-ting Marxian, *Annaliste* or social-scientific modernization theories.

Three interventions in particular by leftist labour historians served as bellwethers. The first was William Sewell's *Work and Revolution in France* (1980).[10] Sewell was among the earliest to shift his attention from quantitative social history, with its silences about people's feelings and beliefs, to cultural anthropology, which provided insights into workers' sym-bolic lives and understandings beyond the dry facts of occupational structure, wage rates and economic exploitation. As he puts it,

I experienced the encounter with cultural anthro-pology as a turn from a hardheaded, utilitarian, and empiricist materialism – which had both lib-eral and *marxisant* faces – to a wider apprecia-tion of the range of human possibilities, both in the past and in the present. Convinced that there was more to life than the relentless pursuit of wealth, status, and power, I felt that cultural anthropology could show us how to get at that 'more.'[11]

The second was Gareth Stedman Jones's 'Rethinking Chartism' (1983), which achieved iconic status in helping initiate the linguistic turn. Stedman Jones pondered why the Chartists in Britain in the 1830s and 1840s continued to use a language of political radicalism (the people against the aristocrats) that could be traced back to the 1790s and beyond, when they were 'supposed' – as class-conscious proletarians – to be talking the language of socialism (workers against capitalists). He argued convincingly that language needed to be taken seriously rather than treated as a simple reflection of the economic base. And the third was Joan Scott's 'Gender: a useful category of historical analysis' (1986), which marked the destabilizing but irresistible arrival of gender in historical circles.[12]

Grand, teleological narratives based upon structural materialism took the brunt of the gathering critique. The cultural and linguistic turns, and the panoply of poststructuralist and postmodernist ideas, began to pose a series of challenges to the social history project. To summarize brutally: first, they cumulatively rejected the commonsensical notion that the biological begat the economic begat the political begat the cultural: culture did not reflect social experience but constituted it; the causal arrow pointed both ways. Second, they shifted emphasis from the material to the linguistic, drawing primarily on anthropology, philosophy, literary criticism and cultural studies rather than the old allies, economics, sociology and political science. Third, they insisted that social categories – including the idea of 'the social' itself – were not external referents, preceding language, culture and consciousness, but dependent upon them. Fourth, they placed new emphasis on mentality, identity and meaning rather than on social structures and economic bases. Fifth, they stressed the transience, fluidity and multiplicity of

identities – and the disturbing but inescapable logic at their centre: while 'identity gives us a provisional place from which to speak', it is 'constructed in history and fatally dependent on difference'.[13] Sixth, in the analysis of power, they undermined the explanatory primacy granted to class and the state by picking up on the Foucauldian notion of power as dispersed and fragmented. And seventh, they exploded any lingering notion that language was a transparent conveyor of meaning from past to present, forcing historians to become more self aware and to interrogate much more forcefully how texts are generated and survive, how archives are ordered, how language serves as a social actor rather than a neutral medium, how categories are constructed and how historians themselves deploy rhetorical strategies in the writing of their own narratives.[14]

If all of this stimulated a range of emotions – unease, outrage, incredulity and incomprehension among them – from those resistant to change, most social historians came to recognize that these challenges also presented a substantial number of opportunities. If the new social history had already considerably expanded the range of legitimate subjects and sources, the cultural turn assisted and accelerated this expansion not only by incorporating histories of 'cultural' topics but also by necessitating the writing of histories of things not previously seen as *having* a history, such as the body, sexuality and emotions. As Keith Thomas puts it, '[E]very aspect of human experience now has its historians, from childhood to old age, from dress to table manners, from smells to laughter, from sport to shopping, from barbed wire to masturbation.'[15] Moreover, with the renewed focus on the individual, first, the contextualized biography as an entry-point to a study of a broader world and, second, psychoanalysis as a means of exploring the interior self, both once largely discredited by social historians, gained new leases on life.

The changes wrought by the cultural turn can be examined in more depth by a focus on three categories: class; gender and sexuality; and nation, race and empire.

## CLASS

Perhaps most social historians had always doubted a schema in which the prevailing mode of production produced an appropriate set of classes, which in time achieved an appropriate consciousness and so propelled history forward. But increasing numbers of historians in the Marxist tradition, those influenced by the more nuanced, agency-restoring Thompsonian version, began to push Thompson to his logical conclusion: if classes make themselves, it is surely possible that they might *not* make themselves (or not be made for long), that a given economic position might not produce a corresponding (indeed, any) class identity or class consciousness.

Detailed empirical research played a significant part in the questioning of the primacy of class, as did the failure of quantitative analysis to discover consistent class patterns across time and space. Such research increasingly revealed complex societies difficult to squeeze into separate boxes labeled with class tags. Even multiple subdivisions could only, at best, hope to capture a simulacrum of the unwieldy reality by stopping the clock at one moment in time, with classes frozen, and scarcely did justice to an individual's weaving in and out of class positions over the course of a lifetime. Nor did class reductionism do justice to the onion-skin status-layerings *within* classes. It became increasingly challenging to explain some of the great events in world history primarily in class terms without performing considerable mental gymnastics. The English, American and French Revolutions, once confidently labeled as 'bourgeois', turned out to have considerable numbers from all classes on both sides and to be seriously complicated by regional and religious affiliations. The Bolshevik Revolution in Russia seemed more like a coup d'état than a triumph of historical inevitability. The partition of Africa by the

European powers in the late nineteenth century seemed to owe as much if not more to non-economic strategic and political thinking than to the machinations of big business in pursuit of capital investments or raw materials. Attempts to pin the blame for the world wars of the twentieth century on particular classes or to undertake a rigorous class analysis of their causes, courses and outcomes proved unconvincing. And so on.

A related problem was that people identified objectively by historians or sociologists as belonging to particular classes often failed to play their expected roles. For example, many in a particular class position supported political parties or movements that appeared ill suited to advance their class interests. It was rather too convenient and patronizing to dismiss working-class Tories, proletarian Nazis, Reagan Democrats or Christian, Jewish and Islamic fundamentalists as the victims of 'false consciousness', presupposing that scholars knew what was better for them than they did themselves, or at the very least failing in the historian's duty to try and empathize. Equally uncompelling was an explanation that they might not yet have attained the necessary level of consciousness – still be Marx's 'potatoes in a sack' – with its assumption that they were somehow preordained to follow a particular teleology, that history could only unfold along one particular trajectory. Consciousness could neither be true nor false nor underdeveloped if identities were cultural achievements rather than social essences; it was simply what it was.[16]

The libertarian turmoil of the late 1960s had propelled increasing numbers of feminists and racial and sexual minorities into the academy, first on the margins but increasingly in the mainstream. The gap between socioeconomic 'realities' and people's discordant identities and political actions resonated particularly strongly for them. Modernization theories with their focus on class and labour seemed to have little or no place for them, pushing them to the explanatory edge or ignoring them altogether. As Carle Hesse puts it, 'Neither liberal modernizationists nor

Marxists could account for the new forms of social solidarity that emerged in the post-colonial and post-civil-rights world: students, black nationalists, feminists, environmentalists, gays and lesbians, left and right Zionists, Christian fundamentalists and so on.' The social history project, positing a relatively 'transparent relationship between social existence and self-understanding, being and consciousness', could no longer cope. The new cultural history stepped into the breach 'because it appeared to offer a means to investigate the question of how social actors are historically constituted, how forms of collective identity and solidarity come into being and how they are transformed.'[17]

What all this amounted to was the notion that people balanced multiple forms of ethnic, gendered, sexual, religious and regional identities, as well as class; that none of these forms of identity was stable or necessarily long-lasting; and that class was not *the* major explanatory tool, *the* fundamental form of identity to which all else could be reduced. Class had no particular explanatory priority in social and historical analysis, but was simply one of a plurality of oppressions (or opportunities), each rooted in a different form of domination – sexual, racial, national or economic. Class was a linguistic construct that had to be thought, talked and propagated. It was thus vulnerable both to alternative discourses that might present themselves as superior ways of explaining the numbingly complicated reality that made up an individual's existence and to discursive reconstructions and remodelings of its own internal coherence.

Faced with these complications, some historians came to reject the use of class entirely. They dismissed it as just another nineteenth-century construct – such as race, gender and sexual orientation – that imposed a bogus simplicity on complex social relations and gradations. Just as all reputable scholars came to reject the 'scientific' separation of people into a hierarchy of races, recognizing that there was nothing natural or essential about these arbitrary classifications; just as

historians of gender and sexuality came to challenge and even demolish binary divisions, claiming that such divisions owed more to social and cultural construction than to biological imperatives: so historians of class found it increasingly difficult to ignore the dissolution of boundaries and bonfire of categories taking place elsewhere. Class was a fiction – maybe a useful, even a necessary fiction in support of a progressive political agenda, but a fiction nonetheless.[18]

## GENDER AND SEXUALITY

In the hands of social historians, the story of the rise of first the bourgeoisie, then of the working class, was overwhelmingly a male narrative. Women, whether as wives, mothers or daughters, were simply assumed to share the class position and consciousness of their menfolk or were ignored as powerless and voiceless. Feminist scholars contended that this was an unacceptable distortion, that traditional studies remained blind to the experiences of 50 percent of the population. It was feminists above all who began to shake up the field from the 1970s. Their own work suggested that the traditional markers of political progress for the aspiring classes, such as the French Revolution or the Great Reform Act of 1832 in Britain, may actually have been regressive for women, and that the highlighting of other less-celebrated advances, such as changes in divorce laws or in property laws for married women or in reproductive rights issues, might produce a very different female-centred narrative.

To be sure, the new social history had opened the gates to the more systematic study of women's experiences, especially of women's labour, and for a time the addition of 'a chapter on women' (or 'add women and stir') became *de rigueur* for any self-respecting survey of social history. As (principally) women historians pushed the boundaries ever further, securing broader recognition that women were a serious topic for scholarly investigation, this meant looking more intently beyond the public and into the private and domestic spheres where they mostly lived their lives. It also entailed a close reading of non-quantifiable sources and a search among letters and diaries and such like for micro-information about individuals, rather than a focus on collective subjects. This sorely tested the elasticity of the social history project, but the real breech came when feminist scholars shifted from the history of women to the history of gender, from analyzing experience to analyzing discourse, a recognition that social categories such as masculinity and femininity, even male and female, were not essential and timeless but discursively constructed. Just as importantly, feminist scholarship taught that every aspect of the public realm, all of the terms of modern legal, political and philosophical discourse and of social and political identity (class, race, nation, religion, citizen) are predicated on binary assumptions about male and female, masculinity and femininity, that cannot be simply accepted as read but need to be deconstructed.[19]

The emergence of what might be called the 'sexual turn' in social historiography during recent years has proven to be one of the most vibrant and illuminating growth areas in the discipline. In the 1970s and 1980s pioneering historians and sociologists, working within a broadly social constructionist paradigm, argued that a recognizably modern homosexual identity was created largely through the power of new medical and legal categorization in the late nineteenth century. Sexology and medical science classified the distinctive categories of first the 'homosexual' (beating out a proliferation of competing terms such as 'invert', 'pervert' and 'Uranian') and then the 'heterosexual', while legislative and moral codes policed the boundaries between 'normality' and 'deviancy' as never before. The 'constructionists' generated dissent from 'essentialists' in a long-running contest that largely played itself out during the 1990s as leading protagonists on both sides gradually abandoned their more extreme positions. Patterns of (homo)sexual expression and desire across time and place are still fiercely

disputed, above all for the ancient world and for the non-Western world, but few historians would now disagree that they have a *history*; they are not timeless; and that premodern valuations of male/male or female/female sex differed markedly from modern ideas.[20]

Much debate has also centred on the negative or positive consequences of the imposition of sexological notions in the late nineteenth century and beyond: the extent to which homosexuals could use these new constructions to their advantage or to which they were controlled by them and trapped within them. Taking Britain as an example, recent scholarship has helped complicate our picture of this new homosexual. These proponents of the 'new gay history' or the 'new queer history' point to the late and partial reception of continental sexological ideas in Britain and downplay the significance of legal changes and high profile court cases. They emphasize not so much Michel Foucault's famous sexual invert as a new 'species' with a distinct identity, psychology and pathology but rather overlapping and colliding discursive formations and social types–multiple ways for men who had sex with men and women who had sex with women to understand themselves and be understood.[21] One of the most intriguing claims is that the notion of distinct, binary opposite, 'homosexual' and 'heterosexual' identities did not take firm hold, in Britain as elsewhere, until the quarter century after the Second World War. Before then, according for example to Matt Houlbrook's account, 'queers' could be roughly divided into three main groupings: the 'queens' or 'queans' who adopted effeminate mannerisms or drag or other markers of their 'inversion'; higher-class men whose gender-identification was strictly masculine and who tended to despise the queans; and working-class 'trade' who did not identify as queer, did not think their masculinity was compromised by having sex with men and who often had sex with women as well.[22] Historians of lesbianism, which was never criminalized, suggest an equally uneven impact of sexology and the multiple, late and fractured construction of lesbian identities.[23]

Such accounts from the frontline of the sexual turn demonstrate well the distance that social history has covered. First, a continuation of the ambition to incorporate the once marginalized – gays and lesbians and, more recently, transsexuals and transgendered people – within the historical fold, fuelled by the gay liberation movement since the late 1960s and the increasing place at the table of sexual minorities within the academy. Second, under the influence of gay and lesbian studies and queer theory, the sociologically inspired and now culturally inflected deconstruction of categories once considered ahistorical, which is as radically unsettling to normative assumptions of majority sexuality and gender expression as it is revealing about the lives of minorities.

## NATION, RACE AND EMPIRE

If contemporary concerns in and out of the academy have deeply influenced the historiographies of class, gender and sexuality, the same Crocean logic applies equally to recent histories of nation, race and empire. A whole host of issues has ensured that they are among the hot-button historical topics of our time, including the resurgence of ethnic nationalism in tandem with globalization, the messy end of the European colonial empires, postwar immigration and the rise of multiculturalism in Europe, the politics of race and ethnicity in the United States and the rise of the 'American Empire'. And overshadowing everything else, the persistent, pressing need to remember the Holocaust, which has served as the major energizer of memory studies, the investigation of how historical events are remembered, twisted and shaped by different groups and different generations.

To suggest that national, ethnic and racial identities are frequently far more powerful mobilizers of lasting loyalties than class is scarcely a contentious assertion nowadays. Again, however, the social history paradigm finds this difficult to accept. In his debunking

of false theories of nationalism, Ernest Gellner facetiously refers to 'the Wrong Address Theory Favored by Marxism':

> Marxists basically like to think that the spirit of history or human consciousness made a terrible boob. The awakening message was intended for *classes*, but by some terrible postal error was delivered to *nations*. It is now necessary for revolutionary activists to persuade the wrongful recipient to hand over the message, and the zeal it engenders, to the rightful and intended recipient. The unwillingness of both the rightful and the usurping recipient to fall in with this requirement causes the activist great irritation.[24]

Gellner's writings contain many pointed debunkings of the pretensions of nationalists, and the 1980s brought a flurry of studies of the ways in which national identity is manufactured rather than discovered, traditions are invented and history distorted in the pursuit of a political goal. Benedict Anderson's *Imagined Communities* was particularly influential in marking the transition from structural/materialist analyses of nationalism to a fascination with the way in which meanings are constructed, emblems and symbols fashioned and memories perpetuated. Equally significant in reorienting social historians was Edward Said's *Orientalism*, which helped many to appreciate both the notion of 'othering' and also the blatant or subtle ways in which empire impacted on the culture of the metropole.[25]

Much of the new work on nation and empire has expanded social history's ambition to rescue subordinate groups from the condescension of Thompsonian cliché. Indeed, the whole thrust of postcolonial and subaltern studies has been to recognize and recover the neglected voices of the indigenous, the colonized and the enslaved. So, too, the historical exploration of race and ethnicity in the United States has been part and parcel of a project of recuperation. American historians, always rather less influenced by Marx and less focused on class than their European colleagues, have made striking efforts to uncover the life experience of African Americans, pre- and post-slavery, as well as the stories of Native Americans,

European immigrants and newer minorities such as Latinos, Asians and mixed race groups. Again, as with feminists and sexual minorities, the assertiveness of many of these groups on the political stage since the 1960s and their arrival in the universities – first on the wings, then moving to centre stage – has proven to be highly significant.

And, once more, the cultural turn has its fingerprints all over this vibrant scholarship. The search for the subjective perceptions of individuals rather than their 'objective' reduction to group statistics; the construction and instability of identities and categories (both indigenous and metropolitan); the creation of hybridities; the gendered nature of the colonial experience; the negotiation of micropower; the impact of difference on ideas of normativity; the borrowings from anthropology, literary criticism and cultural studies; the interrogation of the national or imperial archive: all these have figured prominently in the most arresting and challenging studies of nation, race and empire since the 1980s.

## SOCIAL HISTORY TODAY

Where does all this leave social history today? It is possible to tell the story as one of success, even mission accomplished. F.M.L. Thompson, in his editorial comments for the *Cambridge Social History of Britain* (1990), reveled in the experimental, open-ended, eclectic nature of social history; its lack of methodological certainty or rigidity, he thought, unlike the new economic history, was most definitely an asset. The three volumes of essays he marshaled together scarcely laid claim to the totalizing vision of the 'social history project', but nor did they register a great deal of concern about the challenge to the discipline's epistemological foundations. Authored mainly by academics holding posts in social and/or economic history, or history/modern history *tout court* (but not yet cultural historians, still struggling on the peripheries to gain institutional recognition), they covered a wide swath of topics,

including towns, cities and the countryside; demography; the family; work; housing; food, drink and nutrition; leisure and culture; the state and society; education; health and medicine; crime and authority; religion; philanthropy; and clubs and associations. As reviewers pointed out, the essays collectively summarized the impressive achievements of social history in accumulating information about all aspects of the material environment (heedless of notional boundaries between social, economic and political history), while at the same time sidestepping big and newly assertive questions about gender and sexual identities, and the ideas, emotions, manners and morals animating ordinary individuals.[26]

Fast forward a decade to Scribner's six-volume *Encyclopedia of European Social History* edited by Peter Stearns. 'Wide agreement exists on what social history is as a particular approach to research concerning the past,' Stearns boldly states in his introductory comments. 'Social historians explore change and continuities in the experience of ordinary people. They pursue this focus on two assumptions: first, that groups of ordinary people have meaningful histories that help us better understand both past and present; and, second, that ordinary people often play a major, if unsung, role in causing key developments and are not simply acted upon.'[27] Armed with this wide remit, Stearns throws open the net: his contributors deploy the same kind of methodological eclecticism and breaching of borders championed by F.M.L. Thompson. The gains from the cultural turn are acknowledged (even with separate essays on 'Cultural history and new cultural history' and 'Gender theory') and all the new topics and approaches are trawled together. The variety of subjects is, to borrow Stearns' own description, 'staggering', and very little appears to be off limits. The encyclopaedia's sections, each with many subsections, include: processes of social change; population and geography; cities and urbanization; rural life; state and society; social structure; social protest; deviance, crime and social control; social problems and social reform; gender; the family and age groups;

sexuality; body and mind; work; culture and popular culture; modern recreation and leisure; religion; education and literacy; and everyday life. Some of these recognizably pertain to the 'old' new social history, others are more obviously 'new cultural'; but all, Stearns claims, can sit comfortably under the social history parasol.

The stance of Thompson and Stearns is one way out of the 'crisis': an open-door policy, everyone welcome in the big tent. To switch metaphors, it amounts to a proclamation of victory and then moving on. Geoff Eley's comment, in his survey 'The generations of social history', has an interesting spin on this sense of 'mission accomplished'. After noting that, by 2000, many social historians 'were moving increasingly freely across the old distinctions of the social, the cultural, the political, the intellectual, and so on, allowing new hybridities to arise', he provocatively suggests that, 'A continued willingness to participate in the conditions of its own disappearance may be the greatest mark of social history's success.'[28]

There is also a 'Crisis? What crisis?' variation on the narrative of success. Thomas Osborne lucidly argues that the linguistic turn and greater archival reflexivity are advances and opportunities for social history and should not be seen as constituting a threat. If social history is seen as an ethical outlook – the extension of the boundaries of legitimate history to include the forgotten, hidden or marginalized as a process of inclusion, reclamation and liberation – the demise of one particular social (read: social*ist*) project does not make the vocation of social history redundant. The notion of the social for historians was never a fixed category; its use was always malleable and promiscuous. 'This may mean that we should reconsider the crisis in social history', he writes, 'that to be critical of certain traditions or perspectives within social history, or to want to move social history into new domains – such as those associated with French thought on memory, with the concept of the archive, or with mutations in sociability, identity and

citizenship – is not necessarily to make a judgement about social history as a political or intellectual vocation; it is to continue doing social history by other means.'[29]

The success story may be the main way in which most working social historians who immerse themselves in the practical and are less concerned about the theoretical implicitly situate themselves.[30] But the majority of those historians who are more theoretically inclined or who have registered an opinion have tended to settle on a sociocultural compromise. In the inaugural edition of *Cultural and Social History* earlier referred to, for example, Asa Briggs writes that he does not separate social and cultural history in his own work, and Harold Perkin, once Britain's first lecturer and then first professor in social history, marks the two as 'friendly collaborators', inextricably intertwined: 'The social includes the cultural, and itself is rooted in the culture, which supplies the language and the concepts in which to describe and analyse society.'[31]

A typical rhetorical device among the theoretical reflections is to accept warmly many of the advances of the cultural/linguistic/postmodernist turn, before adding a 'However …'. A case in point is the volume promising to move *Beyond the Cultural Turn* edited by Victoria Bonnell and Lynn Hunt. Their assembled authors have all been profoundly influenced by the cultural turn; *however*, 'they have refused to accept the obliteration of the social that is implied by the most radical forms of culturalism or poststructuralism. The status or meaning of the social may be in question, affecting both social history and historical sociology, but life without it has proved impossible.' The editors maintain that the most fruitful work combines both cultural and social modes of analysis (as impressively exemplified since 1984 in their own series for Chicago, 'Studies in the History of Society and Culture'). What they find most problematic in cultural approaches, which emphasize the demystification and deconstruction of power, is that social contexts or causes are occluded or effaced. They call for a reconfiguration rather than a jettisoning of the social, a restoration of a sense of the 'social embeddedness' of cultures, social groups and individuals, without reinstating the discredited materialist model of causation.[32]

Some writers subscribe to the 'why can't we all get along?' way of thinking. For example, in a review of Hans Mommsen's *The Rise and Fall of Weimar Democracy* and of Rudy Koshar's *Germany's Transient Pasts: Preservation and National Memory in the Twentieth Century*, which he takes as exemplars of social and cultural history respectively, Stefan Berger extols the benefits and critiques the shortcomings of each and calls for a happy eclecticism rather than the hegemony of one over the other.[33] This echoes to some degree John Stevenson's earlier contention that 'definitional disputes within and between disciplines can be some of the most arid intellectually. Whether "all history is social history" or not matters less than that historians, of all kinds, keep an open door to whatever contributions may assist in understanding the past.'[34] A decade later he might have written 'whether "all history is cultural history" or not', but the point still holds.

Nevertheless, among some of the leading thinkers on this issue, the desire to meld the two and to find a way back in for the material and structural has attracted more adherents. Take R.J. Evans in his polemical *In Defence of History*, angrier in tone than in substance. He reels off a familiar list of the ways in which 'postmodernism' has improved the writing of history: it has taken neglected topics seriously; it has complicated models of causation in directing attention to language, culture and ideas; by focusing on gender, the cultural dimensions of power and authority, memory and the like it has not merely added to our range of knowledge but challenged and changed our understanding of some of the big political and social events, from the French Revolution to the First World War. *However*: he is far from abandoning social history. In calling for the continued recognition of connections between people's standard of living, occupation, gender, sexual orientation, ethnicity and social status, their social, moral and political attitudes and the language in which they express them (albeit in a two-way process), Evans falls back on Marx's famous dictum about men (*sic*) making their own history but not in a manner of their own choosing.[35]

Geoff Eley and Keith Nield, more nuanced theoretically, and in a more conciliatory timbre, also laud the achievements of the cultural turn but lament what has been lost. 'We persist in believing that the political formation of subjectivities and the structured consequences of capitalist inequality can both be addressed in the same analysis,' they write. 'There should be ways of combining the poststructuralist critique of knowledge with certain registers of cautious structuralist argument. Both are patently possible. *We do not have to choose.*' They call for hybrid, collaborative history, retaining a materialist perspective – shorn of reductionism and innocent of any intensions to recreate a master narrative, to be sure – but acknowledging the power of the discursive moment. 'Regularities' – a key term for them – in wealth and poverty in capitalisms across time and space *do* exist materially, they insist, even if we can only know them through discourse.[36] Eley argues the falseness of the dichotomy between the social and the cultural, and applauds the ways in which younger scholars in particular have blurred boundaries and produced new hybridities. He laments the way in which the earlier concerns of social historians have been forgotten rather than fruitfully reengaged, especially the loss of confidence in painting the big picture and tackling the subject of society as a whole. With few notable exceptions, historians have ceded most of the terrain of the great debates – revolution, the transition from feudalism to capitalism, the Industrial Revolution and so forth – to either historical sociologists like Michael Mann, Anthony Giddens, Theda Skocpol and John Hall, all unafraid to make sweeping comparisons across broad sweeps of time, but all relatively untroubled by the cultural turn, or, much worse, to ideologues of neoliberalism like Samuel Huntington.[37]

Eley is by no means alone in his nostalgia for a more adventurous and heroic social history. Gareth Stedman Jones, in his extended review of *Les Formes de l'Expérience*, Bernard Lepetit's edited collection of another generation of *Annaliste* scholarship, is left uneasy by the renunciation of all external forms of social determination, combined with the corresponding freedom of action accorded individuals, displayed in the essays. He writes,

> The danger of a view of history that not only rejects the role of the economy or other forms of structural determination, but also substitutes for the regularities of discourse the creativity of idiolects and the microscopic variety of situational semantics is that the resulting ensemble will be too boneless to fulfill the rudimentary requirements of historical explanation. Too great an emphasis upon the resources and competence of actors in the face of structures, and too insistent a focus upon the freedom offered by their liminal location between contradictory belief systems, can lead to the disappearance from view of a whole range of historical phenomena to which this voluntaristic approach offers little guidance.

And this matters for historians *engagés* like Eley, Stedman Jones and presumably most other social historians. As Stedman Jones expresses it, 'the battering of the credibility of history and the loss of historians' self-assurance and 1960s' hope have happened alongside 'the unraveling of the postwar settlement, the unbidden return of so much that was erased from the official memory after the Second World War, and the reemergence in new forms of so many of the nationalist and racist insecurities and hatreds that had once erased the path of fascism', all of which combines 'to remind us just how urgent it is that the moral and intellectual authority of history be renewed and reasserted.'[38]

In similar vein, Manu Goswami contrasts social history's erstwhile expansive optimism with the melancholic introspection of cultural history and its watchwords of contingency, undecidability, difference and fragmentation. The local and the particular supersede analysis of deep structures and large-scale transformation. And yet, since 'cultural history cannot account for the conditions of its own global emergence and resonance without recourse to the forms of historical totalization that it rejected in the reaction formation against social history', she calls for the writing of history attuned to the dynamic interchange between categories of perception and social transformations.[39]

There are two concerns here, rehearsed repeatedly by a number of writers. One is the reinstatement of some aspect of the social in an attempt to explain causation and change over time, once and maybe still the historian's prime duty. The second is a sense of the abdication and powerlessness of historians in face of the global triumph of neoliberalism – and the need to reinstate, yes, some aspect of the social in response. Laura Lee Downs speaks well to the first when she writes *a propos* gender,

> [T]hose historians of gender who would like to take the more purely constructivist route continue to face some very real epistemological difficulties, notably the fact that gender, understood as a purely discursive construct, cannot in and of itself explain change. If, for example, sexual identities are understood to be produced solely through discursive processes, then how are we to account for changes in said identities over time? Without some way of linking discursive process to social experience, historians cannot account for the changing meanings of masculine and feminine.[40]

Gabrielle Spiegel rightly suggests that, as cultural history continued to believe in the objective reality of the social world, 'sociocultural history' would have been a more proper label all along. She sees (and supports) a current trend towards the return of what she calls a 'modified phenomenology'. Drawing variously on Pierre Bourdieu, Michel de Certeau, Anthony Giddens and the later Michel Foucault, among others, she touts the merits of 'practice theory' (a term borrowed from Andreas Reckwitz), which 'asserts the continuing relevance of semiotic insights proffered by the linguistic turn, yet reinterprets them in favor of a rehabilitation of social history by placing structure and practice, language and body in dialectical relation in historical systems.' Again this is the language of compromise: a 'weak version' of poststructuralism, an 'attenuated concept' of discourse: an acknowledgment of the social, contextual determinants of thought and behaviour alongside the mediating role of language and culture in their functioning.[41]

Some scholars hold that this compromise is theoretically untenable. Richard Handler, for example, insists that the attempt to maintain a distinction between the social and the cultural – falling back on the assumption that the social is, after all, 'more real' than the cultural – is unnecessary and theoretically pernicious.[42] Miguel Cabrera, too, in making the case for 'postsocial history', objects to the way in which some social historians see the opening up to culture, emotions and the symbolic as merely complementary to socio-economic histories. He believes that the new cultural history's retention of a determining social – not as the cause of social actions but in setting the possibilities for behaviour and consciousness – is fatally flawed. The contention of postsocial history is that social reality is a discursive construction. He writes,

> Obviously, this does not mean that discourse constructs social reality in a literal sense, as a set of phenomena and material relations. It builds social reality as a *meaningful entity*. That is, it constructs through its mediation, the image, idea, or consciousness that individuals have of it, and according to which they act.

'Articulation' is Cabrera's preferred term, rather than the 'reflection', 'representation' or 'expression' of sociocultural historians; this 'has the express purpose of denoting the constitutive function of language in the shaping of objects, subjects, and practices and of stressing the rhetorical character of any relationship between individuals and their social environment.'[43]

The debates continue. Whether the postsocial will have any traction among historians or whether, as I suspect, most will be content with the sociocultural compromise hammered out by some of the heavy hitters in the field remains to be seen. Social history, modified and chastened or broadened and expanded or possibly both, depending on one's definition,

is clearly not dead, even if the social history project itself has ended up in the proverbial dustbin. But without a project the utility of the label begins to fade, its identity to blur. Social historians of the future may prefer to style themselves as, simply, historians.[44]

## NOTES AND REFERENCES

1   Patrick Joyce, 'The end of social history?', *Social History* 20, 1 (January 1995): 73–91.
2   Asa Briggs, 'Editorial', *Cultural and Social History* 1, 1 (2004): 2.
3   Eric J. Hobsbawm, 'From social history to the history of society', *Daedalus* 100 (1971): 43; Charles Tilly, *Big Structures, Large Processes, Huge Comparisons* (New York: Russell Sage Foundation, 1984); Geoff Eley, *A Crooked Line: From Cultural History to the History of Society* (Ann Arbor: University of Michigan Press, 2005), 25, 71–2.
4   Peter N. Stearns, *Social History* 1 (1976): 3.
5   Eley, *A Crooked Line*, 189.
6   Tony Judt, 'A clown in regal purple: social history and the historians', *History Workshop Journal* 7, 1 (1979): 66–94.
7   Edward Thompson, *The Making of the English Working Class* (London: Gollancz, 1980 [1963]), 14; Emanuel Le Roy Ladurie, *Montaillou: The Promised Land of Error* (New York: G. Braziller, 1978); Carlo Ginsburg, *The Cheese and the Worms: The Cosmos of a Sixteenth-Century Miller* (Baltimore: Johns Hopkins University Press, 1980); Natalie Zemon Davis, *The Return of Martin Guerre* (Cambridge, MA: Harvard University Press, 1984); Robert Darnton, *The Great Cat Massacre and Other Episodes in French Cultural History* (New York: Vintage Books, 1985): Robert Gildea, 'Introduction', in *Writing Contemporary History*, ed. Robert Gildea and Anne Simonin (London: Hodder Education, 2008), xii–xiii, xvi–xviii.
8   Karl Appuhn, 'Microhistory', in *Encyclopedia of European Social History*, ed. Peter N. Stearns (New York: Charles Scribner's Sons, 2001) I, 105–10.
9   Sewell, Jr, 'Crooked lines', 400–1; Patrick Joyce, 'Introduction', in *The Social in Question: New Bearings in History and the Social Sciences*, ed. *idem* (London: Routledge, 2002), 4.
10   William H. Sewell, Jr, *Work and Revolution in France: The Language of Labor from the Old Regime to 1848* (Cambridge and New York: Cambridge University Press, 1980).
11   William H. Sewell, Jr, 'The concept(s) of culture', in *Beyond the Cultural Turn: New Directions in the Study of Society and Culture*, ed. Victoria E. Bonnell and Lynn Hunt (Berkeley and Los Angeles: University of California Press, 1999), 35–6.
12   Gareth Stedman Jones, 'Rethinking Chartism', in his *Languages of Class: Studies in English Working-Class History, 1832–1982* (Cambridge: Cambridge University Press, 1983); Joan Wallach Scott, 'Gender: a useful category of historical analysis', *American Historical Review* 91, 5 (December 1986): 1053–75.

13 Geoff Eley and Ronald Grigor Suny, 'Introduction', in *Becoming National: A Reader*, ed. *idem* (New York: Oxford University Press, 1996), 32.

14 See, for example, Cabrera, *Postsocial History*, ch. 1; Joyce, 'The end of social history?': 82–3; Ronald Grigor Suny, 'Back and beyond: reversing the cultural turn?', *American Historical Review* 107, 5 (December 2002): 1481–8; Carla Hesse, 'The new empiricism', *Cultural and Social History* 1 (2004): 201–7; R.J. Evans, 'Prologue: what is history? – now', in *What is History Now?*, ed. David Cannadine (Houndmills: Palgrave Macmillan, 2002), 6–9; Joyce Appleby, Lynn Hunt and Margaret Jacob, *Telling the Truth About History* (New York: W. W. Norton, 1994), 230; Adrian Wilson, 'A critical portrait of social history', in *Rethinking Social History: English Society 1570–1920 and its Interpretation*, ed. *idem* (Manchester: Manchester University Press, 1993), 22–3; Gildea, 'Introduction', in *Writing Contemporary History*, ed. Gildea and Simonin, xxi–xxiv; Paul E. Johnson, 'Reflections: looking back at social history', *Reviews in American History* 39, 2 (June 2011): 384.

15 Keith Thomas, 'The changing shape of historical interpretation', in *Penultimate Adventures with Britannia: Personalities, Politics and Culture in Britain*, ed. Wm. Roger Louis (London: I.B. Tauris, 2008), 48.

16 Cabrera, *Postsocial History*, 8.

17 Hesse, 'The new empiricism': 204–5.

18 The debate on class can be followed in Patrick Joyce (ed.), *Class* (Oxford: Oxford University Press, 1995); David Cannadine, *The Rise and Fall of Class in Britain* (New York: Columbia University Press, 1999).

19 Laura Lee Downs, 'From women's history to gender history', in *Writing History: Theory and Practice*, ed. Stefan Berger, Heiko Feldner and Kevin Passmore (London: Arnold, 2003), 261–81; Eley and Suny (eds), *Becoming National*, 26; Suny, 'Back and beyond': 1481–2; Ruth Harris, 'What future for gender history?', in *Writing Contemporary History*, ed. Gildea and Simonin, 70–1.

20 See, for example, David M. Halperin, *How To Do the History of Homosexuality* (Chicago: University of Chicago Press, 2002).

21 For overviews, see Joseph Bristow, 'Remapping the sites of modern gay history: legal reform, medico-legal thought, homosexual scandal, erotic geography', *Journal of British Studies* 46 (January 2007): 116–42; Chris Waters, 'Distance and desire in the new British queer history', *GLQ: A Journal of Lesbian and Gay Studies* 14, 1 (2008): 139–55.

22 Matt Houlbrook, *Queer London: Perils and Pleasures in the Sexual Metropolis, 1918–1957* (Chicago: University of Chicago Press, 2005).

23 For example, Laura Doan, *Fashioning Sapphism: The Origins of a Modern English Lesbian Culture* (New York: Columbia University Press, 2001).

24 Ernest Gellner, *Nations and Nationalism* (Oxford: Blackwell, 1983), 129–30.

25 Benedict Anderson, *Imagined Communities: Reflections on the Origin and Spread of Nationalism* (London: Verso, 1983); Edward Said, *Orientalism* (New York: Pantheon Books, 1978); Eric J. Hobsbawm and Terence Ranger (eds), *The Invention of Tradition* (Cambridge: Cambridge University Press, 1983).

26 F.M.L. Thompson, 'Editorial preface', in *The Cambridge Social History of Britain 1750–1950*, ed. *idem* (Cambridge: Cambridge University Press, 1990) I, ix–xi; reviews of ibid: Olive Anderson, *English Historical Review* 107, 422 (January 1992): 146–9; John Stevenson, *History* 76, 248: 418–32; James A. Jaffe, *Journal of British Studies* 31, 1 (January 1992): 89–95.

27 Peter N. Stearns, 'Introduction', in *Encyclopedia of European Social History* I, xix. See also *idem*, 'Social history present and future', *Journal of Social History* 37, 1 (Autumn 2003): 9–12.

28 Geoff Eley, 'The generations of social history', in *Encyclopedia of European Social History* I, 3–30.

29 Thomas Osborne, 'History, theory, disciplinarity', in *The Social in Question*, ed. Joyce, 175–8, 186–7.

30 See Hartmut Kaelble, 'Social history in Europe', *Journal of Social History* 37, 1 (Autumn 2003): 35.

31 Briggs, 2–3; Perkin, 5, *Cultural and Social History* 1, 1 (2004).

32 Bonnell and Hunt (eds), *Beyond the Cultural Turn*, 11, 25–6.

33 Stefan Berger, 'Social history vs cultural history: a German debate', *Theory, Culture & Society* 18 (1) (February 2001): 145–53.

34 Stevenson, *History* 76, 248: 432.

35 Evans, *In Defense of History*, 158–63.

36 Geoff Eley and Keith Nield, *The Future of Class in History: What's Left of the Social?* (Ann Arbor: University of Michigan Press, 2007), 17, 189–201.

37 Eley, *A Crooked Line*, 196–203.

38 Gareth Stedman Jones, 'The new social history in France', *The Age of Cultural Revolutions: Britain and France, 1750–1820*, ed. Colin Jones and Dror Wahrman (Berkeley: University of California Press, 2002), 103–4. For another lament at historians' 'fiddling while Rome is burning', see Jürgen Kocka, 'Losses, gains and opportunities: social history today', *Journal of Social History* 37, 1 (Autumn 2003): 23.

39 Manu Goswami, 'Remembering the future', in 'AHR Forum: Geoff Eley's *The Crooked Line*', *American Historical Review* 113, 2 (April 2008): 420, 422

40 Downs, 'From women's history to gender history', 275.

41 Gabrielle M. Spiegel, 'Comment on *A Crooked Line*', in 'AHR Forum: Geoff Eley's *The Crooked Line*', *American Historical Review* 113, 2 (April 2008): 414–15; *idem* (ed.), *Practicing History: New Directions in Historical Writing After the Linguistic Turn* (New York and London: Routledge, 2005), 22–5; Thomas Welskopp, 'Social history', *Writing History*, ed. Berger et al., 217–18.

42 Richard Handler, 'Cultural theory in history today', *American Historical Review* 107, 5 (December 2002): 1513.

43 Cabrera, *Postsocial History*, 10, 46, 123–6.

44 See Chris Waters, 'Is there still a place for social history?' in *Writing Contemporary History*, ed. Gildea and Simonin, 7–11.

# 15

# Women's History/Feminist History

Judith P. Zinsser

## WHEN WOMEN'S HISTORY EQUALED FEMINIST HISTORY

Women's history has always been feminist history. At its simplest level, 'feminism' means an identification with other women, a sense of their disadvantaged status in relation to men, and a desire to change that situation.[1] If one seeks out the first women writing their own history, one finds a feminist purpose: to prove that contrary to prevailing cultural expectations and dominant attitudes about the sexes, women were valued beings worthy of respect and capable of all of the rational activities reserved for the male mind and body. Similarly, literate, privileged women often came to their feminism through stories of exemplary women from their culture's past. These heroines offered possibilities and gave images of alternative lives. This interplay between emerging feminisms and women's histories has been the pattern throughout modern times, whether in fifteenth-century Europe or twentieth-century North Africa.

Christine de Pizan (1365–c.1430), usually identified as Europe's first feminist historian, declared in *The Book of the City of Ladies*, her collection of exceptional women's biographies: 'There is not the slightest doubt that women belong to the people of God and the human race as much as men and are not another species or dissimilar race, for which they should be excluded from moral teachings.'[2] A successful writer and courtier, with patrons among the rulers of France, Burgundy, and Britain, she thus claimed full humanity for women and rejected the subordinate, dependent, and inferior status assigned to her sex. The wives, mothers, deities, queens, and princesses she then described from Classical, Biblical, and historical sources, proved her assertion and affirmed that women could be models of faith and reason.

### The feminist challenge of the 1970s: goals, methodologies, and sources

The women's history that now fills the shelves of libraries and appears in computer searches had its beginnings in the feminist activism of the late 1960s in North America and the United Kingdom. As in earlier centuries, these Anglo-American feminists believed that valuing women's past would have a direct impact on their and other women's lives. 'Foremothers' to follow, models to emulate, words to inspire – all would give purpose and authority to their endeavor. The indignation, even rage, that gave energy to their writings is understandable when one appreciates their discovery. They, like all but those few prescient early advocates for women, had accepted as authoritative, verifiable truth that, as a respected North American male historian described it, 'the subject matter of history is always men in the midst of other men–men in collectives and groups.'[3] The great power of historians had been their control of this definition, of what was remembered, and by their omissions, what has been forgotten. The insistence of women such as Gerda Lerner in the United States and Sheila Rowbotham in England that history consisted of *two* sexes, both worthy of inclusion in our narratives and analyses of the past, seems so obvious now as to be silly. 'Like so many profoundly important true things ... faintly embarrassing to say or write it,' the North American medievalist, Nancy Partner has noted.[4] That women's inclusion is accepted as self-evident today is the result of this wedding of feminism and history.

Although in the twenty-first century, as the North American historian of medieval England Judith M. Bennett has commented, 'patriarchy talk might be unfashionable,' in the late 1960s and 1970s knowledge of the oppression of women by patriarchal attitudes and institutions across the ages and continents drew outrage.[5] Feminists, both outside and inside the Academy, such as Sheila Rowbotham and Shulamith Firestone in England and Robin Morgan and Lois Banner in the United States, saw the omnipresence of patriarchy as unifying all women, once its victims, and now its opponents. History then offered models of resistance such as the French revolutionary Olympe de Gouges; the German socialist Clara Zetkin and her Russian counterpart Alexandra Kollontai; the suffragists Emmeline Pankhurst and Alice Paul; the women's birth control advocate and international activist Aletta Jacobs of the Netherlands, to name only a few of the exemplars they discovered. The writers Virginia Woolf and Simone de Beauvoir gave the new generations of women activists theoretical explanations for this skewed, gendered society, and vivid images and startling phrases that became shorthand justifications for activism. In *A Room of One's Own* (1938) Woolf imagined Shakespeare's 'wonderfully gifted sister, Judith,' perhaps more gifted than her brother, William, yet never able to use her talents because of the realities of a woman's life in the theater in sixteenth-century London. De Beauvoir's dictum in *La Deuxième Sexe* [The Second Sex] (1946), 'women are not born but are made,' led her to explore biology, mythology, history, and sociology, and to decry Western culture that had enshrined man as the measure of the human; tied a woman's identity to her body and therefore relegated all women to existence as the 'other,' as not male, and by implication a species of lesser beings.[6]

Previous scholarship had been concerned with 'noteworthy' events, 'with those,' according to a pre-eminent English male historian, 'who, whether victorious or defeated, achieved something.' As he made clear in his still popular *What Is History?* (1961), this 'something' was by definition political and by default, the achievement of the few men, the Napoleons and Franklin D. Roosevelts whose choices and actions dominated their eras and thus, according to these men's narratives, accounted for all of the significant events of their time. 'History,' as a French male social historian, explained, 'has no direction of its own accord, for it is shaped by the will of men and the choices they make.'[7] Most men and all but a few women – the wives, daughters, and consorts of these exceptional beings – played no part worthy of recording. When mentioned, these women usually reenforced denigrating images of their sex. Theodora of Byzantium was a manipulative prostitute; Mary, Queen of Scots proved malleable, a victim of her passions in one account, helpless political rival in another; Catherine the Great of Russia achieved more fame because of her lovers than her creation of a centralized Russian Empire. The peasant women, the urban market women, the servants in noble households, the spinners and weavers in the factories, the shop girls in the department stores, the waitresses in the tea rooms and diners were not even significant enough to mention. They disappeared in apparently inclusive terms such as 'peasants,' 'towns-people,' and 'workers.'[8]

For these feminist activists, this study of women's past was their means of creating a collective identity and contributing to what all believed would be a rapid transformation of the traditional histories. Initially, they saw the task as a two-part endeavor: to recover the lost Shakespeare's sisters, and to study the ways in which cultures and circumstances had limited women's lives and opportunities. Rowbotham's *Hidden from History* and *Women, Resistance and Revolution*, published in 1972 and 1973,[9] exemplified this union of feminist history and activism in the name of a new account of Britain's past. As the narratives multiplied, a third goal emerged: a desire not just to chronicle women's achievements when, despite the constraints of their societies they acted as men, but also to value women's designated activities, to give recognition to the role women had played in the continuation of families, and thus of cultures and of all human history. With this addition of the everyday lives of women the narrow parameters of traditional men's history could be avoided.[10]

However, even men's radical histories proved disappointing. For in this project of reclaiming and revaluing women's contributions, feminist historians found themselves both heirs and critics of the new social history of the lower classes associated with the Western European Marxist and demographic historians of the 1960s. For example, Georges Soboul in his work on the *sans culottes* of the French Revolution, E.P. Thompson and Eric Hobsbawm in their studies of the English working class, defined their subjects as exclusively male as a matter of course. Women remained marginal and appeared only occasionally: a widow, a dressmaker, a referent for artisans claiming women's rights; or were subsumed in abstract population increases and declines. When in the late 1960s Rowbotham

and Sally Alexander, another young, English feminist, had suggested a special women's history meeting of the radical socialist Ruskin History Workshop, the others simply laughed.[11] Similarly, the 'New Left' radical and revisionist historians of the United States, such as Eugene D. Genovese, Staughton Lynd, and Howard Zinn, who claimed to be writing the narrative 'from the bottom up,' assumed that when they described men's lives they had also described those of women. As the North American feminist scholar Caroll Smith-Rosenberg noted, when women did appear it was 'as members of families,' that sexually neuter, monolithic institution consisting of parents and children. Women were never seen 'as persons in their own right.'[12]

The French Annalistes' history also remained a masculine phenomenon, its value, according to Fernand Braudel, one of its most famous proponents, determined by 'the extent to which it can explain the life of men as it is being woven before our very eyes, with its acquiescences and reticences, its refusals, complicities, or surrenders when confronted with change or tradition.' Such attitudes, Susan Mosher Stuard, a scholar of early modern Dalmatia, found indicative of complicity with exclusionary traditions that 'call[ed] into question the fidelity of the Annales School to the history of the masses.' It belied their intention to create 'a history that may legitimately claim to be total in its grasp.'[13]

The fall of 1969 saw the publication of Gerda Lerner's article, 'New approaches to the study of women in American history.' It heralded for many feminists in the United States the first of many initiatives to change women's disadvantaged status in past histories and their right to participate in the creation of future histories. The 1970s became the decade for challenge and transformation. The collection edited by Berenice A. Carroll, *Liberating Women's History: Theoretical and Critical Essays* (1976),[14] was typical of these efforts. The topics ranged from historiography and methodology to studies of the economic and social roles of women from the seventeenth century to the present. The authors came from different specialties and different parts of the United States. Hilda L. Smith, for example, was a graduate student in history at the University of Chicago; Asunción Lavrin, a Latin Americanist, taught at Howard in Washington, DC; and Carroll herself was a political scientist. Articles, essays, narrative surveys, and monographs appeared and inspired yet more research and writing that revitalized and transformed the study of women's past. As Joan Kelly, the Marxist feminist historian of the Italian Renaissance, explained, these scholars literally 'open[ed] up the other half of history.' In addition, they envisioned a broader impact: a new history that would speak 'in male and female voices,' that would succeed where social historians, radicals, revisionists, and Annalistes, had failed. Theirs would be inclusive, not exclusive – even by implication or omission – universal, not particular.[15]

Hard though it may be to believe now, in the 1970s it was possible to read everything that had been written about women in English and other European languages. In the seventeenth and eighteenth centuries a few women and men in France, Scotland, the Netherlands, and Germany had published collective sketches of women to appeal to a new, female reading public. In the nineteenth century, these collections became a staple of women's history. Most famous perhaps were those by the English sisters Agnes and Elizabeth Strickland and their best-selling stories of queens and princesses. Women also wrote biography. Marie d'Agoult, a member of the same circles as the prominent nineteenth-century French authors and historians Jules Michelet and Alexis de Tocqueville, chose Mary Stuart and Joan of Arc; Lucretia Mott, the North American suffragist, Florence Nightingale.[16]

Feminism had also motivated previous generations in North America and Europe. Lydia Maria Child's 1835 *Brief History of the Condition of Women in Various Ages and Nations* assumed steady progress for women from the Classical era to her own day. Elizabeth Ellet's two volumes on *The Women of the American Revolution* appeared in 1848

and formed part of the mid-nineteenth century effort to reclaim women's past and to assert their rights. Similarly, in the first decades of the twentieth century classic studies such as Lina Eckenstein's *Women Under Monasticism* (1896), Eileen Power's *Medieval English Nunneries* (1922), Alice Clark and Ivy Pinchbeck's studies of English working women's lives (1919 and 1930), and Julia Cherry Spruill's *Women's Life and Work in the Southern Colonies* (1938) told of other eras filled with opportunities and accomplishment. The 1960s saw the resurgence of interest in works such as Doris Mary Stenton's *The English Woman in History* (1957) and Eleanor Flexner's *Century of Struggle: The Woman's Rights Movement in the United States* (1959).[17]

For a number of scholars in the United States, the most significant predecessor was the feminist writer and activist Mary Ritter Beard – by the 1930s she was the most well-known authority and advocate for women's history in the United States. Beard explained that her militancy on behalf of women came when she was in Manchester, England working with the suffragists. A chance encounter with a drunken, teenage factory worker one night in May of 1900, gave her a harsh glimpse of a young girl's life. She resolved that, from this point on, 'I knew I must do something for women.' Lobbying and writing to preserve the historical record of women's lives and to give value to all that they had accomplished became one aspect of doing 'something for women.'[18]

In the works Beard co-authored with her husband, in her 1934 document collection, *America Through Women's Eyes*,[19] in her efforts to establish the World Center for Women's Archives, her critiques of the new 1940s edition of the *Encyclopedia Britannica*, and finally in her best known work, *Woman as Force in History: A Study in Traditions and Realities* (1946),[20] she made the case for women's significance and the need for their inclusion in the historical record. Unlike her contemporaries, such as de Beauvoir, she had no interest in exploring the origins or effects of patriarchy. She called the concept of women as an oppressed group 'dogma,' 'one of the most fantastic myths ever created by the human mind.' Instead Beard focused on what she identified as the 'duality of women's position in society – women are subordinate, yet central; victimized, yet active.' Lerner called Beard 'my principal mentor as a historian,' and found this apparent contradiction in women's condition a challenge. What particularly appealed to her, however, was Beard's 'central idea: that women have always been active and at the center of history.' As Lerner explained in 'Placing women in history': 'the next step is to face, once and for all and with its complete consequences, that women are the majority of humankind and essential to the making of history.' In addition, Lerner adopted her mentor's interdisciplinary approach (Beard turned to legal, social, and economic methodologies) and her use of a wide variety of sources, including those ignored in traditional political history, such as women's letters, diaries, and fiction.[21]

Subsequent women's historians also followed Beard's methodology, drawing freely from anthropology, sociology, economics, and psychology, to name the most obvious of the social sciences contributing frameworks and analytical tools. For example, North American cultural historian Natalie Zemon Davis' cross-disciplinary *Society and Culture in Early Modern France* (1975)[22] gave an ethnographer's analysis of the lives and values of sixteenth-century artisans and peasants, particularly women's relations with local religious and civic elites. Although this first generation of scholars mined traditional sources and men's histories – for example, French historians' work on manorialism included records of a medieval peasant widow's obligations – they quickly turned to less orthodox texts, and different ways of reading them. Zemon Davis used proverbs to speculate on the values and world view of sixteenth-century Lyons' craftswomen.[23] Barbara Welter in *Dimity Convictions* (1976),[24] her collection of essays on nineteenth-century Euro- and Afro-American women, took

evidence from magazines, novels, sermons, and cookbooks. Similarly, Sarah B. Pomeroy used vase paintings, gravestone inscriptions, and the graffiti on the walls of Pompeii – to name only a few of her sources – to recreate the lives of women in Classical antiquity, in Athens, Rome, and Sparta.[25] For those seeking modern women's history, interviews and oral memory proved invaluable, as have every kind of media source from mail order catalogues to television programs. The Buffalo Women's Oral History Project formed the basis of the study of New York lesbian history. Similar projects have led to histories of Kenyan women's resistance to British laws and European Jewish women's lives during World War II, as well as women's experiences in the partition of India.[26]

## Feminism's new questions and historiographical patterns

Lerner's early published articles posed questions which guided this first decade of modern women's history. It could be argued that they have guided research and analysis in women's and feminist history to the present day. How did the system of inequality originate? How was gender defined in a given period? Where had the ideal images of women come from? How had they affected women's lives? What had women been doing throughout history? Who defined and controlled their sexual lives and how? How did women see their world? How did they relate to other women? How have class, race, religion, and ethnicity affected women in different eras and cultures? Why had women's activities and accomplishments been denigrated or forgotten? Lerner formulated a total of 17 and ended her list with the most far-reaching question of all: What would history be like if seen through the eyes of women and ordered by values they define?[27] It was this final query that has proved the richest, challenging women's and later gender historians across continents, and vastly different methodological and theoretical approaches, even those who questioned the descriptive and substantive validity of the very concept 'women.'

The historiographical patterns of women's history were also categorized by Lerner. These, she explained had governed its evolution in the past. She could not know that these patterns would recur as each new group of feminist scholars, as the historian of African-American women Patricia Hill Collins has characterized it, worked to retrieve their history from the angle of their particular lens. Lerner's first category, 'compensatory history,' told of exceptional women, the queens, regents, maharanis, and empresses who exercised male power. 'Contribution history' identified 'ladies' who had in one way or another affected men's history, such as: the abbesses of Europe's ninth-century double monasteries; the indigenous intermediaries of Europe's colonial conquests in the Americas; the *salonières* associated with the Enlightenment and the Romantic movement; the women of the Chinese Communist Party who accompanied Mao Zedong on the Long March. However, important as these heroines were, Lerner noted that their narratives did nothing to challenge or alter the conceptual framework and criteria of inclusion characteristic of the male, not the female world.

'The true history of women,' she insisted, 'is the history of their ongoing functioning in that male-defined world *on their own terms.*' This she saw as the real task of the feminist historian of women: 'to reconstruct the missing half – the female experience.' This reconstruction Lerner insisted would be different from men's history. It would not be a monolithic past subsuming all women under the rubric of elite history; differences in race and class would be central to these new narratives. This 'transitional history,' as she called it, this history of women '*on their own terms*,' required new analytical categories, new ways to determine what was and was not significant. Words and concepts such as 'roles and functions,' 'marriage,' 'reproduction,' 'sexuality,' 'images and realities,' assumed primacy when women's lives became the focus of the historian's research and analysis. Using

Simone de Beauvoir's terminology, Lerner asked provocatively: 'What would the past be like if men were regarded as woman's "other"?'[28] New narrative histories of European women experimented with ways to meet her challenge. Feminist historians rejected the traditional periodization of men's history and organized women's experiences across eras and political boundaries. Borrowing from anthropology and sociology, in their narrative history of European women, Bonnie S. Anderson and Judith P. Zinsser used place and function in society – women of the fields, women of the churches, and so on – as the defining categories. Others, for similar projects, used stages in a woman's life, as a daughter, wife, and widow.[29]

## Feminist epistemological challenges of the 1980s

In discovering and writing women's history, this generation of feminist scholars challenged more than just the omissions and approaches of past narratives. They queried every aspect of the historian's craft: what questions to pose; what constituted valid sources and authoritative evidence; what methodologies to use; and most significant of all, who legitimated the history produced by these efforts? They sought, as the cultural historian of France, Ann-Louise Shapiro explained, to uncover 'the conceptual and epistemological imperatives embedded in the process and the product.'[30] By the beginning of the 1980s, these North American and Western European women historians had not only destroyed comforting traditional images of the accuracy and stability of 'history,' but had also shown the falsity of claims to the objectivity and political neutrality of its practitioners.[31] For the old history, according to the discoveries of the new feminist-inspired women scholars, had served the interests of patriarchal hierarchies, sustaining images of the female that justified societies in which the denigration and disadvantage of women were taken for granted, and assumed to be part of the 'natural' order. 'Accurate' was the most important word under attack. Whether a monograph or a textbook, traditional histories appeared to present a series of scientific, verifiable answers to obviously significant questions, answers based on information meticulously researched and carefully described in a coherent and self-evident 'true' analytical narrative. Certitude masked the premises that skewed these narratives and analyses. The very definition of history had been narrowed to the concept of 'significance.' The 'significant' in history became the story of the heterosexual male elite and its exercise of power. 'Valid' sources, methods, and analytical tools were only those that illuminated the elite in general and its use of public authority in particular. Any criticism of these choices then had been dismissed as unimportant, incomplete, subjective, politically biased slurs on the work of neutral, objective scholarship. Women's historians were not the first to issue such challenges, but the omission of over half the human race, and a half so obviously different from even the actors of more inclusive men's histories, made 'all history as we know it ... merely prehistory,' as Lerner characterized it.[32]

Once aware, women historians puzzled over their previous failure to see, and described the process that Sheila Rowbotham called a coming to 'historical self-consciousness,' connecting their present to other women's past, and the realization that what appeared to be unique to one individual formed part of the 'general pattern of women's existence.' They marveled at what they called 'academic sleight of hand,' this 'ability to depict a world without women, a world whose existence is clearly denied by the writers' and readers' own experiences.' The North American historian Linda Gordon wrote of her outrage at 'the shameful suppression of knowledge.'[33] They looked to their own specialties and asked new questions of familiar men's narratives and perceived the same omissions and false premises. Most famous and most often quoted, Joan Kelly, an expert on the fifteenth-century humanist Leon Battista Alberti, wondered 'Did women have a Renaissance?'

She concluded that 'the entire picture I had held of the Renaissance was partial, distorted, limited, and deeply flawed by those limitations.' She realized that though men gained increasing liberty in this era, women did not. Even those phenomena usually described as positive developments for women, such as courtly love, had reinforced 'existing institutions and power relationships.' Like Lerner and subsequent feminist historians, she insisted that the study of women demanded new ways of thinking, new categories for research and analysis that reflected women's experiences. Kelly suggested three categories that, like Lerner's questions, have continued to guide feminist historians in all parts of the world into the twenty-first century: study of women's economic, political, and cultural roles; the regulation of their sexuality; and each era's ideology about women.[34] The addition of insights from literary theory added other dimensions to this feminist epistemology. Feminist historians sought to understand not only an era's ideology about women but also a culture's ideological and symbolic uses of the concept of 'woman' and the 'feminine.' For example, the ancient, cross-cultural warrior act of raping the enemy's women traditionally has signified the emasculation of its men; similarly, the sexual purity of daughters has constituted the honor of a man's family in many cultures across the millennia.

## FEMINIST STRATEGIES FOR PROFESSIONAL RECOGNITION

In the United States the passage of the affirmative action legislation of the 1960s and liberal educational loan policies of the same era gained more women admission to graduate history programs, and enabled more of them to complete graduate degree programs in the most prestigious university history departments: Joan Kelly and Gerda Lerner at Columbia University; Natalie Zemon Davis at Michigan; Joan W. Scott at Madison-Wisconsin; Judith M. Bennett at the

University of Toronto; Linda Gordon at Yale. In the 1970s and 1980s this feminist energy led women's historians to fill shelf after shelf with new scholarship. Joan W. Scott, trained in the history of early modern Europe, reminisced about those first decades when 'activism confirmed agency,' and feminist scholars could see themselves as 'producers of new knowledge, transmitters of revised memory, fashioning tales to inspire ourselves and the generations to come.' As the historian of medieval England Judith M. Bennett remembered, there was 'the clarity of that 1970s ideal of a seamless union of history and feminism,' the shared goal, 'to add depth,' in an ever-expanding narrative as more women's lives became known and recorded.[35]

However, the new scholarship went beyond service to their cause, their younger sisters, and in the case of Afro-American women, their race. Their confidence and success as the producers of this new history made it possible to challenge men's hegemony in the Academy. The early leaders reasoned that validity for their work and authority for themselves would come with four changes in circumstances: (1) when journals and university presses published their articles and monographs; (2) when a significant number of them acquired tenured professorships; (3) when traditional graduate and undergraduate curricula included women's history and their feminist perspective; (4) when national professional organizations accepted feminist historians as valued colleagues and elected them as their officers. This constituted the pattern of acceptance won in North America. Although there would be variations, it also proved to be the basic pattern in other parts of the world, as each culture's feminists created their women's history narratives and asserted their right to participate and excel within a particular nation's academic institutions.[36]

## Publications

As early as the start of the 1970s, committed to their feminist agenda and unique multidisciplinary approach, these activists founded journals that published their discoveries, among which the North American *Feminist Studies* (1972), *Signs: Journal of Women in Culture and Society* (1975), and *Frontiers* (1975) were but the first, and were quickly followed by similar initiatives by feminists outside of Britain and North America, such as the Australian *Women's Studies International Forum* (1978) and the French *Pénélope* (1979). Originally, historians made up a significant percentage of the contributors to these publications. As a result, it was not until 1989 that a separate journal devoted exclusively to history was started. *The Journal of Women's History* was founded, as the editors explained, not only because the traditional journals remained reluctant to include women's history (90 percent of the articles concerned men's history) but also because the existing feminist journals simply could not 'accommodate the geometric increase in research and writing in women's history.'[37] Similarly, when the national and regional historians' conferences proved reluctant to accept their panels the younger members of the North American Berkshire Conference of Women Historians (sponsor of an annual networking and social meeting for women in the profession mirroring those of male historians in the American Historical Association) importuned the elder professors to hold the first Berkshire Conference on the History of Women in 1973. Over the decades, participation increased exponentially with the growth of the field. Over two thousand attended the 14th Conference in 2008, including scholars from universities all over the world.

Women's historians had much less difficulty gaining acceptance of their monographs. In the course of the 1980s feminist scholarship in North American and Western European women's history began to appear on the lists of Anglo-American publishers as activists turned their articles into chapters and their dissertations into books. Trade and university presses advertised their new titles in women's history widely and prominently displayed them at historical conventions.

They commissioned survey histories, article collections, dictionaries of individuals and institutions, handbooks, reference guides, and bibliographies of bibliographies. In 1990 titles in women's history made up 10 percent of HarperCollins' total sales. A particularly dependable category, these studies of women's lives brought revenues of over US$10 million a year.[38]

## Professorships and curriculum innovation

When professional historians' organizations in the United States like the American Historical Association (AHA) and the Organization of American Historians (OAH) proved relatively impervious to the new studies of women's past and to its practitioners, feminists formed advocacy groups, and petitioned and pressured their male colleagues. The women's caucus of the AHA, the Coordinating Committee on Women in the Historical Profession (CCWHP), formed at the December meeting in 1969, succeeded in their efforts with the appointment of the Rose Committee whose report the following year began the transformation of history departments in the United States. The study documented women's disadvantaged access to and status within 30 representative women's colleges, and co-educational colleges and universities: fewer admitted to graduate school, fewer gaining PhDs; fewer hired for tenure track positions; fewer advancing beyond the lower ranks of the faculty. Perhaps most dramatic was the revelation that the number of women historians in the Academy had declined in number since the 1950s. In 1965 only 12 percent of professional historians in the United States were female – compared with 20 percent in 1950 – and they were clustered in the lowest ranks at the least prestigious institutions.[39]

Subsequent reports by a new, permanent AHA Committee on Women Historians (CWH) led to the establishment of guidelines for female to male ratios at every stage of the academic process. The CWH also sponsored

two key publications that both appeared in 1975. A *Directory of Women Historians* with over 1,000 short biographical entries answered university department chairs' plaints of wishing to hire women, but unable 'to find any that were qualified.' The now famous *Survival Manual for Women (and Other) Historians* (1975) edited by two historians of the United States, Suzanne Lebsock and Eleanor F. Straub, demystified many aspects of male academic culture and gave practical advice on how to gain acceptance for a conference panel, how to frame a journal submission or a grant request, and how to write a book proposal, all key aspects of a scholar's means to completion of research, publication, and thus advancement in the academic hierarchy.[40] After almost 20 years of activism, CWH reports to the AHA membership showed progress in hiring but continued difficulty in advancing to higher levels. The numbers show the persistence of old patterns. In 1985–86 the number of women full professors in history departments totaled only 33 out of 390 positions in the same three categories of institutions polled. The highest percentage of women, 25.6 percent, occurred at the single-sex women's colleges, but this represented a continuing drop in numbers since 1968–69 as the previous generation of women faculty retired. The lowest occurred at the large co-educational research universities, 5.1 percent, despite the fact that 12.1 percent of their tenured history faculty was female.[41]

Most of these women hires represented acceptance by North American college and university history departments that they must include courses on women and thus needed specialists in this new field. Initially in many parts of the United States and Canada pressure for such programs grew out of feminist activism, often led by graduate students and junior faculty. Under the rubric of 'women's studies' they taught each other in a newly founded women's bookstore, someone's living room, a trailer parked on the campus at Sonoma State College in northern California. Jill Ker Conway and Natalie Zemon Davis taught the first women's history at the University of

Toronto in 1971 at the same time they agitated for day care facilities. Their bibliography of European women's history circulated as purple mimeographed pages before the days of e-mail attachments and websites.[42] The growth and institutionalization of women's studies programs meant the growth and institutionalization of women's history, which, along with women's literature, formed a core component of this emerging field. By 1987 the United States could boast of almost 500 such interdisciplinary programs at the full range of colleges and universities, both public and private. In addition 57 multi-disciplinary research institutions devoted to women's issues (including women's history) had been created, often funded by outside sources. For example, the Ford Foundation helped establish Centers for Research on Women at the University of Washington-Seattle, Duke, the University of North Carolina-Chapel Hill, Spelman College, Memphis State University, and Stanford.[43]

## Professional organizations

With publication and tenure-track appointments, feminist women historians in the United States developed networks, alliances, and strategies that gained them important appointed and elected posts within the professional historian's organizations. Anne Firor Scott, a feminist scholar of southern women's history won the OAH presidency in 1984, Natalie Zemon Davis, the AHA leadership in 1987. If official commitment seemed to weaken, the CCWHP, its title later simplified to the Coordinating Council for Women in History (CCWH), continued to lobby within the AHA and OAH for candidates favorable to women's issues, rules of inclusion for conference panels, the Joan Kelly Prize in feminist history, and institutes on the teaching of women's history, to name only a few of its projects. It was the CCWH that established the affiliation with the International Federation for Research in Women's History (founded in 1987 by the Norwegian feminist historian Ida Blom, Ruth

Roach Pierson of Canada, and Karen Offen of the United States), thus connecting North American and British feminist scholars with those in other parts of the world.[44]

## REWRITING HISTORIES IN NORTH AMERICA AND WESTERN EUROPE

### Successes

By the end of the twentieth century English and other European language women's and feminist historians could point to successes and continuing challenges. Under the rubric of 'women's and gender history' (originally used synonymously in English) the study of the other half of humanity had become a legitimate academic field to which even the most traditional men's historians paid lip service. General histories of European women and collections of articles by North American and British feminist historians were translated into Italian, Spanish, and German. Inspired by these works and also by women's studies' authors, such as the anthropologist, M.Z. Rosaldo of the United States, women historians in these countries, as well as the Netherlands, Belgium, and Russia, also wrote their own monographs and their own national narratives, running to four, to six volumes. They organized their own conferences and *colloques* and found publishers for their presentations. In 1986 the Dutch National Network of Feminist Historians (Landelijk Overleg Vrouwengeschiedenis) sponsored an international meeting on women's history that had over 800 participants and offered over 100 lectures and workshops.[45] Optimistic feminist scholars like Nancy Partner could argue that not only had women been restored to history, but with the end of the 'one-sex model' men's full humanity had been restored as well.[46]

Women's historians presented alternative analyses of, for example, the most male fields of Western historiography, both the political narrative of elite white men's lives and the political and intellectual theories that had justified their power and authority. The Queens, empresses, political hostesses, and leaders of temperance societies, to name only a few categories of women's roles now documented and analyzed, found their way into new general histories, even into school history textbooks and school leaving examinations. Initially, in addition to these 'women worthies,' feminist scholars turned from the narrative to the philosophical canon and described what privileged men had written about women in their political and philosophical texts. The feminist perspective of the North American and British political scientists Mary Lyndon Shanley and Carole Pateman provided the inclusive analysis of theory and lived history that women scholars hoped would replace the traditional narratives and their underlying exclusionary premises. They explained that 'Western political thought rests on a conception of the "political" that is constructed through the exclusion of women and all that is represented by femininity and women's bodies.' Perceptions of sexual difference and men's power over women then became not misogynist aberations but fundamental to understandings of 'the relation between nature, the sexes, reason and politics; ... the domestic, the familial ... and the economy and the state.'[47]

The French feminist historian Michelle Perrot, in her 1984 essay, 'Les femmes, le pouvoir, l'histoire' [Women, the power, the history], had already contributed to this analysis. She critiqued myths, especially in nineteenth-century accounts of French politics, about women's power. Historians like Jules Michelet, she discovered, glorified the female and favored an ideal 'equilibrium' between the feminine and the masculine. However, he identified the female with 'nature' and violence, seeing progress only when the 'male' held sway. Perrot explained that the sociologist, Auguste Comte assumed that men must always hold the power as women never advanced beyond a 'sort of infant state,' and thus, according to his logic, must be confined to the domestic realm of family and household. Such issues, feminist historians argued, were central to any political history in any age and any culture. As Karen Offen, the North American historian of European women, explained, 'the sexual balance of power at the decision-making level lies at the heart of the history of civil societies.'[48]

With these premises revealed, the invented legal exclusions of women in Western history, such as the Salic Law of early modern France, the resubordination of women in Protestantism and in seventeenth century political theory, the false universals of the eighteenth-century revolutions in North America and Western Europe that promised equality to 'all men,' the liberal individualism of the nineteenth century, the primacy of class as defined by male experience in Marxism and the socialist-inspired parties and revolutions of the twentieth century, all depended on the sexed images and single sex reality of the politically active male citizen.[49] In 1998 the English Liverhulme Trust gave its financial support to a three-year British project to enrich and transform the intellectual history of the Enlightenment. The 35 articles of *Women, Gender and Enlightenment* (2005) covered women's activities, intellectual contributions, and a feminist critique of British and French men's political theories during the period.[50]

Other feminist scholars had more ambitious goals. Tjitske Akkerman and Siep Stuurman from the Netherlands have insisted on the equal intellectual centrality of 'feminism,' as it has never been solely concerned with 'women' but with the basic questions of political theory: equality, liberty, and power.[51] More recently, feminist Western intellectual historians analyzed women's reconceptualizations of citizenship and the state, insisting that the writings of Christine de Pizan, Margaret Cavendish, Marie de Gournay, Rosa Luxemburg, Margaret Fuller, and Jane Addams, to name but a few of the best-known examples, be considered not as 'women's texts,' but as contributions equal to those of men and be added to the canon of Western political theory.[52]

These Western feminists did not limit themselves to creating inclusive political narratives and revising documentary canons of political philosophies. Social history and particularly the study of labor also seemed a natural means to transform the mainstream narrative of human history. Women's labor had been one of the earliest topics studied, and male historians, even before these feminist initiatives, had acknowledged women wage-earners, and women's exclusion from the labor movement. Training in social history, combined with the political radicalism and feminism of the late 1960s in Britain and the United States, led a number of feminists such as Sheila Rowbotham, Renate Bridenthal, Linda Gordon, and Nancy Hartsock to turn to Marx's theories of history as the basis for a new synthesis, a method for analyzing both women's and men's lives. As a theoretical model of oppression and exploitation, Marxism seemed promising for a number of reasons. For example, Frederick Engels believed that he had found the origins of patriarchy and the subordination of women in the advent of private property. The English periodical, *History Workshop*, founded in the late 1970s, described itself as a 'Journal of Socialism and Feminism.' When Temma Kaplan, the United States historian of twentieth-century Spain, taught the first women's history course at UCLA (University of California at Los Angeles), she entitled it 'Women and Capitalism.'

Previous women's historians had made connections between women's denigrated status and the emergence of commercial and industrial capitalism. Alice Clark had argued that Europe's medieval urban women had fared better than their early modern rural counterparts.[53] Mary Beard hypothesized that the economic changes of the nineteenth century accounted for the oppression of women as a group rather than a class. Contemporary feminist economists, and legal theorists in the United States, such as Catherine MacKinnon, as well as historians, built on these early authorities and described how capitalism and industrialization had changed families, both urban and rural, from the relative strength of producers to the relative weakness of consumers. They credited Marxism

with a number of theoretical concepts that became commonplace in women's history, in particular, the 'fundamental notion of differences between appearance and reality ... a sense of dialectics and contradiction,' and the belief that 'all historical situations [are] driven by conflict.'[54]

In addition, Marxism, as it had for male workers, made women agents, not just victims. Like the men of E.P. Thompson and Eric Hobsbawm's English working class, they came to 'awareness,' and acted out of their own experiences, not just in reaction to economic forces and structures. But this women workers' 'awareness,' feminist historians discovered, led to more than just consciousness of class. According to the first premise of Marxist analysis, in nineteenth-century industrial societies men's class identification came through their employment, through their relationship to capital. The 'mode of production' determined their role and place in society. However, this was not the case with women. Their sense of function and class came through their relationship to the men of their families rather than through their interactions with the industrial economy. For men, the family acted as a possible unit for resistance; for women, it often was the site of oppression.

Also European and North American urban women's and men's circumstances as waged workers in the nineteenth century were rarely the same. Patterns of job segregation, what the British feminist theorist Juliet Mitchell identified as the sexual division of labor, limited women to certain kinds of tasks, usually the least skilled, lowest paid, and most vulnerable to fluctuations in the economy.[55] In fact, subsequent research, particularly on women's work in England, demonstrated that there had never been the 'golden age' of women's work enshrined in Alice Clark's 1919 monograph. Judith M. Bennett's study of medieval and early English brewsters showed that new products and new markets brought change to women's lives but not transformation. Customs and gendered attitudes prevailed over economic forces. The truisms of women's labor kept them as effectively disadvantaged in terms of skilled, stable, and well-paid labor in one era as in another.[56]

Despite these difficulties, Marxist feminists in Britain and the United States made an important theoretical addition to women's history. Their consideration of the effects of women's gender and sexuality broadened the usual analysis to include not only 'modes of production,' but also what they came to call 'modes of reproduction,' a concept implicit in Marx's writings but never emphasized. Initially, as defined by Mitchell and used by Joan Kelly in her essay on 'The doubled vision of feminist theory,' 'reproduction' meant the control of women's bodies. Subsequent Marxist feminists used the word to signify both women's biological reproductive function and their cultural and social role as nurturers and educators – literally the reproducers – of the next generation of workers. Kelly believed that this female function perpetuated not only capitalism, but also patriarchy. She explained that 'in the poor family [women's waged labor] sustains the working population ...' and 'at the same time, this unwaged and unacknowledged work of women in the home, keeps women dependent on men and bound to a subordinate, servicing role.'[57]

A Marxist perspective had different effects on women's and feminist history in countries where socialist governments controlled university and thus scholarly production such as in Hungary. There 'feminism' was identified exclusively with the women of the bourgeoisie. Thus, women's history, like feminism, took on a negative caste and was seen as divisive and unproductive. Only from the late 1980s with the political transition to multiparty states could feminist scholars in Central and Eastern Europe return to study of women other than those honored as victims of the capitalist system or as activists in the socialist cause.[58] Such socialist attitudes colored historical production in other countries as well. In France, adding what was identified as 'histoire au féminin,' enriched socialist historians' existing studies of labor, the revolutions of 1789, 1848, and 1870, and World War I, but

always women were seen in relation to men, not as independent actors with a separate, particular history. A French woman scholar's earlier effort to include analyses of the family in her women's history course was rejected as adding a 'bourgeois,' and thus unnecessary, model. In fact, a *colloque* of the early 1980s brought together prominent women academics, such as Michelle Perrot, Mona Ozouf, Arlette Farge, and Geneviève Fraisse, to consider the question, 'Is a history of women possible?' In India studies of women's past were affected by Marxism in more subtle ways; for example, leading historians insisted on universal acceptance of Engel's presumption that subordination began with the creation of private property.[59]

## Victory?

These disagreements proved characteristic of the evolution of the field no matter the cultural or political context. Ultimately, each group of academic women came to feminism and women's history by its own particular route, influenced by their own intellectual propensities: for example, via sociology in France and Nigeria, and women's studies in Brazil and India. However, even where women's history had been accepted as a legitimate field in and of itself, this acceptance did not lead to the changes feminist historians had hoped for. Into the first decade of the twenty-first century, mainstream histories remained surprisingly immune to transformation. No inclusive history of women *and* men had evolved. Many political historians in North America and Western Europe accepted the concept of women's oppression in theory and added the bare facts of suffrage movements and modern feminist activism to their national histories. Social historians of Europe saw the ways in which the new research advanced, for example, demographic studies of the early modern family and comparative analyses of twentieth-century social welfare policies. But 'putting women back, as if they somehow slipped out,' remained a partial gesture at best. These accommodations did not, in fact, fit all women back in, and the underlying premises of traditional political, economic, religious, and social history negated a true synthesis. As with the Marxist analyses, female lives had to be fitted to structures, categories, and periodizations created to define and represent men's experiences not women's. This kind of 'integration,' the United States philosopher Elizabeth Minnich has explained, 'is inadequate if it means only including traditionally excluded groups in a dominant system of thinking.' All must accept that: 'You don't simply add the idea that the world is round to the idea that the world is flat. You go back and rethink the whole enterprise.' At worst, traditional men's historians denied the need for any change at all.[60]

Resistance to such suggestions could be startling. Some medievalists continued to question the twelfth-century learned abbess, Heloïse's authorship of her letters to her former mentor and lover Abelard. The North American historian Louise Tilly described the response of 'a crusty old historian of the [French] Revolution' after hearing Joan W. Scott's speech on Olympe de Gouges (author of the Declaration of the Rights of Woman and victim of the Terror). He asked 'in his own eastern twang, "Now that I know that women were participants in the Revolution, *what difference does it make*?"' As described by the Brazilian scholar, Maria Beatriz Nizza da Silva, these men saw this 'as a feminist problem or as a simple curiosity and not worth much attention.'[61]

## THE MANY FEMINISMS AND MANY WOMEN'S HISTORIES OF THE 1980S AND BEYOND

In the United States scholars of feminism and of the evolution of the new field of women's history had not imagined the complexity of their task. They expected recalcitrance on the part of traditional historians, but not the varied perspectives their call for change elicited in their own and other cultures in the 1980s,

from women as well as men. Many who had participated in and shaped the early collaboration between activism and the creation of new knowledge now write nostalgically of the apparent unity of the 1970s. Some were surprised and saddened by the new divisions among North American women's historians. Colleagues echoed the contemporaneous criticisms by French women historians, calling the new narratives, 'essentialist.' This 'essentialism' could mean the portrayal of a seemingly undifferentiated universal woman devoid of race, class, and sexual orientation. Or, it could mean new manifestations of the racism, classism and sexism that had characterized the old men's history. Unintentionally, the research of the new history had produced its own false universal. Just as traditional history had purported to be the story of all 'men,' now the stories of white, Christian, privileged, heterosexual females appeared to be presented as the history of all females.[62]

### The case of the United States

Starting in the 1980s, black feminist scholars formulated the first full-scale theoretical challenges to the history of women in the United States as constructed by Euro-American women activist scholars. Patricia Hill Collins, the African-American feminist theorist and historian, described the way in which she and other black intellectuals like bell hooks came to their own particular consciousness of their female disadvantage, the 'intersection,' as she described it, 'of my unique biography with the larger meaning of my historical times.'[63]

In the 1970s, feminist scholars like Gerda Lerner, though eager to explain and prove from their writings that they did not ignore differences of race, found that their 'Women's history' as usually understood and much publicized was considered to be that of white, privileged women. There could be no identification with this white feminist history of subordination and resistance, as 'oppression' did not have the same meaning for all women. Also, the new histories of the black experience in the Americas told only of black men. As feminist historians and cultural critics Hazel V. Carby in England and Darlene Clark Hine in the United States argued, in these new narratives black women made appearances as the stereotypical 'other': the sexualized 'Jezebel' of white males' fantasies, the foil to equally fanciful images of 'pure' white females; smiling mammies on boxes of pancake mix; domestic servants, as nameless as their enslaved predecessors. Black women's history, therefore, suffered its own form of invisibility, present but imagined and undifferentiated.[64]

In addition, these black historians pointed out that white women in the United States, even contemporary white, feminist scholars, had exhibited their own kind of oppressive behavior towards each other and towards women of other races. Thus, multiple prejudices plagued these minority women as black, and as female, even in African-American universities. Most of the first generation of scholars dealt not only with segregation but also with the triple demands of earning a living, raising children, and completing a graduate degree. Wanda A. Hendricks, a historian of early twentieth-century black women activists, described how even affirmative action could be used to devalue and denigrate. As a student, she encountered unspoken subordination and alienation in the predominantly white educational institutions she attended. As a new faculty member, she found herself the object of resentment, accused of undeserved privilege; her scholarship dismissed as an illegitimate area of historical inquiry.[65]

The poet and activist Audre Lorde warned other black women, 'it is axiomatic that if we do not define ourselves for ourselves, we will be defined by others – for their use and to our detriment.'[66] Self-definition meant the discovery of specific circumstances of subordination and victimization in the past that had continued into the present, including fixed forms of economic exploitation, the denial of political rights, and negative stereotypical cultural images and attitudes.[67] Acquiring and making knowledge of their forebearers available constituted resistance. To validate their new

perspective, they rejected the language and frameworks familiar to the dominant white groups. This gave these women scholars power and, as Collins described the feeling, a sense of being, independent, self-identified individuals.[68] As white feminist historians had challenged the universality of men's experience, the work of scholars such as Elsa Barkeley Brown, Deborah Gray White, and Evelyn Brooks Higgenbotham demonstrated that the history of white domination in the United States was not the defining narrative of the past, only one of many perspectives.[69] In establishing these new analytical approaches, these black feminist women's historians made choices similar to those of white feminist scholars: they sought to value what women had done, for example black women's 'mothering,' both of their own and others' children. They looked to new kinds of sources, for example, the songs of women Blues singers such as Billie Holliday. They used their own experiences as evidence for their analyses and as a means of evaluating more traditional written sources.[70] In fact, creation of their own history demonstrated the 'knowledge validation process' that all women's historians across their differences of, for example, race, ethnicity, and nationality, have followed. In this way back feminist women historians, as Collins explained, provided insight not only into the relationships among women, but also into the choices and mechanisms by which any subordinate group creates 'knowledge that fosters resistance' to dominant historical narratives and to the political realities of subordination.[71]

These feminist historians and the Chicana writer/activists Cherrie Moraga and Gloria Anzaldúa, editors of *This Bridge Called My Back: Writings by Radical Women of Color* (1981),[72] made the intellectual leap that ameliorated the divisive character of these and subsequent divisions among North American feminist women's historians. They endeavored to define themselves and each other but without being exclusionary in turn. They sought interconnections in the 'systems of oppression.' Like Collins, they accepted that theirs was also a 'partial perspective,' only one angle of vision. As the US feminist historian of science Donna Haraway argued, each group or individual produced 'situated knowledge,' creating a history within the context of a community of beings in particular circumstances.[73]

## Feminist women's history: a world-wide phenomenon

From the 1980s onwards, particular feminist narratives of women's histories proliferated as more self-identified groups of women in English-speaking cultures, Western Europe and Eastern Europe; Latin America; North, East and West Africa; East, West, and South Asia followed the pattern inherent in the process of researching and writing women's and feminist history. Many exhibited the same interrelationship between the crafting of a separate identity and a coming to feminist awareness. Striving for equality in the present meant questioning long-lived patriarchal institutions, and examination of all-too-familiar political, economic, religious, and cultural traditions. Thus, these newly active women's historians throughout the world challenged their culture's traditional narratives, and in their research refused to take women's disadvantaged status as natural or fixed. They sought evidence of resistance and activist forebearers. But in the specificity of their discoveries, they also insisted on the specificities of the analyses they formulated. Often this meant questioning the applicability of the histories and theories provided by feminist English and, and in some regions, French, language scholars who initially dominated the world of feminist scholarship.

For example, in Egypt the resurgence of the women's movement in the 1980s led to new research on the nineteenth-century origins of women's activism and a critique of the Western narrative that had attributed feminism to European influence ignoring its coincidental origins within the Ottoman Empire.[74] Similar presumptions about the Western-style equality guaranteed by the new constitution to Indian women at the time of independence from Britain came into question and led to reassessments by women scholars of India's traditional legal and political histories and to diverse, interdisciplinary studies. Indian feminists sought the origins of patriarchy in the Hindu classics, in different historical periods and produced works on the modern era in categories such as: the family, employment, health, and law.[75] Radha Kumar, the writer and peace activist, wrote *The History of Doing: An Illustrated Account of Movements for Women's Rights and Feminism in India 1800–1990* (1993)[76] for a popular audience and, reflecting the Women's Studies orientation of other Indian feminists, took a broad view of women's activism, including not only those seeking political rights, but also nationalists and environmentalists. Mexican feminist scholars first published broad national histories of women in the late 1980s, a result of their efforts to prove to contemporaries women's agency and significance across race and class. The direct and indirect effects of the United Nations Decade for Women (1975–85) have yet to be assessed, but, in Nigeria, the resulting 1985 Programme of Action's directive to include women in the nationalist and development project spurred government sponsorship of programs in women's studies. This, in turn, led to an appreciation of the need to include women in the newly constituted field of African history and, given the paucity of traditional sources, to establishment of the Women's Research and Documentation Centre at the University of Ibadan. The acceptance of particular methodologies such as the peoples' oral traditions and the integration of feminist perspectives has resulted in analyses of women in all periods of Nigerian history.

Women's Studies in Brazil developed in the 1970s also as part of participation in the Decade meetings, feminist initiatives in government and on university campuses. With the founding of women's studies institutes, Brazilian scholars chronicled the ways in which assumptions from the past had shaped their own experiences. The opening of ecclesiastical archives provided the sources for wide-ranging histories of women of every race and at every level of society. Similar institutes in Argentina and elsewhere in Latin America produced essay collections that explore topics such as labor, sexuality, immigration, and the family, and led to the completion of full-scale narrative histories.[77] The first extended history of Korean women was a group scholarly project, published by the prestigious Ewha Woman's University in Seoul. Japanese women had a three-volume general history by the end of the 1950s (translated into English in 1976), but it was as part of the women's movement of the 1960s and 1970s that women scholars and popular authors turned to writing detailed studies of, for example, early twentieth-century women silk factory workers, and the women who went to Southeast Asia to work as prostitutes before World War II. Local and national women's history associations proliferated in the 1970s, and with their conferences and the publication of document collections and a five-volume survey history gave Japanese women's history a wide audience. Two prizes established in the 1980s further encouraged its legitimation. Women scholars in China applauded their government's decision to host the United Nation's Women's Conference in Beijing in 1995. It spurred formation of local activist groups against, for example, family violence, and encouraged translations of Western scholarship, original research and publications narrating Chinese women's past. Since 2000, Chinese academic journals have devoted entire issues to articles about women. In every instance, as Ludmilla Jordanova, the British feminist scholar, has explained, these acts of telling and writing women's histories constituted 'cultural work,' creating identities, inspiring independence, apportioning blame.[78]

## APPROACHES TO TRANSFORMATION OF TRADITIONAL NARRATIVES IN THE 1980S

Despite this cultural function and recognition of the richness of the many new narratives, into the twenty-first century women's history continued to exist most often as a separate narrative. And the burden of proof, the justifications for inclusion remained with feminist women's historians, with those wishing to rethink the telling of the past not with those who rejected and excluded. The United States feminist historian Kathi Kern echoed the fears of French feminist scholars like Arlette Farge, when she described this as 'persistent ghettoization,' women's histories set aside, never central to revision of European, North American, or for that matter, any narrative of the past.[79] Perhaps anticipating these negative attitudes and practices, North American feminists of the 1960s and 1970s had offered a way to value this separation. The historian of the United States, Barbara Welter, in one of the earliest articles in this new scholarship, 'The cult of true womanhood, 1820–1860' (1966), wrote on the prescriptive literature popular in the nineteenth century that glorified the domestic image of the dutiful wife and mother.[80] Welter suggested that this widely disseminated ideology could constrain privileged white women even more effectively than restrictive legal, political, and economic practices and institutions. The idea of women's relegation to the 'private' world of the household and men's access to the 'public' arena of power found easy acceptance as an analytical distinction even in traditional histories for it had echoes in the avowed ideals of contemporary Western culture, and the perceived realities of cultures in Asia and other parts of the world.

### 'Separate spheres'

At first seen as a negative, with more study of North American nineteenth-century women's letters and diaries this apparent separation of women from the 'public sphere' came to be lauded as a positive aspect of their lives. Carroll Smith-Rosenberg described how her research into the correspondence between two close women friends 'radically transformed my approach to women's history.' In the resulting article, 'The female world of love and ritual: relations between women in nineteenth-century America' (1975),[81] she turned to women's own writings, discarded images from men's views of women, and described instead the comforts and strengths they derived from their intimate friendships. The study of women's same-sex relationships, followed naturally: Lillian Faderman's *Surpassing the Love of Men: Romantic Friendship and Love Between Women from the Renaissance to the Present* (1981).[82] Other historians believed that in these separate spaces all women could gain autonomy; that the creation of women's 'private sphere' was an essential nascent mechanism for the beginnings of the women's movement. For example, Estelle Freedman argued that United States women gained their political rights as a direct result of what she called 'female institution building.'[83]

English-language feminist historians and scholars in disciplines like sociology, anthropology, and political science used these distinctions and applied these ideas way beyond that envisioned by their first exponents. Although Smith-Rosenberg was clear in her article that she was writing about only a limited group of women, subsequent readers extrapolated from her sample and imagined a universal female experience. These glorifications of 'women's culture' and evocations of what came to be interpreted as an 'essential' image of 'femininity' and of a 'female' way of life drew criticisms because they glossed over the differences between women and women's experiences. Black women scholars in the United States responded with studies of their own female culture. The novelist and activist Alice Walker coined the term 'womanist' to avoid using the term 'feminist' associated with a movement that did not speak to black women's experiences or goals. White women historians like Nancy Hewitt agreed that 'No such universal sisterhood existed,' and rejected the implications

of the different spaces reserved to women and men. She saw the nineteenth-century idea of 'separate spheres' as yet another mechanism by which women of the socially dominant group imposed their definitions of the family and the household on lower-class women as it had been intended to impose constraints on privileged white women.[84]

Other critics of this approach found it too narrow and dependent on an imagined correlation between rhetoric and reality. This became particularly obvious with the writing of women's history in cultures other than North America and Britain. The imperial Ottoman harem, though in theory a restricted isolated 'separate sphere' for women, did not mean autonomy for all those who lived within its walls, nor isolation and lack of authority in the 'public sphere' of politics. Leslie P. Pierce's research showed that in the nineteenth century hierarchies among the women shifted and changed as favorites vied with each other for influence with the sultan; their male relatives were given court appointments and thus tied key aspects of the bureaucracy to women's manipulations; they controlled money and acted in the law courts through intermediaries when necessary.[85] These histories thus proved the concepts to be unstable spatially and sexually. As the British feminist historian Lenore Davidoff and the United States political scientist Joan Landes argued, the mixing of the Victorian model of 'separate spheres' and of the 'public/private' division often described in human societies, is more symbolic than actual, intentionally gendered constructions. It could be argued, in fact, that Western women's historians had enshrined these differences by their studies, making them seem natural. The United States feminist scholar Linda K. Kerber, in her article 'Separate spheres, female worlds, woman's place: the rhetoric of women's history' (1988), identified these phrases as simplistic rhetorical opposites; she saw historians' task as one of 'demystification.' She called the process, 'deconstruction,' the term now associated with a wide range of historical analyses. Such study of language she believed, left 'power no place to hide.'[86]

## 'Deconstruction' and gender

As early as the 1970s, a number of feminist women's historians in the United States, schooled in the social and cultural history of early modern Europe, influenced by the work of French feminists, and modern literary criticism, had already turned to 'deconstruction' of the language of gender, believing that this approach would provide historians with the inclusive analyses of all human behavior that had so far proved elusive. Often grouped together under the rubric of 'cultural history,' feminists drew on the writings of French post World War II theorists such as the psychoanalyst Jacques Lacan, the philosopher Jacques Derrida, and the sociologist Michel Foucault. Feminist historians were drawn to the emphasis on texts, to the highlighting of the uses made of the binary opposites created by a culture and reflected in its institutions, writings, and images. They could easily see parallels in history of the role and power of language to create dominant–subordinate relationships. In theory, a language system offered many possible meanings, while the practice of that language made definitions specific within a specific social system.

This practice, or 'discourse,' as it came to be identified in subsequent writings in women's and feminist history, the North American medievalist and theorist Gabrielle M. Spiegel, described as the determining force in constructing a society. Feminist anthropologists and historians in the United States and France would add its role in creating not only 'subjectivity' but sexual identity through definitions of 'gender,' of what was 'feminine' and 'masculine.' Feminist readers of the early twentieth-century philosophers, Antonio Gramsci of Italy, Mikhail Bakhtin of the Soviet Union, the French philosopher and historian of the 1970s and 1980s, Michel de Certeau, and the United States anthropologist Clifford Geertz could easily apply their various approaches to both the delivery and the reception of language, making even the most subjective and subordinate members of a society both active and passive participants in its meanings and force. Thus, women as well as men, contributed to the ways concepts of femininity and masculinity were symbolically represented, influenced their lives, and the formulation of subsequent historical descriptions of their thoughts and experiences.[87]

Enunciated initially by Natalie Zemon Davis and Joan Kelly, this linguistic approach, study of the concept of 'gender,' was advanced as a category of historical analysis as essential as religion, race, ethnicity, and class. Zemon Davis explained, 'Our goal is to understand the significance of the *sexes*, of gender groups in the historical past.' The social relations of the sexes,' as Kelly called it in her essay of that name, included discovery of each era's definition of 'feminine' and 'masculine,' the rationale for different roles, the designation of opportunities, access to and use of wealth, and all other kinds of power. Some feminist historians in the United States went so far as to imagine that this was the way to end the 'ghettoization' of women's history, and the traditional, apparent gender neutrality of the past. An analysis of the effects of gender would take all historians away from the histories of 'man' as the universal. Instead men must be described as men, women as women.[88]

Joan W. Scott, known then as a feminist historian of early modern European labor, gave the first systematic explanation of this new synthesis of the history of both sexes. In her widely quoted and reprinted essay, 'Gender: a useful category of historical analysis'(1986), she described gender as 'a constitutive element of social relationships based on perceived differences between the sexes.' This knowledge then operated in a culture to 'establish meanings for bodily difference.' It was, she continued, society's 'primary way of signifying relationships of power.' As Nancy Partner has explained, 'only the most temperate of feminist criticism was necessary to recognize that biological femaleness did not automatically or "naturally" entail femininity when the "Feminine" turned out to be every society's catchall category for transparent male fears, biological fantasies, and crude excuses for systematic domination.'[89]

Zemon Davis advocated that 'Study of the sexes should help promote a rethinking of some of the central issues faced by historians – power, social structure, property, symbols, and periodization.' It had the hoped-for effect. As Scott has noted, analyses of gender and the methods of 'deconstruction' drew historians in North America and Europe, whether feminist or not, into areas that had been resistant to women's historians, for example, the gendered language of nation building and of European colonial empires in the nineteenth century.[90] Study of language has brought the rewriting of history so important to women's and feminist historians. For example, the eighteenth-century North American and French Revolutions, staples of traditional white men's history, now include gender analyses of: revolutionary rhetoric; government policies towards women; public, allegorical representations of the female and the male; definitions of citizenship and of the liberties enjoyed by different categories of women and men; and at the end of the conflicts with reestablishment of peace and order based on male hegemony.

However, this conceptual shift to study of the historical construction of gender difference had a negative consequence for women's history and its ties to feminist activism. Realization of the malleability, incompleteness, and instability of language in relation to women and men, their roles and their sexuality, the contradictions and privileges inherent in such categories, shifted the emphasis to a history of those constructions, not of the groups so described. At its most rigorous, deconstruction focused not on the 'text' itself, but on how the text worked to produce plural and variable effects and meanings.[91] Thus, even the writings of the historian became created, subjective 'texts' that could not be considered certain or fixed languages

with which to describe and represent the past. Critics interpreted this approach to mean that the 'discourse' and representation had replaced lived women's experience and their agency, leaving no place for a coherent study of women's or feminist activism.[92]

Nancy Fraser, the United States feminist theorist, explained the problem from the perspective of women's history: it was as if there were no reality to women's experience, only language describing it. Analyses had gone from the essentialism of 'reifying women's social identities under stereotypes of femininity' to 'dissolving them into sheer nullity and oblivion.' French feminist theorists, Monique Wittig, for example, issuing a challenge on behalf of lesbians, saw even the concept, 'woman' as ideologically constructed to enforce heterosexuality, a social creation 'intermediate between male and eunuch, which is described as feminine,' and imposed on women by men as a means of oppression. Feminist literary theory, as the North American scholar Judith Butler argued in *Gender Trouble: Feminism and the Subversion of Identity* (1989),[93] and by implication its historical equivalent, had shown its own exclusionary homophobia by limiting 'gender' only to the concepts of 'feminine' and 'masculine,' and silencing the full range of alternative meanings.

In the 1980s in Europe and North America, lesbian women had, like women of racial and ethnic minorities, protested their inclusion under the white, heterosexual rubric of 'woman' and now used this theoretical language to describe the historical formation of fixed sexual identities. More recently, the historian of science, Anne Fausto-Sterling, demonstrated the imaginative quality of even the physical reality of 'sex.' This, she discovered, could be constructed as well. The anatomical sexual possibilities of an infant's body, the presence, for example of a penis *and* ovaries, gave a surgeon the power to reconstruct a person as a one-sexed body. As the Norwegian feminist theorist Toril Moi notes about sexual and gender distinctions, 'the meaning of a word is its use,' the relationship between the body and sexuality contingent on circumstance and choice.[94]

Feminist theorists in the United States from political science and philosophy, as well as history, such as Linda Alcoff, Nancy Fraser, and Kathleen Canning, have endeavored to find a way to resolve this ultimate paradox for women's history and women's studies in general: 'What can we demand in the name of women if "women" do not exist and demands in their name simply reinforce the myth that they do?' The answers echo the theories of Donna Haraway's concept of 'situated knowledge.' Alcoff called it 'historicized subjectivity,' meaning that a woman had a real historical identity but that it would be defined in a context that was always shifting. That context as first identified by black feminist theorists, and elaborated upon by subsequent critics of 1970s Western white, heterosexual feminism, had many complex characteristics, not just gender. The identification that resulted was multiple, 'intersectional.' In history as in the present, a particular woman experienced sexism, racism, and any number of practices in her culture which offered possibilities and limitations; having discovered, interpreted, and used their meanings, she became an agent of her own life.[95]

## THE PRESENT AND FUTURE OF MULTIPLE FEMINIST WOMEN'S HISTORIES

Despite the preference among academics in English-language countries and in Western Europe for 'gender history,' women's historians have discovered that the boundaries between this approach and their sex-specific history are easily dissolved, and even ignored. Gender history still often means study from the perspective of women. Even so, women's history has not been integrated throughout the historical narratives commonly constructed whether by women or men. As Judith M. Bennett has explained the phenomenon in the story of women's past, a 'patriarchal equilibrium' reasserted itself.

History, as for other areas of modern culture, seems to have a 'glass ceiling.' A certain amount of women's history can be taken in without disturbing the traditional categories and paths of analysis. Few contemplate the history of women becoming the base narrative, as was true for so many centuries, of men's history. In addition, much of women's histories' feminist energy has been absorbed by women's studies which with its activist/presentist agenda has little time for discussion of context and research into the past. Even its studies of causes rarely consider events before the nineteenth century.[96]

So, women's history thrives, but as a separate field. In Eastern Europe, having rejected the taint of 'bourgeois' Western feminism, scholars have continued to piece together women's past. An international group of historians under the editorship of Francisca de Haan, Krassimira Daskalova and Anna Loutfi recently completed *A Biographical Dictionary of Women's Movements and Feminisms: Central, Eastern and South Eastern Europe, 19th and 20th Centuries* (2006) with hundreds of entries chronicling previously forgotten women's activities.[97] East, South, and West Asian feminist women's historians have critiqued what they see as the cultural imperialism of Euro-American feminists and their definitions of 'feminism,' the way in which global inequalities have affected cross-national analyses. They have rejected the domination of English- and French-language scholars. To counter what they see as white historians' universalizing practices and antagonism to men, they have developed their own theoretical frameworks and analytical perspectives.[98] These better explain the tensions of their cultures; for example on such topics as *sati*, the wearing of head scarves, and footbinding. Africanists dismiss the wholesale application of analytical frameworks from the colonizers' academies; in particular, insistence on a hierarchy of gendered roles and rigid definitions of masculinity and femininity. Japanese women's historians have created an English supplement to their women's history journal so as to disseminate their research more widely, and thus claim their own interpretive authority.

Ironically, women's differentiated initiatives, though originally divisive, have led to the increased sophistication and thus authority of the field. Women's historians in many cultures write of new self-awareness about their research and their writing. As the North American feminist Elsa Barkley Brown explained: 'History is also everybody talking at once, multiple rhythms being played simultaneously.'[99] The totality of their work has highlighted the interdependence of women across their differences and offered opportunities for comparisons. Websites, list servs, journals, pamphlet series, and collections of articles in many languages by scholars from many countries have made possible topical and comparative studies of: the intersections of religion and politics; women's claims to full citizenship; social activism and feminism; control of women's sexuality and reproductive rights; women's labor in industry, as domestic workers, as prostitutes; and diasporas, especially of African women to all parts of the Atlantic and Mediterranean world. In the early 1990s the Norwegian feminist historian Ida Blom supervised the first scholarly world history of women.

Audre Lourde, the poet and feminist activist, quick to point out the flaws in North American women's history and its white feminism, believed that it was not the differences that brought conflict and fragmentation. 'It is rather,' she continued, 'our refusal to recognize those differences, and to examine the distortion which result from our misnaming them and their effects upon human behavior and expectation.' The Indian feminist Chandra Talpade Mohanty, once highly critical of any efforts to record a 'women's history,' also saw the positive in this new rejection of all universals when writing of women's lives. She described instead the 'incorporation' of differences within and across cultures. In *Feminism Without Borders: Decolonizing Theory, Practicing Solidarity* (2003) she encouraged feminist historians to indulge in the richness of comparison and to seek similarities and continuities as well as differences and change.[100] Perhaps the renewed popularity of biography both of women 'worthies,' and of those known only in their own small world, such as Dan Di, famous for her opposition to the 1930s annexation of Chinese Manchuria by the Japanese, and Laurel Thatcher Ulrich's early New England midwife indicate the willingness of feminist historians to embrace the ultimate difference, the reconstruction of an individual woman's life in all the confusion and complexity of her separate context.

Documenting women who led independent lives or who openly opposed male authority remains subversive both of men's authority in the present and of its past history. Similarly, feminist and women's history continues to force reassessment of what was assumed to be the familiar whether of political concepts such as 'democracy' and 'fascism,' of social identities such as 'the worker' and 'the witch,' or traditional narratives such as the evolution of dynastic states, and the founding of the world's major religions. Even the very marginality of women's and feminists' narratives and analytical insights can be a positive, not a negative. Historians know that inclusion often has meant co-option and silencing. Virginia Woolf warned that all scholar feminists must ask themselves on what terms they have joined 'the procession of educated men' and where it will it lead them? In the first decades of the twenty-first century in an intellectual environment that remains by definition exclusionary, and by practice hostile and constraining, perhaps feminist women's history is best served by its separateness. 'Marginality,' bell hooks asserted, can be seen as a choice, a 'site for resistance – as a location of radical openness and possibility.'[101]

## FURTHER READING

See the following collections of key articles, each with a useful introduction:

Karen Offen, Ruth Roach Pierson and Jane Rendall, *Women's History: International Perspectives* (Bloomington, IN: Indiana University Press, 1991).

Judith Butler and Joan W. Scott, eds, *Feminists Theorize the Political* (London: Routledge, 1992).

Robyn R. Warhol and Diane Price Herndl, eds, *Feminisms: an anthology of literary theory and criticism* (New Brunswick, NJ: Rutgers University Press, 1993).

Linda Nicholson, ed., *The Second Wave: A Reader in Feminist Theory* (New York: Routledge, 1997).

Sue Morgan, ed., *The Feminist History Reader* (New York: Routledge, 2006).

For those interested in a more detailed version of the narrative of Women's History/Feminist History, these two surveys are particularly good and have extensive bibliographies:

Mary Spongberg, *Writing Women's History Since the Renaissance* (New York; Palgrave, 2002).

Françoise Thébaud, *Ecrire l'Histoire des Femmes et du Genre* (Lyons: Ens Editions, 2007).

## NOTES AND REFERENCES

1    This simple definition governs the last section, 'Traditions rejected: a history of feminism in Europe,' of Bonnie S. Anderson and Judith P. Zinsser, *A History of Their Own: Women in Europe from Prehistory to the Present* (New York: Oxford University Press, 2000 [1988]), 2 vols. See also Nancy Cott, *Grounding of Modern Feminism* (New Haven, CT: Yale University Press, 1987), 4–5. More recently, Mary Spongberg also allies coming to feminist consciousness with the uses that North American and European women have made of history. See her *Writing Women's History Since the Renaissance* (New York: Palgrave Macmillan, 2002), 8–9.

2    Christine de Pizan, *The Book of the City of Ladies*, trans. Earl Jeffrey Richards (New York: Persea Books, 1982), 187.

3    David Hackett Fischer, *Historian's Fallacies: Toward a Logic of Historical Thought* (New York: Harper & Row, 1970), 217.

4    Nancy Partner, 'Introduction' to the special issue, 'Studying medieval women: sex, gender, feminism,' *Speculum* 68(2) (1993), 305.

5    Judith Bennett, *History Matters: Patriarchy and the Challenge of Feminism* (Philadelphia, PA: University of Pennsylvania Press, 2006), 155.

6    See Virginia Woolf, *A Room of One's Own* (New York: Harcourt Brace and World, 1957 [1929]), 48–50; see also Chapter 5. For a discussion of de Beauvoir's approach, see *New French Feminisms*, ed. Elaine Marks and Isabelle de Curtivron (New York: Schocken Books, 1981), 7. The editors include a selection from the introduction to the English edition of *The Second Sex*, trans. H.M. Parshley (New York: Knopf, 1952), 46–8.

7    E.H. Carr, *What Is History?* (New York: Alfred A. Knopf, 1963), 168. Roland Mousnier, *Social Hierarchies: 1450 to the Present*, trans. Margaret Clarke (London: Croom Helm, 1973), 195.

8    This and the subsequent description comes from Judith P. Zinsser, *History and Feminism: A Glass Half Full* (New York: Palgrave Macmillan, 1993), chapters 2, 3, and 4. At this juncture I would like to acknowledge my debt to Joan W. Scott's commentaries on this field. Citations could be made to one or another of her writings for many sections of this essay. Her best-known early contributions can be found in Joan W. Scott, *Gender and the Politics of History* (New York: Columbia University Press, 1988).

9    Rowbotham, *Hidden from History* (London: Pluto Press, 1973); Rowbotham, *Women, Resistance and Revolution* (New York: Pantheon, 1972).

10   Lucy Maynard Salmon (1853–1927) in the United States and Eileen Power (1894–1940) in England had pioneered such efforts to create a history of everyday women's and men's lives with works such as Salmon's *Domestic Service Since the Colonial Period* (1897) and Power's *Medieval People* (1924).

11   See Johanna Alberti, *Gender and the Historian* (London: Pearson Education, 2002), 28–9.

12   Carroll Smith Rosenberg, 'Hearing women's words: a feminist reconstruction of history,' as reprinted in *Disorderly Conduct: Visions of Gender in Victorian America* (New York: Oxford University Press, 1985), 18; 'The new woman and the new history,' *Feminist Studies*, 3(1 and 2) (Autumn 1975), 89.

13   Fernand Braudel, *On History*, trans. Sarah Matthews (Chicago, IL: University of Chicago Press, 1980), viii. Susan Mosher Stuard, 'Viewpoint: the Annales School and feminist history: opening dialogue with the American stepchild,' *Signs* 7(1) (Autumn 1981), 141, 143.

14   Berenice A. Carroll, ed., *Liberating Women's History: Theoretical and Critical Essays* (Urbana, IL: University of Illinois Press, 1976).

15   Joan Kelly, 'The social relations of the sexes: methodological implications of women's history,' in *Women, History and Theory: The Essays of Joan Kelly* (Chicago, IL: University of Chicago Press, 1984),15.

16   See Brita Rang, 'A "learned wave." Women of letters and science from the Renaissance to the Enlightenment,' in Tjitske Akkerman and Siep Stuurman, eds, *Perspectives on Feminist Political Thought in European History. From the Middle Ages to the Present* (London: Routledge, 2000), 50–66; Suzan van Dijk, 'Early historiography of Dutch and French women's literature,' in S. Van Dijk, Lia van Gememert, and Sheila Ottway, eds, *Writing the History of Women Writing: Toward an International Approach* (Amsterdam: Royal Netherlands Academy of Arts and Sciences, 2001), 81–94.

17   On early European and North American women historians, many of whom wrote about women, see Spongberg; Kathryn Kish Sklar, 'American female historians in context 1770–1930,' *Feminist Studies*, 3(1 and 2) (Autumn 1975); Natalie Zemon Davis, 'Women as historical writers, 1400–1820,' in, Patricia H. Labalme, ed., *Beyond Their Sex: Learned Women of the European Past* (New York: New York University Press, 1980); Bonnie G. Smith, 'The

contribution of women to modern historiography in Great Britain, France, and the United States, 1750–1940,' *American Historical Review*, 89(3) (June 1984). For those mentioned here: Child, *Brief History of the Condition of Wopmen* (New York: C.S. Francis, 1849 ed. on line); Ellet, *Women of the American Revolution* (New York: Baker and Scribner, 1848); Eckenstein, *Women under Monasticism* (New York: Macmillan, 1896); Power, *Medieval English Nunneries* (New York: Biblio and Tannen, rept. 1964); Clark, *Working Life of Women in the Seventeenth Century* (London: Routledge, 1919); Pinchbeck, *Women Workers in the Industrial Revolution* (London: Virago, 1981 reprt.); Spruill, *Women's Life and Work* (Chapel Hill: University of North Carolina Press, 1938); Stenton, *English Woman in History* (New York: Macmillan, 1957); Flexner *Century of Struggle* (New York: Ballantine, 1959).

18  Mary Ritter Beard as quoted in Barbara K. Turoff, *Mary Beard as a Force in History* (Dayton, OH: Wright State University, 1979), 16.

19  Mary Ritter Beard, *America Through Women's Eyes* (New York: Macmillan, 1934 ed.).

20  Mary Ritter Beard, *Woman as Force* (New York: Macmillan, 1946).

21  See Gerda Lerner, *Majority Finds Its Past* (New York: Oxford University Press, 1979), pp. xxi, xxiii; 'Placing Women in History,' in *Majority Finds Its Past*, 159.

22  Natalie Zemon Davis, *Society and Culture in Early Modern* France (Stanford, CA: Stanford University Press, 1975).

23  Natalie Zemon Davis, 'Women in the crafts in sixteenth-century Lyons,' *Feminist Studies*, 8(1) (1982): 47–80.

24  Barbara Welter, *Dimity Convictions: the American Woman in the Nineteenth Century* (Athens: Ohio University Press, 1976).

25  Sarah B. Pomeroy, *Goddesses, Whores, Wives and Slaves: Women in Classical Antiquity* (New York: Schocken Books, 1975).

26  Madeline Davis and Elizabeth Lapovsky Kennedy, 'Oral history and the study of sexuality in the lesbian community: Buffalo, NY, 1940–1960,' *Feminist Studies*, 12(1) (Spring 1986), 7–26; Luise White, *The Comforts of Home: Prostitution in Colonial Nairobi* (Chicago, IL: University of Chicago Press, 1990); Esther Katz and Joan Ringelheim, *Surviving the Holocaust* (Proceedings of 1983 Stern College for Women Conference); Urvashi Butalia, *The Other Side of Silence: Voices from the Partition of India* (Durham, NC: Duke University Press, 2000 [1998]).

27  Gerda Lerner, *Teaching Women's History* (Washington, DC: American Historical Association, 1981).

28  See Lerner, *Teaching Women's History; Majority Finds Its Past*, particularly the introduction, 'Placing women in history,' and 'The majority finds its past.' On the importance of race, class, and ethnicity, see also the three essays on African-American women's history in the same collection. Lerner reformulated her questions somewhat in a 2004 article for the *Journal of Women's History* placing more emphasis on the effects of gender

definitions, 'the tension between reality and image,' but remained committed to the creation of a women's history with its own periodization, and analysis. See Gerda Lerner, 'U.S. women's history: past, present and future,' *Journal of Women's History*, 16(4) (Winter 2004), 25.

29  Anderson and Zinsser, *A History of Their Own*; Merry E.Wiesner-Hanks, *Women and Gender in Early Modern Europe* (Cambridge: Cambridge University Press, 1993). Though published after the1970s both works reflect the innovative thinking of the late 1970s.

30  Ann-Louise Shapiro, ed., *Feminists Revision History* (New Brunswick, NJ: Rutgers University Press, 1994), vii.

31  French critiques were particularly eloquent. Michelle Perrot explained: 'C'est le regard qui fait l'histoire,' and 'Ce regard n'est jamais neutre, il est toujours, au contraire, profondément subjectif. Ceux qui le nient sont dupes de rationalisations plus ou moins factices. [It is the gaze that makes history and this gaze is never neutral, on the contrary, it is profoundly subjective. Those who deny it are dupes of rationalizations that are more or less artificial].' Perrot as quoted in Yvonne Knibiehler, 'Chronologie et histoire des femmes,' in *Une Histoire des femmes est-elle possible?*, ed. Michelle Perrot (Marseilles: Rivages, 1984), 52. Knibiehler called attributing significance to sex in 'the human sciences' an 'epistemologic rupture,' 56.

32  See Gerda Lerner, *The Creation of Patriarchy* (New York: Oxford University Press, 1986), 5; 'Majority finds its past,' in *Majority Finds Its Past*,159. Though Peter Novick became famous for his extensive proof that historians were not 'objective' in *That Noble Dream: The 'Objectivity Question' and the American Historical Profession* (1988), feminist critiques predated his. Also, other male historians had already written of this bias. For example, the intellectual historian H. Stuart Hughes explained in *History as Art and as Science: Twin Vistas on the Past* (New York: Harper Row, 1965) that the historical profession would have to admit that most narrative history was neither objective in its presentation nor comprehensive in its coverage.

33  Sheila Rowbotham, *Woman's Consciousness, Man's World* (New York: Penguin Books, 1987 edn), 28. Dolores Barracano Schmidt and Earl Robert Schmidt, 'The invisible woman: the historian as professional magician,' in Berenice A. Carroll, ed., *Liberating Women's History: Theoretical and Critical Essays* (Urbana, IL: University of Illinois Press, 1976), 54. See also essays by Hilda L. Smith and Sheila Ryan Johansson in the same collection. Linda Gordon, interview, MARHO, *Visions of History*, Henry Abelove, Betsy Blackmar, Peter Dimock, and Jonathan Schneer, eds (New York: Pantheon Books, 1983 ed.), 202–3.

34  Joan Kelly, *Women, History and Theory*, 'introduction,' xii–xiii; 'Did women have a renaissance?,' 20, 27–8.

35  Bennett, 1. Joan W. Scott, 'Feminism's history,' *Journal of Women's History* 16(2) (Spring 2004), 12.

36  This section is largely taken from Zinsser, *History and Feminism*, chapters 5, 6 and 7. For individual United States women's accounts see, for example, *Voices of Women Historians: The Personal, the Political, the*

*Professional*, eds Eileen Boris and Nupur Chaudhuri (Bloomington, IN: Indiana University Press, 1999) and *Telling Histories: Black Women Historians in the Ivory Tower*, ed. Deborah Gray White (Chapel Hill, NC: The University of North Carolina Press, 2008).

37  See 'Statement of purpose,' *Journal of Women's History* 1(1) (1989), 7, 8–9. Similarly, the British *Women's History Review* was not founded until 1992.

38  Interview with HarperCollins editor, Hugh Van Dusen, 15 November 1990, New York City, as quoted in Zinsser, *History and Feminism*, 89.

39  See for a description of the Rose Committee findings, Zinsser, *History and Feminism*, 64.

40  Both were published by the American Historical Association in Washington D.C.

41  The numbers in 1985–86 were: research universities – 15 women out of 295 full professors; coeducational colleges – 8 women out of 56 full professors; women's colleges – 10 women out of 39 full professors. See Zinsser, *Feminism and History*, 64; Table 5.1, 69. The CWH continues to do periodic surveys of women's success within the Academy. In 2003 women represented 41% of new history PhDs but only 32.8% of those hired as assistant professors. As a male colleague remarked to the author in relation to a new search, 'We have enough women, don't we?' Advancement remained a problem particularly for those who had received their doctorates since 1986. Within their departments, women continued to report sexual harassment, unequal service requirements, and glaring disparities in their salaries when compared to men's, and a sense that they must accomplish more to gain recognition and promotion. See www.historians.org/governance/cwh/2005Status/intro_a.cfm and www.historians.org/Perspectives/issues/2008/0809/0809new1.cfm, accessed 29 June 2010.

42  This list became the basis of Natalie Zemon Davis, 'Women's history in transition: the European case,' *Feminist Studies* 3(3–4) (1976), 83–103.

43  Zinsser, *Feminism and History*, 80–81. The Ford Foundation also gave aid in other countries. The Carlos Chigas Foundation in São Paulo, Brazil received grants in the 1970s for women's history projects: a bibliography of women's history (1979) and four successive collections of essays, primarily covering the period 1750–1850. See Maria-Beatriz Nizza da Silva, 'Women's history in Brazil: production and perspectives,' in Karen Offen, Ruth Roach Pierson, and Jane Rendall, eds, *Writing Women's History: International Perspectives*, (Bloomington, IN: Indiana University Press, 1991), 372. Note that institutes and feminist centers were also significant in supporting feminist scholarship elsewhere in Latin America and in Western Europe. See Françoise Thébaud, *Ecrire l'histoire des femmes et du genre* (Lyon: ENS Editions, 2007), Part Two, *passim*.

44  IFRWH/FIRHF, originally conceived of as the women's caucus of the International Congress of the Historical Sciences (CISH/ICHS), also hosts research conferences of its own. A number of other feminist historians played a role in the initial stages of this organization, for example: Sølvi Sogner, Blom's colleague, Gisela Bock of Germany, and Natalie Zemon Davis and Mary Beth Norton from the United States. See the accounts by Blom and Offen on the occasion of IFRWH's 20th anniversary: www.ifrwh.com/id38.html, accessed 29 June 2010.

45  Anna Angerman, 'Preface,' in Anna Angerman, Geerte Binnema, Annemieke Keunen, Vefie Poels, and Jacqueline Zirkzee, eds, *Current Issues in Women's History* (New York: Routledge, 1989), 7.

46  Partner, 'Introduction,' *Speculum*, 306.

47  'Introduction,' in Mary Lyndon Shanley and Carole Pateman, eds, *Feminist Interpretations and Political Theory* (University Park, PA: Pennsylvania State University Press, 1991), 3.

48  Perrot also rejected the glorification of women's indirect power and turning to the work of French anthropologists, applied their accounts of power in French society. See Michelle Perrot, 'Les Femmes, le Pouvoir, l'Histoire,' in Michelle Perrot, ed., *Une Histoire des Femmes est-elle Possible?* (Marseilles: Rivages, 1984), 208–9, 211–12, 214–15; Comte as quoted in Perrot, 215; Karen Offen, 'Feminist campaigns in 'public space' civil societies,' in Karen Hagemann, Sonya Michel, and Gunilla Budde, eds, *Civil Society and Gender Justice: Historical and Comparative Perspectives* (New York: Berghan Books, 2008),100.

49  See on the formation of these exclusions and also for examples of women's active participation: *Political and Historical Encyclopedia of Women*, ed. Christine Fauré (New York: Routledge, 2003 [French edition 1997]). Hilda L. Smith coined the term 'false universals' in *All Men and Both Sexes: Gender, Politics, and the False Universal in England, 1640–1832* (University Park, PN: Pennsylvania State University Press, 2002).

50  Barbara Taylor and Sarah Knott, *Women, Gender and Enlightenment* (New York: Palgrave Macmillan, 2005).

51  See the introduction to *Perspectives on Feminist Political Thought in European History: From the Middle Ages to the Present*, eds Tjitske Akkerman and Siep Stuurman (New York: Routledge, 1998).

52  See, for example, the collection edited by Hilda L. Smith and Berenice A. Carroll, *Women's Political Social Thought: An Anthology* (Bloomington, IN: University of Indiana Press, 2000).

53  Alice Clark hypothesized that the medieval era was a 'golden age' for urban women. She was but one of many women's historians who sought such a halcyon period. Judith M. Bennett effectively argued that such a golden age never existed for city women of England's medieval era. Most important in these discussions has been the realization that the shift from household to commercial production has proved a negative for women in any era and any culture. See Mary S. Hartman, *The Household and the Making of History: a Subversive View of the Western Past* (New York: Cambridge University Press, 2004).

54  See Renate Bridenthal and Claudia Koonz, eds, *Becoming Visible: Women in European History* (New York: Houghton Mifflin, 1977), 5; Linda Gordon, MARHO,

*Visions of History*, eds Henry Abelove, Betsy Blackmar, Peter Dimock, and Jonathan Schneer (New York: Pantheon Books, 1983 edn), 78, 79. Juliet Mitchell's *Woman's Estate* (New York: Pantheon, 1973) and Rowbotham's *Woman, Resistance, and Revolution: A History of Women and Revolution in the Modern World* (1974) initiated the analyses. Articles by the United States historians Bridenthal, Gordon, and Hartsock, the economist Heidi Hartman, and legal theorist Catharine MacKinnon, were published between 1976 and 1982.

55 For an early Marxist feminist orientation, see Juliet Mitchell and Ann Oakley, eds, *The Rights and Wrongs of Women* (New York: Penguin, 1977). For critiques of previous labor history by European and North American feminist historians, see, for example, Joan W. Scott, 'Women's history and the rewriting of history,' in Christie Farnham, ed., *The Impact of Feminist Research in the Academy* (Bloomington, IN: Indiana University Press, 1987); Mary Jo Buhle, 'Gender and labor history,' in J. Carroll Moody and Alice Kessler-Harris, eds, *Perspectives on American Labor History: the Problems of Synthesis* (DeKalb, IL: Northern Illinois University Press, 1989).

56 Bennett, *History Matters*, for a summary of her critique, see chapter 5, 82–107. See also Judith M. Bennett, *Ale, Beer, and Brewsters in England: Women's Work in a Changing World, 1300–1600* (New York: Oxford University Press, 1999).

57 Joan Kelly, 'The doubled vision of feminist theory,' in *Women, History and Theory*, 52.

58 British and United States radical/socialist feminist historians of the 1970s and 1980s have been accused of fostering this same false dichotomy between working-class and bourgeois feminists in their histories of women in the nineteenth and twentieth century. For these developments, see the articles in the section, 'History practice: gendering trans/national historiographies: similarities and differences in comparison,' *Journal of Women's History*, 19(1) (Spring 2007). See for earlier discussions: Sonya Kruks, Rayna Rapp, and Marilyn B. Young, eds, *Promissory Notes: Women in the Transition to Socialism* (New York: Monthly Review Press, 1989). Marilyn J. Boxer, in 'Rethinking the socialist construction and international career of the concept "bourgeois feminism,"' *American Historical Review* 112(1) (February 2007), argued that class differences and party allegiance were not synonymous, nor was there an 'absolute class divide between women's groups.' She concluded that 'bourgeois feminism was invented by socialist women and did not exist as a discrete, identifiable, class-based women's movement.' See especially, 146–47, 156–58.

59 The presentations of the *colloque* were published as *Une Histoire des femmes est-elle possible?* [Is a History of Women Possible], ed. Michelle Perrot (Marseilles: Rivages, 1984) [English trans. by Felicia Pheasant published by Blackwell, 1992]. It presents the French objections to a separate women's history: essentialism; ghettoization; an Anglo-Saxon idea with no relevance for French culture in which negotiation rather than conflict characterized relations between the sexes. See also Offen et.al., eds, *Women's History: International Perspectives*, with chapters on socialist parties' influence on women's scholarship, including in India.

60 See Nancy F. Partner, 'No sex, no gender,' *Speculum* 68(2) (April 1993), 433–4. Louise Tilly, 'Gender, women's history and social history,' *Social Science History* 13(4) (Winter 1989), 439. Elizabeth Minnich, Jean O'Barr, and Rachel Rosenfeld, eds, *Reconstructing the Academy: Women's Education and Women's Studies* (Chicago, IL: The University of Chicago Press, 1988), 43. Elizabeth Minnich, *New York Times*, 23 November 1981.

61 Nizza da Silva, 'Women's history in Brazil: production and perspectives,' in Offen et al., eds, *Writing Women's History: International Perspectives*, 369.

62 See bell hooks, *Ain't I a Woman: Black Women and Feminism* (Boston MA: South End Press, 1980 edn), 81–82. Joan W. Scott explains 'the essentialist notion underlying some identity politics that takes 'women' to be all of us with female bodies all over the world and at any time in history and that assumes therefore, that there are attitudes, feelings and interests that we all necessarily have in common.' Joan W. Scott, 'The tip of the volcano,' *Society for Comparative Studies of Society and History* 35(2) (1993), 439. This was her response to Laura Lee Downs' essay criticizing Scott's advocacy of literary deconstruction in history, 'If "woman" is just an empty category, then why am I afraid to walk alone at night? Identity politics meets postmodern subject,' *Comparative Studies in Society and History* 35 (2) (1993), 414–37.

63 Patricia Hill Collins, *Black Feminist Thought: Knowledge, Consciousness and the Politics of Empowerment* (New York: Routledge, 1991), xii.

64 See hooks, 7; Collins, 68–82. On the continuing importance of this critique, see Marcia R. Sawyer's comments, *Journal of Women's History* 5(1) (Spring 1993), 126–8.

65 Wanda A. Hendricks, 'On the margins: creating a space and place in the academy,' *Telling Histories*, 148–150, 151. See this collection of autobiographical essays for other information on black women historians' experiences in the profession.

66 Lorde, quoted in Collins, 26.

67 See Collins, 6–7.

68 Collins, xiii–xiv, 221.

69 In addition to publication of their books, the work of these scholars appeared in major scholarly journals of the early 1990s: Elsa Barkley Brown in *History Workshop Journal*; Evelyn Brooks Higginbotham in *Signs*; Daphne Clark Hine in the *Journal of Women's History*.

70 Collins, 99–102, 208–12.

71 See Collins, chapter 10. For other US minority women's historians' initiatives, see Ellen Carol DuBois and Vicki L. Ruiz, eds, *Unequal Sisters: A Multicultural Reader in US Women's History* (New York: Routledge, 1990).

72 Moraga and Anzaldúa, eds., *This Bridge Called My Back* (New York: Kitchen Table, Women of Color Press, 1981); see also Collins, 234.

73  Donna J. Haraway, 'Situated knowledges: the science question in feminism and the privilege of partial perspective,' in *Cimians, Cyborgs, and Women: The Reinvention of Nature* (New York: Routledge, 1991), 183–202. Gisela Bock also saw no competition between types of oppression and activism, each was but 'one constituent factor of all others.' See her article 'Women's history and gender history: aspects of an international debate,' *Gender and History* 1(1) (1989).

74  See Margot Badran and Miriam Cooke, *Opening the Gates: A Century of Arab Feminist Writing* (Bloomington, IN: Indiana University Press, 1990), now in its second edition, 2004.

75  See for example, Neera Desai's *Women in Modern India* (1977) and other works described by Arpana Basu, 'Women's history in India,' in Offen et al., eds, 181–209.

76  See Kumar, *History of Doing* (New York: Verso, 1993).

77  Histories of Women in Brazil and Argentina appeared in 1992 and 2000, respectively. Such efforts culminated with publication of Isabel Deusa Morant's four-volume *Historia de las Mujeres en Espana y América Latina* [History of Women in Spain and Latin America] (Madrid: Caterdra, 2005–2006).

78  Information for this sampling of women's history initiatives comes from two principal sources: Offen et al., eds See also the bibliographies of the four-volume *Restoring Women to History* under the general editorship of Cheryl Johnson-Odim and Margaret Strobel (Bloomington, IN: University of Indiana Press, 1999); there are volumes for Asia, Latin America, and the Caribbean, the Middle East and North Africa, and Sub-Saharan Africa, each written by experts in the field. Ludmilla Jordanova, *History in Practice* (New York: Oxford University Press, 2000), 44.

79  For critiques, see Judith Allen, 'Evidence and silence: feminism and the limits of history,' in Carole Pateman and Elizabeth Gross, eds, *Feminist Challenges: Social and Political Theory* (Boston, MA: Northeastern University Press, 1987), 181. Arlette Farge, 'Pratique et effets de l'histoire des femmes [Practical considerations and effects of women's history],' in Perrot, ed., *Une Histoire des Femmes est-elle possible?*, 17–35, and Thébaud, 182–183. Kathi Kern, 'Productive collaborations: the benefits of cultural analysis to the past, present and future of women's history,' *Journal of Women's History* 16(4) (2004), 38. Reflecting on the continuing difficulties for French feminist historians, it was only in 1991–92 that a narrative of French women's history was published, a collection of essays commissioned by an Italian publisher: *Histoire des Femmes en Occident* [History of Women in the West], eds Georges Duby and Michelle Perrot. Ten years after the last issue of *Pénélope* in 1985, *Clio, Histoire, Femmes et Sociétés*, a journal of women's history was established. Only since 2000 have there been national organizations and institutes specifically devoted to women's history, such as SIEFAR (International Society for the Study of Women in the *ancien regime*) and the Institut Emilie Du Châtelet.

80  Welter, 'Cult' in *Dimity Convictions*.

81  Carroll Smith-Rosenberg, 'The female world of love and ritual ...' *Signs* 1 (1) (Autumn 1975) and 'Hearing women's words: a feminist reconstruction of history,' in *Disorderly Conduct: Visions of Gender in Victorian America* (New York: Oxford University Press, 1985), 27.

82  Faderman, *Surpassing the Love of Men* ... (New York: Morrow, 1981).

83  Estelle Freedman, 'Separatism as Strategy: Female Institution Building and American Feminism 1870–1930,' *Feminist Studies* 5(3) (Autumn 1979), 513–14.

84  Nancy A. Hewitt, 'Beyond the search for sisterhood: American women's history in the 1980s,' *Social History* 10(3) (October 1985), 315. The English translation of the German sociologist, Jürgen Habermas' *The Structure of the Public Sphere* [*Strukturwandel der Öffentlichkeit. Intersuchungen zu einer Kategorie der bürgerlichen Gesellschaft,*1962] in 1989 (Cambridge: MIT Press) contributed to the reification of this idea of a private sphere for bourgeois women and a public sphere for men of this social category; the latter, Habermas argued, became increasingly democratic in western Europe from the late seventeenth century on.

85  See Leslie P. Pierce, *The Imperial Harem: Women and Sovereignty in the Ottoman Empire* (New York: Oxford University Press, 1993). The *Journal of Women's History* included a 'Forum' on the concept in 2003, 15(1) and 15(2), with contributions on women of many different times and regions. See also, Joan W. Scott and Debra Keates, eds, *Going Public: Feminism and the Shifting Boundaries of the Private Sphere* (Urbana, IL: University of Illinois Press, 2004).

86  Linda K. Kerber, 'Separate spheres, female worlds, woman's place: the rhetoric of women's history,' *Journal of American History* 75(1) (June 1988), 9–39.

87  See the very useful collection edited by Gabrielle M. Spiegel, *New Directions in Historical Writing after the Linguistic Turn* (New York: Routledge, 2005). Michel de Certeau's *The Practice of Everyday Life*, trans. Stephen F. Randall (Berkeley: University of California Press, 1984,) is considered his most important and influential contribution to the work of North American scholars. The equivalent text by Clifford Geertz is *The Interpretation of Cultures* (New York: Basic Books, 1973).

88  Natalie Zemon Davis as quoted by Joan Kelly in 'The social relations of the sexes: methodological implications of women's history,' in *Women, History and Theory*, 9.

89  Joan W. Scott, 'Gender: a useful category of analysis,' in *Gender and the Politics of History* (New York: University of Columbia Press, 1988). Nancy Partner, 'No sex, no gender,' *Speculum* 68(2) (1993), 423. Note that the English literary scholar, Denise Riley's *Am I That Name? Feminism and the Category of 'Women' in History* (Minneapolis: University of Minnesota Press, 1988), was published in the same year as Scott's essay collection and had a similar effect, bringing into question preconceptions and assumptions about how the concept 'woman' with its attendant stereotypical, binary meanings

had been created by past narratives, not by any reference to reality.

90 Natalie Zemon Davis, 'Women's history in transition,' 90. See also Davis' interview in MARHO *Visions*. Scott, 'Feminism's history,'13. 'Subaltern Studies' as theorized by the members of the South Asian scholarly group founded in the 1980s draws on similar theoretical premises (especially Gramsci) in its efforts to retell the imperial narrative from the perspective of the South Asian subjects, not their British rulers.

91 Joan W. Scott in her study of nineteenth-century French feminisms, *Only Paradoxes to Offer: French Feminists and the Rights of Man* (Cambridge: Harvard University Press, 1996) exposed the limitations, internal tensions and incompatibilities between the language of rights and the concept of the individual, gendered as male. Women might find new languages of protest and justification, but the pattern of exclusion remained intact.

92 In the United States and Britain the arguments extended from the late 1980s into the 1990s, with articles appearing in the *American Historical Review*, *Gender & History*, *Feminist Studies*, *Radical History Review*, *Women's History Review*, and the *Journal of Women's History*. See for example, attacks by Linda Gordon, Laura Lee Downs, Susan Kingsley Kent, and Joan Hoff ('Gender as a postmodern category of paralysis' is a particularly telling choice of title). See, for an indication of the concept's general acceptance in addition to, if not instead of, women's history: 'AHR Forum: Revisiting Gender: a useful category of historical analysis,' *American Historical Review* 113 (5) (2008), 1344–429. For a more international perspective at the beginning of the debate, see Gisela Bock, 'Women's history and gender history,' 7–30.

93 Judith Butler, *Gender Trouble* (New York: Routledge, 1989).

94 Nancy Fraser in *The Second Wave: A Reader in Feminist Theory*, ed. Linda Nicholson (New York: Routledge, 1997), 391; Monique Wittig in Nicholson, ed., 265–6, 271. *Signs* published 'The lesbian issue,' 8(1) (Autumn 1982) to explore many of these issues. See Francisca de Haan, 'Women's history behind the dykes,' in Offen et al., eds; Toril Moi, *What is a Woman?* (New York: Oxford University Press, 1999), 113, 117; Anne Fausto-Sterling, *Sexing the Body: Gender Politics and the Construction of Sexuality* (New York: Basic Books, 2000). Eve Kosofsky Sedgwick's *Epistemology of the Closet* (Berkeley: University of California Press, 1990) gives a systematic explanation of what has come to be called 'Queer Theory,' and the need to study not only the construction of 'sexualities,' but also the role of forced 'silences' in gendered power relationships.

95 See Linda Alcoff, 'Cultural feminism versus post-structuralism: the identity crisis in feminist theory' in Nicholson, ed.

96 See Bock, 8, 17.

97 Francisca de Haan, Krassimira Daskalova and Anna Loutfi, eds., *Biographical Dictionary of Women's Movements and Feminisms* (New York: Central European Union Press, 2006).

98 See for example, Kumar, 'Afterword: in a small personal voice (with apologies to Doris Lessing),' in *The History of Doing*. Perhaps the most famous early statement of these views is by the Vietnamese filmmaker and writer Trinh T. Minh-ha, *Woman, Native, Other. Writing Postcoloniality and Feminism* (Bloomington, IN: Indiana University Press, 1989). White English language feminists have also contributed to this dialogue: see the Australian scholar, Chilla Bulbeck, *Reorienting Western Feminisms: Women's Diversity in a Post-Colonial World* (Cambridge: Cambridge University Press, 1998); Antoinette Burton, '"History" is now: feminist theory and the production of historical feminisms', *Women's History Review* 1 (1) (1992), 25–39. Burton admonishes: 'feminists genuinely concerned about joining history and theory must be mindful of how the historical narratives of feminism are being constructed, contested and recast even as we write, even as we read,' 26.

99 Elsa Barkley Brown, 'What has happened here,' in Nicholson, ed., 274, 275.

100 Audre Lorde as quoted in Sonya O. Rose, 'Introduction to dialogue: gender history/women's history: is feminist scholarship losing its critical edge?,' *Journal of Women's History* 5(1) (Spring 1993), 95. See the last chapter of Chandra Talpade Mohanty, *Feminism Without Borders: Decolonizing Theory, Practicing Solidarity* (Durham, NC: Duke University Press, 2003), 221–51, 270–3. Similarly, Elleke Boehmer, writing from an African perspective, warns of the risks of rejecting the 'globalizing tendencies of feminism,' and calls instead for recognition 'that cultures are fields of interrelationship that exist in dialogue.' She looks to assertion of 'a politically effective even if always provisional consensus about issues in common to be addressed.' Elleke Boehmer, *Stories of Women, Gender and Narrative in the Postcolonial Nation* (Manchester: Manchester University Press, 2005), 13.

101 Virginia Woolf, *Three Guineas* (New York: Harcourt, Brace & World, 1966), 62. bell hooks as quoted in 'Introduction,' in Sue Morgan, ed., *The Feminist History Reader* (New York: Routledge, 2006), 37.

# 16

# Gender I: From Women's History to Gender History

Bonnie G. Smith

The ingredients for women's history have long been in place and women's history itself has an extensive pedigree, going back centuries. Fine observation of political, social, and cultural events in which women were involved was a main feature of initial efforts; in the nineteenth century such endeavors were supplemented and eventually reshaped by professional investigation in archives and other repositories of documents. The rise of feminist movements across the globe also motivated the writing in women's history over the past 250 years, even as the narrative of that history felt the influence of national liberation, civil rights, and post-colonial activism. In recent decades, theoretical concerns stemming not only from politics but from various new ideas found in linguistics, anthropology, psychoanalysis, and other fields have led to postmodernist thought influencing some histories of women. Finally, shaped by all these recent trends in scholarship, gender has emerged as both rival and supplement to the women's history enterprise. Debate encircles and enriches all these developments.

In the eleventh century two Japanese writers, Murasaki Shikibu (1960) and Sei Sonagon (1979), laid the groundwork for a history of women that focused on the cultural and social life they witnessed around them. Each described the customs of the Japanese court and the aristocracy, including accounts of pilgrimages, sexual practices, marriage, and family life. The poetry that passed among men and women showed ways in which the emotions were expressed, while customs such as watching the change of seasons or the appearance of cherry blossoms are shown to have been important moments in women's lives. The gendering of men and women through social, political, and cultural practices implicitly filled the writings of these insiders to Japanese high society. There was little in these astute authors' work that did not provide models for later thinking.

In the fifteenth century the professional writer Christine de Pisan described the lives of important women in her *Book of the City of Ladies* (1982 [1405]), which told the story of courageous, accomplished, and virtuous heroines from preceding centuries and from different cultures. Christine's work was motivated by a sense of the injustice dealt women by learned and other well-known men. These men called women a variety of bad names, piquing Christine to such a point that she had to write a book. Christine chose these women for their accomplishments, their courage, their special fidelity in hard times, and their courage in the face of torture, rape, and other unspeakable trials. However, like a good historian Christine spoke candidly of sexual attacks, not mincing words that might gloss hard truths. She also wrote about heroines who were more enduring on the historical stage than victims of rape and abuse. Joan of Arc was the special topic of another work (1977 [1429]), and although it would be a while before there were similarly sweeping works of women's history, some of the groundwork had been laid.

In the early modern period, displaying an evolving historical sensibility, women wrote family memoirs and collected papers charting both involvement in major events and the details of everyday life. The groundwork for later historical writing also appeared in the political tracts that women such as Mary Astell (1703) and Elizabeth Elstob (18th century; see Ferguson 1985) published, often anonymously or under pseudonyms. When in the seventeenth century Sor Juana de la Cruz (2005) penned her long poem describing the workings and aspirations of her mind, she too created an archive for later investigations of women's intellectual history. Some others of her writings had a decidedly political edge, as they charted the misogynous deeds of churchmen and other leaders. During the English Civil War women chronicled events, including the brave deeds of women in their families, and they collected and preserved family papers. Committing longstanding oral family histories to paper also occurred. Later their historical awareness led them to monumentalize important locales and scenes of battle. Between 1745 and 1750 Louise-Marie Dupin (2009 [c.1750]) of France worked on a massive history of women she hoped to write. Her research assistant during that time was Jean-Jacques Rousseau, and the reading notes for the project and some drafts remain extant at the University of Texas, which bought the papers in the 1950s. These manuscripts show Dupin's concern for the history of all women,

for one of the sources was the Jesuit reports on customs, manners, and ideas in China. Thus, whether through the development of archival materials or the analysis and narration of the past, women's history has evolved from the practices of early times, including not a small amount of political opinionizing.

The Enlightenment sensibility of many authors inspired histories of women. The eighteenth and early nineteenth centuries saw the publication of anthologies of women's writings, including those by Louise Keralio (1786–89) in France, whose other works included her partisan histories of the Bourbons and the French Revolution. The French and American Revolutions were events that crystallized women's opinions about their status and their history. Not only did Germaine did Staël write a paradigm-setting history of the revolution in which her father figured so large, she simultaneously culled material from the past histories of women about whose politics she could comment. Men participated in the overflowing interest in women's past: in Europe, Antoine-Léonard Thomas (1774), William Alexander (1779), and Christoph Meiners (1808) all wrote histories of women between 1772 and 1800, while in China at the same time author Zhang Xuechange produced an influential essay on learned women and their scholarship over the course of many dynasties (*Women's Learning*, 1797/98; see Mann 1992), arguing that their erudition had declined.

Over the centuries so many authors from around the world have mined written records and oral histories to produce their histories that scholars have not yet fully accounted for all of them. In 1831, a learned Chinese woman, Wanyan Yun Zhu (1994 [1831]), published *Precious Record from the Maidens' Chambers*, a history of Chinese women from many walks of life. To produce this work, Wanyan Yun Zhu relied in part on her collection of some 3,000 women poets, for in that same year she also produced an annotated anthology of their works called *Correct Beginnings* (1999 [1831]), edited with the help of her three granddaughters. As readers sent more poems to the family, the granddaughters produced successive volumes – *Correct Beginnings Continued*. The books by Wanyan Yun Zhu and her granddaughters showed a breadth of interest in women poets from all parts of China and Korea, and in women from all times facing a variety of challenges. In Africa, queen mothers were important politically because they were keepers of extensive family histories and genealogies, usually in their own memory.

Interest in the history of women in the wider world also has an early pedigree. Like Wanyan Yun Zhu, who branched out to cover Korean women, others crossed national borders to find fascinating or active women from the past whose stories they could tell. Women novelists and historians in the West used the figures (both known through common memory or researched in secondary works) of African and Asian women from the eighteenth century and earlier on to endorse change, just as the French picked up the idea of free trade from early modern China. Aside from Montagu, eighteenth-century authors Olympe de Gouges and Germaine de Staël were just two who envisioned the lives of women of color in a variety of foreign venues as part of their campaigns for greater freedom for women. De Staël's coverage ranged from powerful Cleopatra and Amazon queens to the enslaved mother Mirza and this disparate cast was emblematic of the importance of variety in the development of a political imagination. In her 1835 two-volume work, *The History and the Condition of Women of the World in all Times*, Child similarly pointed to women of accomplishment such as Assyrian queen Semiramis whom she credited with building Babylon in one year's time or Zenobia who headed her country's armies. Zenobia's learning also impressed Child as did that of Avyar, 'the greatest of Malabar's seven sages,' four of whom were women. Child missed the famed poetry and prose of Chinese and Japanese women authors as well as their accomplishments in the visual arts, but she attributed the invention of spinning and silk production respectively to the wives of Emperors Yao and Hoang-Ti.

The amateur writing of women's history flourished down to World War I in a variety of sub-genres, ranging from political to cultural history and from global to local studies. The Strickland sisters of Great Britain excelled in writing histories of queens (regnant, dowager, and princesses, with their material derived from both private and public archives as well as from secondary sources. These works were so popular that they were reprinted for close to a century, and they formed a foundation for studies of queenship by professionals many decades later (Strickland and Strickland 1851–52). The aura of courtly politics was fodder for these modern amateurs, beginning with writers like Stéphanie-Félicité de Genlis whose volumes on court life shared common ground with Sei Shonagon (Genlis 1785). Where there were no queens, writers like Elizabeth Ellet produced *Queens of American Society* (1869) to explore the relationship of notable women too. Other amateurs focused on social and work life: by the late nineteenth century, African American women were producing biographies of memorable figures in their past, joining a chorus of historians of women (Des Jardins 2003; Hine 1993), and along the way they described living patterns, family life, and work opportunities. Still others, such as Anna Jameson (2005 [1832]), investigated women's involvement in cultural life and the arts, for example as patrons of and models for painters – a social history of the arts that art historians have recently professed to be their own invention.

These amateur efforts, praised and eagerly read by the general public at the time, came to be scorned by professionalizing historians for their subject matter – social and cultural history, not to mention women. In fact, any history not performed by professionals was feminized and thus denigrated and the language of sex infused nineteenth-century declarations of professional standards. US historian Richard Hildreth thought that amateur history was 'tricked out in the gaudy tinsel of meretricious rhetoric. For the sake of our fathers and ourselves, the great characters in American history should be presented unbedaubed with patriotic rouge, without stilts, buskins, tinsel or bedizenment' (Hildreth 1849–52). The *English Historical Review* (1898) promised not to corrupt its readers with 'allurements of style.' It valued works for their rejection of 'tinsel embroidery' and their refusal 'to adorn a tale.' Other professional journals pointed to the 'tawdry trappings' of amateur works – all of these words used to describe women, especially public women. 'Clio is going to be just a gal-about-town,' warned one university historian of amateur writing, 'on whom anybody with two bits worth of inclination in his pocket can lay claim' (Smith 1998).

Meanwhile, professionalizing historians in the nineteenth century proclaimed the masculinity of their own work in archives where they found documents and honed their skills at digging out truthful facts. They described themselves as adventurers, citizens, and heroes as they locked themselves in seminar rooms to compare treatises and documents emanating from the burgeoning nation-state. They did, in the words of one, 'manly work' and they supported the nation – itself 'a large-scale solidarity, constituted by the feeling of the sacrifices one has made in the past ... [the nation] presupposes a past' (Renan 1990 [1882]). In outlining the history of the nation and other similarly grand and masculine institutions such as the papacy, historians made politics their business and the sole focus of their concerns as both men and citizens. As towering, lone intellects, they erased the fact that their wives, daughters, sisters, and mothers often provided the essential work of research, copying, filing, and even composing their works, and emphasized in any number of ways – including refusing women admission to seminars – that the work of the nation's history was for men and it was about politics first and foremost. Any other type of history was degraded, inferior, and feminine.

Nonetheless, professionalization of historical writing and its attendant masculinization from the nineteenth century on also influenced the writing of women's history in two ways. First as it came to characterize all that was wanting in amateur history – a gendered foil (although amateur history was written by women and men alike) to the superior work of the virtually all-male historical profession. As a result, the vast field of social, cultural, and to some extent economic history was developed with a passion by amateurs. Because women's writing and thinking about the past became the antithesis of all that was excellent and above the common herd, women could grab the common herd as its audience. The work of Julia Cartwright, Margaret Oliphant, and Alice Morse Earle plunged into the cultural and social lives of women and their families with a vengeance. In so doing, all the while gaining appreciative audiences, they came to influence the turn toward the cultural that men in the profession would adopt early in the twentieth century and thereafter. Alice Stopford Green, for example, was a major force in getting her hyper-professional husband to write a social history of England (Smith 1998).

Second, professionalization advanced the writing of women's history in the academy, if slowly. The tropes of professional history writing in the nineteenth century included those envisioning the profession as a small republic of elite, if comradely, men. However, the appearance of standards for the development of expertise drew the attention of women who believed that they too had human capacities, even if most men did not agree. There were just enough men in the profession who allowed women into their classrooms to open the doors of professional opportunity. Frederick Maitland mentored Mary Bateson at Cambridge, while she produced expert scholarship in medieval social and cultural history, including a path-breaking article on double monasteries and women's leadership in them (Bateson 1899). Eileen Power also attended Cambridge and although similarly ineligible for a degree did similarly innovative work on the social and cultural history of women in nunneries and women more generally in medieval history (Power 1975). Even more experimental, Lucy

Maynard Salmon in the United States wrote about domestic servants, museum culture, the history of cookbooks, household interiors, and the vernacular landscape. Salmon converted the primacy of government sources into a broad definition of document that allowed ordinary items such as laundry lists and railroad schedules to serve as historical evidence – all of this before World War I (Salmon 1906). Men in the profession began to follow the lead of these professional women historians by venturing beyond their narrow preoccupation with the official record and political history.

## THE REVIVAL OF WOMEN'S HISTORY AFTER THE MID TWENTIETH CENTURY

Women's history experienced an explosive resurgence with the rebirth of feminist activism after World War II. Across the West in the postwar period, civil service and union women made notable demands for representation and comparable wages, continuing the activism of working women in the 1920s and 1930s. Others agitated in the 1950s and early 1960s for the right to birth control information and increasingly effective technologies, most notably diaphragms and the new birth control pill. Since the end of the war activists around the world had also demanded gay rights, beginning with the decriminalization of homosexuality. By the late 1960s feminism had become a mass movement, producing along with significant legal gains a greater number of professional and amateur writers of women's history. As women sought legal rights protecting them in the workplace and home, historians such as Gerda Lerner (1986) and Anne Firor Scott (1970) were investigating the lives of African American women and Southern women, producing two very different scenarios from the past. When Jill Conway and Natalie Zemon Davis launched women's history at the University of Toronto late in the 1960s, they compiled a widely-distributed bibliography (in mimeographed form) of women's history written

over the past centuries. The notable fact, besides the tremendous energy and innovative spirit of the two scholars, was that the bibliography consisted in large part of the work of many forerunners such as Alice Clark and Ivy Pinchbeck – today unacknowledged and mostly forgotten. Thus the claim that women of the 1970s and thereafter 'invented' women's history simply does not stand up to the evidence, which is not to discount that students and professors in the late 1960s and 1970s demanded courses in women's history, founded journals and held conferences, and increased the number of women writing history and those teaching women's history. The institutional power of women's history burgeoned as never before and there was many a new venture such as the anthologies, formal courses, and programs of study that suddenly came into being.

Because so many young historians came from the radicalized universities of the 1960s, there a leftist or populist look at women's past flourished, and this vantage point was also relatively new. Women workers such as Adelaide Popp and Marie Bouvier wrote moving memoirs of their lives in the late nineteenth and early twentieth centuries respectively, but these were hardly shaped by a studied, Marxist historical thrust. In contrast, Sheila Rowbotham's *Women, Resistance and Revolution* (1972) and *Hidden from History* (1974) emphasized and even celebrated women's grass roots activism and their participation in Communist revolution. Professionals published many studies of women and socialism in the 1970s and early 1980s. Interest in women in Russia and China was also strong, as they seemed to offer women greater equality than in other, non-socialist countries. Additionally the admiration for socialism led researchers to inquire into the history of oppressed and working-class women in all historical societies. During the 1970s and early 1980s investigations by Michele Perrot, Alain Corbin, Jane Lewis, Darlene Clark Hine, Judy Walkowitz, and many others led to a wide variety of studies of women's work, working women's sexuality, activism, and relationship to political power.

At somewhat the same time but at a slower pace scholars investigated other issues in women's history. Ann Firor Scott had shown the ways in which the history of middle- and upper-class women could be revelatory. African American professional scholars took to the archives as their amateur predecessors had done 75 years earlier. Their distress at being left out of the burgeoning field of African American history was palpable, the argument being made initially and forcefully in such works as *All the Women are White, All the Men are Black But Some of Us Are Brave* (Hull et al. 1982). Monographs such as Paula Giddings *When and Where I Enter: The Impact of Black Women on Race and Sex in America* (1984) followed and the field of women in African history also opened to more active investigation. Simultaneously critics noted the relative lack of attention to Hispanic women's history and literature and to that of women of color more generally, ultimately leading to anthologies beginning with *This Bridge Called My Back: Writings from Radical Women of Color* (Moraga and Anzaldua 1981) and monographs such as Vicky Ruiz's *Cannery Women, Cannery Lives: Mexican Women, Unionization, and the California Food Processing Industry, 1930–1950* (1987). Variety within studies of race and class became the order of the day by the mid-1980s.

## FOUNDATIONS AND RISE OF GENDER HISTORY

The origin of gender history is a much disputed topic, but one can argue that like women's history its beginnings are complex. A crucial moment in the development of gender theory came in 1949 with the publication of Simone de Beauvoir's bestseller, *The Second Sex* (2009 [1949]). This dense and lengthy description of the 'making' of womanhood discussed Marxist, Freudian literary, and anthropological theories that, according to Beauvoir, actually determined women's

behavior. In her view women, in contrast to men, acted in accordance with men's view of them and not according to their own lights. This analysis drew on phenomenological and existential philosophy that portrayed the development of the individual subject or self in relationship to an object or 'other.' Thus, as Beauvoir extrapolated from a variety of thought, a man formed his subjectivity in relationship to 'woman' as other or object, spinning his own identity by creating images of someone that was not him. Instead of building selves in a parallel way, women accepted male images of them AS their identity. By this view, femininity as most women lived it was an inauthentic identity determined not inevitably, as a natural condition, but as the result of a misguided choice. This insight had wide-ranging implications for future scholarship, notably in suggesting voluntaristic and variable aspects to one's sexual role or nature.

A second extrapolation from existentialism in *The Second Sex*, however, did touch on women's biological role as reproducer. For French existentialists, living an authentic life entailed escaping the world of necessity or biology and acting in the world of contingency. From this creed Beauvoir posited that women were additionally living an inauthentic life to the extent that they just did nature's bidding by having children and rearing them. They should search for freedom and authenticity through meaningful actions not connected with biological necessity. The assertion that women could escape biological destiny to forge an existence apart from the family also opened the way to gender theory. A group of translators in the Northampton, Massachusetts area working under the aegis of H.M. Parshley made *The Second Sex* available to a widespread Anglophone audience in the 1950s, with the project as a whole arousing great excitement in the Smith College community. Small wonder that Betty Friedan, Gloria Steinem, and other Smith alumnae and students at the time were prominent among the pioneers of the feminist movement.

Beauvoir's was not the only French doctrine to lay some of the groundwork for gender theory. During that same postwar period Claude Lévi-Strauss posited in his structuralist theory that people in societies lived within frameworks of thought that constituted grids for everyday behavior. These frameworks were generally binary, consisting of oppositions such as pure and impure, raw and cooked, or masculine and feminine. Binaries operated with and against one another as relationships. One could and did draw from structuralism that in the case of masculine and feminize, these concepts or characteristics were mutually definitional. Lévi-Strauss developed these theories in *The Elementary Structures of Kinship* (1949), in which he took kinship as the fundamental organizing category of all society, to be based on the exchange of women. The American anthropologist Gayle Rubin elaborated on Lévi-Strauss in 'The traffic in women' (1975), an article that further developed gender theory again, using French concepts as its basis. 'The subjection of women can be seen as a product of the relationships by which sex and gender are organized and produced,' Rubin wrote (1975: 171). Her second point extrapolated from Lévi-Strauss was that the most important taboo in all societies was the sameness of men and women. By 1980, it had become a commonplace for US anthropologists, sociologists, and some psychologists in academe to talk about 'the social construction of gender.' To quote a 1978 textbook, 'Our theoretical position is that gender is a social construction, that a world of two sexes is a result of the socially shared, taken-for-granted methods which members use to construct reality.'

Rubin's article also highlighted the work of French psychoanalyst Jacques Lacan, who articulated the symbolic power of the phallus, the relativity of masculine and feminine psyches, and the nature of the split or fragmented subject in even stronger terms than Sigmund Freud had done. Freud had seen the rational, sexual, and moral aspects of the self as in perpetual contest. In an essay on the 'mirror stage' in human development, Lacan claimed a further – different splitting. The baby gained an identity by seeing the self first in terms of an other – the mother – and in a mirror, that is again, in terms of an other. Both of these images were fragmented ones because the mother disappeared from time to time, as did the image in the mirror. The self was always this fragmented and *relational* identity. Lacan also posited language as a crucial influence providing the structures of identity and the medium by which that identity was spoken. In speaking, the self first articulated one's 'nom' or name – which was the first name of one's 'father' – and simultaneously and homonymically spoke the 'non,' the proscriptions or rules of that language, which Lacan characterized as the laws of the 'father' or the laws of the phallus. Lacanianism added to gender theory then developing in the United States a further sense of the intertwined nature of masculinity and femininity, beginning with identity as based on the maternal imago and fragmented because of it. Second, it highlighted the utterly arbitrary, if superficially regal, power of masculinity as an extension of the phallus. Third, the fantasy nature of the gendered self and indeed of all human identity and drives received an emphasis that became crucial to leading practitioners of gender history at its outset.

Under the sign of what came to be known as 'French feminism,' French theorists picked up on Lacanian, structuralist, and other insights to formulate a position that contributed to the development of gender theory in the Britain and the US. For these theorists, such as Luce Irigaray, masculine universalism utterly obstructed feminine subjectivity. What Simone de Beauvoir called 'the Other' had nothing to do with women but amounted to one more version of masculinity – male self-projection. Women thus appeared as erasure, as lack, and in Luce Irigaray's *This Sex Which Is Not One* (1985), as unrepresentable in ordinary terms. The woman was the divided, nonunitary, fragmented self. The result for the writing of social history were such compendia as Michelle Perrot's *Une histoire des femmes est-elle possible* (1984).

I will not go into the influence of Michel Foucault in the United States nor of such historians as Arlette Farge and Alain Corbin on Anglophone theorists of gender, except to point to further steps along the path of seeing gender as enmeshed in a grid of power that produced subjects as they articulated and reproduced the principles of power. Foucault's work gave a sense of bodily behavior as redolent of biopower in the performance of social rules about sex and gender, while downplaying or even dismissing the traditional sense of human agency – an emphasis that could be and was extended to the development of gender theory.

Although many of these theories had more or less influence on the social history of women by the mid-1980s, in 1986 they came together when the historian Joan Scott issued her influential manifesto about gender theory in the *American Historical Review* (Scott 1986). Scott asked historians to transform social scientific and positivist understandings of gender by adding Lacanian psychoanalysis, Jacques Derrida's deconstruction showing the difficulties of assigning definite meanings or truth to texts, and Foucauldian–Nietzschean definitions of power. In her view Marxist, anthropological (aside from Gayle Rubin on which her own theory relied in part), and psychological moves toward understanding gender had reached a dead end because they assigned to the terms male and female essential and enduring characteristics. Nor, for that matter, according to Scott, were feminist scholars who studied patriarchy or sought out 'women's voices' or steadier ground. Despite great progress, even those who now followed the lead of 'binary oppositions' of structuralist anthropology had no convincing way of accounting for men's oppression of women. The rigidity of the male–female categories in any of these systems, especially in the work of those who sought out women's 'voices' and 'values' kept gender from being as useful as it could be.

As a palliative, Scott considered the way the trio of French theorists could overcome the rigidities and insufficiencies of gender theory as it had evolved to the mid-1980s. Lacanian psychoanalysis rested in part on the Swiss linguist Ferdinand de Saussure's understanding of language as a system in which words had meaning only in relationship to one another. For Scott, Lacanianism and all the psychic variation it involved were keys to understanding gender as an exigent, inescapable relationship. Foucault's theory of power as a field in which all humans operated offered another valuable insight. Scott suggested that using Foucault allowed for the introduction of gender issues into political history, thus overcoming the separation that historians had maintained between women's history and the political foundation on which most history writing rested.

Scott, using French ideas almost exclusively, explained that gender could be a category or subject of discussion through which power operated. It could operate thus in several ways. For one, because gender meant differentiation, it could be used to distinguish the better from the worse, the more important from the less important. Using the term 'feminine' articulated a lower place in a social or political hierarchy. Additionally, gender explained or assigned meaning to any number of phenomena, including work, the body, sexuality, politics, religion, cultural production, and an infinite number of other historical fields. Because many of these were fields where social history had established itself and where Scott herself had done major work on France as well, gender theory of her variety came to have steady if often unacknowledged influence.

One could cite the thousands of works that have subsequently been published by scholars around the world using weak, strong, misunderstood, and utterly twisted versions of gender theory or the influential extensions of gender theory by important thinkers such as Judith Butler (1990, 1993). It is also important not to rehearse the many claims to those who mentioned gender history before there was gender history. Moreover, there were other important French people such as Frantz Fanon who further contributed to ideas of difference and an understanding of intersectionality in gender theory. Currently there is much discussion of circulation, routes, and pathways of knowledge, and it seems to me that the development of gender theory around the world – as is now the case – from this French-American connection should be explored in depth as one of the most powerful examples of that circulation in present times.

Gender history surged after 1990, taking two basic directions. One of these involved turning attention to men as sexed and gendered beings, and a rich literature on masculinity has been developed. Studies of men in countries around the world, in sports and the military, in fashion and consumerism, and in the workforce are legion by this time. Historians such as Andrew Rotter have extended the investigation of masculinity to diplomacy and high politics. In his study, Rotter (1994) showed that US foreign policy in the 1950s and 1960s faltered because American leaders had a rigid vision of masculinity, disallowing the possibility that rulers such as Jawaharlal Nehru should be taken seriously because he wore a skirt-like garment and a flower pinned to his jacket. All such studies are exciting to historians simply because they are providing much new archival material and new historical insights. But as Toby Ditz has written most do not address the questions central to more complex gender theory.

More in line with postmodernist theories of gender are works such as Afsaneh Najmabadi, *Women with Mustaches and Men without Beards: Gender and Sexual Anxieties of Iranian Modernity* (2005) and Mrinalini Sinha *Specters of Mother India: The Global Restructuring of Empire* (2006) in which questions of power are central to the analysis. Najabadi begins by drawing a sexual scene in nineteenth-century Iran that allowed for the fluidity of sexual identities, especially embodied in the image of the *amrad* or feminine young male. Contacts with the West, however, uncovered a heterosexual social economy and made heteronormativity appear crucial to modern nationhood. Najmabadi portrays the creation of a modern Iran around a restructuring of relationships among men and between

men and women in the context of the reconfiguration of sex roles. The fantasy of US citizen Katherine Mayo about the condition of women in India in her best-selling book *Mother India* of the 1920s was a global event of such import that it sparked feminists in India to become more active than ever before, constructing a compelling justification for their activism and setting out political claims. Men became as insistent against the fantasy and the women activists as well – serving as yet another lobbying group in the 'Mother India' debate that raged around the world (Sinha 2006). Political power was at stake in the gendered activism controversy over the book launched around the world. Neither of these works takes gender to mean simply the study of men or women or, in many cases, simply the study of women. Rather, much more is at stake as this scholarship operates in the multiple registers of politics, psychology, globalism, sexuality, and identity. It looks at the historical activities of women and men as well as the production of gender

## WORLD HISTORY AND WOMEN'S MODERNITY

As seen in the last two examples, some of the most sophisticated work in women's and gender history over the past two decades has come from scholars studying world and postcolonial history. These two new fields have been shaped by the study of women's and gender history, but they also raise questions. By the early 1990s world history had become a rising teaching field in universities, and by the late 1990s world history had attracted an increasing number of researchers. The new world history of the 1990s distinguished itself theoretically by stating that it considered only interactions and global connections rather than focusing on individual civilizations. In the past, global history meant writing civilizationally about 'women in China' or 'women in Argentina,' and scholars have pursued professional, non-Western civilizational studies of women since the 1970s. A second concomitant of civilizational writing was the specific focus on non-Western women, with the idea that global history should exclude the West. In the new paradigms set by world history over the past two decades, however, the field was defined for many as focused on connections and interactions rather than distinct civilizations. Thus, women sitting at home feeding silk worms is not world history, for world history is not simply an account of those who don't live in the West. It has most vividly been described as the history of men on horseback, in ships, in airplanes, and running artillery used transnationally. 'If you don't cross borders,' said one pioneer of the field, 'you don't belong in world history.' For a while, it seemed that women would have no place in the new world history – except for the facts of Chinese women binding their feet in imitation (perhaps) of Persian dancers.

Engaged scholars challenged the implication that there was no place for women's history in world history, given the guidelines for updating the field. Their argument ran that the work of women at home was often directly tied to global markets. For instance, women spinning or weaving silk for the Silk Road trade, even though they never budged from the inner chambers, had participated in the unfolding of world history. Those sitting at home singing a love song for their merchant husbands crossing continents or soldier sons at vast distances from home were also engaged in world history, though in different ways that cried out for narration and analysis. Even women not connected to men's travel, trade, or soldiering were important topics for study because they dealt in traded commodities, worked for global firms, or raised crops that entered the global marketplace. Issues that might seem personal such as genital cutting had long been global issues and because migration had occurred for millennia such customs traveled. Nonetheless, at the 2009 annual meeting of the World History Association, out of the hundreds of presentations there was only one paper on women in world history.

Scholars amidst this debate in the 1990s and 2000s pursued global investigations at an increasing pace. In the 1980s social scientists recognized women's place in the global workforce, providing statistical and ethnographic information for historians. The study of women's work in relationship to global markets going back centuries has become an important ingredient in women's history. Some historians have taken the opportunity to study women slaves crossing oceans, bringing innovations in agriculture, providing populations around the world with sugar and other innovative products, and even themselves participating in the slave trade. Findings that female slaves from West Africa actually launched and maintained rice production in the American South, it goes without saying, ignited a firestorm of protest from (mostly male) historians invested in a specific gendering of innovation and in a non-agential form of women's slavery (Carney and Rosomoff 2010). Women in Korea hundreds of years ago were transmitters of religions across regions as were those participating in Islamic, Christian, and other pilgrimages (Clancy-Smith 2006). Another way for historians of women in the West to access world history has been through the study of empire, currently an active pursuit, but the other paths being taken are numerous, for instance, in the study of international feminist movements, women's participation in global warfare, and their engagement with global trends in the arts and sciences (e.g. Hawkesworth 2006).

Gender and post-colonial theory, however, have thrown such activism and feminism and even the history of women itself into question. There was an additional international component to women's activism in that colonized women mobilized against foreign oppressors, even as they cited ideas about the improvement of women's condition from theorists in oppressor countries. This trend has recently been called 'colonial modernity.' Briefly put, the embeddedness of women in (unequal) family relationships and traditional obligations became a rallying cry for male reformers around the world seeking to become citizens in and leaders of modern nations. The male goal of modernizing women, which included producing them as individuals and activists in the public sphere and directing that women's actions operate within modernity, produced the category 'woman' and 'women,' which in many cultures had not even existed in languages such as Chinese (Barlow 2004). The aim was to make kingdoms and decaying empires ready for nationhood and modernity in the tradition of the enlightened nations of the West. In Siam, for example, a modernizing and colonizing kingdom used reform of the legal system and of the marriage system, specifically banning polygyny, to consolidate its regime in modern ways (Loos 2006). By this interpretation, feminism more generally, East and West, is seen as part of a colonial modernity that not only produced women but produced them as feminists – all in the name of legitimating the modern nation where women were no longer oppressed drudges but enlightened individuals. The ongoing scholarship around colonial modernity is transforming the history of the world in general and of the West in particular, as its own enlightenment is attached to colonialism (Barlow 2004). For interpretations of feminism the stakes are high.

Women also continued to mobilize internationally, but ironically, if the idea of 'colonial modernity' holds, with an increasing distrust by women from the colonized 'south' toward those coming from the imperial powers, armed with a firm belief in their racial superiority. When German activists at an international meeting of WILPF (Women's International League for Peace and Freedom) sponsored a resolution condemning the presence of black troops in their country after World War I on the grounds that blacks would rape white women, African-American women had to lobby hard to block the motion even though they could not stop the pernicious racist speeches. Indeed, movements were fractious because of racism and ethnic antagonisms. Local women in India, for example, did not want British women with their claims to superiority and omniscience arriving in their country to set up an Indian branch of WILPF. They would do the organizing themselves. Thus although women might seem to have been puppets of modernizing men, other historians counter that women learned organizing and other political skills outside mainstream politics.

Gender theory and post-colonial theory have done additional work. In terms of non-Western scholarship on individual regions and nations, the record in women's history is staggering and the accomplishments wide-ranging. Most interesting has been the experimentation that scholars of non-Western women's history have undertaken to interrogate Western paradigms and in fact to break or confound them. To give just two examples, Dorothy Ko (2005) narrates the history of footbinding (*Cinderella's Sisters: A Revisionist History of Footbinding*) in reverse order, beginning with Christian and reformist attacks on the practice and then moving backwards through men's writings over the centuries to uncover their fantasies. Only near the end of her study does Ko arrive at the bound foot, exploring it through its materiality, that is through a minute look at the shoes, bindings, and structures of the bound foot and women's multiple engagements with the foot and relationships to one another across the practices of it. The foot-bound woman, in Ko's telling, is a production caught between literature and women's engagement with the material body. Likewise, Nancy Rose Hunt's *A Colonial Lexicon of Birth Ritual, Medicalization, and Mobility in the Congo* (1997) looks at objects, rituals, and usages around birthing in the Congo to arrive at a pastiche of reproductive life and its meanings. The account appears disjointed for many readers, leaving behind the familiar, linear structures of the progressive, gendered historical monograph.

By the lights of 'colonial modernity' theorists, sexuality is simply one more category of the progressive, individualist, eugenicist colonial mind. But there are other, more positivist approaches using insights from and tools of inter-disciplinary scholarship that have an equal power to confound. Influenced like most women's and gender history – and indeed like history generally – by contemporary concerns in politics and everyday life, the history of gays and lesbians, transgendered people, and transsexuals has offered an incredible array of data with the potential to radicalize positivism itself. In US history, transsexuals, who were especially prominent after the sex reassignment surgery of Christine Jorgensen in 1952, have served more radical ends in questioning sex roles and gender than feminists have, scholars maintain. The histories of men and women, searching for ways to become physically the sex they felt themselves to be intellectually and emotionally, threw sex into question more than half a century ago. In demanding that their bodies be altered to harmonize with their intimate feelings, these American transsexuals dramatically posed the question of whether sex was physical or mental. In their case, mental sex preceded physical sex. According to scholar Joanne Meyerowitz (2002) feminists in the 1970s and 1980s rejected transsexual women as not 'women born women' – that is, people who had not been born with female genitals, exposing a range of problems in feminism itself. But these breakthroughs have hardly been confined to the West alone: for example, the studies by Evelyn Blackwood and Khaled El-Rouayheb show a wide range of sophisticated and transdisciplary understandings of the sexual past (Blackwood et al. 2009; El-Rouayheb 2005). Blackwood brings us the concept of 'sacred gender,' one hardly fitting the constraints of 'colonial modernity.' The import of works theorizing 'lesbian-like' practices or imported valorizations of a 'third sex' is precisely to show the potential of a more traditional historical methodology for critique (e.g. Bennett 2006).

Historians have introduced the study of fantasies and mental states as a legitimate way to understand history: for example, feminism as a psychological construct and built in part from fantasies that women in various parts of the world have long had about one another. In so fantasizing they can be said to participate in global processes via their imaginations. Joan Scott in an important essay 'Fantasy Echo' (2012) used insights from psychoanalysis to suggest that feminist history and feminist reliance on heroines in the past was based on an imperfect reading – a fantasized echo – of that past that did a great deal of psychic work in determining politics. Applied to other past activists, not only did someone like Mary Wortley Montagu in the eighteenth century describe Ottoman women and imitate them in countless ways, more remote actors who could only read about foreign women wore turbans, bloomers, or unfettered garments in the modern age and in the case of Chinese footbinders picked up habits from women almost a continent away. Such fantasies and imitations were far from meaningless. An entire politics developed in the West over women adopting bloomers, a derivative of Ottoman harem pants or, somewhat later, the slim pants of people in southeast Asia first adopted by men. The precise workings of fantasy in women's history and in women's writing has opened up new terrain for history as a whole that still remains to be sufficiently explored.

The nation as an eroticized construct has also emerged from women's and gender history. Some of the early work in US history, for example, pointed to the gendered iconography of the new American republic. 'Liberty,' figured as a woman, wept at the death of George Washington; in France, Liberty was similarly depicted as a bare-breasted woman leading armed male citizens into battle for freedom. More recently the figuring of women in many national movements has been prominent, while nation-building, like marriage, has been fraught with violence against women. Drawing on insights from the late George Mosse about the eroticization of war, historians of women and gender have recently devised a theory of the nation by which it is constructed out of an eroticized politics and gendered political fantasy (Mosse 1985). George Mosse contributed some of the framework in his evidence about the ways in which men's deaths on the battlefield were turned from simply a death to a fabled sacrifice around which one erected monuments, including those of mothers holding young children or adoring young men. Historians of women and gender such as Sinha and Najmabadi (Najmabadi 2005) both consider that the modern nation as an eroticized entity, operating on both implicit and explicit invocations of sexuality and gender as they rippled with libidinal energy.

## POINTS OF CONTENTION

From the beginning of the 'academicization' of women's history there have been calls for its demise and fences suggested for its confinement. For example, the late Lawrence Stone suggested in a comment some 30 years ago that women's history could only be done in the context of family history (Stone 1977). Outside of the family, women really had no history. Male scholars in Australia became hysterical when Patricia Grimshaw and her co-authors suggested in *Creating a Nation* (1994) that women were at all important in the Australian past. Fifteen years and thousands of books later, British historian David Starkey dredged up the tired tropes of trivialization and femininity used by nineteenth- and early twentieth-century male professionals. In 2009, he told the *Radio Times*: 'One of the great problems has been that Henry [VIII], in a sense, has been absorbed by his wives. Which is bizarre. But it's what you expect from feminized history, the fact that so many of the writers who write about this are women and so much of their audience is a female audience. Unhappy marriages are big box office.' The trivialization of scholarship on women would have been familiar to both amateur and professional women scholars generations earlier.

But where indeed does women's history or gender history stand in truth? A decade ago, Judith Zinsser subtitled her book on the status of women in the profession and women's

history *A Glass Half Full?* (Zinsser 1993). Responding to calls for women's history simply to stop – it had already said more than enough – Alice Kessler Harris gently soothed the still outraged male professionals that after a few decades of scholarship a full picture of women's past was still not in view. Kessler-Harris pointed out in the *Chronicle of Higher Education* that in fact much remained to be accomplished. For one thing, the findings of women's history and the insights of gender history had simply not been mainstreamed, as advocates of dispensing with women's history maintained (Kessler-Harris 2007). Since the founding days of 'second wave' women's history, a variety of commentators have pointed to the disappearance of women's history as a goal. The idea is that women's history is not that important except to fill in material that the historical record has missed. Once that record is filled in – c.7,000 years of history recovered in one or two decades of work, so the thought went – there would be no more need for a 'women's' history but rather history would truly become the history of humankind.

In fact, in the 20 years since the introduction of gender history and the 40 years since the 'take-off' of women's history distinctly new paths have opened in both fields. For example, since the fall of communism in 1989 the history of women in Eastern Europe has taken off among scholars in the region. *The Journal of Women's History* took justifiable pride in carrying articles on eastern European women's history when many saw the area as fundamentally uninteresting because it was allegedly chaotic, racist, and intellectually backward – an 'other' needing basic civilizing, not historical attention. Meanwhile, eastern and southeastern historians of women took on massive institution building, such as founding women's and gender studies programs, writing biographical dictionaries (e.g. De Haan et al. 2006) and founding journals – for example, *Aspasia* – devoted to the studies of women in eastern Europe and the former Soviet Union. Thus, beyond the squabbles, local scholars showed that a trans-European feminist practice actually flourished in the nineteenth and twentieth centuries and that there was contact across borders alongside local practices and debates. 'Any suggestion to the contrary is a denial of the intelligence and human agency of countless women and men,' the editors of the biographical diction- ary of activists in eastern and southeastern Europe maintained (De Haan et al. 2006: 3). Indeed, as a result of this scholarship many Western European and US historians, who had often seen socialism as an answer to the ine- quality of women, were forced to investigate conditions with fresh eyes.

Still another point of contention was and is the inordinate attention paid to US and Euro- pean women's history. In part this complaint is a by-product both of the massive scholar- ship in non-Western women's history and of the wider globalization of the economy and politics. Additionally and more specifically the criticism targets the relentless presentism in the Amero-centric concentration on twentieth- century US women's history. Whereas the Berkshire Conference of Women Historians has cut European panels to accommodate ses- sions on global history, it keeps a strong con- temporary Americanist bias. It is, according to one scholar, worse than the American His- torical Association in favoring nineteenth- and especially twentieth-century history while rejecting medieval and ancient panels. Critics maintain that there is much to learn from the 'deep' past and in particular that there is far more continuity than change in women's wages and in their general status in society (Bennett 2006). Rejecting a deeper past also eliminates the many accomplished women globally, not only those who excelled in crafts such as silk-making but those thou- sands of women poets, novelists, and other authors who were acknowledged in their own time but who in the face of presentism and Amero-centrism are not being publicized as much as the US activists of the twentieth and twenty-first centuries.

What future do historians of women and gender face? Exciting and important findings come from an even deeper past in the activities of women in prehistory and possibly even in big history – as the universe came into being and before there was a written historical record. Researchers have found that in the very distant past male and female skeletons were of approximately the same size, sug- gesting that over the past millennia women were systematically denied food as part of male privilege that remains to this day. Sec- ond (among many observations) the idea of male the hunter, woman the gatherer has also been discredited. Women, researchers now demonstrate, were active hunters in prehis- toric times. As women's and gender history continues to blaze trails for the profession as a whole, one can expect further controversy, innovation in the field, and even revolutions in the writing of history generally.

## REFERENCES

Alexander, William. 1779. *The History of Women, from Earliest Antiquity to the Present Time*. London: W. Strahan and T. Cadell.

Astell, Mary. 1703. *Some Reflections Upon Marriage*. London: Printed for R. Wilkin.

Astell, Mary. 2002 [18th century]. *A Serious Proposal to the Ladies. Parts I and II.*, ed. Patricia Springborg. Peterborough, Ontario: Broadview Press.

Barlow, Tani E. 2004. *The Question of Women in Chinese Feminism*. Durham, NC: Duke University Press.

Bateson, Mary. 1899. 'History of the Double Monasteries.' *Transactions of the Royal Historical Society*, n.s. 13: 137–198.

Bennett, Judith. 2006. *History Matters: Patriarchy and the Challenge of Feminism*. Philadelphia: University of Pennsylvania Press.

Blackwood, Evelyn, Abha Bhaiya, and Saskia E. Wieringa. 2009. *Women's Sexualities and Masculinities in a Globalizing Asia*. London: Palgrave Macmillan.

Butler, Judith. 1990. *Gender Trouble*. NY: Routledge.

Butler, Judith. 1993. *Bodies That Matter: On the Discursive Limits of 'Sex.'* NY: Routledge.

Carney, Judith and Nicholas Rosomoff. 2010. *In the Shadow of Slavery: Africa's Botanical Legacy in the Atlantic World*. Berkeley: University of California Press.

Child, Maria. 1835. *The History of the Condition of Women in Various Ages and Nations*. London: Simpkin, Marshall, and Co.

Christine de Pisan. 1977 [1429]. *Ditié de Jehanne d'Arc*, ed. Angus J. Kennedy and Kenneth Varty. Oxford: Society for the Study of Mediaeval Languages and Literature.

Christine de Pisan. 1982 [1405]. *The Book of the City of Ladies*, trans. Earl Jeffrey Richards. New York: Persea Books.

Clancy-Smith, Julia Ann. 2006. *Exemplary Women and Sacred Journeys: Women and Gender in Judaism, Christianity, and Islam from Late Antiquity to the Eve of Modernity*. American Historical Association.

de Beauvoir, Simone. 2009 [1949]. *The Second Sex*, trans. Constance Borde and Sheila Malovany-Chevalier. NY: Knopf.

De Haan, Francisca, Krasimira Daskalova and Anna Loutfi. 2006. *Biographical Dictionary of Women's Movements and Feminisms: Central, Eastern, and South Eastern Europe, 19th and 20th Centuries*. Budapest: Central European University Press.

Des Jardins, Julie. 2003. *Women and the Historical Enterprise in America: Gender, Race, and the Politics of Memory, 1880–1945*. Chapel Hill, NC: University of North Carolina Press.

Dupin, Louise-Marie. 2009 [c. 1750] A. Hunter. 'The unfinished work on Louise Marie-Madeleine Dupin's unfinished Ouvrage sur les femmes.' *Eighteenth-Century Studies*, 43: 95–111.

Ellet, Elizabeth. 1869. *The Court Circles of the Republic, or The Beauties and Celebrities of the Nation*. Hartford, CT: Hartford Pub. Co.

El-Rouayheb. 2005. *Before Homosexuality in the Arab-Islamic World, 1500–1800*. Chicago: University of Chicago.

*English Historical Review*. 1898. Vol. 13: 167, 125.

Ferguson, Moira, ed. 1985. *First Feminists: British Women Writers, 1578–1799*. Bloomington, IN: Feminist Press.

Genlis, Stéphanie Félicité. 1785. *Tales of the Castle: or Stories of Instruction and Delight*, trans. Thomas Holcroft. London: G. Robinson.

Giddings, Paula. 1984. *When and Where I Enter: The Impact of Black Women on Race and Sex in America*. New York: W. Morrow.

Grimshaw, Patricia, Lake, Marilyn, and Quartly, Marian. 1994. *Creating a Nation*. London: Penguin Books.

Hawkesworth, M.E. 2006. *Globalization and Feminist Activism*. Oxford: Rowman & Littlefield.

Hildreth, Richard. 1849–52. *History of the United States of America*, 6 vols. NY: Harper. Vol. IV, vii.

Hine, Darlene Clark. 1993. *Black Women in America: an Historical Encyclopedia*. Brooklyn, NY: Carlson Press.

Hull, Gloria T., Bell-Scott, Patricia, and Smith, Barbara. 1982. *All the Women are White, All the Men are Black But Some of Us Are Brave*. Old Westbury, NY: Feminist Press.

Hunt, Nancy Rose. 1997. *A Colonial Lexicon of Birth Ritual, Medicalization, and Mobility in the Congo*. Durham, NC: Duke University Press.

Irigaray, Luce. 1985. *This Sex Which Is Not One*. Ithaca, NY: Cornell University Press.

Jameson, Anna. 2005 [1832]. *Shakespeare's Heroines: Characteristics of Women, Moral, Poetical, and Historical*. Peterborough, Ontario: Broadview Press.

Juana de la Cruz. 2005 [17th century] *Sor Juana Ines de la Cruz: Selected Writings*, ed. Pamela Kirk Rappaport. New York: Paulist Press.

Keralio, Louise. 1786–89. *Collection des meilleurs ouvrages francois, composés par des femmes, dédiée aux femmes francoises*. Paris.

Kessler-Harris, Alice. 2007. 'Do We Still Need Women's History?' *Chronicle of Higher Education*, vol. 54.

Ko, Dorothy. 2005. *Cinderella's Sisters: A Revisionist History of Footbinding*. Berkeley, CA: University of California Press.

Lerner, Gerda. 1986. *The Creation of Patriarchy*. New York: Oxford University Press.

Levi-Strauss, Claude. *The Elementary Structures of Kinship*. 1949. Boston, MA: Beacon Press.

Loos, Tamara Lynn. 2006. *Subject Siam: Family, Law, And Colonial Modernity in Thailand*. Ithaca, NY: Cornell University Press.

Mann, Susan. 1992. '"Fuxue" (Women's Learning) by Zhang Xuecheng (1738–1801): China's First History of Women's Culture.' *Late Imperial China*, 13(1): 40–62.

Meiners, Christopher. 1808. *History of the Female Sex: Comprising a View of the Habits, Manners, and Influence of Women*. London: H. Colburn.

Meyerowitz, Joanne J. 2002. *How Sex Changed: A History of Transsexuality*. Cambridge, MA: Harvard University Press.

Moraga, Cherrie and Anzaldua, Gloria. 1981. *This Bridge Called My Back: Writings from Radical Women of Color*. New York: Kitchen Table.

Mosse, George Lachman. 1985. *Nationalism and Sexuality: Respectability and Abnormal Sexuality in Modern Europe*. NY: Howard Fertig.

Murasaki Shikibu. 1960. [11th century]. *The Tale of Genji; a Novel in Six Parts*. New York: Modern Library.

Najmabadi, Afsaneh. 2005. *Women with Mustaches and Men without Beards: Gender and Sexual Anxieties of Iranian Modernity*. Berkeley, CA: University of California Press.

Perrot, Michelle. 1984. *Une Histoire des femmes est-elle possible*. Paris: Rivages.

Power, Eileen. 1975. *Medieval Women*. New York: Cambridge University Press.

Renan, Ernest. 1990 [1882]. 'What Is a Nation?', trans. Martin Thom, in Homi Bhabha, ed., *Nation and Narration*. 1990. London: Routledge, pp. 8–21.

Rotter, Andrew. 1994. 'Gender relations, foreign relations: the United States and South Asia, 1947–1964.' *Journal of American History*, 81: 518–42.

Rowbotham, Sheila. 1972. *Women, Resistance and Revolution*. New York: Pantheon Books.

Rowbotham, Sheila. 1974. *Hidden From History*. New York: Pantheon Books.

Rubin, Gayle. 1975. 'The Traffic in Women: Notes on the "Political Economy" of Sex.' In Rayna R. Reiter, ed., *Toward an Anthropology of Women*. NY: Monthly Review Press. pp. 157–210.

Ruiz, Vicky. 1987. *Cannery Women, Cannery Lives: Mexican Women, Unionization, and the California Food Processing Industry, 1930–1950*. Albuquerque, NM: University of New Mexico Press.

Salmon, Lucy Maynard. 1906. *Progress in the Household*. Boston, NY: Houghton, Mifflin and Co.

Scott, Anne Firor. 1970. *The Southern Lady: From Pedestal to Politics, 1830–1930*. Chicago, IL: University of Chicago Press.

Scott, Joan. 1986. 'Gender: A Useful Category of Historical Analysis.' *American Historical Review*, 91(5): 1053–75.

Scott, Joan Wallach. 2012. *The Fantasy of Feminist History*. Durham, NC: Duke Univesity Press.

Sei Sonagon. 1979 [11th century]. *The Pillow Book of Sei Shonagon*. London: Harmondsworth.

Sinha, Mrinalini. 2006. *Specters of Mother India: The Global Restructuring of Empire*. Durham, NC: Duke University Press.

Smith, Bonnie. 1998. *The Gender of History: Men, Women, and Historical Practice*. Cambridge, MA: Harvard University Press.

Stael, Germaine de. 2008 [ 1818] *Considerations on the Principal Events of the French Revolution*. Indianapolis, IN: Liberty Fund.

Stone, Lawrence. 1977. *The Family, Sex and Marriage in England 1500–1800*. NY: Harper & Row.

Strickland, Agnes, and Strickland, Elisabeth. 1851–52. *Lives of the Queens of England: from the Norman Conquest*. London: H. Colburn.

Thomas, Antoine-Leonard. 1774. *Essay on the Character, Manners, and Genius of Women in Different Ages*. Philadelphia: R. Aitken.

Wanyan Yun Zhu. 1994 [1831] *Precious Record from the Maiden's Chamber*. 1831. in *The Columbia Anthology of Traditional Chinese Literature*, ed. Victor H. Mair. 1994. New York: Columbia University Press.

Wanyan Yun Zhu. 1999 [1831]. 'Correct Beginnings: Women's Poetry of our August Dynasty.' In *Chinese Women Poets: An Anthology of Poetry and Criticism from Ancient Times to 1911*, ed. Kang-i Sun Chang and Haun Saussy. 1999. Stanford, CA: Stanford University Press.

Zinsser, Judith. 1993. *History and Feminism: A Glass Half Full?* New York: Twayne Publishers.

# 17

# Gender II: Masculinity Acquires a History

Karen Harvey

When did masculinity get a history? Women's historians have for some time insisted on the study of men as gendered subjects too.[1] Numerous were the comments about the need to historicize masculinity from the contributors to a special feature of the magazine *History Today* in 1985.[2] Women's history did not exclude men and masculinity, then; on the contrary, women's historians opened up the academic space in which to consider the history of masculinity. Later, as 'gender' developed as a more precise and explicit analytical concept in the 1980s, so men and masculinity were elevated as key concerns. In spring 1989, the editorial of the first issue of the key journal in the field – *Gender and History* – declared an attention to 'men and masculinity as well as women and femininity'.[3] To a considerable extent, therefore, the history of masculinity displays many of the same characteristics as the broader history of gender, a sub-field of which it is often considered a necessary component part. This is because whether characterized by a culturally inflected analysis of meanings, or a socially inflected examination of experience, gender history is essentially a comparative exercise. This feature gives gender history

the potential to transform the discipline. As 'a theoretically informed attempt to bring the two sexes and their complex relations into our picture of the past', writes John Tosh, the history of gender 'is conceptually equipped to attain a fully comprehensive social reach; and on this basis it has the potential to offer a theory of social structure and of historical change.' It promises nothing less than 'to modify the writing of *all* history'.[4]

It would be a grossly inaccurate account of origins and impact, though, to state that the history of masculinity had achieved a presence in the discipline equivalent to that of women's and gender history during the 1970s and 1980s. Statements about the importance of examining men and masculinities as well as women, and about the necessarily comparative nature of gender history, did simply not translate into sustained analyses of the history of masculinity. A coherent and identifiable history of masculinity – with a measurable presence in specialist journals, edited collections, monographs, job titles, statements of research interests, and seminar and module topics – only emerged during the 1990s.[5] And with that distinctive genesis, comes a distinctive historical field; the history of masculinity clearly bears the stamp of its later date of birth.

Coming after the massive changes that women's and feminist history had made to the discipline, and also after the first key theoretical statements about gender, masculinity is a field of history produced out of the productive tensions between poststructuralist theory, social history, feminist theory, women's history, but also (and often less acknowledged) the area of study often known as 'Men's Studies'. Associated with some of these approaches we can identify some of the factors influencing the field's relatively delayed appearance: notably the resistance to 'gender' arose from worries about postructuralist theory, seen as making women less visible, and also from concerns about lending power to men and a new generation of women using a new epithet of 'gender' to get ahead.[6] It is worth making sense of these tensions in the context of 'identity politics', because as a context for the histories of women, gender and masculinity this illuminates some of the many issues at stake for historical practitioners, as well as their views about how History should be practised. Identity politics is a form of late-twentieth-century politics 'based upon group identity, as opposed to interest, reform or ideology'.[7] Such identities are often built upon 'the specificity of each group's history and ideological singularity', and recognition of this helps us understand some of the tensions between these politically charged fields of History.[8] Women's history and men's studies were in part motivated by a desire to forge collective identities for men and women. These fields also emerged at the same time that researchers in politics began to question the role of concepts of women and gender in identity politics. One author saw within the rise of 'political-cultural movements', 'the politicization of gender, the family, and the position of women'.[9] Identity politics was also seen as a process that sought to delimit and control women, and the appropriate response from feminist academics was to interrogate discourses about women as symbols, restoring

them 'as human beings'.[10] Any attempt to construct women in identity politics 'is a struggle to construct an "us" that is said to share a single historical experience'.[11] History has been central to critiques of identity politics, used to expose apparently 'core or bedrock identity' as fictions used to delimit and disenfranchise.[12] And in the history of masculinity (as with the history of women) one aim was to forge an identity for men *as men* in the present, while also challenging normative ideas about what 'men' and 'masculinity' meant in the past. In this cultural context, the history of masculinity was closely linked to politics.

## THE CHALLENGE OF RESEARCHING MEN

Recognizing the roots of the history of masculinity in 'Men's Studies', along with the vigorous dialogue between historians and researchers on modern men during the field's inception, is important to an understanding of some of its key theoretical preoccupations. It is a commonplace of accounts of late-twentieth-century women's history that feminism played a key shaping role. Feminist politics of the 1960s and 1970s made women's history possible (perhaps imperative) and shaped the aims and methods of many women's historians. Indeed, feminists invested in the potential of the discipline of history to transform contemporary experiences. Precisely the same investment in History was made by those engaging in the field of 'Men's Studies' in the 1980s: their aim was to expose men as gendered beings, and as people capable of change, in part by historicizing masculinity. As Victor Seidler stated in his book *Rediscovering Masculinity* (1989), he was 'exploring masculinity as a historically emergent experience', and this was 'a precondition for thinking about whether it is possible for men to change'. For Seidler, this was indubitably 'an issue of political practice'[13] Seidler's primary historical object was an Enlightenment concept of reason that translated into a universal and singular notion of masculinity, and to which 'enormous institutionalized power' accrued. The aim was to expose 'masculinity as a social and historical experience', thus acknowledging many different masculinities while also challenging what had become normal personal relations of power.[14] History enabled general change, but it also drew upon individual personal histories. Lynne Segal's book *Slow Motion: Changing Masculinities, Changing Men* (1990), begins with an account of men in the 1950s; Seidler goes back to Enlightenment philosophers, but also includes an autobiographical account of his own sexual growth from the 1940s onwards.[15] This emphasis on the personal as an intellectual, historical and political resource was important. 'If it is important to recognize in this process that our identities are historically forged, it is also important to retain the substance of our individual experience as a theoretical resource', cautioned Seidler.[16] The opening of his book situates his individual experience at the heart of the analysis: 'This is both a personal and a theoretical book. It is a contribution to an understanding of a particular masculinity in its social and historical formation. It is also the experience of a particular man and his growing up into masculinity.'[17]

Such a position involves reflection on the practice of history and knowledge creation. Drawing on one's individual experience as a theoretical resource is a direct challenge to what Dale Spender had called 'the objectivity of objectivity'.[18] Feminist scholars dispensed with the term 'subjective', preferring 'partial and temporary "truths"'.[19] This feminist stress on the legitimacy of the individual position of the author is a reminder that a relativist stress on multiple meanings is not purely a result of poststructuralism. But my main point here is specifically that this feminist emphasis on the individual and positioned practitioner also emerged in men's studies. More generally some of the feminist challenges to the theoretical underpinnings of historical enquiry were shared by those who first began to explore the history of masculinity. As Victor Seidler explains, feminism 'challenged the forms of our knowledge' and 'the relation of learning to experience, the relation between the personal and theoretical. Our personal experience can no longer be so easily dismissed as "subjective" or "biased", but must be recognized as opening up new ways of locating ourselves within a shared experience of power and subordination. So it is that feminism has implicitly challenged both the methods and the theories that we had inherited within social theory and philosophy.'[20]

As feminism did for women's history, men's studies rooted the historical quest to a living group, rendering it an embodied process and one that foregrounded the materiality of experience. 'The body' as an organizing category and interpretive concept here became important. Examining the changing nature of 'the body' has been key to gender history, exposing – as it can – the discursive nature of the apparently most natural and permanent of categories. Essentially, a gendered history of the body disrupts 'sex' as an organizing category for historical research. For early works on masculinity, 'the body' was a particularly radical concept. The association of men with self-control and domination (over their own and others' emotions, bodies and desires) was seen to disassociate men and their physical bodies.[21] This was regarded as a particularly extreme version of a cultural inability of men to get 'in touch' with their feelings and experiences. Writers struggled to find ways to get men back 'in touch', but also with which to research and examine such experiences. It was in this context that a poststructuralist deconstruction of language was seen wanting, doing nothing to account for the often contrasting experiences of the physical state of being a man. 'Structuralist and post-structuralist theories have failed to illuminate contradictions within our lived experience,' explained Seidler.[22] This became a common theme in work on masculinity. Writing with regards to social relations of power, Bob Pease claimed that men's 'social or institutionalized power may not always correlate with their experience as individual men and their *feelings* of powerlessness'.[23] The same point is made by Jonathan Watson in his study of men's health, when he advises that 'we need to differentiate between the production, reproduction and erosion of patriarchy as located within social structures and institutions, and masculinities as a personal and embodied response to and reflection of these social and cultural values'.[24] Watson examines how men talk about their own bodies, and in this way 'embodiment provides the ground on which the dynamics of gender are made personal and the tensions of agency and structure are realized'.[25]

Some of the principal issues observable in Men's Studies research – the politics of practice, critiques of historical knowledge, identity (whether psychological, individual, or corporate), diversity, power, change over time, the body, and the disjuncture between dominant discourses and individual experience – have all become key to the history of masculinity. This had roots in a political project and was indebted to feminism, sharing some of its key motivations. We will see that as a maturing field of historical enquiry, the history of masculinity is no longer defined by these motivations. Yet it is remarkable that a great many of the concerns of this field can be traced to this early work. Indeed, as I will discuss at the end of this chapter, the political antecedents of the history of masculinity gives it the radical potential to transform History.

## TRACKING THE HISTORICITY OF MASCULINE IDENTITIES

The historical contingency of masculine identity is perhaps the fundamental concern of the history of masculinity. In early works, considerable emphasis was placed on the social construction of roles, manifest in work on, for example, the socialization of boys.[26] The history of masculinity followed some of the first steps of modern feminist and women's history in their challenge to essentialism, establishing early on that dominant notions of

masculinity are socially and culturally constructed rather than 'natural' and unchanging. Now studied from pre-history to contemporary history, masculinity has developed a narrative of change just like any other historical phenomenon, with certain chronological narratives acquiring considerable weight.[27] On the one hand, these signify the identity of the history of masculinity as part of a wider discipline prone to narrative, stressing synchronic norms rather than diversity. On the other hand, some of this work has produced findings that could be considered 'non-traditional'. Notable here is the work on the history of male sexuality, and the argument therein that in pre-modern societies the form of masculinity to which accrued social status and power was not equated with 'heterosexuality'.[28] The role of queer theory and queer history in this work is clear. In fact, these areas have had a palpable impact on the history of masculinity in ways that they do not seem to have transformed women's history. Arguably, there has been a greater tension between homosexuality and masculinity, than between lesbianism and femininity; historically, from the eighteenth century onwards, it seems that lesbianism could be regarded as a kind of hyper-femininity, while homosexuality became opposed to normative masculinity.[29] Evidence of the extent to which the history of masculinity shares intellectual antecedents and academic space with other fields in the discipline – particularly women's history – is the degree to which the narratives of the history of the former have been combined with narratives emerging from the latter. Indeed, this narrative of sexuality defines the history of masculinity for much of the early modern period.[30]

It is not surprising that historical research into male sexuality has fed directly into queer studies. Martha M. Umphrey's landmark article, 'The trouble with Harry Thaw', sought to expose the difficulties of studying historical subjects that fail to fit into the identity categories of the researcher: 'If my recuperable gay man transmogrifies into a site of incoherent and indeterminate sexual identity, that isn't his fault.'[31] Instead of writing Thaw's history as a gay man, she argues for the writing of a queer history, employing a category that suggests something apart from the heterosexual, and that can necessarily 'denaturalize and destabilize public representations of compulsory heterosexuality'.[32] Umphrey draws on Trumbach's 'Birth of the queen' article as a source of alternative identities for Thaw, suggesting that the persona of the eighteenth-century rake or libertine – 'a manly man interested in both women and boys' – is a more appropriate label for Thaw than 'homosexual'.[33] Clearly observable, here, are parallels between the methodological and epistemological issues confronted by scholars of gender and sexual identities, of masculinity, femininity, heterosexuality, homosexuality and bisexuality. These scholars seek to problematize contemporary categories by historicizing them; underpinning these endeavours are assumptions about relativism, historical change, contingency and diversity.

## GENDER THEORY AND MODES OF ANALYSIS

Men's Studies research was undertaken outside the discipline of History, by practitioners in other departments, who published their work in sociology and politics journals. An equally important factor in shaping the history of masculinity was the development of gender as a category of analysis. As noted above, women's historians made statements about the importance of seeing men as gendered subjects of historical analysis, as well as women. However, a theoretical complexity and precision to statements about the relational nature of gender was properly the result of poststructuralist modes of gender analysis. The landmark work is by Joan Scott. Scott's definition of gender was precise: gender is 'the knowledge that establishes meanings for bodily differences'.[34] This knowledge, she stated, had been used to shape social relationships such that these appeared to be based on biological differences.

Crucially, however, the knowledge about bodily differences – the way in which people understood the body – had also been 'a primary way of signifiying power relationships'.[35] Relationships between men and women, but also the character and distribution of political power more generally, has been built upon and legitimized by ideas about gender. This form of analysis took a Derridean method of deconstruction and applied it to gender in language. The influence of Jacques Derrida produced an attention to difference, a critique of dichotomy, and an exposure of processes of 'othering'.

As the founder editors of *Gender and History* noted, such a focus on discourse, on 'the historical construction of masculinity' produced a kind of emptying.[36] While 'men' became an empty category, masculinity became a plural one. This emphasis on plurality, on *masculinities*, is one direct result of a poststructuralist form of analysis. It is a focus central to John Beynon's book, where 'masculinity' is defined as being 'composed of many masculinities'.[37] Lynne Segal's book also stresses plurality, with sections on three sets of 'competing masculinities': manly ideals, homosexuals, and black men. As John Tosh has written, '"Masculinities" fits with the post-modernist vision of the world, with its proliferation of identities and its contradictory discourses.'[38] Despite some shared roots and early statements as to the difficulty of defining 'women', masculinity possesses far more plurality and diversity than does the category of femininity in historical studies.

While the subject of identities has most often been mined using postmodern analyses of language, other scholars have approached this topic in terms of 'subjectivity', sometimes employing psychoanalysis as their analytical tool.[39] Seidler promoted the use of psychoanalysis as one route out of the impasse between discourses of power on the one hand, and men's emotions on the other. He felt that psychoanalysis restored the relationship between experience and language.[40] In doing so, researchers could examine the disjuncture between dominant discourses and individual experience. Whether psycho-analytic in approach or not, this is a central organizing matrix in the history of masculinity, one that has superseded the earlier emphasis on social/cultural constructionism. Instead, the domains of language and experience are invariably regarded as distinct and mutually constructive, and studies of masculinity can examine one or the other, or the complex ways in which they interact. So it is that the editorial of the first issue of *Gender and History* saw gender as both 'a set of lived relations' and 'a symbolic system'.[41] Evidencing the influence of poststructuralist gender theory, recent works in the history of masculinity have given considerable space to cultural representations of masculinity in particular. Laura Lee Downs' account of the field of the history of masculinity, for example, is almost entirely focused on such cultural and discursive approaches.[42]

The predominance of such approaches in this field is manifest in the work on the history of the male body. While researchers in Men's Studies sought to emphasize a concept of embodiment, with its inclusion of the emotional and physical experiences of the human body, historians, by contrast, have tended to concern themselves with the symbolic or discursive. In this vein, historians 'read' the body, often placing it in the context of national or international contexts of politics or conflict.[43] But some work on the body also demonstrates a desire amongst historians of masculinity to incorporate actual male bodies – or a meaningful concept of them – into their research. Christina Jarvis's study of American male bodies during the Second World War begins with the ideal of the male heroic body, but poses the questions 'how were extreme wartime masculine ideals maintained in the face of hundreds of thousands of wounded and damaged masculinities? How exactly *was* masculinity represented during the war? And what role did actual male bodies play in the construction of wartime and postwar masculinities?'[44] In seeking to expose the relationship between 'personal and cultural narratives of male

embodiment', we can observe a widely felt desire to integrate meaning and experience in the history of masculinity.[45]

There is notable dissatisfaction with a discursive approach in this field. Downs regards such analyses as unable to connect 'discourses to their socio-economic contexts'.[46] Historians of masculinity 'wish to complement rigorous dissections of discourse with the social and psychological'.[47] Historians are keen to stress that gender – including masculinity – operates at many levels: 'the psychic, interpersonal, institutional, cultural and social'.[48] Downs similarly states that gender is 'a discursively constructed identity, but also a social and subjective one', arguing that historians of gender should incorporate all levels into their analyses.

The example Downs gives of such a multi-level analysis is John Tosh's landmark article, 'What should historians do with masculinity?' Tosh argues, here, that a new imperial form of masculinity emerged in the late nineteenth century, serving as the focus of identification from a particular lower-middle-class group of male clerical workers, as their economic and social position was threatened by economic and social change.[49] In the tradition of this example of the early history of masculinity, Tosh has continued to stress 'experience' as a key concept, as distinct from discourse, describing his practice thus: 'The analytical family historian deals in abstractions … Individual case-histories not only anchor these abstractions in lived experience … Social history is about the messiness of people's lives, as well as the structure which enable us to generalize about those lives.'[50] Tosh exemplifies what might be considered a newly revived social history of masculinity. The context for this is a series of recent challenges to the academic hegemony of cultural approaches. In the current disciplinary divergence between social and cultural history, Tosh falls on the side of the former, writing 'a more nuanced account of social experience'.[51] It is not the case that the history of masculinity is dominated by analyses of discourse, cut free from socio-economic context, therefore. In fact, there have been many different modes of analysis adopted in the history of masculinity: a gender analysis of patriarchal relations between men and women, a social historical analysis of the interactions between masculinity and social status, an examination of the psychological, selfhood and subjectivity, and finally a cultural historical analysis of masculinity in representation.[52] Just as practitioners emphasize plurality in historical constructions of masculinity, so we should stress the various modes of analysis that these practitioners employ. Notwithstanding the various modes of analysis, there are some recurring issues addressed by historians of masculinity, that further expose some of the conceptual apparatus of this field. Here I will focus on two closely related interpretive concepts.

## HOMOSOCIALITY AND PATRIARCHY

The emphasis in early works in the history of masculinity was on men in homosocial environments. *Manful Assertions*, an important early collection edited by Michael Roper and John Tosh, is striking for its almost exclusive focus on men alone: as workers, fathers and husbands, as imperial adventurers or readers of boys' papers. In this way, the history of masculinity operated in ways similar to early feminist and women's history: serving as a corrective, recovering men as gendered subjects, and restoring them to the historical record. As Tosh outlined in 'What should historians do with masculinity?', homosociality was at the heart of this project. Yet herein we might locate some tension between the conceptual underpinnings of the history of masculinity and gender history more generally. For Tosh, as for many other historians of masculinity, nineteenth-century manliness was a set of values and code of behaviour shaped in large part by relations between men rather than relations between women and men: 'masculinity is as much about homosociality as about patriarchy'.[53] While a commitment to gender as a comparative analytical

category is widely stated, much of the comparative element of the history of masculinity is generally constituted from comparisons between masculine and non-masculine ideas, rather than between men and women. Homosociality as a concept thus links many works on masculinity, from a study of seventeenth-century Cambridge students, to an analysis of men's responses to domesticity in mid-twentieth-century England.[54] This stress on men alone reflects the idea that it is at such homosocial sites that masculinity is shaped or tested or becomes most pronounced.

A second enduring theme is masculine power. Lynne Segal notes that feminists have long been interested in 'the search for an explanation of men's power over women'.[55] In women's history, the resultant problematization of male power has of course emphasized women, examining sites of women's agency, for example. In the history of masculinity, the emphasis is naturally upon men. If women's history and feminist history was in part faced with the challenge of writing the histories of the disadvantaged, the dispossessed, the silent and the unrepresented, then historians of masculinity have been faced with the challenge of writing the histories of the powerful, and of historicizing gendered power relations. The *Gender and History* collective led their editorial discussion of masculinity with this issue of power, referring to men's 'superior position' and 'the more powerful', in contrast to 'the less powerful', 'subordinate groups'.[56] Power, or 'manful assertions', has been the pre-eminent concern of historians of masculinity.

One way in which historians of masculinity have interrogated patriarchy is by exposing the extent to which men's experiences have not mapped neatly onto dominant discourses of male power. Seidler is critical of feminist theories of language, that see the world as organized for the benefit of men, and 'language simply as a one-way mechanism, of domination'.[57] Here we can identify a key strand of the history of masculinity, that seeks to problematize the notion of a one-dimensional patriarchal masculinity. Seidler seeks to 'explore the contradictions of our experience as men';[58] there is a related body of work on the history of masculinity that examines men's inability or even 'failure' to fulfil patriarchal expectations, and the anxieties and tensions that emerge as a result. This is particularly pronounced in studies of the male body, often informed by a psychoanalytic framework, where the phallus serves as the patriarchal symbol which men's real, fleshy, fragile bodies can never match.[59]

Examining this disjuncture between men's feelings and experiences on the one hand, and dominant discourses of male power on the other, historians have problematized the idea of 'patriarchal masculinity'. As Tosh has pointed out, early contributions to the history of masculinity focused on 'whether masculinity was wholly subsumed in patriarchy'.[60] Rather than retain a notion of patriarchal masculinity, albeit one that many men have found difficult to obtain, historians have argued that there are in fact many different types of masculinity, not all predicated on male power. Researchers in this field are thus treading a careful path between acknowledging the oppression of women and also the greater access of some men to power alongside the disempowerment that patriarchy brings for some other men. One important insight of historians of masculinity is that being a man has not always been equated with social or cultural power.

It is in this context that 'hegemonic masculinity' has become so important to the field, serving as the main interpretive concept. The key work is R.W. Connell's *Masculinities* (1995). In this work, 'hegemonic masculinity' was the form that was 'culturally exalted', performed by the political elite and sustaining its authority.[61] One of the strengths of this model is its insistence on the presence of other codes of masculinity – subordinate, marginalized and complicit – that not only coexist with but are defined with reference to the hegemonic form. Plurality is built into this model, although it serves to maintain the dominant status of hegemonic masculinity. Connell's model has been an important

device for historians of masculinity, enabling them to examine the ways in which certain forms of masculinity did not map directly onto power.

As rich a resource as it has been, the model has nevertheless come under scrutiny. This is, in fact, the most notable area in which the history of masculinity has challenged theory. In an important review of early books on manliness and masculinity, David Morgan commented that Connell's concept of hegemonic masculinity had been challenged by a recently published collection on masculinity edited by Mangan and Walvin. First, hegemomic codes were therein shown to be very flexible, accommodating a range of different features at different moments. And second, ideology – of a dominant, hegemonic code of masculinity, for example – did not necessarily translate into practice.[62] Such points are raised by others in later works. Historical research demonstrates that hegemonic codes were 'highly complex, fluid, and full of contradictions'. Furthermore, work has emphasized the extent to which alternative codes were not defined in relation to a hegemonic code, but were 'shaped independently'.[63] Connell's sociological concept has generated considerable debate, therefore, and in its reception in the discipline of History we can observe how 'the history of masculinity has the potential to modify (rather than simply work within) this theoretical framework in the interests not only of greater analytical precision but also of furthering a more dynamic relationship between history and theory.'[64]

Models of hegemonic masculinity have given way to approaches to power that place other key historical categories of identity more fully alongside gender. Arguably, with its greater focus on the public realm and work, the attention to men and masculinity has led to a focus on the intersection of social rank or class and gender. In this way, historians of masculinity – like other gender historians – have sought to expose how apparently 'genderless' notions of power have in fact been thoroughly gendered. Historians of masculinity also examine how masculinity is both illuminated by and inter-sects with race. Race, gender and class were brought together in the important work of Anne McClintock, *Imperial Leather* (1995), a study of empire in the nineteenth and twen-tieth centuries.[65] Her key conceptual inter-vention was that 'race, gender and class are not distinct realms of experience'; 'Rather they come into existence *in and through* rela-tion to each other – if in contradictory and conflictual ways.'[66] Imperial power was not simply expressed through metaphors of sex-uality, but was constructed out of relations of gender. Race was not simply about blackness and whiteness, but was constituted from notions of labour power. These categories interlocked to create social power. 'Patriar-chal power' no longer adequately describes the kind of power that historians of masculin-ity are concerned with; power, now defined as a multi-faceted matrix or grid, is not a result of the dynamic interaction between different forms of masculinity, then, but between a number of different categories of identity.

## RETHINKING INTERPRETIVE CONCEPTS

Because of the particular historical relation-ship of masculinity and social power, histori-ans of masculinity occupy an enviable position in the field. As Tosh has pointed out, the his-tory of masculinity 'does not deal with a neglected group, nor can it be placed under the banner of 'history from the margins. Rather, it is a new perspective which potentially modi-fies our view of every field of history in which men are the principal subject-matter – which is to say the overwhelming majority of written history.'[67] We might accurately view the his-tory of masculinity as not simply a topic of study, then, but as an approach with a some-what distinctive conceptual apparatus. In this final section, I will suggest that the historical proximity of masculinity to power, along with men's historically greater opportunities enables practitioners of the history of masculinity to rethink some central interpretive frameworks of their discipline.

I wish to focus here on conventional dis-tinctions between 'public' and 'private' or 'domestic' arenas, often conceptualized as 'separate spheres'. From its inception, wom-en's historians sought to challenge this dis-tinction. Breaking down the traditional gendered and value-judgements about the appropriate topics for historical study, gender historians also emphasized their focus on 'gender in all places – in the home and in the workplace, in the neighbourhood and in diplo-macy, in play and in war, in private relations and in parliaments'.[68] In early works, the his-tory of the family was one area where the history of masculinity had considerable impact, openly challenging the divide between the public and domestic aspects of men's lives that had long been reinforced by historians.[69] This focus on men and domesticity continues to generate new and challenging research.

Conversely, historians of masculinity have done much to rewrite political history and the history of the public sphere. This focus on the political is by no means all-encompassing; we have seen above how the history of masculin-ity examines the home and 'private' spaces. Yet work on masculinity and politics has inter-rogated those bastions of history, politics and the public, and exposed the profoundly gen-dered bases of their discursive construction and social operation. Despite anxieties about this being the enemy in new clothes – a his-torical 'tootsie' – historians of masculinity are not old-style political historians in new garb, therefore. They have taken gender – as both a cultural and social history – to the very centre of modern political power. An important exam-ple is the collection *Masculinities in Politics and War: Gendering Modern History* (2004), focusing on politics and war from 1750 to the First World War. The challenge to traditional historical frameworks is clear in the structure of the book. Four substantive parts each repre-sent a key aspect of gender history's concep-tual and methodological apparatus: that sexual difference is historically variable and specific; that masculinity and femininity are relational categories, that gender as a symbolic system signifies and articulates relations of power, and that gendered subjectivity involves the interplay between discourse and experience.[70]

In this way, historians of masculinity – in common with other historians of gender – challenge some of the key concepts and precepts of the historical discipline. This was certainly a conscious aim of historians of gender and masculinity. As the editors of *Gender and History* put it, 'For men, one of the great privileges of being in a superior position is being allowed to take that position for granted, to claim that identity as the norm, and to treat that hierarchy as natural. This is as true for the study of history as it is for the historical past itself. Since it is men who have, by and large, been responsible for the doing and writing of history, it is their definition of the legitimate historical project which has prevailed.'[71] Examining the historical construction of masculinity thus means exposing the historical construction of history. In this sense, the history of masculinity has at its heart a self-reflective practice that invites us to scrutinize historical writing and expose its premises, assumptions and claims to question and analysis.

## CONCLUSION

To a considerable extent the agenda for masculinity was set by women's historians. Like its foremother – women's history – this work interrogates some of the key concepts and theories that pattern the Historical discipline, such as public and private, the social and cultural, experience and discourse. Yet arguably the history of masculinity can be more disruptive of historical writing than women's history, and perhaps gender history. Through an emphasis on power and patriarchy, including formal and institutional politics, the history of masculinity has come to occupy a significant and potentially radical space within the discipline. If most history before (after and still) women's history was 'men's history', then it is the history of masculinity

that holds the potential to expose the discipline of history most fully and broadly to gender as an analytical concept.

## NOTES AND REFERENCES

1  Laura Lee Downs, *Writing Gender History* (London: Hodder, 2004), p. 74.
2  Anna Davin et al., 'What is women's history?', *History Today*, 35, 6, (1985), pp. 38–48.
3  'Why gender and history?', *Gender and History*, 1, 1 (Spring 1989), p. 1.
4  John Tosh, *The Pursuit of History: Aims, Methods and New Directions in the Study of Modern History*, 2nd edn (1984; Harlow: Longman, 1991), pp. 179, 180.
5  John Tosh, 'Introduction', *Manliness and Masculinities in Nineteenth-Century Britain* (Harlow: Pearson, 2005), p. 1.
6  Downs, *Writing Gender History*, pp. 73–4.
7  Michael Kenny, *The Politics of Identity: Liberal Political Theory and the Dilemmas of Difference* (Cambridge: Polity, 2004), p. vi.
8  Ibid., p. 7.
9  Valentine M. Moghadam, 'Introduction', in idem. (ed.), *Identity Politics and Women: Cultural Reassertions and Feminisms in International Perspective* (Boulder, CO; Oxford: Westview Press, 1994), pp. 21, 16.
10 Ibid., p. 22.
11 Joan Smith, 'The creation of the world we know: the world-economy and the re-creation of gendered identities', in Moghadam (ed.), *Identity Politics and Women*, p. 27. Smith's argument is that modern capitalism relies on at least two institutions – the modern state and the contemporary household – that are in part predicated on a mythic patriarchal household. So history is here critical.
12 Quote from Kenny, *Politics of Identity*, pp. 23–4, 101.
13 Victor J. Seidler, *Rediscovering Masculinity: Reason, Language and Sexuality* (London and New York: Routledge, 1989), p. 3.
14 Ibid., p. 13. Seidler was by no means alone in this endeavour: the final section of Lynne Segal's *Slow Motion: Changing Masculinities, Changing Men* (London: Virago, 1990), is called 'Beyond gender hierarchy: can men change?'.
15 Segal, *Slow Motion*, pp. 1–25; Seidler, *Rediscovering Masculinity*, passim, and pp. 28–39.
16 Seidler, *Rediscovering Masculinity*, p. 1.
17 Ibid., p. 1.
18 Dale Spender, 'Introduction', in Dale Spender (ed.), *Male Studies Modified: The Impact of Feminism on the Academic Disciplines* (New York: Pergamon Press, 1981), p. 5.
19 Ibid., p. 6.
20 Seidler, *Rediscovering Masculinity*, p. ix–x.
21 Ibid., p. 44.
22 Ibid., p. 185.
23 Bob Pease, *Recreating Men: Postmodern Masculinity Politics* (London: Sage, 2000), p. 9.
24 Jonathan Watson, *Male Bodies: Health, Culture and Identity* (Buckingham: Open University Press, 2000), p. 2.

25  Ibid., p. 107.
26  John Springhall, 'Building character in the British boy: the attempt to extend Christian manliness to working-class adolescents 1880–1914', in James Mangan and James Walvin (eds), *Manliness and Morality: Middle-Class Masculinity in Britain and America, 1800–1940*, new edn (1987; Manchester: Manchester University Press, 1991), pp. 52–74; and Allen Warren. 'Popular manliness: Baden-Powell, scouting and the development of manly character', in Mangan and Walvin (eds), *Manliness and Morality*, pp. 199–219.
27  For a recent summation of work in this field for the British case, see Karen Harvey and Alexandra Shepard, 'What have historians done with masculinity? Reflections on five centuries of British History, circa 1500–1950', in *Journal of British Studies*, 44, 2 (2005), pp. 274–80, along with the other essays in this special feature.
28  The key works here are Alan Bray's *Homosexuality in Renaissance England* (London: Gay Men's Press, 1988) and 'Homosexuality and the signs of male friendship in Elizabethan England', *History Workshop Journal*, 29 (1990), pp. 1–19; and Randolph Trumbach, 'The birth of the queen: sodomy and the emergence of gender equality in modern culture, 1660–1750', in M.B. Duberman, M. Vicinus and G. Chauncey (eds), *Hidden From History: Reclaiming the Gay and Lesbian Past* (Harmondsworth: Penguin, 1989), pp. 129–40; *idem*, 'Sex, gender and sexual identity in modern culture: male sodomy and female prostitution in Enlightenment England,' *Journal of the History of Sexuality*, 2 (1991), pp. 186–203; and *idem*, *Sex and the Gender Revolution: Volume One: Heterosexuality and the Third Gender in Enlightenment London* (Chicago, IL and London: University of Chicago Press, 1998) (who charts the shift away from this model of one of normative heterosexuality).
29  A classic statement on the history of love between women is Lillian Faderman, *Surpassing the Love of Men: Romantic Friendship and Love Between Women From the Rennaissance to the Present* (New York: William Morrow, 1981).
30  I have written about this more extensively in Karen Harvey, 'The history of masculinity, circa 1650–1800', *Journal of British Studies*, 44, 2 (2005), pp. 296–311.
31  Martha M. Umphrey, 'The trouble with Harry Thaw', *Radical History Review*, 62, 8 (1995), pp. 8–23; reprinted in Robert J. Corber and Stephen Valocchi (eds), *Queer Studies: An Interdisplinary Reader* (Oxford: Blackwell, 2003), p. 23.
32  Ibid., p. 28.
33  Ibid., p. 24.
34  Joan Wallach Scott, *Gender and the Politics of History* (New York: Columbia University Press, 1988), p. 2.
35  Joan Scott, 'Gender: a useful category of historical analysis', *American Historical Review*, 91 (1986), pp. 1053–75; quote at p. 1067.
36  'Why gender and history?', pp. 1–2.
37  John Beynon, *Masculinities and Culture* (Buckingham: Open University Press, 2002), p. 1.
38  Tosh, 'Introduction', *Manliness and Masculinities*, p. 3. Charlotte Hooper admires the work of the sociologist Robert Connell – discussed below – precisely because he enables discussion of multiple masculinities, without skating over the issues of male power and privilege. Charlotte Hooper, *Manly States: Masculinities, International Relations, and Gender Politics* (New York: Columbia University Press, c2001), pp. 53–6.
39  Notable is the work of Klaus Theweleit, *Male Fantasies Vol. I: Women, Floods, Bodies, History*, trans Stephen Conway (Cambridge: Polity, 1987) and *Male Fantasies Vol. 2: Male Bodies: Psychoanalyzing the White Terror*, trans Chris Turner and Erica Carter (Cambridge: Polity Press, 1989). More recently, Lyndal Roper has studied early-modern German masculinities from this perspective. See the essays in *Oedipus and the Devil: Witchcraft, Sexuality, and Religion in Early Modern Europe* (London: Routledge, 1994). Michael Roper's recent studies also focus on psychology in the history of masculinity. See Michael Roper, 'Between Manliness and masculinity: the "war generation" and the psychology of fear in Britain, 1914–1950', *Journal of British Studies*, 44, 2 (2005), pp. 343–62; and 'Slipping out of view: Subjectivity and Emotion in Gender History', *History Workshop Journal*, 59, 1 (2005), pp. 57–72.
40  Seidler, *Rediscovering Masculinity*, pp. 9–12.
41  'Why gender and history?', p. 2.
42  Downs, *Writing Gender History*, pp. 75–83.
43  Ina Zweiniger-Bargielowska, 'Building a British superman: physical culture in interwar Britain', *Journal of Contemporary History*, 41, 4, (2006), pp. 595–610.
44  Christina S. Jarvis, *The Male Body at War: American Masculinity during World War II* (DeKalb, IL: Northern Illinois University Press, 2004), p. 4.
45  Ibid., p. 5.
46  Downs, *Writing Gender History*, p. 128.
47  Harvey and Shepard, 'What have historians done', p. 276.
48  'Why gender and history?', p. 2.
49  John Tosh, 'What should historians do with masculinity?: Reflections on nineteenth-century Britain', *History Workshop Journal*, 38 (1984) pp. 179–202. Downs, *Writing Gender History*, p. 83.
50  John Tosh, *A Man's Place: Masculinity and the Middle-Class Home in Victorian England* (New Haven, CT and London: Yale University Press, 1999), p. 199.
51  Tosh, 'Introduction', *Manliness and Masculinities*, p. 2.
52  Harvey and Shepard, 'What have historians done', p. 275.
53  Tosh, Introduction', *Manliness and Masculinities*, p. 5.
54  In a recent article, Martin Francis references the work of Alexandra Shepard on homosociality in early modern England, for example. See Martin Francis, 'A flight from commitment? Domesticity, adventure and the masculine imaginary in Britain after the Second World War', *Gender & History*, 19, 1 (2007), p. 174. See also Alexandra Shepard, *Meanings of Manhood in early modern England* (Oxford: Oxford University Press, 2003).

55  Segal, *Slow Motion*, p. 61.

56  'Why Gender and History?', p. 2.

57  Seidler, *Refashioning Masculinity*, p. 8.

58  Ibid., pp. ix, xv.

59  Segal's section on 'Shrinking the phallus' covers psycho-analysis in the main, and examines the ways in which research was then exploring male subjectivity, in the context of male power, a good deal of it examining the fragility of that power. Segal, *Slow Motion*, p. 60–82.

60  Tosh, 'Introduction', *Manliness and Masculinities*, p. 4.

61  R.W. Connell, *Masculinities* (Cambridge: Polity, 1995), p. 77.

62  David H.J. Morgan, 'Men made manifest: histories and masculinities', *Gender & History*, 1, 1 (Spring 1989), p. 90. The book reviewed was J.A. Mangan and James Walvin (eds), *Manliness and Morality: Middle-Class Masculinity in Britain and America, 1800–1940* (Manchester: Manchester University Press, 1987).

63  Harvey and Shepard, 'What have historians done', p. 278.

64  Ibid., p. 278.

65  Anne McClintock, *Imperial Leather: Race, Gender and Sexuality in the Colonial Conquest* (London: Routledge, 1995).

66  Ibid., p. 5.

67  Tosh, 'Introduction', *Manliness and Masculinities*, p. 2.

68  'Why gender and history?', p. 2.

69  Tosh, 'Introduction', *Manliness and Masculinities*, p. 5.

70  Stefan Dudink, Karen Hagemann and John Tosh (eds), *Masculinities in Politics and War: Gendering Modern History* (Manchester: Manchester University Press, 2004), pp. xii–xv.

71  'Why gender and history?', p. 2.

# 18

# Sexuality and History

Amy Richlin

The urge to write a history of sexuality is relatively recent, a product of major ideological shifts. In a particular place, a brief window opened, and a set of questions became askable. Like women and the body, sex has not seemed, to most historians since historians began, to have a history at all. What changed?

People write the history they need; one major motive for history-writing is self-interest, accelerated by competition. Histories succeed to the degree that they serve a market. The history of sexuality is a product of the sexual revolutionaries of the late twentieth century, and, especially in its Foucauldian manifestations, will continue to seem important as long as their market exists. We cannot know what is coming next but can expect that it will be radically different, due to each generation's need to define itself against the previous generation. The push now, in this subfield as in the field as a whole, is towards globalization, as the writers awake from their dream of themselves. But the whole project of academic history-writing, as of the academy itself, is Western, and will continue to matter only insofar as the Rest is interested. Or, indeed, anybody, as the present takes over (Settis 2007).

Of course self-interest is not the only motive for writing history. Many historians desire the past like lovers, eroticizing or even Orientalizing it, and historians of sexuality desire the desiring past. Chris Waters writes of the 'new British queer history' (2007: 150): 'by rendering the past *other*, by distancing it radically from our own understandings and categories of identity, [writers] have created a world they render desirable.' Joseph Bristow, writing on Matt Houlbrook's case studies of twentieth-century working-class men, says they 'belong to a long-vanished world, and one senses that he has more than a pang of nostalgia for it' (2007: 124). Medievalist Carolyn Dinshaw describes her own work as springing from 'the deep desires for history that many queers (including me) feel' (2001: 202). Note that 50 years work as well as 700 to enable desire, which, as Plato said, is for that which you have not.

Others, myself included, feel a duty to the dead: to memorialize their lives, whether happy, dull, or wretched. Some, like historians of the Holocaust, write to bear witness; thus German historian Clayton Whisnant: 'For the first generation of gay and lesbian activists an important part of confronting homophobia in the contemporary world was uncovering its roots in the past' (2008: 1). Some write to give a voice to the unvoiced; thus transgender historian Susan Stryker, on the relation between oppression and historiography (2008: 150). Such a testificatory impulse can involve a willingness to challenge the idea that history tells a story of change (Bennett 2006: 67–9), thereby confronting historicism itself, as in Catharine MacKinnon's essay 'Does Sexuality Have a History?' (1992: 122–3):

> I would hypothesize that ... the actual practices of sex may look relatively flat. In particular, the sexualization of aggression or the eroticization of power and the fusion of that with gender such that the one who is the target or object of sexuality is the subordinate, is a female, effeminized if a man, is relatively constant. And that hierarchy is always done through gender in some way ... [V]ariation may not be the most prominent feature of the historical landscape .... For such suggestions, feminists have been called ahistorical. Oh, dear.

That 'Oh, dear' marks a significant claim about what history-writing is, and a refusal to be bullied out of it.

For it is a fact that even this most self-consciously avant-garde field has developed orthodoxies, despite the relentless call for something new; for everyone, 'naive' is the most withering term of dismissal. Like etiquette, orthodoxies provide a rulebook amid the proliferation of scholarship – where, as Giulia Sissa likes to say, bibliographies don't communicate. The one thing of which we may be certain, to continue in this Croce-ish vein, is that what we read now is of the now, and will mean something different to our older selves. But will it still be a history of sexuality?

## HISTORY OF THE HISTORY OF SEXUALITY

> This what neglected topic? This strangely what topic? This strangely neglected what?
> (Kingsley Amis, *Lucky Jim*, ch. 1)

Jim Dixon, the ambivalent novice historian, contemplates with gloom the hackneyed opening of his first article: 'In considering this strangely neglected topic.' The three questions he is then impelled to ask himself apply to all academic endeavors, and we might unpack his questions for present purposes as

follows: What is the history of sexuality good for? Why does it matter? To whom? And, if it matters, how can it be written? What is it a history *of*? The project faces two major epistemological problems: the field's own historicity demonstrates that the visibility of the object of study is (like Brigadoon's) historically contingent; and the object of study is itself hard to pin down.

### This what neglected topic?

The importance of this history should not be doubted. To the old war-to-war historians such a project might have looked frivolous, but that would have been a mistake. Sex and gender permeate all aspects of social institutions. How can we fully understand war and empire without understanding how cultures express them in terms of – and by means of – rape? How can we understand slavery without understanding the sexual openness of the slave's body? But bibliographies don't communicate, and although the history of sexuality often deals with politics, political history does not yet often deal with sexuality. The resulting analyses cannot be adequate. Catullus used to be read without the obscene poems that make up a large proportion of his work; the resulting understanding of Catullus was much skewed, but high art had to exclude the low. Catullus's work is now more often read as a whole. History likewise needs to be of the whole, not of the high, or as much of the whole as we can see: always the limit. No – 'needs' marks the narrower limit, because the need is unenforceable: whose need is it?

### This strangely what topic?

Most collections of essays on the history of sexuality begin with the history of the field; particularly good ones may be found in Duberman, Vicinus, and Chauncey (1989) and in Leonard (2006) (see also Richlin 1993, 1997). The following outline reflects my own current work on the history of the circulation of knowledge of ancient sexuality in modern Europe.

Christendom, as the mapping of a religion onto a geography, began in the fourth century CE and continues through the present day. A gap in the blanketing of the West by Christianity opened in the late eighteenth century, soon reclosing, then reopening in the late nineteenth century, widening with World War I into the 1920s, narrowing again, then blasting open in 1968. How soon it will close again is unknown; it always has before, and when it does it will shut down the history of sexuality. Christian dogma provides a complete set of rules for sexuality, built to last, so that, during the long centuries when Christianity had no outside in the West, there could be no public value in knowing other systems. In the West, learned men remained conscious that there had been a different set of rules in place before Christianity, and curiosity about this intensifies during the Renaissance and sporadically thereafter, but history as a discipline itself formed within an academy that was largely Christian. Only the rise of anthropology, hand in hand with colonialism, in the eighteenth and nineteenth centuries – inquiry into the mores of other cultures – enabled historians to begin thinking about a history of their own mores. Well before the rise of identity politics in the 1970s, then, a few scholars had begun to turn to the past for personal reasons. The longing for past difference as sexually liberatory has been a very widely shared motive; rarer has been a desire to understand sex like any other aspect of the past.

The usual list of forerunners of today's field includes Enlightenment curiosity, nineteenth-century philhellenism as an enabler of nineteenth-century homophile culture, the appearance of sexology in the late nineteenth century and of identity politics in the late twentieth; also, within professional history, the rise of the Annales school, legitimizing inquiry into the sordid and quotidian. The particular history of the history of sexuality is made up of interlacing stories. Feminists at least from Mary Wollstonecraft on have incorporated sexual issues into their project of making women visible to history, but the impetus to write about women's sexuality does not really arise until the Second Wave of the women's movement, impelled by formulations like Kate Millett's *Sexual Politics*: power is sexual. Boom: histories of childbirth, of medical advice, of marriage, prostitution, and rape and the laws and customs that policed them, of how sex constitutes the state. Gender itself began to be denaturalized with Simone de Beauvoir's dictum 'On ne naît pas femme: on le devient' (1981 [1949].1: 285), and its undermining continued through Monique Wittig to Judith Butler, founding current queer theory.

Meanwhile, although the rise of philhellenism in the Enlightenment made the history of Greece and Rome a central preoccupation of the nascent academy in the early 1800s, the great difference between ancient and modern sex/gender systems was not part of the mix. B.G. Niebuhr did not want to talk about it; Theodor Mommsen did not want to talk about it; and they set the pattern for others to follow, for German scholarship led the way in the nineteenth century. The early fascination expressed by Winckelmann and Goethe was nipped in the bud by the Napoleonic Wars; Louis Crompton's detective work (1985) uncovered Jeremy Bentham's massive research on sodomy dating from 1774 to 1824, but demonstrated the reasons for its contemporary unpublishability. Standard nineteenth-century handbooks of ancient history do not discuss sexuality. K.O. Müller's 1824 history of the Dorians, now often cited, insofar as it focused on pederasty belonged to a world of German scholarship decidedly outside the mainstream, although much more was written in Germany than elsewhere (Dynes 2005), culminating in the work of Magnus Hirschfeld from the 1890s through the 1920s. Similarly, in the Anglophone world, it was only J.P. Mahaffy, writing in Ireland, who included sections on sexuality in his history of the Greeks (1874) – and these were removed in later editions.

Mahaffy was Oscar Wilde's teacher, and it was in Wilde's time that the world of what might be called 'shadow scholarship' began to coalesce in English. John Addington Symonds' essay *A Problem in Greek Ethics* (1883, 1901) was privately printed, it is true, and circulated as such books did; but the number printed eventually mounted to more than two hundred, and the essay joined such underground classics as Edward Carpenter's *Ioläus* (1902). This was a history motivated by the desire among elite European homophile subcultures to find ancestors in the then-hegemonic classical past. The pervasiveness of this desire among the educated is shown by the recurrent invocations of antiquity in underground publications after World War I, not only in Europe but, at least after World War II, in America (see Richlin 2005; Valentine 2008). This substantial body of writing certainly amounts to a history, but has no academic credentials, and suffers from methodological handicaps ranging from over-reliance on literary sources to a willingness to work from translations, indeed a general lack of access to primary sources.

With the 1960s, things began to change: 1964 produced J.Z. Eglinton's *Greek Love*, in the last flowering of shadow scholarship; 1968 produced the sexual revolution; 1969, Stonewall; 1976, Michel Foucault's *La Volonté de savoir*; 1978, K.J. Dover's *Greek Homosexuality*. John Boswell's *Christianity, Homosexuality, and Social Tolerance* appeared in 1980, and the *Journal of the History of Sexuality* began publishing in 1990. Of these historical works, only two were produced by professional historians – Boswell's book and the journal – but of these works only Dover's, and perhaps the journal, were the outcome of what might be called a basically historical desire to describe how things were. Both Foucault and Boswell wrote as partisans motivated, like Symonds and Edward Carpenter, by an activist agenda. As Jeffrey Weeks, a pioneer in the field, remarks, for some the desire to 'write about sexuality' came first, academic writing being only a means to the end of writing about sexuality so as to 'be listened to': 'Academic awards permit us to

speak with authority; and to make what we say acceptable' (2002: 27–8).

Susan Stryker, however, writing on transgender history, points out how even the radical academy can still exclude those who do not fit (2008). Indeed, partisanship turned the project into (plural) writings of the histories of sexualities, as the writers fought it out in a series of turf wars. This has nowhere been more true than in my own field, Classics, on which Ruth Mazo Karras politely remarked, 'The level of discourse in this discussion has been ... extremely vehement, revealing that these are issues about which scholars care even more than most historians usually care about their subjects' (2000: 1250). Her observation was borne out in the acrimonious debate over James Davidson's *The Greeks and Greek Love* (2007), centered on the sensitive issues of homonormativity and of how closely ancient pederasty resembled what is now called pedophilia (see Davidson 2009 with associated links). At the same time, as interest in sexuality spread throughout the discipline and, simultaneously, in related fields (art history, literature, religion), an ability to read across periods and disciplines became more and more necessary; an ability to do so accurately remains rare, and it clearly remains difficult for scholars to assess the value of arguments based on evidence with which they are unfamiliar.

An overview of the history of sexuality in the West – the first work done in the field – would be useful, but the number of historians writing in the field is now very large, and it is only possible here to list the names of some scholars who have staked out important areas and/or positions (see now Clark 2011). On Egypt and the Near East, Zainab Bahrani, Gwendolyn Leick, Lynn Meskell, Dominic Montserrat; on Greco-Roman antiquity, Kathy Gaca, Thomas Hubbard, Giulia Sissa, and the writers covered in Karras's 2000 review essay (and see now Davidson 2007; duBois 2003; Harper 2011; Sissa 2003; and Skinner 2005); on rabbinic Judaism, Daniel Boyarin and Michael Satlow; on late antiquity and the early Church, Bernadette

Brooten, Peter Brown, Virginia Burrus, Elizabeth Clark, Mathew Kuefler, Stephen Moore (especially 2001), Judith Perkins; on medieval Christendom, Judith Bennett, John Boswell, Carolyn Bynum, Carol Clover, Carolyn Dinshaw, Mark Jordan (especially 1997), Karma Lochrie, Nancy Partner, James Schultz; on early modern Europe, Alan Bray, Judith C. Brown, Joan DeJean, Michael Rocke (especially 1996); on eighteenth-century Europe, Rictor Norton, Randolph Trumbach; on nineteenth-century Europe and America (by far the biggest field), Joseph Bristow, George Chauncey, Anna Clark, Louis Crompton, Lillian Faderman, John Fout, Carroll Smith-Rosenberg, Martha Vicinus, Judith Walkowitz, Jeffrey Weeks; on twentieth-century Europe and America, Allan Bérubé, John D'Emilio, Estelle Freedman, Alison Oram, Kathy Peiss, Ruth Rosen, Leila Rupp, James Steakley. Byzantine history, so crucial as a bridge between the ancient Mediterranean and the medieval Near East, remains short on studies of sexuality due to the difficulty and conservatism of the field and to the anti-sex tilt of most sources, many still not translated; but see James (1999). It is an oddity of the history of sexuality that medieval Islamic cultures, which attracted marked attention in nineteenth-century homophile writing, and which certainly attended to sexual behavior through the hadiths, have elicited no recent body of work comparable to that on Greece and Rome (probably because no one took Arabic in high school; will this change?); but see Arjona Castro (1985), Wright and Rowson (1997), Babayan and Najmabadi (2008), and work on satiric literature by G.H.J. van Gelder.

The name conspicuously missing from this list is that of Michel Foucault, whose late work grabbed the field in the early 1980s and has controlled the direction of inquiry since then. *La Volonté de Savoir* (1976) appeared in English as volume one of the *History of Sexuality* in 1978, and at once caught the imagination of writers already using what came to be called the 'social constructionist' approach (Weeks 2005). Both feminism and gay studies became absorbed in the 1980s in a struggle between social constructionism, which holds that genders are constructed through the socialization of the individual, and what was called (mostly by opponents) essentialism, which holds that sexuality and gender are transhistorical categories. Foucault offered social constructionist arguments so compelling to his followers as to turn into a sort of creed.

In this last major work before he died of AIDS, like so many other great writers in the field (John Boswell, Alan Bray, Jonathan Walters, John J. Winkler), Foucault set out to explain how it was that modern sexuality was both defined and voiced by institutions like medicine, law, and psychology, which built a sexed self; after volume one, he began on the question that had fascinated many – how the Greco-Roman sex/gender system had been transformed after the rise of Christianity. He never got to Christianity (luckily, according to Lochrie 1997); volumes two (translated into English as *The Uses of Pleasure*, 1985) and three (*The Care of the Self*, 1986) discuss sex and the [male] self in, respectively, Greece and Rome. Foucault was, however, a philosopher (Karras notes that many have argued he was 'no historian': 2000: 1253), and volumes two and three are reliable only in patches. But philosophy does not have to be documented, and the persuasiveness of volume one surely stems from the radical imagination of its arguments rather than from its remarks on nineteenth-century French history. Only another philosopher, Judith Butler, has influenced the history of sexuality as much as Foucault.

Two claims from volume one profoundly affected the field. On page 43, Foucault famously said that 'the homosexual' came into existence with the medical characterization of the category in 1870; before this time, there was only the sodomite, perpetrator of 'forbidden acts.' 'The sodomite had been a temporary aberration; the homosexual was now a species.' Julian Carter in 2005 called this 'probably one of the most provocative sentences of the last century' (2005: 8). More temperately, Joseph Bristow (2007: 18): 'This memorable formulation soon became something of a slogan.' In a similar vein, Foucault posited that 'sexuality' itself is a historical construct (1978: 105; cf. Weeks 2002: 29–30). Both claims pulled the rug out from under historians of sexuality, many of them primarily interested in what used to be called 'homosexuality.'

But this did not at all prevent a Foucauldian history of [sexuality] from being written; scholars in droves tried to prove or disprove the nonexistence of sexual identity before the nineteenth century, particularly of identities related to same-sex object choice. The Foucauldian position is now widely accepted, the counter-evidence ignored. David Halperin's book *Saint Foucault* (1995) takes its place alongside his reproachful essay 'Forgetting Foucault' (2002), Jeffrey Weeks' 'Remembering Foucault' (2005), and Karma Lochrie's ambivalent 'Desiring Foucault' (1997). Indeed, so entrenched has this position become that new scholarship looks to dislodge it; it sounds very 1990s. In 1989, Carol Vance referred (approvingly) to social constructionism as 'the new orthodoxy' (cited in Weeks 2002: 39); in 1993, Nancy Partner referred (disapprovingly) to 'the dogmas of a new orthodoxy' (425); in 2000, Ruth Mazo Karras used similar terms (descriptively) of Foucault and social constructionism (1251); in 2005, Linda Garber referred disparagingly to 'Foucauldian Orthodoxy' (35–9) as inadequate to deal with a global history of sexuality. But Foucault is still used as a stick to beat scholars trying to write outside the paradigm he set: thus Kate Drabinski reviewing Kathy Gaca's book (2004: 525): 'This defensive position does not allow Gaca to acknowledge how Foucault's work in many senses enables her work, prompting the questions she is able to ask.'

Orthodox practice has led to some oddities in the literature. Documentation often falls on deaf ears; as Judith Bennett remarks, 'the rebuttals are remarkably ineffective: among modernists, these myths still prosper, even

decades after they have been demolished by credible scholarly research' (2006: 43). Bibliographies don't communicate; there's nothing to keep the most egregious falsehoods from being repeated as gospel, even by scholars otherwise meticulous, eminent in their own fields (see Richlin 1997: 28–9). Thus Jeffrey Weeks argues, following Foucault's volumes two and three in 2005 (199):

> Like us post-Christians, the ancients were faced with the task of elaborating an ethic that was not founded in religion or any a priori justification. Unlike us, however, they did not attempt to codify acts, thereby making sex itself the bearer of values and moral anxieties, nor did they attempt to submit individuals to external laws.

In order to believe this, you have to exclude the Jews from the category 'ancients'; ignore Greek law and the enormous mass of Roman law; and ignore the even more enormous mass of custom enforced by the state (as in the office of censor), religious law (e.g., on ritual purity), moral suasion, and ridicule. The first is easy, since Classics kicked out the Jews in the nineteenth century, and Foucault let that pass; the second two are enabled by specialized training. What Foucault chose to write about in volumes two and three is taken by many to be all there is to know.

One of the saddest losses to dogma has been Freud – hopelessly old-hat to Kim Phillips and Barry Reay, in the introduction to their reader *Sexualities in History* (2002: 5):

> Early historians of sexualities produced works ringing with Freudian theories ... The Freudian influence can be dimly detected in sexual histories long after its mid-twentieth-century heyday, just as other ghosts from the early days of psychoanalysis lingered in the intellectual and popular consciousness.

Compare Susan McCabe, reviewing Kathryn Kent on the formation of lesbian identity from the nineteenth century to the early twentieth, which after all was Freud's time (2005: 128): 'Somewhat troubling, however, is Kent's own transhistorical use of psychoanalysis to describe the ego formation of historicized "proto-identities."' Say what you will about Freud, he is a lucid writer and certainly has a theory of the formation of the sexual self, one predicated on childhood experience rather than on philosophical self-fashioning by adults. Nancy Partner (1993, 2005) ably defends the use of psychoanalytic theory for thinking about medieval people, and the approach remains current, for example in Matt Houlbrook's work. The cryptic Lacan, in contrast, is rarely dismissed.

In short the burst of writing on the history of sexuality since 1970 has become somewhat bogged down in the problem of what are the legitimate terms in which to write. We can anticipate, however, that the problem of writing about the premodern in modern terms will soon fade away, as historians of the premodern themselves recede into history (see Bennett 2006 for statistics).

## This strangely neglected what?

Meanwhile the field has become a minefield of forbidden words, starting with 'sexuality' (as seen above) and 'homosexuality.' The danger remains serious: 'Medievalists know that if they claim to have found "homosexuals" in the Middle Ages they will provoke cries of outrage, and nothing else they say will be heard. So they avoid the term' (Schultz 2006: 14). Yet it is the case that 'homosexuality' is retained in book titles – Dover, writing *Greek Homosexuality* before Foucault, knew no better, but Craig Williams produced *Roman Homosexuality* (1999, 2nd edition 2010) as a committed Foucauldian. This would seem to be just a marketing issue, except that scholars continue to want to write about what the uninformed still call 'homosexuality,' and so must find periphrases, most commonly 'same-sex sexuality' or (better) 'same-sex desire': 'I have spent all this time undermining the term "same-sex sexuality",' says Leila Rupp (2001: 301), 'but, in fact, I think that it is the best one we have.' Writing as a queer theorist, James Schultz remarks shrewdly, 'How different is "same-sex" from

"homosexual" anyway? It still makes sexual object choice the paramount criterion' (2006: 17n15). An excellent overview of the issues involved in 'homonormativity' and the attempt to write a history of a sexuality not defined by object choice is provided by Susan Stryker (2008).

'Lesbian' has fared no better; Judith Bennett valiantly sought to hang onto it by coining the term 'lesbian-like.' As she observes (2000: 11, with notes 27 and 28), the rejection of 'lesbian' as a term now amounts to a claim to 'historical professionalism.' In 1989 Leila Rupp revisited her own essay of 1980 to explore the politics of a refusal to use the term 'lesbian': history-writing includes both the duty to be true to the expressed identity of the object of study and a consciousness of the historian's own location. She judiciously titled her 2009 global overview *Sapphistries* (see discussion of terminology, 2009: 1–6). For Afsaneh Najmabadi, writing in 2006, this argument is over (18): 'Remember the debates over the question, were there any lesbians (or lesbian-like women) in medieval Europe?'

The word 'woman' had itself undergone a similar ban in the late 1980s. The editorial statement in the first issue of *Journal of Women's History* wrestled with the propriety of putting 'women's' in the title (1989: 7); this trend eventually arrived at solipsism as feminism splintered (see Richlin 1993: 276). Nonetheless, this and other journals with 'women' in the title are still publishing, although the word remains endangered; Najmabadi, writing in the *Journal of Women's History*, continues,

> Without replaying that discussion, I want to use it as a way of returning that question to gender: Were there any women in medieval Europe? Try asking this question in your classes and see what a great discussion you get! That we ask the first question with comfort and presume the ease of the answer to the second (well, of course there were women, but defined differently) works on the presumption of the naturalness of woman; that there have always been women. What does it mean that we do not have the same discomfort with presuming the possibility of existence of women in medieval Europe that we have about lesbians?

Surely discomfort with either poses political as well as epistemological difficulties, especially in a field in which sex so often turns out to be men's (see Garber 2005, Sissa 2003, and Richlin 1993: 277 on the 'just-when' problem).

Next to go must be 'heterosexuality,' as argued forcefully by James Schultz in the essay cited above; in his analysis, by the very use of the word to describe sex acts before the nineteenth century 'we do our small part in consolidating the heterosexual norm' (2006: 20). Again, heterosexuality was denaturalized as 'compulsory' by Adrienne Rich in 1980; she did not then hesitate to posit that what was being compelled in periods before the modern was heterosexuality. One of Schultz's points is that heterosexuality needs to be historicized, and I only wish that would happen; what Gayle Rubin (1984: 281) dismissed as 'Good, Normal, Natural, Blessed Sexuality,' however, draws relatively little attention, sex within marriage in particular hardly counting as sex at all, at least in the scholarship. Giulia Sissa's *Eros Tiranno* (2003) marks a deliberate attempt to confront this situation.

If both 'homosexuality' and 'heterosexuality' must go, it is perhaps not surprising that 'normative' is also poised for extinction, now being spoken of as also a nineteenth-century concept (Clark 2005: 141–2). Most of an issue of *Journal of the History of Sexuality* (2001) was taken up with a forum, or mass attack, on Carolyn Dinshaw's book *Getting Medieval*, after which Dinshaw, who writes, as seen above, as a queer theorist, spent most of her response defending herself for defining 'queer' in relation to a norm (206–10). Susan McCabe defines queer studies as claiming 'a more universal as well as diverse effulgence of nonnormative identifications,' depending on 'a paradox: the transhistorical existence of erotic pluralism' (2005: 120–21). It is indeed very hard to see how queerness can hold together as a concept, much less a transhistorical one, without normalness, but we continue to have a history of sexuality without 'sexuality,' after all.

Finally, 'social constructionism' itself is on its way out. Where Leila Rupp in 2001 could proudly swear allegiance ('I take up this task from the perspective of one firmly committed to a social constructionist perspective on sexuality,' 287), we find Jeffrey Weeks in 2005 recanting (187–8):

> The harsh and mechanistic term 'social construction' has become deeply unfashionable since the late 1980s, when the constructionist/essentialist debate collapsed of exhaustion ... and as the cutting edge of queer theorists sought to transcend its dichotomies ... Those of us doomed forevermore to be labeled as social constructionists ... were never what some of our detractors portrayed us as. We were certainly not a conspiracy ...

Scholars who most vociferously denied the existence of sexual identities before the nineteenth century now, moving with the times like the Vicar of Bray, 'have begun to argue that some forms of sexual identities did appear in the premodern' (Clark 2005: 142).

The question of whether, as Mieke Bal puts it, concepts can travel is of course central to the whole project of writing history, and plagues the practice of translation, so necessary to most historians. Epistemological problems are peculiarly difficult for writing a history of sexuality. Materials are abundant but elusive. Private sexual acts leave no trace except, perhaps, on the bodies of the participants, or more permanently in the form of babies; few people write a record afterwards, and when they do no corroboration is possible, while such records are the first to be destroyed by the dying and their heirs. Records of public sexual acts are rarely produced by the performers. Moreover, the deeper we dive into the wreck, the less of this material we find. The attraction of discourse analysis must spring in part from the comparatively enormous amount of it we have to work with, since most cultural products are saturated with sexuality in some way.

As always, women are harder to find out about; in most periods, women's desires are almost impossible to discover. Because the record of desire has mostly not been left by women, or boys, or what the Romans called *cinaedi* (sexually passive and/or effeminate men), it is a rarity in history for adult males to be the ones described in love poetry; before the rise of the novel, we have little trace of what was attractive about them (oh, Mr. Rochester!). Likewise, statements of the pleasures of being penetrated are not common. Slavery had no outside from the earliest known times in the ancient Mediterranean well into the modern period, and in slave societies sexual status and civil status are impossible to separate (see esp. duBois 2003: 82–113; Brooten 2010; Harper 2011: 281–323, 391–462; Heszer 2005), but slave texts are rare, never mind slave texts about sex. If sexual identity did not predate the modern period, the historian of sexuality may find herself unable to identify her object: 'Is there an "it" to study?' said Carole Vance in a 1987 conference paper (cited in Duberman et al. 1989: 6).

'Writing the history of *what*?' muses the historian, wandering with Alice and the Fawn through the wood where things have no name. When things dared not speak their name, what were they? Inside the closet, no one knows you're a homosexual. The existence of same-sex subcultures has been amply documented in many periods before the premodern; plenty of people would have identified each other as 'one of us'; but others could not say, were risking too much by saying anything, or just had no one to talk to about it. We have labels for them, but what did they think they were doing? Sometimes we can see that they identified with the Greeks, but what did that mean to them? The Greeks, in turn, had names for 'sexual perverts,' of which the best known today is *kinaidoi*, but what did *kinaidoi* call themselves? No writer calls himself by that name, although there was a class of performers called *kinaidologoi*. The historian finds herself wondering about the meaning of labels for the labeled, although in no doubt that a brand leaves a scar.

The bias of the field as so far discussed has been increasingly towards the modern, away from the premodern (see Bennett 2006); the focus, predominantly on the Anglophone

world. This being said, historians from other fields can look for help as follows: among general anthologies, *Hidden from History* (Duberman et al. 1989) holds up extremely well, most of its essays coming from major writers; the more recent *Palgrave Advances in the Modern History of Sexuality* (Cocks and Houlbrook 2006) refreshingly divides its chapters into area overviews (demography, sexology, law, marriage and reproduction, race and empire, cities, religion and spirituality, pornography and obscenity, prostitution, childhood and youth, cross-dressing and transgender). Almost all its writers are historians of modern Britain, but then that is not unrepresentative of the field as a whole.

Useful overviews of particular sub-subfields include, among book-length studies, Louis Crompton on homosexuality in the West (2003); Marilyn Skinner on classical sexuality (2005), along with Thomas Hubbard's comprehensive and reliable sourcebook (2003); Ruth Mazo Karras on sexuality in medieval Europe (2005), along with sourcebooks by Conor McCarthy (2004, Anglocentric) and Martha Brožyna (2005; includes Jewish and Muslim sources); and the sourcebook on same-sex love in India by Ruth Vanita and Saleem Kidwai (2000). Articles and review essays of broad scope include Bristow (2007) – new work on nineteenth- and twentieth-century male homophile subcultures; Clark (2005) – marginal identities in European sexuality; Garber (2005) – queer sex in Asia; Karras (2000) – Greece and Rome; Waters (2007) – new British queer history; and special issues of *Journal of the History of Sexuality* on sexuality in late antiquity (10.3/4, 2001), theory and method (14.1/2, 2005), Latin America (16.3, 2007), and modern Germany (17.1, 2008), of *Speculum* on medieval women (68.2, 1993), and of *Journal of Homosexuality* on 'same-sex desire' in classical antiquity and its reception (49.3/4, 2005). *GLQ, Gender and History, Journal of Women's History*, and *Radical History Review* often carry articles and reviews on the history of sexuality; *American Historical Review*, whose website claims it to be the most influential historical journal in the world, does not, and it is sobering to one immersed in this field, which makes such claims for itself (see below), to see how little it registers with the discipline at large.

Despite the best of intentions, however, and the wholesale move of women's studies into the global present (see the 1998 *Gender and History* special issue on international feminism, and compare the Berkshire Conference programs for 2008 and 2011), the history of sexuality remains a largely Anglophone and Anglocentric production; which raises epistemological problems of its own.

> The expected relationships within each sedoretu are:
>
>> The Morning woman and the Evening man (the 'Morning marriage')
>>
>> The Evening woman and the Morning man (the 'Evening marriage')
>>
>> The Morning woman and the Evening woman (the 'Day marriage')
>>
>> The Morning man and the Evening man (the 'Night marriage')

## GEOGRAPHY OF THE HISTORY OF SEXUALITY

> The forbidden relationships are between the Morning woman and the Morning man, and between the Evening woman and the Evening man, and they aren't called anything, except sacrilege.
>> (Ursula K. Le Guin, 'Mountain ways,' 2002)

Ursula Le Guin's work, much influenced by her famous father, the anthropologist Alfred Kroeber, often explores, as here, what it would mean to live in a sex/gender system with sharply defined norms completely different from our own – most famously in *The Left Hand of Darkness*, set on a planet in which individuals' physiological sex can shift between male and female. She sends her imaginary anthropologists and diplomats to live as participant observers in galaxies far, far away, but, as historians do, she writes for home consumption. It should not take science fiction to point out that sexuality varies from culture to culture; this truth has been a basic

preoccupation of anthropology since its origin as a discipline, and indeed a fascination with sex-norm variance goes back to ancient ethnographers like Herodotus and Pomponius Mela: it is true both that they exoticized the Other (particularly the Egyptians, who, they say, reversed gender norms among their other oddities), and that they belonged to a longstanding tradition of relativism that loved to destabilize 'us' by looking at 'not-us.'

Some historians today would like to do the same; historians today, however, inhabit a discipline formed within an academy formed within the realm of the Indo-European languages, emphasis on the 'European' – even the Semitic languages and cultures fell by the wayside in the nineteenth century (Marchand 1996). How is the history of sexuality to get out of its Western rut? Or has it, and we just don't know it, because we don't speak the language? Indeed the academy itself might be viewed as a product of European nationalism, and thus part of the baggage train of colonialism. Still, whereas nonwestern indigenous traditions of thought about sexuality continued, in the Western-style academies that formed around the world (some before the nineteenth century), the appeal of academic publication and the desire to join in the ongoing scholarly conversation have produced, to varying degrees, histories of sexuality in languages other than Indo-European.

Anglophone scholarship has, however, found itself ill-equipped to incorporate even scholarship published in European languages (see Ruggiero 1990 for a polite attempt to draw attention to articles published in *Quaderni Storici* from 1979 to 1984; he had them translated into English in 1990). It is the translation of Foucault's volume one into English in 1978 that is routinely cited as the breakthrough event for the field (Phillips and Reay 2002: 6, 'a pivotal moment'); Anglophone scholars rarely cite Foucault in French. Ramón Gutiérrez, writing in the *Journal of the History of Sexuality* to introduce a special issue on Latin America (2007), does tell the story of the influence of the Annales school in Mexico and cite some work in Spanish, but by and large confines his bibliography to work in English. *Journal of the History of Sexuality* had a Germanist, John Fout, for its founding editor, and now has a medievalist, Mathew Kuefler; Fout voiced support for a 'truly international' approach in his mission statement (1990), and both Fout and Kuefler promised to incorporate primary texts in translation, but this project never really got off the ground, and a survey of both articles and book reviews shows an almost total focus on Anglophone scholars and scholarship and on European modernity, with side trips to the elsewhere and elsewhen.

Does it take one to know one? This problem vexes all fields with spatial and chronological ranges, and we are only beginning to deal with it in the history of sexuality. The problem of the voice of the *cinaedus* (above) is closely implicated in the debate on nomenclature and identity (see Garber 2005: 40–3 on Asian identity debates); and of course this is a longstanding issue within feminist theory and postcolonial theory, as in Michelle Cliff's essay 'Claiming an identity they taught me to despise' (see Richlin 1993 on the ethnographer's dilemma). In any case, we might expect that an essay written by a Chinese person, in China, in Chinese, about the history of sexuality in China would be (different from?) one in English written here (an essentializing assumption?). Gayatri Spivak (1999) writes about the problems of Western histories that feature the 'native informant'; certainly there is a tendency in the field to exoticize the past (e.g. Phillips and Reay 2002: 9, 'In a culture that did not know modern homosexuality ...' – cue tom-toms). But what materials are we to use in writing about the colonized? Scholars repeatedly complain that the archives are themselves the product of colonialism (so Arondekar 2009; J. Sweet 2000). Meanwhile, the former recipients of the attentions of missionaries are not uniformly delighted to receive the Foucauldian good news, as Ross Forman notes (2006: 127): 'In Africa in particular, cultural critics, politicians, and religious authorities alike often have united in their insistence that homosexuality is "un-African" and did not exist before the arrival of Europeans.'

The Rest is indeed writing back, and readers here can take some comfort in reflecting that the size of the British empire plus the tendency for English to be accepted as an international language mean that we will not need to venture outside the Indo-European language group yet. We can, however, expect an argument from people tired of being described by others. In *Sexuality: An African Perspective*, Jennifer Wanjiku Khamasi and Susan Nyambura Maina-Chinkuyu set out to address 'previous works and their inability to address adequately matters pertaining to norms and sex behaviors in the African context' (2005: 1). This slim volume, though not primarily historical in its focus, is surely a harbinger of histories to come (see now Epprecht 2008).

The Dutch publisher Brill has made an important move by launching two new journals, *Hawwa* (*Eve*; from 2003) and *Nan Nü* (*Male Female*; from 1999). *Nan Nü* is subtitled 'Men, Women and Gender in Early and Imperial China,' and frequently carries articles and reviews on the history of sexuality, a hot topic today in Chinese-speaking areas. Articles are in English, many translated from Chinese, and the editorial board mixes scholars from the US, China, and Europe. *Hawwa*, which editor Amira El-Azhary Sonbol in her mission statement (2003: i–iv) describes as the 'first peer-reviewed academic journal to focus on Middle Eastern and Muslim women,' identifies strongly as feminist, being named after Eve as a 'symbolic figure' who 'illustrates ultimate gender equality.' The journal takes as its purview the enormous geographical and historical sweep of Islam, and the contributors come from universities in that world; the journal, however, is published, without comment, in English, the editor noting only that there will be 'occasional room for significant articles in the French language.' Content was projected to focus one-third on the past, two-thirds on the present and policy issues, and indeed volume 4.2–3 is a special issue on rewriting the history of sexuality in the Islamic world (see Semerdjian 2006). Journals on related topics are well-established in Spanish (*La Ventana: revista de estudios de género*, 1995–; *GénEros*, 1993–) and now in Vietnamese (*Nghiên cú'u gia đình & gió'i* [*Journal of Family and Gender Studies*], 2002–). In short the field is about where women's studies was in the 1980s, when writing *about* 'women of color' was replaced by writing *by* the former objects of study.

Again, the list of writers in the field is long and growing. A survey might include: for Japan, Gregory Pflugfelder, Jennifer Robertson, and Miriam Silverberg; for China, Charlotte Furth, Bret Hinsch, and Sang Tze-Lan; for India, Jyoti Puri, Jenny Sharpe, Giti Thadani, and Ruth Vanita; for Asia and the Pacific, the collection edited by Lenore Manderson and Margaret Jolly; for indigenous North America from contact to 1850, the collection edited by Sandra Slater and Fay Yarbrough (2011); for Latin America from prehistory to the modern, Michael J. Horswell, Sylvia Marcos, Dora Dávila Mendoza, Pete Sigal, Maite Zubiaurre, and the writers surveyed in Gutiérrez (2007); for Africa, Khamasi and Chinkuyu (2005) and Murray and Roscoe (1998); for the Near East, Afsaneh Najmabadi on Iran, Muallâ Türköne on Turkey, Dor Ze'evi on the Otto-man empire, the greatly influential and con-troversial Nawal El Saadawi on Egypt, and, on Islam in general, the pioneering work of Abdelwahab Bouhdiba (1982; see above for medieval Islam). The representative mix of cultures and periods in Murphy and Spear (2011) does not reach back before the early modern. Ann Laura Stoler's work has been widely influential in postcolonial studies; Walter Williams' work on the *berdache* and similar identities spans North America and the Pacific (see now Slater and Yarbrough 2011). But a division by regions is inade-quate to deal with transnational issues (including Orientalism itself), as pointed out by writers like Jasbir Puar. The field has also to deal with a bibliographic past that includes items like Felix Bryk's *Voodoo-eros: Ethno-logical Studies in the Sex-Life of the African*

*Aborigines* (1933), or James Cleugh's *A His-tory of Oriental Orgies: An Account of Erotic Practices among the Peoples of the East and Near East* (1968), or *Cradle of Erotica: A Study of Afro-Asian Sexual Expression and an Analysis of Erotic Freedom in Social Relationships*, by Allen Edwardes and R.E.L. Masters (1962). All these titles were (re) printed in the US in the 1960s, and indeed formed part of a discourse of their own (see Furth 2005).

The sheer mass of material suggests that the field might do well to retreat from local theo-retical battles for now and resort to a more Kinsey-like project of surveys. Starting from the issues set out by Foucault has paradoxi-cally limited both research and teaching – a problem well outlined for nonwestern studies by Linda Garber (2005) and in general by Susan Stryker (2008). There still seems to be no escaping debates over categories; as Ulrike Strasser and Heidi Tinsman consciensiously argue (2005: 164): 'Given that so many of gender history's analytical categories were first developed for the European context, how can we make sure that in studying gender systems in other cultures, we do not resort to another form of Eurocentrism...?' Afsaneh Najmabadi asks the same question (2006) in an essay titled, 'Beyond the Americas: are gender and sexuality useful categories of his-torical analysis?' Yet we might reflect on Uma Narayan's reminder (2000: 95):

Insofar as versions of relativism subscribe to these colonial pictures of 'essential differences' between cultures, relativism becomes a danger rather than an asset to feminist agendas. ... Third World feminist political struggles are often painfully aware that there are a number of 'master's houses.' Some of these houses are owned not by 'Western' masters but are part of the local real estate, while others have deeds so intricate that it is difficult to unravel how much they are the prop-erties of 'local' or 'Western' masters.

Qualms about terminology are something of a luxury, even if comparative study of non-western sexual systems can well be used in teaching to decenter not only Western history but Western historiography (so Garber 2005).

Perhaps, in a global perspective, we might think about rural/urban divisions, which surely contributed to the radical change of systems from classical antiquity to Christendom, as John Boswell argued in 1980. Yet, as Matt Houlbrook documents (2006: 150), the Internet is breaking down even this ancient division. The growing field of World History may prompt the next generation of scholars to think in terms of world systems, and not to section off parts of the globe as if they had no influence on each other – an extreme case of which is provided by my own field, which has tended to treat Greece and Rome apart from the world that surrounded them. The case for making the history of sexuality a part of World History is well made by Tony Ballantyne and Antoinette Burton (2005) as well as by Strasser and Tinsman, who provide a detailed course outline.

## NOW WHAT?

> Things duplicate themselves in Tlön. They tend at the same time to efface themselves, to lose their detail when people forget them. The classic example is that of a stone threshold which lasted as long as it was visited by a beggar, and which faded from sight on his death. Occasionally, a few birds, a horse perhaps, have saved the ruins of an amphitheater.
> (Jorge Luis Borges, 'Tlön, uqbar, orbis tertius,' 1964)

E.H. Carr might have been thinking of Borges' Tlön when he explained how all facts are not historical facts; in his parable, Borges reminds the historian how fragile is the tissue of the past. Historians of sexuality have to ask, what's next? What will happen after the children of '68 retire? After queer theory starts to sound ... dated? I hope that, like feminism, the history of sexuality will not be lost again: so passionately desired, so hard to come by for so long, so, against all logic, valuable. Vexed though it has been by epistemological problems, this history still constitutes a noble response to centuries of silence.

Generational shifts have already caused too many schisms. I hated to see Jeffrey Weeks defending himself (2005: 188): 'Far from

creating a new orthodoxy, we saw ourselves as challenging orthodoxy, as subverting traditional ways of presenting sexuality.' Compare Chris Waters, writing on 'the new British queer history' (2007: 152n5): 'more than once I have been accused of being a traitor to my generation.' Reviewing Alice Kuzniar's collection *Outing Goethe and his Age*, Denis Sweet (1998: 519) delivers a lecture on year-appropriate scholarship: 'Unearthing gay saints belongs to the practices and suppositions of another era.' Examples of the fallacy 'they were dumb then, we're smart now' (Richlin 1993: 272) are easy to find; despite the general treatment of Whig history these days as naive, a sort of Whiggishness pervades the field, which loves what's new. So Joseph Bristow on the new historians (2007: 142): 'One can only hope that their scholarly achievements will be remembered more accurately than they have at times chosen to recall those intellectual ancestors on whose work they still rely.'

The field also, despite its failure to make an impression on the *AHR*, maintains illusions about its influence in the culture as a whole. So, with great optimism, Carolyn Dinshaw (2001: 211) writes:

> Since the work of medievalists – particularly feminist and queer medievalists – was made a topic of discussion on the floor of Congress in the mid-'90s, I reasoned, why not occupy that space and use it for our own perverse purposes ... ?

Jeffrey Weeks is less sanguine (2005: 188, speaking of social constructionism): 'what amazes is ... our relative failure. We have not captured the popular imagination' – though his optimism soon springs back up (194). These hopes, after all, arose out of the struggles of many who had to fight to be heard, including many whose academic work was only a sideline on their activism, and many more whose work had to arise outside the academy. We owe it to them to keep the work going.

And this we can do through our one sure forum for activism: teaching. The focus on pedagogy and curricular issues by Ballantyne and Burton (2005) and Strasser and Tinsman (2005) is both timely and welcome. Things change; now that Greece and Rome are no longer the object of widespread awe and emulation, the importance of their historical example will dwindle – although I now must hope that they will not disappear altogether, like Borges' stone threshold. We, living as we are in the very late Roman empire, are trying to learn not to write as if here were everywhere and now were always. The *AHR*, in 1999, did rearrange its table of contents for reviews to lead with the categories 'Methods/Theory' and 'Comparative/World.' The Internet can make big changes: Google lists 348,000 hits for the combination 'Foucault' + 'History of Sexuality' (February 27, 2012); historical websites like that of the Schwules Museum in Berlin open up local histories to the world (Whisnant 2008: 1; see www.schwulesmuseum.de, and compare the list of US archives at www.glinn.com/news/lar1.htm). Even as globalization changes sexualities, it helps historians see what used to be there.

Huge problems remain to be dealt with. One territory I doubt will be commonly explored: age as a variable in the definition of sexual subjects. Writing now, historians have tended to treat Greek and Roman pederasty as if it had nothing in common with what is now identified as a sex crime. In fact it very often involved forced sex with enslaved adolescents. The biggest difference, indeed, between Greek and Roman sex/gender systems and those of the modern West is that in antiquity persons male and female were considered to become sexual actors at puberty. This age line was not a concern of the church, and so it long outlasted pederasty. The historian who rejoices to find queer sex everywhere in the elsewhen may not be so interested in tossing out the age of consent, nor so pleased to find that the founders of Stoicism endorsed not only teacher/student sex but incest (no marriage, no family, no kinship, no problem; Gaca 2003: 81). In any case, it would be difficult to say so; Haworth Press yielded to pressure to remove an article on pederasty from a 2005 special issue on same-sex desire in antiquity.

Projects I think should be undertaken: to understand how Orientalism predated Islam, how women wore the veil for a thousand years and more before Mohammed, and how the map of Christendom, in which we still live today, began to be drawn; to see how slavery has conditioned sexuality in world systems (see Strasser and Tinsman 2005), as the system of ancient sexuality continued on up to the early modern period, and as systems of slavery and human trafficking continue today. There is still work to be done. And if, as I take it, the historian's job is to remember, we must remember this, before the window closes again.

## ACKNOWLEDGMENTS

Many thanks to Joseph Bristow, Charlotte Furth, Nancy Hewitt, Elizabeth Pollard, Nancy Rabinowitz, James N. Schultz, Emily Selove, Giulia Sissa, and Ellen Snyder, without whom my overview would be over a lot less, and above all to Nancy Partner for her kind patience when it wasn't over sooner.

## REFERENCES

Amis, Kingsley. 1954. *Lucky Jim*. London: Gollancz.

Arjona Castro, Antonio. 1985. *Sexualidad en la España Musulmana*. Córdoba: Universidad de Córdoba.

Arondekar, Anjali R. 2009. *For the Record: On Sexuality and the Colonial Archive in India*. Durham: Duke University Press.

Babayan, Kathryn, and Afsaneh Najmabadi, eds. 2008. *Islamicate Sexualities: Translations Across Temporal Geographies of Desire*. Cambridge, MA: Harvard University Press.

Ballantyne, Tony, and Antoinette Burton, eds. 2005. *Bodies in Contact: Rethinking Colonial Encounters in World History*. Durham: Duke University Press.

Bennett, Judith M. 2000. '"Lesbian-like" and the social history of lesbianism.' *Journal of the History of Sexuality* 9: 1–24.

Bennett, Judith M. 2006. *History Matters: Patriarchy and the Challenge of Feminism*. Philadelphia: University of Pennsylvania Press.

Borges, Jorge Luis. 1964. *Ficciones*. Trans. Anthony Kerrigan. New York: Grove Weidenfeld.

Boswell, John. 1980. *Christianity, Homosexuality, and Social Tolerance*. Chicago: University of Chicago Press.

Bouhdiba, Abdelwahab. 1982. *La Sexualité en Islam*. Paris: Quadrige/PUF. Translated as *Sexuality in Islam* by Alan Sheridan, 1985, Routledge and Kegan Paul.

Bristow, Joseph. 2007. 'Remapping the sites of modern gay history: legal reform, medico-legal thought, homosexual scandal, erotic geography.' *Journal of British Studies* 46: 116–42.

Brooten, Bernadette J., ed. 2010. *Beyond Slavery: Overcoming Its Religious and Sexual Legacies*. New York: Palgrave Macmillan.

Brożyna, Martha A., ed. 2005. *Gender and Sexuality in the Middle Ages: A Medieval Source Documents Reader*. Jefferson, NC: McFarland.

Bryk, Felix. 1933 and various reprints. *Voodoo-eros: Ethnological Studies in the Sex-Life of the African Aborigines*. Privately printed for subscribers.

Carter, Julian. 2005. 'Introduction: theory, methods, praxis: the history of sexuality and the question of Evidence.' *Journal of the History of Sexuality* 14: 1–9.

Clark, Anna. 2005. 'Twilight Moments.' *Journal of the History of Sexuality* 14: 139–60.

Clark, Anna, ed. 2011. *The History of Sexuality in Europe: A Sourcebook and Reader*. London: Routledge.

Cleugh, James. 1968. *A History of Oriental Orgies: An Account of Erotic Practices among the Peoples of the East and Near East*. NY: Crown Publishers.

Cocks, H.G., and Matt Houlbrook, eds. 2006. *Palgrave Advances in the Modern History of Sexuality*. Basingstoke: Palgrave Macmillan.

Crompton, Louis. 1985. *Byron and Greek Love*. London: Faber and Faber.

Crompton, Louis. 2003. *Homosexuality and Civilization*. Cambridge: Harvard University Press.

Davidson, James N. 2007. *The Greeks and Greek Love: A Radical Reappraisal of Homosexuality in Ancient Greece*. London: Weidenfeld & Nicolson.

Davidson, James N. 2009. 'Response: Davidson on Verstraete on Davidson, *The Greeks and Greek Love* ...' *Bryn Mawr Classical Review* 2009.11.03. Available at http://bmcr.brynmawr.edu/2009/2009-11-03.html.

de Beauvoir, Simone. 1981 [1949]. *Le Deuxième Sexe*. 2 vols. Paris: Gallimard.

Dinshaw, Carolyn. 2001. 'Got medieval?' *Journal of the History of Sexuality* 10: 202–12.

Dover., K.J. 1978. *Greek Homosexuality*. Cambridge, MA: Harvard University Press.

Drabinski, Kate. 2004. Review of Kathy Gaca, *The Making of Fornication*. *Journal of the History of Sexuality* 13.4: 522–25.

Duberman, Martin Bauml, Martha Vicinus, and George Chauncey, Jr. 1989. 'Introduction.' In *Hidden from History: Reclaiming the Gay and Lesbian Past*, ed. Martin Bauml Duberman, Martha Vicinus, and George Chauncey, Jr: 1–11. New York: New American Library.

duBois, Page. 2003. *Slaves and Other Objects*. Chicago: University of Chicago Press.

Dynes, Wayne R. 2005. 'Light in Hellas: how German classical philology engendered gay scholarship.' *Journal of Homosexuality* 49.3/4: 341–56.

Edwardes, Allen and R.E.I. Masters. 1962. *Cradle of Erotica: A Study of Afro-Asian Sexual Expression and an Analysis of Erotic Freedom in Social Relationships*. NY: Lancer Books.

Eglinton, J.Z. 1964. *Greek Love*. New York: Oliver Layton.

Epprecht, Marc. 2008. *Unspoken Facts: A History of Homosexualities in Africa*. Harare, Zimbabwe: Gays and Lesbians of Zimbabwe.

Forman, Ross. 2006. 'Race and empire.' In *Palgrave Advances in the Modern History of Sexuality*, ed. H.G. Cocks and Matt Houlbrook: 109–32. Basingstoke: Palgrave Macmillan.

Foucault, Michel. 1976. *La Volonté de savoir*. Paris: Gallimard.

Foucault, Michel. 1978. *The History of Sexuality*. Vol. 1: *An Introduction*. Trans. Robert Hurley. New York: Vintage.

Foucault, Michel. 1985. *The Use of Pleasure*. Trans. Robert Hurley. New York: Vintage.

Foucault, Michel. 1986. *The Care of the Self*. Trans. Robert Hurley. New York: Vintage.

Fout, John (1990), 'A Note From the Editor.' *Journal of the History of Sexuality* I: 1–2.

Furth, Charlotte. 2005. 'Rethinking Van Gulik again.' *Nan Nü* 7: 71–78.

Gaca, Kathy L. 2003. *The Making of Fornication*. Berkeley: University of California Press.

Garber, Linda. 2005. 'Where in the world are the lesbians?' *Journal of the History of Sexuality* 14.1/2: 28–50.

Gutiérrez, Ramón A. 2007. 'Introduction to the special issue.' *Journal of the History of Sexuality* 16: 349–54.

Harper, Kyle. 2011. *Slavery in the Late Roman World, AD 275–425*. Cambridge: Cambridge University Press.

Heszer, Catherine. 2005. *Jewish Slavery in Antiquity*. Oxford: Oxford University Press.

Houlbrook, Matt. 2006. 'Cities.' In *Palgrave Advances in the Modern History of Sexuality*, ed. H.G. Cocks and Matt Houlbrook: 133–56. Basingstoke: Palgrave Macmillan.

Hubbard, Thomas K., ed. 2003. *Homosexuality in Greece and Rome: A Sourcebook of Basic Documents*. Berkeley: University of California Press.

James, Liz, ed. 1999. *Desire and Denial in Byzantium*. Aldershot: Ashgate.

Jordan, Mark D. 1997. *The Invention of Sodomy in Christian Theology*. Chicago: University of Chicago Press.

Karras, Ruth Mazo. 2000. 'Active/Passive, Acts/Passions: Greek and Roman Sexualities.' *American Historical Review* 105: 1250–65.

Karras, Ruth Mazo. 2005. *Sexuality in Medieval Europe: Doing Unto Others*. New York: Routledge.

Khamasi, Jennifer Wanjiku, and Susan Nyambura Maina-Chinkuyu, eds. 2005. *Sexuality: An African Perspective*. Eldoret, Kenya: Moi University Press.

Le Guin, Ursula K. 2002. 'Mountain ways.' In *The Birthday of the World*: 91–118. New York: HarperCollins.

Leonard, Sarah. 2006. 'Pornography and obscenity.' In *Palgrave Advances in the Modern History of Sexuality*, ed. H.G. Cocks and Matt Houlbrook: 180–205. Basingstoke: Palgrave Macmillan.

Lochrie, Karma. 1997. 'Desiring Foucault.' *Journal of Medieval and Early Modern Studies* 27: 3–16.

MacKinnon, Catharine A. 1992. 'Does sexuality have a history?' In *Discourses of Sexuality: From Aristotle to AIDS*, ed. Domna C. Stanton: 117–36. Ann Arbor: University of Michigan Press.

McCabe, Susan. 2005. 'To be and to have: the rise of queer historicism.' *GLQ* 11: 119–34.

McCarthy, Conor, ed. 2004. *Love, Sex, and Marriage in the Middle Ages: A Sourcebook*. London: Routledge.

Mahaffy, J.P. 1874. *Social Life in Greece from Homer to Alexander*. London: Macmillan.

Marchand, Suzanne. 1996. *Down from Olympus: Archaeology and Philhellenism in Germany, 1750–1970*. Princeton: Princeton University Press.

Moore, Stephen D. 2001. *God's Beauty Parlor, and Other Queer Spaces in and around the Bible*. Stanford: Stanford University Press.

Murphy, Kevin P., and Jennifer M. Spear. 2011. *Historicising Gender and Sexuality*. Malden, MA: Wiley-Blackwell.

Murray, Stephen O., and Will Roscoe, eds. 1998. *Boy-Wives and Female Husbands: Studies of African Homosexualities*. New York: St. Martins.

Najmabadi, Afsaneh. 2006. 'Beyond the Americas: Are gender and sexuality useful categories of historical analysis?' *Journal of Women's History* 18: 11–21.

Narayan, Uma. 2000. 'Essence of culture and a sense of history: a feminist critique of cultural essentialism.' In *Decentering the Center: Philosophy for a Multicultural, Postcolonial, and Feminist World*, ed. Uma Narayan and Sandra Harding: 80–100. Bloomington: Indiana University Press.

Partner, Nancy F. 1993. 'No sex, no gender.' *Speculum* 68: 419–43.

Partner, Nancy F. 2005. 'The hidden self: psychoanalysis and the textual unconscious.' In *Writing Medieval History*, ed. Nancy F. Partner: 42–64. London: Hodder Arnold.

Phillips, Kim M., and Barry Reay. 2002. 'Introduction.' In *Sexualities in History: A Reader*, ed. Kim M. Phillips and Barry Reay: 1–23. New York: Routledge.

Richlin, Amy. 1993. 'The ethnographer's dilemma and the dream of a lost golden age.' In *Feminist Theory and the Classics*, ed. Nancy Sorkin Rabinowitz and Amy Richlin: 272–303. New York: Routledge.

Richlin, Amy. 1997. 'Towards a history of body history.' In *Inventing Ancient Culture: Historicism, Periodization, and the Ancient World*, ed. Mark Golden and Peter Toohey: 16–35. London: Routledge.

Richlin, Amy. 2005. 'Eros underground: Greece and Rome in gay print culture.' *Journal of Homosexuality* 49: 421–61.

Rocke, Michael. 1996. *Forbidden Friendship: Homosexuality and Male Culture in Renaissance Florence*. Oxford: Oxford University Press.

Rubin, Gayle. 1984. 'Thinking sex: notes for a radical theory of the politics of sexuality.' In *Pleasure and Danger*, ed. Carole S. Vance: 267–319. Boston: Routledge and Kegan Paul.

Ruggiero, Guido. 1990. 'Introduction.' In *Sex and Gender in Historical Perspective*, ed. Edward Muir and Guido Ruggiero: vii–xxii. Baltimore: Johns Hopkins University Press.

Rupp, Leila J. 1989. '"Imagine my surprise": women's relationships in mid-twentieth century America.' In *Hidden from History*, ed. Martin Duberman et al.: 395–410. New York: New American Library.

Rupp, Leila J. 2001. 'Toward a global history of same-sex sexuality.' *Journal of the History of Sexuality* 10: 287–302.

Rupp, Leila J. 2009. *Sapphistries: A Global History of Love between Women*. New York: New York University Press.

Schultz, James A. 2006. 'Heterosexuality as a threat to medieval studies.' *Journal of the History of Sexuality* 15: 14–28.

Semerdjian, Elyse. 2006. 'Rewriting the history of sexuality in the Islamic World.' *Hawwa* 4.2–3: 119–30.

Settis, Salvatore. 2007. *The Future of the 'Classical'*. Trans. Allan Cameron. Cambridge: Polity Press.

Sissa, Giulia. 2003. *Eros Tiranno: Sessualità e Sensualità nel Mondo Antico*. Rome: Laterza. Trans. 2008 as *Sex and Sensuality in the Ancient World*. New Haven: Yale University Press.

Skinner, Marilyn B. 2005. *Sexuality in Greek and Roman Culture*. Oxford: Blackwell.

Slater, Sandra, and Fay A. Yarbrough, eds. 2011. *Gender and Sexuality in Indigenous North America, 1400–1850*. Columbia: University of South Carolina Press.

Spivak, Gayatri Chakravorty. 1999. *A Critique of Postcolonial Reason: Toward a History of the Vanishing Present*. Cambridge: Harvard University Press.

Strasser, Ulrike, and Heidi Tinsman. 2005. 'Engendering world history.' *Radical History Review* 91: 151–64.

Stryker, Susan. 2008. 'Transgender history, homonormativity, and disciplinarity.' *Radical History Review* 100: 145–57.

Sweet, Denis M. 1998. Review of Alice Kuzniar, *Outing Goethe and His Age*. *Journal of the History of Sexuality* 8: 516–19.

Sweet, James H. 2000. Review of Stephen O. Murray and Will Roscoe, eds, *Boy-Wives and Female Husbands: Studies of African Homosexualities*. *Journal of the History of Sexuality* 9.1/2: 205–08.

Valentine, Jody. 2008. 'Lesbians are from Lesbos: Sappho and identity construction in *The Ladder*.' *Helios* 35: 143–69.

Vanita, Ruth, and Saleem Kidwai, eds. 2000. *Same-sex Love in India: Readings from Literature and History*. New York: St. Martins.

Waters, Chris. 2007. 'Distance and desire in the new British queer history.' *GLQ* 14: 139–55.

Weeks, Jeffrey. 2002. 'Sexuality and history revisited.' In *Sexualities in History: A Reader*, ed. Kim M. Phillips and Barry Reay: 27–41. New York: Routledge.

Weeks, Jeffrey. 2005. 'Remembering Foucault.' *Journal of the History of Sexuality* 14: 186–201.

Whisnant, Clayton. 2008. 'Gay German history: future directions?' *Journal of the History of Sexuality* 17: 1–10.

Williams, Craig A. 1999 (2nd edn 2010). *Roman Homosexuality: Ideologies of Masculinity in Classical Antiquity*. Oxford: Oxford University Press.

Wright, J.W., Jr, and Everett K. Rowson, eds. 1997. *Homoeroticism in Classical Arabic Literature*. New York: Columbia University Press.

# 19

# Psychoanalysis and the Making of History

Michael Roper

In mapping the relationships between history and psychoanalysis, we might identify three broad although overlapping fields. Firstly there is now a considerable and rapidly growing body of research on the history of psychoanalysis. This includes cultural histories which tend to be agnostic towards the basic premises of psychoanalysis, regarding it as set of knowledge claims or a technology of the self whose relationship to modernity in the twentieth century needs to be understood.[1] It also includes studies from within the field of psychoanalysis itself, sometimes orientated towards practitioners and reflecting a professional and personal allegiance to a particular form of psychoanalytic thought.[2] Secondly, there are historians who draw on psychoanalytic ideas to illuminate events or people in the past. 'Psychobiography', for example, applies the clinical concepts and insights of psychoanalysis as a means of exploring the motivations of particular historical figures, usually eminent, such as artists, politicians and scientists.[3] Freud's own study of Leonardo da Vinci provides a typical – and typically contentious – example.[4] In addition there are many studies within social and cultural history which have sought to understand collective events, behaviour or states of mind in the past; such as witchcraft, war, political extremism and revolution, by exposing and exploring their unconscious and irrational roots.[5]

In this chapter, however, I am less concerned with the historical development of psychoanalysis, or with the application of psychoanalytic concepts to the past, than with the way in which history itself is made, and the mental processes that contribute to its making. I wish to turn the spotlight of psychoanalytic enquiry onto the historian, to think about the residues of the past to which we expose our feelings as well as our minds in doing history. How, I will ask, does the historian's unconscious bear upon his or her efforts to make sense of the past? There are at least four major schools of psychoanalytic thought and practice, Freudian, Kleinian and Jungian, with Lacanian approaches being less visible in the clinical than the academic setting. In what follows I will draw particularly on the work of Melanie Klein (1882–1960) and her followers, who have had a strong influence within

British psychoanalytic circles since the Second World War. Whilst Klein was keen to stress that her work was an extension of rather than a departure from Freud, her ideas have contributed to a distinctive emphasis on early infancy, primitive emotional states, and the enactment of what Klein termed 'unconscious phantasy', which Klein studied in great detail through observing children at play. My analysis of historical work will be equally selective, relating principally to the development of social history within the Anglo-American context, where the intellectual and emotional and political trajectories have differed somewhat from those within Europe.

## THE UNCONSCIOUS BURDENS OF THE PAST

The past, as the psychoanalyst and cultural historian Karl Figlio remarks, often bequeaths a kind of 'unconscious burden'.[6] What Figlio means by this is that past emotions, although evanescent in themselves, leave traces that trouble the present. Like the deep emotional impulses that Freud thought were all the more crucial to the understanding of human action because largely inaccessible to the conscious mind, the residues of past human dramas are transmitted in ways that later generations may, despite their best efforts, fail to fully comprehend. Freud believed that emotions which could not be worked through within the mind, or brought into consciousness, were apt to be repeated or acted out. Their impact might be especially strong when a past society has, like the patient in psychoanalysis, forgotten, repressed or otherwise failed to deal with them.[7]

This unconscious burden can take a variety of forms. It can be carried widely within the culture, such as the memory of class, patriarchal or colonial oppression, political issues that are debated publicly and to which the historian's own research may respond more or less directly. Or it may be felt in a more immediate and intimate way, being carried in the material *evidence* of the past, such as when we encounter an entry in a letter or diary that suddenly draws us in to the emotional situation of the person or people we are studying. I am sure that many of us have had this experience of sudden recognition, which momentarily seems to bridge the difference between past and present. For me, working as I have in recent years on the letters of First World War soldiers, that feeling is animated by homesickness, loss, anger or despair, feelings that had called out to be attended to by someone else at the moment of being recorded, and which, in feeling moved, I am drawn to work on.[8]

Let me give an example. At a conference held in spring 2008 to mark the retirement of the oral historian Paul Thompson, Alessandro Portelli – who has been crucial to the development of thinking about myth and memory in oral history – gave a paper about the impact of economic globalisation on the steel workers of Italy. What was the subjective experience of steel-making among those who had worked and built communities around steel, he asked; and what was the collective consciousness of their present situation? In the central Italian town of Terni, known for its steel production, and studied by Portelli over the past 25 years, the electrical steel plant was marked for closure: global shifts in capital would soon make these men redundant. At the same time, in another plant in Italy owned by the same multinational conglomerate, seven workers had been killed in a violent explosion and fire. Portelli then went on to quote, translating from the Italian, the testimonies of some of the men who had run to the scene minutes afterwards. They described victims still alive, but whose skin had turned to charcoal, or whose flesh had burnt away, revealing their internal organs, and who would soon die. Portelli did not comment much on their testimony, he simply quoted the witnesses, but the scene that these men had encountered was conveyed to all of us in the seminar room, and there was an almost palpable sense of horror as we imagined what the onlookers had seen. We had not witnessed the event ourselves, we had only heard a story, but the emotional experience seemed, at that moment, to have lost little of its power in being transplanted to a different time, place and language, now heard – and felt – third-hand by an academic audience of oral and cultural historians in Britain.

Psychoanalytic ideas can help us understand what is going on at times such as this when powerful events from the past confront us. The unconscious burden is something that psychoanalysis and history have in common. Both the analyst and the historian are alert to the unresolved residues of the past, what Figlio calls the 'never-conscious/never-remembered', and both seek to work upon and transform this psychic burden.[9] For Freud the point of psychoanalysis was to replace unbidden repetition by memory, and a similar impetus characterises history, which tries to 'bring the past to mind with the aim of resolution'.[10] One of the social purposes of history, as Figlio sees it, is thus to function as a kind of conscience or 'cultural super-ego' in relation to the psychic burden.[11] Historians work upon the unassimilated traces of the past that 'belabour society', seeking in this way to repair the damage caused by previous generations.[12] They, by implication, tend to be the kinds of people who are *receptive* to those residues, who wish to bring the unconscious burden to light and subject it to scrutiny.

Recognition of the unconscious burden is not new. R.G. Collingwood, though careful to distinguish history from psychology, was perceptive about historical knowledge as a psychological process. For Collingwood, the historian's task was to attempt to reconstruct through present thought, the thought of the past. He felt however that this effort was not only motivated by the present circumstances; the past itself had a kind of power to haunt, to re-present itself in order to be subjected to thought. In this way the difference between past and present was diminished:

> historical knowledge is that special case of memory where the object of present thought is past thought, the gap between present and past

being bridged not only by the power of present thought to think of the past, but also the power of past thought to reawaken itself in the present.[13]

Collingwood was clear that the historian's task was to reconstruct past thought as *distinct* from raw and immediate, unreflective experience, which he termed the 'subjectivity of feeling'.[14] 'Of everything other than thought', he said 'there can be no history.'[15] What this conception seemed to do, was bracket off those categories of experience that were least capable of assimilation by the mind. It excluded from historical analysis the very mental phenomena that most interests the psychoanalytically inclined historian: those emotional sensations that cannot be thought but which are communicated nonetheless. Nevertheless what Collingwood had to say about the mechanisms of *transmission* between past and present was as pertinent to emotion as to thought, the power of which, in contrast to Collingwood, I see as the proper object of history in its relation to thought.

## THE HISTORIAN'S UNCONSCIOUS RELATIONSHIPS WITH THE PAST

I would like to make two observations here about the way in which history deals with the emotional sensations of the past, and hence about how the practice of psychoanalysis and of history might be analogous. Firstly, in doing history we place ourselves in a relationship with the past. We are often careful to stake out the differences between history and psychology. History, some say, is concerned with externalities, with economic, social, political and cultural processes, with processes that are shared and not, in Collingwood's terms, with 'mere subjectivity'.[16] History should keep sight of the big picture, the external structures that shape human action and feeling, and it should not descend too far into interior inspection. If it does, the individual life should serve as an illustration of a larger pattern and process, since the

concern with context is what separates history from biography.[17] And yet, in fostering
the empathy that Collingwood sees as necessary to the reconstruction of past thought,
bringing proximate experiences from our
present to the evidence of past thought, we
are in essence creating a relationship with the
past.[18] Historical understanding is, in that
sense, not a million miles removed from the
relationships we conduct with one another,
where empathy counts equally. Moreover, of
course, the vast bulk of evidence before us
has been left by sentient beings, with whom
we can develop a close relationship in the
process of research, even if the ostensible
topic of our inquiries is seemingly impersonal. The question of how we take in the
emotional residues of the past to which we
exposes ourselves, of what, in psychoanalytic terms, is being transferred to us through
the historical record, and what sense we are
then able to make of its residues, is a fundamental matter of historical method.

Secondly, I would like to turn Collingwood's idea of reconstructing past thought
on its head, and say that much contemporary
historical research is animated by precisely
those moments when past thought has *failed*.
The expansive literature on trauma, on the
psychology of evil, on disaster, on manifestations of the irrational such as witchcraft, all
provide examples. These are the moments
when psychic residues were so powerful that
they overwhelmed the capacity of past minds
to assimilate them, being then transmitted in
the letter, diary, court transcript or oral history interview, not in a reflective way as
memories, but as raw projections. I think this
is why the accounts of the witnesses of the
factory disaster related by Portelli struck the
audience so forcibly, being in essence unprocessed fragments of affect, carried in a narrative. In such situations, the unconscious
burden is especially great, and the historian
is often drawn into an attempt to bring to
mind what is unthought, in an effort to mitigate its traumatic force. At the same time, of
course, emotional experiences such as these
are often the most difficult of all to attend to,

and the historian may then simply reproduce
the pain of the past, as if they were themselves in a post-traumatic state.[19]

The psychoanalytic concepts of transference and countertransference can help shed
light on how the historian works on this
unconscious burden. Transference is a key
concept within the clinical practice of psychoanalysis. It refers to the unconscious
aspects of the patient's communication which
are transferred onto the analyst, so that, for
example, in his case-study of Dora, Freud
came to understand his patient's strong negative transference as a repetition of her earlier
unresolved feelings towards 'Herr K', a close
friend of Dora's father. These feelings had
been re-experienced by Dora with such intensity in the analysis with Freud that she had
found it necessary to terminate the treatment
early.[20] For the Kleinian analyst, transference
has a broader meaning, referring not only to
the repetitions of past relationships observed
by Freud, but to enactments of unconscious
phantasy in the present. Everything that the
patient brings in to the psychoanalytic session: her reports of daily life, thoughts,
dreams and so on, is understood in terms of
the transference, even if its subject matter is
ostensibly unrelated to the analyst. It is the
analyst's task to explore, within this intersubjective relationship, why the patient is
presenting material to them in this way at this
particular time. What kind of psychic project,
they will ask, is the patient enacting with the
analyst in the psychoanalytic session?[21]

Most historians – with the exception of
those doing oral history – do not of course
have a direct personal relationship with the
subjects of their research, but when reading a
personal communication such as a letter or
memoir, we must inevitably place ourselves
in some way within the circle of our subject's
relationships with others, as if we are ourselves the object of their transferences. In
reading the letters home of soldiers on the
Western Front, for example, I tried to put
myself into the position of the mother or
father who is being addressed. Why, I asked,
do these sons wish to tell their parents one

thing rather than another, and at this time rather than another? Why did they complain vociferously to their mothers about army food, and remember Sunday lunches with such relish? Why did they write little about their spirits and much about their stomachs? What kinds of emotional states were mothers being asked to hold on behalf of sons; what, in psychoanalytic terms, was being projected into the phantasised mother as the son composed his letter, or into the phantasised son as the mother composed her reply?[22] Such research involves acting to some extent *as if* the historian was the intended recipient of the communication, when in fact – with the notable exception of those who write with more than an eye on posterity and who really *are* addressing the future historian – it was originally intended for others.

For the psychoanalyst, the clue to interpreting the patient's state of mind lies in their own emotional reactions to what is going on in the session. They try to take in emotionally, or 'introject', the patient's unconscious communications. What, they ask themselves, is being lodged in them by the patient? How does the patient make them feel, and what does that in turn suggest about those aspects of the patient's psychic life that they are unconsciously being invited to hold? This, broadly speaking, is what is termed the 'countertransference', and whereas for Freud and for Klein it was seen as a potential problem, within post-Kleinian psychoanalysis it is seen as the main resource for understanding the patient, provided that, in the face of experiences that may be exceptionally difficult to tolerate, the analyst is able to sustain his or her attention and not enact an emotional response.[23]

For the Kleinian analyst Wilfred Bion, the thinking done by the analyst was a form of containing: it involved processing the patient's emotional sensations in such a way as to lessen their toxicity. The original model of containing was the maternal relationship, and the capacity of the mother to take in, and make sense of, anxious experiences on behalf of the baby.[24] It would be trite to say that, as historians, we seek to reverse the generations,

acting as mothers to the past, but I do think that the desire to work on unassimilated experiences, to bring them to light and subject them to scrutiny, and to alleviate the burdens of the past on behalf of the wider society, plays a significant part in animating historical work. One could think here of the contemporary interest in trauma, genocide, slavery, colonialism and dispossessed minorities, and also in political processes such as reconciliation, concerns which simultaneously depend upon and generate historical scholarship and debate.[25] Another way of saying this is that as historians, we often feel a duty to the past to expose ourselves to, or introject, its unconscious burdens, and to work upon them as the mother works upon and mediates the baby's distress. As Collingwood observes, in order for a past thought to become an object of historical knowledge, the historian must be a certain kind of person. He or she must have the kind of mind which is receptive to that thought, or 'pre-adapted to be its host'. In another passage he describes this process in terms which, in their use of domestic metaphors, are evocative of the process of containing described by Bion, where the baby's emotional state is received by the mother. The thoughts being investigated by the historian, says Collingwood, must be 'of such a kind that it can revive itself in the historian's mind; *the historian's mind must be such as to offer a home for that revival*' (italics mine).[26]

In our efforts to offer such a home, we will draw energy from our own personal pasts, and in our historical pursuits we will be prone to repeat the patterns of unconscious response that are familiar to us from our earlier and non-professional lives. If the burdens of the past are too threatening, the historian will not be able to offer a 'home' for them. Then, she or he may well react to the unconscious burden by acting it out. Our subjects, after all, cannot respond to our interpretations as the patient in psychoanalysis does, and most of us do not have the clinician's benefit of a personal analysis and supervision. To take a personal example, one of the most difficult problems I experienced in writing my book *The Secret Battle* was its length. In early drafts I could not strike the right balance between description and analysis; there were simply too many examples. While this is a common problem, it was compounded by the intense longing for home that sons communicated in their letters from the Western Front, and the often intolerable anxiety experienced by mothers as they waited for news. I felt an obligation to these families to keep faith with their suffering, but its very intensity also seemed to produce in me a tendency to enact or dramatise that militated against historical understanding.[27] If, when we read another historian's work, we find ourselves saturated in horror, pain or violence, but lacking the means to understand it; if we identify so strongly with the emotional situation of the subject that the difference between then and now is temporarily obliterated; if the evocation of an emotion seems to have taken the place of interpretation, this may be because the historian is mentally overwhelmed, and can do little more than pass on the original emotional sensation.

Hence, not only do the unconscious burdens of others' pasts call upon the historian, but the historian's *own* unconscious burdens, and how they are dealt with psychically, form an important feature of how she or he seeks to get to grips with history. To state the bald psychic logic, our own unconscious phantasies and defence mechanisms will influence the manner in which we react to the unconscious burdens that our profession throws up. In what follows, I wish to look more closely at the ways in which such relationships might be seen to operate within social history over the past four decades. The psychic burden, I believe, lies particularly close to the surface in social history. This is partly because social history has pioneered the concern with the personal experience of everyday life, a concern that, however, has frequently co-existed with a certain scepticism that unconscious motivations, supposing they exist, can be adequately deduced from the relatively sparse and partial evidence that historians commonly work with; and that they are perhaps not the proper concern of historical

analysis in the first place. This scepticism applies even more to the idea that historical analysis might partly be a product of the historian's unconscious, something which it is thought the biographer, not the historian, must answer for because their subject matter is more obviously individual and psychological.[28] I have also chosen social history because of its sense of moral purpose, for the long-running practical engagement with social movements, with socialist, feminist and post-colonial critiques, and its recurrent call, 'whither politics?', have kept social history in a creative and reflective dialogue with its subject-matter, and hence in close touch with the unconscious burdens of the past.

## RESCUING THE FORGOTTEN: E.P. THOMPSON

In the preface of E.P. Thompson's 1963 edition of *The Making of the English Working-Class* there is a sentence which does not appear in the 1968 edition. It comes immediately after Thompson sets out his disagreements with the static and abstracted conceptions of class adopted by some sociologists, and where he explains his idea of class as a social and cultural process. Then he goes on: 'This book can be seen as a biography of the English working class from its adolescence to until its early manhood.' In the rest of the paragraph, Thompson outlines the key arguments about change in class relationships between 1780 and 1832, such that 'the working-class presence was, in 1832, the most significant factor in British political life'.[29] With the omission of the biography analogy from the 1968 edition the paragraph conforms more closely to the orthodoxies of historical writing, so it moves straight from a discussion of concepts of class to a summary of the book's narrative of change. Readers of the second edition would not encounter that rather revealing paternal expression, which conjures the English working-class *as if* it was a child of Thompson's own making, over whose historical progress he had tended.

We can only speculate on why this sentence, although imprinted on the minds of many readers, is missing from the 1968 edition, but it is emblematic of a larger ambivalence within social history about the subjective sphere. On the one hand what is special about *The Making* is the way it brings alive the sphere of personal experience: Thompson's aim is to document the lives and perceptions of those omitted from the historical record, and he wants us to consider class, not as an abstraction, but as a lived experience, or what he calls a 'relationship'. We are encouraged to develop a sense of empathetic feeling for 'real people' in a 'real context'. Thompson is certainly passionate, and we are invited to share his passion for retrieving a history of 'the lost causes, and the losers themselves'.[30]

On the other hand, Thompson is clearly unsympathetic towards some of the structures of feeling he investigates. He is critical for example of the 'raw emotionalism' of the adherents of primitive Methodism, and his explanation of it in terms of sublimation, a 'displaced' reaction to the psychic pressures of rapid processes of industrialism, draws on psychology less to dignify than to pathologise.[31] The strident authorial style invites support or dissent, but does not allow much space for reflection by the reader on the range of Thompson's feelings towards the men and women whose lives and experiences he is documenting, or about what might have given rise to his desire to champion them, and what affective ends might be being served for the wider society in the historical project of rescue.

Melanie Klein's ideas about the psychic positions adopted by the infant can help to illuminate the unconscious basis of the social and moral commitment that is characteristic of Thompson's work. In the early months, Klein says, the baby is largely stuck in the paranoid-schizoid position. Its mental world is divided. It experiences strong feelings of anxiety, envy and persecution, against which it mobilises a range of primitive defence mechanisms. Fearing the destructive strength of its emotions, it splits the world into good and evil, love and hate, either violently projecting its destructive impulses outwards, or idealising the loved object in the hope of averting destructive impulses from it. In the paranoid-schizoid position the infant has no capacity to understand the workings of its internal world. Thinking is paralyzed. As it develops, however, the infant begins to be able to perceive the world in terms of whole objects, recognise its ambivalence, and see that its external objects such as the mother are neither wholly good nor wholly bad, but a mixture of the two. At that point it enters the depressive position, which is characterised by feelings of guilt and remorse about its destructive impulses, and the recognition and taking of responsibility for the harm that these may have done to its loved objects. It engages in reparative activities, atoning for its earlier envious attacks. As Bob Hinshelwood has pointed out, the depressive position was for Klein a source of creativity, as it was in the reflective working through of the depressive dilemmas that movement and emotional development occurred. It was from the depressive position too, that, in Klein's words, 'social feeling' arose. In the individual's attempt to repair damage to their internal world, reparation becomes, in Bob Hinshelwood's phrase, 'a powerhouse for mature energy and creativity in the actual external world'. It is through humanitarian projects in the external world that reparative impulses are enacted.[32]

Crucially, for Klein, the movement from the paranoid-schizoid into the depressive positions is never conclusively achieved: as adults, we continue to oscillate between the two and we mobilise many defences against the pain of feeling guilt and remorse in the depressive position. Manic defences were of particular interest to Klein. They are ones in which guilt towards the loved object is assuaged by omnipotent attempts to control it. Idealisation, or heightened moral attitudes, Klein says, and sweeping and grandiose efforts to rescue and to make good damaged objects, are characteristic of manic defences.

The historical approach that Thompson developed in *The Making*, and has continued to exert an influence within social history over nearly a half century, resonates with Kleinian ideas. There is a strongly moral aspect to his professed aim to 'rescue the poor stockinger, the Luddite cropper, the "obsolete" hand-loom weaver, the "utopian" artisan, and even the deluded follower of Joanna Southcott, from the enormous conde-scension of posterity'.[33] A double injustice has been done to these people, Thompson believes, firstly in being marginalised within their own lives, and then by history itself, which in concentrating on the successful, and ransacking the past for 'forerunners-pioneers' of the labour movement or Welfare State, compounds this forgetting of 'working people' and of their contributions to history. The programme is certainly an ambitious one, as is suggested by terms such as 'rescue' and 'enormous condesension'. However, recog-nition of the occasionally manic reach of Thompson's thought is suspended by, on the one hand, the pity being aroused in the reader towards history's victims, and on the other, anger towards those historians who have conspired in their neglect. We are invited, in other words, to ignore the psychic mecha-nisms that are being mobilised by Thompson and aroused in us as readers, and to identify instead *with* the 'casualties' (a term that is used twice in the preface) and against their enemies past and present.

This 'rescue' takes the form of exhaustive description, often intended to demonstrate by the sheer depth of historical context, that the customs of working people were not irra-tional or backward-looking, but that they had a sense to them, if only the historian was attentive enough to discover their logic. The achievement of one of Thompson's most well-known essays, 'The moral economy of the crowd', was to show how custom could be creatively drawn on to negotiate, and limit, the encroachments of the market econ-omy.[34] There was an element of nostalgia for pre-capitalist relations, and the motivation was firmly reparative, the aim being, as Craig Calhoun describes it, to 'restore human dignity to those whose practices they were and make them truly meaningful'.[35]

Thompson's approach gave history – and historians – a special place within contempo-rary politics, for they were the ones charged with the task of reparation. In *The Making* he points out that future societies may find 'exemplars' in beliefs and practices that look to us outmoded, unlikely, or downright bizarre, and in essays like 'Time, work discipline and industrial capitalism', he was keen to show how history could be a force against determin-istic thinking. If the process of industrialisa-tion, seen through the 'inward apprehension of time of working people', could take such different patterns in different periods and places, surely it was not immutable and could be resisted.[36] Finally, of course, Thompson was always both an activist and a historian, his other major contribution to public life being the cause of nuclear disarmament. The repara-tive impulse dominated his life and was the essence of his passion. Calhoun's tribute to Thompson as a key figure in 'the immensely intellectually productive and sometimes polit-ically important borderland between academic scholarship and public activism', suggests the creative social force of this impulse.[37] Thomp-son's achievement was to help transform his-tory itself into a social movement.

## ORAL HISTORY AND THE REPARATIVE URGE

The development of women's history and oral history from the late 1960s and 1970s extended the reach of the reparative impulse. Oral history was, from the start, seen not just as a distinctive form of historical method, using interviews rather than documents, but as a movement. According to Paul Thomp-son, who played a key role in its develop-ment within Britain and internationally, the ultimate aim of oral history was not just to broaden the range of source material open to historians, but to transform society itself. That the first chapter of his book *The Voice of the Past* was titled 'Historians and the Community' signalled this ambition. The oral history interview could itself, Thompson felt, be a means of righting wrongs. By giving a voice to the silenced, it could act as a counter-force to the power structure, which 'worked as a great recording machine shaping the past in its own image'.[38] The archival impulse, the motivation to generate new testimony, to add diversity and counter-balance the dead weight of tradition, has contributed to the development of social history, as each generation discovers new constituents who have been omitted or silenced.

But Paul Thompson went further. He not only imagined oral history's ability to enrich and correct distortions in the historical record; he conceived of the interview itself as a reparative act. Through it, he felt, the boundaries between society and the 'ivory tower' could be breached. The usual power relationships between 'ordinary people' and the educated elite could even be reversed: the historian would 'sit at the feet of others who, because they come from a different social class, or are less educated, or older, know more about something'.[39] The act of telling their story would, moreover, be therapeutic, drawing them into social contact and affirming the value of their lives. The interviewee 'can be given a dignity, a sense of purpose, in going back over their lives'.[40]

The success of *The Voice of the Past* – now in its third edition and 30 years on, still the most popular text on oral history – was due in no small part to its proselytising energy. It proceeds by example, demonstrating the potential of oral history not just to broaden the range of topics and records available to history, but to challenge the very suppositions and the methods of history.

Oral history has been a major creative force within social history, but there have also been times when the reparative urge has bordered on the manic. Some oral historians have tended to hold a rather romanticised view of 'ordinary people', the very idea of which revives the condescension it seeks to avoid.[41] Klein's idealisation is apparent. Feelings of envy, rivalry or anger – the analyst's 'negative transference' – have sometimes been difficult to cope with when the oral historian assumed that, while the interviewee

may feel diffident and shy, the empathy would be largely positive.[42] It could be difficult to acknowledge the depth of the social differences that can exist between the interviewer and interviewee, differences which are reproduced within the very encounter itself.[43] There could be a hesitation to probe more uncomfortable aspects of working-class culture such as racism and conservatism. Whereas these aspects could be split off and projected into history's winners, they were more difficult to recognise in the losers, and to contain within the larger project of a rehabilitative history, aimed at restoring dignity.

The reparative urge has continued to be a characteristic feature of social history. In many senses, Raphael Samuel's *Theatres of Memory*, published in 1994, marked a departure from the concerns of the 'new social history' of the 1960s and 1970s. Where its gaze had been fixed firmly on the behaviour of people in the past, Samuel was interested in contemporary culture and its sense of the past: *Theatres of Memory* is a kind of ethnography of popular historical pursuits. Memory and culture, the latter now not necessarily seen in relation to productive relations and social class, were the central concepts. Samuel gently pricks the bubble of E.P. Thompson's ambition in the preface when, in a comment with a decidedly Kleinian twist, he describes Thompson's approach to history as 'a gigantic act of reparation'.[44] At the same time, *Theatres of Memory* is clearly operating within the Thompsonian mould. It is a compendium of popular historical movements, and Samuel is keen to demonstrate the extent of historical knowledge these societies possess, whether the passion in question is children's theatricals, battle re-enactment, steam trains or traction engines, open-air museums or the 'great army of collectors' of old household objects.[45] 'Professional history' is criticised for its narrow elitism, an elitism which makes it hesitant to appreciate this treasure-house of memory. History, contends Samuel, 'is not the prerogative of the historian, nor even, as postmodernism contends, a historian's "invention". It is, rather, a social form of knowledge; the work, in any given instance, of a thousand different hands.'[46] Once again, the recuperative urge is at work here, Samuel making himself the champion of history's bit-part players, and chiding those who arrogantly assume they have centre-stage in the theatre of memory. Professional historians, rather than Thompson's capitalist masters, become the bad objects upon whom indignation is visited.

For all these historians, the idea of reparation hinges on the conviction that the losers have, in Craig Calhoun's acute observation, 'better moral visions than those of the victors'.[47] History becomes an act undertaken on behalf of these others, something done in their name, and oriented at some level towards claiming them as moral exemplars for everyone, present as well as past. It is partly for this reason, I think, that intellectual differences and challenges within social history have often been felt very deeply. When Caroline Steedman, writing about her working-class childhood in 1950s South London, insisted that her story did not fit within the dominant tropes of post-war social history, of strong collective values and loving, selfless mothers, this was a criticism, not just of what she felt to be a distorted vision of the past, but of her fellow social historians and others on the left who had propagated a 'landscape of psychological simplicity'.[48] The maternal landscape about which she wrote, of envy, material desire, and children as an emotional and financial burden, was hardly capable of being worked into a progressive left-wing moral vision. Steedman's exposure of the psychic underpinnings of social history, of its need for comforting moral visions and sometimes impoverished sense of the subjectivity of those it sought to restore to history, is one of the book's creative achievements.

## MANIC SPLITTING AND THE CULTURAL TURN

Another example of the extraordinary emotional ferment that could be caused by differences within social history is the 'cultural turn' which pre-occupied many social historians in the 1990s. Reactions were volatile, and a sub-genre of critique soon developed within the field, an anxiety literature that filled books and special issues of journals.[49] Post-structuralism, for some, was to be opposed not just because of its emphasis on language rather than the material realities of class, but because it appeared nihilistic. I was among those who initially experienced it in this way, as threatening a form of history to whose sense of moral purpose I was deeply attached. The powerful critique of feminist historians such as Catherine Hall and Joan Scott now seemed to reveal E.P. Thompson less as the progenitor of a reparative history, than as the architect of a concept of class which left women on the edge, and so reproduced their oppression.[50] The moral authority of the historian was brought into question: those charged with 'giving a voice' to history's losers, appeared to have conspired in their silencing. I do not have space here to adequately recapitulate these debates, but their heightened emotional vocabulary suggest to me that the post-structuralist challenge was sometimes experienced unconsciously within the paranoid-schizoid position, as a kind of persecutory attack. The title of Bryan Palmer's 1990 book, *Descent into Discourse*, suggests this; as does its depiction of the proponents of discourse as suffering from a kind of psychic malaise whose symptoms include a 'fixation on language' and an 'idealized reading of discourse'.[51] This challenge to social history's moral assumptions could re-kindle raw and defensive feelings, post-structuralism being the bad object which had to be evacuated in order to preserve the humanity and concern characteristic of social history.

However, it was not just the sceptics of the cultural turn who were prone to occupy this kind of position. In part the sceptics were responding to the emotional temperament of the post-structuralist critiques, which were themselves sometimes absolutist in tone. The rejection of 'binary categories' might have been the catch-all of some post-modern historians, but in positioning post-structuralism as a superior paradigm, and employing it to great effect in a critique of Thompson's humanist materialism, they erected a very clear binary opposition. In fact, looked at from the point of view of the psychic impulses at work, there are striking similarities between Thompson and some post-structuralist accounts. For Joan Scott, for example, the concept of gender was the key to revealing hitherto concealed operations of power. The promise of deconstruction was that in showing how concepts such as class or the nation-state were conceived within the terms of sexual difference, and how such conceptions had efficacy in producing certain kinds of subjective identifications, we would gain insight into how, ultimately, certain forms of oppression were perpetuated. The big questions, of power and politics, remained central. History was also given a special place within this kind of enquiry, as the discipline which could best expose these operations. The emotional impact on some readers was little short of revelatory. A review in the *Journal of Social History*, for example, begins: 'This is a radical book, provocative, exciting, and very satisfying.'[52] It goes on to stress the importance of Scott's work in reversing the usual hierarchy of disciplines, wherein physics and the sciences are at the top, the social sciences in the middle, and history at the bottom. Then follows a line which reveals an unconscious affinity with the emotional temperament of Thompson's social history: 'For post-structuralist thought, including feminist theory, makes history the queen of disciplines.'[53] It was E.P. Thompson himself who, as far as I am aware, coined this phrase, and it was now being repeated approvingly of a book that professed a sense of history philosophically opposed to his own. Political and theoretical differences may have run deep, but this reviewer's reactions suggest that both the opponents and the proponents of post-structuralist history were operating from similar psychic positions. Grand moral visions, the excitement of being in the vanguard, and the strong desire to nurture and protect the new 'good object' and expel the bad, would, for Klein, count as signs of being in the grip of manic defences.

## IN SEARCH OF A PAST: THE BRINGING TOGETHER OF INTERNAL AND EXTERNAL WORLDS

So far I have drawn back from speculating on what features in the personal past of the historian might lead to the motivation to want to engage in reparative history. I am not even sure that it would be appropriate or enlightening to embark on such an investigation. In short, I am not advocating the psycho-biographical study of the historian. There are, however – precisely because of the way that social history brought the personal past into the frame of history – some autobiographical accounts by social historians that speak to these issues. In 1984 the oral historian and author of *Blood of Spain*, Ronald Fraser, published an extraordinary memoir of his childhood in 1984.[54] *In Search of a Past* is in one sense a social history of Fraser's own childhood, based on interviews that Fraser undertook in the early 1970s with the servants of the manor house near Aldermaston where he grew up. In a technique that Fraser also uses in *Blood of Spain*, *In Search of a Past* interweaves testimony – from his German nanny Ilse, the head gardener Bert, the stableman Carvell and others – to reconstruct the social relations of the household among the interwar gentry. This technique allows the servants to speak for themselves, reversing the authority relations of Fraser's childhood, when the servants had called him 'master Ronnie'. *In Search of a Past* is wonderfully insightful about deference, its emotional costs and its hard economic realities, such as the fact that it cost more to feed a horse than a stableman. Yet despite Fraser's desire to expose this hidden history of exploitation, his account does not idealise the world of the servants. He clearly feels great affection for Ilse but we also learn how she used to tie him to the potty. The servants speak at length of their arguments with each other, and it is sometimes frustrating to the reader how little resentment some of them feel towards Fraser's family for the way they were exploited.

Rather, what the book does is to convey a sense of the psychic conditions surrounding Fraser's interest in documenting the lives of the servants, and his interest in history itself. At various points he reflects on why he embarked on the project of interviewing the staff who worked at the manor house. Recounting a conversation with his psychoanalyst, he says 'Look, I've spent ten years trying to dispose of the past by committing it to paper. Uselessly, of course, otherwise I wouldn't be here.'[55] Sandwiched in-between the servants' accounts there are passages which record Fraser's sessions in psychoanalysis, where the past begins to be reconstructed from the inside, rather than being evacuated into the external record of the servants' testimony.

The psychoanalytic sessions reveal an internal world divided between the intimate and constant contact with the servants, and the cold and distant world of his own parents: 'Two Manors, under different roofs, I explained, the old at the rear, a place of small, pleasant rooms with bulging beams and walls thick enough to withstand a siege where servants, nanny and children lived; and the superimposed and imposing new Manor at the front, which belonged to the parents.'[56] *In Search of a Past* documents the particularly close relationship between the young Fraser and Bert, the gardener, who showed a warmth and emotional intimacy that Fraser's own father, trained to keep a stiff upper lip, could not. Bert was a socialist and a fierce critic of Fraser's father, and his political outlook was one that Fraser himself would later adopt. It was Bert who gave Fraser his first lessons in politics, which included learning about the Spanish civil war.

Fraser's narrative reveals the emotional conditions under which Freud's 'Family romance' might arise, where, under the pressure of strongly ambivalent feelings, real parents are rejected in favour of idealised replacements. Fraser's activities as a social historian, we begin to see, draw some of their energy from his sympathy with the servants and his hostility towards his parents. In his preface to the book Fraser gives special thanks to those who worked at the manor house, and he apologises to them for not being able to write it earlier. The impulse to want to atone to the servants in some way for the damage inflicted by his own social class, to record those injuries for posterity, and to give back something to the victims in the form of his book, takes a very personal form. It even extends to the parents whose remoteness he blames for his troubles. The book opens with the account of a car journey with his father, back to the manor house. Fraser's father is losing his memory:

> the old man's mind is starred, a shattered windscreen of opaque desires and memories. Where does this road go? He looks without seeing, or sees without recognizing, the distant white house, hull-down on the edge of the flatlands below the fir-crested hill. Have I any friends? In the silence his eyes fix on the road again, and Manor disappears behind Amnersfield wood.[57]

The mood here, born of Fraser's exhaustive efforts in historical reconstruction, and in seeking to understand the inner world through psychoanalysis, is one of sorrow and guilt; and hence of depressive rather than manic anxiety.

## CONCLUSION

Mark Phillips, in an article on 'sentimental history', charts the growing concern among historians in recent decades with trying to reconstruct the everyday experiences and inner worlds of people in the past.[58] The achievement of these historians, believes Phillips, is not just to have documented lives that were largely invisible to history, but to have explored realms of human experience that were previously regarded as beyond the province of history, such as birth, childhood, ageing, madness and death. Phillips, however, sounds a note of caution. Is not the novelist or poet, the film-maker or the photographer better placed to produce such affect? There are costs, Phillips believes, in deliberately narrowing our vision so as to produce in the reader 'an unusual sense of closeness to historical experience'. What has happened to causal explanations, to the study of larger patterns of past life, to the bigger and arguably more important questions? Phillips is critical of the moral impetus of historians such as E.P. Thompson, but his own essay has a strident tone. Empathy, he tells us, 'can lead to some dangerous paths'. The effort to identify with others, with whom we have no immediate and obvious connection, can result in 'self-indulgence or even prurience'.[59] The very best histories of this kind are in some ways the most dangerous, he believes, as they put us in the thrall of emotion, almost for its own sake. Sentiment, says Phillips, 'carries possibilities for facile pathos, or even more disturbingly, for a kind of fellow-feeling that becomes the cover for respectable forms of learned voyeurism.' [60]

Some historians might conclude that this chapter is another sign of the introspective turn within history, its narrowness of vision compounded by the turning back of the empathetic gaze onto the historian. To an extent such criticism is appropriate. 'Sentimental' histories do run the risk of pandering to a modern malaise of disconnection and retreat from action in the world. When so much is beyond our control, we cling to empathy, to the intimacies of past human relationships which can, moreover, make for dramatic narrative. It is sometimes the case that in histories of this kind the social and political context disappears from view. But, at the same time, what I have tried to argue here is that it is not possible to achieve a neutral distance, if by 'distance' we mean a kind of turning of the historian's back on the unconscious burden. Emotional residues from the past will, inevitably, transmit themselves to us. Indeed, they are the very stuff of historical evidence, and it behoves us to cultivate an attitude of receptiveness towards them.

The danger lies, rather, in the failure to examine and to account for empathy, so that our projections are then simply visited on the past. If all we do is to concentrate on the 'external' history, trying to reconstruct the past from the outside as Fraser initially sought to do; and if we seek to conceal the evidence of our own subjectivity, we will leave the emotional residues of the past circulating unthought and unprocessed within the wider culture, or half-digested in manic formulations. In response to those who wish to curb the historian's attentiveness to past emotion, one could ask – with more than a hint of manic triumphalism, to be sure – what kind of psychic project are they acting out? Certainly, in this phantasised programme, the ego would appear to be master of its house, maintaining firm control over the unruly desires of the id. But such an enterprise would surely be rather barren. Collingwood sounds an appropriate note of caution: if the historian 'tries to master the history of a thought which he cannot personally enter', he comments, the result will be 'dry bones'.[61] That accusation could hardly be levelled at social history, for what has made it such a vibrant force over the past half century is precisely its concern with the flesh and blood of subjective experience, its efforts to bring history into an engagement with politics and social action, and its capacity for critical and creative reflection on history as an unconscious project.

## NOTES AND REFERENCES

1   See for example Michel Foucault, *History of Sexuality Volume I* (Harmondsworth, Middlesex: Penguin, 1981); Nikolas Rose, *Governing the Soul: The Shaping of the Private Self* (London: Free Association Books, 1999) and *The Psychological Complex: Psychology, Politics and Society in England, 1869–1939* (London: Routledge, 1985); Mathew Thomson; *Psychological Subjects: Identity, Culture, and Health in Twentieth-Century Britain* (Oxford: Oxford University Press, 2006); Joel Pfister and Nancy Schnog (eds) *Inventing the Psychological: Toward a Cultural History of Emotional Life in History of the United States* (New Haven, CT: Yale University Press, 1998); Eli Zaretsky, *Secrets of the Soul: A Social and Cultural History of Psychoanalysis* (New York: Vintage, 2005).

2   There are numerous such studies, for example Peter Gay, *Freud: A Life for Our Time* (New York: Anchor Books, 1989); the numerous works of Paul Roazen, including *Freud and his Followers* (New York: Alfred A. Knopf, Inc., 1975); Gregorio Kohon, *The British School of Psychoanalysis: The Independent Tradition* (London: Free Association Books, 1985); J. Schwartz, *Cassandra's Daughter. A History of Psychoanalysis* (London: Karnac, 1999); and the journal *Psychoanalysis and History* (published by Edinburgh University Press).

3   For an interesting example of differing approaches to psychobiography, see *The British Journal for the History of Science*, 32/3, 1999. In this issue Brett Kahr, Karl Figlio and John Clay interpret the life of the seventeenth-century scientist Robert Boyle using insights drawn from Freudian, Kleinian and Jungian traditions respectively. Some influential essays in psychobiography are reprinted in G. Cooks and T.L. Crosby (eds), *Psycho/History: Readings in the Method of Psychology, Psychoanalysis and History* (New Haven, CT: Yale University Press, 1987). See also W.T. Schultz, *Handbook of Psychobiography* (Oxford: Oxford University Press, 2005); Alan C. Elms, *Uncovering Lives: The Uneasy Alliance of Biography and Psychology* (New York: Oxford University Press, 1994).

4   S. Freud, 'Leonardo da Vinci and a memory of his childhood', *Standard Edition of the Complete Psychological Works of Sigmund Freud*, XI (London: Hogarth Press, 1953–74), pp. 63–137. For critical commentaries see William Runyan, *Life Histories and Psychobiography. Explorations in Theory and Method* (New York: New York University Press, 1982); David E. Stannard, *Shrinking History. On the Failure of Psychohistory* (New York: Oxford University Press, 1980); Alan C. Elms, 'Freud as Leonardo: why the first psychobiography went wrong', in D.P. McAdams and R.L. Ochberg, *Psychobiography and Life Narratives* (Durham, NC: Duke University Press, 1986).

5   The scope for psychoanalytically history of this kind is outlined by Peter Gay, *Freud for Historians* (New York: Oxford University Press, 1985). See Timothy Ashplant, 'Psychoanalysis in historical writing', *History Workshop Journal*, 26, Autumn 1988, pp. 102–20. See on witchcraft, John Demos, *Entertaining Satan: Witchcraft and the Culture of Early New England* (New York: Oxford University Press, 1982), and Lyndal Roper, *Oedipus and the Devil. Witchcraft, Sexuality and Religion in Early Modern Europe* (London: Routledge, 1994). On revolution, Lynn Hunt, *The Family Romance of the French Revolution* (London: Routledge, 1992); and war, Daniel Pick, *War Machine. The Rationalisation of Slaughter in the Modern Age* (New Haven, CT: Yale University Press); and Klaus Theweleit, *Male Fantasies* (Cambridge: Polity, 1987). The prospects for psychoanalytically informed history are usefully discussed in the contributions to J. Damousi and R. Reynolds (eds), *History on the Couch* (Melbourne: University of Melbourne Press, 2003). See also essays in S. Alexander and B. Taylor (eds), *History & Psyche. Culture, Psychoanalysis and the Past* (Basingstoke, Hants: Palgrave, 2012).

6   Karl Figlio, Historical imagination/psychoanalytic imagination', *History Workshop Journal*, 45, Spring 1998, pp. 203–6; and 'Getting to the beginning: identification and concrete thinking in historical consciousness', in S. Radstone and K. Hodgkin, *Regimes of Memory* (London: Routledge, 2003), pp. 152–67.

7   The concept of a burden, says Figlio, 'suggests a model both of the psyche and of history: thoughts burden the psyche; intentions of earlier times burden a society. In both cases, the burdened organ – psyche or society – has either to assimilate these burdens or discharge them: there must be thinking or action.' 'Historical imagination/psychoanalytic imagination', p. 204.

8   See Michael Roper, *The Secret Battle. Emotional Survival in the Great War* (Manchester: Manchester University Press, 2009) and 'Slipping out of view: subjectivity and emotion in gender history', *History Workshop Journal*, 59, Spring 2005, pp. 57–73.

9   Figlio, 'Historical imagination/psychoanalytic imagination', p. 203,

10  Figlio, 'Historical imagination/psychoanalytic imagination', p. 205.

11  The 'super-ego' in Freud's topographical image of the mind, was an internal representation of authority figures such as parents, and played a key role in mediating both the conscious mind or ego, and the primitive unconscious impulses of the id.

12  Figlio, 'Historical imagination/psychoanalytic imagination', p. 208–9.

13  R.G. Collingwood, *The Idea of History* (Oxford: Oxford University Press, 1951), p. 294.

14  Collingwood, *The Idea of History*, p. 294.

15  Collingwood, *The Idea of History*, p. 304.

16  Collingwood, *The Idea of History*, p. 294.

17  The problem with taking the individual as the unit of analysis, remarks Collingwood, is that 'the tides of thought … flow crosswise, regardless of its structure, like sea-water through a stranded wreck.' *The Idea of History*, p. 304.

18  Collingwood, *The Idea of History*, p. 300.

19  Dominic LaCapra points out the way in which post-traumatic states can create a sense of disorientation in the historian 'whose power and force can be compelling'. He advocates a stance of 'empathic unsettlement', wherein the historian is neither completely identified with the emotional experience of the traumatised, and appropriates and repeats it, nor disengaged and claiming a false neutrality. *Writing History, Writing Trauma* (Baltimore, MD: Johns Hopkins University Press, 2001), p. 46; pp. 40–2.

20  S. Freud, 'Fragment of an analysis of a case of hysteria', *Standard Edition of the Complete Psychological Works of Sigmund Freud*, VII (London: Hogarth Press, 1953–74); R.D. Hinshelwood, *A Dictionary of Kleinian Thought* (London: Free Association Books, 1991), p. 464.

21  See esp. Betty Joseph, 'Transference: the total situation', *International Journal of Psycho-Analysis*, 66 (1985), pp. 447–54; Margaret Tonnesman, 'Transference and countertransference: an historical approach', in S. Budd

and R. Rushbridger (eds), *Introducing Psychoanalysis. Essential Themes and Topics* (London: Routledge, 2005), pp. 185–200.

22 Roper, *The Secret Battle*. Introduction, pp. 1–44.

23 Tonnesmann, 'Transference and countertransference', p. 192.

24 See Wilfred R. Bion, 'Attacks on linking', in W.R. Bion, *Second Thoughts. Selected Papers on Psychoanalysis* (London: H. Karnac, 1987), pp. 93–110; 'A theory of thinking', in *Second Thoughts*, pp. 110–20; and W.R. Bion, *Learning From Experience* (London: H. Karnac, 1991).

25 For an example of the latter see G. Dawson, *Making Peace with the Past? Memory, Trauma and the Irish Troubles* (Manchester: Manchester University Press, 2007).

26 Collingwood, *The Idea of History*, p. 304.

27 The obligation, to 'keep faith' with the victims of trauma, is not unusual, as Dominic LaCapra points out. *Writing History, Writing Trauma*, p. 22–3.

28 For an interesting attempt to put biographers 'on the couch', see Samuel H. Baron and Carl Pletsch, *Introspection in Biography. The Biographer's Quest for Self-Awareness* (New Jersey and London: The Analytic Press. 1985). The unconscious of the historian, by contrast, has been little considered even in the most trenchant defences of the use of psychoanalysis in history, such as Gay's *Freud For Historians*.

29 *The Making of the English Working Class* (London: Victor Gollancz, 1963), p. 12.

30 Thompson, *The Making of the English Working Class* (2nd edn, Harmondsworth, Middlesex: Penguin, 1968), p. 13.

31 Thompson, *The Making*, 2nd edn, pp. 917–18. See also the discussion in Gay, *Freud for Historians*, pp. 141–2.

32 Hinshelwood, *Dictionary of Kleinian Thought*, p. 415.

33 Thompson, *The Making*, 2nd edn, p. 13.

34 E.P. Thompson, 'The moral economy of the English crowd in the eighteenth century', in *Past and Present*, 50/1, 1971, pp. 76–136.

35 C. Calhoun, 'E.P. Thompson and the discipline of historical context', *Social Research*, Summer 1994, p. 5, http://findarticles.com/p/articles/mi_m2267/is_n2_v61/ai_15764915?tag=artBody;col.

36 E.P. Thompson, 'Time, work discipline and industrial capitalism', *Past and Present*, 38/1, 1967, pp. 56–97.

37 Calhoun, 'E.P. Thompson', p. 1.

38 Paul Thompson, *The Voice of the Past. Oral History* (3rd edn, New York: Oxford University Press, 2000), p. 3.

39 *The Voice of the Past*, p. 11.

40 *The Voice of the Past*, p. 11.

41 This kind of romanticisation was not typical however of German work in oral history, which, in response to the legacy of Fascism, tended to have a more critical view of popular politics and values. See for example Gabriele Rosenthal (ed.), *The Holocaust in Three Generations: Families of Victims and Perpetrators of the Nazi Regime* (London: Cassell, 1998); and 'Reconstruction of life stories. Principles of selection in generating stories for narrative biographical interviews', in A Lieblich and R. Josselson, *The Narrative Study of Lives Volume I* (Newbury Park, CA: Sage, 1993).

42 See M. Roper, 'Analysing the analysed: transference and counter-transference in the oral history encounter', *Oral History*, Vol. 31, no. 2, Autumn 2003, pp. 20–33.

43 This point is made forcibly in an essay by Pierre Bourdieu, 'Understanding', *Theory, Culture and Society*, 13, 1996, pp. 17–37.

44 Samuel, *Theatres of Memory* (London: Verso, 1994), p. viii.

45 Samuel, *Theatres of Memory*, p. 19

46 Samuel, *Theatres of Memory*, p. 8.

47 Calhoun, 'E.P. Thompson', p. 18.

48 Carolyn Steedman, *Landscape For a Good Woman. A Story of Two Lives* (London: Virago, 1986), p. 12.

49 Among the many examples see Patrick Joyce, 'The end of social history?', *Social History* 20/1, January 1995, pp. 73–91, and Geoff Eley and Keith Nield, 'Starting over: the present, the post-modern and the moment of social history', *Social History*, 20/3, October 1995. See also A. Marwick, 'Two Approaches to historical study: the metaphysical (including 'postmodernism') and the historical', *Journal of Contemporary History*, 30, 1995, pp. 5–35, and Hayden White, 'Response to Arthur Marwick', *Journal of Contemporary History*, 30, 1995, pp. 233–46.

50 Joan W. Scott, 'Women in *The Making of the English Working Class*', in *Gender and the Politics of History* (New York: Columbia Press, 1988), pp. 68–90; Catherine Hall, 'The tale of Samuel and Jemima: gender and working-class culture in early nineteenth-century England', in *White, Male and Middle Class Explorations in Feminism and History* (Cambridge: Polity, 1992), pp. 124–50.

51 Bryan D. Palmer, *Descent into Discourse. The Reification of Language and the Writing of Social History* (Philadelphia, PA: Temple University Press, 1990), p. 5.

52 Marilyn J. Boxer, Review of '*Gender and the Politics of History*', *Journal of Social History*, 22/4, 1989, p. 788.

53 Boxer, Review of '*Gender and the Politics of History*', p. 789.

54 Ronald Fraser, *In Search of a Past. The Manor House, Amnersfield, 1933–1945* (London: Verso, 1984); and 'In search of the past: a dialogue', *History Workshop Journal*, 20, Autumn 1985, pp. 175–88.

55 Fraser, *In Search of a Past*, p. 5.

56 Fraser, *In Search of a Past*, pp. 4–5.

57 Fraser, *In Search of a Past*, p. 3.

58 M. Phillips, 'On the advantage and disadvantage of sentimental history for life', *History Workshop Journal*, 64, Spring 2008.

59 Phillips, 'On the advantage and disadvantage of sentimental history', pp. 50–1.

60 Phillips, 'On the advantage and disadvantage of sentimental history', p. 56.

61 Collingwood, *The Idea of History*, p. 305.

# 20

# New National Narratives

Kevin Foster

In this chapter I will examine the ways in which British writing about a non-imperial space, Latin America, over almost two centuries, has provided a crucial means of self-analysis and self-assessment; how, in knowing South America Britons have endeavoured to better know themselves. I will argue that South America has occupied a central place in British writing over this period because it has consistently been of use, furnishing a redolent, symbolic space within which the contradictions and anxieties of empire could be held up for inspection. As such, I will explore how, over two hundred years, narrative theory in Britain has intersected with shifting endeavours to articulate, interrogate and promote the nation's identity, anxieties and achievements.

## NARRATIVES AS SOCIALLY SYMBOLIC ACTS

In his introduction to *Identity of England* (2002), historian Robert Colls observed that his book was 'about how the English have thought about themselves. Occasionally, it is about how others have thought about the English' (Colls, 2002: 2). Colls' separation of these processes of self-analysis may imply that thinking about oneself is somehow distinct from how others think about one and how one thinks of them. It is my intention in this chapter to demonstrate that these practices are inextricably linked and their outcomes crucially interdependent; to demonstrate that the English, and Britons as a whole, have often thought most penetratingly about themselves when ostensibly thinking about others. Linda Colley (2002) and David Cannadine (2001), among a host of others, have both written penetratingly on how the British experience of, respectively, captivity at the imperial frontier, and the pageantry of the Indian Raj, have offered important insights into the ways in which the British thought about themselves and their empire. Cannadine's study of British perceptions of the empire, *Ornamentalism* (2001), set out to correct the approach of domestic and foreign scholars who had regarded British imperial history 'as if it were completely separate and distinct from the history of the British nation'. On the contrary, he argued, 'Britain was very much a part of the empire, just as the rest of the empire was very much part of Britain', the two comprising an 'entire interactive system', one 'vast interconnected world' (Cannadine, 2001: xvii). Cannadine demonstrated that the empire was inconceivable in isolation from the metropolitan centre as the domestic environment furnished a model by which the populace might think of and so understand the empire. What this meant in practical terms for those Britons struggling to 'conceive of these diverse colonies and varied populations beyond the seas' was that they began 'with what they knew – or what they thought they knew – namely, the social structure of their own home country' (Cannadine, 2001: 3-4). Through the heyday of the Empire, from the mid-nineteenth century to the end of the Second World War, 'Britons generally conceived of themselves as belonging to an unequal society characterized by a seamless web of layered gradations ... which extended in a great chain of being from the monarch at the top to the humblest subject at the bottom ... and it was from that starting point that they contemplated and tried to comprehend the distant realms and diverse society of their empire' (Cannadine, 2001: 4).[1] As a result, the people's perception of the empire

> was not exclusively (or even preponderantly) concerned with the creation of 'otherness' on the presumption that the imperial periphery was different from, and inferior to, the imperial metropolis: it was at least as much (perhaps more?) concerned with what has recently been called the 'construction of affinities' on the presumption that society on the periphery was the same as, or even on occasions superior to, society in the metropolis. Thus regarded, the British Empire was about the familiar and domestic, as well as the different and the exotic: indeed, it was in large part about the domestication of the exotic – the comprehending and the reordering of the foreign in parallel, analogous, equivalent, resemblant terms (Cannadine, 2001: xix).[2]

Seen in these terms, the empire provided a 'mechanism for the export, projection and analogisation of domestic social structures and social perceptions' (Cannadine, 2001: 10). Where the British Empire was concerned, the imperative to analogisation rescued the nation's vision of its far-flung possessions from trite reductivism, producing a sophisticated understanding of its structural complexities and a genuine responsiveness to the

lives of the individuals who constituted it. Yet when this same sense-making system was applied to British visions of extra-imperial territories, like Latin America, it rendered a disappointing array of familiar stereotypes. Where one promoted knowledge through identification, the other seemed to foster only ignorance. Why was it that an identical process resulted in such contrasting outcomes?

One explanation resides in the cognitive processes involved in making sense of the unfamiliar. If 'acts of perception are really acts of recall', then what the British saw in India, Africa, Latin America and elsewhere, was crucially determined by what they remembered of or had read or heard about equivalent prior experience and the preconceptions they fed (Bartlett, 1972: 14). The effort to order and understand new experiences, to absorb and evaluate unfamiliar states or situations involves a combination of what cognitive scientists term 'bottom-up' and 'top-down' processing. Bottom-up processing involves 'building up a composite meaning on the basis of our perception of its component parts'; top-down processing, as its name implies, draws on the 'expectations, assumptions and prior knowledge' of the interpreter – what Said calls the 'textual attitude' (MacLachlan and Reid, 1994: 70; Said, 1978: 93).[3] While regular contact between Britain and its colonies served to demystify many of the empire's exoticisms, to convert a raft of top-down assumptions into the embodied evidence of bottom-up observation, ongoing and repeatedly professed ignorance about Latin America necessitated a primary – and thereafter habitual – recourse to top-down processes, to prejudice and preconceptions, to the framework of assumptions and expectations they provided, within which experience and observation might be ordered and explained. Like 'Darkest Africa', Britain's popular imagining of South America might have had its origins in geographical ignorance, but as Philip Curtin remarks, as knowledge of the continent grew, it was subsequently 'adhered to out of cultural arrogance' (Curtin, 1964: 293).

The British were not alone in their ignorance about Latin America or their recourse to familiar patterns of response on encountering it. J.H. Elliott notes that the earliest Western encounters with the New World habitually drove Europeans back onto familiar patterns of thought and understanding. Surveying a wide array of texts from the late sixteenth through into the seventeenth century, Elliott observes:

> it is difficult not to be impressed by the strange lacunae and the resounding silences in many places where references to the New World could reasonably be expected. How are we to explain the absence of any mention of the New World in so many memoirs and chronicles, including the memoirs of Charles V himself? How are we to explain the continuing determination, right up to the last two or three decades of the sixteenth century, to describe the world as if it were still the world as known to Strabo, Ptolemy and Pomponius Mela? ...
> The reluctance of cosmographers or social philosophers to incorporate into their work the new information made available to them by the discovery of America provides an example of the wider problem arising from the revelation of the New World to the Old. Whether it is a question of the geography of America, its flora and fauna, or the nature of its inhabitants, the same kind of pattern seems constantly to recur in the European response. It is as if, at a certain point, the mental shutters came down; as if, with so much to see and absorb and understand, the effort suddenly becomes too much for them, and Europeans retreat to the half-light of their traditional mental world.
> There is nothing very novel about the form of this sixteenth-century response. Medieval Europe had found it supremely difficult to comprehend and come to terms with the phenomenon of Islam ... Nor is this a matter for surprise for the attempt of one society to comprehend another inevitably forces it to reappraise itself ... This process is bound to be an agonizing one, involving the jettisoning of many traditional preconceptions and inherited ideas. It is hardly surprising, then, if sixteenth-century Europeans either ignored the challenge or baulked at the attempt. There was, after all, an easier way out, neatly epitomized in 1528 by the Spanish humanist, Hernán Perez de Oliva, when he wrote that Columbus set out on his second voyage 'to unite the world and give to those strange lands the form of our own' (Elliott, 1970: 13–15).

Elliott's vision of sixteenth-century Europeans, dazzled by the prodigality of the New World, retreating to 'the half-light of their traditional mental world' from where they might understand 'those strange lands' by imposing on them 'the form of our own' offers a key image for the processes determining Britain's cultural relations with Latin America and the persistence of its seemingly perennial ignorance about the continent and its peoples. After all, the half-light of ignorance was preferable to the painful glare of novelty. A society engaged in a genuine effort to comprehend another, Elliott observed, must subject itself to an often agonising self-appraisal in which many 'traditional preconceptions and inherited ideas' have to be jettisoned.[4] This is not a process that any community will undertake lightly, and when it does take place it is driven not by altruism or a disinterested desire for greater knowledge of others but by a combination of compulsion and self-interest. In the case of the Spanish conquest of Latin America:

> it was the stimulus of practical considerations – the need to exploit the resources of America and to govern and convert its peoples – which compelled Europeans to widen their field of vision (sometimes in spite of themselves) and to organize and classify their findings within a coherent frame of thought.
> Officials and missionaries alike found that, to do their work effectively, they needed some understanding of the customs and traditions of the peoples entrusted to their charge ... The *visitas* of royal officials to Indian localities therefore tended to turn into elaborate inquiries into native history, land tenure and inheritance laws; and the reports of the more intelligent and inquiring of these officials ... were in effect exercises in applied anthropology, capable of yielding a vast amount of information about native customs and societies (Elliott, 1970: 32–3).

The eagerness of the British to conquer and then exploit their imperial possessions, particularly in India, gave rise to practical considerations of government, commerce and comparative religion comparable to those that the Spaniards had confronted in the New World that enforced a corresponding extension of the conquerors' cognitive boundaries. Yet in Latin America, while the British had extensive resources to exploit they had, beyond the thinly scattered populations of Guyana and Belize, no people to govern and so no need to pretend to an interest in or concern for the locals and their cultures, or any mission beyond the extraction of profits or the exercise of influence. They were, as William Yale put it, at liberty 'to secure [their] imperial interests without assuming the invidious burden of colonial rule' (quoted in Buchan, 2003: 14).[5] Freed from the 'practical considerations' which might demand an uncomfortable cohabitation with the other, the British had no need to expand their settled patterns of thought and perception to make room for the challenges posed by contact with Latin America or its people, and so no reason to subject themselves to a painful process of reappraisal. As such, while Latin America remained of largely commercial interest to the British, their established perceptions of it and the prejudices they fed could survive undisturbed, and the vision of Britain they reflected back remain untarnished.

This suggestion that these stereotypical constructions reveal as much about Britain as they do about Latin America implies one of the principal explanations for their persistence. They survive because they continue to perform a valuable function: they express and manage the nation's 'political unconscious'. According to Frederic Jameson, it is the purpose of the political unconscious to restore 'to the surface of the text the repressed and buried reality of [the nation's] fundamental history' (Jameson, 1981: 20). British stereotypes of Latin America restore to the surface of the narratives that preserve and promote them, voices previously unacknowledged in or consciously excised from the nation's fundamental history. These voices are significant because while they sometimes extolled the glories of the empire they also articulated the anxieties inherent in its extension, management and loss. The consolidation and further expansion of the British Empire in the late eighteenth and early nineteenth centuries coincided with the development and expansion of the revolutionary liberation movements of the Latin American republics. At the same time that the British were coming to terms with the moral and practical dilemmas arising from the extension of their dominion, the peoples of Latin America were throwing off the yoke of colonial government and for the first time enjoying the rights of free men. As a result, at that point and perennially thereafter in the world of English literary culture, Latin America became inextricably intertwined with a range of efforts to understand and mediate the burdens of empire. British narratives set in or centred on Latin America ostensibly concerned with the experience of imperial subjugation can thus be seen as endeavours to address the moral and practical effects of the exercise of imperial power. Patrick Brantlinger notes that while 'Empire involved military conquest and rapacious economic exploitation', it was also characterised by 'the enactment of often idealistic although nonetheless authoritarian schemes of cultural domination. The goal of imperialist discourse is always to weld these seeming opposites together or to disguise their contradiction' (Brantlinger, 1988: 34). Latin America furnished an ideal symbolic space, free from the complications of 'official' rule, within which narrative fiction might unpack and illuminate the contradictions of imperialist discourse. Here the 'buried reality' of imperial affirmation could be exhumed and held up for examination. Here the political, cultural and moral anxieties arising from the establishment, maintenance and decline of the Empire, might be articulated, assuaged or indulged. The resulting re-interpretation of these texts in terms of a 'deeper, underlying and more "fundamental" narrative', their recovered status as excavations of the 'buried reality' of colonial anxiety, transforms them from prejudicial travesties into 'cultural artefacts' whose central value lies in their status as 'socially symbolic acts' (Jameson, 1981: 20, 29). English literary responses to Latin America that employ the continent to engage with the contradictions of imperial discourse and the anxieties they reflect, that employ narratives about Latin America to explore questions of national identity in Britain, thus constitute a significant contribution to the broader historical record of the experience of empire.

## BURDENS OF EMPIRE: NARRATIVES OF LEADERSHIP

Mary Louise Pratt claims that 'By the 1820s', little more than ten years after Napoleon's invasion of Spain triggered a wave of independence struggles within its former colonies, 'the South American revolutions ... had become a source of immense interest in Europe' (Pratt, 1992: 146). In Britain, however, Cedric Watts asserts that neither Latin America nor its liberation struggles 'preoccupied the British consciousness' at any deeper level (Watts, 1979: 44). Despite David Sinclair's claim that 'There was much airy talk of the cause of liberty and republicanism', and that 'leaders of the independence movement ... were fêted as heroes in London', English literature of the period yields not a single portrait of a liberation hero – indeed hardly any mention of Latin America at all (Sinclair, 2003: 48).[6]

Britain's refusal to engage with the origins or processes of the republics' rebellions against Spanish colonial rule made Latin America the ideal locus for examining its own transformation into an imperial power, a perfect site for the objectification and interrogation of its own political unconscious. While Britain's successes in the Seven Years War had vastly extended its 'national prestige and imperial power ... at the end of the day', Linda Colley observes, Britons 'were left wondering if they had overstretched themselves' and were 'made nervous and insecure by their colossal new dimensions' (Colley, 1992: 109). This nervousness finds some unlikely forms of expression. In his epic poem, *Madoc* (1805), a principal literary proponent of Britain's imperial expansion, Robert Southey, employed the eponymous hero's adventures in the New World to address the anxieties raised by the nation's

'colossal new dimensions'. The poem details how Madoc, son of King Owain of Gwynedd, discovers a paradisal land on the far side of the Atlantic. With a faithful band of followers he liberates its people from the barbarous oppression of the Aztecs, and remains to found a new Eden. The brevity of this précis is misleading. The poem comes in at a little under 9,000 lines, a narrative stretch which even Southey's more sympathetic critics felt 'unjustified' (Curry, 1975: 161). Reviewers derided the poem: one found it 'interminable', while another considered it 'as long a labour as any twelfth-century Atlantic crossing' (Williams, 1979: 189, 195).[7] Contemporary critics have found it uninteresting, bloated, contradictory and ideologically inconsistent, with its protagonists dismissed as 'mere righteous ciphers' who neither involve nor engage the reader (Franklin, 2003: 83).[8] Ironically, it is these inadequacies that have come to be regarded as the poem's principal strength. Caroline Franklin has noted that the 'discordant voices' that render *Madoc* an 'artistic failure' also make it 'a poem of great interest to the cultural historian' (Franklin, 2003: 71, 70). Composed through the years of Southey's extended grappling with the effects of the French revolution on British liberty and his resultant transformation from Jacobin firebrand to establishment imperialist, the poem celebrates the nation's expanding colonial role while addressing the disquiet to which it gave rise.[9] The specific fear that Southey addresses in *Madoc*, the buried reality of colonial anxiety that he excavates and dusts off, focuses on a perceived crisis of leadership within the country. The poem asks, and answers the question: did the nation have the personal and collective qualities to conquer and run an empire – could we do it? He was not alone in asking this question.

In the closing years of George III's reign, the many scandals involving the Royal Family, the casual corruptions of political life with its rotten boroughs and 'septennial bribes', fed general distaste for the country's governing classes and the widespread fear that the country was not fit to run an empire (Crabbe, 1905: 123).[10] A popular explanation for the dissolution of standards among the ruling order was the impact of foreign influences on the nation's moral fibre.[11] Where once these influences were principally French, as trade between Britain and the East burgeoned, a corresponding conviction took hold that domestic corruption was the product of moral contamination contracted in the East. 'Viewing immorality as a colonial import', Tim Fulford notes, 'was in one way reassuring: it assuaged Britons' fears that the "infections" of moral and political corruption were endemic to British character. It allowed them to imagine the "infections" as diseases that threatened the nation from without. Displacing them to the East helped recast ... the anxieties of the domestic realm as "anxieties of empire". Extermination of the supposed sources of infection in the colonies then became a mission by which Britons assured themselves of their own purity' (Fulford, 1999: 168). In the early years of the nineteenth century the responsibility for national purification at home and abroad began to shift, as it was felt that the nation's traditional aristocratic governors, endlessly embroiled in political and sexual scandals, emblems of profligacy and moral dissolution, could no longer be entrusted with the task. Literature, history, biography, and more straightforwardly propagandist tracts of the period, increasingly identified the nation's finest qualities with the gentry, the professional classes and the military – in particular the navy: 'In the years between Trafalgar and the accession of Queen Victoria romantic portraits of the navy provided moral exemplars for the domestic and imperial spheres. They promoted the chivalry of the ocean when the chivalry of the land was in doubt' (Fulford, 1999: 162).[12] Southey played a key role in engineering this shift in public attitudes to the military and the aristocracy through his massively popular *Life of Nelson* (1813). Nelson's qualities, initiative, courage, dutifulness, devotion to country and absolute selflessness, had taken a mere parson's son to national prominence and demonstrated that he and those like him were 'fitter to govern than the landed classes who currently held (and abused) power and privilege ... The biography of Nelson, which began as an article in the conservative *Quarterly Review*, was ... intended to show the public how the social order could be preserved by a return to the virtues of a Nelson' (Fulford, 1999: 162, 172–3). These virtues and the ideal of national leadership they enshrined, also had a specific purpose in Britain's role as an emerging colonial power:

> In constructing his myth of the imperial hero, Southey was performing an influential service for a Britain in the process of defining itself as an imperialist nation. Reviving the code of chivalry, he defined British authority in terms of paternalism, duty and disinterestedness tested in battle. He shaped the image of the gentleman as one who commanded effectively because he had a self-command that made him resist Oriental luxury and the feminization of culture. It was a powerful image, because it offered a solution to the anxieties that beset the imperial nation at home and abroad – the solution of war. It is in battle that Nelson redeems the national character: Southey shows his readers that the salvation of Britain and Britishness lies in its military role. The moral fibre necessary for proper government is found in imperial conflict: the empire is necessary as a training ground for government at home (Fulford, 1999: 177).

Victorian leaders and the public enthusiastically embraced Southey's prescription for domestic and imperial captaincy. The *Life* sold in large numbers, going through 13 editions in the four decades after its publication. In *Madoc*, published eight years before the *Life of Nelson*, we can see Southey working towards this position on the nature and qualities of leadership through a focus on imperial conquest as the testing ground of personal and national character. Though nobly born, Madoc turns his back on the privileges of preferment, making his way in the New World as a free man. The loyalty that he inspires in his followers is not due to his royal pedigree but rests on the personal qualities that are foregrounded in his struggle with the Aztecs – high principle, intelligence, courage and piety. Above all, his distinction rests on his demonstrated capacity in action. He takes a leading role, as both strategist and warrior, in the battles against the Aztecs. He bears arms nobly and bravely, hazards his life and proves his mettle, thus affirming his right to lead, to shoulder the responsibilities of command and enjoy the rewards it brings. He is, as such, carefully crafted to exhume, address and assuage the anxieties inspired by the crisis of leadership and the buried colonial realities it hints at. With men like Madoc directing its imperial ventures, Southey assures the public, the nation could rest easy, certain that the extension and management of its frontiers were in capable hands.

## VICTIMS OF EMPIRE: NARRATIVES OF LEGITIMACY

If Britons in the early nineteenth century were principally preoccupied with the crisis of leadership, the further expansion of the empire meant that their grandchildren's anxieties were focused less on the practicalities of leadership than its moral defensibility. After all, Linda Colley asked, 'In what terms could a people who claimed to be uniquely free justify their massively extended dominion to others and to themselves?' (Colley, 1992: 110). Thus the crisis of leadership gave place to a crisis of legitimacy. While the moral and social consequences of this crisis were addressed in a wide range of political, philosophical and religious tracts at the time, it was in adventure fiction that ordinary Britons first encountered the moral dilemmas of empire. The nineteenth-century adventure narratives that argued for or justified the extension of empire were, in Martin Green's well-worn phrase, 'the energising myth of English imperialism. They were, collectively, the story England told itself as it went to sleep at night, and, in the form of its dreams, they charged England's will with the energy to go out into the world and explore, and conquer and rule' (Green, 1979: 3). By the mid-nineteenth century, however, some of

these tales were less likely to bring on a reassuring slumber than they were to engender nightmares. Adventure fiction set in Latin America reveals that 'defensiveness, self-doubt, worries about "fitness", "national efficiency" and racial and cultural decadence' are a consistent presence in the fictional treatment of imperialism from the mid-nineteenth century onwards (Brantlinger, 1988: 33). They arise from a fundamental contradiction at the heart of the nation's imperial vision. Namely, that while denying an interest in formal empire, Britain continued to conquer, dispossess and expropriate with gusto.[13] Despite the position espoused by 'Palmerston and many of his contemporaries' that 'British overseas interests should be secured wherever possible without formal imperialization', the mid-nineteenth century witnessed an exponential growth in the nation's overseas possessions (Brantlinger, 1988: 20). Adventure narratives set in non-imperial regions like Latin America provided a space within which the nation's lust for possession might be balanced against its ambivalence about the moral defensibility of conquest and control. Here, the tensions implicit in these contradictory impulses could be conceded, while the anxieties they engendered might be addressed. Narratives ostensibly about Latin America thus exposed and engaged with the moral and political contradictions that lay at the heart of Britain's conflicted relationship with the ideals and practices of imperialism, contradictions that so crucially shaped its national identity.

For the greater part of the nineteenth century the British were uncomfortable with the idea of themselves as an imperial power: 'Even among those historians who treat empire-building as a continuous economic and political process, the idea still seems prevalent that the early and mid-Victorians were not imperialists in the ideological sense because they were not highly conscious of the Empire as a problem – in other words, because they were not jingoists' (Brantlinger, 1988: ix).[14] It was, as Green notes, 'Austria and Russia, and France under Napoleon, that were empires in the opprobrious sense. England was essentially a trading nation, and the home of liberty' (Green, 1979: 145).[15] Yet as Linda Colley notes, 'The spoils of the Seven Years War made it far more difficult to sustain this flattering contrast between the failed empires of the past and the British empire of the present. And this made for problems of morale as well as practical difficulties' (Colley, 1992: 109). These practical difficulties were most marked at the sharp end of empire, on the imperial frontier, where European adventurers battled native populations for possession of their lands and resources with predictable consequences. The problems of morale engendered by these events, and the buried realities of colonial politics that they brought to the surface, comprise a consistent theme in adventure narratives of the period set in Latin America. These narratives revealed that though the British were confident of their status as emblems of civilisation and progress, their conduct at the imperial frontier and their contact with the primitive peoples they encountered there suggested otherwise.

By 1859, the year of Conan Doyle's birth and, of course, the publication of Darwin's *Origin of Species*, 'the conviction that "inferior peoples" were by nature condemned to extinction' was, as Sven Lindqvist has shown, 'a major element in the European view of mankind' (Lindqvist, 1997: 10). Prominent thinkers in biology, anthropology, race and evolutionary theory had separately concluded that the extermination of primitive peoples by their more civilised brethren was the expression of an irresistible law of nature. If by the mid-nineteenth century genocide was regarded as an 'inevitable by-product of progress', the key question for modern man was not whether to condone or condemn it, but how to arrive at some sort of moral accommodation with it (Lindqvist, 1997: 123). As early as 1850 Herbert Spencer had proposed that the eradication of the unregenerate was not a matter for moral vacillation, but a binding religious obligation: 'The forces which are working out the great scheme of perfect happiness, taking no account of incidental

suffering, exterminate such sections of mankind as stand in their way ... Be he human or be he brute – the hindrance must be got rid of' (Spencer, 1850: 461). In this context, instead of wringing their hands over the plight of the unfortunate victims, it was believed that 'the true compassion of the superior races consisted in helping them on their way' (Lindqvist, 1997: 10).

Not everybody was convinced that the extinction of primitive peoples was inevitable, or regarded genocide as a misunderstood species of Christian charity. Surveying the catastrophic results of modern man's endeavours to improve his primitive brothers, John Howison argued that the real savages were closer to home, and that it was civilised man himself who was most in need of moral reform:

> The continent of America has already been nearly depopulated of its aborigines by the introduction of the blessings of civilisation. The West Indian archipelago, from the same cause, no longer contains a single family of its primitive inhabitants. South Africa will soon be in a similar condition, and the islanders of the Pacific Ocean are rapidly diminishing in numbers from the ravages of European diseases and the despotism of self-interested and fanatical missionaries. It is surely time that the work of destruction should cease; and since long and melancholy experience has proved us to be invariably unsuccessful in rendering happier, wiser, or better, the barbarians whom we have visited or conquered, we may now conscientiously let them alone and turn a correcting hand towards ourselves and seek to repress ... our avarice, our selfishness, and our vices (qtd Lindqvist, 1997: 122).

In *The Lost World* Conan Doyle's strips away the lagging of respectability that science and religion had afforded genocide, exposing the ugly truths about colonial dispossession, and in the process of exploring Howison's theories about the complicated relations between civilisation and savagery, making a clear point about the true nature of British 'civilisation'. Conan Doyle does this by projecting his analysis of the practical implications and moral burdens of empire onto an imaginary Latin American landscape. Here, in the semiotic free fire zone that this setting affords, he can illustrate what happens when civilised man finds his pursuit of land, loot or security obstructed by his more primitive brothers, and how he justifies and lives with the bloody consequences of his actions. Here he can lay bare the repressed and buried realities of the nation's fundamental history, the political unconscious that the nation tries so hard to repress or deny. As such, what looks, in the first instance, like an escapist narrative offers no refuge from the uncomfortable truths of colonial realpolitik. Conan Doyle's central concern in *The Lost World* is to offer an allegorical critique of the moral landscape of British imperialism and its narrative legitimations, to use Latin America to explore and explain a society in which obscure matters of scientific dispute occasion outrage and wild public brawling, while the eradication of whole peoples passes without comment.

The fictional premise that underpins this analysis rests on maverick Professor George Edward Challenger's discovery of an isolated plateau in Brazil, where, cut off from the evolutionary conditions that have shaped the modern world, ancient life forms co-exist with more developed species. When Challenger presents these findings to a meeting of the Zoological Institute in London they provoke uproar. Undaunted, he invites the Institute to dispatch a party to the area to test the veracity of his claims. This group, comprising a Professor of Comparative Anatomy, Summerlee, the gentleman adventurer, Lord John Roxton, and the journalist and narrator, Edward Malone, is duly elected, dispatched, and later augmented in the upper reaches of the Amazon by Challenger himself. The party heads inland, locates and ascends the plateau, and the adventure begins. For all the primeval glamour of this lost world, the narrative centres on the struggle for dominion between the plateau's competing hominid groups – the 'ape-men', primitive, simian and savage, and the more evolved Indians, 'small men, wiry, active ... Their faces ... hairless, well-formed and good humoured' (Conan Doyle, 2001: 151, 163). Despite their evolutionary advantages, the Indians are barely holding their own and when the adventurers encounter them they are fighting for their survival. When the adventurers are attacked and brutalised by the ape-men they decide to take an active role in the conflict and play midwife to evolution (Conan Doyle, 2001: 153). Contributing their strategic insight and modern weapons to the Indians, in a final, climactic confrontation they help them defeat and all but exterminate the ape-men. The particular manner in which the last of the ape-men are dispatched, 'screaming and clawing ... thrust over the precipice, [they] went hurtling down, as their prisoners had of old, on to the sharp bamboos six hundred feet below' is highly suggestive, not least in its biblical allusion to the Gadarene Swine (Conan Doyle, 2001: 174). More pertinently, and more topically, it alludes to a method commonly employed by white settlers in Australia to dispose of aborigines with whom they were in conflict over land or natural resources.[16] Further, the strange clicking talk of the ape-men recalls the languages of the Nama and Herero people of South West Africa, now Namibia, who after rebelling against the cruelty of the colonising Germans were almost entirely exterminated in a 12-month period during 1904–5.[17] These parallels drive home Conan Doyle's point, that though the superior beings may claim to be accidental witnesses to the working out of a natural law, here and all across the globe, they have shown themselves to be enthusiastic participants in the extermination of their fellow men. When Malone and Roxton come across Challenger in the final stages of the massacre he has abandoned all pretence to scientific detachment and is 'strutting about like a gamecock', his eyes 'shining with the lust of slaughter' (Conan Doyle, 2001: 174). If Challenger's regressive savagery comes as a shock, Lord John Roxton's coldly rational determination to settle a personal 'score' with the ape-men – the 'filthy beasts' had 'fingered [him]... all over' – by 'wiping them off the face of the earth', is more deeply alarming (Conan Doyle, 2001: 153, 170). In their efforts to demonstrate their superiority over the brutal primitives of the plateau, the adventurers only reinforce the evidence of their commonality with them.

The key figure linking the seemingly antithetical extremes of civilisation in the novel is the 'splenetic scientist', Challenger (Fraser, 1998: 66). His formidable intellect is strangely yoked to a pathological incapacity to restrain himself – he is forever 'effervescing with fight' (Conan Doyle, 2001: 26). He meets scepticism, or any expression of intellectual difference, with an immediate recourse to assault. When, after his attack on Malone, his exasperated wife describes him as 'a brute', this is no idle rhetorical figure (Conan Doyle, 2001: 28). Every description of Challenger emphasises his squat simian bulk. His affinity with the ape-men is first implied in a glint of teeth. Immediately before he launches an assault on Malone his 'black moustache lifted and a white fang twinkled in a sneer' (Conan Doyle, 2001: 26). This brief glimpse of Challenger's fangs and the bestial instinct they signify has an important echo later in the novel, when Malone is throttled by an ape-man. Drifting into unconsciousness, he recalls that as 'the creature felt me grow limp in his grasp, two white canines gleamed for a moment at each side of the vile mouth' (Conan Doyle, 2001: 166). The uncanny likeness between the scientific *übermann* and the degenerate apes demonstrates that for all the smug assurance of his evolutionary advantages, modern man has not left his more primitive self behind but carries his primordial savagery within him, and the least provocation might bring it to the surface and betray him. Conan Doyle's insistence on the fellowship between civilised man and his primitive forebears demolishes the orthodox scientific and moral vindications of genocide, exposing the uncomfortable truth that for all its cant about civilisation, progress and mission, colonialism involved the dispossession and destruction of men, who, whatever their physical or cultural differences, were inescapably our kith and kin, if not our brothers. The slaughtered ape-men lay bare the long-buried reality of colonialism's fundamental history, betraying the

true nature of its self-denying brutality. Little wonder they haunt us – they *are* us.

## END OF EMPIRE: NARRATIVES OF LOSS AND LONGING

By the early 1970s the British were battling to hold onto their prized conception of themselves as paragons of civilisation. Their fundamental history, it seemed, was less the divinely ordained gospel of moral and political pre-eminence than an irresistible tragedy of dissolution and despair. Britain in the early 1970s was a nation displaying all the marks of terminal degeneration. Its imperial possessions mostly gone and its military in retreat abroad, at home its uncompetitive manufacturing industries, soaring inflation, balance of payments deficits, fissile industrial relations, and deeply entrenched antagonisms of race and class, all revealed that the kingdom was disunited and Britain, patently, no longer great.[18] As the decade unfolded and Britain grappled with the effects of long-term decline, the stock images of anarchy and decay which had once reinforced Latin America's irreducible otherness, came to look more and more like a portent of where Britain itself was heading. As a result, the vision of Latin America as a place of violence and corruption that, in the late nineteenth century, had served to assert British self-confidence, was increasingly employed by writers and historians a hundred years later to articulate the collapse of that confidence and address the anxieties to which it gave rise. The fears that had once been safely stored away in the nation's political unconscious were now rising to the surface and assailing its key narratives of political and moral exceptionalism. Where Latin America had once furnished Britons with a reassuring vision of difference, now when they looked at it they saw a mirror image of themselves.

By early 1974 Britain's manifold economic and social problems required a radical response, and Harold Wilson's newly elected Labour Government appeared ready to rise to the challenge. Within weeks of its election it placated the fractious unions with the promise of pay rises, increased Corporation Tax to fund more generous social security benefits and set up the National Enterprise Board to take over failing private companies. While these modest measures brought respite to welfare recipients and struggling businesses, they sparked panic among right-wing commentators. The *Daily Mail*'s Santiago correspondent detected in Labour's reforms an echo of the radical policies instituted in Salvador Allende's Chile where, 12 months earlier, in the final year of his presidency, inflation had topped 304 per cent, the middle classes had revolted and the military had seized power. Allende's experiment had 'pointed up the dangers a relatively prosperous country faces when it seeks to reform overnight', dangers, the *Mail*'s man in Santiago cautioned, that Britain would do well to heed (quoted in Beckett, 2002: 116).

The suggestion that 1970s Britain might learn something useful from events in Chile underlines Andy Beckett's claim that over the past half-century the two countries have functioned 'as each other's political subconscious', where the most cherished fantasies or deepest anxieties of each might be realised or resisted (Beckett, 2002: 13). At crucial historical junctures, each furnished the other with a compelling narrative justifying radical economic, social or political transformation. Chile's prominence in British political culture has its roots in the recognition of its potential serviceability to key debates at home. Through the 1930s and 40s as civilian and military governments of the right and left attempted various radical policy experiments, observers came to realise that Chile 'offered the full kaleidoscope of politics, in a country small and centralised enough for every ideology to have hopes of success. Its narrow test tube of territory, its concentrated population of less than ten million, its perpetually bubbling inflation and European-style consumer booms and slumps, its endless elections ... seemed to make it an ideal laboratory for new notions from abroad' (Beckett,

2002: 88). It was also an exporter of influential ideas. When Eduardo Frei was elected to the Presidency in 1964 he set out to redress the extreme disparities of wealth and poverty that marked Chilean society. In an effort to broaden economic participation, spread the wealth and ensure decent provision for the poor, he launched the Revolution in Liberty, a moderate program of nationalisation, state planning of the economy and land redistribution. His policies were hailed by social democracies from around the world and especially admired in Britain. From the mid-1960s into the early 1970s politicians, public servants, community activists and student revolutionaries made the journey south to learn, first, from Frei's reforms, and, after his election in 1970, to absorb the lessons from the more radical experiments in economic restructuring and social planning pursued under Salvador Allende's administration.

As Allende's policies polarised Chile and the economy descended into chaos, right-wing commentators in Britain wrung their hands in consternation, convinced that the Wilson government's fidelity to 'the Santiago Model' was taking the country the way of Chile (Beckett, 2002: 190). The military coup of 11 September 1973, which put an end to Allende and his regime, sharpened debate in Britain over how best to respond to the deepening crises at home, recasting political and economic challenges as questions of patriotism and loyalty. The right argued that just as Allende's economic and social policies had all-but ceded control of the country to the Soviet bloc, so the Labour Party's support for Chile brought its loyalty to Britain into question. More extreme elements within the security services spread the rumour that Wilson was a Russian agent, intent on selling out the country to the Kremlin. It is a measure of the gravity of the social and political crises of the day that, by 1974, the contention that the Labour government posed a threat to the nation's values and traditions had spread beyond the shadowy world of espionage and into the mainstream press. In September 1974 the *Financial Times* columnist, Samuel

Brittan, predicted the collapse of the British parliamentary system within a lifetime, while *The Times* warned of what it called a 'last chance parliament' (quoted in Beckett, 2002: 187). A year later, Robert Moss, a former director of the Economist Intelligence Unit, published *The Collapse of Democracy* (1975). For Moss, Britain in 1974 was a mirror-image of pre-coup Chile, perched on the same political precipice that the Chileans had toppled over in 1970 when they elected the veteran socialist to the presidency. Britain now, like Chile then, was 'suffering a crisis of structures and beliefs' as 'disciplined minorities moved by radical ideologies and an equally radical contempt for the past' were working to subvert 'the conventions of the great majority' and 'knock away the bases for a free society' (Moss, 1977: 20, 12–13, 15). The threat was clear. Without a radical rethink in political direction, tomorrow's Britain would look like today's Chile.

That change of direction came when Wilson resigned in 1976 and was replaced by the more pragmatic James Callaghan for whom, as Peter Clarke notes, 'fidelity to socialist dogma ... was simply not [a] priority' (Clarke, 2004: 351). Under Callaghan's leadership the economy struggled back onto its feet, the Government and unions arrived at an uneasy compact, inflation was gradually reeled in, and with that the extreme right's principal bases for anxiety and agitation evaporated. More importantly, 12 months before Callaghan's accession to power, Margaret Thatcher was elected to the leadership of the Conservative Party, where, she made it clear, 'ideas from Britain's radical Right' and those disgruntled by Edward Heath's placatory corporatism would find a warm welcome (Beckett, 2002: 200). In the first instance it was economic radicalism that caught her eye. Through her adviser, Professor Alan Walters, she kept a close eye on the free market reforms instituted in Pinochet's Chile, where a group of Milton Friedman's former students, the 'Chicago Boys', were given the opportunity to put his monetarist theories to the test and rebuild the Chilean

economy. Their reforms included deep cuts in public expenditure, increases in interest rates, the removal of tariffs on imports and price controls on local goods thereby exposing industries unaccustomed to competition to the full blast of market forces. Their 'shock treatment' very nearly killed the patient. The price of staple goods rose steeply, unemployment soared and wages plummeted. With the sudden loss of so much state revenue the welfare state virtually collapsed. However, once the economy had bottomed out, it first tentatively recovered before prospering: interest rates fell, productivity rose, and economic growth far outpaced American and European averages. When Margaret Thatcher was elected Prime Minister in 1979 and Britain embarked on its own economic revolution following the blueprint set by the Chicago Boys, Chile once again returned to the mainstream of British media and political narrative. As in the days of Frei and Allende, enthusiastic visitors queued up for the guided tour, though on this occasion it was right-wing politicians, neoliberal economists, state-modernisers, change managers and their media cheer squad who came to sit at the feet of the country's economic gurus. No longer an admonitory example of the strong medicine that Britain might need to swallow, Chile was now a shining example of the good health of the patient subjected to such a course of political and economic therapy, and a model for the nation's own recovery. Back in Britain, in a reversal of roles from the preceding decade, it was the left's turn to lament the irresponsible extremes of Chile's radical economic and social experiments and bemoan the influence they were exerting over domestic policy. Under the structural reforms of the 1980s, British manufacturing industries collapsed, interest rates spiralled, unemployment mushroomed, and access to social security was restricted, while labour market flexibility was enshrined in law and a whole array of once sacrosanct public enterprises privatised. When the workers resisted the reforms, as they did most iconically on the picket lines at

Orgreave and Wapping, the Government showed its readiness to use violent confrontation to drive home its policy agenda and reinforce its supremacy. The message was clear: those who resisted the triumph of neo-liberal economics would be beaten into submission.

For British politicians and commentators, events in Chile from the 1960s to the 1980s provided a language through which reforms being planned or attempted in Britain could be imagined, analysed and debated. While Allende's experiments offered a vehicle by which the radical right might critique the leftward drift of British politics in the early 1970s, the transformation of the economy under Pinochet enabled the right to push its own agenda for reform at home. At the same time, while Allende's Chile provided the left with a realised utopia of wealth redistribution and land reform, in the wake of its dismemberment by the military it furnished a durable myth of viable socialism and an enduring site of pilgrimage. Seen and used as a proxy for the enactment and resolution of British political debates, Chile has for more than thirty years now given form to Britain's political unconscious. Here the nation's worst fears, the repressed anxieties of imperial decline – economic collapse, political extremism, social fission – can be given form, and then be addressed and assuaged. In the light of this it is no exaggeration to claim that, without Latin America, many British writers could hardly imagine their own country.

## EMPIRE REDUX: NARRATIVES OF REDEMPTION

When the Argentines invaded the Falkland Islands in April 1982, Britons were unexpectedly presented with an ideal opportunity to turn back the tide on a half century of despoliation. In dispatching the Task Force, defeating the Argentines and reclaiming the islands Britain could strike a blow against the varied forces that had conspired over the preceding decades to reduce its power and diminish its

status. Victory in the South Atlantic would return the nation to its long-buried, fundamental history of military conquest and imperial authority, and so restore it to its authentic self. For more than two centuries British writers had journeyed to Latin America in quest of or in flight from the nation's fundamental history. Presented with such a clear symbol of this elusive ideal in the rolling hills of the Falkland Islands, the whole weight of the nation's history and culture drove the Task Force southwards – 200 years of pride powered by 50 years of shame and guilt.[19] The Argentines weren't just resisting Britain's military elite, they were battling the nation's most powerful cultural myths. Standing between the British and the embodied evidence of their essential identity, they never stood a chance. The political unconscious that Latin America had helped frame and articulate now assumed physical form and steamrolled the hapless Argentines. Narrative had rarely assumed a more physical form.

## NOTES

1  For a more detailed discussion of how the British saw their own social system see Cannadine, 2001.
2  Cannadine's assertion that the empire was dedicated to the domestication of the exotic through parallel, analogy and equivalence is, of course, a calculated rebuttal of the theories of Edward Said. Said's reading of the British Empire conceived of it as a bureaucratic and discursive system designed to 'other' and thereby legitimate the oppression of its subject peoples. Cannadine contends that this approach is 'too simplified' and is not alone in his recognition that for all his moral forcefulness – if not because of it – Said's understanding of the relations between coloniser and colonised wanted subtlety, that it was unable to acknowledge 'the extent to which empire was about collaboration and consensus as well as about conflict and coercion' (Cannadine, 2001: xvi). See Said, 1978 and 1993. Bhabha criticised Said's promotion of a static model of colonial relations in which 'colonial power and discourse is possessed entirely by the coloniser', and where there is no room for negotiation, compromise or change (Bhabha, 1983: 200). See also Ahmed's claim that Said offers an homogenised representation of 'the West' and Porter's assertion that Said's reduction of East–West relations to an entrenched system of binaries overlooks the nuances in their shifting relations over a vast historical stretch (Ahmed, 1992; Porter, 1983). See

Dutton and Williams for an analysis of how Said's arguments might be applied to non-Western populations and cultures (Dutton and Williams, 1993). See Loomba 1998 for a synopsis of these debates.

3  For more on this see Said, 1978: 92–110.

4  Peter Winch observes that 'Seriously to study another way of life is necessarily to seek to extend our own – not simply to bring the other way within the already existing boundaries of our own because the point about the latter in their present form, is that they *ex-hypothesi* exclude the other' (Winch, 1967: 30).

5  Brantlinger observes: 'Palmerston and many of his contemporaries believed that British overseas interests should be secured whenever possible without formal imperialization' (Brantlinger, 1988: 20).

6  David Sinclair notes that a portion of Gustavus Hippisley's *The Siege of Barcelona: A Poem in Three Cantos* (1842) was dedicated to the dubious Latin American exploits of 'Sir' Gregor MacGregor (see Sinclair, 2003: 30–1). Edmund Burke, Jose Blanco White and Robert Southey all made passing reference to events in South America in their letters and political writings, and Byron named his yacht *Bolivar*. But MacCalman (1999) contains not a single entry dedicated to South America. By contrast one of the first great works of Latin American independence, the *Repertorio Americano*, 'an attempt to contribute knowledge and vision to the task of founding the new American republics' was published in London and mostly written by Andrés Bello, who lived there for 19 years (Pratt, 1992: 172). In making 'himself a conduit and a filter for European writings that might be useful to the nationbuilding process there' the *Repertorio* offers a model for the one-way intellectual and cultural traffic between Europe and Latin America at this time (Pratt, 1992: 172).

7  Southey's epics did go on. When Shelley made the pilgrimage to Greta Hall to visit his idol, he reportedly 'slipped beneath the table, unconscious with boredom, during Southey's rendition of one of his own epics' (Storey, 1997: 213). For nineteenth-century criticism of the poem see Madden, 1972.

8  For contemporary critical opinion on *Madoc* see Franklin, 2003: 80-84; Pratt, 1992: 149-61; Curry, 1975: 1160-1, and Madden, 1972: 5.

9  For details on Southey's conversion see Franklin, 2003: 60-84, and Mahoney, 2003: 1-33.

10  The royal scandals included the Prince of Wales's bigamous marriage, his gambling and gluttony, and the Mrs Clarke affair, in which the Duke of York's mistress accepted bribes and sexual favours from military officers in return for preferment. For more on this see Fulford, 1999: 166-8.

11  In 1803 the Whig reformer, Henry Brougham, published *An Inquiry into the Colonial Policy of the European Powers* in which he argued that those sent out to rule the empire returned to Britain sunk in 'luxurious habits ... [and the] corruption peculiar to Oriental society' (quoted in Fulford, 1999: 170). For more see Fulford and Kitson; 1998; Leask,

1992. The prime symbol of domestic corruption, the Prince of Wales, had a taste for the oriental. Contemporary satirists often portrayed him in his favourite architectural folly, the Royal Pavilion at Brighton, as a Sultan disporting himself among his harem. See Fulford, 1999: 170; Musgrave, 1959.

12  Colley refers to the emergence of a 'highly selective cult of heroism' over this period (Colley, 1992: 195). See also Fulford, 1999: 162; Colley, 1992: 195-7.

13  Edward Said calculates that while European powers were 'in occupation of approximately 35 percent of the earth's surface' in 1815, by the end of the Great War this had more than doubled to 85 percent, and a significant proportion of this territory was in British hands (Said, 1983: 222).

14  The *Oxford English Dictionary* entry for 'imperialism' notes that its primary signification, 'the rule of an emperor, esp. when despotic or arbitrary' was the common usage in the mid-nineteenth century and that it retained this pejorative sense until well into the 1890s. In its earliest uses it is employed as a synonym for 'Jingoism'. The first use of the term in the more favourable sense of 'The principle or spirit of empire ... seeking, or at least not refusing, an extension of the British empire in directions where trading interests and investments require the protection of the flag' was recorded in 1895 (COED, 1991: 821).

15  The view that the British Empire was a happy accident was famously propounded in Sir John Seeley's claim that 'We seem ... to have conquered and peopled half the world in a fit of absence of mind' (Seeley, 1971: 12).

16  See Schlunke, 2005; Elder, 1988; Reynolds, 1982.

17  For the clicking language of the ape-men see Conan Doyle, 2001: 152, 156, *passim*. For the German massacre of the Herero see Cocker, 2001: 269-371.

18  For the economic difficulties of the early-mid 1970s see Clarke, 2004: 358-400; Bernstein, 2004: 157-228; and Marwick, 1990:184-392. The state of the British economy at this time is summarised in the title of Dell, 1991: *A Hard Pounding*. The most dramatic economic emergency of the period, the Sterling crisis of 1976, is dealt with in Burk, 1992. Historical responses to the 1970s were marked by a sense of the decade's crises. The title of Jeremy Seabrook's study of working people and the idealism of the labour movement was *What Went Wrong?* while Calvocoressi's *The British Experience 1945–75* was in large measure 'a tale of hopes deflated by failures' (Marwick, 1990: 8).

19  See Barnett, 1982 for this particular reading of the islands.

# REFERENCES

Ahmed, L. (1992) *Women and Gender in Islam: Historical Roots of a Modern Debate*. New Haven: Yale University Press.

Barnett, Anthony (1982) *Iron Britannia*. London: Allison and Busby.

Bartlett, Frederick C. (1972) *Remembering: A Study in Experimental and Social Psychology*. Cambridge: Cambridge University Press.

Beckett, Andy (2002) *Pinochet in Piccadilly: Britain and Chile's Hidden History*. London: Faber and Faber.

Bernstein, George L. (2004) *The Myth of Decline: The Rise of Britain Since 1945*. London: Pimlico.

Bhabha, Homi (1983) 'Difference, discrimination, and the discourse of colonialism', *The Politics of Theory*, eds, F. Barker, P. Hulme, M. Iversen and D. Loxley. Colchester: University of Essex Press.

Brantlinger, Patrick (1988) *Rule of Darkness: British Literature and Imperialism, 1830–1914*. Ithaca: Cornell University Press.

Buchan, James, (2003) 'Bitter legacy'. Review of *Sowing the Wind: The Seeds of Conflict in the Middle East* by John Keay. *Guardian Weekly*, 3–9 July 2003.

Burk, Kathleen, and Alec Cairncross (1992) *Goodbye, Great Britain: The 1976 IMF Crisis*. New Haven: Yale University Press.

Cannadine, David, (2001) *Ornamentalism: How the British Saw their Empire*. London: Allen Lane.

Clarke, Peter (2004) *Hope and Glory: Britain 1900-2000*, 2nd edition. London: Penguin.

Cocker, Mark (2001) *Rivers of Blood, Rivers of Gold: Europe's Conquest of Indigenous Peoples*. New York: Grove Press.

Colley, Linda (1992) *Britons: Forging the Nation 1707–1837*. London: Vintage.

Colley, Linda (2002) *Captives: Britain, Empire and the World 1600-1850*. London.

Colls, Robert (2002) *Identity of England*. Oxford: Oxford University Press.

*The Compact Oxford English Dictionary* (COED), 2nd edition (1991). Oxford: Clarendon Press.

Conan Doyle, Arthur (2001 [Original 1912]) *The Lost World and Other Thrilling Tales*. London: Penguin.

Crabbe, George (1905 [Original 1782]) *The Village*, in *Poems*, Volume I, ed., Adolphus William Ware. Cambridge: Cambridge University Press.

Curry, Kenneth (1975) *Southey*. London: Routledge and Kegan Paul.

Curtin, Philip (1964) *The Image of Africa: British Ideas and Action, 1780–1850*. London: Macmillan.

Dell, Edmund (1991) *A Hard Pounding: Politics and Economic Crisis 1974-6* Oxford: Oxford University Press.

Dutton, Michael and Peter Williams (1993) 'Translating theories: Edward Said on orientalism, imperialism and alterity', *Southern Review*, Vol. 26, No. 3 (November 1993), 314–57.

Elder, Bruce (1988) *Blood on the Wattle: Massacres and Maltreatment of Australian Aborigines Since 1788*. Frenchs Forest: National Book Distributors and Publishers.

Elliott, J.H. (1970) *The Old World and the New 1492–1650*. Cambridge: Cambridge University Press.

Franklin, Caroline (2003) 'The Welsh American Dream: Iolo Morganwg, Robert Southey and the Madoc Legend', in Gerald Carruthers and Alan Rawes (eds), *English Romanticism and the Celtic World*. Cambridge: Cambridge University Press.

Fraser, Robert (1998) *Victorian Quest Romance: Stevenson, Haggard, Kipling, and Conan Doyle*. Plymouth: Northcote House.

Fulford, Tim (1999) 'Romanticizing the empire: the naval heroes of Southey, Coleridge, Austen and Marryat', *Modern Language Quarterly*, Vol 60, No. 2 (June 1999), 161–96.

Fulford, Tim and Peter J. Kitson (eds) (1998) *Romanticism and Colonialism: Writing and Empire 1780–1830*. Cambridge: Cambridge University Press.

Green, Martin (1979) *Dreams of Adventure, Deeds of Empire*. London: Routledge and Kegan Paul.

Jameson, Frederic (1981) *The Political Unconscious: Narrative as a Socially Symbolic Act*. London: Routledge.

Leask, Nigel (1992) *British Romantic Writers and the East: Anxieties of Empire*. Cambridge: Cambridge University Press.

Lindqvist, Sven (1997) *'Exterminate All The Brutes'*. London: Granta.

Loomba, Ania (1998) *Colonialism/Postcolonialism*. London: Routledge.

MacCalman, Ian (ed.) (1999) *An Oxford Companion to the Romantic Age: British Culture 1776–1832*. Oxford: Oxford University Press

MacLachlan, Gale and Ian Reid (1994) *Framing and Interpretation*. Melbourne: Melbourne University Press.

Madden, Lionel (1972) *Robert Southey: The Critical Heritage*. London: Routledge and Kegan Paul.

Mahoney, Charles (2003) *Romantics and Renegades*. London: Palgrave.

Marwick, Arthur (1990) *British Society Since 1945*, 2nd edition. London: Penguin.

Moss, Robert (1977 [Original 1975]) *The Collapse of Democracy*. London: Abacus.

Musgrave, Clifford (1959) *Royal Pavilion: An Episode in the Romantic*, revised edition. London: Hill.

Porter, D. (1983) *'Orientalism* and its problems', *The Politics of Theory*, eds, F. Barker, P. Hulme, M. Iversen and D. Loxley. Colchester: University of Essex Press.

Pratt, Mary Louise (1992) *Imperial Eyes: Travel Writing and Transculturation*. London: Routledge.

Reynolds, Henry (1982) *The Other Side of the Frontier* Ringwood: Penguin.

Said, Edward (1978) *Orientalism: Western Conceptions of the Orient*. London: Penguin.

Said, Edward (1983) *The World, the Text, and the Critic*. Cambridge, Mass.: Harvard University Press.

Said, Edward (1993) *Culture and Imperialism*. London: Chatto and Windus.

Schlunke, Katrina M. (2005) *Bluff Rock: Autobiography of a Massacre*. Fremantle: Curtin University Books.

Seeley, Sir John (1971) *The Expansion of England*, ed., John Gross. Chicago: University of Chicago Press.

Sinclair, David (2003) *The Land That Never Was: Sir Gregor MacGregor and the Most Audacious Fraud in History*. London: Review.

Storey, Mark (1997) *Robert Southey: A Life*. Oxford: Oxford University Press.

Southey, Robert (1906) (Original 1813) *The Life of Horatio, Lord Nelson*. London: Dent.

Watts, Cedric, and Laurence Davies (1979) *Cunninghame Graham: A Critical Biography*. Cambridge: Cambridge University Press.

Winch, Peter (1967) 'Understanding a primitive society', *Religion and Understanding*, ed., D.Z. Phillips. Oxford: Oxford University Press.

Williams, Gwyn A. (1979) *Madoc: The Making of a Myth*. London: Eyre Methuen.

# 21

# Cultural Studies and History

Gilbert B. Rodman

... somewhere in the middle of the story. There are, after all, no absolute beginnings. An old (but, of course, by no means the first) version of this argument is Marx's (1978: 595) reminder that people make history, but never in conditions of their own making: that our ability to create new stories (and, in so doing, to remake the world) is always already constrained (and enabled) by the specific social, cultural, political, economic, histori-cal (etc.) circumstances into which we are born.[1] A more recent variation on this theme can be found in Deleuze and Guattari's (1987) theoretical work on the rhizome: the ever-shifting, rootless multiplicity that they offer as a counterpoint to the linear, genea-logical forms of arborescent thought that have dominated (and, in their eyes, damaged) Western culture for far too long. For Deleuze and Guattari, there are no absolute begin-nings or *tabulae rasae*: only intermezzos, plateaus, and sprawling networks of fluid linkages.[2] In cultural studies, this idea appears in many places and takes many forms (including ones explicitly derived from Marx and/or Deleuze), but perhaps its most elegant summation is Larry Grossberg's (personal communication, 1999) observation that the beginnings of the stories we tell are always the endings of other stories that we

have not bothered to tell. We always enter the conversation in mid-sentence. Always.

At its best, cultural studies crafts and tells the kinds of stories that differ significantly from those produced by other intellectual formations. One of the most important such differences revolves around the potentially awkward phrase – 'intellectual formation' – that I am using to describe the kind of thing that cultural studies is. There are other terms that might read more gracefully – 'discipline' and 'field' being the most obvious (and most often used) options – but those terms would also be misleading, since one of the key differences that matter here is that cultural studies is *not* a scholarly discipline unto itself. Over the past two or three decades, numerous people and institutions have tried (and continue to try) to stuff the square peg of cultural studies into the round hole of normative disciplinar-ity anyway (the astonishing proliferation of cultural studies textbooks over the past dec-ade or so is the most obvious example here), but such efforts fundamentally misunderstand what cultural studies is.

A thorough discussion of cultural studies' prickly relationship to the traditional disci-plines is beyond the scope of this essay (though we will return to a small portion of that argument shortly).[3] What I want to focus on instead are cultural studies' answers to the epistemological questions at the heart of this handbook: e.g., how does cultural studies actually know what it claims to know? what does cultural studies consider to be meaningful evidence? and what does it believe that evidence actually demonstrates? To answer these questions meaningfully, however, we first need to wrestle with a more fundamental question: just what is this thing called 'cultural studies'? In part, this extra step is necessary because explaining what cultural studies is (and thus what it *thinks* it needs to know) will make it easier to understand *how* it actually goes about the business of trying to produce that knowledge. More crucially, however, there is already a great deal of misinformation about cultural studies in active circulation (even, unfortunately, among people who claim to do it themselves): enough so that it would be foolish for me simply to treat the definitional question as a given. In fact, the odds are good that what most people think they already know about cultural studies is actually wrong – though this is almost certainly not their fault. There has been a lot of 'the blind leading the blind' when it comes to cultural studies (see Rodman, 1997) and those who have been led astray can hardly be blamed for the poor guidance they have received.

Over the years, a lot of people have tried to define cultural studies,[4] and even a casual examination of such efforts demonstrates that cultural studies is a much trickier enterprise to explain than most traditional academic disciplines. Reading actual cultural studies scholarship may actually exacerbate the average newcomer's confusion since the range of such work is incredibly diverse and varied. Let us take a very quick glance at five major examples of cultural studies research (chosen not quite at random):

- Paul Gilroy's *Against Race* (2000): a complex, thickly layered theoretical argument – with extended detours through both hip-hop and Nazi Germany – about the tight (and perhaps unbreakable) connections between the concepts of race, nation, and fascism.

- Lawrence Grossberg's *Caught in the Crossfire* (2005): an empirically grounded analysis of the ongoing (and largely unacknowledged) 'war on kids' in the US, which ultimately concludes that children have become an accidental casualty of a systematic effort by neoconservative forces to undo contemporary forms of modernity.
- Meaghan Morris' *Too Soon Too Late* (1998): a collection of essays on culture, history, media, and politics that covers topics ranging from suburban shopping centers to former Australian Prime Minister Paul Keating, from popular images of King Kong to a deconstruction of touristic metaphors for scholarly work.
- Janice Radway's *A Feeling for Books* (1997): a far-reaching, multi-method examination of the Book-of-the-Month Club that weaves together extensive archival research, critical literary analysis of selected Club titles, autobiographical narratives, and an ethnographic study of the Club's editorial offices.
- Carol Stabile's *White Victims, Black Villains* (2006): a history of crime journalism and policy in the US that demonstrates the fundamental interrelationship of both major media institutions and law enforcement agencies in forging a cultural and legal climate that fetishizes white womanhood and demonizes black masculinity.

All five of these books are examples of important cultural studies research but, on the surface anyway, none of them appears to resemble any of the others in ways that would make it easy for someone who is not already a semi-fluent cultural studies practitioner to understand how or why they are all part of the same intellectual formation. They don't share objects, methods, disciplinary frameworks, or theoretical underpinnings in any obvious way.

To a large extent, this is because cultural studies has never centered itself around the sorts of core features that most disciplines use to define themselves: it has no primary research object, theoretical framework, or methodological approach to call its own. As a result, there is nothing that works as a 'close enough' soundbite definition (e.g., 'psychology is the study of the human mind') that might help to make cultural studies somewhat intelligible (or at least initially manageable) to newcomers. The most common such shorthand explanations – e.g., 'cultural studies is the study of popular culture,' or 'cultural studies is a particular form of critical theory' – are ultimately more misleading than they are helpful, even by the very low standards of the soundbite genre. While a significant amount of cultural studies scholarship has focused on popular culture and/or embraced various strands of critical theory, there has been just as much (and perhaps even more) work done in the name of cultural studies for which such claims cannot legitimately be made. All five of the books mentioned above, for example, engage with 'theory' and 'the popular' somewhere along the way ... but only Radway's takes a form of popular culture as its primary focus, and only Gilroy's wrestles with intellectual abstractions at enough length to render it 'theory-heavy.'

Nonetheless, if we are going to try and engage with the question of cultural studies and its relationship to historical theory, we have to enter the territory somewhere. And so, drawing on Stuart Hall's (1992: 281) claim (itself derived from the writings of Antonio Gramsci) that the intellectual's job is both 'to know more than the traditional intellectuals do: really know, not just pretend to know, not just to have the facility of knowledge, but to know deeply and profoundly' and to communicate that knowledge effectively 'to those who do not belong, professionally, in the intellectual class,' I offer the following definition:

> Cultural studies is an interlocking set of leftist intellectual and political practices. Its central purpose is twofold: (1) to produce detailed, contextualized analyses of the ways that power and social relations are created, structured, and maintained through culture; and (2) to circulate those analyses in public forums suitable to the tasks of pedagogy, provocation, and political intervention.

I do not have space here to unpack all the pieces of that definition in full (see Rodman, forthcoming), but I do want to map out four key characteristics of cultural studies implicit in that definition, with an eye on how they each help to shape cultural studies' approach to scholarly research, evidence, and analysis: (1) its overtly political nature, (2) its interdisciplinarity, (3) its constructivism, and (4) its radical contextualism.

## POLITICS

Arguably, cultural studies' overtly political nature is what distinguishes it most sharply from traditional academic disciplines. Almost any discipline, after all, can boast that the best scholarship produced in its name involves 'detailed, contextualized analyses.' And most disciplines will at least claim to care about sharing the fruits of their intellectual labors with a broader public. But very few disciplines openly embrace political agendas of any sort, nor do they typically take 'political intervention' to be a common part of their disciplinary missions.[5] (For that matter, 'mission' is a far more directive, politically charged term than most disciplines would claim for themselves.) Of course, even in the most 'neutral' and/or 'objective' disciplines, there are scholars – often prominent ones – who are unabashedly open about the political stakes of their research, but such examples merely represent the ability of individuals to carve out a viable space for political work in fields that, taken as a whole, refuse to define themselves in political terms. Cultural studies, on the other hand, works the other way around: i.e., it *begins* with a strong political commitment of some sort – there is simply no such thing as a politically neutral cultural studies – and then expects individual practitioners to pursue intellectual work that is compatible with that political mission.[6]

The primacy of cultural studies' desire for political engagement is crucial here. Stuart Hall once described the Centre for Contemporary Cultural Studies (CCCS) at the University of Birmingham (arguably, the earliest site where cultural studies actually traveled under that name)[7] as 'the locus to which we *retreated* when that conversation [i.e., the one around the British New Left of the late 1950s] in the open world could no longer be continued: it was politics by other means' (Hall, 1990: 12, emphasis in original). Hall's words can be understood as an exhortation for cultural studies to retain a sharp political edge as it pursues its academic projects, but they are also a pointed reminder that the university was not a place where cultural studies had ever intended to take up permanent residence. If cultural studies has become a primarily academic enterprise since the CCCS was founded – and, arguably, this is the case, even if that is not necessarily a good thing – it has done so accidentally and tangentially, rather than by design.

This is not to deny the value of academic work, nor is it to suggest that cultural studies somehow does not belong in the university at all. Far from it. It is, however, a way of suggesting that cultural studies' approach to scholarship begins from a very different set of assumptions than those commonly underpinning traditional disciplines. Cultural studies is not driven by a sort of encyclopedic desire to produce 'knowledge for knowledge's sake,' or to amass an exhaustive body of scholarly information in the abstract belief that such a storehouse of research will eventually prove itself useful to somebody somewhere. It does not assume that its chosen research objects are somehow intrinsically or self-evidently worthy of study. And it is not interested in the sort of 'internal' projects that matter greatly to researchers working within a particular discipline, but not at all to anyone outside that tiny circle of scholars.[8] Instead, cultural studies is driven by the desire to intervene productively in social, cultural, and political struggles in the larger world, especially insofar as it is able to do so on behalf of (or alongside) those segments of the population who are unjustly disenfranchised, oppressed, and/or silenced.

For example, describing the major reasons that cultural studies should take popular culture seriously as a research object, Stuart Hall writes:

> Popular culture is one of the sites where this struggle for and against a culture of the powerful is engaged: it is also the stake to be won and lost *in* that struggle. It is the arena of consent and resistance. It is partly where hegemony arises, and where it is secured. It is not a sphere where socialism, a socialist culture – already fully formed – might be simply 'expressed.' But it is one of the places where socialism might be constituted. That is why 'popular culture' matters. Otherwise, to tell you the truth, I don't give a damn about it. (1981: 239)

Hall's larger argument here suggests that popular culture is *not* simply the (or even 'a') natural research object for cultural studies. Instead, the worthiness of popular culture is contingent on its role in the political project(s) at stake for cultural studies in any given context ... and, crucially, the nature of those political projects is not guaranteed in advance. In the essay cited above, Hall is most immediately concerned with constituting 'a socialist culture,' but cultural studies as a whole is not inherently or necessarily a socialist project, and Hall would be one of the first (and one of the loudest) to argue that cultural studies' relationship to socialism has always been more of a critical engagement with the Marxist problematic than a doctrinaire adherence to a party line.

This last point helps to underscore a crucial aspect of cultural studies' political nature. In much the same way that there is no predefined set of cultural studies research objects, theories, or methodologies, cultural studies' politics are not easy to predict except, perhaps, in the very broadest and most general of ways. While cultural studies has historically been a leftist – and even a radical – endeavor, that categorization does not help us very much in predicting which political issues cultural studies will actually take up in any given context, or how it will go about doing so. Cultural studies might safely be said to be committed to a variety of progressive political goals: it is hard, for example, to imagine a cultural studies worthy of the name that, taken as a whole, is not actively invested in ending racism, patriarchy, heterosexism, economic injustice, and so on. Those broad commitments, however, do not automatically translate into predictable analyses of specific 'real world' phenomena. Partially, of course, this is because all of those large problems are themselves slippery, shape-shifting, moving targets. Racism, for example, operates in significantly different ways in different geopolitical and historical circumstances, and so what might work as a productive cultural studies analysis of institutionalized racism at a particular point in space and time (e.g., the UK in the mid-1970s: Hall et al., 1978) will not necessarily work well (or even at all) in a different context (e.g., the US in the mid-1990s: Gray, 2005). Even within a particular historical conjuncture, cultural studies recognizes that the multiple fronts on which, ideally, it would struggle with equal vigor are rarely aligned in such a way that cultural studies practitioners' 'predictable' political inclinations can actually be applied to real cases in neat and predictable fashion. A progressive intervention with respect to the politics of gender and sexuality, for instance, may inadvertently reinforce existing forms of racism and classism (see Rodman, 2006).

Implicit in this last point is the notion that cultural studies understands its political and intellectual work to be inextricably intertwined, with each informing and shaping the other in vital ways. While cultural studies necessarily 'begins' (insofar as we can pretend, for a moment, that one can identify an absolute beginning for any given cultural studies project) with questions arising from its 'real world' political concerns, it also refuses to let its politics serve as a substitute for rigorous intellectual work. The world, after all, is rarely as neatly ordered a place as our politics might tell us it is. As such, if your politics tell you the answers to your research questions in advance – e.g., you already know, before actually doing the relevant research, that Hollywood films are racist or that government policies privilege the rich – then you are *not* doing cultural studies. Put a slightly different way, cultural studies' scholarly research should serve as a genuine test of its political values and beliefs: not merely an automatic affirmation of them.

Understanding cultural studies as a necessarily and explicitly political enterprise does not, in and of itself, explain how it goes about the business of gathering, assessing, and analyzing scholarly evidence. But it *does* help us understand the kinds of research questions that cultural studies deems worthy of asking – i.e., questions that require the intellectual project to pass the 'so what?' test as it might be applied by non-specialists (and, perhaps more crucially, by non-academics) – and thus it begins to frame an answer to the question of how cultural studies determines what actually counts as legitimate evidence.

## INTERDISCIPLINARITY

Undoubtedly, part of the reason why cultural studies is so frequently understood as just another (sub)discipline has to do with its longstanding presence within the university. The earliest example of something explicitly called 'cultural studies' was the founding of an academic unit (the CCCS at the University of Birmingham in 1964), the majority of the work done in its name since that time has been produced by professional scholars and/ or graduate students, and its most widely recognized manifestations continue to appear in traditional academic settings (e.g., scholarly journals, books, conferences, departments, etc.). So it is easy to see why – especially to casual observers – cultural studies might appear to be nothing more than a relatively new form of scholarly work. It waddles like a duck, it quacks like a duck...

... or does it? Even in its academic variations, cultural studies refuses to play by the sorts of rules that traditional disciplines normally use to mark their territories. For most disciplines, one can generally apply some relatively straightforward litmus test(s) to determine what does (and does not) belong within their borders: certain research objects, methodologies, and/or theoretical frameworks are clearly on the inside, while others are just as unmistakably on the outside. Even the fuzzy cases (and every discipline has them) often simply underscore which rules truly matter when it comes to distinguishing neighboring disciplines from one another. For example, film becomes a legitimate research object in the disciplinary context of English because of a particular set of analytic tools that treat film as a form of dramatic narrative and artistic storytelling – i.e., something akin to literature – rather than as a type of mass media (which would place film more squarely in communication's territory). So it is not so much film (as a particular kind of object) that 'belongs' to English as it is a set of theoretical and methodological approaches that places a particular kind of film scholarship within English's territory.

Given what we have already established with respect to cultural studies' unconventional ways, it is probably not surprising that one of the major things that marks it as different from 'normal' disciplinary practices is the degree to which it ignores traditional disciplinary boundaries. To be sure, few (if any) individual cultural studies scholars manage to work outside of institutional settings completely, and those settings are typically themselves shaped in significant ways by disciplinary norms: we are trained as communication scholars or historians or anthropologists (etc.), we occupy faculty positions within discipline-specific departments, and these disciplinary relationships inevitably have an impact on the types of intellectual work that we can actually do (Striphas, 1998). Scholars make research, but never in circumstances entirely of our own choosing ...

Viewed as a whole, however, cultural studies is far more fluid and variable than that. Partially, this is because cultural studies is not wholly – or even mostly – contained with any single 'parent' discipline in the way that, say 'media studies' might be considered a particular specialization within the discipline of communication, or that 'twentieth-century British literature' might be understood as a subfield of English. So all those disciplinarily situated cultural studies scholars are still scattered across almost the full range of the humanities and social sciences (though, to be sure, their distribution across that terrain is far from even), and the specific forms that their work takes vary significantly from one disciplinary context to the next. Perhaps more importantly, though, individual cultural studies practitioners who formally work in the context of specific disciplines cannot – and, if they are actually doing cultural studies, do not – view the borders of their 'home' disciplines as inviolable barriers. If anything, cultural studies has tended to question the rationales for the existence of disciplinary boundaries – why, for example, is there a sharp disciplinary separation between who studies 'literature' and who studies 'society,' as if the two do not necessarily and inevitably inform one another in significant ways? – and it has 'made the rounds' of the disciplines, 'poaching' freely and willfully from most (if not all) of the humanities (Hall, 1990: 16).

Faced with a particular research object, then, cultural studies does not simply assume that traditional disciplinary approaches to that object (assuming that those already exist) will effectively answer the questions it wants and/ or needs to ask about the object. Rather than determining (for example) what 'a good sociologist' would do and then being satisfied simply to do good sociology, cultural studies recognizes that the proper determinant of what research questions most need to be asked and which research methods are most suitable to answering those questions is *not* 'the discipline' (whatever that might be), but rather a combination of the *object* and the real world *context* in which the object is situated (neither of which is likely to be much concerned with disciplinary borders anyway). Put a slightly different way, cultural studies goes where it needs to in order to answer the questions the world poses – even if that approach forces it to cross the artificial borders created between disciplines. A cultural studies scholar working from a disciplinary base of, say, anthropology may find that her most important research questions simply cannot be answered without engaging with economic issues ... and, if she is truly doing cultural studies, she cannot (and will not) back away from those questions solely on the grounds that she is not formally trained as an economist.

Most importantly, however, cultural studies' approach to interdisciplinary work is never cheap or easy (Grossberg, 1995). Part of what makes cultural studies' brand of interdisciplinarity *radical* is the rigor with which it approaches the disciplines that it 'raids.' Our hypothetical cultural studies anthropologist (for example) does not live up to those interdisciplinary ideals simply by sprinkling a handful of citations from economics journals into her 'ordinary' research: she needs to engage the disciplinary problematics of economics 'deeply and profoundly' (Hall, 1992: 281). At the same time, however, she cannot simply assume that, as a discipline, economics has already managed to fully answer all the questions that have led her in that direction. The disciplines from which cultural studies 'poaches,' after all, have their own blind spots, biases, and shortcomings. As such, ideally, the challenge that cultural studies poses to economics (or any other discipline) is that it might offer valuable insights about the discipline and its primary object(s) of study that are not readily achievable by scholars working entirely within the discipline's existing confines (Grossberg, 2006, 2010; Hall, 1990).

In essence, then, cultural studies' efforts at scholarly research are always attempts to do the impossible. Having located a particular research object that bears further investigation, the cultural studies scholar then asks of that object, 'what does this have to do with *everything else?*' (Hall, 2007). Cultural studies' impulse is *not* to find ways to simplify the object so that it becomes easier to analyze, or so that it can be shoehorned into the theoretical and/or methodological frameworks already favored by a particular discipline. Rather, its impulse is to examine the object in ways that, as much as possible, approximate the complex nature of its existence *and* the intricate network of mutually determining

relationships with the larger world. One might say that cultural studies came away from its messy and awkward encounter with Althusserian Marxism (see Hall, 1992) by taking the notion of overdetermination more seriously than Althusser himself did. Like Althusser, cultural studies recognizes that there a variety of interlocking forces (cultural, economic, political, etc.) at play in the world that cannot simply be reduced to one another ... but, unlike Althusser, cultural studies is not willing or able to still assume that the economic (or anything else, for that matter) still manages to be the determining factor that, 'in the final instance,' somehow matters the most.

## CONSTRUCTIVISM

Cultural studies takes it as a given that there is a real world out there – one that exists independently of human thought and experience – but it also assumes that people have no unmediated access to that world: that everything that we think we know about the world is shaped in fundamental and unavoidable ways by the culture(s) in which we live. While cultural studies rejects – for many reasons – the notion that a completely objective and unbiased understanding of the world is possible, it nonetheless recognizes that there is necessarily a certain (if variable) level of intersubjective overlap in how people understand the world around them. All of us 'know' certain things to be true about the world because of such intersubjective overlaps (even if such overlap is inevitably imperfect and incomplete). There are, to be sure, multiple institutions and forces that contribute to that intersubjectivity: language, education, government, religion, and the family are all prominent examples (and, at various moments, past and present, cultural studies has taken all of these on as significant sites for research and analysis). In the late capitalist societies where cultural studies has been the most prominent, however, one of the most pervasive, significant, and rapidly shifting such forces over the past half century or so has been the mass media. As such, it is not surprising that a lot (though, again, by no means all) of the work done in cultural studies engages with the media's role in giving a particular shape to the world as we know it.

In early forms of communication and media studies, the media were often treated as if they were a sort of ancillary institution that simply reported on what happened in the 'real' world: i.e., first, there is reality and then, after the fact, there are mediated representations of reality. In this paradigm, the scholar's primary job is to analyze those representations for whatever inaccuracies and/or biases may have crept into the allegedly simple process of moving information from point A to point B. What cultural studies argues (bearing in mind that this insight is neither unique nor original to cultural studies) is that this is not how media representations work at all. That, in fact, since we can never have unmediated access to the 'true' nature of reality (whatever access we have is *always* filtered through the lens of culture), we need to understand media representations as *constitutive* of reality as we know it (Carey, 1989; Hall, 1997).

Here, we might recall Hall's comments on why popular culture matters to cultural studies, and extrapolate a comparable rationale for cultural studies' ongoing (which is not to say 'obligatory') interest in mass media. Cultural studies does not analyze media texts (journalistic or otherwise) simply to figure out 'what really happened' in the world. Insofar as accurate accounts of events can be (re)constructed and/or grossly distorted representations can be unmasked for what they are, of course, cultural studies may very well be interested in taking on such tasks... but it also recognizes that the world we inhabit is *constructed* out of discourse (not just represented by it) and that, as such, an objectivist focus on 'what really happened' often misses the forest for the trees.

As such, one of the recurring research questions for cultural studies is that of *how* particular (discursive) realities come into being. In particular, cultural studies frequently

approaches this question using the concept of 'articulation': a process by which otherwise unrelated cultural phenomena – practices, beliefs, texts, etc. – come to be linked together in meaningful and *seemingly* natural ways. As it is used in cultural studies, articulation is perhaps most clearly explained by means of an analogy of a tractor-trailer truck, which the British refer to as:

> an 'articulated' lorry (truck): a lorry where the front (cab) and back (trailer) can, but need not necessarily, be connected to one another. The two parts are connected to each other, but through a specific linkage, that can be broken. An articulation is thus the form of the connection that *can* make a unity of two different elements, under certain conditions. It is a linkage which is not necessary, determined, absolute and essential for all time. (Hall, 1986: 53)[9]

Articulation is also cultural studies' attempt to explain how something that seems to be ethereal and ephemeral – language, discourse, media representations, etc. – can nonetheless acquire enough solidity and stability to have very real consequences in the material world. The recognition that a given phenomenon is socially constructed (rather than natural) does not obligate cultural studies to see that phenomenon as somehow 'unreal.' To the contrary, cultural studies recognizes that the strength of certain articulations – i.e., the degree to which they are repeatedly and pervasively reinforced, and thus more difficult to break – gives certain socially constructed concepts considerable material impact. Race, for example, is such a concept – there is nothing biological, genetic, scientific, or natural about the multitude of ways that human beings have imposed racial categories onto the world's population – but those discursive fictions clearly have a very real impact on the material conditions of people's lives.

## RADICAL CONTEXTUALISM

I noted above that a combination of the research object and its context helps to determine the appropriate research questions for any given cultural studies project. But that formulation – complicated as it might be – is actually still a bit too simple, as the actual relationship between object and context is far messier than that. As Larry Grossberg puts it:

> An event or practice (even a text) does not exist apart from the forces of the context that constitute it as what it is. Obviously, context is not merely background but the very conditions of possibility of something. It cannot be relegated to a series of footnotes or to an after-thought, to the first or last chapter. It is both the beginning and the end of cultural studies, although the two are not the same point. (1995: 12)

Put a bit too simply, the cultural studies scholar recognizes two key facts about 'the context' for any given research object. First, she recognizes that context matters immensely: that the object's significance depends on the specific historical circumstances in which it is produced, circulated, consumed, and so on. 'Rock 'n' roll' (for example) means something different in the US in 1956 than it does in the UK in 1963, and neither of these is the same as 'rock 'n' roll' in Iraq in 2010. But she also recognizes that 'the context' is not an objective phenomenon that is simply 'out there' somewhere, waiting to be recognized for what it is by the savvy researcher. Instead, 'the context' has to be actively constructed by the researcher. In other words (and returning to the topic of articulation from a slightly different angle), the cultural studies scholar recognizes that the very same historical facts can be stitched together to create very different stories depending on the context(s) in which the scholar chooses to place those facts ... and that there are always a multiplicity of 'legitimate' contexts available for the scholar to choose from. For example, as I have argued elsewhere:

> We can tell very different versions of 'the same' story – i.e., the tale of Elvis' rise to national prominence in 1956 – depending on which historical facts we decide to use in framing and supporting our narrative... If we're especially concerned with the racial politics of the rise of rock 'n' roll, then it might be especially important for us to pay attention to who originally wrote and recorded the various songs on which Elvis built his career, how faithful his versions of those songs were to the spirit of the originals, what the racial demographics of the audiences who bought those records were, who did and didn't receive royalty payments on sales of those records, whether Elvis' success helped boost the popularity of the black artists whose music he performed, and so on. On the other hand, if we're more interested in the rise of youth culture that rock 'n' roll helped to bring about, then we're more likely ask questions about the age of Elvis' audiences, how links were forged between rock 'n' roll and other youth-friendly aspects of the leisure and entertainment industries (e.g., soda shops, drive-ins, etc.), the rise in disposable income among post-war teens, and so on. Neither of these sets of historical questions is somehow 'wrong,' but each will nevertheless put a very different spin on the story that results. (Rodman, 1999: 41)

One of the most significant consequences of radical contextualism for cultural studies scholarship is that it frequently – perhaps even inevitably – produces genuine surprises for the researcher(s) involved. The mutually constitutive interplay between object and context means that, ultimately, both are moving targets. And so cultural studies research projects often reach conclusions that were not at all what the researcher(s) in question originally expected – or even might have imagined.

For instance, the CCCS research team (Hall et al., 1978) who set out to examine the 'moral panic' over mugging that arose in England in the 1970s began from the assumption that they were examining a pattern of politically significant distortions in media representations of (what seemed to be) a new form of street crime ... but their efforts to establish the contextual framework most appropriate to understanding that phenomenon led them in directions that transformed their project significantly. It gradually became apparent that their ostensible research object (media discourses around 'mugging') was actually one of the earliest visible manifestations of a much broader, deeper shift in

British politics – the rise of Thatcherite 'authoritarian populism' – that few (if any) political observers had actually recognized.

## CONCLUSION

Stuart Hall has recently claimed (2007) that history is the one major discipline in the humanities that cultural studies has not taken seriously enough. And there is certainly a case to be made here. In 2001, for instance, the *European Journal of Cultural Studies* put out a special issue on 'History and Cultural Studies'... which was peculiar mostly because of the apparent *need* for such a thing. It would presumably have seemed unnecessary – maybe even redundant – to assemble a themed issue on cultural studies and English or communication, or sociology: not because those disciplines are somehow coterminous with cultural studies, but because, by the late date of 2001, there would have been nothing particularly novel about focusing on the relationship between cultural studies and any of those fields. And while no one has conducted a formal census of where cultural studies lives in the contemporary university, my sense is that history really is underrepresented in the list of disciplines where cultural studies scholars formally take up residence. There are undoubtedly good (or at least understandable) reasons for this gap. The specific circumstances that fueled cultural studies' dramatic growth over the past 20 years or so undoubtedly favored some disciplines and neglected others – to the point where historical accident arguably mattered as much as any 'obvious' or 'natural' intellectual fit between cultural studies and specific disciplinary formations.

That said, it is worth remembering that cultural studies' relationship to the disciplines has always taken different configurations in different national contexts. Cultural studies' extended tussles with sociology over the years owe a lot to the prominence of sociology in the British academy, and to the ways

that cultural studies was often seen to be treading on sociology's turf (Hall, 1990). Cultural studies' love–hate relationship with English arguably owes a comparable debt to the latter's status as the alpha-discipline of the humanities in the US. But, as Meaghan Morris (1997) points out, in Australia, it is history, rather than English, that is generally taken to be the core discipline of the humanities, and Australian historians have generally been more willing to engage with the sorts of theoretical challenges posed by cultural studies than their British counterparts. As such, Australian versions of cultural studies have had a much closer (if not necessarily close) relationship to history as a discipline than has been the case elsewhere around the world.

More crucial, however, is the fact that, wherever it has been practiced, and regardless of whether the scholars involved have been formally trained as historians or not (and, typically, they have not been), cultural studies has arguably *always* been invested in questions of historicity, even when its ostensible focus has been contemporary culture. If nothing else, cultural studies' radical contextualism is also the characteristic that frequently makes 'doing cultural studies' look an awful lot like 'doing history.' Or, perhaps more accurately, it is the characteristic that necessarily forces cultural studies to engage with questions of historicity. And so we might actually be able to reframe cultural studies as an ongoing series of attempts to write a political history of the present: to make sense of the complexities of contemporary culture, to use that knowledge to tell better stories about the world than those we already have, and to use those 'better stories' as a way to build a better world for all of us.

## NOTES

1  Arguably, what Marx means by 'history' in this context revolves around actual events in the world, rather than the stories that we tell about those events ... but, just as arguably, his comments work well both ways.

2   For Deleuze and Guattari, arborescent models of the world are built around central points of origin and, as a result, 'arborescent thought' is inherently essentialist and deterministic in nature. The rhizome, on the other hand, has no singular beginning or ending, and rhizomatic thought attempts to grapple with the world as a shifting multiplicity of interconnected and overlapping forces. For more on the rhizome as it relates to questions of history and historiography, see Rodman (1993).

3   A variety of takes on this issue can be found in Nelson and Gaonkar (1996).

4   Some of the best of these efforts are collected in Grossberg (1997) and Storey (1996). Other notable examples include Bérubé (1994), Felski (2005), Hall (1990, 1992), Morris (1997), Rodman (1997), and Striphas (1998).

5   Significantly, the major potential exceptions to this rule are the various 'area studies' disciplines centered around historically marginalized populations – women's studies, African-American studies, GLBT studies, and so on: i.e., disciplines that were explicitly founded as political acts and that self-consciously took on politically charged subject matter as their core objects of analysis.

6   This fact doesn't prevent many apolitical scholars from claiming that their work is cultural studies – and, in turn, this phenomenon contributes to the broader confusion about what cultural studies actually is. I would suggest – or, more bluntly, insist – that cultural studies needs to be more diligent about calling out such claims for the misappropriations of the 'brand name' that they are.

7   Virtually any 'big' claim about the nature and history of cultural studies is subject to dispute, and pointing to 'the Birmingham school' as cultural studies' point of origin is no exception. Whatever alternate narratives one might choose to consider for where and when something that deserves to be called 'cultural studies' first appeared, however, the fact remains that the first such candidate that actually bears the 'brand name' is *almost* certainly the Centre for Contemporary Cultural Studies. There is some evidence (Carey, 2006) to indicate that, at roughly the same time that the CCCS was getting off the ground in the UK, James Carey independently coined the term as a description for the work he was doing in the Institute of Communications Research at the University of Illinois.

8   Every discipline has its share of scholars who choose to work on questions that are entirely 'inside baseball' in nature: i.e., projects that wrestle with theoretical or methodological problems that generally only matter to other scholars working in the same field. If these projects ever truly matter outside the disciplines from which they spring, it is in a sort of attenuated, 'trickle down' fashion where (for example) clarifying what Scholar X *really* meant when s/he introduced Theoretical Concept Y *might*, at some unspecified and indeterminable future moment in time, allow other scholars to apply Scholar X's work to some 'real world' phenomenon in new and valuable ways.

9   Also see Grossberg (1997), McLeod (2001: 12–16), Rodman (1996: 24–6, 158–60).

# REFERENCES

Bérubé, Michael. 1994. 'Pop goes the academy: cult studs fight the power.' In *Public Access: Literary Theory and American Cultural Politics*, 137–60. New York: Verso.

Carey, James W. 1989. *Communication and Culture: Essays on Media and Society*. Boston, MA: Unwin Hyman.

Carey, James W. 2006. 'From New England to Illinois: the invention of (American) cultural studies.' In *Thinking with James Carey: Essays on Communication, Transportation, History*, ed. Jeremy Packer and Craig Robertson, 199–225. New York: Peter Lang.

Deleuze, Gilles, and Felix Guattari. 1987. *A Thousand Plateaus: Capitalism and Schizophrenia*. (translated by Brian Massumi). Minneapolis, MN: University of Minnesota Press.

Felski, Rita. 2005. 'The role of aesthetics in cultural studies.' In *The Aesthetics of Cultural Studies*, ed. Michael Bérubé, 28–43. Malden, MA: Blackwell.

Gilroy, Paul. 2000. *Against Race: Imagining Political Culture Beyond the Color Line*. Cambridge, MA: Harvard University Press.

Gray, Herman. 2005. *Cultural Moves: African Americans and the Politics of Representation*. Berkeley, CA: University of California Press.

Grossberg, Lawrence. 1995. 'Cultural studies: what's in a name (one more time).' *Taboo: The Journal of Culture and Education* 1: 1–37.

Grossberg, Lawrence. 1997. *Bringing it all Back Home: Essays on Cultural Studies*. Durham, NC: Duke University Press.

Grossberg, Lawrence. 2005. *Caught in the Crossfire: Kids, Politics, and America's Future*. Boulder, CO: Paradigm Publishers.

Grossberg, Lawrence. 2006. 'Does cultural studies have futures? Should it? (or What's the matter with New York?): cultural studies, contexts and conjunctures.' *Cultural Studies* 20(1): 1–32.

Grossberg, Lawrence. 2010. *Cultural Studies in the Future Tense*. Durham, NC: Duke University Press.

Hall, Stuart. 1981. 'Notes on deconstructing "the popular."' In *People's History and Socialist Theory*, ed. Raphael Samuel, 227–240. London: Routledge and Kegan Paul.

Hall, Stuart. 1986. 'On postmodernism and articulation: an interview with Stuart Hall.' *Journal of Communication Inquiry* 10(2): 45–60.

Hall, Stuart. 1990. 'The emergence of cultural studies and the crisis in the humanities.' *October* 53: 11–23.

Hall, Stuart. 1992. 'Cultural studies and its theoretical legacies.' In *Cultural Studies*, ed. Lawrence Grossberg, Cary Nelson, Paula A. Treichler, Linda Baughman, and J. Macgregor Wise, 277–294. New York: Routledge.

Hall, Stuart. 1997. *Representation and the Media* (DVD). Northampton, MA: Media Education Foundation.

Hall, Stuart. 2007. 'That moment and this.' Paper presented at the conference, 'Cultural Studies Now,' University of East London, London, UK, July.

Hall, Stuart, Chas Critcher, Tony Jefferson, John Clarke, and Brian Roberts. 1978. *Policing the Crisis: Mugging, the State, and Law and Order*. New York: Holmes & Meier Publishers.

Marx, Karl. 1978. 'The eighteenth brumaire of Louis Bonaparte.' In *The Marx-Engels Reader*, 2nd edn, ed. R.C. Tucker, 594–617. New York: W.W. Norton & Company.

McLeod, Kembrew. 2001. *Owning Culture: Authorship, Ownership, and Intellectual Property Law*. New York: Peter Lang.

Morris, Meaghan. 1997. 'A question of cultural studies.' In *Back to Reality?: Social Experience and Cultural Studies*, ed. Angela McRobbie, 36–57. New York: Manchester University Press.

Morris, Meaghan. 1998. *Too Soon Too Late: History in Popular Culture*. Bloomington, IN: Indiana University Press.

Nelson, Cary, and Dilip Parameshwar Gaonkar, eds. 1996. *Disciplinarity and dissent in cultural studies*. New York: Routledge.

Radway, Janice A. 1997. *A Feeling for Books: The Book-of-the-Month Club, Literary Taste, and Middle-Class Desire*. Chapel Hill, NC: University of North Carolina Press.

Rodman, Gilbert B. 1993. 'Making a better mystery out of history: of plateaus, roads, and traces.' *Meanjin*, 52(2): 295–312.

Rodman, Gilbert B. 1996. *Elvis after Elvis: The Posthumous Career of a Living Legend*. New York: Routledge.

Rodman, Gilbert B. 1997. 'Subject to debate: (Mis)reading cultural studies.' *Journal of Communication Inquiry* 21(2): 56–69.

Rodman, Gilbert B. 1999. 'Histories.' In *Popular Music and Culture: New Essays on Key Terms*, ed. Thomas Swiss and Bruce Horn, 35–45. Malden, MA: Blackwell.

Rodman, Gilbert B. 2006. 'Race ... and other four letter words: Eminem and the cultural politics of authenticity.' *Popular Communication*, 4(2): 95–121.

Rodman, Gilbert B. forthcoming. *Why Cultural Studies?* Malden, MA: Blackwell.

Stabile, Carol A. 2006. *White Victims, Black Villains: Gender, Race, and Crime News in US Culture*. New York: Routledge.

Storey, John, ed. 1996. *What is Cultural studies?: A Reader*. New York: Arnold.

Striphas, Ted. 1998. 'The long march: cultural studies and its institutionalization.' *Cultural Studies* 12(4): 453–75.

# 22

# Memory: Witness, Experience, Collective Meaning

Patrick H. Hutton

## THE CONTEMPORARY DISCOURSE ABOUT MEMORY AND THE POSTMODERN TEMPERAMENT

Memory as a topic for historians rose precipitously within the scholarship of the 1980s and has maintained a prominent historiographical presence ever since.[1] A marginal, somewhat arcane interest of the new cultural history during the 1960s – notably through Frances Yates' highly acclaimed study of the Renaissance art of memory – memory studies by the turn of the twenty-first century had reshaped the research and understanding of cultural history, enriching both its methods and content. As a new field of historical investigation that matured rapidly, the phenomenon of memory studies sheds light on the way a field of historiography develops – from bold pioneers blocking out new interpretations, to the more cautious specialists who follow, and ironically to latecomers re-presenting the interpretative insights of the pioneers, once the memory of their accomplishment has begun to fade from view. The historiography of memory studies also reveals the way in which initially provocative interpretative forays into a new field of scholarly inquiry are eventually chastened as they are reassessed and integrated into the larger body of historical scholarship.

The historians' preoccupation with memory in the late twentieth century may be attributed to anxieties about the breakdown of long-standing collective identities, undermined by new historical realities that contributed to their dissolution – globalizing economic forces that challenged the primacy of national identity, a social movement for the emancipation of women that reconfigured the politics of gender and complicated gender identities, the fads of fantasy-driven consumerism that blurred the line between fiction and reality, and the perception of the acceleration of time promoted by a media revolution whose capacity to evoke images approached the instantaneous. At the risk of reductionism, one might argue that the waxing interest in collective memory may be understood as a response to the waning authority of traditions that had lent stability to social and cultural identity in the modern age. In this respect, the discourse about memory is closely allied with a parallel one about postmodernism, which likewise addressed issues of dissolving identities amidst the breakdown of long-established traditions.

The memory phenomenon in late twentieth century historiography may be construed as the first serious effort to assess the divide between memory and history as modes of understanding the past. For much of the nineteenth century, historians, like their readers, thought little about their differences, and tended to conflate them in their excursions into the past. They aspired not only to interpret those times but also to convey to their readers some feeling for its imagination. The public came to value the study of history not only for intellectual edification but also for emotional empathy. Long after their work has been superseded by more exacting scholarship, well-known historians such as Jules Michelet and Benedetto Croce continued to be admired for their capacity to evoke the passion in the pageant of the past. Memory and history were thought to cooperate in the quest to approach the impossible dream of its resurrection.

In the professional historical scholarship that emerged in the early twentieth century, memory and history were understood to operate in tandem. History offered itself as the official form of memory. It claimed to provide a rigorously critical interpretation of the remembered past, chastening collective memory by excising its exaggerations and misconceptions. It prided itself on its accuracy, objectivity, dispassion, and critical distance from the past. It confirmed that claim by its appeal to method and to evidence. Historical scholarship was regarded as a high responsibility because it corrects the misperceptions of memory, and so lends stability to human understanding of the past. In its best analyses, history in its modern scholarly guise offered a perspective on the past based on reliable certainties, and so was regarded as a particular kind of science. As French historian Jacques Le Goff put it, 'memory is the raw material of history.' History begins where memory ends. Its authority depends on the historicist proposition that there is an underlying temporal foundation in which all past experience is grounded. The timeline of history serves as the essential frame of reference for a universal 'science of time.'[2]

As for collective memory considered on its own merits, historians of an earlier generation thought of it as the stuff of immemorial tradition.[3] Learned interest in the nature of tradition first surfaced in the mid-twentieth century in the scholarship of the French Annales School of historiography, notably as its historians addressed questions about collective mentalities within the context of social history. Lucien Febvre and his student Robert Mandrou sought to account for the inertial power of the habits of mind, customs, and other cultural conventions that resisted the initiatives and innovations of the long-range trend toward modernization from the sixteenth century.[4] Most late twentieth-century students of memory, however, stressed not tradition's stubborn resistance to change but rather its protean nature. The watchword of recent historical scholarship on memory is its fragility. As a faculty of mind conspicuous for its elusive nature, memory for today's historians is of particular interest for its susceptibility to manipulation.[5]

Signaling this changing scholarly stance on the nature and significance of collective memory was Eric Hobsbawm and Terence Ranger's *The Invention of Tradition* (1983).[6] The use of the term 'invention' was meant to be provocative, underscoring memory's constructive nature. The authors contended that the appeal to immemorial tradition by nineteenth-century European statesmen lay in its authority to further their immediate political objectives. Tradition, far from ingenuously reaffirming respect for a venerable past, was pressed into service to legitimize practical projects of nation-building. The book was wildly successful. Ten years after its publication, Ranger pointed out that it had been mentioned in every grant application to major American funding agencies in the social sciences during that interval.[7]

The term 'collective memory' in contemporary scholarly discourse includes more than a single meaning. The historiographical phenomenon of memory studies might better be characterized as a convergence of interests, derived from different sources and based on different models. As a starter, one must distinguish episodic from semantic memory. Episodic memory concerns the evocation of particular events; semantic memory deals with commonly shared habits of mind. But their relationship is more complex because episodes frequently recalled over time tend to conflate into abstract images. To put it differently, episodic memory passes imperceptibly into semantic memory, in which memories of actual experience are absorbed into larger fields of imaginative representation. In this way, collective memory is eventually integrated into collective mentalities, suggesting why Annales historians were initially drawn to the topic.[8] Some scholars contend that such collective images are not memories at all, but rather signatures of commonplace social and cultural attitudes that have evolved over time. This seems an exaggeration, for personal testimony about lived experience is invariably the deep source of collective memory, however much its imagery may have been altered over the course of time. Still, the proposition that remembered experience is eventually reduced to its idealized representations has become a central proposition in historical studies of memory. Since memory imports the past into the contexts of the present, it is vulnerable to refashioning to suit present needs. There is, therefore, a politics to memory, and historians today study commemorative representations of the past to unearth the secrets of the political agendas they hide.

The historians' late twentieth-century interest in the dubious reliability of collective memory led to their re-acquaintance with the seminal studies by the largely forgotten French sociologist Maurice Halbwachs during the 1920s.[9] Halbwachs argued that all personal memories are localized within social contexts that frame the way they are recalled. Without such social support, they tend to fade, for the way individuals remember is a function of the relative power of the

social groups to which they belong. Moreover, the particularities of personal memories in often repeated behavior are eventually worn down into social stereotypes. Only their most salient features stand out as these remembered episodes are telescoped into present times. The long-range effect is to transform mnemic images into eidetic icons. In this sense, collective memory is only residually the recollection of actual experiences, as its images are reconfigured to conform to contemporary cultural conceptions. Halbwachs tested his thesis in a case study of the localization of an imaginary landscape of the Holy Land by European pilgrims visiting Palestine from the fourth to the fifteenth centuries. Redeployed in the scholarship of the late twentieth century, his model came to serve as a prototype for method in this field.[10]

In the 1920s, Halbwachs approached the workings of memory as a refutation of the teachings of Sigmund Freud. Freud believed that individual memories remain intact in the recesses of the unconscious mind, from which they may be recovered through psychoanalytic technique. His method involved 'working through' idealized 'screen' memories that blocked access to troubling experiences that had induced a traumatic forgetfulness. Recovery of these repressed memories was the surest route to self-knowledge. In his later years, he expanded his theory to encompass collective memory, though scholars debate whether he explained adequately how such imagery is transmitted over time. His findings about the resurfacing of repressed collective memory, of the sort he presents in his *Totem and Taboo* (1913) and *Moses and Monotheism* (1939), flirt with the notion of a collective unconscious, one that today seems naïve in light of all that we have since learned about cultural communication. The Freudian-inspired field of psychohistory, briefly prominent in the scholarship of the 1960s, eventually slipped to the margins of academic interest.[11] While Halbwachs' claims for the social foundations of all memory may be exaggerated, his focus on memory's dynamic character was better attuned to late twentieth-century worries about memory's unstable nature. Still, the appeal of Freud's approach has persisted, particularly in the examination of unresolved issues of the era of the Second World War. Coming to terms with the historical significance of the Holocaust became a major scholarly preoccupation during the 1980s, and Freud's theory was initially invoked to deal with it. The panorama of late twentieth-century memory studies, therefore, may be read as a tension between the prototypical models devised by Halbwachs and Freud.

Now, decades after their inauguration, memory studies have been institutionalized in a myriad of specialized applications. Issues of memory now occupy a prominent place in doctoral research, where case studies in such scholarship abound. Conferences devoted to the memory phenomenon are regularly convened around the world. At least two internationally recognized learned journals, *History and Memory*, and *Memory Studies* are exclusively devoted to the topic, and there is now a website, H-Memory, for intellectual exchange among researchers in this field.[12] Its subject matter continues to diversify. But one can still trace the royal roads along which such scholarship initially traveled. Here I note three major pathways: the uses of memory in relation to the invention of new technologies of communication (from manuscript literacy to media culture); the politics of commemoration (concerned with anchoring or contesting identities); and the relationship between trauma and memory (problems pertaining to the historical representation of disordered emotional experience).

## MEMORY AND NEWLY INVENTED TECHNOLOGIES OF COMMUNICATION

There is a history of the uses of memory that correlates closely with inventions in the technologies of communication that date from the primordial past. Historians have long been interested in the prodigious memories of the Homeric rhapsodes of ancient Greece.

Early in the twentieth century, pioneering scholars Milman Parry and Harry Lord showed how storytellers in this milieu of primary orality relied on resources of memory largely abandoned today. Trained for the recitation of long epic poems, the Homeric rhapsodes displayed formidable powers of recall. These were enhanced by mnemonic techniques for stitching together episodes into a basic plot line with the help of formulaic phrasing. No one ever told the same tale in exactly the same way. Over centuries of oral recitation, moreover, these epics must have evolved imperceptibly with the changing realities of the times, for oral memory is a present-minded expression of a dynamic imagination. Parry and Lord buttressed their argument by observing Serbo-Croatian storytellers of their own day, who used the same mnemonic techniques and whose powers of recitation weakened dramatically once they were introduced to literacy.[13] The storytellers' uses of memory, they showed, are closely related to the technologies of communication available to them.

The scope of such studies expanded and diversified during the 1960s. Originally of interest only to classicists and folklorists, the topic came to stimulate broad scholarly interest across the social sciences, thanks to the visibly expanding presence and ever more intrusive influence of media culture in the contemporary world. Scholars could see that the move from cultures of primary orality into those of manuscript literacy was but the first in a series of revolutions in the technologies of communication across two millennia that had transforming effects on perception, the uses of memory, and the organization of knowledge. In this heuristic perspective on technology as a force of change in the broad sweep of cultural history, scholars noted a long-range process of relocating reliable knowledge from the memory banks of a well-ordered mind into external archives available for public consultation. In each transition, the methods for organizing human knowledge were re-invented and the understanding of human memory reconceived.[14]

The principal faculties of memory – imagination and preservation – originally so closely bound, over time came to be thought of as powers apart.

Elements of this far-ranging approach to cultural history emerged piecemeal. An early pioneer was the Russian psychologist Alexander Luria, who during the 1930s conducted field studies of the effects of literacy on previously illiterate populations in central Asia.[15] He noted rapid cognitive changes from a concrete to an abstract mindset with the advent of literacy. Historians of orality/literacy have learned much, too, from the field work of anthropologists who have studied twentieth-century African communities in the midst of their passage from orality into literacy.[16] The clearest explanation of the changing psychology attending the move from poetical orality into prosaic literacy – a shift of the primacy of perception from ear to eye – may be found in the studies by the late Walter Ong, a professor of rhetoric at St Louis University and once a student of Marshall McLuhan.[17]

Not surprisingly, research in this field clustered around these times of transition between old and newly invented modes of communication: notably that from orality into manuscript literacy in antiquity (seventh century BCE to first century CE); and from manuscript to print literacy in the early modern era (sixteenth to eighteenth centuries). At each threshold, ideas about memory were reformulated. Each transition marked a significant departure from the modes of memory in cultures of primary orality, as Parry and Lord had earlier explained. The reorientation of Homeric studies to illustrate the cultural consequences of the transition from orality into literacy first appeared in Eric Havelock's *Preface to Plato* (1963), which traced the changing mindset of the Athenians from the Mycenaean (twelfth to tenth centuries BCE) to the Classical Age (sixth to fifth centuries BCE). Ideas expressed poetically in the speech of Homer were recast in a philosophical idiom in the writings of Plato, so that the meaning of the former was incomprehensible to the latter. In this way, Havelock explained why Plato came to believe that Homer 'told lies about the Gods.'[18]

Biblical scholars, too, took advantage of memory studies for identifying oral residues in the New Testament. Noteworthy is the work of the Jesus Seminar, directed by Robert Funk and Roy Hoover. In their preface to *The Five Gospels: What Jesus Really Said* (1993), they invoked Halbwachs' methods to explain how the manuscript gospels incorporated the idealizations of the oral tradition of primitive Christianity. Jesus of Nazareth was a Jewish teacher speaking to a society in moral crisis, they argued, and his sermons were ethical, not messianic. As a preacher, moreover, he never wrote anything down. The writings of the Evangelists, who exposed his life and thought, were composed some 40–60 years after his death. In these texts, testimony of the sayings of Jesus is intermixed with later interpretations of their meaning. Funk and Hoover convened a group of eminent research scholars to study the gospels as literary artifacts that encoded two generations of oral testimony. Participants in the seminar wrestled with these juxtapositions of first-hand testimony and later remembrance, seeking to factor out the pithy aphorisms that Jesus may have uttered from more elaborate idealization of his intentions in the oral tradition perpetuated by his followers.[19] For several years, seminar scholars debated their relationship by casting color-coded ballots for each passage of the major gospels. This sorting process became a basis not only for understanding the historical Jesus but also for fixing the dates of composition of these texts devoted to his memory on the basis of the degree to which they idealized his life and transformed his ethical sayings into theological prophecies.

The manuscript culture of the Middle Ages served as the context for the prestige of the art of memory as an essential skill of rhetoric. As a mnemonic technique, the art had been invented on the threshold of manuscript literacy in the Greco-Roman world. It would play an essential role in education throughout the Middle Ages, whose culture remained heavily dependent on the protocols of orality for the organization and dissemination of knowledge. The classical art of memory held pride of intellectual place in medieval councils of learning, an instrument well-suited not only to the needs of accurate public exposition but also for a society that believed imagery to be the medium connecting empirical and transcendental knowledge.[20]

This interest in the art of memory as a method for intellectual speculation serves as the setting for understanding the historiographical significance of the work of Frances Yates, almost always cited as a founding figure in contemporary memory studies. Yates' book on the art of memory, published in 1966, was the first to examine the intellectual uses of the art in its cultural contexts. But Yates' work had nothing to do with the issue of fragile collective identities that gave memory studies their distinctive appeal in the late twentieth century. Rather, she focused on the belief in memory's powers to interpret the cosmos within the intellectual tradition of Renaissance idealism. She explained the uses of the art by neo-Platonic philosophers, with particular attention to their speculative purposes. Sixteenth-century magi, such as Giulio Camillo, Giordano Bruno, and Robert Fludd, believed that their ornately decorated memory palaces mirrored the structure of the universe, and so contained the keys to its understanding. Celebrating the harmony between divine and human power of mind, their architectonic designs might be regarded as supernova of the intellectual quest of a waning philosophical idealism. As Yates pointed out, all such philosophical speculation about the hermetic knowledge contained in mnemonic schemes was eclipsed by seventeenth-century empiricism, and the art of memory as a resource of learning began to fade with the invention of the printing press.[21]

The spread of print culture in the early modern era is the other major venue to which students of the technologies of communication gravitated, all the more significant because it signaled the crucial transition from ear to eye in the uses of memory. These studies opened a new perspective on the nature of the Enlightenment, shifting interest from the *philosophes* of this intellectual renaissance to the rapidly expanding cadre of readers eager to digest their teachings in a culture in which the printed word made knowledge more accessible to the public than ever before. Intellectual historians of an earlier generation once made much of the efficacy of the print revolution of the fifteenth century, for it was a factor in the success of the German Reformation. But today's students of the coming of print culture prefer its interpretation as a long revolution in the democratization of reading. Only by the eighteenth century was the subject matter of print culture sufficiently diversified and its public adequately literate to make manifest its far-reaching cultural effects. The Enlightenment, once studied for its writers, has for these scholars become as important for its readers, and it is out of their mindset that the modern uses of memory came to the fore.[22] In the creation of a reading public, the Enlightenment witnessed the emergence of a 'republic of letters' as a newly imagined community.[23]

The cultural effects of print literacy were evinced in two ways. On the one hand, printed matter moved facts to be remembered into books and encyclopedias, more accessible to far more people than had been the manuscript archives of an earlier age. In a subtle way, the active evocation of public memory through ready recall gave way to its private consultation in these compendia of knowledge. Robert Darnton is the most readable of the students of print culture. His early scholarship concerned the making of the *Encyclopédie* as the key tool for the organization and preservation of knowledge in the modern era of print culture.[24] But his best-seller, *The Great Cat Massacre* (1984) reached a wider audience. In a series of artfully told stories, he canvassed the new social types born of the emerging age of print literacy: printers, hack writers, editors, clerks, and readers of novels.[25]

On the other hand, the vastly expanded archival capacities of book culture freed the literate mind for a new kind of introspection.

The search for the self turned on new uses of personal memory, which writers of the day portrayed as the deep source of identity. William Wordsworth and Jean-Jacques Rousseau inaugurated a Romantic cult of introspection in their autobiographical writings.[26] The modern novel, too, became a mirror for self-reflection, deepening the valuation of personal identity in the modern age. The novel as an aid to self-analysis received its most profound statement in Marcel Proust's *A la recherche du temps perdu* (1913–27), which extolled the illuminating power of involuntary recall to transform the memory of a single incident into an entire milieu of remembrance.[27] The modern cult of private memory as soul-searching for personal identity would eventually acquire a scientific gloss in the psychoanalytic techniques of Sigmund Freud, who elevated the intuitive insight of the Romantics into a Positivist scientific principle.[28] This emerging divide between private and public memory reinforced the modern distinction between private and public life.

Today we wonder whether print culture is dwindling into insignificance, given the overwhelming influence of media culture. The invention of the World Wide Web has vastly accelerated the long-range trend toward the externalization of memory's resources for preservation and retrieval of information, further obviating the need for a well-ordered mind for data recall. The display of powers of rote memory through the memorization of poetry and apt quotations has long since lost the esteemed place it once held in pedagogy, and has been relegated to televised game shows as an impressive if inessential talent in a culture in which so much information is immediately available online.[29] But digital technology has also come to provide stimulating forums for unleashing memory's imaginative powers to fashion imagery in a newly created cyberspace in which the boundary between memory and fantasy is easily traversed.[30]

The effect of the passage from print to media literacy on the uses of memory is just beginning to receive scholarly attention. There are some provocative forays. In his study of the memory banks of the World Wide Web, Jay David Bolter has pointed out how the digital organization of knowledge in websites mimics the places and images of the classical art of memory.[31] One visits websites as one once followed the topics of the rhetorician. At these places of memory, one clicks icons on a computer screen as one had once located eidetic images on a mnemonic design. Each subsequent click on a newly appearing screen leads deeper into the recesses of knowledge encoded in cyberspace. Triggered by icons, topics displace alphabetical indexing as the basic mode for organizing knowledge.

Electronic culture has created its own anxieties about memory. These have surfaced most frequently in a discourse about biology. Longer life spans in the affluent societies of the Western world have been accompanied by rising worries about maladies of memory in the aging brain. But voicing them also suggests visceral uneasiness about the loss of the need to remember in a culture in which innovation is so greatly valued and heritage so easily trivialized in the kitsch of commercial advertising.[32] Without minimizing its brutal ravages as a pathology of the aging brain, Alzheimer's disease has become a metaphor for contemporary fears about collective as well as individual amnesia.

More upbeat is the argument advanced by essayist Nicholas Carr concerning the resilience of human memory in the face of the digital revolution. A humanist who writes about the cultural effects of new technologies, he offers a lucid overview of recent research in the neuroscience of memory. He cautions against drawing an analogy between biological memory and the artificial intelligence of electronic storage and communication. Having become accustomed over two centuries to housing data we wish to remember in external archives, we are tempted to liken the workings of our memories to those of a data processor. The metaphor of such 'outsourcing,' he claims, has led us astray. Our brains are not machines; nor are our memories simple aggregates of information. Biological memory, he explains, involves ongoing mapping and remapping of neural networks, and is fundamentally different from, indeed incommensurable with, computerized memory. Drawing on the research of neuroscientist Eric Kandel (among others), he explains that biological memory is dynamic and boundless, adapting and even growing through its creative improvisations to meet the challenges of the existential world. Computer memory, by contrast, is static and self-contained. His point is that our growing dependence on the Internet, far from freeing our minds for imaginative play, enthralls us in distractions that disrupt the concerted attention needed for reflective interaction with others and within ourselves.[33]

## THE POLITICS OF COMMEMORATION

Studies in the politics of commemoration began to appear in the late 1970s, prompted by challenges to the primacy of national identity in world affairs.[34] In an age of tightening political connections worldwide, the nation-state as the principle referent of collective identity was beset by competing allegiances at both the global and the local level. It is not surprising that these early studies of commemoration were pioneered by French scholars, for France was a nation perplexed by its identity in the contemporary world, conflicted over issues of the waning of its revolutionary tradition, the fading of its past glories as a great nation, and its uncertain future as but one among many partners in an emerging European confederation. Preeminent among these ventures was the elaborate study of the French national memory, *Les Lieux de mémoire* (1984–92) edited by publisher Pierre Nora. A collaborative venture of some 50 scholars, the project was designed to inventory the myriad of topics that had contributed to the making of the modern French identity since the Middle Ages. In organizing the study, Nora reversed the

timeline of history, descending from the present into the past, much as one might trace a family tree. In keeping with the postmodern temper of the times, Nora and his colleagues de-constructed the French national memory genealogically, digging deep into the diversity of its cultural heritage. In the process, they set aside the modern grand narrative of French history that centered on its eighteenth-century revolution. Plans for its bicentennial were then underway, and Nora's project signaled mixed feelings about the meaning of the celebration.[35] Scholarly contributors to this project hardly mention the French Revolution, which, in the ardent historiographical debates about its legacies carried on over two centuries, had served as the moral touchstone of modern French identity. Historian Steven Englund has noted the elegiac quality of Nora's editorial prose, and one might argue that the objectives of the project get lost in Nora's lofty rhetoric.[36] This novel effort to complicate the issue of national identity nonetheless whetted the historians' interest.[37] It inspired like projects about memory and collective identity not only in France but around the world.

From the practical perspective of professional scholarship, such studies in the politics of commemoration have appealed to historians for the certainties they promise to report about commemorative practices themselves. While collective memory may be elusive and commemorative rhetoric tendentious, historians recognized that they could systematically inventory and describe the practices themselves – the monuments, museums, eulogies, rituals of commemoration, and iconic pictorial representations of martyrs and heroes. While memories evolve, these artifacts remain anchored in fixed times and places. The interpretative interest lies in explaining how these places of memory were invested with changing meanings over time, particularly if they became objects of contested identity in light of changing constellations of political power.

It would be impossible in an essay of this length to inventory, let alone analyze, the specialized contributions to scholarship on the politics of commemoration. Such studies are now legion, most of them devoted to the role of official remembrance in the making of public identities. They draw attention to the commemoration of dramatic events or celebrated personalities. Early topics especially favored by historians include memorials of the First World War, remembrance of the American Civil War, and iconic personalities, such as Abraham Lincoln.[38] But the list now extends far beyond, reaching into the intriguing recesses of mnemonic souvenirs.[39]

Exemplary as a model in this genre is Yael Zerubavel's *Recovered Roots* (1995) for her explanation of the way national memory is created and refashioned over time. She shows how leaders of the newly created nation-state of Israel constructed an official heritage by juxtaposing widely removed and unrelated episodes in Jewish history, two ancient (Masada, Bar Kokhba) and one modern (Tel Hai). She traces the evolution of Israeli national memory from sacred to profane conceptions in a politically charged cycle – from veneration of these episodes to their comic deflation once the foundations of this fledgling nation-state were secure.[40] Her study suggests that the perennially popular notion that history moves in cycles actually concerns the cyclical dynamics of the cultural recourse to memory. In a somewhat different vein, the sociologist Mary Douglas visits this theme in her study of the way institutional memory in modern bureaucracies tends to run in cycles, as practices are invented, modified, and then forgotten, only to be invented anew.[41]

## TRAUMA AND MEMORY

The third and for a time the most intensely studied approach to memory studies concerned the historical task of recovering memories of the Holocaust, both personal and collective. In the decades since the end of the Second World War, the genocide of European Jews by the Nazis has taken on greater moment among historians as an 'unmasterable past' that demands careful reflection and study as a prelude to writing its history.[42] In light of the intensity of the controversy about 'historicizing' the suffering of the victims of the Holocaust, the relationship between trauma and memory came for a time to overshadow other approaches.[43] The learned journal *History and Memory*, launched in Israel in 1989, was during the following decade largely devoted to this topic.

Memory in Holocaust studies is now a vast field of scholarship. But a good place to begin is the early work of the Israeli historian Saul Friedländer, who explored the relationship between memory and history in his own efforts as a Holocaust survivor to recover his lost childhood identity. A Czech refugee, he wrote a memoir about his survival as an adolescent in Vichy France during the war years under an assumed identity, and of his immigration to Palestine after the war to take on a new identity in the incipient Israeli nation. His memoir is about the way his memories of his childhood came back in middle age in fragments, little by little.[44] The need of survivors like Friedländer to work through the trauma of their ordeal gave new life to Freud's theory of psychoanalysis.[45] Freud's method of working through repressed memory as a preliminary step to writing histories of the Holocaust served as a central tenet of work in this field.[46]

The 'Historians Controversy' (*Historikerstreit*) in West Germany during the mid-1980s dramatized the argument about the necessity of attending to memory before turning to history. Ernst Nolte, a scholar well known for his studies of fascism, proposed that 50 years after the Holocaust it was time to 'historicize' its memory. A number of scholars challenged his proposal, contending that any such interpretative assessment was premature. Frankfurt School scholar Jürgen Habermas, for example, argued that the narrative of German history, derived from the imperial ambitions of the Wilhelmine era, was itself in need of thorough-going re-conceptualization.[47] It was not yet time to locate the Holocaust within any narrative context. Too many unresolved moral issues still needed processing, he contended. The controversy raised the question of whether the meaning of the Holocaust could ever be adequately treated through historical interpretation, given the exceptional nature of its atrocities. In this way, the Historian's Controversy of the 1980s led into a debate about the limits of representation during the 1990s. Friedländer, Habermas, and their colleagues pondered how and to what degree historians could adequately convey the suffering that victims knew. Here was a realm of memory that seemingly defied historical representation.[48]

The French historian Henry Rousso offered a parallel study of the relationship between trauma and collective memory as a legacy of the Holocaust in France. In some ways, the French case was more difficult to confront, for the French in the postwar era had been more reluctant than the Germans to admit their complicity in the Nazi's project. But Michael Marrus and Robert Paxton's well-documented study of the plight of Jews in Vichy France, published in 1981, obliged French historians, and the French public, to take a hard look at their morally compromised past.[49] Their book raised issues that led belatedly to some sensational prosecutions, and exposed the way in which Vichy's complicity in Nazi policies vitiated the careers of some of France's eminent politicians, even the highly regarded socialist president François Mitterrand.[50] It was for this reason that Rousso's *Vichy Syndrome* (1989) had such a profound effect on French studies of the war years. Like the German scholars, he cast his argument in psycho-analytic terms. He argued that after the war French leaders put away their unhappy memories in the name of starting over under the banner of national reconciliation. Some apologized for Philippe Pétain's pliant collaboration as a necessary expedient for a defeated nation, and all agreed that it was better to move on. The repressed memories of unresolved issues relating to the war, however, continually resurfaced in its aftermath with undiminished vehemence. In each postwar crisis, and most ardently in that over the future of Algeria, the 'Vichy Syndrome' stirred up unrequited controversies. As Rousso and his co-author Eric Conan entitled a follow-up book on the subject, this was 'a past that would not pass away,' a troubling memory that defied historical evaluation that would put it to rest.[51]

Scholars agree that the Holocaust was an exceptional event, unprecedented and of a magnitude of infamy impossible to match. But cultural historian Alon Confino has recently challenged the notion that its history remains an 'unmasterable past.' As an historical episode, he explains, it resides on the extremes of human suffering, but from a historical standpoint is no more inscrutable than any other historical event. He argues that the discussion of the Holocaust in history is overdetermined in its recourse to psycho-analytic vocabulary and to its exaggerated claims about repressed memory. We do not master the past by arriving at a consensus that brings 'closure,' i.e., settles all problems for all time. Rather we learn from the experience of the past to which we may never be completely reconciled, and each generation must do so anew. He wonders whether Holocaust memory was ever as completely repressed during the immediate decades after the war as some scholars have argued, and suggests instead that it is rather a growing awareness of the historical magnitude of the evil of the Nazi's project that has become more evident over time. Certainly, there was more discussion of the Holocaust during the 1970s and the 1980s, but that may have to do with the way its memory was publicized in films, books, and other exposés that made the public aware of its proportions as an atrocity. But during the decades immediately after the war, there were less publicized assessments and historians today face the neglected task of evaluating their historiographical importance.[52]

Studies of trauma and the memory of the Holocaust have maintained a staying power.[53] Recent work, however, has moved on to issues attending the integration of the memory of the Holocaust into historical narratives about coming to terms with its legacies. The sociologist Jeffrey Olick has traced the way the West German government over the course of nearly a half century struggled to integrate acknowledgment of the evils of Nazi atrocities into formal rituals of atonement, a symbolic reckoning with Germany's past calculated to spare younger generations from association with the crimes of their ancestors.[54] In a sensitively written and thoughtful memoir dealing with memory's reconfigurations over time, Canadian essayist Eva Hoffman explores the changing meaning of the Holocaust for descendants of its survivors as they take up responsibility for imparting its moral lessons to posterity.[55]

Among students of memory, the Holocaust would in time become a reference for interpreting other genocides, which if not of the same proportions, were nonetheless comparable in their cruelty or indifference to fundamental human values. In 2001, Michael Roth and Charles Salas published the proceedings of a conference on diverse twentieth-century atrocities around the globe as a way of understanding history from the vantage point of the extreme margins of experience – from the atrocities in Rwanda to the bureaucratic indifference of Chinese governmental leaders to the suffering of their citizens, to the devious cruelty of Stalinist agents in quelling the uprising in Hungary in 1956. Holocaust studies remained the anchor of this venture, and the volume returns to Germany in its conclusion in essays by Friedländer and Jörn Rüsen about the way historical perspectives on the Holocaust have changed over several generations. The Holocaust may have been unprecedented. But even in its singularity, it came to be viewed as a point of reference for genocides that have followed, sobering portents for the future of humankind.[56]

As a fitting postscript to all the work on memory and history in Holocaust studies, historian Gabrielle Spiegel has offered an insightful perspective on the tendency among these scholars to accord to memory the status of history.[57] Drawing on the work on Jewish religious tradition by Yosef Yerushalmi, she sets memory and history apart on the basis of

their opposing conceptions of historical time. Collective memory evokes the presence of the past. Particularly in its ritual expressions, it contributes to a sense of reliving the past as an act of renewal. Its understanding of time is accordingly cyclical. History, by contrast, establishes a distance between past and present. It insists on the singularity of events that occur but once and for all time. As a conception of time, therefore, history is linear.

Spiegel pursues this distinction in two contexts of Jewish religious thought: that of the Middle Ages and that of the era of the Holocaust and its aftermath. In the earlier era, the distinction between memory and history was clear. Religious Jews thought in terms of sacred time, a realm apart from historical time. All events, even those of suffering and unhappiness, were integrated into the cycles of Jewish tradition in hope of their eventual redemption. In the era of the Holocaust, such a conception of the redemptive quality of collective memory within tradition ceased to offer consolation to its survivors. The Nazi project of genocide included the obliteration of all memory of the Jews.[58] It was a historical event impossible to integrate into the sacred time of remembered tradition. Holocaust memories, therefore, took on the singularity of history, 'fugitive memories' outside living tradition and history alike. The strategy of some Holocaust historians, Spiegel contends, was to privilege the privatizing of such memories. For Holocaust survivors, their memories stood apart from the collective memory of shared faith. In the memory/ history controversy, therefore, the possibility of historical understanding was compressed between inaccessible private memories and historiographical discussion of the limits of historical representation.

Spiegel further notes that this discussion of the Holocaust between memory and history permits comparison with Nora's project on the French national memory. Nora, too, addressed collective memory at the end of and apart from the traditions in which it was once immersed. Memories divorced from living tradition cannot bind people collectively but rather isolate them individually. They come to be perceived as discrete episodes, belonging neither to tradition nor history, but only to topical places in historiographical schemes of the sort that Nora devised. The question is whether the structures of time that appear as constants in Spiegel's interpretation have since been recast in the historiography of the memory phenomenon. Memory studies point to the de-stabilization of the structures of historical time, drawing history closer to memory in the presentist perspective toward which it gravitated in the late twentieth century. This perspective has led to reflection on the mnemonics of historical time.

## MEMORY'S NEWFOUND CLAIMS UPON THE PAST

In its many venues, the intense interest in the history of memory had the unintended effect of unsettling long-established conventions of historical narration. Historians justifiably profess impartiality and dispassion in their research and writing. But memory studies called attention to subjective factors in historical interpretation that challenge their claims to objectivity. History and memory may be of a different order. But as the ongoing discussions of the relationship between them have revealed, they impinge on one another today in self-conscious ways.

Historiographical discussion of the memory phenomenon could not help but highlight the mnemonic character of historical interpretation. Phrased in the parlance of memory studies, historians provide mnemonic cues to their readers in the way they write history. Historians have the power to frame what the public recollects out of the past. If historians are the guardians of public memory, they are its arbiters as well. They not only sanction the past that is to be remembered but also shape the way it is presented. As a minimum, memory studies led some historians to suggest that problems of interpretation be addressed with greater modesty by acknowledging the realities of bias, psycho-analytical factors in

authorship, and the limits of historical representation. As a maximum, such studies raised broader issues about historical narration, historical time, and the representation of the experience of the past.

The changing tenor of historiographical discussion of the issue of historical objectivity is evident in Peter Novick's *That Noble Dream* (1986), widely adopted as a basic text in graduate historiography courses in American universities.[59] Challenging the 'noble dream' of historical objectivity, Novick sought to expose the bias, distortions, and omissions in the master narratives of American history. He pointed out how American historians with a certain naïveté had long presented a past they wanted to remember. From the founding of the American Historical Association in 1884 until well into the twentieth century, eminent historians tended to favor a patriotic view of American identity that denied the divisive realities of class conflict, racial and ethnic discrimination, and the diverse viewpoints of an expanding immigrant population. He drew attention to the near impossibility of obtaining such detachment, and to the insidious temptation to treat objectivity as if it were no more than a consensus of viewpoint promoting professional harmony. The noble dream of historical objectivity, he maintained, is an illusion when tested against the actual debates about the past that have impassioned American historiography since its inception. As this historiography of patriotic consensus fragmented from the mid-twentieth century, he pointed out, a new generation of practicing historians sought to reclaim the forgotten past of women, African Americans, Native-Americans, and other marginalized groups, while those with a theoretical bent proposed new categories of conceptualization to frame a more complex historical memory, notably through models for gender studies, the history of collective mentalities, and global history. In the process, they subverted the political identities previously highlighted by modern American historiography. Implicit in his presentation of historiographical controversies from across

American history is the notion that it is better to understand and accept contested interpretations than to deny them in the name of a specious objectivity.

In problematizing history's subject matter, memory studies have contributed to the widening interest in historiography since the 1980s. Once a technical subject dealing with methods for laboring in the archives, historiography has been reborn as a study of the conceptual schemes in which history is framed. Put differently, memory studies have played a role in the shift from a preoccupation with problems of evidence in historical research to those of rhetoric in historical writing. Historiography, once focused on issues about finding and evaluating sources, has been reoriented toward those of strategies for plotting narrative. Historiography today, therefore, operates at a far remove from Jacques Barzun's *The Modern Researcher*, the essential primer for historiography courses during the 1960s, for the memory phenomenon raised new issues about the interplay between memory and history and so permitted historiography to assume center stage.[60] This postmodern historiography highlighted three themes: the uses of rhetoric in history; periodization as a mnemonic device; and the quest to draw closer to the experience of the past.

## THE RHETORICAL TURN IN HISTORIOGRAPHY

Hayden White's pathbreaking *Metahistory* (1973) transformed thinking about the historiographical significance of narrative. White was the first historian in a century to deflect attention from the science of research to the art of rhetoric. He argued that styles of historical narration are acts of imagination deeply grounded in memory. History's storylines follow patterns of emplotment embedded in an ancient poetics of representation. His theory is indebted to eighteenth-century Neapolitan rhetorician Giambattista Vico's 'new science' of the deep structures of language.[61] The ancient tropes of poetical expression, White explained, still shape the modern narratives of historical writing. To adduce his argument, he de-constructed the styles of narration of a number of famous nineteenth-century philosophers of history, from the metaphorical mode of Friedrich Nietzsche to the ironical style of Benedetto Croce, via the metonymy of Karl Marx and the synecdoche of Georg Hegel.[62]

While independently conceived, White's approach to the rhetoric of historical writing intersected with the then current interest of philosophers and literary scholars in the de-construction of texts under the banner of what was loosely called post-structuralism, and later postmodernism. Before influencing historiography, what has come to be characterized as 'French theory' had a major impact on literature and cultural studies during the 1970s, especially in the United States. In French theory, textual representation blocks direct access to the existential memory of experience. Representation is the medium through which the experience of the past is of necessity filtered. Its imagery cannot be construed as a transparent reproduction of the experience it signifies. Nor can the mindset of authors be read directly out of the texts they write.[63]

The mediator between White's theory of tropes and postmodern literary theory was the French scholar Michel Foucault. A philosopher by training, Foucault possessed a historian's bent, and he made his reputation through a series of historical studies about public commentary on madhouses, hospitals, prisons, and other forms of social management. Foucault was interested in the discourses about the practices of these institutions rather than the practices themselves. The proposition that historians deal in representations rather than realities became the signature of his method. Foucault's editor once included the term 'counter-memory' in the title of an anthology of his writings. Foucault himself never employed the term. But he did propose what might be characterized as counter-narratives with profound implications for the way historians revisit the past. The representations that most interested him were those that disrupt rather than confirm what we perceive to be the flow of experience. In his *Archaeology of Knowledge* (1973), he rejected the method of historians of ideas – tracing the development of ideas from their origins – and called instead for a genealogical reading of intellectual discourse backward from the present. The effect was to challenge the idea of intellectual continuity – construed as a heritage upon which the present builds – in favor of highlighting discontinuities in intellectual representation, and so dissolving long-standing notions about the relationship between past and present in cultural history. The patterns of the past, he maintained, are to be found not in its cultural traditions but rather in the way the texts of the past are imported into the discourse of the eternal present. History is the record of such cultural production.[64]

For Foucault, therefore, there can be no appeal to a master narrative. History cannot be grounded in an ontological timeline, but only in the patterns that may be constructed out of its representations. We read the phenomena of the world as if they were texts. In searching for connections within this web of intertextuality, historical interpretation is an ongoing project of construction and reconstruction, and the form an historian's narrative assumes reveals the give and take of relating textual references. Odd textual juxtapositions, moreover, may conjure up new histories, in which discordant perspectives encounter one another to generate new meanings. [65] Foucault was lionized for his provocative ideas and his original approach to interpreting history, to such a degree that he became an intellectual celebrity for his times.[66] His work, and that of the postmodernists whose spokesman among historians he turned out to be, introduced a strong, and for many a suspect, note of relativism into historical scholarship. Each age, Foucault proposed, reinvents the past in its textual narratives, dispelling the illusion of continuity and challenging each age to wrest from the past usable representations for explaining its present predicament.

Understandably, many historians were suspicious of narrative theorizing, trained as they had been to stay close to their evidentiary sources and to look skeptically upon the idea that representation is something other than an honest effort to give direct expression to experience itself. Scholars turning to the rhetoric of historical writing, therefore, have been accused of succumbing too readily to the contrived separation of form and content implicit in postmodern theory, diverting attention too tendentiously from the realities of the past to the discourses in which they are put on display. Still, students of rhetoric obliged historians to recognize that their power to frame the past carries with it a moral responsibility for the way they bequeath their understanding to posterity.[67] They play a decisive public role in their choices about what and how we shall remember the past.

## THE MNEMONICS OF TIME

Issues about narration in postmodern theory also raised issues about time. Among these theorists, French philosopher Jean-François Lyotard was the first to speak directly to this historiographical issue. His key to the postmodern temper of the 1980s was the repudiation of the idea of history as a grand narrative of the rise of Western civilization.[68] It was not just that Marxism as a philosophy of the progressive avant-garde was on the wane. Liberalism, too, with its mid-twentieth-century commitment to the making of the welfare state through governmental responsibility for social planning, was falling back on the political attitudes of its nineteenth-century beginnings, which favored private initiatives and self-reliance. The age that gave wings to memory studies was also one that witnessed the revival of neo-conservatism.[69]

To dismiss the grand narrative as the essential timeline of modern historiography, however, was to open the way for an exploration of its mnemonic underpinnings, which

embodied a particular conception of historical time. The German historiographer Reinhart Koselleck was the first to examine the
'semantics of time' in the modern historical
era. His work focused on the refashioning of
the conception of historical time during the
Enlightenment. It emphasized future prospects and so cast history as a saga of progress, with recognizable origins tending
toward an anticipated future. The making of
this idea was furthered by the birth of ideology at the end of the eighteenth century, with
its programmatic schemes for the improvement of the human condition. The grammati-
cal mode of such an understanding of history
is the future perfect. History is written as if
there were an expectant past preparing the
way for its eventual fulfillment. In such a
scheme, the present becomes a place marker
in history's march toward its denouement.[70]
To put this argument in more modest terms,
a goal-oriented history cues the search for
origins, and casts the present as but a stage
along the way toward a foreseeable destiny.
Koselleck further argued that modern historical consciousness betrays an ongoing tension
between experience and expectation, or alter-
natively, between memory and hope. Experience is conceived spatially in its references
to places of memory; expectation, by contrast, is conceived temporally as a horizon of
future possibilities. Koselleck proposed an
inverse relationship between the two: the
greater the expectation of the future, the
more past experience contracts into a more
precisely defined niche on the sequential
timeline of modern history.

Historian Peter Fritzsche has explored this
modern conception of historical time from the
vantage point of its reverse mode – nostalgia
for a lost past. Nostalgia, he contends, is a
nineteenth-century invention. It makes manifest a growing awareness of the distance
between past and present, and the need to
savor the memory of a world that is fast disappearing and cannot be retrieved. Beginning
with the French Revolution, he explains,
precipitous change disrupted the lives of vast
numbers of people, toppling long-established

political regimes, driving social groups into
exile, and in the process accentuating popular
awareness of the widening divide between
old and new ways of living. In the new world
of rapid political, economic, and demographic
upheaval, the experience of the past was
no longer a reliable guide to present choices.
Concomitantly, the accelerating pace of change
led to unsettling anxieties about what the
future might hold.[71] Ideas about time were
being transformed, and in its midst nostalgia
became the prevailing mode of memory.
Fritzsche challenges scholars who dismiss
nostalgia as a disabling melancholia to reconsider its complexity as an emotional response
to life in turbulent times. While harboring the
sadness of irreversible loss, memory in the
guise of nostalgia can also quicken the resolve
to deal creatively with an indeterminate future
in which one's resources of hope may triumph over psychological resignation to irrep-
arable loss. Nostalgia may sometimes have
been more remedy than malady in the face of
realities that denied the once reassuring con-
stancy of tradition.[72] Herein lies the interest of
the study by the Russian-born literary critic
Svetlana Boym, *The Future of Nostalgia*
(2001). In light of the collapse of the Soviet
Union as a failed experiment in the making of
the good society, she investigates the resurfacing of discarded visions out of the past
about what the future might hold. In other
words, her interest is not in elegy for a world
that we have lost but rather a reverie for one
that might have been. Transporting past
dreams of the future once denied into a more
appreciative present, nostalgia takes on a utopian allure.[73]

Boym's notion of nostalgic time-travel correlates with the thinking of some present-day
philosophers of history for whom the modern
conception of historical time is now behind
us. The German intellectual historian Lutz
Niethammer has traced the historical rise of
the concept of 'posthistory' as emblematic of
the exhaustion of the 'modern' way of thinking about historical time, which grounded
modern history in a narrative of the struggle
of the bourgeoisie to reshape the world to

conform to its vision of a better future. Post-historical thinking about the time of history, he argues, asks less of the future and more of present possibilities.[74] French historiographer François Hartog has elaborated upon this presentist perspective in contemporary historical consciousness. Taking his cue from Koselleck, he argues that as the expectant future recedes from view, past and future are drawn out of that temporal context into the space of present concerns. A historian of antiquity, Hartog reviews what he characterizes as changing 'regimes of historicity' across the intervening ages.[75] We are timeful beings, and as such our thinking about the human predicament is informed by an existential awareness of time in its historical moments of past, present, and future. Our understanding of the past changes depending upon the temporal moment we choose to privilege. Each conception of historical time fosters a different understanding of the relationship between memory and history.

Hartog portrays the present age – roughly the period since the 1960s – as a new epoch of historical time, one that highlights the primacy of the present moment. He surveys the symptoms of a breakdown in the modern sense of continuity with the past, citing examples of a dearth of practical objectives in the 'revolution' of 1968, the economic crisis of the 1970s, and the waning enthusiasm for the welfare state during the 1980s. For such a present, he concludes, the historicist model of a directional modern history has become an inadequate guide.[76] Couple these events with a sense of accelerating time promoted by the media revolution, and the horizons of expectation collapse into the immediacy of present concerns. British anthropologist Paul Connerton, commenting on powerful economic trends promoting cultural amnesia in the present age, arrives at a similar conclusion. As we discard and hence lose touch with traditions in which we once invested our wisdom, the past escapes its timebound sequencing to become a more open-ended resource for historical interpretation. The vertical timeline of history implodes

into a vastly extended horizontal plane, freeing the historian to time travel to those events that seem most immediately relevant to our current situation.[77]

Such presentism in contemporary historiographical understanding implies a move away from a diachronic conception of historical time toward a synchronic one – from history's storyline to history's topics. The grand narrative breaks up into mini-narratives, each located at a different topical site of memory. In light of this disruption of temporal continuity, discrete experiences lifted out of the past and imported into the present take on new historical meaning. This topical landscape of the remains of memory underscores the complexity of identity, and suggests why Lyotard's proclamation of the demise of the grand narrative and Nora's study of the French national memory aroused such widespread historiographical interest. In such a present-minded conception of historical time, the affinities between memory and history readily present themselves. Both reverse the ordering of narrative and topics and seek to evoke the presence of the past. Both are open to revisiting the past in no particular sequence. Both turn our attention from events to images – that is, from events identified to identities imagined.

For all of its speculations, the historiographical discourse about the mnemonics of time provides insight into why the topic of memory came to the fore in the late twentieth century. The temporal framework of modern history, the official memory of the modern age, had fragmented into the debris of its textual leavings.[78] Given the authority that storyline had once enjoyed about what should be remembered, its dissolution meant that the past was open to more diverse, even personal, interpretation, as evinced in the essays of *égo-histoire* in France during the 1980s.[79] The hold of modern history on the present age was growing weaker. Many pasts pressed for recollection. As a time of dissolving traditions, questions about identity presented themselves in the guise of anxieties about what should and what would be remembered of a vanishing modern age. For this reason, Eva Hoffman has characterized the late twentieth century as an 'era of memory,' by which she means an age of transition in which the old narrative of modern history has dissolved yet no new 'meta-narrative' has been put in its place. This time in history without a script, she suggests, has created nostalgia for history, and scholarly obsession with the topic of memory is its manifestation. Today we long for a past worthy of remembrance. Our memories of the modern age have only diminished powers to renew us.[80]

While most historians continue to write historical narratives as they always have – with an Aristotelian appreciation of a clearly defined beginning, middle, and end – some have been open to experimentation with new strategies of narration. Exemplary as a practical method of exploding the historicist timeline in favor of a synchronic model of historical time is Matt Matsuda's study of modern memory in its historical context. He builds his study of the culture of late nineteenth-century France around topics rather than a sustaining narrative. His history interprets the past at salient places of memory in late nineteenth-century French culture.[81] So too has the art historian Simon Schama, whose personal reminiscences serve as topical points of departure for his journeys into varied contexts for the cultural appreciation of nature.[82]

## NEGOTIATING THE BOUNDARY BETWEEN REPRESENTATION AND EXPERIENCE

Nearly all the work in the historiography of memory studies has focused on issues of historical representation. But as historians explore its possibilities, some have come to reflect on its counterpoint – experience as representation's existential ground.[83] If there are limits to historical representation, they ask, may that boundary be pressed to draw us closer to the past as it was experienced by its historical actors?

The lure of vicariously reliving the past is an old if impossible dream. Nineteenth-century historians had little compunction about enhancing their analysis of evidence with the imaginative reach of their prose, and professional historians today are well aware that what once passed for history in these sometimes florid writings would now be labeled imaginative fiction. Even today, the desire to recapture the past as a living experience persists in many domains, revealing a divide between professional and amateur historians. History buffs continue to be taken with the evocation of an imagined past. Reviewers in popular newspapers and magazines of commentary still praise historians who write about topics of perennial historical interest – for example, the lives of the American 'founding fathers' – in a way that makes them 'come alive again.' The public longing to re-experience the past finds expression in the popular cult of historical reenactment of signal events, usually military battles of the American Revolution or the Civil War. Practitioners of historic preservation are likewise faced with the need to attract the public by drawing them into a reconstructed milieu in a way that conveys the illusion of time traveling into the past.[84] Today's mass tourism industry is based on the proposition that the return to physical places of memory quickens a feeling for what once transpired there. Good teaching in schools, moreover, is often equated with a teacher's capacity to engage students in an emotional involvement with their subject matter, for example by showing up in period costume. The appeal of the image-making of television programming, notably on the History Channel (its now rare depiction of historical subject matter notwithstanding), originated out of just this need.

It is understandable that professional historians have looked with skepticism upon history as imagined re-enactment. They contend that the quest to relive the past is a misguided appreciation of what history can tell us about it. Such techniques for promoting vicarious identification with the past are rather arts of memory, stimulating memory's flights of imagination, not history's grounded empirical analysis. The quest to re-experience the past is fraught with temptation to stray from hard evidence into soft fantasy.[85] Still, memory studies make manifest that poets, novelists, and artists – as well as historians – have something profound to say about the appreciation of the past, and that history as a discipline operates within a field of creative ways to extract its varied meanings.

The breakthrough study about the relationship between these creative efforts to envision the past and the work of professional historians is Jean-Marc Largeaud's *Napoléon et Waterloo* (2006). The definitive fall of Napoleon in the battle of Waterloo signaled the end of French hegemony in Europe. But its memory in French popular culture, Largeaud explains, was over time transfigured into a 'glorious defeat,' an emblem of devotion to duty, loyalty, and patriotism invoked to foster national renewal in times of adversity. Largeaud inventories the remembrance of the event across a century of its depiction, including the testimony of witnesses, its passage into commemorative remembrance, and eventually the emergence of evidence-based historical reconstruction. His most original perspective, however, lies in his account of the way the battle was converted from history into memory once more by novelists, poets, playwrights, and painters, all of whom sought to re-enchant the battle by re-imagining it in ways that embodied some edifying meaning. In his presentation of Waterloo revisited, therefore, Largeaud situates the work of history between two kinds of collective memory: one that stressed commemoration, the other the moral imagination. In reaching for the historical sublime, the fictional accounts of the latter turned history into myth once more.[86]

The last meditation of the late French philosopher Paul Ricoeur configures the relationship between memory and history from the vantage point of our contemporary concerns. His study *La Mémoire, l'histoire, l'oubli* (2000) provides a comprehensive phenomenology of the place of memory in contemporary historiography, and in its way visits the major issues that we have addressed in this essay: orality/literacy, commemoration, trauma. It also serves as a counterpoint to Largeaud's approach. Largeaud showed how the realities of a historical event of violence and suffering may gradually be obscured by memories that extol human virtue through aesthetic idealization. Waterloo, had become remote from military strategy by the turn of the twentieth century. The denouement of its remembrance was a 'happy memory' conjured up out of forgetfulness of the death and destruction of the battle itself. Whereas Largeaud dealt in the aesthetics of memory, Ricoeur dwells on issues attending its ethics. The memory of the Holocaust haunts his narrative, for it remains too close to our worries about man's capacity for inhumanity toward his fellow man to be set aside. He strives to remain faithful to its memory by keeping the realities of history in mind. As he explores the many routes into the history of memory, he returns continually to his thoughts on the question that so preoccupied a generation of historians of the Holocaust: how may we reconcile remembrance of a traumatic event (acknowledging the past that was) with the need to move on (caring about a past that is no longer). An event as infamous as the Holocaust, he cautions, may find consolation in memory only by acknowledging history's truth.

To explain what is at stake, Ricoeur journeys back into those primordial depths out of which the distinction between memory and history initially emerged. He locates that parting of the ways at the threshold at which orality yielded a place to literacy. He bases his analysis on the first philosophical effort to address its implications for the uses of memory: Plato's Socratic dialogue *Phaedrus* (circa 370 BCE). It is the most ancient reflection on the puzzle of memory's relationship to history, here couched in a conversation about the effects of writing on the human imagination. Socrates poses the question: is writing a remedy or a poison as an aid to memory? His answer lies not in choosing one or the other, but rather in considering how the invention of a new technology of communication transforms our understanding of memory's resources. History, Ricoeur explains, may be counted among the first arts of memory. It holds the past fast, memory in its preservationist mode. History, therefore, may be regarded as a kind of commemoration. It is our most informed route toward a critical understanding of the past, but comes at the price of conferring determining limitations on what and how we shall remember. Memory in its mode as imagination, by contrast, must be treasured as an unbounded power of mind. In its inspiration, it emboldens new beginnings; it is, as Ricoeur puts it, 'a little miracle' that transcends history in its capacity for creative renewal. In acknowledging the paradox of its faithfulness to the remembrance of inhumanities out of the past – forgiving yet never ceasing to care all the while – memory may be reconciled with the bleakest historical realities. Here memory quickens out of history's record, a resource that sustains our hope for the redemption of an errant past.[87]

## THE ASSIMILATION OF MEMORY STUDIES INTO CULTURAL HISTORY

Memory studies, like all historiographical fashions that preceded it, have over time diversified and expanded their range of inquiry into ever more specific realms of cultural practice. Alon Confino and Peter Fritzsche teamed up to offer an overview of the 'work of memory' at the outset of the twenty-first century.[88] They see the early studies of the politics of commemoration as too tendentiously committed to exposing political subterfuge and too preoccupied with memory as mere representation.[89] Much of the early work, they argue, factored memory out of the ensemble of its symbolic and cultural relationships. They urge their colleagues to 'move out of the museum and

beyond the monument' to explore the way memory is embedded in social and cultural (as well as political) practices, and more importantly, how they shape them. Memorialists do not seek to remember the past passively but rather to shape it actively. These efforts to fashion a usable past include not just the politics of the memory of great events but also that of ordinary people who appeal to the past to give meaning to their private lives. In advancing this perspective, these scholars invoke the importance of the early twentieth-century studies by Halbwachs and by Aby Warburg on the constructive nature of social memory, and so reaffirm the ancient notion that memory is the seat of the creative imagination. In all of the fields of memory studies that we have examined, there is today more attention to the way memory is a faculty of mind that enables humans to fight back actively against the forgetfulness that postmodern consumerism promotes so aggressively through media. All stress the importance of the remembered past. All stress the creative resources of remembering for imagining a different future. All note the cultural clearings that the active memory opens for doing so. All seek to show how memory's resistance to the eclipse of the past is a remedy for ordinary people as well as for the elites who promote official commemorations.[90]

In this respect, Jay Winter offers an expansive reassessment of the politics of memory in his several studies of the commemorative practices that were a legacy of the First World War.[91] He sees the discussion of differences between memory and history not as a threat to history's integrity but as an opportunity to advance our understanding of cultural history. He attributes the memory phenomenon to the emergence over the course of the twentieth century of a 'creative space' between memory and history. This was a place for historical remembrance to satisfy the need to come to terms with the violence and suffering ushered in by the First World War and that continued relentlessly through the rest of the century. It served as a bulwark against all of the forces of change that threatened to obliterate the memory of this experience in the name of moving on.

Winter turns attention from the passive worries about dissolving identities toward the active work of remembering through the creation of a vast array of 'signifying practices.' These include not only the more obvious symbols of remembrance – monuments, museums and holiday rituals – but also personal souvenirs, including diaries, letters, poetry, novels, and plays. Beyond these agencies of memory, he extends his inquiry to canvass legal tribunals, movies, and television productions that have been put to use in the 'struggle against forgetting.' The projects of historical remembrance, he explains, have opened the past to the voice of the people. Historians are an important group furthering this project. But it has invited the participation of many players, including architects, lawyers, film producers and directors, as well as the ordinary people who have sought to leave some trace of their experience of war. As an expression of the memory phenomenon, historical remembrance provides a kind of theater, a medium through which those who hark back in time actively engage in the work of preserving a memorable past.

From a different vantage point but with a similar purpose in mind, Andreas Huyssen addresses the issue of cultural amnesia in terms of the changing role of the museum in the age of media.[92] He proposes a dialectic between vague fears about the eclipse of the remembered past and the vigorous renewal of public interest in the more imaginative art exhibitions and other cultural spectacles promoted by museum directors. He contends that this revival signals a reaction against a media culture that associates remembrance with obsolescence. A remembered past that stimulates the popular imagination, he explains, has come to serve as an antidote to the fetish of innovation that emerged out of early twentieth-century aesthetics. In the face of the virtual reality of cyberspace that beckons toward fantasy, the museum provides reassurance about the tangible reality of a past that anchors us in the material world. Huyssen argues that the postmodern museum has been reborn as a creative forum for evoking the past as an imagined presence. Given the numbers that flock to the spectacle of their exhibitions, the public would seem to agree.

One might argue that historiography over the past decade has tamed the insights of memory studies to more conventional patterns of historical interpretation. Scholars today favor the integration of memory studies into cumulative historical knowledge over provocative departures into uncharted realms. Memory studies would appear to be assimilating within the larger project of the new cultural history that has developed over the course of the last half-century. The old divide between politics and culture has broken down, as has that between high and popular culture. Memory studies have contributed greatly to our understanding of the nature of cultural communication, and so have provided a remedy for a major inadequacy in earlier versions of cultural history, which often invoked vague notions of the 'spirit of the age' or conjectural recourse to a 'collective unconscious.'

Thanks in part to the memory phenomenon, historical understanding has become more complex, as it tilts toward the social and the cultural. While politics will always be prominent in historical writing, it is unlikely that a political narrative will ever again serve as the backbone of history. The grand narrative of modern political history was focused on understanding a Eurocentric civilization that has since been marginalized by the global forces at play in contemporary history. Henceforth we are likely to live with many narratives, not all of them congruent. Nor will historians ever again be so naïve as they once were about the role of memory in the historical reconstruction of the past. As history becomes the official remembrance of many pasts, history's debt to memory may henceforth be more readily acknowledged. The idea that memory studies is a historiographical matrix, however, may eventually grow more obscure, as a more encompassing cultural history loses sight of the memory phenomenon's role in its own development.

## NOTES AND REFERENCES

1   For perspectives on the rise of memory studies, see Kerwin Klein, 'On the emergence of memory in historical discourse,' Representations 69 (2000), 127–50; Wulf Kansteiner, 'Finding meaning in memory: a methodological critique of collective memory studies,' History and Theory 41 (May 2002), 179–97; Gavriel D. Rosenfeld, 'A looming crash or a soft landing? Forecasting the future of the memory "industry",' Journal of Modern History 81 (2009), 122–58. For a comprehensive compendium of the principal scholarly literature on the subject, see Jeffrey K. Olick, Vered Vinitzky-Seroussi, and Daniel Levy, eds, The Collective Memory Reader (Oxford: Oxford University Press, 2011).

2   Jacques Le Goff, History and Memory (New York: Columbia University Press, 1992), xi, 214.

3   See J.G.A. Pocock, Politics, Language and Time: Essays on Political Thought and History (London: Methuen, 1972), 237–8.

4   Lucien Febvre, 'La sensibilité et l'histoire: comment reconstituer la vie affective d'autrefois,' Annales d'Histoire Sociale 3 (1941), 5–20, and Le Problème de l'incroyance au XVIe Siècle (Paris, 1947), esp. 1–18, 491–501; Robert Mandrou, 'L'histoire des mentalités,' Encyclopédie Universalis 3 (1968), 436–8, and Introduction à la France moderne: essai de psychologie historique (Paris: Albin Michel, 1974), 75–104.

5   Daniel Schacter, The Seven Deadly Sins of Memory (Boston: Houghton Mifflin, 2001), 1–11. Memory is also a frontier of research on the human brain, and there are interesting parallels in the models that neuroscientists and humanists have developed. See Gerald Edelman, Neural Darwinism: The Theory of Neuronal Group Selection (New York: Basic Books, 1988). The best history of the development of the neuroscience of memory is the autobiographical memoir by Eric Kandel, In Search of Memory: The Emergence of a New Science of Mind (New York: Norton, 2006).

6   Eric Hobsbawm and Terence Ranger, eds, The Invention of Tradition (Cambridge University Press, 1983).

7   Terence Ranger, 'The Invention of Tradition revisited: the case of colonial Africa,' in Legitimacy and the State in Africa, ed. Terence Ranger and Megan Vaughan (London: Palgrave, 1993), 62–3.

8   Kandel, In Search of Memory, 129–33, 279–81, uses the terms 'explicit' and 'implicit' to characterize this distinction.

9   Maurice Halbwachs, Les Cadres sociaux de la mémoire (1925; New York: Arno Press, 1975), and the anthology

10  Maurice Halbwachs, La Topographie légendaire des évangiles en Terre Sainte (1941; Paris: Presses Universitaires de France, 1971). On Halbwachs as historian of memory, see Patrick Hutton, History as an Art of Memory (Hanover, NH: University Press of New England, 1993), 73–90.

11  An exception is Peter Gay's skillful integration of Freudian insight into his work on European cultural history. See esp. his Freud for Historians (Oxford: Oxford University Press, 1985).

12  The learned journal History and Memory began publication in 1989; Memory Studies in 2008. H-Memory, online for several years, has become an invaluable bibliographical resource for identifying current research.

13  For an overview of the work of Parry, Lord, and other early students of orality/literacy, see John Miles Foley, The Theory of Oral Composition (Bloomington: Indiana University Press, 1988), 2–10.

14  The changes in mentality have also been plotted by the anthropologist André Leroi-Gouhran as a five-stage process. These include oral transmission, written tables, file cards, mechanical writing, and electronic sequencing. See his Le Geste et la parole: La Mémoire et les rythmes (Paris: Albin Michel, 1964), 65.

15  Alexander Luria, Cognitive Development: Its Cultural and Social Foundations (Cambridge: Harvard University Press, 1976).

16  Jack Goody, The Interface between the Written and the Oral (Cambridge: Cambridge University Press, 1987); Jan Vansina, Oral Tradition as History (Madison: University of Wisconsin Press, 1985).

17  Walter Ong, Orality and Literacy: The Technologizing of the Word (London: Methuen, 1982). He was once a student of Marshall McLuhan, the prophet of the media age.

18  Eric Havelock, Preface to Plato (Cambridge: Harvard University Press, 1963).

19  Robert Funk and Roy Hoover, eds, The Five Gospels: What Did Jesus Really Say? (New York: Harper Collins, 1993), 1–38.

20  Mary Carruthers, The Book of Memory: A Study of Memory in Medieval Culture (Cambridge: Cambridge University Press, 1990), 46–79; Mary Carruthers and Jan Ziolkowski, eds, The Medieval Craft of Memory (Philadelphia: University of Pennsylvania Press, 2002), 1–31.

21  Frances Yates, The Art of Memory (Chicago: University of Chicago Press, 1966), esp. 129–59, 368–72.

22  See Elizabeth Eisenstein, The Printing Press as an Agent of Change (Cambridge: Cambridge University Press, 1979).

23  Michael Warner, The Letters of the Republic: Publication and the Public Sphere in Eighteenth-Century America (Cambridge: Harvard University Press, 1990).

24  Robert Darnton, The Business of the Enlightenment: A Publishing History of the Encyclopédie, 1775–1800 (Cambridge: Harvard University Press, 1979).

of his work: Maurice Halbwachs, On Collective Memory, ed. Lewis A. Coser (Chicago: University of Chicago Press, 1992). On Halbwachs, see Jan Assmann, 'Collective memory and cultural Identity,' New German Critique 65 (1995), 125–33.

25 Robert Darnton, *The Great Cat Massacre and Other Episodes in French History* (New York: Basic, 1984). See also his *The Literary Underground of the Old Regime* (Cambridge: Harvard University Press, 1982).

26 James Olney, *Memory and Narrative: The Weave of Life-Writing* (Chicago: University of Chicago Press, 1998).

27 On involuntary memory in Proust's novel, see Daniel Schacter, *Searching for Memory: The Brain, the Mind, and the Past* (New York: Harper Collins, 1996), 26–8.

28 Patrick Hutton, 'Sigmund Freud and Maurice Halbwachs: the problem of memory in historical psychology,' *The History Teacher* 27 (1994), 146–8.

29 On present-day efforts to redeploy the practice of the art of memory as a mind-game exercise, see the memoir by Joshua Foer, *Moonwalking with Einstein: The Art and Science of Remembering Everything* (New York: Penguin, 2011).

30 Jay David Bolter and Richard Grusin, *Remediation: Understanding New Media* (Cambridge: MIT Press, 2000), esp. 53–84

31 Jay David Bolter, *Turing's Man: Western Culture in the Computer Age* (Univ. of North Carolina Press, 1984), 157–64.

32 On the devaluation of memory in contemporary culture, see David Gross, *Lost Time: On Remembering and Forgetting in Late Modern Culture* (Amherst: University of Massachusetts Press, 2000), 133–53.

33 Nicholas Carr, *The Shallows: What the Internet is Doing to Our Brains* (New York: Norton, 2011), 177–97.

34 An early example of this genre is Maurice Agulhon, *Marianne into Battle: Republican Imagery and Symbolism in France, 1789–1880* (Cambridge: Cambridge University Press, 1981).

35 For the controversy, see Steven Kaplan, *Farewell Revolution: The Historians' Feud* (Ithaca: Cornell University Press, 1995).

36 Steven Englund, 'The ghost of nation past,' *Journal of Modern History* 64 (1992), 299–320.

37 Charles Maier, 'A surfeit of memory? Reflections on history, melancholy and denial,' *History and Memory* 5/2 (1993), 136–52.

38 Excellent studies include Daniel J. Sherman, *The Construction of Memory in Interwar France* (Chicago: University of Chicago Press, 1999); Barry Schwartz, *Abraham Lincoln and the Forge of National Memory* (Chicago: University of Chicago Press, 2000); Jay Winter, *Sites of Mourning: The Great War in European Cultural History* (Cambridge: Cambridge University Press, 1995); and Allen Douglas, *War, Memory, and the Politics of Humor* (Berkeley: University of California Press, 2002).

39 Noteworthy are Michael Kammen, *Mystic Chords of Memory: The Transformation of Tradition in American Culture* (New York: Knopf, 1991); W. Fitzhugh Brundage, *The Southern Past: A Clash of Race and Memory* (Cambridge: Harvard University Press, 2005); Peter Homans, ed., *Symbolic Loss: The Ambiguity of Mourning and Memory at Century's End* (Charlottesville: University Press of Virginia, 2000).

40 Yael Zerubavel, *Recovered Roots: The Making of Israeli National Tradition* (Chicago: Chicago University Press, 1995).

41 Mary Douglas, *How Institutions Think* (Syracuse: Syracuse University Press, 1986).

42 For an overview, see Charles Maier, *The Unmasterable Past: History, Holocaust, and German National Identity* (Cambridge: Harvard University Press, 1988).

43 See the synthesis of scholarship on the leading issues in Daniel Levy and Natan Sznaider, *The Holocaust and Memory in the Global Age* (Philadelphia: Temple University Press, 2006).

44 Saul Friedländer, *When Memory Comes* (1978; Madison: University of Wisconsin Press, 2003). See also his *History and Psychoanalysis* (New York: Holmes & Meier, 1980). Among other refugees from the Holocaust who have reflected on their personal route toward this topic, see Raul Hilberg, *The Politics of Memory: The Journey of a Holocaust Historian* (Chicago: Ivan Dee, 1996).

45 One of Friedländer's first books addressed this Freudian-inspired historiography, *History and Psycho-analysis* (New York: Holmes & Meier, 1978).

46 A provocative counterpoint to the psycho-analytic approach to the memory of the Holocaust was offered by University of Chicago historian Peter Novick in his *The Holocaust in American Life* (Boston: Houghton Mifflin, 1999), esp. 1–15. He introduced issues about the politics of memory into the discussion. Employing the Halbwachian model, he argued that Jewish-American leaders, responding to the identity politics of the 1980s, publicized Holocaust commemoration strenuously for fear it might otherwise be crowded from public attention.

47 Martin Brozat and Saul Friedländer, 'A controversy about the historization of National Socialism,' in *Reworking the Past: Hitler, the Holocaust, and the Historians' Debate*, ed. Peter Baldwin (Boston: Beacon Press, 1990), 102–34; James Knowlton and Truett Cates, eds, *Forever in the Shadow of Hitler? Original Documents of the Historikerstreit* (Atlantic Highlands, New Jersey: Humanities Press, 1993).

48 Saul Friedländer, ed., *Probing the Limits of Representation: Nazism and the Final Solution* (Cambridge: Harvard University Press, 1992), 1–21.

49 Michael Marrus and Robert Paxton, *Vichy France and the Jews* (New York: Basic, 1981).

50 Pierre Péan, *Une Jeunesse française: François Mitterrand, 1934–1947* (Paris: Fayard, 1994), 202–27, 317–25.

51 Eric Conan and Henry Rousso, *Vichy, un passé qui ne passe pas* (Paris: Gallimard, 1996). See also Joan B. Wolf, *Harnessing the Holocaust: The Politics of Memory in France* (Stanford: Stanford University Press, 2004).

52 Alon Confino, *Germany as a Culture of Remembrance: Promises and Limits of Writing History* (Chapel Hill: University of North Carolina Press, 2006), 21.

53 For the continuation of the discussions emerging out of Holocaust studies, see Wulf Kansteiner, *In Pursuit of German Memory: History, Television, and Politics after*

*Asuchwitz* (Athens, OH: Ohio University Press, 2006); Andreas Huyssen, *Present Pasts: Urban Palimpsests and the Politics of Memory* (Stanford: Stanford University Press, 2003). On further reflections on the Vichy syndrome, see Richard J. Goslan, ed., *Fascism's Return: Scandal, Revision, and Ideology since 1980* (Lincoln, NE: University of Nebraska Press, 1998), 182–99. For the Holocaust in Poland, see Jonathan Huener, *Auschwitz, Poland, and the Politics of Commemoration, 1945-1979* (Athens, OH: Ohio University Press, 2003).

54  Jeffrey K. Olick, *The Politics of Regret: On Collective Memory and Historical Responsibility* (New York: Routledge, 2007), 55–83, 139–51.

55  Eva Hoffman, *After Such Knowledge: Memory, History, and the Legacy of the Holocaust* (New York: Public Affairs, 2004).

56  Michael Roth and Charles Salas, eds, *Disturbing Remains: Memory, History, and Crisis in the Twentieth Century* (Los Angeles: Getty Research Institute, 2001), 1–13.

57  Gabrielle Spiegel, 'Memory and history: liturgical time and historical time,' *History and Theory* 41 (2002), 149–62.

58  Pierre Vidal-Naquet, *Assassins of Memory: Essays on the Denial of the Holocaust* (New York: Columbia University Press, 1992), 57, 102.

59  Peter Novick, *That Noble Dream: The 'Objectivity Question' and the American Historical Profession* (Cambridge: Cambridge University Press, 1988).

60  Barzun's book is now in its 6th edition (Florence, Kentucky: Thomson/Wadsworth, 2004).

61  Hayden White, *Metahistory: The Historical Imagination in Nineteenth-Century Europe* (Baltimore: Johns Hopkins University Press, 1973), 265–425. For the sources of White's method, see his 'The tropics of history: the deep structures of the *New Science*,' in *Giambattista Vico's Science of Humanity*, ed. Giorgio Tagliacozzo and Donald Verene (Baltimore: Johns Hopkins University Press, 1976), 65–85;

62  White also employs an alternate analysis of nineteenth-century historians based on Northrop Frye's theory of genre emplotment, from Michelet (Romantic) to Jacob Burckhardt (Satirical), via Leopold von Ranke (Comic) and Alexis de Tocqueville (Tragic). *Metahistory*, 133–264.

63  François Cusset, *French Theory: Foucault, Derrida, Deleuze & Cie et les mutations de la vie intellectuelle aux Etats-Unis* (Paris: La Découverte, 2003), 43–63, 110–39.

64  Michel Foucault, *The Archaeology of Knowledge* (New York: Harper & Row, 1972), 135–48.

65  Issuing from Foucault's line of inquiry was the 'new historicism' movement, a venture whose leading spokesmen were literary critics rather than historians. The term is a misnomer, for this historiographical current was not the old historicism revisited, but rather repudiated. Catherine Gallagher and Stephen Greenblatt, leading proponents, called attention to the cultural negotiation involved in the interplay among textual references. Catherine Gallagher and Stephen Greenblatt, *Practicing the New Historicism* (Chicago: University of Chicago Press, 2000), 1–19.

66  Patrick Hutton, 'The Foucault phenomenon and contemporary French historiography,' *Historical Reflections* 17 (1991), 77–102.

67  On the moral imagination in historical writing (with particular attention to Hayden White's work), see David Harlan, *The Degradation of American History* (Chicago: University of Chicago Press, 1997), 25, 105–26.

68  Jean-François Lyotard, *La Condition postmoderne: rapport sur le savoir* (Paris: Editions de Minuit, 1979), 11–17, 63.

69  Tony Judt, *Ill Fares the Land* (New York: Penguin, 2010), 106–19.

70  Reinhart Koselleck, *Futures Past: On the Semantics of Historical Time*, trans. Keith Tribe (Cambridge: MIT Press, 1985), 246–88.

71  Peter Fritzsche, *Stranded in the Present: Modern Time and the Melancholy of History* (Cambridge: Harvard University Press, 2004), 11–54.

72  Peter Fritzsche, 'How nostalgia narrates modernity,' in *The Work of Memory: New Directions in the Study of German Society and Culture*, ed. Alon Confino and Peter Fritzsche (Urbana: University of Illinois Press, 2002), 62–85; idem, 'Specters of history: on nostalgia, exile, and modernity,' *American Historical Review* 106 (2001), 1587–618. See also Philippe Ariès, *Le Temps de l'Histoire* (1954; Paris: Seuil, 1986), 33–43, who explains how his family's nostalgia for the traditions of old France served as his path into history.

73  Svetlana Boym, *The Future of Nostalgia* (New York: Basic Books, 2001), 57–71.

74  Lutz Niethammer, *Posthistoire: Has History Come to an End?* (London: Verso, 1992).

75  François Hartog, *Régimes d'historicité: présentisme et expériences du temps* (Paris: Seuil, 2003), 11–30.

76  François Hartog, 'Temps et histoire, "Comment écrire l'histoire de France?",' *Annales HSS* no. 6 (November–December 1995), 1219–36.

77  Paul Connerton, *How Modernity Forgets* (Cambridge: Cambridge University Press, 2009), 77–8.

78  Theorist Perry Anderson expressed it as the 'loss of any active sense of history, either as hope or as memory,' in his *The Origins of Postmodernity* (London: Verso, 1998), 56.

79  Pierre Nora, ed., *Essais d'égo-histoire* (Paris: Gallimard, 1987). These were personal accounts by leading French historians about how they had made their way toward intellectual independence in the profession by emancipating themselves from the tutelage of conventional schools of historiography.

80  Hoffman, *After Such Knowledge*, 241–44, points out that the prosperity and comparative tranquility of the late twentieth century gave historians time to reflect on the cataclysms of its early decades. 11 September 2001, she explains, has shaken that secure world from its moorings. It may signal a move out of the era of memory back into history.

81  Matt Matsuda, *The Memory of the Modern* (New York: Oxford University Press, 1996). See also Patrick Hutton, 'Mnemonic schemes in the new history of memory,' *History and Theory* 36 (1997), 378–91.

82  Simon Schama, *Landscape and Memory* (New York: Knopf, 1995).

83  The philosopher of history Frank Ankersmit has taken up this topic in his *Sublime Historical Experience* (Stanford: Stanford University Press, 2005).

84  Diane Bartel, *Historic Preservation: Collective Memory and Historical Identity* (New Brunswick: Rutgers University Press, 1996).

85  Among professional historians, Harvard art historian Simon Schama is a master at drawing history as representation as closely as possible to history as experience, as in his *Landscape and Memory*. Schama has his critics. In a review of Schama's *Dead Certainties* (New York: Random House, 1991), historian Gordon Wood chides him for straying too close to fiction. 'Novel history,' *New York Review of Books* 38/12 (27 June 1991).

86  Jean-Marc Largeaud, *Napoléon et Waterloo: la défaite glorieuse de 1815 à nos jours* (Paris: La Boutique de l'Histoire, 2006).

87  Paul Ricoeur, *La Mémoire, l'histoire, l'oubli* (Paris: Editions du Seuil, 2000), 3–4, 167–80, 642–56

88  Confino and Fritzsche, 'Introduction: noises of the past,' in *The Work of Memory: New Directions in the Study of German Society and Culture*, 1–21.

89  In this respect, see the reply to Hobsbawm/Ranger's thesis about invented tradition in the anthology edited by Mark Salber Phillips and Gordon Schochet, *Questions of Tradition* (Toronto: University of Toronto Press, 2004), esp. Phillips' essay 'What is tradition when it is not "invented"? A historiographical introduction,' 3–29.

90  For new directions in understanding the role of memory in cultural practices, two recent anthologies of work by German scholars stand out: Hans-Jürgen Grabbe and Sabine Schindler, eds, *The Merits of Memory: Concepts, Contexts, Debates* (Heidelberg: Universitätsverlag Winter, 2008); Astrid Erll and Ansgar Nünning, eds, *Cultural Memory Studies: An International and Interdisciplinary Handbook* (Berlin: Walter de Gruyter, 2008). In her introduction, pp. 7–8, Erll takes the long view, arguing that the scholarly interest in cultural memory is more than a century old, and that research since the 1980s may be interpreted as its 'new wave.'

91  Jay Winter, *Remembering War: The Great War Between Memory and History in the Twentieth Century* (New Haven: Yale University Press, 2006), 1–13, 275–89.

92  Andreas Huyssen, *Twilight Memories: Making Time in a Culture of Amnesia* (New York: Routledge, 1995), 13–35.

# 23

# Postcolonial Theory and History

Benjamin Zachariah

## INTRODUCTION

One of the central difficulties in writing about 'postcolonial history' is that no one is sure what it is, or when it is. 'Postcolonial-*ism*' is a label worn uneasily by practitioners of 'postcolonial theory', of 'postcolonial history', 'postcolonial criticism' or (more non-committally) of 'postcolonial studies'. The 'ism' maintains (in some uses) pejorative connotations, as does the 'theory', especially for some critics whose commitment to the discipline of 'history' is construed as a practical rather than an abstract one, with 'theory' being construed as necessarily abstract. (As this is a handbook of historical theory, not too much space will be given to the anti-theorists' false dichotomy.) The 'history' part is in some readings also problematic, given that history as a discipline is itself seen as complicit in 'Western' power/ knowledge constellations.[1] (This may be a matter of *naming* rather than of something essential to the discipline of history itself, which is far from the monolithic entity that some practitioners of postcolonial criticism sometimes make it out to be.) Terminological embarrassments, therefore, make for the first set of engagements and difficulties with

'the postcolonial', another label that belongs in the cluster of terms.

For purposes of initial (and artificial) clarity, we can treat 'postcolonial history' as a subset of 'postcolonial studies'. What, then, is post-colonial studies? There is no coherent set of positions or theoretical engagements that can define it as a field. It refers, in a most general sense, to the consequences of empire, in and for the (former) colonies, and also, in a broader reading, in and for the (former) metropolitan countries, in the latter instance in the form of diasporas, diasporic identities, 'multi-cultural' societies, or more generally the presences of the colonies in the metropoles. It has been extended to include parts of the world that were not subject to formal colonialism but had experiences that could be considered related to colonialism: areas of informal empire such as China or Latin America; then, as 'postco-lonial' became a more theorised and self-conscious set of positions, this justifies its expansion and application to unlikely times, places and peoples. The prefix 'post', in a word which has gradually lost its hyphen, does not refer necessarily to a chronological period after (formal) colonialism (this it has in common with 'the postmodern', from which it borrows much); it refers also to 'going beyond' colonial modes of power/knowledge relations, in which 'the tension between the epistemological and the chronological is not disabling but productive'.[2] It seeks to 'deconstruct' Eurocentric modes of reading and writing history, whether explicit or implicit.[3] Its engagements tend to be 'cultural', related to the sensibilities and subjectivities of the colonised in their encounter with colonialism; 'identity' and 'difference' are thus central themes to be studied. Some commentators nevertheless claim, standing against the 'cultural turn', that the term 'postcolonial' grew out of an engagement with the problems of conceptualising the economic and political aftermath of formal colonialism that nonetheless saw a continuation of imperial control by other means. This is part of a longer debate within postcolonial history of the place of Marxist and materialist readings of history within the concerns of postcolonialism;[4] and indeed, an earlier generation of scholars, such as Stuart Hall or Benita Parry, were centrally involved in political struggles and engaged closely with Marxism, with socialist theory and politics, and only ambivalently (if at all) embraced the increasingly decontextualised 'culturalism' of 'postcolonalism'.[5]

Postcolonialism draws upon an eclectic series of theoretical interventions in the social sciences and in philosophy, and it often does so unsystematically, in an allusive and elusive manner. At its best, it engages politically where it discerns a need, using theory to legitimately claim an academic space from which to make a political intervention. Here, postcolonialism needs to distinguish itself from postmodernism, which is generally seen as being in favour of a multiplicity of readings of 'texts', and is often agnostic about truth-claims.[6] Postcolonialism, as it uses many of the tools of postmodernism to expose the complicity of dominant discourses with oppressive (power/knowledge or political) regimes, but being interested in making interventions with political implications, cannot afford quite the same level of agnosticism. Hence, postcolonialism often needs to fall back upon what Gayatri Spivak has called 'strategic essentialisms' as first pre\mises upon which to ground an argument.[7]

Postcolonial *history*, then, is not fully separable from postcolonial studies except as a matter of relative emphasis and of the need to engage with the disciplinary rules of the historian's profession – the renegotiation of these rules remain one of its central concerns. It is interdisciplinary, but this is an indisciplined interdisciplinarity; its borrowings are eclectic, sometimes playful: it uses poststructuralism via Foucault, Derrida, Lacan; anthropology, critical theory, literary criticism, heterodox Marxism (somewhat guiltily), psychoanalysis, semiotics, feminist theory. It is often difficult to ground the theoretical basis of a particular intervention in specific statements by any particular thinkers. The *mood* is what counts, and the theory is often a kind of received common sense, for which the sources are by now forgotten.

Critiques of postcolonialism are inherent in the field of postcolonialism, and critics who engage with the field are, whether they like it or not, incorporated into the field. Postcolonialism is therefore to some extent the victim of its own success: if we are all postcolonial now, a counter-hegemonic project has succeeded, at least within academia; outside academia is quite another matter.[8] Thus, sceptics or opponents find themselves implicated in the terminological constellations of the 'postcolonial', with the consequence that they are part of the legitimating frameworks they seek to problematise. Central debates often hinge upon the nature of one's political engagement, with the result that positioning oneself politically sometimes becomes central to an argument. This of course can be seen as a logical and legitimate consequence of the death of 'objectivity': we are all interested parties, the personal is political, and our emotional cathexes are integral to our utterances.[9] There is, however, also a tendency for the structure of arguments to reduce speakers or writers to their origins, in a manner reminiscent of forms of stereotyping and essentialisation that, it has been argued, are a feature of colonial thought.

At its best, postcolonialism's political project is to change the ways in which colonialism and its consequences are thought about and written about. One could argue that the partial successes of postcolonialism in achieving recognition in public arenas outside the academic world are based on a formulaic engagement with the more academic debates, and make their appearance mainly as various politically correct formulations – which is still an improvement, as it has discredited certain explicit forms of racism, sexism and cultural discrimination as forms of publicly acceptable behaviour. The question of whether postcolonialism has replaced some forms of discrimination with the axiomatic privileging of the subjectivities of 'victim communities', historically defined and with self-proclaimed inheritors of that victimhood taking centre-stage as their retrospective spokespersons, needs to be kept in mind. It must also be said that postcolonial theorists are very keen on writing their own histories and their own genealogies, in a kind of self-monumentalisation as sites of memory for the downtrodden.[10] Since no one person holds any of the positions that can be attributed to a *mood*, the denials and rejoinders retreat from some of the corollaries of their theories with which they are no longer entirely comfortable. Equally problematically, a good deal of debate takes place at a metatheoretical level: much energy is expended on a critique of 'modernity' (in some versions 'Western modernity' or 'post-Enlightenment modernity'), but there is little agreement and little coherent theorisation on what these categories might mean.

## THEMES, CONCERNS, LOCATIONS: A PARTIAL INVENTORY

'The postcolonial' is too large to be a unified field, as it is evident that it could take in the world as a whole as its geographical area of concern.[11] As it retrospectively defined itself, it claimed a set of solidarities with the marginalised, the victimised and the downtrodden[12] – which are solidarities by intuitive analogy rather than academic engagements. Some versions of postcolonial history run the risk of creating pure victims, as in Ashis Nandy's claim to defend the 'innocence' of the colonised.[13]

It was the Anglo-(North)American (and in the first instance North American) academic world that was integral to the development of postcolonialism, although ostensibly the subject-matter was about areas in the periphery. Postcolonialism found a good reception at a time of the exploring of subjectivities, and the decentring of 'mainstream' history that followed feminist histories, 'history from below', histories of homosexuality, of native Americans, and so on, from the 1960s through to the early 1980s, although in some instances, the institutional bases were not North American in the first instance: for example, the Subaltern Studies group operated for a while out of the Australian National University, Canberra, and later Sussex University, when its founder, Ranajit Guha, taught and worked there. In some ways it remains a phenomenon of the Anglo-American world, although adopted in some centres of intellectual activity in the periphery, the former colonial world. Despite postcolonialism's use of much French theory, its reception in France has been frosty; the belief in France's civilising mission in the colonies has proved remarkably resilient. It was, at least until recently, more American than British; Britain was a reluctant latecomer, having followed the American lead. 'Imperial history' was resolutely old-fashioned and resilient, surviving the need for self-reflexivity in its bases in Oxford and Cambridge, resisting, or sometimes merely ignoring, the onslaught of the 'new imperial history' – which, to a large extent, is British domestic history projected onto a larger backdrop, and arguably defeats the purpose of its alleged 'newness'.[14]

Much of the theory and many of the debates on postcolonialism originated in departments of literature, most often in metropolitan or North American universities; but this literary endeavour took hold in departments of *English* literature in the former colonies, which had a particular need to justify or rethink their existence if they were not simply to reify a canonical set of English (in a national sense) texts rather than texts *in* English; the study of writing in English by writers from the colonial and former colonial world then provided a route into understanding the sensibilities of the colonial imagination. From this starting point, comparative transnational studies of colonial literature, both in English and in translation, led to the highlighting of certain common themes in the literatures of colonies and former colonies, and came to be compared with the literatures of subordinated groups elsewhere (native Americans, African-Americans, homosexuals); and departments of *English* literature increasingly became departments of literature.

This genesis of postcolonialism in literary criticism is important to note. The issues that postcolonialism *history* addresses are most elusive in traditional archival sources, which are dominated by institutional, and particularly statist, imperatives. The legitimacy of the jumps in imagination that the literary critic is permitted to make then provides certain insights which a historian might then be encouraged to substantiate in terms of the methodology of that discipline. But this crossover also changed the rules of historical writing – forcing it to acknowledge the point that history is a genre that makes truth-claims, but is in fact not very different from other literary pursuits that frankly acknowledge the role of imagination and arbitrary reconstruction.[15] This insight has been around since at least the beginning of the 1960s;[16] postcolonialism cannot do without it, as it relies so often on exposing the hidden assumptions behind a 'discourse' and asking whether these assumptions are legitimate.

It is also therefore to be noted that disciplinary boundaries are consequently weakened:

some would argue that rules of evidence according to the demands of the historian's profession have consequently also been weakened. But these 'rules of evidence' have also been subject to renegotiation within the 'historian's profession'; the counterargument would be *either* that postcolonialism is an important attempt at such a renegotiation; *or* that History itself is tyrannical, tainted with 'Western' 'hegemonic' assumptions and teleologies, and must be abandoned in favour of Other ways of seeing the past.[17]

Postcolonialism contains much theory that is variously taken from European thinkers in translation, often pertaining in the first instance to the metropolis, but subjected to decentred and sometimes eclectic readings.[18] It is possible to argue that this theoretical basis robs postcolonialism of its claim to provide alternatives to Eurocentric models, and that it merely provides a critique of the limitations of some of this theory. For instance, the claims to universalism of what has been referred to as 'the Enlightenment' were exposed as particularistic and often oppressive. Romantic reactions to the Enlightenment, however, were subsumed within the term 'post-Enlightenment', a term that appeared often in 1980s and 1990s writing. This discursive violence done to 'Western' thinking was not considered carefully; and after Edward W. Said's powerful critique of 'Orientalism' – arguing that the 'Orient' did not actually exist, but was the necessary Other in the 'Western' imagination that confirmed the self-congratulatory narrative of the 'West'[19] – it ought to have been clear that 'West' and 'East', if rhetorically operational historical categories, cannot afford to be the analytical categories of academic writing.

An unanswered set of questions waits in the wings. What is the place within postcolonial history of aspirations to universal frameworks of understanding? Can there be a critique of the *pretensions to* universality of certain frameworks of understanding that lead to a more universal framework, the qualifier 'more' then establishing that the 'universal' is an absolute abstraction that is not achievable but is nevertheless an aspirational category? There are tendencies now manifesting themselves, in what we can tentatively call a post-postcolonial moment, where the polarities 'universal' and 'local' have given way to a concern with interconnected histories, and with the co-constitution of subjectivities of the coloniser and colonised, rather than with a Europe versus non-Europe, East and West, universalist-tyranny-versus-particularist-liberationist-subjectivity set of frameworks; but perhaps it is too early to tell how far this will go, and whether some of this runs the risk of inventing a new triumphalist narrative of 'transnational history', 'global history' for an age of 'globalisation', projected backwards in time, and of 'cosmopolitan sensibilities'.

An inventory of important influences on postcolonial history would have to include Michel Foucault, Jacques Derrida and Jacques Lacan, as thinkers who can assist in the study of representations of colonised subjects, of their 'Othering', 'deconstructing' 'colonial discourse'. These theorists are often the presiding deities that no longer need to be explicitly cited. At its reductionist minimum, what this amounts to is the borrowing of the idea of a 'discourse' from Foucault, in the sense of a set of implicit assumptions that structure ways in which the world is seen, but which remain powerful by remaining implicit. Edward Said famously borrowed 'discourse' from Foucault and twinned it with the Italian Marxist and anti-Fascist Antonio Gramsci's concept of 'hegemony',[20] 'hegemony' being a state of affairs where people are ruled with their apparent consent because an explicit resort to coercion is not required: people have internalised the disciplinary regime.[21] This internalised disciplinary regime is an aspect of 'biopower', to re-translate to a Foucauldian idiom: a form of political control that encompasses everyday practices and even bodily practices of a population.[22] And it becomes necessary to speak of Foucault's conception of 'governmentality'

or 'governmental rationality',[23] as a result of which a concern with 'colonial governmentality' has now become part of a concern with 'colonial discourse'. Does this run the risk of too static and structuralist a view of 'colonialism'? From Derrida, postcolonialism chiefly uses 'deconstruction', and the slogan 'there is nothing outside the text', the latter being used to justify the reading of texts to render history, and to read all things as text.[24] From Lacan, 'the Other' makes its continuous and mostly unacknowledged appearance, often in conjunction with an attempt to understand the vicissitudes and dynamics of 'race'.[25] Then there are postcolonialism's very own theorists – Edward Said, of course, but also perhaps Gayatri Chakravorty Spivak and Homi K Bhabha. Robert J.C. Young called them the 'Holy Trinity' of postcolonial critics.[26]

The recovery of earlier generations of anti-colonial thinkers (Frantz Fanon, Aime Cesaire, Amilcar Cabral, Albert Memmi, perhaps also Steve Biko), though often stripped of much of their political radicalism, has also come to be part of postcolonial history and theory (thus we have Homi K. Bhabha's Fanon as opposed to Fanon the Marxist).[27] Postcolonialism is particularly ambivalent about Marxism, which often makes its appearance as a rigid system of thought that 'imposes closure' and is, after Edward Said, an 'orientalist' framework.[28] But there is still a concern with Marxism running through postcolonialism in some respects, sometimes explicit, often disavowed, sometimes in dialogue with the earlier selves of the writers who disavow it.

Much of the early work that has (retrospectively, at least) been incorporated into the genealogy of postcolonialism, for instance Subaltern Studies (of which, more below), was part of a cluster of concerns with peasant societies, with which left-wing intellectuals engaged closely in the 1960s and 1970s. Not a long time later (and it is tempting to connect this explicitly with the so-called 'fall of communism', c.1989–1992),

Marxism was seen in many ways to be another European and Eurocentric metanarrative. This highlights another potential problem of postcolonial history: anachronistic readings based on the (often moral) values of a different context in space and time are projected onto the past, according to which standards the past is always deficient (and in this sense, postcolonial history, despite its denials, is a theory of 'progress'). Karl Marx, listening to the debates in Parliament on the East India Company's Charter should somehow have anticipated late twentieth century critiques of Eurocentrism – and later Marxist theory that rejected, for instance, the 'Asiatic mode of production' does not recover Marxism for a non-Eurocentric reading as a result.

Postcolonial history is counter-canonical; but it increasingly operates without a canon to counter, content with de-centring that which is no longer at the centre. Arguably this is itself a result of the success of postcolonial histories: the (neo)colonial attitudes that (once) underpinned the writing of (some) history are no longer legitimate. However, this can be also be attributed to the larger set of contemporaneous trends that challenged mainstream histories from the 1960s: feminist histories, histories from below, postmodernism, and to some extent gay and lesbian histories (though these have been relatively little used in postcolonial fields, for reasons that we shall not have space to enter into). There is now a danger of the creation of a canon from the counter-canon of 'postcolonial thinkers', whose self-referentiality and collusive footnoting of one another has much to do with this.

Lest it be imagined that these sets of characterisations and criticisms are merely external and hostile, a clarification is in order. The field of postcolonialism has been, as befits its concerns, quite relentlessly engaged in self-criticism; its agenda changes with time, and it reorients its engagements. All of the difficulties outlined above have been to a greater or lesser extent acknowledged among the

practitioners of postcolonialism, and have been the subject of vigorous internal debates. However, these have also been the lines of external criticism to postcolonialism. Hostility of this kind has been expressed very often in the periphery itself, often in terms of the location of the postcolonial strongholds (North America) and a perceived lack of political engagement on the part of the anointed theorists of postcolonialism with important issues at a local level (geographically and temperamentally distanced as they are from the peripheral country that their scholarship is ostensibly concerned with).

## (POST-)MARXISM AND THE LOST HISTORIES OF LIBERATION: THE CASE OF *SUBALTERN STUDIES*

It is now so ingrained in hearts and minds that *Subaltern Studies* (*SS* for short) was at the vanguard of the postcolonialism wave that it comes as a surprise for those who came in late to learn that *SS* in its origins was actually a late wave of the 'history from below' movement of the 1960s and 1970s. Its models were the British Marxist historians, notably E.P. Thompson, a man quite hostile to 'theory'.[29] *SS*'s main theoretical engagement was with a heterodox Marxism, in particular following Antonio Gramsci. Gramsci's lament, following the Fascist seizure of power in Italy, was that the left had not really bothered to understand the Italian peasantry, which had seemingly betrayed its own interests by siding with the Fascists; the *SS* group similarly sought the basis of 'subaltern consciousness'.[30] Of particular importance was Gramsci's idea of a 'passive revolution', in which major social changes do not accompany the transition from (the remnants of) a feudal order to capitalism: an older elite assists in the transition with minimal or limited support from a working class, thereby presiding over its own continuity as an old aristocracy merges with and identifies with an emergent bourgeoisie, who in turn do not need to invoke solidarities (through the 'national' idea) with classes lower down the social order. The resultant political order is devoid of the experience of popular participation in revolutionary change, in contradistinction to the 'classical' revolutionary trajectory of the French Revolution. Hence the 'passive revolution'.[31] This model was important in that it explained the top-down nature of the transition to 'modernity' in India (castes and estates rather than classes, a strong state, state capitalism, 'pre-capitalist' survivals, and so on, although the debate on 'modernity in India/Indian modernity' is an ongoing one). An attempt to 'recover the voices' of the 'subaltern', a term that loosely meant 'non-elite' and therefore was the acknowledged Other or stranger to the historian's alleged Self, was later to give way to a reduction of the 'subaltern' to a cultural symbol that legitimated the historian as its cultural spokesman even as 'the subaltern' ceased to be considered by its self-appointed representatives as a real person.

Among the important work to come out of the early period of *SS* was a set of critiques of 'the colonial archive', notably on how subsequent historians of divergent ideological persuasion were in danger of reproducing the assumptions of the colonial state.[32] *SS* quickly had to face the problem of sources for nonelite voices, as with most histories from below. The 'colonial archive', often the only written source available, was according to Ranajit Guha to be 'read against the grain', but this was only possible with a jump in the historian's imagination taking the place of 'hard' evidence, by altering or reversing the assumptions of the ruling elite whose reports, written in the 'prose of counter-insurgency', filled these archives.[33] One could, of course, argue, that a rather static view of 'the archive' dominated such writing, where the active role of the historian in constituting the relevant archives for particular questions was not taken into account. The models, however, for the forms of social history reconstructed painstakingly from difficult archives, are not difficult

to recognise: they are Carlo Ginzburg's *The Cheese and the Worms,* Emmanuel Le Roy Ladurie's *Montaillou* and Natalie Zemon Davis's *The Return of Martin Guerre.*[34]

*Subaltern Studies* worked with conceptions of class from a quasi-anthropological perspective: class and caste were regarded as akin to each other, and class and religious affiliation tended to be difficult to separate, with distinctions not easy to draw from an emic perspective.[35] Bernard Cohn, historical anthropologist from Chicago, who made a contribution to *SS* in Volume IV, was largely responsible for the insight that colonial social dynamics created the very units of society in the colony that were apparently ancient and long-standing (variation on the 'invention of tradition' argument, a volume in which Cohn had a contribution).[36] Cohn was not a long-term member of *SS*, and had been writing since the 1950s; Nicholas Dirks later claimed that Cohn had anticipated Michel Foucault by several years in showing the impact of colonial discourse in the power/knowledge constellations within which political and social life was lived.[37]

There was also a strong set of interventions on the allegedly incomplete development of the Indian working class[38] – in part emerging from the 'mode of production debate' of the 1970s that had taken place outside and before *SS*: was there an incomplete transition to capitalism in a colony or an ex-colony, contrary to Karl Marx's formulation that colonial rule would inadvertently be progressive, because it would destroy the 'Asiatic mode of production', static and village-based? Was there indeed an 'Asiatic mode of production' that survived?[39] These were part of a cluster of concerns with the potential of peasants to become the social basis for revolutionary or socialist regimes that emerged around and during the Vietnam War and the Chinese Cultural Revolution;[40] they thus amounted to a sort of radical-developmentalism-and-its-alternatives approach. (A surprising absence in this set of concerns is Mao Zedong himself, although some members of the *SS* collective were practising Maoists before they were academics.) Dipesh Chakrabarty postulated an 'incomplete transition' to capitalism because the Indian worker's 'mentality' was still pre-capitalist; rural loyalties and 'communal' (religious) consciousness remained central to his being.[41] Chakrabarty was then very much a part of what he would later criticise as the theory of the not-yet, of India and the 'non-West' more generally being seen by the standards of 'Western' history as incomplete, as in the 'waiting room of history'.[42] It is curious that Chakrabarty sought a model of a working class in Karl Marx's theoretical writing, in *Capital* rather than in his historical writings – as his reinvented self ought to have told him. These earlier genealogies of *SS*'s concerns were soon to be repressed, although the repressed returned periodically in strange distorted forms.

One of the points of continuity from this early phase to the later phases of *SS* can be said to be an investment in the 'national' – although *SS* claimed to be challenging elite and top-down views of a national elite directing the masses, and of most communist narratives similarly showing the party leading the people. It also challenged what it saw as neo-imperialist readings of imperial rule providing progress and modernity, leading to a modern nation-state. Allegedly following Gramsci, *SS* sought to understand peasant consciousness; it also set out to find popular versions of the 'nation', and popular contributions to 'nationalism' – expecting to find this.[43] That there was no popular version of the nation was discomforting. Gramsci's idea of a 'passive revolution', however, proved important in that it seemed to explain the top-down nature of the Indian state and the inadequate development of a national-popular consciousness, in which the limited participation of the 'masses' in revolutionary activity led to the continuation of pre-independence institutions and elites rather than their displacement in the new, non-revolutionary order.[44] As we shall see, this concern with nationalism among *SS* scholars who never

quite succeeded in abandoning national frameworks of analysis, provided something of a justification for the subalternists' claim to the right to speak for the subaltern.[45]

Early *SS* was criticised for not being adequately theoretically oriented – a charge that in retrospect seems strange indeed.[46] Gayatri Spivak entered the project in Volumes IV and V, published in 1985 and 1987.[47] The following year, she published the now iconic 'Can the subaltern speak?', addressing the problem of representation as a problem of the historian appropriating the experience of someone else and rendering it in the language of history. Thus the subaltern could not speak – in the language of history – except when spoken for, which mediation made the project of the 'recovery' of subaltern voices impossible. Subalternity, in Spivak's reading, was a pure state of voicelessness, and her ideal-typical subaltern was a woman. Her statement that the speaking for colonised women was a way in which the coloniser legitimated his role was also central to one of her central lines of argument – 'white man saves brown woman from brown man' was her pithy summary of the claim.[48] Which of course left open the question why 'brown elite woman' speaking for 'brown subaltern woman' was a more legitimate form of representation.

In Partha Chatterjee's coinage of the possibility of the 'subalternity of an elite', a relational rather than an absolute subalternity was established.[49] The (dis)advantage of this turn of phrase was that it potentially enabled the rendering of elites as victims of colonialism, obscuring their own role as oppressors (although this is not necessarily the way he meant the phrase). This is a non-problem if one insists on the *relationality* of the category 'subaltern'; but gradually, 'subaltern' as a term seemed to lose anything like a stable meaning as programmatic statement followed programmatic statement among the protagonists of the movement that were prone to programmatic statements, in all of which the 'subaltern' took different shapes.[50] Some critics pointed out that 'subaltern' was Gramsci's term used to avoid the Fascist censors, and it made no sense that *SS* used it without the need to hide their politics. But the term served them well after their Marxism had been underplayed, disavowed or forgotten. 'Subaltern' became a shorthand for all the oppressed, for peasants, for non-Westerners, and thus was blurred, imprecise, a literary device, a metaphor or metonymy, etc.

> The peasant acts here as a shorthand for all the seemingly nonmodern, rural, nonsecular relationships and life practices that constantly leave their imprint on the lives of even the elites in India and on their institutions of government. The peasant stands for all that is not bourgeois (in a European sense) in Indian capitalism and modernity.[51]

It is unnecessary, for the purposes of this essay, to map the journey of 'subaltern' from peasant to symbol;[52] nor is it necessary to try and trace exactly when the decentring of elite narratives gave way to the centring of the subaltern*ist* as spokesman for the subaltern (variously construed), with the subalternist-symbolic-subaltern combination taking on the 'Western'. It might also be noted in passing that History itself, in some readings, was abandoned as a sort of Western, post-enlightenment form of discrimination,[53] and other forms of reading the past had been anointed as co-equal ways of seeing: 'I take gods and spirits to be existentially coeval with the human, and think from the assumption that the question of being human involves the question of being with gods and spirits.'[54] It might instead be noted that a project of understanding 'subaltern consciousness' – understanding the subaltern who was, initially, the stranger, the Other – gave way to a self-evident appropriation of the right to represent that Other as a sort of extension of the Self, against a new Other, variously conceived as 'the West', 'the oppressor', or 'History' itself. The implicit subjecthood and nationalisation of that new Self against an increasingly 'Western' Other – whether that 'West' lay in 'discourse' or elsewhere – needs to be noted here.

*Subaltern Studies*'s coupling with 'postcolonialism' was announced in a monumentalising publishing venture a mere six years into the *SS* project: *Selected Subaltern Studies* in 1988, with an introduction by Spivak that had initially been a part of *SS IV*, 'Subaltern Studies: deconstructing historiography',[55] and a foreword by Edward W. Said attesting to the importance of the project.[56] Ranajit Guha edited a *Subaltern Studies Reader* in 1997,[57] and subsequent publications by members of the collective have kept the brand-name alive. In many ways, *SS* and 'postcolonialism' were separate developments that moved closer in mutual recognition. *SS* had Gramsci; Said himself used Gramsci and Foucault in his similarly iconic *Orientalism* (1978);[58] *SS* followed.

As *SS* began to epitomise the success and possibilities of a counter-hegemonic project against the tyrannies of an academic establishment, it became somewhat of a model for the historiographies of Other regions. But what part of it? By the 1990s, the divergence between a radical liberationist approach and an increasingly textual one could no longer be ignored or regarded as easily bridgeable. Latin American supporters of *SS*, as they modelled themselves on their Indian colleagues, found themselves faced with this problematic of whether to concern themselves with the recovering of the life-worlds and experiences of the 'subaltern' as a historical figure a la Gramsci, or whether to focus on the deconstructing of 'Western' modes of thought relating to Latin America – two projects that, it was increasingly apparent, were methodologically and politically incompatible.[59]

## DECOLONISING THE SELF

Edward Said's *Orientalism* described a strategy of representation: the Orient did not exist as such, but was a creation of the 'West' that was in need of a strong Other to define itself; the 'Orient', passive, decadent, feminine, was what the 'Occident', active, vigorous, virile, was not. Thus, Orientalism was a form of power/knowledge that enabled the impe-rial endeavour to succeed.[60] Said chose to use the term despite the fact that it referred already to a set of scholarly endeavours as well as to a political position among colonial administrators in colonial India (i.e. those who opposed the imposition of European principles of governance and society on India and preferred to govern in an 'Oriental' man-ner); he therefore used the term in an extended way.[61] Said could, as later debates in which he participated confirm, be accused of 'occidentalism' in that he flattened the 'West' into an unproblematic and relatively monolithic set of discourses (it is not really a place).[62] This is nowhere more evident than in his tracing 'Western' discourses about the 'east' back to ancient Greece, which is only possible by accepting European myths of its own origins that make Greece 'Western' and 'European' – as the *Black Athena* debates soon afterwards were to underline.[63]

But Said is symptomatic of a quest for a voice that decentres – 'provincialises' in cur-rently fashionable terms – Europe, or at least the Eurocentric imagination. This Eurocen-tric imagination is not peculiar to Europeans, the argument goes, but could be internalised by the colonised. Said's own work is in many ways a rebellion against his own colonial education – his *Culture and Imperialism* seeks to demonstrate how the classic texts of the European canon are complicit in imperi-alism.[64] Said's doctoral student, Gauri Vishwanathan, showed how English litera-ture as a discipline that glorified the English and Englishness developed in the colonies rather than the metropole.[65]

The rediscovery for postcolonialism of earlier anticolonial voices that wrestled with the internalised coloniser was a part of the same dynamic: Frantz Fanon, Aime Cesaire, Leopold Senghor, Steve Biko, or Ngugi wa Thiongo, the artiste formerly known as James Ngugi.[66] The reference to a period of self-strengthening, of the acquisition of cultural self-confidence among the dispossessed before they can *regard themselves* as equals, is common to these texts. Among the dangers

that attend this process is the risk of seeking the authentically 'indigenous'. And as with many stage-ist arguments – another one being the Marxist argument that 'national liberation' must precede 'socialism' for the colonies – we all seem to be stuck in the immediate stage and never succeed in pro-ceeding to the next one. The discursive con-test continues; 'we' wrest the right to write 'our' 'histories' (or to tell our pasts differ-ently) from 'them'; 'they' are no longer the possessors of Universal truths.[67] What hap-pens, then, when there appears a need for a universalism of sorts?

Historians might also wish to note that many of these texts emerge from a rather schematic reading of French colonial rule, for which the myth of the civilising mission was far more directly important than for other European empires, British, Dutch, Portuguese or Belgian. Aime Cesaire, for instance, writing in 1955, seeks to demolish precisely this claim: 'colonisation works to *decivilise* the coloniser, to *brutalise* him in the true sense of the word, to degrade him, to awaken him to buried instincts, to covet-ousness, violence, race hatred and moral relativism.'[68] Furthermore, 'the very distin-guished, very humanistic, very Christian bourgeois of the twentieth century' needs to be told that:

> without his being aware of it, he has a Hitler inside him ... what he cannot forgive Hitler for is not *crime* in itself, *the crime against man*, it is not *the humiliation of man as such*, it is the crime against the white man, the humiliation of the white man, and the fact that he applied to Europe colonialist procedures which until then had been reserved exclusively for the Arabs of Algeria, the coolies of India, and the blacks of Africa.[69]

In addition, the importance of understanding 'the value of our old societies' was stressed:

> They were communal societies, never societies of the many for the few.
>
> They were societies that were not only ante-capitalist, as has been said, but also *anti-capitalist*.
>
> They were democratic societies, always.

They were cooperative societies, fraternal societies. I make a systematic defence of the societies destroyed by imperialism.[70]

This rather romanticised 'defence' of an idealised precolonial society reappears more often in writing in postcolonial mode from the 1980s onwards. And although sometimes phrased in a quasi-leftist language, borrowing some of the language of Marxism, it demonstrates the absence of class, of social stratification, and of power relations in the invocation – rather than analysis – of 'precolonial' societies. As 'precolonial', 'colonial' and 'postcolonial' become the terms of analysis, colonialism becomes the most important set of facts about a society. This is despite the fact that only the first of the terms is unambiguously chronological in its significance.

Such a position tends easily towards a defence of the 'innocence' of the colonised and a search for the 'authentic' 'native' style in a cultural nationalism that is untainted by 'Western' or other 'foreign influences: Ashis Nandy's Gandhi, for instance, is the authentically national anticolonial in his rejection of things and civilisations 'Western', his alleged use of 'feminine' resources of the self, thereby rejecting hypermasculine Western masculinities.[71] The obvious problem with this interpretation is that 'indigenist' readings of colonial rule are responses to colonial rule, and thus reifications or inventions of 'indigenism'.[72] 'It is the colonialist who becomes the defender of the native style', Frantz Fanon wrote perceptively in *The Wretched of the Earth*,[73] and versions of 'tradition' borrowed for anticolonial polemics could easily be the self-Orientalisation of the 'native', strategic or otherwise.

Postcolonial historians themselves run the risk of reproducing such a move in their own recounting of these histories of the 'indigenous'. An awkward or ambivalent relationship to anticolonial or 'Third World' nationalisms marks much anticolonial history-writing – the postcolonialists' ability to speak a nationalism at second remove, but also a disavowal of the narrowness of any nationalism and at least a rhetorical identification with national liberation movements elsewhere in the world. That the 'liberation' is legitimated by the 'national' makes it difficult for a consistent disavowal of all nationalisms to be made: an alternative axis of legitimate identity that will serve to justify a place in an international world of nation-states does not materialise.

Thus, difficult questions, for instance of internal colonialism within the boundaries of a 'postcolonial' state, of gender issues (in which women are subordinated to the building of a 'nation'), or indeed of class exploitation, do not always get the attention they deserve – which itself becomes a matter of strong (internal) dispute among (people who have been classified as) postcolonial thinkers or historians. By contrast, metropolitan nationalisms have been subject to the criticism that they discount the diversity of culture and identity in their midst, and attempt to discipline identities into rigid, homogeneous and more or less racially characterised nationalisms. Metropolitan nationalisms are explicitly seen as forms of oppression, and thus intolerant of diversity of human experience and desire. Why such criticisms are far less often levelled at their non-metropolitan versions is not a matter of logical consistency.

The question of who the spokespersons for a 'culture', a people, a 'nation' are raises itself here, in particular by claiming a privileged position as (post)colonised to (re)present '"Indian" pasts', 'African pasts' and so on. It has not gone unrecognised that this, and at times only this, is in danger of becoming the 'project' of postcolonial historiography: '… a certain postcolonial subject had … been recoding the colonial subject and appropriating the Native Informant's position.'[74] 'We cannot fight imperialism by perpetuating a "new orientalism".'[75] These dangers are manifested in the necessity to explicitly distance oneself from the implications of postcolonial argument: to deny the charge of indigenism, and to point out that the postcolonial intellectual writes from within the 'inheritance' of a 'universal and secular vision of the human' that 'is now global'.[76]

That many of the identitarian journeys mapped by postcolonial writers are personal as much as they are historical or political is not denied by them. 'For objective reasons that I had no control over, I grew up as an Arab with a Western education.'[77] 'I have lived all my conscious life in the framework of institutionalised separate development.'[78] Coming to terms with the past, and with forms of writing about the past are thus ways of coming to terms with oneself: 'the black man has become a shell, a shadow of a man, completely defeated, drowning in his own misery ... The first step therefore is to make the black come to himself; to pump back life into his empty shell; to infuse him with pride and dignity ....'[79] A return to universalism can only take place once this vital move has taken place.

## THEME AND VARIATIONS: WRITING HISTORY AND THE (POST)COLONISER

One theorist identified with a new postcolonial canon who has resisted the search for the 'indigenous' has been Homi Bhabha; his insistence on the 'hybridity', the 'ambivalence', the 'in-between-ness' and 'fluidity' of human experiences, and his search for comparable examples in other contexts, however, have still been within the framework of seeking the subjective experiences of fellow victim communities.[80] The ambivalence that Bhabha describes makes its presence felt, for instance, in the 'mimicry' of the colonial subject of the 'post-Enlightenment' norms of the coloniser: '... colonial mimicry is the desire for a reformed, recognisable Other, as *a subject of difference that is almost the same but not quite.*'[81] The colonial subject's mimicry slides easily into mockery, subversive in that the Anglicised native is not, cannot be, English; and is a reminder that the principles articulated for the metropolis, not intended for the colony, are, when appropriated, disruptive of the existing order.

If we were to use this principle to read the writings of postcolonial theorists rather than just postcolonial situations in the historical past (and one of the characteristics of postcolonial theorising is an anachronistic set of readings that demand the past be read in the light of present perceptions and sensibilities), then we can trace the oscillation between the nativist tendencies of seeking 'authenticity' (in community, culture, 'nation') and the attempt to find standpoints that are generalisable and defensible outside of the subjectivities of the colonised, or of their retrospective interpreters and representatives.

Postcolonial histories are of course many, and to draw an axis of differentiation between the 'colonial difference' theme, which was important earlier on, to the 'entanglements' and 'co-production' of colonial and metropolitan societies theme that has of late been more prevalent might be useful, although the division proposed here is too schematic and presupposes a 'progress' from the former to the latter that is difficult to sustain if one looks at everyday writing in postcolonial mode, now the hegemonic common-sense of much well-meaning academic writing. The latter theme is represented in the so-called 'New Imperial History'. The 'new' is a critique of metropolitan nationalisms often implicit in writing 'old' imperial histories, or imperial histories of imperialism, as we might call it.

The trend that has come to be called 'the New Imperial History' (hereafter NIP) provides a strong critique of, for instance, 'Little Englander' histories of Britain, which underestimate or ignore the impact of the empire on British domestic life. An early and programmatic statement of this position was provided by Catherine Hall:

In Britain, the traces of those imperial histories appear everywhere – in the naming of streets, the sugar in tea, the coffee and cocoa that are drunk, the mango chutney that is served, the memorials in cemeteries, the public monuments in parks and squares.[82]

This is not particularly dissimilar to the Manchester revisionism of the 1980s, led by John MacKenzie, who insisted that if Empire was not always a central issue in domestic British affairs, this was because its ubiquitous presence made it always visible and therefore invisible[83] – an argument close to Edward Said's in *Culture and Imperialism*,[84] though MacKenzie, an anti-Saidian, might not have appreciated this.[85] That the plea for a 'new' imperial history was made alongside a plea for the relevance of imperial history in the history of Britain should not blind us to differences: the 'nation' (British? English?), in the 'new' argument, was not merely *shaped* by the experience of empire, but was unthinkable without it. The argument that there was a core 'Englishness' or 'Britishness' at 'home' impervious to the experiences and cross-currents of the perambulations of colonial subjects, diasporas, migration, consumption patterns, etc. was implausible; the myth of the 'national' core, contemporaneously as well as retrospectively among Little-England histories and 'old' imperial historians alike, was a refusal to acknowledge that the Empire was always also at Home.[86] It might be noted in passing that the NIP was more sceptical of a *metropolitan* national imagination than it was of the 'national liberation movements' that set themselves up in opposition to (but also at least in part on the model of) metropolitan nationalisms; and NIP was more sceptical of nationalisms, nation-states or states than *SS* was.

What this amounted to was a critical approach to British 'national' history, exploring lines of tension. The outsider within; the importance of empire in constructing norms of masculinity and femininity; the similarities of race and class as discursive categories; the imperialism of early (British, imperial) feminist projects; race, sexual anxieties, miscegenation; the exclusions of the liberal imagination – all became themes for exploration.[87]

Paul Gilroy is notable in resisting a trend of opting for a cultural counter-nationalism in opposition to metropolitan nationalism or parochialism:

> As a supplement to existing formulations of the diaspora idea, the black Atlantic provides an invitation to move into the contested spaces between the local and the global in ways that do not privilege the modern nation state and its institutional order of the sub-national and supra-national networks and patterns of power, communication and conflict that they work to discipline, regulate and govern.[88]

Gilroy coined the term 'The Black Atlantic': 'my own provisional attempt to figure a deterritorialised, multiplex and anti-national basis for the affinity or "identity of passions" between diverse black populations.'[89] He thus stands against a counter-nationalism of a black variety,[90] invoking Homi Bhabha's ideas of the 'in-between-ness' and 'hybridity' of cultural forms.[91] Gilroy never loses sight of the fact that the arguments about being a nation were invoked consciously due to the legitimacy of national paradigms on a world stage, rather than treating 'nations' as inevitable entities (even when imagined or invented).

The paradox for NIP is, however, that it needs the nation for its own structure: 'By now it is paradoxically axiomatic that obituaries of the nation are premature.'[92] Thus, identities, subjectivities, and the colonial impact on the production of identities and the control of those identities end up being studied, more often than not, in the context of metropolitan nationalisms. That the tone of writing about such nationalisms is not one of approval makes little difference to the process of reification.

## SOME CONCLUSIONS

Postcolonial history's sensitivity to 'discourse' and to the cultural dynamics of how colonialism disciplines the Other appears for some years now to have reached a *cul de sac*. At its worst, 'postcolonialism' descends to the politics of comparative victimhood, where an assertion of solidarity with the oppressed, generically, takes the place of rigorous intellectual engagement. At its worst, again, in centring the academic voice that claims the right to speak for the downtrodden, it privileges the identity of the academic speakers themselves. If 'postcolonial history' remains relevant, it can only be by historicising itself.

No single intellectual or academic would accept the charge that their writing has produced a valorisation of 'authenticity', a freezing and reification of identities, an imprisonment of the individual in a pre-defined collectivity and her surrender to the authority of self-proclaimed custodians of 'culture' and 'tradition', recognised as such by states and governments. But indeed, this is what appears to have happened.

The claiming of a privileged position as (post)colonised to (re)present the subjectivities of one's fellow downtrodden subjects requires an identification that is as uncertain as that of the inheritor of the (historically defined) perpetrator community (the colonisers, the white races) identifying with the victim community (the colonised, 'Indians', 'First Nations', women) and writing from that perspective. A trend set in motion is difficult to arrest – the notoriously autonomous text, perhaps? And is it possible to draw back from the implications of the project without surrendering the cultural authority that has been won for oneself, and is sustained, by that project?

The acknowledgement of diversity, plurality and a multiplicity of voices is now considered common sense; it is 'difference' rather than similarity that is assumed when two people not of the same 'culture' come face to face. This is differently problematic; it is a semi-coercive assumption of alterity that produces conversations in which one assumes that the 'stranger' does not speak one's language.

And as to the dangers of universalistic claims that yield an oppressive cultural imperialism when left unquestioned: the new 'Western' conservatives operate not by continuing to assert the universality of 'Western'

thought and therefore the right of the 'West' to export its values by force to a reluctant world that must be administered the painful cure to an illness it is ignorant of; they operate by *acknowledging* diversity and difference and by fighting that diversity in the name of the *right* of the 'West', self-proclaimedly *particular* rather than universal, to *impose* itself on its Others – as a matter of its *survival*.

Samuel Huntington's notorious 'clash of civilisations' argument identifies several 'cultures', among them the 'Western', whose contending subjectivities must battle for survival, and he therefore argues that the 'West' must defend itself or be destroyed.[93] So the decentring of the 'Western' claim to universalism and to a monopoly of standards of 'progress', 'modernity', 'rationality', etc. has arguably created a new situation in which, shorn of such universalist pretensions, 'Western man' must defend his subjectivity – and his potential loss of power and therefore his own (potential) victimhood – in the same way as the Native American (or the First Nations), or the Chinese, or the 'Islamic', civilisations, have to. In another book, Huntington argued that 'Western' culture did not require being born 'Western', merely an acceptance of 'Western' values.[94] But he did argue that this culture would have to be defended resolutely against the cultural relativism of our times – other cultures would similarly defend themselves in their own territories. (Huntington expects 'civilisations' to behave like states, and consequently to make war on other civilisations that presumably would also organise themselves like or as states.) Structurally, Huntington's is a nearly-classical postcolonial argument, in many senses; he has only to establish the victimhood, actual or impending, of the 'West', to perfect it.

The bulk of the significant or formative debates in postcolonial history occurred in the period from the late 1980s to the early 1990s, which makes many of them between 20 and 30 years old. The *terminology* of the postcolonial interventions have acquired a certain currency and legitimacy, in particular, the term 'subaltern'. The arguments have gradually lost their opponents, and some of them appear to be exercises in tilting at windmills. The term 'postcolonial' increasingly appears to be devoid of the polemical and political charge that it once carried.

And although there is now a tendency to think of postcolonialism as conducive to enabling an understanding of the (post)colonial Other by the (post)colonising Self, or by analogous victims by perpetrators, postcolonialism was in the first instance a model of *conflict*, a challenge to the right of the (post)coloniser to continue to represent the (post)colonial subject as if s/he did not have a voice. In fact, we may note in parentheses that many of the challenges posed to postcolonial theory and theorists came from a position that claimed a *different axis of confrontation* – the argument was that internal conflicts among the (post)colonised, for instance on 'class' lines, were being brushed under the carpet, and a form of unproblematic and unified 'identity' of the postcolonial was being celebrated instead.

The way out of this conflict between (post)coloniser and (post)colonised was for the (post)coloniser to shed some of the burden of her inheritance of historic-guilt-as-perpetrator by *accepting the subjectivities of the (post)colonised*. This was a sort of vicarious redressal of grievances, an academic version of state apologies and reparations for alleged or actual historic wrongs; but perhaps it has proved its limitations as an approach to writing history.

## NOTES AND REFERENCES

1 Dipesh Chakrabarty, 'Postcolonialism and the artifice of history: who speaks for "Indian" pasts?', *Representations* 37, *Special Issue: Imperial Fantasies and Postcolonial Histories* (Winter 1992), pp. 1–26.
2 Stuart Hall, 'When was "the post-colonial"? Thinking at the limit', in Iain Chambers and Lidia Curti (eds), *The Post-Colonial Question: Common Skies, Divided Horizons* (London: Routledge, 1996), pp. 242–60: 254.
3 'Deconstruction' came into postcolonial theory from Jacques Derrida, *De la Grammatologie*, translated into English by Gayatri Spivak, considered one of the main theorists of 'the postcolonial'. Jacques Derrida, *Of*

*Grammatology*, trans. Gayatri Chakravorty Spivak (London: Johns Hopkins University Press, 1976).
4 See Aijaz Ahmad, 'Postcolonialism: what's in a name?' in Roman de la Campa, E. Ann Kaplan and Michael Sprinker (eds), *Late Imperial Culture* (London: Verso, 1995), pp. 11–32.
5 Benita Parry, *Delusions and Discoveries: Studies on India in the British Imagination, 1880–1930* (London: Allen Lane, 1972) was a pioneering work in focusing on British imperial attitudes to Empire; criticisms of her by (among others) the emerging heroes of 'postcolonial theory' led to a first round of polemics. For a contextualisation of some of these debates, see Michael Sprinker, 'Foreword', to Benita Parry, *Delusions and Discoveries* (new edition, London: Verso, 1998), pp. vii–xiii; Benita Parry, 'Preface' to the new edition, pp. 1–28.
6 Thus, the contention by Michel Foucault that there are always contending 'regimes of truth' is inadequate for the purposes of postcolonialism – see Michel Foucault, 'Truth and power', in Michel Foucault, *Power/Knowledge: Selected Interviews and Other Writings 1972–1977*, ed. Colin Gordon (New York: Pantheon, 1980), pp. 109–33. Again, there is no consensus on what 'postmodernism' really is, and the label is often disavowed by thinkers associated with it. But there is by now a readily recognised set of characteristics attributed to it by outsiders who know they are outside.
7 Gayatri Chakravorty Spivak, 'Introduction: Subaltern Studies: deconstructing historiography', in Ranajit Guha and Gayatri Chakravorty Spivak (eds), *Selected Subaltern Studies* (New York: Oxford University Press, 1988), pp. 3–24; Sara Danius, Stefan Jonsson and Gayatri Chakravorty Spivak, 'An interview with Gayatri Chakravorty Spivak', *boundary 2*, Vol. 20, No. 2 (Summer, 1993), pp. 24–50, in which Spivak says she no longer wants to use the term.
8 On the potential divergences, see Edward W. Said, *Covering Islam: How the Media and the Experts Determine How We See the Rest of the World* (revised edition, London: Vintage, 1997) [1981], still quite relevant today.
9 The phrase 'emotional cathexes' is the phrase used in the English translation of Sigmund Freud, *Introductory Lectures on Psychoanalysis* (trans. J. Strachey) (Harmondsworth: Pelican, 1974) [1915–17].
10 Gyan Prakash, 'Writing post-Orientalist histories of the third world: perspectives from Indian historiography', *Comparative Studies in Society and History*, Vol. 32, No. 2 (April 1990), pp. 383–408; Gyan Prakash, 'Subaltern Studies as postcolonial criticism', *American Historical Review*, Vol. 99, No. 5 (December 1994), pp. 1475–90; Dipesh Chakrabarty, 'A small history of Subaltern Studies', *Habitations of Modernity: Essays in the Wake of Subaltern Studies* (Chicago: University of Chicago Press, 2002), pp. 3–19, etc. Rosalind C. Morris (ed.), *Can the Subaltern Speak? Reflections on the History of an Idea* (New York: Columbia University Press, 2010), is among the latest monumentalising efforts.

11  That which is referred to as postcolonial history is now so large a set of fields that it is impossible for any one individual to treat it as a whole. It is therefore necessary for the author of this essay to declare his perspective as in the first instance a historian of South Asia, interested in intellectual histories and the movements of ideas. The case studies selected for the purposes of this essay are intended to be illustrative rather than comprehensive; and far longer works treating postcolonialism(s) are readily available should a reader be interested in fields or sub-fields not adequately treated here. See for instance Robert J.C. Young, *Postcolonialism: An Historical Introduction* (Oxford: Blackwell, 2001).

12  Gyan Prakash, 'Can the subaltern ride? A reply to O'Hanlon and Washbrook', *Comparative Studies in Society and History*, Vol. 34 (1992), pp. 168–84; Homi K. Bhabha, 'Introduction: locations of culture', *The Location of Culture* (London: Routledge, 1994), pp. 1–18.

13  Ashis Nandy, *The Intimate Enemy: Loss and Recovery of Self Under Colonialism* (Delhi: Oxford University Press, 1983), p. ix.

14  See for instance Kathleen Wilson (ed.), *A New Imperial History: Culture, Identity and Modernity in Britain and the Empire, 1660–1840* (Cambridge: Cambridge University Press, 2004); the appearance of such metanarratives can be seen as an important step towards the creation of a (counter?-)canon.

15  The work of Hayden White is influential in this regard: see for example 'The value of narrativity in the representation of reality', *Critical Inquiry*, Vol. 7, No. 1 (Autumn, 1980), pp. 5–27; 'The question of narrative in contemporary historical theory', *History and Theory*, Vol. 23, No. 1 (Feb., 1984), pp. 1–33; and other essays collected in Hayden White, *The Content of the Form: Narrative Discourse and Historical Representation* (Baltimore: Johns Hopkins University Press, 1987).

16  See for example E.H. Carr, *What is History?* (2nd edn, reprint, Harmondsworth: Penguin, 1990) [1961], esp. pp. 22–5.

17  Dipesh Chakrabarty, *Provincializing Europe: Postcolonial Thought and Historical Difference* (Princeton: Princeton University Press, 2000).

18  See for instance Ranajit Guha on Asia, and India, being outside Hegel's Universal History. Ranajit Guha, *History at the Limit of World History* (New York: Columbia University Press, 2002).

19  Edward W. Said, *Orientalism* (New York: Pantheon, 1978).

20  Said, *Orientalism*.

21  Antonio Gramsci, *Selections from the Prison Notebooks*, ed. and trans. Quintin Hoare and Geoffrey Nowell Smith (London: Lawrence and Wishart, 1971).

22  Michel Foucault, *The History of Sexuality, Vol. 1: An Introduction* (New York: Pantheon, 1978); Thomas Lemke, '"The birth of bio-politics": Michel Foucault's lecture at the Collège de France on neo-liberal governmentality', *Economy and Society*, Vol. 30 No. 2 (May 2001), pp. 190–207.

23  Michel Foucault, 'Governmentality', in Graham Burchell, Colin Gordon, and Peter Miller (eds), *The Foucault Effect: Studies in Governmentality* (Chicago: University of Chicago Press, 1991), pp. 87–104.

24  Derrida, *Of Grammatology*.

25  Jacques Lacan, *The Four Fundamental Principles of Psychoanalysis* (London: Hogarth Press, 1977).

26  Robert J.C. Young, *Colonial Desire: Hybridity in Culture, Theory and Race* (London: Routledge, 1995), p. 163.

27  Homi K. Bhabha, 'Foreword: remembering Fanon', in Frantz Fanon, *Black Skin, White Masks* (London: Pluto Press, 1986); Cedric Robinson, 'The appropriation of Frantz Fanon', *Race and Class*, Vol. 35 No. 1 (July 1993), pp. 79–91.

28  Said, *Orientalism*, pp. 155–7.

29  See E.P. Thompson, *The Poverty of Theory* (London: Merlin Press, 1995) [1978], his long polemic against Louis Althusser. On Thompson's importance to *SS*, see Sumit Sarkar, 'The relevance of E.P. Thompson', and 'The decline of the subaltern in Subaltern Studies', for his understanding of the changes – for the worse – in the *SS* project – both in Sumit Sarkar, *Writing Social History* (Delhi: Oxford University Press, 1997), pp. 50–81 and 82–108 respectively.

30  David Arnold, 'Gramsci and peasant subalternity in India', *Journal of Peasant Studies* Vol. 11, No. 4 (1984), pp. 155–77; Antonio Gramsci, *Selections from the Prison Notebooks*, ed. and trans. Quintin Hoare and Geoffrey Nowell Smith (London: Lawrence and Wishart, 1971).

31  Antonio Gramsci, 'Notes on Italian history', *Selections from the Prison Notebooks*, pp. 1–44.

32  Ranajit Guha, 'The prose of counter-insurgency', in Ranajit Guha (ed.), *Subaltern Studies II* (Delhi: Oxford University Press, 1983), pp. 45–88; Shahid Amin, 'Approver's testimony, judicial discourse: the case of Chauri Chaura', in Ranajit Guha (ed.), *Subaltern Studies V* (Delhi: Oxford University Press, 1987), pp. 166–202; Gyanendra Pandey, 'The bigoted Julaha', *The Construction of Communalism in Colonial North India* (Delhi: Oxford University Press, 1990), pp. 66–108.

33  Ranajit Guha, 'The prose of counter-insurgency', in Ranajit Guha (ed.), *Subaltern Studies II* (Delhi: Oxford University Press, 1983), pp. 45–88;

34  Carlo Ginzburg, *The Cheese and the Worms: The Cosmos of a Sixteenth-Century Miller* (London: Routledge & Kegan Paul, 1980) [1976], Emmanuel Le Roy Ladurie, *Montaillou: Cathars and Catholics in a French Village, 1294–1334* (Harmondsworth: Penguin, 1980) [1975], Natalie Zemon Davis, *The Return of Martin Guerre* (Cambridge, MA: Harvard University Press, 1983). These became central to the project of teaching students how to write social history with problematic sources; and they formed models for work such as Shahid Amin, *Event, Metaphor, Memory: Chauri Chaura, 1922–1992* (Delhi: Oxford University Press, 1995), and later, in a book that sits awkwardly with the theoretical directions of *SS*, Partha Chatterjee, *A Princely Impostor? The Strange and*

*Universal History of the Kumar of Bhawal* (Princeton: Princeton University Press, 2002).

35  Partha Chatterjee, 'Agrarian relations and communalism in Bengal, 1920–1935', in Ranajit Gua (ed.), *Subaltern Studies I* (Delhi: Oxford University Press, 1982), pp. 9–38.

36  Bernard S. Cohn, 'The command of language and the language of command', in Ranajit Guha (ed.), *Subaltern Studies IV* (Delhi: Oxford University Press, 1985), pp. 276–329.

37  Nicholas Dirks, 'Foreword' to Bernard Cohn, *Colonialism and its Forms of Knowledge: The British in India* (Princeton: Princeton University Press, 1996), pp. ix–xvii.

38  Dipesh Chakrabarty, *Rethinking Working Class History: Bengal 1890–1940* (Princeton: Princeton University Press, 1989).

39  Stephen P. Dunn, *The Fall and Rise of the Asiatic Mode of Production* (London: Routledge & Kegan Paul, 1982).

40  For the genealogy of these concerns, see Henry Bernstein and Terence J, Byres, 'From peasant studies to agrarian change', *Journal of Agrarian Change*, Vol. 1, No. 1 (January 2001), pp. 1–56. Thus, Friedrich Engels, *The Peasant War in Germany* (1850) was a key text, as was the 1966 translation of A.V. Chayanov, *The Theory of Peasant Economy* (Homewood, IL: The American Economic Association, 1966) (first published in 1920); in Ranajit Guha, *Elementary Aspects of Peasant Insurgency in Colonial India* (Delhi: Oxford University Press, 1983), a breathtakingly wide array of examples from across the world, in different times and spaces, are brought into play; the influence of Eric Wolf's *Peasant Wars of the Twentieth Century* (New York: Harper and Row, 1969), of Teodor Shanin, *Peasants and Peasant Societies* (Harmondsworth: Penguin, 1971); of ongoing debates in the *Journal of Peasant Studies*, of Karl Marx's letters to Vera Zasulich late in his life which talked of the possibility of a radical peasantry as the vanguard class instead of the proletariat, all need to be acknowledged. Much of this could be said to have essentialised 'the peasantry' as broadly comparable worldwide – a point acknowledged in Bernstein and Byres, 'From peasant studies to agrarian change', p. 7.

41  Chakrabarty, *Rethinking Working Class History*.

42  Chakrabarty, 'Postcolonialism and the artifice of history', recycled eight years later as Chapter 1 of Dipesh Chakrabarty, *Provincializing Europe: Postcolonial Thought and Historical Difference* (Princeton: Princeton University Press, 2000), pp. 27–46, when the argument proposed had few, if any, academic opponents.

43  Ranajit Guha, 'On Some Aspects of the Historiography of Colonial India', in Ranajit Guha (ed.), *Subaltern Studies I* (Delhi: Oxford University Press, 1982), pp. 1–8.

44  Partha Chatterjee, *Nationalist Thought and the Colonial World: A Derivative Discourse?* (London: Zed Books, 1986).

45  I have made this argument in more detail elsewhere: see Benjamin Zachariah, 'Residual nationalism and the Indian (radical?) intellectual: On indigenism, authenticity and the coloniser's presents', in Debraj Bhattacharya

(ed.), *Of Matters Modern* (Calcutta: Seagull Books, 2008), pp. 330–59.

46  See for instance Rosalind O'Hanlon, 'Recovering the subject: *Subaltern Studies* and histories of resistance in colonial South Asia', *Modern Asian Studies*, Vol. 22, No. 1 (1988), pp 189–224, a review article on the first three volumes of *SS*.

47  Gayatri Chakravorty Spivak, 'Discussion: Subaltern Studies: deconstructing historiography', in Ranajit Guha (ed.), *Subaltern Studies IV* (Delhi: Oxford University Press, 1985), pp. 330–63; Gayatri Chakravorty Spivak, 'A literary representation of the subaltern: Mahasweta Devi's *Stanadayini*', in Ranajit Guha (ed.), *Subaltern Studies V* (Delhi: Oxford University Press, 1987), pp. 91–134.

48  Gayatri Chakraborty Spivak, 'Can the subaltern speak?' in Cary Nelson and Lawrence Grossberg (eds), *Marxism and the Interpretation of Culture* (Basingstoke: Macmillan, 1988), pp. 271–313.

49  Partha Chatterjee, *The Nation and its Fragments: Colonial and Postcolonial Histories* (Princeton: Princeton University Press, 1993), p. 37.

50  Reviewers have pointed out that despite *SS*'s claims to being a movement or a school of thought, many writers who have published under its banner have made no programmatic claims.

51  Chakrabarty, *Provincializing Europe*, p. 11.

52  For a recent non-subalternist narrative of this kind, see David Ludden, 'Introduction: a brief history of subalternity', in David Ludden (ed.), *Reading Subaltern Studies: Critical history, contested meaning, and the globalisation of South Asia* (London: Anthem Press, 2001), pp. 1–27.

53  Chakrabarty, 'Postcolonialism and the artifice of history'.

54  Chakrabarty, *Provincializing Europe*, p. 16.

55  Gayatri Chakravorty Spivak, 'Introduction: Subaltern Studies: deconstructing historiography', in Ranajit Guha and Gayatri Chakravorty Spivak (eds), *Selected Subaltern Studies* (New York: Oxford University Press, 1988), pp. 3–24.

56  Edward W. Said, 'Foreword', to Ranajit Guha and Gayatri Chakravorty Spivak (eds), *Selected Subaltern Studies* (New York: Oxford University Press, 1988), pp. v–x.

57  Ranajit Guha (ed.) *A Subaltern Studies Reader 1986–1995* (Minneapolis: University of Minnesota Press, 1997).

58  Edward W. Said, *Orientalism* (New York: Pantheon, 1978).

59  Latin American Subaltern Studies Group, 'Founding statement', *boundary 2*, Vol. 20, No. 3 (1993), pp. 110–21; Florencia A Mallon, 'The promise and dilemma of Subaltern Studies: perspectives from Latin American history', *American Historical Review*, Vol. 99, No. 5 (December 1994), pp. 1491–515; Daniel Mato, 'Not "studying the subaltern," but studying *with* "subaltern" social groups, or, at least, studying the hegemonic articulations of power', *Nepantla: Views from South* Vol. 1, No. 3 (2000), pp. 479–502.

60  Said, *Orientalism*.

61  See e.g. SN Mukherjee, *Sir William Jones: A Study in Eighteenth-Century British Attitudes to India* (Hyderabad: Orient Longman, 1987); Martin Moir and Lynn Zastoupil (eds), *The Great Indian Education Debate: Documents*

*Relating to the Orientalist-Anglicist Controversy, 1781–1843* (Richmond, Surrey: Curzon, 1999).

62   Ahmad, 'Orientalism and after' summarises some of these debates.

63   Martin Bernal, *Black Athena* (2 vols, London: Vintage, 1991); the debate thereafter is too long to summarise, but see for instance Jacques Berlinerblau, *Heresy in the University: the* Black Athena *Controversy and the Responsibilities of American Intellectuals* (New Jersey: Rutgers University Press, 1999); Martin Bernal, *Black Athena Writes Back: Martin Bernal Responds to his Critics* (ed. by David Chioni Moore) (Durham: Duke University Press, 2001).

64   Edward W. Said, *Culture and Imperialism* (London: Vintage, 1994) [1993].

65   Gauri Vishwanathan, *Masks of Conquest: Literary Studies and British Rule in India* (London: Faber, 1990).

66   See e.g. Frantz Fanon, *Black Skin, White Masks* (New York: Grove Press, 1967) [1952]; Frantz Fanon, *The Wretched of the Earth* (Harmondsworth: Penguin, 1967) [1961]; Aime Cesaire, *Discourse on Colonialism* (New York: Monthly Review Press, 1972) [1955]; Leopold Sedar Senghor, 'Negritude: a humanism of the twentieth century', in Wilfred Carty and Martin Kilson (eds), *The African Reader: Independent Africa* (New York: Vintage, 1970), pp. 179–92 [1964]; James Ngugi, *A Grain of Wheat* (London: Heinemann, 1967); Steve Biko, *I Write What I Like: A Selection of his Writings* (London: Heinemann, 1979) [1969–78].

67   See Ranajit Guha, *An Indian Historiography of India: A Nineteenth-Century Agenda and its Implications* (Calcutta: KP Bagchi, 1988), reprinted with revisions in Guha, Ranajit, *Dominance without Hegemony: History and Power in Colonial India* (Cambridge, MA: Harvard University Press, 1997), pp. 152–214; and Ranajit Guha, *History at the Limit of World History* (New York: Columbia University Press, 2002), for a remarkable continuity of concerns.

68   Cesaire, *Discourse on Colonialism*, p. 13.

69   Cesaire, *Discourse on Colonialism*, p. 14.

70   Cesaire, *Discourse on Colonialism*, p. 23.

71   Nandy, *The Intimate Enemy*.

72   See E.J. Hobsbawm and T.O. Ranger (eds), *The Invention of Tradition* (Cambridge: Cambridge University Press, 1983).

73   Fanon, *The Wretched of the Earth*, pp. 195–6.

74   Gayatri Chakravorty Spivak, *A Critique of Postcolonial Reason: Towards a History of the Vanishing Present* (Cambridge, MA: Harvard University Press, 1999), p. ix.

75   Gayatri Chakravorty Spivak, 'The question of cultural studies', *Outside in the Teaching Machine* (New York: Routledge, 1993), p. 277.

76   Chakrabarty, *Provincialising Europe*, pp. 4–5.

77   Said, *Culture and Imperialism*, p. xxx.

78   Biko, 'We blacks', *I Write What I Like*, p. 27.

79   Biko, 'We blacks', *I Write What I Like*, p. 29.

80   Homi Bhabha, *The Location of Culture*, especially 'Introduction: locations of culture', pp. 1–18, and 'Of mimicry and man: the ambivalence of colonial discourse', pp. 85–92.

81   Bhabha, *The Location of Culture*, p. 86.

82   Catherine Hall, 'Histories, empires and the post-colonial moment', in Iain Chambers and Lidia Curti (eds), *The Post-Colonial Question: Common Skies, Divided Horizons* (London: Routledge, 1996), pp. 65–77: 66.

83   See for instance John M. Mackenzie, *Propaganda and Empire: The Manipulation of British Public Opinion, 1880–1960* (Manchester: Manchester University Press, 1984); John M. Mackenzie (ed.), *Imperialism and Popular Culture* (Manchester: Manchester University Press, 1986).

84   Said, *Culture and Imperialism*

85   John M. Mackenzie, *Orientalism: History, Theory and the Arts* (Manchester: Manchester University Press, 1995).

86   For a programmatic statement, see Antoinette Burton, 'Who needs the nation? Interrogating "British" history', *Journal of Historical Sociology*, Vol. 10 No. 3 (September 1997), pp. 227–48. See also Catherine Hall, *Civilising Subjects: Colony and Metropole in the English Imagination, 1830–1867* (Chicago: University of Chicago Press, 2002); Catherine Hall (ed.), *Cultures of Empire: Colonizers in Britain and the Empire in the Nineteenth and Twentieth Centuries: A Reader* (London: Routledge, 2000); Catherine Hall and Sonya O Rose (eds), *At Home with the Empire: Metropolitan Culture and the Imperial World* (Cambridge: Cambridge University Press, 2006).

87   For instance Frederick Cooper and Anne Laura Stoler (eds), *Tensions of Empire: Colonial Cultures in a Bourgeois World* (Berkeley: University of California Press, 1997); Mrinalini Sinha, *Colonial Masculinity: The 'Manly Englishman' and the 'Effeminate Bengali' in the Late Nineteenth Century* (Manchester: Manchester University Press, 1995); Antoinette Burton, *Burdens of History: British Feminists, Indian Women, and Imperial Culture 1860–1915* (Chapel Hill: University of North Carolina Press, 1994); Antoinette Burton, *At the Heart of Empire: Indians and the Colonial Encounter in Late Victorian Britain* (Berkeley: University of California Press, 1998); Philippa Levine, *Prostitution, Race, and Politics: Policing Venereal Disease in the British Empire* (London: Routledge, 2003); Anne Laura Stoler, *Race and the Education of Desire: Foucault's History of Sexuality and the Colonial Order of Things* (Durham: Duke University Press, 1995); Anne Laura Stoler, *Carnal Knowledge and Imperial Power: Race and the Intimate in Colonial Rule* (Berkeley: University of California Press, 2002); Mary Louise Pratt, *Imperial Eyes: Travel Writing and Transculturation* (London: Routledge, 1992); Sudipta Sen, *Distant Sovereignty: National Imperialism and the Origins of British India* (London: Routledge, 2002); John Marriott, *The other empire: metropolis, India and progress in the colonial imagination* (Manchester: Manchester University Press, 2003); Adele Perry, *On the Edge of Empire: Gender, Race, and the Making of British Columbia 1849–1871* (Toronto: University of Toronto

Press, 2001); Alan Lester, *Imperial Networks: Creating Identities in Nineteenth-Century South Africa and Britain* (London: Routledge, 2001).

88  Paul Gilroy, 'Route work: the Black Atlantic and the politics of exile', in Chambers and Curti (eds), *The Post-Colonial Question*, pp. 17–29: 22.

89  Gilroy, 'Route work', p. 18.

90  Paul Gilroy, *The Black Atlantic: Modernity and Double Consciousness* (Cambridge, MA: Harvard University Press, 1993); also Paul Gilroy, *Between Camps: Nations, Cultures and the Allure of Race* (Harmondsowrth: Penguin, 2001).

91  Bhabha, *The Location of Culture*.

92  Antoinette Burton, 'Introduction: on the inadequacy and the indispensability of the nation', in Antoinette Burton (ed.), *After the Imperial Turn: Thinking With and Through the Nation* (Durham: Duke University Press, 2003), pp. 1–23; quote from p. 1.

93  Samuel P. Huntington, *The Clash of Civilizations and the Remaking of World Order* (New York: Simon & Schuster, 1996).

94  Samuel P. Huntington, *Who are We? The Challenges to America's National Identity* (New York: Simon and Schuster, 2004).

# PART III

# Coda. Post-postmodernism: Directions and Interrogations

Nancy Partner

## INTRODUCTION

First, the term 'post-postmodern,' used to demarcate this section of chapters, clamors for explanation and perhaps even justification. After all, it is hard to think of a conceptual or chronological term more awkward than 'post-postmodern' with its lurching double stumbles forward anchored back to something 'modern.' Admittedly, not a happy locution, and we consider it a place-holder, a temporizing makeshift pointing to a real change whose exact nature has not yet clarified itself sufficiently to generate a better name. It has been true for some time now that the kind of energy that pushed forward the many investigations of the linguistic turn has subsided along with the contentiousness that threatened, or invigorated, long-held assumptions about the stability of historical knowledge. As a matter of disciplinary atmospherics, as occasioned by conferences, round tables, special seminars, and other academic venues for assertion and debate, the canon of postmodern issues that predictably raised the temperature and temper of discussion a few

years ago (deconstruction, semiotics, non-empiricist epistemology, tropes, fictionality) are no longer on the agenda of things demanding immediate attention, much less denunciation. Historians always, and correctly, are engaged in a process of argumentation, testing and revising, but the swirl of contestation that surrounded postmodernist debates with a sense that the entire discipline was either under foundational attack or undergoing radical self-emendation has cooled. There certainly continue to be historical subjects, issues of interpretation and assertion, at the center of intense debate, but not the entire historical enterprise, the very integrity of historical knowledge that seemed to be at stake during some phases of postmodernism. 'Theory' doesn't have the irritant bite of a fighting word any longer; it has settled into a niche in history's normal vocabulary.

It is impossible to say precisely when this shift in attitude, more a recalibration of response than a change of substantive ideas, took place. As is always the case with these amorphous movements, it seems to have happened somehow *before* anyone noticed it enough for comment. So to inquire when exactly did postmodernity end and post-postmodernity begin is to propose a question about something real but which inevitably evades a real-time answer. Indeed, if the linguistic turn taught us anything, it is that chronological markers (into ages, eras, Middle Ages, Modern, Early Modern, Late Early Modern!) are surely our most artificial of disciplinary fictions, however earnestly they are endorsed in college curricula, and however indispensable they are in practical ways. Nonetheless, in terms of historical theory some sort of passage in intellectual life has been repeatedly noted. A stage of stock-taking, assessment and consolidation, a looking about and noting where we are now – states of mind not conducive to words with 'ism' suffixes – is what this feels like.

Just as the 'post' of postmodern did not mean for history that the methodological rigor and demanding training of the discipline's modernist advance had been left behind or discarded, so the 'post' of post-postmodern does not abandon postmodernism. If anything, the subsiding of theory-driven conflicts has freed up a positive attention to mainstreaming those postmodernist insights and techniques of interpretation that have become the 'new normal' of the discipline. This kind of 'post-ness,' in the accelerated life of our academic culture seems a pause for consolidation, practical testing, and various adjustments and fine-tuning of analytic instruments for practical use, for 'doing history' in a phrase many historians still prefer for their work. The chapters in this section are evidence of this stage and contributions to it. They could assuredly have been more numerous and different; undoubtedly a few years more of discussion and the integration into professional life of people now in graduate training, will suggest what we might have chosen instead, or in addition. The guiding ideas here are: central features of historical study that were most challenged by postmodernism and have reasserted and redefined themselves; kinds of evidence and technologies of information that demand serious interpretive evaluation; the meeting of ancient

and postmodern insights on the permanence of narrative form.

The critical scrutiny of foundational elements of history has been re-energized and reoriented in the wake of the radical challenges of 'theory' in its many postmodernist guises. The first chapter in this section returns to the defining issue of epistemology for history in modernity: representation. Taking full account of the effects of deconstruction on naive positivism, John Zammito demonstrates that the encounter of history and science can be reformulated now with a sharper sophistication, aligning history and science in 'a far more disunified, situated and contingent theory of empirical inquiry which suits *both* the natural and the human sciences.' Historians tend to overlook the fact that postmodernism has had an impact on science as well as the humanities, and its older style of rigid ahistorical empiricism has encountered acute objections and undergone some very interesting reformulations. Acts of interpretation, in this post-positivist account, are the inevitable mediation between observer and the object of inquiry (the 'world') for the scientist as much as for the historian who share more than we may recognize. Frank Ankersmit confronts the basic issue of *what* is represented by historians and how with a radical reappraisal of the concept of experience. Here again, the historical theorist accepts and integrates postmodernism into his critique: 'in my view, the linguistic turn cannot be undone – and we should not try to do so. But it may be that the linguistic turn has its own blind spot and that its very successes hide from view things we cannot afford to ignore.' Ankersmit argues that experience, considered as a pre-linguistic mediating process between subject/viewer and linguistically embedded object, deserves a serious reconsideration, especially in light of the many challenges offered to the idea of anything pre-linguistic by the linguistic turn.

Deeply connected to fundamental questions of representation are questions concerning evidence, especially in forms that were little used or unknown when history became modern. The elements of the historical construct are first encountered as trace, what is left as the present moment passes, and are then restated by the historian in a different assemblage of parts in an interpretive key: trace becomes document and documents become history. This is the historian's work in its most pared down description: to take the fragments we can know of past actuality and transmute them into the complex and meaningful artifact that deserves the name of history. From antiquity onwards, this process of reading, interpretation and construction has evolved in response to cultural pressures and continues to do so. Currently, the very nature of what counts as a document and the techniques required to discern what it documents are under new pressures. The two chapters in this section address the photograph, a nineteenth-century technology whose problematic allure still eludes the control of our evidentiary technique, and digital records whose very recording processes undermine the concept of the document itself. From their extreme poles on the spectrum of 'evidence,' the photograph and the digital record are post-postmodern icons of the ungraspability of information: the photograph freezes a moment of time into mute permanence lacking past, future, and contextual surround; the digital record can morph into endless versions and locations and evanesce.

Using iconic images from the Holocaust, Judith Keilsbach lays out the hermeneutic conundrum of the photograph: that it offers the promise of unmediated reality in its most intense form and yet confronts the historian with a 'reading' problem in equally acute form as the fixed and mute image requires historicist explanation. The relation of truth, and the adjudication of the kind of truth, to a photographic image is complex in the extreme. Valerie Johnson and David Thomas survey the theoretical and technical problems of digital records: 'What is a digital record and is it different from a paper record? Indeed, what is a record?' These are not questions that might seem immediately theoretical, but the drastic shifts in the production and media of information from material to electronic mark a point at which change demands entirely new

concepts. The very concept of the archive, so crucial to the professionalization of history, is undergoing seismic shifts, both technical and conceptual: 'This postmodernist turn in conjunction with the digital has resulted in challenges to the objectivity, authority, impartiality and nature of the archive ....'

The post-postmodernist back-to-basics scrutiny is trained on the self, agency, and the location of interiority in the social-liguistic matrix by David Gary Shaw. Concepts of agency, intention, human action with its causes and outcomes remain central to the project of historical knowledge, emphatically when we accept the reality of intention without classical rationality, marked by 'desire more than rationality.' In the wake of deconstruction, Foucault, and generalized social constructionism, the self remains a surprisingly durable presence in our understanding of history: 'the effective human agent will persist in being a sort of self.' But, in Shaw's taxonomy, that sort of individual self is a social self: 'It turns out that to understand social selves we need to understand what was "in their minds" and the particular historical circumstances and its concrete social conditions will determine what was possible.'

And as a slightly ironic coda to a postmodernism that presents itself as emphatically part of late-modern self-awareness, Aristotle's *Poetics*, the first systematic analysis of the complex artifacts made of language (what we call 'literature') in the Western tradition is offered to historians as their, our, foundation text for metahistorical theory. This chapter is a historian's *vade mecum* through the core elements of the *Poetics*, pointing out the ways in which the central procedures for assembling materials into long, coherent, meaningful narratives, so cogently and presciently laid out by Aristotle, are 'about' history, as much as, or even more than fictional stories. 'Aristotle's Narrative Theory,' my suggested alternative title for the book that never did have its own name, laid out the central elements of the linguistic turn for history at the very inception of history and conceptual thought in the Western world.

# 24

# Post-positivist Realism: Regrounding Representation

John H. Zammito

When historical theorists of the 'postmodern' school pronounce the utter irrelevance of 'epistemology' to the practices of history, and indeed insist that history not be regarded as a 'science' or even a 'discipline' but only as a 'discourse,' they are, in my view, invoking long-since abandoned notions of epistemology and science, hangovers of a positivism that has been discredited within the most advanced precincts of the philosophy of science and of epistemology generally.[1] To take up a formidable exemplar, I detect in Frank Ankersmit's postmodern philosophy of history an acutely ambivalent reaction-formation vis-à-vis natural science: both an uncritical affirmation of some of its ('scientistic' or 'positivist') pretenses and an unbounded aversion to its projection onto the humanities.[2] Were he seriously to consider the recent revolution in philosophy of science and language, he would discover that neither the positivist pretenses, affirming the unique authority of natural scientific method, nor the hegemonic projections of preposterous standards upon the humanities – the covering-law model of historical explanation, most notoriously – have survived the revolution.

Foremost among the casualties is the notion that philosophy is authorized to impose a priori rules upon empirical inquiry, a notion that Joseph Rouse has called 'epistemic sovereignty.'[3] As Philip Kitcher has noted, virtually nothing survives of such a priori conceptions in current philosophy of science, epistemology, or philosophy of language.[4] The work of the last 50 years has demolished the unified theory of 'science' which logical positivism/empiricism *projected* upon actual natural-scientific practices and *presumed* to discredit the very idea of the human sciences.[5] No unified theory of science – and a fortiori not the positivist one – stands. In its place we have a far more disunified, situated and contingent theory of empirical inquiry which suits *both* the natural and the human sciences.[6] The grand-scale 'normative' prepossessions of the 'Received View' in philosophy of science (think of Hempel's 'covering law' claim) have proven ultimately incongruous with *any* effective descriptive or explanatory investigations of concrete areas or problems. In the words of Mary Hesse, 'What has in fact happened is that, far from philosophy providing criteria for history, all forms of historical investigation, internal as well as external, have led to radical questioning of all received philosophical views of science.'[7] As other commentators have it, such 'philosophical models of proper evaluation are irrelevant to the historian's task. Indeed, with their typical stress upon the formal, abstract properties of verbal argument, they can even impede an adequate naturalistic understanding of actual judgments ....'[8]

Over the past 50 years revolutions in science studies have brought to the fore a conception of investigation and warrant – of methodology and epistemology – which is profoundly congenial to historical practice. There is now a real prospect of fundamental rapprochement between the 'two cultures' that does not begin by consigning historical inquiry to essential inferiority, as was the case with positivism. I propose to articulate how historicism finds support in the dramatic mutations which have taken place in philosophy of science leading to *naturalism* in epistemology.[9] Naturalism's return in philosophy of science is timely for those of us who seek to affirm the soundness of historicism against not only its old-fashioned positivist, but equally against its postmodern critics.[10] Under these new auspices, I seek a reconciliation between the human and the natural sciences – both to open out the 'hermeneutic' dimensions of actual natural scientific inquiry and to retrieve a sense of disciplinary legitimacy for the human sciences, and specifically history, against what I take to be hyperbolic if not hysterical postmodern characterizations of its linguistic dissolution.[11] Postmodern 'theory' has trumped up 'positivism' as a reductive simplification of empirical verification, to discredit connection between history and evidence or warrant and thus arrogate history to fiction. If we first dispense with the positivist delusion of what science *must be*, as well as with the postmodernist delusion that language can *never refer* in any cognitively worthwhile manner, we can turn to the question of what

historical inquiry *can be*, and put the methodological and epistemological questions of historical practice back into a sane context. My endeavor to bring these decisive insights to bear upon the discussion of historical practice is hardly to seek to place it under the old positivist yoke, but rather to demonstrate the liberating implications of the demolition of this old positivism for historical inquiry, on the one hand, and, on the other, to reaffirm *shared* canons of empirical inquiry that have been dangerously obfuscated in these hyperbolic postmodern formulations.

## POST-POSITIVISM AND NATURALIZED EPISTEMOLOGY

Within philosophy, positivism is finally dead: Willard van Orman Quine presided over its interment, dogma by dogma.[12] The collapse of traditional philosophy of science, and with it the old illusion of 'first philosophy' that there exist a priori standards against which philosophers could hold scientific achievements to assay their worth, is patent.[13] As Philip Kitcher has observed, 'the failure of appeals to conceptual truth, to analyticity, is fully general.'[14] Accordingly, 'virtually nothing is knowable *a priori*, and, in particular, no epistemological principle is knowable *a priori*.'[15] Since, instead, 'knowledge is embedded in the history of human knowledge, and not detachable from it,' we are 'ineluctably dependent on the past.'[16] He concludes, 'the denial of the *a priori* thus leads ... to a position whose emphasis on the growth of knowledge invites the title "historicism."'[17]

How does this affect what we wish to understand about science? Traditional philosophy of science has been concerned to justify the truth-claim of its products: theories or laws. But one could also be interested in science as *process*, and in the link between that process and success. The traditional concern sets out from the premise that there is a standard *higher* than science for the ascertainment of knowledge or truth. That standard was traditionally associated with *logic*.[18] But one of the ways to construe post-positivism in the study of science is to see it as the displacement of this ideal of logic by a concern with rational intelligibility.[19] The essential question then becomes: what *is* rationality? Is rationality independent of science (as process) and criterial for it? And above all, can it always have been the same? The key here is *change*.

The decisive starting point for post-positivism has been the recognition of a tacit collusion between positivism and relativism: first, that, in the absence of *absolute* certainty in cognitive assertion, 'anything goes,' and second, more insidiously, that, in accordance with the fact/value dichotomy, *all value-judgments are (equally) arbitrary*.[20] As soon as one abandons the foundation of a priori principles, *both* traditions have affirmed, there is no stopping on the slippery slope to total relativism, to the 'death of epistemology' or indeed of philosophy.[21] Once one begins to 'de-transcendentalize,' in Richard Rorty's terminology, there is no place *left* for epistemological questions.[22] With the failure of the claims to absolute certainty (to foundationalism), it has been all too facile to infer a radical historicism or relativism. But this was wrong-headed from the outset.[23] The 'place' from which such absolutes could be pronounced – pro or con – was *no human place*. Humans are always already situated. This is what it means to reject a 'view from nowhere.'[24] Therefore, with Thomas Nickles, I am 'forced to reject [such radical historicism], historicist though I am, as an untenably strong form of historicism.'[25] With Nickles, too, I believe the project now is to 'temper our historicism with a dose of (pragmatic) naturalism,' and achieve thereby a 'more Deweyan sort of balance.'[26]

In Kitcher's terms, 'the central question is whether [there is] any way to save the traditional meliorative project of epistemololgy.'[27] Admittedly, normative naturalism remains empirical, but it does not follow that it cannot be critical. In the words of David Hull, 'The stories that historians tell are theory-laden but not so theory-laden as to be useless.'[28] Hull makes the essential rebuttal: 'No matter how strongly one's general views color one's estimations of data, sometimes these data can challenge the very theories in which they are generated.'[29] This idea of 'resistance' or 'constraint' operates to keep both substantive empirical inquiry *and* the meta-inquiry into its justification from the total arbitrariness associated with radical relativism. It is the key to moderate historicism.

The post-positivist view of inquiry suggests at the very least that epistemic norms are immanent in cognitive development, that there can be an *iterative* normativity, if not an ultimate one. Ronald Giere has summarized the current arguments against naturalized epistemology, first and foremost the familiar 'vicious circle' argument.[30] Logicists claim that, without some *prior idea* of good or successful science, a naturalist reconstruction could never even get off the ground.[31] Thus, G.H. Merrill argues that history of science cannot do without a prior logical concept of science (what Karl Popper called the 'demarcation problem').[32] He insists it requires some 'more basic logical and philosophical' criteria, 'appropriate canons of reasoning' that 'may be identified and elucidated through philosophical analysis.' No such philosophical canon has withstood criticism, however, and one of the most compelling critiques from science studies has been that such models are woefully incongruent with the successes we can discern in science. The response to Merrill is that beyond an absolute skepticism, which it is pointless to debate, the emergent and immanent standards that the moderate historicist proposes represent the best available accounts of the growth of knowledge and the constitution of empirical inquiry.[33] Merrill himself acknowledges that 'science is thought of as a paradigm epistemic enterprise.'[34]

I agree with Ronald Giere that 'attempting to draw a fundamental distinction between rational and irrational activities is itself not an effective way to understand science, or any other human activity,' and, I would add, especially if the idea of rationality that is in play here should be what Jürgen Habermas long ago called the 'positivistically halved idea of reason,' reason stripped of its pragmatic and creative, its dynamic and dialectical character.[35] But there are other traditions of thought about rationality: most promising is a convergence of pragmatist naturalism in the spirit of Dewey with elements in dialectical historicism in the vein of Hegel. At the very least, we need to think about how history can be *rationally understood* to change reason.[36] Rather than presuming rationality independent of, and criterial for science as process, we should be concerned with the *dynamics of changing rationality*, with the historicity of reason. That is, we must consider rationality immanent in the growth of knowledge, as emergent in and through the process of science.

Giere thrusts the traditionalist scruple about circularity back upon the critics themselves. Every foundationalist formulation has fallen into infinite regress, so that it hardly seems that theirs is a superior epistemic stance.[37] In Harold Brown's apt words, 'a priori epistemology faces problems that are at least as serious as those faced by naturalized epistemology.'[38] The circle is vicious only if one privileges the foundationalist ideal of absolute certainty, which itself has proven perennially inept against skeptical pressures demonstrating internal inconsistency and infinite regress.[39] James Brown argues that as soon as one recognizes that philosophy of science is not foundational, the circularity argument against normative naturalism becomes only a 'pseudo-problem.'[40] By carefully distinguishing between the use and the accreditation of a theory in the construction of an account, Brown shows that it is possible both to utilize theory in empirical research and then to critique its result and work toward a more plausible theory.

Not every circularity is necessarily vicious, particularly not the hermeneutic circle in interpretation. The core idea of the hermeneutic circle has been that, via a process of successive approximations against wider and wider resources of application, interpretation achieves an immanent and self-correcting rigor.[41] Two strengths of the naturalist circle are its embrace of success in science, however approximate we may have to be at the outset about both science and success, and the more general principle of growth of knowledge, of *learning itself*, as the most discernible basis for any idea of rationality we might hope to find. We have no higher warrant for rationality than the success of inquiry. Naturalism in epistemology seeks to use empirical success to warrant legitimacy.[42] If this leap from 'is' to 'ought' appears to violate the sacrosanct 'fact-value dichotomy,' ostensibly upheld from Hume forward, then that is simply grounds for viewing the 'fact-value dichotomy' as merely the 'last dogma' of positivism, to be consigned to the ashheap with all the rest.[43] That success is always an immanent and emergent principle is just what it means to adopt an anti-foundationalist, historicist approach.[44] As Nicholas Rescher puts it, 'Science *as we have it* – the only "science" that we ourselves know – is a specifically human artifact that must be expected to reflect in significant degree the particular characteristics of its makers.'[45]

We have compelling historical evidence, as Dudley Shapere has shown, that change has taken place in 'scientific goals, methods, criticism of appraisals, *etc.*, and not just empirical and theoretical content.'[46] Thus it becomes possible to conceive reason as an emergent – ontogenetically as well as phylogenetically – and to ascertain its structure from within the circle of its own emergence. As Harold Brown argues, 'A consistent empiricism requires that even truths of logic have [a] kind of empirical prehistory ....'[47] That is, 'norms, in the form of both ends for science and methodological imperatives, are introduced and evaluated in the same ways as theoretical hypotheses, experimental designs, new mathematics, and other features of the so-called content of science.'[48] He explains: 'To be sure, these truths are deeply embedded in our present conceptual system, but this need show only that such elementary principles as noncontradiction and *modus ponens* are so simple and so useful that they were built into our language in the distant past; that they have been passed down from generation to generation through the normal means of cultural transmission; and that no reasons have appeared to cast them out.'[49]

Larry Laudan is a primary proponent of such a normative naturalism.[50] It is a crucial feature of Laudan's normative naturalism that methodological rules are strictly *hypothetical*, not *categorical* imperatives; they are always 'directives for achieving scientific ends.' Moreover, Laudan argues that 'history shows that there are no fixed ends for science and that the available background knowledge also changes. Thus there can be no fixed, categorical methodological directives for the pursuit of science.'[51] As Adam Grobler puts it, 'Laudan's offer consists in fact of replacing the hierarchical model of scientific rationality by a reticulated one. The three levels – the factual, the methodological and the axiological – are mutually related there.'[52]

Taking up a phrase from Charles Peirce, science is essentially the story of *how we learned to learn.*[53] In the words of Larry Briskman, 'we want an epistemology which allows that we can *learn to be more rational* – that we can learn to pursue better (or more rational) aims and can equally learn to pursue these aims better (more rationally).'[54] Nickles, Briskman, and others have termed this 'a broadly "bootstrap" account of the growth of knowledge.'[55] In the words of Shapere, 'we learn *what* "knowledge" is *as* we attain knowledge, ... we learn *how* to learn in the process of learning.'[56] As Nickles puts it, 'a defensible historicism does not rule out a bootstrap account of the development of knowledge; on the contrary, it requires it!'[57] That is, 'a moderate historicism itself implies that any adequate account of the growth of knowledge will be broadly circular. The growth of knowledge will have the character of a self-transforming, ultimately self-supporting or "bootstrap" process.'[58]

This implies a 'multi-pass conception of science,' i.e., an iterative process of adjustment, for which the term *dialectical* is not

inappropriate.[59] 'Human knowledge has grown by means of a self-transforming, dialectical or 'bootstrap' process, rooted in variation, selective retention, and triangulation of historically available resources.'[60] Nickles affirms a Deweyan Hegelianism here: embracing 'Hegel's "methodological" insights, his anti-dualism, and his historicist and sociological tendencies.'[61] This pragmatist-naturalist reception is, he aptly affirms, only '*weakly* Hegelian because ... it presupposes no transcendent Reason that shapes the overall developmental process.'[62] 'Bootstrap' rationality is emergent intelligibility. It should be understood as 'autopoeisis,' systemic self-organization.[63] Rationality, then, becomes not the *cause* of our success, or even a supratemporal *standard* for it, but rather the *tentative harvest* of our history of discovery. That is simply what it means that 'philosophers take scientific activity as somehow paradigmatic of rational behavior.'[64] That, in my view, is the 'living' heritage of Hegelian dialectics.

This moderate historicism is, I submit, highly *robust* and sustainable. The want of totality does not betoken want of concreteness. Hilary Putnam evokes the key caution from John Austin: enough is not everything, but enough can be enough.[65] The whole idea of dialectic is that one never starts from nowhere.[66] A problem is inconceivable without a context; it is always already mediated. If there is no ultimate *foundation*, there is always some *platform*. And that platform is far more elaborate than a congeries of 'data':

> Problem contexts include much more than empirical datum constraints on adequate problem solutions. Large, conceptual problem contexts contain constraints of many kinds, many of them previous *theoretical* results, which function as consistency conditions, limit conditions, derivational requirements, etc.[67]

Scientific problems emerge from 'a structure of constraints (on the problem solution) plus a general demand, goal, or explanatory ideal of the research program in question that certain types of gaps in those structures be filled.'[68] These constraints 'constitute a rich supply of premises and context-specific rules for reasoning toward a problem solution.'[69] Thus every problem is an emergent, in a situation, and the constraints that situate the emergent problem also equip the inquiry with (some of) the terms for its solution. Moreover, this whole syndrome must be taken as a dynamic, not a static process, resulting in 'successively sharper reformulations of a problem.'[70] Such reformulations can result in radical departures, and it has been empirically the case that 'it frequently takes science a good deal of time and effort after a discovery to say what exactly has been discovered.'[71]

If this contextualist, thickly descriptive approach to the genesis and pursuit of a scientific problem is one harvest of the naturalization of epistemology, another is the recognition that intelligibility entails more than overt logical operations. 'Not all of our rational activities and capacities can be made intelligible in terms of a fully conscious deliberation, but that does not make them any less rational.'[72] This was what Michael Polanyi was seeking to articulate by 'tacit reasoning.'[73] It also embraces what Marx Wartofsky has invoked as the 'heuristic tradition,' namely non-inferential judgment, the 'craftsmanlike skill ... exemplified in legal, clinical, aesthetic, and historical judgment.'[74]

Two points can be established. First, *retrospectively* we can trace the routes of (some of) our insights. Second, making *intelligible* those successes can empower us, both psychologically and methodologically, to undertake new inquiries. Not only can we be confident that 'problems and constraints do not fall out of the sky,' but we can be hopeful that we can reiterate at least some of the moves that led us through prior solutions and *learn* how to attempt new ones.[75] Rationality is the concept we can articulate to affirm that science has indeed found a way of 'bootstrapping stabilized past results and practices into the future.'[76]

Scientists *learn* and they *use* what they learn: 'Once a scientific claim is reasonably settled, they do not hesitate to use the newly accepted entities and processes in new research.'[77] There is nothing frightening or

illegitimate about this, even if some interpreters have called such presumptions 'black boxes.' As Nickles rightly asserts, 'Something already black boxed can later be used.' Indeed, that is what 'progress' – or, less complacently, cumulation – betokens:

> Often the most successful steps [in human learning] have become 'black boxed' and taken for granted by later generations, who employ these capacities and their products as 'givens' rather than items that were once constructed. In these cases the apparatus of construction and maintenance has become invisible and remains so as long as things work well enough.[78]

The shift of focus from science as product to science as process, from the context of justification to the context of discovery, from logic to rational intelligibility, from timelessness to historicity – all these betoken the robustness of a naturalist, historicist, evolutionary epistemology. This is the great harvest of post-positivism in science studies.

## POSTMODERNISM: 'DISCOURSE' VS. 'DISCIPLINE'

In 1969 the historian of science Bernard Cohen stated what he took to be the conventional wisdom of all practicing historians:

> The historian's job is ... to immerse himself in the writings of scientists of previous ages, to immerse himself so totally that he becomes familiar with the atmosphere and problems of that past age. Only in this way, and not by anachronistic logical or philosophical analysis, can the historian become fully aware of the nature of the scientific thought of that past age and can he really feel secure in his interpretation of what that scientist may have thought he was doing.[79]

But *can* a historian 'become fully aware?' *Can* a historian 'really feel secure?'[80] Are there such ubiquitous canons or historiographical techniques whereby anachronism is avoided or accuracy assured?[81] The 'postmodern' crisis of historical understanding arose out of such anxieties.

Barry Barnes has made the case eloquently:

> If the individual historian cannot write other than selectively, and with prior tendencies of interpretation, how can we articulate an ideal which stresses the primacy of evidence, documentation and 'what actually happened' as though the problem of selection and bias did not exist or could simply be overcome?...
>
> The constraints upon the historian arise from his status as a member of a culture with a pre-existing common vocabulary, and a shared set of patterns, structures and forms of representation. This large and diverse set of cultural resources does define what the historian is able to represent the past as constituting, and to a large extent it restricts how the past can be perceived...[82]

For many postmodern theorists, this would suffice to plunge historical inquiry into inescapable aporias. But that is not what Barnes, one of the most important post-positivist practitioners of science studies, infers. Rather, he continues, this situatedness

> implies nothing substantive... [it] involves no necessary 'bias' in the old-fashioned sense. One *finds out* what best describes the past, by empirical study and documentary method. This is why it is possible to *learn* from history.
>
> By retaining a broadly empiricist ideal of history, and insisting that 'what actually happened' is to be decided by concrete investigation, we make our available cultural resources and representations compete as a means of understanding the past. As a consequence, the results of historical enquiry can surprise us, challenge us, and educate us.[83]

This simultaneous articulation of the 'situatedness of the historical subject' and insistence upon the possibility of learning, of disrupting presupposition, is the essence of a robust hermeneutical historicism. To uphold it, we need to address the hyperbolic anxiety of postmodernism and deflate it into proper epistemological and methodological implications. 'Discourse,' to be sure, will remain a very important concern, but 'discipline,' and the notion of a normal/normative practice for the disciplinary community of historians, needs to be defended.

One of the most prominent and persuasive postmodern theorists is Richard Rorty, and just because some historians have even regarded his positions as congenial to historical practice, I would like to use his view to exemplify and then to deflate the postmodern, 'discursive' conception of history.[84] In *Philosophy and the Mirror of Nature*, Richard Rorty poses the central epistemic issue for historical method in terms of moments of rupture 'where we do not understand what is happening' (PMN: 321) – i.e., 'the transitions between the "archaeological strata" which Foucault discerns' (PMN: 322) or the 'paradigm shifts' of Kuhn – moments best captured, Rorty claims, by Kuhn's notion of *incommensurability*.[85] He adds a crucial elaboration:

> The historian can make the shift from the old scheme to the new one intelligible, and make one see why one would have been led from the one to the other if one had been an intellectual of that day. There is nothing the philosopher can add to what the historian has already done to show that this intelligible and plausible course is a 'rational' one. (PMN: 272)

The crucial issue between Kuhn and his critics, according to Rorty, was whether 'philosophy of science could construct an algorithm for choice among scientific theories' (PMN: 322), that is, 'some criteria for knowing when and why it was rational to adopt a new conceptual scheme' (PMN: 270–1). The core of Rorty's claim is: 'change was not brought about by "rational argument" in some sense of "rational" in which, for example, the changes lately brought about in regard to society's attitude toward slavery, abstract art, homosexuals, or endangered species would *not* count as "rational" ...' (PMN: 332). 'As soon as it was admitted that "empirical considerations" ... incited but did not require "conceptual change" ..., the division of labor between the philosopher and the historian no longer made sense' (PMN: 272). Philosophy has nothing to add.[86]

Shifts and difference in discourse merely happen, according to Rorty, and what remain available to us for interpretation at such junctures are only intellectual history or ethnography. 'There is no point in trying to find a general synoptic way of "analyzing" the "functions knowledge has in universal contexts of practical life", [because] cultural anthropology (in a large sense which includes intellectual history) is all we need' (PMN: 381). 'We need a sense of the relativity of descriptive vocabularies to periods, traditions and historical accidents. This is what the humanist tradition in education does ...' (PMN: 362). Rorty resists the idea that there might be any norms governing the passage from one discourse to another: 'there is no discipline which describes it, any more than there is a discipline devoted to the study of the unpredictable, or of "creativity"' (PMN: 320). 'For solving difficult cases in historiography, anthropological description, and the like ... nothing save tact and imagination will serve' (PMN: 293). Intellectual historians and cultural anthropologists, according to Rorty, should practice not 'epistemology' but 'hermeneutics.'

In Rorty's usage, '"hermeneutics" is not the name for a discipline, nor for a method ..., nor for a program of research ...' (PMN: 315). 'Hermeneutics is not "another way of knowing" – "understanding" as opposed to (predictive) "explanation"' (PMN: 356). Indeed, hermeneutics should disown 'knowing.' Rorty uses 'hermeneutics' as 'an expression of hope that the cultural space left by the demise of epistemology will not be filled' (PMN: 315). While epistemology seeks commensuration, 'hermeneutics is largely a struggle against this assumption.'[87] He proposes to strip hermeneutics of its methodical significance and reorient it to an overall conversational style, appropriate to what he calls 'abnormal discourse.' 'Contributing to an inquiry,' as he sees it, falls under the constraint of a disciplinary community and its 'normal discourse,' but 'participating in a conversation' need not. The course of a conversation is not governed by the terms of a given subject. It can continue by 'changing the subject.' Hence it can turn into 'abnormal discourse,' and 'the product of abnormal

discourse can be anything from nonsense to intellectual revolution' (PMN: 320).

'Hermeneutics sees the relations between various discourses as those of strands in a possible conversation, a conversation which presupposes no disciplinary matrix which unites the speakers, but where the hope of agreement is never lost as long as the conversation lasts' (PMN: 318). Hermeneutics is simply 'discourse about as-yet-incommensurable discourses' (PMN: 343). For Rorty 'commensurable' means: 'able to be brought under a set of rules which tell us how rational agreement can be reached on what would settle the issue on every point where statements seem to conflict' (PMN: 316). He contends that 'the dominating notion of epistemology is that to be rational, to be fully human, to do what we ought, we need to be able to find agreement with other human beings' (PMN: 316), but any effort at 'truth' as 'ultimate commensuration' is 'to see human beings as objects rather than subjects' (PMN: 378). Instead, 'keeping the conversation going' is a way of resisting 'proposals for universal commensuration through the hypostatization of some privileged set of descriptions' which is all that he thinks can be meant by 'objective truth' (PMN: 376). He goes so far as to allege that 'to look for commensuration rather than simply continued conversation – to look for a way of making further redescription unnecessary ... is to attempt to escape from humanity' (PMN: 376). He sees such proposals for commensuration as inevitably a 'freezing-over of culture' and 'dehumanization of human beings,' and vehemently objects to any enterprise – and a fortiori to Habermas' specific enterprise – to formulate the 'transcendental conditions,' the necessary, prior rules for conversational progress. '"Transcendental hermeneutics" is very suspicious ... a way of seeing freedom as nature' (PMN: 380), i.e. of rendering human subjects into objects.[88]

In the extraordinary pathos of these lines Rorty's panic seems to be that should all discourse be reduced to normal discourse, creativity would dry up. Why must we accept

Rorty's suggestion that 'we would do well to abandon the notion of certain values ("rationality", "disinterestedness") floating free of the educational and institutional patterns of the day' (PMN: 331)? Does Rorty intend 'tact and imagination' to stand as irreducibly 'irrational'? Is that what 'edifying discourse' means? *Is* the search for consensus the aspiration to stasis? *Is* the inevitable outcome a fixity of all human enterprise? Why must we believe that? The question is whether we could not broaden the concept of rationality, rather than forsake it.

We cannot leave 'hermeneutical *phronesis*,' the skills involved in being hermeneutical, completely unreflected, as if they were utterly separate from reason.[89] We must seize from Rorty's own words the decisive starting-point: 'the possibility of hermeneutics is always parasitic upon the possibility (and perhaps upon the actuality) of epistemology' (PMN: 320). 'Hermeneutics is the study of an abnormal discourse from the point of view of some normal discourse – the attempt to make some sense of what is going on' always and invariably from some particular vantage in some particular moment (PMN: 320). 'The fact that hermeneutics inevitably takes some norm for granted makes it, so far forth, "Whiggish." But insofar as it proceeds nonreductively and in the hopes of picking up a new angle on things, it can transcend its own Whiggishness' (PMN: 321). Here Rorty acknowledges that while we are always *initially* culture-bound, we can accept and integrate novelty, which is the movement Gadamer calls a 'fusion of horizons.'[90] The 'Whiggishness' with which hermeneutics commences is its burden, not its privilege. It cannot be shrugged off (that's the point of 'holistic' radical interpretation and the 'hermeneutic circle' alike) but it can, patiently and with openness to the possibility, be 'compromised and transcended.' Everything hinges on what it means to 'be able to find agreement with other human beings' (PMN: 316).

We cannot dispense with the principle of 'hope of agreement.' When Rorty disparages in epistemology 'the hope of agreement as a token of the existence of common ground,

which, perhaps unbeknownst to the speakers, unites them in a common rationality' (PMN: 318), he is in fact denying the only coherent sense of the phrase even for his own hermeneutics. To be sure, to be rational in the hermeneutic sense 'is to be willing to refrain ... from thinking that there is [*already established*] a special set of terms in which all contributions to the conversation should be put' (PMN: 318). Precisely because there is no shared premise at the outset, the only hope of agreement is in this move, but that is what makes it a *rational* move. Hermeneutics must presume that *some* common ground will be found through dialogue, or the 'hope of agreement' is fatally compromised and the benefit of conversation over estrangement is lost. Dialogues cannot be undertaken without affirming the possibility of 'reaching understanding.' To be hermeneutical is to aim at commensuration, and not as failure, foreclosure or freezing of all creativity, but precisely as *community*. The idea of a 'hope of agreement' is the very essence of the 'rationality' principle animating authentic hermeneutics, which both dares to suspend prior disciplinary assumptions *and* seeks to establish some common understanding.

To bring this problem back squarely to the problems of historical practice, this Rortian extremity of 'abnormal discourse' or 'incommensurability' puts in intense question how historical narratives, as exercises in hermeneutics, can possibly be composed. Essentially, what is the procedure by which ethnographers and intellectual historians transport us intelligibly across ruptures? The question is how historians or anthropologists *can* account – even descriptively – for shifts in paradigm. *How is it* that intellectual history can 'make ... intelligible, ... make one see why ...' (PMN: 272) – i.e. *persuade*? What makes hermeneutics *actualizable*? We are faced with essential questions regarding how and why such accounts claim plausibility or explanatory reliability. Practicing historians will certainly acknowledge that to understand is only possible if one can explain, i.e., offer a fuller account in one's own terms which reveals factors which historical figures simply took for granted as well as conflicts and confusions of which they appeared unconscious. Thus, intellectual history, as a normal discourse of 'hermeneutical *phronesis*,' acknowledges, at least as a regulative ideal, the familiar phrase, 'to understand the author better than he understood himself.'[91] Such understanding *situates* the historical object in a diachronic frame, in which, to be sure, what comes after can be quite revelatory. More typically, it is the diachronic past more than the future that proves crucial in understanding or explaining a text's project and even its perplexities. The point is, I think, to distinguish historical reconstruction, which via 'thick description' seeks to establish what meanings can be imputed to texts for the arguments they articulate or obfuscate, from various forms of appropriation for contemporary relevance, 'genealogical' debunking, or 'strong misreading' as creative criticism.

Rorty's celebration of hermeneutics as 'abnormal discourse' clashes irretrievably with his evocation of the efficacy of intellectual history (and cultural anthropology), because these *disciplines* undertake their hermeneutic procedures precisely as *normal science*. Historical hermeneutics *is* 'normal science,' rational procedure undertaken and policed (yes) by a 'disciplinary community.'

## DISCIPLINARY COMMUNITY AND A PLATFORM FOR INQUIRY

Though it is no occasion for complacency, William McNeill was right when he observed that our 'practice has been better than [our] epistemology.'[92] The 'normal scientific' practice of disciplinary history, since its establishment in the early nineteenth century in Germany, has been *historicism*.[93] As Frank Ankersmit, has noted, almost all current professional history is written under the tacit auspices of historicism.[94] A recent, powerful affirmation of history as normal science – Aviezer Tucker's *Our Knowledge of the Past* – holds that historicism does not exhaustively

warrant historical practice, but it provides a paradigmatic core.[95]

When the 'Received View' in philosophy of science abandoned the 'context of discovery' to the serendipitous, it left a major *theoretical* matter to be clarified, namely how it was that history and the other empirical human sciences were to proceed and to appraise their own efficacy.[96] Without accepting the distinction of context of discovery from context of justification as such, I want to focus on just that open epistemological question. Nickles notes, 'historians and philosophers *have* succeeded in making intelligible the routes to several important discoveries.'[97] *How* did they do that? What does *intelligible* signify? If historians go about 'making intelligible to reason (insofar as possible)' by offering 'accounts,' how is that done, and with what claim to reasonableness? What *is* 'historical *explanation* as opposed to mere chronicle or anecdote?'[98] It is not just condescending but obscurantist to write this off to mere ad hoc groping in the inductivist dark, even if so grand an authority as Karl Popper insinuates it.[99] On the other hand, no one is really trying to propose that there is some deep *algorithmic* theory to be discovered.[100] That is, historical practice presumes that 'reasoning [concerning concrete problems of change] usually is so complex and context-specific' that it is pointless to seek a universal algorithm.[101] That does not make it pointless, however, to take methodological bearings, to theorize the endeavor, and to use, in our theorizing, the exempla of 'intelligibility' which we appear to possess.

Taking up three key insights of postpositivist epistemology into a reconsideration of disciplinary historical practice may help resituate it as authentic empirical inquiry and rescue it from the hyperbolic anxieties that characterize much postmodern rhetoric about historical method. In my monograph, *A Nice Derangement of Epistemes*, I offered a historical-critical clarification of (1) the theory-ladenness of data, or the condition that all knowledge entails an element of cultural-linguistic construction, which does not, however, signify the impossibility of cognition or of its improvement, (2) the underdetermination of theory by evidence as a condition of all empirical inquiry, which does not preclude the evaluation of theoretical merits on other criteria, and (3) the situatedness of claims to knowledge within the practices of a disciplinary community with its ongoing, contingent, and fallible yet discriminating standards.[102] I believe that a proper appreciation of these three principles would rescue the epistemological and methodological discussion of history from the debilitating delusions of radical incommensurability and indeterminacy of language. There have been important efforts in this direction already, which I would like to invoke.

Mark Bevir sets out from a key epistemological tenet of post-positivism: the theory-ladenness of observation. 'Because our experiences embody theoretical assumptions, our experiences cannot be pure, and this means that our experiences cannot provide unvarnished data for determining the truth or falsity of our theories.'[103] Following a familiar argument from Quine he infers:

> If an observation disproved a favorite theory, we could rescue the theory by insisting that the observation itself rested on a false theory; and, if an observation proved a detested theory, we could jettison the theory by insisting that the observation itself rested on a false theory.[104]

But it would go too far, as Quine himself insists, to think that this proceeding can be followed inveterately. 'There is no point in our attacking a web of interpretations unless we also champion a suitable alternative.' The standard is not absolute, Bevir insists: 'historians make sense of the past as best they can; they do not discover certainties.'[105]

Raymond Martin has noted aptly that 'we still do not know how historians do, or should, decide among competing historical interpretations.'[106] For Martin, there is a question as to 'the extent to which evidence can resolve disagreements among competing interpretations.' He offers the idea that 'confirmation in historical studies is a holistic affair.'[107] He elaborates: 'Often we do not have access to the

evidence we need to determine what happened: too much of it may be lost or hidden. Or we may not be clever enough or have the relevant theoretical apparatus we need to interpret properly the evidence we do have.'[108] But the problem goes deeper: 'competition among interpretations sometimes cannot be resolved regardless of how much access we have to the evidence.'[109] Martin recognizes Michael Krausz's claim that 'often there is more than one ideally admissible historical interpretation of a given phenomenon.'[110] Krausz calls this view 'multiplism,' and connects it to the thesis of the underdetermination of theory by evidence advocated by Quine.

Yet underdetermination does not betoken incommensurability. As Lionel Rubinoff correctly avers: 'points of view overlap, and it is this overlap which contains the possibility of reconciliation and synthesis. The overlap thus holds forth the promise of a new value system which retains some elements of its dialectical predecessors and competitors and discards others.'[111] Rubinoff tries to develop this idea of 'translation' as an approach to the adjudication of interpretations:

> if different historians, working with precisely the same evidence, produce different pictures or accounts of the past, because of their different points of view, to regard each result as equally objective is equivalent to claiming simply that it should be possible to translate one interpretation into another.[112]

Moreover, there are grounds to consider such interpretations in terms of other cognitive and cultural values which would allow a discrimination of their relative merits.

Invoking French post-structuralism (in particular Michel Foucault), David Boucher claims 'interpretative constraints emanate not so much from the object, or text itself, but from the discursive formation and the interpretative communities which inhabit it.'[113] He elaborates:

> The interpretative community is a constraint on interpretation. The institutional structures of the community authorize only a limited number of legitimate approaches to the text. There is a form

of tacit agreement within the community, not on the meanings of texts, but on the manner in which meanings can be arrived at.[114]

While Boucher intends this to advance a postmodern scruple, this connection with the disciplinary community is essential to a post-positivist notion of 'objectivity.' Aviezer Tucker argues that a disciplinary community may make plausible claims to collective knowledge if three constraints are satisfied: the consensus must be *uncoerced*, it must involve a *large number* of participants, and a significantly *heterogeneous* group must reach a *unique* common judgment.[115] While the claim to knowledge is contingent and fallible, it nevertheless is the best explanation of the consensus. Once this consensus is achieved, a disciplinary community achieves 'normal science' or a paradigm, in Kuhn's terms.[116] Tucker indeed develops one of the most impressive defenses of disciplinary historical practice as a normal science.

The notion of the underdetermination of theory by evidence plays a major role in Tucker's theory of historical practice. Tucker contends that historical practice has a 'scientific core' or paradigm, but that it is not *altogether* a normal science. 'Historiographic core theories constrain the possible range of interpretations, but parts of historiography are still underdetermined' (OKP: 21), largely for lack of sufficient evidence (OKP: 146–7). 'Cognitive values may not be sufficient for discriminating among some historiographic hypotheses, and inconsistent evidence may not disprove some historiographic theories because historians add different ad hoc hypotheses to save them' (OKP: 146). Hence the discipline entails elements both of determinacy and of underdetermination, but he insists that is no license for radical incommensurability, or the indeterminacy thesis regarding historical knowledge (OKP: 179; 258). 'Insufficient evidence does not imply that historiography is indeterminate, that anything goes, because the evidence may still be sufficient for eliminating many improbable

hypotheses, while conferring equal probability on several competing underdetermined historiographic hypotheses' (OKP: 142).

An empirical science, in Tucker's view, is what 'generates probable knowledge' (OKP: 1); the 'modern sense' conceives such practices as 'stochastic, probabilistic, with limited powers of prediction, and irreducible to another science' (OKP: 211). According to Tucker, modern historiography is 'scientific' in this sense, and Bayesian probability theory explains why. The discipline of history is faced with the irretrievable absence of the past. There are only *traces* in the present which become 'evidence' only under a theory. 'Historiography makes no observations of historical events, but presents descriptions of such events in the presence of evidence' (OKP: 17). The theoretical core of 'scientific historiography' is the 'attempt to infer information about a cause from relevant similarities among its putative effects, the evidence, by inferring the information-causal chains that connect the cause, the alleged source of the information, with its effects, the alleged receptors of the information' (OKP: 74). The practice of historiography is 'inference from evidence to a common cause.' 'Historians are interested only in particular types of causal chains, the ones that preserve information' (OKP: 94). The decisive role of Fred Dretske's information-theory of epistemology is clear in this formulation.[117] Tucker elaborates: 'the actual theories and methods that historians use habitually are about the transmission of information over time, from event to evidence' (OKP: 21). 'The selection of evidence according to its information-preserving qualities is theory-laden' (OKP: 106); only theory elucidates how evidence shows 'information-preservation' or *fidelity*. 'Historians must use theories to know where to search for relevant evidence, to recognize relevant evidence once they discover it, and to interpret nested evidence to generate the kind of evidence that is useful for them' (OKP: 95). Thus, 'confirmation and explanation require more than historiography and evidence; they require theories that connect historiography with evidence and identify the evidence as such in the first place' (OKP: 93).

Bayesian theory establishes 'the degree of probability the evidence confers on the hypothesis,' hence it is central to 'warranting claims based on partial evidence' (OKP: 96). Tucker argues that 'background information and theories can evaluate prior probabilities of separate causes that are tokens of a single type of cause' (OKP: 113). That is, even if not quantifiable precisely, the order of magnitude of difference in the probability of separate causes relative to a common cause can be sufficient. In the measure that they share (even tacitly) these theories linking evidence with event (and process), historians are scientific, in Tucker's estimation. Tucker affirms that Bayesianism 'is the best explanation of the actual practices of historians' (OKP: 96; see 21; 120; 134). He argues, indeed, that 'Bayesian formulae can even *predict* in most cases the professional practices of historians' (OKP: 134; my emphasis). 'Explanations of descriptions of events in paradigmatic historiography are ... the best explanation of a range of evidence, given background information and theories' (OKP: 188). Clearly historians do not actually calculate Bayesian probability; it can only be tacit in their reasoning, Tucker acknowledges. 'Historians do not quantify fidelities... Since there is no set of algorithms for evaluating fidelities, historians exclude evidence that does not achieve a threshold of fidelity for whatever reason' (OKP: 121). Hence the importance of corroborating evidence (OKP: 114). 'Historians ... must bootstrap their evaluations of the fidelity of particular evidence by other evidence' (OKP: 123). The distrust of an uncorroborated evidential claim is 'taught as part of the historiographic guild's right [sic] of passage' (OKP: 123). And in just this sense he affirms 'historians are able to agree on much of historiography because they agree on theories and evidence' (OKP: 142). This 'normal science' within historiography is robust, as Tucker elaborates: 'epistemically, we can distinguish the evidence for historical processes from the evidence for

events that compose such processes ... We can possess knowledge of events, without thereby knowing some of the processes they are parts of' (OKP: 13) and conversely, 'even when evidence for many of the links on the information-causal chain is missing, it is possible to infer with high probability the properties of some of the missing links and the cause' (OKP: 75).

According to Tucker, in appraising the fit of evidence with theory, historical practice 'is not substantially different from biology, geology, or physics' (OKP: 8). A 'colligatory concept' in historiography is not epistemologically different from a theoretical term in physical science: 'There is no difference between the use of such theoretical concepts to explain evidence and the use scientists make of theoretical, unobservable concepts to explain a range of evidence ... Neither the atom nor the Renaissance are directly observable; they are extremely useful and well-confirmed theoretical concepts' (OKP: 138). Thus, 'another advantage of the Bayesian interpretation of historiography is the elimination of apparent historiographic anomalies when compared to science' (OKP: 137).

## ROBUST HISTORICISM VS. POSTMODERNISM: DEBATE WITH ANKERSMIT

The issue of 'colligatory concepts' brings us to the crux of the conflict between postmodern approaches and the post-positivist approach to method, namely the relation between language and the world. Rather than rehearse the endless debates about French poststructuralist notions of 'free-floating signifiers,' I would like to engage in defense of the possibility of judging intersubjectively the 'fit,' however 'loose,' of linguistically articulated historical interpretations (e.g., 'colligatory concepts') with evidence about aspects of the actual world, which I take to be the essential practice of disciplinary history. Such an approach, I believe, corresponds to the more moderate and justifiable forms of 'semantic holism' which Willard van Orman Quine and Pierre Duhem represented as viable reformulations of simplistic, term for term, verification schemes in empirical research.

For more than a decade, now, I have been engaged in debate with the figure I regard as the most rigorous and brilliant of the postmodern philosophers of history, Frank Ankersmit, on just these issues.[118] In summarizing our debate I hope to elucidate the difference between the post-positivist stance I embrace and the postmodernism that Ankersmit, with waxing and waning enthusiasm, has been advocating. Where, then, does our failure to agree arise? Ankersmit asserts that what a historical representation ascribes to 'an aspect of the world' cannot qualify as 'reference' simply because reference can 'from a logical point of view' only be associated with 'picking out uniquely' individuated things. His claim excludes the use of 'reference' to conceive any ascription to the world of more complex or implicated processes or states. Such conceptions, he argues, are strictly linguistic: in his argot, 'speaking about speaking.' He takes this to be the thrust of Quine's 'semantic ascent,' that is, he assimilates his view to Quinean indeterminacy of language. But Ankersmit's 'epistemological asceticism'[119] is not consistent with the semantic holism central to the linguistic turn since Quine.[120] It would be more accurate to say that Ankersmit commits himself to a *pre*-Quinean instrumentalism, with its entrenched suspicion of 'theoretical terms' and credulity regarding 'observational' ones.[121] I contend this drastically impoverishes the reach not only of ordinary language but of the theoretical languages of all empirical sciences – human and natural.

Existence exceeds the terms of Ankersmit's stipulated ontology. How, then, shall we *denote the excess*? From a pragmatic epistemological vantage, what are we to make of Ankersmit's insistence that historical representations are 'about' some 'aspect of reality?' By 'aboutness,' Ankersmit recognizes we are forced to work with the 'fit' of larger chunks of language with larger chunks of actuality. I believe we must begin from the recognition that historical texts are proposals to an interpretive community to discriminate meaningfully some aspect of actuality, however contingent or fallible ('indeterminate'). What has been central to our controversy is my insistence that colligatory concepts in historical writing entail some intersubjectively discriminable connection to (an aspect or part of) the actual past such that historians can then appraise and contest the warrant of the attribution in any account invoking them. For Ankersmit, such colligatory concepts could refer if and only if they exhaustively identified a unique entity in the world. All concepts, with the exception of proper names – and, in his view, 'uniquely identifying descriptions' – are radically indeterminate, in that no concept can be so exhaustively specified as to denote a singular instance to the exclusion of all possible others (a result that has, incidentally, widely discredited *intension* as 'uniquely identifying description' within recent philosophy of language).[122] All type terms, including natural kinds, are ineligible for reference, according to him, because they are 'indeterminate' in this sense. Most process terms and system relations are similarly ineligible for reference because of their ontological indeterminacy. Thus, on Ankersmit's proposal, language is crippled in its ability to denote any but the most obvious 'middle-sized dry goods,' to borrow a telling phrase.

Epistemologically, I believe *reference* can be widened to conceive *all* operations which (contingently and fallibly) impute to actuality (or its 'aspects') some intersubjectively ascertainable character. I suggest that most interesting empirical inquiry in history, as in natural science, has to do with such 'aspects,' whether 'colligatory concepts' or 'theoretical terms.' What I care about is the degree of intersubjective ascertainability possible in historical accounts – an epistemological, rather than a 'logical' desideratum. Indeed, Ankersmit is quite right to see the thrust of my argument as privileging the pragmatics of historical and scientific explanation over what he calls 'logic.' If existence does not *somehow* constrain reference, we can never learn anything about the world, because we can never encounter the resistance that makes an account *wrong*. If notational systems are unquestionably human artefacts, the world exerts constraint on the applicability of these notational systems. States of the world can impose or evoke certain considerations of importance or relevance. Whether a mushroom is toxic certainly *can* be regarded as neither important nor relevant *if* one does not propose to eat it. But it would be a *defective* 'notational system' in gastronomy which stipulated that a toxic mushroom need not be *considered* toxic, or which dismissed toxicity as irrelevant to the eating of mushrooms.

Let us bring this directly to bear upon historical concepts. The practice of historical representation is caught up with selection and construction. Representations organize evidence to advance unique proposals. For Ankersmit, there is nothing available for historians to debate other than these representations. That is, in Ankersmit's preferred language, the *extension* of 'Renaissance' is restricted to representations that employ it. There are as many 'Renaissances' as there are historical representations using that term – and 'Renaissance' exists *only* in these representations. Ankersmit himself writes, 'of course the Renaissance is to be associated exclusively with things taking place in fifteenth- and sixteenth-century Italy.'[123] But he questions whether such crude gestures, however *necessary*, can ever amount to a *sufficient* condition of successful reference. I think that what is necessary and sufficient should be an empirical determination of historical practice, not something to be stipulated a priori. That colligatory concepts *can* be merely heuristic is something that practicing historians might concede, without going all the way with Ankersmit to the posture that they are *always and only* heuristic, that there is never any 'chunk of reality' that they denote and in terms of which, accordingly, they can be confuted. Whatever actuality might be embodied in the term 'Renaissance,' Ankersmit makes a strong

argument that 'Mannerism' seems strictly a heuristic label whose necessary and sufficient characteristics for application have been unceasingly debated since the term's origination in the technical discourse of art history.

To elucidate his notion of historical representation, Ankersmit invokes Arthur Danto's discussion of pictorial representations of Napoleon.[124] Ankersmit underscores the distinction between 'an individual human being (such as Napoleon)' and any 'representation of the historical personality in question'.[125] Representing Napoleon 'as' a Roman emperor, for example, is not only a *metaphoric* intervention, substituting 'represented-as-Roman-emperor' for Napoleon, but this 'represented as' catches only an 'aspect' and not the full, individuated actuality of Napoleon. One can make sense of Ankersmit's claim by presuming that a portrait accentuates an *aspect* of the sitter so decidedly as to render itself inadequate as a reference to the whole person.

I am not persuaded that this settles the matter. Consider caricature: distortion for a point is the heart of the enterprise. Yet I would hold that the enterprise is point*less* if we do not recognize the sitter behind the caricature. We *learn* something from the distortion in caricature, just as we learn something from the 'aspect' highlighted in a portrait painting, and – Ankersmit notwithstanding – it is *about* the sitter. Without that, the specific point of portrait or caricature as genres of representation is lost. Concretely, what does *portrait* mean in the phrase 'portrait-painting'? What difference does it make that a painting is a *portrait*? To be sure, we can recognize the artistic brilliance of the form in itself, accentuating its aesthetic meaning and artistic merit as *expressive* painting. Consider the contrast of *representational* with *abstract* painting. Not all painting *is* representational. There are inordinately rich aesthetic representations making no *cognitive* claim whatsoever. This is the glory of painting as pure aesthetic expression. But there is *something else* going on, I submit, when we are talking about portraiture or representational painting.

Surely historians may take up different representations-of-Napoleon in order to ascertain (aspects of) Napoleon, the actual historical figure, and it makes all the sense in the world to seek as many as offer insight into this enigmatic figure. This is to privilege the *portrait* element in 'portrait painting,' without denying its character as *painting*, as an artistic work. Even in portrait painting and crucially in historical representation, our intention is to make a credible claim about something actual. Let us look to historical representation directly to clarify this. There is clearly an element in our appreciation of great works of historical writing that parallels this appreciation for the aesthetic and formal aspect of painting. Historical writing *can be* a form of art. But it is not *only* a form of art. Historical writing is a cognitive pursuit, not just an aesthetic one. It strives to be empirically valid, that is, to persuade others of its insight into actuality. I think this is where Ankersmit's otherwise fruitful analogy with portrait painting goes awry by ignoring its disanalogies.

Ankersmit invokes what Willard van Orman Quine termed 'ontological relativity,' the 'looseness of fit' of language (and theory) to the world, in order to distinguish history from natural science.[126] The point of the new philosophy of science and language, however, is that natural science as empirical inquiry faces the same indeterminacy.[127] The complexity of the epistemic situation cannot be evaded in the direction either of purely linguistic or of strictly material determination. Quine's whole point was to render *all* language (including the privileged proposition of logical atomism) indeterminate, and to thrust us back upon a far more contingent, empirical and holistic 'looseness of fit' between language and world. En route, Quine *demolishes* Ankersmit's logical atomist notion of reference. Quine affirms the 'inscrutability of reference' only to assert the necessity of *some reference scheme* in order for language (and *meta*-language) to be possible *at all*. 'Semantic ascent' – what Ankersmit calls 'speaking about speaking'– is

*not* a philosophical endeavor to dissolve ('reduce') the referent into language (as might be said of Davidson or Rorty, and more plausibly of Derrida), but instead to elucidate from within language the ineluctable contingency of all referential systems and to problematize the elevation of any one to ultimate standing. Linguistic holism does not obviate ontology; it only localizes it to the referential scheme of some 'home language,' whereupon ordinary language and theoretical language must and do carry on.

Philosophy of science has taken the 'linguistic turn' in an important direction, both affirming the 'theory-ladenness of observation' – the inevitability of a 'conceptual scheme' *constructing* contingently and fallibly what phenomena can signify – *and* insisting on a crucial element of *constraint* by the object of inquiry (the 'world') which does not permit just any projection to *fit*.[128] But this means that natural scientific inquiry *shares* with historical and hermeneutic inquiry the need always to *interpret* in a crucially reflexive manner: recognizing the cultural ('subjective') component in the conceptual (theoretical-linguistic) construction projected, and recognizing the natural ('objective') component of material constraints – not only in the object but in the apparatus of investigation, including the very materiality of the embodied inquirer (a line of thought that links the 'Duhem-Quine Thesis' with new theories of 'hybridity' in Latour, Haraway and Barad).[129]

By suggesting that colligatory concepts – and historical representations containing them – have a referential component, a cognitive, and not merely a formal intention (however contingent and fallible), I am arguing for the robustness of historicism. If historical practice is rational, as Ankersmit has always professed, this historicism – commonplace among practicing historians on Ankersmit's view as much as on mine – deserves to be philosophically explained, not discredited 'logically.' With Aviezer Tucker, I maintain that historicism *is* the rational core of the historical discipline. To be sure, that rational core leaves a great deal underdetermined.

But that, as Quine has taught us, represents the condition of all human understanding of actuality. Both for philosophers and for historians, 'providing intelligible descriptions and explanations of [change]' is extremely difficult.[130] Consequently, *localizing* inquiry holds the best prospect for substantive outcomes. All historians and many philosophers of science have acknowledged this by their practices: grand theory of science as a whole has come increasingly to be displaced by situation-specific methodological and epistemological study.[131] Much if not all that is interesting in current science studies is pursued *locally or situationally* within ongoing empirical scientific sites of practice.[132] Complexity and highly local, concrete mediations call for 'a historical vocabulary that leaves scientific practice neither utterly divorced from its cultural context nor relegated to a mere puppet of other forces,' in the words of Peter Galison.[133] We need to develop a historical language with the dialectical richness to articulate what Andrew Pickering has called the topology, the temporality and the materiality of practice.[134] Such accounts set out to register the *entrenchment* of practices, apparatus and concepts as heterogeneous and patchy structures – a congeries of 'black boxes,' if you will – which are nonetheless real and binding, hence a theory of *constraints*. And such accounts seek to register *emergence*: the radical novelty that erupts at the concrete level of event and agency in history.

## NOTES AND REFERENCES

1  For a comprehensive anthology of the postmodern debate in history, see Keith Jenkins, ed., *The Postmodern History Reader* (London/New York: Routledge, 1997). Key works within the disciplinary historical conversation include: Hayden White, *Metahistory* (Baltimore: Johns Hopkins University Press, 1973); White, *Tropics of Discourse* (Baltimore: Johns Hopkins University Press, 1978); White, *The Content of the Form* (Baltimore: Johns Hopkins University Press, 1987); Frank Ankersmit, *Narrative Logic* (The Hague: Nijhoff, 1983); Ankersmit, *History and Tropology* (Berkeley & LA: University of California Press, 1994); Ankersmit, *Historical Representation* (Stanford: Stanford University Press, 2001); Hans Kellner, *Language and Historical Representation: Getting the Story Crooked* (Madison: University of Wisconsin Press, 1989); Dominick La Capra, *Rethinking Intellectual History* (Ithaca: Cornell University Press, 1983); La Capra, *History and Criticism* (Ithaca: Cornell University Press, 1985); La Capra, *Soundings in Critical Theory* (Ithaca: Cornell University Press, 1989); Robert Berkhofer, *Beyond the Great Story: History as Text and Discourse* (Cambridge: Harvard University Press, 1995); David Roberts, *Nothing But History: Reconstruction and Extremity after Metaphysics* (Berkeley, Los Angeles, etc: University of California Press, 1995).

2  Ankersmit is fiercely committed to the autonomy and indispensability of the humanities and historical writing, to the urgency of their cultural-political mission today. Hence his adamant resistance to any rapprochement between the human and the natural sciences. This is particularly vivid in his latest book, *Sublime Historical Experience* (Stanford: Stanford University Press, 2005). 'The battle lines between those who really wanted to get to grips with history, the humanities and political realities of the present and the future, and those who have only science before their eyes now seems to be have been erased' (77), he laments. He is hostile even to any endeavor to seek the similarities rather than the differences: 'In what way is the cause of our understanding of the natural and the human sciences furthered by merging them together into one indiscriminate cognitive soup?' (31). Nothing is more uncongenial to Ankersmit than 'the demand for history to be a science' (171, citing Nietzsche). 'Models borrowed from the sciences are useless ... The historian does not speak the language of science or of theory' (53). 'History and historical experience belong to the domain of the craftsman ... rather than that of the scientist' (111–12). 'History has stubbornly remained what it has always been, namely, something halfway between a craft and an art' (190). Ankersmit takes his stand 'against a scientistic interpretation of historical writing' (54), against 'all these ambitious scientistic attempts to violate the nature and purpose of historical writing' (190). 'Science has recently lost a good deal of terrain to art,' he avows (6). Against the truth purveyed by science, we need to recover 'aesthetic' (and historical) truth.

3  Joseph Rouse, 'Beyond epistemic sovereignty,' in Peter Galison and David Stump, eds, *The Disunity of Science: Boundaries, Contexts, and Power* (Stanford: Stanford University Press, 1996), 398–416. See also Rouse, *Engaging Science: How to Understand Its Practices Philosophically* (Ithaca/London: Cornell University Press, 1996); and Rouse, *How Scientific Practices Matter: Reclaiming Philosophical Naturalism* (Chicago/London: University of Chicago Press, 2002).

4  Philip Kitcher, 'The naturalists return,' *Philosophical Review* 101 (1992), 53–114, citing 76.

5  Zammito, *A Nice Derangement of Epistemes: Post-Positivism in the Study of Science From Quine to Latour* (Chicago/London: University of Chicago Press, 2004).

6   Peter Galison and David Stump, eds, *The Disunity of Science: Boundaries, Contexts, and Power* (Stanford: Stanford University Press, 1996).

7   Mary Hesse, *Revolutions and Reconstructions in the Philosophy of Science* (Bloomington/London: Indiana University Press, 1980), 7.

8   Donald MacKenzie and Barry Barnes, 'Scientific judgment: the biometry–Mendelism controversy,' in Barry Barnes and Steven Shapin, eds, *Natural Order: Historical Studies in Scientific Culture* (Beverley Hills/London: Sage, 1979), 191–210, citing 191–2.

9   The kinship of historicism and naturalism is not new. See Robert Brandom, 'Vocabularies of pragmatism: synthesizing naturalism and historicism,' in Brandom, ed., *Rorty and His Critics* (Oxford: Blackwell, 2000), 156–183. It was in recognition of that kinship and in its repudiation as 'mere psychology' that figures as different as Frege and Husserl launched, at the close of the 19th century, a major endeavor to revive a logically autonomous philosophy. Hence there is a fundamental kinship, too, between phenomenology and logical positivism, the dominant forms of foundational philosophy of the twentieth century. Richard Rorty observes: 'seventy years after Husserl's "Philosophy as Rigorous Science" and Russell's "Logic as the Essence of Philosophy," we are back with the same putative dangers which faced the authors of these manifestoes: if philosophy becomes too naturalistic, hard-nosed positive disciplines will nudge it aside; if it becomes too historicist, then intellectual history, literary criticism, and similar soft spots in "the humanities" will swallow it up.' (Richard Rorty, *Philosophy and the Mirror of Nature* (Princeton: Princeton University Press, 1979): 168; hereafter cited in text as '(PMN: page)').

10  I take Philip Kitcher's essay, 'The naturalists return,' as the clearest account of that decisive revival.

11  For instances of postmodern hyperbole in philosophy of history, see Sande Cohen, 'Structuralism and the writing of intellectual history,' *History and Theory* 17 (1978), 175–206; David Harlan, 'Intellectual history and the return of literature,' *American Historical Review* 94 (1989), 581–609; Keith Jenkins, *Re-Thinking History* (London/NY: Routledge, 1991); Jenkins, *On 'What is History': From Carr and Elton to Rorty and White* (London/NY: Routledge, 1995); Jenkins, *Refiguring History: New Thoughts on an Old Discipline* (London/NY: Routledge, 2003); Alun Munslow, *Deconstructing History* (London/NY: Routledge, 1997). For my characterization of this as 'hyperbolic,' see my essay 'Are we being theoretical yet? The new historicism, the new philosophy of history, and "Practicing historians,"' *Journal of Modern History* 65:4 (Dec. 1993), 783–814. I continued this argument against Ankersmit in his most postmodern posture in: 'Ankersmit's postmodern historiography: the hyperbole of "Opacity,"' *History and Theory* 37:3 (Oct. 1998), 330–46. I make another effort on these lines, engaging Dominic La Capra and Joan Scott: 'Reading "experience": the debate in intellectual history among Scott, Toews and LaCapra,' in Paula M.L. Moya and Michael R. Hames-Garcia, eds, *Reclaiming Identity: Realist Theory and the Predicament of Postmodernism* (Berkeley, Los Angeles, etc.: University of California Press, 2000), 279–311.

12  Quine got to the heart of what giving up positivist foundationalism means: 'scruples against circularity have little point once we have stopped dreaming of deducing science from observations' (Quine, 'Epistemology naturalized,' in Quine, *Ontological Relativity and Other Essays* (NY: Columbia University Press, 1969), 69–90, citing 75–6). In highlighting Quine's role in finally killing off positivism, I do not want to deny or diminish the role of others, such as Ludwig Wittgenstein or Wilfred Sellars. Quine's place in this account is exemplary – but in all the senses of that term.

13  '[M]ethodological foundationalism is a hopeless program and thus ... naturalism, in spite of the circle argument, is our only alternative' (Ronald Giere, 'Philosophy of science naturalized,' *Philosophy of Science* 52 (1985), 331–56, citing 336).

14  Kitcher, 'The naturalists return,' 63. Bonnie Tamarkin Paller observes similarly: 'The failure to provide adequate rules ... has encouraged many philosophers to conclude that there are no unchanging, essential, and transcontextual rules which are discoverable a priori' (Paller, 'Naturalized philosophy of science, history of science, and the internal/external debate,' *PSA 1986*, Vol. 1, 258–68, citing 258).

15  Kitcher, 'The naturalists return,' 76.

16  Ibid., 72, 75.

17  Ibid., 72n. 'The "naturalized turn" commits one to the rejection of the claim that the proper philosophical method is a priori conceptual analysis ... Then, since philosophers do not have privileged access to normative truths, any answer to the normative question is going to have to come through the only other available methodology, this sort of a posteriori methodology, specifically beginning with an historical analysis of particular cases' (Paller, 'Naturalized philosophy of science,' 259).

18  Rudolf Carnap, *Meaning and Necessity* (Chicago: University of Chicago Press, 1956); Karl Popper, *The Logic of Scientific Discovery* (London: Routledge, 2002); Carl Hempel, *Fundamentals of Concept Formation in Empirical Science* (Chicago: University of Chicago Press, 1952).

19  Ronald Giere, 'Kuhn's Legacy for North American Philosophy of Science,' *Social Studies of Science* 27 (1997): 496–8.

20  Guy Axtell captures this well: 'it is not mistaken to see skepticism and foundationalism as flip-side images of this received view in empiricist philosophy' ('Normative epistemology and the bootstrap theory,' *Philosophical Forum* 23 (1992): 329–43, citing 334). Elsewhere he elaborates: 'The logicist's overstatement of the objectivity of metascientific discourse and the subjectivity of normative ethical discourse has exacerbated a dualistic approach to meta-level discourse that is antithetical to

pragmatism' for 'pragmatism has always advocated opening epistemology onto a plane of psychological, social and historical conditioning that cuts *across* these neat divides' (Axtell, 'Logicism, pragmatism, and metascience: towards a pancritical pragmatic theory of metalevel discourse,' *PSA 1990*, Vol 1, 39–49, citing 46).

21 Giere, 'Philosophy of science naturalized,' 334. The second argument brought forth against naturalized epistemology, according to Giere, is the distinction of description from prescription. The final objection to naturalized epistemology trades on dread of a slide into relativism. The claim that it is impossible 'to take a middle road between the old logical empiricism and the new historical relativism' (J. Kegley, 'History and philosophy of science: necessary partners or merely roommates?,' in *History and Anti-History in Philosophy*, ed. T.Z. Lavine and V. Tejera (Dordrecht: Kluwer, 1989), 237–55, citing 244) I reject unequivocally.

22 This is the conclusion that Rorty has drawn from Quine, Kuhn et al., and it signifies for him, as Kitcher phrases it, 'the death of philosophy ... [whereupon] succession passes variously to history, sociology or literary theory' ('The naturalists return,' 113). On this important notion of 'de-transcendentalizing' and Rorty see Nickles, 'Scientific discovery and the future of philosophy of science,' in *Scientific Discovery, Logic, and Rationality*, ed. Nickles (Dordrecht: Reidel, 1980; Boston Studies in the Philosophy of Science, Vol. 56), 1–59, citing 48.

23 '[D]oubt is not criticism. Moreover, the logical possibility of an alternative is not itself an alternative ... But while doubt is cheap, criticism is not. The *non*justificationist, having renounced proof in favour of improvement, acknowledges that alternatives and doubt are always possible but insists that generalized doubt and the possibility of alternatives be translated into concrete criticism and actual alternatives before they need be taken seriously' (Larry Briskman, 'Historicist relativism and bootstrap rationality,' *Monist* 60 (1977), 509–39, citing 521).

24 Thomas Nagel, *The View from Nowhere* (NY: Oxford University Press, 1986).

25 Nickles, 'Good science as bad history,' in Ernan McMullin, ed., *The Social Dimensions of Science* (Notre Dame: Notre Dame University Press, 1992), 88.

26 Ibid., 116, 89. Axtell refers to 'Dewey's emphasis on the generation of criteria for problem-solving through the 'method of intelligences' and the study of the mutual conditioning of means and ends' ('Normative epistemology and the bootstrap theory,' 336–7). 'Dewey's pragmatic-normativism eschews both justificationism and relativism of value judgments, including axiological judgments' ('Logicism, pragmatism, and metascience,' 46).

27 Kitcher, 'The naturalists return,' 113.

28 David Hull, 'Testing philosophical claims about science,' *PSA 1992*. Vol. 2, 468–475, cited from 473.

29 Ibid., 471. He puts it pithily in another context: 'reality has a way of forcing itself on us independent of our

beliefs' ('In defense of presentism,' *History and Theory* 18 (1979), 1–15, citing 12). Harold Brown makes the same point: 'it is not the case that there are no checks on the range of possible interpretations ... the range of possible ways of understanding it is limited by the properties of that object' ('For a modest historicism,' 552).

30 Giere, 'Philosophy of science naturalized,' 331–56.

31 Axtell, 'Normative epistemology and the bootstrap theory,' 334, refers to Feigl, Reichenbach and Ayer as employers of the 'vicious circle' and 'infinite regress' arguments and makes the important point that such arguments 'helped them to insulate theoretical science, including its norms, from the metaphysical, the noncognitive, and the merely pragmatic. It allowed them to define scientific disagreement as disagreement resolvable by logic and evidence alone ...' (Ibid.).

32 G.H. Merrill, 'Moderate Historicism and the Empiricist Sense of "Good Science",' *PSA 1980*, vol. I., 223-225. On Popper's 'demarcation problem' see W. W. Bartley, 'Theories of demarcation between science and metaphysics,' in *Problems in the Philosophy of Science*, ed. Imre Lakatos and Alan Musgrave (Amsterdam: North Holland Pub. Co., 1968), 40-64; Larry Laudan, 'The demise of the demarcation problem,' in *Physics, Philosophy and Psychoanalysis*, ed. Robert Cohen and Larry Laudan (Dordrecht: Reidel, 1983), 111-127.

33 Here, Toulmin's idea of a '"common law" model' which works 'by the collection and restatement of precedents' seems to offer a promising alternative to the 'statutory law' of 'general, timeless recipes' which grounded the orientation of the earlier philosophy of science and still monopolizes the very idea of law in their estimation (Toulmin, 'From form to function: philosophy and history of science in the 1950s and now,' *Daedalus* 105 (1977), 143–62, citing 154). See also James Brown, 'Explaining the success of science,' *Ratio* 27 (1985): 49–66.

34 Merrill, 'Moderate historicism.'

35 Giere, 'Philosophy of science naturalized,' 342–3. See Jürgen Habermas, 'Gegen einen positivistisch halbierten Rationalismus,' *Kölner Zeitschriften für Soziologie und Sozialpsychologie* 16 (1964): 635–659.

36 While it would be too sanguine to take emergentism as established, evolutionary epistemology opens new prospects here that must not be foreclosed dogmatically.

37 Giere, 'Philosophy of science naturalized,' 333.

38 Harold Brown, 'Normative and naturalized epistemology,' *Inquiry* 31 (1988): 53–78, citing 55.

39 In the terms of Karl-Otto Apel: 'Any attempt at ultimate grounding leads to a trilemma: either there must come about an infinite regress, or a logical circle, or else the grounding-procedure has to be broken off by axiomatizing or, better, dogmatizing certain premises' (Apel, 'Types of rationality today: the continuum of reason between science and ethics,' in *La Rationalité Aujourd'hui* (Toronto: McGill University Press, 1980), 310).

40 James Brown, 'History and the norms of science,' *PSA 1980*, Vol. 1, 236–48, citing 243.

41 Richard Palmer, *Hermeneutics* (Evanston: Northwestern University Press, 1969); David Hoy, *The Critical Circle: Literature, History, and Philosophical Hermeneutics* (Berkeley, Los Angeles, London: University of California Press, 1978); Paul Ricoeur, *Hermeneutics and the Human Sciences* (Cambridge: Cambridge University Press, 1981).

42 Kitcher, 'The naturalists return,' 113. John Passmore put it as follows: 'To pick out from what scientists have done the strategies which make possible the emergence of science as a successful enterprise entails looking carefully at what has happened, contrasting successful and unsuccessful science and asking how far the failures were the result of the use of bad strategies as distinct from ignorance of crucial facts, experimental limitations and so on' (Passmore, 'The relevance of history to philosophy of science,' in *Scientific Explanation and Understanding*, ed. Nicholas Rescher (Lanham, MD: University Press of American, 1983), 83–105, citing 92).

43 See Hilary Putnam, *The Collapse of the Fact/Value Dichotomy and Other Essays* (Cambridge: Harvard University Press, 2002); Jack Nelson, 'The last dogma of empiricism?' in *Feminism, Science, and the Philosophy of Science*, ed. Lynn Hankinson Nelson and Jack Nelson (Dordrecht: Kluwer, 1996), 59–78.

44 'What is given up is an unworkable supra-historical a priori conception of rationality and what is sought is, in Wartofsky's words, "the sources of its *intrinsic* normativeness"' (J. Kegley, 'History and Philosophy of Science,' 253), referring to Marx Wartofsky, 'The relation between philosophy of science and history of science,' in *Models: Representation and Scientific Understanding*, ed. Wartofsky and Robert Cohen (Dordrecht: Reidel, 1979; Boston Studies in the Philosophy of Science, Vol. 40), 119–39, citing 134.)

45 Nicholas Rescher, 'Extraterrestrial science,' *Philosophia Naturalis* 21 (1984), 400–424, citing 413.

46 Dudley Shapere, 'The character of scientific change,' and 'What can the theory of knowledge learn from the history of knowledge?' in Shapere, *Reason and the Search for Knowledge* (Dordrecht: Reidel, 1984; Boston Studies in the Philosophy of Science, Vol. 78), 205–60 and 182–202, as Thomas Nickles summarizes (Nickles, 'Scientific discovery and the future of philosophy of science,' 45).

47 Brown, 'Normative and naturalized epistemology,' 61.

48 Ibid., 69.

49 Ibid., 61.

50 Laudan, 'Progress or rationality? The prospects for normative naturalism,' *American Philosophical Quarterly* 24 (1987): 19–31; 'Relativism, naturalism and reticulation,' *Synthese* 71 (1987): 221–34; 'Normative naturalism,' *Philosophy of Science* 57 (1990): 44–59. For criticism, see, e.g., Alexander Rosenberg, 'Normative naturalism and the role of philosophy,' *Philosophy of Science* 57 (1990): 34–43; Jarrett Leplin, 'Renormalizing epistemology,' *Philosophy of Science* 57 (1990): 20–33; Harvey Siegel, 'Laudan's normative naturalism,' *Studies in History and Philosophy of Science* 21 (1990): 295–313; Gerald Doppelt, 'Laudan's pragmatic alternative to positivist and historicist theories of science,' *Inquiry* 24 (1981): 253–71; 'Relativism and recent pragmatic conceptions of scientific rationality,' in Nicholas Rescher, ed., *Scientific Explanation and Understanding: Essays on Reasoning and Rationality in Science* (Lanham, MD: University Press of America, 1983), 107–42; 'Relativism and the reticulation model of scientific rationality,' *Synthese* 69 (1981): 225–52; 'The Naturalist conception of methodological standards in science: a critique,' *Philosophy of Science* 57 (1990): 1–19.

51 Brown, 'Normative and naturalized epistemology,' 65.

52 Adam Grobler, 'Between rationalism and relativism: on Larry Laudan's model of scientific rationality,' *British Journal for the Philosophy of Science* 41 (1990): 493–507, citing 496.

53 Nickles, 'Scientific discovery and the future of philosophy of science,' 7.

54 Briskman, 'Historicist relativism and bootstrap rationality,' 521.

55 Nickles, 'Good science as bad history,' 91. See also: Nickles, 'Remarks on the use of history as evidence,' *Synthese* 69 (1986): 253–66.

56 Shapere, 'What can the theory of knowledge learn,' 185.

57 Nickles, 'Good science as bad history,' 116.

58 Ibid., 117.

59 'The pragmatic conception of belief and attitude is *dialectical* ...' (Axtell, 'Logicism, pragmatism and metascience,' 47) 'What we need ... is a dialectical history of science. But having said this, it should be clear that the norms of such a science must be derived from the historical context itself and cannot be imposed upon it by philosophical fiat, or by some supra-historical a priori conception of rationality ... It requires, I think, a characterization of the *historical enterprise* called science, in a new way, in order to see in it the sources of its *intrinsic* normativeness.' (Wartofsky, 'The relation between philosophy and history of science,' 134)

60 Nickles, 'Good science as bad history,' 117.

61 Nickles, 'Integrating the science studies disciplines,' in Steven Fuller, ed., *The Cognitive Turn* (Dordrecht: Kluwer, 1989), 225–256, citing 248.

62 Nickles, 'Good Science as Bad History,' 117.

63 Humberto Maturana and Francisco Varela, *Autopoeisis and Cognition: The Realization of the Living* (Dordrecht: Reidel, 1980; Boston Studies in the Philosophy of Science, Vol. 42); Susan Oyama, *The Ontogeny of Information: Developmental Systems and Evolution* (2nd edn, Duke University Press, 2000); Oyama, Paul Griffiths and Russell Gray, eds, *Cycles of Contingency: Developmental Systems and Evolution* (Cambridge: MIT Press, 2001).

64 Nickles, 'Scientific discovery and the future of philosophy of science,' 32.

65 Hilary Putnam, 'The craving for objectivity,' *New Literary History* 15 (1984), 229–239, citing 239.

66 'The dialectic does not simply set to work in a blind and immediate fashion, but proceeds rather from the indispensable insight that a beginning must always be made at a specific and determinate point, if indeed a beginning is to be made at all' (Rüdiger Bubner, 'Closure and the understanding of history,' in Bubner, *The Innovations of Idealism* (Cambridge: Cambridge University Press, 2003), 179).

67 Nickles, 'Scientific discovery and the future of philosophy of science,' 35.

68 Ibid., 37.

69 Ibid.

70 Ibid., 38.

71 Ibid., 22.

72 Ibid., 18.

73 Michael Polanyi, *The Tacit Dimension* (NY: Doubleday, 1966).

74 Wartofsky, 'The relation between philosophy and history of science,'; Nickles, 'Scientific discovery and the future of philosophy of science,' 39.

75 Nickles, 'Scientific discovery and the future of philosophy of science,' 39. This is Kuhn's point about the exemplarity of paradigms, and reasoning by analogy.

76 Nickles, 'Good science as bad history,' 107.

77 Ibid.

78 Ibid., 113.

79 I.B. Cohen, 'History and the philosopher of science,' in *Structures of Scientific Theories*, ed. Frederic Suppe (2nd ed.; Urbana: University of Illinois Press, 1977), 308–349: 346.

80 'The critical historian must use some standard by which to judge whether or not he has been successful – successful, that is, at reconstructing the contemporary problem situation accurately. That is, he must decide how he will tell if his efforts to overcome the parochial and unfavorable modern bias have been sufficient... A ready standard in this endeavor is the attainment of clarity and consistency.' Thus, 'the need for an independent standard transforms the aim of "seeing a theory in its own time" into "seeing a theory as clear and coherent in its own time"' (Lynn Lindholm, 'Is realistic history of science possible? A hidden inadequacy in the new history of science,' in *Scientific Philosophy Today*, ed. Joseph Agassi and R.S. Cohen (Dordrecht: Reidel, 1981; Boston Studies in the Philosophy of Science Vol. 67), 159–86, citing 181). That is, 'historians do not know if they *can* declare a view unclear or incoherent in its own historical context' (Ibid., 167). 'Whenever a seemingly unclear or inconsistent view presents itself, the critical historian is led almost irresistibly to the view that the weakness is one in his reconstruction' (Ibid., 182).

81 See the apt comments in David Hull, 'In defense of presentism,' *History and Theory* 18 (1979): 1–15. And see also Nicholas Jardine, 'Philosophy of science and the art of historical interpretation,' in *Theory Change, Ancient Axiomatics, and Galileo's Methodology: Proceedings of the 1978 Pisa Conference on the History and Philosophy of Science*, ed. Jaako Hintikka, David Gruender and Evandro Agazzi (Dodrecht: Reidel, 1978), Vol. 1, 341–8.

82 Barry Barnes, 'The vicissitudes of belief,' *Social Studies of Science* 9 (1979): 247–63, citing 252–253.

83 Ibid.

84 'If Rorty's reform of his own discipline were to be actually carried out, the voice of philosophy would begin to sound rather like the voice of intellectual history' (David Hollinger, 'The voice of intellectual history in the conversation of mankind: a note on Richard Rorty,' in *In the American Province: Studies in the History and Historiography of Ideas* (Bloomington: Indiana University Press, 1985), 167–175; 215–16; cite from 169). Anthony Cascardi links Rorty with Lyotard: their approaches, 'although historicist insofar as they assert the contingency of all discourse, constitute further refusals of the attempt by history to mediate and thereby recuperate the differences among divergent accounts of human nature or the world...' (Cascardi, 'An afterword: the lines redrawn,' in Reed Way Dasenbrock, ed., *Redrawing the Lines: Analytic Philosophy, Deconstruction, and Literary Theory* (Minneapolis: University of Minnesota Press, 1989), 219–20). For a very insightful discussion of Rorty's 'historicism' see D. Hall, *Richard Rorty: Prophet and Poet of the New Pragmatism* (Albany: SUNY Press, 1994), 14–64, esp. 54ff, where Hall explores the question whether Rorty 'may have stretched the word "historicism" beyond usable limits.' Hall concludes that Rorty 'ought to reconsider his claim to be a historicist ...' since 'Rorty's historicism is a poeticized one' and Hall finds it 'better ... to take full responsibility for one's literary pretensions than to mask them by claims to historicist practice' (p. 63).

85 On Kuhn and incommensurability see my *Nice Derangement of Epistemes*.

86 This is the language which inspired Hollinger's appraisal of Rorty.

87 As Harold Bloom puts it, 'The strong imagination comes to its painful birth through savagery and misrepresentation' (Bloom, *Anxiety of Influence* (NY: Oxford University Press, 1997), 86).

88 For Rorty's criticism of Habermas see Rorty, 'Habermas and Lyotard on Postmodernity,' in R. Bernstein, ed., *Habermas and Modernity* (Cambridge: MIT Press, 1985), 161–75, 224–5; Richard Rorty, *Contingency, Irony and Solidarity* (Cambridge: Cambridge University Press, 1989), 65–9.

89 Richard Bernstein has noted that 'sometimes Rorty writes as if any philosophical attempt to sort out the better from the worse, the rational from the irrational (even assuming that this is historically relative) must lead us back to foundationalism and the search for an ahistorical perspective' (R. Bernstein, 'Philosophy in the Conversation of Mankind,' in Hollinger, ed., *Hermeneutics and Praxis*, 78).

90 Hans-Georg Gadamer, *Truth and Method* (New York: Crossroads, 1989). Rorty thoroughly misinterprets Gadamer, but that is a matter for another context.

91  On this classic phrase of hermeneutics, see Ernst Behler, 'What it means to understand an author better than he understood himself: idealistic philosophy and romantic hermeneutics,' in *Literary Theory and Criticism: Festschrift Presented to René Wellek in Honor of His 80th Birthday* (Bern, Frankfurt, NY: P. Lang, 1984), Vol. 1, p. 69–92; and Klaus Müller-Vollmer, 'To understand an author better than the author himself: on the hermeneutics of the unspoken,' *Language and Style* 5 (1972), 43–52.

92  William McNeill, 'Mythhistory, or truth, myth, history, and historians,' *American Historical Review* 91 (1986), 8.

93  I an not going to elucidate this concept here. I presume that it is familiar to historical theorists.

94  Frank Ankersmit, *Historical Representation* (Stanford: Stanford University Press, 2002). See my essay, 'Ankersmit and historical representation' *History and Theory*, 44 (May 2005), 155–181.

95  Aviezer Tucker, *Our Knowledge of the Past*.

96  The distinction is generally traced to Reichenbach, but whatever its genesis, the consignment of the 'context of discovery' to happenstance is pervasive in the Received View. See Paul Hoyningen-Huene, 'Context of discovery and context of justification,' *Studies in History and Philosophy of Science* 18 (1987), 501–15, for a discussion of the contrast and its fate.

97  Nickles, 'Scientific discovery and the future of philosophy of science,' 30.

98  Ibid., 31.

99  Popper, *The Poverty of Historicism* (Boston: Beacon, 1957).

100  Nickles, 'Scientific discovery and the future of philosophy of science,' 7.

101  Ibid., 16.

102  Zammito, *A Nice Derangement of Epistemes*.

103  M. Bevir, 'Objectivity in history,' *History and Theory*, 33 (1994), 328–344: 331.

104  Ibid., 331.

105  Ibid., 331.

106  Raymond Martin, 'Objectivity and meaning in historical studies,' *History and Theory* 32 (1993), 25–50, cited from 29.

107  Ibid., 37.

108  Ibid., 30.

109  Ibid., 38.

110  M. Krausz, 'Ideality and ontology in the practice of history,' in W.J. Van der Dussen and L. Rubinoff, eds, *Objectivity, Method and Point of View* (Leiden, NY, etc: Brill, 1991), 97–111.

111  Rubinoff, 'Historicity and objectivity,' 147.

112  L. Rubinoff, 'Introduction: W.H. Dray and the critique of historical meaning,' in Van der Dussen and Rubinoff, eds, *Objectivity*, 8.

113  D. Boucher, 'Ambiguity and originality,' in Van der Dussen and Rubinoff, eds, *Objectivity*, 28.

114  Ibid., 41.

115  Aviezer Tucker, *Our Knowledge of the Past* (Cambridge: Cambridge University Press, 2004); hereafter cited in text as '(OKP: page)'.

116  For Tucker, historiography attained this in the early nineteenth century in Germany under the auspices of Ranke. Historiography did not achieve its paradigm autochthonously; instead, it adopted a successful paradigm from predecessor inquiries, then elaborated this paradigm in its own domain. Tucker makes the important point that evolutionary biology followed historiography in adopting the essential features of this paradigm and deploying them to constitute its own 'normal science.'

117  Fred Dretske, *Knowledge and the Flow of Information* (Cambridge; MIT Press, 1981).

118  Zammito, 'Ankersmit and historical representation.'

119  Frank Ankersmit, *Historical Representation* (Stanford: Stanford University Press, 2002): 135.

120  Quine, 'On empirically equivalent systems of the world,' *Erkenntnis* 9 (1975), 313–328. On the proliferation of notions of semantic holism see Jerry Fodor and Ernest Lepore, *Holism: A Shopper's Guide* (Oxford: Blackwell, 1992).

121  On Instrumentalism or anti-realism, Bas van Fraasen, *The Scientific Image* (Oxford: Clarendon, 1980); Nelson Goodman, *Ways of Worldmaking* (Indianapolis: Hackett, 1978).

122  Stephen Schwartz, ed., *Naming, Necessity and Natural Kinds* (Ithaca: Cornell University Press, 1977).

123  *Not* 'exclusively,' however: there was a Northern Renaissance, and an Elizabethan one; there is the Harlem Renaissance, and effort has been made to find one in the twelfth century. That is, the historical concept can be transferred (and transformed).

124  Ankersmit on Danto: Frank Ankersmit, *Historical Representation* (Stanford: Stanford University Press, 2002), 80.

125  Quine, 'Ontological relativity,' in Quine, *Ontological Relativity and Other Essays* (NY: Columbia University Press, 1969).

126  Ankersmit, *Historical Representation*, 190.

127  N. Katherine Hayles, 'Constrained constructivism: locating scientific inquiry in the theater of representation,' in George Levine, ed., *Realism and Representation* (Madison: University of Wisconsin Press, 1993), 27–43. The entire volume is appropriate; and see Jay Labinger and Harry Collins, eds, *The One Culture? A Conversation about Science* (Chicago/London: University of Chicago Press, 2001). See, finally, the new journal, *Configurations*, for which this issue is the guiding thread.

128  See the aptly titled *Construction and Constraint: The Shaping of Scientific Rationality*, ed. Ernan McMullin (Notre Dame, IN: University of Notre Dame Press, 1988), and see the debate between Andrew Pickering and Peter Galison in *Scientific Practice: Theories and Stories of Doing Physics*, ed Jed Buchwald (Chicago/London: University of Chicago Press, 1995).

129  On hybridity, see: Bruno Latour, *Science in Action* (Cambridge: Harvard University Press, 1987); Latour, *The Pasteurization of France* (Cambridge: Harvard University Press, 1988); Donna Haraway, 'Cyborg Manifesto,' in Haraway, *Simians, Cyborgs, and Women: The Reinvention*

*of Nature* (NY: Routledge, 1991), 155–61; Hararway, 'The promises of monsters: a regenerative politics for inappropriate/d others,' in Lawrence Grossberg, Cary Nelson and Paula Treichler, eds, *Cultural Studies* (NY: Routledge, 1992), 295–337; Karen Barad, 'Meeting the universe halfway: realism and social constructivism without contradiction,' in L.H. Nelson and J. Nelson, eds, *Feminism, Science, and the Philosophy of Science* (Dordrecht: Kluwer, 1996), 161–94; Barad, 'Getting real: technoscientific practices and the materialization of reality,' *Difference: A Journal of Feminist Cultural Studies* 10 (1998), 87–128; Barad, 'Agential realism,' in Mario Biagioli, ed., *The Science Studies Reader* (NY/London: Routledge, 1999), 1–11. And for a historically adept application of this insight see Christopher Lawrence and Steven Shapin, eds, *Science Incarnate: Historical Embodiments of Natural Knowledge* (Chicago: University of Chicago Press, 1998).

130  Nickles, 'Scientific discovery and the future of philosophy of science', 17.

131  Philosophy of science has increasingly opted to work within the local domain of a scientific specialty. Indeed, Steven Fuller proclaimed 'the future of the philosophy of science lies either in some other branch of science studies (especially history and sociology) or in the conceptual foundations of the special sciences' (Fuller, *Philosophy of Science and Its Discontents* (Boulder, CO: Westview, 1989), xii).

132  See Mario Biagioli, ed., *The Science Studies Reader* (NY/London: Routledge, 1999).

133  Peter Galison, 'Context and constraint,' in *Scientific Practice: Theories and Stories of Doing Physics*, ed. Jed Buchwald (Chicago/London: University of Chicago Press, 1995), 13–48, citing 17.

134  Pickering, 'Beyond constraint: the temporality of practice and the historicity of knowledge,' in *Scientific Practice: Theories and Stories of Doing Physics*, 42–55, citing 55.

# 25

# Historical Experience Beyond the Linguistic Turn

Frank Ankersmit

## INTRODUCTION

Three stages can be discerned in the philosophy of history since World War I. The first stage gave us the discussion of the covering law model as initially defined by C.G. Hempel in his famous essay of 1942. The second stage was hermeneutics. It was introduced in the Anglo-Saxon philosophy of history by William Dray in his *Laws and Explanation in History* of 1957, which gave Collingwood's thought a much wider audience than it had hitherto had. Discussion of this topic gradually petered out with teleological explanation, the so-called 'logical connection argument' as presented by G.H. Von Wright and the debate on reasons versus causes. Recently, however, the interest in Anglo-Saxon hermeneutics seems to be on the increase again. Much the same story can be told for German hermeneutics, as developed in the tradition going from Schleiermacher, via Droysen, to Dilthey. The impressive *finale* was Gadamer's *Truth and Method* of 1960. That tradition also lost its impetus in the 1970s. But like Anglo-Saxon hermeneutics it presently seems to be undergoing a

certain renaissance, too – above all because of the affinities discerned by some theorists between Gadamer's hermeneutics and Donald Davidson's philosophy of language.

The third and last stage began in the 1970s, when the adherents of the covering law model and of hermeneutics – whether of German or Anglo-Saxon origin – had to clear the road for the protagonists of the linguistic turn, most notably Hayden White. The adherents of the linguistic turn gained a quick and easy victory over their opponents. All the more so, since only with them did the philosophy of history seem to be quite up to date again. They demonstrated why language matters to the philosophy of history and thus brought the discipline in line with contemporary philosophy of language.[1]

Since then not much has changed, but I think one can safely say that the paradigm of the linguistic turn is still the dominant one. We should be happy with this, for it cannot be doubted that many aspects of the use of language in historical writing still need to be explored. I am thinking here especially of a cross-fertilization between the philosophy of history and the philosophy of language. Both parties stand to win a lot from that. The notion of representation certainly would be a good starting point here.

Nevertheless, one may ask oneself what topics could usefully be addressed after the linguistic turn and have not yet, or only very rarely, attracted the interest of philosophers of history. When asking this question I have in mind topics where the achievements of the linguistic turn are accepted rather than questioned. In fact, in my view, the linguistic turn cannot be undone – and we should not try to do so. But it may be that the linguistic turn has its own blind spot and that its very successes hide from view things we cannot afford to ignore. As I hope to show below, much of this is true of the notion of historical experience. That will be my topic, then, in this chapter. And, again, this is a going beyond rather than against the linguistic turn. Hence the chapter's title.

## THE MAGRITTE CONCEPTION OF HISTORICAL WRITING

There is a series of paintings by René Magritte called *La Condition Humaine*. All the paintings in the series have something in common. They depict part of visible reality – a landscape, a city, a street – and part of our view of that reality is blocked by a painting. For there always is a depiction of a painting on these paintings; they are partly paintings of paintings. The funny thing, though, is that what you see on *that* painting is exactly the same that you would see if there was no painting, if the painting were removed and you had an unobstructed view of what was hidden behind it. So with these paintings it is just as if you were moving around in your room, or outside your house, with a picture frame – and then seeing part of the world through the (empty) frame and the rest of it outside the frame.

But there is an interesting asymmetry here. Magritte imitates (or produces) this effect with a painting and *not* with a painting's frame. Obviously, this would not work in reality itself. If we walked around our house with

a painting, we would never be tempted to confuse what we saw on the painting with that part of the world that was obscured from view by it – even if by some strange coincidence what was depicted on the painting were to be exactly identical with what could be seen behind the painting. The explanation, of course, is that Magritte used a painting to achieve the effect intended by him. In order to see this, let us distinguish between painting 1 and painting 2; where painting 1 denotes the Magritte painting itself and painting 2 the painting that is so insidiously shown on painting 1. And, indeed, the painter can then arrange things in such a way that what is seen on painting 2 is exactly identical with how painting 1 would depict reality if there were no painting 2 on painting 1. Since reality itself is not a painting, no painting could relate in a similar way to what we see in reality.

Magritte's painting can be seen as a comment on the illusionism of figurative painting. Figurative painting wishes to provoke in us an illusion of actual visual reality, so that when we look at the painting within its framework it's just as if we were looking outside through the 'window' of the framework. This endows the figurative painting with a peculiar paradox: of course you look *at* the painting, but you are invited to react to this as if you were looking right *through* it, just as you may look through the glass of a window to the landscape outside. Put differently, it's just as if the painting exists only in order to efface itself. It's just as if all of the tremendous effort in making a figurative painting is aimed at the self-destructive purpose of making the viewer *forget* that it is there at all. The more successful the painting is with this, the less you will be aware of its very existence. And the ideal figurative painting is the painting whose existence has dwindled to nothingness.

Painting may often suggest useful and unexpected insights into the nature of historical writing. And so it is here. For most of the traditional and commonsensical beliefs of historians about the old and venerable issue of subjectivity versus objectivity can be elucidated in terms of Magritte's paintings. Recall the famous anecdote about Fustel de Coulanges who suddenly became worried by the spell he had cast on his audience by the power of his eloquence and then exclaimed: 'Messieurs, ce n'est pas moi, mais c'est l'Histoire qui vous parle!' Fustel distrusted what he told his audience about the early Middle Ages not because he had any doubts about the truth of what he was saying. Fustel was confident that the key to the scientific knowledge of the past had finally been discovered in his age and he was neither a sceptic nor a historical relativist in the way that is true of so many historians in the twentieth century. His worries were of a more dramatic nature: the mere and ineluctable fact that historical knowledge needs a historian and historical language, for its being expressed made him uneasy and fear that his language might be an obstacle rather than a bridge to the past. Even more illuminating is Ranke when lamenting in the preface to his *Englische Geschichte*:

> It has been my wish hitherto in my narrative to suppress myself as it were, and only to let the events speak and the mighty forces be seen which, arising out of and strengthened by each other's action in the course of centuries, now stood up against one another, and became involved in a stormy contest, which discharged itself in bloody and terrible outbursts, and at the same time was fraught with the decision of questions most important for the European world.[2]

Just like Fustel Ranke wanted to erase himself, to wipe himself away from his writing, because his presence in his writings would compromise the objectivity of his account of the past. His text should not speak to his readers, but the past itself. Only this could guarantee its objectivity; and as soon as any trace would remain of himself and of his own language subjectivity would triumph over objectivity. The same kind of worry inspired one of the weirdest historical texts ever written: Prosper de Barante's *Histoire des Ducs de Bourgogne* (1824–6).[3] Barante actually wanted to achieve what Ranke had only believed to be an unattainable ideal. For

when composing the history of Burgundy from 1364 to 1477 he effectively tried to 'wipe himself out' by presenting only quotes from the sources he had used (e.g. the *Chronique de St. Denis*, and the writings of historians such as Froissart, Olivier de la Marche or Commynes). Stephen Bann most appropriately characterizes Barante as a 'taxidermist'.[4] And, indeed, Barante wanted to show the past by making use of remnants of the past itself.[5] Of course even Barante, however ingenious his method was, did not really pull this off: he had to select from his sources and write texts connecting his quotes. So even he was still most powerfully present in the historical text compiled by him.

Fustel, Ranke and Barante shared what one might call the 'Magritte conception of historical writing'. The historical text is here conceived of as the surface of a figurative painting that should provoke in the spectator the illusion of not actually looking at a painting but at reality itself. Obviously, this is what Magritte had wanted to suggest with his Condition Humaine series, since there would be no difference between what we saw on the painting and what we would see if the painting was not there. Similarly, the historical text should evoke in us the illusion that we are looking at the past itself instead of at the text. And to the extent that the text is successful in achieving this effect, we can say (with Ranke) that the historian has 'wiped himself out', with Fustel that his audience is not listening to him – or the historian generally – but at the past itself and, with Barante, that the historian's text truly is the past itself.

## THE MAGRITTE CONCEPTION OF HISTORICAL WRITING AND THE LINGUISTIC TURN

Self-evidently, the Magritte conception of historical writing is wrong: we only need to think of it in order to realize ourselves that we do not look *through* paintings or texts but *at* them. Nevertheless, in this chapter I shall take the intuition behind the Magritte conception seriously. First, though they were well aware that their audiences knew how to discern illusions from reality, a great number of artists (since Giotto) and theorists of the visual arts (since Vasari) have aimed at creating this illusion of reality in their paintings – and were remarkably successful in this. I shall be the last to maintain that their successful illusionism was these great painters' best claim to eternal fame, but nobody can deny that it often was part – and a most respectable part – of their artistic effort.[6] So the role of illusionism in art may prevent us from dismissing the Magritte conception of historical writing out of hand. Perhaps there is some truth in this conception after all.

Next, we should not underestimate the enormous a priori appeal that the Magritte conception has always had. Intuitively almost everybody immediately subscribes to it. So much becomes clear already when we realize ourselves that the conception was only effectively discredited by the so-called linguistic turn. Think of what historiography (the history of historical writing) was before Hayden White and what it became after the publication of *Metahistory*.[7] Traditional pre-Whitean historiography was textually naive: it operated on the assumption that you could always look through the historical text to the past itself, and compare the two in the way you could compare the relevant part of a Magritte painting with what was really behind it. And then you could establish where the historical representation was correct or not, just as you would immediately recognize where what you saw on the Magritte painting (dis)agreed with actual reality itself (i.e. that part of visual reality that was obscured by the painting). Precisely this enabled the historiographer to show what progress had been made by historians in their attempt to satisfactorily account for the past. And, next, what political and moral prejudices had prevented the (great) historians from the past from getting to the 'Truth' about the past. Put differently, the illusionism of the historical text was taken seriously – or, I'd better say, the unwitting embrace of illusionism went unnoticed.

Then Hayden White came along and told us how things really are, namely that we do not look *through* texts but *at* them and that we must recognize that the historical text is an instrument meant to generate historical meaning. As he went on to say, the historical theorist's primary task is to explain how the historical text can have this most remarkable capacity of generating meaning. Just as we have every reason to be deeply surprised that such humble things as mere little dots of paint on a canvas can generate pictorial meaning and be the material basis for the genius of the Rafaels, the Da Vincis, the Titians, the Rembrandts, and many others.

This was nothing less than a complete revolution in historical thought. For this suddenly made historical theorists (and some historians) aware of the fact that there *is* – whether we like it or not – something that always stands in the way between the historian (and his/her audience) and the past itself. Namely, the historical text. White – and all the others having accepted the linguistic turn and all its consequences – pitilessly insisted on the inevitability of the historical text as the medium between us and the past. No text, then no access to the past at all. And they rudely (but justly) imparted to us the message that you might be entirely right when condemning each effort to translate the past into a text as inevitably subjectivist, but that this only means that you will have to live with subjectivism. The aspiration of objectivity arises from the albeit understandable, but impossible and hopelessly inconsistent desire to represent the past in the absence of a *text* representing the past.

If seen in this light, the linguistic turn added one more dimension to our awareness of the differences between the sciences and the humanities – such as history. Certainly, the sciences (and the reflection on the sciences) have known their own struggle with subjectivism, skepticism and relativism. Most of the philosophy of science and of language deals with it. But these have always been discussions about truth and falsity and about how to distinguish between them. It was always taken for granted here that we should use language when dealing with the secrets of nature. Language, as such, was never questioned. And this is different in what separates those historians and historiographers before White still living in happy oblivion of (historical) language, on the one hand, and the language-wise adults we have become since the linguistic turn, on the other. In the sciences the issue is how to discern between linguistic truth and falsity; in history the issue is language as such, between the past itself as a no less linguistic category as trees and tables, on the one hand, and the irrevocably linguistic nature of the historical text, on the other. To put it simply, the sciences have to do with the distinction between truth and falsehood, whereas discussion in the philosophy of history since the linguistic turn put the issue of language, as such, on the agenda. This is what distinguishes the adherents of the linguistic turn from their linguistically naive predecessors. The sciences and the reflection on the sciences don't have their counterparts in the Fustel de Coulanges, the Rankes and the Barantes wanting to make nature speak for itself, and *not* through the voice of the physicist, out of fear that the phycisist's language should inevitably and irrevocably distort nature itself and thus introduce the phycisist's 'subjectivity'. This, then, is where the reflection on history and historical writing problematizes language in a way not having its parallels elsewhere.

We can now also understand the popularity of so-called representationalism in the philosophy of history. The idea here is – as the term 'representationalism' suggests – that the historical text is a representation of the past, and where the term carefully retains what is suggested by its etymology. Hence, a making present again of what is absent. And a representation succeeds in performing this remarkable feat by being a kind of substitute or replacement of what it represents. In the well-known words of Ernst Gombrich:

> the clay horse or servant buried in the tomb of the mighty takes the place of the living. The idol takes the place of the God. The question whether it represents the 'external form' of the particular divinity or, for that matter, of a class of demons does not come in at all. The idol serves as the substitute of the God in worship and ritual ...[8]

So A is a representation of B if it can function as a substitute for B, so that A has on us the effect of B somehow being around. Of course we then primarily think of representations in the narrow sense of the word: in the way that someone being far from his or her beloved may feel that the beloved is somehow present in a photo (representation) of the beloved. But it need not necessarily be a photo; it could also be a ring, a handkerchief, a comb, or whatever. Anything can be a representation of anything else. The implication is that in historical theory one must distinguish between the linguistic turn (as exemplified by Hayden White) on the one hand and representationalism on the other. It is true: both are critical of the disregard of the historical text one will find amongst adherents of Collingwood or theorists discussing causality or socio-scientific approaches to historical writing.

But whereas the linguistic turn requires us to analyze the historical text (as done by White himself, and by Roland Barthes, Lionel Gossman and so many others), for representationalists the historical text is merely just one way of representing the past, of making the past present again. And they will insist that historical novels, films, history paintings, objects left from the past and so on may also represent the past. Here the emphasis is on making the past present again and not primarily on how a text may account for part of the past. In fact, representationalism still retains a memory of the Magritte conception of the past as exemplified by Fustel, Ranke or Barante. These nineteenth-century historians wanted to make the past speak for itself. Representationalists know this to be impossible, but are willing to settle for the next best thing, i.e. for a representation of the past that is the best, or most believable substitute for the actual past itself. They will acknowledge that people with a cognitivist bend of mind will then primarily look at historical texts, but representationalists will agree that this certainly is a good idea (if only because of the sheer amount of historical writing we presently have and could not possibly afford to ignore); but they are also prepared to consider alternative representations. The implication is that language is not taken for granted here (as in the philosophy of science and of language), considered from a perspective outside language itself, so that a number of questions now can be asked, such as what non-linguistic relationships we may have to the world (or to the past) and how these compare to what we can expect from language. In this way representationalism may help us answer the question of what might lie beyond, or after, the philosophy of language. Or, at least what a philosophy of history might look like that does not focus exclusively on the relationship between the historian's language and the past described in it.

## HUIZINGA'S NOTION OF HISTORICAL EXPERIENCE

Needless to say, such a post-linguistic philosophy (of history) will be of all the more interest if it succeeds in making clear how it is related to linguistic philosophy (of history) – hence to the paradigm preceding it. When having to deal with this issue, help can be expected from the Dutch historian Johan Huizinga. And above all from Huizinga's project for a dissertation in linguistics[9] that he devised in 1895 after having finished his study of Sanskrit in Groningen and before he turned to history a few years later. The main idea of the project was to use synaesthesia for a better understanding of the words for sensory experience in Indo-Germanic languages; hence, the words we use for colors, sounds or what is given to the sense of touch.

Locke was the first philosopher to become interested in synaesthesia, mainly thanks to a letter he had received from William Molyneux (1656–98) and from which he quoted in *An Essay Concerning Human Understanding* the following passage:

suppose a man born blind, and now adult, and taught by his touch to distinguish between a cube and a sphere of the same metal, and nighly of the same bigness, so as to tell, when he felt one and the other, which is the cube and which is the sphere. Suppose then the cube and the sphere posed on a table, and the blind man be made to see: quaere, whether by his sight, before he touched them, he could now distinguish and tell which is the globe, which the cube.[10]

Locke argued that the blind man[11] had no experience of how cube or sphere would affect his sight and, hence, he would be unable to tell them apart by sight alone. He conceived of the subject of experience as if it were a kind of metropole and where each of the senses was one of terminal-stations in the metropole, without there being a metro-network connecting these terminal-stations with each other. So any kind of synaesthetic interconnection between the senses was out of the question for him. Kantian imagination ('Einbildungskraft') produced the 'metro-network' that was still absent in Lockean empiricism. And then the imagination might make the formerly blind man recognize which is the cube and which the sphere, when seeing these forms for the very first time.

Huizinga develops his own theory of synaesthesia in a discussion with the influential nineteenth-century philologist Fritz Bechtel (1855–1924), who had discussed a problem similar to the one that Locke had put on the agenda.[12] Locke had discussed cubes and spheres, whereas Bechtel dealt with the perception of colors and sounds. Locke/Molyneux investigated the synaesthesia of the senses of sight and touch, whereas Bechtel addressed the senses of sight and hearing. To take Bechtel's own example: would we relate the sound of a trumpet to the color red rather than to any other, or not? And, if so, why? Bechtel's answer was affirmative: there is a synaesthetic quality that the sound of the trumpet and red do have in common and that makes us relate them. The synaesthetic quality in question is that both are *penetrating* – and this explains the synaesthetic affinity of red and the sound of the trumpet.

Huizinga agreed with Bechtel about all this, but he considered Bechtel's argument to be unsatisfactory. When accounting for synaesthesia, Bechtel requires us to consider a set of sounds and a set of colors; and each time we hear one sound from the set of sounds and see a color from the color-set, we jot down on a piece of paper the adjective best capturing the experience. And then – such is his argument – we shall discover that the adjective 'penetrating' is used for both the *sound* of a trumpet and for the *color* red.

Huizinga observed that in this approach the phenomenon of synaesthesia is merely *established* rather than *explained*. Bechtel did empirical research on synaesthesia, but never asked himself how to account for the data he had discovered. In order to remedy Bechtel's shortcoming, Huizinga suggested to replace Bechtel's 'horizontal' approach with a 'vertical' one. Bechtel's approach can be described as 'horizontal' since he was content to observe that most people will associate the adjective 'penetrating' with both the color red and the sound of the trumpet – and this allows him to pair off the color red and the trumpet sound. Huizinga, however, preferred the 'vertical' approach, where the idea is that 'penetrating' is the adjective used for describing an (synaesthetic) experience, say E, that the color red and the trumpet sound have in common. And E therefore reduces us to a stage where sensory experience has not yet been split up into sounds and colors. E is permanently present in our sensory experience of the world, but we never notice it, since we neatly divide up all our sensory experiences in sounds, colors, smells, tastes and feels. Only when we try (vertically) to explain synaesthetics, do we suddenly become aware of its presence. Finally, we observe that we associate the adjective 'penetrating' with the color red and the sound of a trumpet – and there is no a priori reason why we should also do so with E – which is, after all, not the experience of a color or a sound. So for describing the experience of E we will need another word than 'penetrating'. Huizinga proposes the word 'fierce' ('fel' in Dutch).

Huizinga derives some amazing conclusions from this. In the first place, it follows that the word 'fierce' succeeds in doing what Bechtel's word 'penetrating' still failed to do: it will bring us to a level of experience – the level of synaesthesia – where the differentiation between sounds and colors has *not yet* taken place. Clearly so, since 'fierce' describes what the experience of sounds and colors do still have in common. From this it follows, again, that we can categorize terms like 'fierce' and 'penetrating' in categories that are either *closer* to the world ('fierce') or *less so* ('penetrating'). Put differently, 'fierce' is suggestive of a more direct and immediate contact with the world than the word 'penetrating'.

I would not hesitate to applaud this is as a most revolutionary discovery, for no philosopher of language has ever used synaesthesia (or any other property of language) to uphold the claim that we can discern these layers in language, legitimating the claim that some words in ordinary language are closer to the world than some others. The phrases 'close to the world' or 'remote from the world' are meaningless, if not simply nonsensical within the framework of contemporary philosophy of language.

Though Huizinga never returned to this dissertation-project, it was the background for much of his later writings on history, historical writing and, especially on what Huizinga referred to as 'historical sensation' – and hence what we might call historical experience. This is a most fortunate coincidence, since it will enable us to see how these abstract musings about synaesthesia may help us to clarify our relationship to the past. Crucial here, again, is Huizinga's 'verticalization' of the relationship between language and ourselves, on the one hand, and the world, on the other. We, and the language we use, can move closer to the world or opt for distance. Indeed, there always is a distance between us (and our language) and the world – and epistemologists investigating the relationship between the subject, or language, and the world certainly dealt with a real and important problem. But this distance is not fixed – as, perhaps, the ideal of scientific objectivity invites us to think – on the contrary, it may increase (with terms such as Bechtel's 'penetration'), or decrease (as with Huizinga's 'fierce'). And it is the axis of experience on which we can measure this amount of distance. Synaesthesia made us aware of this axis – and of the fact that the term 'fierce' expresses an experience of the world where subject and object, ourselves and the world, have come closer to each other than is the case with the term 'penetration'. Experience then becomes the decisive variable, for the vertical axis of experience will decide our use of language. An intense experience of the world, a closeness of subject and object, will give us terms like 'fierce', as well as that section of language and semantic meaning of which 'fierce' is part. The weakening of experience, the relative absence of ourselves in what we experience and say, will give us terms such as 'penetration'. So now language follows experience, and not the other way round as in Rorty's slogan 'language goes all the way down', and where experience is the meek and obedient servant of language, where language always guides the way and determines experience.

Following the Dutch literary critic Lodewijk van Deijssel (1862–1954) Huizinga discerned three marks on the scale of experience: (1) observation, and where experience has the role it has in the sciences; (2) impression, to be associated with the phenomenalism of impressionist painting; and (3) sensation, where subject and object come closest to each other, where you may have an actual fusion of subject and object and a kind of *unio mystica* of the two. And, indeed, in agreement with the primacy of experience to language, each of the three would invite the kind of language most appropriate for expressing experience. Language (and theory) do not determine experience here (as we have all been taught), but experience determines language. Experience acquires here an absolute priority over language. Recall Huizinga's argument that synaesthesis produces a vertical axis between subject and object, and that the language we use (e.g. 'penetration' or

'fierce') has to docilely follow experience on its movement along the axis between 'normal' and synaesthetic experience.

Huizinga's re-arrangement of our traditional epistemological intuitions must have implications for how to conceive of the old issue of subjectivity versus objectivity. Obviously so, since Huizinga's rendering to the subject its freedom of movement (denied to it by epistemology) must put a wholly new complexion on the old problem. More specifically, if the historical subject of experience possesses this freedom of movement on the 'vertical' axis between the subject and the world, we can conceive of subjectivity (and objectivity) in two ways, instead of just one. Subjectivity may be understood in the traditional sense of the illegitimate projection of properties of the subject onto the object; but we can also take subjectivity to mean the resonance of the past in the historian (as exemplified by Huizinga's 'sensation' of the late Middle Ages). For here the historian's subjectivity blends, more or less, into the past itself. So could one possibly be more subjective than that? However, at the same time we can *also* describe this situation as the *ne plus ultra* of objectivity. For this resonance of the past in the subject of experience is only possible on the condition that it is not distorted by aspects of the subject alien to the object, i.e. to the past itself. And, as we have seen, this most remarkable epistemological feat can only be accomplished in terms of moods and feelings.

Finally, I said a moment ago that the vertical axis Huizinga had introduced between subject and object also implied the untimely claim that language had to follow experience and not the reverse, as everybody nowadays would chorus. The adherents of the linguistic turn being most vociferous of them all. But what might this mean? How can language follow experience? This is where Goethe's *Theory of Colours* of 1808 is surprisingly helpful.[13] Self-evidently, nobody will take seriously for a moment Goethe's pretension to offer with his *Theory of Colour* a believable alternative to Newton's optics. But we might read Goethe as follows.

There are colors – and we can then do either of two things. We can establish – with Newton – the physical properties of light of different colors and what effect these properties have on our retina. The successes of this strategy are, of course, indisputable. But we might also ask ourselves how we *experience* colors. And this question is just as irreducible to Newton's as states of consciousness are irreducible to states of our neuro-physiological apparatus (assuming the present *communis opinio* on the mind/body problem to be correct). Goethe argues that then a systematic uncertainty will arise in the relationship between colors and the language we use for expressing our experience of them (no such thing is the case, of course, with the Newton strategy). The experience of the color is there – as clear and well-defined as an experience could possibly be – but only gropingly can we try to make language capture the experience, without ever being wholly successful. Of specific interest is Goethe's characteristic of how we try to make language do what we want:

> The necessity and suitableness of such a conventional language where the elementary sign expresses the appearance itself, has been duly appreciated by extending, for instance, the application of the term polarity, which is borrowed from the magnet to electricity, &c. The plus and minus which may be substituted for this, have found as suitable an application to many phenomena; even the musician, probably without troubling himself about these other departments, has been naturally led to express the leading difference in the modes of melody by major and minor [para. 757]. For ourselves we have long wished to introduce the term polarity into the doctrine of colours [para. 757].[14]

In order to do justice to how we experience colors we will rely on polarities, differences and contrasts between different colors. There are no 'pure' colors, but only colors such as red-yellow, yellow-red, red-blue, blue-red or a 'bloody red', 'a threatening led-grey', 'a false cupper shine', to add examples from Huizinga, which are quite appropriate in the present context. And Goethe lengthily describes some of these mixtures of colors. But there never is a natural, fixed and immutable

link between language and experience here; so the only alternative left to us is to start to 'paint' with words, so to speak, and try to find that mix of words that comes closest to the experience. Here, then, experience is lord and master, whereas language breathlessly runs after experience in a forever vain effort to keep up with it.

Goethe's theory of color has a most welcome empirical confirmation in a cognitive defect known as 'color anomia':

> Patients with color anomia perform normally on tasks that require discrimination of colors but cannot name colors or point to colors named by the examiner. There is a distinction between color perception versus color recognition.[15]

So patients suffering from this defect have no problem with experiencing colors: they experience them just as we do. But they are systematically unable to *name* their experience since there are no exemplary examples for fixing unambiguously the relationship between the language for colors and experience in the way we do have such exemplars for words like 'square' or 'circle'. When we have explained to somebody what squares and circles are and have shown him/her a few exemplars of them, and if he/she even then is incapable of correctly recognizing squares and circles, we can only conclude that something must be wrong with his/her perceptive faculty.

But there's nothing wrong with the perceptive faculty of these people suffering from color anomia; they are not color-blind. Rather, they have a problem with words (for color). They did not succeed in internalizing the way words for color are used in the culture of which they are part. Their defect is not cognitive, but a cultural defect. It is as if they have always continued to live in the state of nature for this aspect of the human condition. All this suggests that at our language for colors must somehow be defective and that this is why it is for some people impossible to learn. However, this 'defect' of our language for colors should not be taken to mean that it sadly failed to achieve the referential perfection that the language for squares and circles is capable of. That would be too normative a reaction; it's not so that the language for colors ought to succeed in achieving what the language for squares and circles does un-problematically. It's rather that a different logic is involved in our speaking about our *experiences* (of colors) than when we are speaking about squares and circles. And within this logic language has lost all its former pride and traditional arrogance; it now shows itself as the lame and awkward servant of its lord: experience.

Color is one of the most banal, pedestrian and unexciting aspects of the world; they are permanently around and seem to harbour little secrets. If language can stumble over so simple a phenomenon, one may feel less confident about its achievements elsewhere as well. Especially when experience enters the scene. This is most likely to be the case when we have to do with the world of culture, art, poetry, music, emotions – and, yes, of history. It is probably no coincidence that Huizinga so heavily relied on color words for expressing his historical experience of the Middle Ages.

## EXPERIENCE VERSUS EPISTEMOLOGY

Now, it is true that Huizinga was no philosopher and, even more so, he never felt even the slightest temptation to join issue with philosophers. He believed them to be a strange breed, that one had best avoid as much as possible. So we might decide to dismiss Huizinga's theoretical musings as the irresponsible speculations of someone who does not know what he is talking about. Nevertheless, I'd prefer to take him more seriously as a philosopher than he would have probably considered appropriate himself. Indeed, in the remainder of this chapter I'd like to put in a word for the category of experience generally and for Huizinga's notion of historical experience in particular.

I am well aware that this is going to be an uphill fight, since Western philosophy has never been kind to the notion of experience.

It is illustrative that it would be impossible to write a narrative of Western philosophy with experience as its hero, whereas this role is most becoming for philosophical notions such as Reason, Being, knowledge, truth, language, mind and matter. The 'grand narrative' of the history of philosophy cannot be told in terms of the notion of experience. As Martin Jay put it:

> For it will quickly become apparent to anyone seeking a meta-narrative of this idea's history [i.e. of the notion of experience], that no such single story can be told. Rather than force a totalized account, which assumes a unified point of departure, an etymological archè to be recaptured, or a normative telos to be achieved, it will be far more productive to follow disparate threads where they may lead us. Without the burden of seeking to rescue or legislate a single acceptation of the word, we will be free to uncover and to explore its multiple and often contradictory meanings and begin to make sense of how and why they function as they often have to produce so powerful an effect.[16]

Just as any other history, the history of philosophy is also the history of the victors. And experience surely does not belong to those victors, since it has no patents of nobility and can claim no significant victories over its competitors, Reason, Being, truth, etc. Experience has always been the underdog, it is the most 'proletarian' in the ranks of philosophical notions.

Surely, one will now protest that I have left empiricism out of my account and that no one could possibly doubt the importance of the empiricist tradition in the grand narrative of Western philosophy. However, as it happens, nothing illustrates my case better than empiricism. It is true that empiricism emphasized the role of experience in our quest for knowledge, but empiricists have always insisted that experience can never be more than the humble and docile servant of the mind, or of reason. Bacon himself had already pointed out that experienced answers our questions only after we have asked them; and hence the priority of the inquisitive mind. Half a century later Robert Boyle was even more explicit:

experience is but an assistant to Reason, since it doth indeed supply information to the understanding, but the understanding still remains the judge, and has the power or right to examine and make use of the testimonies that are presented to it.[17]

So in empiricism experience can never tell you anything really new, never make you into a person different from whom you are now, it can never give you new ideas, but only tell you whether the ideas you already have are either right or wrong. In sum, with a friend like empiricism, experience no longer needs enemies.

Little has changed since the days of Bacon and Boyle. Though Boyle's 'Reason' has had to yield to 'language' in the course of time, experience still is in the same subaltern position. For if there is one thing that all contemporary philosophers, of whatever denomination, agree about, this is that language determines experience, and not the other way round. The idea that experience might be prior to language was rejected by Sellars' attack on 'the Myth of the Given', by Quine's attack on the two dogma's of empiricism, by Donald Davidson's holism, by Gombrich in his criticism of 'the Myth of the Innocent Eye', by the thesis of the theory ladenness of empirical facts, by Richard Rorty's slogan that 'language goes all the way down', by Derrida's condemnation of what he referred to as the 'metaphysics of presence' – and so one might go on for quite some time. Even more so, in the sciences the memory of the 'hard facts' of the experiment was never wholly forgotten, whereas historians have always been (painfully) aware that in their discipline facts are unpleasantly malleable and unstable. They are like unfaithful lovers, always eager to make love with others. The linguistic turn in historical theory explained and justified these intuitions by insisting that the constraints of fact and experience are virtually nil in comparison with the constraints of language. So if little authority was left to experience even in philosophy of science and of language, experience more or less disappeared from the discourse of contemporary philosophers of history.

The unpopularity of the notion of experience in Western philosophy is not hard to explain. Though the history of Western philosophy in the last three to four centuries is immensely complex, few will doubt that the theory of knowledge (or epistemology) has been Western philosophy's core business since Descartes, Locke, Hume and Kant. Philosophers wanted, above all, to answer the question of what we can know, of what are the condition and the limits of our knowledge of the world. And, as this formulation makes clear already, the two central entities then had to be the (knowing) subject and the object (of knowledge). Put differently, epistemology dealt with the question how the subject, the mind, could have certain knowledge of the object, or the world. In actual philosophical practice this compelled philosophers to draw an imaginary line between subject and object, and next, to determine where the sphere of influence of the one ends and that of the other begins. The very nature of this discussion implied that the protagonists of the subject (the Cartesians, the Kantians, the idealists) wanted to claim for the subject most of the trajectory between the subject and the object, whereas the protagonists of the object (the realists, the materialists, the positivists, the physicalists, the behaviorists) wanted to do the same in the name of the object. So whatever one might wish to discover between subject and object always became immediately the object of contention between the advocate of the subject and those of the object.

Now, experience self-evidently is the natural inhabitant of this middle ground between the subject and the object; experience mediates between them, the subject becomes aware of the object thanks to experience. So as soon as any substance was granted to experience, the advocates of the subject and of the object all greedily pounced upon it in order to distribute it amongst them, while trying to capture the fattest bits for themselves. Schopenhauer already recognized the mechanism: 'They share a common border: where the object begins, the subject ends.'[18] Subject and object directly border upon each other: there is no 'no man's land' between the two of them. And they will not suffer anything to grow up in this narrowest of narrow borders between the two of them, which is why experience is always drained of any content in epistemology and why epistemology and experience must remain each other's mortal enemies.

## HISTORICAL EXPERIENCE

We saw in the previous section that episte-mology has the innate tendency to crush experience to death between subject and object. So we can only get hold of experience if we can think of a world in which subject and object have to sing a little quieter than in the tradition of Western epistemology. But epistemology is a good example of what one refers to as 'gesunkenes Kulturgut'. We have all become epistemologists and find it very hard to think of a world in which subject and object have lost much of their present promi-nence. But just think of history – and of how 'we' relate to it. Is it clear here what is the subject and what is the object?

Admittedly, we can ruthlessly and mind-lessly apply the epistemological matrix – and then we get on the one hand the historian (the individual historian, or all historians, or a historical transcendental ego) and, on the other, 'the past' as investigated by him/her. But as we all know – and Gadamer even bet-ter than all of us – we're part of the past and the past is part of us. In the world of history and of culture the demarcation line between subject and object is typically unstable and, in fact, impossible to define. Can you say where you, yourself 'end' and where history 'begins' (or the other way round) )? The past is within us, much in the way that our super-ego is the 'garrison' (to use Freud's memora-ble metaphor) that civilization has quartered upon us so that we behave like nice and responsible people. So it's history we should primarily think of when wondering where to look for a fair balance in the relationship between subject, object and experience.

When pondering this balance there is no better start than Walter Benjamin's essay on the work of art in the age of its technical reproducibility. This is probably the best known text Benjamin ever wrote; so it's use-less to rehearse all of the argument here and I therefore restrict myself to what is relevant in the present context. And that is Benja-min's notion of the aura. The idea is that with the possibility of its technical repro-ducibility the work of art lost its aura; it is now merely the first item in a possibly endless series of replicas that may even be indiscern-ible from the original itself. Moreover, find-ing Leonardo's *Mona Lisa* or Rembrandt's *Nightwatch* on biscuit-tins, on supermarket-bags, on bath-sheets, in advertisements, etc., cannot fail to rub off somehow on the origi-nals themselves and reduce them to the sta-tus of trivial vignettes of modern civiliza-tion. This is how and why these great works of art gradually lost their former aura. The crucial part is that people were not aware of the great work of art's aura before it lost it. Only after the great works of art became reproducible do we become aware of the fact that they must have once possessed this aura. So before the age of technical repro-ducibility the work of art had its aura, but nobody noticed. Only now, after the aura has gone, do we conclude that the work of art must once have had this aura.

I never found Benjamin's argument particu-larly convincing: before Daguerre one was undoubtedly very much aware of the aura of great works of art and in spite of their being reproduced billions of times, they still have retained all of their aura. Perhaps even more so (suppose a father saying to his daughter upon entering a museum: 'And now you will finally see the real thing!'). But Benjamin has a similar argument for the human face: that lost its aura with photography. And there might, indeed, be some truth in this conjec-ture. The mechanism is familiar enough: many people (like myself) only notice a clock's ticking once it has stopped, or you only realize what being healthy is after you get a toothache or what it means to be young when you are getting old and are no longer young. In sum, Benjamin has in mind the kind of situation that you become aware of something at the moment that it ceases to exist – and when it has become a thing of the past.

The mechanism described here by Benjamin can be elucidated by using increased self-understanding as foil.[19] Supposed you attended a party and felt unusually happy there; and the event may then suddenly make clear to you how much of a socializer you actually are. Or take the reverse, you found the evening pretty awful though nothing was really wrong with it – and you discover how much of a solitary person you actually are. Or you hear a piece of music, and you get an idea of the emotional centre towards which all your moods naturally gravitate (as happens to me when listening to Max Bruch's symphonies). In all such cases the event in question may result in an increased self-understanding. Indeed, you understand yourself better than you did before, but there is no rupture or caesura in the continuity of your self-understanding.

This is different with the Benjamin mechanism. There is an event, such as the discovery of photography, the toothache or the event that makes you realize that you are no longer young – and, indeed, this also results in a better self-understanding. You become aware of something about yourself that you did not know before the event. But now there is a rupture: a discontinuity arises that separates the former self from the new self. And this can be specified. The clarity you get about yourself is clarity about a former self, about a self that you are no longer. And, indeed, there is a gain here: for you get to know something about yourself, that you were hitherto not aware of. At the same time, this explicitly is an increased knowledge of a former self and, hence, also indicative of something you do not know about your 'new' self. When the toothache makes you realize what it means to be healthy, the world of having pains and of being ill still remains to be discovered. Or when there is an event in your life that makes you realize that you are no longer young (such as the girls are no longer

interested in you or you discover that jogging is not what it used to be), then you know for the first time with an overwhelming clarity what it was like to be young (or, rather, what it must have been like); but what it is like to be old is still a big question mark. So there is, on the one hand, what now has become a past reality and that has acquired the sharp and clear contours of objective reality. But, on the other, it is precisely this new past reality, with its so very clear contours, that pushes you in the unknown void of the present and of the future, the void that you have become after having secreted a former self.

So it is the presence of a rupture that distinguishes the more trivial moments of increased self-understanding from what Benjamin had in mind. And the ingredients in this rupture are the following. There must always be an event triggering the mechanism. Next, this event powerfully demarcates a stage prior to it – the past – from a later stage – the present and the future. And where the past takes on the features of the world of objects, offering themselves for further scrutiny thanks to its newly acquired fixity and stability, whereas the present and the future have the openness and the lack of determination we always associate with what it means to be a 'human subject'. But, most importantly, there is the moment of the revealing event itself. Of that moment you can say that you belong to neither the past nor the present; you then move from the one to the other. At that moment there only is the experience of the event – and the codes for reading the experience are still not there. These codes become available only when you have moved on the stage after the event in question. So at that moment there is only the still nameless and still ineffable experience – and the domain of both object (the emerging past) and subject (of the emerging new self) are still in the dark. At that moment you are outside time itself. But after the moment a new past has come into being – waiting to be investigated – and a new self eager to start working on the job. This, then, is how the past originates. And this is why in historical experience the notion of experience has acquired the status and power to boldly resist epistemological speculation. For now experience is the lord and master, while subject and object are temporarily relegated to the background. So this is where the philosophy of history may add a new and still unwritten chapter to the book of contemporary philosophy.

There are two more things that deserve our attention. One of the more amazing consequences is that selfhood and knowledge of the self never coincide; whereas we are at first sight inclined to believe that selfhood is the *conditio sine qua non* of all knowledge of the self. This is, of course, the assumption of much of hermeneutics and, more specifically, of Collingwoodian hermeneutics. For there the idea is that re-enactment may carry the historian into the mind of the historical agent and that exactly this will enable him to explain the agent's actions. These are now as transparent and as accessible to investigation as our own actions. But the picture I painted a moment ago suggests that it is the other way round. Our own self is where mystery prefers to dwell whereas only the not-self, the human past, lends itself to objective investigation. We are never at home with ourselves, so to say, and as soon as we think we are, we have become a different self (and with which we are, again, not at home). As Arthur Danto says: 'to put it with a certain dash of paradox, we do not occupy our own interiors. We live, rather, naively in the world'.[20] Only a basically later self can indeed get to our interior; but when we succeed in ever getting there, this is also the indubitable sign that we have moved on to a later stage of ourselves relating to the former as the present relates to the past. And then we have objectified historically our former self in the way that we objectify others – and whom we self-evidently exclude from what or whom we are.

There is a striking asymmetry, Danto goes on to say, between how we construct our own relationship to the world and how we do this for others. When I say that 'X is the case', I take this to be a statement about the world; but when I say that P believes that 'X is the case', I see this statement as part of how P represents the world. Put differently, we construct our own opinions as being *world-related*. But the opinions of others we include into their representations of the world; hence, they are for us not world- but *mind-related*.

This may help us see how historical experience and the notion of historical representation hang together. It will be obvious that historical representation presupposes historical experience. For representations can only come into being after historical experience has separated a former self from a (historically) later self, and that can be accounted for by means of historical representation. Hence, historical meaning, as expressed by historical representation, is irrevocably intensionalist. For historical representations are not world- but mind-related. Any effort to reduce historical meaning to truth is thus doomed to failure. Davidsonian semantics – attempting to do just this[21] – can therefore never be of any use for historical representation. Put differently, Davidsonian's semantics is still part of a radically a-historicist worldview and in which historical experience had not yet separated the domain of the subject from that of the object (the past).

A second observation. Historical experience always involves loss. Quite naturally so, since a former self is exchanged for a later one. And this may be quite painful (almost literally so, as in the case of health). How sad is the day you realize that youth has gone forever – all the more so because this is exactly what made you aware for the first time in your life what it must have meant to be young! Such are the treacherous workings of the Benjamin mechanism: joys and happiness only manifest themselves for what they are to a self for whom they are no longer accessible. Nevertheless, these sorrows are always softened by continuity elsewhere. They can therefore always be taken up in the matrix of increased self-understanding discussed a moment ago and that I used as foil for historical experience. There is simple bodily continuity and which already puts severe restraints upon what havoc historical experience might create in our lives.

## CONCLUSION

At the outset of this chapter I discussed the Magritte conception of history – as exemplified by Fustel de Coulanges and Ranke – and what is wrong with that conception from the perspective of the linguistic turn. Though fully agreeing with this criticism, I nevertheless ventured the conjecture that, perhaps, there might be a kernel of truth in the Magritte conception after all. And, if so, this might reveal to us the eventual shortcomings of the linguistic turn, what is its blind spot and what we may expect to discover 'beyond the linguistic turn'. As I have argued in this chapter, the notion of historical experience is a promising candidate.

Let me put it this way. What Fustel and Ranke apparently were hoping for was a contact with the past carefully respecting 'as it has actually been', so that our speaking about the past is as good as an encounter with the past itself. Or a Michelet-like 'resurrection of the past'. Speaking and writing about the past should be a kind of time-travel – and as one could with Goethe, Burckhardt, Mommsen and numerous others take the coach or train to Italy, so one could listen to the historian and visit the actual past itself. That was their ideal; and we should recall that the Fustels, Rankes, etc., lived in a time when one had just begun to discover the secrets of history. Small wonder that the past still was so much of a new and fascinating reality for them that they believed to be possible what we find hopelessly naive.

But the notion of historical experience gives us at least part of what the Fustels and Rankes had so desperately hoped for. For historical experience gives us an authentic encounter with the past in which past reality still is untainted by language. For historical experience reduces us to a stage prior to the subject/object dichotomy and where language has not yet cut up the world in historical language, on the one hand, and a past as it can be discussed in language, on the other. And all this is less weird and counter-intuitive than it may at first sight seem. For only historical experience can explain how the past comes into being, what happens when we divide a still diffuse and all-encompassing present into a past and a present, and why this happens.

## NOTES AND REFERENCES

1  Though it must not be forgotten that in the philosophy of history the linguistic turn drew its inspiration from literary theory rather than from philosophy of language.
2  L. Ranke, *A History of England Principally in the Seventeenth Century*. Translated by W. Boase et al., Oxford 1876; 467.
3  P. de Barante, *Histoire des Ducs de Bourgogne de la maison de Valois. 10 Vols.*, Bruxelles: Grégoire 1839.
4  S. Bann, *The Clothing of Clio*, Cambridge: Cambridge UP 1984.
5  S. Bann, *The Clothing of Clio*, Cambridge 1983.
6  This was, of course, the main inspiration of E.H. Gombrich's *Art and Illusion*, undoubtedly his most important book.
7  H. White, *Metahistory. The historical imagination in nineteenth century Europe*, Baltimore: Johns Hopkins UP 1973.
8  E. Gombrich, 'Meditations on a hobby horse', in M. Philipson and P.K. Gudel eds., *Aesthetics Today*, New York: New American Library 1980; 175.
9  J. Huizinga, *Inleiding en opzet voor een Studie over Licht en Geluid*. Red. Jan Noordegraaf, Amsterdam 1996.
10  J. Locke, *An Essay Concerning Human Understanding, Vol. I*, London 1965; 114.
11  Molyneux's blind man was the English mathematician Nicholas Saunderson (1682–1739).
12  F. Bechtel, *Ueber die Beziehungen der sinnlichen Wahrnehmungen in den indogermanischen Sprachen*, Weimar 1879.
13  J.W. von Goethe, *Theory of Colours*. Translated by C.L. Eastlake, London 1840.
14  Goethe, op cit.; 303.
15  See www.nanonline.org/nandistance/mtbi/ClinNeuro/agnosia.html.
16  M. Jay, *Songs of Experience. Modern American and European Variations on a Universal Theme*, Berkeley 2005; 2, 3.
17  R. Boyle, *The Works of the Honourable Robert Boyle, Vol. 5*, London 1672; 171.
18  A. Schopenhauer, *The World as Will and Representation Vol. 1*. Translated by Judith Norman, Alistair Welchman and Christopher Janaway, Cambridge 2010; 26.
19  I am referring here to Jon Elster's notion of 'mechanism'. See J. Elster, *The Nuts and Bolts of the Social Sciences*, Cambridge 1988.
20  A.C. Danto, *Narration and Knowledge*, New York 1985; 339.
21  D. Davidson, Truth and Meaning, in *idem., Inquiries into Truth and Interpretation*, Oxford 1985; 17–37.

# 26

# Photographs: Reading the Image for History[1]

Judith Keilbach

There are many photographs we all know well. The frequency of their reproduction brought them before our eyes time and again, and thus these pictures have become a part of our memory. Photographs are able to give us a sustainable image of events we were not personally involved in. Beyond that, as images of the collective memory, they grant that these visual imaginations are shared by others; hence they can underwrite a mutual interpretation of certain events. Photographs undoubtedly impact our imagination and definition of the past.

Likewise, our imaginations of the Holocaust – despite the problem of how to depict the Holocaust, a problem I will come back to later – are shaped by photographs that are part of our cultural memory. Although we can assume the number of available pictures of this event to be immense, the repertoire of 'Holocaust' pictures that we can actually recall is comparatively small. The same pictures have been continuously reproduced and recycled in books, exhibitions and films, and it is this repertoire of pictures that shapes our memory and knowledge of the events. The reasons for the repeated reproduction of certain photographs can be found in their availability, their aesthetic quality, the motifs they present, as well as in the fact that they allow for adaptation to the relevant interpretation of the incident. As photographic pictures they promise to show historical reality, but due to their widespread usage they have turned into symbolic images and have come to signify meanings that are abstractions and become detached from what the pictures really show. To what extent photographs are able to depict historical reality at all and how they can be transformed to symbolic images is a question I would like to explore in this essay.

In order to do so, I will start by presenting several theoretical positions analysing the relationship of photography and reality or truth, then show different categories of Holocaust photographs, before ultimately analysing three examples of symbolic images to investigate the difficulties and possibilities inherent to symbolic images.

## PHOTOGRAPHY, HISTORY AND HISTORICAL REALITY

The particular relationship between reality and (analogue) photography results from the nature of the latter's technical production: analogue photographs are, as we all know, products of physical and chemical processes. They are produced by capturing the light emitted or reflected by an object on the light-sensitive carrier of a film or a photographic plate through a lens. The exposure itself happens completely 'without the creative intervention of man' who 'enters into the proceedings only in his selection of the object to be photographed and by way of the purpose he has in mind' but who does not play a part in the actual production process.[2] This automated production grants all photographs particular powers of evidence and persuasion. Due to the absence of the human, 'photography affects us like a phenomenon in nature' and gains objectivity from its very production process.[3] At the same time it assures us of the existence of the object depicted as this is a necessary prerequisite for the photo-chemical process. As a 'sign which refers to the Object that it denotes by virtue of being really affected by that Object',[4] each photograph has an indexical quality which inextricably connects reality and photograph.

The objects or persons thus depicted are a '*necessarily* real thing which has been placed before the lens, without which there would be no photograph'.[5] It is this indexical relation to the depicted object which makes photography appear as 'the world being inscribed onto a light-sensitive surface', even though the exposure is preceded as well as succeeded by 'deeply-rooted cultural, coded gestures which entirely depend on decisions made by humans'.[6] This inscription is the cause of the special power of evidence confirming our knowledge about the world because, as Roland Barthes puts it, 'every photograph is a certificate of presence'.[7] Moreover, as photography brings time to a standstill it thus always refers to the past. Irrespective of the prior structuring of reality for the camera, which Barthes indicates, each photograph freezes the moment in which it was exposed and captures a moment of time that is already a part of the past the second the shutter shuts. Therefore, the present documented through photography's indexical nature is already a moment in time now past: photography connects

reality and the past. In Barthes' words, after photography it can never be denied 'that *the thing has been there*'.[8]

Due to these qualities, photography seems to be an extraordinarily suitable medium for historiography. In private use, photographs recall memories of past experiences (and often trigger tales about them). If they are used as historical documents, they evidence incidents or situations of the past: heads of state meeting, historic town views, horrible disasters or enormous triumphs. Photos are especially able to inform on matters of everyday life as they capture the way people work or live at a specific time. Their immediate power of evidence helps photographs support the displaying of history, as they may be used to illustrate descriptions or to reinforce explanations of why and how events unfurled the way they did. However, the function of photos to establish the power of knowledge, to constitute subjectivity, and to facilitate social regulation should not be overlooked.[9]

Despite the particular relation between photography and the past, many theorists involved in analysing photography doubt its usefulness for *history* or even refuse this idea altogether. Because although photographs may confirm a past presence, it is often not possible to completely decipher the captured incidents or the situation in which they were taken. To learn about the past from images viewers need to know more about the context in which the picture was taken. This leads to the more general theoretical question of how meaning is assigned to images and if this meaning actually has anything to do with history itself.

Walter Benjamin adumbrates this problem in his *Small History of Photography*, written in 1931. After discussing the different phases and styles of photography, he points to the necessity of additional, written information in order to properly 'read' photographic images which claim to be authentic (contrary to photography used in art or advertising). At the end of his essay he quotes Brecht, who said that 'less than ever does the mere reflection of reality reveal anything about reality. A photograph of the Krupp works or the A.E.G. tells us next to nothing about these institutions. Actual reality has slipped into the functional'. In order to show a reality that is no longer explicit, Brecht pleads that 'something must in fact be *built up*, something artificial, posed'.[10] Following this argument, Benjamin advocates a constructivist photography because he considers it to be able to reveal reality and 'grasp the human connexions in which it exists'.[11] However, he also remarks that even these photographic constructions 'must remain arrested in the approximate' unless they come with captions.[12] His question 'Will not the caption become the most important part of the photograph?' implies that he considers the written word crucial to both shed light on the context of the depicted situation and to ensure the decipherability and legibility of images.[13]

While Benjamin focuses on the waning visibility of the social world (e.g. structures and connections), Roland Barthes, who also studies photographs in his writings on semiology, uses a different approach, asking how images convey messages. Assuming that images are polysemic he on the one hand points to the connotation that 'is elaborated at different levels of photographic production'[14] (through several procedures such as selection, technical treatment, cropping, etc.), and on the other hand to the accompanying text, stating these two limit the possible meanings of a photograph. For Barthes, captions are a technique to '*fix* the "floating chain" of signifieds' and to anchor the meaning of images.[15] Unlike Benjamin, however, he does not understand captions as signposts helping the reader to perceive photographs as 'evidence for historic occurrences'.[16] With their distinct approaches Barthes and Benjamin are concerned with different questions, and although both authors study the relationship of text and image while scrutinizing the potential of photographic pictures, they identify different difficulties: according to Barthes, who underlines the polysemic meaning of images, pictures contain an *overflow of information*; according to Benjamin, photographs show *too little reality*, i.e. not enough structures and context.

Susan Sontag also assumes that 'any photograph has multiple meanings' and 'cannot [in itself] explain anything'.[17] Based on the notion that photographs involve 'a view of the world which denies interconnectedness' and continuity,[18] she formulates her doubts about their suitability for historical purposes due to their temporal structure. Accordingly she does not describe photography as a medium of historiography, but instead as a *memento mori*, as 'all photographs testify to time's relentless melt'[19] and are thus 'a token of absence'.[20] Since the camera records a standstill of time and freezes a moment, it 'makes reality atomic'[21] and

> reinforces a nominalist view of social reality as consisting of small units of an apparently infinite number – as the number of photographs that could be taken of anything is unlimited. Through photographs, the world becomes a series of unrelated, freestanding particles; and history, past and present, a set of anecdotes and *faits divers*.[22]

For Sontag, however, knowledge of the world cannot manifest itself by depictions, only by the understanding of functions, and 'functioning takes place in time, and must be explained in time. Only that which narrates can make us understand'.[23] Analysing the temporal structure of photography, Sontag shifts the emphasis to the atomizing and mortifying qualities of pictures, two qualities which have the effect of preventing any explanation of historic events and do not in any way do justice to the processuality of history. Unlike Benjamin and Barthes, who were both looking into the *relationship* between images and words, Sontag strictly opposes any such relation,[24] and following her argument one may come to the conclusion that 'photography shows neither history nor stories, but, on the contrary, suspends history and renders each form of historic representation impossible'.[25]

The objections raised by these three theorists already illustrate that in order to come to any conclusion about the relation of photography to history, it is necessary to first clarify the terms 'history' and 'social reality'. Nineteenth-century historicists, for example, did not regard photographs as sources because historiography was mainly interested in public figures and their activity in political history; photography could not document their acts of will as its automated production did not produce any 'traces of the human spirit or the human hand'.[26] However, the increasing interest in topics of social and cultural history has resulted in photographs being entered into the canon of acceptable sources; additionally, methods of historical picture research have been established that – analogue to the standard methods of source criticism – can help to interpret or decipher pictures. Despite this methodological interest, however, the assumption still remains that photographs are neither able to depict the processuality of history nor the structural and causal interconnectedness of occurrences.

In an essay published in 1927, Siegfried Kracauer tried to answer the question of how to interpret 'history' and 'reality' by drawing an analogy between photography and historicist thinking, and opposing both to history. Noting that photography seems to lack the essence of the original, he compares it to historicist thinking, whose advocates seem to 'believe at the very least that they can grasp historic reality by reconstructing the series of events in their temporal succession without any gaps'.[27] Kracauer, however, believes otherwise: 'The truth content of the original is left behind in its history; the photograph captures only the residuum that history has discharged'.[28] Whereas both photography and historicism record the appearance of events without considering their significance, according to Kracauer, it is the (incomplete) memory that grasps actual meaning and thus that which 'has been perceived as true'.[29] As a consequence, photography might be able to illustrate 'the spatial configuration of a moment' but not its truth.[30] This concept radically distinguishes reality and truth as two different ideas, a similar distinction as the one made between historicist thinking and history or between photography and memory.

In *Camera Lucida*, Roland Barthes likewise distinguishes between reality and truth when he describes the moment he is looking at photographs and believes to find his recently deceased mother's essence depicted in one special picture. The *noema* of the photograph, its 'that has been', nourishes hope for a revelation of truth, but usually pictures are only 'chafed by reality'.[31] On the other hand, any connection of reality and truth, something Barthes experiences when looking at this photograph, is rare and occurs only when the truth of an object entwines with the truth of a subject. Such a connection always requires an emotional investment as it happens at a point 'where affect (love, compassion, grief, enthusiasm, desire) is a guarantee for Being'.[32] Thus it is no coincidence that both Kracauer and Barthes use photographs of loved ones to trace the truth of photographic images, and that both judge them against their own memories. But whereas Kracauer did not find himself able to encounter his grandmother in a photograph, Barthes claimed to recognize his mother's essence in one. This may be the reason why Barthes (contrary to Kracauer's early writings) does indeed deem photography able to contribute to gaining knowledge, even though this might happen in a different way from the standard procedures of historical studies.

Barthes shows the form in which photographs can release historic knowledge by a portrait taken by Richard Avedon with the title *William Casby, born a slave*. This photo witnesses the reality of the past 'not by historical testimony but by a new, somehow experiential order of proof', as Barthes puts it, 'a proof no longer merely induced: the proof-according-to-St.-Thomas-seeking-to-touch-the-resurrected-Christ'.[33] The basic assumption seems to be that only by touching an object are we able to assure ourselves of its physical reality. Thus Barthes comes to the conclusion that from now on, 'the past is as certain as the present, what we see on paper is as certain as what we touch.'[34] This interpretation is based on the concept of the photograph being a print of light, a concept linked to the idea that we may gain assurance by touching an object, as this gesture confirms the physical reality of the depicted object. Photography, as André Bazin has it, is like a fingerprint, 'a kind of decal or transfer' of the object itself, and therefore 'shares, by virtue of the very process of its becoming, the being of the model of which it is the reproduction; it *is* the model'.[35] Due to this idea of physical touch that results in a photographic depiction, the lack of materiality any object has in a photo moves to the background; one might even say that this lack is part of a means to substantially transfer reality into a medium or another reality. It seems that photography enables a direct access to past reality.

According to Barthes, Avedon's portrait, like a photo of a slave market, 'certifies that slavery has existed, not so far from us';[36] thus photography contributes to historical knowledge. This knowledge about history, however, does not result from a critical discourse of historical documents. Rather, its evidence is brought along in an experiential way to the extent that photographs enable an immediate access to the past. By enabling this to happen, photography undermines traditional historical methods, which claim that history cannot be accessible without the intermediary of a historian. The historic reality of slavery, as Barthes puts it, 'was given without mediation, the fact was established *without method*'.[37]

Summing up, I would like point out that photography is not simply a copy of a past reality. If we follow Barthes's phenomenological ideas, then photography does indeed have the capability of illustrating historic truth. This is, on the one hand, based on the prerequisite that the pictures can be deciphered or read, i.e. that they signify meaning and can be put into the context of a historical narrative. On the other hand, it is also necessary to have already gained knowledge about the social reality or historical event in order to encounter it 'again' in photographs. This knowledge may result from one's own experience (memories) or from obtaining historical knowledge; in the latter case it should be noted that these images are largely understood in the knowledge gained from viewing other photographs.

## PHOTOGRAPHS OF THE HOLOCAUST

After having noted this principal difficulty in visualizing historical reality through photographic depictions, the Holocaust provides an even stronger challenge to the reliability of the photographic image. A number of arguments even object to the possibility of photographically representing the Holocaust at all. These objections also result from the different conceptions of the event itself. Replying to the statement that 'there are no images of the Shoah', Georges Didi-Huberman pinpoints these differences, arguing that if we understand the Holocaust (or the Shoah) as 'the absolutely specific operation and moment of the gassing of Jews' then 'indeed, we know of no single photographic image'.[38] However, advocating a conception in which '"the destruction of the European Jews" [...] is an infinitely large, complex, ramified, multiform historical phenomenon' and taking into account the many different techniques 'for bringing the "Final Solution" to its fruition' leads him to the conclusion that 'there were indeed – and in considerable numbers – images of the Shoah'.[39] But a conception of the Holocaust that takes into account the successive deprivation of rights and the manifold forms of persecution down to the systematic destruction of the Jews still faces the problem of visualizing something that, quoting Brecht, has 'slipped into the functional'. The total extinction (*Endlösung*) was preceded by decisions and acts, the rules of law and bureaucratic administration that allowed different institutions to interact and guarantee a smooth and seamless procedure of dispossession, resettlement and murder. It can be said that the Holocaust was marked by the fact that different layers of politics and administration were interlocked – something that is difficult to depict through photographs.

In his *Theory of Film: The Redemption of Physical Reality* of 1960 Kracauer touches on pictures showing the 'litter of tortured human bodies' taken shortly after the liberation of the concentration camps. Believing that their concreteness and 'experienceability' help to redeem physical reality, as the subtitle of his book claims, he hopes these images are able to 'redeem horror from its invisibility behind the veils of panic and imagination' because these 'mirror reflections of horror [...] beckon the spectator to take them in and thus incorporate into his memory the real things too dreadful to be beheld in reality'.[40] However, considering the inherent visual limits to the Holocaust as complex, multilayered occurrence, one may doubt Kracauer's hope. These images are unable to show the scope and the tracelessness of the extermination of the European Jews that can be understood as main features of the Holocaust. At the same time, these features seem to make any photographic visualization impossible as visualization seems to imply the visibility of the object to be depicted. As Gertrud Koch reminds us:

> The concretism of visual plasticity (*Anschaulichkeit*) that must attach itself to an extant object – the image – is intrinsically opposed to a portrayal of that which constitutes *mass* destruction. Thus arises a horrifying hierarchy extending from the mountains of corpses of those whose bodies remained to be captured on film, to the people who literally went up in smoke, having left behind them no visual mnemonic trace that could serve their redemption.[41]

By pointing out that the pictures taken in the concentration camps are 'misleading' as they show the camps 'at the moment the Allied troops marched in', Hannah Arendt brings forward another argument. Especially the sights which upset the allied soldiers so much and which constitute the horror of the camps, i.e. human beings reduced to mere skeletons, 'were not at all typical for the German concentration camps; extermination was handled systematically by gas, not by starvation'.[42] That calling up these photographs of the liberated concentration camps is the only way people remember (instead of recalling a story) is a problem Susan Sontag

also discusses. Stating that 'this remembering through photographs eclipses other forms of understanding, and remembering. The concentration camps – that is the photographs taken when the camps were liberated in 1945 – are most of what people associate with Nazism and the miseries of the Second World War' she implies that the Holocaust is part of a whole clutch of decisions, structures, ideologies and events that are not retained in people's memories because no pictures exist.[43]

Despite these general problems in capturing the systematic destruction of the European Jews in photographs, there do exist copious photographs that depict the Holocaust in isolated moments. Similarly to Didi-Huberman, who speaks of a 'considerable number' of images, Marianne Hirsch points out 'that the Holocaust is one of the visually best-documented incidents in the history of an era marked by a plenitude of visual documentation'.[44] These pictures were either taken for official purposes by the perpetrators, or as snapshots or souvenirs; or they were taken after the concentration camps had been liberated. In addition, there also are some pictures that were clandestinely taken by Jewish photographers and resistance fighters.[45] All these photographs show only a minuscule excerpt of an occurrence whose structure and scope simply cannot be visualized through photographs; nevertheless they allow, as Jürgen Zetzsche puts it, 'human imagination to envisage what people experienced in these death camps. The photographs of the Holocaust achieve an explicitness in their historical statements that reaches beyond the gap between what really happened and its representation in photographic pictures'.[46]

The major part of photographs documenting the Holocaust was taken by the perpetrators. The function and use of the pictures was manifold, stretching from official assignments to secretly taken snapshots. For official purposes pictures were taken in the concentration camps and ghettos – among other reasons – to supply visuals for reports in the illustrated press which described concentration camps as 'education camps'[47] or justified the ghettoisation by pointing out the Jews' 'appalling' way of life and their 'hygiene standards'.[48] The reports from the concentration camps served to disprove any rumours on how badly the prisoners were treated in the work camps: thus the photographs recorded how the prisoners worked or spent their spare time.[49] These illustrated features make use of the credibility of photography as a medium in order to deceive and spread untruths (after the war this would contribute to diminishing the power Holocaust photographs have as visual evidence). The reports on the ghettos contributed to the constitution and reinforcement of anti-Semitic stereotypes by visually supporting associations such as 'lack of personal hygiene', 'layabouts' and 'criminals'. The fact that these stereotypes were given a visual reality by Nazi politics (ghettoisation, prohibition to work, etc.) explains their long-lasting impact on the one hand and also hints at the difficulty one faces when using these pictures again.

Most of the pictures taken of the camps and ghettos, however, were not intended for publication. They served official purposes instead and were commissioned to, for example, document the construction of camp buildings in Auschwitz (archive of the *Bauleitung*, i.e. construction office), the medical experiments or the prisoners' suicides. There were internal activity reports, too: in his final report on the Warsaw Ghetto uprising in May 1943, Jürgen Stroop, for example, included more than 50 captioned photographs. The pictures document, for instance, how blocks of houses were set on fire in order to force the resisting inhabitants to leave their hiding places; and how these people were then rounded up, arrested and deported. One of the best-known Holocaust pictures originates from this report, a picture I will refer to later: that of the little boy who, together with other ghetto inhabitants, is being rounded up on the street by SS-men armed with machine guns.[50] Likewise, a leather-bound album from Auschwitz, the original purpose of which has never been clarified, documents a horrific deed: it contains 193 photographs showing the arrival and

selection of Jews deported from Hungary. The pictures are sorted into systematic units (e.g. 'deployable men', 'deployable women', 'non-deployable men', 'non-deployable women'), and their arrangement emphasises the efficiency of the selection performed on the Auschwitz-Birkenau platform.[51] The majority of the official photographs, however, was taken for the purpose of registering the concentration camp inmates, i.e. prisoners who were not killed immediately after their arrival were recorded in a prisoner register and photographed for that purpose. Of Auschwitz alone, 39,000 of these portraits remain.[52]

Apart from the official photographs there also are copious amateur pictures showing single aspects of the Holocaust. These pictures were taken by German soldiers on off-duty excursions to the Warsaw Ghetto, for example. Like tourists they recorded their impressions in photographs. Their pictures show typical street scenes and can be read as documents of the Jewish population's systematic isolation and their insufficient supply of food and other necessities. The Warsaw tram, a recurring motif, is marked by a star of David and thus refers to the segregation within the spheres of living and of public facilities; the barricades and the checkpoints emphasize the internment of the ghetto inhabitants; and pictures which show people dressed in rags, begging on the streets or lying exhausted on the pavement, clearly underline their isolation and starvation.

Yet amateur photographers not only used their cameras on such excursions. Private snapshots were taken too – despite their explicit prohibition – of executions and hangings, and of the humiliation of the population in the occupied regions. There thus are pictures of Jewish men forced to pose for 'funny' group pictures together with German soldiers. On other photographs, soldiers standing proudly behind a row of bodies lying on the ground seem to present these bodies as some kind of trophy. Beside these posed shots there are numerous pictures which document murder – often through a series of photographs – in which the action is not performed for the camera: the depicted people focus on their activities which are fixed by the photographer. These pictures were personal snapshots to remember events, as the place of their discovery reveals: 'Most of these photographs were found in the wallets of dead or captured soldiers or SS-men, often together with pictures of their mothers, fiancées and families. Like these, the snapshot plays a fetish-like role in the owner's personal balance of memories and emotions'.[53] Some of these amateur pictures have gained a wider publicity over the last years. Since the mid-1990s they have been shown as part of an exhibition on the *Wehrmacht*, the former German army, in several German and Austrian towns. The aim of the exhibition was to document that the *Wehrmacht* carried out a war of destruction in the former Soviet Union. This central thesis contradicted the image of a 'clean army' which had been popular up to then, i.e. an army that had acted purely on a military basis and adhered to both the law of war and the law of nations.[54]

As I mentioned before, these personal souvenir pictures of executions and hangings were all made despite the explicit prohibition to photograph such activities or to report about them. On 14 August 1940, a decree signed by SS-lieutenant general Krüger on the 'Implementation of Executions' states that 'any participation of spectators or photography is forbidden'.[55] In 1941, Otto Woehler, Chief of Staff of the 11th Army, threatened punishment and ordered the confiscation of all amateur pictures taken of executions:

> No photographs will be made of such abominable excesses and no report of them will be given in letters home. The production and the distribution of such photographs and reports on such incidents are looked upon as undermining the decency and discipline in the armed forces and will be severely punished. All existing photographs and reports of such excesses are to be confiscated together with the negatives.[56]

Likewise, Reinhard Heydrich, head of the *Reichssicherheitshauptamt* (Gestapo and Security Service combined), repeated the prohibition of photography and, in 1942, specifically interdicted 'the taking of pictures at mass executions and requested that the commanders of the Order Police hunt for pictures, films, or plates circulating among their own men'.[57] That so many amateur photographers ignored this prohibition despite the unmistakable threat of punishment can be explained either by their curiosity or as an act of separating oneself from the documented action by 'emptying the gaze', as Hüppauf would have it.[58] In any case, the specific situation and its breaking of the taboo on the inviolability of human life and dignity seem to have required the production of photographs in order to be able to better remember what happened. Although they are now used, as in the case of the 'Wehrmachtsausstellung', as historical documents these amateur photos were only in exceptional cases taken with the intention to document for historical purposes.

The pictures that were taken after the liberation of the concentration camps constitute a second large field of Holocaust photography. When the allied soldiers entered the camps they were confronted with scenes so unbelievable that they reached for their cameras to authenticate the horrible sight of scattered corpses, piles of dead bodies and living skeletons. After having visited the Ohrdruf concentration camp, General Eisenhower requested soldiers, journalists, politicians, and local citizens in the vicinity of the camps to visit the liberated camps and witness the atrocities. In the course of these visiting tours, official as well as amateur photographers took pictures. As many visitors initially perceived the camps as unreal the pictures were considered as attesting to the reality around them: *LIFE* magazine photographer Margaret Bourke-White speaks of an 'air of unreality' and recalls: 'I kept telling myself that I would believe the indescribably horrible sight in the courtyard before me only when I had a chance to look at my own photographs.'[59] Joseph Kushlis, one of the soldiers liberating Ohrdruf, likewise returns to the pictures he took to make sure the events he remembers were real.[60]

Paradoxically, the photographs were needed to substantiate what the liberators and visitors saw with their own eyes. The camera itself thus became a more reliable witness and confirmed what the eyewitnesses saw through a kind of duplication process. At the same time, taking pictures helped the photographers to rationalize and integrate the atrocious scene around them into familiar patterns of perception and behaviour. 'Using the camera was almost a relief,' Bourke-White stated, 'it interposed a slight barrier between myself and the white horror in front of me.'[61]

These photographs played an important role in the Allied information campaign aimed at 'letting the world see' the atrocities that were perpetrated in the camps. The pictures not only bore evidence of the Nazis' barbarity, they at the same time 'made everyone into a witness'.[62] They were published in newspapers and magazines all over the world, distributed to Germans in the form of booklets and printed on posters exhibited all over Germany.[63] Despite the indexical nature of these photographs many viewers found them hard to believe: in Britain and the US some thought the newspaper reports about the camps had been exaggerated,[64] and in Germany the population was even more sceptical – hardly a surprise, as the pictures contradicted everything they knew before and were taken by the victorious enemy that was now using them for 'propaganda' reasons. If nothing else, the Nazis' visual manipulation taught many Germans to doubt the authenticity of officially displayed photographs.[65] Furthermore, the pictures demanded a sense of guilt and responsibility that many Germans refused to assume (which in turn resulted in them disputing the credibility of the photographs and reports about the concentration camps).

A number of photographs seem to anticipate these doubts by emphasizing the act of witnessing. Barbie Zelizer describes an 'array of representations of witnessing', like pictures of official delegations shown around the camps, soldiers examining torture set-ups, dead bodies or cremation ovens, or German civilians forced to look upon stacks of corpses.[66] These photographs echo the eyewitness reports, a genre to which many journalists turned in order to describe the horrors of the camps. Barbed-wire fences, crematorium chimneys, ovens, abandoned possessions, skulls, masses of dead bodies and corpses that look particularly grotesque are other recurrent motifs. Analysing the compositional features of these images, Zelizer homes in on the victims' gaze: many photos showed survivors looking directly in the camera (or staring at a point behind the photographer), or 'portrayed the unseeing eyes of the dead'.[67] Another feature has to do with the numbers of people: 'The photos oscillated between pictures of the many and pictures of the few', she states, concluding that taken together these images suggested that 'the depiction of each individual instance of horror represented thousands more who had met the same fate'.[68] All these photographs taken after the liberation of the concentration camps attest to the atrocities committed by the Nazi regime. However, since taking pictures always implies an objectification these images at the same time reified the victims once again.

## SYMBOLIC IMAGES

Photographs play an important role in informing and educating about the Holocaust. While images of the liberated camps were published within the framework of the Allied information campaign, pictures taken by the perpetrators gradually surfaced as well. Today they are a significant part of the visual memory of the Holocaust. But 'although more than two million photos exist in the public archives of more than 20 nations', as Sybil Milton stated in 1986, 'the quality, scope and content of the images reproduced in scholarly and popular literature has been very repetitive'.[69] Despite the growing global attention to the Holocaust that accompanied films and television programs such as *Holocaust* and *Schindler's List*, the building of the United States Holocaust Memorial Museum in Washington, the introduction of Holocaust courses in colleges and universities and the like, her statement regarding the constant recurrence of the same pictures is still valid. Given the numerous existing photographs the repertoire of published images is indeed very small.

This is not to say that the selection of images that was circulated did not change. On the contrary, the selection of photos published in newspapers, schoolbooks or exhibitions definitively changed over the course of time and differed depending on the 'national' meaning of the Holocaust. The selection of the photos' subjects offers an interpretive frame that fits the political and ideological landscape at that time and corresponds with the respective conceptualization of the event. Discussing the pictures that were published shortly after the war, Cornelia Brink argues that it was particularly the specific combinations of pictures and their captions that imbued them with political meaning. She for example states that the use of contrasting images – pictures indicating the inhumanity with which prisoners had been treated, and pictures of their rescue by Allied soldiers – contributed to legitimate the Allied victory: these images supported the depiction of Germans as cruel sadists and of the Allied forces as fighting for the cause of humanity, an interpretation that granted the latter not only the military but also the moral victory.[70] Placing photographs of individual survivors next to images of piles of dead bodies similarly emphasizes the definition of this war as a rescue operation.[71] However, the general accusation against all Germans (through captions such as 'These infamous actions: you're to blame!') soon disappeared. In line with the changing political landscape, different photographs were starting to be published. Amongst the photographs that have lost their prominence over the course of time are the images that emphasize the act of witnessing. On the one hand frontal group shots of survivors became more prominent, on the other hand the 'equipment' that had enabled the mass murder (ovens, gas chambers) was increasingly shown.[72] Replacing explicit depictions of mass murder with images of still-standing survivors not only supports the interpretation of events as a successful liberation; these photographs are at the same time better suited to commemorate the victims, to glorify resistance fighters or to evoke the miracle of survival than depictions of piles of dead bodies or Allied soldiers helping survivors who are in a pitiful state.

The changing subjects of the circulating images not only correspond with the different 'national' meanings of the Holocaust but also with the altering definition of the event itself.[73] After the war, the atrocities in the concentration camps were first perceived as one of the many horrors committed during the war. Their understanding as genocide and systematic murder emerged only later, just as the conception of the Holocaust as the traceless destruction of the European Jews. A selection of corresponding photographs accordingly reinforced these changing interpretations. Pictures of men behind barbed wire or in barracks that were taken shortly after the camps' liberation, for example, echoed images of POW camps and thereby contributed to the interpretation of the atrocities as war crimes. The changing conception of the events as acts of systematic extermination in turn led to the increasing publication of images that emphasized the industrial nature of the Holocaust, whereas pictures of landscapes and empty places started to accentuate the tracelessness of the extermination and reflect the impossibility of their photographic depiction.

However, the referentiality of the photographs that were sought to provide evidence of mass murder and the inhuman treatment of people weakened bit by bit. Despite photography's indexical quality, the pictures paradoxically came loosened from the concrete situation they depict. Gradually they started to signify abstract conceptions such as 'Holocaust', 'cruelty' or 'history'. Hints at such separation can already be found shortly after the liberation and sometimes resulted from the photographs themselves. By framing individuals in close-up, for example, they were removed from the concrete space and time of the photographic moment and thereby transformed from an individual with a particular fate at a particular moment in history into an unspecified 'victim'.[74] Even when the photographs didn't de-contextualize their motifs themselves, many of them were used to refer not just to the singular event that was depicted but to the occurrence of thousands of similar instances (for example, by means of combining an image of an individual body with one of piles of corpses), suggesting that to get an idea about what happened in the concentration camps it is necessary to look past what is concretely depicted and add the sheer scale of the occurrences. Likewise images of piles of suitcases, eyeglasses and hair refer to something beyond the objects that they visually depict. Seen as traces of systematic extermination, these images of personal possessions and exploitable parts of the human body are metonymies symbolizing the great many number of the disappeared.

But the weakening of the photographs' indexicality is also an outcome of their repetitive reproduction. On the one hand the pictures are emptied of their information because, as Clément Chéroux has it, mass reproduction causes details of time, context and actual motif to be less and less precise.[75] As a historical source photographs can thus lose their accuracy. According to Chéroux, due to this loss of information the pictures are degraded from a document containing context to a symbol lacking substance.[76] On the other hand the recurrent use of the same pictures gives rise to an abundance of meaning. We know that photographs receive a crucial part of their meaning from their contextualization. Dependent on the captions, the combination of images and their publication context, they can signify highly diverse things and with each new usage the meaning of a photograph shifts. If pictures start to circulate more sparsely, the meaning it once emphasized can fade away,[77] whereas the constant recurrence of the same images in different contexts and usages results in several overlapping meanings. Eventually, recurrently reproduced photos have come to signify abstract ideas, their

indexical referentiality diminished as the materiality in their depiction is no longer perceived. They are nothing more than 'familiar visual cues'.[78] Their high profile as symbolic images assures that they will be recognized when reproduced or cited which makes them into highly suitable objects for popular and artistic processing, what Marianne Hirsch calls the 'work of postmemory'.[79] However, despite their transformation into symbolic images, these pictures are still able to invoke historical knowledge. Even if these photographs that everybody recognizes 'encapsulate common ideas of significance and trigger predictable thoughts, feelings', as Susan Sontag states, pointing critically to the power of ideologies that 'create substantiating archives of images',[80] they still call upon existing knowledge and are able to unlock the (hi)story in our minds.

The changing motifs, loss of information and diminishing indexical referentiality can be illustrated with three examples. The first one is a black and white photograph that, according to Sybil Milton, is one of the 'two images [which] have come to symbolize the complex series of events now known as the Holocaust'.[81] The meaning of this picture does not exactly correspond with what is concretely depicted, and the picture thus allows for a demonstration of the loosening of a photograph's indexicality. 25 years after Milton's analysis, however, the picture is no longer reproduced very often. This can be seen as resulting from a shifting conception of the Holocaust. At the same time its 'disappearance into the archive' cleared its former meaning and makes it possible to have a fresh look.

What we can see in the picture is a bulldozer clearing a pile of dead bodies; the bulldozer is placed in the centre of the photograph and seen in full-frontal view. The bodies in the foreground make up a small pile. In the background of the picture a barrack stretches away, running parallel to the top and bottom edges of the picture thus visually dividing the site and the sky in two equal parts. The bulldozer is driven by a man whose

Source: Imperial War Museum, negative number BU 4058

slightly inclined head is covered by a cap. The frontal view of the machine, the presence of its driver, and the position of the dead bodies in particular – partly cut off by the frame, leaving the impression that their extremities continue outside the frame at the bottom left corner of the picture – evoke the impression that the bodies stretch out to the beholder of the picture.[82] In its explicit display of human bodies and extremities the photo – if studied closely – is an extremely unsettling and shocking one.

In his critical discussion of symbolic images, Clément Chéroux uses this photograph to show how falsely photographs may be perceived if they do not receive an appropriate historical context: the photo described, which was published in copious books and journals, is used as a symbol of the industrial murder carried out by the Nazis. But the photo was neither made by one of the perpetrators

nor does it show a moment of organized extermination; instead it was taken by Sergeant Oakes, a British photographer with the No. 5 Army Film & Photographic Unit, on 19 April 1945, i.e. four days after Bergen-Belsen had been freed.[83] In fact, the picture documents how the Allied soldiers buried the dead bodies lying everywhere in the camp in order to prevent an epidemic. 'What is shown is not the inhuman way the Nazis treated their victims even after they had died', but a photographic documentation of the sanitary precautions taken by the Allied forces.[84] Nevertheless the picture can serve as a symbolic image of the Nazi atrocities once it has been removed from its contextual frame (prohibition of photographs by the Nazis, time of origin, etc.) and is not studied closely (the driver's cap makes clear that he is not a member of the SS, the mouth protection indicates the epidemiological hazard, etc.). In this case, the lack of context and the brief glimpse of the actually depicted scene lead to a fundamental misreading of the picture. Chéroux states: 'Thus the object which is documented by the picture is the very opposite of what is symbolised by it.'[85] Beside its clear composition, the track record of the picture as a Holocaust photograph can mainly be traced back to the fact that it offers a plausible visualization of how we interpret the Holocaust. As a symbolic image, i.e. if the image is understood as the remains of an extermination programme that had not been brought to its end, the photo may still, despite its misreading, trigger historical knowledge of the Holocaust.

Another photograph that has become a general symbol of the Holocaust is the picture of a boy who is being arrested together with other people in the Warsaw ghetto. This example illustrates how the particular context of a moment in history can vanish, changing the picture from a visual document of the suppression of the Warsaw Ghetto uprising to the depiction of an innocent victim. What we see in the picture are a number of people coming out of a house on to the street with their arms raised, guarded by SS men. They are led by a woman in a black coat moving diagonally to the right towards the photographer and the beholder. In that move she is turning her head to the left so that we get a good look at her profile. On her left walks a small boy, also raising his arms. Under his cap his face is clearly visible as he was photographed in a nearly frontal view. Under his buttoned-up coat his naked legs are visible, his stockings seeming to slide down. The woman and the boy walk side by side, but there is a small distance between them that distinguishes the boy from the group of people forming a unit closely behind the woman in the background. This distance, located nearly in the centre of the picture, divides the photograph into two halves, additionally separating the boy from the other 'arrested' people. One of the SS men in the far right corner of the picture, shown frontally, points his gun's

*Source*: United States Holocaust Memorial Museum, photograph #26543

barrel at the boy. Likewise, the woman's glance is directed at the boy; every item in this composition focuses attention on the boy.

Originally, the photo of the boy was part of the Stroop report, which described how the uprising in the Warsaw ghetto (19 April to 16 May 1943) was put down. Labelled with the caption 'Mit Gewalt aus Bunkern hervorgeholt' ('Pulled from the bunkers by force'), the picture served as evidence of the German troops' successful 'clearance' operation, searching all the houses in the ghetto, tracing numerous hide-outs and arresting the people hiding there. As a symbolic image, however, the picture has left the context of its origin as well as the context of its original usage; it has come to symbolize the defencelessness and innocence of the victims of national socialism. The little boy serves as the perfect representative, as his young age (comparable to Anne Frank's) suggests exactly these qualities.[86] Here, too, the documentary content of the picture is quite different, as the arrest depicted in the photograph was preceded by an act of resistance. Whereas the historical contextualization of the picture underlines that the residents of the ghetto were not fully defenceless but indeed fought their deportation for days, the symbolic image lacks any hint at the uprising itself. Similarly, the innocent child representing all victims of the National Socialists entails a significant reduction of the victims' diversity. But just like the photograph of Bergen-Belsen analysed above, the photo of the small boy may also help recall the historic events and their complexity. The moment captured in the photo may trigger speculations on what happened to these specific people; in turn, these may connect to historical knowledge about the Holocaust and be able to give an idea of the historical reality of what happened.

The photograph of the arrest was also widely published, however, often incompletely: the chosen cropping usually centred on the little boy, with the size of the cropping varying so that sometimes only the little boy is visible, sometimes also the woman beside him, and sometimes even the man in the background who seems to be pointing his gun at the boy. These changes of scale not only remove the situation or environment the boy is shown in, but also the visual signs that would allow readings other than the victims' innocence and defencelessness. Clipping the picture especially favours the way (West) Germany dealt with its National-Socialist past. Stripped of any political and social context, the Holocaust becomes a catastrophe without any actors or, rather, with the Gestapo and SS as the only actors in this symbolic image. At the same time, the innocent child's face releases feelings of empathy and enables a feeling of guilt which is removed from any actual analysis of historical responsibility. The offer of feeling guilty without having to reflect upon one's own involvement in the incidents explains the picture's success in West Germany in particular.[87]

A third photograph, also very well known, supports this de-contextualization even more strongly, as it shows neither victims nor perpetrators. The picture in question is the one showing the gate of Birkenau that all deportation trains passed when arriving at the camp. What we see are rail tracks that stretch from the foreground of the photo into its depth. They are linked by switches, and the construction of the photo in central perspective increases the impression of the tracks meeting each other at the vanishing point of the picture which is placed exactly in the dead centre of the gate's frame. The gate is located in the centre of the building under a tower flanked by low wings on the left and right. The long building takes up the whole upper half of the photo and runs parallel to the top and bottom edges of the picture. The passageway is clearly visible due to the contrast between the dark building and its bright snow-covered surroundings. Scattered across the tracks in the foreground of the picture we can see plates and bowls slightly covered by, or filled with, snow.

*Source*: Mémorial de la Shoah/CDJC, photograph XCVII_36

The picture was taken shortly after Auschwitz was liberated (27 January 1945) as part of a Red Cross status report. It was taken by Stanislav Mucha, a Polish photographer who accompanied a unit of the Red Cross, and whose photographic documentation of Auschwitz-Birkenau – apart from the gateway – also contains elements such as the crematorium ruins, dead bodies and parked railcars. However, only the picture described above managed to gain a high profile. Its motif is often compared to a gaping abyss, an association based on the assumption that the picture shows the entrance to Birkenau. But once more, as Chéroux informs us, this is a misreading, as the picture does not show a view from outside the premises, but was taken inside the camp and thus shows its exit. The impression of being devoured, however, is evoked by the picture independently of knowing the 'right' direction of the gaze, as the central perspective of its construction pulls the beholder 'inside'. At the same time it communicates a feeling of desertedness created by the vastness of the area, the snow and the absence of people. Especially the lack of human bodies enables the beholder to see the picture removed from what the Holocaust actually meant to each victim. The presentation of an empty place deserted by people, however, can also be read as a hint at the tracelessness of the incident, implying the impossibility of its photographic depiction. As a result, the photograph seems to offer several readings (de-contextualization and abstraction of actual events, reflection on the problem of presentation) and thus appeals to different types of viewers. This potential is another reason for the frequency with which certain pictures have been published.

Yet the high profile of this picture cannot only be measured by looking at the number of its publications. In addition, it has served as a model, because many visitors of the memorial have adopted the picture's viewpoint. The power of Stanislav Mucha's photograph, however, not only results from its perspective: it succeeds in rendering an atmosphere of desertedness especially because of the snow-covered crockery which implies that this place has not always been empty and depopulated.

The scattered plates also contribute to a deferral of concreteness or 'delay of density',[88] as they cannot be instantly recognized as such. A close study of the picture is necessary in order to identify the objects under the cover of snow. The anticipation of what might be buried under the snow alone already provides an approach to the historical truth.

All three photographs described above can be categorized as symbolic images. Their meaning has been removed from the concreteness of the photographed scenes and come to symbolize something quite different from the situation they document. However, the Bergen-Belsen photograph does point to the fact that bringing the recurrent publication of symbolic images to a stop can after a while clear them of their fixed meaning and facilitate a fresh close look at what they really depict. But even if they have lost their indexical quality and signify abstract concepts, these pictures by no means inhibit the evocation of knowledge about the Holocaust. Depending on what one already knows, symbolic images are able to unlock this historical knowledge regardless of whether they have been placed in their correct historical context. It seems that the visual access to history does not so much require contextualization or a high profile, but is rather a matter of perception and reception.

## FOUR PHOTOGRAPHS

Even if the suitability of particular photographs to become symbolic images can be explained by their content, aesthetic design, possible readings, and their ability to be integrated into specific policies of memories and commemoration, there still remains the matter of the other pictures. Among the millions of photographs stored in archives there are undoubtedly a high number of photographs that meet these criteria. Nevertheless they are hardly utilized – if at all – a fact which has to be discussed in light of the different economies to which the pictures' circulation is tied. Despite the fact that many photos

have been already processed in databases, detailed research would still be necessary in order to trace these more unknown pictures; an effort many photo editors will not make. The picture's decipherability, its storage of historical knowledge, etc., does require a certain 'investment' (research of context, explanations, captions, etc.) in order to provide the photographs with a meaning that will recall the symbolic images immediately and remove the need to read them closely.[89]

Among the pictures which have only recently come to the attention of the public are four highly unusual photographs, i.e. photos taken by prisoners in August 1944 with a camera that had been smuggled into the extermination camp of Auschwitz-Birkenau. Two of the pictures show many burning bodies outside; a third shows an unrecognized view between trees, several naked women can be seen in one corner of the photo; the fourth is overexposed by back light and makes one sense

*Source*: The State Museum Auschwitz-Birkenau in Oświęcim

rather than see tree tops. The lack of picture quality these photos have may be one reason why they are hardly used: they are partly blurred and details are only recognizable in some parts of the shot. The two photos of the burning bodies, for example, have been taken from inside a building so that where one part of the picture shows the view outside, the rest of the picture remains black.[90] Thus a blow-up was made of one of these pictures, and this blow-up was actually published several times. The unusual framing alone leads to an initial confusion that provokes a closer study of the pictures. But even in the blow-up of one detail, i.e. after removing the formal confusions, the picture provokes a 'delay of density'. The rising smoke obstructing the view, and the posture of individual people standing among the bodies in the centre of the picture guide the viewer to the actual situation depicted. The visibility of the labour necessary to exterminate people and the matter-of-factness with which this was executed cause quite a shock. The explicitness of this photo or of the blow-up, respectively, seems to be too high to turn it into a symbolic image.

These four photographs were to be seen in public as part of the exhibition *Mémoire des camps* in 2000. In the catalogue of the exhibition there is a text on these four photographs by Georges Didi-Huberman, who describes them as an act of resistance in which the prisoners tried to defy absolute extermination on the one hand, and to counteract the unimaginability of the event on the other. In France, Didi-Huberman was fiercely attacked for his position, which led him to state it more precisely in a quite polemic response to his critics, a response that was then published as a book together with the catalogue text in 2003. The publication of the book, which also contains the four photographs in question (the German edition shows one of the pictures of the burning bodies on the cover), increased their publicity and the knowledge of their original context. If it is true that photographs can be transformed into symbolic images by their recurring use, then we might be witnessing such a process here.

Didi-Huberman not only submits the photos to a close reading, he also formulates a grander theory of the image in which he focuses on the historic truth of images on the one hand and specifies the relevance of reception on the other. Following Hannah Arendt's argument, he sees the four photographs as 'instants of truth':[91]

> The four photographs from August 1944, of course, *don't tell* 'all of the truth' (it would be very naïve to expect this from anything at all – things, words, or images): they are tiny extractions from such a complex reality, brief instants in a continuum that lasted five years, no less. But they *are* for us – for our eyes today – truth itself, meaning its vestige, its meagre shreds: what remains, visually, of Auschwitz.[92]

Whether the pictures will really be perceived as truth depends once more on the way they are viewed, as Didi-Huberman speaks of two ways of 'being inattentive' to these images, one in 'wanting to make them *icons* of horror', the other in seeing in them 'no more than a *document* of horror' and 'making them more *informative*' than they are.[93] Instead he claims the effort of *archaeological work* and the *time* to *work on the images* that are 'acting ceaselessly one upon the other by collision or fusion, by ruptures or metamorphoses – all of them acting on our own activity of knowledge and thought'.[94] Only by doing so can truth surface in these photographs.

## NOTES AND REFERENCES

1  An earlier version of this text was published in *History and Theory*, May 2009.

2  André Bazin, 'The ontology of the photographic image', in *What is Cinema?* (Berkeley, Los Angeles, London: University of California Press, 1967), 9–16, 13.

3  Bazin, op. cit., 13

4  Charles Sanders Peirce, 'Nomenclature and divisions of triadic relations, as far as they are determined', in *The Essential Peirce: Selected Philosophical Writings, Vol. 2 (1893–1913)* (Bloomington and Indianapolis: Indiana University Press, 1998), 289–299, 291.

5  Roland Barthes, *Camera Lucida: Reflections on Photography* (New York: Hill and Wang, 1981), 76.

6  Philippe Dubois, *Der fotografische Akt: Versuch über ein theoretisches Dispositiv* (Amsterdam, Dresden: Verlag der Kunst, 1998), 54 [transl. from German].

7  Barthes, *Camera Lucida*, 87

8  Barthes, *Camera Lucida*, 76

9   Cf. John Tagg, *The Burden of Representation: Essays on Photographies and Histories* (Minneapolis: University of Minnesota Press, 1993).

10  Cited after Walter Benjamin, 'A small history of photography', in *One Way Street and Other Writings* (London, New York: Verso, 1979), 240–57, 255.

11  Benjamin, 'History', op. cit., 255.

12  Benjamin, 'History', op. cit., 256.

13  Ibid.

14  Roland Barthes, 'The photographic message', in *The Responsibility of Forms Image, Music, Text* (London: Fontana Press, 1977), 15–31, 20. Here Barthes refers in detail to trick effects, pose, objects, photogeny, aestheticism and syntax.

15  Roland Barthes, 'Rhetoric of image', in *Image, Music, Text* (London: Fontana Press, 1977), 32–51, 39.

16  Walter Benjamin, 'The work of art in the age of mechanical reproduction', in *Illuminations* (New York: Schocken Books, 1999), 211–44, 220.

17  Susan Sontag, 'In Plato's cave', in *On Photography* (New York: Doubleday, 1977), 3–24, 23

18  Ibid.

19  Sontag, op. cit., 15.

20  Sontag, op. cit., 16.

21  Sontag, op. cit., 23.

22  Sontag, op. cit., 22f.

23  Sontag, op. cit., 23. In her reflection on images of suffering Sontag is even more explicit, stating that photographs 'are not much help if the task is to understand. Narratives can make us understand. Photographs do something else: they haunt us'. Susan Sontag, *Regarding the Pain of Others* (London: Penguin, 2003), 80.

24  Referring to the discussion about the possibility to visually represent the Holocaust Jacques Rancière problematizes such a radical opposition, c.f. Jacques Rancière, 'The intolerable image' in *The Emancipated Spectator* (London, New York: Verso, 2009), 89ff.

25  Bernd Stiegler, 'Zeigen Fotografien Geschichte?', *Fotogeschichte*, 95 (2005), 3–14, 3 [translated from German].

26  Johann Gustav Droysen, *Historik*, ed. Peter Leyh (Stuttgart: Frommann-Holzboog, 1977), 87 [translated from German].

27  Siegfried Kracauer, 'Photography', *Critical Inquiry*, 19(3) (1993), 421–36, 424f.

28  Kracauer, 'Photography', op. cit., 429.

29  Kracauer, 'Photography', op. cit., 426.

30  Kracauer, 'Photography', op. cit., 431.

31  Barthes, *Camera Lucida*, op. cit., 115.

32  Barthes, *Camera Lucida*, op. cit., 113.

33  Barthes, *Camera Lucida*, op. cit., 79f.

34  Barthes, *Camera Lucida*, op. cit., 88.

35  Bazin, 'The ontology of the photographic image', op. cit., 9–16, 14f.

36  Barthes, *Camera Lucida*, op. cit., 89f.

37  Barthes, *Camera Lucida*, op. cit., 80.

38  Didi-Huberman responds to Gérard Wajcman who has fiercely criticized Didi-Huberman's text about four photographs from Auschwitz (and the exhibition *Mémoire des camps* for whose catalogue Didi-Huberman had written his text) by objecting 'there are no images of the Shoah'. Georges Didi-Huberman, *Images in Spite of All: Four Photographs from Auschwitz* (Chicago: University of Chicago Press, 2008), 58.

39  Ibid.

40  Siegfried Kracauer, *Theory of Film: The Redemption of Physical Reality* (Princeton University Press, 1997), 306.

41  Gertrud Koch, '"Not yet accepted anywhere." Exile, memory, and image in Kracauer's conception of history', *New German Critique*, 54 (1991), 95–109, 104.

42  Hannah Arendt, *The Origins of Totalitarianism* (New York: Harcourt Brace Jovanovic, 1973), 446.

43  Susan Sontag, *Regarding the Pain of Others* (London: Penguin, 2003), 79.

44  Marianne Hirsch, 'Surviving images: Holocaust photographs and the work of postmemory', *The Yale Journal of Criticism*, 14(1) (2001), 5–37, 7.

45  A first distinction of the photographs can be found in Sybil Milton, 'The camera as weapon: documentary photography and the Holocaust', in: *The Simon Wiesenthal Center Annual*, 1 (1984), 45–68.

46  Jürgen Zetzsche, 'Beweisstücke aus der Vergangenheit. Photographs des Holocaust und ihr Spuren in der Literatur', *Fotogeschichte*, 39 (1991), 47–59, 50 [transl. from German].

47  *Münchener Illustrierte Presse*, 16 July 1933; *Illustrierter Beobachter*, 3 December 1936.

48  *Illustrierter Beobachter* 24, 1941; *Berliner Illustrierte Zeitung*, 24 July 1941.

49  For a more detailed discussion of these press articles cf. Habbo Knoch, *Die Tat als Bild: Fotografien des Holocaust in der deutschen Erinnerungskultur* (Hamburg: Hamburger Editionen, 2001), 75ff.

50  On the Stroop report cf. Richard Raskin, *A Child at Gunpoint: A Case Study in the Life of a Photo* (Aarhus: Aarhus University Press, 2004).

51  On the Auschwitz Album cf: *The Auschwitz Album: The Story of a Transport*, ed. Israel Gutman and Bella Gutterman (Jerusalem: Yad Vashem, 2002).

52  Didi-Huberman, *Images*, op. cit., 24.

53  Dieter Reifarth and Viktoria Schmidt-Linsenhoff, 'Die Kamera der Henker: Fotografische Selbstzeugnisse des Naziterrors in Osteuropa', *Fotogeschichte*, 7 (1983), 57–71, 59 [transl. from German].

54  Therefore it came hardly as a surprise that the exhibition faced massive opposition. One point of criticism was the use of these very amateur photographs. Their presentation was dismissed as highly suggestive and a lack of context was criticized. It was, however, the allegation of their wrong historical placement that led to an investigation of their sources by an expert commission and consequently to a revision of the exhibition. But this allegation did not only challenge the way the curators of the exhibition critically assessed their sources; implicitly the historians who uttered such criticism doubted in general whether photographs may serve as a historical source. For more information on the exhibition cf. www.verbrechen-der-wehrmacht. de/docs/e_archiv/archiv.htm (last visited: 6 July 2011).

55 Cited after Reifarth and Schmidt-Linsenhoff, 'Die Kamera der Henker', 62.

56 Cited after Milton, 'The camera as weapon', op. cit., 48.

57 Cited after Ibid.

58 Cf. Bernd Hüppauf, 'Emptying the gaze: viewing violence through the viewfinder', New German Critique, 72 (March 1997), 3–44.

59 Margaret Bourke-White, 'Dear Fatherland, Rest Quietly'. A Report on the Collapse of Hitler's 'Thousand Years' (New York: Simon and Schuster, 1945), 73.

60 Cf. Cornelia Brink, Ikonen der Vernichtung. Öffentlicher Gebrauch von Photographs aus nationalsozialistischen Konzentrationslagern nach 1945 (Berlin: Akademie Verlag, 1998), 31.

61 Bourke-White, Fatherland, op. cit. 73.

62 Barbie Zelizer, Remembering to Forget: Holocaust Memory through the Camera's Eye (Chicago: Chicago University Press, 1998), 139.

63 Cf. British and American press Zelizer, Remembering, op. cit. and for publications in Germany Brink, Ikonen, op. cit., 47–78.

64 Cf. Zelizer, Remembering, op. cit., 141ff.

65 Cf. Brink, Ikonen, op. cit., 84ff.

66 Cf. Zelizer, Remembering, op. cit., 100ff.

67 Zelizer, Remembering, op. cit., 115.

68 Zelizer, Remembering, op. cit., 110, 111.

69 Sybil Milton, 'Photographs of the Warsaw Ghetto', in Simon Wiesenthal Center Annual 3 (1986), 307.

70 Ibid., 39f.

71 Cf. Brink, Ikonen, op. cit., 49.

72 Zelizer, Remembering, op. cit., 161f.

73 cf. Daniel Levy and Natan Sznaider, Holocaust and Memory in the Global Age (Philadelphia: Temple University Press, 2006); Peter Novick, The Holocaust in American Life (New York: Mariner Books, 2000).

74 Cornelia Brink describes this detachment in more detail and argues that in terms of their visual composition these photographs often reminded of Christian motifs which add to their abstract meaning of 'guilt' and 'sacrifice'. Cf. Brink, Ikonen, op. cit., 57f.

75 According to Chéroux the loss of information involves both the quality of the picture which is diminished by its reproduction, as well as the contextualization, cf. Clément Chéroux, 'Du bon usage des image' in Mémoire des Camps: Photographies des camps de concentration et d'extermination nazi (1933–1999), ed. Clément Chéroux (Paris: Marval, 2001), 11–21, 13.

76 This is how Nicole Wiedenmann summarises Clément Chéroux' position in her essay '"So ist das, was das Bild dokumentiert, das Gegenteil dessen, was es symbolisiert." Holocaustfotografie im Spannungsfeld zwischen Geschichtswissenschaft und Kulturellem Gedächtnis', in Die Macht der Geschichte, ed. Fabio Crivellari et al. (Konstanz: UVK, 2004), 317–49, 324.

77 Allan Sekula states that archive serve as a kind of 'clearing house' and 'liberate' images 'from the actual contingencies of use'. Allan Sekula, 'Reading an archive', in Blasted Allegories: An Anthology of Writings by Contemporary Artists, ed. Brian Wallis (Cambridge/London: MIT Press, 1989), 114–27, 116.

78 Zelizer, op. cit., 158

79 Schindler's List for example restages well-known film footage to authenticate the narrative and Art Spiegelman's Maus quotes many photographs. On Schindler's List cf. Miriam Hansen, 'Schindler's List is not Shoah: Second Commandment, popular modernism, and public memory', in Spielberg's Holocaust: Critical Perspectives on Schindler's List, ed. Yosefa Loshitzky, (Bloomington, Indianapolis: Indiana University Press, 1997), 77–103. On Maus and postmemory cf. Hirsch, 'Surviving images', op. cit., 5–37.

80 Susan Sontag, Regarding the Pain of Others (London: Penguin, 2003),76f.

81 Milton, 'Photographs', op. cit., 307.

82 In the film footage that also exists of this scene and which is incorporated e.g. in 'Nazi Concentration Camp' by George Stevens (1945), the dead bodies move indeed towards the spectators.

83 According to the details stored in the database of the Imperial War Museum.

84 Wiedenmann, op. cit., 324.

85 Chéroux, op. cit., 16.

86 See also Marianne Hirsch's discussion of images of children in Holocaust memory: Marianne Hirsch, 'Projected memory: Holocaust photographs in personal and public fantasy' in Acts of Memory: Cultural Recall in the Present, ed. Mieke Bal, Jonathan Crewe and Leo Spitzer (Hanover: University Press of New England, 1999), 3–23.

87 On the relationship between photographical and political discourse regarding the national-socialist past of West Germany cf. Habbo Knoch, 2001.

88 Roland Barthes, 'Shock-photos', in The Eiffel Tower and Other Mythologies (Berkeley, Los Angeles, London: University of California Press, 1997), 71–4, 73.

89 The picture of a shooting in Pancevo where 18 hostages were executed on 22 April 1941 by members of the Wehrmacht as retaliation for the killing of a SS man is another 'new' symbolic image. The photograph shows how a soldier kills a hostage who was not immediately dead with a shot to the head. It is on the cover of the book documentation accompanying the exhibition Vernichtungskrieg. Verbrechen der Wehrmacht 1941–1944 that was shown in different cities between 1995 and 1999. Taken by the German propaganda company photographer Gerhard Gronefeld, it was widely published in newspapers and magazines to discuss the highly controversial exhibition and symbolizes today the crimes of the German Wehrmacht.

90 For Didi-Huberman's reasoning it is important to point out that this indoor room is the interior of a gas chamber.

91 Didi-Huberman, op. cit., 31.

92 Didi-Huberman, op. cit., 38.

93 Didi-Huberman, op. cit., 34.

94 Didi-Huberman, op. cit., 116.

# 27

# Digital Information: 'Let a Hundred Flowers Bloom …' Is Digital a Cultural Revolution?

Valerie Johnson and David Thomas

## INTRODUCTION

The seemingly sleepy and unchanging world of archives, records and information has seen a paradigm shift in recent years. The dominance of parchment and paper has been challenged – and overthrown. During 2009–10, there were nearly 24 and a half million visits to The National Archives' website, in comparison with over 90,000 onsite visitors to The National Archives' reading rooms in Kew.[1] Over 131 million documents were downloaded: over 220 times the number of original documents delivered onsite.[2] In today's world, access to information is primarily online. The age of the digital record has arrived with a vengeance.

## THE NATURE OF THE BEAST

But what is a digital record, and is it different from a paper record? Indeed, what is a record? This is less arcane and more relevant a question than first appears. In the paper world, a

record is seen by archivists as having specific characteristics. Seminal archival theorist Hilary Jenkinson, whilst acknowledging that the word 'document' was 'difficult to define', decided to 'be dogmatic', going on to describe documents as:

> all manuscript in whatever materials made, all script produced by writing machines, and all script mechanically reproduced by means of type, type-blocks and engraved plates or blocks: adding to these all other material evidences, ... which form part of or are annexed to, or may be reasonably assumed to have formed part of or have been annexed to, specific documents thus defined.[3] (italics in original)

Jenkinson further distinguished a document which could be considered to belong to an Archive by a further definition:

> one which was drawn up or used in the course of an administrative or executive transaction (whether public or private) of which itself formed a part; and subsequently preserved in their own custody for their own information by the person or persons responsible for that transaction and their legitimate successors.[4] (italics in original)

By defining a document in this way, Jenkinson established an archival school of thought that views an archive as textual and linguistic, with an emphasis on the recording of some administrative transaction. Concepts of authenticity and originality are also of crucial importance. Though Jenkinson was writing in the 1920s, this tradition has survived with little substantive challenge, and remains the dominant theoretical paradigm, so that in contemporary discussions, the same concepts are evident. For example, The International Organization for Standardization (ISO) currently defines records as 'information created, received, and maintained as evidence and information by an organisation or person, in pursuance of legal obligation or in the transaction of business'.[5]

## RIPPLES AND WAVES

The digital represents a powerful and unsettling challenge to this paradigm.

In the digital world, records are not simply digital equivalents of those found in the paper world. Though there are digital documents that have clear paper analogues, there are also new information vehicles, such as text messages, audio streams, wikis, blogs or tweets. It is unclear what status these new forms have, and how they relate to each other and to paper. Can born-digital records, such as emails, websites or datasets, be seen as records in the same way as paper? In the early days of electronic documents, many information professionals were clear – they were not. As Richard Cox reports, 'most archivists either ignored what were then called machine-readable records ... or more adamantly declared the early electronic records to be non-records and, therefore, not their responsibility.'[6]

Archivists of the past had stressed the unchanging nature of the true record, so how could the constantly shifting website possibly be seen as analogous? With websites described as a 'performance', consisting of all the text, images, links, running banners, adverts, video and audiostreams and so on, it

is easy to see how archivists struggling with new forms of records found 'that the classic concept of record [sic] had limited their capacity to understand electronic systems containing a variety of complex entities that do not correspond to it'.[7] What had happened was that the *nature* of records had changed, so that in the digital context, records could be dynamic, created from multiple sources and existing in multiple locations in different versions.[8]

This is particularly true of datasets, databases and other sets of data that exist in a fluid state. Archivists have already had to face up to the consequences of this. For example, under British company law, companies have to maintain a record of members or shareholders, and records of these shareholdings are seen as one of the core series of records in business archive collections.[9] Today, with millions of shares changing hands electronically every day, there no longer exists a fixed record of the shareholdings of large companies. The result is that what was viewed as one of the key records of business effectively cannot exist in a physical format. All the archivist can do is to take electronic snapshots, but even these are out of date by the time they are downloaded. The current record itself is in a state of constant flux, and this demands a new definition of what a record is. Instances such as this have even led some authors to ask whether records are ever actual.[10] In such a context, and with a blurring of records and information, it has become necessary to ask: is there such a thing as a record any more? Should we abandon trying to shoehorn a new paradigm into the concepts of the old, and instead seek to develop new concepts for a new paradigm?

Some archival theorists have responded to this novel uncertain world by trying to find or impose certainty, via the introduction and use of stringent definitions – not always successfully. The prestigious and authoritative Society of American Archivists' glossary defines a record as:

1. A written or printed work of a legal or official nature that may be used as evidence or proof; a

document. – 2. Data or information that has been fixed on some medium; that has content, context, and structure; and that is used as an extension of human memory or to demonstrate accountability. – 3. Data or information in a fixed form that is created or received in the course of individual or institutional activity and set aside (preserved) as evidence of that activity for future reference ....[11]

However, in the accompanying text, the requirement for fixity of form is immediately contradicted by notes that focus entirely on fixity of content: 'Records may be in any format, including text, images, or sound. However, the concept of record is ultimately independent of any specific carrier or format. Paper records may be microfilmed, and electronic records may be transferred from memory to disk to paper.' Fixity is itself described as 'the quality of *content* being stable and resisting change'[12] (our italics). If the US professional body can appear so confused, it is little wonder that others have sought clarity of their own. One major project concluded that 'in order to be defined as records, digital entities must be affixed to a medium and have stable content and fixed form, as well as explicit linkages to other records inside or outside the digital system (i.e. an archival bond), five necessary persons involved in its creation (i.e. author, writer, originator, addressee and creator), an action in which they participate or which they support, and five necessary contexts of creation (i.e. juridical-administrative, provenancial, procedural, documentary and technological).[13] Could *any* digital content be accepted as a record under such a stringent definition? Another categorical approach has been to the other extreme: to the inclusive. This can be seen in one author's statement that 'records are created during administrative activities ... This characteristic identifies records and distinguishes them from stored information in general.'[14]

Yet this unhelpfully covers almost everything. Others have focussed on a distinction between form and content, collapsing the Society of American Archivists' ambivalence

into certitude. Louise Craven, for example, has claimed that,

> the fundamental distinction to be drawn between paper records and electronic records is this: with paper records, the *paper* (or parchment or vellum) must be preserved, for this is the authentic record; with electronic records, it is the *information* which must be preserved, for that is the authentic record.[15]

Some archivists have explored with vigour and relish this new world, emerging with new and invigorating theoretical breakthroughs, such as the post-custodial paradigm 'in which analysis of the characteristics of individual documents is replaced by understanding the business functions, transactions, and workflows that cause documents to be created',[16] and where the records do not exist as physical entities, instead, as mentioned earlier, 'superseded by a virtual concept or 'performance' where the idea of a record having a sole physical location becomes meaningless'.[17]

The picture that emerges therefore is one of wrestling with the unfamiliar. Yet others view the change as altogether less apocalyptic, seeing little change in *principle*. Randall Jimerson for example, is almost dismissive, commenting that,

> In looking at these new technologies, it is essential to recognize that electronic records and computer applications are simply a new generation of tools with which people order, manage, and document their interactions and their ideas. Technology alters how we communicate and how we work, but it does not fundamentally alter the basic needs and reasons we do so.[18]

Though there are difficulties with definitions, it is still easy to conceive of a digital document, email, website or dataset, as a record. It may be that archives are now approaching a place explored by the library and information studies field as early as the late nineteenth century, when there was a move to pull together the management of documents under the field of 'documentation'. This raised the issue of what a document was: 'If printed works, then also manuscripts; if manuscripts, then also maps and images; if maps, then also globes; if diagrams then also models; and so on.'[19] The work of Paul Otlet, who described sculptures as 'three-dimensional documents' and Suzanne Briet, who focussed on documents as signs and representation, was pioneering, and has been rediscovered as of renewed relevance in the digital era.[20] Concepts such as that of 'bounded variability' (where changes to the form are 'allowed' though limited and controlled by set rules)[21] have started to pave the way for a more sophisticated apprehension of the record in the digital world, and there is evolving an understanding that sees a digital record as a set of digital components or elements, plus their metadata.

## ORIGINALITY, PROVENANCE AND TRUST

Yet issues remain. Digital objects are in some elements at least radically different from paper analogues. One issue is that of originality. This is a crucial element in the paper world, but may not even exist in the digital world. For example, if a person sends an email, where is the original: on the creator's computer, on the email supplier's system, on the recipient's computer, or nowhere? Discussion also needs to embrace the hybrid that is the digitised document, in other words, an 'image' of a record. A large proportion of the digital resources online consist not of 'born-digital', but of digitised material. Yet as neither original digital nor original paper, this documentary Frankenstein has an even more fragile identity.

The other major problem of digital records centres round authenticity and trust. It remains true that it is much easier to change and falsify a digital document. Governments and other bodies such as the Open Knowledge Foundation have put huge efforts into making data available for use by members of the public.[22] However, this effort will be wasted if the data is not trusted. Unfortunately, trust and authenticity are much harder and slipperier concepts in the digital world. Most people

are, rightly, suspicious of much material they see on the internet. Moreover, most of the traditional assurances associated with physical records can no longer be relied on. Physical records could be trusted because they were produced on paper or parchment of the right period, using the right technology for their date (ink, manual or electric typewriter, ball point pen, etc.) and their existence could be traced from their creator through their transfer to an archive.

In contrast, consider UK government websites: these are created electronically by government departments, then captured, stored and delivered by the Paris-based Internet Memory Foundation. The National Archives at Kew holds back-up copies and provides access through its website. In this complex situation, most of the early proofs of authenticity no longer exist. There is no physical object and no simple transfer from creator to archive. Rather ironically, given that this was a keystone in the Jenkinsonian paradigm of nearly a century ago, in the digital era, authenticity is often seen to lie in the concept of provenance (where it has come from). This concept has now re-emerged as of enormous importance to the web.[23] New forms of authenticity are being developed based around trust in the holding institutions and appropriate metadata. In Nicole Convery's words, the concept of authenticity 'is no longer rooted in the material cultural artefact, and thus in physicality, but in the way it is used and contextualized'.[24]

## CHALLENGING THE CONCEPT OF THE ARCHIVE

If digital documents challenge the nature of what is a document, do they also challenge the very concept of the archive? In the digital world, can there be such a thing as an archive repository? Are there not simply caches of information? Certainly, the concept of archives and libraries distinguished by the difference between manuscript as against published material is collapsing, as component concepts of the record and of originality come under strain. Once again, does it matter: does the user know if the digital information they seek is held by an online library or archive, and do they care? Ian Wilson, Librarian and Archivist of Canada has rightly described a new generation, 'a clientele who care less about the source of information and more about whether or not they have access to it'.[25] Others go much further, claiming that 'by undermining the stability of the historical record, digital technologies also undermine the role of the archive'[26] and 'the security of a knowable past'.[27]

There are other challenges to archives that are more fundamental still. Convery discusses how, 'recordkeeping methodologies and practices are no longer "just" challenged by the format of records but much more by the way that information is used, accessed and consumed both by the individual and society as a whole.'[28] Her use of language denotes a seachange in the way archives and information are viewed: a consumer durable, or possibly unendurable. Society's attitude to information has radically changed in the digital age: this change is both cultural and one that cannot be reversed.

Complicating the picture is the impact of theoretical revolutions in other disciplines. At the same time as the digital revolution, and in tune with other disciplines, the archival world experienced its own 'cultural turn'. Indeed, Jacques Derrida himself graced the archival sphere with an influential publication, *Archive Fever*, on the nature of the archive.[29] This postmodernist turn in conjunction with the digital has resulted in challenges to the objectivity, authority, impartiality and nature of the archive, from archivists themselves, as well as historians, particularly in the discipline of postcolonial studies and in imperial history.[30] Once again many archivists have embraced this new world, exploring its implications with energy and insight, welcoming an archival world, that though uncertain, embraces a wider variety of people, documentation, interpretations, versions and histories.

Yet here too, there remain others who see continuity, not chaos. Cook claims that:

> Archivists are now perceiving that a world of relational databases, of complex software linkages, of electronic office systems, of hypermedia documents, of multi-layered geographical information systems, is, when all the high-technology rhetoric is put aside, still a world of information relationships, of interconnections, of context, of evidence, of provenance. Re-creating such relationships for complex electronic records should be no different for the archivist, at a conceptual and theoretical level, than unravelling the interconnections of the many series of records that were typical of the nineteenth-century office.[31]

## THE FUTURE ARCHIVE

So the future remains on a knife-edge of revolution against evolution. Who will own information? And whose will be the choice to retain or to destroy? In the world of the web, can information truly be taken down or destroyed, when it may have been copied or archived? Where new media are concerned, are new formats influencing content and how is the 'democratic' nature of social media tools influencing the way information is communicated, shared and used?

Will concepts of documents as a single entity still exist, in an environment where information and data is constantly combined and re-used? With the proliferation of digitised and digital records on the web, will the paper record simply become a poor cousin that is too hard to access? Will people speak, as some do now, of the digital dark ages, of the 'dark side' of information, of the 'problems' caused by data deluge, information overload and 'infobesity'?[32] Or will the flood of information be seen as a wonderful opportunity?

Closer to the archival arena, will the proliferation of information mean, ironically, that appraisal becomes redundant, 'if everything can be kept and everything searched and found, with relative ease and trivial cost'?[33] There have been and still are adherents of the argument that we should keep everything, and indeed, unlike the situation in the paper world, digital documents are often not subject to selection. The

National Archives, for example, keeps all government websites.

Will the same become true of cataloguing and description? For why catalogue, when there is Google? The archival discipline of original order and arrangement is fast disappearing in a digital world, and with ever more technically sophisticated resource discovery tools, is it necessary or even possible to catalogue? Indeed, one can go further. When the document is born-digital and delivered online via a full-text search, where does the catalogue end and the document begin?

On a wider scale, is what we are really seeing the loss of control of the archive from the archive profession? Will everything be done outside the official record and will we all effectively be archivists; or, on the contrary, will professional archivists become more important as guardians of authentic data? Community archives and user participation are already making inroads into the professional sphere, blurring the distinction between the expert and the crowd and enabling users to create their own values for information, their own definitions of what is worth keeping, and who is permitted to keep it.[34]

At the same time, there have always been inconsistencies in archival theory and practice, and of course in the records themselves. In the words of one writer, archives 'may be deceptive, elusive and often plain wrong'.[35] New digital standards have emerged,[36] yet the postmodernists have made their mark and there is a new awareness that digital standards too, though they may appear stringent, are themselves no more than 'human constructs that have been shaped within a particular historical and cultural context', and that 'the meaning and value of records extends far beyond their status as reliable and authentic evidence of action'.[37]

## IMPACT AND IMPLICATIONS FOR RESEARCH

Whilst archival practitioners await the future with expectation, historians and researchers are still coming to terms with the present. Many have yet to adjust to the impact of these documentary changes on research access, methods and methodologies. These changes are both substantial yet, paradoxically, for many historians, relatively unexplored.

Access, for example, has been transformed. For example, the publication of texts of historical manuscripts has been a fundamental aspect of historical scholarship since the Renaissance. The nineteenth and early twentieth centuries were the high water mark of this activity, with broad agreement on tools and approaches to editing, including the use of footnotes, annotations and commentaries. This period saw the development of some of the great series of texts: in the UK these included the Calendars of State Papers and the publications of the Historical Manuscripts Commission. More recently, university presses and other publishers have also developed series of edited texts, such as Oxford Medieval Texts, or the Loeb editions of ancient Greek and Roman material. However, cost and financial pressures have meant that publishers are increasingly unwilling to take on such projects while, in the UK at least, central government is no longer able to fund the editing or production of scholarly editions of archives. The United States is in a more fortunate position with the National Historical Publications and Records Commission continuing to support the publication – mainly online – of significant historical records. [38]

However, the disappearance of government funding for the traditional editing of historical manuscripts has been more than replaced by the emergence of funding streams for digitisation. In the UK there are at least four separate funding streams. First, many institutions do some digitisation using their own resources. The National Archives, for example, has digitised its collection of wills using its own funds. Some records digitised in this way are provided free, others for a modest charge for downloading individual items. Second, come the funding bodies: in the UK these originally included the national lottery, but this has largely withdrawn from funding digitisation to leave the Research Councils and the Joint Information Systems Committee (better known by its acronym JISC) to fund academic digitisation projects and the creation of digital resources, largely for academic research. Third are the academic publishing companies – Gale, Adam Matthew, Proquest, and others – who often digitise specialised collections and rely on selling them in small volumes but at high prices. Fourth come the family history publishing companies – Origins, Ancestry, Find My Past and others – who digitise records of interest to genealogists and whose business model relies on a mixture of subscriptions and selling high volumes of individual documents at low prices.

There is a similar situation in the United States where the big family history companies (notably Ancestry), the leading academic publishers and some federal funding bodies, all carry out digitisation. The National Endowment for the Humanities has funded a range of projects ranging from Aegean Dendrochronology to Women's Writing.[39] The major difference between the two countries is that the USA has a number of independent charitable funding bodies, including Mellon and the Getty Foundation, who have put resources into digital humanities, whereas in the UK such bodies are fewer in number and, apart from the Wellcome Trust, less well resourced than their American counterparts. The situation is even more complex in the world of book digitisation since we have the work of Google, the Internet Archive and the wonderful Project Gutenberg which relies heavily on volunteers and generates revenue from voluntary donations.

Scholars at every level now have access to an unimaginably large information resource. The Internet Archive is well on its way to making three million items available online. Its two millionth item was *Homiliary on Gospels from Easter to first Sunday of Advent* by Heiric, of Auxerre, who lived ca.841–ca.876.[40] The sheer volume of available material means that ever more sophisticated questions can be asked. The celebrated Culturomics project developed by Erez Lieberman-Aiden and

Jean-Baptiste Michel makes it possible to trace the ways in which words and phrases appear and disappear in the five million books digitised by Google. Culturomics discovers anything from the time it takes words in general usage to change their forms to the speed with which individuals become famous or drop out of sight.[41] In Dan Cohen's book *Equations from God*, he argued that, up to 1800, mathematics was generally considered a divine language but it was 'secularized' in the nineteenth century. Part of his evidence was that mathematical treatises, which often contained religious language in the early nineteenth century, lost such language as the years went by. Cohen was writing in the pre-Google Books world and his argument was based on treatises by leading mathematicians. As he recognises, had he been writing now, he would have been able to do a much more comprehensive survey of the use of religious language in Victorian mathematical writing.[42]

In recent years scholars have begun to consider the possibility of using digital technology to create new forms of editions. The clearest explanation of what those might be like has come from classicists. They envisage creating an *apographeme* of classical Greek and Latin – an analogy to the *genome*, representing the complete record of all Greek and Latin textual knowledge preserved from antiquity, ultimately including every inscription, papyrus, graffito, manuscript, printed edition and any writing-bearing medium. Within the *apographeme* every text would be a multitext, with dynamic editions linked to visual representations of the manuscripts, inscriptions, papyri and other sources. Each source will be linked to the background data needed to understand it – a transcription, information about the particular type of Greek or Latin script and its abbreviations, and about where it was produced.[43] This project is ambitious and is only realisable because the volume of literature from the classical period is limited, but its ambition offers a clear road map for funding bodies. There have been some similar, but slightly less ambitious plans by historians, for example, the British Academy funding for online versions of Anglo-Saxon charters or the Old Bailey Online project which digitised all the surviving records of the central London court.[44]

Future technologies offer even more exciting possibilities. It is possible to imagine systems which could learn from themselves. An editorial system could learn from a small body of structured data – training sets, machine actionable dictionaries, linguistic databases, encyclopaedias and gazetteers – with heuristics for classification, and then use this learning to analyse a much larger body of content for which only scanned text and catalogue level metadata was available.[45]

Sadly, such transformative approaches do not come cheaply. As Peter M.W. Robinson said, 'Making a real electronic scholarly edition is far, far harder than writing a book, and takes far, far longer.' Part of the problem lies in the fact that there are not yet standard tools to enable the creation of complex digital editions and there is a relatively small pool of experts to draw on.[46] The Oxford-based Electronic Enlightenment Project probably represents the current state of the art for digital images – it has a sales pitch of *Scholarship with added value* and says of itself that EE 'is not simply an 'electronic bookshelf' of isolated texts but a **network of interconnected documents**, allowing you to see the complex web of personal relationships in the early modern period and the making of the modern world.' However, it cost Mellon US$2.7 million dollars in grant funding. Until standard tools become more readily available, then the possibility of producing scholarly editions which fully exploit the possibilities of digital technology will remain limited. [47]

## COLLABORATION

One way of expanding the amount of online digital material while operating within limited budgets is to use volunteers to assist with the creation of scholarly editions. In London the *Transcribe Bentham* project provided software to enable volunteers to transcribe manuscripts of the English political writer Jeremy Bentham. The project had limited funding, but during the six months in which it was fully operational, about 400 individuals transcribed over 1,000 manuscripts. There were difficulties: one major problem was that many volunteer editors struggled with Bentham's handwriting and most ended up working on one or two documents and then disappearing.[48] The challenge has been taken up the London's Institute of Historical Research whose *ReScript* project which was launched in 2011 will build a prototype editing facility to allow online collaboration on the editing of four significant historical texts – Clarendon's *History of the Rebellion*, John Aubrey's *Brief Lives*, Joseph Foster's *Alumni Oxonienses* and the St. Botolph Aldgate Parish Clerk's Memorandum Books.[49]

One of the great potential advantages of online scholarly editions is that they can make it easier for different scholars to annotate texts. They can thus become valuable tools for a different sort of collaboration: scholarly collaboration. There is currently some concern about the technologies available. Scholars wanting to annotate have to learn a different software system for each new collection of texts and have no easy way to integrate comments made by colleagues using other tools. One project, The Open Annotation Collaboration, with partners from the universities of Illinois, Queensland and Maryland, as well as the Los Alamos National Laboratory and JSTOR is seeking to develop interoperable technology.[50] Even without this standard approach, there is currently a range of interesting projects. The University of Texas has created an online version of all five editions of Edward Fitzgerald's *Rubaiyat of Omar Khayyam*. Users can add their own annotations and comments on the text.[51] The same approach is taken in the Pynchonwiki, which allows interested people to comment on every page of all Thomas Pynchon's novels.[52]

One current issue in the digital humanities is that of isolation. Traditionally, unlike scientists, historians have tended to be lone scholars. If they are to exploit the possibilities of the digital world then historians may need to learn to become more collaborative. Writing in 2011, Anthony Grafton, President of the American Historical Association, commented that, 'As new forms of scientific research offer historians research possibilities that complement the textual record, as digital archives and exhibitions expand and digital research methods become more accessible, historians will have to learn how to form and work in teams.' He also suggested that new forms of teams involving multiple forms of organisations – partnerships as well as hierarchies – might take shape. In order to achieve this, historians will need to find ways to award credit to multiple creators for a single project and to create physical and social spaces, as the natural scientists at every major university already have, where interdisciplinary collaborative research can take place.[53]

The development of digital resources and of programmes for annotation and collaborative editing has greatly enhanced the possibilities of collaborative research by historians. Truly these are tools for conviviality. However, because the use of digital resources and tools is very new, in most cases less than ten years old, then this approach to scholarship has not become part of the mainstream. Indeed some scholars who use these approaches appear to identify themselves as digital humanists rather than scholars who make use of material online. According to Christine Borgman, 'Digital scholarship remains a backwater in much of the humanities. Concerns about publishing, tenure, and promotion for digital humanities scholars are a continuing theme in the conferences and in the literature of the field.'[54] It is a new world and it is to be hoped that over the next decade a new generation of historians will see the use of digital resources as a commonplace, and will employ online material with as much ease and familiarity as their predecessors used medieval charters and rolls.

So far humanities researchers have not gone as far in tapping the potential of online collaboration and annotation as their scientific colleagues. One of the most successful collaborative scientific projects has been GalaxyZoo where thousands of volunteers have characterised the images of galaxies from the Sloan Digital Sky Survey. It turned out that not only were these volunteers as accurate at characterising galaxies as professional astronomers, but in a few cases they managed to highlight potential future areas for astronomical research.[55] Collaborative techniques, including crowd-sourcing, have also been successfully used to create historical archives. One of the most successful of these is The Hurricane Digital Memory Bank, which uses electronic media to collect, preserve and present the stories and digital records of Hurricanes Katrina and Rita. It is a joint project between George Mason University's Center for History and New Media, and the University of New Orleans in partnership with the Smithsonian Institution's National Museum of American History.[56]

## SUSTAINABILITY

The existence of so many models for digitisation and so much material being digitised at such expense leads to some questions about the sustainability of digitised collections. Both grant-funded and commercially funded resources are at risk. There are two significant threats to the survival of digital collections – financial and technological. Large funding bodies insist that grantees have to guarantee that their material will be available for, typically, seven years. Guarantees of the long-term availability of materials given with great enthusiasm and genuine commitment when the grant application is being completed can ring a bit hollow seven years down the line when the money has long since run out. The National Archives of the UK has recently been approached by one large grant-funded project for which the funding has now been used up and the team is dispersing. The organisers would now like The National Archives to take responsibility for the resources that they have created. In fact, the funding model for academic digitisation is contributing to the problem: it is relatively easy to obtain funding for a new, exciting project which pushes the boundaries of scholarship and creates significant digital resources. There is simply no source of funding to maintain those resources once they have been created.

Analysis of some statistics reveals the scale of the problem. Of the 155 projects funded by the New Opportunities Fund in the UK between 1998 and 2003 at a cost of £55 million, 25 can no longer be found, while there have been no changes or enhancements to a further 83. Of the 155, there are only 30 which have been enhanced or added to since the launch. So in less than ten years, 16 per cent of resources have been lost and 53 per cent have, at best stagnated.[57]

Commercial organisations have different imperatives since they need to keep their resources available online to generate revenue and some of the early commercial digitisation projects, such as the 1901 Census of England and Wales, still survive. However, commercial organisations cannot guarantee to be around for ever. Proquest, originally known as University Microfilms, has been around since the 1930s but other major microfilm houses have disappeared over the years. Moreover, corporate policies change: in 2008, Google began work on a major plan to digitise newspapers, but in May 2011 they announced that they were not going to add any new features or functionality to the site nor were they planning to accept any more microfilm or digital files for processing.[58]

There has been some interesting work by the Strategic Content Alliance on business models to ensure the survival of digital collections. A 2009 report produced by the Alliance found that

projects are experimenting with and have deployed a wide range of revenue generating models while at the same time finding ways to minimize their direct outlays by reducing the scope of their work or by taking advantage of opportunities for assistance and subsidy from host institutions and outside partners. So, at this stage of their development, most of the projects covered in this collection of

case studies rely on a mix of generated revenue and host support. While a couple of them have been around long enough to demonstrate financial viability, for most of the cases we studied it is too early to tell whether the mix of sustainability strategies employed will succeed over the long run.[59]

As well as exploring business models for sustaining digital resources, the funding bodies need to consider technological issues. It seems likely that in some cases digital resources will have to be transferred to institutions other than the creating ones in order to ensure their survival. This produces particular difficulties when images are stored and delivered using complex proprietary software. If successful transfer is to happen then funding bodies need to insist that projects meet minimum standards for resource creation using open-source software, with the aim of ensuring that digitised records can easily be transferred to a new holder in the future. Yet the cost of ensuring the survival of such systems might be prohibitive particularly in the absence of any source of funding to support this.

Some funding bodies are already working on this. For example, the Economic and Social Research Council (ESRC) recently launched a new data policy that focuses on a commitment to the long-term sustainability of data and requires that '[research] data must be made available for preparation for re-use and/or archiving with the ESRC data service providers within three months of the end of the award otherwise we will withhold the final payment'.[60] Yet there is still some way to go. In 2010, The National Archives were sent a grant application where the applicants were proposing to meet the sustainability requirement by simply sending The National Archives a database on a CD. The sustainability problem is not a theoretical computing issue – it is a live problem now. A 2004 University of Illinois study examined website citations in three top online journals and found that about half of the URLs cited in their articles no longer pointed to the authors' source material.[61] Web addresses have become so unreliable that the Modern Language Association recently stopped

requiring authors to cite URLs when refer-
encing web-based resources.[62]

Equally problematic is the apparent
reluctance of some traditional libraries to
fully engage with web-based resources.
Columbia University collects papers that
Non-Governmental Organisations publish
and distribute, but web-only material has been
largely ignored: at a 2011 conference presentation, the Columbia librarians noted that of
40 documents published on the website of
Refugees International – a group that regularly publishes papers and field reports on
displaced populations in 27 countries – none
had been archived by Columbia's Center for
Human Rights Documentation and Research,
while only 10 were listed by the Online
Computer Library Center (OCLC), an international library cooperative.[63]

## RISKS AND ISSUES

There are risks and issues in the proliferation
of digital texts. To some extent, the choice as
to what is digitised is determined by the funding priorities of funding organisations. This
has led some scholars to raise concerns.
Randall Jimerson made the point that whilst
the digitisation of material increases access,
the choice of what to digitise still privileges
what is available as opposed to the silent mass
of the undigitised.[64] Certainly Jimerson has a
valid point. Because most institutions can
only digitise a vanishingly small proportion of
their archives and special collections, there
will, inevitably, be selection bias. Most material is digitised commercially and is selected
for digitisation because somebody hopes to
make a profit from reselling it, hence the huge
bias towards family history-related records
and popular sources for undergraduate level
research; for example early newspapers.
Even digitisation projects driven by the
academy might have unintended consequences. Tim Hitchcock, Robert Shoemaker
and the British Library have created a fabulous set of digital resources for anyone working on eighteenth-century British history – Old

Bailey Online, the Burney Collection of newspapers and London Lives.[65] These resources
are amazingly easy to use, but are London-
centric, and focussed on the poor and on
crime. Does their existence bias the choice of
undergraduate essays, Masters theses and
PhD topics?

The huge corpus of digital material now
available to scholars raises a number of
difficulties. Despite the development of
Culturomics, some scholars have complained
at the lack of sophisticated research tools.
According to Christine L. Borgman, 'Until
analytical tools and services are more sophisticated, robust, transparent, and easy to use
for the motivated humanities researcher, it
will be difficult to attract a broad base of
interest within the humanities community.'[66]
Equally, while this gigantic volume of data
has clearly brought many benefits, it has the
potential to cause problems for the less
sophisticated user. One problem is the Google
issue. Anyone interested in a particular subject
can try simply 'Googling' it. In the world of
mass digital resources, there is a fair chance of
being taken to a resource without any explanation as to its context and research value.

As John Updike said in his defence of the
book:

> In imagining a huge, virtually infinite word-
> stream accessed by search engines and popu-
> lated by teeming, promiscuous word snippets
> stripped of credited authorship, are we not
> depriving the written word of its old-fashioned
> function of, through such inventions as the writ-
> ten alphabet and the printing press, communi-
> cation from one person to another – of, in short,
> accountability and intimacy? Yes, there is a ton
> of information on the Web, but much of it is
> egregiously inaccurate, unedited, unattributed
> and juvenile.[67]

Indeed some of the comments on the Rubaiyat
site or the Pynchonwiki do not add greatly to
the sum of human understanding. Does
knowing that in 1997 vandals daubed the
University of California with images of
muted posthorns help greatly – beyond of
course proving that *The Crying of Lot 49* is
still read in California?[68]

This new world requires a new approach to historical scholarship. In future, researchers will require new skills. They will need to have a good understanding of the technologies required to make the best use of online resources – text mining, the use of geographical information systems and other analytical tools. There is some feeling that academics have so far failed to adjust to this new reality. Writing in the *Times Higher Education*, Cathy Davidson commented, 'Our education systems so far look as if the internet hasn't been invented yet. Scratch most conventional academic departments and you will see little hint of restructured courses, let alone restructured thinking.'[69] In December 2010 a group of Digital Humanities students at Bloomsburg University were so concerned about the situation that they published a manifesto for Digital Humanities education. It said, 'It is baffling why the concepts of DH are not being taught more broadly at the undergraduate level. Digital Humanities is about not only learning and accepting the digital ways of our world, but also about how to apply these strategies to our education.'[70] And yet, many archivists hear urban legends about people who waste huge amounts of time and mental effort pursuing false trails – basing an argument on a known forgery or spending ages analysing financial records without understanding the basis on which they were created. How many more opportunities are there for these sorts of errors in the digital world? The new world of history requires a high degree of technical sophistication, but more than ever it requires old fashioned scholarly values about understanding the meaning and significance of sources.

## ACCESS

Taxpayers have to a large extent funded digitisation of humanities resources. Consequently it is worth exploring whether digital has increased broad-based access to original source materials. Can those outside the academy and those only loosely affiliated use a wider range of resources for their own research pursuits? Even before the internet, technological developments such as microfilm made it much easier for people to see records and publications. Some scholars have argued that the development of microfilm in the 1930s reduced the costs of doing historical research. This made it possible for students and junior scholars to undertake research that would have formerly required costly travel to libraries and archives.[71] The same process occurred in the family history community where the creation in the 1970s of microfiche editions of British parish registers by the Genealogical Society of Utah made it much easier for ordinary people to access these records from a central location rather than having to visit local archives and churches round the country. More recently, the provision of online access to family history records for a modest charge has greatly enhanced their use, and today very many family historians begin their research by using the big family history databases such as Ancestry. On the other hand and probably inevitably, the commercially funded academic projects are only of benefit to those who have access to university or national libraries, thus excluding family historians, school teachers and others outside the academy.

The picture for digitisation projects funded by the major academic funding bodies is on the whole fairly good. The authors tried to access a large sample of resource enhancement projects funded by Arts and Humanities Research Council (AHRC) in the UK. There are some splendid and freely accessible sites, including Old Bailey Online, Fine Rolls of Henry III and the Nottingham University Place Name Tool amongst many others. Sadly a small number leads to broken links or cannot be tracked down. A very few just do not understand democratic access. The Newcastle Electronic Corpus of Tyneside English 'is available for non-commercial use by individuals or groups that can demonstrate a *bona fide* interest'.[72] Hard to know what a non-*bona fide* interest might be and anyway you can hear a pretty good corpus of

Tyneside English in the streets outside the university. You need to submit a brief description of your proposed research to the University of Edinburgh to access the Calum Maclean collection of Scottish Gaelic folk tales.[73]

Contrast this English and Scottish desire to control with the recent statement by the Mellon Foundation:

> There are important public policy reasons for ensuring the broad reach of the humanities, and many of the library and scholarly resources and publications that the Mellon Foundation has supported are accessible and useful to a wide range of people from advanced scholars to students and teachers in kindergarten through 12th grade and the general public.[74]

Could there be a better definition of democratisation of access?

## CONCLUSION

The digital age has caused a paradigm shift in the documentary world, with the very nature of records and the archive under attack. From the researcher's point of view, although digital documents are much easier to find and access than analogue ones, the demands and skills required to use them well are greater than in the traditional paper world. Awareness needs to be raised and training increased properly to equip present and future researchers to optimise the amazing opportunities that the digital opens up, but also to negotiate a path through the challenges of these new records – a quicksand of shifting content and context.[75]

In 2010 when two Harvard scientists, Erez Lieberman-Aiden and Jean-Baptiste Michel suggested a ten-year programme for the digitisation of the complete written record of the human race, the response of the incoming President of the American Historical Association was 'It's a wonderful plan, but also one impossible to realize in their proposed time frame.'[76] His response exemplifies the major challenge facing those involved in the creation of online historical resources – the lack of a compelling vision for the future.

It is easy to find excuses, and the funding models are partly to blame. It is, again, easy to define relatively small digitisation projects to answer specific research questions, but a large-scale and overarching vision requires interoperability, standards, national and international co-ordination that at present do not exist. The classicists have their *apographeme* – an all embracing corpus of Latin and Ancient Greek material – and it has been recently pointed out that 'the dream of collecting all kinds of media in one repository of knowledge can be traced back to the ancient origins of information and documentation', with the authors citing the Mouseion of Alexandria as the common ancestor for archives, museums and libraries. Perhaps it is to this compelling vision of the co-ordinated portal and point of access that historians and archivists need to return.[77] And there are some good signs. In the United Kingdom, British History Online a joint initiative of the Institute of Historical Research and the History of Parliament Trust showcases core printed primary and secondary sources for the medieval and modern British history.[78] The *Europeana* project, launched in 2008 with funding from the European Commission, has the goal of 'making Europe's cultural and scientific heritage accessible to the public' via a single internet portal, allowing people 'to explore the digital resources of Europe's museums, libraries, archives and audio-visual collections'.[79] In North America, the Canada Project, the first initiative under the Canadian Digital Information Strategy, has a goal to 'To make accessible all Canadian knowledge to all Canadians' through a digital 'knowledge platform'.[80] More of this kind of innovative and inter-disciplinary collaboration is needed. As Ian Wilson, Librarian and Archivist of Canada has said, 'when we make use of the Web, we must make sure that we are not recreating, repeating and perpetuating online the boundaries and practices that have developed in the physical world ... It is up to us to invent a new, seamless kind of knowledge institution.'[81] This new kind of institution should bring not only librarians and archivists together, but historians and researchers from a wide range of disciplines to explore and share learning around the implications of this new world. For example, beyond the academy, the internet and the availability of cheap digital cameras has made it possible for communities and individuals to save and make accessible documents that might otherwise have been lost or languished hidden in private hands.[82]

Some have seen a division between two fundamentally different views of archives – what has been called the evidence-memory dichotomy. On the one side of this divide are records creators and archivists who place an emphasis on legal and business accountability. On the other, researchers and users who emphasise historical and cultural value.[83] Digital records can help to bridge this divide, with some records such as corporate websites clearly existing in both mental worlds (with both formal accounting and governance material as well as commercial and advertising matter).

This is an archival brave new world 'characterized by the increasing irrelevance of constraint of place, time and medium'.[84] But perhaps it is also still the age of the dinosaur when it comes to digital records.

To return finally to Lieberman-Aiden and Michel, a more appropriate response might have been 'It's a wonderful plan, let's try ...'.

## NOTES AND REFERENCES

1 Statistics from The National Archives (June 2010).
2 These figures relate to 2009–10. Statistics from The National Archives (May and October 2010).
3 Hilary Jenkinson, *A Manual of Archive Administration* (London: Percy Lund, Humphries & Co Ltd, 1966, re-issue of the second edition), p.5.
4 Jenkinson, *A Manual of Archive Administration*, p.11.
5 *Information and Documentation. Records Management. General*, BS ISO 15489-1:2001 (October 2001).
6 Richard J. Cox, *Archives and Archivists in the Information Age* (New York: Neal-Schuman Publishers Inc, 2005), p. 211.
7 Luciana Duranti, 'Reflections on InterPARES. The InterPARES 2 Project (2002–2007): an overview', *Archivaria*, 64 (Fall 2007), 113–21; quotation p.114.
8 Caroline Williams, 'Government information: what to keep', unpublished internal paper, Version 7:2, The National Archives, 8 October 2008.
9 Lesley Richmond, 'Corporate records', in Alison Turton (ed.), *Managing Business Archives* (Oxford: Butterworth-Heinemann,1991), pp.100–27; this discussion pp.119–20.
10 Terry Cook, 'What is past is prologue: a history of archival ideas since 1898, and the future paradigm shift', *Archivaria*, 43 (Spring 1997), 17–63.
11 See the term 'Record' at www.archivists.org/glossary (accessed 12 May 2011).
12 Ibid.
13 Duranti, 'Reflections on InterPARES', 113–121; quotation p.120.
14 Angelika Menne-Haritz, 'Managing and archiving administrative records in the digital era – the instrumentality of electronic records for administration communication', in Niklaus Bütikofer, Hans Hofman, Seamus Ross (eds.), *Managing and Archiving Records in the Digital Era: Changing Professional Orientations* (Baden: hier+jetzt, 2006), pp.31–8.
15 Louise Craven, 'From the archivist's cardigan to the very dead sheep: what are archives? What are archivists? What do they do?', in Louise Craven (ed.), *What are Archives? Cultural and Theoretical Perspectives: A Reader* (Aldershot: Ashgate, 2008), pp.7–30; quotation p. 21.
16 Eric Ketelaar, 'Archival theory and the Dutch manual', *Archivaria*, 41 (Spring 1996), 31–40; quotation, p.33. Cook, 'What is past is prologue'.
17 Adrian Cunningham, 'The postcustodial archive', in Jennie Hill (ed.), *The Future of Archives and Recordkeeping: A Reader* (London: Facet, 2011), pp.173–89.
18 Randall C. Jimerson, *Archives Power: Memory, Accountability, and Social Justice* (Chicago: Society of American Archivists, 2009); quotation p.319.
19 Niels Windfield Lund and Michael Buckland, 'Document, documentation and the document academy: introduction', *Archival Science*, 8, 3 (2008), 161–64; quotation, p.161.
20 Windfield Lund and Buckland, 'Document, documentation and the document academy', p.162. Also Michelle M. Tourney, 'Caging virtual antelopes: Suzanne Briet's definition of documents in the context of the digital age', *Archival Science*, 3, 3 (2003), 291–311.
21 Term used by Duranti in her article, 'Reflections on InterPARES', p.120.
22 See http://data.gov.uk for the UK Government initiative; http://okfn.org/about for the Open Knowledge Foundation (accessed 12 May 2011).
23 For example, the World Wide Web Consortium (W3C) has a specific Provenance Working Group, one of the aims of which is to 'publish W3C Recommendations that define a language for exchanging provenance information among applications'. See www.w3.org/2011/prov/wiki/Main_Page (accessed 15 June 2011).
24 Nicole Convery, 'Information management, records management, knowledge management: the place of archives in a digital age', in Jennie Hill (ed.), *The Future of Archives and Recordkeeping: A Reader* (London: Facet, 2011), pp.191–212. This quotation p.193 also uses the work of Tredinnick.

25  Ian Wilson, 'The State of Canadian Confederation: to know ourselves'. The Extraordinary Symons Lecture, Toronto, 28 February 2008. At: www.collectionscanada. gc.ca/about-us/012-216-e.html (accessed 16 June 2011).

26  Luke Tredinnick, *Digital Information Culture: The Individual and Society in the Digital Age* (Oxford: Chandos, 2008), p.161.

27  Tredinnick, *Digital Information Culture*, p.156.

28  Convery, 'Information management, records management, knowledge management'.

29  Jacques Derrida, *Archive Fever: A Freudian Impression*, trans. Eric Prenowitz (Chicago & London: University of Chicago Press, 1995).

30  See for example amongst an increasing archival literature, Joan M. Schwartz, '"Having new eyes": spaces of archives, landscapes of power' and other articles in the Special Section on Archives: Space and Power, in *Archivaria*, 61 (Spring 2006), 1–104. In imperial hsitory, see, for example, the work of Ann Laura Stoler and Antoinette Burton.

31  Cook, 'What is past is prologue'.

32  See Tredinnick, *Digital Information Culture*, pp.153–6 for discussion of the digital dark ages; for other information 'problems', see David Bawden and Lyn Robinson, 'The dark side of information: overload, anxiety and other paradoxes and pathologies', *Journal of Information Science*, 35, 2 (2009), pp.180–91.

33  Richard N. Katz and Paul B. Gandel, 'The tower, the cloud, and posterity: documenting in a digital world', in Terry Cook (ed.), *Controlling the Past: Documenting Society and Institutions, Essays in Honour of Helen Willa Samuels* (Chicago: Society of American Archivists, 2011), pp. 217–38.

34  James Surowiecki, *The Wisdom of Crowds: Why the Many Are Smarter Than the Few and How Collective Wisdom Shapes Business, Economies, Societies and Nations* (London: Little, Brown, 2004).

35  Andrew Prescott, 'The textuality of the archive', in Louise Craven (ed.), *What are Archives? Cultural and Theoretical Perspectives: A Reader*. (Aldershot: Ashgate, 2008), pp. 31–51.

36  For example, in the United States, The National Archives and Records Administration endorses the Department of Defense (DoD) 5015.02-STD RMA Design Criteria Standard which can be found at http://jitc.fhu.disa.mil/recmgt/standards.html; whilst the European Commission published its Model Requirements for Electronic Records and Document Management (MoReq) in 2001, an updated MoReq2 in 2008, and most recently a MoReq 2010; see www.moreq2.eu (both accessed 23 June 2011).

37  Heather MacNeil, 'Trusting records in a postmodern world', *Archivaria*, 51 (Spring 2001), 36–47; this quotation p. 46.

38  See www.archives.gov/nhprc/ (accessed May 2011).

39  See the National Endowment for the Humanities, Online Humanities Projects, www.neh.gov/projects/online.html (accessed May 2011).

40  See www.archive.org/details/toronto (accessed May 2011).

41  Anthony Grafton, 'Loneliness and freedom', *Perspectives on History* (March 2011), at www.historians.org/Perspectives/issues/2011/1103/1103pre1.cfm (accessed May 2011).

42  Daniel J. Cohen, *Equations from God – Pure Mathematics and Victorian Faith* (Baltimore, MD: Johns Hopkins University Press, 2007); Dan Cohen, 'Is Google good for history?', notes for talk given at *American Historical Association Annual Meeting, 7 January 2010,* at www. dancohen.org/2010/01/07/is-google-good-for-history (accessed May 2011).

43  Gregory Crane et al., 'Classics in the million book library', *Digital Humanities Quarterly*, 3, 1 (Winter 2009), section 10. See http://digitalhumanities.org/dhq/vol/003/1/000034/000034.html (accessed May 2011).

44  For Anglo Saxon Charters, see www.trin.cam.ac.uk/chart-www/charthome.html. For the Old Bailey Online, see www.oldbaileyonline.org (accessed May 2011).

45  Crane et al., 'Classics in the million book library'.

46  Peter M.W. Robinson, 'The ends of editing', *Digital Humanities Quarterly*, 3, 3 (Summer 2009), section 20, at: www.digitalhumanities.org/dhq/vol/3/3/000051/ 000051. html (accessed May 2011).

47  For information on the Electronic Enlightenment project, see: www.e-enlightenment.com/info/about. Between 2001 and 2008, the Mellon Foundation awarded the project eight grants totalling US$2,742,100. See also the Ithaka Case Studies in Sustainability review of the project at www.ithaka.org/ithaka-s-r/research/ithaka-case-studies-in-sustainability/case-studies/SCA_BMS_CaseStudy_EE.pdf (accessed May 2011).

48  Marc Parry, 'Facing budget woes: prominent crowdsourcing project will scale back', *Chronicle of Higher Education*, 11 March 2011; at: http://chronicle.com/blogs/wiredcampus/facing-budget-woes-prominent-crowdsourcing-project-will-scale-back/30322. The Bentham project's website is at www.ucl.ac.uk/Bentham-Project (accessed May 2011).

49  IHR Digital, Rescript, the collaborative editing of historical texts, at www.history.ac.uk/projects/ReScript/ See also Jane Winters, 'Approaches to digital editing', unpublished conference paper, April 2011, at http://sas-space.sas.ac.uk/2855/1/Approaches_to_digital_editing.pdf (accessed May 2011).

50  The Open Annotation Collaboration project website is at: www.openannotation.org (accessed May 2011).

51  See The Collaborative Rubaiyat website at http://scholar. hrc.utexas.edu/rubaiyat/texts/1889/1?    show=tags (accessed May 2011).

52  For the Pynchonwiki website, see http://pynchonwiki. com (accessed May 2011).

53  Grafton, 'Loneliness and freedom'.

54  Christine Borgman, 'The digital future is now: a call to action for the humanities', *Digital Humanities Quarterly*, 3, 4 (Fall 2009), section 4. See www.digitalhumanities. org/dhq/vol/3/4/000077/000077.html (accessed May 2011).

55  See *The Story So Far*, available from the GalaxyZoo website, at www.galaxyzoo.org/story (accessed May 2011).

56  See The Hurricane Digital Memory Bank website, at http://hurricanearchive.org/about (accessed May 2011).

57  A 2009 survey by Alastair Dunning of the websites created by The New Opportunities Fund digitisation projects 1999–2004 can be found at http://web.me.com/xcia0069/nof.html (accessed May 2011).

58  Matt McGee, 'Google shuts down ambitious newspaper scanning project', *Search Engine Land*, 20 May 2011, at http://searchengineland.com/google-shuts-down-ambitious-newspaper-scanning-project-77970 (accessed May 2011).

59  Nancy L. Maron, K. Kirby Smith and Matthew Loy, *Sustaining Digital Resources: An On-the-Ground View of Projects Today*, Ithaka Case Studies in Sustainability, 2009, p. 4, at www.jisc.ac.uk/media/documents/publications/general/2009/scaithakaprojectstoday.pdf (accessed May 2011).

60  See *ESRC Research Data Policy*, September 2010, available at www.esrc.ac.uk/about-esrc/information/data-policy.aspx (accessed 22 June 2011).

61  James Ho, 'Hyperlink obsolescence in scholarly online journals', *Journal of Computer-Mediated Communication*, 10, 3 (2005), article 15, at http://jcmc.indiana.edu/vol10/issue3/ho.html (accessed May 2011).

62  Purdue Online Writing Lab, 'MLA works cited: electronic sources (web publications)', http://owl.english.purdue.edu/owl/resource/747/08 (accessed May 2011).

63  Steve Kolowich, 'Archiving the web for scholars', *Inside Higher Ed*, 6 May 2011, at www.insidehighered.com/news/2011/05/06/libraries_try_to_preserve_and_archive_websites_for_academic_study#Comments (accessed May 2011).

64  Jimerson, *Archives Power*, p.322.

65  For Old Bailey Online, see www.oldbaileyonline.org. The Burney Collection is available through Gale – Cengage, at http://gale.cengage.co.uk; London Lives at www.londonlives.org (accessed May 2011).

66  Borgman, 'The digital future is now', Section 5.

67  John Updike, 'The end of authorship', *New York Times*, 25 June 2006; at www.nytimes.com/2006/06/25/books/review/25updike.html?pagewanted=2 (accessed May 2011).

68  See http://cl49.pynchonwiki.com/wiki/index.php?title=Main_Page (accessed May 2011).

69  Cathy Davidson, 'So last century', *Times Higher Education*, 28 April 2011, at www.timeshighereducation.co.uk/story.asp?sectioncode=26&storycode=415941 (accessed May 2011).

70  Bloomsburg University Undergraduates, *Manifesto on Digital Humanities*, at http://humanistica.ualberta.ca/bloomsburg-u-undergraduate-manifesto-on-digital-humanities. A search on Google reveals a number of other similar manifestos (accessed May 2011).

71  'History, people, and informatics: a conversation between Sharon Irish and Wendy Plotkin', *Digital Humanities Quarterly*, 4, 2 (Fall 2010), at www.digitalhumanities.org/dhq/vol/4/2/000086/000086.html (accessed May 2011).

72  See http://research.ncl.ac.uk/necte/corpus.htm (accessed May 2011).

73  See www.celtscot.ed.ac.uk/calum-maclean/access/register.html (accessed May 2011).

74  See Helen Cullyer and Donald J. Waters, 'Priorities for the Scholarly Communications Program', *Andrew W Mellon Foundation, Annual Report, 2008*, 34, at www.mellon.org/news_publications/annual-reports-essays/annual-reports/content2008.pdf (accessed May 2011).

75  Initiatives like the introduction of an MA in Digital History run by the University of Essex is a very positive step forward in this space.

76  Grafton, 'Loneliness and freedom'.

77  Thomas Kirchhoff, Werner Schweibenz and Jörn Sieglerschmidt, 'Archives, libraries, museums and the spell of ubiquitous knowledge', *Archival Science*, 8, 4 (December 2008), 251–66; quotation p. 252.

78  See www.british-history.ac.uk (accessed 20 June 2011).

79  See www.europeana.eu/portal (accessed May 2011).

80  Under the Canada project Library and Archives Canada, the University of Waterloo, Open Text Corporation, Bibliothèque et archives nationales du Québec and the Canadian Association of Research Libraries are joining forces 'to incite institutions, organizations and businesses across the country to pool their contents to create a unique showcase of our nation's ingenuity, and a made-for-Canadians digital space to learn, dialogue, innovate, create, and drive our economic competitiveness in coming decades.' Ian Wilson, 'The state of Canadian Confederation: to know ourselves'. The Extraordinary Symons Lecture, Toronto: 28 February 2008. At: www.collectionscanada.gc.ca/about-us/012-216-e.html (accessed 16 June 2011).

81  Wilson, 'The state of Canadian Confederation: to know ourselves'.

82  See Michael Moss, 'Jonathan Oldbuck's cat', in Niklaus Bütikofer, Hans Hofman, Seamus Ross (eds.), *Managing and Archiving Records in the Digital Era: Changing Professional Orientations* (Baden: hier+jetzt, 2006), pp.115–126; discussion p.116.

83  For example, Jennifer Meehan, 'The archival nexus: rethinking the interplay of archival ideas about the nature, value, and use of records', *Archival Science*, 9, 3–4 (2009), 157–64; in particular p.158.

84  Eric Ketelaar, 'Everyone an archivist', in Niklaus Bütikofer, Hans Hofman and Seamus Ross (eds.), *Managing and Archiving Records in the Digital Era: Changing Professional Orientations* (Baden: hier+jetzt, 2006), pp. 9–14.

# 28

# Recovering the Self:
# Agency after Deconstruction

David Gary Shaw

The question of historical agency grows from the factual quartet that in the past people wanted, willed, tried and suffered. Agency occurs whenever a person generates some event or idea, a word or deed, possibly something unique, and pushes on because of it. In small acts of going to work, caring for friends, marching, or riding to meet your Waterloo, people do; and the springs and significance of their doing are the core of what historians should care about. At the base, such action is akin to animals, say the horses pulling carts and cannons or carrying men at Waterloo. But human agency is at its most interesting when it reaches beyond the animal desires and strivings for meaning, self-reflection and interpretation. This chapter will explore the sort of agency that has opened up for historical examination, reflecting on the postmodernist moment that highlighted our doubts about free human action before going on to our more recent context for analysing human action historically, the framework of human significance.

While historical agency – how people purposefully create their history – has always been a great background issue for historians,

it has rarely been a central historiographical concern, even in the discipline's most theoretical moments. Twentieth-century developments in historical theory typically gave only a small place to agency as an explicit theme, so my present goal is to orient historians towards a viable engagement with agency in theory. On the way, I shall argue that postmodern history was continuous with the trajectory of preceding historical work in trying to limit most sorts of historical agency; that our present historical agency has surprising variety and possibilities and is soon likely to embrace more kinds of historical agents. Moreover, this new phase of agency will encourage historians to reconsider the place of experience and language, even as they hold fast to the importance of narrating the self for understanding historical action. Crucially, however, among the array of possible historical agents, the effective human agent will persist in being a sort of self, nested in the centre of deliberation, interpretation, and narrative. The practice of history will require thinking more often about the social and dynamic selves that constitute societies by their actions, but these will be culturally and historically determinate selves.

Before proceeding, a tentative definition, or location, is in order. 'Agency' implies, in Thomas Sewell's words, 'the efficacy of human action.'[1] For the present, we should add that human action might just be collective but is certainly also individual. It should be meant, but needn't be the result of a complex plan. It requires desire more than rationality. Moreover, analysing agency need not indicate or recommend individual*ism*, methodological, political, or ethical, but if the social system as a whole or a group as a whole or other forces (general or hidden) are the sole actors, we are unlikely to consider it a sort of historical agency.[2] It may be, however, that animals have agency too and we shall glance at what the animal within the human may tell us about action. The reader will be quickly aware that in following the grain of most discussions of historical agency, we do not focus on theorising historical action in its totality or on much of the philosophy of action. We examine rather the contingencies in which selves form, act, and may be understood rather than focussing narrowly on the agent-as-cause-of-effects alone.

## CHALLENGES TO AGENCY

Even before the advent of a palpable postmodern challenge to the idea that individual people controlled their historical agendas, the mainstream of historical work and reflection in social history and then cultural history had already penned the individual agent up into a sometimes quite small place. This was partly because the nineteenth century had often advanced not just the individual but the great and exceptional male individual as a crucial mover of history. As Carlyle put it:

Universal History, the history of what man has accomplished in this world, is at bottom the History of the Great Men who have worked here. They were the leaders of men, these great ones; the modellers, patterns, and in a wide sense creators, of

whatsoever the general mass of men contrived to do or to attain; all things that we see standing accomplished in the world are properly the outer material result, the practical realization and embodiment, of Thoughts that dwelt in the Great Men sent into the world: the soul of the whole world's history, it may justly be considered, were the history of these.[3]

While agency in Carlyle is in fact much more complicated and interesting than many credit, there can be no doubting the centrality of the great men in his conception and how little they owed to the many women.

Across most of the historical discipline in the twentieth century, however, the 'great man' theory was roundly rejected. The entire drive of Marxist inflected historiography was to demonstrate the dynamic of class and the determinisms of social relations and their economic apparatuses. Human agency existed but was highly constrained and often minimised.[4] Social historical sources very much favoured such an approach, since they were often strikingly poor, episodic or otherwise difficult to handle if a rich sense of the individual person was a goal. This did not necessarily dampen interest in the particular human, but it was little more than a rhetorical flourish. This school's more sensitive writers represented powerful individuals as mouths of movements and classes, as in Christopher Hill's renderings of Cromwell or Bunyan or Milton.[5]

Scholars have recently argued that social history had an underlying conceptual bent against the autonomous agent. 'To speak of subjectivity in social history can only refer to a reflection or expression of the social context .... The *causes* of actions have nothing to do with autonomous individual agency ...' (my emphasis).[6] This is a strong reading of social historical practice and E.P. Thompson noted and resisted it. Working against the grain, he argued that individual initiative and freedom were compatible with the great historical structures.[7] The anti-individual tendency moved on to cultural history but the effects on intellectual history were perhaps the most drastic. To remain vital, intellectual historians urged themselves to join with the cultural historical movement and to displace authors, those conceptual actors, from the discipline's centre.[8]

Historians were, in other words, already theoretically primed for a movement away from the belief in or at least the depiction of autonomous and effective people, away from agency. By the time Michel Foucault's work ascended to orthodoxy, explicitly valuing the human-as-actor in history was a distinctly balkanised and old-fashioned pursuit. For a key time, Foucault was undeniably the chief general in the agentless army of postmodernism, who was admired in many sub-disciplines of history in part just because he had already relegated individual agency and, more importantly, the individual, to a background position and he believed little in the psyche of his subjects. As Terry Eagleton noted, Foucault had a 'positivist distaste of interiority,' the supposed anchor of richly human agency.[9]

While Foucault's early and mid-career texts are deeply intelligent and almost brutally attractive, he gave very little sustained attention to any particular human. Foucault's are unpeopled landscapes. Rhetorically, this is a coup. Humanity suffers in his pages but the individual almost never does. It is telling in this respect that his most concentrated analysis of an individual in a classic like *Discipline and Punish* is of the condemned Damiens' body undergoing old regime punishment. The new world provides much less individuality and Damien has no humanity, save the little that came from corporal empathy, the community of imagined pain.[10]

Foucault does, however, frequently refer to the generic 'individual' and sometimes quite ominously. As he put it in *Discipline and Punish*, considering the origin of a society of individuals:

> The individual is no doubt the fictitious atom of an 'ideological' representation of society; but he is also a reality fabricated by the specific technology of power that I have called 'discipline' ... [P]ower produces; it produces reality; it produces domains

of objects and rituals of truth. The individual and the knowledge that may be gained of him belong to this production.[11]

The individual was an historical effect, not an essence, not a sort of atom from which the whole was composed. As a subject, this individual was a type, paradoxically not an individual at all: 'subjects are gradually, progressively, really and materially constituted through a multiplicity of organisms, forces, energies, materials, desires, thoughts.'[12]

Foucault alarmed and charmed readers into a strange sympathy with the non-individuals depicted, those constructed, typically nameless subjects, who seem all too like his readers, denizens of the structures of modernity. From the theoretical point of view, some considered Foucault potentially incoherent or in effect a pessimistic determinist. Both criticisms involved claims that the ability to resist and the possibility of directed change and of free human actions were drastically curtailed. The philosopher Charles Taylor was just one of the most prominent to doubt that Foucault had the intellectual warrant to deny a place to free action within his historical world.[13] But many historians were inspired by power and its slippery ways.

The extreme quality of Foucault's conception, coupled with topics that tended to focus on people who were typically thought vulnerable – the sick, the mentally ill, the criminal, but noticeably not women – stimulated a reaction to Foucault that did as much as anything else to revive a theory of effective historical agency. Theorists such as Nancy Fraser set up historians such as Carolyn Dean, Kathleen Canning, and Lyndal Roper to question the way that Foucault's work cut off the possibility for distinguishing power's culprits and beneficiaries from those who had suffered most at its hands.[14] Part of the problem was that, for Foucault, suffering at the hands of modernity was uniform: the poor didn't have it worse; women never got their moment. The other part was that the place for blame as for liberation had shrunk to almost nothing. Foucault's later works revealed a very different picture, but their influence was small and things had already started to change within the discipline.[15]

There were many strident voices who were effective in yelling down postmodernism but it is worth noting that their concern was often for the loss of human agency within the dominance of structure.[16] While there is something in Sarah Maza's claim in the mid 1990s that, 'The best historians have always shared [a] preoccupation with balancing structure and agency,' many historians were in fact less convinced of the importance of individual agency to begin with, and so striking the right balance had meant starting with structure, assuming modest agency, but only coming to examine it in depth when it was subaltern agency.[17] Still, many feminists didn't want to give up the historical possibility of female autonomy and so they became crucial to keeping the independent agent alive and resisting the claims of power/knowledge and discourse. So as it turned out, postmodernism was not the first but rather the last in a series of critiques of the individual's agency, and it was the one that finally catalysed a wider reaction.[18]

## TOWARDS A THEORY OF HISTORICAL AGENCY: THE STRUCTURE–SELF–DISCOURSE PROBLEM

Foucault was just a late part of those reflections that proved that our traditional ideas of human historical freedom beg questions. The lessons that crystallised in historiography with Foucault and haunted its perimeters with Derrida included the claims that the basis of the historical agent was the subject (perhaps the individual) and that that entity was not what it seemed, was not as durable or certain as both commonsense and theoretical perspectives supposed and as Descartes had laboured to prove.[19] The traditional individual's importance is very hard to credit if the self and subject are taken to be artificial constructs not

of a person's own making, if, in other words, you are something else's creature. Foucault doubted that the modern subject was in any sense an autonomous entity; Derrida suggested that the subject as typically understood was a creation of metaphysics that needed constant deconstruction, at best. In his cheeriest moments, he allowed that it was 'an incontrovertible fact' that 'there are subjects, "operations" or "effects" of subjectivity' – people, perhaps he meant – but the trouble came in thinking that there was stability or durability to them.[20]

As importantly, historians could forget that throughout the twentieth century their colleagues in philosophy and psychology had come to recognise the peculiar and surprising quality of the self. As much as doubting that persons were subjects, those disciplines started to doubt that persons were simple or atomistic. The psychoanalytic self was fundamentally divided and other tendencies in psychology have converged to stress the psyche's internal borders and the differential awareness 'we' have of our psychological contents. In philosophy, Derek Parfit criticised the importance of self-identity to personhood, by arguing that the crucial element was psychological continuity, not identity.[21] At present and beyond postmodernism, there is near consensus on the flexible, fluid and fragmentary qualities of whatever self there is and realization that the 'protean' self grapples with the world in order to know and make itself, a lesson best learned from the shrewdest and most careful theorist of the self, Paul Ricoeur.[22]

In total, this constitutes a very important orientation away from a merely subjective self towards a person understood as intersubjective, dependent on the world, on others, and therefore vulnerable to them in sometimes-intense ways. The mess of history is this complex of subjects and selves. At this pass, we see again the postmodern view looming, the opinion that the tangle of people cancels individual agency, that the subject is compromised and not the independent person at all. Some even argue that we may need to abandon notions of the individual, 'that wonderful, windowless monad,' as Elizabeth Ermarth has called it.[23] For Ermarth, as for Miguel Cabrera, it is the new, 'discursive condition' that compels this change rather than any yearning for the individual or the subject. I think, however, that the self remains irrepressible for our analysis of agency and the world, of self dealing with structure, of people coping in history.

At the start of one of the best considerations of this problem by a historian, (who might also be considered a sociologist), William Sewell considered the term 'structure' itself, noting that it 'empowers what it designates.'[24] It is revealing that social scientists have been happier with such a term (or entity) than they have been with 'individual.'[25] Helpfully, however, Sewell argues that structures should be thought of not as entities per se but patterns that repeat themselves at least until affected by an event, which potentially alters the pattern.[26]

Sewell's conception of historical agency illustrates a thoughtful, moderate position that many historians will recognise as theirs and one that links well with the practice of history, the noticing of what repeats and the excitement about the appearance of change. Sewell worked to cope with sociologist Anthony Giddens' influential but schematic account of agency. Within his theory of structuration, Giddens conceived of the individual's role as an essential and irreducible element in the social structure. This is in distinction to the view that sees the person as a sort of leftover in social and historical life, a place where people's actions matter only when they occur in a small nook – known as contingency – still ultimately structured by the larger partner of society, system, language, or whatever. In analysing revolutions, for instance, Rod Aya only slightly caricatures Theda Skocpol's influential social science theory, by remarking that:

> This theory ostensibly explains the events by structure (with an assist from culture) and explains change of structure by the events ... But it brings human agency back in to do the rough stuff. As

the explanation unfolds, structure constrains agency to make the events ... Agency is the Third Man between structure and event who does the killing and coercing.[27]

The implication is that in the normal, non-revolutionary course of events agency may be relatively quiescent. However, within the Sewell–Giddens frame, it is a constant function of social life, not the remainder.

According to Sewell, for instance, part of the meaning and role of structure is to make social action possible. He argues that 'Structures ... are sets of mutually sustaining schemas and resources that empower and constrain social action and that tend to be reproduced by that social action.'[28] Essential to social patterning is what Giddens calls the 'duality of structure,' which Sewell also embraced in recognition of the role individual people play in making history happen. The mechanisms of duality suggest hydraulic or biological imagery: people are part of the fluid in the system that provides the nutrients and the energy and the pressure to allow the system to exist. The element that is most productive, going well beyond Marx's idea of people's autonomy, is the recursive character of agency within structure. In other words, each element makes and changes the other, the individual pressed by the system but also changing that system by his or her action. Within a social framework, therefore, there was a theoretical basis for giving standing to the individual who would process and adjust the structural features of the world in order to make things happen, not just as a Third Man, but as a vital node in the vast network of society.

The social choices people made in this structuration approach are only part of its power, however. Giddens and Sewell both also lay considerable stress on knowledge, as in some moments Foucault also had, albeit with almost sinister intent. Sewell speaks of agency very much in terms of the use of social knowledge, knowledge of the structure in which the individual is embedded. Choice is based largely on knowledge. While such a stress could be taken too far, were we to define the actor solely as the knower, for instance, there is no question that the actor with information and inclination, however crude or unrefined, is a key part of historical doing. Getting the relevant knowledge right is a key part of an historian's understanding of action. On the continuum of structure and agent, Sewell and Giddens are a fair way along towards the agent side of the equation. They provide more latitude for an effective actor than Mead's social interactionism did.[29] Moreover, while the influential theory of Pierre Bourdieu also shares the similarity of factoring the individual agent into the mix, mediated by the *habitus*, in the final analysis Bourdieu's agent has little significant freedom.[30] For him, choice is a sham.

While it remains the case that for Sewell at least structure retains the upper hand over the agent, structure in his work came to have less to do with society and somewhat more to do with discourse. For many others too, structure would cease to mean society or the social and come to be the linguistic, symbolic, or discursive. However, this part of the linguistic turn did not necessarily demand surrendering agency. The agent or the subject might somehow remain active with a primarily logistic or verbal structure. Taking such lessons seriously, one could speculate that human agency might primarily become semantic agency, doing things with meanings. For some historians this was exciting, for others threatening a cut off from 'real' action, even the 'real' world.

In its freer moments, poststructuralism's actor or speaker might have occupied this position, as in Elizabeth Ermarth's variation, which has a strong sense of the Romantic self-fashioning self.[31] As productively, however, we might look at the historians who moved beyond the unsettling 'aporias' of postmodernity to try to make the linguistic turn pay its way, perhaps even creating a new paradigm. Miguel Cabrera has recently articulated such a view and laid out its pedigree from social and cultural history, giving it the rubric of *postsocial* history. It is characterised by a focus on discourse rather than society or culture

and the crucial feature of this aspect of the linguistic turn is the commitment to the way that the social world and socio-political history are causally dependent on discourse and language. Critically for our purposes, however, Cabrera identifies the postsocial – I would argue in contradiction to many brands of postmodernism – as committed to a productive and not merely ironic or critical agenda. Moreover, included in the postsocial historian's interests is situating an individual and his or her roles within discursive regimes that still allow people some autonomy.

While there are several important elements of Cabrera's summary of the state of play, we must focus on the nature of the actor and its context. Central perhaps is the claim that

> For postsocial history, it is not only that social practice is always inscribed in a particular discursive regime, but that the latter also operates as a real causal foundation ... Individuals assess or reproduce their living conditions or draw up their projects for the future always within a world – which includes themselves – that has been meaningfully constructed.[32]

Cabrera asserts that discourse itself established the conditions for action and the timbre of particular acts, but 'individuals do not use discourse as a means of action.'[33] This is to say that discourse is playing the role of structure here, of *discours*, **not** *parole*, and that this structural limit on what can be said or done, is not in any simple or direct sense controlled by the individual actor.

It is worth stressing the ways in which Cabrera goes beyond the postmodern rhetorical prejudices. He is in the first place quite unashamed to speak of individuals, but they must be understood as historically constructed subjects and it is the latter not the individual as natural kind, as barebones, that are the actors. Agency is 'a capacity they acquire when they are constituted as subjects.' This in and of itself does not promise a break from a Bourdieu-like mere semblance of free agency. What does, however, is Cabrera's appreciation that discursive categories provide an 'imaginary' through which individuals 'make a diagnosis of their place in the world and thus acquire the set of beliefs, intentions, feelings, passions, aspirations, hopes, frustrations or expectations that motivate, underlie, accompany, justify or confer sense on their actions.'[34] There is in this new history just enough room for the individual to act, but the springs of action are in the processing of discourse.[35]

Before accepting this summary, however, we need to doubt two things. First, the systemic nature of discourse: we might believe that people make discourse by the act of speech, rather than the opposite. In other words, structuration applies here too. Secondly, we should question the supposed relationship between language and reality, and consider demoting language a rank. Much theory supports the view that while we can describe almost everything in language, we don't create everything by our collective speech. There is much outside the text, but we might see language's limits most usefully by more directly examining our understanding of the agent.

## DEFINING THE AGENT: THE DOG AND THE HORSE

The historiographical and theoretical traditions friendliest to agency tend to start from the vast richness, intricacy and possibility of chatty and discursive human life, but I think this is an analytic error. We should not move too quickly towards the actor's greatest possibility, as we are very likely to lose our balance and make into norms what should be taken as historically specific characteristics, apt for particulars not for general claims. To some extent, this sort of error has been typical of theory of all sorts. Alasdair Macintyre has pointed out how distorting it can be in explaining how our ethical theories – long before Nietzsche – were anchored on a model of the strong, independent, fully resourced man, a real enough figure but not nearly so characteristic of human life – being at best only a phase of a lucky life of a particular sex – as might be supposed. The realities of disability and dependence, even happy, typical

dependence, become minimised.[36] Historians are perhaps particularly aware of the diversity of humanity as well as how the facts of the archive hide loquacity. Agency needs modelling from a minimal base and we might follow Macintyre in considering animal agency to set a foundation.

In 'Silver Blaze,' Conan Doyle's famous story, Sherlock Holmes is called in to investigate a homicide, for which a suspect has been arrested who looks to be guilty according to a variety of circumstantial evidence. Holmes surprises all by blaming the victim – the dead horse trainer. A key actor in the homicide is the valuable racehorse itself, but Holmes also builds important parts of his case on the famous 'curious incident of the dog in the night time.' This incident was that 'The dog did nothing in the night-time,' but he *ought* to have barked or attacked the intruder who took the horse according to the prevalent but wrong theory. This same dog had earlier been shown to be the sort one could set upon intruders, but he did nothing at this crucial moment because, the implication goes, he knew the night walker, who was the victim. *Did* the dog act?

The victim got by the dog easily enough, therefore, and as easily avoided the drugged stable boy. He took the racehorse away, intending to maim it surgically and mildly, the game being a gambling fix.

> Once in the hollow, he had got behind the horse and had struck a light; but the creature frightened at the sudden glare, and with the strange instinct of animals feeling that some mischief was intended, had lashed out, and the steel shoe had struck Straker full on the forehead.

The horse killed him. Did the horse act? Does instinct, the flow of habituated feeling, count as an action? It is at least an element common to all actors. Choosing with some knowledge of the situation, however, is what we expect. Thus, we cannot be sure how much Silver Blaze did what he did on purpose but the dog certainly understood the situation and acted appropriately.

Like the dolphins that Macintyre particularly investigates, horses and dogs are among the most intelligent animals, sociable and able to communicate beyond the minimum imaginable. They understand a good deal and indeed a good deal of language. Can they act? They certainly seem to be able to do so. You may train a dog to fetch a ball, but he won't always do so. He may be too tired, too excited, too suspicious to want to. Scientists have often worried about anthropomorphising animals, but while one can do that, it is a peculiar myopia that thinks that action would be limited to people. We could blame Descartes again, he who thought that animals were something like automata, lacking a soul and reason, but more importantly, horses and dogs, among others, choose and do and may enter history as such.[37] It is worth noting that my minimal conditions for acting don't require elaborate intentions. Soldiers firing their weapons under orders are acting, even those that don't much understand the army's collective goals, their own beyond that moment in time. While horses drawing artillery or carrying officers weren't trying to win the Battle of Waterloo, horses don't always do what their riders want; they can throw them off and flee or look for grass. The point is not exactly that animals are thus made actors; it's that human actions are often of this 'animal' sort and I don't want to rule out the ordinary. A horse at Waterloo is a little like a medieval apprentice blacksmith carrying water under orders. He could risk a hiding and run; he may not see the big picture, but he still acts.[38]

Animal actions can be contributing causes, as can gunpowder and galleons, but it would seem in familiar and plausible micro-situations like Conan Doyle's that the dog who didn't bark, like any sentinel who could have but didn't, contributed as an actor in an action-situation. Silver Blaze's homicidal kick would seem to be less certainly an action, even if it was part of an event of human importance. The horse was 'frightened' and we are not so inclined to admit mere fear and emotion as a proof of the presence of an actor, but then 'with the strange instinct of animals feeling that some mischief was intended', 'lashed out.' Much is hidden from the historian, but

the attribution of an instinct, which was in this case a mode of knowledge, is not unlike the attributions of perception or habit that historians often make. Conan Doyle is plainly uncertain about explaining why the horse struck someone he did know, but the horse may well have noticed or felt the strangeness of the entire nocturnal situation. As R.G. Collingwood supposed, the historian's job can be very much like the detective's. We collate our evidence with reasons and stories. The horse may have acted. The dog certainly was in an action situation.

Plainly, the Conan Doyle story comes in a fictional genre and a discursive package but it is a familiar and easily appreciated one. What it assumes about these animals is pretty much what we would still consider. The animals might act and they might understand some language but it would be very hard to claim that their actions were based on their discursive abilities. Even an exceptional dog will understand only some dozens of words, but he will understand many situations and many possibilities for doing within those situations. Oddly, dogs would appear to be part of language games, as Wittgenstein called these circumstances.[39] Horses certainly appreciate some human social situations too and react to words within contexts that are plainly not dependent solely or primarily upon the words themselves. Language in these cases is plainly part of the context of acting but is *not* constitutive of them. Our ability to provide an endless discursive fabric for all situations is not the same as supposing that language is required for understanding to take place. Be quiet with a domestic animal, no words uttered, and you'll get on just fine, so long as you act appropriately.[40] We are animals too. The historical actor, one supposes, need not be a linguistic animal nor a rational one, but it may be harder to imagine its not being an emotional one. Strangely, perhaps, the pursuit of historical agency has taken us towards the idea that it is not a simple subset of human agency. It is conceivable that historical agency embraces only certain sorts of human agency, a small amount of animal agency, and possibly other sorts of sentient causes that inhabit the borderlands between human and other.

## FROM ACTION TO AGENCY

Language can go all the way down touching and describing all that can be thought or perceived, but it needn't do so and we shouldn't forget that what writers and theorists prize is not what actors require. Agency can exist without the linguistic and it is probably the case that human beings can be actors without being powerfully enmeshed in linguistic schemes, which is not to say that they wouldn't be part of myriad language games and other cultural protocols, more or less discursive, at other moments. Agency need not emerge from or even with discourse or language, but in fact, historical agency usually does. Action most often occurs within a very rich situation in which a great number and variety of conditions and forces are at play, affecting the human beings involved. The thing about animals is that their agency is relatively simple, whether or not conditions, like involvement in a war, the Duke of Wellington's horse carrying him across the line of fire at Waterloo, make an animal's role crucial.[41] The thing about humans is that their actions are often complex, cooperative and self-conscious. Being cooperative and self-conscious tends to force them to have complex intentions. One wants to survive the battle, as well as support one's brothers-in-arms. A particular action taken – to kneel now and prepare to fire, notwithstanding the brave horses (and riders) apparently bearing down on you – may carry these intentions, these assumptions, as well as many others.

Since complexity is a key feature of most human and historical agency, few notions should be more appealing to historians than William Reddy's action situation. He works partly in a psychological tradition for which the individual remains absolutely central, but as with many strains of social scientific and humanistic thought, the actor is not a simple individual but a mass of thought activity embedded in a world of material and interpersonal possibilities. Crucially, 'the logic of action is serendipitous and combinative'[42] and 'even most unimportant decisions ... involve consideration of multiple factors and multiple effects.'[43] The place of verbalization, as of explanation, is somewhat curtailed by the situation itself, for we verbalise reasons best when we have departed from our normal action or when the decision was especially difficult. Even so, the tendency is for our statements to simplify or summarise what had mattered. This is of course part of why historians always care about what people *said* their reasons were for a past action but they rarely are content to leave it at that and not to pursue other avenues of explanation. Reddy's point, however, is to warn us against simplifying action situations through the habitual *action* of theorising, which is an abstracting and simplifying process. In any given moment of decision and action, there are a great number of factors to bear in mind, and humans, by all signs unlike horses, are aware of a staggering variety of them, albeit only some clearly.

The richness of action situations from an individual's point of view is crucial. Events are formed often enough out of a large mix of egocentric actions and deliberations. Collective action comes into it here – the similarity of action situations – but perhaps most crucially what helps to control the relevance of various factors that condition an action and are therefore relevant to the historian are the effects of *attention* and *emotion*. Reddy notes the extent to which cognitive psychology has analysed the complexity of attention – the focussed consciousness – and its need to give various factors their due in any circumstance. This is a sort of subconscious and unconscious and conscious all rolled into one, but it is also a world of somewhat conscious channel surfing for the mind. What is important about this analysis, I believe, is that we are near to the core chamber of structuration, the place where the modes and codes of the world grapple with life's plentiful predicaments. I use the term *world* here in something like its phenomenological sense, the range of meanings and concerns calling to the historical individual.

Examining the agent in this light turns the historian towards the fusion of emotion, information and decision. Emotion does not stand aside from deliberation but it keys it, provides impetus to establish what is important for that person, what he or she cannot but give attention to. By the same token, I would add that within this structurating process language, symbols, experience, know-how all are available to play their parts. It is no wonder that the human sciences, history included, are bewilderingly difficult. The inputs are vast and no one is in a position to be sure what was operative. Why did you unlock the side door to the house before going on vacation ? We typically have more than one answer, not just your fear of locking the dog-sitter out. Why didn't the dog bark? Holmes' story is only one theory. The available sources challenge historians to form plausible answers but specifying the relevant is a key part of the historian's account of agency.

The richness of action situations means that they can be teased apart, analysed in various ways, but to repeat, they don't require a single-focussed, utterly grounded subject at the base of this activity. If the theory of historical agency will do well to consider action situations and actions, it will do as well to ease itself towards the putative doers of actions. There are so many things to hand that in any given situation the supposed doer may indeed be too distracted, too fragmented, too unsure of what's what to deserve much independent credit as a cause. But, it is a self nevertheless, which is why agency must usually float on selves. Even, then, however, the *failure* to be much of an effective cause – an actor in the classic sense – still interests the historian, in part because the personal circumstances that lead to historical *inactivity* can be of some importance. This may be again for reasons of the non-barking dog sort. Someone should have attended to an emerging crisis but was distracted by his sleepiness, by a tempting dinner heating nearby, by his fears that she meant to betray him after all, or by his hopes that he

was only imagining an ominous clamour outside the door.

Inactivity interests us also because it relates as well to the counterfactual historical investigations that have in recent years reversed that little bit of methodological orthodoxy that warned historians of the futility of asking what if. 'What-if' questions at least test our understanding of the range of factors at work in an action situation and our guesses about the causal elements at play.[44] In addition, however, one person's inactivity is usually that same person's *activity* of the wrong sort for a given narrative or explanatory line. This recalls that Maréchal Grouchy, Napoleon's wandering general, was following the Emperor's orders when he missed the Battle of Waterloo. His actions and decisions rendered him inactive in the main story, however central he was in his own tale and however much his doing nothing explains the result at Waterloo. As we'll see, from the historian's point of view action usually occurs as part of a *narrative* context.

## THE SELF AS THE HISTORICAL AGENT

First, however, I should make clear that action points back to the actor, which is most often and interestingly a historical self. The Self is a capacious, less tendentious term than the much-criticised subject and that is part of the reason for its contemporary and historiographical usefulness. The sort of self possible in a given historical moment ought to be one of the crucial axes of almost all historical investigations. Not to do the work of describing historical selves is tantamount to yielding up the claim to be doing history.

We needn't demand too much from any given historical circumstance, but the self should usually be viewed as a highly localised site of awareness, often the clear vicinity of action, of deliberation, of meaning-making, and of suffering. Most sorts of historical explanation will need to be more or less aware of the nature of selves at a particular historical moment and what aspects of their situation they are likely to give the most attention and the most emotional commitment.[45] An under-conceived notion of the self may be said to be a major flaw within many brands of history, very notably social, cultural and economic histories.

As an actor, the self we have been describing is functionally a series of concurrent processes within a variety of action situations. In other words, there is always a lot going on with a self, only some of which the historian can pursue, but history is in part working out the dynamism of areas of action. Agency is almost the essence of history and more of the reason is now apparent: actions engage selves in the effort through time, in the attempt, sometimes long planned and strenuously imagined, of bringing something else into existence and so connecting one time to another by generating that little differential of change that is the true marker of historical time. This is the difference that matters most to historians. People doing often means intending and plotting and at the least means *semantic agency*, the doing or suffering that transforms meanings, even by a little, and therefore changes the individual and the people around. Semantic agency is *cognitive* change and to be a person is to operate in this domain.

As a radical first step, historians must be aware that there may be moments of real difference, in which it may not be right to say that a culture has selves at all. The second and more common move, however, will be to qualify and perhaps even quantify these modes of agency. For historians, special significance should attach to the *social self*. This concept has the appeal of a certain naturalness in academic discourse, since one knows immediately what it might mean, but below I try to develop it in a specific direction so that it maintains within it the recursive qualities of structuration, the in-and-out of social processes that must go *through* the semantic agency of the individual. Agency works not through atomistic individuals, but through social selves. Analysing these lays the stress on finding out how the self works *with* other selves and especially *in* social interaction, which unquestionably provides much of an individual's identity and the framework of interests and values in which agency takes place and that will affect particular action situations.

The social self is useful in overcoming historians' tendencies to focus either on an individual and his or her ideas or on a particular aspect of a social class and social circumstance. The social self reminds us that we must, in the final analysis, mix the self with a world and its action situations in order to understand the constraints and significance of action.

While no term of analysis, self or society included, should be considered ahistorical and useful for all historical situations, the social self can take us through a great variety of historical circumstances. It may have special utility in examining the pre-modern world or the contemporary non-Western world or worlds that possess thinner access to individual selves. To focus on what it might do best, we should look to its possibilities in the domain of social history, or now postsocial history, the world of people difficult to know in detail. Let us consider very abstractly the problem of religion during the English Reformation period. To determine the agency of a given individual with respect to religious choice is not only to determine whether or not he or she chose the radical action, for instance, of joining the Pilgrimage of Grace – a rebellion against Henry VIII in 1536 – perhaps as a statement of his or her anger over the Protestant changes in religion.[46] Following a specific individual through a life to that choice would include this sort of analysis, but often we would be sketching the contexts that that *type* of person would face. This act of rebellion would be explored in a specific milieu, bounded at least by geography and propinquity, i.e. the physical fact of people being together, then extended carefully to cultural propinquity, the fact of their having converse together by direct knowledge of each other or by the assimilation of selves through common knowledge. Geography and knowledge may not seem to be the usual starting points for social history but once we realise that mere class markers rarely tell us enough in order to understand a person's role, it is incumbent on historians to build up the actual social groupings that were at play. These are unlikely to represent unities, i.e. groups of people who acted identically, but they represent semantic milieux, zones in which the possibility of a particular action, i.e. a social or political action situation, is likely to be shared and in which, therefore, a similar problem or question is likely to be faced.

Knowing the social self means knowing the background socio-ethical assumptions for actions. The social context must be joined to the context of probable ideas and memories that people had and along which lines they might have acted or reacted. To pursue the example of the Pilgrimage of Grace, for instance, we would need to define the background political and religious assumptions. Often when dealing with a preindustrial world, this question will have to take the form, what is the sort of thing that these people knew was relevant, what hermeneutical framework shaped their reception of recent events and new ideas? Plainly, something like cultural history can be of the first importance here, but our understanding must be built as well on the deep and general mental assumptions of that historical world. It turns out that to understand social selves we need to understand what was 'in their minds' and therefore the particular historical circumstance and its concrete social conditions will determine what was possible. To this extent, the methodology of the social self may sometimes have the character of the linkage between conceptual history and social history that Reinhart Koselleck sought.[47]

It is, however, incumbent on historians to make sure that the assumptions they raise were actually available in that historical world. The difference between this approach and typical postmodern approaches is that there is no assumption here that the input is monolithic or even hegemonic even if it is much repeated and typically provides the platform for current elaboration and future reactions. Specifying

within any moment the relevant ideas and issues is of course one of the most challenging of historical problems. Some things are made explicit, but others are sometimes opaque, as indeed Catholicism itself might be in the run-up to the Pilgrimage of Grace, if only because State power had proscribed it. Social assumptions will be paramount to understanding rebelliousness at any point in history. We know rebellion is an option, but did *they* think it was? What was needed to justify such a radical action is always a crucial question.

The Pilgrimage of Grace failed and the government was lenient with those who had risen. Were we pursuing the social self of the pardoned rebels at that point, we might wonder whether people's social positions explained their participation or attitude towards the rebellion as much as their ideas did. As usual, the relative failure of class analysis forces us to sub-class interrogations and small group interactions, the places where actors actually are. Linking the small group and the social network to larger events will often be frustrating, but a key aspect of the social self is to see that how people decide to act on the historical questions that present themselves is bound up with their small-scale social location, with what Giddens calls 'the routines of day-to-day life.'[48] For any given action situation, we really need to know how people were knit together. One of the questions of thought we need to unravel, therefore, is what importance did people attribute to a particular social link. It is one thing to establish that each of us is part of a social network running through the mail carrier, for instance, another to claim that this is a sufficient proof that we are a politically active group or that the mail carrier is our leader. The priest or the magistrate of the sixteenth century, however, deserves just such prejudice. He may be a network leader and a word or action from him might first raise the question of rebellion and tend to persuade some people, one way or the other, that the cause or time was right. Thus, we need to establish the latent power of interactions and relationships and be sensitive to the fact that social networks can be crucial to possible and actual chains of action.

Such a possibility, however, will develop more readily into an actuality if that social network was already sufficiently established to create a group identity for some of its members. Social history has proved repeatedly that some people will still go their own way, so the task is again only determining the questions a person is *most likely* to face in trying to make a decision, if things come to a head. The action situation, however, can be understood without our necessarily being able to explain the minutiae of the particular decision itself. Sources sometimes fail us, especially in remote times, but it is an advantage of the model that it can still produce a plausible general account through the linkage of cultural matter and specific social circumstances. The social self can be sketched generally and held as part of the context of the sorts of action situations through which the Pilgrimage of Grace came into being and disappeared.

Actions, even events, and their 'causal' decisions are often arbitrary enough, especially from the point of view of one person, one village, one anything. The consequences of actions can of course be immense, but the place of action's greatest consequence may well be around the self, which goes on perhaps a little, perhaps a lot, differently after events, more than in the midst of them, that moment when a person is more like horse than we might like to suppose. That is to say, when a person's reasons may be as opaque as his actions were clear, when he may be an agent rather more like a horse at Waterloo. Afterwards, however, and unlike the horse, people may interpret their experiences and change themselves. Semantic agency, even narrative agency, as often must look backward as forward. Moving through time and experience, selves change and change the ground for their next actions by interpretation and habituation, by scarring.

As I've described it before,[49] the social self is part of the social historian's remedy for certain typical weaknesses in the evidence.

One can work the social self up even when archives don't really support nuanced examination of a full individual self – pre-modern histories around the world, extending in some historiographies to the present time. But in fact, the social self ought to be present even when records are sufficiently rich and it may be thought the failure of many a biography to go it alone with their subjects, taking them sometimes too seriously, whether at face value or as an effect of the narrowest of contexts, the buried self and the family. Yet, all these things – deep self and family romances – might matter greatly and it is here perhaps that the psychological and experiential claims most obviously deserve their due, as we seem to drill down from general social idea and specific social circumstance to the ego, even the private self. What is necessary, however, is that no self should be treated as an atom or an island. Social or psychological atomism is probably the real bane of theorising the self, as much as the related notion of the subject.[50] Selves are necessarily social selves, infused with language, social relations and symbol systems as well as bound up in bodies. But selves are also transformative on their own: they change themselves (and sometimes others) by semantic agency and the narrative of experience and meaning that gives selves their vaunted but tenuous continuity.[51]

## EXPERIENCING THE SELF

Semantic and reflective agency produces density of self. One of the crucial differences between a horse and a person is the density of the agency involved. Density through time is a perhaps strange way to measure a historical self and actor, but it does speak of the quality and quantity of will, the psychic thrust into the world of doing, that historians have to assess in an acting person. It doesn't at this level explain the total psychology so much as the motivation and drive behind action. Such density across time takes us back to questions of how to account for the impact of an actor within an action situation and the pressure upon an actor. This is an area where the concept of experience is relevant.

Historians have been suspicious of experience for nearly 20 years, but it deserves revival since it is a sort of synonym for the accumulated density of a self: some social selves are bigger than others; everyone's personhood is distinctively shaped by his or her particular past, the experienced past. After the eightieth hearing, we start to understand how to use the word aporia. After a couple of strolls down the bridle path, we learn to avoid the puddle that is deeper than it looks. We may eventually become bored with both these activities and look for greener and more level pastures, verbal or herbal. Part of the nature of a human actor is the myriad ways that experience shapes the person and the ways that experiences are themselves complex. Past action situations determine some and only some of the action situations of the future, including the amount of attention they might require, the amount of emotion they generate. This sort of experience is slightly different, slightly anterior, to that famously criticised by Joan Scott. She was warning against a willingness to give first-person *claims* from experience special epistemological status, including the power to trump some discussions and to obstruct others, especially that of discourse. She worried that: 'Questions about the constructed nature of experience, about how subjects are constituted as different in the first place, about how one's vision is structured – about language (or discourse) and history – are left aside.'[52] This may be true, but is hardly an argument against caring about experience, especially if one sees discourse as but one player within a historical complexity, one which doesn't exist except as it works through people and their reiterative and generative use of language. We might say that discourse is partly produced and wholly sustained by experience, by the situated selves who use it. This is especially clear if we lean on an idea of experience as having an 'active, inquisitive dimension,' an old idea but still alive in our sense of seeking experiences that are adventurous.[53] Even in Scott's

formulation, the 'problem' is with overvaluing the *account* of experience and assuming that experience is simply felt and simply reported.

There have been other concerns about experience from scholars who unlike Scott are trying to understand what we could call self-centred agency. Jay Smith worries that, 'connecting experience to action actually obscures the fundamental cognitive processes that lie behind political choice.'[54] Smith sees the difficulty in the fact that recourse to experience often implies the separation between it and thought, whereas what is needed is a full integration. Thus, he sees that experience as a concept may well rely on the distinction that Scott also authorises, between words and world, between structures and emotions. To move behind this postmodern-antipostmodern antithesis, Smith argues that if one examines particular cases, one can demonstrate the inadequacy of relying on either an emotional formulation based on experience alone or a model of discursive dominance. Rather, he suggests it will be necessary to go back to specific human consciousness and to ideas and beliefs. This is a trajectory that links back to the social self insofar as the ideas and assumptions of consciousness are not the preserve of intellectuals and can be found in the evidence of socio-cultural life, but insists they need to be found in order to understand things like political action.[55]

There is plainly a risk in systematically separating and valorising either the emotional or the intellectual.[56] Yet, as we have argued in this chapter, an understanding of action requires an appreciation of the intersection of emotions and beliefs, language and self. It is not necessary to understand the concept of experience as a binary term, an ally or synonym for feeling-in-action.

As Martin Jay has recently reminded us, in the thought of a key figure like Dilthey, 'Experience is knowledge on the basis of perception' and it comes to fruition in meaning and through concepts that are necessarily about the world.[57] Moreover, as Derrida put it: '"Experience" has always designated the relationship with a presence.'[58] There is no experience conceivable without change, outside time, or with only one thing. In other words, to conceive of anything to which the term experience can apply is to find that there is diversity, time, and indeed difference of some sort. In a way, Ricoeur's sense that the way to the self was through the other is recapitulated in the notion that experience exists only where there is a conscious bit, maybe a bit of self, and something *else*, something else that is at least open to examination and not only by that individual person.

Experience deserves some reconsideration by those interested in agency because it plays a dynamic role in the making of the self. As Fionola Meredith says:

> If we reintroduce the category of experience conceived as process, as the continual weaving of the cord which connects consciousness (in the form of values, feelings, intuitions, desires and so on) to a world which is forever 'incorrigibly plural ... and more of it than we think' we overcome the stasis endemic to all structuralisms.[59]

Such experience is that of the variable self upon which theorists and historians have tended to converge. In practice, however, it suggests that historians need to seek out the effects of experience upon an agent. By this I mean that experience amounts to the conditioning and transformative effects of the world upon an individual. Those effects may be shaped discursively, but they may also arrive and be represented in discursively opaque or crude shapes as well – Scott's concern. Experience tends to condition subsequent reactions and this means of course that what has happened before tends to affect what can follow. Presumably, one of the special qualities of good equine warriors was the ability to perform boldly and better, even after first facing the sensory attack of battle. This sort of experience probably cannot be reduced to belief, even if it can perhaps be translated, as Jay Smith might like, into terms of consciousness. Events and actions in their contexts constitute the experiences that condition selves and one of the key factors in allowing historians usefully to differentiate one actor or sort of actor from another will be giving due weight to *processed experience*, which needn't be subservient to first-person accounts. Bourdieu's *habitus* is embodied experience.

While social history may have failed in showing that social position determines, social position that is inflected by experience and factored through a particular social self and psychological channel will start to give a much richer picture by which to understand agency. This experiencing person is always in the midst of events and reactions thereto. Bodily experiencing work or war, touching and seeing, are the natural cocoons of actions. Often enough they will be accompanied by related speech acts but shouldn't be reduced to language or assumed to exist only where there is the language for the job. Action, as we have already seen, doesn't require language, even human action. Experience points at least a little to the non-linguistic, maybe physical, possibly deeply psychological. As such, it points as well to the possible significance of *presence* as the non-linguistic. Taking the non-verbal seriously as a mode of facing human action may well be very important in working out the freedom of the many for whom words were not so highly valued as they are today. But it might be wisest and safest to look to see that the presence that the historian can be most sure of is akin to Heidegger's 'readiness-to-hand' and that would suggest that historians take material culture seriously as an important part of the self's framework. In other words, self-fashioning and the exercise of the self often work through active or passive engagement with places and things. In fact, one suspects that much of the undertheorised interest in material culture in recent years grows from the intuition of the ways that this domain bears on the self, social or otherwise. This is the presence we can be sure of. Experience is about the acting body and the things of the world as much as the word and discourse.

## NARRATIVE AND PERSPECTIVE

If I am suggesting that some elements of experience and presence might be developed by historians to enhance their understanding of agency, partly as a counter to their professional prejudice in favour of the word and the story, this is only to set up a conclusion on the most broadly validated topic and tool for understanding historical agency: narrative. We cannot look to Silver Blaze here because language in its narrative form remains an exclusive marker of human selfhood and agency and a characteristically powerful feature of action and its analysis; no other animal tells stories. Since the topic has been treated all over the humanities and psychology, I will concentrate on only a couple of issues, especially questions about the seams constructed or ripped out between one story and another, tales sometimes within one person, sometimes across cultures, sometimes between historians now and actors then.

Narrative has often been a central means for conceiving of human action among philosophers, psychologists, literary scholars of all stripes, but it is practicing historians who rely on making narratives. Their theorists, however, have more often used narrative to show the manner by which the historian-as-creator fashions, construes or otherwise makes up the meaning of historical evidence. Prominent has been the place of the writer of history rather than the agents within it. This point of view, in effect re-founded by Hayden White 35 years ago, provided an important plank in the vessel of constructivist thought that surrounded historical and other literary studies.[60] Louis Mink, however, was at the same time stressing the special status of holistic thinking or 'comprehension' generally and saw that narrative might be a central mode of comprehension for people, irreducible to other ways of representing.[61] On this theoretical foundation, much can be built, even if for many scholars such narrative understanding blurs with White's slightly thinner conception.

Yet, the focus of narrative now needs to be on what it reveals about the acting and suffering self. In this respect, narrative for historians of agency may be thought of as learning to use the stories that historical selves told and were told and the role that such telling plays in deliberating and doing. In other words, their stories, not ours. All the elements we have discussed – social selves and experience, language and materiality – wash through the channels of the self and may be told as tales. Lives might even come to have a narrative substance.[62] As Nancy Partner summed it up: 'We will persist in telling our stories.'[63] Must we, must everyone? Mark Johnson thinks so and claims, 'There exists an intimate connection between life stories and the structures of rationality. These stories are our most basic contact with rational explanation.'[64] Robustly stated, such narrative is neither an option nor an ornament for the selves in the past, but a cognitive means by which they made sense of the social world and their place in it, as well as of the particular actions they took or planned to take. The narratives are part of the contents of history, something historians need to find in order to do the best job at representing past agents.

This isn't easy to do, even where evidence is favourable. Agents are unstable. All that we have suggested about the inchoate and fragmentary quality of the self and of experience tells us that stories are in various ways works of art and artifice and accident. They may multiply prolifically, even within one person. The fullest stories people might tell do become like histories, heavily thought out, understandably rationalising and potentially ever distant from the earliest presentation. The early and later version of a story reveal much about someone but not all. The Waterloo despatch and Wellington's later claims don't always agree. Cortes never mentions his terrifying dogs, which other sources suggested affected the Aztecs. Whatever narratives are provided by the past through evidence, it will still be the historian's job to assess them and put them to the question, where necessary.[65]

For the purposes of understanding agency, the historian brings hermeneutic and forensic criticism to bear upon the narratives and narrative structures of the past.

Even if narrative is taken to be tantamount to a cognitive universal, its role in particular historical situations will be vastly different. Medieval historians had a long, now old discussion of individualism, mainly eager to prove that the Middle Ages created it and it was not a renaissance achievement. In looking back at that debate, we can see it was partly asking how people told stories about themselves then, how often and in what terms?[66] Such questions are about the way that beliefs, stories and ideas shape selves and thus determine meaning and action. Did they make a narrative when people in another place and time would make a prayer or do a dance? Did it seem like an option for them, a choice to use narrative about themselves as opposed to a requirement to? Cultures differ, individuals differ, and one of the tasks for historians is to mark the standing of narratives of self-explanation and their milieux within any particular historical person's context. If we believe with many philosophers that a particular sort of ethics develops upon particular narrative resources, then establishing the importance of such things historically is crucial. We may even say that alongside other concepts of the social self, the propensity to narrative for moral understanding ought to be constantly investigated.

Even if the stories people tell vary by their sense of context and their training, they still may not reveal the individual actor so much as a general social identity or merely elements of a particular sort of action situation. The psychologist Dan P. McAdams does 'not believe that we learn much about ourselves by discovering that we are of a certain "type"' and therefore seeks the individual element within personal narratives of identity. Historians, however, may often find themselves unable to find material suitable to sketch a personal myth, in which case the typological, calibrated to the evidence, may still be a useful means of delineating a social self.[67]

Indeed, historians often do not want or need to study individuals as such but just as types and exemplars. Where history is about the typical, it may have recourse to the typological narrative as a guide to past minds in action.

Developing narrative for psychological, moral, military or other deliberative purposes is a skill as much as an effusion of self. Those taught to have narratives of self-understanding will find their considerations in their action situations seriously divergent from people for whom language is less associated with doing. If virtue must be taught and cultivated before it can be knowingly acted upon, the same goes for the sort of narrative that is its historical accompaniment.[68] For some cultures, there will be other modes. In some respects, historians have tended to make too much of selves like Augustine and Abelard who speak so well to us that they obscure what it meant to their contemporaries. If psychologists have recently discovered that those with great experience of managing and making narratives are best at integrating difficult matters like psychotherapy into their personal narratives, we should also expect that those with few narrative skills will operate very differently. We should expect and explore the different selves that are achieved depending on the prevalence of narrative and its valuation within a historical culture or sub-culture.[69]

The people of the past, the cultures of the past, and present historians all have their narrative imperatives and they combine to bring us to one of the most challenging questions: To what extent does the historical self's own narration have historical priority? This would not be a problem in considering animal agency, although whether the historian has an obligation to giving priority to the perspective of the actor would revive that question. Allowing that it is common enough for people to have stories and understandings to tell about themselves, is finding these stories out and depicting the self understanding of the past the crucial goal of history? Is priority to be given to the semantic or hermeneutical agency of the past, i.e. people's own accounts of their doings? There cannot be a simple answer of course but the question that has been strikingly raised by Brad Gregory and others is: What did it mean to them?[70] Is the crux of the revival of agency to give this question its due, so that the people of the past are not reduced merely to objects of history, mere gears in the machine, or suffering nodes of time? This is close to what Joan Scott worried about, namely, that this perspective would dominate historical analysis. But, as Gregory argues, in some situations we shall be unable to get a convincing story for ourselves if we do not take seriously the self-accounts of the past and their semantic evidence. The Pilgrimage of Grace was at least partly a matter of the self-image of the agents as Catholic loyalists and one needs to know that to understand their actions.

The special hermeneutic problem of the self and agency, therefore, is how the historian and reader negotiate the space between our current ideas and theirs. Gregory's kernel question: 'what did it mean to them?' presses forward and if we also adopt Charles Taylor's view that human agents are 'self-interpreting animals,' able to reflect on their goals and values and history as they make their plans for the future, we see that the challenge is a steep one.[71] In considering agency finally, we are facing at some level the fiction of other human beings, the dead perhaps, but still the human. Do we give their narratives, their meanings, and their words priority in understanding their actions? Do we do it just because we would like to be so treated ourselves? Can we do it critically? The answer to all these questions is, I think, yes. It is possible to try, in the way of continuities, to connect our conceptions to theirs, but one may with equal justification approach their agency from a perspective less involved with our own current conceptions just because the gaps are too large or uncomfortable and might be thought to distort what we can know about the past. Thus, even if the story of the past is a function of the present, because meaning is always in the present, it must be recognised that that present has the intellectual resources to hold aspects of today in abeyance while

we ask about the past, not on our own terms, but in conscious dialogue with *their* terms.[72]

With this approach, we can expect to produce interpretive narratives that can absorb the past's strangeness, its difference from us and other pasts, with due empathy. In all important matters, the present and past may well have seriously divergent views about agency or morality. The nature of the world is such that the past must make itself known through the actions – typically thinking and writing and reading, but also often viewing as in art or film – of the historical interpreter. The historian is the skilled interpreter and it is incumbent on him or her to face self consciously the question of the place and role of his or her own assumptions about agency. The problem is more acute in studying agency than elsewhere because in analysing it an admirable empathy bumps up against hard-headed explanation or hard-hearted ethical critique. Giving the past's people and stories their due is to give them their hearing, but we can never assume they deserve the last word.

Given this general posture of conscientiousness, the historian will still inevitably approach the historical agent and historical actions from one or another perspective and level of analysis. In some cases, these assumptions will move actions very near to the status of events, in which issues of the self are very likely to be peripheral or irrelevant. Certain forms of historiography, for instance world history or environmental history, are these days quite likely to take up agency from a high-level perspective in which selves matter less because the difference among selves is less likely to yield refinement in analysis. This is different, by the way, from the systematic poststructuralism from which we started. Arguably, that movement just omitted the self even where it is easy to imagine that knowing more about it would have changed our understanding of the incident. Somehow, to know more about Damien the regicide might indeed have altered the meaning of Foucault's *Discipline and Punish*. Both postures are matters of historiographical agency but they are not both determined merely by decision or prejudices about the scale of history.

The civil hearing of the agents of the past, the people, is part of what makes us turn so many events into actions and actions into matters that will be illuminated by knowing historical selves better. We could resist this sort of turn, but we should never do so casually or automatically. Historians now, regardless of topic or era, should always ask after the agent, imagining the selves that acted, the world those selves worked on, their semantic and practical agency, managing and manipulating culture and matter around them. Caring about what it meant to people, their high values and small desires both, is the only way to understand why people did what they did and so why history came out as it did, felt as it did, and was told and remembered as it was. Animals may act and do so in history, but to *read* and *write* and *exist* historically, to act historically, is pure human.

# NOTES AND REFERENCES

1  Thomas Sewell, *The Logics of History* (Chicago: The University of Chicago Press, 2005), 124.
2  To this extent, we see how agency and causation start to part company.
3  Thomas Carlyle, *On Heroes and Hero-worship and the Heroic in History* (BiblioBazaar: Charleston, South Carolina, 2007, orig. 1841), 11.
4  Henry French with Jonathan Barry, *Identity and Agency*, 'Introduction,' 1–4.
5  See Christopher Hill, *God's Englishman: Oliver Cromwell and the English Revolution* (Dial Books: New York, 1970); *A Tinker and a Poor Man: John Bunyan and His Church* (Knopf: New York, 1989); *Milton and the English Revolution* (Viking: New York, 1978).
6  Miguel Cabrera, *Postsocial History* (Lexington Books: Lanham, MD, 2004), 2.
7  E.P. Thompson, *Customs in Common* (New York, 1993), 8–15; and French, *Identity and Agency*, 4–13.
8  William Bouwsma, 'From history of ideas to history of meaning,' *Journal of Interdisciplinary History* 12, 'The new history: The 1980s and Beyond (II)' (Autumn, 1981), pp. 279–91; John E. Toews, 'Intellectual history after the linguistic turn: the autonomy of meaning and the irreducibility of experience,' *American Historical Review* 92 (1987): 879–907; see Dominick LaCapra, 'History, language and reading: waiting for Crillon,' in *History and Theory: Contemporary Readings*, ed. Brian Fay, Philip

Pomper, and Richard T. Vann (Malden, Mass.: Blackwell, 1998), 90–118.
9  Terry Eagleton, 'Self-undoing subjects,' in Roy Porter, ed., *Rewriting the Self: Histories from the Renaissance to the Present* (Routledge: London 1997), 265.
10  Michel Foucault, *Discipline and Punish: The Birth of the Prison*, tr. Alan Sheridan (Vintage: New York, 1979), 3–7.
11  *Discipline and Punish*, 194.
12  Michel Foucault, 'Two lectures,' in *Power/Knowledge: Selected Interviews and Other Writings, 1972–1977*, ed. Colin Gordon (New York: Pantheon, 1980), 97.
13  Charles Taylor, 'Foucault on freedom and truth,' in *Philosophy and the Human Sciences* (Cambridge University Press: Cambridge, 1985), 152–84.
14  These scholars had very different things to say but agency was explicitly on their minds: see Carolyn J. Dean, 'The productive hypothesis: Foucault, Gender, and the history of sexuality,' *History and Theory*, Vol. 33, No. 3. (1994), 271–96; Kathleen Canning, 'Feminist history after the linguistic turn: historicizing discourse and experience,' *Signs* 19 (1994): 368–404.
15  His effect upon the study of sex and sexuality is thoughtfully and critically assessed by Dean, 'Productive hypothesis.'
16  Keith Windschuttle, *The Killing of History: How Literary Critics and Social Theorists are Murdering our Past* (New York: Basic Books, 1996); Joyce Appleby, Lynn Hunt, and Margaret Jacob, *Telling the Truth about History* (New York: Norton, 1994). The defence of a theory of truth was certainly the anchor of reaction and the connection between truth and agency is often reached via complex links through theories of language.
17  Sarah Maza, 'Stories in history: cultural narratives in recent works in European history,' *The American Historical Review* 101, (1996): 1501. Compare the account of Miguel Cabrera, *Postsocial History*, 1–18.
18  The slow emergence of Actor Network Theory within historical studies might be adding another piece to this development. For the approach, see John Law and Michel Callon, "After the Individual in Society: Lessons in Collectivity from Science, Technology and Society," *Canadian Journal of Sociology* 22 (1997), 165-82; John Law and John Hassard (eds), *Actor Network Theory and After* (Oxford: Blackwell, 1999); and Bruno Latour, *Reassembling the Social. An Introduction to Actor Network Theory* (Oxford University Press: Oxford, 2007). I thank Laura Stark for alerting me to the importance of this approach or ontology in sociology and science studies.
19  As Ethan Kleinberg has recently made clear, Derrida's impact on historiography was a very peculiar one, since Derrida was apparently rarely read or understood. See 'Haunting history: deconstruction and the spirit of revision,' *History and Theory* 46 (2007): 113–43; see also Gabrielle Spiegel, *The Past as Text* (Baltimore: Johns Hopkins University Press, 1997), 29–43; and Spiegel, 'Revising the past / revisiting the present: how change happens in historiography,' *History and Theory* 46 (2007): 1–19.

20 In choosing to cite Derrida's words from an interview, I realize that I run the risk of allowing his remarks to misrepresent his work, but the directness of his words are in this respect irresistible: Richard Kearney, 'Deconstruction and the Other,' in *States of Mind: Dialogues with Contemporary Thinkers* (New York University: New York, 1995), 175. The interview was in 1981.

21 Derek Parfit, *Reasons and Persons* (Oxford, 1984), 219–44.

22 His fullest engagement with Freud is *Freud and Philosophy: An Essay on Interpretation*, tr. Denis Savage (Yale University Press: New Haven, 1970); and the masterful *Oneself as Another* (University of Chicago Press: Chicago, 1992, orig. 1990), which deserves more consideration than I am able to give it here.

23 Elizabeth Deeds Ermarth, 'Agency in the discursive position,' *History and Theory* 40 (2001): 44.

24 Sewell, *Logics of History*, 124.

25 There has been something of an over-reaction against methodological individualism, the one fully atomistic school of social theory, and in favour of the large concepts of structure or culture or language. For the sociological side of things, see James S. Coleman, *Foundations of Social Theory* (Cambridge, Mass.: Harvard University Press, 1990), 1–23.

26 Sewell, *Logics of History*, 218–19.

27 Rod Aya, 'The third man; or, agency in history; or, rationality in revolution,' *History and Theory* 40 (2001): 144.

28 Sewell, *Logics of History*, 143.

29 A useful survey of the issue in social science is Caroline B. Brettall, 'The individual/agent and culture/structure in the history of the social sciences,' *Social Science History* 26 (2002): 429–45.

30 See Pierre Bourdieu, *Outline of a Theory of Practice*, tr. Richard Nice (Cambridge University Press: Cambridge, UK, 1977, orig. 1972); *The Logic of Practice*, tr. Richard Nice (Stanford University Press: Stanford, 1990, orig. 1980); and the critique by Judith Butler, *Excitable Speech. A Politics of the Performative* (Routledge: New York and London, 1997), 142–8.

31 Ermarth, 'Agency in the discursive condition.'

32 Cabrera, *Postsocial History*, 98–9. I have put my own spin on this sort of embedded agency in *Necessary Conjunctions: The Social Self in Medieval England* (Palgrave-Macmillan: New York, 2005).

33 Cabrera, *Postsocial History*, 99. He draws here as well on the work of Keith Baker, one of the intellectual historians who rose most quickly to the challenge of the linguistic turn. See, for instance, Baker's, *Inventing the French Revolution: Essays on French Political Culture* (Cambridge: Cambridge University Press, 1990).

34 Cabrera, *Postsocial History*, 97–8.

35 For Cabrera, the centrality and virtual autonomy of the discursive is the major point at issue, upon which he argues against Sewell; agency is clearly a secondary issue.

36 Alasdair Macintyre, *Dependent Rational Animals* (Duckworth: London, 1999).

37 Miguel Leon-Portillo, ed., *The Broken Spears. The Aztec Account of the Conquest of Mexico* (Beacon Press: Boston, 1992), 30 and passim.

38 This is probably contentious and deserves more extended treatment. In essence, the distinctive part of human agency consists in its self and its self-understanding. It is not action that makes humans distinct; it is reflection through a self and interpreting action.

39 Wittgenstein made use of animal analogies, famously in *Philosophical Investigations*, tr. G.E.M. Anscombe (Oxford: Basil Blackwell, 1958), 25: 'It is sometimes said that animals do not talk because they lack the mental capacity. And this means: "they do not think, and that is why they do not talk." But – they simply do not talk. Or to put it better: they do not use language – if we except the most primitive forms of language. Commanding, questioning, recounting, chatting, are as much a part of our natural history as walking, eating, drinking, playing.'

40 Of course, domestic animals used to living with us probably expect and respond to many verbal cues, but if we imagine a cat here rather than a dog, the point should be clear.

41 Wellington said of his horse Copenhagen, 'There may have been many faster horses, no doubt many handsomer, but for bottom and endurance I never saw his fellow.' Christopher Hibbert, *Wellington: A Personal History* (HarperCollins: London, 1997), 65.

42 William Reddy, 'The logic of action,' *History and Theory* 40 (2001): 12. See also his *Navigation of Feeling. A Framework for the History of Emotions* (Cambridge: Cambridge University Press, 2001).

43 Reddy, 'Logic of Action,' 13.

44 See Johannes Bulhof, 'What if? Modality and history,' *History and Theory* 38 (1999), 145–68; Niall Ferguson, ed., *Virtual History* (London, 1997). The relation between agency and the logic and utility of what-if questions is, I suspect, closely related and worth further attention.

45 This may be related to Karsten Stueber's view that 'empathy' ought or does play a large role in the historian's consideration of past human beings. See 'Reasons, generalizations, empathy and narratives: the epistemic structure of narrative explanations,' *History and Theory* 47 (2008): 35–40.

46 There were many other reasons that might have encouraged support for the rebellion, but suppose this is the one that our actor had bouncing around his mind most often. See M.L. Bush, 'The Tudor polity and the Pilgrimage of Grace,' *Historical Research* 80 (2007): 47–72; R.W. Hoyle, *The Pilgrimage of Grace and the Politics of the 1530s* (Oxford University Press: Oxford, 2001); and C.S.L. David, 'Popular religion and the Pilgrimage of Grace,' in A.J. Fletcher and J. Stephenson, eds., *Order and Disorder in Early Modern England* (1985), 79–88.

47 Reinhart Koselleck, '*Begriffsgeschichte* and social history, in *Futures Past*, tr. Keith Tribe (Columbia University Press: New York, 2004), 75-92; and 'Social history and conceptual history,' in *The Practice of Conceptual History*, tr. Todd Samuel Presner et al. (Stanford University Press: Stanford, 2002), 20–44.

48 Anthony Giddens, *The Constitution of Society. Outline of a Theory of Structuration* (University of California Press: Berkeley, 1984), 64.

49  Shaw, *Necessary Conjunctions*, 1–20.
50  For a classic expression of this view in its political side, see Charles Taylor, 'Atomism,' in *Philosophy and the Human Sciences* (Cambridge, 1985), 188–210, and from the standpoint even of cognitive psychology Mark Johnson, *Moral Imagination: Implications of Cognitive Science for Ethics* (University of Chicago Press: Chicago, 1993).
51  Cf. Parfit, *Reasons and Persons*, 199–456.
52  Joan Scott, 'The evidence of experience,' *Critical Inquiry* 17 (1991), 777.
53  Thus, it was still in Grimm's Germany according to Reinhart Koselleck, 'Transformations of experience,' *The Practice of Conceptual History*, 46.
54  Jay Smith, 'Between *discourse* and *experience*: agency and ideas in the French pre-revolution,' *History and Theory* 40 (2001): 121.
55  Smith, 'Between *discourse* and *experience*,' 141.
56  Certain strains of what I call presencism come close to the opposite view as well, marking entire significant domains that are beyond and apparently above the word, that matter greatly and yet are not pure emotion alone, but rather closer to pure being. This deserves further discussion, as this is my term for this diverse group of writers, including notably Eelco Runia and Michael Bentley, but Gumbrecht is most influential and apposite here. See Hans Gumbrecht, *Production of Presence: What Meaning Can't Convey* (Stanford University Press: Stanford, 2004); E. Runia, 'Spots of time,' *History and Theory* 45 (2006): 305–16.
57  Martin Jay, *Songs of Experience* (University of California Press: Berkeley, 2005), 227.
58  Jacques Derrida, *Of Grammatology*, tr. Gayatri C. Spivak (Johns Hopkins University Press: Baltimore, 1998; orig. tr. 1976), 60.
59  Fionula Meredith, *Experiencing the Postmetaphysical Self: Between Hermeneutics and Deconstruction* (Palgrave-Macmillan: London, 1995), 108.
60  Hayden White, *Metahistory: The Historical Imagination in Nineteenth-Century Europe* (Johns Hopkins University Press: Baltimore, 1973); *The Content of the Form. Narrative Discourse and Historical Representation* (Johns Hopkins University Press: Baltimore, 1987); Noel Carroll, 'Interpretation, history, and narrative,' in *History and Theory: Contemporary Readings*, ed. Brian Fay, Philip Pomper, and Richard T. Vann (Blackwell: Oxford, 1998), 34–56. For a recent review and defence

of narrative, see David Carr, 'Narrative explanation and its malcontents,' *History and Theory* 47 (2008): 19–309.
61  See Louis Mink, 'The autonomy of historical understanding,' *History and Theory* 5 (1966): 24–47; and 'History and fiction as modes of comprehension,' *New Literary History*, 1 (1970): 541–58.
62  This is to borrow and shift a bit Frank Ankersmit's term for the gluing thing within the narrative: see his *Historical Representation* (Stanford University Press: Stanford, 2001), 136–8.
63  Nancy Partner, 'Making up lost time. writing on the writing of history,' in *History and Theory: Contemporary Readings*, ed. Brian Fay, Philip Pomper, Richard T. Vann (Blackwell: Oxford, 1998), 71. The quotation may refer only to historiographical agency.
64  Johnson, *Moral Imagination*, 179. See also Alasdair Macintyre, 'Epistemological crises, dramatic narrative and the philosophy of science,' *Monist* 60 (1977): 453–72.
65  History as inquisition or detection is a theme famously given by R.G. Collingwood, *The Idea of History*, ed. Jan van der Dussen (Oxford University Press: Oxford, 1994), 249–82.
66  See Colin Morris, *The Discovery of the Individual, 1050–1200* (London, 1972); Jakob Burckhardt, *The Civilization of the Renaissance in Italy*; and Stephen Greenblatt, *Renaissance Self-Fashioning: From More to Shakespeare* (Chicago, 1980).
67  Dan P. McAdams, *The Stories We Live By: Personal Myths and the Making of the Self* (Guilford Press: New York, 1996; orig. 1993), 12.
68  See Alasdair Macintyre, for instance, *Three Rival Versions of Moral Inquiry: Encyclopedia, Genealogy, Tradition*. (Notre Dame, 1991).
69  Jonathan M. Adler, Joshua W. Wagner, and Dan P. McAdams, 'Personality and the Coherence of Psychotherapy Narratives,' *Journal of Research in Personality* 41 (2007): 1179–98.
70  Brad Gregory, *Salvation at Stake: Christian Martyrdom in Early Modern Europe* (Harvard University Press: Cambridge, 1999); see also David Gary Shaw, 'Social selves in England,' *Writing Medieval History*, ed. Nancy Partner (Hodder-Arnold: London, 2005), 3–21.
71  See Charles Taylor, 'Self interpreting animals,' in *Human Agency and Language* (Cambridge, 1985), 45–76.
72  See the classic paper by Thomas Haskell, 'Objectivity is not neutrality: rhetoric versus practice in Peter Novick's *That Noble Dream*,' in *History and Theory: Contemporary Readings*, 299–319.

# 29

# The Fundamental Things Apply: Aristotle's Narrative Theory and the Classical Origins of Postmodern History

Nancy Partner

So it is clear on these grounds that the poet must be a maker of his plots rather than [merely a maker] of verses, particularly if he is [considered] a maker in terms of his mimesis and if what he represents is actions (praxeis). And indeed even if it turns out that he is making [his work] out of actual events, he is none the less a poet – a maker: for nothing prevents some actual events from being the sort of things that might probably happen, and in such a case he is the maker of those events. (Aristotle, *Poetics*, p. 83)

## THE LINGUISTIC TURN IN CLASSICAL GREEK

It is, I think, instructive and important to see the way that Aristotle's *Poetics* stands as a foundational prolegomenon to the entirety of the linguistic turn, and to modern narrative theory in particular. The grounds for this assertion are all here in the epigraph passage from about the middle of Aristotle's book, summed up and tossed off as an incidental corollary to the analysis he had built from the first definitions of *Poetics*, something I will discuss further on. We generally don't see the connection between classical literary theory and modern historical practice; it took a long time in the history of history for metahistory, both the concept and Hayden White's breakthrough book, to happen.

The fact that in the longue durée history of literary analysis, the structural armature of historical writing went uninterrogated and taken for granted until very recently, is self-explanatory. Open fictional invention within historical works was a rhetorical commonplace from classical antiquity through the medieval period and persisted into the eighteenth century. Narrative form, vaguely associated with epic, was equally unremarkable to readers. Stringent demands on history for entirely verifiable content presented with transparent and balanced argumentation are entirely the product of history's professionalization in the nineteenth century. Research methods, techniques for handling primary sources, training, and standards took decades to work out as history changed from an intellectual literary avocation to a credentialed professional discipline. An exacting attention directed to the complex language structures which contain and present the new archival evidence certainly had to wait its turn; that delay was nothing surprising in itself. But there hovers around linguistic analysis of historical writing using methods shared with literary studies a sense of something entirely new, even intrusive, an incursion from alien fields of cultural production whose central concern is not truth, at least not in the same sense as history. The idea that language is primary and constitutive, not a transparent vessel of objective fact, and that narratives are narratives, not segments lifted from pure reality, feels very modern, hyper self-aware and reflexive, just the kind of idea 'we' would come up with. So it is clarifying to see things from the perspective that greater distance in time allows: that postmodern narrative analysis of history is grounded in the classical philosophic tradition in the earliest dissection of mimetic activity.

Aristotle's extreme limit case, the fictional narrative made entirely of historical events neatly identifies the node where the formal power of language meets past actuality and leaves the ineffaceable mark of fiction on history as the price for intelligibility, coherence, and meaningfulness. And it is, as we say, very good to think with. Each of the key concepts in the epigraph passage (in chapter 9 in the traditional editions) has already been precisely defined: *mimesis* is the covering category for cultural artifacts; the 'poet' is the author of narrative fictions, verse or prose; the action/*praxis* is the lengthy sequence of meaningful events; the plot/*mythos* is the carefully assembled sequence of events, exhibiting internal logic and meaning.[1] Plot dominates all other elements and the poet, in this special Aristotelian sense, is the plot-maker, maker of narrative form. Thus, even in the somewhat unlikely case (to classical Greek sensibility) of the plot whose constituent events were all historically true, the plot-making author retains his title to being the 'poet' of everything he writes.

This originary insight into the conceptual 'place' where history, in the sense of the attempt to respect the reality of the past and expose its kind of truth or meaning, is inextricably knotted together with fiction, what we make with language alone, was the 'problem' that the linguistic turn recovered and pushed to the foreground of intellectual debate when postmodernism took aim at history, along with all the other language-embedded humanities. This, in essence, is the content of the form, to use Hayden White's most tellingly acute book title.[2] Narrative form gives articulate voice to the vanished events of the real past, while narrative form unavoidably imprints the touch of culture on the objective nature of events in time.

As students in my seminar on historical theory effortlessly recognize when we discuss this passage, the artifact alluded to by Aristotle that results from the 'poet' making his plot from actual events is assuredly what we mean by history: verifiable contents held together in an emplotted structure whose skeleton is causal logic. The writer in this special case called by Aristotle 'the poet,' a term of praise for disciplined achievement, is what we now call 'the historian.' And yet it is important to see how Aristotle was, at least by implication, including the historians among the writers of fiction. The postmodernist conundrum seen as so irritating and insulting to the claims of the modern historical discipline – that the results of evidentiary rigor in research, and disciplined impartiality, can only attain meaningful expression through operations with language that are identical and shared between invented fictions and history – was an incidental throwaway subconclusion in the first work of literary criticism in ancient Greece. No amount of repeated readings can entirely dull the sheer astonishment of contemplating this.

## WHAT ALCIBIADES DID: ARISTOTLE'S HISTORIAN

History, per se, in the fifth century BCE only recently given its name, *historia*, by Herodotus in the first line of his big book about the Persian invasion of Greece, is occasionally summoned up, more or less in the margins of the discussion, when Aristotle wants, in categorical fashion, to stress what *poiesis* is not. These few comments Aristotle made explicitly about history have the understandable effect of directing our attention away from the importance of the *Poetics* for historical writing and knowledge. History, in Aristotle's reductive description, is merely chronological and empirical; the historian 'tells what happened.'[3] The poet (alias: fiction writer) wields control, selection, discernment, and logic over his emplotted narrative. The historian dutifully tags along after events and records them, or some time segment of them, his work helplessly open to coincidence, happenstance, pointless simultaneity, inconsequence, incoherence. The poet finds the plot. The historian submits to reality. 'What Alcibiades [for example] [actually] did or what happened to him.' is the solitary example of historical 'particulars,' unfiltered by a plot-building principle.[4] Interesting enough, extremely interesting in the case of Alcibiades, but no guarantee of those qualities of likelihood, necessity, probability, and generalized application that secure the superior state of 'seriousness' that Aristotle famously awards to fictional composition.[5]

Aristotle admits no deviations from this strict binary, even though appreciative readers of Herodotus's ingenious narrative schemes have to feel indignant at this imperceptive and unjust account. The category, history, seems doomed here to an early demise by undiluted realism. The process of locating what the inchoate mass of events are 'about,' at a higher level of abstraction, belongs to fiction because fiction owns the plot, the mythos, as its self-definition. Historians, in this severe scheme, are committed to actuality on its own terms, albeit not the terms a writer of any sort would choose.

There is a compliment of a sort built into this reduced position for history: the strong suggestion that the historian stands committed to reality, to that kind of truth, to telling 'what happened' at whatever cost to intellectual and artistic achievement. This kind of truth, close correspondence with 'what happened,' which we respect as commitment to factuality, was not the Greek standard for serious worthwhile knowledge. It was too chancy to be a reliable instance of permanent patterns worth remembering. Serious knowledge had to have some claim on generality and permanence, and the writer who would render real knowledge from the shards and tendrils of events had to exert aggressive mental operations to find and display the causal trajectory of the meaningful movement in time. In recognition of the difficulty of that work, Aristotle insists on calling such a writer the 'poet,' the maker, a club that excludes the historian, by definition. This line of reasoning is plainly reasonable in its own strict terms. As we have seen, one conclusion apparent to us is that if historians refuse to be mere chroniclers and act like the writers they are, they too become 'poets,' i.e. fiction makers. There are overwhelmingly strong reasons proceeding from the cultural and epistemological responsibilities of history to decline to accept this classification, but nothing is compromised by merely recognizing that it follows logically from Aristotle's fine-edged definitions.

Thus, Aristotle's book has not been centrally important to the mainstream of historical self-understanding. Historian readers don't see themselves and their work in Aristotle's descriptions. The great exception to this is of course Paul Ricoeur's monumental work, *Time and Narrative*, which embraces Aristotle's narrative construction, the plot, as the shared property of fiction and history. Ricoeur's book, especially volume 1 in which he unpacks and extends Aristotle's treatment of plot as a permanent and universal feature of telling events in time, should be the historian reader's first stop after the *Poetics* itself.[6] Indeed, I consider this essay on simply reading *Poetics* from a historian's perspective as a possible vestibule into the illuminating richness of *Time and Narrative*. But even Ricoeur, whose knowledge and attention to the detailed nuance of philosophic discourse were near exhaustive, did not point out the full significance of Aristotle's 'poet of the actual.' History, with Herodotus as a named author, functions in Aristotle's analysis as the programmatic opposite to *poiesis*. The philosophic approach primarily finds and defines categories: the category *poiesis* is defined by the *praxis*/plot structure, the necessary condition of intelligibility and meaning. Since *poiesis* is fiction in this definitional sense, the categorical not-*poiesis* has to lack the defining qualities – by definition. So it follows, in logic if not in actual practice, that history, the not-fiction mode of recording events, has to lack plot and all the meaningful selection implied by emplotment. But historians know that Aristotle's *praxis*, plot, causal logic, and selection, belong to them, to us.

## THE HISTORIAN AS ARISTOTLE'S MAKER OF THE ACTUAL

The epigraph passage (see page 495) comes about halfway through Aristotle's short untitled work usually called *Poetics* from its opening words, '*peri poietikes*.' The words stemming from the Greek root verb, poiein (to make, do, fashion, perform) and its derivatives such as poietike, poietic, *poiesis*, have shifted radically over time away from their classical Greek meanings based in a craftsman's verb of hands-on making or fashioning as they evolved into the modern vocabulary for poetry, versifying, and fictional creation. [7] Although the sound of the Greek root words has stayed remarkably audible in their English derivatives (poet, poetry, poetics), their culturally embedded meanings have almost completely reversed from the Greek sense of intelligent workmanship into romantically infused ideas of inspiration and creation. George Whalley, the translator and commentator of the edition from which I have quoted, strives throughout his translation to preserve and accentuate the weight of Aristotle's own conceptual terminology in what was the first work of literary analysis in the Western tradition: 'poiein (to make, do, fashion, perform) – is a strongly active verb that will dominate the whole discussion in the sense of "to make." (Emphatically, it does not mean "to create".) … Aristotle does not recognize a distinction between "art" and "craft."'[8] This crucial restoration of Aristotle's specific conception of how artifacts are made with language brings into sharp visibility the important, and permanent, implications of this foundational work for the mode of writing we recognize as history, and for the intellectual operations underlying historical knowledge. With its central concepts understood as Aristotle lays them out, *Poetics* speaks to historical writing as much as fiction. As a historian, I think our claim to Aristotle's *Poetics* as the foundational classic of our discipline is long overdue.

I realize this may seem an unlikely assertion about a book whose primary example is tragic drama, but Aristotle's book was emphatically not about poetry in the modern sense or even in the classical Greek sense. It was the first exacting analysis of what is required of an author (his poet, an all-purpose designation) to make, to craft, from some complicated, various, overlapping congeries of events a single coherent written account of something meaningful: the 'poet,' in this sense, turns the miscellany of events (pragmata) into a logically unified complex action (*praxis*) following a trajectory from beginning to resolution (telos). The examination he begins with the words, 'peri poietikes,' is what we now call narrative theory. In fact, the book conventionally titled *Poetics* could, without distortion, and with considerable gain in accuracy, be called Aristotle's Narrative Theory.

His analysis is rigorously formal. In anachronistic terms, Aristotle reverse engineers the successfully achieved work back to its basic elements of authorial selection and placement – the deceptively simple beginning, middle, and end of the organically unified plot or mythos. From mimesis to *poiesis*, from category to subcategory in philosophic analysis, Aristotle immediately defines the major modes of mimetic activity, differentiated by their matter (as for music, painting, writing), their subjects of representation, and their methods of deploying their matter. He efficiently arrives at, assembles, and defines the components of the subcategory at issue: *poiesis* or the kind of mimesis done with language representing complex actions.[9] Following Whalley's prompt, I am using the unfamiliar Greek *poiesis* hoping to avoid some of the high aesthetic, versifying, fiction-only baggage of 'poetry;' probably impossible to carry off, but worth a try. The taken-for-granted hierarchy of Greek culture places tragedy in the foreground of Aristotle's discussion, his chief example of serious literary achievement, with comedy and epic in for frequent mention, and history standing in the margins as the counter-example of what *poiesis* is not. For reasons to be discussed, history, in Aristotle's definitional categories, was not conceded a share in the formal and intellectual operations of *poiesis*. For the moment, it is sufficient to note that the minimal definition of *poiesis* does not specify any special sort of action as appropriate for representation, or where the author was to find his materials. Tragedy is the obvious useful example; it does not define the subject.

'A tragedy, then, is a mimesis of an action [*praxis*] – that is, it is [morally] serious and purposeful, having magnitude ...' – an early conclusion – and he repeats soon after, 'Since [tragedy] is a mimesis of an action ....'[10] Or as Whalley notes: 'Praxis (action) is a keyword that Aristotle uses consistently ... not just any action, but an action arising from choice, directed towards and implying a telos, to which other subsidiary movements may be attached without deflecting it.'[11] Giving *Poetics* a historian's reading, attentive to its many implications for the core elements of historical writing, it is obvious that the centrality of the

*praxis*, a protracted complex series of events imbued with human intentionality and of compelling seriousness and importance, takes the discussion right into our turf. And, one has to notice, of all the aspects involved in the successful mimesis of an action worth telling, fictional invention, making things up, is completely absent.

This is a notable absence since tragic drama functions as Aristotle's main test case throughout the book, bringing to mind its many and varied component elements, including speech, character, choral song, and stage effects to present a story that arouses pity and terror. One might expect that brilliant originality in the art of fictional invention would compel attention here. But all the parts of tragedy are subordinated to one single overarching and defining activity – plot-making: 'the putting together of the events.'[12] 'The plot is the mimesis of the action,' Aristotle declares in an early summary section, and we should read that line with a heavy accent on 'plot.'[13] Plot or mythos, 'the putting together (?structuring) of the events,' yields the integrated complex sequence determined by the intricate, multilevel, causal relations among its component events. This sequence assembled from only those particular events which belong in the logically meaningful train, nothing happenstance or without effect in the larger movement, emerges as the exact equivalent of the mimesis, this special kind of mimesis – the achieved work itself. 'The plot' – nothing else, however floridly dramatic or gripping, not even the characters like Oedipus or Agamemnon, defines the mimesis of the action. Aristotle sweeps away everything distractingly colorful or emotionally rending with a breathtaking austerity, and locks a rigorous attention on the intellectual operations that extract meaning from the inchoate rush of human experience. No plot, no mimesis. That is what his mimesis in language, the *poiesis*, is about, 'about' in the deep sense, nothing else.

With only a slight adjustment, we can cast this directly into historian's terms: the coherent and intelligible written account (the mimesis) of a complex series of events (the *praxis/ action*) is essentially its plot. Emplotment is primary to both coherence and meaning, if these qualities are to emerge from any written account of events. Aristotle underscores this primacy of plot over and over again: plot stands in *Poetics* as achieved intellectual control over contingency and accident. Plot, 'the putting together of the events,' the writer's talent and labor so simply summarized, is what the writer, the 'poet,' must do successfully to justify his claim to achievement. Plot and meaningfulness, in the most exacting sense, are virtually interchangeable.

'So it is clear on these grounds …' – the primacy of emplotment – that the author generically called 'the poet' is somehow the 'maker' of actual historical events once he configures them into a plot.[14] What Aristotle means is plain:

> So Reader, if you now grasp the key concept terms as I have defined them (mimesis, *poiesis*, plot/*mythos*, *praxis*), if you grasp their categorical relations to one another, and have followed the logical steps of my analysis of the subject up to this point, then you have to see, as one of our corollary conclusions, that what I say next is indubitably the case. Logic demands your acknowledgement: it follows.

And what he says next is an astonishing precursor insight into the core of the postmodernist challenge to empirical history, tossed off as a corollary conclusion of the larger analysis of literary composition, and one of very little concern to classical Greek culture. Aristotle merely notes that the 'poet,' (the fiction writer is the only modern equivalent for Aristotle's usage) deserves his status by virtue of his controlling decisions in formulating the structure of his plot, emphatically if he is depicting a complex sequence of events over a longish time, an action or *praxis*, and his status as the 'maker,' the one source and authority from whose mind the work proceeds is unaltered even if he chooses to make this plot from actual events, historic events. The integral formal structure, the narrative structure or plot, not invented characters or

speeches or imagined events, much less diction or metrical lines, is what makes a work in its entirety a work of *poiesis*, of narrative fiction, the linguistic artifact that Aristotle, first among philosophers, was here examining and defining. Of all the elements that make up a mimesis in language, whether tragedy or epic – character, speech, events, dramatic additions – 'the most important of these is the putting together of the events … and so the [course of] events – the plot – is the end/telos [the defining purpose] of tragedy, and the end/telos is what matters most of all.'[15]

Throughout the first half of *Poetics* where Aristotle defines and classifies the central concepts for understanding mimesis in language (prose or verse – he makes no distinction), he repeatedly stresses the primacy of plot, the putting together of events into a coherent, logically entailed sequence, intelligible as a unified whole. This capacious, demanding concept of plot (mythos in Greek) takes precedence over any and all other contributions to the written work's finished state. The fact that there are even forms of this mimesis that make do with language alone, without the help of scenery or music, and that this mode is 'an art that happens so far to have no name' is noted by the way. We, however, can note that this language-alone art sets up the framing category for history. The writer whose judgement and intelligence can arrange a multiform array of events into intelligible narrative is the sole maker of those events, as they stand arranged in that form, in that plot, the 'poet.' And if those events happen to be real historical events, their author remains their 'poet' or maker, insofar as they can only be understood in terms of his plot.

Aristotle's breathtakingly brilliant insight driving his foundational taxonomy of the artifacts of language, was that the author's formal construction was the defining activity: the form is the 'fiction' in its Latin sense of something made. Everything else is secondary. It is hard to overstate the importance of this insight. Versifying, making metrical lines, is emphatically dismissed out of hand by Aristotle as qualifying a writer as a 'poet' in this special sense. Aristotle's 'poetry' (*poiesis*) is not formal verse by definition. Beautiful speeches, thoughts and feelings, tragic characters, all are useful, even indispensable for some purposes, but none are definitive. Even the status of the component episodes, as fact or invention, is entirely secondary in Aristotle's analysis which obsessively focuses on what makes the telling or writing of series of events meaningful, intelligible, about something more than mere registration of something that happened. The telos, the resolution point of the plot in linear terms, and 'the point' of the plot in terms of meaning, is a function of emplotment. This recognition that narrative form is the conveyor of meaning, and that narrative is made, not found, even when comprised of historical events, was self-evident to Aristotle, and non-controversial because high Greek culture was minimally interested in verifiable details of fact, maximally interested in generalizable knowledge. Yet this marginal variant of Aristotelian poiesis, a well-constructed narrative made of actual events, offhandedly brought into the *Poetics* to underscore the point about the importance of plot, is history. What else could it be?

Aristotle is firmly underscoring the idea that making coherent plots, the selecting and arranging of events and other narrative information into verisimilar but meaning-intensive sequences, is so fundamentally and overwhelmingly important to *poiesis* (alias: fiction) that even in the most extreme, slightly absurd, limit case – that of the 'poet' choosing all his narrative pieces from actual history – the result is fiction and the writer is the 'poet' or maker of that work in its entirety. This is a radical insight, using 'radical' in its originary 'rooted' sense. Nothing could be more radical from the point of view of historical knowledge and its epistemological claims to establish stable knowledge of the world outside the text, the real past.

I cannot be the only reader to notice how Aristotle's scalpel-fine logic, which defines the function and importance of literary elements – that the overarching structure or plot is primary to meaningfulness in a way that no

character, singular event, or any component of a complex action (*praxis*) can be – is a recognition that has immense and permanent repercussions for history as a mode of written information about the real past. If this passage has not gotten the attention it deserves it is because it is overshadowed by the far more controversial paradoxes, to us at least, of the immediately preceding passage comparing history and fiction. Among the most frequently quoted remarks from *Poetics* are Aristotle's award of the prize of higher seriousness, intellectual importance or philosophic status (the translation seems exceptionally difficult) to 'poetry' (alias: fictional composition not necessarily in verse form) over history as he defined it. In Whalley's translation: 'That's why in fact poetry is a more speculative and more "serious" business than history: for poetry deals more with universals, history with particulars.' The fiction writer or 'poet' does the difficult intellectual work of selecting and arranging events to expose the inner workings of human behavior as exhibited under moral stress and conflict – the permanent features of human character and political life, knowledge of enduring value: 'poetry deals more with universals, history with particulars.' The historian, merely records what reality presents, however contingent or one-off trivial. As Whalley puts it: 'Aristotle's point, by implication, is that the historian observes and records, the poet discerns and constructs, making his construction even when the materials are "actual."'[16] It is in the following passage, just wrapping up a curious logically entailed point, that the radical implication of history's embrace within emplotted language is underscored, however many centuries before its full import acquired any cultural significance

## WHAT IS IT ABOUT?
## THE *PRAXIS*: THE SHAPE
## OF DESCRIBABLE REALITY

The deep permanent structures of narrative composition, as central to the modern research-based discipline of history as to its earlier modes, are the *praxis*, the protagonist, and telos or end, and these deserve some specification of their functions. 'The plot is the mimesis of the action [*praxis*],' Aristotle states clearly, putting plot and *praxis* into a kind of equivalence.[17] The sort of emplotted sequence Aristotle analyses is, or requires, or takes as its subject matter – difficult to settle on an adequate verb for this relation – a particular kind of action whose characteristics are collected in the term, *praxis*. Once laid out for inspection, the Aristotelian *praxis* is immediately recognizable as a typically 'historical' kind of reality: the historically significant convergence of events playing out over time, with lasting effects beyond the immediate surround, a course of events that speak to the aspects of life we care about, what historians write about. As definitions go, this is admittedly somewhat circular, but what makes any course of events loosely worth writing about is what constitutes the classical *praxis*.

The *praxis* and the *mythos*, alias: the action and the plot, are really the same thing regarded from somewhat different viewpoints. Thinking about plot directs our attention to the formal configuration of a coherent and comprehensible narrative of events. The *praxis*, comprised of exactly the same emplotted events, directs our analysis to the question of how those events, those and not others, were recognized and assembled in the first place. What is it that makes all those events connect and bring to light something both real and important? In a condensed way, the *praxis* is the answer to a direct and sensible question addressed to any written history: What is it about? The answer inevitably occupies two levels, as: What is it about? It is about the American Civil War. But what is it really about? It is about the impact of slavery in the secession of the Confederate States. Or – This book is about the textile industry in medieval Bruges; but it is *really* about the formation of bourgeois self-awareness as a social and economic collective during the twelfth century. One level of 'aboutness' points to the literal contents of a

narrative, and a next level of 'about' pushes further to an abstracted thread of causation or meaning, the level that extends the significance of the subject at hand out to a larger world. The *praxis* is that collection of historical information that can sustain the second level query into what it is 'about.'

There is nothing new here; this is common practice in academic history. The professional historian, the graduate student seeking the topic for a thesis that will make an impact, are alert to the presence of the second level significance implicit in the evidentiary record of 'what happened' – as Aristotle reductively gestured at the historian's work. It is that inferred or intuited sense of the seriously meaningful, abstractable level of significance that attracts the historian to one subject rather than another, and that sense of the significance inhering somehow 'in,' not on the visible surface of, events is the sensitivity that locates the true *praxis*, singles out the *praxis* from other chronological, more or less connected series of events.

The *praxis* always feels found, and always is made. The historian's procedure of deploying that sharpened sense for the immanent meaning of events as the filter that collects in, and excludes from, the relevant contents of a work of history is both true-to-evidence and authorial in its control. The effect, on historian-author and reader, when it works best, is that of discovering, of uncovering, the true meaning of 'what happened.' The Aristotelian poet's *praxis* is our earliest progenitor.

## THE PROTAGONIST'S PRIVILEGE: THE NAME OF THE REAL

Narrative is the form that maintains coherence over historical duration, and narrative form requires some central subject to accomplish that. A crucial operation in forming a narrative is locating a subject that (or who) undergoes change over time and yet remains a recognizable entity by virtue of its main identity markers. The traditional narrative subject is a human protagonist – Aristotle's hard to translate 'men in action' or 'men of action in action' or 'men acting,' (but not in the sense of actors on a stage), all indicating intentionality, choice, goal-directed acts, a thickly populated social and political scene.[18] Tragedy needs individual protagonists, but we should note that Herodotus placed The Greeks as collective Protagonist for his history. The Greeks occupy a collective subject position that narrows down to Athens as the big action proceeds. A *praxis* requires a protagonist as the focal nexus for acting, being acted upon, cohering qualities into an identifiable something, a something that can undergo change, development, internal tension, confront resistance and opposition and yet remain recognizable.

Within the formal makeup of a historical *praxis*, the protagonist is a function of causal logic; something must cause and be the locus of effects. The protagonist, regarded in this formalist way, is a narrative position, but never a static one. Without something (more often a some thing these days than a some one) occupying the protagonist position, history can't be about anything, can't achieve the degree of specification required for knowledge. The answer to the second level 'about' inquiry is usually the name of the protagonist connected to a verb (as, for example, 'the rise of the middle class'). Narrative form itself is a highly persuasive mode of argumentation, arguing for the actuality of whatever is related intelligibly and fully, and nothing benefits more from this intensified reality effect than the narrative protagonist.

When history underwent its modern professionalization during the later nineteenth century, the *praxis* that spoke most clearly to intellectual and political gravity was the development of the nation state. The Name of the nation designated the protagonist whose formation could be traced from its earliest expression through all stages of emergence until it achieved sovereign statehood: state formation was the organic life course of the national protagonist in standard-setting 'scientific' works like William Stubb's *Constitutional History of England*, first published in the 1870s. To nineteenth-century historians, to name the nation was indubitably to name something real, something 'there' in reality even before it found expression in actual institutions, law, designated borders, and the recognition of others outside it. We don't find this as convincing, but the proliferating national movements of the post-cold war age benefit from the same manipulation of linguistic reality. National entities such as Estonia and Slovakia, which can claim actual statehood for only a very few years, act as the protagonist of exaggeratedly longue durée histories reaching back to Roman times, their ethnicized shards of continuity held together in a single plot chiefly by the power of the protagonist function to assert reality of its name. The invisible, and usually unremarked, privilege of the protagonist position in a narrative of actual events (even when there is scarcely anything that qualifies as an event) is to impute reality to itself. This too is built into the structure of the *praxis*.

## THE END MARKS THE BEGINNING: CONTROLLING TIME

To satisfy the basic conditions for a plot, a sequence of events cannot be merely chronological; the sequence must be meaningful, intelligibly connected, every component standing in some logical relation to the others. Here is Aristotle's essence of this complicated requirement:

> A 'beginning' is what does not necessarily have to follow anything else, but after which something naturally is or happens; an 'end,' the other way round, is what naturally is after something else, either of necessity or usually, but has nothing after it; a 'middle' is what comes after something else and has something else after it. Well-constructed plots, therefore, must neither begin at an accidental starting point nor come to an accidental conclusion, but must have followed the principles we have given.'[19]

Beginning, middle, end – Aristotle's necessary conditions for emplotted events – can seem far too simple to be good to think about, much less to think with, our peculiar academic mode of praise. But, unsurprisingly, this simplicity is not simplistic, not thinned or flattened out. The profundity results from discarding all superficial elements, then removing the useful expendables, until only the irreducible necessary minimum remains. These narrative elements of beginning, middle, and end are so fraught with operative meaning that explaining how they work unfolds and expands into layer after layer of the narrative operations that produce the logic and meaningfulness of reported events. Aristotle's succinct definitions only begin the process.

From the historian-author's point of view, the beginning never comes first. 'Beginning' describes the logical-relational placement of a certain event inaugurating everything that follows; this 'beginning' locates a reasonable and sufficient starting point for the entire sequence the author wants to relate. The process of deciding on that inaugurating point can't possibly start there: everything is a 'beginning' of some tellable series, or more than one. Just starting off from some historical 'thing' is too open-ended and slack, lacks any principle for control, lacks a sense of trajectory. Beginnings never come first, not logically and not to the historian. The beginning can only be perceived as an answer to a question formulated around some resolution or 'thing that has come to be.' Where did it start? In this sense, all historical narratives are teleological in some overarching sense, and resisting the pressure and temptation of teleology, or at least recognizing it, is the mark of the well-trained modern research historian.

Beginnings are conceptually possible only as a function of endings: the end, the telos in the classic Greek sense, determines the beginning. In a fundamental way, all narrative constructions are teleological. It is better to admit this head-on and deal with the implications than deny it flatly in the hope of expelling ideological determinism from history. Student historians are taught, quite correctly, to recognize and resist the lure of teleological determinism – the blinkered seeing in the array of evidence only what resembles and

thus supports a predetermined outcome. But there is an important difference between a rigid determining telos which suppresses and evicts all contradictory information on the way to its hegemonic outcome, and a provisional or contingent telos which provides an intelligible form while remaining open to new formulations if the pressure of recalcitrant evidence grows strong enough. All narrative form requires a 'sense of an ending' to find its intelligible duration. In that sense, without telos there can be no beginning, no principle of relevance for evidence. But history does not have to sacrifice its corrigibility, its openness to valid alternatives, its sense that every history is a version, in using telos, the teleological anchor point, to produce comprehension. The historian's telos has a strong reality connection.

## WHY SHOULD A BOOK CALLED '*POETICS*' BE OUR FOUNDATION TEXT?

Thinking about history through the optic of Aristotle's *Poetics* brings into focus the way that historical narrative is always the solution, the provisionally best solution, to a massive and intricate series of problems. Every forward-moving element in the historian's narrative construction is a solution to a small-scale problem (this piece of evidence, this works here) understood as a component of the large-scale problem – how to see and place the pieces in relation to the big subject. Thinking of an intelligibly formed narrative as the final product emerging from the cumulative little solutions to a complex series of problems is thinking about the writer's work. A narrative, taken as a whole, is the end solution to a large number of problems, and each part of the narrative is the solution arrived at to solve some specific problem. This foregrounds the real meaning of what we call 'the process of selection,' and brings out the real possibility of all the other possible solutions hovering, silent and invisible, around the ones chosen.

What many of us call in the classroom 'the principle of selection' when explaining to students what the historian-researcher does when turning all the potential evidence into a coherent work of history is probably the most intuitively straightforward of all the operations in professional history. At least it sounds like a method, with decisions governed by relevance, causal logic, context, sufficiency, correct weighting, and other rational standards. And it is a method, not a science-based replicable method, but a rational process. 'Selection,' however, places all the stress on the correct choices, or at least the intention to make correct choices, and doesn't quite get at the adjudicatory process at the heart of narrative construction which is the problem solving. For historians, the constructedness of the historical account is most readily explained and understood in terms of the 'principle of selection.' Historians readily accept that the state of the evidence supporting knowledge for any series of events is always imperfect, from the historians point of view. There is always too little, or too much, or an uneven distribution over even very short periods of time, and even for times and events for which the evidence is sparce and inadequate, every last piece of whatever there is still cannot be merely shuffled into some logical order, or chronological order, and all included. This still does not get at the entirety of the procedures involved in narrative construction.

Each narrative component stands in place of the (suppressed, disqualified, rejected) contenders for that position, alternates for some visible presence and weight in the narrative sequence. This sensitized awareness we bring as reader or writer, that every event, every person, every detail of the social or political context, the depth or sketchiness of descriptive detail, that make up the historical account is the winner in a now invisible contest for inclusion, is quite possibly the single most important effect of knowing the skeletal construction of narrative, the poetics of narrative. The alternates, the failed competitors in the push towards inclusion in the story, or at least the fact of their existence if not their exact nature, touch the awareness of the theory-informed reading, disabused forever

of the naive idea that history comes in one version only.

Facts, even with their halo of skepticism as 'facts,' are not lost to poetics. Postmodernist revisions to our conceptions of how language refers to things did challenge the small-scale stability of knowledge by demonstrating that the relation of words to extra-linguistic reality was not a simple alignment of a sound (a word) with direct perception of reality, but a far more complex process involving the programmatic relations among words themselves within a signifying system. Nonetheless, our concept of 'the fact' emerged, nuanced and self-conscious, but largely intact. In Hayden White's taxonomy of the fact (with acknowledgement to Arthur Danto): 'a fact is an event under a description' – where 'description' can be understood as consisting of a perspicuous listing of attributes of the event … by which an event is assigned to its proper kind and, usually, given a proper name.' 'An event cannot enter into a history until it has been established as a fact.'[20] Even events turned into facts remain problems. Reality is the problem; narrative is the solution (however provisional and incomplete every historical narrative solution is).

In general, historians pay little or no attention to narrative theory for obvious, and blameless professional reasons, the same reasons that explain why historians of post-Soviet Estonia pay scant attention to the scholarship on ancient Greek prostitution. Specialization is the defining strength of modern historical research, and only a personal inclination or the chances of graduate training direct attention to linguistic-based theory in an evidence committed field. An inclination towards theoretical analysis is itself a specialist practice in contemporary academe. Nonetheless, narrative form is always already 'there,' and after at least a quarter century of the linguistic turn, it is no longer outrageous to say that historians are generally conscious of narrative as a form not found, but made. They may not know exactly how it is 'made,' or the implications of the component pieces that make up a narrative, but few academics are prepared to assert that the single coherent version is the veritable shape of past reality.

The central realization caught in Aristotle's passage about the poet as maker of the actual was the driving insight of the entirety of *Poetics*: that deploying language into complex forms that make time and action intelligible is how humans turn the stuff of reality into knowledge. The form is what renders the meaning from the content: the content may be found but the form is always made. This insight, worked out in Aristotle's book, locates the source of knowledge produced by fiction, and at the same time, as an ineluctable corollary, locates the special kind of fiction in history. This insight, about form and content, the made and the found, if accepted with full knowledge of the component logic that leads to it, is the first and yet permanent realization of the 'problem' of language and the representation of reality in the Western tradition. But just because narrative is endemic, pervasive, and unavoidable, it cannot be neutral or naively transparent on extra-narrative reality. It makes a series of special demands, and just because we effortlessly and without resistance accede to them, does not mean that they do not bring special distortions, their own shaping of reality to meet the demands of narrative coherence and movement. Narrative, as a formal mode of organizing and presenting information about events in a period of time, remains a permanent and central aspect of historical knowledge because narrative permeates individual identity and group identification at every scale from kinship, small community, through tribe, ethnicity, religious affiliation, on up to the nation, the nation-state, and the multi-national state: in other words, the subject and protagonist position of nearly all historical accounts.

The elements of narrative form are separable for the purposes of analysis. They can be assigned names and their functions can be specified and distinguished from one another. Thus: action/*praxis*; beginning, middle, end; plot/*mythos*. But in the writer's practice, and correctly understood as elements of a complex and integrated armature, rendering events and causation intelligible over time, none of the elements of a narrative can stand alone, or do its work alone. Each entails and implies the other, or only exists as a function of the rest of the working components of a narrative. The beginning exists logically as a function of its telos. A *praxis*, to be narratable, has to have some focal entity to act, be acted on, be the subject of change or continuity: a protagonist, however impersonal or abstractly conceived (i.e. the middle class, urbanization, feudalism). *Praxis* entails protagonist – a narrative function combining coherence and the ability to undergo change. The kind of scrutiny that deserves to be called theoretical belongs to history because the foundational elements for imposing form on time, for locating and naming a subject, for the filtering of evidence as relevant or not, all occur at a stage logically prior to nearly all the critical operations that make history a rigorous discipline. The history has to be about something, something that can assume at least provisional shape with some descriptor name (say, Anglo-Saxon kingship) before the evidence for it can be regarded as evidence of anything, before any assertion can be arguably true or false. Aristotle's singling out of the *praxis*/action and its expression in a coherent plot leads directly to these considerations. The obvious sensible question about any historian's research project – i.e. 'What is it about?' – takes us right back to the core elements singled out by Aristotle in the foundational book of our discipline.

## NOTES AND REFERENCES

1  Aristotle's *Poetics*, translated and with a commentary by George Whalley, edited by John Baxter and Patrick Atherton (Montreal & Kingston: McGill-Queens University Press, 1997), p. 83/traditional chapt. 9.

2  Hayden White, *The Content of the Form: Narrative Discourse and Historical Representation* (Johns Hopkins University Press, 1987).

3  *Poetics*, p. 81/chapt. 9: 'For the distinction between the historian and the poet is not whether they give their accounts in verse or prose ... no, the [real] difference is this: that the one [i.e. the historian] tells what happened,

the other [i.e. the poet] tells the sort of things that *can* happen.'

4  *Poetics*, p. 83/chapt. 9.

5  *Poetics*, p. 81/chapt. 9: 'That's why in fact poetry is a more speculative and more "serious" business than history: for poetry deals more with universals, history with particulars.' We should note that the universals referred to here are plainly not the highest level of philosophic abstraction, but the middle level of generalized observation about social and political life, what 'a certain kind of person tends to say or do' – the ordinary subject matter of history.

6  Paul Ricoeur, *Time and Narrative*, Vol. 1, translated by Kathleen McLaughlin and David Pellauer (Chicago & London: University of Chicago Press, 1984).

7  Aristotle's *Poetics*, p. 83/traditional chapt. 9.

8  *Poetics*, Whalley's annotation, p. 44, n. 1. This translation with commentary, made by George Whalley as a teaching text at the University of Toronto is exceptionally useful for non-classicists; he deliberately preserved as much as possible of the original language and syntax, and uses the Greek *poiesis* throughout in order to show as clearly as possible that this term does not mean poetry in a modern or ancient sense. The chapter numbers added to page numbers indicate the traditional numbering in Greek editions.

9  *Poetics*, p. 51/chapt. 2.

10  *Poetics*, p. 67, 71/chapt. 6.

11  *Poetics*, Whalley annotation, p. 66, n. 9.

12  *Poetics*, p. 73/chapt. 6.

13  *Poetics*, p. 71/chapt. 6.

14  *Poetics*, p. 83/chapt. 9.

15  *Poetics*, p. 73/chapt. 6.

16  *Poetics*, Whalley annotation, p. 80, n. 70.

17  *Poetics*, p. 71/chapt. 6: '...the plot is the mimesis of the action (for I use "plot" in this sense – the putting together of the events)'.

18  *Poetics*, p. 51/chapt. 2, and p. 50, n. 19.

19  *Poetics*, p. 77/chapt. 7.

20  Hayden White, 'The historical event,' *Differences: A Journal of Feminist Cultural Studies*, 19(2) (2008), p. 13.

# Index

art
  history as 204
  of memory 354, 358, 359, 360
  and science 203, 204, 205
articulation (cultural studies) 349, 350
artifacts of language 498, 500
*Aspasia* (journal) 278
Astell, Mary 267
audience (rhetoric) 150, 151–3
Auerbach, Erich 85, 112, 113
Austin, John 405
authenticity (documents/records) 459, 460, 461
authority in history 59
Aya, Rod 478

Bachelard, Gaston 174
Bacon, Sir Francis 24, 30, 31, 54, 82, 433
Bakhtin, Mikhail 209–10, 212
Bann, Stephen 159, 426
Barad, Karen 416
Barkan, Elazar 215
Barnes, Barry 407
Barnes, Julian 193
Barthes, Roland 121, 150, 205–6, 209, 210,
  440–1, 442–3
Barzun, Jacques 366
Bateson, Mary 269
Battle of Trafalgar example 54, 62
Baudrillard, Jean 159
Bayesian probability and historiography 412–13
Bazin, André 443
Beard, Charles A. 20, 34, 35, 36, 86, 94
Beard, Mary Ritter 241–2, 249, 258
Bechtel, Fritz 429–30, 431
Becker, Carl 20, 34, 35, 36, 86, 88, 94, 197
Beckett, Andy 336–7
beginning, middle, end (Aristotle) 370, 499,
  503, 504, 506
Below, Georg von 19
Benda, Julien 73
Benjamin, Walter 435–6, 437, 440, 441
Bennett, Judith M. 239, 245, 299, 300
Bentham, Jeremy 167
Bentley, Michael 4
Berger, Stefan 234
Bergson, Henri 71, 72
Berkhofer, Robert 148
Berkshire Conferences 245, 279, 303
Berlin, Isaiah 88
Bernheim, E. 26, 32, 33
Berr, Henri 15, 19, 68, 76
Bevir, Mark 411
Beynon, John 286
Bhabha, Homi K. 382, 389, 390
*Bildungsroman* story type 109
biography 70, 207, 217
  vs history 314
  women's 238, 241, 246, 258, 259

Bion, Wilfred 315
biopower (Foucault) 167, 168, 173, 273, 382
*Birth of the Clinic* (Foucault, 1973) 164, 165, 166
Blackwood, Evelyn 277
Bloch, Marc 34, 36, 67–9, 71–2, 74–5, 76, 94, 95
Blom, Ida 259
body, history of 211
'the body' (gender history) 284, 285, 286, 287
Boltanski, Luc 71
Bolter, Jay David 360
*Book of the City of Ladies* (Pisan/Pizan,
  1405) 238, 266–7
bootstrap account of learning 405, 406, 413
born-digital records 459, 461, 463
Boswell, John 297, 306
'bottom up'
  history 'from the' 5, 95
  vs 'top down' processing (cognition) 327
Boucher, David 411–12
Boulard, Henri 74
boundaries of history 202–19
Bourdé, Guy 75
Bourdieu, Pierre 71, 136, 479, 488
Bourke-White, Margaret 446, 447
Boyle, Robert 433–4
Boym, Svetlana 368
Brantlinger, Patrick 329, 332
Braudel, Fernand 67, 68, 69–76, 100, 102,
  155, 187, 188, 195, 225
Breivik, Anders 183, 185, 189, 192, 197
Briggs, Asa 99, 102, 225, 233
Brink, Cornelia 448
Briskman, Larry 405
Britain
  and its empire 326–41
  in the New World 328
  in the 1970s 335–7
British History Online 470
British in Latin America 326–41
Brittan, Samuel 336–7
Brown, Harold 404
Brown, James 404
Brucker, J.J. 82
Buckle, Thomas Henry 12–14, 30, 33, 85
Buffalo Women's Oral History Project 242
Burckhardt, Jacob 87
Burke, Peter 212, 213
Burns, Ken 197
Burtt, E.A. 87
Butler, Judith 257, 273
Butterfield, Herbert 87, 204, 205
Byzantine history (sexuality) 298

Cabrera, Miguel 236, 478, 479
Caesar, Julius 57
Callaghan government (UK, 1976) 337
Cambridge Group for the History of
  Population and Social Structure 99

Hoffman, Eva 364, 370
Holliday, Billie 252
Holocaust 115, 215–16
    and denialism 203, 214
    and gay/lesbian activists 294
    and memory 158, 159, 357, 362–4, 371
    and narrative history 191, 195
    photographs of 443–7, 449–55
    symbolic images of 447–54
Holocaust photographs 439
Holocaust studies 362, 364
homonormativity 297, 300
homophobia and feminism 257
homosexuality 230, 285–6, 297, 299–302, 304
homosociality 288
hooks, bell 251, 259
Hoover, Robert 358
Houlbrook, Matt 230
Howison, John 333
Hubert, Henri 74
Huizinga, Johann 86, 429–31, 432, 433
Hull, David 403
human action 474, 475, 476, 481, 489
human agent/agency 474, 475, 478, 479, 481, 491
human sciences (Foucault) 165, 176
humanism (Foucault) 165, 167, 176, 179
humanities 15, 401
humanity, history of 204, 217, 218
Hume, David 27, 37
Hunt, Nancy Rose 276
Huntington, Samuel P. 391
Hurricane Digital Memory Bank 466
Husserl, Edmond 137, 138
Hutton, Patrick 224
Huyssen, Andreas 373

ideality of history 42, 45, 46
ideas, history of 81, 86, 169
identity
    in Foucault 171
    sexual 299, 302
    in social history 227, 228, 229, 230, 231
identity politics 283
ideology (Abu-Lughod) 217
idiosyncrasy (Abu-Lughod) 217
Iggers, Georg 15
illusionism 425, 427
imagination and constructive history 60–1
immanent meaning 502
'immobile' history 69
imperialism, British/English 332, 334
*In Search of a Past* (Fraser, 1984) 321–2
incapsulation of thoughts 52
incommensurability (Kuhn) 407, 409, 411, 412
indigenous peoples 202, 215
indirect speech 53
individual (Foucault) 476
individual agency 475, 476, 477

individualism 475, 490
inference 55, 58, 61
information
    access to 458
    and archives 461–3
    as consumer durable 462
    and records 459–60
information vehicles 459
infotainment as genre 129, 130
inquiry, logic of question and answer
    as theory of 55
inscrutability of reference (Quine) 416
intellectual history 5, 81–92, 408, 409–10
intelligible form (telos) 504
intention/intentionality 13, 16, 399
interdisciplinarity (cultural studies)
    346–8
International Federation for Research
    in Women's History (IFRWH) 247
*International Review of Social History* 99
Internet Archive (Google) 464
interpretation 3, 7, 204, 206–7, 209, 215,
    218, 221–2, 397, 398–9, 404, 407,
    411–12, 413, 416
    and (anti-)postmodernism 212, 214
    in Derrida 207
    of evidence 57–8
    of historical document 58
    in White's work 110–11, 112, 114–15
introjection 315
invented speech 213
invention (rhetoric) 151, 154–5
*Invention of Tradition* (Hobsbawm/Ranger,
    1983) 355
irony (White) 124, 130
'Is history a science?' (Villari, 1891) 13
Isenberg, Michael T. 153
Islamic sexuality 298, 304–5

Jacobs, Aletta 239
Jaeger, Werner 89
Jakobson, Roman 150
Jameson, Anna 268
Jameson, Frederic 329
Jarvis, Christina 287
Jay, Martin 433, 487
Jellinek, Georg 18
Jenkins, Keith 124, 125, 154–5
Jenkinson, Hilary 458–9, 461
Jews/Jewish 215, 216, 299, 362, 363, 364
Joan Kelly Prize 247
Johnson, Mark 489
Johnson, Paul E. 96
Johnson, Valerie 399
Joint Information Systems Committee
    (JISC, digitisation funding) 464
Jordanova, Ludmilla 254
Jorgensen, Christine 277